I0139027

THE

Law-French

DICTIONARY

Alphabetically Digested;

Very useful for all young STUDENTS in the *Common Laws* of *ENGLAND.*

To which is added,

THE

Law-Latin Dictionary:

Being

An *Alphabetical Collection* of such *Law-Latin* Words as are found in several *Authentic Manuscripts*, and Printed *Books* of *Precedents*, whereby *Entring-Clerks*, and others, may be furnished with *fit* and *proper Words*, in a *Common Law Sense*, for any thing they shall have occasion to make use of, in *Drawing Declarations*, or any parts of *Pleading*. Also, a more *Compendious* and *Accurate Exposition* of the *Terms* of the *Common Law* (interspers'd throughout) than any hitherto extant, containing many *important Words* of Art used in *Law Books*.

Collected out of the best Authors, by *F. O.*

THE LAWBOOK EXCHANGE, LTD.
Clark, New Jersey

ISBN 978-1-58477-377-1

Lawbook Exchange edition 2004, 2018

The quality of this reprint is equivalent to the quality of the original work.

THE LAWBOOK EXCHANGE, LTD.
33 Terminal Avenue
Clark, New Jersey 07066-1321

Please see our website for a selection of our other publications and fine facsimile reprints of classic works of legal history:
www.lawbookexchange.com

Library of Congress Cataloging-in-Publication Data

F.O.

The law-French dictionary alphabetically digested, to which is added the law-Latin dictionary: very useful for all young students in the common laws of England / collected out of the best authors by F.O.

p. cm.

Definitions given in English for Norman-French and Latin terms.
Originally published: London: Isaac Cleave/John Hartley, 1701.
ISBN 1-58477-377-4 (cloth: alk. paper)

1. Law—England—Dictionaries—Anglo-Norman dialect—Early works to 1800. 2. Anglo-Norman dialect—Dictionaries—English—Early works to 1800. 3. Law—England—Dictionaries—Latin—Early works to 1800. 4. Latin language—Dictionaries—English—Early works to 1800. I. Title.

KD313.F1262003
340'.03—dc2l 2003052783

Printed in the United States of America on acid-free paper

THE

Law-French DICTIONARY

Alphabetically Digeſted;

Very uſeful for all young STUDENTS in the *Common Laws* of *ENGLAND*.

To which is added,

THE

Law-Latin Dictionary:

Being

An *Alphabetical Collection* of ſuch *Law-Latin* Words as are found in ſeveral *Authentic Manuſcripts*, and Printed *Books* of *Precedents*, whereby *Entring-Clerks*, and others, may be furniſhed with *fit* and *proper Words*, in a *Common Law Senſe*, for any thing they ſhall have occaſion to make uſe of, in *Drawing Declarations*, or any parts of *Pleading*. Alſo, a more *Compendious* and *Accurate Expoſition* of the *Terms* of the *Common Law* (interſpers'd throughout) than any hitherto extant, containing many *important Words* of Art uſed in *Law Books*.

Collected out of the beſt Authors, by *F. O.*

LONDON,

Printed for *Iſaac Cleave*, at *Serjeants-Inn* Gate in *Chancery-Lane*; and *John Hartley*, over-againſt *Gray's-Inn* in *Holborn*. 1701.

THE PREFACE.

Forasmuch as the reading of the Later and Modern Reports, without the knowledge of the Ancient Writers of the English *Laws, will hardly shew the true grounds and reasons of them; and since most Students are at a loss to find the true Interpretation and Meaning of many Words (used by Authors who have Written thereof in the* Law French) *which are taken in a different sense, and no* Dictionary *of this kind being yet made publick; I have therefore, for the Use and Ease of all Young Students in the* Common Law, *collected out of many Authors, and composed Alphabetically, all or most part of the Words generally used by them as* Law French, *and given the meaning thereof as near as I could in* English. *It cannot be expected that they should be Grammatically declined or put into all Cases and Tenses; but in some places I have shewn the several Tenses of divers Verbs, as the Word* dier, *to say,* &c. *by by which others may be eaſily gueſſed at. And becauſe ſome Words are diverſly uſed by ſeveral Authors, I have therefore ſet down the ſeveral ways, whereby they are uſually accepted and expreſſed, and have added the Author's Names and Folios, and the ſeveral Impreſſions of their Books. So that the Student may have recourſe thereunto, and may the better apprehend the true Sence of the Words as they were intended.*

F. O.

THE
Law-French
DICTIONARY

A. To, *a ſcavoir*, to know *a dire*, to ſay.

A, by, *a Tort*, by wrong; and from, *a Ceſtuy* from him.

A, at, *Tenant a volunt*, Tenant at will.

A, for, *a cauſa de cy*, for this reaſon. *Covient a, eux*, it is neceſſary for them. *per Perkins* 55.

A fils et a fits d' roy, For the King's Daughter or Sons.

A, Is the third Perſon ſingular of the Verb. Viz. *J'ay*, I have, *tu as*, Thou haſt, *il a*, He hath, *ſi ayes*, if ye have. *per Crompton* 223 b.

Le Reigne, *a*; the Queen hath, *ſi a de bien*, if he hath Goods, *En ſon Ewe que a*, in his Waters which he hath, *per Crompton* 162, b.

A la Ville, to the Town, *a*, is alſo taken for like or after, as *Alamode*, after the Faſhion.

A, is ſometimes taken for *In* or *E n*, in the faſhion.

A la Preſence, in the Preſence.

A, is ſometimes uſed for *Avec*, with, viz. *a peu perd*, with ſmall loſs.

Que a, who hath, *p. Crompt. Jur. Cur.* 188, a.

Aage, age, *Laage de ung an*, a Year old, *Tout ung Aage*, all one Age, *Eſt pluis Aage q'autre*, he is older than the other.

Abaiſſer, to bring low, caſt down or abate.

Abbaiſſer, idem.

Abbandon, leaving, *abbandoner aſcun*, to deſert or leave one, *abandonaunts*, idem.

Abaſaunts, debaſeing.

un Abathie, an Abbey, *un Abby*, idem.

Abbe, an Abbot, from *Abba*, ſignifying Father.

Abbeſſe, an Abboteſs.

Abater & Abatre, to quaſh, deſtroy, beat down, or pull up by the roots.

Abbatu, thrown down, proſtrated, *Boys abate*, Wood cut or fallen, *p. Coke, Rep.* 5, 25, a.

Abbater, to demoliſh or throw down, *Abbater arbres*, to fell trees, *Abatre*, idem. *per Plowd. Com.* 316, b. & *p. Briton* 31, a.

Abatue & *Abatus*, thrown down.

Abatu per vent, blown down, *p. Nov. Narr.* 16, b.

Abate, is alſo a term in Law, uſed upon a wrongful entry, or detaining the poſſeſſion of Lands.

Abatement, wrongful entring, it is alſo a Term in Heraldy, denoting ſome mark or ſtain in Arms.

Abatement, of a Writ or Plaint for uncertainty, *Miſnomer*, &c.

Un abator, is he who wrongfully enters upon Lands or Tenements upon the Death of Tenant in Fee; He who ſo enters upon the Death of Tenant for Life or Years, is called an Entruder.

Abbaiaunce, reſpite, or in expectation, *abayance*, idem.

Abaizance idem, *ſicut in nubibus*, a thing in the conſideration of the Law, or in its diſpoſition. 2. *Hen.* 7, 13. a.

Abaſaunts, abaſeing.

Abeiſſe & *Abbeiſſe*, abated, Leſſened, *p. Nov. Narr.* 7, a.

Abbayer, to bark as a Dog, *abbaye*, barking as a Hound, when a Deer turns head, he is ſaid to be at bay.

Abbeſſed, caſt down, humbled, *p. Phillips.*

Abece, the Alphabet.

Abbreyer, to ſhorten, contract, or epitomize.

Abbrege, ſhortned, contracted.

Abbettours, aiders, aſſiſtants, *abbettaunts*, aiding or aſſiſting, *abbettaſt*, had aſſiſted or abetted. *p. Plowd. Com.* 390. b.

Abbuver, to give Water, *abruver les Chevaux*, to water Horſes.

Un abbrevoir, a Watering place.

Abdicate, to renounce or refuſe,

Abhorrer, to deteſt.

Abject, caſt down, *choſe abject*, a vile thing.

Abille, & *Abiller*, vide, *Habille* & *Habiller.*

Ablution, waſhing away, cleanſing.

Abjurer, to forſwear, to recant, or deny.

Abjurement, denying renouncing.

Aboler & *Abolir*, to root out, to aboliſh.

Aboli hors d'uſage, aboliſh'd, out of uſe.

Aboliſſement, aboliſhing.

Abogen, bowed.

Abominer, to deteſt, to abhor.

Abondant, moreover, furthermore.

Aborder, to apply to, to arrive at.

Aborderment, bordering, or arriving at.

Aboutir; to draw to, alſo to ſet or make boundaries or limits of Lands, &c.

Les Aboutiſſants, the limits or bounds.

Aboutiſſements, idem.

Abſcondre & *Abſconder*, to hide.

Que abſents, who are away.

Abrogée, put away, *Abroger*, to put away.

Abſince, & *abſcynte*, Wormwood.

Abſouldre & *Abſoul*, to forgive or pardon.

Abſouls & *abſoulbs*, forgiven, pardoned.

Abſtenir, to forbear.

Aſtrus, & *Abſtruce*, hidden, difficult.

Abſurd, inconvenient, fooliſh.

Abuſion,

Abusion, abuse, *p. Mirror Instit. Wrong*, Cap. 5. Sect. 2.

Un abysme, a bottomless Pit.

A C.

Accrester, to happen, to accrew.

Accreste, encreased, accrewed.

Puit accreste, may happen, *p. Fitzh. nat. brev.* 185, a.

Accesser, to assess, *Accessont sur enquest*, the Jury assess, *p.* 2. *Edw.* 5. 3.

Accerte, found. *p. Nov. Narr.* 65, b.

Accordant, agreeable, according to.

Accort, heedy, wary.

Accoller, to embrace.

Accomplir, to finish or fulfil.

Accomplice, fulfilled.

Accoster, to draw near, to be familiar with.

Accoucher, to lye, *Accouchement*, lying down.

Accoutre, to dress, deck or adorn, *accouster*, idem.

Accreve, encreased, *acereu* idem.

Achemine, went along with, proceeded. *p. Coke, rep.* 9. 120 b.

Achater, to buy, *achator*, a buyer, *acheter*, idem.

Achate, bought, purchased, *achapt*, idem.

Achete, idem. *achatamus*, wee bought.

Acheson, hurt, damaged.

Accoinct, very necessary or familiar.

Accomoder, to lend, *accomoda*, lent.

Accompaigner, to keep company with.

Accompter, to reckon, *vous accomptes*, ye shall be accompted, or reckoned with. *p. Kitchin* 54, b.

Accorder, to agree, *d'accorder*, of the agreement.

Accordant, agreeing, *doit accorder*, ought to agree.

Accoster, to prop or hold up.

Accoustomer, to be used or accustomed.

Accoustomee, used. *p. Coke, rep.* 9, 120.

Accresser, to happen, vide *accrester*.

Accrest, to encrease or grow.

Accrust, hath happened or accrewed. *p. Plowd. Com.* 203.

Accrocher, to apprehend, to pull or draw to, to hook, vide *Encroche*.

Acenseur, a Farmer, *acensement*, a letting to Farm.

Acertes, in good earnest, truly.

Aceres, Maple trees. *p. Coke. rep.* 4, 62.

Achevement, an obtaining or acquiring.

Achemine, accomplished.

Acheteur vide, *Achator*, a buyer

Acier, Steel.

Acoup, sudden, or suddenly

Serra accouple, shall be joyned.

Acquerir, to get, to obtain.

Acquis, got or obtained. *Biens acquis*, goods gotten or obtained.

Acquisser, to receive, gather, *p. Fitzh. gr. abr.* 2. *pt. fol.* 5. a.

Acre, sharp in tast. *Acrimonie*, sharpness.

Acquiter, & *Aquiescer*, to acquit, also to agree to, or stand to.

Acqueister, to pacifie or make quiet.

Acrestra, shall fall or happen, *p. Briton* 92, b.

Un acte, an authority of Court.

Actif, busie, active.

Actuel, ready, speedy, effectual.

Actuelment & *actualment*, presently, out of hand.

Accomplissement, fulfilling.

Aquitte, released, absolved, *acquite de son serement*, absolved of his Oath.

Accrust, accrewed, happened.

A D.

Ad, hath and had.

Ad ewe, hath had.

Ad a fair, had to do.

Ad este, hath been.

Adage, an old saying, *cest un conion adage*, it is a common saying.

Adayer, to provoke.

Adayement, a provocation.

Addonne, given to.

Un addoubeur, a promoter, or setter up of Causes.

Addoulcir, to asswage or mitigate.

Addoulciment, mitigating or asswaging.

Addoulcissement, idem.

Ades, by and by, anon.

Ademain, to morrow.

Adeprimes, at the beginning, at first.

Adiprimes, idem. *p. Termes Ley.* 240, a.

Adderere, belonged unto, *p. Nov. Narr.* 65. b.

Adereign, put in order, tryed, arraigned.

Adevant, before, before such time, *p. Plowd. abr.* 18.

Adieu, farewel. *p. Kitchin* 7, a.

Adherer, to stick or cleave to.

Adjourner, to give, or appoint another day.

Adire, to say, or speak to.

Adjouster, to put to, add, or reckon, to make even, *adjuster*, idem.

Adjoust, added, set right. *p. Plowden's preface.*

Adjudger, to give Judgment, *adjudgera*, shall judge.

Adjoignant, joyning unto.

Adresser, to resort unto, to have recourse unto, *Adress*, idem.

l'Admirante, the Admiralty.

Admis, admitted, *Admetre*, to admit.

Administer, to direct, dispose, or govern.

Administrateur, he that doth direct or administer.

Admoneste, charged, admonished warned, *p. Brit.* 60. b.

Adjure, to swear to.

Admirablement, wonderfully.

Adonc, then, at that time, *adonques*, idem.

Adopter, & *prendre a filz*, to adopt or make one his son, *adoptif*, chosen, adopted.

Adorer, to worship, *adorateur*, a worshiper.

Adosser, to lean against any thing.

Adroit home, a right or fit man.

Adnuller, to make void or destroy.

Adowel, ought to have.

Advenir, to happen, or fall out.

Advertizer, to give notice.

Adventure, chance accident.

Advenant, according, fitting, *Il est jeune* & *Gaillard a l'advenant*, he is young and lusty accordingly.

Advenu, come to pass, *advenement*, happening also, a chance.

Advenues, the passages, or entries, *Garder les advenues*, watch the access or entries.

Advint, happened.

Advowterer, an adulterer, *un adultere*, idem.

Advowry, vide *avowry*.

Advertir, to give notice, or to admonish.

Advertissement, admonition.

Adveu, faith or fidelity.

Advover, to vouch, confess, or own.

Advover quelque crime, to a vow any fault.

Adyre, to say, or speak. *p.* 1. *Hen.* 7, 9. b.

A E.

Ael, a Grandfather, *ail*, idem.

Aele, a Grandmother.

Aererer, to plow or plowing, vide *airer*.

Aerin, brass, *airaine* idem. & *airain*, idem. *p. Termes de Ley.* 179, & 251.

Aeier, steele, *aery*, the nest of Hawks, *airy*, idem.

Aestime capitis, a forfeiture in case of Murther. It is said by *Blunt*, that in an Assembly at *Exeter*, King *Athelstan* declared that the Mulct for killing the King should be 30000 *Thrimsæ*, of an Arch-bishops head or Princes 15000, of a Bishop or Senate, 8000 of a Priests or Thanes head, &c. and that a *Thrimsa* was the 4th part of a *Saxon* shilling.

A. F.

Affaire, to be had, made, or taken. *p. Fitzh. Nat. brev.* 167, a.

Affair, business.

Affame, famished, starved.

Affectate, wilful. *p. Plowd. Com.* 12, a.

Affermer, to make sure, to stablish, to fortify; also to let to Farm. *affirmer*, idem.

Affiert, it behoveth, or belongeth. *p.* 2. *Hen.* 7, 9, a.

Affier, set, taxed, assessed, confirmed.

Afferer, to tax or assess. *p. Coke rep.* 8, 39, a.

Afferont, they belong.

Affectuous, desirous. *p. Plowd. Com.* 306. b.

Affiont, trusting. *p. Kitchin.* 174, b.

Affirrours, Persons who tax or assess such amerciaments as are set in inferiour Courts.

Affins, kindred by Marriage.

Affinage, refining Metals.

Affraies, fightings, assaults.

Affranchir, to set free.

Affries, implements, tools.

Affries de son carve, implements of his Plough, *termes de ley* 246.

Afgodess, impiety, ungodlyness. *Saxon. p. Phillips.*

A G.

Agast, dismaid with fear, also wasted.

Agait, waiting, *gist en agait*, he lyeth in wait.

Agaitz, Idem.

Agard, awarded, *le agard*, the award.

Agir, to go, *agisant*, lying.

Agister, to put into, to go in or to depasture or lay in, *agist*, Idem.

Agistment, is the laying in of Cattle, to go and depasture or feed by the month or week, and is called *tacking*.

Aggregation, a gathering or assembling together, *aggreger*, to assemble, or gather.

Aggrandir, to make great, to enlarge.

Agglue, joyned or congealed.

Aggravee, vexed, made hainous.

Aggresseur, the first who does the offence, or gives cause of it.

Agrarian law, a Roman law to distribute lands among the common People.

Agreeont, they agree.

Agrestical, clownish, rude.

Agneau, a Lamb, *agnels* & *agnes*, lambs, *agneler* to yean or bring forth lambs.

Aguir, to guide. *p. stat. confirm. Cart.* 25. *Edw.* 1.

Aguille, a Needle.

Agniser, to acknowledge, *agnize* & *agnise*, acknowledged. *p. Coke* 8, 116.

Aguillet, a point or sharp end.

Aguiser, to sharpen whet or grind.

Ahontir, to shame, *ahonter un home*, to abash or make one ashamed.

Aherda soy, joyned himself unto. *p. Plowden.* 262, a.

A. I.

Aid prier, to pray in aid or assistance.

Aider, to help or assist, *aidre*, idem.

Al aid de dieu, the help of God.

Si vous aid dieu, so help ye God.

Jeo aie, I have. *p. Fitzh. nat. Brev.* 184. b.

Ajants, having, *nientayant*, they have not.

Aiet, he shall have. *p. Crompt. Jur. Cur.* 17, b.

Come ait este dit, as hath been said.

Aincientment, anciently.

Qui aid, he who helpeth.

Lever aids sur le sujets, to raise aids upon the Subjects.

Un aigle, an Eagle.

Aigre, sharp, eager.

Ailours, elsewhere, otherwise.

Aillours, ailleurs, & *aylors*, idem *p. Briton.* 32, a.

Ail, a Grandfather, vide *ael.*

Ailess, a Grandmother, *aele*, idem.

Ainsi, even so, after the same manner, so that, unless.

Ainsi come, even as it were.

Dit ainsi, he said so, or thus, *ainsi*, thus.

Ainsi soit il, so be it, *il estainso*, it is so.

Aimant, a Loadstone,

Taillours des aimans, cutters of Diamonds. *p. stat. art. sup. Cartas Cap.* 20.

Aimer, to love, *amer*, idem.

Aireau, a Plough, *airant*, Plowing, Tilling.

Airaine, brass. *p. termes de Ley*, 180, b.

Ais, a board.

Aier, steele.

Aile, a wing, *aile de Oyseau*, the wing of a Bird.

Aire, the nest of a Hawk or Bird of game.

Ait, he hath.

Aisne, first born, *aisne fitz*, eldest Son.

Aisnee fille, eldest Daughter.

Aisnesse le droit, the right of the first born.

Aisement, speedily, quickly.

A. L.

Al, to, *al mon pre*, to my meadow. *p. Kitch.* 35, a.

Ala, goeth, *est ala*, he is gone, *Fitzh. Nat. brev.* 97, a. and also brought.

Il

Il alaſt, he went, or he goeth, *p. Coke rep.* 8, 37, a.

Alaſſent countre, they ſhould go againſt. *p. Mirr. Inſt.*

Alant avant, they have gone forth.

Avers alantes, Cattle going.

Vous alaſtes, ye have gone, *ale* gone, went.

Ale & tout defail, gone and quite ſpoiled.

Alangeor vide *Languer.*

Aleblaſtre, Aleblaſter.

Aleigeance, fidelity, alſo alledging.

De aler, of the other. *p. Hen.* 6. *annal.*

Aleconner, an Ale-taſter, an Officer who takes care of the Aſſize of Ale and Victuals.

Aler & aller, to go, or to take a Journey.

Leſſe aler, let go, *alera* ſhall go.

Aler en quelque lieu, to go to any place.

Aller a port, to go to the gate.

Aller verſui aſcun, to go towards one.

Alay vide *Aloy.*

Le aler, the bringing, *de ny aler*, not to go.

Alegent, they ſhall alledge.

Aliener, to ſell, *aliene*, ſold, vide *Eſtranger.*

Alienee, the buyer, *alienation*, ſelling.

Allee & venue, to go and come.

Alience, confederacy combination, *Aliaunce*, idem.

Almoignes, *Alms*, *pour almoigne*, for Alms.

Almoygne & almognez, idem. *almner*, vide *aumoner.*

Alme, Soul, *almes*, Souls.

Alont hors, they went out, *alomus* we went.

Alodium, a free manner, *p. part* 1. *Inſt.* 5, a.

Alt, high.

Alveys, Alder-trees, vide *poſtea.*

Alloynd, ſtolen, hid, concealed or chaſed away.

Alloyners, they who hide, ſteal, conceal, &c. *p. Briton* 26, B.

Alloyner, to chaſe or drive away.

Aylienont, they put off, or deferr.

Alien, one born out of the King's dominions.

Allies & alliez, Kindred, confederates.

Alors, there, at that time, or in that place.

Aloy, a value on Gold or Silver, or addition of ſome baſer Metal, the Mixture, or temper of Metals.

Alternif, that which is done by turn, one after another.

Alternativement, by courſe or turn.

Alterquer, to wrangle.

Alun, Allom.

Alveys ſegs, flags, alſo Alder-trees. *p. Nov. Nar.* 5, a.

Allyeant, they bind.

Alleynours, they who make ſale.

Altercation, controverſie, diſpute.

A. M.

Amer, to love, *aimer*, idem. *amer* is alſo bitter.

Ama d' aler bravement, love to go fine.

Ament, they love, *de amer*, for to love.

Ames, Friends, *amies*, idem.

Amiee, beloved.

Ambu-

Ambages, a circuity of words, or a long idle or foolish discourse. *p. Coke rep.* 11, 29.

Ambideux, both.

Ambrey, a Cup-board.

Amene, brought, *ameni*, idem.

Amena, idem, *sera amenus*, shall be brought.

Amender, to make better, *ne amenisse*, may not be amended, *amendez* in modern *French* is to buy.

Amercie, amerced, *amercy*, idem. *sont amercies*, are amerced, *estre-amercie* to be amerced.

Amestie, freindship, kindness.

Amnestie, a forgetting injuries.

Amesna, brought also lead or carryed away or drove, *amesne*, idem, *est amesnable*, to be brought or carryed. *p. Fitzh. Justice*, 12, b.

Amesner, to bring, lead or drive.

Vous amesneres, ye may bring.

Amesnera, shall bring, carry, &c.

Il amenusoit, he may bring. 21. *Hen.* 7, 28, a.

Amesner son host, to lead his Army.

Amasser, to heap up or lay together.

Amour love, *a mort* dead, thence.

A la Mort, sitting Melancholy,

Amoler, to melt, *amollir*, idem. and to make soft, *amolir*, idem. *p. termes Ley.* 116.

Amortizer, to alien lands to a body Politique.

Ample, broad, large.

Amplier, to encrease, to enlarge.

Amputer, to cut, *amputation*, cutting.

Amortir, to alien Lands to a Corporation.

Amont & a mount, upwards.

Amplie, encreased,.

Amplement, largely, fully.

Amuzement, gazing.

Amuzer ascun, to put one in a study, or to busy one's thoughts.

Amenuiser, to make thin, or lean, or to be slender, *amoindrir*, idem.

Amortissement, giving lands to a Corporation or body Politick, being then said to be in dead hands, against which the statute of *Mortmain* was made.

A N.

An, a Year, *Anne*, idem. *le an*, the Year, *ung an*, one Year, *deux ans*, two Years, *de an in an*, from Year to Year, *demi an*, half a Year, *de anten*, of the last Year.

Annates, the first Years Fruit paid out of the Church-livings.

Anarchie, a common Wealth without a Chief.

Ancelle, a Maid-sevant.

Ancestres, ancestors.

Ancien, old, *le pluis ancien de touts*, the oldest of all.

Antique temps, old time, *antic*, idem.

Ancre, an Anker.

Angleterre, England.

Ankes, Geese. *p. Brokes Gr. abr.* 144.

Anient & Anyent, defeated, recovered against, also barred and annulled. *p. Greg.* 296, b. & *Parkins.*

Aniente, void, being of no force. *p. Fitzh. Nat. brev.* 214. b.

Aneantir, to make void.

Anient anslerment, utterly void.

Anienter, to defeat, stop, or throw out. *p.* 3. *part. Inst.* 119.

Anientisment,

Anientisiment, destruction, making void or annulling, *anichilling*, making void.

Anuels livers, year books of the Laws.

Anuels livers, idem.

Anuel, a Ring, *anel*, idem.

Anuels & anneux, Rings.

Anuelment, yearly, *annuele*, idem.

Anuelx & annuelx, Rings, *p. Parkins* 17, b.

Anz, years, vide *ans*.

Anoya, hurt, mischief,

Anyent idem, *ut aniont*.

Anguille, an Eele.

Anui, to day.

Annexee, joyn'd, coupled.

Aoust, the month of *August*. vide *Aust*, idem.

Aore, now. *p. Plowd.* 12, a.

A. P.

Aparluy, by himself, *aperluy*, idem.

Apanage, the settlement given to the young Children of Princes, *apennage*, idem.

Apay, contented, satisfyed. *p. Fitzh. Nat. brev.* 186, b.

Apparels, ready provided, fitted.

Apparust, had appeared.

Come apparoissoit, as it appeared. *p. Coke. rep.* 9, 120.

Apeu, a few, *apee* one foot.

Aper, a Boar, *p. Coke* 8. *rep.* 138.

Appergeront, they appear, *apperge*, shall appear. *p. Coke part.* 10, 100. *Plowd. Com.* 63, b.

Apertment, openly, publickly, also severally, a-part.

Aperceu, perceived, found. *p. Britton* 139, a.

Aperluy, by himself, *Coke rep.* 5, 58.

Apeler & appeller, to Cite or call before a Judge.

Apprimes, first.

Appel, called, or cited; also where one sues, being next of kin to a Person Murthered, which Appeal must be brought within a Year and a Day after the fact is committed.

Appellomus, we cite or call before.

Aportet, it ought, or needeth, *come aportz*, as it ought.

Appellant, he that cites or calls, *appelle*, he that's cited.

Appeller, vide *approver*.

Jeo appelloi, I have called, *sont appelles*, are called.

Appels, called or cited.

Violont apelle, they would cite. *p.* 1. *Hen.* 7, 5. b.

Appeller dieu a testimoignage, to call God to witness.

Appellement, calling or citing.

Appenses, hung, fixed.

Appent, belonging to, *appendant*, idem.

Apenage, vide *Apanage*.

Il appient, it belongeth, *il appent*, idem, also it ought.

Appent a la journes, belonging to their Oaths, *p. Coke rep.* 8, 39, a.

Il appiert & appert, it appeareth, or is manifest.

Il apierge, idem.

Apperoit, he should appear. *p. Britton* 47.

Appetite, desire, *appetant*, desirous, greedy.

Appier, to appear, *ne appiert*, he doth not appear.

Apposes, questioned, demanded, interrogated.

Appoſer, to queſtion, demand, &c. *eſteant appoſe*, being queſtioned, &c. *p.* 4. *Hen.* 7, 2. a.

Appoincter, to direct, appoint, *appoinct*, directed.

Apres, after, *venir apres*, to follow after.

En apres, hereafter, afterwards, moreover, farthermore.

Apres que, after which, *cy apres*, after that.

Apprender, to learn, to apprehend.

Apprendre, to take, *proffit, apprendre*, taking or receiving profit.

En apprent, it is taught or ſaid.

Nous apprenons, we have advice.

Apprendes, learn ye, underſtand ye.

Appreſter, to prepare, *appreſt*; prepared.

Appreſmidi, afternoon.

Approver, to proſecute, to prove or give evidence, *un aprover*, is one that takes upon him to juſtifie or prove a Crime, to be done, either by battel, or in a Writ of right, or otherwiſe by proof in criminal Cauſes.

Approve, vouch'd, or currently owned.

Appriſe, learned, ſkill'd, *appriſe in la ley*, learned in the law, *appriſes*, idem.

Apris, underſtood, alſo valued, appriſed. *p.* 1. *Hen.* 7, 5. a.

Apprompter, to borrow, *Apprompt*, borrowed, *ad aprompt*, hath taken, borrowed, or truſted with. *p. Yelverton* 22.

Approcher, to draw nigh.

Approper, to appropriate, or order to a particular uſe.

Apprope, any thing ſo ordered, *appropre*, idem.

Approperment, properly.

Appropriation, when Tithes or Lands are in the hands of Spiritual perſons, they are ſaid to be appropriated.

Lour appries, their own proper.

Approwe, to improve or make better by tilling Land, or incloſeing. *p. Fitzh.* 149. *Nat. brev.*

Aptment, fitly, aptly.

Appeter, to deſire, to wiſh for.

Appenſer, to think or conſider.

Appenſe, forethinking, or conſidering.

Aqueous, wateriſh, *Aquoſity*, wateriſhneſs.

Aquatiques & *Aquatile*, that live in the Water.

Aqueduct, a Conduit that conveys water by a Pipe, &c.

A R.

Arable, plowed Land.

Arace, to deface.

Arage, Mad, Diſtracted. *Brit.* 39.

Arages, Mad-men. *p. Brit.* 17. a.

Arain, Braſs.

Aracher, to root up, to tear up, *arache*, pull'd up by the roots, *arachement de bois*, ſtocking up Wood. *p. termes de Ley*, 27, b.

Arayer, to put in order, *aray*, Apparel.

Arbitrer, to award, *un arbitre*, an award.

Arbitreront, they awarded.

Arbre, a tree, *Arbres*, trees, *arbres fruictiers*, fruit-trees, *arber*, a wood alſo.

Archives, ancient Records, and alſo the places where they are kept.

Archievesque, an Archbishop, *archieveshies*, Archbishopricks. *p. Fitzh.* Justice, 188. b.

Arcter, to force, to bind, to compel, *arcts*, bound or forced, *arctera*, shall bind or force.

Arctable, forcible, *sont arctes*, are forced. *p. Compton* 5. *Jur. Cur.* 42, b. b. 43.

Arc, a Bow, *ark*, idem, *arc tend*, bow bent.

Arc de un pont, the Arch of a Bridge.

Un arcenal, an Armory, or Store-house for Arms.

Arche, a Chest, or Box.

Arden, a Wood, or Woodland.

Arder, to burn, *arda*, burned, *ardè*, idem.

Ardant, burning; *Ferveux arde*, burning hot.

Ardus, burned, *arses*, idem, & *arse*, idem.

Arere, again, behind, back, or left.

Aremain, idem, *aler in arrere*, to go backwards, or behind.

Aret, an Account, *arretted*, charg'd with a Crime.

Arere luy, behind him. *p. Coke.*

Arerissement, hindrance, *arress*, idem. *p. Coke, rep.* 8, 128, b.

Arrerie, hindred. *p. Britton*, 35, a.

Arene, Gravel.

Arroy & *array*, ordering or accoutring Soldiers.

Armes de quel, with what Weapons.

Arranger, to put in order, *arraine*, idem.

Arete, taken or charg'd with some Crime.

Aret & *areste*, idem, & *arret*, idem, *arretted*, idem. *p. nov. narr.* 59. b.

Array Challenge, is excepting against a Jury Empanelled or Arrayed, *i. e.* put in order; as when a Peer is Party, and no Knight Retorned or Unpanelled.

Argent, Silver, also Money, *vif argent*, Quicksilver.

Argent est cause de ceo, Money is the Cause of all this.

Argil, Clay, Lime, and sometimes Gravel, also the Lees of Wine, gathered to the hardness of Stones.

Argoil, idem.

Arquebuse, a Hand-gun, a Caliver.

Arguer, to Dispute.

Armie, Armed.

Arpen, an Acre, *arpent*, idem, also a Furlong. *p.* 1. *Part. Insti.* 5. b.

Arorez, Fodder, Soil, Compost. *p. Kitchin.* 59. a.

Arondelle, a Swallow.

Arras, earnest given in part on a Bargain.

Arrer, to Plow, *arer*, idem.

Arre, Plowed.

Arrect, imputed to, or charged with. *Coke* 7, 6, b.

Arester, to detain or withold one from Liberty.

Arrestres, ye should take into Custody.

Arundinetum, a place where Reeds grow. *Instit.* 4.

Arser, to burn, *arsure*, burning, *le arsar le maine*, the burning the Hand.

Arte vide *arcte*, forced. 2 *Rich.* 3, 14.

Artique, North, *artic*, idem.

As, to, into, amongst.

As, joyn'd to a Plural is Plural, and signifies to.

As Justices, to the Justices, *as tu cel*, hast thou this, *as*, is the plural of *A*.

Asne, an Ass.

Aspirer, to breath, *respirer*, idem.

Aspre, sharp, tart.

Asavoir, to be known, or understood.

Assavoir & *ascavoir*, idem, also (to wit) *cest ascavoir*, (that is to say). p. *Parkins* 62, a.

Fet ascavoir, to be made understand.

Ascun, some one, any, *vide aucun*.

Ascuns & *aucuns*, plurals.

Assay, try, *assayed*, tryed to bear the Test.

Assoy, idem, *en assaiant de harneis*, in trying or fitting of Armour. p. *Crompt. Jur. Cur.* 72, b.

Assaut, Assault.

Ascavanter, to certifie, or make known.

Asceverer, to affirm.

Ascriber, to write.

Ascient, knowing.

Assess, rated, set, limitted, *ass* & *assesse*, idem. p. 1 *Hen*. 5, 3.

Assetz, enough or sufficient, *assez*, idem.

Teignount Asietz, they hold it sufficient. *Plowd. R.* 16, b.

Assembler, to come together, *assoner*, idem.

Assentont, they agreed.

Assentez, agreed, assented.

Assart, eraced, *assert terres*, are lands joyning to a Forest or Chase, and converted into Tillage, or Pasture, formerly woody Ground Stock'd up and enclos'd, being *assart*, i. e. eraced by the Tenants, also Land improv'd.

Pour assertez, for converting Wood-lands into Arable or Pasture, *de asser*, to improve. p. *Brit.* 184. & 40.

Un assees, a Woodcock.

Assiduement, frequently, earnestly.

Assigner, to assign.

Est assise, is affirred, or assessed.

Assoicierant, they go or gather together.

Assoiler, to Absolve, or forgive.

Assoile, Absolved, forgiven. *Coke rep.* 8, 68.

Assoiles a Moy, pardon me. p. 2. *Rich.* 3. 14.

Assouther, to acquit, *assouth*, acquitted.

Assoynounts, Concubines. p. *Brit.* 248. b.

Assuredment, assuredly, certainly.

Asseu, fished, or sewed. p. *Nov. Nar.* 48.

Aster, and *home aster*, a Man that is resident; it seems to come from *astre*, or *atre*, an hearth. p. *Britton* 151. & p. *Nov. Nar.*

Astre, in Modern *French* is a Star.

Asur, Blue, Sky-Colour.

Astrint, costive, bound.

Astre, by *Britton* is an Hearth, *atre*, idem. p. *Nov. Nar.*

Asyle, a Sanctuary, or place of refuge for Offenders.

A T.

Atcheivement, performing some great exploit.

Attainder,

Attainder, to Impeach or Accuse in Court, or to convict of high Crimes.

Attaine, brought, Commenced. *p. Britton.* 120.

Attaindre, to bring to pass, or attain to.

Attacher, to fasten on, to arrest.

Attache, fixed unto. *p. Plowden* 323. *attachent*, they take or arrest, *serra attach*, shall be taken.

Attaints, Convicted, Attainted.

Attempter, to go about any Act, *Ne attempteroit*, he should not attempt. *p. Mirror Justic.*

Attempt en action, a Suit brought *de un attemptate*, of one who designs to bring or do. *p. Plowden.*

Attender, to wait, to follow, *attent*, belonged to, *attient*, idem, *atteigne*, idem. *p. Parkins.* 115. a.

Attourner, to become tenant, to *attorne.*

Attreit, drawn unto. *p. Coke rep.* 11. 34.

Attamined, depending, or in being, brought. *p. Coke. rep.* 5. 47. b. *Chimins*, ways, *chimins male attyres*, ways out of repaire. *p. Britton* 31. a.

Attrapper, taken, seiz'd, *ne les peuvent pas attrapper*, they could be taken or apprehended. *p. Coke rep.* 9. 120.

A U.

Au, until, at, to, by, also, for.

Au ceo temps, until this time.

Au pluis, at most, *au quel*, to whom, *au fine*, to the end, *au temps*, at the time.

Au amone, for Alms, *au dernier*, at the last.

Availe, advantage, *Person availe*, for his advantage.

Avance, preferr'd. *p. Greg.*

Avant, before, *avant le temps*, before the time.

Avanthier, the day before, or Yesterday.

Avant que il, before that. *Plowd. Com.* 313. b.

Avant maine, before hand. *p. Fitzh. Justic.* 20. b.

En avant, henceforwards, to come hereafter, *de icy en avant*, from this time forwards. *Plowd.* 309. b.

Suist avant, he sued forth.

Avenage, vide *appenage.*

Avage le Seignieur, let the Lord go. *p. termes Ley.* 174, b.

Le Availe, the benefit or profit. 26 *Hen.* 8, 9. b.

Audace, bold.

Avec, with, *avec se*, with that or this.

Avec quel, with whom. *p. Kitchin.*

Avecques, together with, *avec soy*, with him.

Avener, to come, *puit aveigner*, he may come.

Aveign, cometh, happeneth, *aveignes*, idem. *p. nov. nar.* 7. b.

Avenants, coming or happening. *p. Plowd. abr.* 16.

Avenage, rent Oats. *p. Phillips. avenor*, the King's Officer to provide Oats.

Avenes, Oats, *vide aveynes.*

Avegler, to blindfold, *aveagle*, blind.

Aver,

* *Aver*, to have; *avoir*, idem, *in Mod. French.*

Avera & avra, ſhall have, *averes*, ye ſhall have.

Est de aver, it is to ſay. *p. Coke.*

Re aver, to have again, *en avoir*, in having.

Vous aves imprist, ye have taken upon you.

Poit averer, he may have.

Averomus, we have, *jeo averay*, I may have, *jeo averoy*, idem, *avoy*, have had, *avomus*, we have. *p. Coke*, *avoyent*, they ſhould have. *p. Plowden.* 303. a.

Vous aves, ye have, words uſed in Court when Jurors appear, *i. e.* ye have appear'd.

Avers, Beaſts, Cattle.

Averpeny, Money contributed towards the King's Carriages.

Average, ſervice by Cattle, or Horſe Carriage, alſo Merchants, *retorne in Average*, to thoſe whoſe Goods are thrown overboard for the ſafety of the Ship.

En averuſt, in doubt or fear, *vide avroust.*

Aves, Birds.

Aveynes, Oats, *Avens*, idem, & *aveines*, idem.

Auferance, taking away.

Avel, broken off, cancelled. *p. More. rep.* 30.

Aventure, a thing fell out by chance.

Avenue, happen'd. *p. Britton* 3. b.

Augurim, foretelling, alſo Arithmetic. *p. Plowd.* 287.

Aviener, to come, *aviendra*, ſhall come or happen, *il avint*, it happen'd.

Avient, it cometh; alſo they have. *Plow. Com.* 396.

Avide, greedy, covetous.

Aujourdhuy, to day, this day.

Aviſement, Conſidering, Directing, Adviſing.

Aviſe, Adviſed, *vous ſois aviſes*, be ye Adviſed. *Brit.* 2. b.

Aule, a Hall, *vide Sale.*

Aulnegeor, he who Seals Woollen-cloth.

Aumone, Almes, *aumoigne*, idem. *p. Brit.* 2.

Aumoner, the King's Officer to diſtribute Alms to the Poor.

Aume & aulm, a Soul.

Un aulne, an Ell, *aulner*, a Meaſurer by the Ell, *aulnage*, Ell Meaſure.

Aunes, Meaſures, Gallons. *p. Brit.*

Arbre aulne, an Alder-Tree.

Aunceſter, the Father, Grandfather, or other Perſons under whom the Heir claimeth.

Auncient demeſne terres, are Lands contained in Domeſ-day Book, held of the Crown; which Book was compiled in the time of *Edward* the Confeſſor.

Avoidera, ſhall eſcape or avoid.

Avouch, to juſtifie, or maintain.

Aune, a word uſed for *inned* or carry'd, as Corn in Harveſt, *a barne* to Barn or Stack.

Avolſont le ſpics de frument, they gathered the Ears of Corn. *p. Plowd.*

Aupres, near, at or nigh, *aupres luy*, about him.

Aucun, ſome one, *aucuns*, ſome Plural.

Aucune ſoits, ſometimes, *aucunement*, ſomewhat.

Avengle, blind, *avenglement*, blinding.

Aveignont, they come.

Aulmosnier, an Almner, or *Almoner*.

Avises, discreet. *p. Stat. Art. sup. chart.*

Avissi, also, in like manner, *ausci* & *ausi*, idem.

Un auge, a trough.

Avower, to own, to justify, to maintain, *avowry*, owning or justifying, acknowledging, *il avowera*, she shall avow or justify, *de sa avowry demesn*, of his own confession or having owned, *avowastes*, ye have avowed.

Advouzen, *avowson*, or *advouson* the right of presentation to a Church. Note that an *advowson* will not pass in a Fine, under the title of Tenements. *p. Greg.* 282.

Au quel, to which.

Aurel & *auril* & *avril*, the month of *April*.

Auront, they have, *il aura*, he shall have. *p. Crompt. Jur. Cur.* 155, a.

Auricula, an Ear, *aures*, Ears.

Aust, the month of *August*, *Britton* 151, b.

Autant, as much, equal, so much, like as.

Autant il devoit, he ought as much, *ces choses sont autant al ung que a l'autre*, these things are as much to the one as to the other.

De autant pluis, so much the more.

Auter, other, *de auter* of the other.

Autiel forme, such a manner. *Coke* 5, 42.

Autour, about.

Autre, the other, *L'auter de apres*, next unto.

Auter foitz, other times, heretofore, some time past, *auterfoiz*, idem.

Les autres, the others, *autres*, idem.

D' autre part, of the other side.

En autre, to another, *a un autre foits*, at another time, *auter foits marie*, marryed again.

Autrement & *auterment*, otherwise. *p. Coke.*

Qui est autre, which belongeth to another.

Autryseer, surveyed. *p. Britton.*

Avens, Penthouses.

Un autheur, an Authour.

Autre soyl, another's Ground.

Aveugle, puzzle. 1. *Hen.* 7 15. b.

Automne & *Automnale*, Harvest time,

Autiel, another such, *Autielx*, such like. *Parkins* 112.

Avoid serra, shall be avoided.

Aux, to them, and *aux nous*, towards us. *p.* 2 *pt. Instit.* 639.

Auxi hault, so high, and as high. *Coke* 5, 26, a.

Aux quels, to which, or wherewith.

Auxi bien, as well as, so also besides. *Parkins* 180.

Auxi bien, so well.

Auxinct, and also, whereas.

Awaits, ambushments, vide *agayts*.

Awrusts, doubts, fears, *awroust*, doubtful.

Awrons, doubtful. *Plowd. Com.* 349.

En aweroust, in doubt, in fear.

En awer & *aweir*, idem.

Ayde vide *aid*.

Aydants, aiding.

Aye, have, *jeo Aye*, I have.

Ayant & *Aynt*, having.

Ayent,

Ayent, they have; *Ayet*, he should have. *p. Cromp. Jur. Cur.* 39. b.

Ayle, Grandfather, vide *aile.*

Ayeles & ayele, Grandmother.

Ayeul, idem, in Modern *French.*

Aylours, besides, elsewhere, otherwise.

Aylors vide *ailors.*

Ayrer, to Plow, vide *arrer.*

Ayres, Plowed.

Ayront, they sit to hatch or breed. *p. Coke rep.* 7, 17, b.

B. A.

B*Aailler*, to gape or yawn.

Baaillemont, gaping or yawning.

Babillard, a babler, or prater, *balatron*, idem.

Bague, a reward or bribe.

Bailwick & Bail, a County, liberty and jurisdiction.

Bailer, to commit, deliver or pawn.

Pur baile, for to deliver, *termes Ley*, 30, a.

Bail de seizin, livery of seizin *p. Britton*, 102, a.

Baila, delivered, *bailment*, delivering.

A bailer, to deliver, *bayler*, idem. *p. Kitchin* 136, a.

Bail, is derived from the Greek verb Βάλλω, id est *Mitto*, to let pass, *car celluy que beille. Mittit a se. bailes hors*, delivered out, *traditur in ballivo*, delivered upon bayl or keeping.

Bailours, sureties. 20 *Hen.* 7, 2, a.

Bagage, carriage, *bale*, a pack, *ballats*, little packs.

Baisser, to humble, to bring low, to stoop.

Baiser, to Kiss, *baise*, a Kiss, *baiseur*, a Kisser.

Baisa, Kissed. *p. nov. nar.* 7, a.

Baisement, Kissing.

Baiser la test, to bow the head.

Un bal, a daunce, *ballades* songs.

Un bale, a pack of Goods, &c.

Balen a Whale, *balaine & balene*, idem. *p. Britton*, 7, b.

Un balk, a ridge between two furrows of Land.

Un Baley, a broom or besom.

Bander, to tye, to bind,

Banir, to banish or put in exile.

Banissement, banishing.

La banque, the place to exchange Money, or the Bank, *banquier* a Banker.

Un banqueroute, a Person broke or decayed in his Estate a Bankrout.

Banquetement, feasting, *banqueter* to feast to banquet.

Barat, deceit, subtilty, wrangling.

Un baretter, a wrangler, one who setteth others at variance, *barateur* idem, and in the Law is one who stirs up suits and strife.

Barbaudier, a Brewer.

Balen, a Whale, *Balens*, plural. *balain & balene*, idem, *vide antea.*

Bandoner, to leave, to abandon.

Bandon, left to ones self, leaving.

Bank, a bench.

Bans, the publishing in the Church before Marriage, also the proclaiming any thing in publick places.

Barbe, a Beard, also Sheep.

Barbier, a Barber to shave.

Barbits barbytes, berbes, Sheep also.

Barbuytes & berbectes, idem.

Le

Le Barges, the roof of a House. *p. Coke. rep.* 5, 101, a.

Barcaria & Bercaria, a Sheep-coat.

Barkaria, a Tan-house.

Barkery, a liberty to take the barks of Trees.

Barateur a barater, a mover and maintainer of Suits, Quarrels, &c.

Barter & Baretre, to exchange.

Bareyes de Maison, the eaves of a House.

Barreaux de Maison, the bars or grates of a House.

Baron, a Husband, also a Peer of the Realm.

Prist baron, took to Husband.

En bar, in stay or stoppage.

Barrera, shall stop, stay, or barr.

Barreroit, should or ought to stay.

Un barton, a Mannor-house, also demesn Lands and the Fold-yards or Rick-yards thereof.

Barrets, quarrels. *p. Coke rep.* 8, 37, a.

Bas, low, humble, ignoble. *p. termes Ley* 12, b.

Basilique, a Royal Palace.

Un lieu bas, a low place.

Chambre bas, a Jakes.

Basseur, Lowliness, Humility.

Bas Cur, an out-yard or base Court.

Bastarder, to Basterdize.

Un bast, a Pack-saddle.

Un bastille, a Fort or Castle.

Un bastiment, a Building.

Baston, a Staff, Club, or Cudgel; also it is taken for a Pledge, or Security, also a Waiter upon a Prisoner. *p. Coke rep.* 9, 36.

Batel, a Barge, Boat or Trough. *p. Brokes gr. abr.*

Battel & batails, a Barge, Boat or Barges. *Coke* 5, 107.

Batella mare, Sea-banks.

Bater, Batre & Batter, to beat.

Battel, a form of Tryal by *Duell. lib. assize* 1. a.

Batus & Batu, beaten, *Bate*, id. *Coke* 7, 44, a.

Batture & batement, beating, *batante*, idem. *p.* 1 *Hen.* 7, f, 7, b.

Batist, hath beaten, *qui est batu*, he that is beaten.

Batures, stripes, blows.

Batewe & Batue, a boat or barge, *Bateux*, Boats or Barges. *p. Kitchin* 191. *bateau*, idem, in Modern French.

Baudemont, openly, fairly, *Britton* 140, a.

Un Baudroyuer, a currier of Leather.

Bayler, to deliver, idem *ut bailer*.

Ils bayleront, they delivered. *Plowd.* 391. a.

Baylerent, they should deliver. *p. Plowden.*

B E.

Beat, Blessed, *bearers*, in the Law, are Abetters or Maintainers. *p. Philips.*

Beal, well, *pluis beal*, very well, and by *Coke* 'tis more lawful. *rep.* 5, 31. a. and by some, is the most fair or fairest, *viz. p. Parkins* 97. a. And *fort beau*, very fair, vide *belle*.

Beau temps, a clear Season, fair Weather.

Beau coup moins, much less.

Beucoup, very much, *p. Coke rep.* 9, 121.

Bedell, an Aparitour, Messenger or Summoner, from *beadeau*.

Belement, idem. *ut baudement*, i. e. fairly.

Bele, well, in Health.

Belier, a Ram.
Beins, Goods, *beins & biens import*, goods carryed, *byens*, idem.
Benigne, favourable.
Bery & bury, the chief ſeat of a Mannor.
Berluſſer, a Gaſh or Cut. *p. termes Ley*, 179, b.
Berquerium & Bercueria, a Houſe to lay Tann in. *Coke* 5, f, *Inſt.*
Belle, fair, *belment*, fairly, *belement*, idem.
Un beofe & beufe, an Ox, vide *boefe.*
Beovets, Steers.
Berbits vide *barbits* Sheep, *un berbe*, a Sheep.
Beſants, talents of Gold, *p. Mirror Juſt.* alſo an ancient ſort of Coyn.
Beſoigne, needful, needeth, *Beſoignable*, needful, *beſoignes*, needs, buſineſs.
Si beſoigne, if need bee, *que il beſoignera*, if it ſhall need, *ne beſoigne*, it needs not.
Beſogne, Work, Workmanſhip, *beſognes*, the plural, *eſtre en la beſogne*, to be in the Work, *beſayle*, great Grandfather.
Beu, drank. *p. Britton* 42, b.
Bever, to drink, *beverer*, idem. *de bever*, idem. *p. Parkins* 43, a.
Bevent, they drink, *bevrage*, drinking.
Sans beyver, without drink. *p. Britton* 136, b.
Ne beyvent, they drink not. *p. eund.*
Il ad bever, he had drank.
Beutre, Butter, *buerre*, idem.
Ne aye beu, I have not drank. *Britton* 42, b.
Beliſtrer, to beg.
Benir acun, to bleſs one, or wiſh one well.
Un beovier, an Ox or Neat Herd.
Beſtiails, all manner of Cattle.

B I.

Bien, well, *byen*, idem.
Bien toſt, ſoon after, *lib. aſſize.* 213. b.
Biens vide *beins*, Goods.
Un biche, an Hound, vide *brache.*
Bienfacteur, well doing, doing good.
Bienvienner aucun, to welcom any one.
Un biere, a Bier or Coffin.
Bigamie & bigame, twice Marrying.
A bigot or *bigotted*, Superſtitious, Ceremonious.
Bigotiſme, Superſtitions in Ceremonies.
Bigottizing, to be fooliſh in Superſtitions.
Un billet, a Letter, and by *Kitchin* a Warrant. 279, a.
Biſayle vide *Beſaile.*
Biſextie, twice ſix.
Bitumie, Glue or Pitch, of a Roſinary quality, and more particularly called *bitumen.*
Bis, Bread or Bisket, *pur payſer le bis*, to weigh the Bread or Bisket. *p. Crompton Jur. Cur.* 87, b.

B L.

Blanc, white, *blanke*, idem. and *blanche*, idem. *p. Coke rep.* 7, 15, b.
Blancher & blanchir, to make white.
Qui eſt blanchet, which is whiteiſh.
Blancheur, whiteneſs.
Blandir, to allure one by fair words.
Blandiſſement, alluring, flattering.

Blasoner, to display Arms in Heraldry.

Ble, Corn. *Blees*, idem.

Blees scies, Corn cut. *p. lib. an. Hen.* 8, 2, b.

Blemeur, to blemish, *p. Britton* 49. a. *tout sort de ble*, all sorts of Corn.

Batre la Ble, to thrash Corn.

Degast ses Blees, his Corn trod down, eat up, or spoyl'd. *p. More rep.* 421.

Blesme, pale, bleak.

Lour Blesseures, their Wounds.

Blessus, Wounded. *Blessa*, shall Wound. 21. *Hen.* 7. Fol. 28, a.

B O.

Boefe, an Ox, *boefs* plural.

Boier, to drink, *ils boierunt*, they drank.

Boy, drink, *boyer*, to drink, *ad boya*, hath drank.

Bonne, good, *bon*, idem. *Bonte*, goodness.

Bois, Wood. *Sub bois*, underwood. *Boies*, Woods.

Bois abate, Wood cut down. *Coke, rep.* 5, 25, a.

Boscos, wood ground. *p.* 1. *pt.* Instit. 4, b.

Boscage, liberty of taking wood, also woody places.

Bote, & *boot*, aid, help, advantage, such as, *hedgbote*, *haybote*, *ploughbote*, &c.

Ne Bota, it helps not, or boots not. *Britton.* 26, a.

Bote, by *Brokes* abridgment is, added, or put unto, also an amends, or recompence. Fol. 220.

Boiste, and *boist*, a Box. *p. nov. narr.* 41.

Boisseau, a Bushel. *Boisseaus*, plural.

Bolivre, a lip.

Bonne, a Hat, Cap, or Bonnet.

Bouche, the Mouth, also the Cheek, *p. Coke.* 5, 10, b.

Un Bouche, a Mouthful.

Bordlanders, Tenants holding the Demesnes which the Lords keep in their Tenure for maintenance of their Board, or Table.

Bordeaus, Stews, Brothel-Houses.

Bordarii, Cottagers, Husbandmen. *Borduani*, idem.

Bouc, a Goat. *Bouquin*, a Kid.

Jeo sue bote & espernonne, I am Booted, and Spur'd.

Le Bouche de la playe, the Orifice, or Mouth of the Wound.

Un Bouchier, a Butcher. *Boucherie*, Slaughter,

Bovate terre, as much Land as six Oxen may Yearly till. *Vocat.* six Ox gangs and a Plough Land. *p. Cromptons, Jur. Cur.* 200.

A Boucher, to speak.

Bouger, to give out. *Ne bouger*, to stand to it, not to budge.

Botes hors, to put out. *p. Britton.* 245. a.

Boteles, without help, or amends.

Boundes, limits, also Merestones.

Bousment, stopping. *Bouschement*, idem. *p. Britton.* 48. b.

Boute, shew forth, *se boutent*, they intrude themselves. *Boutent hors*, they put out. *p. Britton.* 18, a.

Bougre, a Buggerer, *bougrerie*, buggery.

Boviller, to boyl, or seeth.

Bourg, a Town, or Burrough.

Un Bourse, a Purse. *Burs*, and *Burse*, idem.

Boucher, to stop. *Bouschement*, stopping.

Bourges, a Free-Man, or Denizon.

Bourgessors, and *Bourglarers*, House-breakers. *p. Britton*, 17 a.

La Boute de Rue, the end of the Street.

Boutefeu, an incendiary.

Ad Boy, hath drank. *p. Coke rep.* 8, 146. b.

B R.

Brache, an Arm, also a Hound. *p. Kitchin*, 60.

Braces, and *Bras*, Arms. *p. nov. narr.*

Brace, an Arm. *Bras de Mer*, an Arm of the Sea.

Braceresses, Brewers. *Bracerases*, idem. *p. Brit.* 77, a.

Brachonner, and *Braconer*, a Hunter, or Deer Stealer.

Bracheator, a Brewer, also a Hunter, or Fowler.

Brachier, idem. *p. Kitchin.* 11, b. and 14. b.

Braire, to Cry, or Bray like an Ass.

Brant, burned. 21. *Hen.* 7, 27, b.

Brayard, a cryer, or lamenter.

Brebes, Sheep. Vide *Barbits*.

Brevage, drinking, idem ut *Bevrage*.

Brees, Wheat, Bread-Corn.

Brider, to bridle. *Un Bride*, a Bridle.

Brief & *Brefe*, a Writ.

De Brief, shortly, *brievement*, idem.

En Brief, in short.

In Brigam, in contention, an old word for wrangling. *p. Coke.* 1 Instit. 3, b.

Broches, spits, also Gallons. *p. Termes de Ley.* 33. a.

Brique, brick, *briqueterie*, brick-work.

Un brochet, a Pike.

Bruarium, heath ground.

Brumal, Winterly, or winter-like.

Brusors, Brokers.

Bruse, a purse or pocket, *burs*, idem.

Evacuation del bruse, emptying the Pocket, *Coke. rep.* 5, 126.

Bruere, heath ground, or heath. *brusey*, heathy.

Bruyere, & *Bruierie*, idem. *Bruiier*, modern French for heath.

Bruer, brewing, *pour brewer* & *pister*, for brewing and baking.

Brua, doth brew, *p. Greg.* 29.

Bruit, a Report, *il court bruit*, there runs a Report.

B U. B Y.

Buant, drunkening, *p. Coke* Inst. 138. and by *Plowden*, a Bull, or Bulling. *Com.* 304. b.

Burglares, vide *Bourglares*.

Un Buccine, a Trumpet.

Buffe, a blow, or Stroke.

Burse, idem, *ut Bourse* & *Bours*.

Bumbard, a sort of Gun.

Bumbaseen, Cotton, Fustian.

Buizart, & *Buissart*, a Kite, or Buzzard.

Butin, spoil, pillage.

Byen, vide *bien*, well.

Byen publique, the Commonwealth.

Bye, a dwelling place. 1. *part* Inst. 5, b.

Byens, vide *biens*.

Bysants

Bysants, vide *besants*.

Byan, to dwell, *p. Coke*. 1. Instit. 5.

C A.

Ca, here, *ca* & *la*, here and there, also hither and thither, also wandering.

Courir la & *la*, to run here and there.

Cabale, a particular Assembly, informing and advizing each other.

Cablicia, brush wood. *p. Crompton Jur. Cur.* 195.

Cacher, to hide, *Cachement* hiding.

Cache, hid. *Se cachoit*, he hid himself.

Cachette, secretly, privily.

Cachetter, to sign, or seal.

Cachet, a signet, or seal.

Cader, to fall, *cade*, fallen. *Voit cader*, would fall. *Cadet*, a younger Brother, or yongest Child.

Calculer, to compute, or reckon.

Calcul, accounting, computing.

Calendes, the first Day of the Month.

Un calsay, a Causey. 12. *Hen.* 8, 2, b.

Calme, quiet, tranquill.

Camera, & *camere*, a Chamber.

Cambre, Ceiled, Vaulted.

Chameraire, a Chamberlain, in the Modern French, *Cubiculair*, & *chambellan*.

Un campane, a Bell, *pulsure de campane*, ringing of the Bell. *p. Fitzherbert's* Just. 41, b. *Campane environ le col. del beof*, the Bell about the Oxes neck, *p. Plowden*. 229. *Coment*. a.

Camp, & *Campaign*, a Field.

Campesters, idem plural, and pastures. *p. Plowd*. 316. b.

Le camp, an Army in Tents, or in the Field encamp'd.

Campaigne del Roy, the Queen Consort.

Campaine Royne, idem, *p. Coke. rep*. 5.

A Canceller, to deface, to cancel. *p. eund. rep*. b. 46. a.

Cantaria, a *chauntry*, a place to Sing Mass.

Canal, a place dug for a Water course, also a Kennel, or place for Dogs.

Canape, hemp, *Canope*, idem. *p. Kitch*. 21, b.

Un Captiff, a Prisoner, a Captive.

Capitaine en cheif, a General, or chief Head. *Plowd. Com*. 268. a.

Capax, capable. *p. Brokes abr*. 288.

Caquet, much tongue, pratling, scolding, or one much used to it.

Car, for, because, for that.

Carbons, Coals.

Domus carneletta, a Castle, 1. *pt. Instit*. 5, a.

Caressé, chearing, welcoming, complement.

Care, Flesh, vide *chare* & *chair*.

Carol, or Song, in Consort, & *Carolle*, idem.

Carve of Land, *carucata terre*, as much Land as may be Tilled by one Plough in a Year, or a hide of Land. *p. Phillips*.

Car entant, forasmuch.

Cart, paper, *Carte*, writing.

Carve, a plough, *carew*, idem.

Carew de terre, a plough Land.

Catarre

Catarre, a Rheum distilling.

Casser, to put out, to cashiere,

Castigation, Punishment.

Caste, chast.

Caverne, a Cave, or hollow place.

Causare, to cause, *causeroit*, may cause.

Causera, shall cause.

Caut, wary, *cautement*, warily. *par Cautels*, by cunning or craft.

Cautels, warnings, cautions.

Cave, beware, *caveont*, they take heed.

Cautelle, guile, craft.

Caveola, a Cage. *p. terms Ley.* 172.

A Causa, by reason of, because, for.

C E.

Ce, this, that, *ceo*, *cetty*, *cecy*, *cel* & *celuy*, signify that, this, these, &c. *Ceo* & *cet*, are masculines, *cetty* feminine.

Cest. that is, *ce est*, idem:

Ce terme this term. *Cet home*, this Man, *cetty feme*, this Woman, *ces homes*, these Men.

Est ce elle, ou non? Is this She, or not.

Ce signifie que, this declares that.

Ceans, here within.

Est il ceans? Is he within?

Ce cy, this here, *Ce cy mesme* this very same thing.

Ceder, to fall, to give place, vide *Cader*.

Je te cede, I give thee place.

Ceduls, Seats or Pews in a Church. *p. Kitchin.* 194. a.

Ceo est cest, this is it, or that is t, vide *cestuy*.

Ceindre, to girt, or gird.

Ceinct & *cinct*, girt or bound.

Cel, this, and also that. *p. Cromp. jur. cur.* 221. a.

Ce la, this same, and that same.

Celebrer, to extol or magnify, to celebrate.

Celebres, celebrated. *p. Parkins* 53, b.

Celeront, they divulge, or discover. *Briton*, 9, b.

Celer, in modern French is to hide.

Celement, privily.

Celle, she, *celuy*, him, & *celui*, idem.

Celuy la, that same Man, vide *cestuy*.

Per celuy outiel, by such or such. *terms de Ley* 57.

Cendre, Ashes, *encendre*, in the Fire. *p.* 3. *part Instit.* 44.

Un cengle, a girt.

Cense, a Farm, *censeour*, a Farmer. *Nos poit censomous*, we may judge, 1. *Hen.* 7. *Annals*, 25, b.

Centre, the middle part or Center.

Cent, a hundred, *cent foits*, a hundred times, *cent foits double*, 200 times, *cent foit trois*, 300 times, &c.

Cens deux 200, *trois cens*, &c.

Huict & *huit cens* 800. *cens neuf* 900.

Centeinors, *hundredors*, or Men of the same hundred. *p. Mirrour Just.*

Centeine, to divide by the hundred.

Mettres per centaines, to put by hundreds.

Ceps, a pair of Stocks.

Un ſep, a Stock or Root.

Cependent, in the mean time.

Cercher, to ſeek out, to enquire.

En cerchent, in ſeeking, *la cerche*, the ſearch, *cerches*, ſought for.

Ceps de arbres, the ſtocks of Trees or Roots when felled. *p. Coke rep.* 5.

Un cerf, a Hart or Stagg.

Ceo, this, *pur ceo*, for that, alſo becauſe, and therefore, *ceo en avant*, from henceforth.

Ceole, Heaven.

Cerisiers, Cherry-trees.

Cere, wax, *Cerot*, a Serecloth, *ſerot*, idem.

Cere, is alſo a Lock.

Certes, verily, truely.

Deſtre certaine, to be a Captaine. *p. Coke rep.* 7. 9, & 37.

Certainment, aſſuredly, without doubt.

Cervois, Bear, Ale, *hauſt de cervois*, a draught of Beer.

Ceſtuy, him, he, *ceſt*, it is, and that is.

Ceſtaſſavoit, (that is to ſay) *p. Parkins.*

Ceſtaſcavoit, idem. *p. eund.* 131, a.

Ceſtuy cy meſme, his own ſelf here.

Ceſtie, him, *ceſtuy la meſme*, he, himſelf.

qui eſt ceſtuy ci? who is this here?

En meſme ceſtuy, in this ſame. *p. Coke rep.* 7, 33.

Ceſtuy que, he who, or who is, or he whoſe.

Ceruſe, white-lead.

Ces & ceux, theſe, and thoſe.

Ceſſer, to ſtay, to abate, to ceaſe. *p. Coke rep.* 6. 32.

Un ceſſure, a Receiver, a Bayliff, or one ſo deputed. *p.* 16, *Edw.* 6, 8.

Le ceſſe, the forbearance or the ceaſing.

Le ces, idem. *ſans ceſſe*, without intermiſſion, without ſtay, alſo preſently.

Ceſſera, ſhall abate, ſtay, & *ceſſion*, ſtaying, alſo ſitting, *ceſſer de parler*, to forbear ſpeaking.

Ceſſe de braire, hold your yawling or crying.

Ceſtaſcavoit, that is to ſay. *p. Dyer & Parkins*, 131.

Ceſtaſſavoir, idem. *p. Coke*, idem. *ut ceſtaſſavoit.*

Ceſt, this, *ad ceſt*, hath this.

Cet, that, *ceux*, thoſe, theſe, *per ceux ou ceis*, by thoſe or theſe.

Le ceur, the Heart, *ceurs plural*, *cuer & cueur*, is a Heart in modern *French*.

A certifier, to certifie.

Ceynture, girding, *ſuns ceynture*, without a girdle, or ungirdled. *p. Britton.* 11. b.

C H.

Chacun vide *chaſcun*.

Chair, Fleſh, *chare*, idem.

Chare, Deer, Veniſon, vide *cher*.

Trop chare, too dear. *p. Crompton Juſtice*, 7, b.

Chair envenomee, Veniſon.

Chair de porc, Swines fleſh.

Chair de berbits, Mutton, *chair de veau*, Veal, *chair de cheureau*, Goats fleſh.

Chair de ſerf, red Deer, or Stags fleſh.

Chair de leporina, Hares fleſh.

Charneu, fleſhy.

Chaleur, Heat.

Chambre, a Chamber.

Chaffed, chaſed.

Champerty,

Champerty, is the buying Lands contrary to the Statute, 32 *Hen.* 8. and alſo compriſeth maintainance in carrying on Suits at Law, on condition to have part thereof recovered.

Champ, a Field, *champs plural*, vide *camp. playn campe*, an open Field.

Champeſtre, an open Country uninclosed.

Le chancellerie, the Chancery.

Un chandelle, a Candle.

Chandeler, Candlemas.

Change tout, alter all.

Chaunter, to ſing, *chanter*, idem.

Chauntant & chantant, ſinging.

Ad chaunt, hath ſung.

Et jur chanta pour le plt. and the Jury gave Verdict for the Plantiff. *Mich.* 8. *Hen.* 6. *chaunte*, ſung, *chauntu dulciment*, ſung ſweetly.

Le chauntry, the Muſick or the Singing.

Doit chaunter, ought to be ſung.

Un chanel, a Sink or Drain, vide *canol*.

Charier, to draw, or drive.

Chares, Charets, Carts, Waggons. *p. Nov. Nar.* 52, b.

Un charret, idem.

Charets, is ſometimes taken for Cart-loads. *Kitchin* 241.

Charters, Writings, Charts.

Le charter, the Driver or Carter.

Un chariot, a Waggon, *charietz. plur.* 2. *Hen.* 7, 1. a.

Charnels amies, Kindred in Blood. *Briton* 135, a.

Avec charnelles, with battlements. *p. eund.* 31, a.

Un charme, a Spell.

Charbons, vide *carbons*.

Chaperon, a Hood or Bonnet.

Un charbonnier, a Collier.

Chaume, Straw.

Chardon, a Thiſtle.

A charger, to charge.

Chaſer, to Drive or Hunt, *chaſſer*, idem.

Chaſe, Drove, Hunted. *p. Coke rep.* 6. 14, a.

A chaſer & rechaſer, to drive backwards and forwards, *p. chaſement*, by driving, &c.

Chaſera, ſhall Drive, Hunt, &c.

Chaſſe idem *ut chaſe*.

Chaſes, Drivings, *enchaſes*, idem.

Charve idem *ut carve*.

Chaſcun idem *ut cheſcun*.

Chaſtaigne, a Cheſnut.

Chaſtellain, the Owner or Captain of a Caſtle.

Un chat, a Cat, *p. Brokes grand abridgment, tit. wreck.*

Un chate idem. *p. Coke rep.* 5, 107, b.

Chattells, are all Goods moveable and immovable, alſo Leaſes, &c.

Chateus, Goods. *p. termes de ley*, 208.

Chatelx real, Chattles real. *p. Parkins*, 109, a.

Chateux, Chattels. *p. Kitchin*, 243, & *Plowd.* 277.

Chate, brought.

Un chateaw, a Caſtle.

Chauld, Hot.

Chapon, a Capon. *p. nov. nar.* 2, a.

Chavoucher, to ride, *Chavaucher*, idem.

Chavauchant, they ride.

Chavauche, ridd.

Chaſtier, to geld. *caſtre* gelded.

Chaulx, Lime.

Le chief, the head, the top. vide *test.*

Chein, a Dog. vide *chien.*

Chemin, a way, vide *chimin.*

Checke, controul, command. *p. termes de Ley.* 102. b.

Chemise & *chemyse*, a Coat, Smock, or Shift.

Chemyse de lynge, a Linnen Smock. *p. nov. nar.* 71, b.

Cher, Dear, *chiere* idem. *p. Parkins*, 115.

Chercheut, they sought, *chercher*, to seek. *p. Cokes Report.* 9, 120.

Cherir ascun, to flatter one.

Un cherve, a Cherry.

Cheftaine, Captain.

Cherte, Charity, also dearth.

Chet, doth happen, or fall out. *p. Britton* 200, b.

Cheser, to happen, *chese*, happened. *p. eund.* 128. b.

Chesent, they happening. *p. eund.* 84.

Chescun, every one, each. *p. Coke* 9, 83. & *chescun*, by *Greg.* is over and above, in the Mote Book, fol. 220.

Chesne, an Oak, in Modern *French.*

Chevisance, obtaining, purchaseing, vide *chivisaune.*

Cheval, a Horse, *chival*, idem.

Chevaler & *chevalier*, a Horseman, a Knight.

Cheveres & *chevers*, Horses. *p. nov. nar.* 13, a.

Chevaucher, to ride, *chevauche*, ridd.

Chevauchement, riding.

Cheu, happened, fallen out.

Chez, at, with, near.

Cheut, a fall, *sa cheut*, his fall, *Coke* 9, 122.

Chier, to fall, *p. le chier*, by the fall.

Chiet, doth fall, *chia*, fallen, *que chia*, which fell. *p. Brokes abr.*

Chirra, shall lie, or fall, *chira*, idem.

Chient, they fall.

Chien, a Dog, *chyen*, idem, *chienne*, a Bitch.

Chierographorum, of Writings, vide *Chyrograph.*

Chimin, a way, *le haut chimin*, the high way.

Chiminage, a Toll taken towards repairing high ways, in Forests, Chases, and some other places, paid by the Passangers.

En ses chiminant, in his journey or passage on the high waies.

Mal chival, a jade Horse.

Chivaler, a knight, *service en chivalry*, is Knights service to attend the King in his Wars.

Chivisaunce, Tradeing Trafficking.

Chivalks & *chivaulks*, Horses, *a chivaulx*, to grind or work in a Horse-mill. *p. Coke rep.* 11, 50.

Chivancher, to ride, *chivauchomus*, we rode.

Chivanchant, riding, or they ridd, *chivauchomus*, we rode.

Chivauchea, rode, *chivancha*, idem.

Chole, Anger, Choller.

Chivers & *chyvers*, Goats.

Un chorde, a String.

Chose & *chos*, a thing, *choses*, plural.

Choise idem. *ut chose. p. Fitzh. gr. abr.* 2. *pt.* 5, a.

Chrestien, a Christian.

Choniques, Annals, Chronicles.

Chymen idem. *ut chimin.*

Chyvers idem. ut *chivers.*

Un chyrograph, the Indentnre of a Fine. *p. nov. nar.* 43.

C I.

Ci, here, *ci pris cy mis*, as ſoon ſaid as done. Modern French.

Ci davant, heretofore, *ci longement*, ſo long.

Cibien, as well, ſo well, *Cybien*, idem. *p. Coke* 8, 85.

Cices, Pulſe, Vetches,

Ciens, hither, here, *ceiens* & *cienz*, idem. *p. Coke* 9, 37. b.

Ciel, Heaven, vide *Ceole*.

Un cigne, a Swan, *cignes*, Swans, *cignets* young Swans, *cygnits*, idem.

Cil idem, *ut celuy*.

Cimitorie, a Burial place or Church-yard.

Cinque, five, *cinque foits*, five times.

Cinquieme, the fifth, *cinquieſm*, idem.

Cinquantie, fifty, *cinquantieſme*, the fiftieth.

Cips vide *Ceps*, the Stocks.

Cire idem, *ut cere*.

Ciste, a Cheſt, *cest*, idem.

Cisti, him. *p. Parkins* 131.

Citoſt, as ſoon as, as oft as.

Citius, rather.

Un cimiterre, a crooked Sword,

Cirier, a Wax-chandler.

Cite, a City, *al Cite*, at the City. *p. Plowden*, *Com.* 300. b.

Ciphis, Cups. *p. an. Rich.* 3.

Un ciphe de vin, a Cup of Wine. *p. Coke* 9, 86.

Cirer, to Seal, vide *cerer*.

C L.

Un claud, a Ditch.

Un clave, a Horſe-ſhoe, alſo a Horſe-nail. *p. Fitzherb. Nat. brev.* 49.

Clayes, Hurdles, Stakes for folding Sheep. *p. Coke Report.* 8, 125, b.

Cler, clear, *clerte*, clearly.

Un cler, a Clark.

A fair cler, to make clear or bright, *pur cleanſer*, to make clean *clerement*, clearly.

Clere, Clergy.

Clete, Hurdles to fold Sheep.

Cleiſ, a Key, *cleifs* & *clifs*, Keys.

Clief, alſo a Key. *Coke rep.* 5, 91, b.

Cloche, a Bell, alſo a Trumpet.

Clocher, to ſhut, and from thence a Cloiſter.

Clos, ſhut or incloſed, *un clos*, an incloſed Ground, fenced about.

Cloie, pricked with a Nail.

Cloier mon chival, to prick a Horſe in ſhooing, *Cloy*, pricked, lamed, *cloya*, idem.

Clou, is modern French for a Nail.

Clough, a Valley between Hills.

Cloſture de hayes, incloſeing with hedges.

C O.

Courcter, to force, *coherter*, idem. *Coke* 7, 24.

Coerts, forced, *cohert*, idem. & *cherc*, idem.

Coherter, to force, or to compel,

Cohertera, ſhall force.

Fait cohert, was forced.

Coneu, known.

Conuſter, to know, *conuſtre*, idem.

Coeur,

Coeur, a Heart, alſo the Breſt. *p. Coke* 8, 157.

Cognom, a Sirname.

Cognizance, confeſſing, acknowledging.

Cognuzance, having knowledge.

Coigne, Coyn, Mony.

Coigner, to Coyn. *p. Plowd. Com.* 116, a.

Coleberti, Tenants in free Soccage.

Coiler, to gather, *Collier*, idem.

Collyer & Coller, idem.

Collegee, gather ye, *colige*, idem.

Coillers & coillours, Collectors.

Coilliot, *p. Coke* 8, *rep.* ſeems to be a lock of Wool, taken as Toll.

Colier, a collecter? *Collecteres*, ye ſhall gather, *beincollye*, well gathered.

Colle, a Neck, *col*, idem. alſo Glue and Paſt.

Collateral cheſes, things by the by, Securities, over and above, afterwards.

Collateral, alſo is what's equal on either ſide in Kindred, ſuch are Brother and Siſters, Children and their Iſſue.

Colluſion, deceit,

Colucanis & collarii, are Cottagers.

Columbes, Doves, Pigeons.

Columbarie, a Dove-houſe, *columbare*, idem.

A combat, to fight, *combatre*, idem.

Combatier, idem, *combatant*, fighting.

Un combe, a Valley betwixt two Hills.

Combien, although, *combien que*, although that.

Combien eſte? How many are ye?

Combieny a il? how long is it ſince?

Combien, how much, how well, and how many. *p. termes Ley*, 113, a.

Combien vaillant, how much are they worth? *p. Britton*, 185.

Come & Comme, as, where, alſo how and even as.

Comburer, to burn, *eſtre combre*, to be burned, *Comberts*, burned.

Comment, although, notwithſtanding, albeit, when, how.

Coment ce la? how ſo?

Comencer, to begin, *comencera*, ſhall begin.

Comence, begun, *comenceroit*, it ought to begin.

Comenſant, beginning, *comenſeant*, idem. *Comenſement*, & *comenſiant*, idem.

Comeder, to eat, *comederoit*, ſhould eat. *p. Plowd.* 19.

Comide, eaten. *p. Plowd. eod. fol.*

Comenge, excommunicated, or accurſed.

Comengement, excommunication.

Comettre, to commit, *que fuit comiſe al Priſon*, who was committed to Priſon. *p. Coke.*

Commiſes, committed, acted, done, *comiſe*, idem.

Cominaſſe, to have common, *ne cominaſſent*, they ſhould not common. *p. Nov. Nar.* 53.

Cominer, to eat with, alſo to converſe.

Commorant, dwelling, or abideing.

Commineront, they aſſembled together. *p.* 1, *Hen.* 7, 5, b.

Un commote, a great Seignior, or Lord.

Commoigue, a fellow Monk.

A comparer, to appear.

Compertment, appearing, alſo preſenting.

Com pernaunt, ſet forth, comprehending, or compriſing, *compernans*, idem.

Compeſter, to dung Soil, alſo to fold Sheep upon Land.

Compeſt, & *Compoſt*, dung Soil.

Compromiſe, a mutual undertaking, or promiſe.

Compter, to reckon, to number, or count.

Comunement, commonly.

Comenſaſt, he had begun.

Comenſant, & *comenciant*, beginning.

Compier, a Godfather. *p.* 10. *Hen.* 7, f, 7, a.

Comon de ſhack, is to be taken after harveſt till Corn re-ſowed. Meadows called Lammas Meadows, are alſo ſubject to that *Comon* after the Hay is off.

Compartir, to divide, or ſhare.

Commorant, ſtaying, abiding.

Compenſer, to recompence, *compenſe*, recompenſed, rewarded.

Compatir, to ſuffer together.

Compatible, abiding together, or agreeing.

Un complice, a Companion in Wickedneſs.

Comportement, behaviour.

Comprendre, to perceive.

Il comprents, it contains. *p. Plowd. Com.* 197.

Comprometre, to put to Arbitration.

Compromis, an Arbitriment, a conſent thereto.

Communement, the Commonalty. *p. Kitch.*

Communer, to diſcourſe, to confer.

Con, known, diſcovered, *p. termes de Ley* 18, b.

Conceder, to grant.

Concevoir, to think, to ponder, alſo to bring.

Conation, endeavouring. *p. termes Ley*, 136.

Conceve, brought forth, or perfected. *Plowd.*

Conceave, conception, or an opinion.

Concur enſemble, come, or agree together.

Concurrant, a Rival.

Concubeant, a lying together. 1. *Hen.* 7, 6.

Condampner, to give judgment againſt.

Condigns, Worthy.

Confeſſer, to acknowledge.

Confeſſomous, we own, *confreers* Brothers in a Religious Houſe.

Confier, to truſt, *confrairie*, brotherhood, fraternity.

Confiſquer, to bring goods as forfeited to the publick Treaſury.

Conge, *Coungee*, & *Congee*, leave, licence.

Conge d'eſlier, leave to chooſe.

Voil done a moy conge? Will you give me leave?

Conge de accorder, licence of agreement.

Congeable, lawful, with licence.

Conglutiner, to join together, *conjoindre*, idem.

Congreger, to gather together.

Congruement, agreeably.

Coniers, Warrens. *p. Britton.* 185.

Conynges,

Conynges, Conies, *coninges*, Shillings.

Un conroieur, a Currier of Leather.

Le concile, the Council.

Condoloir, to mourn together.

Conduite, leading.

Confirmer, to eftablifh.

Les confins, the bounds, or limits,

Confisquer, to forfeit goods to the ufe of the King. Vide *antea*.

Confrerers, fellows, or brothers of one Society.

Couqueftre, to overcome, *Conquis*, conquered.

Un coquine, a henrooft, alfo a kitchin. 4. *pt. Coke* 86, *Inftit.*

Confifter, to truft, or ftand together.

Confoler, to Comfort.

Confute, fixed unto, annexed. *p. Coke* 5, 41, b.

Contrariant, being againft.

Conftituter, to appoint.

Contenue, contained. *p. le contenue*, by the contents.

Contamus, we declare, or count.

Conteke, ftrife, contention.

Controve, contrived, *controver*, to contrive.

Neint contrifteiant, & *neint contriftient*, it doth not otherwife appear, notwithftanding.

Conteignes, contained.

Conter, & *Contre*, againft.

Contingencie, happening by chance.

A Contradire, to gainfay.

Counter, to declare, to count.

Contraband, prohibited.

Contremont, upwards. *p. Nov. Narr.* 71, b.

Controvor, a contriver of falfe reports.

Contrepanel, a counterpart. *p. Parkins* 112, a.

Convenable, neceffary, fit, *convenablement*, conveniently.

Convainquus, convicted, *Coke* 9, 121.

Conus, acknowledged, known, owned, *conu*, idem.

Ne conus, not known, *fi conus foy*, if he own himfelf. *Cokes rep.* 5, 117, b.

A conufter, to know, *poit conuftre*, may know.

Conufans, knowing, acknowledging, *conufant*, idem.

Il conut, he owns, or acknowledgeth.

Le conufans, the acknowledging.

Il conufoit, he may own.

Ne poit conufer, he may not acknowledge.

Il conuftra, he will acknowledge.

Conufomus, we own, or acknowledge.

Connying, knowledge.

Copped, laid in heaps, or cocks, *cope*, a hill.

Blees en coppe, corn in cocks.

Contecker, to join in ftrife, *conteckent*, they ftrive.

Contekours, brawlers. *p. Fitzh. Juft.* 201, a.

Conteks, differences, *contekes*, idem. alfo fuits.

Convenable, agreeable.

Un cordiner, a Shoemaker.

Corie, Leather, *corye*, idem. *p.* 1. *Rich.* 3d.

Un cord de lane, a load of Wool.

Cornue, a horn, *corner*, to wind a horn.

Corne, hunted. *p. Britton* 33, a.

Cornele,

Cornele, the crown of the head, alſo a Crow.

Corodie, a proviſion of dyet, and apparel.

Coraage, a Cuſtom of paying certain meaſures of Corn.

Cordage, Stuff to make Ropes.

Corone, a Crown, *coronement*, Crowning.

Corps, a Body, *lour doux corps*, their two Bodies.

Cors, a Body; *il eit cors*, he hath a Body. *p. Britton*. 230.

Corps incorporate, bodies incorporated.

Corſues, corporal, *p. Britton* 142.

Corſepreſent, a Mortuary.

Corrupte & brief parlance, by the haſty and ſhort pronounciation. *p. termes de Ley*.

Corriger, to correct, to chaſtiſe.

Corrigee, & *corige*, corrected.

Corrumper, to break, to violate.

Coſinage, kindred.

Coſces, & *Coſceti*, Husbandmen. *p. Cokes Inſtit*. 1 *pt*.

As Coſtages, at the charges, or coſts.

Coſtes, ſides, *Demicoſtes*, the mid ſides.

Coſte, by, preſent, near.

Eſtoit coſte, ſtanding, or being by, alſo a rib. *p. Fitzherbert* Juſt. 21, a.

Coſteins, neighbouring, bordering.

Contenir, to contain.

Contentieux, full of ſtrife.

Contreſte, to withſtand.

Un Coq, a Cock.

Contremettre, to lay againſt, or impoſe upon.

Contriſter, to be ſorrowful.

Cottel, a Knife, *Cotel*, idem.

Coteau, idem, alſo a Sword.

Cotures, little Houſes, Cottages, alſo coverings. *p. Brit*. 148.

Coquiner, to beg.

Coterelli, Cottagers, 1. *pt. Inſt*. 5, b.

Coucher, to ſet, or lie down.

Coucher de ſoel, Sun ſet.

Couchant, lying.

Couche, lyeth.

Eſtre couche, to be laid along.

El couche, ſhe lay.

Coulpe, a fault, *coulp*, idem.

Covenable, fitting.

Covert, hidden, covered.

Feme Covert, a Marryed Woman.

Terres covert, wood lands.

Covrir, to cover.

Coverture, the condition of a Married Woman, or continuance in Marriage.

Pound covert, a Pound in a by place, or not publick, as in a Man's own Yard, &c.

Pound overt, the Pariſh Pound.

Covers, covered.

Chival covert, a Horſe arrayed, or harneſſed.

Covertment, tacitly, or impliedly.

Covient, it behoveth, or they ought.

Covin, fraud.

Counter, idem, *ut conter*, to declare, &c.

Ad count, hath declared, *countaſt*, idem.

Un count, a Declaration.

Count, alſo is an Earl, *countee*, idem, *Countau*, idem.

Un countour, a Serjeant at Law, or Councellor.

Coungee, vide *congee*.

Counterface,

Counterface, counterfeit.

Counterpalais, A County Palatine.

Countera, ſhall or will declare.

Countermand, to forbid, to recall.

Countervault, countervailed.

Counterdiſt, forbidden, denyed, *p. Plowd.* 68, a.

Le counterdit, the forbidding. *p. eund.* 141.

La coupe, the fault. *p. Britton*, 62, & 245, b.

Coupe & recoupe, cut and cut again.

Coup & coups, cut, *couper*, to cut.

Coupes, Strokes, Blows, or Slaſhes.

Couper le tayle, to dock, or cut off the Entayle.

Courre, to run, *curree*, idem. *courey*, running, alſo ready, *courrage*, running, *courge*, idem.

Ne courge, it runs not, or goes not, *ne court*, idem.

Courir a & la, wandering here and there.

Court, conſtrained, forced, alſo ſhort.

Un courſair, a Pyrate, *Un courratier*, a Horſecourſer.

Courtement, ſhortly.

Coupables, guilty.

Coupure, cutting, lopping, *coupart*, idem.

Courtilage, a piece of Ground, or Garden near a Houſe, a void piece, or Yard.

Courant, running, *coraunte*, idem.

En coupant boyes, in cutting Woods.

Coyly, gathered, a *coyler*, to gather or collect.

Coylours vide *coilours.*

C R.

Cracher, to Spit, or put upon a Spit.

Crainer, to refuſe, *crainent ſon Company*, they refuſe his Company. *p. Yelverton*, 150.

Crampus, Lame, *Britton*, 36.

Credence, belief.

Cretaine, fear, *cretaine de ewe*, fear of Water. *p. Plowden. crainte* is fear in modern French.

Cree, Created.

Creance, belief, perſwaſion, truſt, credit, faith.

Credence, belief alſo.

Faux creance, falſe faith, infidelity.

Creies, believe ye.

Creanſor & creanſour, a Creditor. *p. Fitzherb. Nat. brev.* 28, a.

Creſſer, to grow, *ne creſſera*, ſhall not grow.

Que creſſe, which groweth, *creſt* doth grow.

Creſſaunt & creſſaunts, growing. *creſſoient*, they grew.

Crever, to thruſt, *creva l' Oeil*, thruſt out the Eye. *p. Coke, rep.* 9, 120.

A croir & a crier, to believe, *croire*, belief.

Croy moy, believe me. *jeo ne croy paſs*, I do not believe, *ne creu*, not believe, *jeo croy*, I think, I take it to be, *ne croyeront*, they believe not, *jeo penſe que tu le croies*, I think that thou believeſt.

Fuer crible, were debated, *cribler*, to argue, debate, ſcan. *p. Plowden*'s Preface to his Comment.

Un

Un croise & *croisse*, a Cross, *croix*, Crosses.

De crepute, Lame. *p. Fitzh. Nat. brev.* 25, b.

Crestein idem *ut Cresteine*.

Creve, shook, ratled, also encreased. *p. Fitzh. Justice*. 160, b.

Crere, to believe, *rien crere*, to believe nothing. *p. Britton*, 13, a.

C U.

Cule, Dung, Filth.

Cueiller, to gather or reap.

Cuer, a Heart, or Mind, vide *coeur*.

Cuers, plural, p. cuer, by heart, or without book.

Cuir, Leather.

Curtiver, to Plowe.

Currir, to run, *currist*, he runneth.

Curge, run, *curgera*, shall run or happen.

Ne curroit, hath not run, *curgera ove la terre*, shall go with the Land, *Coke* 5, 16, b. *curge*, happeneth, runneth, ariseth with, *curgeront*, they run.

Un cursitor, an Officer who makes out Original Writs in Chancery, or Writs of Course, the number of such Officers are 24.

Curve, crooked.

Custos, Keeper.

Cul prit, ready to prove the guilt or the issue upon not guilty pleaded.

Cunicules & *cunicles*, Coneys.

Le cure, the care.

Cuttle & *Cuttel*, vide *Cottel*, a Knife, & *conteau*. idem.

Curt temps, short time.

Cumuler, to keep up, to lay together in Heaps or Cocks.

La cuisse, the Thigh.

Cule nuict, the night season.

Curtiner, to fence in, to inclose.

Cultiver, to Till.

Curer, to cleanse.

Un Cartilage, a backside, or small piece of Ground, near a Messuage, commonly used for Hemp, Flax, Beans, &c. vide *curtilage*.

Custodire ne poit, may not keep. 12 *Hen.* 8. 3, a.

C. Y.

Cy, here, so, as.

Cy pris, so near, *cy tant come*, as much as.

Cy insuit, here followeth.

Cy apres, hereafter,

Cy devant, before this, heretofore.

Que cy, that it is, that is here.

Cy court, so speedy. *Coke* 7, 36.

Cy eu je suis, here in this place.

Cygne, a Swan, vide *Cigne*.

Cygnets, young Swans.

Cyel, heaven, vide *ceole*.

Cysors, Cutters, *cysours de bourses*, Cutpursers.

Cylindre, a thing long and round.

Cypress, Cypresses.

Cy vivement, so lively. *Plow. abr.* 72.

Cybien, as well.

Sont cy, they are here.

Cy long, as long.

Cy avant, as well before.

Et il dit que cy, and he said it was thus, or so.

Cy eins, here within, in this place.

D A.

DA, a word affirmative for yes.

Ouy da, yea verily, *dea* idem *ut da*.

D' abatus, to be thrown down.

D' agister, to lay in or take Cattle at Grass, or Hay.

Daigner, to vouchsafe, to think worthy.

Un dagg, a small Gun, a hand-gun, vide *baque*.

D' aler, to go, *vide aler*.

D' alvey Seggs, Rushes, flag Ground, also Alder-trees. *p. Nov. Nar.* 5, a.

Dam, loss, damage, *damoiouse*, idem. *p. Britton* 54, a.

Dame, a Lady, also a Doe, or Female Deer.

D' amesner, to go, or bring.

Damner, to condemn.

Damosells, Maidens.

Dans, within, into, vide *deins*.

Darrain, latter, last, *darraigne* idem.

Al darrain, at last, from the French word, *dernier*, i. e. *ultimus*.

Darreinment, lastly, lately, *darrenment*, idem. *p. Fitzh. Just.* 77, a.

Un dague, a poinard, a Dagger.

D' aventure, perchance.

D' avantage, vide *avantage*.

D' avers, of Cattle, vide *avers*.

Datif, a thing in gift.

D' avoider, to put by, to avoid, also to go away, or out of.

Date, dated.

D' autiel, of the like, or such.

Un dard, a Dart.

Dauphin, a Dolphin Fish.

Un dagge, a Pistol, or short Gun.

D E.

Debater, to strive, to debate.

Deable, Devill, *diable*, idem.

De, of, for, from, *dien de le eglise*, I come from Church.

De la, from that, beyond, over.

Debase, to bring low, *debase*, *les pountes*, below the Bridges. *p. Cromp. Jur. Cur.* 88, b.

Debassa, downwards.

Debonerte, good will, likeing, *p. Britton*, 104, a.

Deboter, to depose, to deny, hinder.

Debote, hindered denyed. *p. Britton* 104.

Debouche & corns, is by *Brit.* put for huy and cry. f, 20.

Debility, weakness.

Debruser, to break or tread down, or throw down.

Debruse, thrown down, *debruise*, idem.

Deca, on this side, *deca & dela*, hither and thither.

Dela mer, over the Sea.

Decela, discover. *Coke* 9, 121.

Dedens, within, *dedeins*, idem. and there within. *dedans* idem ut *dedens*.

Deca le mer, on this side the Sea.

De la mer, over the Sea. *per* 3 *part. Instit.* 39.

Deceu, deceived, *dechavoir*, unknown.

Deceder, to Dye.

Decess & decez, defunct, deceased.

Dedire, to gainsay, *ceo ne poimus dedire*, this we cannot deny or gainsay.

Ne dedit, it cannot be denied. p. *Plowd.* 179. b.

Est dedit, it is denied, *ad dedit*, dath denied, *soit dedits*, be denied.

Deceners & deciners, are they who reside within the Tything or Mannor, who ought to swear Allegiance at the Leet, from which Knights, Clerks and Women are exempted, also such as oversee and govern them.

Decenier, a Tythingman.

A dozoner, is one who ought to be Sworn at twelve Years of Age or above.

Decret, a Decree.

Deciens, since, or in time past.

Decise, cut off. p. *Plowden.* 252. b.

Decrepute, Lame. p. *Fitzherbert.*

Deschyre, to tear off, or to fall off. p. *Britton.* 7.

Dechasser, to drive off, to drive away.

Dechasse, driven away, *Decassement*, driving.

Declarissement, declaring. p. 3. *part Instit.* 1.

Decolle, beheaded.

Decouper, to cut down, *decoupe* cut off or from, or docked. *Plowd.* 252.

Defaile, Default, *defally*, vide, *Postea.*

Defairer, to deface, undo.

A defair, to defeat, to make void, or to reverse.

Defaitera, shall defeat.

Defawchez, to mow, or reap or cut off.

Defaucher, idem. p. 12 *Hen.* VIII. 2. b.

Defeater, to put by or hinder.

Defendre, to Defend.

Deferer, to put off, *delateur*, idem, and to lay to ones Charge.

Defeazance, a Liberty to undo or make void.

A definer, to expound.

Decimes, Tythes, vide, *dismes.*

Decorer, to deck or adorn.

Dedie, Dedicated.

Defailer, to wear away, to languish, wither, to spoil, *tout defaile*, all spoil'd.

Un defaut, a neglect of appearing or pleading in Court.

Deflurer & deffleur, to deflower.

Defrisher & defrischer, to work by Tilling the Ground.

Defover, to dig up or dig again.

Defoss, dig'd up.

Deforcer, to put out of Possession by force, also to keep such possession though without force by him who hath not Title to the same.

Defowlez & defoules, trod down, spoil'd.

Defower, to uncover.

Neiut defeat, undefeated.

Defally, defeated.

Degages, replevined, or deliver'd out upon Bail. p. *Nov. Nar.* 53.

Degast, wasted, spoiled, destroyed, *degaste*, idem.

Degaster, to wast, *a fair degast*, to commit waste.

Degasta, shall wast or spoil.

Degata, wasted, destroyed. p. *Fitzherbert.* 24. a.

Degaſtement, waſting.

Debault, over or above.

Debors, out, without.

Deiu, God.

Delaiſſer, to leave, forſake, *delaiſſe*, left.

Deia, dyed. *p.* 2 *Rich.* 3. *annal. deja*, idem, alſo likewiſe.

Dillonque, then, there, vide *illonq;*.

Dejecter, to caſt off, *dejecte*, caſt off, dejected.

Dejet, thrown down.

Dejettement, a caſting off.

Deins, within.

Dela, idem, *ut de ca*, and from thence.

Delegation, a Power conferred or given upon another.

Deliberer, to purpoſe, to think, to conſult.

Ils delibere, they conſulted.

Delire, vide, *deſlire*.

Delict, an Offence, a Fault.

Delinquer, to commit an offence, *il a Delinque*, he hath done amiſs.

Delecter, to delight.

Demaiſnes, *demaines* & *demeſnes*, the Lord's peculiar Lands kept in his Hands.

Ses demean, his own, *en lour demeſne*, as their own. *p. Stat. Gloceſ. cap.* 4. *demean*, idem.

Demaine, to Morrow, *le jour apres demain*, the day after to Morrow. 5. *Edw.* 3. 23.

Demaunder, to ask, requeſt, *demaunda*, asked, *demaundomus*, we require, or ask.

Deme, to be. *p. termes de Ley.* 95.

Deluge, a Floud, *deluvie*, idem. *p. Britton.* 77. b.

Demenge, paſt, gone over, elapſed.

Son demeſne, his own.

Demie & *demy*, the half.

Dementiers, in the mean time, alſo forthwith.

Demiſe, *demiſt*, let go, let to Farm, to part with.

Demiſe le Roy, the Abateing or Death of the King, *Que ſoy il dimiſt*, for that he is Dead or gone, as by entring into a Religious Profeſſion, he left the World.

Demit & *demitte*, left, *demiſterent*, they left. *p. Mirror.*

Demittable, *demiſeable*, or to be letten.

Demitter, to let go, to put away, vide, *dimitter*, to part with.

Democratie, a Commonwealth, or Government by the People.

Demonſtrer, to ſhew.

Demorger, to ſtay, reſide continue or dwell, *demorgent* & *demoergent*, they reſide, dwell, &c. *il demoerge*, they remain or dwell. *p. Stat.* 28. *Edw.* 1.

Demurrants, inhabitants, *demoerrants*, idem, ſuch as ſtay or dwell.

Demurrer, to ſtay, to abide, alſo a Plea in Law, demanding the Advice of the Court.

Demurge, left, ſtaid.

Il demurra, he ſhall remain or ſtay.

La demurraſt, he ſtaid there. *p. Plowd.*

Il ad demurr, he hath dwell'd.

Demeure, in *Mod. French* is to abide or dwell.

Demurrant, remaining, abiding.

Il demurt, it remaineth or belongeth unto.

Denariata terre, the fourth part of an Acre of Land which is a *Fardingdale* or *Farundale*, *denie*, forbidden.

Dene & *denne*, a Valley or Dale, also a place inhabited. *p. Cokes Inst.* 1. p.

Un denier, a Peny, *deniers*, Money, *denires*, idem.

Denommer, to Name or Nominate.

Denombrement, numbring.

Denoter, to make known.

Dent, a Tooth, *dentes*, Plural.

Denouncer, to declare.

Departir, to divide, also to rejoyn in Pleading, other matter than at first Pleaded unto, also, to leave.

Departibiles, dividable, *departissement*, dividing, a Partition.

Deplayer, to wound, *deplaye*, wounded.

Depriver, to take away, *deprist*, took away.

Deposer, to testifie, also to put down.

Deprimer, to bring one low.

Depeller, to pull down, or thrust down.

Depriver, to put by.

Depuis, since, *depuis le temps*, after the time, afterwards, lately.

De quoy, wherewith, of which.

Deraigne, Dishabited, Unapparelled, *deraigner* to displace, to turn out of Order, vide, *daraine*.

Au dernier, at last, *le darnier*, the last.

Derniermert, lastly, lately.

Deraign & *dereyn*, to prove, try, also to put out of Order.

Deroguer, to Abrogate, to diminish.

Derompe, to break, to burst.

Derecherf, further, moreover.

Derompement, breaking, bursting.

Derriere, backwards, behind, again, vide, *arrier*.

Derire moy, behind me. 2. *Hen.* VII.

Derise, Mocked, Laught at.

Des, from, *des le commencement*, from the beginning, *des* Plural of *de*.

Desaccuastomee, unwonted, not usual.

Desafubler, to undeceive. *p. Britton*. 39.

Desaventure, mischance.

Desarray, to put out of Order.

Desbourser, to expend or lay out.

Descrie, perceived, *descryer*, to discover.

Descroistre, to grow less.

Deschuer, to fall out, to happen, *descheur*, idem, also to fall down. *p.* 12. *Hen.* VIII. 1. a.

Desdire, to gainsay to recant.

Desesparer, to Despair.

Desgorger, to Vomit.

Desgarnys, unwarned.

Desarmee, Disarmed.

Desastre, a hard Chance.

Desjoindre, to separate.

Desheriteur, to Disinherit.

Desboucher, to unstop, to set abroach, also to dispark.

Descinct, ungirded.

Deschire, torn, rent.

Descoller, to behead one.

Disco-

Discovrir, to uncover, *discovertes*, uncovered.

Desempestrer, to get out of a Snare, to unentangle.

Deshabiller, to undress one.

Deshonte, without Shame.

Deslier, to Choose, Elect, also to unbind, or set free, *deslie*, loose, unbound, freed.

Desmaintenant, from henceforth, even now.

Desmettre, to misplace, to put out of joynt.

Desgarner, to unfurnish.

Desnigrer, to defame, to speak ill of.

Desnuer, to make naked.

Desnue de amies, void or destitute of Friends.

Desoler, to ruin, to make desolate.

Desormais, hereafter, compounded of *des & Mais*, *i.e.* from thence, *vide desormes*.

Despendre, to spend.

Desplier, to unfold, to make manifest.

Desouth, under, *desorbes*, from under.

Desraciner, to root out.

Despores, Spurrs. *p. Parkins* 148.

Desroy, to be out of Order.

Le deserte, the Banquet, or after course.

Dessevrer, to put asunder.

Dessus, above, aloft.

Les dessus de touts choses, the uppermost part, or face of all things.

Destendre, to stretch out, *destendu*, stretch'd, and sometimes, loosned.

Destiner, to appoint.

Destruere, to destroy, to wastes,

Destruict & gaste, destroyed and wasted. *p. Plowd.* 191.

Desordre, confusion.

Desore, from hence, *desere*, idem. *p.* 2. *part Instit.* 639.

Desormes, hereafter.

En despitant, in spight.

Despitousment, despightfully.

En despite le Cur, against the Rule of the Court, or against their will in spight of them. *Brit.* 223. b.

Desouth, beyond, *desouth la Mer*, beyond Sea.

Desouth p. Kitchin, is above, and likewise by him in some places, for under.

Desoubs, is under, *Mettre desoubs*, put under and to submit unto. *p. Eundem.*

Destoier vide estoier, to stand to, and to abide by.

Dessus quoy, upon which, *la dessus*, thereupon. *p. Coke Rep.* 9. 120.

Destopper, to open.

Ne destour, not gone back or stirred.

D'estre, to be.

Desurder, to raise.

Desuis, above or before.

Desus, idem. *p. Britton.*

Desuis est dit, aforesaid, abovesaid.

Il destruist, he destroyeth. *Plowden.*

Desyra, took away, spoild. *p. nov. nar.* 47. b.

Desveloper, to unfold, or unwrap.

Desvelope, unfolded.

Desvester, to undress, or uncloath, and by *Coke* 'tis, to put off or discontinue. *rep.* 5. 80. idem *ut devester*, *devestre*, idem.

Detenus,

Detenus, withheld, *detence*, kept withheld.

Determinera, shall end.

Detrahe, withdrawn, or held back.

Devant, before, *va devant jeo te suy aray*, go before I will follow thee.

Cy devant, heretofore, before this time.

Detracter, to backbite, to speak ill of one.

Deu, a debt, and *duement*, duly.

Devantq; before that, *devant & darrer*, before and behind.

Devent que jours, before which days.

Devenir, to become.

Deveign, become, *deveign Lye*, become bound.

Devenus, become, *devenont*, they became.

Deveignont, idem, *deviendra*, shall become.

Ils dever, they ought, they came.

dever estre, ought to be, vide, *deves*.

Deyve, ought, *ne deyvent*, they ought not.

Devient & devoyent, idem, *ne deves*, ye ought not.

Devises, Shares, Dividends, Divisions. *p. Britton* 185.

Devers, against, towards, *negard devers moy*, look towards me, *deves*, ye ought, *devers orient*, towards the East.

Devove, appointed, *devover*, to appoint or to give unto.

Deux, two, *deux a deux*, two by two.

D'eux, of them, *deulx*, idem, also, from them.

Devestre, to put off, *devest*, put off.

Devie & devia, dieth, *devier*, to dye.

Devient, they die; *devierent*, they are dead.

Devierviant, they should dye.

Le devison, the Division.

Devises ouster, put forth, put out.

Sont devises, are given or devised.

Ne Devestua, shall not be put by. *p. Greg.* 288.

Devoyer, endeavour.

Dew & dieu, God. *p. Brit.* 1. a.

Devolute, happened, became, devolved. *per Nov. Narr.* 61. b.

Dextre & dexter, the right Hand.

Dextrement, nimbly, aptly.

Deyvent, they ought, idem, *ut devient*. *p. Britton* 27. b.

D I.

Diable, vide, *deable*.

Diametre, the middle.

A dicelle, from henceforth. *p. Stat. sup. Chart.* 28, *Edw.* 1.

Die, say, declare. *p. Britton* 8. b.

A dire, to say, *jeo die*, I said, *dit*, doth say.

Est ditz, it is said, *vous dires*, ye shall say.

Jeo aye dit, I have said, *diomus*, we say.

Disont & diont, they said, *voir dire*, to speak truly.

Dillonques,

Dillonques, from thence, from that time.

Dict, a Word.

Dirra & *dirray*, ſhall ſpeak or ſay.

Diſtu, ſpeak thou, *diſant* ſaying.

Il diſt ainſi, he ſaid ſo.

Dicel, of this ſame.

Un dilapider, a Lapidary.

Dimitter & *dimeter*, to leave, *ne dimit*, doth not leave.

Dimetter, alſo, to Leaſe out.

Dirute, thrown down, deſtroyed.

Diſeame, unſowed.

Dieu, God, *dieu tres puiſſent*, Almighty God.

Dieu te gard, God ſave thee.

Differer, to delay, to put off, *differer de jour en jour*, to put off from day to day.

Digerer, to digeſt.

Dign, worthy, *dign de Loyer*, worthy of reward, *dignement*, worthily.

Digit, a Finger.

Dimenche, Sunday, *dimenches*, Sabbath days, *dimence et dimanche*, Sunday. *p. Mirror Juſtice*, *cap.* 5.

En dimentiers, in the mean time. *p. Britton* 10. b.

Dimiſont, they Demiſe, or Leaſe out, or let go.

Dimittant, Leaſeing or letting go.

Dilliours, of Electours. *p. Plowd. Abr.* 23. a. vide, *illors*.

Diminuer, to leſſen, or take away from.

Dicy, from hence, *de icy*, idem, *dicy en avant*, from henceforwards.

Diriger, to direct, *directres*, ye direct.

Directe, directly and directed, *directement*, directly.

Dirept, took away.

Dirupt, broke down.

Diſcendre, to go down, diſcend.

Diſcendue, deſcended, *diſcendus*, idem.

Diſcendiſt, doth deſcend.

Diſcinct, ungirded, unbound.

Diſcerner, to diſcover.

Diſliver, to diſplace, *diſlieu*, diſplaced.

Diſavaile, diſadvantage. 35. *Hen.* 57. a.

Diſcomoder, to make unprofitable, to do Damage.

Diſcovert, not within the bands of Matrimony, alſo a Woman unmarried, or Widow.

Diſannexe, unjoyned.

Diſcontinuer, to ceaſe.

Diſconus, unknown. *p. Hen.* 8. 26. 2. b.

Diſcretement, prudently, or wiſely.

Diſcrepance, variance. *p. Plow. Com.* 190. b.

Diſcombrance, Diſturbance. 1. *Hen.* 7. 7. b.

Diſcowrer, to cleanſe.

Diſcriver, to diſcover. *p. Fitzh. Nat. br.* 42. b.

eſt diſcerne, is ſeen.

Diſcuſſe, decided.

Diſdeinance, diſpiſeing.

Diſetteuſe, Poverty, want, beggery. *p. Coke rep.* 11. 53.

Diſgrade, degraded.

Diſjoinctive, not joyntly.

Diſſemblable, unlike.

Diſmarries, unmarried. 35. *Hen.* 6. 40. b.

Diſmer,

Dismer, to Tythe.

Dismes, Tythes.

Le dise, part the Tythe, or tenth part, *p. More* 485.

Disoient, vide *antea*, & *dysoit*.

Come disoi, as I said, 2. *Rich.* 3. *ann.*

Disoitisme, the 18th part. *p.* 18*th. Edw.* 3. 6. *p.* 7.

Disistz, ye said. *p. Plowd.*

Dispenser, to distribute.

Dispencer, to discharge, or acquit.

Dispenser le leyes, to dispence with the Laws.

Dispendu, put off, hindred, avoided.

Dispend, depend. *p. Coke rep.* 8.

Disputomus, we will dispute, 43. *Hen.* 3, 23. b.

Dispuny, unpunished, *dispunis*, idem.

Disseteux, destitute.

Dissimuler, to dissemble.

Dissiper, to spread abroad.

Distorne, diverted. *p. Kitchin.* 21, b.

Dist, said. *p. Britton* 38, b.

Son dist, his Speech, *p. Plowd.*

Distre, idem, *ut de estre*, to be.

Distreiner, to take by distress.

Ne destreinera, shall not distrain.

Distraire, to draw back, or withdraw.

District, the bounds of a Territory, wherein the Lord hath right to distrain.

Districte, restrained or hindred. *p. Nov. Narr.* 16, b.

Distruer, to destroy.

Disturber, to hinder.

Dites ceo, speak it, or speak ye. *p.* 20. *Hen.* 7, 5. *annal.*

Diviner, to foretel, *divinance*, foretelling.

Diveller, to throw off, to pull off.

Divell, pull'd, or thrown off.

Diviser, to separate, or divide.

Diverter, to turn away, also to fix one's thoughts on new matter.

Divers, differing or different.

Divers moult, differing much. *p. Termes Ley.*

Diversement, diversly, severally. *p. Plowd. Com.* 378.

Divorser, to separate from Marriage by a Spiritual Sentence.

Un divorse, such a separation.

Divulguer, to declare openly, or publish secrets.

Divulguee, the thing so published.

Dix, ten, *diz*, idem, & *dize*, idem.

Dise sous, ten Shillings.

Dise quater, fourteen.

Dizeime, the tenth, *dixisme*, idem.

Disme, idem.

Disoitisme, the eighteenth. 2 *part Instit.* 639. *tempore Edw.* 3*d. en le act p. dismes.*

Dizaine, containing ten.

Le Dixiesme, the tenth.

Dix size, sixteen.

Dix trois, thirteen.

Dix neufiesme, the nineteenth.

Dizesinque, fifteen.

Dix butiesme, & *dix butieme*, the eighteenth.

Diminue, lessened. *p. Plowden.*

Dize, ten, *p. Plowd.*

Le dize, the tenth, *p. Coke.*

Dycel, of this, of it.

Docker, to cut off, to dock or barr.

Doce, the back, *dos*, idem. 2. *Hen.* 7, 8, a.

Doet, he ought, *doet & poet*, he ſhould, may, or ought.

Doet a moy, he oweth to me.

El doet, ſhe ought.

Doit, oweth, and ought.

Doit demurrer, he muſt ſtay.

Doyes, do ye.

Vous doyes, ye ought.

Doient, & *Doyent*, they ought, or are, *doint*, idem.

Ne doit, he owes not.

Docile, eaſy to be taught.

Un document, a precept, or inſtruction.

Un Doigt, a Finger, idem, *ut digit.*

Dol, grief, alſo deceit.

Doler, to grieve.

Doleur aver, to have grief.

Doleur, pain, or grief.

Doleance, grieving.

Doles, Hogſheads. *p. Fitzh. Nat. Brev.* 88. a.

Un docenary, & *docener*, one admitted as a Reſiant in a Mannor to be ſworn.

Domeſman, a Judge, one that giveth Sentence.

Dommage, loſs, damage.

Porter dommage, to bring, or ſuffer loſs, or hurt.

Dommageable, hurtful.

Domer, to tame.

Domeſtes, tame things. *p. Stat. reſt.* 1. 20.

Donaiſon, vide *denizon.*

Donner, to give, & *doner*, idem.

Donant, giving.

Si nos donoremus, if we ſhould give. *p. Plowd.* 97. b.

Done, & *dones*, given.

A donner un don, to give a gift.

Donnera, ſhall give.

Donement, giving.

Eſteant done, being given.

Donez, given.

Donc & *donque*, then, therefore, *donques*, idem.

A toy donques, to thee therefore, *adieu donc*, farewel then.

Un donizon, a gift. *p. Nov. Narr.* 17.

D'ont, whereof.

Dont il appiert, by which it appeareth.

Dont, alſo, whence, and whereby.

Dormir, to ſleep.

Dormie, ſlept and ſleepeth.

Dormant, ſleeping.

Dorp & *thorp*, a Village.

Dors, a back, idem *ut dorce* & *dorſe.*

D'or, gold.

Dore & *doree*, gilded.

Dorra, would give, or do.

Jeo te doray, I would give thee. *p. Britton*, 62.

Doſſes, ſhoulders, alſo backs.

Dotkins, an old Coin about a Farthing value.

Dout, fear.

Doutent, they feared.

Dowtous, doubtful, or doubted. *p. Fitzh.* 222. *Nat. brev.*

Douze, twelve.

Douzain, a dozen.

Doudize, twelve.

Doudize deniers, twelve Pence.

Douze milliares, twelve miles. *p. Termes de Ley.*

Douſter, vide *ouſter.*

Douns, Gifts.

Jeo doy, I owe thee. *p. Brit.* 174.

Dote, dower.

Breve de dote, a Writ of dower.

Douteuse, doubtful.

Doux, gentle, tractable, also smooth.

Un doyn, a Dean.

Doyenne, a Deanship, or Deanry.

Je doyne, I give thee. *p. Britton.* 94, b.

Ne tu doynes, thou dost not give. *p. eundem.*

Ne doyent, they ought not. *p. Plowden.*

D R.

Dragme, & *drachme*, a dram weight.

Drap, & *drape*, Cloth.

Seant de south drap de estate, sitting under a Cloth of state. *p.* 13. *Hen.* 7.

Drap bien drappe, Cloth well wrought.

Drappes, plural.

Un drappier, a Clothier.

Dras, Wares. *p. Brit.* 38, & 33, a.

Drenchs, free Tenants of a Mannor.

Droit & *droict*, right.

Mere droit, a direct, or meer right.

Droitement, directly, rightly.

Droitural, & *droiturel*, rightful.

Sons droiturel, indirectly, without right.

Droiturement, & *droiturelment*, rightly.

A Droiture, to do rightly.

En droiture, in doing right.

Drus, a Tooth, vide *dent.*

Druf, a Thicket of Wood, *dru* idem.

Drusden, & *drosden*, idem.

Du, from, of, out, by, in.

Du chimin, by the way.

Du cost d'orient, from the East.

Du Arabie, from Arabia.

Du touts, in the whole.

Du quel, of which.

Duc, a Duke, or Leader, or General.

Duche, a Dukedome.

Dunum, *duna*, & *dun*, a Hill.

Duritie, hardness.

Dur, hard, *dure*, hard.

Durer, to last, to continue.

Durer jesque a la fin, to continue to the end.

Durette, hardness, *durement*, hardly, continually, also fiercely.

Duresse, force, also hardship.

Durham, in the year Books called the *Franchise de werk*,

Duit, he ought.

Duist estre, it ought to be.

Il duist tue, he hath killed. 3. *Hen.* 6.

Duissoit, he ought.

Duissoient, they ought.

Ne duist mitter, he ought not to send, or put.

Que duict, who ought.

Dulce, fresh, sweet.

Dumes, brambles, thorns. *p. Fitzh. Nat. brev.* 59, b.

Ust duy, had died. *p. Coke Rep.* 8, 76, a.

Le dyst, the said.

Dysont, they said.

Dyzant, saying, *dysant*, idem.

Dyker, to Ditch. *p. Fitzh. Justice* 75, a.

E *Age*, age, vide *aage*.

Eau & eaue, Water, vide *ewe*.

Eawes, Waters.

Eare, to Plowe.

Ealra, all, a *Saxon* word.

Ealrawitena gemot, a Councell or Court of all the Wisemen.

Ebrie & ebriee, drunk.

Ebrietie, drunkeness.

Ebulition, boyling, bubbling up.

Echelle, a Ladder.

Eclypser, to vanish, to hide.

Ecloy, Urine.

Edict, an ordinance, or command.

Edite, set forth.

Edovart, Edward.

Edifier, to build.

Effacer, to blot out, to deface.

Effacement, defacing obliterating.

Ees, Bees, *p. Britton*. 85.

Effect, Force, Vertue.

Effoder, to dig up, *effode* dug up or out.

Effrayer, to affright, *estre affray*, to be frighted.

Effraye, fear, terror.

Effunder, to shed, spill. 3 *Hen.* 7, 1, b.

Effundes, spilt or shed.

E G.

Egal, equal, *sont egales*, are equal.

Egual, idem in mod. French.

Egaler, to make equal.

Egality, equality, *Egalitie*, idem.

Engalement & engalment, equally.

Eglise, the Church, vide *Esglise*.

Egalisement, making equal.

Egrotant, sick.

Eguiser, to happen.

E I.

Eide, aid.

Eiant, having, vide *Eyant*.

Eins, in within, and by *Yelverton*, but, 113.

Eins concela, but hide, or conceal.

Vous vient eins, come ye in, *p. Parkins*.

Eins, within. *p. Gregory* 281.

Soy tent ens, kept himself in. *p. Coke rep.* 8.

Einsi, being, vide *ainsi*.

Einsi oustre, being ousted, or outed. *p. Fitzh.* grand Abridgment. 152 a. *ceo vindra eins*, this shall come in. *p. Coke Report*, 5, 69.

De eins, Eyes, *p. Nov. Nar.* 116.

Eies, forwards, *p. termes Ley*, 156.

Eign, old, eldest, *plus eigne*, older.

Eisne, eldest.

Eignesse file, eldest Daughter, *einesse*, idem. *p. Britton* 57, b.

Eire, to hatch, or sit over, *eire de espernons*, young brood of Hawks.

Il eit, he hath, *eient*, they have.

Eyent & eyant, they have.

Eit, may have. 2 *Hen.* 7, 15.

E L.

El & sa, she and her.

Elle, her and she, *ele*, idem. *p. Parkins*.

Eliser, to choose, *poet eleyer*, may choose.

Elisors, electors, *eliew*, chosen *elews*, idem.

Eloigner, to filch, to imbezle, *esloigner*, idem.

Eloignment, filching, stealing.

Eloinement & elongation, a removeing a great way, from or off.

Elopement, is, when the Wife leaves the Husband, and goes with the advouterer.

Ellupe, idem *ut elope*.

E M.

Emanciper, to set free.

Un emancipe, he that is set or made free.

Embellies, set forth, shewed, alsо decked or trimmed, *p. Mir. Just*.

Emer, to buy, *un emer*, a buyer, *le emer*, the buyer.

Eme, brought, *ema*, idem. *emont*, they bought, or they buy.

Emanet, he came forth, he arose from.

Emailler, to Enammel.

Embas, below, *ou en bas*, or below.

Un ambassade, a message.

Embler, to steal, *ad emblee*, hath stolen.

Embeasiler, to filch, idem *ut esloignee*.

Embiller, to deck or trim.

Emblements, profits of Land.

Emblerr, stealing, *embleea*, stolen.

Ad embleai, hath sowed, *emblee*, idem. *p. Hen. 6. annal. emblea*, idem. *p. Coke*, *Report* 5.

Embleya, shall sow, *p. Parkins* 109.

Un embleer, a seedsman, or sower.

Le embleyer, the sowing. *p. Parkins* 109.

Embler, to sow, *emble & ere*, to Plow and Sow.

Embleement, sowing, *embleyment*, idem.

Embleements & emblements, Corn, Grass, and other profits of Lands, vide *antea*.

Per embles, by stealing, *p. termes de Ley*, 131.

Emblees, *p. Brokes* grand Abridgment, is, stolen, 320.

Emboir, to drink up.

Embraser, to burne, vide *arser*.

Embrase, burned.

Un embracer, he that labours in a Cause in Law without Fees, also one that informs or perswades Jury-men.

Embu, distayned, dyed, drunk up.

Emmurer, to wall about.

Emolluments, profits, advantages.

Emont, they bought, *p. Plowd.* 379, a.

Emparka, impounded, *Emparkes*, idem.

Emperkment, impounding.

Emparlance, liberty and time to advise upon, or together.

Emptre, to make worse, *Empere*, idem. *p. Britton* 143.

Emporcel & enporcel, in Pigg, or great with Pigg, *Empechement*, hindrance.

Emporter, to carry, or bring, *emport*, carryed.

Emporta, idem. *emportees*, ye carryed.

Jeo emport, I bear or carry.

Emprendre

Emprendre, to take upon.

Emprant, took also borrowed. *p. Termes*, 246. b.

Emprent, comprehended.

Il emprist, he took upon him, or undertook.

Empris, taken in hand.

Emprisoner, to put in Prison.

Emprisont, takeing, also they took. *Plowd.* 91, a.

Emprisoner soi mesme, to put himself in Prison.

Emprisonera, shall imprison.

Emprister, to take upon him.

Empriteront sur eux, they took upon them. *p. Parkins*, 115, a.

Empraunt, borrowed, or borrowing.

Emption, buying.

Emsemblement, in like manner, together, with. *p. Nov. Nar.* 7, b.

Empeche, hindered, also accused.

Empeschement, hindring, *empeschemints*, hindrances, *p. Coke, Rep.* 9, 121.

Emplir, to fulfill, *emplee*, fulfilled.

E N.

En, in, by, within.

En ce, in this or that.

En chimin, by the way, and in the way.

En apres, hereafter, afterwards.

En oultre, furthermore.

Encheson, by the reason of, or cause.

Encepper, to take again, *Br.* 125, b.

Enapres illont este icy, there may be hereafter.

Enbeverer, to water, *droit de enbeverer*, right of watering, or taking water for Cattle. *p. Britton* 156, b.

Enbrever, to write down in short, also put into writings. *p. eund.* 7, a.

Ency, therein. *Plowd.* 80.

En quoy ay jeo offence, wherein have I offended.

En quater ans, whithin four Years.

En pu temps, within a little time.

Enblai & enblee, idem *ut emblee*.

Enbleier, to steal, *pour le enbleier*, for the stealing, 26 *Hen.* 8.

Encaver, to beware.

Enchaser, to Hunt, Drive, or Course.

Enchasemus, we Hunted, &c.

Enchasa, *enchaca*, & *Enchasea*, Hunted, Drove, Chased, *enchasiastes*, ye chased.

Encharger, to give in Charge or Command.

Pur enchason vide *encheson*.

Enchison idem. or for which cause or matter. *p. Coke Rep.* 5, 100, b.

Auter encheson, other cause.

Enchison, *p. Coke*, *Rep.* 5, hapned.

Encombre, to hinder, disturb, also to possess a Church.

Encombent, he that possesseth, the Person or Vicar thereof.

Enclaimant, claiming.

Encient, with Child.

Encoupe, accused, charged with, also endited, appealed. *p. Britton*, 11, 12.

Enclowe, pricked by a Nail in shewing a Horse.

Enclume, an Anvill. *p. termes Ley*, 164.

Encountree, to be against.

Enclore, to impark inclose.

Encore, vide *uncore*.

Encrochement, fencing in building upon enclosing, or overcharging the Commons, also where the Lord doth overcharge the Tenants in Rents, or Services.

Encru, encreased.

Incur, to run into, hapned.

Endebter, to owe.

Endeges, wanting Age. *p. Britton*, 62.

Endowement, giving, setling upon.

Endocer, to endorse, or write upon the backside.

Endoce, endorsed.

De infanter, to be with Child, or breeding.

Inferrer, to put in Irons, or Fetters.

Enformer, to teach.

Pur enformer, for teaching.

Enfraunchiser, to make free.

Enfreinder, to break.

Enfreint, broken.

Enfreind, breaking.

Enfrenge, broken.

Enfurer, to run, or fly away.

Enfua, shall fly, or run.

Enfues, driven away. *p. Cromp.* 168.

Enfue, fled. *p. eund.* 141.

Enfuont, they fly.

Enfuant, flying, or runing away.

Se enfuyoit, he was fled. *Coke Rep.* 9, 120.

Enfuis, have been, *enfuys*, idem.

Engarnies, with-held. *p. Mirror Cap.* 5, 2.

Engendre, to beget.

Que engender, who begot.

Engendrure, begetting, also having Issue.

Engendrure a nestre, Issue to be born. *p. Britton* 91.

Engendre, is also, begotten.

Engetta, ousted or outed.

Engette, cast out.

Engettement, putting out of possession. *p. Brit.* 93.

Engettre, *Engetter*, to eject, or throw out, also to lay or put.

Engettement le mains, laying on of hands.

Engleterre, England.

Englois, an English-Man.

En englisheirie, in English. *p. Brit.*

Enhabler, to enable.

Pur enginer, to beguile. *p. Stat. Westm.* 1. *Cap.* 29.

Enhaunce, & *enhausen*, to raise up.

Enhaute, exalted, set up.

Enhault, on high.

Enheriter, to inherit.

Enheritera, shall inherit.

Encre, Ink.

Enjont, enjoyning.

Enjoindre, & *Enjoinder*, to enjoyn, to command.

Enjetter violentz mains, to lay violent hands.

Enjetter ascun orderrs, laying, or throwing dung or filth. *p. Fitzh. Nat. brev.* 176, b.

En lieu, instead of.

Enlever, to advance higher, to lift up.

Enombrager, to shadow, hide, or cover.

Ennoyter, to annul, to make void, alter. *p. Brit.* 1, a.

Enpantes, carryed away. *p.* 13. *Hen.* 7, 9, b.

Enpire, made worse, vide *Empire*.

Enprendre, & *enprender*, to take upon one.

Enpaine, & *Eupoin*, in hand.

Enpirsant,

Enprisant, taking in hand, or upon one.

Enprower, to improve, also to enclose.

Jeo vous enprie, I desire you. *Park*. 170, a.

Enfreindre, & *enfraindre*, to break.

Enlever, to lift up.

Ennobler, to make noble.

Enracier, vide *postea*.

Enracive, rooted, vide *erace*.

Le enquest, a Jury to enquire into.

Les enquest, their verdict.

Vous enquires, ye shall enquire.

Enquis, & *enquise*, required.

Pur enquirer, for enquiring.

Equerage, enquiry.

Enquer, ask, enquire.

Enracer, to pull up by the roots, to demolish.

Enrollment, entring upon record.

Ensient, being with Child, *insient*, idem.

Ensient engrossement, great with Child.

Ens, within, *eins*, idem, *ens cy*, here within.

Ensemble, in like manner, also together.

Ensiment, also.

Ensuant, pursuing.

Ensuer, to pursue.

Esealast, sealed.

Enseares, locked.

Ensemblement, uniting together.

Ensement, likewise, in like manner. 1. *Hen*. 7, 10.

Ensevilir, to bury.

Ensevelie, buried.

Soit cors ensevely, let the Body be buried. *p. Britton*. f. 18.

Enserve, kept, reserved.

Ensier, to mow, or reap.

Ensoy, in it self.

En est ensuivi, in what followeth. *p. Coke Rep*. 9.

El ensuits, it followeth.

Cy ensuiant, they here follow or pursue.

Ensuera, shall follow, or shall happen.

Entant que, in as much. 1 Inst. § 283.

Entend, conceive, understand.

Enterrer, to lay, or bury in the Earth.

Enterre, buryed.

Enterment, burying.

Entre, between, among.

Entre deux, between hand.

Entrelasser, to put between, to interline.

Enterlaise, & *enterlease*, & *enterlesse*, omitted, left out. *p. Plowd*.

Ent, thereupon. *nat. brev*. also of them.

Entant, so that, forasmuch, *entent*, idem.

Enterlassement, interlining.

Enterlaise, also mingled.

Entendre, to understand, to think, to be mindful.

Soit a entendre, it is to be understood. *p. Littleton*.

Entend, a purpose to do.

Entende, understood.

Vous entendes, perceive ye, mind ye.

Entendment, waiting, also understanding.

Entermedle, mingled, mixed.

Entermellent, they use, occupy.

Entrepennent, they consulted among themselves, Enterprizing. *Coke* 2, 120.

Enterpend, purposed.

Entegris,

Entegris de tanners que fount, of Tanners who use fresh Bark and old Bark together, and deceitfully Tan Leather. *p. Britton.* 33.

Entier, the whole, *entiertie*, idem, *Entirement*, wholy.

Entour, round about, *entowre*, idem.

Eontourer, to go a Compass about. *p. Kitchin.*

Entromitter, idem, *ut intromitter*, to meddle with.

Entover, to walk about, *entorement*, wholly. *p. Brit.*

Entour les ovres, about their works.

Entrer, to enter in, *entrent*, they enter.

Entramous, we entred.

Entruder, he who wrongfully enters upon Tenants, or Lands upon the Death of Tenants for Life, or Years. He who so enters upon the Dearh of Tenants in Fee is called an *Abator*.

Envenemer, to Poison, *envenome*, Poisoned.

Envers, against.

Enveigleroit, may pre-possess, or enveigle.

Environ, to compass about.

Envoyer, to send one a Message, *Ad envoye*, hath sent, *Envoyes*, Messengers, Ambassadors.

Envoieront, they sent forth. *p. Mirror. Cap.* 2. *Ser.* 15.

Enuer, to work, to use.

Enuera, shall work to the use.

Enuront, they work, or enure.

Envellope, wrapped, folded.

Environ, about.

E P.

Epiphanie, the Day when the Star appear'd to the Wise Men at Christ's Nativity, generally called Twelf Day.

Epitomie, an Abridgment.

E Q.

Equiture, to ride.

Equinoce, equal Day and Night.

Equivoque, a double understanding.

Equivalent, of like value.

Equipollent, idem. *p. Coke Rep.* 5, 89, b. and 8, 93. b.

E R.

Eracer, & *erescer*, to root out.

Erace, rooted out, vide *enrace*.

Erainent, leaving off, or avoiding. *p. Yelverton* 153.

Erberage, provision for Cattel, Victuals, vide *herberage*.

Errer, to go astray.

Il erver, he travelled, *eroer*, idem, or journeyed. *Mirror Cap.* 2.

Errance, wandering, *Errassent*, they should wander.

Erer, to Plough. *p.* 2. *Hen.* 8. *annal.*

Ere, idem, *p. eund. si jeo voil ero*, if I will Plough. *p.* 12. *Hen.* 8, 2, b.

Erreur, Error.

Ert, it shall be, also it is.

Ert estable, it shall be firm. *Brit.* 49. b.

Un ermit, a Hermit.

Erberger, to lodge, or harbour one. *Herberger*, idem.

Eriger, to raise up.

Erudic, learning, *erudice*, learned.

Erudition, learning, *erudier*, to learn, *les erudite*, the learned.

E S.

Es, signifies, in, plurally *p.* 3. *pt. Instit.* 39.

Es, thou.

Esceppe & *eskep*, Shipped, vide *eskepper*.

Esheat,

Esheat, a forfeiture to the King or the Lord of the Mannor, in a criminal cause, also for want of Heirs, *eschea*, happened.

Eschaper, to escape.

Eshetour, he that seizes for the King in such Case, by vertue of his Office.

Escheter, to fall or happen unto.

Eschevins, Sherriffs.

Eshuer eshire & eshure, to fall or happen or fall out, *eshuera*, shall fall out, also to avoid or shun.

Eshie & eschy, happened, befell.

Enchest & enchuist, hath happened or befell.

Eshevier, to fall out, in Mod. *French*.

Eskippe, shipped.

Escient, knowing, also they knew. *p. Britton* 4, b.

En eshuant, in avoiding.

Eschaude, famished, also choak. *p. Britton* 4.

Esclander, to defame.

Escoce, Scotland, *escosse*, idem.

Escoter, to contribute unto.

Escowrer, to cleanse.

Esclairees, cleared.

Escripts, writeings.

Escrier, to write, *escrie*, written.

Escryeurs, Writers.

Escriera, shall Write.

Escrie, written, *escript in le cuer*. written in the Heart. *per Kitchin.*

Escrit, written, *escripture*, writeing.

Jeo escrivera, I have written.

Escriemus, we write, *escront*, they write.

Escrivener, a Scribe.

Le escrier, the writer, *in escrivant*, in writing.

Escries, discovered, known. *p. Fitzh. Just.* 146, b.

D' escocher, to shoot.

Escole, a School.

Esclaves, Slaves, *esclairees*, cleared.

Eschorcheours, they who flay Cattle for their skins. *p. Brit.* 63.

Escrovet, a scrowl.

Escrowe & escrowle, a writeing which is not to take effect but on some condition or Act to be performed.

Eschues, Shields.

Eschews, Wind-fallen Trees.

Pur eshure, for avoiding, also befalling.

Un escossois, a Scotch-man, or Scottish.

Eskipper, to Ship, *escipt*, *eskipt*, & *escippe*, ship'd, *eskirpe*, idem. *p. Crompton Jur. Cur.*

Eskippeson, shipping.

Esglise, Church, *esglis*, idem.

Eslier, to choose, to elect, *eslieu*, chosen.

Eslius, idem. *esliera*, shall choose.

Esliors, electors, *esliant*, chooseing.

Esloigner, to take away privily, to embezle.

Esloignes, strayed, embezled.

Esloignment, straying, or making away.

Eslus, *eslues*, & *eslien*, chosen, elected.

Esmerveiller, to wonder, to admire.

Esnecy, a right of Primogeniture.

Esposent, they married.

Espandue, shed, spilt, *sanke espandue*, Blood shed, *sank espank*, id.

Especialment, chiefly.

Espee & espe, a Sword.

Espee, by *Britton*, a thigh and ſometimes a Leg.

Esperer, to hope, to truſt in.

Espier, hope, truſt, *espoier* idem, *on espere*, it is hoped.

Esperitual, Spiritual, Divine.

Esperver, a Hawk, *esperons*, Hawks.

Esprever in Mod. French, is a Hawk.

Esperons ſpurs, *esperons de Or*, gilt Spurrs. *p. Coke Rep.* 7. 13.

Espine, a Thorn.

Espingles de boys, pins of Wood.

Espirit, a Spirit.

Que espier, who informs. 1. *Hen.* 7. 3. a.

Esplees & esples, are the Profits of Lands, and generally taken for the whole Profits.

Esplee le Huiſſes, Bolt or Lock the Doors.

Esploir, to requeſt earneſtly with Tears.

Espoier, to hope, to wiſh, to truſt to.

Mon espoier, my Truſt or Hope.

Espoirant, hoping, *avoit espoier*, he had hopes.

Eſſay, a Proof or Tryal.

Eſſarter vide *Aſſarter*.

Espouſer, to Wedd, to Marry.

Espouſels, Marriage, *espouſelx*, idem.

Le espoux, the Bridegroom.

Espouſee, the Bride, *espouſe*, Married.

Eſſoyn & eſſoin, to have a further day given for Appearance in Court, *eſſon* idem, excuſed.

Eſſoient & eſſoint, they had been.

Estagn, a Pool or Pond, *estrang p. terms Ley* idem.

Estable, made firm, *establir*, to confirm.

Estandord, the chief Enſign in War.

Estaine, Tinn, *estagne & estayne* idem.

Un estraunge, a ſtrainger, *Estrange* idem.

Est, he is, *estre*, to be, *estoit*, he was.

Eſſoient, they were, alſo, they ſtood, *ad estre*, hath been.

Estoia, ſtandeth, *estoier*, to ſtand, or abide.

Estoierent, they would ſtand, *estoiroit*, ſhould ſtand or be.

Estoit de coſt, he was near.

Est tant adire, 'tis as much as to ſay.

Esteant, being, *esteaunt*, idem.

Estee, been, *il ad este*, he hath been.

Estes, ye be, *ad Son este*, hath his being.

Ne est de estre, Not to be, or not ſo accounted.

Este, Summer. *p. Nov. Nar.*

La mi este, Midſummer.

Establie, eſtabliſhed, *estable*, idem.

Estatute, is that which is made a Law by King, Lord and Commons.

Estende, to be, alſo to extend.

Esteven, Stephen, *esteynerye*, Tinworks. *p. Plowd.* 328.

Estemans, liking, eſteeming, valuing, *estimans* idem.

Estimures, Robbers, Rovers, Pyrates.

Estoyer, to ſtand to, idem *ut estier*.

Eſtoyera, ſhall ſtand, *poit bien eſtoir*, may well ſtand, *eſtoyent*, they ſtand.

Eſtoyſe le brief, let the writ ſtand or be. *p. Plowd.* 287.

Eſtoyſent, they ſhould remain or be.

Il eſtoyt pris, he was arreſted.

Eſtoper, to bar, ſtop, *eſtopper*, idem.

Deſtopper, to throw open.

En eſtopel, in ſtay, *eſtopel*, is an impediment in an Action proceeding from a Man's own fact.

Eſtoilles, Starrs. *p. Brit.* 42.

Eſtoyels, idem. *p. Lambert*, *eſtoyers*, idem.

Eſtovers, are the Advantages of Hedgbote, Firebote, Plowbote, Commoning.

Eſtovers, en viver & veſture, the benefit of Eating and Clothing. *p. Stat. Glouc.* cap. 4.

Eſtranger, to Alien, or Sell.

Un eſtrange, a Pool. *p. termes de Ley*, 177.

Eſtreats, Penalties ſet in Court to be levyed by the Bayliff, or a true Liſt thereof.

Il eſtreyte, ſtop it. *p. Hen.* 7. alſo ſtreightned.

Eſtreitz, Streets. *p. Fitzh. nat. br*, 185.

Haut Eſtrete, the High-ſtreet, or Way.

Eſtrier, Writing. *p. Crompton Jur. Cur.*

Eſtreiont, they wonder, or go aſtray.

Eſtraitment, ſtrictly, *eſtreitment*, ſtreighrning.

Eſtreps, pulled down.

Eſtrepement, Spoyl made in Houſes, Lands or Woods in prejudice of him in Reverſion.

Eſtrepes, ſtript, pulled off.

Eſtrayted, forced. *p.* 9 *Hen.* 7. *Annal.*

Eſtreit hors, drawn out. *Plowden.*

Eſtreit de haut Chimia, ſtreightned the High-way.

Eſtudier, to Study, *un eſtude*, a Study.

Eſturgon, a Sturgion.

Eſtauncher, to ſtop, to ſtaunch or ſtay.

Eſtancher le ſang, to ſtop the Blood.

Eſtaunckement de ſoif, quenching the Thirſt, or allaying Thirſt.

Eſtendue, ſtretched forth.

Mains eſtendues, open hands.

Le eſtincel, the Spark. *p. Plowden's* Preface.

Eſtroicter, to inſtruct.

Eſtues & eſtuves, the hot Houſes or Stews, alſo Bawdy Houſes.

Et, and, *& ainſi*, and alſo.

E U.

Evacuer, to make void, or empty.

Evader, to eſcape, to ſlip away, to put by.

Evagation, wandring abroad.

Le evangel & evangile, the Goſpel.

La lumiere evangelique, the Light of the Goſpel.

Euchariſts, the Sacrament, alſo Thankſgiving.

Eveſque, a Biſhop, *eveſquerie*, a Biſhoprick, *eveſchery & eveſchie*, idem.

Exerwick, York, *everwickscire*, Yorkshire.

Eust, had been, *ceux eunts*, these being.

Euf, vide *eof*, an Egg.

Eviter, to shun, avoid.

Ne eust estre pris, had not been taken. *p. Coke Rep.* 9, 145.

Evulser, to throw back.

Ewe, Water, vide *eau*.

Ewe, had, *ad ewe*, hath had, *d'este ewe*, to be had.

En ewer, in doubt.

Ewelles, Geese.

Un molin eweret, a Water-mill. *p. Nov. Nar.*

Eux, them. *ent euximes*, amongst them.

Eux mesmes, themselves.

E X.

Son execute, his Executor.

Excomenge, Excomunicated.

Excomengement, Excommunion, a Censure of the Church.

Exequies, Funerals.

Explorer, to bewail, also to make diligent search. *Explorater*, a Scout or Spy.

Exprimer, to press.

Extorquer, to put out by force, vide *deforcer*.

Expressement, directly, expressly.

Exchewe, to fall down, to avoid, vide *eschew*.

Expire, to end, to go out, to dye.

Ne extenderoit, should not extend to, or exceed.

Extinguisher, to put out, to avoid.

Extientisement, extinguishing,

Extiensmes, idem.

Extienter, to extinguish.

Entinsement, extinguishment, *p.* 2, *pt. Fitzh. gr. abr.* 112, b.

Extraict, vide *estreits*.

Extrairer, to draw out.

Exteint, put out.

Exaggerer, to make worse, to aggravate.

Exclus, shut out, *exclusivement*, not including.

Exemption, a freedom or liberty.

Exile, banishment.

Un exorcize, a Conjurer.

Explees, vide *Esplees*.

Exquis, excellent, *exquiement*, exactly.

Eyette, ye have, *p. Fitzh. gr. abr.* 27, a.

Eyre, a Court of Itinerent Judges, also a Court of the Forrests, *eire*, idem.

Eyns & *Eyans*, having, *eyant*, idem.

Eyde, help, vide *eide*.

Eyes, ye have. *p. Britton* 95.

De eyre, to sit, brood, or hatch.

Eyt, he hath, vide *eit*.

Eyrer, to Plow, also to hatch or bring young Birds, chiefly of *Goshawks*.

Eyent, they shall have, *eyens*, ye have.

Eyera, shall hatch or sit upon Eggs.

Ey, a watery place, also water.

Eyens, but. *p. Plowd.* 231.

F A.

F*Ablesse*, weakness, lib. *Assize* 6.

Fabes, Beans, vide *febue*.

Un fable, a feign'd thing.

Fabloir, to devise stories, to prevaricate.

Fachon, the likeness the fashion.

Falast, failed, *fait*, deed, *en fait*, in fact.

Facile,

Facile, easy, *facilement*, easily.

A fair, to do, *face*, made, *faces*, ye made.

Jeo face, I made, *facerant*, they made.

Si faceroy, if I made, or should do.

Faisance, making, *faizance*, making or doing.

A leo fair, to do this. *Fair ascovoir*, to give notice.

Jeo fair luy scaver, I will have you to know.

Fair vous voil estre fait, do ye as you would be done unto, *faires*, ye make or do.

Fait comise, a deed done, *fait & fact* a deed.

Faiture, making, doing, *faitours*, evil doers, so in the *Stat*. 7. *Rich*. 2*d*.

Un Faisaunt, a Phesant, *faisance*, doing, *fezance*.

Falsifier, to do falsly, also to adulterate.

Faix, a burthen, or load.

Faixime, deceit.

Nief de faix, a Ship of Burthen.

Falesia & falaize, a Bank, or Hill by the Sea side, *Coke Inst* .5. *fatigue*, weariness.

Un farse, a Comedy, an idle Story.

Fairaginous, Maslin, or mingled Corn.

Farou, Pig'd, Farrowed.

Un fardel de terre, a fourth part of an Acre.

Farundel, *fardingdeale*, *ferdingdale*, idem.

Faut, omitted, wanted, needful, *Faat forme*, wants form.

Un Fau, a Beechen Tree, *fain* in modern French, idem.

En fany, in the manner, *ove le fany*, with the manner, or in the taking.

Faonatio, fauning.

Faucher, to cut, to mow.

Fauchement, cutting, mowing, *fauche*, mowed, cut.

Faud, a Fold, or Penn for Sheep, *faulde*, idem, *& fraud*, idem, *faux* false, *fauxifira*, shall falsify.

Faulter, *& faulder*, or default.

Que faudra, who make default.

Faudra, wanteth, or needeth.

Faudroit, should want, or it behoveth.

Faultont, complaining.

Faulser defoy, to break his trust, or faith.

Fausine, falsly, *fauseours*, counterfeiters.

Ne fault, it needs not, *faut* want, *fault*, idem.

Cest ma ist ta faut, this mine, that is thy fault.

Faut date, wanting date.

Fauxim, faulty, *fauxisme*, falsity, *fauximent*, idem.

Fauxiers de seal du Roy, counterfeiters of the King's Seal, *fauxity*, *& fauxitie*, falseness.

Fauxere, to counterfeit.

Fayront, they should do.

Faytours, Vagabonds, idle Persons.

F E.

Feal, faithful, *fealment*, faithfully.

Feale, fealty.

Fealty, faithfulness.

Feaule, idem.

Febue, Peanes.

Feasors, doers, makers.

Fesants,

Fesants, idem, *ut faisance*.

Feizoit, he hath done or made, *feizoyent*, they have done or made.

Feint, feigned, ſlackned.

Feine & *fene*, hay, graſs, *foine*, idem.

Felle, Gall, bitter.

Felon, a Felon, *feloniſſement*, Feloniouſly.

Felo de ſe, he that kills himſelf.

Femme, a Woman, *feme Covert*, a Married Woman.

La femme, & *la feme*, the Wife.

Femeles, Girls.

Fendue, ſtrook, *feru*, idem.

Fenſe month, the Month wherein young Deer fall.

Feneſtre, a Window.

Ferre, Iron, *en ferges*, in Irons, *ferres*, Irons.

Ferrure, Iron, allſo ſhowing Horſes.

South ferreur, under lock.

Fermalx, ſhut up, *feriſt*, ſtrook.

Pur ferrer, to ſhoe.

Fere, to be Mad, Diſtracted, alſo to be done.

Ferra, ſhall do.

Feries, Marts, Fairs.

Fermer, to ſhut, to cloſe up, *ferme* & *firme*, idem.

En fermes, cloſe in, ſhut up cloſe, or in, *p. Britton*.

Feres, wild Beaks, Beaſts of the Foreſt.

Ferra, ſhall make or do.

Ferra vous vouſtre ſuit, do your Suite.

Ferroit, he ſhould make or do, alſo might ſtrike, *ferromus*, we do.

Feront, they do, *feroyent*, they ſhould do.

Ferres, ye make or do.

Soit fery, be ſtrook or wounded. *p.* 4. *Hen.* 7.

Ferue, ſtrook, wounded. *p. Plowd. feru*, idem.

Ferve, great Heat.

Feriont, they ſtrook or aſſaulted, *fiereront*, they are aſſaulted or ſtrook.

Feruſt, ſtrook, *feruſt al terre* ſtrook to the Ground.

Feſors, vide, *feaſors*, makers, Doers, *feaſome*, doing.

Feriours, Aſſaultours.

Feſoit, he would make or do, *feſoyent*, cauſed or made.

Feaſors de draps, Clothworkers or Clothmakers.

Feſoient & *feſoyent*, they would or ſhould, make or do, *feſomus*, we make.

Jeo feſoy, I made it.

A fezer, to make 12 *Hen.* 8. *Annal.*

Il que feſoit, he who made.

Pur voyer Feſaunt, for true making.

Feſte, a Feaſt-day, *le feſte de touts ſaincts*, the Feaſt of all Saints.

Feſtination, haſtening, *feſtine*, quick, ſpeedy.

Fet aſcavoir, to be made know or underſtand.

Feve, late, *p. Coke Rep.* 9. 121.

Feiie, idem, in *Mod. French. Feve*, Zeal. *p. Coke Rep.* 9.

Un feud, a Fee or Reward.

Le feu, the fire, *fewe*, idem.

Feverer, the Month of *February*.

Furier, idem, *feve*, late, *fewe*, burned, *fewes*, a ſort of light Wood.

Feves,

Feves, Pulse. *p. nov. nar.*

Fester, to keep Holy-day, to Feast.

Un feure, a Smith, vide, *Foigeron.*

F I.

Fiance, truth, faith, affiance, assurance.

Fiancer, to wed, to betroth.

Fief, a fee, a Freehold.

Neint fiant, or *fyant*, not trusting. *p. Plowdens* Preface.

Fiestes, ye had made, *fistes*, idem.

Figer, to fasten.

A que fies, to which you may put trust.

Fieu, Fire, *fiew*, idem. *p.* 1 *Hen.* 7. 10. vide *Feu.*

Finer, to end, to conclude, determine.

Le file, the thread, *filer*, to spin, or twist.

En fin, in the End, *al fine*, at last.

Au fine, to the end, *finist*, ended.

Finie, ended, *finalment*, lastly.

Filacetum, a place wherein Brakes and Fern grow.

Fiene, hay, vide *Foyne.*

Fiew, Fire, *fieu*, idem.

Fine, in the *Terms of the Law*, 240, is put for force, or of necessity.

Fier, to trust to, to put, also to be arrogant.

Figuree, described.

Finy, ended, *finyment*, ending.

Un fil, a Bank. *p. Brit.* 111.

Fimes, Mudd, *p. Fitz. nat. br.* 185.

Fimez, a Drayn or Pitt.

Filaser, an officer who makes Process in the Common Pleas Court, who are in Number 14.

Fils, Sonnes, *file* & *fille*, a Daughter.

Firma, vide, *Ferma.*

Firma le huis, shut the Door.

Firmer, to shut, *le firme*, the shutting, *done Firmitie*, gave strength.

Firme, kept and maintained, *p. divers Authors.*

Fist, made or done, *fist fait*, he hath made a Deed, *fit*, he made. *p. Coke Rep.* 5.

Vous ne fiste, ye may not make. 26. *Hen.* 8.

F L.

Flair, to blow. *p. Cromp. Jur. Cur.*

Cornestre flaye, a Horn to be blown. *p. eund.*

Un fleche, an Arrow.

Flecher, to bend, vide, *postea.*

Fluvie, a River, *fluve*, idem.

Fley, a River. *p.* 16, *Hen.* 7. f. 14.

Flechir, to bend, *flecher*, idem. also a Bowyer.

Flourie, flourished, *un fleur*, a Flower.

Le fleuret, the foyle or foyn. 9. *Cap. Rep.* 120.

A flurerer, to flow, also to flower.

Un flambeau, a Torch or Link.

Flot, a floud, *la flot de la mer*, the flowing of the Sea.

Flot & *reflot*, Ebbing and Flow-

Flux & *reflux*, idem.

Flotter, to Flote or Swim, *me flotement*, Floting or Swimming on the top of the Water.

Flotages, such things as so Swim.

Fliche de lard, a side or Flichin of Bacon, *Fleicke*, idem.

Fled-

Fledwite, a Mulct for freedom of Fugitives.

Flemest wite, a liberty to challenge Goods of a Fugitive.

F. O.

Foder, to dig, also digging.

Foyder, to dig.

Foder, also is to feed, *pur foder de dames*, for feeding of Deer.

Pour Fodder, idem, thence foddering of Cattle.

Foible, feeble, weak.

Foine, vide *Foyne*.

Foits, times, *un foit*, once, *tout foits*, at all times, *quelque foits*, sometimes, *par fois*, betimes, *foits*, idem ut *foits*, *ascun foits*, sometimes, *sovent foits*, oftentimes.

Fol, a Fool, an Idiot.

Folier, to do Foolishly.

Foils, Leaves, *foiles*, idem.

Folement, foolishly, madly.

Folkland, & *Folcland*, Copyhold Lands, so call'd by the *Saxons*.

Folkmote, the County Court, or Sheriffs Turn.

Un Fond, a Ground, or Land Tax.

Fong, before, fore Teeth.

Fondeur, a Melter of Mettels.

Font & *fount*, they made, or did.

Forbanir, to Banish, or Exile.

Foreprise, except, saving to himself.

Bon foreprise, a good exception. *p. Parkins* 135.

Forepris, excepted, saved, *forspris*, idem.

Un forcelet, a Fort, or small Castle. *p Stat. Westm.*

Formage, Cheese, *formee*, formed.

For, with its compounds, for most part, signifies out as.

Foreclose, to shut out, *forpris*, &c.

Forfaict, forfeited, *forfaitera*, shall forfeit.

Forjure, to renounce, forswear.

Fors, but, *fors toy*, but only thee.

Fort bien, very good, *forsque*, except.

Un fort latron, a strong Thief, *fortment*, strongly.

Fortuiment, by chance.

Forger, to frame, to fashion.

Forgeron, a Smith.

Forsque, only, until, but.

Forsque solement, but only.

p. Fort maine, by strong hand.

Fortment, strongly, forceably.

Un fosse, a Ditch, a Pit, *fosses*, plural.

Fosse soubs terre, a Current under Ground.

Un fosseur, a Digger, or Delver, *fossoyour*, idem.

Un foss debruse, a ditch thrown down or into.

Un foster, a Park-Keeper, or Ranger, *forster*, idem.

Foundee & *foundus*, founded, or cast.

Estre foundre, to be melted, cast. *p. Plowden*. 313.

Le founder, the Occasion, Original, Ground, or Cause.

Ils fount, they do, or did, or make.

Fourcher, to delay, put off, prolong, *fourch*, idem.

Fourches, Stocks, or Pillory, *fourche* in modern French is forked.

Fovir, to dig, vide, *foder* idem.

Feo;

Jeo fowdra, I ſhall dig. *fowe*, digged.

Fovagle, digging. *p. Nov. Narr.*

Pur fower, for cutting down, alſo carriage.

Fourmage, Cheeſe, *formage*, id.

Fouler, to tread down, *fowler aux pees*, to tread under foot.

Foy, faith, *foyal*, faithful.

Doner foy, to give credit, *p. Coke* 5. *Rep. I.* 43.

Foyne, Hay, alſo Graſs.

Pur foys, the agreement, or covenant. *p. Nov. Nar.*

Un fournaiſe, a Furnace.

Foyder, to dig. *p.* 12. *Hen.* 8, 2.

Poit foyer, may dig. *p. eundem.*

F R.

Fra, ſhall make, or do.

Fra la, ſhall make there. *p. Plowd.* 334, a.

Fracture, breaking.

Fraine, a Bridle, *freine*, idem.

Un fraile, a Basket.

Franchement, freely, *frankment*, idem.

Franci plegii, Free-ſuiters, or pledges. *p. Coke. Inſt.* 73.

Franc, free, *franktenements*, Free-holds, *frank bank*, free bench.

Franchienment, making free, franchizing.

Frank tenant, a Free-holder.

Frankelmoignes, Free-Alms, *Francois*, French.

Fraude, foldage, *frankfaud*, free-foldage.

Faud, *faudra*, a Fold, or Pen, for Sheep.

Levaſt fraude, ſet up a Fold. *p. Coke Rep.* 8. 125.

Fraunches, liberties, *franches*, idem.

Frateral, Brotherly.

Fraxines, Aſhen Trees.

Fraſſetum, & *Fraxinetum*, a Wood of Aſh Trees.

Freines, young Aſhen Trees, Saplings.

Freſn, an Aſh Tree in Modern French.

Frees, Brethren.

Terre giſer freſhe, Land laying untilled.

Friſche, & *freſhe terre*, untilled ground. *p. Stat. Glouc. Cap.* 4.

Frener, to Bridle.

Freinder, to break.

Frere, a Brother, *freres*, Brothers.

La frere mon aile, my great Uncle.

Freres gimaulx, Twins.

Freſhment, preſently, freſhly.

Friburgh, a free Burgeſs. *p. Termes de Ley*, 102. alſo a Burrough Town, and by *Blunt* the ſame as *frank pledge*.

Frounts, they make, or do. *p. Brit.* 3.

Froidement, coldly.

Fruict, fruit, *Fruiteux*, fruitful.

Frument, Wheat Corn.

Un friperer, a Seller, or furbiſher of old Clothes.

Fruſtrum terre, a ſmall piece of Land.

Fruſtrer, to diſappoint, or make void.

Fryth, a *Saxon* word for Peace, alſo a Plain between two Woods.

F U.

Füer, to fly, *jeo fua*, I fly.

Fua, fled or gone, *fuont*, they fled.

Fuir, flying, and ſometimes, *fuer*, idem.

En ſon fuer, in his flight. *p. Coke Rep.* 5, 99.

A fuer, to fly.

Fuors al Sanctuarie, flyers to the Sanctuary.

Un futise & futive, one that is fled.

Est futive, is fled, *de fuy*, fled. *fuyt*, idem. *p. Britton* 86. also flight, *p. eund.* 120.

Un fuyeur, a run away, *fuite*, flight.

Furitſs, Fugitives. *p. Mirror. Justice.*

Fuayl, Fuel. *p. Nov. Nar.* 50,

Fuistes, ye were, *fuist & fut.* it was.

Fut un foits, it once was, *fuissoyent*, they were, *jeo fuy*, I was *p. Coke Rep.* 5, 36.

Fueille verd, a green Leaf.

Funerailles, Funerals.

Fundus, a Farme. *p.* 1 *part. Inst.* 5.

Un furet, a Ferret.

Fureur, anger, rage.

Furches & furca, gallows and Forks, idem. *p. Fitzh. Justice*, f, 17.

Furches, by *Britton*, 30 & 31; is used for stocks, vide *Fourches*, and for all such things as are to punish offenders in a Leet, vide *juices*.

Il fust, he fled, *Coke Rep.* 9, 121.

Furer, to steal, *furt*, theft.

Furtivement, theevishly, or by stealth.

Fundements, chief rules, or grounds for reasoning.

Fuser, to shed, to spill, *fuse*, shed.

Fuse sang, bloodshed.

Fusile, meltable and melting.

Fust, a Clubb or Staff, *un crois de fust*, a wooden Cross, *per Britton*, 25.

Fut, he was. *p. Yelverton.* 40.

Fueilla, leaffy or full of leaves, *fueilleur*, idem.

Fumee, smoakey.

Fumier, a Dunghill, *fumage*, Dung, or manuring with Dung.

Arbres fustage, old high Trees of the Forest.

Fustain, Cotton, *bumbasine*, id. & *Fustian*.

Futur, in time to come, *futise* a Fugitive.

Fussent, they should be, *fust*, was and had been. *p. Coke Rep.* 9, 120.

Fynyeroit, should end. *p. Plowd.* 304.

Poies fyer, ye may trust. *per eund.* in the Preface.

Furnage, a Tribute paid to the Lord of the Mannor, by the suiters for the use of his Oven.

G A.

UN *gage*, a pawn, also a surety or pledge.

Gage battel, to wage Warr, *gager de ley*, to wage Law.

Gager, to deposite, to put or lay down, also to engage or undertake, *Gagera*, shall engage.

Bailer en gage, to deliver or put in pawn.

En gage, is also betrothed, by some Authors.

Gager contra ascun, to fight, also to lay a wager.

Gages, wagers, *pris ses gage*, took his Fee. *Hill.* 3. *Hen.* 6. & *Fitzh. Justice*, 158, a.

Gages, suretys, *p. Gregory*.

Gaigner & gainer, to get, to obtain by Husbandry.

Il ad gaigne, he hath gained, *p. Parkins*, 176.

Est gaine, is gotten, *p. Coke, Rep.* 6, 25.

Que gaine, who Plow or Till, 4. *Rep. Coke* 37.

Gainage & *wainage*, things belonging to the Plow and Cart, *gaignage*, idem, or the benefit arifeing by Tillage, alfo Arable, *p. Crompton* 200.

Gaignarie or *gainery*, idem, i. e. profit by Tillage.

Gainure, Tillage, *gaignont*, they get, or manure.

Gales & *galeys*, Wales, *galois*, Welch, *p. Plowden* 126.

Gales gents, Welchmen, *per eundem, fol.* 23.

Un gaille, a Jayl or Gaol.

Galines, & *Galynes*, Cocks, or Capons. *Gelines*, Poultrey.

Gants, & *Gaunts*, Gloves. *Gantier*, a Glover.

Garbes, Sheafs of Corn, and fometimes the fame as *Herbas*.

Un garbe, a Sheaf or Bundle, *p. Termes de Ley*, 170.

Garder, to keep, to beware, to look to.

Gardes, kept; *Gards*, idem. *Fait gard*, doth keep. *per Coke Report.* 5, 89. *Gardera*, fhall keep.

Gardes, look ye to, beware, have a care.

Bien foy gard, let him take care, or heed well.

Preignes gard, take heed, *per Coke* 5. *Rep.* 25.

Bien gardus, well kept, *per Crompt. Jur. Cur.* 165.

Un gard, a Ward. *Un gardien*, a Warden, or Guardian.

En le gardure, in the keeping. *Plowd.* 373.

En le gardeincy, idem. *per Termes Ley.*

Cur de Gardes, the Court of Wards.

Le Garden, The Keeper. *per Coke Rep.* 7, 36.

En garde, in Cuftody, or Wardfhip.

Seignour garden, the Lord-keeper.

Un Gardrobbe, a place for Apparel, a Wardrobe.

Gardes voustre challenges, look to your Challenges; the which the Clerk of the Crown and Clerk of Affizes fay to the Parties, when the Jury is about to be fworn.

Garner, to warn, *est garnee*, is warned, or fummoned, *garnisher*, to warn. *p. Kitchin* 6.

Garnishment, fummoning, *garnye*, idem. *Garnis*, idem.

Est garnish, he is fummoned or warned.

Garnisht, idem, alfo kept.

Ne garnee, not kept or warned, *garnishee*, is he in whofe hands Mony is attached.

Garrons, warning, fummoning, *garnement*, idem.

Garrantly, warrantly, *un garrant*, a warrant.

Garrenteront, they fhould warrant.

Garrein, a warren for Conies, &c. *p. Kitch.* 59.

Garren et garene, idem. *p. Coke Rep.* 7, 23.

Garrayne, idem. *p.* 12 *Hen.* 8, f, 9.

Garniture, furniture, trimming.

Garson, a Boy, or young fervant.

Garsion, idem. *per Fitzh. Just.* 25.

Garſons Chauntement, & *Garſons Chauntant*, Singing Boys. *p. Coke Rep.* 8. 45.

Garſettes, Girls.

Un Garth, a Yard, Garden or Backſide, alſo a ſmall Homeſtal. *p. Blount.*

Garſonent, they draw, as in Fiſhing.

Soit garant, let it be granted, *garunt*, idem.

Gartier, a Garter.

Gaſter, to waſt, to ſpoil.

Les gaſtes, the waſts, *gaſtines*, waſt ground.

Gaſtment, waſting, ſpoiling, Depredation.

Gayner, to Sowe or Till, or the profit thereby.

Tu Gaynes ma terre, thou doſt Sow or Plow my Land. *p. Britton* 142.

Gaſcher, to Row, as in a Boat.

Un gay, *un geay*, the Bird called a *Jay*.

Gauche, the left ſide. *p. Coke Rep.* 9. 120.

Gauche mamelle, they left Pap or Dugg. *p. eund.*

Gavel, Tribute, Toll.

G E.

Un geaſt, a Gueſt. *p. Kitchin*, 176. *Geſtes*, Gueſts.

Generallement, generally, *gentilhome*, a Gentleman.

Geners, Kinds, Species.

Un geant, a Giant.

Geler, to Freeze, vide *glace*.

Gelee, Froſt, *gele blanche*, white or hoary Froſt.

Gelement, Freezing, *gelure*, Ice.

Geline, a Hen, alſo a Capon. *p. Brit.* 151.

Gelines, Poultry.

Gentes, *Gents* & *Gens*, Common People, Lay-men, alſo a Country or Nation.

Gens de Meſtier, Handy-crafts Men.

Gens de Egliſe, Churchmen, the Clergy.

Genus & *genues*, Knees.

Il ne genulera, he ſhall not Kneel.

Gentilhome, a Gentleman.

Gentifeme, a Gentlewoman.

Gentileſſe, the Nobility.

Geole, a Cave, a Priſon.

Geolier, a Jayler.

Germines, young Branches, or Sprouts of Trees.

Ils germine, they ſpring, or ſprout out.

Germe & *germaine*, ſtock, kindred.

Engendre de meſme germe, came of the ſame ſtock, or Kindred or Root.

Germer, to bud, to ſprout.

Germement, budding, ſprouting.

Les gentiles, the Heathen.

Geſir, to lye, vide, *giſer*; *geſine*, lying.

Le geſte, the behaviour, *geſte*, put, caſt in. *p. nov. nar.* 47.

Gette, idem, *p.* 21. *Hen.* 7. 40. alſo caſt from.

Il Poet gette, it may lie, *Poet eſte gette*, it may be gotten. *p. Fitzh. nat. brev.* 28. *gettes*, idem.

Gerbee de blee, a Sheaf of Corn, vide *garbe*.

Gevement, grieving. *p. Stat. Weſtm.* 1.

Geures, kinds. *p. Plowd.* 332.

Geſt, vide *guſt*.

Gigner, to beget, *Gignets*, begetting.

Gild, a Fraternity combined in Orders, &c.

Gildable, Tributary or lyable to Taxes and Orders.

De gilours, of such. *p. Britton* 24. a.

Cy gist, here lyeth, *pur giser*, to lay or expose, *giser*, to lye, *gisant*, lying.

Girdland, a *Saxon* Word for Yard-land. *p. Coke*.

Gisont en agait, they lye in wait.

Gisoient, they lye. *p. Parkins* 29.

Gira, shall or will lye. *p. Coke Rep*. 5. 13.

Girra, idem, *p. eund*. 6. 25.

Girroit, should lye.

La git, there lies. *p.* 20 *Hen*. 7. 9.

Poit giser les deniers in le Curt, may lay or bring Money into the Court.

Gisure, Lodging, *p. Termes de Ley*, 77.

Gisnats, lying, *p. Parkins*, 93.

Gisants, idem.

Gist, lyeth.

G L.

Glacer, to freeze, *Glace*, Ice

Glace de tout costes, iced, or frozen about.

Un glave, a Sword; vide *Espee*, *p. Coke Rep*. 5, 122.

Glaire, Gravel, Sand.

Glaire de un Oeuf, the White of an Egg.

Glans, Mast, Acorns, *p. Brit.* 143. Also all manner of Nuts, Haws, Hipps, *p. Stat. Glouc.*

Glebe, a piece of Earth, or Turf, *p. Broke's Abr*. 303.

Gleab-lands, Church-lands.

Gason, in modern *French*, is a Turf, or piece of Earth.

Glisser, to slide, or slip, *glissant*, slippery.

Glisement, sliding, slipping.

Glaunts, swimming, *p. Brit*. 6.

Gloir, Glory.

Glu, Glue.

Glyn, a Valley.

G O.

Gors, a Stream or Pool, *gort*, idem.

Gorse, a watry place; and by such Name a Weare or Soil may pass by Deed, *p. Plowd*. 151. Also a Pool or Fish-pond, *p. eund*.

Gote, a Ditch, Sluce, or Gutter, *p.* 23, *Hen*. 8.

Gorse leves en ewes, Ditches thrown or cast up in watry places. Also Pits, *p. Britton*. 32.

Goule Aoust, vide *Gule d'Aoust*.

Gomme, Gumm.

Un Gorre, a Sow.

Le goust, the Taste, *Gouster*, to taste.

Gourt & *Goor*, a watry place.

Un govette, a Drop.

Goutteux, Gouty.

Goule, vide *Gule*.

G R.

Graces, Thanks, *p. Plowd*. 307.

Graine, Corn of all sorts.

Grainer, to Till, or Sow, *grayner*, idem.

Le Grammair, the Grammer.

Graffer, a Notary or Scrivener, *p. Stat*. 5. *Hen*. 8.

Grange & *graunge*, a House or Farm of Husbandry.

Grangier, a Farmer.

Grava, a Wood or Grove, properly a little Wood.

Grand, great, *grand fuir*, much a-do.

Grandement, greatly, very much, *grandeur*, greatneſs.

nul graund, no Lord or Grandee. *p. Kitch.* 203.

Graunter, to grant, *grantus* & *grantuz*, granted.

Al Grantant, at the granting.

Grantaſtes, ye have granted. 49 *Edw.* 3. 1. a.

Grauns, given. *p. Brit.* 4.

Gratis, freely for thanks.

Gree & *gre*, conſent, good likeing.

Sans gree, without agreement. *p. Coke Rep.* 8. 125.

En bon gre, in good part.

Encounter ſon gre, againſt his will. *p. nov. nar.* 71.

Que il poit fair gree, that he might make agreement or ſatisfaction, *uſt fair gre*, he had given ſatisfaction or made agreement.

Greviouſment, greivouſly.

Le greff or *greve*, an Officer who hath the Power of a Sheriff or chief Conſtable.

Gerefa, idem, *Greve* in *Saxon* is a Buſh.

Sherereve, *Portgreve*, Chief Officers.

Grith, Peace. *p. termes Ley.* 178.

Grith breach, Breach of the Peace. *p. eund.*

Grithſtole, a Sanctuary.

Grosboys, a great Wood. *bois gr.* idem.

Greit, greeteth.

Greinder & *greynder*, greater.

Greinder enqueſt, the Grand Jury.

Greive, greivous, *grever*, to greive.

Greindement enſient, great with Child. *p. Coke* 6. 35.

Que eſt greve, who is dammaged, *p. Hen.* 6. 5.

Ne grevement, they grieve not. *p. Stat. Weſtm.* 1.

Gros, Fat, *groſſier*, to grow big, *le groſſure*, the greatneſs, bigneſs.

Groſſes Diſmes, great Tythes, *i. e.* of Corn and Hay.

Groſſement enſient, great with Child, *groſſe de enfant*, idem.

Groſſone, a Fine at Entrance. *p. lib. aſſ. fol.* 64. a.

Groſſes nyeffs & *nyefes*, great Ships.

Grot, a Den or Cave, alſo a ſhady woody place, with Springs of Water.

Greſſler, to Hail, *greſle*, Hail.

Griffs, Claws, or Talons of Birds, &c.

Grue, a Crane.

Gruarii, the chief Officers in a Forreſt.

G U.

Guerr, War. *Rep.* 8. 166. a.

Guerdon, a reward, vide *Gurdon*, idem. *p. Coke Rep.* 9. 121.

Guſe, a Pit. *p. termes de Ley.* 176.

Gurge, a Pond or Pool.

Gurgite, a Watery Place, *gurges*, idem.

Guerre, War, *guerres*, plural.

A leve guerre, to raiſe or make War.

Guerrine, Warlike.

Guſt, *Bracton* uſeth it for a ſtranger that lodges the 2d night a Gueſt, *geſt*, idem. *p. Lambert.*

Guiſes, Faſhion, Uſages.

Le gule, the Throat, *trencha luy en le gule*, cut his Throat.

Gule de aouſt, the firſt-day of *Aug.* which is St. *Peter ad vincula.*

Le guelle & *gueule*, the Wind-Pipe or Gullet.

Guetter,

Guetter, to watch.
Un guydon, an Ensign or Standard bearer.
Gyser, to lye, *gysant*, lying, *gisoit*, it lyeth.
Gyzer, to lay or sit, as a Swan to hatch.
Gyses, Geese, 10, *Hen.* 8, 2.

H A.

H*A*, hath, *qui ha*, who have.
Habile, able and fit, *hable* idem.
Habilitie, aptitude, hability.
Habiller, to Dress, to Array.
Habilliment, clothing, arraying.
Habile de corps, light of Body. active.
Habiter, to dwell, to inhabit.
Habite, inhabited.
Des habits, the Inhabitants.
Habitue, used, accustomed.
Hache, an Axe, also hewed, cut.
Hada, a Haven or Port.
Hables, Havens, Ports.
Haga, a House in a City or Burrough.
Haits, lively, active.
Un hale, a Hall.
Haine, hatred, spite.
Hair, to bear Malice.
Qui hait, who hateth.
Haies, Hedges, Mounds.
Haies levye, ou abatu, Hedges made up or cast down.
Halener, to breath.
Hallamsheire, a part of *Yorkshire*, where *Sheffeild* now stands.
Ham, a Habitation or Town.
Un hamel, a Hamlet or Village. *p. Plowd.* 337.
Hamsel & Hamstal, an ancient Messuage in decay, or a Toft, *i. e.* a place where a House had stood.
Hanap, a Cup, Pot, or Tankark, *Hanapper*, *p. Parkins*, 43.
Hanap, idem. a Hamper.
Hanser, to accuse.
Hanter, to frequent or use.
Happe, obtained gotten. *per Cromp. Jur. Cur.* 48.
Happeroit, should chance or happen.
A happer, to chance or fall out.
Happa, shall chance or befall.
Ceo happa, it fell out, *p. Coke*, *Rep.* 7, 10.
Haqueene, an ambling Nag, or pad Nag.
Un hayne, a small Gun not a yard long.
Haquebut, a bigger Gun.
Un harangue, an oration.
Harrasser, to tyre, to weaken.
Harasse, tyred, weakened.
Halimote, a Court Baron.
Harer, to stirr up, move or provoke.
Harier, to importune, to urge, also to provoke.
Hariot & heriot, is that which is given or paid to the Lord of the Fee upon the Tenant's death and is commonly the best Goods or Beast, vide *heriot*.
Harneis, Armour, furniture of Arms.
Hassarders, Gamesters, Lottery-men.
Haster, to make haste, *hastivity*, hastiness.
Hastif & *hastive*, presently, quickly.
Hastifment & *hastivement*, idem.
Harbiger vide *herberger*, *harberger*, idem.
Un hart, a Stag of 5 Years old.
Le haunche, the Hipp.
La haute, the point, also high.

Hault,

Hault, high, *plus hault*, higher.

Hau, a voice of calling.

Haust, a draught, *haust de servois*, a draught of Beer.

Haure, a Haven or Port, *per Termes Ley*. 95.

Haut vey, the High-way, *haut streat*, idem.

Hautement & hautment, proudly, arroganrly.

Haulment, idem. *hauliement*, highly.

Hautenesse, highness, greatness, *hautess & hautness*, idem. *hautain*, lofty.

Tres haut & treshault, most high.

Lever en hault, to raise up on high.

Haunge, contrivance, *p. Brit.* 48.

Havement, greedily.

Hautainment, loftily.

Haulteur et hauteur, height.

Haulser, to set up.

Haulser le prix, to raise the prise.

Havoir & avoir, to have.

Haw, a small piece of Land near a House, and sometimes a Mansion-house.

Haugh, a Valley. *p.* 1. *pt. Inst.* 5.

Un hay, a Hedge, Mound or Fence.

Hayson, the fencing or hedging time.

Un camp bien hay, a field well Hedged.

Hayes, plural, *en haye*, in ranks, or rows.

Haybote, necessary stuff for Hedging.

Hayn, vide *hain*, hatred, *hay*, envious, malicious, *estre hay*, to be malicious.

Heint, hate.

Heriot & heriet service, is a duty from Tenant, in fee to the Lord, payable at the Death, and is usually double the Annual Quitrent, vide *hariot custome, antea.*

Herault, a Herald at Arms.

Herberger, to lodge, harbour or entertain.

Moy herberger, ro lodge me, *p. Fitzh. Just.* 209.

Herberge & herbage, Victuals, Provision or Entertainment, *p. Coke Rep.* 5.

Herbeger ne voet, would not Entertain. *p.* 5, *Edw.* 4. *pas An. lib.*

Soit herberge, he entertained, lodged. *p. Coke Rep.* 8, 23.

Un herberger & herbiger, an Inn-keeper. *p. Kitchin*, 126.

Heritage, an Inheritance.

Hereditaments, such things as go with the inheritance, to the Heir, and not to the Executor?

Helas, Alass.

Hebette, dull, blockish.

Healder, an old *Saxon* word for Tenant, or Occupyer.

Heure, an hour, *heures*, plural.

Bon heure, a good hour, good luck.

Mal heure, the contrary.

De le heure, from such time, or that time.

A cest heure, at this time present, *al heure*, in time, *del heure que*, since, 42, *Edw.* 3. 20.

Le heynoste, the hainousness, *p.* 2. *R.* 3, 13, b.

Heureusite, happiness, blessedness. 1. *Rep. Coke* 1.

Heureux, happy, fortunate.

H I.

Hibon, an Owl, *hulotte*, idem.

Hideux, horrible, dreadful.

Hier, Yesterday.

Hirst, a Wood, vide, *hurst*.

Histoire, History.

Un hide de terre, is a Plow Land computed to be 100 Acres. *p. Crompt. Jur. Cur. fol.* 200.

Hidage, anciently a Tax upon every Hide of Land.

Hine, a Servant in Husbandry.

Hidel, a place of Sanctuary or Protection.

Hirciscunda, a Division of Inheritances amongst Heires.

H O.

Home & homme, a Man.

Homicide, Man-slaughter.

Home de Guerre, a Soldier or Man of War.

Homage, Obedience, and by tenure to be true to the Lord of whom Land is held.

Holt, a Wood, *Saxon.*

Holm, an Island or grassy Ground compassed with Water, also a River Island, *Saxon.*

Hoo, a Hill, *Sax.*

Hoir Mod. French, for heir.

Homesoken, an immunity from forceable Entries.

Hont & honte, Shame, disgrace. *p. Coke* 4. *Rep.* 5.

Sans hont, Impudent, *pur hont*, for Shame.

Ne fuer honte, were not Ashamed.

Honteux, Blushing, *estre honteoux*, to Blush or be Ashamed, *chose honteuse*, a thing causing Shame or Blushing.

Hors, out, without, *hors de Sence*, Mad.

Hors de temps, untimely.

Hort date, bearing Date.

Un horologue, a Clock. *p. Coke Rep.* 5. 1.

Hostelle, the Houshold.

Hostel de Roy, the King's Houshold.

Un hostelier, an Inn-keeper, also an Hostler.

Hoch pot, to mingle together, so where a Man dyes and leaves several Children, some of whom are preferred in his Life time, what they have had of their Father is to be put in and valued with what is left in *hoch pot*, and all equally to be divided amongst all the Children.

Hostile, Enemy like.

Hovement, Digging, or Delving.

Un hove, an Iron Instrument to dig or delve.

Hoyan, so called in *Mod. Fr.*

Howgh, a Valley, *Brittish.*

Hockettor & hocqueteur, a Knight of the Post, a decayed Man.

H U.

Hu & hute, an Outcry.

Hueis, idem. *p. Fitzh. Just.* 200.

Hure, an Hour, vide, *heure*, also time. *p. Plowd. Abr.* 32.

Hui & huy, to day.

Huile, Oyl, *Huille*, idem. *p. Coke Rep.* 7. 37. a.

Hulet & hewlet, an Owl.

Huis, a Door or Porch.

Huis & huse overt, the Door open.

Huisse, idem.

Huisser, the Usher, or Porter.

Huit & huist, eight.

Huist çens, eight Hundred.

Le hutieme partie, the eight Part.

Huistime, idem.

Humecter, to moisten.

Humer, to suck or draw in.

Humers Plein de eau, full of watery Humours.

Le humble, the Belly.

Hurst, a Wood or Grove of Trees.

Un hunter de tavernes, a Hunter or frequenter of Taverns. *p. Coke Rep.* 5. 58.

Hutesium & hutestum, a hue and cry. *p. Fitzh.* 17.

Hutesium, is also an Outcry, or Proclamation, from thence *husteium* the Hustings in *London*, where Proclamation is made upon Exigents, *&c.*

Huyer, to cry out, or Proclaim.

Huys, idem, *ut huis.*

Huy, to day in *Mod. French.*

De huys en huis, from Door to Door.

Un Hutte, a little Cottage.

Hydropique, Dropsical.

Hypocrier, to Dissemble.

Hythe, a Wharf, little Haven or Port, as *Queenhyth*, *Lambhyth*, &c. *p. Blunt.*

Hyver, Winter. *p. Britton*, vide *Iver & Yver.*

Hulm vide *holm.*

Huscarle, a domestick Servant, *Saxon.*

Huseans, Buskins, from *houseau*, a kind of Boot, or any thing worn over Stockins.

I A.

JA, now, already, or from hence.

Ja deux ans, now two Years since.

Ja soit que, although, that.

Ja failli, I have fail'd, thence *Jeoffailes.*

Jades, lately, even now, also heretofore.

Jadis, idem. *per Coke Rep.* 6. 23.

Jaloux, Jealous.

Jalemanes, however, notwithstanding, nevertheless, *Jalemaeynes*, idem. *p. Plowd. Com.* 304. *p. Plow. Abr.* 57.

Jademain & jalemens, always. *p. Brit.* 4. a. also *p. Stat. Glouc. cap.* 8. for ever.

Jammes & jamais. per Sat. Westm. 1. 20. never, and *per termes de Ley.* 6. presently, and *p. eund.* 84. *sile.*

Jamais, *a jam & magis*, at this time and further.

A jamais & a jammes, forever. perpetual, always, still. *p. al. Authores.*

Jammes devant, never before.

Jambes, Thighs,

Jampnum, furse, gorse.

Les jareds, the Hammes, also Thighs. *p. termes Ley.* 179.

Janvier, the Month of *January.*

Jarcer, to cleave, also Cleft.

Un jardin, a Garden.

Jaulne, Yellow Colour. *per Plowd.* 339.

Jeo jay, I have, *javera*, I shall have. *p.* 2 *Hen.* 7. 11. b. and by *Cromptons Jur.* 22. I may have.

Ja ent ad Cess, hence it hath been passed, or gone, or times past, also hath for born doing. *per nov. nar.* 56. b.

Jaun, idem, *jampnum*. i. e. furse.

I C.

Icel, this. *per Coke Rep.* 8. 157.

De iceux, of them. *p. Plowd.* 276. b.

Iceluy, he, the same Man.

Icelle, She, or the same Woman.

En icellez, in these same. *Plowd.* 349.

De icel, of it. *per Coke Rep.* 6. 26. also of the same. *per Crompt.* 221.

Jeo voil icy dire, I will here tell you, *icell* is generally taken for it, and the same.

Jecter, thrown, cast, vide, *jette & jetta*.

Jectment, throwing, casting.

Jectes en Mouldes, cast into Moulds.

Ject Commaundements, laid Commands.

Jeady, the Day, also *Thursday*.

Jeo, I, *jeo aye*, I have.

Jeo ne poy, I cannot.

Jeo soy, I be, or am.

Jeo sue, I have been, also I am.

Jeoffailes, Faults, Mistakes, *Misprisions*, over-sights in Pleaing, vide, *jay failli*.

Jeopardie, hazard.

Jemin, a Yeoman. *Saxon*.

Jesq; & jesques, to, unto, or until.

Jesquez, idem.

Jeusdy, Tuesday, vide, *Juisde*.

Un jeu, a Play or Game.

Jean, John.

Jeuner, to fast.

Jeudi & jeaurdie, Thursday.

Jeune, Young, *Jeune Garson*, a Young fellow.

Jeunes, Young Persons.

Un jeune fille, a Young Maiden.

Lour jenuesse, their Youth, *Jeunesse*, Youthful. *per Coke Rep.* 11.

Jerint, they have gone.

Jetsen & jetson, Goods, or things cast into the Sea to preserve the Ship.

Jetter, idem, *ut jecter*.

Jette & jetta, idem.

Ils jetteront, they threw down. *p. Plowd.*

I G.

Ignote, unknown.

Ignier, to burn, *ignyer*, idem.

Ignye, fired, burned.

Ignorer, to be Ignorant of, not to know.

Ignorement, Ignorantly.

Ignominieux, reproachful, dishonorable.

Ignominieusment, reproachfully, shamefully.

Jit tout ceo fuit, all this was. *p. termes de Ley.* 24. b.

Il, he and it. *Il ferra*, it shall be.

Il est ainsi, it is so.

Il jia, they are.

Ou il est il, where is it, or where is he.

Il puisse, he may have.

Il y ad sicome sont, as if there are. 1 *p. Inst.* 167.

Illeonques, thither, also there & thence, *deillonque*, from thence.

Il Fault, it behoveth.

Illec, thither, there. *p. illec* that way.

Illegitime, unlawful.

D'illours, Electors. *p. Plowden.* 23.

Illusion, Deceit, beguiling.

Illoyal, unfaithful.

Illustre, famous, eminent.

Illustrer, to make clear, or evident.

I M.

Imbatler, to enclose. *p. More's. Rep.* 119.

Imbase, made worse.

Imbu, instructed, endued, also wetted.

Imbuent, they drank, or they swallow'd.

Imbezile, to Steal, Pilfer.

Impanel, to write down in order, as in returning Jurors Names.

Imparker, to impouud, *imparks*, impounded.

Impeach, to accuse one of Crimes, to hinder.

Imperer, to Command.

Imperite, unskillful, unlearned.

Imperites, idem.

Impedier, to hinder.

Implicative, implicitly.

Implead, to commence a sute, to sue for.

Implier, to fill up. by *Fitzh. Nat. Brev.* 88. also to fullfil, by *Brokes Abr. gr.*

Pur impleer, for the fulfilling.

Implede, filled. *p. Cromp. Jur. Cur.* 223. b.

Impartir, to Communicate.

Imbecile, weak, also to purloyne.

Immeubles, Goods not removeable.

Immonde, unclean.

Impiteux, unmerciful.

Immunitie, Exemption, Priviledge.

Impersoneé, one inducted to a Benefice Ecclesiastick, also a Dean and Chapter are Persons *impersoneé* of an impropriation or a Benefice appropriated to them. *p. Blunt.*

Implorer, to ask or desire earnestly.

Impierment, prejudicing, impairing.

Implements, things necessary for a Trade or Furniture of a House, or used in Husbandry.

Improwment, making better, or of more value.

Imposer, to put upon. *p. Coke Rep.* 5. 49.

Import, brought in, carried.

Imprender, to take upon one.

Imprendra & imprendera, took upon him.

Imprise sur Luy, took upon him. *p. Coke Rep.* 5. 13. b.

Impristeront, they took upon them, also they put forward.

Impregnant, filled with, containing, or being with Child.

Imprimee, Printed, *imprime*, idem.

Impro-

Impropriation, Tythes in Lay-Mans Hands, but *appropriation* are ſuch in Spiritual Perſons Hands.

Impudique, without Shame.

Imputer, to Charge with, to Impute.

Impunee, impuniſhed.

Imprimeur, a Printer.

Impoſture, deceiving, *un impoſteur*, a deceiver.

Imprecation, Curſing.

Ne impediera, ſhall not hinder.

Improprement, unproperly.

Impliquer, to entangle.

Impoſt, Tribute, Tollage or Cuſtoms.

Imprimerie, the Art of Printing, alſo an Impreſſion and a Printing Houſe.

I N.

Inapres, then after, alſo from thence.

Inacouſtume, not uſed, unaccuſtomed.

Inadvertence, Unadviſedneſs.

Inanere, to make void or null, to defeat.

Incapacitie, inability.

Incedent, are ſet forth or Publiſh'd. *p. Coke Rep*. 8. 19. a.

Incender, to Burn, or ſet on Fire.

Inceſſament, always, or continually.

Incongruitie, unagreableneſs.

Inchaſe, drove. *p. Coke* 8. 66. b.

Incident, a thing not to be ſeparated as a Court Baron, from a *mannor*, alſo a thing hapning or falling out of neceſſity.

Inciter, to ſtir up, or to provoke.

Inciſer, to cut.

Incite, provoked.

Incumbrant, encumbring.

Incumbent, he who is poſſeſſed of a Church with care of Souls, who bends all his Study to his Cure.

Incurgera, ſhall forfeit, ſhall incurr.

Queux Incurgera, which ſhall happen or fall out. *p. Coke* 5. 118. b.

Incurre, happened, alſo encreaſed. *p. More Rep*. 116. *incurra*, idem.

Ne incurr, run not into.

Indeu, indebted.

Incluſivement, comprehending, *excluſivement*, the contrary.

Incogna, unknown.

Incommoder, to hinder.

Inchanter, he who Sings Verſes to Charm.

Inleaſed, enſnared, intangled, in Modern French *Enlaſſe*.

Un juge, a Judge.

Inconſiderament, raſhly.

Incontinent, immediately.

Incorrectement, Faultily.

Incuter, to ſtrike, *ne voil incuter*, will not ſtrke. *p. Fitzh. Juſt*. 11. a.

Indire, to declare, alſo to endite, *indict*, endited.

Indices, Signs, Tokens.

Indoctement, unlearnedly.

Indomit, boiſterous, untameable and ungovernable. *p*. 1. *part Inſtit*. 124.

Inducer, to bring in.

Infect, undone, not accompliſh'd. *p. Plowden* 250. b.

Infreint, broken.

Infantes, Children.

Ingen, wrong, deceit, *pur Ingen*, for wronging or deceiving. *p. Kitchin* 144. a.

Ingenie,

Ingenie, Wit, Ingenuity.

Indeciz, undetermined, undecided.

Indemne, ſaved, harmleſs.

Indignement, unworthily.

Individu, not to be divided.

Per indivis, as not divided.

Indiviſum, in Law is when two or more hold in Common without Partition.

Injuſtement, wrongfully.

Indult, Young, not of Age.

Ineffable, unutterable.

Infreinder, to break, *infreint*, broken.

Male ingene, ill Will, *Coke* 3. *Rep*. 83.

Inique, Wicked, *iniquement*, Wickedly, *les ingenyes*, their Wits. *Plowd*. 82. a.

Ingendres, begotten.

Inhabile, unfit, unable.

Inhiber, to forbid.

Inhumer, to bury.

Injurieux, hurtful, or wrongful.

Ing, a watery Place, 1 *part Inſt*. 5.

Ingyſt, thrown out. *p. Fitzh. gr. abr.* 1 *pt. fol*. 238.

Injecture le Maines, laying Hands on one.

Injurer aſcun, to wrong one.

Injunction, a Prohibition, or command, alſo a Writ ſo called out of the Court forbidding to Act.

Inorer, vide, *Ignorer*.

Inſient, vide, *enſient*.

Inſient, pregnant, quick with Child.

Inſient priviement, newly with Child.

Inſient groſſment, great with Child.

Inraſer, vide, *enraſer*.

Inracera, pull'd down, thrown down.

Inquiſe, enquired unto. *per Kitchin*. 4.

Al inſpection, upon View or Sight. *p. Fithz*. 134.

Infamer, to ſcandalize.

De infame, of ill Name.

Inegal & inegual, unequal.

Inſtainement, preſently, vide, *maintainant*.

Inſurge, roſe up.

Inepte, unfitly, fooliſhly.

Inſtruict, inſtructed.

Inſuer, to purſue or follow.

Inſuiſt, following, and he followed.

Inſuera, ſhall follow or purſue.

Intaunt, foraſmuch, inaſmuch.

Intromit, medled with, *Intrimitter*, to meddle with, and, *come jeo intend*, as I think or conceive.

Intendement, thinking, conceiving.

Intelligence, knowledge.

Interleſſer, to put between, alſo to leave out or omit.

Interleſſe, left out, omitted, *interleſſant*, interlined.

Inover, to invent a new, to change.

Inopine, ſudden, unlook'd for.

Inſciement, ignorantly, without one Knowledge.

Inſtigateur, a provoker, a ſtirer up.

Inſolu, unpaid.

Interjecter, to caſt or put between.

Intermettre, to diſcontinue, *intrometter*, idem.

Interoguer, to queſtion, to demand.

Intervalle, a ſpace between, alſo a ſpace of time, &c.

Les intestines, the Intrails, or Bowels.

Intime, inwardly, *mon intimie amie*, my dear, or inward Friend.

Intrication, intangling.

Intrusion, unlawful entry into possession.

Intruder, vide *Entrader*.

Inveigner, to find, *inveigne*, found.

Inveignant, finding, *serra inveigne*, shall be found.

Inventer, to find out.

Investe, possessed.

Invenigne, vide *envenome*, Poison.

Inviter, to shun, to be unwilling.

Ipso Invito, against his will.

Inviter, is also to provoke.

Invironer, to compass about.

Ale inviron, to go about.

Invalider, to weaken, to make void.

Inventorier, to inventory, or write particulars.

Inutile, unprofitable.

J O.

Joua, played. *p. Coke Rep.* 9. 120.

Jovant, playing. *p. eund.*

Joindre, to join, to couple.

Joialx, Jewels. *p. Stat. Art. sup. Chart. Cap.* 20.

Joignant apres, joining unto, or hard by.

Joinct, joined, *jouc* play'd.

Jonges, Yokes, *p. Plowd.* 276.

Un jonc, a Rush, *joncaria*, rushy places, *juncaria*, idem.

Jour, a Day, *touts jours* for-ever.

Ce jour, to Day, *en quel jour*, in what day, *le jour demaine*, to morrow, *touts les jours*, daily, *jourment*, idem.

Journante, day breaking. *p. Britton* 209.

Journallement & journalment, daily. *p. Plowd.* 378.

De jour en jour, from day to day.

Jour, is also an Oath, *que appent a la journee*, which belonged to their Oath. *p. Coke rep.* 8. 34.

Poit estre jouree, may be sworn. *p. eund.* 9. 40.

Joitement, Wording. *p. Coke* 5. 99. a.

Joyesement, merrily, cheerfully, *p. eund*, 7, 17.

Un jou, a Cock, *jo*, idem.

Joung, a Yoke, vide *Juge*.

Jouste, hard by, joining, *jouxte*, idem.

Joyeux, Merry, joyful.

Joyntenants, they who hold by the same Title without Partition.

Joesdie, Thursday, *p.* 1. *Hen.* 7. 5. a.

Joeudi, idem in mod. *French*.

Joyaux, Jewels, *per Stat.* 28. *Edw.* 1.

Jotson, vide *Jetson*.

Joyeusment,, Joyfully.

I R.

Ire, Wrath, Anger. *Iracund*, angry.

Qui est ire? Who is angry?

Ire, Also to go, to pass, to journey.

Ire ad largum, to go or be set at liberty, to escape.

Ira, shall go, or journey, *p.* 19 *Hen.* 8. 10. b.

Irra, idem, *p.* 21. *Hen.* 7. 27. a. from *aler* to go.

Ne irroit avant, he should not go or pass before this time. *per Plowd. Abr.* 22. b.

Irrount,

Irrount, they go, &c.

Irruer, to pull, or throw down.

Irreprehensible, blameless.

Irrite, unjust, unlawful. *p. Coke rep.* 8. 56.

Irrites, void. *p.* 2. *pt Institutes* 665.

Irriter, to provoke, to stir up.

Irruption, breaking in.

Irrevokeablement, not to be revoked.

Irresourme, unreformed.

Irrepleviable, not to be delivered upon Sureties, or Pledges, a distress to remain.

I S.

Un Isle, an Island.

Isser & *issir*, to go forth.

Isseroit, should issue forth.

Issist, he went forth, or issued out, *Issuist*, idem.

Issuont, they spring forth, or issue out.

Istuants, issuing, *issuant*, idem, *issaut*, idem. *p. Coke* 8. 87. & *p. Parkins* 125.

Issauntes, idem.

Issint, so. *p. Fitzh. nat. br.* 40, also they be. *p. Parkins* 125, a.

Issi, thus, and so. *p. termes de Ley* 55, b.

Issue, Children.

Item, also, it being an Article.

Isliera, shall choose. 32. *Hen.* 6, 20.

Isser, to issue, out to go.

J U.

Cel juge, this Yoke, *un juge* a Judge.

Juillet, the Month of *July*.

Juises, *p. Fitzh Justice* 201. seems to be Nusances, or Stanks to turn the Water out of its Course.

Juiff, a Jew.

Jusne, Young. *p. Coke Rep.* 11. 53.

Junes, Young People. *p. eund.*

Lourt junessa, their Youth. *p. Plowd.* 303, b.

Jument, a breeding Mare, a Colt, also a Bullock. *p. Gregory* 30. & *p. eund.* 323, b.

Jugum terre, is taken to be half a Plough'd Land, or as much as a Yoke of Oxen can till.

Juncaria, Rushy places, *Joncaria*, idem.

Juns, a Man's Scull. *p. Nov. Narr.* 69.

Jure, sworn, also an Oath.

Jumpna, a waterish place, 1. *pt. Instit.* 5.

Jures, ye are sworn, also Oaths.

Pur jurer, for to be sworn.

Jnrement, Swearing, *Jurye*, Sworn.

Serra jure, shall be Sworn.

Estre poient jures, ye may be.

Juries, idem ut *Jures*.

Jurgent, they shall Swear. *p. Britt.* 9, a.

Juisdie, vide *Jeusdye*. Tuesday. *p. Nov. Nar.* 53.

Jubile, a Pardon, a Year of rejoicings given every fiftieth Year by the Pope.

Jurisconsultes, Councellors in the Civil Law.

Jusques, until, unto, *Jesque*, idem.

Jusques a ce lieu la, unto this place, here.

Jusquei a maintenant, till this present.

Justement, uprightly.

Justes,

Justes, contentions in Arms, and with Spears on Horseback.

Jousts, in Modern French.

Se justefier, to purge himself of a Crime.

Justifiont, they justify'd or maintain'd.

Juvences, Heifers, also Steers.

Juvence, a Steer.

Jusne, Younger.

Junes, Young ones. *p. Britt.* 169, a.

Juvent, Young, *juvents & juvens*, idem.

June shovellers, young Quoists, or Pigeons.

Juvenches, Calves. 39. *Hen.* 6. 22, b.

K A.

Kallender Month, is 30, or 31 Days, but saying twelve Months, it shall be computed according to 28 Days *per* Month. *Coke rep.* 6. 61, b. a twelve Month singularly is all the Year. *p. eund.*

Kantref, in Wales includes a hundred Villages.

Karle, a Man Servant, or Clown.

Karrata feni, a Cart load of Hay.

Kay, a Wharf to land Goods.

Kayage, Toll paid for such landing, or loading.

K E.

Keins, idem ut *keyne*.

Kidells, Weres where Fish are caught. *p. Coke* 2. *pt. Instit.* 38. *kopen*, idem.

Kernellata domus, a Castle.

Un kerver, a Carver. *p. Parkins* 23.

Kernes, idle Persons, Vagabonds.

Keyns, Oaks, also Young saplings of Oaks, the Modern French is *chesnes*.

Keynez, Oaken Trees. *p. Plowd. abr.* 75.

K N.

Knol, a Hill. 1 *pt. Instit.* 5.

Knout, a Knight. *p. Britton.* 200, b.

Un kne, idem ut *knol*.

Knave, anciently a Man Servant, also a Male Child. *p.* 14. *Edw. 3d Stat.*

L A.

LA, is a sign of the Femenine Gender for the, as *la feme*, the Woman.

La, is also an Adverb of place, as, *la ou tu es*, there where thou art.

La, is also a Relative, rehearsing the thing spoken of, but most often stands for there.

L, the Letter is very often used for *le*, the, before any word, as *L'espousels*, the Marriage, *l'issue*, &c. *L'adite*, *l'adict*.

Si la, so long until, *p. Brit.* 136, a.

Labeurer, to labour, *labeur*, labor.

Labourage, Husbandry work, Tillage.

Jour labour, day work.

Laict, Milk, *lac*, idem, also a *Lake*.

Laborieux, painful, laborious.

Lacerer, to tear in pieces.

Lacerta, a fathom. *p.* 1. *pt. Inst* 4.

Laces, Gins, Snares.

Laches, negligence, slackness, default, omission.

Lacher, to be idle, negligent, lazy, to loyter.

Lacheſſe, idem. neglect.

Lache, idleness, laziness, from *lasche*, modern French, careless, slothful.

Lader, to Ship, or lade on Board.

Lafferent, they belong.

Laies gents, Lay-Men, *lays gens*, idem. i. e. they who are not of the Clergy.

Laganes, Gallons, *Lageons*, idem. *Cromp. Justice* 33. *un lagon*, a Gallon. *p. Coke Rep.* 6. 61.

Lai, where.

Laghlite, a Mulct for Breach of the Law. *Saxon. biens lagon*, goods at the bottom of the Sea.

Ligan, idem.

Laieur, breadth. *p. Fitzh. Nat. Brev.* 225, b.

Laiſant, leaving, *lature* & *laicture*, idem.

Lain & *lane*, Wool.

Leynes peals, Wool fells. *p. Stat. Weſtm.* 1. 59.

Layſer, to leave, *laiſe*, left, *laiſer*, idem, and to relinquish, and forsake. *p. Coke* 7, 15, and 6, 76.

Laiſſer la feme, to put away the Wife, or leave her.

Laiſſe le huis overt, left the Door open.

Eſt laiſe, is set forth or left.

Layſe, idem ut *laiſe*.

Un laiz, & *un lezs*, a Legate.

Evoy laiſe, I had left. *p. Plowd. Preface.*

Lamena, led, carried.

Il langue, the Tongue.

Couper la langue aſcun, to cut out one's Tongue.

Languer, & *langur*, Weakness, Sickness.

Languir, to languish, *languiſant*, languishing.

Languorouſment, faint, languishingly.

Lannemannus, the Lord of the Mannor. 1. *pt. Inſt.* 5, a.

Un lapidaire, a Jeweller.

Laps de temps, loss of time.

Lays gens, vide *lays gens.*

Lay poiar, Lay-power.

Loyſomus, let us rest, or leave off, *Coke Rep.* 10. 37.

Larges, encreased, enlarged.

Larges ou eſtraits, encreased, or diminished. *p. Britton* 143, b.

Large, wide, *fort large*, very wide.

Large ouſter, over measure.

Largeſſe, a Gift, or Reward.

Mettre large ou vaſt, to let go at large.

Larroneux, Thievish.

Larceny, Theft, *Laron* & *Larron*. a Thief, or Felon.

Lareyns, Thefts.

Un Laſi, one of the Lessees. *p. Coke Rep.* 5, 9, a.

Laſer, a Leprous Person.

Laſſer, to tire, to make weary.

Las, weary.

Laſſe, wearied, *Laſette*, weariness.

Laſtals, Dunghils, or places to throw Filth, or Dung.

Laſtels, stays, hindrances, stops.

Lattre, the side.

Latrine, a Sink, Jakes, or House of Office.

Laten, Brass.

Lature, breadth, *Leaure*, idem.

L'autre, the other.

Laver, to wash.

Lave, washed, *Lavement*, washing, *Levera*, shall wash.

Lawe, a Hill, *lawnd* & *lound*, a Plain between Woods.

Lagette, a Chest, Box, or Drawer.

Laynesse, greatest, largest, biggest. *p. nov. narr.* 61.

Layseront, they leave. *Coke Rep.* 6, 12, b.

Lay gents, common People.

L E.

Le, is an Article before the Masculine Gender signifying, the, as *le home*, the Man.

Les, is put as a plural, as *le un*, the one, *les auters*, the others.

Lea & *Ley*, Pasture Ground.

Leal, vide *Loyal*, i. e. faithful, &c.

Lealment, faithfully, lawfully. *p. Brit.* 184.

Leaument, idem *p. eund.* 18.

Leans, within. *p. Stat. Westm.* 1.

Leaure, the breadth. *p. nov. nar.* 68, b.

Un lease, a Leash wherein Grayhounds are led.

Leaz, leased, demised.

Lecteur, reading, also read.

Leger, to read, *bien poit leer*, could well read. *p. Coke Rep.* 11, 35.

Lecte, a Bed, *lede*, hurt.

Leicher, to lick, *licher*, idem.

Leide, aid.

Un leez, a lease. *p. Parkins* 157, b.

Leger, & *legier*, sudden, hasty, also violent and notorious. *p. Fitzh. Just.* 147, a.

Legerte, hastily, suddenly, violently. *p. Brit.* 237.

Leigerment, lying. 1 *Hen.* 7. 1. and 31, also easily. *p. Rep.* 3 26. also dormantly, or by the bye. *p. Plowd.* 303, b.

Rewle legerment, a standing Rule.

Un legion, a number of Armed Men, containing by some 6500, by others 12500 Men.

Un legat, an Ambassador.

Legislature, a Declaration of the Laws in Writing or Print.

Legitime, lawful.

Le lendemaine, the next day after, or the morrow.

Defferer en lendemaine, to put off till to morrow.

Le quel, the which, *lesquels de deux qui que ci soit*, which of the two soever it be.

Lendemaine, is sometimes used for out of hand, and presently, and afterwards.

Lee, read, *lees* plural. *leisure*, reading.

Leigne & *leygne*, the Elder.

Lembleier, to steal.

Lenir, to mitigate, to asswage.

A lenvoy, to convoy, or send. *p. Brit.* 19.

L'envers, the inside, or within.

Lendroit, without, outwards.

Leser, to hurt.

Lesus, hurt.

Lese, let.

Lese a bail, let to bail. *Rep.* 10, 99.

Lesion, hurting, also wounding.

Ad less un a large, hath set one at liberty.

Lessa, left, leased, let out.

Lesse, idem.

Ne lessent, they leave not. *p. Brit.* 204.

Ne lessez, ye shall not fail, or omit. *p. eund.*

Ne lerrount, they omit not, or fail not. *p. eund.* 9.

Lenrase, vide *enrace.*

Lentier, the whole.

Lerra, shall hinder, omit, or let.

Leront, they lye. *p. Coke* 9, 66.

Lepre, a Leper.

Leschewes, Trees fallen by chance, windfals. *p. Brokes Grand Abr.* 341.

Lescheker, Exchequer.

p. Leaser, by falsifying, leasing.

Lesse, a Mainprize let out upon bayl.

Lessance, bayling, *lessant*, id.

Less aler, let go, *a lesser hors*, to let out.

Leswes & *Lesues*, Pasture Ground. *p.* 1. *pt. Inst.* 5.

Ne pur lesser ascun arrest, nor for staying any arrest. *p. Fitzh. Justice* 193.

Lesglise, vide *eglise.*

Un lettre, a letter, *bailler lettres a porter*, to deliver Letters to be carryed.

Lever, to raise, or set up.

Se lever du lict, to raise ones self up in Bed.

Pur lever un mese plus haut, for building a House too high. *p. Fitzh. nat. brev.* 184.

A lever un molin, to build a Mill.

Leve, lifted up, *leva le main*, hold up the hand, *leve en le nuict*, rose in the Night.

Le court leve suis, the Court Rose.

Levain, Yeast, Barm, Leven.

Leve, built, *leva le fesaunt*, spring the Pheasant. *p. Kitch.* 59, b.

Leu, a Bed, vide *lect* & *lict.*

Leverer, a Lurcher, or small Gray-Hound.

Levere, idem, *leuriers*, Gray-Hounds, *levers*, idem.

Un leveret, a young Hare, *leural*, idem.

Lieure, a Hare, *Leures*, Hares.

Leve, raised.

Levorer, a tumbler Dog. *p. Kitch.* 59, b.

Levesque, a Bishop, vide, *Evesque.*

Leveschrie, a Bishoprick.

Lewes, a Mile, sometimes taken for a Furlong.

Lewkes, Miles, *p.* 2. *Hen.* 7, 10, a.

Leuks, idem. *p. Coke Lib.* 10, 72, but is more properly *leagues*. *p. Phillips.*

Aler tres lewes entour, to go three Miles about. *p. nov. nar.* 52, b.

Tient lew, held, or took place. *p. Cromp, Jur. Cur.* 57, b.

Leyre, the Heir. 4. *Hen.* 7, 1, a.

Leuvad, a Forest, or Park. *leuved*, idem, *leuve*, idem, & *leuca*, idem. *p.* 1. *pt. Instit.* 5.

Leyed, hurt, vide *lede.*

Leyn, Woolen Cloth. *p. nov. nar.* 31.

Leynes, Wool, *pealtz lanuts*, Wool Felts. *p.* 3. *pt. Instit.* 39.

Ley, Law, *leyes*, plural.

Leys gens, Lawyers. *p. Brokes gr. abr.* 288.

Lez & *les*, those, these.

Lez, is also nigh, or near unto.

Lict,

Lict, a Bed, vide *Lect*.

A lier, to read, *lia*, read, *lie*, idem.

La lie, the Dregs the Lees.

Lie, bound, *lye*, idem, also read. 2. *Rep. Coke* 9.

Lier, to bind, knit, tye.

Liera, ſhall bind, &c. *lyera*, idem.

Qui lie, who bind, *liant*, they bind, *liont*, idem.

Lieiſon, bound, *liement*, binding, *lien*, idem.

Lieges, Miles or Leagues. *per Fitzh. Juſt.* 146.

Lieues, idem. *p. Britton.*

Lien, a Cord or String, or Line.

Lief & *leof*, rather, *Saxon*.

Ne poit lier, could not read.

Lieus, places, *ſeunt en lour lieux*, ſitting in their Places 13. *Hen.* 8. 11. b.

En auter lieu, elſewhere, in another Place.

Lieux, *p.* 2. *Hen.* 7. *Weſtm.* b. Places.

De lieu a lieu, from Place to Place.

En lieu, inſtead, in place of, *au lieu*, idem.

Un liewe, a place. *p. Greg.* 202.

Lieux, Miles. *per nov. nar.* 53. b.

Liewxz, idem. *p. Plowd.* 87, b.

Lige & *ligne home*, a Vaſſal, a Subject, *liege*, idem.

Liger, to tye, *liga*, tyed. *p. Fitzh. Juſt.* 23. a.

Lignage, Parentage, Kindred, Linage.

De meſme lignee, of the ſame Blood, Kindred, &c. *Ligon*, vide *Lagon*.

Licher, to lick.

Limitter, to bound, define, limit.

Linquer, to leave, *linquy*, left, *linquiſt*, leaveth.

Lin, Flax, *line*, idem, *linarium*, a flax Ground.

Ling, Linnen, *linthes*, Sheets. *p. Cromp.* 32.

Lingues, Tongues.

Il lirroit, it ſhould be Lawful. *p. More Rep.* 27.

Bien lirroit, well lawful. *per Plowd. Abr.* 9. a.

Bien liſt, idem.

Lite & *lyte*, a Bed, vide *lict*.

Ligne, a Line, *fait a la ligne*, *ou cordeau*, made with a Line and Level.

Lign, is alſo a League.

Un Linier, a Flax or Hemp-dreſſer.

Veſtu du ling, clothed with Linnen.

Liqueur, Liquor, *lyſt*, Lawful, idem *ut liſt*.

Un lis, a Flower de Luce.

Litige, Strife, Debate, *Litigeux*, contentious.

Livrer, to deliver, *liver*, delivered.

Livre, a Book, *lieur*, idem.

Un liver, a pound Weight, *livers* Plural, *p. More* 648.

Lyera, ſhall bind, or tye.

L O.

Loins, farr off, 2 *lib. Aſſ.* 190. a.

Lore, hire, reward, *lower*, idem, alſo a bribe. *p. Fitzh. grand Abr.* 199. b.

Pour lour loier, for their Fee. *p. Mirror.*

Londres, London.

Loggis, a Lodging, *logis*, idem. *un loge*, a Lodg, or Cabbin in a Ship, *loggis*, alſo is, it behoves.

Il eſt loiſible, it is lawful, *loiſt*, lawful, legal.

Loin Pluis, very far.

Longure,

Longure, length, *a la longue*, at length.

Longueur, idem, *ut longure.*

Longayne, a Sheep walk, or Fold course, *longaine*, idem. *p. nov. nar.* 16. b.

Cy longement, thus long, as long as. *p. Plowd.*

Pluis longement, longer, more long.

Lostel & *losteil*, vide, *hostel.*

Lourd, blockish.

Lors, then, at that time. *per Stat. Westm.* 1 *cap.* 20.

Lorsq; and then.

Lovage, hireing.

A lover, to Praise.

Lotoix, a Washer-woman, *loture*, Washing.

Lotux, gives Suck, suckles.

Lothenoit, *quasi lecherwit*, amends given for lying with a Bond-woman.

Loup, a Wolfe.

Lou, where.

Sans lower, without reward or Fee.

Lower, gain, also a Fee or Bribe. *p. Brit.* 38. a.

Lourgulary & *lourderie*, Inhumanity, also any Villanous Act.

Lour, their, theirs, *loer*, idem.

Lour, in Modern French, is to praise.

Lovanger, idem.

Lowage, possession, *en lowage de Mese ou toft*, in Possession or Occupation of the House or Toft. *p. nov. nar.* 2. a.

Loyal, Faithful, True, Lawful, *loyaux*, idem.

Loyalment, Faithfully.

Loyes, Laws, *loyx*, idem. *per nat. brev.* 42.

Loynteines & *loyntens*, a Collateral Heir. *p. Brit.* 91.

En pluis loyntime degree, in the more Collateral degree. *p. eund.* 189.

Un loyer, a reward, or gratuity.

Loz, Praise.

L U.

Lu & *leu*, Light, *lever*, Lightning.

Luce, a Pike, a Jack Fish.

Et luce est & *luse est*, the Use is, or the Custom is. *p. Coke* 5. 39. b. & *p. Plowd. Abr.* 21. b.

Lucratif, Profitable, Gaining.

Luiere, to Shine, *Luminere*, idem.

Luissant, Shining, also Lightning.

Lue, read, *lues*, idem. *p. Brit.* 9. *fuit lus*, be it read. *p. eund.* 101. a.

Lumiere, Light, *lumineux*, giving Light.

Lunitique, Frantick.

Lunedie, *lundy* & *lundie*, the day called Munday, *le lune*, the Moon.

Lunettes, Spectacles.

Lung & *lune*, the one.

Un lupe, a Wolf, vide, *loupe.*

Luder, to play, *tiels que lude*, such who Play.

Luse, playing Cards.

Luy, him, he, the same Man, *el*, her. *p. luy*, by it self, or himself, *sur luy*, upon him.

Luy, is also, who and where. *p. Coke Rep.* 5. 39. b.

Luy, is sometimes taken both for him and her.

A luy & *de luy*, to and from him and her.

A luy ceaux, to him or them.

Lupulicetum, a Hop-Yard, or Ground where Hops grow.

L'une & *l'auter*, the one and the other.

Lut & *lute*, Dirt, Clay.

Luter, to dawb with Clay, or Morter or Line.

L Y.

Lye, read, vide, *lie*.

Lye, *p. Fitzh. Justice* 176, is bound or tyed.

Lyant, vide, *liant*.

Lyeront, they are bound.

Lyer, *p. Brokes grand Abr.* is to tye bind or Fetter, and by *Kitch.* 26. b. 'tis to read.

Lynge, Linnen, idem, *ut linge*.

Ne lyst, not Lawful. *p.* 13 *Hen.* 7. 9. b.

Lyte, by some Authors is a Bed, idem, *ut list*.

Lyre & lyer, to alledge, to declare for, also to oblige, or bind.

Lyver, idem, *nt livre*, and *p. Dyer*, 6. b. and *Plowdens* Preface

Lyeur, is a Brook.

Un lyre, a Harpe, *lyvers*, is also Pounds.

Lyeges, Subjects. *p. Fitzh. Just.* 149. a.

M A.

M*A*, my, *feminine*, *mon*, my, Masculine, also mine.

Ma amie, my She Love, *mon amie*, my Lover or He Love.

Machecollata domus, a Castle. *p.* 1. *pt. Inst.* 5. a.

Machiner, to devise Evil, or go subtilly or cunningly about it, *machination*, devising Evil.

Maerisme, Timber, *merisne*, idem.

Macegriefs & *macegrefs*, such as buy and sell stolen Flesh. *p. Blount.*

Un magicien, a Diviner, Magician.

Maign, great, *magnifique*, stately, August.

Magi, the Art of Enchantment.

Un machine, an Ingine.

Majhem, maimed.

Macular, to spot or blot.

Mahim, a hurt, whereby one loseth the use of some Member.

Maines, Hands, *le maine dextre*, the right Hand.

Maines estendues, open hands.

Oustre le maine, out of hand.

Ma mainy, my Family, *p.* 19. *Hen.* 6. fol. 1.

Bailler ses maines, to give his Hands.

Mainz, idem, *ut maines*, *per Dyer* 7. a.

Maignasium, a Brasier's Shop.

Mainpernour, a surety.

Mail, a small Coin, less than a Peny. *p. Kitchin* 12 & 61.

Un mail, is a half Peny. *per termes de ley*. 331.

Mainprize, Bayle, *mainpernable*, Baylable.

Less ad mainprise, let to Bayle. *p. nat. br.* 299. b.

Mainorable, tenable, demiseable, also habitable.

De main in main, from hand to hand.

Maincraftes, Handycrafts.

Mainoverer, to manure, *meynovera*, shall Manure. *p. termes ley*. 174. b.

Mainovre,

Mainovre, handy-work, *p.Brit. Cap.* 62.

Maintenant, now, at this present.

Makement, contrivance, practice, 42, *Edw.* 3, 2, b.

Maintenir, to hold, to keep, to maintain.

Maintenera, ſhall keep, &c.

Manites foitz, often, divers times.

Jeſque mantenant, hitherto.

Maintenus, held, kept.

Maintainor, he who maintains or ſeconds a ſuit in Law.

Maiſne vide *puiſne*, Younger.

Mainorants, remaining.

Un Maire a Mayor of a Town.

Meieur, idem, in modern *French*.

Mais, but, vide, *Mes*.

Mais, is alſo more, *Il a mais de quarante ans*, he is more than forty Years.

Maiſonner, to build.

Maiſon, a Houſe.

Maiſonnement, Building.

Maiſtre, Sir, Maſter.

Malade, ſick, diſeaſed, *eſtre fort maladie*, to be very ſick.

un Maladie, a Sickneſs.

Maladif, ſickly, ſick.

Male, Evil, Miſchief, Hurt. *Males*, plural.

Malement, evilly, or miſchievouſly.

Maledef, afflicted, *p. More's Rep.* 878.

Maleadventure, ill Fortune.

Maleadviſe, unwary, imprudent.

Male iſſues, Sons.

Male denier, a Half-penny, *p. Termes Ley*, 157. b.

Malefeſant, ill doing, *Malifice*, idem.

Malegree, againſt ones will,

Malveiſt apert, an open offence, *p. Stat. Weſtm.* 1, 15.

Malveis & Malves, ill will, *malveſnes*, idem. *per Plowden*, 360.

Malavis, unadviſedneſs.

Malvois, Evil. *p.* 3. *part. Inſt.* 39.

Malediction, a Curſe.

Malfacture, guilty of doing ill. *maleſeſance*, idem.

Ala mal heur, at an ill hour,

Malveiſnes, illneſs, wickedneſs *p. Plowd.* 75, b.

Malvoillance, ill-will, malice.

Malleable, pliant to the Hammer.

Maltolt & maltault, toll, import, but properly any unjuſt exaction. *per. Stat. Weſtmon.* 1, 58.

Manaſſer, to threaten, *pur manaſſer* for threatning.

Manas, threatned, *manaſſes*, threatnings.

Manaſſera, ſhall threaten.

Mancke, a ſleve or glove.

Mamelles, Breaſts, Duggs.

Mander, to ſend, *il mandra*, he ſent.

De mander, of bringing, *per Fitzh. Nat. Brev.* 23.

Mandement, a command.

Mande vide *maunde*.

Un manque, *a maihme*, a wound. *p. Coke* 9, 120.

Manger, ro eat, to feed.

Bailler a manger, to give food.

Mange, eateth, *maunge*, eat, *ils mangeront*, they eat, *puis manger*, after dinner. *p. Hen.* 7, 26.

Un manteau, a Cloak, or Mantle.

Mainor, a Lordſhip, or Mannor; alſo a chief dwelling.

Manſion,

Mansion, the chief house, *manning*, a days work. *p. Blount*.

Manse, a Farme, *manses*, hides of Land.

Manumisse, set free.

Manumitter, to enfranchise or set free.

Manurer, to dung, soyl, or fold upon Lands, to order husbandly.

Manuester, to filch or take away privily, also to thieve.

Manuestes, thievings.

Merchander, to Traffick, to Commerce.

Un marche, a Market, *march* & *marche*, idem.

Marches, Markets, *per Britton* 53.

Marces, Marks in tale of Money.

Marchet & *merchet*, Moneys paid the Lord in ransom of Virginity, or for License of his Tenants Daughters to Marry.

Marcher, to walk, go or march.

Marier, to Marry, *marie*, maryed.

Si vous maryes, if ye marry, *p. Plowden*, 303.

Maryeres, Ye shall marry. *p. eundem.*

Marisdie, & *Mardie*, Tuesday, vide *Juisdie*.

Mariscbal, an Officer, or Keeper of the King's Bench Prison; also the Earl Marshal, Knight Marshal, Judges Marshal, &c.

Maries, Marsh-ground.

Marettum, idem, from *Maret*, French.

Marys, idem. *p. nov. nar.* 2. a.

Masle, Male-kind, *petit masles*, Boys.

Marquer, to note, or set down in writing.

Manicles, Gyves, Fetters.

Manie, Madness. *un Manique*, a Madman.

Marches, the Bounds and Limits of a Country; also Markets, *p. Britton* 53.

Le marge d'un livre, the Margent of a Book.

Mare, the Sea, *la marine* & *marin*, of or belonging to the Sea.

Maritime, the Sea-Coast.

Jure maritime, the Rights or Laws of the Sea.

un Marque, a Marquis.

Mois, a Month.

Le mois de Mars, the Month of *March*.

Martyre, Martyrdom.

Massacre, killing or murthering of any.

Massoner, to sing Mass.

Masure terre, Ground containing about four Oxe-gangs,

Maten & *Matin*, morning, *matutine*, early.

Matine. early, *le matyne*, the morning, *p. Fitzh. Just.* 86, b.

Mature, ripe, come to Perfection, *matures*, idem, *per Parkins* 109.

Matrimoigne, Marriage.

Magre, & *maugre*, in despight of, against.

Maugre sa soen, against his Will.

Maugre son test, whether he will or no.

Maulgre, id. in mod. *French*.

Mauger, notwithstanding, 1, *Hen.* 7.

Maulx, Evil.

Maunder, to send, *maunde*, sent.

Ont maunde, they have sent. *p. Termes Ley*, 87.

Maundera, shall send. *p. Plowd.* 313.

Per maundement, by command.

Maunger, to Eat, also Food.

Maunge, eat ye, also eateth.

Mauvesse, guilt, fault, *per Britton*, 10.

Mauvaise, ill, base, bad, *per eundem. Maus*, idem.

Mauvayse gard, ill kept, *per Coke* 11, 49.

Pur mausesheure, for avoiding ill. *p. Britt.* a.

Mauvesement, maliciously, *p. Britton*, 37, b.

Mauvaisement, idem. and wickedly.

Un mat, a sot, a fool.

Maxime, a rule in Law, a principle not to be disputed or denyed.

Maynourable, Tenantable; also tillable. vide *mainorable*.

Mayhem, the loss of some Member of the Body, *p. Coke Rep.* 5. 50.

Le maz d' un neuf, the Mast of a Ship.

M E.

En le meane, in the manner, *p. Plowden*.

Mean, vide, *Mesne*.

un Mease, a Messuage, *Mese*, idem, *Mees*, idem.

Le meason, the House, *p. Greg.* 336, a.

Medlesse, affraies, strife, quarrelling.

Medsee, a reward or bribe, something in compensation.

Meer, the Sea, *mer*, idem.

Meen & mesne, the Tenant between the Lord and the undertenant. *p. Britton* 58.

Melieur, better, *melious*, best.

Meinder, fewer. *p. Kitchin*, 7, a.

Meins, less, *meindre*, idem.

Le meignee, the Family, or Houshold, *p. Stat. Art. sup. Chart.* 28, *Edw.* 1.

Mein mine, *miens & mines*, somewhat, *veint meines*, nevertheless.

Al meins & au meins, at least, *al meinst*, idem. *Kitch.* 7, a.

Meint foits, seldom.

Meir, Mayor, *p. Plowd.* 36, b.

Meime, a Family, Houshold.

Meistre, Matter or cause, also the means.

Meister, requisite, necessary.

Meit, the one half, the *moity*.

Melle & miel, Hony.

Du miel celeste, Manna.

Que nul se mellera, that none shall meddle, *p. Plowd.* 313. b.

Melieux, better, also knowledge, *meliour*, idem.

Le melieur, the middle.

Per le Melieu, through the middle.

Menacer, to threaten.

Menceur, he that threatens.

Menacement, threatning.

Mendica, begging, *un Mendicant*, a beggar.

Soit menant, they be dwelling or resideing.

Mene, a Houshold Servant also a Family.

Soient menes, they are brought *p. Britton* 10, b.

Menserges, lyes, *p. Crompton*, 35, b.

Mener, to walk about, to lead.

Mene, lead or drove, *Menes*, go, plurally.

Menus, small, *menu*, idem. slender.

Mengent

Mengent, they eat. *per Britton* 10.

un Mesonger, a lyer, *menteur*, & *mentour*, idem.

Le mesoigne, the lye, *mesonges*, lyes.

Ment, a Mind, *ove un ment*, with one mind.

Sans ment, a Sot a Fool.

Eyent mentu, they have lyed, *mentent*, they lye.

Menterie & *mentery*, slander, false reports.

Mentir, to speak falsely, to lye.

Mehme mehime, vide *Mayhme*.

Menage, carryage, burthens.

Per le menu, by small parcells, by retayle.

Mere & *mera*, only absolute.

Mere droit, cheif right, meer right.

Mercie, thanks, also pity.

Jeo vous mercie, I give you thanks.

Mercredie, Wednesday, *merkerdie*, idem.

Merkedy, idem, *merdie*, Tuesday.

Mere, Mother, *mere de ma feme*, my Grandmother, *ma mere grand*, my great Grandmother.

Le mere bank, the Sea shore.

Merger, to drown, *merging*, drowning.

Merge, drown'd, *mergera*, shall drown.

Meridinal, Southward.

Mermesettes, Monkeys. 12, *Hen*. 8. 4, b.

Merisme, Timber, vide *maerisme*.

Meremium, is the Latin, in Law us'd for Timber, *mertlage*, speaking of Martyrs. *p*. 9. *Hen*. 7, 14.

Meriter, to deserve.

un merrour, a Lookinglass, *merroar* idem.

de ce merture, of this matter. *Coke* 9, 121.

Merveille, wonder, *mervileux*, wonderful.

Mesavenir & *mesaveign*, to come amiss, to mishappen, *mesaventeur*, an ill-chance.

mescreant, a faithless Person, an Unbeliever, vide *Miscreant*.

Mesconuster, to misunderstand, *mesconustre*, idem.

Mesdire, to speak amiss of one, to backbite.

Mesquerdie, Wednesday.

Mesle, mingled.

Meseaus, Leprous. *p. Britton*, 88, a.

Mesteaux, idem. *per Mirror*. *Just*.

Meschet, it fell amiss, or contrarily. *p. eund*. 191.

Meslauge, Mixture.

Mes is sometimes put for my, as *mes avers*, my Cattle, *mes* also for mine, *de mes reports*, of my Reports, *p.Coke* 9, 36. b.

Messarius, a Mowyer. *per Fleta* 2. *cap*. 75. a Harvest-man.

Messor, idem.

Mestilo, Munkcorn, Maslin, Wheat and Rye mingled.

Se mecoignostre, he knows not himself.

Mescrus, suspected or fled for fear, also guilty.

Mescru, idem, and mistrusted, *per Britton*. 4. 6. and 2. *part Inst*. 633.

Mescreables gents, People denying, or not believing the Faith in Religion.

Mesnage, Houshold, *mesnagement*, Houswifry, also Thriftiness.

Mesprendre, to mistake, to do amiss.

Mosprenants, mistaking. *Coke* 9. 121. *Misprision*.

Mespriser, to do amiss, to contemn.

Le messe, the Mass, *Messes* Plural.

Le mesme, the same, *luy mesme*, himself.

Eux mesmes, themselves, *ce mesme*, this very same.

Eulx mesme, they themselves. *p. Greg.* 281.

Le enfant mesmer, the Infant himself.

Que jeo mesme, than I my self. 2 *Hen.* 7. 15. a.

Mesme in *Termes de Ley*, is sometimes put for although, vide, f. 267. b.

Le mesme, vide, *meen*.

Estre mesnes, to be carry'd, brought. *per* 3 *pt. Inst.* 39.

Mesq; albeit, although.

Mesaveigner, mischance.

Mesle, mingled, *meslange*, mingling, *p. Plow.* 339.

Messurer, to move.

Messoignes, lyes, false Stories. *per Termes de Ley* 104.

Mestive, harvest, *en temps de mestives*, in time of Harvest.

Mestiver, idem *ut messarius* & *messer*.

Ou mestier, where it needeth or is requisite, also need, *per Kitch.* 17, b, and needful.

Mester & *mestre*, idem, *i. e.* need.

Si mestier soit, if need be.

Meyes, a Month, *mete*, idem. *per Brit.* 62, b.

Met, sent, put, *mette*, idem. *per Crompt.* 56.

Mettre & *metter*, to put, *de mestre*, of putting.

Mettre hors de sont heritage, put out of his Inheritance.

Metter, to shew forth.

Mettre aucun, to rest one, or take repose.

Se met, doth put himself, *per Britt.* 232. b.

Mettre en contraire, to oppose or set himself against, *p. Plowd.*

Met, he put or brought, *mettont* plural.

Ne mettre, did not bring. *per Hen.* 6.

Mettre en Dieu, put himself upon God, *p. Nov. Nar.* 3. b.

Meere a fin, brought to an end.

Meurs, Demeanour, Manners, Behaviour.

Meur, Ripe, ready. *p. Plowd.* 36. b.

Soit meu, he moved or stirred up.

Meus, moved, stirred up, *per Britt.* 240. b.

Meutre, Murther, *per Coke* 9. 121.

Meurture, idem. *p. eund. meurtre*, idem.

Meurtrier in modern *French* is a Hangman.

Meux, the best, *meulx*, better, also rather.

Meyndre, lesser, smaller, *meindre*, idem.

Meys idem ut *meis*.

Meyn, a Hand, *p. Parkins* 161, vide *Maine*.

Avant maine, before-hand, *per Britton* 106.

Meyney, a Family, *per Lambard*.

Meynovera, shall manure or dress in a husbandlike manner.

Meynorable,

Meynorable, vide, *mainourable*, ſometimes 'tis put for Tillage.

Meubles, moveables houſhold-Stuff.

Meurir, to ripen.

Meyndre, vide, *meinder*.

M I.

Mi, the halfe, the moity, alſo the middle, vide *my. per mi*, amongſt, *Coke* 9. 120.

Mi, mixt, alſo put. *p. termes de ley*. 75. a.

Mi lieu, the middle place.

Mie & *my*, a negative Note or Denying.

Ee midi, Noon, Mid-day, *midy*, idem.

Midivint, Midnight, *Coke* 9. 120.

La mi eſti, Midſomer.

Miel hony, *mielleux*, Sweet as Hony.

Michaelm, Michaelmas.

Al miens, at leaſt, *meis*, idem.

Miendre, vide, *meinder*.

Ou mieſter ſera, where need ſhall be. *p.* 3 *pt. Inſtit.* 39.

Mier, Mother, idem, *ut mere*.

Mieulx, *mieux*, vide, *meux* & *meulx*.

Mieux engendres, better reconciled or agreed with. *Coke* 5. 34. a.

Le milieu, the middle. *p. Cromp*.

Mien elle eſt mien, ſhe is mine.

Mient, better, beſt.

Minovery, Treſpaſs done by the Hand, as by cutting Wood in a Foreſt or the like.

Meinoverer, by *Britton* is to manure Lands. *cap.* 40.

Miſaventure & *Miſadventure*, an unfortunate Action.

Miſe, Expence, Disburſement, *mis*, idem. vid. poſtea.

Miſe, put.

Mille, a Thouſand, and alſo a Mile.

Le millieme partie, the thouſand part.

Milliares, Miles.

La Miene, the Countenance, *Mine*, idem.

Miner, to dig, *ne minera*, ſhall not dig.

un Mineral, a Mine or Quarry. *Miniere*, idem.

un Minour, one under Age.

Miniſh, to make leſs.

Miniſter, to offer, to ſerve.

Minues diſmes, ſmall Tythes.

Minuict, Midnight, *Minuit* & *Mynute*, idem.

Minuict is alſo a Minute.

Midi, Noon, *le Vent Midi*, the South Wind, being the Sun at Noon is always South.

Mis, Expence, alſo put, ſet down, taken, *p. Coke* 11. 6.

Miſconuſant, unknown.

Miſes fuerunt, were put. *per Fitzh. nat. brev.* 42.

Misfeaſours, Miſdoers.

Mis fait, he did amiſs, or wrong.

Miſfaits, Wrongs, Offences, Miſdeeds.

Miſpriſel, Wrongful or miſtaking.

Miſpriſteront, they miſtook.

Miſpriſe ſur lui, took upon him amiſs, or by miſtake.

Miſnomer, to miſname.

Miſſives, Epiſtles, Letters.

Miſconus, Unknown, *myſconus*, id.

Miſagarde, Unduly awarded, 2, *Rich.* 3.

Miſtioner, to mingle or mix together.

Miſtion, mingling, mixture.

Miſt, ſent, *ne miſt*, put not.

Se miſtrent, they put themſelves. *p. Brit.* 5, b.

Miſtier,

Mistier, need, vide, *mestier*.

S'il est mistier, if need be.

Mister, need. *per* 27 *Hen.* VII.

Misteront, they put. *p. Mores Rep.* 578.

Ne mistera, shall not put, *mistera*, idem, *mittera*, idem. *per Crompton* 70.

Mistermyng, miscalling. *per Plowd.* 141, b.

Mislyer & *mislier*, to choose the wrong or mistake. *per Kitchin* 67, a.

Doit mistee, might or ought to put, *esteant misse*, they being sent home.

Mitter, to send or put, *mittre*, idem.

Mittomus, we put, *mittont*, they put or sent.

Mitter a large, to set at Liberty. *per Crompton Jur. Cur.* 70.

Mit, sent, put.

Mynute, vide *minuist*, idem. *per Brook gr. Abr.* 209.

M O.

Mocquer, to Scoff, to deride.

Mocquerie, Division, Scoffing.

Moeryer, to dye, *moerge*, dead. *per Brit.* 18. *cap.* 95.

Moebles, moveables.

Moign, a Monk, *moignes* Plural.

Moinder, idem *ut meinder*.

Moys, a Month, vide *meys*, *moies* & *moyes* idem, also *moise* idem. *per* 2 *Rich.* 3. 14, b.

Moissoner, to Reap. *per Coke Rep.* 11. 53. *moissonner*, idem.

Le moit, the half, *moitz*, halves, moieties.

Moler, to grind, *mol*, a Mill, *molins*, Mills.

Moliner, a Miller, *dentz moliers*, the Teeth called Grinders, *pur moliek*, Grinding.

El molera, she shall Grind. *per Parkins* 87. b.

Molt, much, *moult* idem. *per Kitchin*, *per moltez*, by many, *Plowden* 132, b.

Moins, less, vide *mien*, *rien moins*, nothing less.

Moindre, least.

Mon, my and mine.

Le mound, the World, *mond*, idem.

Mondain, a worldly Man, *du monde*, the People.

Monopoler, to get into ones Hands, what ought to be for the Publick.

Vie monastique, the life of a Monk.

Monstrer, to shew, *monstra*, sheweth, *monstrans*, shewing, *ne monstres*, ye shew not, *monstremus*, we will shew, *monstra*, shall shew. *per Parkins* 186.

Mordre, to bite, to nipp, *morsure*, biting.

Mora a Moor, or Boggy Ground or Barren.

Monsier, Sir, Lord.

Mort, Death, *il est mort*, he is dead.

A la mort, unspirited, heavy.

Morier, to dye, *moront*, they dyed, *moreaunt*, idem.

Morant, dying, *morera*, shall die.

Mort d'auncester, the Death of the Ancester.

Ne pas morier, cannot die.

Poet morier, may die, *morust*, died, *morarent*, they died. *per Britton* 30, b.

Morue, Death. *per Parkins* 109.

Mortmain, a dead hand, *i. e.* when Lands are given to or purchased by a Convent of Religion, or other such Corporation or to their Use, against which there is now an Act of Parliament.

Mot, a word or Speech, *mote*, idem, *mots*, words.

Mote, in the old *Saxon* signifies a Court, from whence *Swainmote*, *i. e.* the Freeholders Court, *Wardmote*, and several others.

Ne dire mot, not a word, be silent, *de mote en mote*, word for word. *Motes* is also Words, and *motes* is likewise moved.

Moucher to hide, *moucha*, hid *p. moucher*, by hiding, *p. Comptons Justice* 27, a. *moucher* in Mod. French, is to blow ones Nose.

Morceau, a piece, parcel or lump of any thing.

Morceau de pain, a peice of Bread.

Mouldre, to grind, *moulture*, grinding, *sans moulture*, without toll or paying for grinding, *ne moulda*, not ground or grinded.

Moult, much, many, *molt*, idem, *divers moult*, very desiring.

Moulder, to cleanse, *moundes*, clean, clear.

Le mounde, the World, *mound*, idem. *p. Kitch.* 3.

Moundre, to Fence, or enclose.

Mountant, ariseing, amounting unto.

Mous, we, vide, *nous*, we or us.

Mourir, idem *ut morier. per Coke* 9. 121.

Move, contained or come in Question.

Moves, months, *size moves*, six Months. *p. Termes de Ley* 70. b. vide, *moyes* & *mois*.

Movoit, hath moved, *moyen*, Means.

Moyn, a Monk, vide *moigne*.

Pur moyen, by reason of, or means of.

Moy, my and I, *moy & mes ancessors*, I and my Ancesters, *moy mesme*, I my self, *a moy mesme*, to my self.

Moyen, indifferent, mean, also temperate.

Moyenment, indifferently, temperately, moderately, meanly.

Per ce moyen, by this means, *les moyens*, the means.

M U.

Muer, to change, *mue*, changed, *muet*, idem.

Home muable, an unconstant Man.

Muance, changing.

Mult, idem *ut moult*, *multz*, idem.

Muet, dumb, speechless, *mutus*, idem. *per Parkins* 9.

A mulcter, to set a Fine, *mulcter*, is also a grist, *mulveyn*, middle. *per Brit.* 212, b.

Muillere, & *mulier legittimate*, *muliertie*, those that are Legitimate, or Lawful Issue.

Muins, warned.

Multure, vide *moulture*.

Mulnes, fullness, *mullnesse*, idem.

Mulnes soer, the second Sister, or the middle between two. *per Plowd. Com.* 333. & *per Coke* 1 *pt. Instit.* 23, b.

Munder,

Munder, to cleanse, *mundes*, cleansed.

Mundera, shall cleanse, vide, *mounder*.

Muner, to warn, *muni*, warned.

Muniments, Deeds, and commonly called *miniments*.

Le mure, the Wall, *mure*, walled, *les murs*, the Walls, *novel mure*, a new Wall. *per Coke* 5. 16.

Murger, to perish, to die, *murgent*, perished.

Muruvont, they have died. *p. nov. nar.* 62.

Murra, shall die. *p. Britton* 186.

Murrerant, they die, *murrust*, died.

Murrant, dying.

Murrust, Homage, the Jury or Homage is respited or staid or remaineth. *p. nov. nar.* 30.

Mushe, hidden, *Mussue*, idem.

Pur mussetes, by stealth, privily, secretly.

Muscettes, idem, *musser*, to convey away privately, also to hide.

Pur murage, for repairing Walls.

Viel mur, an old Wall.

Muis, a Bushel, *mus*, idem.

Munier, to fortifie, to defend.

Muy, a Tun, or great Vessel.

Mutiner, to mutiny, *mutin*, Tumultuous.

M Y.

Mystiquement, mistically.

Sons myses, are put. *p. Parkins*, 66, a.

Mye & *my*, are generally used in the negative or denyal, like the Word, *pas*, not any.

Ne serra mye, shall not be, *ne Poet my*, may not be, *Parkins*, 69. a.

Ne voet my vener, would not come at all. *p. Coke Rep.* 5. 25, a.

Per my & per tout, by every part and the whole. *per eund.* 5. 10. and *per* 1 *part Inst.* 186.

Per mye tout, all through. *per eund.* 7, 17, a. and 8, 125, b. and throughout all. *per Plowd.* 179.

My tout, all parts, *nest my compleat*, not wholly or fully. *p. my*, through. *per Greg.* 219, and *per my*, by *Coke* 9, *Rep.* 29. by part.

Myer, Mother. *per nov. nar.* 22.

Mystie, needed, *per eund.* 53.

Myscrue, absconded. *p. Fitzh. Just.* 213. b.

N A.

N*Aam*, to lay hold on, to distrein. *per mirror. Sect.* 13.

Naidgaits, lately, sometimes.

Naidgayers, idem, and *naidgacres*, idem, and *naidgaris*, idem, and *nadgares*, idem.

Nad, hath not, *nay*, have not.

Que na, who hath not.

Navera, shall not have.

Nailours, not elsewhere.

Nappent, doth not belong.

Nayer, to Swim, *nayement* & *nagement*, Swimming.

Nad este resiant, hath not been Resident.

Naif, a Woman Slave, vide *naif*, *naiste*, Villainage.

Naufer,

Naufre, assaulted, beaten.

Poit naufre, may beat.

Navouera, shall not vouch, own, or justify.

Nase, a Nose.

Nees, is sometimes also put for Nose.

Naistre, to be born.

Nasquist, born.

Ou il naysquist, where was he born. *p. Greg.* 338.

Faux naistres, Bastards. *p. Mirrour.*

Namender, not to amend, or better.

Narrer, to declare.

Narracon, a Declaration.

Un natural, an Idiot, a fool, *nastres*, idem. *p. Britton* 17, a.

Natants, swimming, *naiant*, idem.

Nau, a Ship, vide *nyef*.

Naufrage, Shipwrack.

Naufrer, & *naufter*, idem ut *naufre*.

Naufra, wounded, beaten, *naute*, idem.

Naviger, to Sail, to Navigate.

Navant & *navoient*, they had not. *p. Yelverton.*

Nassele, a Barge.

Naif, natural, lively.

Naisance, Birth, *naisant*, being Born.

Natte, a Mat.

Narine, the Nostrils.

Un navet, a Turnip.

Naute, wounded, hurt.

Naurure, idem in Modern French.

N E.

Neese, a Nose, also born. *p. Plowd.* 23, b.

Nee, a Native, also born.

Ne, not, *ne l'un ne l'auter*, neither the one nor the other.

Ne cecy, *ne ce la*, neither this, nor that.

Ne, nor, no, *ne ansi*, no truly, or not also.

Ne unque, never, not at any time.

Neint, nothing, *neant*, idem.

Necessaire, necessary.

E after *N* is oft cut off before a Vowel, as *n'avoit*, *n'osa*, *n'est*, &c.

Nef, *neef*, *neif*, a Ship.

Neif, is also a Bond-woman, *niefe*, idem, *nefe* idem.

Le neif, the ninth.

Neifty, Bondage, Villainage.

Breif de neifty, a Writ of Neif or Villainage.

Neglegement, negligently.

Negocier, to be busy, *negoce*, business.

Neiger, to Snow, *neige*, Snow.

Nerfe, a Sinew, *nerveux*, full of Sinews, Strong.

Neghesithseld ne geld, hath not any thing given, or paid, are words of the *Saxon* Language used in our Law.

Neifture & *neifure*, Nativity.

Neint contristeant, notwithstanding.

Neint meins, nevertheless.

Nemport riens, nothing carrying.

Nemy, none, & *que nemy*, and what not.

Nemi & *nei*, not, *nemie*, idem.

Ou nemie, or not. *p. Brokes gr. abr.* 213.

Nepurquant, nevertheless. *p. Brit.* 212.

Nequedont, & *uequedent*, idem. *p. eund.* 16, and 45.

Neque, neither.

Nequedant vener, they cause to come. *p. Mirrour.*

Nevement, closely, nearly.

Nescries, not discovered.

Nese & *nez*, vide *nase* & *nose*.

Nessens, Ignorance.

Le nessans, the growing, rising, the birth or breeding, and bringing forth.

Nesture, the birth, *nester*, idem.

Nestre, not to be, *neysture*, idem, *p. nestre*, by the birth.

Nestres. p Britton 17, a. is an Idiot.

Nest que forme, 'tis only form. *p. Coke Rep.* 5, 35, a.

Nestroit, not known. *p. Mirror. Just.*

Nesques, only.

Vous nestes, ye are not, or know not. *p.* 26. *Hen.* 8, 8, a.

Net, clean, neat.

Nettement, cleanly.

Nettete, cleanliness.

Net ore, fine Gold. *p. Plowden* 319, b.

Also *net*, is put for clear, apparent, *p. eund.* 37, and 170, a.

Neuf nine, *le neufieme*, the nineteenth.

Neufiesme, idem, *neur neuf*, nine a Clock.

Nieufme, the ninth.

Neysture, birth, idem, ut *nesture*.

Neye, drowned. *p. Britton.* 5, a.

Nead, a knot, or knob.

Neatre, not to side with any.

Neze, Nose. *p. Mirrour* of Justice, 4. *part.*

Ni, is put for *Ne*, neither, and nor.

Un ni, a denying, or saying nay.

Nid, a Nest, *un nid de oyseau*, a Bird's Nest.

Nides, Nests.

Nicher, to build Nests, to nestle.

Nicol, the ancient name for *Lincoln*.

Neice, a Brother, or Sisters Daughter.

Nief, vide *neif*, a Bondwoman.

Niefs, Ships.

Nieufe, the ninth.

Niez, a foolish nice Person.

Nient meins, nevertheless, albeit, notwithstagding.

Nient pluis, nothing more, vide *neint*.

Nient, to deny.

Niement, denying.

Niant, a denyer.

Niger, black.

Nifle, a thing of no value, or trifle.

Nisser, not to issue out, or go forth. *p. nov. nar.* 108.

Nive, Snow.

Nief, nine, idem ut, *neif*, or *neuf*. *p.* 21. *Hen.* 7, 27, b.

N O.

Noier, black.

Noircer, to wax black, or make black.

Noier, to hurt.

Ne noira, shall not hurt.

Noix, Night, also a Walnut.

Noet, Night. *p. nov. nar.* 16, b.

Noel, Christmass.

Noitz, Nights. *p. Parkins* 176, b.

Noblisse,

Noblesse, the Nobility, Nobles.

Noyer, to drown, *noye*, drowned.

Nom, vide *nosme*.

Noms nosmes, Names named. *p. Britton* 7. b.

Nommement, namely.

Nosement, idem.

Nombre, numbred, reckned, told.

Nommer, idem ut *nommement*.

Non, not, nay. *Non certain*, uncertain.

Nonantie, ninety, *nonantiesme*, the ninetieth.

Nout & *nount*, they have not.

Nonchosant, knowing nothing.

Nonchalant, carelesʃs, negligent.

Nonante & *neuf*, ninety nine.

Non pluis, nothing more.

A Norir, to nouriʃh, to breed up.

Norissent, they nouriʃh, *per Britton*, 166. b.

Nouriture, Nouriʃhment, or Food.

Norie & *norye*, Education, Suʃtinence, Breeding.

Norices, Nurʃes.

Non sue, non-ʃuited, as when the Plantiff is called in Court, and doth not appear.

Le Nord, & *le Nore*, the North.

Nosme, Name, *nosmez*, names, *p. Parkins*, 116.

Nosmera, ʃhall name.

Nosmeamt, & *nosmant*, namely naming.

Ne nosment, not naming, 31, *Hen.* 8, 14.

Nosast, he durʃt not, *nosast aler enter ses besoignes*, durʃt not go about his Buʃines. *p. Coke Rep.* 5, 28, a. vide *osast*.

Jeo nosa, I dare not.

Nosest, knows not, *que il nosest*, that he knows not how.

Noster & *nostre*, our, *nostres* ours.

Nous, wee, us, *nous mesmes* our ʃelves.

Noter, to note, *notaire*, a Notary.

Notoire, manifeʃt, publick plain, notorious.

De novel, of late, *fait novel* newly made.

Novelment, newly, *novels*, news.

Noel, in *Modern French*, is God with us, *novel*, idem.

Noveulx masons, new Houʃes.

Novelle, new, *p. Fitzh. nat. brevium*, 50. *nove*, idem.

Novembre, the Month of *November*.

Novies foits, nine times.

Nourir, to nouriʃh, *nourit*, he that is fed or nouriʃhed, *nouriture*, food, alʃo *alimony*.

Un nourisse, a Nurʃe.

Nowel, Chriʃtmas, *novel*, id. *p. Plowd.* 112.

Novel, new, late.

Noyer, to hurt, *ne noyera*, ʃhall not hurt.

Nouns, names, *nous*, we, our.

Noyer, black, alʃo hurt.

Ne noyer, knew not, alʃo hurt not. *p. Coke* 5, 60.

Un noys, a Nut, *le noyau*, the kernel of a Nut. *noz*, our. *p.* 2. *part. Instit.* 639.

Nuds, naked, *nud*, idem, *nue*, idem.

Nuçe, a Nut, *nuces*, Nuts.

Nuee, Clouds, Cloudy.

Nuire, to hurt.

Pur nurrer, for preserving, *p.* 4, *pt. Instit.* 26.

Nuit, night, *nuict*, idem. *nuyt.* idem.

Nul, none, *nully*, no one, no body.

Nullement, in no wise, by no means.

Nunqs never.

Pur rurture, idem. *ut nourture.*

Nudite, nakedness.

Nuage, Clowdy.

Nuisant, hurtful, *nuissance*, annoyance.

Nusance, idem. also offence, damage.

Nusant, idem. *ut nuisant.*

Sans nusance, without hurt innocently.

Nute, vide *nuict* & *nuit.*

Nussoit, had not, should not.

Puy uurtraire, for sustainance, vide *nurtiture.*

Nust estre, hath not been, *il nust mis*, he hath not put. *per Fitzh. Justice*, 97, a.

Nutante, before night. *p. Brit.* 122, a.

Nyefe, vide *neif*, a Ship.

Nyent avaut, they having none before.

Nyef idem *ut neif*, a Woman, Villain, or Slave.

Nye, a nest. *per Britton.* 85, vide *nie.*

Nuyte, night. *p.* 1. *Hen.* 7, 34, b.

Ny, a Note of Negation.

O B.

O *Moy*, oh me.

Obediement, obediently.

Obeier, to obey, *obeissant*, obedient.

Obeissance, obedience.

Objicer, to lay to ones charge, to object.

Objecter, idem.

Obit, Dead, *obites*, forgotten.

un Obit, a Duty paid as a Mortuary; also Dirges, Funeral Song, Obsequies, Trentals.

Obliger, to bind, *obliger corps & beins*, to bind Body and Goods.

Obligor, the Person bound. *Obligee*, he to whom.

Oblie, Forgot, *oblites*, idem, *p. Coke* 1. *Rep.* 136.

Oblies, idem, *p. Fitzh. gr. abr.* 187. b.

Oblique, a-wry, a-thwart.

Obsecrer, to beg, to crave, to ask for.

Obmittes, Left out, omitted.

Soit observes, be it taken notice of.

Pluis observe, more remarkable.

Observa, kept, 2. *part. Fitzh. gr. Abr.* 112. b.

Obsolete, Out of use, antiquated.

Obteneres, Ye shall obtain, *Obteyneres*, idem.

Objurger, to rebuke, to reprehend.

un Oblation, an Offering.

Oblicter, to sport, to rejoice.

Oblivieux, forgetful.

Obscur-

Obscurcir, to darken, to obscure.

Obscur, dark, *obscurissement*, obscurely, darkly, also obscuring.

Obsequies, Funerals.

Ostant, hindring, leting, standing against.

Non obstante, notwithstanding.

Oblier, to forget, *oblie*, forgotten, *obliant*, forgetting, *obliance*, forgetfulness.

Obstine, obstinate, *obstinement*, obstinately.

Obsister, to oppose, to stand against.

Obtenue, that which is gotten.

Obtrectation, ill report, slandering.

Obvier, to prevent.

Obumbrer, to shadow.

O C.

Occasionellement, occasionally, by reason of.

Occidental, the West part.

Occider, to kill, *occide*, killed. *p. Mirror, cap.* 2, 15.

Occist, hath killed. *p. Plowden ab.* 16, b.

Octante, eighty, *octantiesme*, the eightieth.

Octobre, the month *October*.

Occulter, to hide, *occultement*, hiding.

Occluder, to shut, *il occlude*, he shut.

Occire, to kill, or slay, *occiant* slaying.

Occision, slaughter, *occiser*, killing. *p. Coke* 5, 13.

Occurrent, happening.

Occulair, that which is plainly seen or evident.

Occlairment, visibly, or evidently.

O D.

Odeur, a Smell, *Odeur mau plaisant*, an unpleasing Smell.

Odeur plaisant, a sweet Smell.

Oderment, Smelling.

Odieux, odious.

Odible, idem.

O E.

Oefs, Wild Fowl, also Geese, *p. Britt.* 48. a.

Oes, Use, or Benefit. *p. eundem* 33.

Oels, Eyes.

Oegles, idem, & *Ogles*, idem.

un Oil, an Eye.

Oiele, idem. *avec l' oil sur ascun*, to watch over one, to have an Eye upon him.

Oeps, Need, also Use, Trust.

Oeps demesne, own Use.

As oeptaz, they have wished, also needed. *p. nov. narr.* 6. b. so craved.

Ohe? Is it so?

O F.

Offenser, to offend, *offendans*, offending.

Offendre, idem. also to endammage.

Offrir, to offer, *offre* & *offra*, shall offer or tender, *p.* 2, *Hen.* 7, 9.

Offres, offered, or tendred.

Un official, a Bishop's Chancellor; or the Arch-deacon's substitute.

Offusquer, to darken.

O I.

Oier, to hear.
Oies, heard.
Ceo oies, hear ye this.
Oiera, ſhall hear.
Oiant, hearing.
Ne oirires, ye ſhall not hear.
Le oire, the hearing.
Oil, yes, alſo, I will.
Ois certe, yes truly. *p. Fitzh. abr.*
Oindre, to annoint.
Oinct, annointed.
Onguent, Ointment.
Oiſeau, a Bird, a Fowl, *oiſel*, idem.
Oiſeuſe, ſloth, idleneſs, *oiſif*, idem, and ſlothful.
Oiſeux, idem, *oiſivete*, idleneſs, *p. Coke Rep.* 11, 53.
Oiſeleur, a Bird Catcher, a Fowler.
Oiſon, a Gooſe.

O L.

Olet, ſmelleth.
Ne olet pas, it ſmells not. *p. termes de Ley* 58, b.

O M.

Ombre, a ſhadow, *ombrayer*, idem, *ombre*, is alſo ſhade. *p. Plowd. Com.* 379, a.
Ombragement, ſhadowing.
Omettre, to neglect, to omit.
Omis, left undone, omitted, *omiſſe*, idem.
Ne omitteres, neglect ye not.
Omiſe, left out, forgotten to be inſerted.
On, it, *on*, in modern French is often put for *homo*.

O N.

Un on, an Ounce.
Oncle, Uncle.
Onques, ever, vide *unques*.
Ont, they have, they uſe. *p. Plowd. abr.* 5, a.
Ont dit, they have ſaid.
Un ongle, the Nail of the Finger.
Onze, eleven, *onze foitz*, eleven times.
Onzieme, the eleventh.

O P.

Operer, to work.
Ops, need, uſe, vide *oeps*.
Oppoſer, to ſet againſt.
Opprober, to reproach.
Opiner, to think, to deem.

O R.

Orail, an Ear, *orelle*, idem. *p. Brit.* 16, b.
Oraiſons, Prayers.
Ordure, filth.
Ordir, to be filthy, ſluttiſh.
Ord, filthy, ſluttiſhneſs.
Ordurs, dung, filth.
L'orde, the method, the order.
Un ordinary, a Spiritual Judge.
Ordonner, to ordain.
Ordeynment, ordaining.
Fuit ordine, it was ordained *p. Brit.* 77, b.
Grand ordure, a ſtink, or filthy ſmell. *p. termes de Ley* 87, a.
Ore, Gold, *or*, idem, *de orbs*, of Gold. *p. Crompt.* 22, b.
Ore, is alſo, now, *ores*, idem:
Orfeure, a Goldſmith.
Les orfeours, the Goldſmiths. *p. Stat. Art. ſup. Chart. Cap.* 20.
Orfeurerie, Goldſmiths Work.
Orieiller, to give Ear unto, to hearken.

Done

Done orielle, give Ear. *p. Plowden's Preface.*

Orphan, a Child without living Parents.

Orfelin, idem in modern French.

Orges, Barly.

Pain de orge, Barly Bread.

Orier, to riſe up.

Orier, the riſing, *p. Fitzh. Juſt.* 86.

Oriſons, vide *Oraiſons*, *Oriſonz*, idem.

Orguel, pride, *les orguellons*, the proud, the rich, the lofty. *p. Brit.* 1, a.

Orial, vide *oraile*.

Orrount, they hear. *p. eund.* 106, a.

Un orme, an Elm Tree.

Orne, adorned, decked. *p Coke* 9, 121.

Orner, to deck, to trim.

Ortiels, Toes, Claws.

Ortelles chiens, Dogs claws. *p. Kitchin.*

O S.

Os, a Bone, *oſſe* idem, *oſſes*, Bones.

Oſer, to dare, *ne oſa*, dare not.

Il ne oſt, he durſt not.

Ne oſa aler entour ſes beſoignes, he dares not go about his buſineſs.

Oſeau, a Bird, vide *oiſeau*, 12. *Hen.*

Oſtelle, a Houſhold.

Oſtier, a door.

Oſtyers, doors. *p. Kitchin*, 45, b.

Oſtre, ſhewed, alſo moreover, farthermore. *p. Brit.* 119, b.

Oſtage, vide Hoſtage, *Bailler oſtages*, to give pledges.

Oſtement, putting out, putting away.

Oſter, idem ut *ouſter*.

Oſter, is alſo to take away, to remove, to diminiſh.

Oſte, taken away, &c.

O T.

Ottrie, given, reſtored, anſwered for. *p. Stat. Weſtm. Cap.* 4.

O U.

Ou, where, whether, alſo *or*.

Ou pur, or for, *de ou*, from whence, alſo whereof.

Ou il eſt, ou non, either it is ſo or not.

Ou va tu? whither goeſt thou?

Oucunq; whereſoever, whenſoever.

Overt, publick, open.

Overtes opentide, i. e. when Corn is carried out of the Common Fields. *p. Brit.*

Ove, with, *oveſq;* with us, alſo by which.

Oveſques, together with.

Oves, Eggs.

Ovel, equal.

Ovelmemt, equally.

Ovel, is alſo new. *p. Plowd.* 13, b.

Overeche, goes beyond, *p. eund.* 281.

Over, work, labour, *overage*, idem.

Overages, Carriages, also days works.

Overaines, idem. *p. Plowd.* 334, a.

Un overage, an undertaking, *p. nat. br.* 42, b.

Overer, to work, to labour, *ovrer*, idem.

Overs, works, *un overier*, workmen.

Ovres, idem, *ut overs.*

De over le huis, to open the Door, *p. Coke*, 5, 21, b.

Il over, he openeth, *que over*, who opened, *p. Cromp.* 29.

Ne poet overer, may not open, *overtment*, openly.

A overer, to be wrought or worked.

Over le charitie, a deed of charity. *p. Termes de Ley*, 109.

De overer en vous, to open or shew you. *p. Cromp.* in his Preface, *serront overts*, they shall be opened. *per eund.*

Main overer, to Manure.

Overages & ovrages. p. Fitzh. Justice 173, & *per Coke rep.* 8, 106, a. are days works.

Outre, further, besides, *outre ce*, besides this, or besides that, *outre pluis*, furthermore.

Outre pluis, idem. *oultre*, beyond, also furthermore, & *oultre ce la*, and besides this further, *en oultre*, furthermore, vide *oulster* & *ouster*, *en aler pluis oultre*, to go no further. *Coke* 9, 120.

Overt, open, *overtment*, openly.

Overture, an opening, also a proposal.

Se fair overture, he opened his mind.

Ount, they have, *ount estre*, they have been.

Ount lieu, some place, any place, *p. Kitchin* 17, a.

Ount ceo, ensue, they have followed. *p. Plowd.* 305, b.

Ouq, and that, where.

Ouelx, equal, *p. Parkins* 59, b.

Ovils & oveilles, sheep.

Ovres, acts, deeds. *per Coke* 8, 131, a.

Que nul oure, that none gild, *p. Stat. sup. Art. Chart. cap.* 20.

Oustre & ouster, out, beyond, besides, farther, vide *oultre*, also over and more.

Le ouster, the uppermost, over.

Oustd, outed, *ouste*, idem.

Il oust, he put out, or outed.

Ousterment, altogether, more than that.

Oustrement, idem, and utterly *p. Fitzh. nat. br.* 97.

Oustes, yee outed.

Ouster eit, went away. *p. Coke* 6, 41 b.

Main overer, manuring, also to make better.

Outerment, putting forth.

Outragious, excessive, unreasonable.

Outrageousment, unreasonably, without measure, *outratouse*, id. *p. Britton* 137, a.

Ouy, yea, ſo, alſo.

Ouyez, crying out, publiſh ing, proclaiming.

Oweltie, right, alſo due, owning.

Owel, equal, *owels parts*, equal ſhares. *p. Coke, Rep.* 5, 18. *Owelx*, idem.

Owelment, equally, *p. emid.* 7. 45.

Oweltie, equallity, *p. emid.* 5. 95. *b.*

Owels, Goods. *p. Greg.* 299. *b.*

En Owel miſchief, in equal miſchief. *p. Coke*, 5.

En owel Eſtate, in the ſame State or Condition, *p. Greg.* 284. alſo his own Eſtate.

Owel Remede, the like, or proper Remedy.

Ower, Oar, Miner Oar, to dig Oar.

Owres de Argent, Oars of Silver, *p. Plow.* 311.

Owaijles, Sheep, alſo Sheep of the Fold, *Nov. nar.* 63. and Lambs.

Owells, Eyes, *vide Oiles, p. Fitzh. nat. b.*

Ouſter des Owells, to put out the Eyes.

Owells, p. Nov. nari. is put for Geeſe.

Owell, equal. *Owelty*, partition.

Oyer, to hear, *il oyer*, he heareth.

Oya, ſhall hear, *Oye*, heard, *Oyes*, hear ye.

Jeo aye Oye, I have heard, *jeo oyeroy*, I have heard, *p. Plowd.* Preface.

Oyera, idem. *p. eund.*

Vous ſeara Oyes, ye ſhall be heard.

Oye, yes, aye. *Jeo Ocroy*, I heard.

Oyl, Sr. hear ye Sir, 1 *Hen.* 7. 16. *b.*

Oyel, idem, alſo hear ye, 14 *Hen.* 8. 25.

Oyel certes, yes truly, *p. Plowd.* 365.

Ceo Oyes, hear this, *Oye moy*, hear me, *oyeramus*, we have heard, *oyant*, hearing, 26 *Hen.* 8, 4, *a.*

Oyſels, Hawks, *p. Brit.* 84 *b.*

Oyſeauxe, Birds, *Oyſeaux*, id.

Un Oyſea, a Bird.

Un Oyle, an Eye, *par termes Ley.* 298. *b.*

Oyſons, Geeſe, *Oyes*, idem.

Oyez, heard, alſo a Term uſed when any thing is Cried. *Coke*, 8. 35.

Oyers, hearing, *p. Stat. Glouc.*

P A.

Un PAct, a Contract, an Agreement.

Paction, idem.

Pain, Bread, *Pain blanche*, white Bread.

Pain groſſe, brown Bread.

Panes, Loaves of Bread, *p. Coke*, 8. 49. *b.*

Un pani, a penalty, amerciament, *p. Greg.* 233. *a.*

Paiſtre, & *paſtre*, to feed, alſo to depaſture.

Le pais, the Country, *paiſes*, Countries.

Pais voisins, neighbouring Countries.

Paor, power.

Le Panche, the Belly, the Stomach.

Pauvage, Mast, also the benefit of Feeding Swine in Forests or Chases.

Pannage, pavement. Pannage *idem. p. Coke, rep.* 8. 47. *a.*

Un Pantofle, a Slipper.

Le Pape, the Pope.

Par, by, *par-la*, thither, that way.

Par de la, by the same, *p. Crompton*, 31. *b.*

Par cy this way.

Parramount, above *parramount la terre*, over the Land, *p. Plowden*, 309. *a.*

Par dessus, from above, *par mi*, by half.

Paravaile, lower, under, he who takes the Profits.

Par *ou*, which way, *paravant*, former, *Coke* 10, 37.

Pard, loss, and losing, also hindrance, *p. Fitzh. nor. bind.* 21.*a parde*, lost. *p.* 2 *Hen.*7.11 *b.*

Parder, to lose, *il pardist*, he lost.

Pardices, Patridges.

Parosse, Parish.

Parel, danger, *p.*12*Hen.*8. 3 *a.*

Un Paillard, a Whore, a Harlot.

Parasite, a Flatterer.

Un Parc, Parker, a Keeper of a Park.

Parler, to speak, to converse with. *ne parla*, speak not. *pariance*, speaking.

Pariel, alike, equal, *nest pas pariel*, unlike.

Pares, of like degree, equal.

Parier, perjured. *prieurement* idem.

Pariet, a Wall.

Un Parke, a Pound to keep in Cattle. *Comen Parke*, a common Pound.

Parlez, speak ye. *parlante*, speaking, *parlance*, idem.

Parlance, is also Speech Language, *parlont*, they speak.

Parle, spoke. and speak. 10 *Hen.* 8. w. a.

Le Parliament, the great Assembly of the Nation, and of the three Estates.

Parlire, to read through.

Parolle, & parol, giving ones word, a word.

Parolx, words, *belle parolles*, fair words.

Par, in mod. *French*, is sometimes put for work.

Parount, whereby. *par quoy*, idem, and for which.

Parquer, to enclose, to impark.

Parimpler, to fullfil, *vide perimplisher.*

Parimplies, fulfilled, *parimple*, idem, *p.* 1 *Hen.* 7, 5. *a parimplishment*, fulfilling.

Parceners, are who hold a joint Estate from the same Ancestor, several Daughters are but one Heir and Partners.

Par quoy doncque, for what cause, also, then, and therefore.

Parches, pieces, parcells, 1 *Edw*, 5, 3.

Partir, to devide, *partiment*, division.

Les

Les Parrowes leſchequer, the Barons of the Exchequer, 1 *Hen.* 7, 8. *a.*

Parfaitment, readily, perfectly.

Parmy, amongſt, *parmy les rues*, abroad in the Streets *parnes*, take.

Le Parroſſiens, Inhabitants of, or within a Pariſh.

Paroier, to appear, to ſhew ones ſelf.

Apart, aſide, *quelque part*, ſomewhere, ſome part.

Un Participant, an acceſſory, a partaker.

Particulierement, ſpecially, particularly.

Particularizer, to ſhew in particular.

Paſcage, graſing, feeding of Cattle.

Paſher, to feed, *paſcer*, idem.

Paſche, Eaſter, *paſque*, idem. *p. nov. nair.* 21.

Pas, not, no, and in many places 'tis ſet as a word formally to deny and contradict what is before expreſſed, alſo a confirmation of a Negative. *Nil pas force*, of no force or of no value.

Pas trop mal, not very ill.

Pas a pas, leiſurely.

Un paſſe, a degree, a ſtop.

Paſſants, Paſſengers. *p. Brit.* 32. *b.*

Paſſable, tolerable.

Paſſe, gone beyond, exceeded.

Paſſer, to go over. *paſſes*, gone.

En temps avant paſſes, in times paſt.

Paſturer, to depaſture, to feed.

Paſſont, they fed, *p. nov. nar.* 53.

Paſtors, Shepherds, *paſteurs*, idem.

Paſquerages, paſture Grounds.

Paſſetemps, Games, Paſtimes,

Un Paſſereau, a Sparrow.

Paſſe le age, above the age.

Paſlant, beyond, above, over.

Patent, open, evident.

Lettres patents, are ſo called, becauſe they are not cloſed with wax, as *Subpœnas* and original writs, & *dedimus poteſtatem*, &c.

Paumont, laying hands upon *p. Briton*, 135.

Patron, a Protector, Defendor, or who has right to preſent to a Church.

Pavoir, Fear.

Paumage, & *Paunage*, the benefit of Skins and Horns of Deer in a Foreſt, *p. Brit.* 185. *a.*

Pawnage, *p. Crompton*, is the feeding Swine in Woods, &c. in maſt time, *i. e.* the Money paid for it. 166. *a.*

Un Pau, a Stake.

Pax, & *paix*, Peace, *paics* is ſometimes put for it.

Payer, to pay, *payerez*, & *payeres*, ye ſhall pay.

Le pays, the Country, a Region, *paiz* & *paize*, Countries.

Pawnage de avers, by *Coke*, 8. 56, *b.* is the agiſting Cattle.

Paver, Fear, *pavour*, & *pavor*, idem.

Payens, Heathens, Pagans.
Payenic, Heathenish.

P E.

Un Pe, a foot, *pee*, *peas*, idem.

Pees, Feet, and sometimes put for Peace.

Peace, *p.* the Stat. of Fines, 18 *Edw.* 1. is put for concord or agreement, *peax*, peace, *p. nov. nar.* 31. *b.*

Peau, a Skin, *vide pel.*

Peautre, Pewter, *p. Brit.* 24. *a.*

Pealtzlanuts, Woolfels, *p.* 3 *part Instit.* 39.

Pecher, to commit a fault, to sin, *p. mirour Justice.*

Peche, a fault, an offence, *pech*, idem.

Pechers, offenders, *p. Coke*, *rep.* 7. 44. *a.*

Pecheront, they are accused, *p. Brit.* 10 *b.*

Peeres, the chief Nobility.

Pein, Penalty,

Peise, Weight.

Peison, feeding, depasturing.

Pejer, worse.

Pellota, & *pelote*, the Ball of the Foot.

Penne, a Pen.

Pel, a Skin.

Peleryn, a Pilgrim, *p. Brit.* 96. *a.*

Pelerinage, Pilgrimage, *p. eund*, 108.

Peles, Issues arising from, or out of, *p. Fitzh.* Justice, 205.

Penance, Punishment.

Penon, a Standard, Banner, or Ensign of War.

Un peigne, a Comb, *peigner*, to comb.

Pen, a Hill, *Brittish*, sometimes a Bay.

Penticostals, Oblations made at *Whitsontide.*

Pendre, to hang, *pendue*, hanged, *pende*, & *pendu*, idem. *pender* to consider.

Pendant, continuing, abiding, depending.

Penser, to think, *il pensoit*, he thought, *pensant*, & *pensy*, & *pensement*, thinking, *pense*, thought.

Ne pensoient, they thought not, *pensoremus*, let us consider, *p. plowd.* 305.

Il pensist, he thinketh or thought, *pensoit*, idem.

Pense vous, think ye, consider, *pense*, idem.

Pege, pitch.

Peinct, painted.

Per, through, *percase*, by chance.

Perbien, very well, *percas*, perhaps.

Tenant peravaile, and under Tenant, *vide paravaile.*

Percusser, to strike, *percuse*, strooke, wounded.

Percusse, idem.

Il percust, he stroke, or cut, *percute*, strook.

Peramount, vide *paramount*

Perclose, the conclusion, or latter end, *p. kitch.* 199, *a.*

Voile perdre, will lose, 18 *Hen.* 8, 2. *b.*

Pertices, Partridges, *perdices*, idem, *vide pardices.*

Perdes, loſt, *perdue*, idem, *perdre*, to loſe, & *perder*, idem, *ad perd*, hath loſt, *perdu*, loſt.

Perd, loſs, *p. plowd. Com.* 305, *b.*

Pere, Father, *per de la*, elſewhere, ſometimes, 'tis for beyond Sea.

Peres, Stones, alſo *Peter.*

Perenter, between.

Perier, to periſh, *perie*, dead, *perre*, periſhed, *periera*, ſhall periſh.

Perimpliſher, to fulfill, *ſerra peremplies*, ſhall be fulfilled, *perimpliſh*, fulfilled, *vide parimpler.*

Perimpliſhment, fulfilling.

Perfundeſſe, depth.

Perfunder, to pour out.

Permuter, to exchange.

Permanable, durable.

Permetter, to ſuffer, *fuit permiſe*, 'twas ſuffered.

Permiſes, ſuffred, *permis*, idem.

permiſe. allowed, *p. plowd.* 190, *b.*

Permettre, idem, *ut permitter.*

Permutation, exchanging.

Pernance, taking.

Perilleux, dangerous.

Periſſables biens, periſhable Goods.

Perentoirment, preſently.

Perunt, & *perount*, by which, alſo, whereupon they.

Perquiſites, profits and advantages over and above the yearly Rents.

Perount, is alſo put for diſcerning, *p. plowdens preface.*

Perquirer, to obtain, *perquirera*, ſhall obtain.

Perpretes, committed, done, *perpetrer*, to commit.

Un pernour, a taker, a *recever*, *pernours*, plural.

Pernor, to take, *pernes*, ye take. *p.* 3, *part Inſtit.* 81.

Pernont, they take, *pernant*, taking.

On pernacie, in the taking.

Perpendiculairement, ſtreight down, perpendicularly.

Perſuader, to entice, to perſwade.

Perenter, between, *perenter*, idem.

Peiſer, to weigh.

Peront, whereby.

Pertant, inaſmuch, *vide portant.*

Peſage, a cuſtom paid for weighing wares and merchandizes.

Peſſons, Fiſh, Fiſhes, *vide poyſons.*

Peſcherie, Fiſhery, *il peſha*, he fiſhed.

Peſſons Royal, are Sturgions, Dolphins, &c.

Peſche, Fiſh, *p.* 12 *Hen:* 8, 3. *a. piſce*, idem.

Peſtez, a Baker, *peſtour.* idem, *p. Brit.* 76, *a.*

Peſtre, to feed; *en peſſant de avers*, in feeding of Cattle, *p. nov. narr.* 2. *a.*

Peſiblement, peaceably, *p. emid*, 31, *a.*

Perteignant, belonging alſo, they belong unto.

Pertient,

Pertient, & *pertinent*, belonging, appertaining.

Petit, ſmall, little, *petitement*, ſmally, *per petit & petite*, by little and little.

Petite *hommes*, mean Men.

Peu, few, *a peu pres*, almoſt, ſcarce enough.

Al trop peu, a very few, in *plowd. pref. tres peu*, idem.

Peu a peu, idem, *ut petit & petit.*

Ne peuvent, they could hardly, *Coke* 9, 120.

Ne peut, he cannot, *p. nov. nar.* 5. *a.*

Il peult, he may, or can.

Un Peuple, a Nation, a People.

Ville fort peuplee, a Town that is very populous.

Pew, few, *p. Coke*, *rep.* 8, 22 *b.*

Peyes, weights, *p. Brit.* 2 *a.*

PH.

Phaiſants, Pheaſants.

Un philtre, an amorous Potion.

Pheon, the head of a Dart or Arrow, a Term in Heraldry.

Philiſer, vide *Filaſer.*

P I.

Piccage, Money paid in a Fair or Market, for ſetting up Booths.

Pier des Roylme, a Peer of the Realm, *vide pere.*

Pier, a Tyler, *p. Kitchin*, 25, *a.*

Pier, is alſo a Father, *p. Coke, rep.* 6, 32, *a.*

Seynt pier, holy Father, *p.* 1 *Hen.* 7, 10, *a.*

Pierre, & Pierres, Stones, Gravel.

Un pier, a Stone, *p. plowd.* 339.

Piers, Pears, alſo Pear-trees.

Piere, is alſo Peter. *p. nov. nar.* 5, *a.*

Piers, is ſometimes put for pieces, as p. 2. Edit. 4. *piers de Lane*, pieces of Cloth.

Il piert, he appears. *p. Brit.* 96 *a.*

Sicome piert, as it doth appear.

Pire, worſe, *pier*, idem. *p.* Stat. art. ſup. Chart. 28. *Edw.* 1.

Un pile, a Ball.

Pied, vide *pe*, a Foot.

Un pedſtal, de un Columne, the Foot of a Pillar or Column.

Piſcharries, Fiſhings, *un piſcharie*, a Fiſh pond, *piſcharers*, Fiſhers, *un piſher*, a Fiſhmonger, *piſched*, fiſhed.

Piſhons, & *poiſſons*, vide autea *peſhons.*

Peſſons, & *peſchieries*, &c.

Le peſce, the Fiſh, p. 12 *Hen.* 8, 11, *a.*

Pour *piſter & bruer*, for baking and brewing.

Piſtor, vide *peſtor*, *perter* baking, *p. Brit.*

Un pitle, a ſmall encloſed piece of Land, *pightle*, idem.

Pirat, a Robber at Sea.

Piquant, ſharp, *avoir pique*

contre

contre auccun, to have or bear malice or rancour againſt one.

P L.

Un placard, an Order or Decree of the Prince, a Licence, or Mandate, *placart*, idem.

En plai, in full, *p.* 1 *Hen.* 7, 5. *b.*

Un plage, a Wound, plague, *idem*, *plages*, wounds.

Plaider, to plead, *plaint*, a Suit commenced.

Plair, to pleaſe, *ſi vous plair*, if you pleaſe.

Plainment, fully. *p.* 1 *Edw.* 5. *playe* a wound.

Planchir, to floar, to plank.

Plaiſance, pleaſure, alſo pleaſing.

Playn champ, an open Field, 16 *Hen.* 7, 10, *b.*

Pleroit, ſhould pleaſe, or think good, *plerra*, ſhall pleaſe.

Plerres, Gravel or Stones, *p. nov. nar.* 48.

Plegij, Pledges, alſo Suiters, *p. Coke*, 2 pt. Inſtit. 73.

Pleder, idem, *ut plaider*, *pledera*, ſhall plead.

Pledaſt, he pleadeth, *pledent*, they ſhould plead, *vorra pledra*, would plead.

Ple, pleaſe, *ſil pleiſt*, if he pleaſeth.

Quel luy pleiſt, which he pleaſeth, *Coke* 6. 25. *b.*

Plein, full, *en plein vie*, in full life.

Pleinment, fully, *pleigrent*, idem.

Pleynment, idem.

Pleinertie, the Church having an Incumbent, or Parſon, *&c.*

Plier, to fold, alſo to pleat.

Pleurer, to weep, *plourir*, idem.

Plevies, Sureties, Undertakers, *p. Mirror.*

Plevyes, idem, *p. eund ſect.* 177.

Plomb, Lead, *un plombee*, a plummet or pellet of Lead: *plombe* alſo, is Lead.

Un plombier, a Plummer.

Pluvie, Rain, *pluye*, idem. *pluvine*, idem.

Pluvieux, rainy, *pluvial*, like to rain, *il pluera*, it ſhall rain.

Un plume, a Pen; *plumes*, Feathers.

Un plumaſſier, a Feather-maker.

Plus, more, *ou pluis*, at the moſt.

Pluſtoſt, moſt, or moſt often, *pluiſtoſt*, idem. alſo rather, and more of, *p. Coke*, 5, 10 *a.*

Pluſtoſt-que, as well as, *a pluſtoſt*, as ſoon as, and *pluiſtoſt*, *p. plowd.* 290, *a.* is rather then, *au plus*, at moſt, *p. Cromp.* 222.

Plus longement, furthermore.

Pluſers, many, *pluſors*, idem. *pluſiers*, idem. *ave pluſors avers*, with more Cattle.

Pluſors fois, oftentimes.

Pluſors, *p. plowd.* 102, *b.* is put for many.

Pluicoſtre, furthermore.

P O.

Poche, a Sack, also a Pocket.

Poir, vide *poyar.*

Poiez, ye may, *poit*, he may, *poient*, they may.

Poiene, idem *ut poient*, *p. parkins* 15, *b. ne poimus*, we may not. *p.* 2 *Hen.* 7, 11.

Un poign, a Hand, *en poign*, in hand.

Pont, a Bridge, *pontage*, & *pointage*, contribution for repair of Bridges.

Poinons pendants, Streamers, *vide poynons.*

Un poire, a Pear, *vide pire*, *un poirier*, a Pear-tree.

Point, none, not; *ne prist point*, had not took any. *point* is a word used to make the denial more express or absolute, like as the word *pas.*

Poises, weights; *en le poise*, in the weight, *poids*, idem. *vide poyses.*

Pois, *peason*, also weight, *poitz*, *points*, *poit*, may, *poy*, idem. *poiastes*, might.

Ponce, Fingers, *pointz*, idem. *ponce* idem. *p. nat. nar.* 69. *a.*

Poisson, Fish, *termes de Ley*, 189.

Pollice, a Thumb.

Poleyns, Colts.

Poler, to dress up.

Pomes, Apples, *pommes*, idem.

Pomers, Apple-trees.

Pondue, weighed.

Poignant, pricking, sharp, tart.

Un poignee, a Handful.

Un poignard, a Dagger.

Pointes, Fingers.

Polypragmon, a principal Offender, an arch Knave, *p. Coke* 8, 37, *a.*

Un popingay, a Parrot. 12 *Hen*: 8, 3, *b.*

Porca terre, a ridge of Land.

Un porceaux, a Hog, *porcells*, Pigs, Porks, Hogs. *porces*, idem. *p. Coke* 9, 58, & *Greg: mote book.*

Un poison, a Vessel called a Hogshead.

Poinson, idem, *poinson de vin*, a Hogshead of wine.

Poix, pitch.

Port, Behaviour, *bone port*, good Behaviour.

Porteres, ye shall bear or carry, also behave.

Un port, a Gate, a Porch.

Portes, Doors, Gates, *ports*, idem.

Porten, carryed, bore, *p. Brit.* 7. *b.*

A porter, to bear, to carry, also to bring.

Portera, shall bear, &c. *porterant*, they bear, &c.

Porteront, they have bore, &c. *portount*, they bear. *quant al porter*, as to the bearing, &c. *Coke* 8. 88, *a.*

Portant, bearing.

Pose, put the Case, also set, placed, 2 *Rich.* 3d, 14, *a.*

Possedera, shall possess.

Potencie, might strength.

Po-

Poture, drinking, *vide beverage*.

Polir, to poliſh, to cleanſe.

Polie, poliſhed, *poli*, idem.

Poliement, ſmoothly, brightly.

Poligamie, having more wives than one.

Pount, idem *ut pont*.

Poſthume, that's born after the Fathers Death.

Poſtuler, to plead, to argue, alſo to demand.

Potage, broath, porridge.

Pouces, Fingers, *p. nov. nar.* 70.

Pouldre, duſt, *pouldreux*, duſty.

Poulter, a Falconer, alſo a Poulterer.

Pour, for, *pour autant*, forasmuch.

Pour, power, *vide poyar*.

Ne pot, may not, 2 *Hen.* 7 14, *b*.

Pover, poor, as *povers*, to the poor.

Provers, idem, *ut povers*.

Povre, idem, *ut prover*.

Poults, poultry, *poulſins*, Chickens.

Pourcheſer, to buy, to obtain.

Pourmener, to go or walk about, *pouralle*, idem.

Pourquoy, idem *ut parquoy*.

Pourmenement, walking about.

Pourtanque, becauſe, for that, foraſmuch.

Pour ce, for that cauſe, therefore.

Pourpreſture; an Encloſure, by encroaching upon the Kings or Lords waſts; alſo an obſtructing the High-way, or Water-courſe. alſo nuſances.

Pour neant, for nothing, or nought.

Pourpartie, is a ſhare in diviſion of Lands or Tenements held formerly in parcenary.

Pouvrete, poverty, need, neceſſity.

Pouvrement, poorly, needily.

Pourpenſer, to bethink one ſelf, to deviſe.

Purpenſe, forethought, deviſed.

Pourquoy non, why not, wherefore: *pour ce que*, for that, becauſe.

Pour ſemer, to ſow.

Un pourtraicte, a Draught, an Image.

Ne nous povons, not in our power, 16 *Edw.* 4.

Ne pouvoit pas, he could not, *p. mirror*.

Poyes, ye may, *joo poy*, I may, or can, *ne poyes*, ye may not.

Poyer, to, can, or may, *poyent*, they may.

Poyar, power, alſo *poyer*, idemr *p.* 1 *Hen.* 7, 16.

Ouut poyer, they have power, *p. Greg*: 301, *b*.

Poyſons, idem *ut poyſons*, Fiſhes.

Nount poyar, & *poier*, they have no power.

Poyſer, to weigh, *Cromp.* 222, *b*.

Poyſes, weights, *vide poiſes*.

Poynons, vide *poinons*,

Par poy, & *par pay*, Brit. 133, *b*.

Poyomus, we may, p. *plow*.

En poyne, idem. *ut en poigne*.

En son poygnes, in his hands, *p.* 12 *Hen.* 8, 1, *a.*

P R.

Prandre, to dine, *prander*, idem.

Practiquer, to practice, *per practique*, by subtlety.

Jeo preia, I desire, I pray, *ils preiont*, they pray.

Un pre, a Meadow, *un pree*, idem, also *un pra* is sometimes put for a Meadow.

Les prez, the Meadows, *preine*, take, took.

Preceder, to go before, *preceda*, goeth before, *precedera*, shall go before, *predecesser*, who died before, or who was before in place or estate: *preferrer*, to put before.

Predire, to foretell.

Prefect, advanced, promoted.

Predial, belonging to Mannors, Farms, &c.

Preche, discoursed, *preche overtment*, talked publickly, *p. Coke rep.* 7, 44, *a.* & *Fitzh. Gr. abr.* 1 pt. *fol.* 287, *a.*

Jeo preigne, I take, *preigne vous*, take ye, *preignont*, they take, *preignant*, taking.

Preignes, it behoveth, *preignes gard*, take heed.

Ne prenent, they shall not take, *p. Yelverton*, 141.

Ne preignent, they may not take.

Un prelate, a dignified Clergy-man.

Premis, put before, premised.

Le premier, the first or chief, *premier*, is also a reward.

Raisons preignant, having force and weight.

Prendre, to take, *prender*, idem. *prent* & *pris*, taken, altook, *prendront*, they take.

Pren, profits taken, *p.* 2 part Inst. 506.

Prense, taking, *prendra*, took.

Prendreyt, should take, *prendroit*, idem.

Prendoient, they may take, *prendrance*, taking.

De luy prender, to take him.

Si prendroit Issu, if he should take or join Issue.

En prender, such things as the Lord of a Mannor should have before Attornment, as Wardships, Escheats, &c. but such as lie in Rents Reliefs, Heriots, &c. Attornment ought first to be.

Prennent, they take, *prenderent*, idem.

Prepens, forethought.

Pres, near, nigh, *apres*, idem.

Estre au pres, to be present.

A peu pres, within a little, almost.

Cy pres, as near, so nigh.

Pressieux, pretious, 1 *Edw.* 5, 3.

Presenteres, ye shall present, *p. Kitchen.* 3, *a.*

Presentement, presently, p. *plowd.* 309.

Prest, took, *prestes*, take ye.

Prest, is also ready, p. *Davies rep.*

Pretende forethought, p. *Fitzh.* Justice 20.

Preterite temps, former times.

Prest-money, is given to bind the Taker to be ready at all times appointed.

Un prester, a priest, *presters*, priests.

De prester, to lend.

Prepense, forethought.

Prevaile, overcome.

Pur le preve, for the relief, *p. Stat. art. sub. Chart.* 28 *Edw.* 1.

En grand prev, in great apprehension or fear, *p.* 2 part Instit. 506. *preu* is also set for honest.

A prie, to pray or desire, *ne soit prie*, not been ask'd; *p.* Stat. *Westm.* 1. *prie*, pray, ask: *prier*, prayer, p. *eund* Stat. cap. 51. *priera*, shall pray, *prieront*, they pray. *poet priera*, may pray, p. *Greg*: 315. *prie estre resceu*, pray be received.

Prescrire, to appoint, to prescribe.

Presque, almost, well nigh; *presque touts*, near all.

Pressant, enforcing, urging.

Prestement, readiness.

Prestre, vide *prester*, *j'avoye prester*, I have lent.

Pretendre, to make shew, or pretence.

Preterite, past, gone, expired.

Pretexte, by colour of.

Prevariquer, to deal doubly.

Pur prier, for to request, pray, or ask.

Priomus, we pray, *prismus*, we take.

Pris, taken, *pria*, took, *priz*, took, *vide postea.*

Al primes, at first, *prime facie*, at first view.

Le primers, the chief, *en le primes*, in the beginning.

Printemps, the first time.

Primerment, formerly in the first place.

Solement jeo pria, only I wish, *p. termes Ley*, 266.

Gist pris, lies near, *cy pris*, so near.

Prisel, taking, *beins prises*, Goods taken, *p. art. sup. Chart.* 28, *Edw.* 1.

Prisance de ses parol, taking his word.

Terres prises, Lands taken; p. 5 *Hen.* 7, 5.

Le prisor, the Taker.

Encore prist, always, and yet ready.

Il prist, he took, *pristeront*, they took or were ready; *pristera terre*, they landed, *p. termes de Ley*, 181, *b. prit*, ready.

Priaunt, they praying, or asking for.

Priants, idem. *p. Coke* 9, 120.

Priver, to spoil, or take away.

Privie, deprived, *person privie*, is who has an interest in the thing demanded.

Privities en sank, alliance in blood.

Le privitie fuit determine, the privity or consent was determined.

Privitie

Privitie en tenure, as by Lord and Tenant, *&c.*

Probes, honeſt, *probitie*, honeſty.

Prochein, near, next, *le procheins Villes*, the next Towns ;

Prochain, *& prochein*, ſignify Neighbourhood.

Prochientie, being nigh.

Le procheins terres, the next Lands.

Procreer, to beget, to engender.

Procreanter, idem.

A proeeder, to proceed,

Ne procedez, ye proceed not.

Proceſſions, *ſupplications*, prayers by way of perambulation.

Prode, produced.

Producer, to ſhew, *jeo aye producer*, I have ſhewed *p. plowd.* in his preface.

Sont prodes, are produced, ſhewed, *prode*, idem. *prode*, is alſo, put, *p. plowd. com.* 106, *a.* & 161, *b.*

Produiment, ſetting forth.

A prover, to prove, *un proveur*, an Evidence, a Proſecutor, alſo a Challenger.

Proditorie, Treaſon, *p. Fitz.* Juſtice, 40, *a.*

Proditeur, a Traitor.

Profer, *offred*, brought, alſo preferred.

Produiant, ſhewing forth, *produire*, to ſhew or to produce.

Prowe, profit, *profet*, idem. *p.* 3. *partem Inſtitut.*

Le commen prowe, the publick good or profit.

Proyer, to put off, *p. mores. rep.* 842.

Prohiber, to forbid, *prohibe*, forbidden.

Projecteront, they throw.

Promitter, to promiſe, *promitte*, promiſed.

Promit, idem. *promitta*, ſhall or may promiſe.

Promeſſe, a promiſe.

Promptre, to lead.

Prompt, ready, *promptiment*, readily.

Prodige, a ſtrange thing, a progedy

Proeſme, a Neighbour, *proſme*, idem, *p. Britton*, 237, *a.*

Produire, to bring forth, alſo to alledge.

Praeme, a preface, a prologue.

Promener, to walk, *vide pourmener.*

Promeu, advanced, promoted.

Propice, merciful

Propre, own, *de ſon propre malice*, of his own or proper malice.

Ma propre main, my own hand.

Properment, properly,chiefly, *propement*, idem, *ſes propres biens*, his own Goods.

Un proprietaire, an Owner.

Proroguer, to defer, to prolong,to put off.

Proſcription, an attainder.

Proſtrerner, to throw down.

Proſtration, falling at ones Feet, alſo throwing to the Ground.

Proſtituer, to ſet open to all.

Jeo

Jeo protest, I protest, *p. plowd.* preface.

Provendre, a prebendary, *provander*, idem.

Proveignaut, coming, arising. *provenient*, idem.

Provant, proving.

Provenant hors, coming out, *p. Davies rep.* 4 *b.*

Proveignants, issuing out of *p.* 1 *Hen.* 7, 8, *b.*

Provers hommes, poor Men, *p. Kitch.* 3, *a.*

As provers, to the poor, *p. eund.* vide *povers.*

Prou, much, enough, *vous prou?* have ye enough?

Prove, a proof, a tryal, essay.

Pryse, idem, *ut*, *prise*, taken.

Pryst, ready, *vide prist*, *plowd.* 276, *b.*

P U.

Publie, *publee*, & *publyee*, published.

Puer, to spoil, *puir*, idem. *pues*, spoiled.

Puant, stinking, perishing, spoiled.

Herbes pues, grass spoiled, or trodden down.

Puantise, Filth, *p. nov. nar.* 16, *a.*

Ne puet, he could not, *ne puit*, idem, *p. eund*, 5, *a.*

Pugisa, shall deflower, or defile, *p. Crompt.* 73.

Pugner, to fight, *pugnant*, fighting.

Puis, afterwards, since.

De puis, from thence, after that.

Puisue, *apounger*, *petty*, later, *puisue*, *temps*, later times.

Pucelle, a Maid, a Virgin.

Pucellage, Virginity, Maidenhead.

Puissant, strong, mighty.

Puissance, power, authority.

Puissamment, mightily, vigorously.

Il puet este, it may be.

Puist estre, it ought to be.

Puissoit, he might, *puissent*, they might.

Jeo puisse, I might, or could. *ne puit*, he ought not, *ne pussoient*, they ought not.

Pulles, the young of any thing, commonly put for Colts; 18 *Hen*: 8, 2, *a.*

Pulles esperners, young Hawks.

Pulter, a poulterer.

Pulsure, striking, knocking.

Pulsa le huis, knock'd at the Door.

Punees, younger Sons.

Une punee, a younger Daughter.

Punie, punished; *punir*, to punish.

Punisher, idem, *ut punir.*

Puniera, shall punish.

Serra punis, shall be punished.

Punies, punished, *punique*, idem, *punyque*, idem.

Punyshe, *p.* 12 *Hen.* 8, 1, is punished.

Pur, for, *ne pur venir*, not to come: *pur* in Mod: *French*, is pure, neat, clean.

Purger, to cleanse.

Purgement, purging, cleansing, *purge*, *idem.*

Purgiser, to deflower, to ravish, to defile, *p. Brit.* 16, *b*, and 39 *a.*

P*urpartie*, a ſhare by partition.

P*arpart*, partly.

Je ne purpulay, I have not ſpoke.

P*urpulaſtes*, ye have not ſpoke, *p. Brit.* 42.

P*urpenſe*, conſidered of before, forethought, *vide pourpenſe.*

A purpris, to take from another what is not the Taker's own.

Purpriſe, & *purpris*, are words uſed for *purpreſture*, which is the encloſing waſts, or commonable places, digging therein, or other publick nuſance in them, *vide pourpreſture.*

Purra, ſhall or may, *purra eſte*, may be.

Jeo purray, I may or can, 26 *Hen.* 8, 1, *a.*

Purraile, the ſame as *purlue*, & *purlay*, i. e. the venue, or borders of a Foreſt or Chaſe, *vide Cromptons Jur. Cur.* 153.

Purroit, ne may, *purrount*, they may.

P*ourrount eſte mis*, they may be put.

Comme il purront, as they might or could, *p.* P*arkins*, 167, *b.*

P*urvey*, provided, *p.* 14 *Hen.* 8, 30, *b.*

P*urvieu*, idem, alſo proviſion by way of ſome condition, *p. plowd.* 251.

P*urveyance*, proviſion *de purveyer*, to provide, *purveiſt*, he provided, *purveyer*, to provide, *purview eſt*, it is provided, *purviewes*, proviſions, *purvieus*, provided.

P*urſuer*, to proſecute, alſo to follow.

Puſel, a little Girl.

Puſeit, he may, *puſſent*, they may or can.

Le publique, the Commonwealth.

Pus, afterwards, after.

P*uſſe*, idem. alſo, may or can, *p. Brit.* 126.

Un putaine, a Whore, a Harlot.

P*uteine*, idem, *p. Coke rep.* 5, 51, *a.*

P*utages*, Whoredoms.

P*utatif*, taken, eſteemed, thought.

P*uys*, a watry place, an ouzy place, *p. Britton*, 6, *a*,

P*uz*, idem, *ut pus*. i. e. after.

Q. Q.

QEN, in what, *p*, 3 pt. *Inſtitut.* 1.

Qi, who, *qils*, they, who, *p. eund.* 93.

Qu, becauſe.

Quadrangulaire, Four-ſquare.

Quadruple, Four-times.

Quand, when, *quand ſerra ce?* When ſhall this be?

Quadrageſime, Lent-ſeaſon, *p. Plowd.* 89, *b.*

Quadragenaire, forty Years of age.

Un Quadran, a Sun-dial, and Mathematical Inſtrument

Quadrer, to fit well, juſtly agreeing.

Quant

Quant a ce, as for this.

Quant & quant, forthwith, therewith.

Quantes foits, how often, oftentimes.

Quantiesme, how much, what number.

Quaquet, prating, babling.

Quant, when, when as, how much.

Quaunt, idem. and according to, and as much, *p. Plowd.* 262, & *Davies rep.* 4, *b.*

Quadratata terre, a farthingdale of Land.

Quadrugata terre, a teeme Land.

Quash, to overthrow, make void, annul.

Quant al, as to, *quant al moy?* what is it to me?

Quant la est, where there is,

Quantieme, the whole, the quantity.

Quarrere, a quarry.

Quar, for; *p.* 1 *Edw*, 5, *a.*

Quarentiesme, the fortieth; *quarentieme*, idem.

Quarante foits, forty times.

Le quarrant, the fortieth; *qvarante*, the fortieth.

Quarentene, is 40 Days allowed a Widow to enjoy the chief House before the Heir entreth.

Quarentena, a Furlong. *p.* 1 *partem* Instit. 5, *b.*

Quaresme demi, Midlent.

Quatorze, fourteen; *quatre*, four.

Quarreur, square.

Le quart, the fourth.

Quaterment, fourthly.

Quatre vings, eighty; *quatre vings & dix*, ninety in modern *French*.

Quassa, made void, annulled qu shed.

Quasi presque, near, almost.

Que, that, which, to, and than, and then.

A que, to whom, whereby.

Que est ce la? what is that there?

Que fais tu? what doest thou?

A que son Baron, other than her Husband, *p. Crompt.*

Pur que, for what, why; *Kitch.* 7, *a*,

A que est ses Avers, whose Cattle are these?

Que quant, that when.

Que voil, which will, and which was.

Que versus, against whom, *p.* 4 *Hen:* 7, 1, *a.*

Nount que de Lease, they have nothing but of Lease.

Quccunque, & *quelcunque*, whatsoever, wheresoever.

Quel, what, which, who, how; *quele*, idem.

Quel home, what Man, which Man.

En quel maniere, in what manner.

Le quel, the which, whether, *Coke* 3 37.

A quel, to what, *p. eund.* 5, 89, *a.*

Quelque, whatsoever, something.

Quelque un, some one, any one, *p. Coke* 9, 120.

Quelque

Quelque chose, any thing, ſomething.

Quelcunque, whoſoever.

Quelque partie, every part, the whole.

Quelque foits, ſometimes, *p. Hobart*, 2.

Par quel, by which, by whom.

Quel grand? how great? *quel eſt maiſtre, tiel eſt ſervaunt*, as is the Maſter, ſo is the Man.

Le quel, the which, *pour quel raiſon?* for what cauſe?

Querces, Oaks, *quercez*, idem. *p.* 13 *Hen.* 7, 9.

Querir, to ſeek, to call for, to fetch, *querer*, idem.

A querer, to get, to obtain.

Voil querer, will enquire, ſeek for.

Quis, ſought. *quer ſon viver*, to get his Living.

La queſt, vide *Enqueſt*.

Querant, enquiring, ſeeking, *querance*, idem.

Queraſt, he enquired, he ſought.

Querge, ſeek thou, enquire.

Queſte, an enquiring after.

Le queſt, the which.

Querele, a Complaint, a Quarrel.

Querelles & querellez, plural.

Querks, idem. *ut querces*, querkes and querques, idem.

Quetment, quietly, peaceably, *quitment*, idem.

Queve, a Tail.

Queus, whom, *as queus*, to whom, *le queus ont*, who have.

Queux, which, whom, *en queux*, in what, in which, *p. Kitch.* 4. *plowd:* 9.

Qui, who, what, whence, whom, whoſe.

A qui eſt tu? from whence art thou?

A qui, to whom, *p. Rich.* 3.

En qui maines, in whoſe hands; *p. Brit.* 106, 8.

Qui que ce ſoit, whoſoever he is.

Et qui pluis eſt, and which is more.

Qui ce qui la, now here now there.

Qui dez vous? do you imagine?

Quicunque, vide *quecunque*.

Quils, they, thoſe, that they.

Quint, the fifth, *quindix*, fifteen.

Un quiſſour, a Collector, Gatherer, a Receiver; *p. Fitz. gr. abr.* 2 part. 5, *a*.

Quinze, the fifteenth, *le quinzime*, idem.

En le quinzime, five Days after; *p. Plowd:* 255.

Quinquageſima, the fiftieth: Quinquageſima Sunday, about 50 Days before *Eaſter*.

Quitment, freely, acquitted, *p. Greg.* 299.

Quire, leather; *quirs*, Skins, Hides, alſo Pelts; *p. Brit.* 33 & 38, & 3 part Inſtit. 39.

Blauncheours de quirs, Whittawers; *p. eoſd.*

Quiſent chairs, they expos'd Fleſh to ſale; *p. Brit.* 33.

Quivre, Copper; *p. Plowden* 56.

Quivres, Skins, Pelts. *p. Stat.* Westm. 1. *cap.* 20.

Quiter, to acquit, to discharge.

Quictance, a quittance.

Quore, of whom, which; *quor*, for.

Quoy, look ye; *pur quoy non*, why not; *p. Coke* 9, *rep.* 120, also for what reason.

De quoy, where with, 2 part *Instit.* 166. *Quotidien*, daily.

Pour quoy is also wherefore; *a quoy*, to which.

Si'l neit de quoy, if he have not wherewith, *p. Fitzh.* Justice, 167, *b.*

Quy'l, that would, *p. nov. nar.* 45.

Quy'l garderoit, that he would keep, *p. eund.*

Quyvre, vide *quivre*.

Quyur, Copper, *p. Plowd.* 311, *a.*

R A.

R*Abbaiser*, to pull down; *Rabais*, abated pull'd down *Rabbatre de pris*, beat down the price.

Rachater, to redeem, to make compensation for Thievery.

Raboter, to plain to make smooth.

Racinetter, to root, *un racinette*, a root.

Un Race, a Family, Kindred.

Radchemistres, & *radmans*, Tenants in free soccage, by free Rent; *p. Coke*, 1st part Instit. 5, *b.*

Rad, firm, stable; *rede* idem *p. eund.*

Radechenistres, Free-men, *p.* Domesday *lib.*

Races, pull'd down, *rases*, idem. *p. Greg.* 332, *b.*

Racióciner, to Reason to Discourse.

Racourcir, to shrink together; *racourci*, shrunk.

Rachasser, to drive back, or again.

Racines, Roots.

Racler, to rake.

Railler, to jest, to joque; *raillerie*, jesting.

Raison, reason; *Raisonnaturelle*, the Law or Reason we are born with, and unwritten.

Raisoner, to reason, to argue.

Raisins, roots, 1 *rep. Coke*, 124.

Ramasser, to gather, to collect; *ramass*, gathered.

Ramage, wild, untamed; *Espervier ramage*, a Hawk among the Woods wild.

Ramens, boughs, branches, lops of Trees, *Plowd.* 470, *a.*

Ramans, idem; *ramailes*, idem.

Rameau, a branch or arm of a Tree.

Ramure, idem, *rames*, boughs.

Ramper, to creep.

Ramis, torn, *p. Brit.* 66, *a.*

Un Rame de papier, a Ream of paper.

Un Rame is also an Oar.

Range, order, *mettre du rang*, to put into order, to array.

Ramener, to bring back, or again; *reamesuer*, idem.

Ramilles, small twigs or sticks.

Ramu, full of boughs.

Ramollir, to soften any thing.

Rapt, snatched; *un Rape*, a force upon a Woman to ravish her.

Rapporter, to carry or bring back.

Rapport, relation.

Rapell, called again.

Raser, to stock up, to dig up; *rasé*, destroyed.

Measons rase, Houses pull'd down.

Rasement, destroying, pulling down.

Rasure, idem; *rase*, torn; *rasins*, roots.

Raser, to shave; *rase*, shaved.

Raser un Ville, to lay a Town even with the ground.

Rarement, seldom, rarely.

Rater, to assess, to set a value or rate upon.

La Rate, the Spleen.

Rapprehendre, to learn again, also to talk again.

Rancumpanne, Cloth not well fulled, or dress'd, *p. Kitch:* 174, *a.*

Ravager, to spoil, *ravage*, spoil, or destruction by Enemies.

Un Rave, a Turnep.

Ravir, to ravish, or take by violence.

Ravie, ravished; *ravi*, idem.

Ravissement, ravishing; *ravisant*, idem.

Un Ravisseur, a Ravisher.

Rauson, a ransom, or thing given for freedom. *p.nov.nar.*6,*b.*

Ray, *le 'ray*, the array, or panel of the Jury, or arraying an Army, *viz.* putting in order, *vide Array.*

R E.

Re, compounded, and put before other words, signifieth again, or back.

Rebaille moy, give me again, *rebailler*, to redeliver.

Rebaisser, to kiss again.

Rebattre un clou, to drive a nail back.

Realx, real; *Chatelx realx*, Chattels real.

Real, Royal.

Realment, really, truly.

Reaver, to have again.

Read, had again; *realt*, he had again.

Reaus, residing, resident.

Reamesner, to take again, to bring back.

Reamesne, brought back.

Recent, now of late, newly.

Rebealx, disobedient, *p.* 3 part, *Instit.* 39.

Reblancher, to whiten again.

Rebouche, stopped up.

Reboucher, to cloy, to make dull.

Rebouchement, dully, taking off the edge of any thing.

Rebutter, to repel, to bar, vide *Termes de Ley*, 233, *b.*

Rebouter, to repulse, to drive back.

Rebut, *rerebote*, casting out, rejecting.

Recel-

Recellement, withdrawing himſelf, hiding.

Rechaſſer, to drive back by force.

Recherche, to ſearch again.

Recheute, a falling down.

Recheif, furthermore, again, alſo, *p. Art. ſub. Chart.*

Rebaptizer, to baptize again.

Recetters, receivours, *p. Brit.* 19, *b.*

Que recetteront, they who receive.

Receut, he would receive, *p. nov. nar.* 35.

Receiter, to receive; *recettement*, receiving.

Receitement, harbouring.

Eſtre reſceu, to be received; *receu*, idem.

Rechoir, to fall again.

Reciproque, one for another.

Recognoſtre, & *rcognoiſtre*, to acknowledge,

Recognaiſſance, acknowledging.

Rechate, marketing, buying.

Recheſt, extended unto.

Reconquiſe, recovered again; *reconquis*, idem.

Recoupe, kept back.

De recouper, to recover; *recoupe*, recovered.

Recourir, to run back.

Recoveres, obtained, recovered.

Recreant, cowardly, faint-hearted.

Recreſſer, to increaſe, to grow again.

Reclamer, to recall, alſo to gainſay.

Reclus, encloſed, ſhut up.

Le Recluſes, ſuch as are ſhut up, *viz.* Religious Perſons in a Monaſtery.

Recombatre, to fight again.

Recomencer, to begin again.

Recouvrer, to recover, to obtain.

Recuiller, to gather together.

Recognuſtre, to acknowledge,

Recuſer, to refuſe.

Recreu, tyred.

Rectores, Parſons of Churches, &c. Alſo Governours.

Redimer, to redeem.

Reddition, ſurrendring.

Redubbours, Brokers, Chapmen, Saleſmen; alſo ſuch as buy Cloaths which are ſtolen, and alter the Shapes. *p. Brit.* 33, *a.*

Redarguer, to check, to controle.

Reedifier, to build again.

Reeve, a Baylif of a Franchiſe or Mannor. *Greve*, idem.

Refreinder, to bridle, to reſtrain.

Refroidit, he recanted, or grew cold, *p. Coke*, 9, 120.

Refuſer, to deny.

Refourbir, to poliſh, to make bright.

Regarder, to look to, to behold.

Un Regarder, is an Officer of the Foreſt, to look to Ver , and what belongs to the browſe of Deer.

Regardes, intents, purpoſes; Re*gardant*, belonging to.

At touts tegardes, to all intents or purpoſes,

Regales,

Regales, the Rights and Ornaments of the Crown.

Regalia, idem.

Regallement, Royally.

Regermer, to ſprout out again, or ſpring.

Regner, to reign, to rule.

Regenter, idem; *Qui reigne*, who reigneth.

Regrators, Huckſters, *i. e.* ſuch as buy quantities of Victuals and Proviſions, in the Market, and ſell it again at higher prizes.

Refroid, cooled, 4 *rep.* 120, *a.*

Reints, reſts, remains; *Illonque reintz*, there remains, or reſts, *p. Brit.* 145, *b.* & 49.

Reis, Nets, *p. nov. nar.* 43, *a.*

Rejaler, to rebound, to give back, to recoile.

Rejouir, to be glad.

Rejecter, to refuſe, to caſt off.

Rejecte, refuſed, caſt off.

Les reins, the Kidneys or Reins.

Par rein, by a ſtream, 13 *Hen.* 8, 16, *b.*

Reintegration, a renewing.

Rejoyndre, to rejoyn an anſwer to a replication pleaded.

Relaſher, to releaſe; *un relaſh*, a releaſe.

Un Relateur, an Informer on the King's behalf, a rehearſer of ſomething concealed.

Relever, to raiſe up again; alſo to deliver back.

Releif, a profit coming unto the Lord, upon the death of a Tenant in Fee, commonly double the chief rent.

Relinque, left; *Relinquiſh*, idem; *relinquiſt*, idem.

Relinquiſher, to leave; *relinquy*, left.

Relinqueant, leaving.

Relire, to read over again.

Un Remaindre, & *remainder*, is an Eſtate in Lands, that ſhall remain after the particular Eſtate, (be it for Life or Years) is expired or determined.

Remercie, thanks, thank ye.

Remeint, reſted, *p. Miror of Juſtice*, Cap. 2. Sect. 15.

Remeyent, idem, *p. Brit.* 188, vide *reminant.*

Remeigne, & *remene*, brought back, *p. eund.* 54, *b.* & 122, *a.*

Remarquer, to note, to make obſervations.

Rembarquer, to take ſhipping back again.

Rembourſer, to pay back what one has expended.

Rembourſement, reſtoring back Money laid out.

Remiſe fuit, was had or recevied back.

Remis, idem, alſo negligent.

Remiſtrent, they remained, they reſted.

Reminant, remaining, alſo inhabiting, *p.* 19, *Hen*: 5, 1.

Remitte, took back.

Remener, to bring again.

Remitter, & *remetter*, to reſtore again to the firſt or moſt antient Eſtate.

Remetion, removing.

Remplir,

Remplir, to fill again; *rempli*, filled.

Rempliſſement, filling again.

Remuer, to remove, to ſtir up. *p. Brit.* 4. *b.*

Remue, removed, *p. eund.* 53, *b.* & 56.

Remeuement, removing.

Remunerer, to reward, to recompence.

Renable, reaſonable; *renables*, idem. *p. Brit.* 27.

Renaiſtre, to be born again.

Rencaria, Lands full of briars and brambles. *p. Coke.*

Rencounter, to run upon one, to meet againſt.

Render, to reſtore; *rendus*, reſtored.

Rendue, paid, given, reſtored; *rendſt*, idem.

Un Renee, a renouncer, a denyer; *renees*, plural.

Reneign, denied, renounced; *renier*, to deny.

Renegade, denying his Faith.

Renome, renowned, chief, principal; *renomez*, idem, *p. Brit.* 143, *renomme*, idem.

A repairant, a going unto; *repairer*, to repair.

Repareyler, idem; alſo, to go unto, *p. Coke*, 11, 57.

Rent a volunt le Roy, fined or taxed at the will of the King.

R*entes ſoient*, they ſhould be fined, *p. Stat.* Weſtm. 1.

R*eappel*, recalled, revoked.

Bien reparel, well repaired.

R*epariller*, to repair; *repareler*, idem.

Pur reperiller, for repairing, *p. Parkins*, 135, *b.*

R*epeller*, to put back.

R*epaiſtre*, to feed; *repue*, fed; alſo a bait, a refection.

R*eforcir*, to wax ſtrong; *renforce*, ſtrengthened.

R*envoye*, a ſending back, a diſmiſſion.

R*enforci*, idem, *ut renforce.*

R*enouvator*, to renew; *renoveler*, idem.

R*enouvele*, renewed.

R*epenſant*, conſidering; *repenſer*, to call to mind.

R*entrer*, to go in again.

R*enomme*, renowned.

R*eplegiare*, to redeliver, to make replevin.

R*epleiviſables*, baylable.

R*eplete*, filled.

R*epenſer*, to call to remembrance.

R*epeſer*, to weigh again.

R*epoſer*, to reſt; *repos*, quiet, reſt,

R*epris*, to take again; *repriſe*, idem.

R*epriſes*, reſumptions taking back.

R*epeller*, & *appeler*, to apeal; *repelle*, appealed.

R*eprimender*, to rebuke, to check.

Un reprimaund, a rebuke; *reprimend*, idem.

R*eprendre*, & *reprender*, to retake.

R*epriont*, reprieved, *Plowd.* 101, *b.*

R*eprent*, retook; *reprent*, idem.

R*epriſomus*, we retook: *repriſt*, he retook.

R*epreſt*, idem; *ont repriſter*, they took back.

Repri-

Repriteront, idem; *repristeront*, idem.

Reputer, to esteem.

Repudier, to forsake, to reject.

A reprier, to reprieve; *repriont*, they reprieved, *p. Plowd. abr.* 18, *a.*

Requiert, he required, or asked for.

Requirast, idem; *requises*, requested.

Resayla le Ewe, the water run back.

Resceus, received; *resceaux*. idem. *p. Brit.* 10, *a.* & 9, *b.*

Rescue, idem, *p. Kitchin.*

Fuit resceu, was received, *p. nov. nar.* 5, *b.*

Res sua, his Substance, *p. Termes de Ley*. 100.

Rescous, forced away.

Rescourrer, to rescue or force from, also to recover back; *recussa*, rescued, *rescusa*, idem.

Reservant, reserving.

Resemee, sowed again.

Reseme, sowing.

Resider, to continue, to abide.

Resoule, resolved.

Resiants, they who inhabit or abide.

Resiancy, an abiding or continuing.

Respi, delay, putting off.

Respondre, to answer; *respons*, an answer.

Respoignans, answering; *respoignant*, idem.

Deveit respoigneront, they would answer, *p. Plowd.* 378, *b.*

Resort, to come unto, to be with.

Se resoult, he resolved with himself.

Respoignable, answerable for.

Restregn, restrained.

Resuscitate, revived, rose again.

Resusciter, to revive, &c.

Resembler, to be like; *resemblement*, likeness.

Restablir, to bring to the former Condition.

Restituer, to restore; *estre restitus*, be restored: *p. Coke*, part 2d, *parte Instit.* 639.

Resumer, to take again.

En retargement, in hindring or staying.

Ret, guilt; *rett*, idem, and suspition of guilt.

Rettes, suspected, also guilty. *p. Fitzh.* Justice, 147 *a.*

Sont rettes, they are guilty, *p. Fitzh.* Justice, 147, *a.*

Rette, guilty, *p. Briton* 82 *b.* also, reputed, accounted.

Rethes, nets, *p. Plowd. com.* 16, *a.* *rete*, a net.

Reteiner, to keep; *retention*, keeping.

Retiendra, shall retain, *Plowd.* 296, *b.*

Retinue, kept, *p. nov. nar.* 53, *a.*

Retarder, to hinder.

Retirer, to go back.

Retray, withdraw, gone back, also refused.

Retre, withdrawn, *p.* 13 *Hen.* 8. 12, *a.*

Retound, cliped, rounded.

Re-

R*etraiƈter*, to withdraw, to take back.

R*etreiƈt*, withdrawn, took back.

Se retreit, he withdrew himſelf.

R*etret*, idem, *retreit*, idem.

R*etarder*, to defer, to put off, to delay.

R*etenu*, retained.

R*etraire*, to pull back.

R*etour*, returning again.

R*etrencher*, to cut off, to leſſen.

R*etrencher le Gages*, to leſſen the Wages.

R*etribuer*, to reward.

R*evanche*, revenged: *p. Coke, rep.* 9, 120.

R*everter*, to return; *revertera*, ſhall return.

R*eveign*, come back; *revenu*, idem.

R*evienderont*, they are come back.

R*evenir*, to return.

R*evenir a ſoy*, to come to himſelf again.

R*evenue*, rent, *l'revenu d'aucun*, any mans rent.

R*everdir*, to wax green.

R*everſeront*, they reverſe, or bring back.

A revers, backwards.

R*evivre*, to bring back to life.

R*eveve*, to view again, or look diſtinctly over.

Le An revolu, the Year gone about.

R*ewle legerment*, a ſtanding rule or order, *p.* 1 *Hen.* 7, 31, *a.*

R*evoquer*, to call back, to revoke.

Un R*evolution*, a change, a turning about.

R*e*, guilt; *reyes*, faults, *p. Brit.* 83. *a.*

R I.

R*icheſſe*, wealth, goods riches, as riches to the Rich; *p. Kitch.* 3, *a.*

R*ibaus*, the Mob, the Rabble, alſo Boors. *p. eund.* 49, *b.*

Un R*ibaud*, a Rogue, a Whoremonger, alſo a ſturdy Beggar.

R*ibaulde*, a Whore, one of evil fame.

R*iblerie*, to keep ill rule, abroad, or in the ſtreets.

R*idiger*, to reſtore.

R*ien & riens*, nothing; *il n'eſt rien ſi facile*, there is nothing ſo eaſy; *rien pluis*, nothing more,

R*ien cul*, not guilty; *navoit nunquam riens*, never had any thing.

R*ien vault*, avails nothing.

R*ipes*, banks; *ripes de le Riviere*, the banks of a River.

Un R*ieu*, a ſmall Brook

R*ieur*, Laughter; *ris*, idem.

R*iguer*, ſternneſs, rigour.

R*igoreux*, rough, cruel, ſharp.

R*ifler*, to ſpoil or take from.

R*iouteux*, riotous, exceſſive.

R*ire*, to ſmile to laugh.

R*iſee*, laughing.

Rieur, a Gigler, one ufed to laughter.

Rifques, chances, haps, tryals.

R O.

Un Robe, a Gown or upper Garment; *robbe*, idem.

Roabes, Apparel, *per termes de Ley*. 131.

Roborer, to work, alfo to ftrengthen.

Robufte, ftrong, mighty.

Le Roignon, the Kidney.

Rompre, to break, to burft afunder.

Rompa, broken; *rompure*, a breach.

Rompement, breaking.

Ronceux, full of brambles, briers.

Un Ronce, a bramble; *rence*, idem.

Roncaria, briery Land, vide *rencaria*.

Rond, round; *rondement*, roundly.

Le Roigne, the Queen; *Royne*, idem.

Royner, to clip, or pare round.

Roffe, heath, *ros*. idem.

Rofeau, a reed.

Rofee, Dew.

Rovefouns, rogation time, *p. Stat*. Weftm. 1 cap. 51.

Rouge, red Colour; *rouguer*, rednefs.

Rouffir, to wax red, vide *ruge*.

Un Rout, an affembly of many together, or above three, to do fome unlawful act; *Rot*, in *Brittifh*, alfo in the *German* Languages.

Roy, a King, *Royal*, Kingly, Majeftick; *Royes*, Kings.

Roylment, Princely, Royally.

Royaulme, a Kingdom, *Royaume*, idem.

Royalty, the Dignity of a King.

Rouler, to fold, to plait.

Rotundre monie, to clip Money, *p. Brit*. 16, *a*.

Le Route, the ftreiks of a Cart-wheel.

R U.

Rumper, to break, vide *Rompre*.

Leverer Rump Jon leufe, a Greyhound broke his Leafh.

Rubie, ruddy, very red.

Rufe, heat, alfo craft, deceit.

Rue, a Street; *Ruelle*, a Lane.

Ruer, to throw down.

Ruge, red, *p. Plowd. Com*. 339, *a*.

Ruineux, ruinous, in decay.

Rugir, to roar.

Un Ruche, a Bee-hive, *p. Brit*. 85, *a*.

R Y.

Ryen, vide *rien*.

Ryen fair, to do nothing.

SA, is Feminine, and signifies her; sometimes it is his, as *sa possession*, his possession, for that *possessio* is femenine, *vide Fitzh. nat. brev.* 182, *b.*

S'abati, abate.

Sablon, gravel, sand; *sable*, idem.

Sable, is also black.

Sablonneux, gravelly, sandy.

Sacher, to know; *saches*, know thou; *sachez*, know.

Sache, understood, known.

Sachant, knowing; *sachent*, idem, also they know; *ne sachera*, shall not know.

Sacha, know; *sachast*, had known.

Sachantement, knowingly, wittingly: *p.* 3d part *Instit.*

Sacree, consecrated.

Un Sachet, a Pocket, a Bag.

Sac, is a Penalty, or Forfeiture in the Lord's-Court.

Saccager, to spoil, to sack.

Saccagement, spoiling, pillaging.

Sacrer, to make holy; *sacre al Dieu*, consecrated to God.

Sacree, enstalled, anointed with holy Unction; also sworn: *p. Coke*, 8, 69, *a.*

Sacrer un Evesque, to consecrate a Bishop.

Un Sacre, a kind of Hawk; also a piece in Artillery.

Sacriledge, stealing things dedicated to holy uses.

Sage, wise; *sagement*, wisely, advisedly.

Moins Sage, unwise, indiscreet.

Sagesse, Wisdom.

Sagette, an Arrow; *sagit*, idem.

Sagitter, to shoot an Arrow.

Sagitta, shot.

Sain, sound, healthful; *sane*, idem.

Sani & entier, whole and sound.

Saigner, to let blood.

Saignee, letting blood.

Saigneux, bloody.

Un Sainct, a Saint, also one that is holy.

Sainctement, holily.

Sailler, to leap, to dance, also to issue forth.

Voil Salier, would leap, *p. Crompt.* 154. *b.*

Sakeber, a Back bearer; *soit oye le Sakeber*, let the Back-bearer be heard, *p. Brit.* 22, *b.*

Saisissement, seizing, laying hold on, attaching; *saisons*, idem, *p. eund* 14.

Saisin, vide *seisin*.

Un Saller, a Sadler.

Saler, to salt, to season with salt.

Sale, Salt; *salwre*, powdering, salting.

Salee, idem, *p. Coke* 10, 139.

Salmure, brine; *sale* is also salted.

Salace, lascivous.

Salive, spittle.

Un Sale, a Hall; *salle*, idem.

Le grand Sale de Pallais, Westminster-hall.

Saliver, & *saliva*, a Salt-pit, or place for making Salt by the Sea coasts; also a Boillery.

Sal peſtre, Salt-peter.

Salaire, a Reward; *ſalarier*, to reward one.

Pour Sallery, for Reward, for Hire.

Pour Salvation, for ſaving.

Pour le Salute, for the health, or ſaving.

Saliꝺaire, wholſome.

Pour le ſalute, for the health.

Sauvacyon, ſaving: *p. Brit.* 1, *a.*

Salubre, healthful.

Salver, to ſalute or accoſt one.

Salve, greeting, *p. Kitch.*

Samedy, Saturday; *Samadie*, idem, *Samedi*, idem.

Sanneyes, Sallyes, withy Trees: *p. Coke*, 8, 47.

Saner, to heal; *ſane*, ſound.

Sanable, which may be healed.

Sauces del mer, Creeks of the Sea: *p. Fitzh.* 216.

Sanke, blood; *Sanc*, idem; *Sang*, idem.

Sanguillant, bloody; *Sanglante*, idem.

Sangulant, idem, *p. Coke*, 9. 122.

Sanke eſpendue, blood-ſhed.

Sang eſpendre, idem, in mod. *French*.

Sank fin, the end of the Kindred, or Line.

Le demi Sank, of the half blood.

Sans, without, beſides; *ſauns*, idem.

Sans fin, for ever; *ſans mein*, immediately.

En Sanitie, in health; *ſante*, health, welfare,

Sant, holy.

Le Sapient, the wiſe.

Sarcler, to rake, to leaſe, alſo to weed.

Un Sarclet, a Rake.

Sarclement, raking, weeding.

A Salter, to leap, to dance; *ſaulter*, idem.

Satisfair, to make amends.

Un Sas, a Seive; *ſaſſer*, to ſift.

Savage, wild, *lour ſavage*, their wildneſs, or being at liberty abroad, as Doves in flight, Fiſh in rivers.

Sauvaigaine, wandring, ſtraying, *ſauvaigne*, idem.

Sauvagine, is alſo Veniſon.

Saunte, ſound, healthful, wholſome, *p. Brit.* 33, *a.*

Un Saulx, a Withy or Willow-tree.

Saulices, Willows, Withies; *Sawres*, idem.

Savant, reſerving, excepting, ſaving.

Sauvant, idem; alſo a Proviſion.

Savement, ſafely: *p. Brit.* 168.

Un baſton de Saudre, a wooden Club, a Staff.

Saverount, they know, *vide Scaver*.

Sauver, to keep, to ſave.

Savour, taſt; *ſans ſaveur*, inſipid, without taſt.

Savorer, to taſt, alſo to ſave.

Sauces, Creeks, *vide*, *ſances*.

Ne Savoi, I know not: 21 *Hen.* 7. 35, *b.*

A Savaete, to, or for the health: *p. Brit.* 77, *a.*

Save-

Savement gardes, ſafely kept.

Ne Savoyent, they know not,

Saufie, ſaved.

Pur ſoy ſauvete, for his ſafety, *Coke* 9, 121.

Say, know, *p. Plowd.* 178, *b.*

S C.

Scarcement, ſcarcely.

A Scaver, to know; *ſceu*, known.

Ne Scavoir, know not; *ſcavoir*, is alſo knowledge.

Poies Scaver, ye may know.

Scavage, is a Toll paid for ſhewing Wares in Fairs.

Ne Scavoit, he knew not.

Ne Scay, know not.

Par le Scavient, interpretationes, by the known, or wiſe interpretations.

Vous Scaves, ye ſhall know.

Scavoir paravant, to foreknow.

Scavois, ye know, or learn.

Ceſt a Scavoir, that is to ſay.

Ils ne point Scavoir, they cannot know.

Scavoita, may know; *a ſcier*, to know.

Que ſcait, he who knoweth.

Scavamment, prudently, knowingly.

Sceit, doth know; *ſcieroit*, may know.

Un Sceau, a Seal; *Gardian de grand Seau*, Keeper of the great Seal.

Si il ne Sceit, if it be not known; *ſcier*, to know.

Sciaſt, he had known; *ſcient*, knowing, alſo to cut.

Scies, Cut.

Scachant, knowing; *jeo ſcie*, I know.

Scavoient, they may know; *ſcavoies*, ye knew.

Que jeo Scavoy, as I know.

Scinder, to cut; *blees ſcies*, Corn cut.

Science, Skill, Knowledge.

Skan & ſcan, argued; *bien skanne*, well argued.

A Scriver, to write.

Un Scrowe, a writing; *priſt ſcrow*, took a writing not executed.

Un Scippe, a Ship; *d'ſcippe*, to ſhip or lade Goods.

Scoles, Schools: *p. Fitzh. nat. br.* 40.

Scrutiment, ſearching.

Schime, Hereſy, Diviſion from the Church.

Scyer, to cut, or mow; *ſcier*, idem.

Jeo voil Scyer, I would know: *p. Plowd.* 97, *b.*

Sciera, ſhall cut.

Scintiller, to ſparkle; *ſcintillation*, ſparkling.

Un Scye, a Sythe, alſo a Saw.

S E.

Se, with a Verb, is termed a Verb reciprocal, as, *un Vicaridge ſe voida*, a Vicaridge became void: 44 *Edw.* 3, 16.

Un Seare, a Lock; *ſeares*, Locks.

Seame, ſowed; *ſeme*, idem.

Seant,

Seant, ſitting; *ſea*, ſate; *Cur fut ſeant*, the Court was ſitting: *p. Mores, rep.* 33. *Se jant*, they ſate.

Sejant ſouth le drap de Eſtate, ſitting under a Cloth of State: 13 *Hen.* 8, 11. *b.*

Seera, ſhall ſit; *ſeiance*, ſitting; *a ſeer*, to ſit; *de ſeer*, idem.

Secus, blind.

Sec, dry; *rent ſec*, dry rent; *i. e.* whereof no diſtreſs may be taken.

Secherеſſe, dryneſs, drought; *ſecheres, ſecular.*

Secrement, ſecretly, privily.

Secunderment, ſecondly.

Un Seer, a Governour, a Superintendant.

Le Seigneur, the Lord; *un Seigneurie*, a Lordſhip.

La Seignioreſſe, the Lady.

Seingle, Corn of Rie; *ſeigle, & ſegle*, Rie; *Pain de ſeigle*, Rie Bread.

Seiſie, ſeized; *ſeſies*, plurally; *ſeizin*, poſſeſſion.

Seizera, ſhall ſeize.

Avoit, Seiſined, hath ſowed, or tilled: *p. Parkins*, 110.

Seel, wax, *p. Coke*, 8, 28, *b.*

Selda, a Salt-pit.

Selies, Wares, Merchandizes.

Segon, in purſuance of, according to: *p. Coke, rep.* 9, 120, *ſelonque*, idem.

S'el, if ſhe.

Un ſelion de terre, is the ground ariſing between two Furrows, *i. e.* one ridge; *ſellon*, idem.

Seillonner, to ridge land or ground.

Seicher, to wither, to make dry.

Seine, himſelf; or one returned to his Senſes from Dotage: *li. Aſſ.* 123, *b.*

Selda, a Wood of Sallys, or Willows.

Le Sein, the boſom.

Semaunces, Seeds: *Coke*, 8, 37, *b. Semence*, idem.

Un Semaine, a Week; *ſemaignes*, Weeks.

Semaines, idem.

El Semble, it ſeemeth; *el ſemblee*, idem.

Moy ſemble, it ſeems to me, methinks.

Semblable, agreable; *ſemblables tiels*, ſuch like; *tiels ſembles*, idem.

Semblont, they think, or ſeem.

Ne Sembloit, it ſeems not: *p. Stat.* Weſtm. 1. *cap.* 35.

Semer, & ſeminer, to ſow; *ſemy*, ſowed.

Semeur, a Sower; *ſemer*, idem, a Seeds-man.

Ne Sema, ſhall not ſow.

Semencer, ſowing, ſeeding, alſo beginning: *p. Coke, rep.* 11. 53.

Seudes, Sellers, Vaults: *p. nov. nar.* 16, *a.*

Selonc, & ſelon, according to, agreeable with.

Sente, a Path-way, alſo thinking.

Se ſente, think themſelves: *p. Brit.* 195.

Cesty qui soy sente, he who thinks: *p. Coke, rep.* 11. 64.

Seneschal, a Steward; *south Seneschal*, an under Steward.

Senestre, the left; *Senestre-main*, the left hand.

Senfue, fled away.

Sengliers, boors, labourers, hinds: *p. Crompt.* 146, *b.*

Sens, since.

Sensuit, it followeth.

Sentir, to feel, to perceive.

Se sentit, he bethinks, or perceives himself.

Sentif, an ability of perceiving; *sentive*, idem.

Seount, they sit: *p. nov. nar.* 102.

Seps, Stocks, vide *Cipps*.

Separer, to divide, to separate.

De cel Sep, of the same Stock or Root: *p. Brit.* 78, *a.*

Septe, seven; *sept*, idem.

Septiesme, the seventeenth; *septieme*, idem.

Septantie, seventy.

Septentrion, the North.

Septembre, the Month, *September*.

Sepulte, buried; *sepulture*, burial.

Sequerens, following.

Sequestre, to take into ones hand, to seize.

Serra, shall be; *ne serromus*, we may not be: *p. Rich.* 3, 14, *b.*

Sereine, calm, quiet, fair, clear.

Serenitie, brightness, clearness.

Sere, late.

Serement, swearing, an Oath.

Pur Sercler, for sowing, for to sow: *p. Brit.* 151, *b.*

Serfe, a Slave, a Servant, a Villain.

Serfe, is used by *Britton*, for a Man-slave, and *Naife* for a Woman-slave, and *Serfe*, by *Coke* is used for a Bond-man.

Serfs, Stags: *nov. nar.* 74.

Demorast Serfe, he should remain a Slave: *p. Brit.* 77.

Serjant, & *Serjaunt*, are used by *Britton* for Servant, 70. and by *nov. nar.* for a Champion, also a Proxy: 6.

Serroit, should be; *serroyt*, idem, *seroient*, & *serrount*, they should be; *serres*, ye shall be.

Server, to keep; *ne serva*, shall not keep: *p. Greg.* 301, also to serve.

Server Dieu, to serve God.

Ne servera, shall not serve.

Servages, services: *p. Brit.* 118, *a.*

Serveres, ye shall serve.

Ne fuit serve, was not served.

Un Serve, a stroke: *p. Term. de Ley*, 110.

Queux, Servant, they who serve.

Service de Chivalry, Knights Service.

Servois, Beer and Ale, vide *Cervois*.

Servage, Slavery, Bondage.

Eumener en Servage, to carry into Captivity.

Serrir,

Serrir, to lock, to ſhut up.

Serre, ſhut, or lock'd up; *ſerra*, ſhall be.

Serail de le Huis, the ring of the Door.

Ses, his, alſo her, if join'd to a plural.

Set, knoweth, vide, *ſcet*; alſo, *Set*, an Arrow.

Setter, to ſhoot, alſo ſhooting; *ſetta*, ſhooting.

Il ſetta un Set, he ſhot an Arrow.

Settles, ſtands, benches.

Ne Sevent, they knew not; *p. Brit.* 211, *b.*

Severeument, ſeverally; *ſeveralment*, idem.

Severe, parted aſunder, cut.

Severs, idem; *ſoit ſey*, be cut.

Seurs, Siſters: *p. Crompton* 142.

Seyettes, Arrows; *p. Brit.* 137.

Seynt, holy: *p.* 1 *Hen.* 7, 10.

Seyer, to ſit, *vide Seer.*

Seya, ſhall ſit; *ſeyant*, they ſit, alſo ſitting.

Il ſeyiſt, he doth ſit.

Seyus, Furrs: *p.* 1 part *Fitz. gr. abr.* f. 53, *b.*

Seyvaſt, hath ſeen: *p. Cromp.* 21.

Sextement, the ſixth time.

S H.

Shack, is a ſort of Commoning after Harveſt, for all ſorts of Cattle: By *Blount*, a Common for Hogs, uſed in *Norfolk*, in all mens grounds, after Harveſt till Seed-time.

Shaw, is a Wood or Grove.

Shovellers, wood Pidgeons; Quoiſts.

June Shovellers, young Quoiſts: *p. Coke rep.* 7. 17, *b.*

Shovelets: *p. rep.* 7. 17, *b.* Gos-hawks.

Shroud, lopp'd, cut.

Shotta, ſhut.

Pur Shower, to ſhoe.

S I.

Si, if, ſo, even, or, as.

Si fort, ſo ſtrong; alſo therefore; *ſi comme*, ſo as, and even as; *ſi non*, unleſs, except; *ſi nonque*, ſaving that; *ſi que*, in ſuch ſort; *ſi la*, until; *ſi bien*, & *ſi byen*, as well; *ſi come*, as it were: By *Britton*, 136.

Si come, as if: *p. eund.* 83, *ſi non*, unleſs.

Sicce, dry; *ſiccitie*, drought; *ils ſicces devenent*, they became dry or withered.

Un Sie, a Saw; *ſier*, to ſaw; *ſcie*, ſawed; *ſies*, ye ſawed or cut.

Le Sien, his own; *garda le ſien*, to keep his own.

Siglaunte, ſailing: *p. Brit.* 6, *b.*

Signer, to ſign, *ſignal*, a ſign, a token.

Signature, ſigning.

Un

Un Signet, a Seal: *p. Terms de Ley*, 14.

Signifier, to give notice, to ſhew.

Que ſignifie ce cy? What meaneth this? or what doth this ſignifie or import?

S'il, if he, *s'ils*, if they.

Sillours, Cutters; *ſillours de bourſes*, Cut-purſes: *p. Fitzh. Juſtice*, 200, *b*.

Simony, ſelling Eccleſiaſtical Preferments.

Le Simoniaque, he who bargains or ſells ſuch.

Singulent, *idem*, ut *ſanguillant*, i. e. bloody: *p. Coke, rep.* 9, 122.

Sinke, five, *vide cinque*; *ſinkement*, fifty.

Siniſtre, vide *ſyniſtre*.

Simplement, ſingly; *ſimpleſſe*, ſimplicity, fooliſhneſs.

Sinoth, Synod, *Saxon* word.

Simulation, diſſembling; *un ſimulateur*, a Diſſembler.

Sinder, to cut; *ſiement de Ble*, cutting of Corn.

Un ſing manual, a Handwriting.

Un ſinge, an Ape, *p. Plowd. Com.* 104, *b*.

Siſſables Arbres, Trees uſed to be cut or loppen, or Copſes.

Situer, to place; *ſitue*, placed, put.

Sidre, Cyder.

Size, ſix; *ſixieme*, the ſixth; *dix ſize*, ſixteen.

Slipper, frail.

Slethe, a bank of a River; *ſlede*, idem. *p.* 1*ſt.* part Inſtit. 52.

S O.

Sobre, temperate, continent, ſober; *ſobrement*, temperately, &c.

Sodeinment, ſuddenly, quickly.

Soc, a Plowſhare, or Coulter.

Soccage, is a Tenure performed by Services in Husbandry to the Lord; alſo a Tenure of Free-hold by a certain Rent for all Services, and to pay upon the death of the Anceſtour, a double Rent for a releif, and to be free from Wardſhip or Marriage: *Socmans, & ſokemans* are ſuch Tenants.

Sodomes, Buggerers, Sodomites.

Le Soel, the Sun; *ſeeil*, idem.

Soliel, Sunday; *jour ſoel*, idem.

Soen, ones own; *que ne ſont ſoens*, which are not ones own: *Plowd.* 260, *a*.

De ſon ſoen teſt, of his own head: *Cromp.* 163.

Maugre le ſoen, againſt his will: *p. Greg.* 211.

Soeſe, ſweet; *ſoeſvement* ſweetly.

Soer, Siſter, *ma Soer*, my Siſter; *ma ſeur*, idem.

Soerts, ſorts: *Plowd.* 332.

Soeffre, to ſuffer; *ſoeffrent*, they ſuffer.

Soet, be it, *vide ſoit*.

Soiſ.

Soif, thirſt; *avoir ſoif,* to be thirſty or a dry.

Soimeſme, himſelf; *ſoymeſme,* idem.

Soient, let them be, they ought to be.

Soies, ye ſhall be; *ſois,* ye be, ye are.

Soit, be it; *ſoit ce,* be it his, or thus.

Soivent, ſeveral.

Ou que nous ſoions. or where we be: *p. Brit.* 43, *b.*

Soigner, to take care, to attend.

Soigne, care, diligence; 9 *rep.* 120, b.

Soigneux, giving attention, being careful.

Soilet, he ought: *p. Plowd.* 334.

Le Soir, the Evening; *touts les ſoirs,* every Evening.

Sois ſoit, be thou; *ſoit ainſi,* be it ſo.

Soixante, ſixty.

Ils Soij, if they be; *p. Fitz. nat. br.* 210, *b.*

Sokemaines, Plow-men, and by *Kitchin,* 81, ſuch as plow their Lords Lands.

Un Soke, a Plow, alſo the liberty of holding a free Court of his Tenants within a liberty.

Soliel, the Sun, and Sunday.

Sole, & *ſoile,* ground, land.

Soliers, ſhoes, *vide ſolyers.*

Eſtre ſoleit, wont to be.

Soloit, eſtre, ought to be; *ſoloyt,* idem.

Que ne ſoloyent, they who ought, or uſe not.

Solement, only, *tant ſolement,* all, only.

Sole, alone, ſoly; *ſoule,* idem; *ſoeil,* idem.

Soleint, they were wont, or accuſtomed to.

Solonque, according.

Si vous ſoies, if ye be.

Soloyt, wanted to; *ſoleit,* idem.

Soloions avoir, we were wont to have, or we ought to have: *2do parte Inſtit.* 639.

Jeo Soley, I uſed.

Un Solyer, a Shoe-maker.

Solyers, ſhoes: *p. Fitzh.* 46, *a.*

Solz, Shillings.

Somnelents, Swoundings, faintings: *Brit.* 66.

Somcrie, briefly; *en ſomcrie,* in ſhort.

Solenniſer, to Celebate, to Solemnize.

De ſon, ou ſa, of his, or her.

Sont, are; *ſount,* idem.

Solicitude, carefulneſs.

Soluiſt, he ought, he is wont: *Coke* 9, 38.

Somme, ſleep; *ſommeil,* ſlumbering.

Songer, to dream; *ſonge,* dreamed.

Soraſes, Mice, *vide ſouraces.*

Sorciers, Sorcerers.

Sorcireſſes, Women ſorcerers.

Sorceler, to bewitch.

Un ſort, a lot; *de ſorte,* after the manner,

De

De ceſt ſorte, after this manner.

Sortilege, Witchcraft.

Un ſot, a Fool, an Idiot.

Sottement, fooliſhly; *ſotye* folly.

Sottie, Fondneſs, Dotage.

Soubdaine, ſudden; *ſoubdainment*, ſuddenly.

Soublever, to heave up, to lift up.

Soubminiſter, to ſerve under another.

Soubs, under; *ſoubz*, idem. *ſoubez*, under.

Soubſcrire, to under-write.

Soubtraire, to with-draw, or take from.

Subz umbre, under ſhew, under pretence, or ſhadow.

Souffire, to ſuffice.

Souffrir, to bear or ſuffer; *ſouffrance*, ſuffering.

Soillure, ſoil, alſo filth, dung.

Sotize, fooliſhneſs; *ſotiſe*, idem.

Souhaite, wiſheth; *ſouhaitant*, wiſhing: *p. Plowd. pref.*

Southaler, to undergo: *p. nov. nar.* 74.

Soubmettre, to ſubmit unto.

Soulement, only: *p.* 12 *Hen.* 8, 2, *a.*

Sourd, deaf; *ſourdeſſe*, deafneſs.

Sourdant, ariſing, ſpringing out.

Souvent, often; *auxi ſouvent*, as oft as.

Soven, often: *p. Crompt. Jur. Cur.* 84.

Sovent foits, often times; *pluis ſovent*, more oft; *il me ſovent*, he remembers me; *ſouvenance*, remembrance; *ſouvenu*, remembred.

Soy tient eins, kept himſelf in.

Souffrette, want, indigence.

Un Soulze, a ſhilling; *un ſous*, idem.

Soul, alone; *Feme ſoul*, a Woman unmarried.

Soule, idem; *ſount*, idem, *ut ſont.*

Soulfre, Brimſtone.

Souraces, Mice; *ſouri*, a Mouſe.

Sourdra, idem, *ut ſurdra*; *ſourdant*, they aroſe; *ſourd*, idem, *ut ſurd.*

Soulment, idem; *ut ſolement*: *p. Fitzh. gr. abr.* 1 part, 54.

South, under; *ſouth bois*, under wood.

South Vicount, under Sheriff, *ſouth-ſeneſchal*, Under-ſteward; *de ſouth la Mere*, beyond the ſea.

Southminer, to undermine; *ſouthmina*, undermined.

Souts, idem, *ut ſouth.*

Un ſoute, a ſuit, alſo a petition, alſo a petitioner: *p. Brit.* 206, *b.*

Fair ſouvenir, to put in mind, *jeo ſouvenir*, I remember: *p. Plowd. pref. Il me ſouvient*, he put me in mind.

Souſpecon, ſuſpition.

Ne ſoune, goes not: *p. Plowd. Com.* 11, *b.*

Ils ſowne a un effect, they are all to one purpoſe: *p. eund*, 86, *a.*

Sowne, p. 2 *Rich.* 3, 13, is put for noise, or sound.

Soy, him, also he, sometimes put for her.

Soy mesme, himself, also her self.

Soyment, idem; *si jeo soy*, if I be.

Vous soyez, ye be: *p.* 26 *Hen.* 8, 3, *b.*

Jeo soy, I am; *jeo sue*, idem, *p. Coke*, 6, 31, *a.*

Soyent, they are, or be, also being.

En soye, in themselves: *p. Plowd.* 313, *b.*

Soy leve, lifted himself, also was raised: *p. eund.* 228.

Soyer, sister: *p. eund.* 8, 87. vide *soer.*

Ne nul de soyens, nor none of his: *Stat. Art. sup. Chartas* 28 *Edw.* 1.

S P.

Spaul, spittle, and spitting: *p. nov. nar.* 70.

Spediment, quickly, speedily.

Specifier, to make mention of.

Les Spousells, the Marriage.

Spolier, to make spoil, also to strip one.

Spoliation, spoiling.

Spinster, an addition to all unmarried Women, from the Viscounts Daughter, downwards, but in the 2d part of the *Instit.*, *fol.* 668, Sir *Edward Coke*, says that *Generosa*, to those who may claim, is a more proper addition, and for want thereof, an Indictement, &c. may be quashed; this is cited by *Blount.*

S T.

Stable, firm, constant; *stall*, idem, and established.

Staunche, sound, firm, whole.

Stanlawe, a rocky Mountain or Hill: *p. Coke, Instit.* 4.

Stirile, barren, fruitless.

Stigmatiser, to burn with a hot Iron.

Stimuler, to stir up, to provoke.

Stagne, a Pool, a Pond, a Lake.

Stange, idem.

Sterver, Death; *ce sterveth*, it dieth.

Le steppes, the way, the path.

Ensuera le hue & steppes, to follow or pursue the cry: *p. Fitzh.* 168, *a.*

Stipuler, to interrogate, to demand, to undertake, to agree with: *p. Plowd. Com.* 82, *b.*

Stipulations, Agreements, Covenants.

Un Stipulateur, an Agent, an Attorney.

Les stirpes, the roots.

Stoure, stocked; *stoure cum Avers*, stock'd with Cattle.

Stow, a House, *saxon.*

Le ſtreat, the way, the ſtreet.

En haut ſtreat, in the High-way.

Straict, diſtracted; *homme ſtraict*, a Man out of his Wits.

Streitment, ſtrictly; *ſtraitment*, idem.

Stupid, drowſy, ſenſeleſs, amazed, drowzineſe.

Studieux, ſtudious.

Sturroit, put, alſo forced.

Stultifier, to make a Fool: *rep*. 4. 125, *a*.

Le Style, the manner; *le ſtyle deſcrive*, the manner of Writing.

Stiptick, binding, coſtive; *ſtiptique*, idem.

Stultifier, to make fooliſh: *p. Coke*, 4 *rep*. 123.

S U.

Sua, ſued, impleaded.

Sue, followed: *p. Brit*. 101, *b*. Alſo become, and to ſeem to be.

Jeo ſue, I am: *p. Brooks grand Abr*. 169. Alſo I was: *p*. 1 *Hen*. 7, 10, *b*.

Bien ſue, well followed; *ſuaſt hors*, hath ſued out: *Plowd. Abr*. 7, *a*.

Suant, & *ſuante*, following.

Subſequer, to follow.

Suader, to perſwade, to adviſe.

Subtraher, to withold; *ſubſtrahe*, witheld, drawn back.

Subit, forthwith, preſently.

Suborner, to inſtruct, or cauſe another to ſwear falſely; *ſuborne*, ſuborned.

Swave, vide *ſuave*, ſweet.

Soudainement, ſuddenly, inſtantly.

Subjuger, to overcome, to ſubdue.

Sublime, high, honourable, lofty.

Submerger, to drown, to oveflow.

Submerge, overflown, drowned: *p. Coke*, 5. 106.

Subroguer, to make a Deputy; *ſurroguer*, idem, and to act in anothers place, by his authority.

Le ſubſtitu, he that is ſo appointed or authorized.

Subterfuges, ſleights, cunning, craftineſs.

Subridendre, to ſmile, to laugh behind anothers back in ſcorn.

Subvertir, to overthrow.

Suc, juice; *ſucement*, ſucking; *ſucer*, to ſuck.

Succider, to cut.

Succidier, to ſucceed; *ſucceder*, idem.

Jeo ſue, I have been: *p. Crompton*. 23.

Si jeo ſuis, if I am.

Que jeo meſme ſue, than I my ſelf have: *p*. 2 *Hen*. 7, 15, *a*.

Sues, ye ought: *p. Coke rep*. 6. 45.

De ſuer, to follow, alſo to ſweat, to ſue.

On eſtre ſues, have been ſued or proſecuted.

Voil

Voil suer, will prosecute: 12 *Hen.* 8. 4.

Suerie, sweat; *suant*, sweating.

Un succes, an event, chance, hap.

Ne suffist, it sufficeth not

Il suffist, it is enough; *suffit*, idem; *ut suffit*: *p. Brit.* 120, *b.*

Sufferance, permission, leave. Tenant at sufferance, is he who holdeth beyond or over his term at first granted without disturbance.

Suffisament, & *sufficientment*, sufficiently.

Suffre, to suffer; *soeffre*, idem.

Suffreit, doth suffer; *suesfrire*, idem. *p.* 3 part *Instit.*

Suient, they serve: *p. Brit.* 3.

Feasant suist a son Molyn, doing suit to his Mill: *p. Parkins*, 134, *b.* Also, *suist*, he sueth; *pur son suist*, for his suit: *p. eund.* 17, *b.*

Sugets, subjects; *sujets*, idem.

Jeo que suis, I that am.

Suis, am; *jeo suis mort*, I am kill'd: *p. Coke*, 9, 120.

Per mains tiens suis, by hands held up: *p. Plowd.* 129, *b.*

En suis, upwards, above, *p. Mirror.*

Suis dits, above said; *suist dit*, aforesaid; *part*, 63.

Suis faits, above done, or made: *p. eund.* 217, *b.*

Ou de suis, or above: *p Termes de Ley.* 9, *a.*

A luy prender suis, to take him up: 20 *Hen.* 7, 2. *a.*

Suivant, following; *suivants*, followers, servitors: *p. Coke*, *rep.* 9, 120. *A suiver*, to follow: *p. eund.* 10, 73.

Suffist, it sufficeth.

Summariment, briefly, chiefly.

Summament, especially: *rep.* 3, 73, *b.*

Sumerger, vide *soubmerger*; idem.

Sullings, Elder-trees; *alneti*, idem.

Superbe, Proud; *superbitie*, Pride.

Suprimer, to suppress, also, to take away.

Suprime, suppressed.

Sur, upon; *sus*, idem; also against: *Coke*, 9, 120.

Sullerye, a plow Land: *p.* 1st. part, *Instit.* 5.

Sur toutque, and above, or before all.

Surder, to arise; *surdans*, arising; *surdant*, idem.

Surderoit, should arise: *p. Mores*, *rep.* 342.

Surde, arose,

Superficie, the outer-most part of any thing.

Supputation, reckoning, counting.

Surachater, to over buy.

Surcharger, to over lade; *surcharge le Comen*, to overstock the Common.

Sur-

Surcesser, to leave off; *ne sursessera*, shall not omit, or leave off; *surcease*, over stay.

Surdirent, they were risen; *surdant*, arising.

Surdus, deaf,; *surds*, idem; *surdite*, deafness.

Surmitter, to suppose, to surmise; *surmitte*, surmised, *p. 1 Edw.* 5, 3; *surmittant*, surmising.

Surmittera, shall surmise.

Ne surmittera, shall not be supposed.

Surmit, put upon; *el ad surmitte*, she hath put her self upon: *p. Coke*, 5, 10, *b*.

Surjetter, to cast over; *surjettement*, casting over.

Surmounter, to overcome.

Surnom, a firname; *surnosme*, idem.

Le surpluis, the remainder, over.

Surprins, taken before one is aware.

Sursemer, to sow upon.

Surrounder, to drown; *surround*, drowned.

Destre en peril surround, to be in danger of drowning.

Surround mesme, drowned himself: *p. Plowd.* 258, *a*.

Sursanes, putrid, rotten: *p. Brit.* 33, *a*.

Surque, whereupon.

Sursist, forbore, neglected: *p. Brit.* 52, *a*.

Survequist, & *survesquest*, he surviveth: *p. Coke*, 8, 88, *b*, & *Plowd. Com.* 252, *b*.

Survivre, to survive, in Mod. *French*.

Sus, idem; *ut sur*.

Susteiner, to uphold.

Susciter, to raise up, to stir up.

Suspense, doubt; *estre suspense*, to be in doubt.

Suspectes, suspected.

Suspendue, hanged.

Sustreits, & *sustrits*, withheld, withdrawn.

Suthdit, hereafter said, or here under said, also following.

Suthtry, withdrawing; *sustrete*, withdrawn.

Un suter, a shoemaker; *seuter*, idem: *p. 3 Hen.* 7. 1, *a*.

Survesque, survived.

Surveyer, to view, to look earnestly upon.

Surlary, salary: 50 *Edw.* 3. 21, *a*.

Suyvre, to follow; *suyvant*, following.

Le jour suivant, the day following.

Suye, followed: *p. nov. nar.* 62. also sued.

Swanimote, a Court of the Forests.

Suyte, a Train following; *tout de suyte*, following all in order.

S Y.

Synistre, the left, vide *sinistre*.

Symerement, purely, simply, sincerely.

Synod, an assembly of the Clergy.

Synodal,

Synodal, pertaining to ſuch aſſembly.

Syre, Sir, Father.

T A.

Un T*Abor*, a ſmall Drum uſed by Pipers; *tabour*, idem.

Tache, tied, knit, fixed unto.

Un Tacke, in the North, ſignifies a Farm: *p. Coke*, 1, 5.

Tacher, in Mod. *French*, is to ſpot, or ſtain.

Tacite, ſilent, not expreſſed in words.

Taciſſer, to cough.

Tailler, to cut off, to dock, alſo to notch.

De Tailer un Villain, the taking or recovery of a Villain departed.

Taile, recovered: *p. Kitch.* 99, *b.*

Taillours des Aimons, Cutters of Diamonds: *p. Stat. Art. ſup. Chartas*, *Cap.* 20.

Taille, notched, cut.

Tailles, Acquittances, Diſcharges, *p. Fitzh. Juſtice*, 199, *a.*

Tailes, idem.

Tailler les Arbres, to crop Trees.

Tailer, in Mod. *French*, *eſt quaſi couper*: *p. Plowd.* 251.

Un bois taillez, a Wood, or Copſe uſed to be cut, ſuch as *Silva Cedue*; *tailliz bois*, under-wood.

Tais toy, hold thy peace, be ſilent.

Taire, to be ſilent, to hold ones peace.

Qui eſt taiſt, he who is ſilent.

Tani, Freeholders; *Tainlands*, Freeholders-land.

Tanche poiſſons, Tench Fiſhes.

Tanque, ſo long, until.

Tantadire, as much as to ſay.

Tantſolement, only, only ſo.

Tantolement, idem.

Tant ſoit peu, how little ſoever it be.

Tanque, until; *tanc*, idem.

Tant, as, foraſmuch, until, ſo, how, which.

Tant Impudente, with what Impudence.

Tant petit, ſo little, as little.

Tant come, as much as.

Tantamount, idem.

Tantoſt, forthwith, preſently; *tantoſt*, idem.

Tantoſtque, ſo ſoon as: 29 *Hen.* 6, 1, *a.*

Tarde, late; *trop tarde*, too late.

Pluis tarde, very late.

Tarder, to delay, *vide targer.*

De temps tardiſe, of late times.

De tardif temps, idem; *tantius*, idem.

Tardant, ſtaying, lingering, long.

Tardement, flowing, ſlackening.

Home

Home tardif, a ſlow Man.

Tare, droſs, waſt in Goods, or Merchandizes.

Targer, to ſtay, to abide, to tarry or delay.

S'il targer, if he ſtay; *targement*, ſtaying.

Targeſt, ſtaid, hindred.

Un Targete, a Shield; *Targue*, idem.

Un Taſſe, a cock or heap; *un Tas*, idem, alſo a ſtack or rick

Taſſes, cocks, heaps, alſo ſheaves; *per taſſes*, by heaps, or cocks.

Mettre tout en un Taſſe, to put all in one cock or heap.

Un Taſs a boir, a Cup to drink out of.

Un Taverner, a Vintner.

Tauntoſt, *p. Brit.* 137. & *alijs locis*, is put for when as, that then, and ſo oft.

Taxer, to tax, to rate, to put a value on.

Un Taulpe, a Mole, a Wont.

Taure, a Bull.

Tayl, Payment, Tally; *ſans fair tayl*, without making payment.

Per Tayl, by Tally: *p. Greg.*

T E.

Teſt, covered; *toiſt*, idem.

Le teſt d'un Meſe, the covering, or the roof of a Houſe.

Teigner, to hold; *teign*, held.

il ceo Teignoit, he ſhould hold.

Soy Teign, held himſelf; *Teygne*, idem, *ut teign*; *tenus*, idem.

Teil, ſuch; *tel*, idem, vide *tiel*.

Le teirce, the third; *teircement*, thirdly.

Teinſt, died, coloured; *teincture*, colouring.

Tellement, ſuch like, in ſuch ſort.

Temeraire, raſh; *temeritie*, raſhneſs.

Temerairement, raſhly.

Temeratement, idem. *p. Coke, rep.* 10, 40.

Un Temple, a Church.

Le temps, the time, *bon temps*, good time.

Il eſt maintenant temps, it is now time.

Long temps devant, long time before.

Perdre beau temps, to loſe a fair opportunity.

Ce temps ci, this preſent time.

Tende, offered: *p. nov. nar.* 32. *b.*

Tend, bended; *tendu*, idem.

Tend arc, bow bent; *tendiſt*, tendered.

Tenebres, darkneſs.

Tenellata Domus, a Caſtle.

Tenir, to hold; *ne teniſt*, & *ne tenſiſt*, he ought not to hold, not held: *p. nov. nar.* 46, *a.*

Teneres, ye ſhall hold; *tenomus*, we hold: *p.* 20 *Hen.* 7, 5, *b*,

Tenir pur suspect, to have in suspition.

Tien, taken, held.

Tenus, bound, also held; *tenues*, idem.

Tenue, thin; *tenuement*, thinly, also weakly.

Terre, Ground, Land, Earth.

Un Terrier, a particular in writing of several Lands, with buttals and boundaries.

Testmoigner, to bear witness, to give evidence; *un Testmoigne*, a Witness.

En Testemoinance, in witness: *p.* 2d part *Coke*, Institut. 639.

Testmoignant, witnessing; *testimoignant*, idem.

Tesmoignes, Witnesses: *p. Kitch.* 66, *b.* Also testimonies.

Testimoign al porter, to bring witness.

Testimoignage, testimony; *testimoignage que le Esprit appoint en un ascun*, i. e. Conscience.

Terminer, to end.

En Tessaunt, in witnessing: *p. Brit.* 242.

Est terme, is called.

Testament nuncupate, a Will by word of mouth, not put in writing, till after the Testator's Death.

Terrene, Earthly.

La Teste, the Head; *le Test*, idem.

T H.

Thack, thatch; *thak*, idem, *Saxon*.

Thanus Regis, a Baron: *p. Coke*, Instit. 1. 5, *b.*

Thewe, is a Cucking-stool: *Saxon*.

Thingus, a Knight, a Freeman, also a Noble.

Theyn, idem, *ut Thane*.

Then, a Servant: *p. Fleta. Lib.* 1. *Cap.* 47.

Theftbote, receiving stolen Goods.

T I.

Tiel, such; *tiels*, idem.

Tient, holdeth, keepeth.

Ils tient, they hold; *que tient*, who hold.

Tiendra, shall hold; *tiendront*, they hold.

Tien, thine; *ce la est tien*, this is thine.

Tien, is also put for *tinne*.

Tieis, the third, vide *teirce*.

A Timer, to fear; *timidiment*, fearfully.

Tieux, such; *tieux breifs*, such writs: *p.* 2d *partem. Institut.* 639.

Tinta, rung, as Bells are; *tinter*, to ring.

Tinters, Tinkers.

Un Tipler, an Ale-house-keeper.

Tirer, to draw, to pull, *tire*, drawn.

Tirant, drawing; *tira*, shall draw: *p.* 21 *Hen.* 7, 27.

Se tira en arriere, he drew himself back.

Se tirer pres, to draw himself near.

Tireurs,

Tireurs, de Ore, Gold-wier Drawers.

Tisser, to weave; *tisseur*, weaving.

Tissier, a Weaver.

Tissu, weaved.

T O.

Toddels de lane, tods of wool, *i. e.* 28 *l.* weight each.

Un Toge, a Gown; *togue*, idem.

Togues, & toges, Gowns.

Toge, is alſo a Coat or Cloke. *p. Brook's grand Abr.* 228.

Toft, ſoon; *plus toft*, as ſoon as.

Pluis toft que, rather than: *p. Plowd.* 185.

Doient pluis toft avec, ought ſooner to have, *vide toſt*.

Le Toict, the roof or covering of a Houſe: *vide Tect.*

Toll'd, barred; *tollent*, they are barred or took away, alſo they take away.

Eſt tolle, is taken away: *p. Plowd. abr.* 21, *b.*

Un Toile, a ſnare; *toil*, idem, alſo a net or gin.

Tolnet, toln, & toll, a duty taken for grinding Corn, alſo for paſſage in ſome places.

Ad Tolle, hath taken away: *Termes de Ley*, 4. *b.* *Tollir*, idem, alſo to make void.

Tolt, is a Writ to remove a real Action out of a Court Baron, to the Sheriffs Tourne, which may afterwards be removed from thence, by a Writ called a *Pone*, into the common Bench, and the Tenant may remove it by *Recordare*.

Tome, a Volume, a great Book.

Ton, thy; *ton corps*, thy Body: *p. Brit.* 94, *b.*

Tonder, to ſhare, to clip, to ſhave.

Un Tondour, a Barber; *Tondure*, idem.

Tondure, ſhaved; *il tonde*, he ſhav'd, or barb'd: *Coke*, 4, 80.

Tonſure, ſhaving.

Tonner, to thunder.

Tonnel, a Veſſel, or Vat: *p. Crompt. Jur. Cur.* 68, *a.*

Torcious, wrongful; *torcenouſe*, idem. *p. Brit.* 68, *b.*

Tourcoiuſment, wrongfully; *tort*, wrong.

Tourcenouſes, wrongs; *a tort ou a droit*, by right or wrong.

Tors chemin, the wrong way, out of the way.

Toſt, rather, preſently, quickly; *ſi toſt*, as ſoon as.

Un Toſale, a Hog-ſtie: *p. Coke*, 9. 58.

Totalement, wholly, effectually, altogether.

Toucher, to touch; *touchant*, touching.

Tourbes, turfs: *p. nov. nar.* 13, *b.*

Tozaile, a Brick-kilne, or chimney: *p. Kitch.*

Toſaile, idem.

A Tour, to compaſs about; *a Tower*, idem.

Un Toor savage, a wild Bull: *p. nov. nar.* 66, *b*.

Tout, all, altogether; *tout un*, all one.

Tout, the whole; *tout foits*, always; *tout temps*, idem; *du tout*, in the whole; *tout autant*, even as, *a touts*, to all: *Brit.* 77, *b*.

Tout par tout, every where; *tout a pluis*, at most.

Tout incontinent, by and by.

Au tout, or more, *p. Stat. Art. sup. Chartas*, Cap. 15.

Tounders de barbits, Sheep-shearers: *p. Brit.* 33, *a*.

La Toux, the Cough; *en tousant*, in coughing,

Un Toyson, a fleece of wool: *p. Termes Ley*, 6, *a*.

Toy, thee, thou; *avec toy*, with thee.

Toy mesme, thy self; *a toy mesme*, to thee, to thy self.

T R.

Le Trac, the trace or path of Man or Beast.

Tracasser, to range, to rome up and down.

Tracement, seeking after, traceing.

Tradicire, to translate.

Trader, to deliver unto.

Traffique, Commerce, Trade.

Traits, & *Tracts*, things drawn.

Traher, to draw, *traicter*, idem.

Trahe, drawn, brought.

A Travers, athwart, across.

Tray, drawn: *p. Plowd.* 272, *a*.

Treyne, idem; *p. Brit.* 16, *a*.

Trayeront lour espees, they drew their Swords: *p. Plowd.* 98.

Trahe al bar, brought to the Bar, also drawn at the Bar: *p. Termes, Ley*, 74, *b*.

Treit, doth draw; *traict* idem; *pur traher*, for Drawing; *ne tray*, not drawn.

Traitment, Drawing.

Trahir, to betray; *Trahison*, Treason.

Traison, idem; *trahi*, betrayed, in Mod. *French*.

Trans, over, also cross.

Trans chimin, cross the way, over the way.

Traverser, to go cross-wise, or over-thwart, also to contradict, to deny, oppose.

Travaile, work, trouble, vexation; *travayle*, idem: *p. nov. nar.* 5.

Traversera, shall oppose or traverse.

Traversant, opposing, traversing, also putting upon trial or issue; *un travers*, idem.

A Travers, a cross: *p. Kitch.* 43, *a*.

A travers mon chimin, a cross my way: *p. Fitzh. nat. br.* 184, *b*.

Traverres, ye cross over.

Transcrire, to write over.

Transmuer, to change.

Transgresser, to do trespass.

Treyte, idem, *ut treit*; *treit son*

Cotel,

Cotel, he drew his Knife: *p. Coke*, 9, 13.

Treits, withdrawn: *p. Plowd. abr.* 17, *b.*

Treat, idem; *p. Greg. ut treit.*

Un Trebuchet, a Pit-fall, or Snare: *p. Kitchin*; also a Tumbrel or Cucking-stool: *p. Cokes* 3 part *Institut.* 39.

Trebucher, to fall down, also to offend: *p. Coke, rep.* 9. 13.

Trencher, to dig, to cut; *trenches*, maims, wounds, cuts.

Le Trenche, the Ditch: *p.* 12 *Hen.* 8, 2.

Trenche lui en le Gule, cut his Throat.

Jeo ne trenchera, I shall not dig.

Trenche a tout, it strikes at all, or it has relation to all: *p. Fitzh.* Justice, 39, *b.*

Il trenche, it enureth unto: *p. Plowd.* 316.

Ne trent lieu icy, it shall not take place here, *p. eund.* 42, *b.*

Trencha, it strikes at, or sticks unto: *p.* 13 *Hen.* 7. 21, *b.*

Que trenche, which falls to, or takes place: *p. Coke*, 5, 24, *b.*

Trenty, thirty; *trentieme*, the thirtieth.

Trent, also thirty. *p. Plowd.* 326, *a.*

Troyseime, thirty, *p. termes Ley.*

Tres foitz & foits, thrice, also three times.

Tresieme, the thirteenth.

Trentiseme, the thirtieth.

Treturement, traitourously.

Trestons, every one: *p. Brit.* 171, & 91, *b.* Also the more part: *p eund*, 145, *a.*

Trestons le ferries, every of them shall bear or carry: *p. nov. nar.* 8, *a.*

Ewes Tresturnes, Waters turned: *p. Brit.* 32, *b.*

Treyteront, they drew, they traced.

Treyner & pendue, drawn and hanged.

Tres beau, very fair; *tres bon*, very good.

Tres bien, excellent: *p. Plowd. preface.*

Tres cher, very dear; *tres hastivement*, very quickly: *Tres* is always used in the superlative degree, as *tres haut*, most high.

Trois, three; *trois cents*, three hundred.

Troize, & tresieme, thirteen.

Troisiesme, the thirteenth: *Coke*, 9. 74.

Troessent, they find: *p. Brit.* 117, *a.*

Le Troue, the Beam of Scales: *p. Coke*, 8, 46.

Tronage, Passage, or Carriage by Barges, &c.

Trope, too, also, too much; *trope tarde*, too late; *trope chare*, too dear.

Un trope tost faict, an over-hasty act.

Trope dure, too hard: *p. Plowd. ab.* 13, *a.*

Trom-

Tromper, to beguile, to deceive.

Trocquer, to barter, to exchange.

Troc, bartering, changing.

Un troupe di Haleques, a shole of Herrings.

Troupe, is put for many, or a multitude.

Trover, to find: *troveres*, ye shall find; *troverount*, they find.

Trove, found; *trovers*, idem; also ye find.

Trovours. Finders; *trovors*, idem.

Pour trover, for finding: *p. Davies, Rep.* 4.

Troveurs, things found: *p. Brit.* 7, *b.*

Un Trowe, a Sow: *p. Greg.* 324, *b.*

Al Trowe, to the Sow: *p. eund.*

Truye, in Mod. *French*, is put for Sow.

Tromperies, vain foolish frauds, cheats.

Ne Truff, he cannot find.

T U.

Un Turbarie, a place where turfs are digg'd: *p. nat. brev.* 183. *A fower turbes*, to dig turfs.

Un Tunicle, a Coat: *p. Park.* 170. *tunicel*, idem.

Tuer, to kill, or slay; *le tuer*, the killing.

Este tue, to be killed; *Tuors*, Slayers.

Tuers, idem; *tua*, killed, slain.

Ne Tuast, he should not kill; *tuast*, also, had killed, *qui est tue*, who is slain; *tueront*, they killed.

Tuerie, slaughter; *tuement*, slaying.

Tutele & Tutel, Government, Guardianship: *p. Plowd.* 293 *b.*

Pur Tuition, for Instruction, also for safegard.

Pur Tutele, idem.

Twaite, Wood grubbed up, and Land made arable.

Tumber, fell down: *Coke*, 9. 120.

Twesdie. vide *Mardie.*

T Y.

Tyent, they held; *tynt*, holden: *p. Brit.* 246.

Un Tyrount, a cruel Lord.

Tyelx, such: *p. Coke*, 6, 52. *b.*

Tyrannuquement, tyranically.

El Tyent, she held: *p. Fitzh. Justice*, 19, *a.*

V A.

VA, go; *va devant*, go before.

Jeo va, I go; *tu vas*, thou goest; *il va*, he goeth; *va per cy*, go this way.

Va, va, go, be gone; *vaer*, to go.

De Vaer, idem: *p. Plowd. abr.* 15, *a.*

Vaont,

Vaont, they go; *vaera*, shall go.

Va pur le voy, go by the way.

Vaant, going; *vaount*, idem.

Que vaant, who go.

Vacant terre, waste ground.

Vache, a Cow, or Heifer.

Vacarie, a Dairy; *vaccaria*, idem; or a Cow-house: *p.* 4 parte *Coke*, 86.

Un Vache sterile, a barren Cow.

Vaches, Cows.

Vail, under *Tenant paravaile*, an under Tenant.

Vagabond, one who hath no place of Habitation.

Vadelets, Men-servants, Officers of houshold: *p. nat. brev. Fitzh.* 230.

Valet & Varlet, idem. *ut vadelet.*

Vagueront, they wander.

Ne vaile, nothing worth, of no value: *p. Brit.* 24. *a.*

En vailance, in value: *p. eund.* 138.

Vaisselle, a Vessel.

Vanter, to boast; *se vanter follement*, to insult or boast foolishly; *vanterie*, boasting,

De Valoir, of worth, of value.

Ne vault, it avails not; *ne vaut*, idem.

Vaulte, worth, value: *p. Parkins*, 115.

Vault riens, it nothing avails: *p.* 26 *Hen.* 8. 4. *b.*

Le Valure, the worth.

Valuist, valued.

A la vailance, to the worth: *p. nov. nar.* 40.

Il vaust, it goeth, it enureth.

Vaont, they go: *p. Coke*, 8, 18.

Vanie, vanished; *p. Terms Ley*, 55. *b.*

Vant, when: *p. eund.* 99. *a.*

Varier, to differ, to disguise, to change.

Varia, shall change.

Ne variera, shall not alter, or change.

Vast, wast; *vastant*, wasting.

Vancre, to overcome, to win, to vanquish.

Vanque, vanquished, overcome.

Vanquise, overcome: *p. Coke*, 10. 24.

Values arguments, Arguments of force or weight.

Valider, to confirm, to strengthen.

Estre pluis valable, to be of more force.

Valitude, health: *p.* 12 *Hen.* 8, 4. *a.*

Vacant, void, empty; *un Benefice vacant*, a Church void of an Incumbent.

Varectum, fallow ground: *Coke*, 5, 15.

Vassalage, vide [*Villeinage.*

Vau, a Valley or Vale.

Vaulx, Valleys, Vales.

Un Vaultenant, an Unthrift, one that is nothing worth.

Vaudra, shall go: *p. Brit.* 95 *a.*

V E.

Un Veau, a Calf; *chare de veau*, Veal.

Veaus, Calves: *p. Fitz. nat. br.* 69, *a.*

Nous ne veerons, we hinder not, nor ſtay: *p.* Stat. *Glouc.* Cap. 8.

Vegle, blind, alſo *a veile*: *p. Kitch.* 174. *a.*

Le vele, the ſhadow: *p. Plowd. Com.* 64.

A veir, to ſee, to behold.

Vous veies, ye ſee.

Doit veier, ye might ſee.

Veiſte, ſee ye; *veit*, he ſeeth; *veyet*, idem.

Poies veier, ye may ſee.

Veiſt, he hath ſeen; *veiomus*, we ſee.

Veieres, ye ſhall ſee; *il vieaſt*, he hath ſeen: *p. Plowd.* 17. *b.*

Le vee, the force: *p. Brit.* 55. *b.*

Veet, he goeth: *p. eund.* 176. 6.

Vee, *p. Mirror*, is forbidden, Cap. 2. Sect. 16. *vide* 2d parte *Inſtit. Coke*, 141.

Veif, a Widow; *vefve*, idem in Modern *French.*

Vefues, Widows: *p. Termes de Ley.* 160. *b.*

Veifuage, Widowhood.

Veign, come; *veignont*, they come.

Deveignomus, we become.

Veignera, ſhall come; *veignants*, coming.

Veiller, to watch, to look to.

Veilles, old; *p. nov. nar.* 50.

Veillement, ſeeing, watching, viewing.

Veillant, idem.

Ou veieſtes, where you ſee, or find.

Veoir, in Mod. *French*, to ſee.

Le Veirge, the Circuit or Bounds limited to the King's Court; *i. e.* twelve Miles round the ſame.

Veiſyns, Neighbours: *p. Brit.* 112. *b.*

Le veia, the ſight; *le veve*, idem.

Veia, ſeeing: *p. Park.* 167. *b.*

Vei, ſaw.

Veer, to ſee: *p. Brit.* 42. to view.

Veiſnus, we have ſeen.

Veie, ſee; *veye*, idem: *p. Brook, gr. abr.* 321.

Veieſtes? did you ſee?

Vellours, Velvet; 12 *Hen.* 8, 3. *b.*

Velloit, he will; *ne voylant*, they will not.

Veyl, will.

Venaunts, coming: *p. Park.* 114.

Venaiſon, Veniſon.

Vendenges, Vintages: *p.* Stat. *Weſtm.* 1 Cap. 51.

Veniſmus, we come.

A Vender, to ſell; *vendre*, idem.

Eſt Vendue, is ſold; *pour vender*, for ſale.

Vendus,

Vendus, ſold; *un vendour*, a ſeller.

Vendible, ſaleable; *vendition*, ſelling.

Sale, idem. *p. Coke* 5. 90, *b.*

Vente, idem. *en vente*, in ſale.

Ventes, Woods marked for ſale.

Venderdie, *Friday*; *vendredie*, idem.

Venredi, idem. and *p. Fitzh. Juſt.* 146.

Venerdy, & *venerday*, idem.

Vengeance, revenge.

Venelle, a Lane; *venelles*, Lanes.

Vener, to hunt; *un veneur*, a Huntſman.

Veneric, hunting.

Venir, to come, to approach unto; *en temps*; *vener*, in time to come.

Doient venir, they ſhould or ought to come.

Poit venir, may come, *voet venir*, would come, *ſont venu*, are come; *venients*, coming: *p. Kitch.* 17, *a. venera*, ſhall come.

Venies, coming; *veniſent*, they ſhould come.

Veniſtes, ye have come; *venus*, come.

Venuſt, he had come: *p. Plowd. com.* 268, *a.*

Venime, poyſon.

Le Vent, the Wind; *ventier*, to blow Wind.

Vent, *p. nat. brev.* 48, is ſale or ſold.

Ventilent, they blow: *p. Cromp. Jur. Cur.* 88, *a.*

Ventre, a belly; *venter*, idem.

Il vente, it bloweth.

Venteux, windy.

Verd, green; *verdir*, to wax green.

Vert, alſo green, alſo whatever beareth Leaves, or is green within the Foreſt, *p. Kitchin* 59. and ſometimes taken for Veniſon.

Vert bois, live Wood: *p. eund.* 170.

Verdoyer, to be green; *verdoyant*, flouriſhing.

Verdeur, greeneſs.

Verge, a Wand, rod, alſo a yard.

Del venue, of the coming or appearing.

Verayment, truly; *verament*, idem.

Vrament, idem; *verage*, true; *verye*, idem.

Verye tenant, the true lawful Tenant.

Veray, idem. ut *verye*.

Verreis, truth: *p. Brit.* 106, *b.*

Verreyes, idem: *p. eund.* 12. *b. vereye*, true: *p. eund. very*, true: *p. Plowd.* 199. *a.*

Veritie, truth; *veritable*, truly.

Vierge, vide *verge*.

Viergier, he that carries the ſtaff or rod in Cathedral Churches.

Verrons, ſeeing, *verront*, they ſee: *p. Brit.* 106, and 25, *Edw.* 1.

Verſer

Verser, to turn, alſo to pour out; *vers*, towards; *vers le fin*, towards the end; *vers que*, againſt whom: *p. Coke* 5, 77. *a.*

Regard vers moy, look towards me.

Vervactum, fallow ground: *p. Coke* 5. 15.

Veſquirent, they live: *p.Brit.* 77. *b.*

Veſcie & veſce, Vetches, a ſort of Pulſe.

Auters ves, otherways: *p. Coke rep.* 5. 33. *b.*

Le Veſpre, the Evening; *veſpers*, evening prayers.

Veſtes, waſt; *vaſtes*, idem. and waſt ground.

Veſture, clothing, alſo the herbage of Ground growing thereon; *veſtir*, to cloath, to put on.

Veſtiments, Garments, alſo the Wood growing on Land.

Veſter, to be, to veſt, to enure.

Veſtre, your; *veſtre demandes*, your requeſts.

Le Veſtrye, the place for laying the Prieſts Veſtments and Ornaments of the Church, and alſo where the Civil affairs of the Pariſh are diſcuſſed.

Le Veſtiare, idem.

Un veu, a Vow; *veu*, is alſo ſeeing, alſo ſeen: *p. Brit.* 223.

Veu que, for as much.

Veut, would; *le Roy le veut*, the King wills it.

Il veult, he will; *veut*, idem.

Jeo vey, I ſee; *veyet*, he ſees; *jeo veiw*, I have ſeen; *veyant*, ſeeing; *veyeront*, they ſaw.

Veygner, to come; *ne veygneſſent*, they ſhould not come: *p. Nov. nar.* 53, *a.*

Veyn, void, frivilous: *p. Brit.* 3, *a.*

Veſte, ſetled: *p. Coke rep.* 5, 84, *b.*

Veſtue, idem; *Ceo veſtue*, veſted this: *p. Plowd. abr. de veſt*, put by.

Veyle, old: *p. Crompt Jur.* 175.

Vetere, old: *p. Broke Gr. abr.* 144, *a.*

Veus, auncient, alſo long ſince: *p. Brit.*

Veyſins, Neighbours, vide *veiſins.*

Veve, a Widow; *veves*, Widows.

Le veve, the ſight: *p.Cromp.* 54, *b.*

Veuſage, Widowhood: *p. Nov. nar.* 33, *b.*

Si un veyeſt, if one ſhould ſee: *p. Plowd.Com.* 98, *a.*

Vevers, Widowers.

Veyer eſt, is to be ſeen: *p. Coke* 5, 80.

Veux, vide *vieux.*

Veves de Frankpledg viewes of the Frankpledge: *Brit.* 27.

Veyeromus, let us ſee: *p. Plowd.* 19, *b.*

V I

Jay view, I have ſeen.

Viende,

Viands, repasts, sustenance, meat, &c.

Un Vichel, a Heyfer.

Vicaire, a Vicar; *Vicarie*, a Vicaridge.

Vicier, to corrupt; *vicie*, corrupted.

Vicont, a Sheriff; *vicount*, idem. *south vicont*, under Sheriff.

Vicountels, things whereof the Sheriff has cognizance in his Court.

Vicine, a neighbour; *vicinage*, neighbourhood.

Vicines & vicenes, Neighbours.

Viduity, Widow-hood.

Vie, Life; *il est en vie*, he is alive.

Vif, life; *viffe* living; *un vife home*, a live Man: *p. Plowd.* 262. *vies*, lives.

Viel, old; ancient; *vieul*, idem, *p. Coke* 5. 22.

Vieller, to wax old.

Viellement, anciently; *viellesse*, old age.

Vieulx, old, ancient; *vieux*, idem. & *vieul*, idem.

Un vierge, a Maiden.

Vief, vide *veve*.

Vient, they come; *il viet*, he cometh, also seeth.

Vient vous eins, come ye in.

Vieant, coming; *viendra*, shall come: *p. Coke* 6. 69.

Viel, seeth; *al vieront*, they look to.

Ad vieu, hath seen; *jeo aye view*, I have seen.

Vivement, lively.

La Vigile, the evening; *vigilance*, watchfulness.

La vielle, the evening.

Vigne, a Vine; *vignoble*, a a vinyard.

Vigueur, strength.

Vil, low, base; *vil pris*, a low price.

Villenage, a base tenure, whereby the Lords claim the Persons and Goods of their Villains.

Ville, a Town, a Village.

Vingt, twenty; *vint*, idem.

Vingtieme, the twentieth; *vinte*, idem. *vingt foits*, twenty times; *Vint quatre*, 24: *p. terms Ley*. 9.

Vinteront, they tie, or bind: *p. Plowd. Com.* 307.

Vin, Wine, *Vine*, idem.

En le vint, tierce, in the 23th *p. eund.* 105.

Un, one; *unisme*, the Eleventh; *ungjesme*, idem.

Un foits, once.

Unement, unanimously.

Virilement, manly, strongly.

Viseur, the Face; *le visage*, idem.

Viscount, vide *vicont*, & *vicomtels*.

Vise, seen; *Il visoit*, he seeth.

Visez vous, see you *p.* 1 *Edw.* 5. 3.

Viewes, seen: *p. Cromp. Jur.* 48.

Visinage, vide *vicinage*.

Vieffes, Widows: *p. Fitzh. nat. br.* 175. vide *veves*.

Vit, a Calf; *vitel*, idem. *vitule*, idem.

Vit is alſo Man's Yard.

Vinagre, Vineger.

Le viſne, the neighbourhood or place whence a Jury is ſummoned, the *venue* : *p. Coke* 5. 19.

Vivement, lively : *p. Plowd. abr.* 72.

Viffe, alive: *p. Brit. tit. wreck.*

Il viſt, he hath ſeen : *p. eund.* 4, *a.*

Viver, victual, diet: *p. nov. nar.* 45.

En viver & veſture, in meat, or eating, and clothing: *p. Stat. Glouc. cap.* 4,

Vivers, & vyvers, vivaria, Warrens, Parks, Fiſh-ponds, &c.

Un vivarie, a place where living things are kept, either in Land or Water : *2dem partem Coke Inſtit.* 100.

Vivands, vide *viands.*

Vivera, ſhall live, *vivara*, idem.

Vivre, to live, alſo living.

Lour viver, their living.

Come il vive, as he lives : *p. Coke* 5. 52.

Vive voys, by word of mouth : *p. Brit.* 131, *b.*

Vivies, victuals; *pour lour viver*, for their livelihood, *Coke* 8. 46.

Ul, any : *p. Stat. Weſtm.* 1 *cap.* 16.

U N.

Un foits, once ; *un*, one ; *ung*, idem.

Ung ou deux, one or another.

Ung Dieu, ung Roy, Cokes, Motto.

Unificence, making one, uniting.

Unement, only, unanimouſly, *Coke* 5. 16.

Unzieſme, the Eleventh, *unzime*, Eleven.

Uncore, yet, *unques*, idem. & *unquore*, idem : *p. Fitzh. nat. br.* 211.

Unque, ever ; *ne unques*, never.

Ne unque viet, he never ſaw.

Uniter, to put together, to join.

Uniement, equally, alſo in one, in union.

Ad uncore, hath yet : *p. Coke* 5. 7. *b.*

Un uln, an Ell in meaſure ; *un ulme*, idem.

Ulmes, Ells, alſo Elm Trees.

Umbre, the ſhadow.

Un meſme, the ſelf ſame, one and the ſame : *p. Coke* 5. 15, *a.*

V O.

Vodroient, they would : *p.* 3 *partem Inſtit.* 39.

De vocer, to call.

Voguer, to call again, alſo to return.

Voguement, paſſing, returning.

Voet, ſheweth forth, willeth, teſtifieth, alſo would : *p. Kitch. primo* and *p. Perkins*, 117, *b.*

Le Roy voet, the King willeth it, vide *veut*.

Vodra, would, *vodra aver*, would have.

Vodront, they would; *ne voet*, will not.

Voire, truly; *voier*, & *voiar*, idem: *p. Plowd. abr.* 6. *b.* also true.

Voirement, truly: *p. Coke*, 9. 47. *Voierment*, idem.

Vous ditz voier, ye said truly, or well.

Voire dire, to say or speak the Truth.

Est a voier, is to be seen: *p.* 14 *Hen.* 8, 1, *a.*

Voier, by *Brooks* Grand abridgment, is put for well and good; *voillet*, would; *voier*, true.

Voiez, vide *voy*, ye see: *p. Greg.* 327.

Voil, will; *voil porte*, will bring; *que il voile*, where he will.

Voilloms, we will: *p. Brit.*

Ne voilomus vener, we will not come.

Tenant a volunt, Tenant at will.

Voilont, they would; *voit*, he will.

Voilles, ye will; *voiet*, & *voet*, would,

Jeo voyes voluntaries, I would be willing.

Si voilet, if he should or would: *p. Plowd.* 379.

Voile, would: *p. Fitzh. gr. abr.* 77.

Ne voille, would not: 21 *Hen.* 7, 31, *b.*

Voiloit veier, would see; *si voit*, if he will.

Voille, will: *p. Coke*, 5, 25. *a.*

Voisines, Neighbours.

Ne voit me vener, he would not come to me.

Jeo voil, I will: *p.* 12 *Hen.* 8, 21, *b.*

Voilent, they would; *s'il voit nemy*, if he would or no; *voit este*, it would be: *p.* 14 *Hen.* 8, 4, *b.*

Voisinage, vide *vicinage*.

Voicine, idem, *ut vicine*.

La voix, the voice.

Voler, to fly; *il vole*, he flyeth: *p. Cromp.* 149.

Ne poient voler, they cannot fly.

Volatiles Royal, Birds Royal: *p. Coke*, 7, 16.

Nous voluns, we will: *p. Brit.* 1. *b.*

Volage, unconstant, unstable.

Volatiles de Ciel, Birds of the Air: *Coke*, 1. 134.

Bone Volour, good Will: *p. Plowd. Com.* 300. *b.*

Vomer, to vomit, also to plow.

Vomissement, vomiting.

Vorra, would: *p. Coke*, 6, 21. *a.*

Vostre, yours; *en vostre case*, in your case.

Vover, to vow; *vove*, a vow.

Voudront, they would, or should; *vodra*, should: *p. Mirror*, Cap. 2. Sect. 19.

Bien

Bien Voulant, good Will.

Vous, ye; *vous doies*, ye ought.

Vous estes, ye be; *vous fues*, ye were.

Vous aves, ye have, words used to Jurors when they appear on calling: *vous mesmes*, your selves.

Il Voucher, he calleth; *vouche*, calls, voucheth; *voucha*, shall call: *p. Park.* 183. *b.*

Vouche, is a Term used in common recoveries, when one is called to warrant Lands, *&c.*

Vouchent, they shall vouch, or call: *p. Brit.* 30.

S'il voet vouche bien save; if he would, bid him welcome: *p. Park.* 174.

Come voudra, as you will, or see good. *Vouloyt moildre*; would have grinded.

Voy ci, see here, see this, look ye.

Voyer, to see: *p. Cromp.* 220. *b.*

Voymus, we may see.

Un Voyager, a Traveller.

Voysent, they go, they be; also they go free, or are acquitted: *p. Brit.* 136. *b.*

Voysent sans jour, they go without further day: *p. eund.* 145, *a.*

Pais voisins, neighbouring Countries.

Ou voylant, or would: *p. Coke*, 6. 40. *a.*

Un Voy, a way or path; *voie*, idem.

Ceo voy, this way: *p. Plowd. Com.* 10. *b.*

Il est hors de la voye, he is out of the way; *va par voy*, go by the way.

Jeo voye, I see: 12 *Hen.* 8. 2. *b.* vide *voie.*

D'estre voye, to be seen: *p. Plowd. Com.* 102. *pr. an.* 1671.

Que voyle, which was: *p. Greg.* 284.

Hault voyes, High-ways; *voyes*, also means: *p. Termes de Ley*, 18. *b.*

Voyer, true, *vide voier.*

Par voyes feasant, for true making: *Coke*, 5, 63.

Nest pas voyer, it is not true.

Voyertie, Truth; *voyerment*, truly; *p. eund.* 5, 25.

Voyagement, travelling.

Jeo aye voye, I have seen: *Kitch.* 5. *a.*

Si un voyt, if one would: 2 *Coke*, 34.

U R.

Vray, true; *vrayment*, truly; *verament*, idem.

Ure, practice, use; *fortment ure*, strongly put or enforced: *Coke*, 5. 60. *a.*

Ure, burned; *soit ure*, may be burned.

Uera, shall burn.

Urera, shall enure, or be to the use.

Ne urera, shall not vest or work: *Park.* 131.

U S.

Vser, to use; *usa*, used, also useth.

Vsance, usage; *usont*, they used.

Vsage, custom, use; *solonque le usage*, according to the custom.

Vst, had, and had been: *p. Plowd. abr.* 12. *a.*

Vssomus, & *ussumus*, we had.

Vsses, ye had; *Jeo ussey*, I had: *p. Plowd. preface.*

Vssent, they had been; *ussont*, idem; & *ussont*, idem: *p.* 21 *Hen.* 7, 27. *b.* And *Coke* 8, 77. *b.*

Si *jeo ussey*, if I had: *Plowd. Com.* 160. *b.*

Que ils ussoient distes, that ye had said: *p. Coke*, 1. 106.

Vssoit estre, would be: *p. Plowd. abr.* 14.

Mes ussoit, but had he been: *p.* Termes *de Ley.*
75.

Vsure, Usury.

U T.

Vtleve, the escape of Felons: *p. Fleta*, Lib. 1. Cap. 47.

Le Vtes, & *utas*, the octaves, or the eighth Day after a Feast, &*c. Plowd. Com.* 227.

Vtensile, a thing of necessary use about or in a Family, or in Husbandry.

Henricus le ute, Henry the eighth: *p. Plowd.* 212. *b.*

Vtlage, Out-lawed, or one who is so, is out of the Protection of the Law: *Vtlages*, Persons that are Out-lawed:

Vtlaghe, idem, *ut Vtlage.*

Que Vtter, who give out, or publish; *uttermost*, outward.

Vtile, profitable; *utilement*, profitably.

Vtus, eight, the eighth day, in the old Books called, *Vstaves.*

V U.

V*uyder*, to make void, V*uide*, void.

Vulgaire, common, publick, also trivial.

Vulgairement, commonly.

Vulgarlie, commonly, also trivially.

V Y.

V*yncles*, bonds fetters: *p. nov. nar.* 21. *a.*

V*yne*, wine, vide *vin.*

V*ynt*, came, went, also attained.

Il V*ynt son age*, he attained his age.

V*yver*, a River, a Pond; V*yvers*, vide V*ivers.*

V*yent*, they came: *p. Coke, rep.* 6. 54. *a.*

W. W.

W*Arden*, vide *Gardien.*

Wacrus, corrupted, spoiled, tainted: *p. Brit.* 77. *a.*

Wainaga, gain, profit or benefit, especially by plowing and erring of land.

Wainable, that may be plowed or manured.

Waiva, left; *wave hors*, left out: *p. Termes Ley*, 358. *a. wavia*, idem.

Wallois, the Welsh People.

Waive, a Woman Out-lawed, the Law leaveth or waiveth her Protection.

Warectum, fallow Land; *wareccum*, idem: 1 *part Instit.* 5. *b.*

Weigher, to weigh.

Weyver, leaving.

Werust, doubt, *vide Awrust*: 32 *Hen.* 6. 19. *a.*

Wranglands, are pollard Trees, or crooked, and used to be cropt, not fit for Timber.

Un Windowe, a blank place, or space.

Wild & weld, a large woody place.

Wombes, Bellies.

Whote, hot, *Saxon.*

Wedues, Widows: *p. Brit.* 29. *b.*

Withernam, vide 2 *part. Institut. Coke*, 141. A taking other Cattle or Goods for what was before wrongfully taken, *&c.*

Wic, a place or dwelling on the bank of a River or Seashore: *p.* 1 *part Instit.* 4.

Wike, in *Essex*, is Farm.

Witenamot, or *witenagemot*, amongst the *Saxons*, was a great Convention like our Parliament or a meeting in Council of their chief wise Men.

Wold, a Plain, a Down, or open Country, Hilly, and void of Wood, as *Coteswold.*

Weald, is the contrary; *i. e.* a woody Country.

Worth, a watry place.

Y. Y.

Y', It, there; *y' est*, it is: *p. Plowd. Com.* 280. *b.*

Y' it is a Relative of things and places.

Y' sont, there are, they are: *p. eund.*

Y' soit, there be, be it so: *p. Fitzh. nat. brev.* 282.

Yalemaines, at the least, however: *Plowd.* 219.

En Ycel, in it; *il y ad*, there hath, also there is.

Sil y ad, if there hath; *Nat. brev.* 24. *b.*

De Ycel, of it, of the same.

Yceux, them; *en yceaux*, in them: *p. Mores Rep.*

Yeulx, Eyes, vide *Oils.*

Nous Yeux ont veves, we have lived to see it.

Ysoit, therein be: *Nat. brev. Fitzh.* 22. *b.*

Al Ycel, to it, to the same: *p. Crompt. Justice*, 19.

Y' aver, there were: *p. Greg* 182. Cap. 10.

Yver, Winter: *p.* 12 *Hen.* 8, 2. *a.*

Yeme

Yeme & *Yemali*, words anciently used for Winter, *viz. tempore Edw.* 3.

Fort grand Yver est aspre, a very sharp Winter.

Jour de Yver, a Winters day.

Froidare Yver, a frosty Winter.

Yvernagium, Winter season, or the Winters Seed-time; from *Hivernee*, Mod. *French.*

Yvises, services, service: *p. Fitzh.* Justice, 201. *a.*

Yvre, Drunk: *p. Plowd. Com.* 19. *a.*

Yveroynes, Drunkenness: *p. Brit.* 66. *a.*

Yverongnerie, idem in Mod. *French.*

Sur Yceaux & *yceux*, of them: *Plowd. preface.*

Il y a, there are: *p. Fitzh. preface* to his *natura brev.*

Il yra, he shall go: *p. Cromp. Jur. Cur.* 47.

Yeme, is often put for *Hyeme.*

Yeven & *Yeoven*, are put for given.

Yeman & *Yeoman*, from *Gemen*, a Teutonick word, signifying a common Person.

FINIS.

The Impressions of some of the Authors cited in this BOOK.

	Printed *Anno*.
Fitzherbert's *natura brevium*,	1567.
Fitzherbert's *Grand Abridgement*,	1516.
More's *Reports*.	1688.
Kitchin *of Courts*,	1592.
Britton *by* Wingate,	1640.
Dyer's *Reports*,	
Nove Narrationes,	1561.
Articuli Nar. & Diversite de Courts,	1551.
Coke's *fifth Part of his Reports*,	1624.
His sixth Part.	1621.
His seventh Part,	1629.
His eighth Part,	1626.
Plowden's *Abridgment*,	1607.
Gregorie's *Moote Book*,	1599.
Termes de Ley,	1641.
First Part of the Institutes,	1670.
Third and fourth Parts of the Institutes,	1644.
Brook's *Grand Abridgment*,	1576.
Edward *the* Vth's *Year Book*,	1559.
Richard *the Third*,	eod. Anno.
Henry *the seventh*,	1555.
Henry *the eighth*,	1556.
Henry *the sixth's*, 1st Vol.	1570.
Henry *the sixth's 2d* Vol.	1567.
The second Part of the Institutes,	1642.
Crompton's *Jurisdictions of Courts*,	1594.
Hobert's *Reports*,	
Fitzherbert's *Justice*,	1587.
Siderfin's *Reports*,	
Manwood	
Littleton's *Tenures*,	1585.
Parkins,	1541.
Mirrour of Justice.	
Plowden's *Commentaries at large*,	1571.
Lord Coke's *Rep. in one Volume*,	1672.
Philip's *World of words*,	1662.

Statutes in *French*, viz. Stat. *Westm.* 1. Stat. *Glouc.* Stat. Confirm. Chart. Stat. Art. sup. Chart. *Lambard's* Archeion. *Davies* Reports. *Yelverton's* Reports, Lib. Assizes.

THE

Law-Latin Dictionary:

BEING AN

Alphabetical Collection

OF

Such *Law-Latin* Words as are found in ſeveral *Authentic Manuſcripts* and *Printed Books* of *Precedents*;

WHEREBY

Entring-Clerks and others, may be furniſhed with *fit* and *proper* Words in a *Common Law Senſe*, for any thing they have occaſion to make uſe of, in *Drawing Declarations*, or any *Parts* of *Pleading*.

ALSO

A more *Compendious* and *Accurate Expoſition* of the *Terms* of the *Common Law*, (interſperſed throughout) than any hitherto extant; containing many *important Words* of *Art* uſed in *Law Books*.

Collected from the Best Authors.

LONDON,

Printed for *Iſaac Cleave*, at *Serjeants-Inn* Gate in *Chancery-Lane*; and *John Hartley*, over-againſt *Gray's-Inn* in *Holborn*. 1701.

TO THE
READER.

AMongst the several Authors of late that have imployed their time in Compiling Law Dictionaries, *none of them have taken care to furnish the* Pleaders *and* Entring-Clerks *with apt* Latin *Words, to insert in their* Declarations *and* Pleadings; *so that they have been most of them constrain'd to make use of common* Dictionaries, *and those that are mean Scholars, or bad Grammarians, have made use of Words of Equivocal Construction, very little to the purpose, not to be helpt by an* Anglice, *or* Anglice vocat' *(as they vainly imagine) of which many instances are frequently found in the late Reports.*

For Remedy of which Mischief for the future, I having been a Collector of Entries, *of* Declarations *and* Pleadings, *and Corrected the same; together with the* Entries *of Judge* Winch, *Serjeant* Thomson, *Mr.* Aston, *and the famous Mr.* Andrew Vidian, *for above thirty Years last past, have thought fit at last to Publish my Notes of such* Law-Latin *words, as occurr'd in my Reading the* Entries *above named, supplying the rest with select* Dictionary *words, which (as near as I could find) had but one genuine signification; and to make the Collection more compleat, have added to the same, an Exposition of the Terms of the* Law, *that all* Pleaders *(but the Country Clerks especially) may have in one Portable Volume, whatever is material to be understood upon this Subject.*

THE
Pleader's Dictionary.

A. B. A. B.

A Aron (a Man's name) *Aaron*, *onis*, m.

A B.

To abate, *Abato*, are. To enter into Lands, or to destroy or beat down.

Abatement, *Abatamentum*, *i*. n. *Co.Lit.* 277. Destroying, beating or pulling down an House, also the entering into Lands or Tenements by a Tortious or wrongful Title. Abatement is twofold, *viz.* abatement of the Writ, and abatement of the Action or Plaint, the causes whereof are these six, 1. Want of sufficient or good matter. 2. The matter not certainly alledged. 3. The Plaintiff Defendant, or place misnamed. (except in Assize, *vid. Dyer*, fol. 84. b. pl. 83. 84. *Plow.* fol. 90. a. b. 91. *a per Cur*) 4. Variance between the Writ, Specialty or Record, or between the Writ and the Action or Plaint. 5. Uncertainty, or want of Form in the Writ Count or Declaration. 6. Death of the Plaintiff or Defendant. Terms *del Ley.* fo. 1. b. *Dyer* fo. 175. *Pl.* 24. *Co. lib.* 5. fo. 61. a. b.

To *Abate* an House, *abatare Tenementum*. *i. e.* to destroy or Raze it down level with the Ground.

To *Abate* a Writ *Casso*, are. *i. e.* to destroy it by Pleading.

Abatement of a Writ. *Cassatio brevis*, *i. e.* when upon some default, the Plaintiffs Suit ceases for a time.

Abaft, the Poup or Stern, the hinder part of a Ship, *Puppis*, *is*, f. Abaft, towards the Poup, a *Puppi*, *à tergo*.

Abeiance, *abeiancia*, æ. f. *Spel.* 6. *Lex.* 1. *i. e.* Expectance *viz.* where the right of Fee-simple lies in Abeiance, that is, only in the remembrance, Intendment and consideration of the Law: For according to the general Rule or Maxim of the Law, there is Fee-simple in some person, or it is in Abeiance, *i. e.* in *nubibus* or Expectancy. *Co. Lit.* l. 3. c. 11. Sect. 646.

Abel (a man's name) *abel*, *lis*,

An Abbey, *abbatia*, æ. f. *abbathia*, æ. f. Lex. 1.

An Abbess, *abbatissa*, æ. f.

An Abbot, *abbas*, *atis*; m.

Abdias (a mans name) *Abdias*, æ. n.

Aberconway (in *Wales*) *Conovium* or *aberconovium*.

Aberdeen (in *Scotland*) *aberdona* and *aberdonia*, æ; f. *Davana*, æ; f.

B *Aber-*

Aberdore (in *Scotland*) *Aberdora*, æ; f.

Aberdour (in *Scotland*) *Aberdura*, æ; f.

Aberford (in *England*) *Carcaria*, æ; f.

Aberfraw (in the Isle of *Anglesey*) *Gadiva*, æ, f. ;

Abergavenny (in *Monmouthshire*) *Abergennium*, *Gobannium*.

Aberneth (in *Scotland*) *Abrenethæum*.

Abertivy (a River in *Wales*). *Ratostatybius*.

To *Abet*, *Abetto*, are. Ra. Ent. 24. *Spel.* 5. Lex. 1. *i.e.* To take part with or assist.

An *Abetting*, Abettans, *ntis*, an assisting.

Abetment, Abettum, i; n. *Pry.* 20. 33. 2 *Inst.* 383. 386. *Reg.* 134.

An *Abettor*, Abettator, oris; m.

Abigail (a Womans name.)

Abigail, Indec. or lis. f.

Abimilech (a Man's name.)

Abimilechus, i; m.

Abinadab (a Mans name.)

Abinadab. Indecl.

Abington (in *Berkshire.*)

Abindonia, or *Abendonia*, æ; f.

Abinoam (a Man's name.)

Abinoam. Indec.

To *Abjure* (Forswear.)

Abjuro, are.

Abjured (Forsworn.)

Abjúratus, a, um.

An *Abjuring* (Forswearing.)

Abjuratio, onis; f.

Abner, ris. m. (a Man's name.)

To be A-board, in Navi esse.

To go A-board, Navem conscendere.

To *Abolish*, Abóleo, ui. itum, *or* evi, etum.

Abolished, Abolitus, a, um.

To *Abort*, (miscarry) Abortio, ire.

Abortive, Abortivus, a, um.

An *Abortive Birth*, Abortus, ûs; m.

Above (beyond or more than the sum of, *&c.*) Ultra Summam.

Above (in a *Deed*) abovementioned, Superius mencionatus.

Above, *a Room*, Supra Rom eam

Abovesaid, Supradictus, a, um.

As Abovesaid, ut Supradictum est.

About, Circa.

Aboy (in *Ireland*) Aboya, æ. f.

Abraham (a Man's name.) Abrahamus, i; m.

To *Abridge*, Abridgio, are. *i. e.* To make shorter in words, holding still the same Substance; and sometimes it signifies the making a Declaration or count shorter by Substracting or Severing part of its Substance, as Abridgment of a plaint in Dower.

An *Abridgment* (short writing.) Abbrēviātura, æ; f.

Abroad (in the open Air, from home or not within) *Foris*. *Sub dio*, in Publico, or aperto. Subdialis, le.

To *Abrogate*, Abrŏgo, are. i. e. To disannul, take away, Repeal.

An *Abrogating*, Abrŏgātio, onis. f.

Abrogated, Abrŏgātus, a, um. i. e. Repealed.

Absalom (a mans name.)

Absalon, onis, m.

An *Abstract*, Abstractum, i; n.

Absurd, Absurdus, a, um.

Absurdly, Absurdè adv.

To

To *Abut*, Abutto, are. i. e. To bound or border upon.

Abutting, Abuttans, antis, partic. pres. Bordering upon.

Abuttaled, Abuttatus, a, um. *Spel.* 7. 1 *Mon.* 532. 2 *Mon.* 998.

Abuttalatus, a, um.

A. C.

Acceptance, Acceptantia, æ; f.

To *Accept*, Acceptor, aris.

Accessory, Accessorium, ii, *n. Fin.* 7. 1. Before the Offence or Fact, is he that commandeth or procureth another to do Felony, and is not there present when the other doth it; but if he be present, then he is also a Principal. 2. After the Offence, is he that Receiveth, Favoureth, Aideth, Assisteth, or Comforteth any Man that hath done any Murder or Felony, whereof he hath knowledge. He which Counselleth or Commandeth any Evil Thing, shall be judged Accessory to all that followeth of this Evil Act, but not of another distinct thing. In the lowest and highest Offences, there are no Accessories, but all are Principals, as in Riots, Routs, forcible Entries, and other Transgressions, *vi. & armis*, which are the lowest Offences: And so in the highest Offence, which is *Crimen lesæ Majestatis*, there be no Accessories, but in Felony there are both before and after. *Co. Lit. l.* 1. *c.* 8. *Sect.* 71.

Achilles (a Man's name) Achilles, ei, & is.

To *Acquit*, Acquieto, are. i. e. To discharge or keep in Quiet, and to see that the Tenant be safely kept from any Entries or Molestation for any manner of Service, issuing out of the Land to any Lord that is above the Mesn, hereof cometh *Acquital & Quietus est.* *i. e.* he is discharged, and he that is discharged of a Felony by Judgment, is said to be acquitted of the Felony, *Acquietatus de felonia*, and if it be drawn in Question again, he may Plead, *auterfoits acquite.* *Co. Lit. lib.* 2. *Sect.* 142.

An *Acquittance*, Acquietancia, æ, f. litera acquietancialis, *Ra. Ent.* 513. *Lex.* 2. It is a discharge in writing of a Sum of Money, or other duty, which ought to be paid or done. This word differeth from those which in the Civil Law be called *Acceptitatio*, or *Apocha*, for the first of these may be by word, without writing, and is nothing but a feigned payment and discharge, though payment be not had. *Apocha* is a writing, witnessing the payment or delivery of Money, which dischargeth not unless the Money be paid.

Accomplishment, Accompliamentum, i; n. *Co. Ent.* 227.

An *Account*, Computus, i; m.

Ballance of Account, Examen computi.

A Book of Accounts, Diarium, ii. n.

A caster of Accounts, Calculator, oris; m. Computista, æ, f.

Of his own accord, Sponte.

An *Acorn* Glans, ndis, f.

According to, Secundum.

According to ones own desire, Optato, adv.

An *Acre*, Acra, æ. f. Denariata terræ. & Nummata terræ. arpennus, i. m. Acre is a certain parcel of of Land that containeth in length 40 Perches, and in breadth 4 Perches, it comes from the *German* word (*Aker*) *id est*, Ager.

Half an Acre, Dimidium unius acræ. Obolata Terræ.

Ten Acres, the fourth part of a yard Land. Ferlingata Terræ.

Acre by Acre, Jugeratim, adv.

Publick Acts Registred, Acta, orum, n.

An *Action*, Actio, onis; f. an Action is a Right of Prosecuting in Judgment of a thing which is due unto any one. It may well be called an Action, *quia agitur de injuria*, for it is a complaint of an Injury received. There be two kinds of actions, one that concerns Pleas of the Crown, the other that concerns Common Pleas, which are called Actions Real, Actions Personal, and Actions Mixt. *Co.* 1. *Inst.* 284. *b.* Sometimes *Loquela* is used for an Action, as in the Entry of a Judgment in Debt, Trespass, &c. by *non sum informatus. Et idem attornatus dicit quod ipse non est informatus per eundem Defendentem Magistrum Suum de aliquo Responsu pro eodem Defendente præfato quærenti in Loquela prædicta dando*, &c.

An *Action Personal*, Actio Personalis.

An *Action of Trespass*, Actio de Transgressione.

An *action of Covenant*, Actio conventionis fractæ.

An *action withdrawn*, Actio Sublata.

An *act of general Pardon*, Amnestia, æ, f.

An *actor* (Stage Player) Histrio, onis; m. mimus, i; m.

An *actress*, Mima, æ. f. Actrix, cis.

Of an actor, Histrionalis, le.

The art or Science of acting, Histrionea, æ, f.

Accused, Rectatus, a, um. Arrectatus, a, um. *Spel.* 53. i. e. Suspected.

An *accusor*, Accessitor, oris. m.

Accustomed, Accustomatus, a, um. *Ra. Ent.* 657.

Co. Ent. 69. Accustomabilis, le *Plo.* 285.

A. D.

Adam (a Man's name.) Adamus, i; m.

An *adder*, Coluber, bri; m.

A *Water adder*, Hydra, æ, f.

Adders Tongue (Herb) Ophioglossum, i; n.

Addice (a Cooper's Tool) Dolabra, æ; f.

An *addition*, Additio, onis; f. In the Law it signifies a Title given to a Man, over and above his Christian and Surname, denoting his Estate, Degree, Mystery, Trade, and Place of dwelling.

An *Addition or Dependance*, Appendicium, ij, n. *Mon.* 553. 555. 606. Appertinentia, 2 *Mon.* 588.

To *adjourn*, Adjorno, are. i. e. To put off.

An *adjournment*, Adjornamentum, i; n. i. e. When any Court is put off, and assigned to be kept again at another Place or Time.

Adjourned, Adjornatus, a, um.

Things adjoyning, Adjacentia, 1 *Mon.* 805.

To *admit*, Admitto. Sis m.

Ad-

Admission, Admissio, onis, f. It is when one that hath right to present to a Church being void, doth present him to the Bishop of the Diocess, in which the Church is, who upon Examination finding him *Idonea Persona*, that is, capable and able, doth consent that he shall be Parson, and saith, *admitto te habilem*. *Co. on Lit.* 344.

To *Administer*, Administro, are, Administrationem committere.

An *Administrator*, Administrātor, oris; m.

Administrator is he to whom the Ordinary (id. est. the Bishop doth commit or give power to dispose and administer the Goods and Chattels within his Diocess belonging to any Person that is dead, without Executor, for the benefit of such Persons, or if the Party make a Will and Executor, and they all refuse or the Executor be within the Age of 17 years. *Co.* 5. *fo.* 29.

An *Administratrix*, Administratrix, cis; f.

An *Administration*, Administratio, onis; f.

An *Admiral*, Admirallus, i. m.

The admiralty, Admiralitas, atis, f.

A Writ to admit a Clerk, *Breve de admittendo Clerico*. It is granted to him who hath recovered his Right of Presentation against the Bishop. *F. n. b. Reg.* 33. *a.*

To *adnull*, Adnullo, are.

An *adnulling*, Adnullatio, onis; f.

To *adorn*, Orno, are.

An *adorning*, Ornatio onis f.

An *adorner*, Ornator, oris, m.

Adrian (a Mans name) Adrianus, i; m.

An *advancement*, Advanceamentum, i; n. 1 *Co.* 78. Dict. Prōmōtio, onis, f.

Advance Money, Pecunia præparatoria.

An *advantage*, Advantagium ij. n. *Co*, *Ent.* 484.

Advantages, Advantagia, orum. n. pl.

To *adventure*, Adventuro, are.

An *adventure*, Adventura, æ; f. 2 *Mon.* 615. Periclitātio, onis, f. Dict.

An *adventurer*, Periclitātor, oris; m.

An *adversary*, Adversarius, ij, m.

Advent, Adventus, i; m. It is the time from the *Sunday* that falls either upon St. *Andrew*'s day, or next to it, till the Feast of Christ's Nativity.

An *adulterer*, Adulter, eri, m.

An *adulteress*, Adultera, æ, f.

Adultery, Adultērium, ii; n. *quasi ad alterius Thorum*, properly spoken of married Persons, but if only one of the two by whom this Sin is committed, be married, it makes adultery, which was severely punished by the ancient Laws of this Land. *Vid. Claus.* 14. *Regis Johannis Memb.* 2.

An adviser before a work is done, Præmonstrator, oris; m.

To *advise*, Adviso, are.

Advice, Advisamentum, i, n. *Spel.* 22. avisamentum, *i*; *n. Ry.* 43. 299. 601. *Pry.* 85. 230. Avisatum. *Ry.* 303.

An *advocate*, Advŏcātus, i, m.

Advowson, Advocatio, onis, f. It is the right of Presentation or Collation

lation to the Church, it is called Advocatio, because the right of presenting to the Church was first gained by such as were Founders, Benefactors or Maintainers of the Church. 1. *Ratione Fundationis*, as where the Ancestor was Founder of the Church, or, 2. *Ratione Donationis*, where he endowed the Church, or, 3. *Ratione Fundi*, as where he gave the Soil whereupon the Church was built, and therefore they were called *Advocati*, and thereupon the Advowson is called *Jus Patronatus*.

A. E.

An *Aery of Hawks*, Aeria accipitrum, *Fle.* 92. The proper word for Hawks, for that we generally call a Nest, in other Birds: Chase Forest *anno* 9. 83. *ca.* 13.

Aeiton (in *Berkshire.*) Aquædunum

Aeton (in *Berkshire.*) *Ætonia.* near *Windsor.*

A. F.

Affeerers, Afferatores, um; m. pl. who are appointed upon Oath in Court Leets to settle and moderate the Fines of such as have committed Faults, Arbitrarily Punishable, and have no express Penalty set down by Statute, *Vid. Kitch.* 46 & 25. *Ed.* 3. *Stat.* 7.

Affeered, Afferatus, a, um. Spel. 24. *Lex.* 41. *Fo.* 165.

An *Affidavit*, Sacramentum, i; n. It is compounded of the Præposition *ad* and the old verb *fido*, as some will have it, but rather of the three words, *dare fidem ad*, and signifies an Oath or Deposition. The Clerks of the Exchequer, use the word *Affidatio*, *vid.* Compendium of the Exchequer, *Fol.* 353, and elsewhere in the same Book.

To *Affirm*, Affirmo, are, a word much used in feigned Actions upon Issues directed out of Chancery.

Aforesaid, Prædictus, a, um. usually, and Præfatus, a, um. most properly *Prædictus* is attributed in Pleadings to Defendants or Tenants, Places, Towns or Lands; *Idem* to Plantiffs or Demandants declaring or Pleading; *Præfatus* to Persons named, not being Actors, but if the same Persons Lands, &c. come very neerly again to be named or mentioned in Pleadings, 'tis most proper and Clerk-like to use *Idem*.

As Aforesaid, ut Præfertur, ut Predictum est, ut Præmittitur.

To *Afforest*, Afforesto, are. *Spel.* 25. *Lex.* 5. *i. e.* To turn Ground into a Forest.

To *Affranchise*, Manumitto, donare Libertate, m.

An *Affray*, Affraia, æ, f. *Ra. Ent.* 662. *bis.*

After, Post adv.

Afterwards, Postea adv.

The *After-birth*, Secundinæ, arum.

The *Afternoon*, Tempus Pomeridianum.

Afternoon, Post meridiem.

Of or in the Afternoon, Pomeridianus, a, um.

A. G.

Again, Iterum.

Against, Contra, præp. Versus, præp.

Against

Against (over against) ex adverso.

Agamer (in *Ireland.*) Agamerium.

Agatha (a Womans name.) Agatha, æ, f.

An *Age*, Ætas, atis; f. Sēcŭlum, i, n.

Old Age, Senecta, æ, f.

Aged, Grandævus, a, um.

Great age, Grandævĭtas, atis, f.

To become aged, Consĕnesco, ere.

Agedly, Vetustè adv.

Under age, Minōritas, atis, f.

Of the same age, Coævus, a, um.

Of one years age, annĭcŭlus, i, m.

Of ripe Age, Puber, eris, d. g. pl. caret.

There are diversity of Ages, which the Law takes notice of. A Woman hath seven ages for several purposes appointed to her by Law, as seven years for the Lord to have aid, *pour file marier*, nine years to deserve Dower, twelve years to consent to Marriage, untill fourteen years to be in Ward, fourteen years to be out of Ward, if she be attained thereunto in the Life of her Ancestor, sixteen years to tender her Marriage, if she were under the age of fourteen at the death of her Ancestor, and twenty one years to alienate her Lands, Goods and Chattels. *Co. on Lit. l.* 2. *c.* 4. *Sect.* 103. *Lit. Ten. Tit. Dower* & *l.* 2. *c.* 4. *p.* 22.

A Man also by the Law, for several purposes hath divers ages assigned unto him; *viz.* Twelve years to take the Oath of Allegiance in the Leet, fourteen years to consent to Marriage, and for the Heir in Socage to chose his Guardian, and fourteen years is also accounted his age of discretion, fifteen years for the Lord to have aid, *pour fair Fitz Chiveler*, under twenty one to be in Ward to the Lord, by Knights Service, under fourteen to be in Ward to a Guardian in Socage, and one and twenty to be out of Ward of a Guardian in Chivalry, and to Alien his Lands, Goods and Chattels. Before the age of twenty one years, a Man or a Woman is called an Infant. Full age regularly is twenty one years, for a Man or Woman to enable them to Seal any Bond or any Deed whatsoever; a Man cannot Lawfully be Impannelled in a Jury before that age, and at seventeen years he may Administer as Executor. *Co. Lit. l.* 3. *c.* 1. *Sect.* 259. *Lit. Ten. l.* 2. *c.* 4. *p.* 22, *&c.*

To *Agist*, Agisto, are. *Spel.* 26. *i. e.* To Feed or Depasture, Aceciam permitteret Equam illam agistare in pasturis ipsius quer. &c. *Ro. pl.* 32.

Agistment, Agistamentum, i, n. *Ro. pl. ib.* i. e. Feeding or Depasturing.

Agle (in *Lincolnshire*) Segelocum or Segelogum.

Agmundisham (in *Buckinghamshire*) Agmundishamum.

Agnes (a Womans name) Agnes, etis, f.

To *Agree*, Agreo, are.

An *Agreement*, Agreamentum, i, n. *Spel.* 26. *Lex.* 5. Agreement (saith *Plowden*) is a word compounded of two words, *aggregatio* and *mentium*, i. e. Agreement of minds, it is a consent of Minds in something done or to be done. Ab aggredien lo dicitur, saith *Spelman*, *Plow. Term. Pasc. Anno.* 4. *E.* 6.

Agrimony (Herb) Agrimonia,
An *Ague*, Febris.

A. H.

Ahab (a Mans name) Ahab Indecl.

Ahazuerus (a Mans name) Ahazuerus, i, m.

Ahaz (a Mans name) Ahaz Indec.

Ahazia (a Mans name) Ahazias, æ; m.

A. I.

Aid, Vid. Ayd.

Aire (in *Scotland*) Vidogara.

A. K.

Akil (in *Ireland*) Achilia.

A. L.

Alabaſter, Alabaſtrum, tri, n.

An *alabaſter Box*, Myrothecium, ij. n.

Alan (a Mans name) Alanus, i, m.

An *Alarm or Signal to Battle*, Signum Bellicum, ci, n. Claſſicum, i. n.

To *Sound an alarm*, Signum Bellicum or Claſſicum canere, Tubâ Signum dare.

Alban (a Mans name) Albanus, i, m.

Albert (a Mans name) Albertus, i, m.

Alberry (in *Hartfordſhire*) Aula, or Villa Antiqua.

Aldborough (in *Yorkſhire*) Iſubriagutium Iſſurium.

A. L.

An *Alderman*, Aldermannus, i, m.

Aldermanſhip, Aldermanry, Aldermanria, æ, f. i. e. The Office of an Alderman. Declaramus quod omnes & ſinguli Aldermanni electi in Civitate prediƈta (i. e. *London*) "quolibet anno imperpetuum "in Feſto Sanƈti Gregorii Papæ ab "Officio Aldermanriæ ſuæ penitus "& preciſe ceſſent, & inde totaliter amoveantur, & amoti, anno "proximo ſequenti ad Officium Aldermanriæ nullatenus re-eligantur, ſed loco illorum ſic ceſſandorum & amovendorum alii diſcreti concives ſui bonæ famæ & "illeſæ per eaſdem Gardas de quibus alii ſic amoti prius Aldermanni fuerunt ſingulis annis "imperpetuum eligantur. Chart Civit London dat. 22°. Nov. 50. *E.* 3.

An *Alder-Tree*, Alnus, ni, m.

The Place where Alders grow, Alnetum, i; n.

Aldred (a Mans name) Aldredus, i; n.

Ale, Cerviſia Illupulata.

Strong ale, Cerviſia vălĭda.

Small ale, Cerviſia Tenuis.

Stale ale, Cerviſia vetula.

An *ale-houſe*, Cerviſiarium, ii, n. Caupona, æ; f. Popīna, æ, f.

An *ale houſe-keeper*, Caupo, onis, m. Pŏpinārius, ii. m.

Alen (a River in *Dorſetſhire*) Alenus.

Alesbury-Vale (in *Buckinghamſhire*) Eilecurium vallis.

Alexanders or Aliſander (Herb) Hipposelinum.

Alexanders of Creet (Herb) Smyrnium, ii. n.

Alexan-

Alexander (a Mans name) Alexander, dri, m.

Alexis (a Mans name) Alexis, is, m.

Alfred (a Mans name) Alfredus, i; m.

Algernoon (a Mans name) Algernon, onis, m.

All-heal, or woundwort Panacea, æ; f.

Ale-hoof or Ground Ivy. Hedera, arborea Terrestris.

All-hallontide, Festum omnium Sanctorum.

Alhallows Barking, Parochia omnium Sanctorum de Barking.

Alhallows Breadstreet, Parochia omnium Sanctorum in vico Pistorum.

Alhallows Honylane, Parochia omnium Sanctorum in Mellis viculo.

Alhallows Lumbardstreet, Parochia omnium Sanctorum in vico Longobardico.

Alhallows Staining, Parochia omnium Sanctorum Pictorum delibuentium.

Alhallows the Wall, Parochia omnium Sanctorum supra murum.

Alkanet (Herb) Anchusa, æ, f.

Alice (a Womans name) Alicia, æ, f. Adeliza, æ. f.

An *alien*, Alienigena, æ, c. g. alien is derived from the Latin word *Alienus*, and according to the Etymology of the word, it signifies one born in a strange Country, under the obedience of a strange Prince, such an one is not capable of Inheritance within *England*. 1. Because the secrets of the Realm may thus be discovered. 2. The Revenues of the Realm (which are the Sinews of War and ornament of Peace) shall be taken, and enjoyed by strangers born. 3. This will tend to the destruction of the Realm. If he be naturalized by Act of Parliament, then he is not accounted in Law, *Alienigena*, but *Indigena*, as a natural born Subject, and may purchase and maintain actions as *Englishmen*. *Coke*, *l*. 7.

An *Alienation*, Alienatio, onis, f.

To *Alien*, Alieno, are. It signifies to transfer the property of any thing to another Person.

To Alien in Mortmain, alienare in Manum mortuam. It is to make over Lands or Tenements to a Religious House or other Body Politick.

To Alien in Fee, alienare in Feodo. It is to sell the Fee-simple of any Lands or Tenements, or of any Corporeal Right, *W*. 2. *C*. 25. 13. *Ed*. 1. 3.

Alimony, Alimonia, æ, f. Nourishment, Maintenance: in a Modern Legal sence, it signifies that portion or allowance which a married Woman sues for upon any occasional separation from her Husband, wherein she is not charged with elopement or adultery.

Alive, Vivus, a, um.

An *Almanack*, Fasti, orum. m. Calendarium, ii. n.

An *Almond*, Amygdălum, i, n.

An *Almond-Tree*, Amygdălus, li, f.

Almondbury (in *England*) Camulodunum.

An *Almoner*, Eleemosynarius, ii. m.

A Lord Almoner, Eleemosynarchus, i, m.

Alms Eleemŏsyna, æ, f.

An

An *Alms-house*, Xenodochium, ii, n.

Of Alms, Eleemosynarius, a, um.

Almost, fere adv.

Alneland (a River in *Northumberland*) Alaunius.

Alne (a River in *Warwickshire*) Alenus

Alone, Sŏlus, a, um.

Alphage (a Mans name) Alphegus, i. m.

Also, Item, adv.

To *Alter*, altero, are. *Ra. Ent.* 413. *Co. Let.* 357.

An *Altering*, Alteratio, onis, f. 1. *Co.* 109.

Although, Etsi adv.

Always, Semper, adv.

Altarage, Altaragium, ii. n. *Spel.* 32. *Lex.* 6. Obventio altaris. Offerings and all small Tythes due to the Priest Spel.

All, Totus, a, um. omnis, ne. Integer, ra, rum. as Totum illud messuagium, all that messuage. Omnis & quælibet Persona & Personæ, All and every Person and Persons. Integra Tenementa. Omnes illæ Terræ.

Allaway (in *Scotland*) Alana.

To *Alledge*, Allego, are.

An *Allegation*, Allegatio, onis, f.

Allegiance, Ligeantia, æ, f.

Allerton (in *Yorkshire*) Cataractonum.

An *Allie by Marriage*, Affinis, is, c. 2.

Alliance by Marriage, Affinitas, atis, f.

Alliance of Blood, Consanguinitas, atis, f.

Allom, Allumen, inis, n.

To *Allot*, Alotto, are. or set out ones share.

Allotted, Allottatus, a, um. *Ra. Ent.* 487.

To *Allow*, Alloco, are.

An *Allowance upon Account*, Allocatio, onis, f.

An *Alley in a Town*, Angyportus, ûs, or, i, m.

All Souls day, Festum omnium animarum.

A. M.

Amain (a Sea term for come on Board) Accedite.

Amain (for the Mariners to lower their Sails) Demittere vela.

Amata (a Womans name) Amata, æ, f.

An *Ambassador*, Orator, oris, m.

Ambleside (in *Westmorland*) Ambegianna.

Amber, Succinum, i, n.

Ambresbury (in *England*) Ambrosia, Ambrosii mons.

Ambrose (a Mans name) Ambrosius, ii, m.

An *Ambush lying in wait*, Insidiæ arum, f.

A lyer in Ambush, Insidiātor, ōris, m.

To lie or be in Ambush, Insidior, ari.

An *Amends*, Emenda, æ, f. Emendals, so much in Bank for repairing of Losses. *Hil.* 4. *E.* 3. *Placito.* 25. 1. *Fo.* 360, 361. *Spel.* 230.

An *Amendment*, Emendatio, onis, f. It imports the Correcting of an Error, either in Process or Pleadings.

An *Amerciament*, Amerciamentum, i, n. Misericordia, æ, f. Wita Wyta, æ; f. It is called in Latin *Miserecordia*, because it ought to be assessed mercifully, and this ought to be moderated by Affeerement of his

his Equals, or else a Writ *de moderata misericordia* doth lie, or because the Party which offendeth putteth himself on the mercy of the King. A Fine is always imposed and assessed by the Court, but Amerciament by the Country. *Co. Lit. Lib.* 2. *c.* 11. *p.* 194. *Term. of Law. Co.* 8. *Rep.*

Amerced, Amerciatus, a, um. Spel. 34. Pry. 53.

Amersham (in *England*) Agmundishamum.

Amesbury (in *Wiltshire*) Ambrosia, Ambrosii burgus.

An *Amethyst stone*, Amethystus, i. m.

Aminadab (a Mans name) Aminadab.

Amongst, Inter.

To *Amortize*, Amortizo, are. i. e. To put Lands into Mortmain.

Amortizement, Amortizatio, onis, f. *Spel.* 34. *Lex.* 7. *Ra. Entr.* 68. 137. i. e. The putting of an Estate into Mortmain.

Amortized, Amortizatus, a, um, Put into Mortmain.

An Amorous Potion, Philtrum, i, n.

Amos (a Mans name) Amos Indec.

Ammunition, Armorum copia.

Of Ammunition, Militaris, re. Castrensis, se.

An *Amulet*, Amuletum, i, n.

Amnon (a Mans name) Amnon.

Amwell (in *Hertfordshire*) Fons Amnensis.

Amy (a Womans name) Amicia æ, f.

A. N.

Anandale (in *Scotland*) Vallis Anangia.

Annanias (a Mans name) Ananias æ, m.

Anarchy, Anarchia, æ, f. Confusion, lack of Government.

An *Anatomy*, Anatomia, æ, f. Sceleton, i, n.

An *Anatomist*, Dissĕcātor, oris, m.

Anatomizing, Dissectio, onis, f.

To *Anatomize*, Dissĕco, ui, ctum.

Annates or first Fruits, Annates, um. f. pl.

Ancaster (in *Lincolnshire*) Crocolana.

An *Ancestor*, Antecessor, oris, m Ancestor is derived from the Latin word *Antecessor*, and in Law there is a difference between *Antecessor* and *Predecessor*, for *Antecessor* is applied to a natural Person, as *J. S.* & *Antecessores sui*; but *Predecessor* is applied to a Body Politick or Corporate, as Epis. Lond. & *Predecessores* sui; Rector de D. & *Predecessores* sui.

Unlike his Ancestors, Dĕgener, eris.

Ancestry, Prosapia, æ, f.

Derived of the Ancestors name, Patronymĭcus, a, um.

An *Anchor*, Anchora, æ, f.

Belonging to an Anchor, Anchorarius, a, um.

To *Anchor, cast Anchor*, Anchoram jacere.

To weigh Anchor, Anchoram Sublevare.

To ride at Anchor, ad Anchoram stare.

Riding at Anchor, Fluctuans ad Anchoram.

The Cable of an Anchor, Anchŏrale, is ; n.

To More at Anchor, Morari ad Anchoram.

An *Anchor Smith*, Faber Anchorarius.

He

He that hath the charge of the Anchor, Anchorarius, ii, m.

Ancorage, Ancoragium, ii; *n. Lex. 7.* a Duty that Ships pay in the Haven when they caſt anchor.

Anchoves, Enchraſichŏli, m. pl.

Anchoves Sawce, Oxygărium, ii. n.

Ancient, Antiquus, a, um.

An *Ancient Man*, Sĕnex ĕnis.

To grow Ancient, Invetĕraſco, ere.

Grown Ancient, Inveteratus, a, um.

And, et, ac, necnon.

And alſo, Aceciam for ac etiam.

And not, Non autem.

And if, Etſi, quod ſi.

And withal, Simul.

And yet, Tamen.

And therefore, Proin, Proinde.

An *Andiron*, Andela, æ; f. Subex Focarius.

Andover (in *Hantſhire*) Andŏvera.

Andrew (a Mans name) Andreas, æ; m.

St. Andrew's Cape (in *Scotland*) Veruvium.

St. Andrew's day, Feſtum Sancti Andreæ apoſtoli.

Angelet (a Womans name) Angeletta, æ, f.

Angelica (Herb) Angĕlĭca, æ; f.

An angle or Corner, Angŭlus, li, m.

A right angle, Orthogŏnus, i, m.

Conſiſting of right angles, Orthogonius, a, um.

To *Angle*, Ineſto, are.

An angler or Fiſher with Hooks, Hamātor, oris, m.

An *angling*, Arundinis moderatio.

An *angling line*, ſeta, æ, f.

An *angling rod*, Arundo, inis.

Angleſey (Iſland) Angleſega, Mona.

Angus (part of *Scotland*) Anguſia.

The *Ankle*, Malleŏlus, i, m.

The *Ankle Bone*, Talus, i, m.

Anne (a Womans name) Anna, æ. f.

To *Annex* (joyn to) Annecto, xi, um.

Annexed, Annexus, a, um.

Annis (Herb) Aniſum, ſi, n.

Anniverſary (yearly) Anniverſarius, a, um.

Annual (yearly) Annuus, a, um.

Annually (every year) Quotannis, adv.

An *Annuity* (yearly ſtipend) Annuus Redditus, Annuitas.

Another, Alius, a, um.

Another mans, Aliēnus, a, um.

Anſelm (a Mans name) Anſelmus, i, m.

To *Anſwer*, Reſpondeo, di, ſum.

An *Ant* (Piſmire) Formica, æ, f.

An Ant hill or Neſt, Formicētum, i, n.

Anthill (in *Bedfordſhire*) Antiliā.

Antholin (a Mans name) Antholinus, ii, m.

Anthony (a Mans name) Antonius, ii, m.

Saint Anthony's Fire, Eryſipelas, atis; n.

Anticks, or Images of Building, Perſonæ, arum.

An *Antidote*, Antidotus, ti. f.

Antimony, Antimonium, ii, m.

An *Anvill*, Incus, ŭdis f.

An *Anvils ſtock*, truncus Incudis.

To ſtrike upon an Anvil, Incudo, ſi, ſum.

A worker on an Anvil, Incudo, onis.

Faſhioned at the Anvil, Incuſus, a, um.

Any, Ullus, a, um.

A. P.

Apart, Separatim.

Apart from, Separate, Sejunctus, a, um.

To stand apart, Distito, are.

An *Ape*, Simia, æ; f.

Apelles (a Mans name) Apelles, is.

Apollo (a Mans name) Apollo, inis, m.

Apology (excuse) Apologia, æ; f.

An *Apoplexy*, Apoplexia, æ.

An *Apothecary*, Apothecarius, ii, m. 1 Mon. 938. Pharmăcŏpola, æ, m.

An *Apothecary's Shop*, Pharmăcŏpōlium, ii, n.

An *Apparator*, Apparator, oris, m. i. e. a Messenger to the Spiritual Court.

An *Apricock*, Malum Præcox.

An *Apricock-Tree*, Malus Armeniaca.

April, Aprilis, is, m.

An *Apron*, Præcinctorium, ii. n. Ventrale, is, n.

To *Appear*, Appareo, ui, itum.

An *Appearance*, Apparentia, æ; f. idem quod Comparentia. *Ra. Ent.* 347. *Doctor and Stu.* 30.

Doth more fully Appear, Plenius apparet, (vox sepius placitando usitata) A Phrase often used in Pleading Indentures and other Writings.

Doth manifestly appear, Liquet manifeste.

It Appears, Constat Imp.

Apparel, Vestitus, ûs, m.

Apparelled, Vestitus, a, um.

A suit of apparel, Indumentum, i. n. Series apparatus, habitus vestitum,

Apparelled gallantly, Concinnātus, a, um.

Apparelled meanly, Vili veste Tectus.

Apparelled in Mourning, Pullātus, a, um.

Apparalled handsomly, Cultus, a, um.

Apparalled unhandsomly, Incultus, a, um.

An *apparelling*, Appărātio, onis, f.

To *apparel*, Vestio, ire.

Apparent, Manifestus, a, um.

Apparently, Manifeste.

To *appeal*, Appello, are.

An *appeal*, Appellum, i, n. Brac. 140. Appellatio, onis, f. *Co. Lit.* 287. An Appeal to a Superiour Court for the removing a Cause out of an Inferiour. Also an Accusation, at the Suit of the Party, his Wife or Heir (and not at the Prosecution of the King) in a Criminal Cause, as an Appeal of Mayhem or Robbery, brought by the Party, or an Appeal of Murder by the Wife or Heir.

An *appellant*, Appellans, antis, f.

An *Appellee*, Appellatus, i; m. *Spel.* 42.

Appendant, Appendens, tis, adj. i. e. That belongs to another by Prescription.

To *appertain or belong*, Pertineo, ere.

It Appertains, Pertinet.

Appertaining, Pertinens.

An *apple*, Pomum, i, m.

A *Genting, or Summer apple*, Pomum Præcox.

A *Summer Golden apple*, Pomum Sanguineum.

A *St. John apple, or Winter fruit*, Pomum Serotinum.

A *Cats-head, or Costard apple*, Pomum decumanum.

A *Queen apple*, Pomum Claudianum.

A Crumpling or little Apple, Pomum nanum.

An Apple soon rotten, Pomum fugax.

An Apple-Tree, Pomus, i; f.

Bearing Apples Pōmĭfer, a, um.

Full of Apples, Pōmōsus, a, um.

An Apple Core, Volva, æ, f.

An Apple-Loft, Pomarium, ii. n.

An Apple-Keeper, Pomo, ōnis, m.

An Apple-Seller, Pomarius. ii, m.

Appleby (in *Westmorland*) Applebera, Abaliaba.

An Apprentice to a Trade, Apprenticius, ii. m. *Spel.* 43. *Pry.* 13.

An Apprentice to the Law, Apprenticius Legis, i. e. a Barester or Councellor.

An Apprenticeship, Apprentisagium, ii; n. *Spel.* 64. Apprenticiamentum, i; n. 2. *Fo.* 11.

To *Appoint*, Statuo, ui, utum, Appunctuo, are.

Appointed, Appunctuatus, a, um.

To Appoint in another's Place, Substituo, ui, utum.

To Appoint Bounds, Termino, are.

By Appointment, Jussu.

To *Apportion*, Apportiono, are. i. e. To divide a Rent into parts according as the Land, is shared amongst the Tenants.

An *Apportionment*, Apportionamentum, i; Lex. 8. or dividing of Rent, as aforesaid.

To *Appropriate*, Approprio, are.

An *Appropriation*, Appropriatiŏ, onis, f. *Lex.* 8. Appropriantia, 1. *Mon.* 942. Appropriamentum, i, n. 37. *Ass.* 17. It signifies the severing of a Benefice Ecclesiastical to the proper and perpetual use of some Religious House, Bishoprick, College, &c.

To *Apprise*, Apprecio, are.

To *Approve*, Apprŏbo, are.

An *Approver*, Approbātor. oris, m. Lex. 8. One who confesses Felony and Appeals or Accuses others also of the same, which he was bound to prove by Combat, or by the Country.

The King's Approvers, Approbatores Regis. They who had the letting of his Demesns to the best advantage.

Approved, Apprŏbātus, a, um.

An *Approving*, Approbatio, onis, f.

An *Appurtenance*, Pertinentia, Brac. 36. 1 Mon. 555, 586. ter.

With their and every of their Appurtenances, Cum eorum & cujuslibet eorum pertinenciis.

A. R.

Arable, Arăbĭlis, le.

An *Arraignment*, Arainamentum, i; n. 2. Inst. 48.

Arraigned, Arainatus, a, um. A Prisoner is said to be arraigned when he is Indicted, and put to his Tryal, *T. of Law.* One arraigned upon an Indictment of Felony or Murder, shall have no Counsel, but the Judges shall so instruct him in all things that pertain to the order of Pleading, that he shall run in no danger by his mispleading. *Dr. and Student*, c. 48. This is altered by a late Act of Parliament.

To Arraign an Assize, Arrainare assisam. Spel. 21. Ry. 403, bis. i. e. To Prosecute by such a Writ.

To *Array*, Arraiare.

An *Array*, Arraiamentum, i; n. Co. Lit. 156. i. e. The order,

Array

array or range of the names in the Pannel of the Jurors for the Tryal of a Cause.

To Challenge the array of the Pannel, Calumniare arraiamentum.

Commissioners of Array, Arraiatores, m. pl. *Lex.* 9.

Arbella (a Womans name) Arbella, Arabella, æ, f.

To *Arbitrate,* Arbitro, are. i. e. To Judge between.

An *Arbitrement,* Arbitrium, ii. n. awardium, ii. n. *Spel.* 63. It is called Arbitrement, because the Judges Elected therein, may determine the Controversie, not according to the Law, but *ex boni viri arbitrio,* or else because the Parties to the Controversie have submitted themselves to the Judgment of the Arbitrators, not by compulsory means, but *ex libero arbitrio,* out of their own accord. It is a power given by the Parties litigant to some to hear and determine some matters in Suit between them, to whose Judgment they bind themselves to stand. There is a diversity between it and concord, for that an Arbitrement may be Pleaded although the time of performance of it be not yet come, but a Concord ought to be executed and satisfied before the Action brought, or it is no good Plea. *Dyer Term. Mich. Anno Sexto. Ed.* 6. 75. Five things are incident to an Arbitrement,

1. Matter of Controversie.
2. Submission.
3. Parties to the Submission.
4. Arbitrators.
5. Rendring the award, which may be either.

1. By word or,

2. By writing. *Dyer* 217. *Pl.* 60.

An *Arbitrator,* Arbitrator, oris, m. Arbitrary, Arbitrarius, a, um.

An *Arbitratrix,* Arbitratrix, icis, f.

An *Arbour,* Topiarium, ii. n.

An *Arbour-maker,* Topiarius, ii; m.

Arbour-making, Topiaria, æ; f.

An *Arch in building,* Arcus, ûs, m. fornix, icis, m.

A *Flat Arch,* Archus planus.

Arched, Arcuatus, a, um.

Arched like a Bow, Arcuatus, a, um.

An *Arch in a Cloyster,* Archa in Claustro. 1 Mon. 933.

Archery, Archeria, æ, f. Co. Lit. 107.

Hollow and arched upwards, Recavus, a, um.

Arch-work, Arquatura, æ, f.

The Arches of a Bridge, Constrata Pontium. Pontis fornices.

An Arched-Roof, Tectum laqueatum.

The Arching of a Roof, Arcuâtûra, æ; f.

To make an Arch Roof, Fornico. are.

The Court of the Arches, Curia de arcubus, i. e. The Arch-bishop of *Canterbury*'s consistory Court.

An *Arch-bishop,* Archiepiscôpus, i, m.

An *Arch-bishoprick,* Archiepiscopatus, ûs, m.

The Arch-bishop of Armagh *in* Ireland, Archiepiscopus Armachanus.

The Arch-bishop of Canterbury, Archiepiscopus Cantuariensis.

The Arch-bishop of York, Archiepiscopus Eboracensis.

An

Arch-Deacon, Archidiaconus, i. m.
An *Arch-deaconship*, Archediăcōnatus, us, m.
Archilaus (a Mans name) Archelaus, i, m.
An *Archer* (Bow-man) Sagittarius, ii, m.
Archibald (a Mans name) Archibaldus, i, m.
An *Architect* (master-Builder) Architectus, i, m.
Architecture (Building) Architectura, æ, f.
Architect-like, Affabrè adv.
Archive, Archivum, i, n. a Chest where the Rolls and Records of the Crown and Kingdom are kept.
Arclo (in *Ireland*) Arclovium.
Ardee (in *Ireland*) Ardracum.
Ardemouth-head (in *Scotland*) Norantum promontorium.
Ardragh (in *Ireland*) Ardracum.
Are (a River in *Yorkshire*) Arus.
Argile (part of *Scotland*) Argathelia.
Arglas (in *Ireland*) Veluntium.
To *Argue*, Argumentor, ari.
An *Argument*, Argumentum, i. n.
A firm Argument, Demonstrātio, onis, f.
A Cunning Argument, Sophisma, atis, n.
Full of Arguments, Argumentosus, a, um.
To hold an Argument with one, Dispŭto, are.
Arias (a Mans name) Arias, æ. m.
Aristarchus (a Mans name) Aristarchus, i. m.
Aristotle (a Mans name) Aristoteles.
Aristophanes (a Mans name) *Aristophanes*.
Aristocrasy, Aristocratia, æ, f. i. e. Government by Nobles.

Arithmetick, Arithmetica, æ, f.
Arithmetical, Arethmeticus, a, um.
An *Arithmetician*, Arithmeticus, ci, m.
Specious Arithmetick, or the Art of Equation, Algebra, æ, f.
An *Arm*, Brachium, ii, n.
A little Arm, Brachiŏlum, li, n.
Of an Arm, Brāchiālis, le.
The Brawn of the Arm or Thigh, Lăcertus, i, m.
An *Arm-pit*, Ala, æ, f.
An *Arm-hole*, Axilla, æ, f.
Of the Arm-holes, Axillaris, re.
An Arm of the Sea, Vide Sea.
To Arm, Armo, are.
A Man at Arms, armed Cap-a-pee, Catăphractus, i, m. i. e. A Cuirasier.
To arm Cap-a-pee, Perarmo, are.
An arming Cap-a-pee, Perarmatio, onis, f.
Armagh (in *Ireland*) Armacha, Ardinacha.
Of Armagh, Armacensis, Armachanus.
Armanoth, (part of *Scotland*) Armanothia.
Armed, Armatus, a, um.
Armed with a Buckler, Scutatus, a, um.
Armed with a Javelin, Pilatus, a um.
Armed with a Sword, Ensatus, a, um.
Armed with a Coat of Mail, Loricatus, a, um.
Armour, Armatūra, æ, f.
A Coat of Armour, Palūditamentum, i, n.
An entire Suit of Armour, Panoplia, æ, f.
Armour for the Thigh, Fĕmŏrāle, is, n.

Cloaths

Cloathes under mens armour, Subarmalia, ium, n.

An armourer, Armamentarius, ii, m.

An armourer's shop, Officina armaria.

An armory, Armamentarium, ii, n.

Arms, weapons, instruments, Arma, orum, n.

Shewing of armour, training, &c. Armiluſtrum, i, n.

An armour-bearer, Armiger, i, m.

Linnen armory, Armatura Linea.

Armourers of linnen armory, Merchant Taylors of London, Armararii linearum armiturarum Moo. 576.

To be in arms, Arma tenere.

They are up in arms, In armis ſunt.

Arms (Coat of Arms) Inſignia, ium, n.

To bear arms, Arma induere, in armis eſſe.

To lay down Arms, Ponere arma.

A man of arms, Vir bellicus.

Deeds of arms, Geſta, orum, n.

By force of arms, Manu forti, or vi & armis.

An army, Exercitus, ûs, m.

To lead an army, Agmen ducere.

To marſhal an army, Aciem ordinare, dirigere.

A wing of an army, Cornus, ſis, m.

Arnold (a mans name) Arnoldus, i, m.

The arſe, Podex, icis.

The arſe-gut, Inteſtinum rectum.

Arſenick, (Ratsbane) Arſenicum, i, n.

Arſeſmart (Herb) Hydropiper, eris, Perſicaria, æ, f.

Art or ſcience, Ars, tis, f.

Made up by art, Factitius, a, um.

An artery (Pulſe) Arteria, æ, f.

The great artery, Aorta, æ, f.

Of the arteries, Arterialis, le.

Arthur (a mans name) Arthurus, i, m.

An article, Articulus, i, m.

To article, Articulo, are.

Article by Article, Articulatim, adv.

An artichoke Cinara, æ, f.

An artificer, Artifex, icis.

To forge or work artificially, Fabrifacio, eci, ere.

Artilleries, Machinæ bellicæ.

Furniſhed with artillery, Machinis bellicis inſtructus.

A train of artillery, Machinarum apparatus.

The artillery yard, Paleſtra, æ, f.

Arun (a River in *Suſſex*) Arunus.

Arundel (in *Suſſex*) Arundelia, arundellum, aruntina vallis.

Arundel (the Family) Arundelius, Arondellius de Hirundine.

Arras (Hangings) Tapes, etis, m.

Figured arras, Pictura Textilis.

Arrerages, Arreragia, orum, n. Arreragium, ii, n. *Spel.* 53, *i. e.* Moneys behind upon an Account.

To arreſt, Arreſto, are. Arreſt is derived, as ſome think, of the *French* word *Arreſter*, to ſtay; or from the *Greek* word ἀρεστον, a decree or ſentence of the Court. Arreſt is when one is taken and reſtrained from his liberty,

berty,

berty, by Power or Colour of a Lawful Warrant. Arreſt ſignifieth properly a Decree of a Court, by virtue of which a Man is Arreſted, &c. The Perſon of a Baron which is a Peer of the Parliament, ſhall not be Arreſted in Debt or Treſpaſs by his Body, for none of the Nobility which is Lord of the Parliament, and by the Law ought to be tryed by his Peers, ſhall be Arreſted by his Body. The Law intends they aſſiſt the King in his Counſel for the Common weal, and keep the Realm in ſafety by their Prowess and Valour, and they are intended to have ſufficient in Lands whereby they may be diſtrained. This Priviledge extends alſo to Women who are Baroneſſes by Birth or Marriage, if thoſe by Marriage loſe not their Dignity by Intermarriage with any under the Degree of Nobility. They ſhall not therefore be put in Juries although it be in the ſervice of the Country. An Arreſt in the night is Lawful: For the Officer ought to Arreſt a Man when he is to be found, for otherwiſe peradventure he ſhall never Arreſt him, *Quiſq; qui male agit odit lucem.* And if the Officer do not Arreſt him when he findeth him and may Arreſt him, the Plaintiff ſhall have an Action upon the Caſe, and recover all his Loſs in damages. No Man ſhall be Arreſted upon the Lord's day, except in Criminal matters. *Cook* 6. *Rep.* Counteſs of *Rutland*'s Caſe. *Cook* 9. *Rep*, Earl of *Salop's* Caſe. *Cook* 9. *Rep.* *Makally's* Caſe.

An arreſt, Arreſtum, i, n. Arreſtatio, onis, f. *Reg.* 106. *Spel.* 58. *Pri.* 21. 24. 27. 73.

Arreſted, Arreſtatus, a, um.

To arrive, Arrivo, are, 1 *Co.* 28.

An arriving, Arrivatio, onis, f. i. e. A coming to.

An arrow, Sagitta, æ. f.

A little arrow, Sagittella, æ, f.

A broad forked headed arrow, Trăgŭla, æ, f.

An arrow head, Cuſpis, ĭdis, f. Spiculum, i, n.

A broad arrow head, Uncĭnus, i, m.

The neck of an arrow, Crena Sagittæ.

The feathers of an arrow, Plumæ Sagittæ.

Of or like an arrow, Sagittarius, a, um.

To ſhoot an arrow, Sagitto, are.

Shot with an arrow, Sagittus, a, um.

A ſmall engin to ſhoot poyſoned arrows, Scorpidium, ii, n.

Bearing arrows, Săgittĭfer, a, um,

A. S.

The biſhop of St. Aſaph, Epiſcopus Aſaphenſis.

Of St. Aſaph (in *Flintſhire*) Aſaphenſis.

Aſarabacca (Herb) Aſarum, i.

As abovesaid, Ut ſupra dictum eſt.

Aforeſaid, Ut præfertur, ut prædictum eſt.

As soon as, Tam cito quam.

As if, Acsi.

As yet, Adhuc, adv.

Ascension day, Festum ascensionis Domini.

An ash-tree, Fraxinus, ni, f.

A wild ash, Ornus, i, f.

Ash (the family) de Fraxinis.

Ash-bridge (in *Hertfordshire*) Jugum Fraxinetum.

Of ash colour, Cineraceus, a, um.

Ashen, Fraxineus, a, um.

An ash-grove, Fraxinetum, i, n.

Ash-wednesday, Cineralia, orum. Dies Cinerum.

Ashwel (in *Hertfordshire*) Fons inter Fraxinus.

Ashes, Cinis, eris, m.

Buck-ashes, Cinis ad Lixivium.

To burn to ashes, In cineres redigere.

To bring a-shoar, Subduco, xi, ctum.

Asked, Interrogatus, a, um.

An asking, Interrogatio, onis, f.

An asking of advice, Consultatio, onis, f.

Assenden (in *Hertfordshire*) Caverna viperina.

Male asphodel, Asphodeli albuci maris.

Female asphodel, or king's spear (Herb.) Asphodeli, hastæ regiæ, fæm.

Astrology, Astrologia, æ, f.

An astrologer, Astrologus, i, m.

Astronomy, Astronomia, æ, f.

An astronomer, Astronomus, mi, m.

Astronomical, Astronomicus, a, um.

Asunder, Separatim, adv.

To take asunder, In partes tribuere.

To cut asunder, Disseco, ui, ctum.

To put asunder, Sejungo, xi ctum.

An ass, Asinus, ni, m.

A little ass, Asellus, li, m.

A she ass, Asina, æ, f.

A wild ass, Onager, is, m.

An ass colt, Pullus asini.

Of an ass, Asinarius, a, um.

Like an ass, Asinalis, le,

An ass dresser or driver, Agaso, onis, m.

An ass-herd, Asinarius, ii, m.

To assart, Assarto, are. i. e. To Glade, or make Glades in a wood, to make plain, to grub up or clear ground of Bushes, Shrubs, &c. Forest Law word.

An assart, Assartum, i, n. *Lex*. 9. *Carta de foresta*, *ca*. 4. *Ry*. 2. 21. 50. *Assartæ tot acræ*, 1 *Mon*. 403. 483. 513. 814. *Assartatio*, onis, f. 1 *Mon*. 585. *Essartum*, i, n. *Spel*. 240. i. e. Land assarted.

To assassin, Percutio, ssi, ssum.

Assassinare, Law word.

An assassin, Percussor, oris, m.

An assassination, Interfectio, onis, f.

To assault, Insultum facere.

An assault, Assultus, ûs m. Insultus. ûs, m. Assault is from the Latin word *Insultus*, which denoteth a leaping or flying upon a Man, so that it cannot be performed without the offer of some hurtful Blow, or at least some hurtful Speech, and therefore to rebuke a Collector with foul words, so that he departed for fear without doing his office, was taken for an Assault. To strike at a Man although he

 were

were neither hurt nor hit with the Blow, was adjudged an Assault. Assault doth not always imply necessarily a hitting, and therefore in Trespass, for Assault and Battery, a Man may be found guilty of the Assault, and yet excused of the Battery. 40. *Ed.* 3. 4. and 25. *Ed.* 3. 24. 27. *Ass. Pl.* 11. 22. *lib. Ass. Plea*, 60.

Assaulted, Insultus, a, um.

To assay, Assaio, are. Pry. 196.

To assay (make tryal of) Tento, are.

The assay master of the mint, Assaisiator, oris, m. He is an Officer of the Mint for the due tryal of Silver, indifferently appointed between the Master of the Mint, and the Merchants that bring Silver thither for Exchange.

An assay, Assaia, æ, f. i. e. Of Measures and Weights.

The assay and assise of bread, Assaia & Assisa panis, *Lex.* 10. *Ry.* 659. Assaiator Cambiorum Regis, *Lex.* 10.

The assay and assise of Wine and beer, Assaia & assisa vini & Cervisiæ.

To assemble, Assemblo, are. i. e. To meet together, Congrego.

An assembly of the Clergy about Church affairs, Convocatio, onis, f.

An assembling, Assemblatio, onis, f. Coadunatio, onis, f. 9 *Co.* 56.

An assembly of people, Assemblatio gentium, Vid. *Rast. Ent. Tit. Huy and Cry.*

An unlawful assembly, Assemblatio Illicita. It is the meeting of three or more persons together, with force, to commit some unlawful act, and abiding together, though not endeavouring the Execution of it: as to assault or beat any Person, to enter into his House or Land.

To assent unto, Assentior, iri.

An assent, Assensus, ûs, m.

To assess or tax, Assideo, ere.

An assessment or tax, Assessamentum, i, n. Law term.

Assessments, Assessamenta.

An Assessor, Assessor, oris, m. Assisor, oris, m. i. e. An assessor of publick taxes, as two inhabitants in every parish were assessors for the Royal Ayd, *anno.* 16, *and* 17. *Car.* 2. *Cap.* 1, and rated every Person according to the proportion of his Estate.

Assets, Omnia defuncti bona personalia. Law term.

To assign over, Assigno, are.

An assignee, Assignatus, i, m.

Assigned, Assignatus, a, um.

An assignation, Assignatio, onis, f.

Assin (a River in *Scotland*) Itys.

An assise, Assisa, æ, f. *Spel.* 56. *Lex.* 10. Redditus Assisæ. 2 *Mon.* 423. 614. An Assise or Sessions of Judges and Justices. Assise cometh of the Latin word *Assideo*, which is to associate or sit together. It is *nomen æquivocum* (saith *Littleton.*) Sometimes it is taken for a Jury, for in the Record of an Assise, the word is, *Assisa venit recognitura*, &c. which is the same

as

as *Jurata venit recognitura*, and in a Writ of right the Tenant putting himself on God and the great Assise, is the same as upon God and his Country, *viz.* the Jury. But most properly it is taken for a Writ or Action, and it lieth where a Man is put out of his Lands, Tenements or any profit to be taken in a certain place, and so disseised of his Freehold. At the Common Law Assise was *remedium maxime festinum*, for in this the Defendant shall not pray the ayd of any but the King, also *maxime beneficiale*, for in no Action at the Common Law, a Man shall recover Land it self and Damages, but only in an Assise against the Disseisor. There be four Assises, *viz.* an Assise of *Novel disseisin*, of *Mort d'ancester*, of *Darrein presentment*, and of *Juris Utrum*. There are several Writs (in case of Disseisin) so called, as *Assisa mortis Antecessoris*, *Assisa ultimæ præsentationis*, &c. It also signifieth the sise, quantity or scantling of any thing.

Keepers of assise, Assisores, m. pl. *Spel.* Also Jurymen.

To assise masures, Assisare mensuras, *Ry.* 569.

To assoil, Absolvo, ere. *Lex.* 12.

To assume or promise, Assumo, psi, tum.

Assumpsit (of the Latin *Assumptio*) is a voluntary promise made by word, by which a Man assumeth and taketh upon him to perform or pay any thing to another. It holds good in Law, where there is something laid down in consideration: For a promise without consideration will not bind in Law to performance, but is called *nudum pactum ex quo non oritur actio*.

The feast of the assumption of the blessed virgin, Festum assumptionis beatæ mariæ virginis.

To assure, *Insure*, Assuro, are. *Bri.* 16. Assecuro, are. *Reg.* 107. *Spel.* 55. 2 *Mon.* 653. 659.

An assurance, Assurancia, æ, f. Securantia, æ, f. *Co. Ent.* 30.

Policy of Assurance, Assecuratio, onis, f.

A. T.

At, Apud. præp.

At another time or place, Alias, adv.

At the first of all, Principio, adv. Primo adv.

At a day Ad diem.

At a place, Apud locum.

At that time, Tunc temporis.

Atheism, Atheia, æ, f.

An atheist, Atheos, i, m.

Athelney (in *Somersetshire*) Adelingia.

Athern (in *Ireland*) Athra.

Athol (part of *Scotland*) Atholia.

To attach, Attachio, are. It signifies to take or apprehend a Person by Commandment or Writ.

An attachment, Attachiamentum, i, n. *Spel.* 58. *Lex.* 12. It differs from an Arrest or Capias, for an Arrest proceeds out of the Interiour Courts by Precept, and Attachmeut out of the Superiour Courts by Precept or Writ, and that a Precept to Arrest hath these formal words *duci facias*, &c. and a Writ of Attachment these, *Precipimus tibi quod attachies*, A. B. & *habeas eum coram nobis*, &c. whereby it appears, that he who arrests, carries the Party arrested to another higher Person to be disposed of forthwith, but he that attacheth keeps the Party attached, and presents him in Court at the day assigned in the attachment, *Lambert's Eirenarcha, lib.* 1. *Ca.* 16. Yet (by *Kitchin fol.* 79.) an attachment sometimes issues out of a Court Baron, which is an Inferiour Court. There is also another difference in that an arrest lies only upon the Body of a Man, and an attachment sometimes on his Goods, which makes it in that particular differ from a Capias in being more general, for (by *Kitchin fo.* 263.) a Man may be attached by an hundred Sheep, but the Capias takes hold of the Body only.

Attachment by writ, Attachiamentum per breve. It differs from a Distress or Distringas in this, That an attachment reacheth not to Lands, as a Distress doth, and that a Distress toucheth not the Body (if it be properly taken) as an attachment doth, yet are they divers times confounded, howbeit in the most common use, an attachment is the apprehending of a Man by his Body to bring him to answer the Plaintiff's Action. A Distress without a Writ, is the taking of a Man's Goods for some real cause, as rent service, or the like, whereby to force him to Replevy, and so to be Plaintiff in an Action of Trespass against him that distrained him.

Attachment out of the Chancery, Breve de attachiamento è Curia Cancellariæ emanans. It is a Writ which is had of course upon an Affidavit made that the Defendant was served with a Subpena, and appear'd not, or it issueth upon not performing some order or decree after the return of this Attachment by the Sheriff, *quod defendens non est inventus in balliva sua*, &c. Another Attachment with Proclamation issues out against the Defendent, and if he appears not thereupon, then the Plaintiff shall have a Writ of Rebellion against him, *West Symboleography* 2. *part. Tit.* Proceedings in *Chancery*.

Attachment of Peiviledge, Breve attachiamenti de privilegio. It is by virtue of a Man's priviledge to call another to the Court whereto he himself belongs, and in respect whereof he is priviledged to answer some Action. *New Book of Entries, verbo privilege fo.* 431.

Foreign attachment, Attachiamentum forensicum. It is an Attachment of Goods or Money found within a Liberty or City, to satisfie some Creditor of his, within such City or Liberty, and by the Custom of some Places, as *London*, *Exceter*, &c. a Man may attach

attach Money or Goods in the hands of a ſtranger, whilſt he is in their Liberty, as if *A.* owes *B.* 5 *l.* and *C.* owes *A.* 5 *l.* *B.* may attach this 5 *l.* in the hands of *C.* to ſatiſie himſelf for the debt due from *A.* *Calthrop's Cuſtoms,* fo. 66.

Attachment of the foreſt, Attachiamentum foreſtæ. It is one of the three Courts there held, the loweſt is called the Attachment, the next *Swammote*, and the higheſt the Juſtice in Eyre's Seat. This Court of Attachment ſeems to be ſo called becauſe the Verderors of the Foreſt have therein no other Authority but to receive the Attachments of Offenders againſt Vert and Veniſon, taken by the reſt of the Officers, and to Enroll them, that they may be preſented or puniſhed at the next Juſtice Seat. *Manwood part* 1. fo. 93. And this Attaching is by three means, by Goods and Chattels, by Body, Pledges and Mainpriſe, or by the Body only. This Court is kept every forty days throughout the year: *See Crompton's Juriſdiction of Courts. Tit.* Court of the Foreſt, for the diverſity of Attachments: *See Regiſter of Writs*, verbo attachiamentum.

An attainder, Attinctura, æ, f. It is when a Man hath Committed Treaſon or Felony, and after Conviction, Judgment hath paſſed upon him: the Children of a Perſon Attainted cannot be Heirs to him or any other Anceſtor. If he were Noble and Gentile before, he and his Poſterity are made Baſe and Ignoble, in reſpect of any Nobility or Gentry which they had by their Birth. This corruption of Blood cannot be ſalved but by Authority of Parliament, the King's Letters Patents will not do it. *Co. on Lit. l.* 3. *c.* 13. *Sect.* 745.

An Attaint, Attincta, æ, f. *Spel.* 58. *Lex.* 13. *Pry.* 31. 47. It is a Writ that lies after Judgment againſt a Jury that hath given a falſe Verdict in any Court of Record, for 40 *s.* debt or damages, or more; the reaſon why it is ſo called, is, becauſe the Party that obtains it endeavours to touch or ſtain the Jury with Perjury, by whoſe Verdict he is grieved, and if the Verdict be found falſe, the Judgment anciently was, that the Juror's Meadows ſhould be Ploughed up, their Houſes broken down, their Woods grubbed up, and all their Lands and Tenements forfeited to the King, but if it paſs againſt him that brought the Attaint, he ſhall be Impriſoned and grievouſly ranſomed at the King's Will. *Co. on. Lit. fo.* 294. *b.*

Attainted, Attinctus, a, um. It is uſed particularly for ſuch as are found guilty of ſome Crime or Offence, and eſpecially of Felony or Treaſon, yet a Man is ſaid to be Attainted of Diſſeiſin, *Weſtm.* 1. *ca.* 24. & 36. *anno.* 3. *E.* 1. A Man is Attainted by two means, *viz.* by appearance or by proceſs, Attainder by appearance is by Confeſſion, by Battle or by Verdict: Attaint by by Confeſſion is twofold, one at the Bar before the Judges, when the Priſoner upon the Indictment read, being asked guilty? or not guilty? anſwers guilty, never putting himſelf upon the Jury: the other is before the Coroner in Sanctuary, where he upon his Confeſſion was in former times conſtrained to abjure the Realm, which from the effect is called Attainder by Abjuration. Attainder by Battle is when the Party is appealed by another, and chuſing to try the truth by Combat, rather than by Jury is Vanquiſhed. Attainder by Verdict is when the Priſoner at the Bar anſwering not guilty to the Indictment, hath an Inqueſt of Life and Death paſſing upon him, and is by their Verdict pronounced guilty. Attainder by Proceſs, i. e. Attainder by Default or Outlawry, is where the Party flies or doth not appear, until he hath been five times publickly called in the County Court, and at laſt upon his default is pronounced or retorned Outlawed. There is a difference between Attainder and Conviction, the firſt being larger than the other, Conviction being only by the Jury, and Attainder by Judgment: Yet by *Stamford*, *fo.* 9. Conviction is ſometimes called Attainder, for there he ſays, the Verdict of the Jury doth either acquit or attaint a Man, and ſo it is in *Weſtm.* 1 *ca.* 14.

To attempt, Attempto, are. 1. *Co.* 80. Attento, are. *Reg.* 40. 41. i. e. To endeavour.

An attendant, Attendens, ntis. It ſignifies one that owes a duty or ſervice to another, or depends on him, as where there is Lord Meſne and Tenant, the Tenant holds of the Meſne by a Penny, the Meſne holds over by two Pence. The Meſne releaſeth the Tenant all the Right he hath in the Land, and the Tenant dies; his Wife ſhall be endowed of the Land, and ſhe ſhall be Attendant to the Heir of the third part of the Penny, and not of the third part of the two Pence, for ſhe ſhall be endowed of the beſt Poſſeſſion of her Husband, and when the Wife is endowed by the Guardian ſhe ſhall be Attendant to the Guardian, and to the Heir at his full Age, *Kitchin* 209. *Perkins Tit. Dower*. 424.

Atteriſh (in *Scotland*) Trimonium.

The attire or ornaments of a womans head and neck, as a bonnet, French hood, knot, &c. Redimiculum, i, n.

To attorn, Attorno, are.

An attournment, Attornamentum, i, n. *Co. Lit.* 309. *Brac.* 41. It is an Agreement of the Tenant to the Grant of the Seigniory, or of a Rent or of a Donee in tail, or by Tenant for Life or Years, to a Grant or Reverſion, or remainder made to another. It is an ancient word of Art, and in the Common Law ſignifieth a turning or attorning from one to another. A Grant to the King or by by the King to another, is good without Attornment by his Prerogative. Also where one doth grant a Rent, Reversion, Remainder, Service, or Signiory to another by way of Devise, by a last Will and Testament. So when the thing granted doth pass by way of use, as where one levieth a Fine, bargaineth and selleth, hath Inrollment or Covenants to stand seised of a Reversion, &c. to the use of another, there needeth no Attornment. Conusee of a Fine of a Signiory, Rent, Reversion, &c. before Attornment, cannot maintain an Action of Wast, nor a Writ of Entry *ad Communem legem*, or in *Casu proviso*, or in *Consimili Casu*, upon the alienation of the Tenant, Escheate upon the dying of the Tenant without Heir, or Ward upon dying, his his Heir within age, therefore by force of the Ingrossement of the Fine, if it be of a Seigniory, he may compell the Tenant to attorne by a Writ called a *per quæ Servitia*, or if a Rent, by a Writ called a *Quem Redditum Reddit*, and if a Reversion, or remainder of a Tenement for Life, then by a Writ called a *Quid Juris Clamat*. *Cook on Lit. l.* 3. *c.* 10. *Sect.* 551.

An *attorny*. Atturnatus, i, m. attornatus, i, m. *Spel.* 58. It is an antient English word, and signifieth one that is set in the turn, stead or place of another. Of these some be private, and some be publick, as Attorneys at Law, whose Warrant from his Master is, *ponit loco suo talem attornatum suum*, which setteth in his turn or place, such a man to be his Attorney, *Co. on Lit. l.* 1. *c.* 7. *Sect.* 59. Those that be private are sometimes by writing, sometimes by word, to make or take Livery or Possession, to make claim to Lands, to enter, to sue, &c. and it is a rule that where the Attorney doth less than the authority and commandment, all that he doth is void, but where he doth that which he is authorized to do, and more, it is good, for so much as is warranted, and void for the rest. *Perk.* 187.109. If a man be disseised of black Acre, and white Acre, and a Warrant of Attorney is made to enter into both, and make Livery, and the Attorney entereth only into one and maketh Livery, it is void for all. So if a Letter of Attorney be made to deliver Seisin upon a Condition, and he doth it without a Condition, it is void, because he did less than his Authority. But if one have authority to deliver Seisin to *J. S.* and he do it to *J, S.* and J.N, that is good as to J.S. because no more than his authority.

The King's Attorney General. Attornatus Domini Regis Generalis.

The King's Attorney of the Dutchy. Attornatus Domini Regis Ducatûs sui Lancastriæ.

A *Letter of attorney*, Scriptum attornatorium. *Co. Ent.* 683.

To

To make an attorney, Constituere attornatum.

A. U.

Avens, or herb Bennet Caryophillata.

Available, Vălidus, a, um.

Audience Court, Curia audienciæ Cantuariensis. It is a Court belonging to the Archbishop of *Canterbury*, and held in his Palace, of equal authority with the Arches, although inferior both in dignity and antiquity. *vid.* 4. *Inst.* f. 337.

Audiendo & Terminando, is a Writ or Commission directed to several persons (when any Insurrection or Misdemeanor is committed in any place) for the appeasing and punishment thereof, *Fitz. nat. brev. fol.* 110.

Audita Querela, is a Writ that lies against one who having taken a Statute Merchant or Recognizance in nature of a Statute staple, or a Judgment or Recognizance of another, and craving or having obtained Execution of the same from the Mayor or Bailiffs, before whom it was acknowledged at the complaint of the party who acknowledged the same, upon suggestion of some just cause why Execution should not be granted by the Lord Chancellor of *England* (or Lord Keeper of the Great Seal) upon view of the Exception suggested to the Judges of either Bench, praying them to grant Summons to the Sheriff of the County where the Creditor is, for his appearance at a certain day before him. *Vide veiel nat. brev. fo.* 66. & *Fitzh. nat. brev. fol.* 102.

An *auditor*, Auditor, oris, m. He is an Officer of the King, or some other great Personage, who yearly by examining the accounts of all under Officers accountable, makes up a general Book, which shews the difference between their Receipts or Charge and their allowance, commonly called Allocations, as namely the Auditors of the Exchequer take the accounts of those Receivers who receive the Revenue of the Augmentation, as also of the Sheriffs.

Audrie (a Womans name) Audria, æ. f.

Etheldreda, æ, f.

Aven (a River in *Scotland*) ave.

Aven-lisse (a River in *Ireland*) Modonus.

Avennon (a River in *Ireland*) Dabrona.

Average, averagium, ii, n. a service due from the Tenant with Horse or Cart, also a small Duty Merchants pay to the Master of the Ship for his Care of their Goods. *Spel.* 60. *Lex.* 14.

An *Augre*, Terebra, æ, f.

A *little augre*, or wimble. Terebellum, i, n.

August, Augustus, i, n.

Avice (a Womans name) Avisia, æ, f.

Avin (a River in *Scotland*) Avinus.

Avington or aventon (in *Gloucestershire*) abone, abonis.

Aukland (in *Durham*) Archelandra.

Auldby (in *Yorkshire*) Derventio.

Aulerton (in *Nottinghamshire*) Segelocum.

An *Aunt by the Father's side*. Amita, æ, f.

An *Aunt by the Mother's side*. Matertera, æ, f.

A *Great aunt by the Father's side*. Proamita, æ, f.

A *great aunt by the Mother's side*, Promatertera, æ, f.

To *averr*. Verifico, are.

An *averment*. Verificatio, onis, f. *Co. Lit.* 362.

Averdupois-weight. Libra sedecim unciarum.

Avery (a Man's name) Albericus, i, m.

Avola (in *Scilly*) Hybla major.

Avon (a River in *Wilts* and *Northamptonshire*) Avona. Alannius.

Avendale or Oundale (in *Northamptonshire*) Avonæ vallis.

Austin (a man's name) Augustinus, i, m.

An *avowry*, Advocare, is, n. advocatio. It is a manifestation or maintenance of a thing formerly done, and cometh of a French word *Advour*, and it is used in our Law, when one hath taken a distress for Rent or other thing, and he who is distrained sueth for Replevin, and he that took the Distress doth Justifie.

Auxilium, ad filium militem faciendum, & ad filiam maritandam, is a Writ directed to the Sheriff of every County where the King or other Lord hath any Tenants to Levy of them reasonable aids towards the Knighting of his Son at 15 years, or the Marriage of his Daughter at 7. At the Common Law it was not limited, yet ought to have been *rationabile auxilium*, but now it is limited to 20 *s.* for a Knights Fee, and so for 20 *l. per annum in Soccagio*. Regist. Orig. fol. 87. Glanvil. l. 9. cap. 8. West. 1. 30 Ed. 1. 25. Ed. 3. 11,

Authentick. Authenticus, a, um.

An *Author*: Author, oris, m.

The *author of a Law*. Legislator, oris, m.

To *authorize*, Authoriso, are.

Authority, Authoritas, atis, f.

Autumn or Harvest, Autumnus, i, m.

Auvagdoune (in *Ireland*) Achadia.

Aurum Reginæ, a duty belonging to the Queen, amounting to a tenth part of the Fine paid upon a Grant of the King.

Auxilliary Forces, Auxilia, orum.

Auton or non (a River in *Northamptonshire*) Ausona, antona.

A. W.

To *award* or Issue Writs. *Emanare vel dirigere Brevia.*

An *award*, vide Arbitrement.

The award, Judgment or Determination of such a Judge, Arbitramentum, i, n.

Awbrey (the Family) Aubræus, aubericus.

A *Shoemakers Awl*, Subŭla, æ. f.

An

An *awm of wine*, Menſura circiter 360. libras, amphora vini.

A. X.

An *Ax* (for Execution) Sĕcūris, is, f.

A *Carpenters broad ſquaring Ax*. Dolābra, æ. f.

A *Battle Ax*, Bipennis, is, f. ſecuris bellica.

A *Poll-Ax*, Ceſtra, æ, f.

A *Chip Ax*, Aciſa, æ. f.

An Ax to cut both ways, Securis anceps.

A *Pick-ax*, Rutrum, i, n, marra, æ, f.

An *Axle-tree*, Axis, is, m.

A hole in the Nave for the Axle-tree, Rotæ Tubus,

A. Y.

Ayd, Auxilium, ii, n. Ayd is where a particular Proprietor is Impleaded, and not being able to defend the thing for which he is Impleaded, he prayeth Ayd of ſome better able, and it is two ways. 1. In a Plea real. *Tenens petit auxilium de* A. B. *ſine quo Reſpondere non poteſt*. 2. In a Plea Perſonal, and then the Defendant *Petit auxilium ad manutenendum exitum* 4. *H.* 30.

Azarias (a Man's name) Azarias, æ. m.

An *azure-ſtone*, Lapis lazuli.

B A C.

A *Bachelor* (or unmarried man) Cælebs, ibis.

Bachelorſhip. Cælibatus, ûs, m.

A *Bachelor of Art*, Baccalaureus, artium.

A *Bachelor of Divinity*, ſacræ Theologiæ, Baccalaureis.

To back a Horſe at firſt, equum dŏmitare.

The back of a man or beaſt. dorſum, i, n. Tergum, i, n.

A *little back*, dorſiculum, i. n.

The back bone, ſpina dorſi.

Of *or pertaining to the backbone*. Spinalis, le.

To *break ones back*. Delumbo, are.

Brokenback't. Elumbis, be.

To *ſplit the back of any thing*. Exdorſuo, are.

The *back of the hand*. Metacarpium. ii, n.

A *ſaddle-back*. Subſidens tergum.

On the backſide, retro, adv.

That dwelleth on the backſide. Poſticus, a, um.

A back-door. Poſticŭm, ci, n.

A little back-door. Poſtĭcŭlum li, n.

Back-doors, oſtia retrorſa.

Backs for Chairs. Terga cathedralia.

Backs of Leather. Præſegmina corii. Terga corii.

The back-ſtairs. Poſtica pars Palatii.

Bacon (the Family) De Beda. De Bajocis.

Bacon, Lardum, i, n.

A flitch of Bacon. Succidia, æ, f.

A gammon of bacon. Perna, æ, f, Petăſo, onis, m.

A

A little gammon of bacon. Petasunculus, li, m.

Bacon-Grease. Axungia, æ f.

Rusty-bacon. Lardum rancidum.

B A D.

A badge or cognizance. Bagea, æ. f. West Licences. 550

A badger (or Grey) melis, is, f.

A Badger. Emax. ācis. adj. One that carrieth Corn, or like Provision from one place to transport it to another for Gain. See *Stat.* 5. *Eliz.*

B. A. G.

Bagley. Bagileganæ Sylvæ.

A bag. Baga, æ, f, *Lex.* 29. *Cow.* 170. *Pry* 49. bis.

A *bag of Leather*, ascopera, æ. f.

A *money bag.* Sparteum, ei, n. Loculus nummarius.

A *sealed bag*, Sacculus signatus.

A *cloak bag.* Pēnŭlārium, ii; n. pera, æ. f.

A *meal bag*, Saccus frumentarius.

A *bag or sack-bearer*, Saccārius, ii, m.

That which is put or carried in a bag. Saccarius, a, um.

Bagged up. Saccātus, a, um.

That which is strained thorough a bag. Saccatus, a, um,

A *Bag-Pipe*, Utrĭcŭlus, i, m. Tibia utrĭcŭlāris.

A *Bag-Piper.* Utrĭcŭlārius, ii. m.

To truss up bag and baggage, at the removing of a Camp. Sarcinas & saccas colligere. Sarcinis aut vasis collectis proficisci.

Bag and Baggage. Sarcinæ; arum. f. Utensilia.

Baggage (Trumpery or lumber) Scruta, orum, n.

He that selleth baggage (or old stuff) Scrūtārius, ii, m.

B. A. I.

Bail. Ballium, ii, n. *Spel.* 69. It signifies the freeing or setting at liberty of one Arrested, or Imprisoned upon an Action Civil or Criminal, under Security taken for his Appearance at a day and place certain. Or it is safe keeping or protection, and thereupon we say, when a Man upon Surety, is delivered out of Prison, *Traditur in Ballium*, he is delivered into Bail, i. e. into their safe keeping, or protection from Prison. It is derived from the French word *Bailler*, and that also cometh of the Greek βαλλεῖν. They both signifie to deliver into hand, for he that is bailed, is taken out of Prison and delivered into the hands of his friends. *Cook on Lit. l.* 1. *c.* 10. *Sect.* 79. What kind of Offenders may be bailed. See *Cook* 2. *part of Inst. c.* 15. Bail is said to be sometimes Special, and sometimes Common. Special Bail is where the Debt or Damages amount to Twenty Pounds or upwards by Stat. of 13. *Car.* 2. Tho since by the rules of Court of either Bench, Special Bail is taken where the Debt or Damges amount to Ten Pounds or higher. Common Bail is for small sums, under Twenty Pounds, by the said

Act appointed for Special Bail, and since under Ten Pounds by the aforesaid Rules of Court. Bail differs from Mainprise, for that he that is bailed, is by the Law accounted to be always in the custody of those persons that bailed him, but he that is Mainprised, is always at large, to go at his own liberty from the time he is Mainprised, till the day of his appearance, *vid.* 2 *Inst. fol.* 78.

Bailment, is a delivery of things, Writings, Goods, or Stuff to another. The Intendment of Law in cases of Bailment, is that it resteth indifferent, whether he be guilty or not until Tryal. *Vid.* Terms of Law. *Dalton.*

A *Bailiff.* Ballivus, i, m. This word Bailie (as some say) cometh of the French word *Bailiff*, but in truth, *Bailie*, is an old *Saxon* word, and signifieth a safe keeper or protector, the Sheriff that hath *custodiam comitatus*, is called *Ballivus*, and the County *Balliva Sua*, when he cannot find the Defendant, he returneth, *non est inventus in Balliva mea* Cook on Lit. *l.* 1. *c.* 10. *Sect.* 79. *Id. l.* 3. *c.* 1. *Sect.* 248. A Bailiff is a subordinate Officer under the Sheriff, of which there be two sorts. Bailiffs Errant, or Itinerant, and Bailiffs of Franchises.

Ballivus Itinerans, a Bailiff Errant is one whom the Sheriff appoints to go up and down the County to serve Writs, Summon the County Court, Sessions, Assises, &c.

A *Bailiff of a Franchise*, Liberty, *Hundred*, Ballivus Franchesiarum, Libertatum, Hundredi. He is one that is appointed to do such offices within the Liberty or Franchise, which the Bailiff Itinerant doth at large in the County.

A *Bailiff* of a *Leet, Court Baron, Mannor.* Ballivus Letæ, Baronis, Manerii. He is one that is appointed by the Lord or his Steward within every Mannor to do such offices as appertain thereunto, as to summon the Court, Warn the Tenants and Resiants; also, to summon the Leet and Homage, Levy Fines, and make Distresses, &c. of which you may read at large in *Kitchins* Court Leet and Court Baron.

A *Bailiwick*, Balliva, æ, f. *Spel.* 67. *Pry* 14. 51, 53.

Bainbridge (in *Yorkshire*) Bainus Pons.

To Bait at an Inn. Diverto, is, si, sum, ere.

A *Baiting place* (or Inn) Diversorium, ii, n.

That which serveth to bait (*or lodge in*) Diversōrius, a, um.

To lay baite for Fishes or Birds. Inesco, are. Obesco, are.

A *bait for Fish or Birds.* Esca, æ. f.

Baize (or fine Frise) Villosus pannus.

B. A. K.

To *bake*, Pinso, is, si, & ui, itum, sum, & stum, ere, i.e. in furno coquere.

Baked

Baked, Pinſitus, a, um.

Baked in a pan, Teſtaceus, a, um.

Baked under the aſhes. Subcineritius, a, um.

Eaſie to be baked, Coctilis, le.

Baked on a ſudden in a Furnace, or Oven, Clibanicus, a, um. in Clibano coctus.

Baked meat. Pinſum, i, n.

A *baker*, Piſtor, oris, m. Fornacarius, ii, m.

A *baker of ſpiced-bread.* Piſtor dulciarius.

A *baker of Pies.* Paſtilarius, ii, m.

A *baker of white meate.* Lactarius piſtor.

A *bakers brake.* Frangibulum, li, n.

A *bakers Shovel, or Peel wherewith bread is ſet into the Oven*, Infurnibulum, i, n.

A *baker's kneeding-trough.* Formaſtra, æ, f.

A *bakers-Wife* (or *Woman baker*). Panifica, æ f.

A *bake-houſe.* Piſtrinum, ii, n. Panificina, æ, f,

A *bakers trade.* Panificium, ii, n.

A *baking pan.* Teſtus, ûs, m.

A *braſs baking pan.* Artopta Ærea.

B A L.

To *Balaſs a Ship*, Săburro, are.

Balaſſed, Saburrātus, a, um.

A *balaſs (or ſtay wherewith Ships are poiſed to ſail upright)* Saburrra, æ, f. ſabulum, li, n.

A *balaſſing (or counterpoiſing)* Libramen, in, is; n.

A *bale of goods*, Bala, æ. f. *Ra. Ent.* 15. *Fle.* 33. *Bala cujuſlibet averdupois Pry* 197.

A *balcony.* Menianum, ni, n. Subdiale, is, n.

Balconies. Projecta, orum, n.

Balſom. Balſamum, i, n.

To make a balk or ridge in earing of land. Imporco, are. Liro, a, f.

A *balk (or ridge between two furrows)* Parca, æ, f. Lira, æ. f.

A *making a balk in eiring*, Imporcatio, onis, f.

A *ball*, Pila, æ. f.

Of a ball, Pilaris, re.

A *cunning toſſer of balls (a Jugler)* Pilarius, ii, m.

A *Foot-ball.* Harpaſtum, ti, n. Pila pedalis.

A *Waſhing-ball*, Smegma, atis, n. magma, atis, n.

A *Seller of Waſh-balls*, Smegmatopola, æ, m.

Balls made by Apothecaries. Paſtilli, orum, n.

Sweet balls, Pilæ oderiferæ.

A *Printers Ink-ball*, Tudes, itis, m.

To ballance (or weigh any thing) Pendo, dis, pependi, ſum, ere.

A *balance (or Pair of Scales)* Bilancea, æ. f. *Reg.* 270. *Hanſards Pleadings*, 32. Mr. *Townſend* in the firſt Impreſſion of his Preparative to Pleading *fol.* 49. unadviſedly makes *Balancea* a balance, and *Quotes Prinns* Records of the *Tower*, *fol.* 196. for his warrant, wherein there is no ſuch word (I ſuppoſe he means *Prinns Animadverſions*, on the Lord *Cook's* 4. *Inſt.*) and afterwards makes uſe of *Bilanx* in *Goldman's Dictionary*, for the ſame purpoſe, without mentioning the Writ *de Bilanciis deferendis* in the

the Regifter, *ut fupra*, where you have thefe words. *Nos fupplicationi prædictæ annuentes. Mandamus quod bilancias & pondera*, &c. *ufque portum de gippewico deferri*, &c.

A *great pair of balances*, Trŭtīna, æ, f.

A *little pair of balances*. Trutinella, æ,

A *Goldfmith's balance*, Statēra, æ. f.

The beam of a balance, Librile, is, n. jugum, i, n.

The tongue of a balance, Examen, inis, n.

The hole or hollow wherein the tongue of the balance turneth, Agina, æ. f.

The handle of a balance, Anfa, æ, f.

The fcale of a balance, Lanx,cis, f. That which is put into a balance, to make even weight. Săcōma, ătis, n.

B A M.

Bamborough (*in the north*) Bebba.

B A N.

Ban River (in *Lincolnfhire*) Banus fluvius.

To divide into bands or companies Decurio, are.

A *band of Soldiers*, Banda Militaris. *Spel.* 70.

A *band or troop of Soldiers*, Comitiva Soldariorum. *Co. Ent.* 436. *Comitativa. Stat. de malefactoribus in parcis.*

A *band of Men*, Exercitus foldariorum.

Of or belonging to the fame troop or band. Turmalis, le.

A *band or hoft of foot-men.* Peditatus, ûs, m.

Small bands of Men. Cohorticulæ, arum, f.

By-bands or companies. Turmatum, adv.

A *band* (*or thing wherewith any thing is tied*) Ligatura, æ,f. Ligamentum, i, n.

A *Neck-band*, or Shirt-band. Collare, is, n.

A *Hat-band*, Spira, æ, f.

A *Head-band*. Anadēma, ătis.

A *Swathing-band*, Fafcia, æ, f.

A *Swathing-band for Children*, Fafciale, lis. Fafcia Cúnabulorum.

A *Withy-band* , Vinctus , ûs, m.

A *Little-band* (*or Swaithing-cloath to tie up wounds.*) Fafciola æ, f.

Banns of Matrimony. Banna, æ, f. *Ra. Ent.* 178. *Cow.* 33. *Lex.* 15.

To banifh. Relēgo , are, in Exilium Relegare.

Banifhed, tranfported.
Foris-judicatus, a, um.
Banitus, a, um.

A *banifhment*, Bannitio, onis, f. Reg. 312. *Spel.* 73.

A *banifhed perfon*, Exul, ulis, c. 2. Extorris, is, c. 2.

A *banifter*, Columella tornata. Columna parva & brevis.

Banchor or bangor (in *Flintfhire*) Bonium feu bovium.

Of *Bangor*, Bangorenfis.

Bifhop of Bangor, Epifcopus Bangorenfis.

A *bank of the River*, Ripa, æ, f.

A *bank (or hillock)* Tumulus, li, m.

The Sea-bank, Littus, ŏris, n.

Of the Sea-banks, Littōralis, le.

A *little water-bank*, Ripula, æ, f.

A bank with poles, boards, &c. to keep off the water from the Wharf, Pila, æ. f.

A *bank or down by the Sea side*. Falesia, æ. f.

High banks made of green Turfs, raised one above another to keep out the Water overflowing, that Cattle may be safe. *Tribunalia, orum, n.*

The banks brink, Margo Ripæ. Crepīdo, inis, f.

That dwelleth on the water banks, Riparius, a, um.

Places before the banks of a River, Præripia, orum, n.

From bank to bank, Ripātim. adv.

He that looks to the banks. Riparius, ii, m.

A reward given to maintain water banks. Ripātum, ti, n.

To put money in the bank. Collibo pecuniam curare, vel mittere.

The sum in the common bank, wheremany have a share. Sors, tis, f.

A *banker*. Nŭmŭlārius, ii, m. argentarius, ii, m. One that maketh gain by changing of money, or letting it out to Usury.

A *bankers Table or Shop*. Argentaria, æ, f.

A *bank of Exchange*. Taberna argentaria.

A *Table whereon a banker telleth money*. Trapeza, æ, f.

The loss or gain of money in bank. Collybus, bi, m.

A *bankruptsie*. Bankruptia, æ, f.

A bankrupt. Decoctor, oris, m.

A *Knight Banneret*. Bannerettus, i, m. *Spel.* 71. He is a Knight made in the Field, with the Ceremony of cutting off the Point of his Standard, and making it a Banner. They are allowed to display their Arms in a Banner in the King's Army as Barons do, *vide*, *Smith*'s Commonwealth, *Cambden*'s Britan, 109. *Stat.* 14. *R.* 2. *ca.* 11. 5. *R.* 2. *Stat.* 2. *C.* 4. 13. *R.* 2. *Stat.* 2. *C.* 1. & 4. *Inst. fol.* 6.

A banner. Bannerium, ii, n. *Spel.* 70.

Bannes-down (near Bath in Somersetshire) Mons Badonicus.

To *banquet together*, Convivor, aris

A *banquet*. Epulum, i, n. pl. Epulæ, arum, f.

A *banqueting-house, or place*. Convivarium, ii, n. Epŭlārium, ii, n.

Bansey, or *Bean Castle (in Scotland)* Banatia.

BAR

To *Barb (or shave)* Tondeo, es, di, sum, ere, & part. ens. Rado, is, si, sum, ere.

A *Barber*. Tonsor, oris, m. Barbitonsor, oris, m. Rasor, oris, m.

A *Barber Chirurgeon*. Tonsor Chyrurgicus.

A *little barber*. Tonstriculus, li, m.

A *barbers Shop*. Barbitorium, ii, n. Tonſorium, ii, n. Tonſtrina, æ, f.

A *barbers baſon*. Concha Tonſoria. Pelvis Tonſoria.

A *barbers caſe of Inſtruments*. Ferrementa Tonſoria.

A *barbers pair of Sciſſers*. Forpex, ĭcis, m.

Belonging to a barber. Tonſorius, a, um.

To barb (*or dreſs Horſes with Trappings*) Phalero, are.

Barbs (*or Horſes Trappings*) Phălĕræ, arum, f.

Barbed (*Trapped*) Phălĕrātus, a, um.

To barb (*or beard Wooll*) Extremitates vellerum tondere.

A bare plat without Corn or Graſs. Glabretum, i, n.

Bardeſey Iſle (on the Coaſt of *Wales*) Adros, vel Andros, vel Andrium Edri.

Bardolph (the Family) Bardulphus, De Batonia, De Beaumois, De Beleſmo.

To Bargain (*to agree upon a price*) Barganizo, are.

A Bargain. Bargania, æ, f. Chævifantia, æ, f.

A *bargaining*. Barganizatio, onis m.

A *bargain-maker*. Pactor, oris, f.

Bargeney (*in Carrict in Scotland*) *and a Creek there*. Berigonium. Rerigonium. Rherigonium. Rhetigonium.

A *barge*. Barga, æ, f. *Spel.* 73. *Bargea*, æ, f. *Co. Ent.* 536.

A *barge, or Ship for Grain*. Navis frumentaria.

A *barge or Ship that Noblemen uſe for Pleaſure, with gorgeous Chambers and other ornaments*. Navithalamus, i, m.

A *Barge-man*. Barcellarius, ii, m.

A *Barge-mote*. Berghmota, æ, f. Conventus ſeu Curia de Rebus metallicis. *A Court belonging to Mines*.

A *Duty paid by barge-men to the owner of the Ground where they tow their barge*. Towagium, ii, n.

A *bark* (*Ship*) Barca, æ, f. *Spel.* 75.

A *ſmall bark*. Navicula, æ, f. I Fo. 135. Navigiolum, li, n. Lembunculus, li, m.

A *bark which is very light or ſwift of Courſe*. Lembus, i, m. Dromo, onis, m.

A *bark-man* (*the Maſter of the bark*) Naviculator oris, m.

To bark or Pill trees. Cortico, are. Decortico, are.

Barked or Pilled. Delibratus, a, um.

A *barker of trees*, delibrator, oris, m.

The barking of a tree. Decorticatio, onis, f.

The bark of a tree. Cortex, ĭcis.

The inward bark of a tree, Liber, bri, m.

A *little or thin bark*. Corticula, æ, f.

A *bark or tan-houſe*. Barkaria, æ, f. Cerdonarium, ii, n.

That hath a thick bark. Cortĭcōſus, a, um.

Having a rind or bark. Corticatus, a, um.

Barley

Barley. Hordeum, ei, n. pl. nom. acc. & voc. Hordea.

Barley growing upon the Mountains. Amphicaustis.

Barley-meal. Alphitera vel alphiton.

Barley flour dried at the Fire, and fried after it hath been soaking in the water. Polenta, æ, f.

Great barley (or beer barley) Zea vel Zeia. Zea deglubita.

A kind of barley having two rows in each ear. Calaticum hordeum.

A kind of barley having two rows of ears. Distichum Hordeum.

Of or belonging to barley. Hordeaceus, a, um.

Barley water. Ptisana, æ, f.

Barm or Yest. Spuma vel flos Cervisiæ.

A barn. Horreum, ei, n.

A barn for the threshing of Corn dry. Nūbĭlar, āris, n.

A barn floor. Area, æ, f. Scuria, æ, f.

A *barn for Hay.* Fœnile, is, n.

A *little barn.* Horrĕŏlum, ii, n.

A *barn Keeper.* Horriarius, ii, m.

Of a barn. Horreatitus, a, um.

A *barnacle (an Instrument to set upon the nose of an unruly Horse.)* Pastomis, idis, f.

Barnet (in *Hertfordshire*) Sulloniacæ. Sullonicæ.

A *baron.* Baro, onis, m. *Spel.* 76. The lowest degree of Peerage in *England*, a degree next to a Viscount, anciently the Lord of a Mannor.

Barons or Judges of the Court of Exchequer. Barones Scaccarii.

Lord Chief Baron of the Exchequer. Capitalis Baro Scaccarii Domini Regis. There are four Barons of that Court, of whom he is Principal and the other three are his Assistants in Cases of Justice between the King and his Subjects, touching matters appertaining to the Exchequer and the King's Revenue. Their Office is to look to the Accounts of the Prince, and to that end they have Auditors under them, as also to decide all Causes appertaining to the King's Revenue, coming into the King's Revenue by any means.

A *Baron of the Exchequer.* Unus Baronum Scaccarii Domini Regis.

Barons of the Cinque Ports, Barones de quinque Portubus.

Barons of London. Barones Londoniæ. The Chief Magistrates of *London* were so called, before there was a Lord Mayor. *Vide Cartam Regis Hen. tertii Concess. Civibus London.*

A *baroness* (or *baron*'s Wife) Baronissa, æ, f.

A *baronet.* Baronettus, i, m. *Spel.* 88. A degree of Honor under Peerage, that takes place of all Knights.

Belonging to a baronet. Baronatus, a, um. 1 *Mon.* 851.

A *barony.* Baronia, æ, f. The Dignity, Territory and Fee of a Baron, under which notion are comprehended not only the

Fees and Lands of Temporal Barons, but of Bishops.

To *bar* (*or set with bars*) Clāthro, are. Pessulum foribus obdere.

A *bar or bolt to make fast doors or gates.* Obex, icis, m, or f. Rĕpāgŭlum, li, n. Rexaciculum, li, n. Pessŭlus, li, m.

To bar the door. Opessulo, are. Obdere pessulum ostio.

A *bar or lever.* Vectis, is, m.

A *little bar.* Pessellum, li, n.

A *bar with an Iron Point.* Vectis rostratus.

A *bar to turn the wheel of a Wine-press.* Sūcŭla, æ, f. Rĕmissarius vectis.

A *cross bar.* Clathrus, thri, m.

Cross-barred. Cancellatus, a, um.

Barred, bolted. Oppressulatus, a, um.

To break open the bars. Repagula convellere.

A *bar where Causes are pleaded, also a bar to an Action.* Barra, æ, f. *Co. Lit.* 372. *Ra. Ent.* 654. *Lex.* 17. Barrandum *Ra. Ent.* 619. barrata placita. *Cow.* 91. pro *præcludendum.* Barre is a word common as well to the English as to the French, of which commeth the Noun a Barre, Barra. It signifieth legally destruction forever, or taking away for a time of the action of him that hath Right, it is called a Plea in Barre, when such a Barre is Pleaded. *Cook.* on *Lit. l.* 3. *c.* 13. *Sect.* 708.

To bar or foreclose. Barro, are.

To be barred or foreclosed, Barrandum, ger.

Barred (foreclosed) Barratus, a, um.

Barratry, Barratria, æ, f. 8. *Co.* 36, 37. in Epistola, *fol.* 5.

A barrel, Cadus, i, m. Barellus, li, m. *Vet. Int.* 235. *Prynn's* Tower *Records* 185. *Ra. Ent.* 16. 204. 653. 1. *Bul.* 126. *Hct.* 93. *Item Barillatus*; as *Barillatum vini continentem Jalonem,* Fl. 70. A barrel or vessel of wine containing a Galon.

The barrel of a gun, Tormenti fistula.

A barrel maker, Vietor, oris, m.

To make barren (to take all the fatness or substance of Land away) Desrugo, are.

To wax barren, Stĕrĭlesco, ere.

Barren, Stĕrĭlis, le.

Very barren, Permacer, cra, crum.

Barrenly, Steriliter, adv.

Barrenness, Sterilitas, atis, f.

A barrester at law, Barresterius, ii, m. (i. e.) a Councellor. Vide Apprentice of the Law.

An utter barrester, de gradu de exteriori Barra, &c.

A barretor, Barrectator, oris, m. A Common mover and exciter or maintainer of Suits, Quarrels or Parts, either in Courts or elsewhere in the Country, in Courts of Records or others, as in the County, Hundred, or other Inferiour Courts. In the Country in three manners, 1. In disturbance of the Peace, in taking or keeping of Possessions or Lands in controversie, not only ly by Force, but alſo by Subtilty. 2. And moſt commonly in ſuppreſſion of Truth and Right. 3. By falſe inventions and ſowing of Calumniations, Rumours and Reports, whereby diſcord and diſquiet may grow between Neighbours. He is never quiet but at variance with one or other. The word is derived of Barret, which ſignifieth a Quarrel, a Bar-troubler, or Bar-offender. *Co. on Lit. l.* 3. *c.* 13. *Sect.* 701.

A common barreter, or Bar-offender, is a common Quarreller, mover or maintainer of Quarrels, either in the Court or Country. Some derive it of the *French* word *Barrateur*, which ſignifieth a Deceiver, others of the Latin word *Baratro*, which ſignifieth a vile Knave, or Unthrift. Some of two legal words *Barra*, which ſignifieth the Bar in Courts where Cauſes are debated, and *Rettum*, which ſignifieth a Crime or Offence. He is *Seminator litium & pacis domini regis perturbator. Cook* 8. *Rep. Barrets Caſe. p.* 37.

Barrow river (in *Ireland*) Brigus, Birgus.

A hand-barrow, Carrus manualis.

A wheel-barrow, Pabo, onis, m. Carrus unirotis, vehiculum truſatile.

A barrow to carry out dung, Vecticula, æ, f.

Barrow-greaſe, Adeps porcina.

A barrow pig, Verres, is, m.

A barton, Bartona, æ, f. *Spel.* 92. Bartonum, i, n. (i. e.) a Court or Yard to keep Poultry in. *Prædictus C. C. per, &c. Conceſſiſſet. infeofaſſet & Conveiaſſet prædicto E. H. hæred, &c. Omne illum Bartonum ſuum & dominicas terras, &c. Trin.* 28 *Car.* 2. *Regis Rotulo* 1999 *cum Robinſon in Com. Banço in actione Conventionis fract. in Cornub. inter Boſcawen & Herlequer & Cook Def.*

Barwick *upon* Tweed (in the North) Abbrevicum, Barvicus, Barwicus, Berwicus, Borcovicum, Borcovicus, Tueſis.

B A S.

Baſing (in *Hampſhire*) Baſenga, Baſingum.

A basket, Sporta, æ, f. Călăthus, m.

A hand-basket, Corbis, is, f.

A wicker basket, Ciſta texta.

A wicker basket wherein fiſh are kept, Fiſcella, æ, f.

A basket or skuttle to carry Earth, Cŏphĭnus, i, m.

A basket or panier to carry bread in, Panariolum, li, n.

Grape gatherers baskets, Quali vindemiatorii.

A basket of oſiers out of which Wine runneth when it is preſſed, Qualum, li, n.

A duſt basket, Doſſuaria Corbis.

A little basket to carry meat, Sportella cum obſoniis.

A ſhoulder basket, Corbis Dorſuaria.

A basket (or pannier) made of oſiers, Caniſtrum, tri, n.

Seed baskets, Satoria Quala.

A little basket of Osiers, Quasillum, li, n.

A twig basket, Reticulus, li, m.

A basket made of bulrushes or such like thing, Scirpiculum, li, n.

A little basket, Sportella, æ, f. Sportŭla, æ, f. Calăthiscus, ci, m. Corbŭla, æ, f.

A basket bearer, Sportularius, ii, m. Circinator, oris, m. Cistifer, ri, m. Circŭĭtor, oris, m.

A basket wench, Ancilla quasillaria.

A basket maker, Cophinarius' ii, m.

A bason to wash hands in, Malluvia, æ, f. Trulleum, ei, n.

A bason to wash ones feet in, Pelvis, is, f. Pelluvia, æ, f.

Basspole Isle (on the *French* Coast) Barsa.

A male bastard, Bastardus, i, m. Bastard is he that is born of any Woman not married, so that his Father is not known by the order of the Law, and therefore by the Law he is sometimes called *filius nullius*, the Son of no Man, sometimes *filius populi*, the Son of every Man, *Cui pater est populus, pater est sibi nullus & omnis. Cui pater est populus, non habet ille patrem.* The Civil Law doth Legitimate the Child born before Matrimony, as well as that which is born after: And giveth unto it Succession in the Parents Inheritance. But to the Child born out of Matrimony, the Law of *England* alloweth no Succession. The *Civilians* say, *Matrimonium subsequens tollit peccatum prius, Matrimonium subsequens legitimos facit quoad Sacerdotium* (because they are legitimate by the Canon Law) *non quoad successionem, propter consuetudinem regni quæ se habet in contrarium.* The Bishops were instant with the Lords that they would consent that all such as were born afore Matrimony should be Legitimate, as well as they that be born within Matrimony, as to the Succession of Inheritance; because the Church accepteth such for legitimate. *Et omnes Comites Barones una voce responderunt, Nollumus Leges Angliæ mutare quæ huc usque usitatæ sunt & approbatæ:* And all the Earls and Barons with one voice answered, That they would not change the Laws of the Realm, which hitherto had been used and approved. If a Man take a Wife, which is great with Child by another, which was not her Husband; and after the Child is born within the Espousals, then it shall be said the Child of her Husband, tho' it were but one day after the Espousals solemnized, according to that, *Pater est quem nuptiæ demonstrant*, for whose the Cow is (as it is commonly said) his is the Calf also. *Smith's* Commonwealth of *England.* Terms of Law. There was an Act made *ann.* 21. *Jacobi Regis*, to prevent the destroying and murthering of Bastard Children, and it was continued 3 *Caroli, c.* 4. If any Woman be delivered of any

any Issue, which by the Laws of this Realm should have been a Bastard, and shall endeavour by drowning or secret burying, or any other way by her self or others to conceal the death thereof, whether it were born alive or not, the mother so offending shall suffer death as in case of murder, except she can prove by one witness at least, that the same Child was born dead. A Bastard having gotten a name by Reputation, may purchase by his reputed or known name to him and his Heirs, although he can have no Heir, unless it be the Issue of his body. *Cook on Lit. l.* 1. *c.* 1. *Sect.* 1. A Man makes a Lease to *B.* for Life, remainder to the eldest Issue Male of *B.* and the Heirs Males of his body: *B.* hath Issue a Bastard Son, he shall not take the remainder, because in the Law he is not his Issue, for *Qui ex damnato coitu nascuntur inter liberos non computentur.* The Justices of the Peace shall commit Lewd Women, which have Bastards to the House of Correction, there to be punished and set on work during the term of one whole year, there to remain till she can put in good Sureties for her good Behaviour not to offend so again, *Septimo Jacobi c.* 4.

A female bastard, Bastarda, æ, f.

Bastardy, Bastardia, æ. f. *Lex.* 17. *Brac.* 12. *Spel.* 93.

To baste meat, Degutto, are.

To baste with lard, Lardo, are.

A basting of meat, Liquamen, inis, n.

B A T.

Battains, (Boards of Timber sawed or cloven shingles) Assamenta, orum.

Battained, Pŏlītus cum assamentis.

Batersey (in *Surrey*) Batersega.

To bath, Balneo, are.

A bath (a washing place, a private washing place) Balneum, ei, n.

Bathes (or Stews, Publick places to wash in) Balnea, orum, n.

A warm bath, Tepidarium, ii, n.

Warm baths, Thermæ, arum, f. Sing. caret.

A bath (Stew or Hot-house) Vaporarium, ii, n.

A bathing place, Balnearium, ii, n. Lavatorium, ii, n.

A little bath, Balneolum, li, n.

A place to bath in cold waters, Frigidaria Cella.

A bathing vessel to wash in, Baptisterium, ii, n. Labrum, ri, n.

A place where men laid their clothes when they bathed, Consternium, ii, n.

He that for a reward keepeth the Clothes of them that be in baths, Capsarius, ii, m.

A bath-keeper (*the master of the bath*) Balneator, oris, m. Balneanus, ni, m.

A mistress (*or dame*) *of the bath*, Balneatrix, icis, f.

The bishop of Bath *and* Wells, Episcopus Bathoniensis & Wellensis.

Money paid for going into the bath,

bath, Balneaticum, ci, n. Balneare, ris, n.

Pertaining or serving to baths, Balnearius . a, um.

Bath city (in *Somersetshire*) Aquæ Calidæ. Aquæ solis, Badiza, Balnea, Bacha, Bathonia.

Battle abby (in *Sussex*) Monasterium de bello.

A battle, Prælium, ii, n.

To join battle (*to fight a battle*) Confligo, is, xi, ctum, ere. in Prælium descendere. Signa conferre. Collatis signis pugnare. Prælia conserere. Audere Prælium.

To bid battle, Bellum indicere.

To begin battle, Velitor, aris.

To set in battle array, Instituere aciem.

To march in battle array, Quadrat agmine ire.

In battle array, Turmatim, adv.

A set battle, Pugna stataria.

The beginning of a battle, Velitatio, onis, f. Pugnæ præfusio.

A sea battle, Naumăchia, æ, f. Pugna Navalis.

To fight hand to hand with his enemy, Confligere manu cum hoste.

A battle between two, Duellum, li, n.

Of a battle, Præliaris.

A little battle, Præliolum, li, n.

A battle waged between light harnessed men, Pugna velitaris.

A battle wherein they that before had gotten the victory are now overcome, Osculana Pugna.

A battle before a city or town, Bellum antarium.

An onset in battle, Impressio, onis, f.

The second ward in a battle where both noble and common Soldiers are, Principia, orum, n.

The wing of a battle, Cornu, indecl.

He that is sent out before the battle to defie or provoke the enemy, Emissarius, ii, m.

Battles (*or Idots*) *in Colleges or Inns of Chancery*, Refectus, uum, pl.

Battlements or pinacles in walls, Murorum summitates. Minæ, arum, f. Minæ murorum. Pinnæ muri.

To batter or beat down with great guns, Pulso, are. Concutio, is, ssi, sum, ĕre. Confringo, is, egi, actum, ere. Quasso, are.

To batter downright, Quatere mænia Tormentis.

A batterer, Pulsātor, ōris, m.

A battering, Concussio, onis, f. Verbĕrātio, onis, f.

Battered, Quassatus, a, um. Lăpĭdātus, a, um.

A battery, Ruina fenestra.

A *battery* (*Bulwark*) Agger, ĕris, m.

A battery, Batteria, æ, f. *Spel.* 93. *Fle.* 65. Verbĕrātio, onis, f. Battery is the wrongful beating of one; but if a Man will take away my Goods, I may lay my hands upon him and disturb him, and if he will not leave, I may beat him, rather than he shall carry them away, for that is no wrongful beating, Menacing beginneth the breach of Peace, Assaulting increaseth it, and Battery accomplisheth it. *Dalt. Just. of P.*

B A Y.

A bay of building, Baia, æ, f. *Co. Ent.* 707. Menſura viginti quatuor pedum.

A bay (road for ſhips to reſt in) Statio, onis, f. Statio navium.

A bay (Cerek) Sinus, ûs, m.

A bay (Dam) Pila, æ, i.Moles, is, f.

Baynards caſtle (in *London*) Bainardi caſtellum.

Bays (Cloath) Pannus baius. Pannus villoſus.

B E A.

A beach (or ſea-ſhore) Acta, æ, f. Littus, oris, n.

A beacon (or becon) Spĕcŭla, æ, f.

A burning beacon, Trulla ferrea, ignis ſpeculatorius.

Beacons, Signæ, arum, f.

To watch at a beacon, Obſervare de ſpecula, ſpeculor, aris.

A watcher at a becon, Speculator, oris, m. Excubĭtor, oris m.

Beaconage, Beconagium, ii, n. *Spel.* 94. *Money paid for maintenance of a beacon.*

A bead, Sphærula, æ, f.

A necklace of beads, Monile ex gemmulis.

A ſtring of beads for the arm, Armilla, æ, f.

A beadel, Bedellus, i, m.

A beadellary, Bedellaria, æ, f. *Lex.* 18. *Ra. Ent.* 191. 8. *Co.* 11. 2. *Ra.* 73.

A *beadel in Univerſities*, Accenſus, i, m.

A beadel of beggars or Bridewell, Fuſtuarius, ii, m. Flagellarius, ii, m.

A beagle, Catellus venaticus, Catulus ſagax.

The beak of a ſhip, Roſtra, orum, n.

The beak head of a ſhip, Extremitas proræ.

A beak, nib or bill of a fowl, Roſtrum, i, n.

Beaked, Roſtratus, a, um.

A beam (or great piece of timber) Trabs, bis, f.

The principal beam of an houſe, Lăcūnar, aris, n.

The wind beam of an houſe, Columen, inis.

A beam which hangeth with candles in a Merchants Hall, Lăcūnaria, æ, f.

The beam of a Crane about which the rope is twiſted in drawing any thing up, Sŭcŭla, æ. f.

A weaver's turning beam, Inſūbŭla, æ, f.

A yarn beam, or weaver's beam, Liciatorium, ii, n. Jugum, i, n.

The beam of a wain or draught tree whereon the yoke hangeth, Temo, onis, m.

The beam between coach horſes, Limo, onis m.

The beam of a balance, Bilanx, ncis.

The laying of beams or rafters from one wall to another, Immiſſum, ſi, n.

The end of the beams that appear under the walls of a houſe, Prŏcēres, um, m.

A wind-beam, or draw-beam, Ergata, æ, f.

Beams

Beams joyned together with divers pieces, Trabes compactiles.

Well wrought beams, Trabes everganeæ.

Belonging to a beam. Trăbālis, le.

That is made of a beam or rafter, Trabicus, a, um. Trabarius, a, um.

A bean, Faba, æ, f.

A little bean, Fabŭla, æ, f.

A French bean, Phaseŏlus, li, m.

The black of a bean being like an eye, Hilum, i, n. Fabæ hilum, nigrum in summa faba.

A bean cod, Siliqua.

A bean stalk or husk, Fabæ tunica vel concha. Valvulus, li, m. Operculamentum, ti, n.

A bean stalk, Fabale, lis. Fabacium, ii, n.

Bean baulm or straw, Stipula fabalis. Fabago, inis, f.

Bean chaff, Fabulum, li, n.

A bean cake, Fabacia, æ, f.

Bean meal, Lomentum, ti, n.

A bean plat (or place where beans grow) Fabetum, ti, n.

A bean bruised, broken or sprouting in the ground, Faba fresa vel fressa.

Bean pottage or buttered beans, Conchis, is, f.

Bean castle (in *Scotland*) Banatia.

To bear (or carry) Bajulo.

A bearer (porter) Corbŭlo, onis, m.

That beareth or supporteth any thing, Sustentācŭlum, li, n. Fulcrum, cri, n.

That bears a great burthen on his back, Dorsuarius, a, um. Dossuarius, a, um. From thence comes the *English* word (Dossers)

To bear arms against, Ferre arma contra.

A bear, Ursus, i, m.

A she bear, Ursa, æ, f.

A sea bear, Ursus marinus.

A little bear, Ursulus, li, m.

A little she bear, Ursula, æ, f.

A bear baiting, Ursi cum cane certamen.

A bear dog, Canis ursarius.

A bearward, Ursarius, ii, m.

A beard, Barba, æ, f.

A great beard, Barba promisca.

A little beard, Barbula, æ, f.

A goats beard, Spirillum, li, n.

The beard of corn, Spica, æ, f. Arista, æ, f.

To turn beasts into rank corn to feed, Impesco, cis, ere. Impescere in lætam segitem.

All kind of beasts, Pĕcus, ŏris, n.

A beast, Bestia, æ, f.

A great and terrible beast, Bellua, æ, f.

A little beast, Bestiola, æ, f.

A wild beast, Fera, æ, f.

A tame beast, Bestia domestica.

An herd of beasts, Pecuare, n. Sing. pl. Pecuaria, orum. Armentum, ti, n.

A beast for service, Jumentum, ti, n. Vehilla, æ, f.

Beasts of chace, Feræ Campestres.

Beasts of forest, Feræ Sylvestres.

Beasts yoked or coupled together, Bijugi, orum, n.

The shoulder of a beast, Armus, mi, m.

Of

Of a beast, Bestiarius, a, um.

Belonging to beasts, Bestiālis, le.

A keeper or breeder of beasts, Pĕcŭārius, ii, m.

A place where beasts are kept, Bestiarium, ii, n.

A pasture or place where beasts go, Pecuaria, æ, f.

A tax within a forest to be paid for horned beasts, Horngelda, æ, f.

A description or painting of beasts, Zoographia, æ, f.

To beat (or smite) Cædo, cĕcīdi, cæsum. Verbero, are.

To beat black and blue, Sūgillo, are.

To beat to the ground, Affligo, is, xi, ctum. Affligere ad Terram.

To beat to death, Oblīdo, dis, di, sum, ere.

To beat with the fist, Alapizo.

To beat with a staff or cudgel, Fustigo, are.

To beat back, Rĕpello, is, puli, pulsum, ĕre.

To beat or bruise any thing to make it longer, less or thinner, Prōcūdo, is, di, sum, ere.

To beat out, Extero, is, trīvi, trītum, ere.

To beat down, Demolio, is, ivi, ire.

To beat down walls, Exparieto, are.

To beat with an hammer, Pertundo, dis, tŭdi, tūsum, ĕre.

To beat on an anvil, Acudo, is, di, sum, ĕre.

To Beat or Pound in a Mortar, Tundo, is, tutūdi, sum, ere.

To beat or knock at the door, Pulso, are.

To beat aparley, Tympani signo ad colloquium evocare.

To beat as the waves, Illido, is, di, sum, ere.

To be beaten, smitten or knocked, Vāpŭlo, are.

To be beaten to the ground, Collābisio, is, ere.

Beaten, smitten or knocked, Verbĕrātus, a, um.

Beaten much, or sore beaten, Conflictatus, a, um.

Beaten black and blue, Sūgillatus, a, um.

Beaten with a staff, Fustigātus, a, um.

Beaten back, Repercussus, a, um.

Beaten to death, Oblisus, a, um. Occisus, a, um.

Beaten out, Excussus, a, um.

Beaten down, Disturbatus, a, um.

Beaten or stamped together, Stipātus, a, um.

A Beater, Verbĕrātor, oris, m.

A Beater out of any work, Excusor, oris, m.

A Beating, Verbĕrātio, onis, f.

A Beating of one thing against another, Collīsio, onis, f.

A Beating against, Illisus, ûs, m.

A Beating down, Demolitio, onis, f.

A Beating black and blue, Sūgillātio, onis, f.

A Beating back, Repercussio, onis, f.

A beating with a cudgel or staff, Defustigatio, onis, f. Fustigatio, onis, f.

A Beating stock, Subĭcŭlum, li, n.

Beau-

Beaufoe (the Family) De Bello Fago.

Beauchamp (the Family) De Bello Campo.

Beaumont (the Family) De bello Monte.

Beaupre (the Family) De Bello Prato. De Bensto. De Beverlaco.

B E C.

Because, Quia, quoniam.
Because of, Ergo, prout.

B E D.

A Bed, Lectus, ti, m. Cubile, lis, n.

A Truckle-Bed, Parabystum, i, n. Forŭlus, li, m.

A Flock Bed, Culcitra, æ, f. Culcitra tomentitia.

A Feather Bed, Pulvinus, ni, m. Culcitra Plumea.

A short Bed, Cămina, æ, f.

A bride Bed, Tŏrus, ri, m. Lectus genialis.

A little Bed or Pallet, Lectŭlus, li, m.

A Bed furnished, Lectus appărătus.

A Bed-stead, Fulcrum, i, n. Sponda, æ, f.

A Bed-maker, Lectarius, ii, m. Clinŏpēgus, i, m. Lectistrator, oris, m.

A Bed-chamber, Cŭbĭcŭlum, li, n. Dormitōrium, ii, n.

Bedcloaths, as Sheets, Blankets and Coverlets, Stragulum, li, n. Lodix, icis, f. Torale, lis, n. Strata, orum, n. Lectualia, n. pl. Fascia Lecti.

Bed-staves, Bacilli tornati.

A Beds testern, Conopeum, ei, n.

The valence of a Bed, Ornamenta pro Lecto.

Bed time, Canticinium, ii, n.

A Bed in a garden (a Bed for herbs) Areŏla, æ, f.

A leek Bed, Porrina, æ, f.

A Bed-fellow, Consors Lecti.

Bedford (in Bedfordshire) Bedfordia, Bedefordia, Budeforda, Lactodorum, Lactodurum, Lactorodum, Lactocudum.

Bed-rid, or so weak that one cannot rise, Clinicus, ci.

A Bedlam (or mad body) Insanus, a, um. Furiosus, a, um.

Bedlam (a place where mad persons and such as are out of their wits be kept and bound, or the Bed or Chamber whereon they fling and tumble themselves) Gyrgathus, i, m.

B E E.

A Bee, Apes, is, f.

A little Bee, Apĭcŭla, æ, f.

Young Bees before they fly, Nymphæ, arum, f. Apum pulli.

The sting of a Bee, Aculeus, ei, m.

A Bee-master, Apiārius, ii, m. Mellarius, ii, m.

A Bee-hive, Alvearium, ii, n. Apiarium, ii, n. Castra Cerea.

A place where Bee-hives are set, Mellarium, ii, n.

A swarm of Bees, Exāmen, inis, n.

Fit for Bees, Apianus, a, um.

The

The driving of the Bee-hives to make honey, alſo the time when it is done, Mellatio, onis, f.

Bee wax, Cera, æ, f.

A Beech tree, Fagus, i, f.

A grove of Beeches, Faginetum, i, n.

Collered Beef, Tŭcētum, i, n.

Beef, Caro būbŭla vel bovina.

Beer, Cerviſia lupulata. Potus lupulatus.

Strong Beer, Cerviſia lupulata, fortis vel primaria.

Small Beer, Cerviſia lupulata, tenuis vel ſecundaria.

Beer veſſels, Dolia Cerviſiaria.

A Beetle, Malleus ligneus, tŭdes, itis, m.

A paving Beetle, Păvicŭla, æ, f.

A little Beetle, Tudicŭla, æ, f.

B E F.

Before (in time) Ante, præp.

Before that, Antequam.

Before (or in preſence) Coram, præp.

Before this time, Antehac.

A little before, Paulo ante.

B E G.

To beget (or Ingender) Procrĕo, are. Gĕnĕro, are.

To be Begotten, Gignor, eris.

Begotten (or Ingendred) Genĭtus, a, um. Procreātus, a, um.

A ſon lawfully Begotten, Mulieratus filius.

To Begin, Incipio, epi, eptum.

A Beginning, Commenſatio, onis, f.

In the Beginning, In principio.

At the Beginning, Primo.

B E H.

To Behead, Decapito, are. Decollo, are.

To be Beheaded, Obtruncor, aris. Plector vel Mulctor capite.

Beheaded, Decollatus, a, um.

A Beheading, Decollatio, onis, f. Truncatio, onis, f.

Behind in payment, Aretro.

Behind and unpaid, Aretro & Inſolutus.

Behind a houſe, Poſt domum.

Behoof, Intereſſe. opus.

It Behoveth, Oportet.

B E L.

To believe or give credit unto, Credo, is, didi tum.

That is Believed, Creditus, a, um.

Not to be Believed (Incredible) Incredibilis, le. Fidei abſonum.

That cannot be Believed as a Witneſs, Inteſtabilis, le.

Beldeſert (in Warwickſhire) Bello deſertum, Bellus locus, Beaudeſert.

Belingſgate, Belinus ſinus.

Bellow (the Family) De Bella Aqua.

Belvoir *or* Beavoir *Caſtle, or near it* (in *Lincolnſhire*) Margidunum, Margitudum.

A Bell, Campana, æ, f.

A little Bell, Tintinnabulum, li, n. Campānŭla, æ, f.

A Paſſing Bell, Mortinola, æ, f.

A Bell (or Chime keeper) Nolæ curator.

A Bell Founder, Campanārius, ii, m. Fusor aramentarius.

The Clapper of a Bell, Nolæ malleus.

A Bell frame, Fabrica campanæ.

A Bell-frey, Campanile, is, n.

A Bell Tower (or Steeple) Basilica f. Pyramis, idis, f. Turris fictarata.

The Bell-weather that goes before the Flock, Sectarius vervex.

Bellows to blow the fire with, Follis, is, m.

A pair of Bellows, Par follium.

The nose of the bellows, Acrophysium, ii, n. Crater follis.

Smiths Bellows, Follis fobrilis.

A Belly (or Paunch) Venter, tris, m.

A little Belly, Ventriculus, li, m.

The Belly of a Swine stuffed, Scrotellus, li, m. Sartutillus, li, m.

The outward part of the Belly from the Bulk down to the Privy Members, Epigastrium, ii, n. Abdomen, inis, n.

The fore part of the Belly and Sides about the short Ribs, and about the Navel, under the which lieth the Liver and the Spleen, Hypochondria, orum, n.

The pain of the Belly or Womb, Hysteralgia, æ, f. Tormina, um, n.

Troubled with the belly-ach, Alvinus, a, um.

That ingendereth pain in the belly, Tormināis, le.

To belong (or appertain to) Pertineo, es, ŭi, tum, ere.

It belongeth (or appertaineth) Pertinet.

A belt (or girdle) Balteum, ei, n. Cingulus, li, m. Subcingulum, i, n.

A belt or sword girdle, Lumbare, ris, n. Lumbatorium, ii, n.

B E N.

A bench (or form to sit upon) Scamnum, i. n.

A little bench (or form) Scamnulum, ii, n. Scamnellum, li, n.

Done with benches one by another, Scamnatus, a, um.

A bench (or seat of judgment) Bancus, i, m. Bank is a *Saxon* word, and signifieth a Bench, or high Seat, or a Tribunal, and is properly applied to the Justices of the Court of Common Pleas, because the Justices of that Court sit there in a certain place, and legal Records term them *Justiciarii de Banco* : Another Court there is called the Kings Bench, both because the Records of that Court are stiled *Coram Rege*, and because Kings in former times have often Personally sate there.

Benches (in a barge or ship) for the Rowers, Transtra, orum, n.

To bend (crook or bow) Curvo, are. Flecto, is, xi, xum, ĕre.

To bend like a bow, Arcuo, are.

To bend backward, Recurvo, are.

To bend forwards, Prōclino, are.

To

To bend a little or incline, Acquinisco, is, xi, ere.

To cause to bend or lean to, Annecto, xi, is, um.

Bending to, Inclinans, tis, P.

Bending down on every side, Convexus, a, um.

Bending forward, Vergens, tis, P.

Bending from (or downward) Dēclīvis, ve.

Bending (or leaning) Innītens, tis, P.

Bent or bowed, Tensus, a, um. Curvatus, a, um.

Bent many ways, Sĭnŭātus, a, um.

Bent like a bow, Arcuatus, a, um.

Bent backward, Rĕcurvus, a, um.

Bent to, Projectus, a, um.

A bending or bowing, Curvatio, onis, f.

A bending from or downwards, Declinātio, onis, f.

Bending forwards, Proclinātio, onis, f.

Bending downwards or unto, Inclinatio, onis, f.

Bendings or turnings, Diverticula, orum, n.

A bending round about, Circumflexio, ōnis, f.

A place bending downward, Rĕclīnātorium, rii, n.

The bending down of any thing, Clivum, i, n.

The bending of a board or table, Tabulæ vel Mensæ clivus.

That cannot be bent, Inflexibilis, le.

Easie to bend, Flexibilis, le.

Bending wise, Acclīnē, adv.

Bent like a bow, Arcuātim, adv.

Beneath (or that is beneath) Inferus, a, um.

Beneath, Infra, subter, &c.

From beneath, Inferne, adv.

A benefice, Beneficium, ii, n.

Beneficed, Beneficiatus, a, um. Beneficiarentur, *Ra. Ent.* 599.

The gift of a Benefice by a Bishop, which he hath in his own Right or Patronage, Collatio Beneficii.

The voidance of an Ecclesiastical Benefice by promotion of the Incumbent, Cessio, onis, f.

A Benefice which being void, is committed to the care of another Clerk to supply the Cure till it be full, Commenda, æ, f.

Benefit of Clergy, Beneficium Clericale.

Benevolence, Benevolentia, æ, f. It is used for a voluntary Gratuity given by the Subject to the King. *Vid.* 11. *H.* 7. *c.* 10. & 13. *Car.* 2. *c.* 4. & *Co. lib.* 12. *fo.* 119, 120.

B E R.

Bergeney (in *Scotland*) Berigonium.

Berkely (in *Gloucestershire*) Bercheleia, Berklea.

Berking (in *Essex*) Berechingum.

Berkshire, Bearrocscira, Berceia, Berkeria, Bercheria.

Of Berkshire, Berchensis, Beruchensis.

Berkshire *men*, Attrebatii.

Bermondsey (in *Surrey*) Bermundi insula.

Bernards *Castle* (in the Bishoprick of *Durham*) Bernardi Castellum.

A berry, Bacca, æ, f.

A little berry, Baccŭla, æ, f.

BES.

Besides, Præter, juxta.

Besides that, Præterquam.

To besiege (*beset or inviron*) Obsideo, es, edi, sum, ere. Oppugno, are.

Besieged, Obsessus, a, um. Oppugnatus, a, um.

A besieger (*he that layeth siege*) Obsessor, oris, m. Oppugnator, oris, m.

A besieging, Obsessus, ûs, m. Obsidium, ii, n.

A rendering up of the place besieged, Dedĭtio, ōnis, f.

A besom (*or broom to sweep houses withal*) Scōpæ, arum, f.

Best, Optimus, a, um.

BET.

To betake (*or commit and deliver*) Trădo, is, didi, itum, ĕre.

To betray, Prōdo, dis, didi, ditum, ere.

Betrayed, Proditus, a, um.

A betrayer, Prōditor, ōris, m.

A betraying, Prōdĭtio, ōnis, f.

To betroth (*or promise in marriage*) Despondeo, es, di, sum, ēre.

Betrothed (*or ingaged by fealty*) Affidatus, a, um.

To be betrothed to a Woman, Affidare mulierem.

The betrothing of a Woman, Affidatio, onis, f.

To make better, Emendo, are.

Made better, Emendatus, a, um.

It is better, Præstat.

The better right, Superior causa.

A better bargain, Potior conditio.

Better, Melior & hoc melius.

Meliùs, adv.

Between, Inter, Præp.

BEV.

Beverley (in *Yorkshire*) Beverlea. Fibrilega, Fibrelega, Petuaria P[illegible]siorum.

Of Beverley, Beverlacensis.

BEY.

To go beyond, Transeo, is, ivi, itum, ire.

Beyond the Sea. Transmarinus, a, um.

Beyond, Ultra, trans.

BIB.

A bib (*or mucketer set on a Childs breast*) Fascia, æ, f. Fasciola pectoralis.

BIG.

Big with young, Fœtus, a, um. Prægnans, ntis.

Bigamy, Bigamia, æ, f. A double marriage, or the marriage of two Wives. It is used as an Impediment to be a Clerk, *Anno*, 4. *E*. 1, 5. but that is abolished by 1. *E*. 6. *c*. 12. & 18. *El*. *c*. 7. which allows to all Men that

that can read as Clerks (tho not within orders) the Benefit of the Clergy, in case of Felony, not especially excepted by some other Statute.

B I L.

Biland (in Yorkshire) *Bellelanda.*

To break-out or cause to break out into a bile. *Ulcero, are.*

A bile (or Ulcer) *Ulcus, eris, n. Phyma, atis, n.*

A breaking out into biles. *Ulceratio, onis, f.*

Full of biles. *Ulcerosus, a,um,*

The ach of a bile. *Ulceris ustus.*

A Bill is when one of the Parties, &c. *vide Heaths Maxims. Page* 212.

A Bill (Obligatory or Declaratory) *Billa, æ, f.* A Declaration, a Bill of Charges. *West. Symbol. Tit. supplications.*

The bill is true. *Billa Vera.* The Grand Inquest Write *Billa Vera* upon all bills presented to them which they find, and *Ignoramus* upon all those bills they do not find, or give any order to it.

A bill (or billet of delivery of a Writ) *Billettum, i, n. Stat.de Westm.* 2. 39. *Ry.* 121. *Fle.* 151.

A bill of Exchange. *Billa Excambii.*

To set a bill on a thing to be sold. *Proscribo, psi, ptum.*

A bill (or hook) *Falx, cis, f.*

An Hedging bill. *Runca, æ, f.*

A little bill (or Hook) *Falcula, æ, f.*

A bill to lop trees. *Falx arboraria, vel Sylvatica.*

A Twy bill. *Bipennis, is, f.*

A bill-man (he that useth a bill) *Falcarius, ii, m.*

Pertaining to a bill. *Falcarius, a, um.*

To thrust in the bill, or beak as birds do. *Rostro, are. Rostrum impingere.*

That hath a bill. *Rostratus, a, um.*

A bill or beak. *Rostrum, tri, n.*

A billet (or Shide of Wood) *Truncus, ci, m. Bacillus, li, m. Talea, æ, f.*

Billets of Gold. *Massa auri.*

B I N.

Binchester (*in the Bishoprick of* Durham) *Bimonium. Binonium. Binovia. Binovium. Viconia. Vinonium. Vinovia. Vinovium.*

To bind (or tye up) *Ligo, are.*

To bind or fasten to something. *Astringo, is, xi, ictum.*

To bind together. *Colligo, are.*

To bind by Covenant. *Obligo, are.*

To bind or fasten underneath. *Subligo, are.*

To bind ones Legs. *Præpedio, is, ivi, itum, ire.*

To bind upon another thing. *Superalligo, are.*

To bind hard or tye fast. *Religo, are.*

To bind with twigs as Coopers do Vessels. *Vieo, es, evi, etum, ere.*

To bind up as Women do their Hair. *Texo, is, ui, vel, xi, xtum, ere.*

To bind one by Oath to do service. *Obstringo, is, xi, ctum, ere.*

To bind one with an earnest penny. *Obæro, are.*

To bind himself by promise to do or perform a thing. *Stĭpŭlor, aris.*

To bind a Vine. *Palmo, are.*

A binding (or tying) *Ligātio, ōnis, f.*

A binding or tying together. *Colligatio, onis, f.*

A binding by Covenant. *Obligatio, onis, f.*

A binder (one that bindeth or tyeth) *Alligator, oris, m.*

A bin (or hutch to keep Chippings of bread in. *Mactra, æ, f. Cerialum, li, n.*

B I R.

A birch-tree. *Betŭla, æ, f.*

A bird. *Avis, is, f.*

A great bird, *Ales, ĭtis, c. 2.*

A little bird. *Avicula, æ, f.*

A young bird. *Avis Pullus.*

Young birds unfeathered. *Implumes Pulli.*

Birds that cannot fly. *Involucres Pulli.*

A bird Cage. *Volucritium, ii, n.*

A Woody place where birds haunt. *Aviarium, ii, n.*

A birding Net. *Rete aucupatorium.*

Bird-lime. *Viscum, ci, n. pl. caret.*

To go a birding. *Aucŭpor, aris.*

A bird Catcher. *Auceps, upis, c.*

A birding (or fowling) *Aucŭpātio, onis, f.*

A birding place. *Aucupium, ii, n.*

The birds gotten by fowling. *Aucupia, orum.*

Fit or appertaining tō takē birds. *Aucŭpātōrius, a, um.*

Belonging to birds. *Avitius, a, um.*

A bird-keeper. *Aviarius, ii, m.*

A bird Merchant. *Avĭcŭlārius, ii, m.*

Carrying birds. *Avigĕrŭlus, a, um.*

To pull birds. *Aves deplumare.*

To draw birds. *Aves Exentĕrare.*

The birth of a Child. *Nativitas, atis, f. Partus, us, f.*

Ones birth-day. *Dies Primigenius. Natalis dies.*

Birth (the after-birth) *Secundinæ, arum, f.*

Untimely birth. *Abortus, us, m. Abortivum, vi, n.*

That causeth untimely birth. *Abortum facere.*

That birth which is cast forth by Medicines. *Aborsus venter.*

By birth. *Natu. Abl. Sing.*

Birth-right (or eldership.) *Eisnecia, æ, f. Law-terms.*

B I S.

Bisham (in *Berkshire*) *Bishamum, Bustelli domus.*

A Bishop. *Episcopus, pi, m.*

A Bishop of the Chief City. *Metropolitanus, i, m.*

To become a Bishop. *Episcopor, aris.*

A Bishop's Vicar, or Suffragan. *Suffraganeus, ei, m. Episcopi Vicarius.*

A Bishops house or mansion-Palace. *Episcopium, ii, n.*

A Bishop's place without the Wall, joyning to the City. *Proxĭmum, mi, n.*

A Bishoprick. *Episcopatus, ûs, m.*

The Bishop's Dignity. *Patriarchātus, ûs, m.*

A Bishop's Miter. *Mitra, æ, f.*

A Bishop's Seat or Chair. *Asfidēla, æ, f.*

Of a Bishop. *Episcopalis, le.*

Deckt with a Bishop's Miter. *Infulatus, a, um.*

The Bishoprick of the Hebrides and of Man-Isle. *Sodorensis.*

Bisket. *Panis nauticus, Panis biscoctus.*

Bissextile. Bissextilis, le. Leap-year, so call'd, because the sixth Calends of *March* are in that year twice reckoned (*viz.*) on the 24*th* and 25*th* of *February*, so that Leap-year hath one day more than other years, and is observ'd every fourth year, and to prevent all doubts and ambiguities that might arise thereupon, it is provided by the Stat. *de anno Bissextili* 21. *H.* 3. That the day increasing in the Leap-year, and the day next before, shall be accounted for one day, &c. *vid. Dyer* 17. *El.* 345.

B I T.

A Bitch. *Canis Fœmina.*

A bitch with Puppy. *Canis Prægnans.*

To bite. *Mordeo, es, mŏmordi, sum, ere.*

To bite off, *Dēmordĕo, es, di, sum, ere.*

To bite to the Quick. *Admordeo, es, di, sum, ere.*

To bite by the Hair. *Obmordeo, es, di, sum, ere.*

To bite again. *Remordeo, es, di, sum, ere.*

To bite softly or privately. *Submordeo, es, di, sum, ere. ere.*

To bite often. *Morsĭto, are.*

To hurt by biting, *Mordico ere.*

To be bitten, *Mordeor, aris.*

Bitten. *Morsus, a, um.*

Bitten round about. *Ambesus, a, um.*

A biting. *Morsus, ûs, m.*

A bite with the Teeth. *Morsus, ûs, m.*

Biting hard. *Mordicùs, adv.*

Biting. *Mordax, acis.*

Very biting. *Mordacissimus, a, um.*

That is apt to bite. *Morsilis, le.*

Biting one another. *Morsicātim, adv.*

Bitingly, *Mordacitèr, adv.*

A bit (or morsel) *Bŏlus, li, m. Frustum, ti, n. Morsellum, li, n.*

A little bit. *Buccella, æ, f. Morsiuncula, æ, f.*

A bit, (or Snaffle) *Chamus, i, m.*

Belonging to a bit. *Sălīnāris, re.*

The bit of a bridle. *Lŭpātum, ti, n. Lŭpus, pi, m.*

The part of the bit which is put into the Horses mouth. *Orea, æ, f.*

The sharp part of a bit writhen like the scales of a Fish. *Squamata, æ, f.*

To make bitter, or soure. *Acerbo, are. Amarico, are.*

To wax bitter. *Inămāresco, is, ĕre.*

Bitterness. *Amāror, ōris, m. Amarities, ei, f. Amārĭtūdo, inis, f. ămārŭlentia, æ, f.*

E 2 Bitter

Bitter. *Amarus, a, um.*

Full of bitterness. *Amaracosus, a, um.*

Very bitter. *Amarŭlentus, a, um.*

Somewhat bitter. *Subamarus, a, um.*

Most bitterly. *Amarissimè, adv.*

B L A.

To make black. *Denigro, are. Nigrefacio, is, ere.*

Shoe-makers black. *Atramentum sutorium.*

To become black. *Nigreo, es, ui, ere.*

To wax black. *Nigresco, is, ui, ere.*

To be somewhat black. *Nigrico, are.*

A making black. *Denigratura, æ, f.*

Made black. *Atratus, a, um.*

Blackness. *Nigredo, inis, f.*

Black. *Niger, a, um.*

Black and blue. *Lividus, a, um.*

Very black. *Perniger, gra, grum.*

Somewhat black. *Subniger, gra, grum.*

Half black and blue. *Sublividus, a, um.*

Of a black colour. *Atricŏlor, oris, Adj.*

Having black interlaced with other colours. *Internigrans, tis, Partic.*

Cole black. *Melanius, a, um, Anthracinus, a, um.*

Black as Soot, or with Soot. *Fuligineus, a, um.*

A black-more. *Æthiops, opis, m.*

A black-bird. *Merŭla, æ, f.*

Blackmore (in the north riding in *Yorkshire*) *Blacamora.*

Blackney (in *Norfolk*) *Nigeria.*

Blackwater River (in *Essex*) *Idumanum. æstuarium. Idumanus fluvius.*

Growing to a blade. *Herbescens, ntis.*

The blades (or Wheel) to wind Thread with. *Girgillus, li, m.*

The breast blade (or the bone above the mouth of the stomach) *Os Ensiforme.*

The Shoulder-blade. *Scapula, æ, f.*

A blade of Corn. *Culmus, i, m.*

A bladder. *Vesica, æ, f.*

A little bladder. *Vesicŭla, æ, f.*

A bladder blown or puffed up. *Utris.*

The Gall bladder. *Vesicula fellis.*

To blame (or lay the fault upon one) *Imputo, are. Culpo, are.*

To blame again one that rebuketh us. *Retaxo, are.*

To blame in words. *Premo, is, ssi, ssum, ere.*

To be blamed. *Arguor.*

Blamed. *Culpatus, a, um.*

A blamer (or reprehender) *Criminator, oris, m. Reprehensor, oris, m.*

Blame (or Fault) *Crimen, inis, n.*

A blaming (or reprehending) *Crīmĭnātio, ōnis, f. Reprehensio, onis, f.*

Blamableness. *Noxietas, atis, f.*

Blameful (or culpable) *Noxius, a, um.*

Worthy of blame. *Culpabilis, le.*

Blameless (or faultless) *Inculpatus, a, um.*

Blame-

Blamelesly (or without blame) *Inculpaté.*

Blank-Castle (*in* Monmouthshire) *Blancum Castrum.*

To blanch (or pull off the rind or pill.) *Reglubo, is, bi, bitum, ere. Excorio, are.*

To blanch or make white. *Dealbo, are.*

The blanching of Mason's work. *Albivium, ii, n.*

Blanch'd Almonds. *Amygdala dealbata.*

Blanch (or white Coat) *Leucon.*

Blandford (in *Dorsetshire*) *Blancoforda.*

A blank, an unluky cast, *Jactus Supinus.*

Blanks. *Spacia.*

A blanket. *Stragulum, li, n. Lodix, icis, f.*

A little blanket. *Lodicula, æ, f.*

Childrens blankets. *Cūnābŭla, orum, n.*

A pair of blankets. *Par Lodicum lanearum.*

To blaspheme, (Curse or speak evil of) *Blasphēmo, are.*

Blasphemy (or ill report) *Blasphemia, æ, f.*

A blasphemer. *Blasphemus, i, m.*

Blasphemously. *Blasphemè, adv.*

To blasten (or sear.) *Fulgŭro, are. Uro, is, ssi, stum, ere.*

To be blasted. *Fulminor, aris,*

Blasted. *Fulguratus, a, um.*

A blasting or striking with a Planet. *Sideratio, onis, f.*

A blasting in Corn or Trees. *Uredo, inis, f.*

A blasting with Lightning. *Fulguritum, ti, n.*

A blast of Wind. *Ventus, ti, m, Flatus, us, m.*

A blast that over-throweth Trees and Houses. *Proflatus, ûs, m.*

A great blast of Wind. *Perflatus, ûs, m.*

A blast of wind turned from the earth upward. *Turbo, inis, m.*

A contrary blast. *Reflatus, ûs, m.*

A blast (or sound of an Instrument) *Flamen, inis, n.*

Much blasted. *Rubiginosus, a, um.*

To blaze abroad. *Divulgo, are.*

To blaze out as Fire. *Efflammino, are.*

The blaze (or blast) of Fire. *Flamma, æ, f.*

A blazing-star, *Cometa, æ, m.*

A blazer of Fame abroad. *Famigerulus, li, m.*

B L E.

To bleach in the Sun (or make Cloaths white abroad in the Sun) *Dealbo, are.*

A bleaching in the Sun. *Dealbatio, onis, f.*

A bleaching place. *Insolatorium, ii, n.*

Blear Ey'd. *Lippus, a, um.*

To bleed. *Sanguino, are.*

A bleeding. *Fluxio, onis, f. cursus sanguinis.*

Bleeding at the Nose. *Narium profluvium. Sanguinis è Naribus eruptio.*

Bleeding that cometh by opening the end of a Vein. *Anastomosis.*

To blemish (or spot) *Maculo, are.*

Blemiſhed (or ſpotted) *mă-cŭlatus, a, um.*

A Blemiſh (or ſpot) *mă-cula, æ, f.*

A Blemiſh (or ſpot to ones Credit) *In famia, æ, f. mă-cŭlātio, onis, f.*

Great blemiſhes (or ſpots) *Tu-bera, orum, n.*

A ſmall blemiſh (or ſpot) *Labecula, æ. f.*

Full of Blemiſhes, *Măcŭlōſus, a, um.*

To blew (or black and blew) Li-veo, es, ere.

Blew (or blew of colour) Li-vidus, a, um. Cæruleus, a, um.

B L I.

Blindneſs or dimneſs of ſight, Cæſitas, atis, f.

Pur-blind, Myops.

Pur-blindneſs, Myopia, æ, f.

Stark blind, Cæcus, a, um.

To make blind, Cæco, are.

Blind born, Cæcĭgĕnus, a, um.

Blind in one eye (or having but one eye) Monoculus, li, m. Luſ-cus, ci, m.

Half blind, Cæcutiens, ntis, Partic.

Sand-blind, Nyctilops, Luſco-ſus, a, um.

Blith *River* (in *Staffordſhire,* and another in *Northumberland*) Blithus.

A bliſter (or bile) Puſtŭla, æ, f. Papŭla, æ, f.

A little bliſter, Ulcuſculum, li, n.

A bliſter (moſt properly that which riſeth on bread in baking) Puſula, æ, f.

B L.

A bliſtering, Inflammatio, o-nis, f.

Fullneſs of bliſters, Papuloſi-tas, atis, f.

A bliſter in the eye, Ophthal-mia, æ, f.

That maketh bliſters, Ulcerari-us, a, um. Ulceroſus, a, um.

Full of bliſters, Puſtuloſus, a, um.

B L O.

A block (or ſtem of a Tree) Trun-cus, ci, m.

A block-houſe, Munitorium, ii, n.

They which keep a block-houſe, Burgæ, arum, f.

Blood, Sanguis, inis, m. pl. caret.

To let blood, Phlebotomo, are. Sanguino, are.

To ſtanch blood, Sanguinem ſi-ſtĕre.

Blood-ſhotten (or rayed with blood) Cruentatus, a, um.

The blood of a wound, Cruor, oris, m.

A little blood (or blood whereof Puddings are made) Sanguiculus, li, m.

Black blood, Tabum, i, n.

Corrupt or tainted blood, Sa-nies, ei, f.

Full of corrupt blood, Sănioſus, a, um.

An Inflammation of blood, Phlegmone, es, f.

Blood-ſhed, Sanguinis emiſſio.

The letting of blood out of a Vein, Phlebotomia, æ, f.

A

A letter of blood, Phlebotomator, oris, m.

Spitting of blood, Hæmoptyſis, ſanguinis expuitio.

He that ſpitteth blood, Hæmoptoicus.

A flux of blood, Hæmorrhœa, æ, f.

An immoderate flux of blood, Hæmorrhagia, æ, f.

Bloody (or full of blood) Sanguineus, a, um.

Bloody (all over in blood) Cruentus, a, um.

Bloody (deſirous of blood) or red as blood, Cruentatus, a, um.

Bloodily, Cruentè, adv.

The track of the blood, Nota cruenta.

To imbrue in blood (to fetch blood of) Cruento, are.

A blood-ſtone, Hæmatites, æ, f.

Bloody-flux, Dyſenteria, æ, f.

Without blood, Exſanguis, gue.

Not ſtained with blood-ſhed, Incruentatus, a, um.

With more effuſion of blood, Cruentior, ius.

To bloſſom (bloom or bear flowers) Floreo, es, ui, ere. Germĭno, are.

To bloſſom before due time, Præfloreo, es, ui, ere. Prægermĭno, are.

A bloſſom or bloom, Flos, oris, m. Quintilia, æ, f.

The bloſſoms or flowers of trees, Quintinæ, arum, f.

To blot out (wipe away or deface) Deleo, es, evi, etum, ere.

Blotted out, Deletus, a, um.

He that blotteth out, Deletor, oris, m.

A blotting out, Deletio, onis, f.

A blot or blur, Litura, æ, f. Labes, is, f.

To blow (or breath) Flo, as, flāvi, ātum, are, Spiro, are.

To blow away (or down) Deflo, are.

To blow again, Reflo, are.

To blow up (or full) Sufflo, are.

To blow to (or upon) Afflo, are.

To blow out, Efflo, are.

To blow vehemently (or throughly) Perflo, are.

To blow an Inſtrument, Inflo, are.

To blow (or wind a horn) Cornicino, are. Cornu inflare.

To blow a trumpet, Cango, is, xi, tum, ĕre, ſono, as, ŭi, ĭtum, are.

To blow or ſpring out as a flower, Effloreſco, is, ŭi, ĕre.

To be blown, Floreo, es, ui, ere.

To be blown down, Diffloreo, es, ui, ere.

To be blown again, Reconfloreo, es, ui, ere.

Blown (or breathed) Flatus, a, um. Inſpiratus, a, um.

Blown (or puffed up) Anhelatus, a, um.

A blower (or breather) Spirator, oris, m.

A blower (or winder of a horn) Cornicen, ĭnis, c. g.

A blowing (or breathing) Inſpiratio, onis, f.

A blowing up, Sufflatio, onis, f.

A place wherein many winds do blow, Conflāges.

Full of blowing, Flatuoſus, a, um.

That may be blown through, Perflabilis, le.

Eaſily blown. Flabilis, le.

To give one a blow (or buffet) Alapizo, are.

A blow (or buffet with the hand) Alapa, æ. f.

A blow (or ſtroke) Ictus, ûs & i, m.

Blows (or stripes) Offerumentæ, arum.

B L U.

To make blunt the edge of any thing, Obtundo, is, ŭdi, ūsum.

To be blunt (or dull) Hĕbĕo, es, ere.

To wax blunt (or dull) Hebesco, is, ere.

Blunt, Obtūsus, a, um.

Bluntness (or dulness) Hĕbĕtudo, inis, f.

A blunt or rude invention, Crassa, æ, f.

Bluntly, Obtusè, adv.

To bluster as the wind, Furo, is, ere. Ut furit ventus.

A blustring, Sonitus, ûs, m.

Blustring (or raging) Procellosus, a, um.

Blustring winds, Irrumpens ventus. Procellosus ventus.

B O A.

To board (or lay boards) board a floor, Tabulo, are. Asso, are.

A board (or plank) Asser, ĕris, m.

Boards of timber sawed, Assamenta, orum, n.

A board in a Kitchin whereon pots or vessels are set full of water, Urnārium, ii, n.

A board on the upper part of the Organ, whereupon the Pipes stand, Pinax.

A cottoning or frizing board, Gossupinarium, ii, n.

A boarding (or planking) of a floor, or laying of boards together, Tăbŭlātio, ōnis, f.

A boarded floor, Tabulatum, i, n. Transitus tabulatus.

That whereof boards are made, Tabularis, re.

Boarded (planked) Tăbŭlātus, a, um.

To plain (or polish) boards, Edŏlare tabulas vel asseres.

Boards (or rafters) laid a cross, Transversaria, orum.

A wild boar, Aper, pri, m.

A tame boar, Verres, is, m.

A little boar, Aperculus, li, m.

The neck of a boar, Glandium, ii, n.

Of or belonging to a boar, Verrinus, a, um.

Of a wild boar, Aprinus, a, um.

A boat, Batus, i, m. Cymba, æ, f. Ratis, is, f.

A little boat, Batellus, li, m. *Lex.* 17. *Ra. Entr.* 32. *Mon.* 281. 1005, *Spel.* 931. Batellagium, ii. n. *Mon.* 754. Cymbŭla, æ, f. Lintriculus, li, m. Scaphŭla, æ, f.

A ship boat, Scapha, æ, f.

A Ferry boat, Trajectum, i, n. *Spel.* 264. Ponto, onis. m. Navis vectoria.

A Ferry boat to carry over horses, Hippāgo, inis, f.

A sculler boat, Linter, tris, m. Acatis phaselis.

A passage boat, Navis vectoria. Navicula vectoria.

A fly-boat, Celo, onis, m. Velox navis.

A fisher boat, Horia, æ, f. Præa, æ, f. Navigiolum piscatorium, vel navis piscatoria.

A little fisher boat, Horiola, æ, f.

Pleasure boats, Cubiculatæ naves.

Wicker boats, Naves vitiles.

A boat or bridge of logs pinned together for the present occasion, Schædia, æ, f.

Boats (or ships) calked with Tow, Serilla, orum, n.

A kind of spy-boats, Geseoreta.

A great

A great boat-pole (an Instrument for thrusting forward, off or down, Trudes, is, f. Contus, i, m.

The space between the Oars in a Boat or Gally, Interscalmium, ii, n.

To hale a boat ashore, Cymbam subdúcere.

To go by boat, Naviculor, ari.

A boatswain, Prorĕta, æ, m. Pausarius, ii, m. Portisculus, li, m.

A boat-man (or rower) Remex, igis, m. Scapharius, ii, m. Linterarius, ii, m.

A boat-mans craft (or science) Nāvĭcŭlāria, æ, f.

B O D.

Womens bodies, Thorax muliebris.

A bodkin (or fine instrument that Women use to curl their hairs with) Calamistrum, i, n. Crinale, lis, n. Discriminale, lis, n.

A bodkin or big needle to curl or crisp the hair withal. Discerniculum, li, n. Acus crinalis.

A hole made with a bodkin, Punctura, æ, f.

Bodiham (in *Sussex*) Bodiamum.

Bodman (in *Cornwall*) Voliba, Voluba.

Bodvary (in *Flintshire*) Varis.

A body (all manner of substance) Corpus, oris, n.

A little body, Corpusculum, li, n.

The body of a tree, Caudex, ĭcis, m. Crus arboris.

A body without head, Truncus, ci, m.

The state of the body, Corporatio, onis, f.

No body, Nemo, inis c. g. Nullus, a, um.

Some body, Aliquis.

The being without bodies, Incorporalitas, atis, f.

That hath a body, Corporeus, a, um.

Bodiless (or that hath no body) Incorporeus, a, um.

B O G.

A bog (or fennish place) Pălus, ūdis, f.

B O L.

A bole or bowl, Pocŭlum, li, n. 2 *Mon.* 666. 1042.

A bole to wash hands in, Trulleum, ei, n.

A bole (or dish) to drink in, Patĕra, æ, f. Crater, eris, m.

A wash bole, Catinus ligneus.

A bolster for a bed, Cervicale, lis, n.

Little bolsters good to carry burthens upon the shoulders, Tomices, pl.

To bolster up, Sustĭneo, es, ui, entum, ere.

A bolstering on every side, Stipatio, onis, f.

A bolt (such as is shot) Catapultarium, ii, n.

A bolt of a door, Pessŭlus, li, m, Obex, icis, m.

Bolted gates, Pessulatæ fores.

Bollen (the Family) Bononius.

B O N.

To be in bondage, Servio, is, iri, itum, ire.

To deliver into bondage, Mancipo, are.

Bondage (or servitude) Servitium, ii, n.

That is in bondage, Servus, a, um.

Of or belonging to bondage, Servilis, le.

To become ones Bondman, Emancipo, are.

To make a bondman free, Mănŭmitto, is, isi, ssum, ĕre.

A bondman, Servus, vi, m.

A bondman or woman, born and brought up in our house, of our bondman or woman, Nativus, i. Nativa, æ, f.

A bondman or prisoner taken in War, Mancipium, ii, n.

A bondman overseeing Cattle, or one dwelling in a Farm, and given to Husbandry, Villanus, i, m.

A bondman or tenant in villanage, Cŏlōnārius, ii, m.

A multitude or company of bondmen, Servi, orum, m. Servitia, orum, n.

The making of a bondman free, Manumissio, onis, f.

He that setteth a bondman free, Patronus, i, m.

A bondman made free, Libertus, i, m.

A bondwoman made free, Liberta, æ, f.

A bond with a distinct condition endorsed or joyned thereto, Obligatio, onis, f.

Bonvill (the Family) De Bonavo.

To pluck out, or break the bone, Exosso, are.

A bone, Os, ossis, n.

A little bone, Officulum, li, n.

The back-bone of a Man or Beast, Spina, æ, f.

The jaw-bone, Mandibula, æ, f.

The great bone of an arm, Ulna, æ, f.

The hip (or buckle-bone) Coxendix, icis, f. Ischium, ii, n.

The bones which are nuder the eyes, Hypopia.

The spindle bone in the shank, Părastătæ.

The uttermost bone in the shank of the leg, Paracnēmium, ii, n.

A bone or gristle that cometh before the mouth of the stomach, for defence of the same, Chondros xiphoides.

The roundness or knots of the bones in the knee, ancle, elbow, or buckle, Condylus, li, m.

Bones that fall from the table, Analecta, orum, n.

To scale rugged bones, Ossa scabrata rădere.

An house where bones are kept, Ossuaria, æ, f.

When the end of a bone is broken, where it joyneth with another, Apagina, æ, f.

The breaking of bones, Ossifragium, ii, n.

That hath the bones of his shoulder blades, standing out like wings, Pterygodes.

That hath his bones pulled out or broken, Exossatus, a, um.

The gathering of bones, Ossilegium, ii, n.

He that gathereth bones, Ossilegus, gi, m.

Boneless (or without bones) Exossus, a, um.

Of a bone (or like a bone) Osseus, a, um.

Splents used by bone-setters, Ferulæ.

A bone-setting, Mochlia, æ, f.

One bone from another, Officulatim, adv.

A bone-fire, Pyra, æ, f. Ignis exstructus in testimonium gaudii.

A bongrace to keep off the sun, Umbella, æ, f. Umbrăcŭlum, li, n.

A bonnet (or under cap) Redimiculum, li, n. Galericulum, i, n.

B O O.

A book, Liber, ri, m.

A little book, Libellus, li, m.

The cover or strings of a book, Syttiba, æ, f.

Books of divers arguments, Pandectæ, arum, f.

Books wherein Laws, Decrees of the Senate are written concerning the Nobility, Elephantini Libri.

A book of Medicines, Antidotarius, ii, m.

A book wherein old customs are written, Annāles, ium, m.

The books of common customs, Rituales libri.

Books of the Holy Scripture, Biblia, orum, n.

Books of Physick, Iatronicæ, arum, f.

Books negligently written, Oscitationes.

A note book, Exceptorius liber.

A book of Memorandums, a posting book, Adversaria, orum. n.

A reckoning book wherein expences are noted in Journeys, Itinerarium, ii, n.

A book of remembrance, Commentarium, ii, m.

A book to instruct one, Protrepticus, ci, m.

A Merchants book noting things for every month, Calendarius, liber.

A book of remembrance declairing what is done daily, Diarium, ii, n. Hemerologium, ii, n.

A book whose Author is not known, Liber Anonymus.

Books set forth under false names and titles, Libri subdititii.

A book Printer, Typographus, phi, m.

Book Printing, Typographia, æ, f.

A book-binder, Biblĭŏpēgus i, m.

A bookseller, Bibliopola, æ, m.

A booksellers shop, Taberna vel Officina Libraria.

Pertaining to books, Librarius, a, um.

To wear (put on) boots, Ocreo, are. Inocreo, are.

Booted (or wearing boots) Ocreatus, a, um.

A boot, Ocrea, æ, f.

A pair of boots, Par Ocrearum.

Boot-hose tops, Ornamenta Ocrealia.

Boot-hose, Caliga ad Ocreas.

A boot

A Boot of neats leather, Pedibovita, æ, f.

Boots for Plough-men (called Okers) Capatinæ, arum, f.

A booth, stall or standing in a Fair or Market, Botha, æ, f. Tabernaculum, i, n.

Booths (cabins or standings made in Fairs or Markets to sell Wares or Merchandize,) Præstega, æ, f. Attĕgiæ, arum, f. Velarium, ii, n.

Booth-cloaths, Velaria, orum, n.

Belonging to such booths, Velaris, re.

A boorder, Communiarius, ii, m. Asht. 108.

Boord or diet, Commensalis, le, adj. Pro Communibus pro Commensali. For Commons, for Boording, Tabling or Dieting, *Vet. Int.* 240.

B O R.

To border upon, bound or to be situate nigh unto, Adjăcĕo, es. Confinio, is.

The borders of a Country, Confinium, ii, n.

A borderer, dwelling by, or that cometh out of one Country and dwelleth in another, Accŏla, æ, c. g.

A bordering upon, Finitimus, a, um.

Bordering near together, Confinis, ne.

Pertaining to such borders, Limitāneus, a, um.

The border (or brim) of any thing, Crepido, inis, f. Prætextum, ti, n.

The border (or brim) of a river, Fibra, æ, f.

A border (or hem) Fimbria, æ, f.

A border (or lace of a Womens gown) Institа, æ, f.

That is full of borders and brims, Labrosus, a, um.

That hath borders or tails finely wrought with many small pieces, Segmentatus, a, um.

That hath a border (or margin) Plutealis, le.

The border of a Garment, Limbus, i, m.

Borders of Garments, Extremitates vestium.

To bore (or make an hole with an Augre or other Instrument, Tĕrĕbro, are. Foro, are.

To bore (or pierce through) Perterebro, are.

To bore (or pierce) round about, Circumfero, are.

Bored (or pierced) through, Perfŏrātus, a, um.

A borer (or he that boreth) Forator, oris, m. Perforator, oris, m.

A boring (or piercing) Foratio, onis, f. Terebratio, onis, f.

To be bored, Foror, aris.

That may be bored, Forabilis, le.

Borlace (the Family) Borlasius.

To be born, Nascor, eris, nātus sum, nasci.

To be born of, Enascor, eris, natus sum, sci.

To be born before his time, Aborior, iris, vel eris, ortus.

To be born nigh unto, Adnascor, eris, natus sum.

A Child

A Child born at the ſun riſing, Lucius, ii, m.

Born after the death of his Father, Poſthŭmus, i, m.

Born and Bred in the ſame Country, Place or Town, Indigena, æ, f.

Born after us (Off-ſpring) they that live after us, Poſtĕri, orum, m.

Born, Natus, a, um.

Born (or deſcended of a ſtock or linage) Oriundus, a, um.

Born in the Country, Rurigena, æ, c. 2.

Firſt-born, Primogĕnĭtus, a, um.

Elder-born, Antegenitalis, le.

Born together, Congenitus, a, um.

To be born (or carried) Feror.

To be born up (or holden) Fulcior, iris, vel ire.

Born up, Suſtentatus, a, um.

That is born (or carried) Geſtatus, a, um. Latus, a, um.

Born or (carried over) Superlatus, a, um.

To be born, Fĕrendus, a, um.

Born (or brought up) Allatus, a, um.

Born (or carried about) Circumlatus, a, um.

To be born down (or ſuppreſſed) Deprimor, eris.

Born down, Oppreſſus, a, um.

To be born withal (or ſuffered to do any thing) Indulgeor, eris.

Born withal (or ſuffered) Indultus, a, um.

A Borough, Burgus, i, m. *Lex.* 22.

A Borough (or City) Court, Burghmota, æ, f.

Borough Goods, Bona municipalia.

To borrow, Mutuo, are.

To borrow or take money to uſury, Fœneror, aris.

Borrowed, Mutuatus, a, um.

Borrowed ſo long as the lender pleaſeth, Precarius, a, um.

A borrowing, Mŭtuātio, onis, f.

A borrowing of one to pay another, Verſura, æ, f.

A borrower or he to whom any thing is lent, Mutuator, oris, m.

B O S.

To put in ones boſom, Inſinuo, are.

A boſom, Sinus, ûs, m.

A boſs (or ſtud) of a girdle or bridle) Bulla, æ, f.

The boſs of a book, Umbĭlīcus, ci, m.

The boſs of a buckler, Umbo, onis, m.

Boſſed, Gibbus, a, um.

Boſcage, Boſcagium, ii, n. i. e. *Maſt and Browze for Cattle in the Woods.*

B O T.

A botch (or bile) Ceramium, ii, n.

Botches, Bubones, m. pl.

A botch coming of Inflammation, Carbunculus, li, m.

The cauſing of a botch, Ulceratio, onis, f.

A botch (or courſe of ill humours) Abſceſſus, us, m.

Cauſiug

Causing botches, Ulcerarius, a, um.

To make a botch, Ulcĕro, are.

Full of botches, Ulcerosus, a, um.

To botch (piece, mend or repair) Resarcio, is, si, ere.

A botcher (or mender of old garments (Sartor, oris, m. Interpŏlātor, oris, m. Pictatius, ii, m.

A botchers shop, Sutrina, æ, f.

A botching (or mending) Interpolatio, onis, f.

Boteley (near Oxford) Botelega.

Both, Ambo.

Both severally, Uterque.

He that playeth on both sides, Ambidexter, tri, m.

Both together, Amplexim, adv.

On both sides, Utrinque, adv.

Both ways, Ambifariam, adv.

A bottle, Uter, utris, m.

A little bottle, Ampulla, æ, f.

A bottle (or vessel to carry drink in) Brochia, æ, f.

The mouth of a bottle, Orificium, ii, n. Lura, æ, f.

Glass bottles, Ampullæ vitreæ.

A maker of bottles (or viols) Ampullarius, ii, m.

Made like or pertaining to bottles, Ampullaceus, a, um.

The bottom (or foundation of any thing) Fundum, i, n.

The bottom of the Sea, Profunditas maris.

The bottom of an earthen pot, Cymbum, i, n.

The bottom of a ship, Carina, æ, f.

From the bottom of the heart, Ab imo pectore.

At the bottom, Penitior, ius, issimus.

B O.

Without bottom, Immensus, a, um.

The very bottom, Funditus, a, um.

A bottom of thread, Glomus, mi, m.

A little bottom, Glomicellus, li, m.

Bound like a bottom of thread, Glomerosus, a, um.

A bottomless place, Vorago, inis, f. Abyssus, ssi, f.

B O U.

A bouget, Vidulum, i, n. Bulga, æ, f.

A bough (or branch) of a tree or herb. Rāmus, mi, m.

A little bough (or branch) Ramulus, li, m.

A bough which is dead, cut or seared, Rāmāle, lis, n.

Of a bough, Rameus, a, um.

Full of boughs, Ramōsus, a, um.

To lop the under boughs, Subluco, are.

Bought, Emptus, a, um.

Bought again, Redemptus, a, um.

Bought for a low price, Ademptus, a, um.

Things bought at advantage to sell again, Promercalia, orum, n.

That may be bought, Emptivus, a, um.

A boul (or any thing that is round) Globus, li, m.

A little boul, Globŭlus, li, m.

A bouling (or playing at bouls) Sphæromachia, æ, f.

A boul-

A Bouling Alley, Sphæristerium, ii, n.

To boult (or range meal) Cribro, are.

To boult (or sift out) Limo, are.

A boulter (or meal sieve) Reticulum, li, n. Cribrum pollinarium.

A fine boulter, Subcerniculum, li, n.

A boulting house, Domus Farinaria.

A boulting cloath, Polintriduum, ii, n.

A boulting trough or tub, Arca pollinaria. Arca cribraria.

He that boulteth, Pollintor, oris, m.

To bound (or limit how far a thing goeth, Limito, are.

To set bounds (to measure) Metior, iris, mensus sum, metiri.

To bound (or border upon) Collimitor, aris, atus sum, ari.

Bounded (or bordered together) Collimitatus, a, um.

Bounded (or bordered, or limited) Limitatus, a, um.

A bound-setter between Land and Land, Place and Place, Finitor, oris, m. Mensor, oris, m.

A bounding (or setting up bounds) Limitatio, onis, f.

A bound, Bunda, æ, f. Spel. 102, Lex. 21.

Bounds, Confinia, orum, n.

A division between two bounds, Bifinium, ii, n.

The bound (or border) of a Country, Margo, inis, f.

Bounds or limits of Land directed to the East, Prorsi, orum, n.

A bound-stone (or mark between mile and mile) Milliarius lapis.

A bound or mark to distinguish one man's ground from another, Terminalis lapis.

The meeting of bounds, Collimium, ii, n.

The meeting of the bounds of three fields, Trifinium, ii, n.

They whose Lands bound together, Consortes.

Bounding (or bordering) near together, Conterminus, a, um.

Of or belonging to bounds, Limitaris, re. Terminalis, le.

Full of bounds (or limits) Terminosus, a, um.

To be bound, Teneor, eris. Obstringo, is, xi, ctum, ere.

To be bound with sureties for payment of money (or performance of Covenant) Obligor, aris.

Bound by Bond (or Covenant) Obligatus, a, um. Tentus, a, um.

Bound by duty for a good turn already received, Devinctus, a, um.

Bound (or tyed) Ligatus, a, um. Vinctus, a, um.

Bound together, Colligātus, a, um.

Bound up, or in, Deligatus, a, um.

Bound under, Substrictus, a, um.

That is bound with Iron, Præferratus, a, um.

Boverton (in Glamorganshire) Bonium, seu Bovium.

Bourton (the Family) De Bortana sive Burtana.

B O W.

To bow (or bend) Curvo, are. Torqueo, es, si, tum, ere.

To bow down (or make stoop under a burthen) Pando, are.

To bow round, Circumflecto, is, xi, exum, ĕre.

To bow inward, Incurvo, are.

To bow back in a compass (or circuit) Regyro, are.

To bow the Knee, Ingeniculor, aris.

To Bow (or wax crooked) Curvesco, scis, ĕre.

To Bow (or incline down) Declino, are.

To Bow to, Acclino, are.

To Bow backward, Reclino, are.

To Bow between, Interclino, are.

To Bow together, Convergo, is.

To be Bowed, Curvor.

To be Bowed the contrary way, Formicor, aris.

Bowed (or Bent) Pandus, a, um. Conflexus, a, um.

Bowed (or Bent) backward, Repandus, a, um.

Bowed upward like an arch roof, Subvexus, a, um.

Bowed downward, Devexus, a, um.

Bowed about, Circumflexus, a, um.

Not bowed, Indeflexus, a, um.

A bowing, Curvatio, onis, f. Flexura, æ, f.

A bowing round about, Circumflexio, onis, f.

A bowing back, Recurvitas, atis, f.

A bowing downward as under a burthen, Pandatio, onis, f.

The bowing in an arched roof, Absis, dis, f. Absidia, æ, f.

A bowing made in roofs of houses like a circle, Haspis, ĭdis, f.

He that boweth the knee (as in making of Courtesie) Suffraginator, oris, m.

Easie to be bowed, Flexibilis, le.

Bowingly, Proclivè, adv.

A Bow, Arcus, ûs, m.

A little Bow, Arculus, li, m. Arcellus, li, m.

A Bow (wherewith they play on a Fiddle or Viol) Plectrum, i, n.

To unbend (or unstring) a Bow, Arcum denodare.

A Cross-Bow, Balista, æ, f.

A Steel-bow (or Tiller) Chalybea balista.

A Bow-bearer, Præfectus Forestæ.

An Ox-Bow in a Plough, Arquillus, li, m.

To bend a Bow, Arcum lúnare vel Tendere.

A bow-man (Archer) Sagittarius, ii, m.

A Bowyer (or Bow-maker) Arcuarius, ii, m.

A Bow-string, Chorda, æ, f. Amentum, i, n.

A Bow-Case, Corytus, i, m. Theca arcuaria.

To make like a Bow, Arcuo, are.

To bend like a Bow, Arcuor, ari.

Of a Bow, Arcuarius, a, um.

Bow-like, Arcuatim, adv.

A Bowyer's shop, Fabrica arcuaria.

A Bow-net, Nassa, æ, f.

To bowel (embowel, or draw out the Garbage or Guts) Eviscĕrō, are. Exentĕro, are.

Bowelled (or Embowelled) Evisceratus, a, um.

The Bowels (or Intrails) of Man or Beast, Intestina, orum, n. Viscera, um, pl.

A bowelling, Exenteratio, ōnis, f.

By Bowels (or Intrails) Visceratim, adv.

To Bowge (or Pierce) Pĕnetro, are.

To Bowge (or Pierce) a ship with shot, Pĕnetro, are.

Bowged (or Pierced) Perforatus, a, um.

A Bowging (or Piercing) Perforatio, onis, f.

A Bower, Umbrăcŭlum, li, n.

Bowes *upon* Stanmore *(in Richmondshire)* Lavatres, Lavatris,

B O X.

A box-tree, Buxus, i, f.

A box, Pyxis, ĭdis, f.

A little box, Pyxidŭla, æ, f. Cistula, æ, f.

A box to keep spice in, Myrothecium, ii, n.

A box to keep Jewels in, Annularium, ii, n.

Made like a box, Pyxidatus, a, um.

A Sand box, Pulveraria Theca.

A box for the balance and weights, Trytodoce, es, f.

A box-maker, Scriniarius, ii, m.

A tinder box, Ignarium, ii. n.

A Printer's Composing box, Lōcŭlāmentum, i, n.

A round box, Capsa rotunda.

An Oval box, Capsa Ovalis.

A dust box, Pyxis vel Theca pulveraria.

Grocers boxes wherein they put their Spice, Nidi, orum, n.

Boxes wherein sweet Perfumes are kept, Olfactoriola, orum, n.

A box to throw dice on the table, Orca, æ, f. Tritillus, li, m.

A box (or pot) to put lots in, Sitella, æ, f.

Poor mens boxes, Cistulæ pauperum.

Box-bearers, Cistiferi, Pyxiferi, orum, m.

Boxley (in *Kent*) Boxleia.

B O Y.

A boy, Puer, ĕri, m.

A little boy, Puellus, li, m.

A boy under 14 *years of age*, Impūber, ĕris, adj.

A boy about 14 *years of age*, Puber, ĕris.

A boy tending upon common harlots, Aquāriŏlus, i, m.

A boy with a bush-head, Comatulus, i, m.

Boys attending upon an Host to carry baggage, Calones, m. pl.

Boys games, Pupillaria, orum. Puerilia.

Boyishness, Puerilitas, atis, f.

Boyish, Puerilis, le.

Boyishly, Pueriliter, adv.

A boy of an anchor, Index ancoralis.

To boyl (or seeth) as Cooks do, Coquo, xi, ctum. Elixo, are.

To boyl before (or parboyl) Præcŏquo, xi, ctum.

To boyl again, Recoquo, xi, ctum.

To boyl much (or throughly) Percoquo, xi, ctum. Excoquo, xi, ctum.

To boyl away, Decoquo, xi, ctum.

To boyl (or seeth) together, Concoquo, xi, ctum. Collixo, are.

To make to boyl, Fervefacio, ere.

To boyl new wine, Defruto, are.

To boyl often, Coquito, are. Coctito, are.

To boyl as a Pot boyleth, Bullio, is, ivi, itum.

To boyl over, Ebullio, ire. Efferveo, ere. Effervo, vi, ere.

To begin to boyl, Effervesco, ere. Bullio, ivi, itum.

To be boyled, Incoquor.

Boyled (or sodden) Coctus, a, um. Elixus, a, um.

A boyling, Elixatio, onis, f.

Throughly boyled, Excoctus, a, um.

Often boyled (or boyled again, Recoctus, a, um.

Boyled before (or too much boyled, Præcoctus, a, um.

Half boyled (or parboyled) Semicoctus, a, um.

Boyled a little, Subfervefactus, a, um.

Easily boyled, Coctilis, le.

A boyling (or seething) Coctio, onis, f. Coctura, æ, f.

A boyling up, Ebullitio, onis, f.

Boyled meats, Aulicoqua, orum, n.

A boyler, Coctor, oris, m.

A boyler or boyling Cauldron, Ahenum, ei, n.

That is boyled in an earthen pot, Testuaceus, a, um.

To boyl as the Sea, Undo, are. Exæstuo, are.

Boyled in Broath, Jurulentus, a, um.

Boyn river (in Ireland) Boanda, Boandus, Buvindus.

Boys (the Family) De Bosco, de Braiosa.

B R A.

A Brace to fasten to beams in building, Fibula, æ, f.

A brace under a beam, Uncus, ci, m.

Braces in building, Cupiæ, arum, f.

A brace of dogs, Bini Canes.

A shooters bracer, Brachiale, is, n.

A Bracelet, Armilla, æ, f. Torquis, is, m. & f.

A Bracelet to be worn on the right hand, Dextrale, is, n.

A Bracelet for Women, set with precious stones, Dextrocherium, ii, n.

A bracelet of Pearls, Linea Margaritarum.

A little Bracelet, Spintherulum, li, n.

That weareth Bracelets, Armillatus, a, um.

Brackley (in *Northamptonshire)* Brachilega.

Bragget (or bracket) a kind of drink, Promulsis, idis, f.

A bragget (or stay) cut out of stone or timber to bear up the summer. In Masonry called a Corbet, in Timber work a Bragget or shouldring piece. Mutulus, li, m.

Brag-

Braggets (*or supporters of rafters*) Prŏcĕres, um, m. pl.

The brain, Cerebrum, i, n.

The hinder part of the brain (*or a little brain*) Cerebellum, li, n.

To dash out ones brains, Excerebro, are.

He that dasheth (*or beateth out*) *the brains*, Excerebrator, oris, m.

The Cauls (*or Films*) *of the brain*, Pia mater, dura mater.

A brake (*such as bakers use*) Frangibulum, li, n. Artopta, æ, f. Mactra, æ, f. Vibra, æ, f.

A brake for flax or hemp, Linifrangibula, æ, f.

A brake (*or heckle*) Linibrium, ii, n.

Brampton (near *Huntington*) Bramptonia.

Brampton (in *Cumberland*) Brementuracum.

Branchester (in *Norfolk*) Brannodunum.

To branch out, Germĭno, are. Progermino, are.

To have branches, Frondeo, es, ŭi, ēre.

To begin to have branches, Frondesco, is, ui, ĕre.

Branched (*Leaved*) *or sprung out*, Frondatus, a, um. Ramosus, a, um.

Branching (*or springing out*) Germinatus, a, um. Frondens, ntis.

A running into fruitless branches, Fruticatio, onis, f.

A branch (*bough or arm*) *of a tree herb or young twig*, Germen, inis, n. Lex. 119. Frons, dis, f.

A little branch (*or young twig*) Rāmŭlus, li, m. Frondicula, æ, f. Coliculus, li, m.

A branch which beareth no fruits, Stŏlo, onis, m. Spădo, onis, m.

A branching, Germinatio, onis, f.

Of a branch, Frondeus, a, um. Sarmentitius, a, um. Rameus, a, um.

A dead branch cut from a tree, Ramale, is, n.

Full of branches, Sarmentosus, a, um. Pampinosus, a, um.

That beareth branches (*or leaves*) Frondifer, a, um.

A brand of fire, Torris, is, m.

A brand of fire quenched (*or put out*) Tĭtio, onis, m.

A brand-iron (*or trivet*) Chytra, æ. f. Chytropus, i, m.

Brann, Furfur, uris, m. Excretum, i, n.

Brann of wheat, Canica, æ, f. Cantabrum, i, n.

Of or belonging to brann, Furfuraceus, a, um.

Full of brann, Furfurosus, a, um.

To brasen (*to mix or counterfeit or cover with brass*) Æro, are. Subæro, are.

Brass, Æs, æris, n.

Brass-work (*or that which is made of brass*) Ærĭficium, ii, n. Æramentum, ti, n.

A brass pot (*cauldron or kettle*) Æneum, i, n. Ahenum incoctile.

A little brass pot (*or posnet*) Ænulum, li, n.

A kind of mixt brass, Ollaria, æ, f.

Brass oar, Onychitis, Ærarius lapis.

Covered with brass, Æratus, um.

Bearing (or bringing forth) brass, Ærifer, a, um.

A brass Mine, Ærifodina, æ, f.

Of brass, Æreus, a, um. Æneus, a, um.

A brasier, Ærarius, ii, m.

A brasiers shop, Maignagium, ii, n.

A place where brass is made, Chalceutice, es, f.

That wherein is brass, Ærosus, a, um.

That is brass within, and gold and other small metal without, Subæratus, a, um.

Brasen types (belonging to Printers) Typi Ærei.

To be hard of flesh (or brawned like a boar) Concallĕo, es, ŭi, ere.

Brawn of a wild boar, Aprugnum vel Aprinum callum.

Bacon of a tame boar, Callum verrinum.

The brawn of the arms and thighs, Tori, orum, n. Lăcertus, ti, m.

The brawn of the legs, Musculus, li, m.

Plenty of brawn, Callositas, atis, f.

Full of brawn, Callosus, a, um.

Bray hundred (in *Berkshire*) Bibrocassi, Bibroc.

B R E.

A breach, Incursio, onis, f. Frussura, æ, f.

A breach between men, Seditio, onis, f. Simultas, atis, f.

The breach of a promise, Punica fides.

Bread, Panis, is, m.

Bread corn, Farr, rris, n. Frumentum, i, n.

Sweet (or unleavened bread) Azymus panis.

Leavened bread, Panis fermentātus, Zymites, æ, m.

Bread a little leavened, Acrizymus.

Bread made of new wheat, Sitanicus panis.

Bread made of wheat, Panis Tritĭceus, Apluda, æ, f.

Rie bread, Panis secaliceus.

Barley bread, Hordeāceus panis.

Oaten bread, Panis ăvēnāceus.

White bread, Panis Silĭgineus.

Cake bread, Dulciarius Panis, Panis artolaganus.

Bread to eat oysters with, Panis Ostrearius.

Hasty bread, Panis spensticus.

Bread baked in an oven, Panis Furnaceus.

Simnel bread, Simnellum, i, n. *Pry*. 71.

Simnel, Wastel, &c. Panis de Wastello, Coketto, Simnello, Treete, Dulcello. Stat. Panis & Cervisiæ 51. *H*. 3.

Cracknel (or Simnel) bread, Similagineus panis. Panis aquaticus, vel Parthicus.

Manchet bread, Collyris, idis, f.

Ranged wheat bread (or houshold bread) Cĭbārius panis. Panis secundarius.

Bread of beans, Panis Fabārius.

Sugar bread or march pane, Saccarites panis.

Saffron

Saffron bread, Panis crocatus.

Bread made of wheat bran (*or horse bran*) Panis furfuraceus.

Brown or course bread, Panis gregarius vel Domesticus. Agelaus panis.

Great loaves of brown bread, Culicii Panes. Aglei panes.

Bisket bread, Panis nauticus. Panis biscoctus.

Dole bread, Tradilis panis.

Mouldy (*or vinowed bread*) Panis mucidus.

Bread baked on the ashes or hearth, Subcineritius panis, Focarius panis.

Bread baked under a pan, Panis testuaceus, Artopticus panis.

Bread baked on a Gridiron, Escarites panis.

Bread not well baked, Panis rubidus.

Light bread, puffed up with yest or barm, Panis spongiosus.

The crust of bread, Crustum, sti, n. Crustulum panis.

A crust of bread, Crustula panis.

The crumb of bread, Medulla panis.

A crumb of bread, Mica panis.

A loaf of bread, Panificium, ii, n.

A roul of bread, Pulpido, inis, f. Torta, æ, f. Tortula, æ, f.

Fine bread, Cyrites panis.

Indian bread, Yucca, æ, f.

A bin for bread, Panarium, ii, n.

The making of bread, Panificium, ii, n.

Breadth, Latitudo, inis, f. Amplitudo, inis, f.

The being of one breadth, Æquilatio, onis, f.

Of one breadth, Æquilatus, a, um.

Of two hands breadth, Didorus, a, um.

To break (*or tear*) Frango, is, egi, actum, ere. Rumpo, ūpi, ptum, ĕre.

To break in pieces, Comminŭo, is, ŭi, utum, ere.

To break asunder (*or in two pieces*) Interrumpo, is, rupi, ptum, ĕre.

To break off, Abrumpo, is, ūpi, uptum, ĕre.

To break (*or burst open*) Rĕfringo, is, egi, actum, ĕre.

To break open violently, Expugno, are.

To break up, Dirumpo, is, ūpi, ptum, ĕre.

To break down, Diruo, is, ui, utum, ere.

To break down an hedge, Dissĕpio, is, sepi, vel psi, ptum, ire.

To break one thing against another, Adfringo, is.

To break (*or bruise small*) Tero, is, trivi, tritum, ere.

To break under, Suffringo, is, egi, ctum, ere.

To break (*as when one breaketh a Law*) Violo, are.

To break often, Ruptito, are.

To break with a Flail, Tribŭlo, are.

To break up a Writ or Letter, Resigno, are.

To break (*or tame*) *a wild beast*, Dŏmo, as, āvi & ŭi, ātum & ĭtum.

To break in, Irrumpo, pis, rupi, uptum, pĕre.

To

To break out, Erumpo, is, upi, ptum, ere.

To break out as the sea doth, Exundo, are.

To break out (as a mans face doth with heat) Pustulas emittere.

To break forth (as water out of a spring) Scăteo, es, ui, ēre.

To break his Oath, Fidem violare.

A breaker (or burster) Ruptor, oris, m.

A breaker (or burster of doors and locks) Effractor, oris, m.

He that breaketh (or violateth) Violator, oris, m.

A breaker (or tamer of horses and colts) Domitor, oris, m.

Good breakers of horses, Hyppothedicæ, arum, m.

A breaker of a League, Fœdifragus, a, um.

A breaking (or bursting) Fractio, onis, f. Ruptura, æ, f.

A breaking in pieces, Fractio, onis, f.

A breaking in sunder, Diruptio, onis, f.

A breaking off, Abruptio, onis, f.

A breaking (or bursting open) Effractura, æ, f.

A breaking (or violating) Violatio, onis, f.

A breaking in, Irruptio, onis, f.

A breaking down, Excisio, onis, f.

A breaking through, Perruptio, onis, f.

A breaking (or taming) of an horse, Domitura, æ, f.

One that breaks as bankrupt, Decoctor, oris, m.

A breaking out into a scab, Ulceratio, onis f.

A breaking out (or bursting out of waters, Scaturies, ei, f.

A breakfast, Jentaculum, li, n,

The breast, Pectus, ŏris, n.

A little breast, Pectusculum, li, n.

A Womans breast (or nipple) Mamma, æ, f. Papilla, æ, f.

A little breast, Mammŭla, æ, f. Mammilla, æ. f.

The breast bone, Sternon, scutum cordis.

A breast cloath, Mammillare, is, n.

A breast-plate (or Gorget) Thŏraca, æ, f. Pectorale, is, n.

Belonging to the breast-plate, Pectoralis, le.

That hath a great breast, Pectorosus, a, um.

That is narrow and strait breasted, Stenothorax, acis.

That weareth breast-plates, Thōrăcatus, a, um.

To breath, Spiro, are.

To draw breath with difficulty, Anhelo, are.

To breath out (or cast forth a breath or fume) Exhalo, are, Vaporo, are.

To breath (or air) Sicco, are.

A breathing, Respiratio, onis f.

A breathing with difficulty, Anhelatio, onis, f. Asthma, atis, n. Dyspnœa, æ, f.

A breathing upon, Afflatus, a, um.

Breath, Hālĭtus, ûs. Spiritus, ûs, m.

A short breath, Suspirium, ii, n.

A moist breath (or air) Vapor, oris, m.

A dry breath (or fume) Exhalatio, onis, f.

Thickness of breath, Dascia, æ, f.

The passage whereby the breath issueth out, Respiramen, inis, n.

A breathing hole, out of which breath, wind, air or smoak passeth, Spiraculum, li, n.

Short breathed, Asthmaticus, a, um.

That breatheth, Spirans, tis, Part.

That whereby we breath, Spirabilis, le.

The breech, Podex, icis, m.

Breeches (slops or long hose) Braccæ, arum, f. Subligaculum, li, n. Femoralia, ium, pl.

A pair of breeches, Par subligaculorum.

Mariners breeches (or slops) Braccæ, arum, f.

Breeches of linen to wrestle or run in, Campestre, is, n. Vestis Campestris.

Breeches (or flop makers) Braccarii, orum, m.

He that weareth breeches, Braccatus, a, um.

To breed (or wax with young) Genero, are.

To breed teeth, Dentio, is, ivi, itum, ire.

A breeder, Fructuarius, a, um.

Breeding, or breed of Cattle, Incrementum, i, n. Co. Ent. 361.

Of the race or breed of horses, Decime de araciis Equorum, 2 Mon. 967.

A breed or flock of Swine, Haratium, ii, n.

A breeder of Cattle, Pecuarius, ii, m.

The bread or increase of Cattle, Pecuaria, æ, f.

A breeding of teeth, Dentio, onis, f.

A breeding place, Pecuarium, ii, n.

Pertaining to breeding, Fructuarius, a, um.

A breeding, Prægnatio, onis, f.

Breeding (or great with young) Fœtus, a, um

Brecknock (City) Brechinia.

Bred in one naturally, Innatus, a, um.

Bred (or brought up) Educatus, a, um.

Breviatures, Siglæ, arum, f.

Brevity, Brevitas, atis, f.

A breve (or brief) Breve, is, n.

Brentford (in *Middlesex*) Brentæ vadus.

Brentwood (in *Essex*) Cæsaromagus.

Breten *spring, or near it (in Suffolk)* Combretonium, Cambretovium, Comvetronium.

Brettenham (in *Suffolk*) *or the same with* Cambritonium, Combretonium Cambretovium.

To brew, Pandoxor, aris vel are. Braxo, are. Potum vel Cervisiam concoquere.

Brewed, Concoctus, a, um.

A brewer, Pandoxator [illegible] Cervisiarius ii, n. Braxator, ris, m.

A brew-house, Pandoxatorata ii, n. Cervisiarium, ii, n.

A brewing Brasium, i, n. Spe 116.

Brewing subs, Cupa Pandoratoriæ.

 Brewess,

Brewess, Ofella, æ, f. Offulæ adiaptæ. Panis madidus. Panis jure emolitus.

B R I.

To bribe (or corrupt with gifts) Perverto, is, ti, sum, ĕre. Largione vel muneribus animum corrumpere, Munera largior.

To bribe (or solicit men to give their voices and consent, Prenso, are. Prehenso, are.

To labour for an office by giving bribes, Ambio, is, īvi, & ii, itum, ire.

To poll by receiving bribes, Deperulor, aris.

Bribed, Corruptus, a, um. Sordidus, a, um. Captus auro.

A briber, Corruptor, oris, m. Largitor, oris, m.

A bribing, Corruptio, onis, f.

A bribe, Largitio, onis, f.

Bribery, Repetundæ, Gen. Repetundarum, Abl. Repetundis. Latrocinium, ii, n. Corruptio, onis, f.

That will be bribed, or sell his faith for money, Venalis, le.

Accused of bribery, Repetundus, a, um.

Pertaining to bribes, Muneralis, le.

With taking bribes in dishonest matters, Corruptè, sordidè, depravatè.

Brick-work, Opus lătĕritium.

Brick-layers work, Opus laterale.

A Brick, Later, eris, m.

A little Brick, Laterculus, li, m.

A Brick-maker, Lătĕrārius, ii, m.

A Brick Kiln, Lateraria, æ. f. Fornax lateritia.

Brick making, Argillatio, onis, f. Cænofactoria, æ, f.

A Brick wall, Sepimentum lateritium. Murus coctilis.

That is made of Brick, Lateritius, a, um.

A rubbed Brick, Later frictus.

A Bridal (or Marriage) Nuptiæ, arum, f. Nuptatorium, ii, n.

He that beareth sway at a Bridal, Paranymphus, i, m.

A Bride-cake, Summanalia.

Pieces of Bride-cake thrown out among the people, Emissitiæ, arum, f.

A Bridegroom, Sponsus, i, m.

A bride (or woman new married) Sponsa, æ, f.

The Bride-house, Nuptorium, ii, n.

The Brideman that leadeth the Bride to Church, Prōnŭbus, i, m.

The Bridemaid, Prōnŭba, æ, f.

A Bride-Chamber, Thălămus, i, m.

Bridewel (in *London*) Fons Bridgidæ.

Bridewel, Pistrinum, i, n. Ergastulum, i, n.

The master of Bridewel, Pistrinarius, ii, m. Ergastularius, i, m.

To make a Bridge, Ponto, are.

A little Bridge, Ponticulus, li, m.

A draw-bridge, Pons versatilis. Cătăracta, æ, f. Ponstratus, i, m.

A Bridge made in haste for a time and shortly removed, Schedium, ii, n.

A Bridge of wood, Pons roborius, vel Ligneus.

Money

Money given for the maintaining of Bridges, Pontagium, ii, n.

The bridge of a Lute, or other Instrument that holdeth up the strings, Magadium, ii, n.

To bridle (or curb) Fræno, are.

To be bridled, Frænor, ari.

Bridled, Frænatus, a, um. Obfrænatus, a, um.

Not bridled, Effrænatus, a, um.

A Bridler, Frænator, oris, m.

A bridling, Frænatio, onis f. Refrænatio, onis, f.

A Bridle, Frænum, i, n. pl. Fræni, orum, m. & Fræna, orum, n.

A little Bridle, Frænulum, li, n.

A bridle rein, Lorum, i, n. habena, æ, f.

The headstall of a Bridle, Orea, æ, f.

Bearing a Bridle, Frænigerus, a, um.

She that Bridles, Frænatrix, icis, f.

To be brief or short in speaking or writing, Laconizo, are. Compendiosè loqui.

Briefness (or Brevity) Brevitas, atis, f.

A brief (or short writing) containing the sum of a thing, Abbreviatio, onis, f.

A brief rehearsal of things treated of before, Recapitulatio, onis, f.

A brief sentence, Sententiola, æ, f.

Brief (or Compendious) Concisus, a, um. Compendiarius, a, um.

Briefly (or Compendiously) Concisè, Compendiosè.

Brig-Casterton (in *Lincolnshire*) Causennæ, Causennis, Gausennæ, Gausennis.

A Brigandine (or Coat of Mail) Lorica, æ, f.

A Brigantine (Pinnace or little Ship) Celox, ocis, f. Paro, onis, m.

A Brigantine (or Rovers ship) Navis Prædatoria.

The least kind of Brigantine, Myoparo, onis, m.

A Brigantine set to espy, Episcopium, ii, n. Navigium Speculatorium.

To be bright (or to shine) Fulgeo, es, si, ere.

To make bright, Elucido, are.

To wax bright, Lucesco, scis.

It is bright, Lucet.

It waxeth bright, Lucessit.

Brightness (or clearness) Splendor, oris, m. Fulgor, oris, m.

Bright (or clear) Lucidus, a, um. Cŏruscus, a, um.

Very bright, Perlucidus, a, um.

Brightly (or clearly) Lucidè, Splendidè.

To brim a sow, Subo, are.

A brimmed sow, Sus subata.

The brim of a bank, or any thing else, Ora, æ, f. Margo, inis, f.

The brim of a sieve (or streiner) Telia, æ, f.

That hath great brims, Marginatus, a, um.

That hath no brims, Achilus, i, m.

Belonging to brims, Marginalis, le.

Brimstone, Sulphur, ŭris, n.

Natural brimstone, or brimstone digged out of the Earth and that never felt fire, Sulphur vivum & fossile, Ignem non expertum.

A place

A place where brimstone is made or boyled, Sulphŭrāria, æ, f.

A maker (or worker) of brimstone, Sulphŭrārius, ii, m.

A dressing with brimstone, Sulphŭrātio, onis, f.

A match made with brimstone, Sulphŭrātum, ti, n.

Dressed with, aired or smoaked in brimstone, Sulphŭrātus, a, um.

A place where brimstone lieth, Sulphŭretum, i, n.

Of or belonging to, mixed with, or of the colour of brimstone, Sulphureus, a, um.

To season with brine, Sălio, is, ui, ii & aliq. ivi, ire, Saltum. Salsedine Condire.

Brine (Liquor that is salt) Aqua salsa. salsedo, inis, f.

Brine with dregs and all, Alex, ecis, f.

Being long in brine, Muriarius, a, um.

Brinish, Salsus, a, um.

To bring, Duco, is, xi, ctum, ere.

To bring by force or violence, Attraho, is, xi, ctum, ere.

To bring from one place to another, Defero, fers, tuli, latum, ferre. Deporto, are.

To bring (or carry over) or on the other side, Trādūco, is, xi, ctum, ĕre.

To bring in, Infero, fers, tuli, latum, ferre. Inporto, are.

To bring in one in place of another, Substĭtuo, is, ŭi, ūtum, ĕre.

To bring back again, Redūco, is, xi, ctum, ere.

To bring forth, Educo, is, xi, ctum, ere.

To bring forth as females do their young, Părio, pĕpĕri, partum.

To be ready to bring forth, Parturio, is, ivi.

To bring forth before the time, Abortio, is, ivi. Aborto, are.

To bring forth flowers, Floreo, es, ŭi, ere.

To bring forth plenteously, Fundo, is, fudi, fusum, ĕre.

To bring forth, as one bringeth forth witnesses, Evŏco, are. Testes producere.

To bring up or nourish, Educo, is, xi, ctum, ere.

To bring together, Conduco, is, xi, ctum, ere.

To bring up in, Innūtrio, is, ivi, itum, ire.

To bring over, cover, or bring against, or a-thwart, Obduco, is, xi, ctum, ere.

To bring somewhat to nothing, Adnĭhilo, are.

To bring under, Subjicio, is, eci, ctum, ĕre.

To bring privily, Supparo, are.

To bring to pass, Efficio, is, ēci, ctum, ĕre.

To bring aside, Seduco, is, xi, ctum, ĕre.

To bring tidings, Nuncio, are.

To bring word again, Renuncio, are.

To bring (or cause) ill luck, Obscævo, are.

To bring into a narrow room or space, Cŏarcto, are.

To bring into presence, Repræsento, are.

To bring often, Perducto, are.

To bring to destruction, Prŏfligo, are.

A

A bringer of one against his will, Perductor, oris, m.

A bringer from one place to another, Traductor, oris, m.

A bringer back again, Reductor, oris, m.

He that bringeth a man to a place, Deductor, oris, m.

A bringer up, Educator, oris, m.

He that bringeth a thing to pass, Effector, oris, m.

A bringer of tidings, Rumigerulus, li, m.

A bringer to naught, Perditor, oris, m.

A bringer forth in sight, Subjector, oris, m.

A bringing, Portatus, ûs, m.

A bringing up (or Education) Educatio, onis, f.

A bringing from one to another, Translatio, onis, f. Traductio, onis, f.

A bringing in, Importatio, onis, f. Inductio, onis, f.

A bringing back, Reductio, onis, f.

A bringing forth (or abroad) Prolatio, onis, f. Productio, onis, f.

A bringing forth of young, Fœtura, æ, f. Procreatio, onis, f.

A bringing together, Collatio, onis, f.

A bringing under, Subjectio, onis, f.

A bringing to pass, Effectio, onis f.

Bringing Gold, Aurifer, fera, rum.

Bringing forth many stalks, shoots or shrubs, Fruticosus, a, um.

Bringing forth fruit twice a year, Biferus, a, um.

Bringing forth fruit thrice year, Triferus, a, um.

To bristle (or set up the bristles) Horreo, es, ui, ere. Setas erigere.

To bristle, put a hair on a shooemakers thred, Inseto, are.

A bristle, bristil (or big hair) Seta, æ, f.

A little bristle, Setula, æ, f.

Bristled, or that hath bristles on his back, Setiger, a, um. Hirsutus, a, um.

Full of bristles, Setosus, a, um.

Setting up the bristles, Horrens, tis, Part.

Bristol (or Bristow City) Bristolia, Bristolium, Bristowa.

Of Bristol (or *Bristow*) Bristoliensis, Bristowensis.

Bishop of Bristol, Episcopus Bristoliensis.

Britain (the Isle of Great Britain) Albion, Alvion, Pridania, Britannia, Pritanniæ, pl. Brutania, Pritania Samothea.

The British *Sea*, Mare Britannicum.

A Britain, Brito, onis, m.

Brittle (or soon broken) Fragilis, le.

Brittleness, Fragilitas, atis, f.

Not brittle, Infragilis, le.

Brittlely, Fragiliter, adv.

B R O.

To broach (or tap) Relino, is, evi & ivi, itum, ere.

A broach, Terebratus ad promendum.

A broach (or spit) Veru, Sing. Indecl.

A little

A little broach, Vĕrŭcŭlum, li, n.

Brockley *Hill near* Elleſtrey (in *Hartfordſhire*) Sulloniacæ, Sullonicæ.

To make broad, Dilato, are.

To wax broad, Lateſco, is, ĕre.

To lay abroad, Pando, is, di, ſum, ere.

A broad way, Platea, æ, f.

The broad end of an oar, Scalmus, i, m.

Broad, Lātus, a, um. Spacioſus, a, um.

Very broad, Perlatus, a, um. Latiſſimus, a, um.

Broad leafed, Latifolius, a, um.

That cannot be made broad, Illatabilis, le.

Broadly, Late, perlate, vaſte.

Brocage, Brocagium, ii, n. Fo. 162. Tranſactio, onis, f. Broctagium, ii, n. *Ry.* 593. 597. (i. e.) Money paid to a perſon for ſelling Goods.

To be broken, Rumpor.

Broken (or burſt) Fractus, a, um. Ruptus, a, um.

Broken in pieces, Comminutus, a, um.

Broken or burſt aſunder, or in the middle, Interruptus, a, um. Interciſus, a, um.

Broken off, Abruptus, a, um. Deſciſſus, a, um.

Broken open, Refractus, a, um.

Broken up, Diruptus, a, um.

Broken down, Dirutus, a, um.

Broken before, Præfractus, a, um.

Broken or violated, Violatus, a, um. Temeratus, a, um.

That may be broken, Fragilis, le.

Broken (or burſt) in the Loins, Dēlumbis, be. Delumbātus, a, um.

B R.

That cannot be broken, Infragilis, le.

Broken out by violence, Proruptus, a, um.

Broken or Bankrupt, Decoctor.

Broken (or tamed) Domitus, a, um.

Not broken (or tamed) Intractatus, a, um.

To broil, Torreo, es, ui, ſtum, ēre.

To be broiled, Torreſco, is, ere.

To broil on a Gridiron, Torrere ſuper crātĭcŭlam.

Broiled on the coals, Toſtus, a, um. Carbonatus, a, um.

A broil (or tumult) Tumultus, us & i, m.

A broker (or bargain maker) Tranſactor, oris, m. Prŏpōla, æ, m. Proxĕnēta, æ, m.

A pawn broker, Brocarius, ii, m. Broccator, oris, m. *Ry.* 593. 597.

Brokers, Brocarii, *Lex.* 21.

A pawn broker, Hypothecarius, ii, m.

A broker that ſells Garments at ſecond hand, Scrutarius, ii, m.

Bromfield (in *Denbighſhire*) Bromfelda.

To ſit on brood Incŭbo, as, ui, itum, are, ans, andus.

Set on brood, Incŭbātus, ûs, m.

A ſitting on brood, Incŭbātio, onis, f.

A brood of Chickens, Pullĭtĭes, ei, f.

A brook (or little river) Torrens, tis, m. Rivulus, li, m.

Little brooks, Irrigua, orum, n.

Broom, Geniſta, æ, f.

A broom field, or the place where broom groweth, Scopetum, i, n.

Of

Of or belonging to broom, Sparteus, a, um.

A broom (*or besom*) Scōpæ, ārum, f.

Broth (*Pottage*) Jusculum, i, n.

Broth (*or liquor to be supped*) Sorbitio, onis, f.

Stewed in broth, Jurulentus, a, um. Jusculentus, a, um.

A maker of broth, Juscularius, ii, m.

A brother, Frater, ris, m.

A little or young brother, Fratercŭlus, li, m.

A brother of one father and mother, Germanus, ni, m.

A half brother, Semigermanus, i, m.

A brother by the fathers side only, Frater Consanguineus.

A brother by the mothers side, Frater uterinus.

A husbands brother (*or brother-in-law*) Lēvir, ĭri, m.

A sisters brother, Sororius, ii, m.

A foster brother, Collactaneus, Homŏgălactus, i, m.

Brothers born at once, Gemini, Gemelli.

A brothers son, Fratrinus, i, m.

A brothers wife, or daughter, Fratrina, æ, f. Fratria, æ, f. Fratissa, æ, f. Frateria, æ, f.

A brothers child, Patruelis, is, c. 2.

Brotherhood, Frāternitas, atis, f.

Brother-love, Philadelphia, æ, f.

The killing of a brother, Fratricidium, ii, n.

He that kills his brother, Fratricida, æ, m.

Of or belonging to a brother, Fraternus, a, um.

After the manner of brethren, Fraternè, adv.

Brotherly, Fraternus, a, um.

A Grandmothers brother, Avunculus magnus.

A great Grandmothers brother, Avunculus major.

The great Grandfathers brother, Abavunculus, li, m.

An Estate coming by a brother, Fratrimonium, ii, n.

Broughham (in *Westmorland*) Braboniacum, Brocavo, Brocavum, Broconiacum, Brovonacis, Brovonacum.

Broughton (in *Hantshire*) Brige vel Brage.

Brought, Allatus, a, um. Advectus, a, um.

To be brought into the World, Procrĕor, āris.

To be brought to pass, Efficior.

Brought by force, Appulsus, a, um.

Brought in, Illatus, a, um.

Brought in another place, Substitutus, a, um.

Brought back or again, Reportatus, a, um.

Brought forth, productus, a, um.

Brought forth (*or born*) Procreatus, a, um.

Brought up, Educatus, a, um.

Brought up wantonly, Delicatus, a, um.

That hath lately brought forth, Effœtus, a, um.

Brought together, Collatus, a, um.

Brought under, Subjectus, a, um. Domitus, a, um.

Brought to pass, Actus, a, um. Effectus, a, um.

Brought to naught, Exĭnānitus, a, um.

A brow,

A brow, Supercilium, ii, n. Palpebra, æ, f.

The space between the brows, Glabella, æ, f.

Having hairy brows, Palpebrosus, a, um.

He that hath brows, Blĕpharo, onis, m.

Bending of the brows, Superciliorum contractio.

To make brown. Obfusco, are.

He that maketh brown colour, Fuscator, oris, m.

Brown (dark colour) Fuscus, a, um.

Somewhat brown, Subfuscus, a, um.

Brown (or natural colour) Pulligo, inis, f.

B R U.

To bruise (or break small) Tundo, is, tŭtŭdi, sum, ere. Quasso, are.

Bruised (or made small) Contusus, a, um. Quassus, a, um.

Half bruised, Semitritus, a, um.

Bruised against something, Illisus, a, um.

A bruising, Contritio, onis, f.

To brush, Verro, ri, sum.

Brushed, Versus, a, um.

A brusher, Converritor, oris, m.

A brush, Verriculum, li, n. Muscarium, ii, n.

A little brush, Scopula Vestiaria.

A brush of bristles to brush Velvet, Muscareum Petaceum.

A brush of bristles to make pots clean withal, Echinus, i, m.

A Painters brush or pencil, Scōpŭla, æ, f. Penicillum, li, n.

A Plaisterers brush (or brush to white with) Penicillus Tectorius.

A dry brush to kindle fire with, Cremium, ii, n.

Brush-wood, or Browse-wood, or rather wind-faln-wood, Cablicia, n. pl.

B R Y.

De Bryer (the Family) De Bruera.

B U C.

A Buck (or Doe) Dama, æ, f.

A bucket. Cēlōnēum, ii, n. Sitŭla, æ, f.

A Well-bucket. Cratera, æ, f. Mergus, oris, n.

A little bucket. Sitella, æ, f. Urnŭla, æ, f.

A bucket with a beam. Telomodiolus, i, m.

Buckets or any thing serving to quench fire, Siphones incendiarii.

Buckingham, Boccinum.

Buckenham, Buckinghamia.

Of Buckingham, *Buckingensis*.

To buckle, Pluscŭlo, are.

Buckled, Plusculatus, a, um.

A buckle (or clasp) Pluscŭla, æ, f.

A Shooe buckle, Fibula calcearia.

A buckle-maker, Plusculariu*s*, ii, m.

A Bucking stock, Lixivarium, ii, n.

A bucking tub, Lixivatorium, ii, n.

A Buck-

A Buckler (or Shield) Clypeum, ei, n. Scutum, ti, n.

A Buckler-maker, Clypearius, ii, m. Scutarius, ii, m.

A Buckler or Shield makers work-house, Fabrica scutaria.

A Buckler player, Oplematicus, i, m.

He that beareth a Buckler, Scutatus, a, um.

B U D.

A Budget, Vidŭlum, li, n.

A Smiths Budget for nails, Follus, i, m.

B U E.

Buelth (in *Brecknockshire*) Bullæum Silurum.

B U F.

Buff-leather, Aluta bubalina.

B U G.

Buggery, Pæderastia, æ, f. Buggery committed with Mankind or Beast is Felony without benefit of Clergy, it being a sin against God, Nature, and the Law, and in ancient times such Offenders were to be burned by the Common-Law. There are two Statutes for it, 25. *H.* 8. revived 5. *Eliz.* 17. One describeth this offence to be *Carnalis copula contra naturam & hæc vel per confusionem specierum, sc.* A Man or a Woman with a Brute Beast, vel *Sexuum*, sc. A Man with a Man, a Woman with a Woman. See *Levit.* 18. 22, 23. *Fitz. Nat.* brev. 269. *B. Dalton.*

A Buggerer, Pæderastes.

To commit Buggery, Pædico, are.

B U I.

To build (or set up) Struo, xi, ctum. Ædifico, are.

To build to (or joyn one house to another) Astruo, is, xi, ctum, ere.

To build of marble, Marmoro, are.

To build in, Inædifico, are.

To build under (or lay a foundation) substruo, xi, ctum.

To build round about, Circumstruo, ere.

To build before, Præstruo, xi, ctum.

To build again, Reædifico, are.

To build up, or finish the building, Perædifico, are.

To be built, Ædificor.

Builded (or Built) Ædificatus, a, um. Conditus, a, um.

Builded upon, Inditus, a, um.

Builded before, Præstructus, a, um.

Builded hard by, Coædificatus, a, um.

Very well builded, Exstructissimus, a, um.

Builded further than a Mans own Ground, Proædificatus, a, um.

Builded (or made) of divers things, Structilis, le.

A builder, Edificator, oris, m. Conditor, oris, m.

A chief (or master) Builder, Architector, oris, m.

An over building, Superædificium, ii, n. 2 *Mon.* 242.

A Building, Ædificium, ii, n. Ædificatio, onis, f.

A Building up, Extructio, onis, f. Exædificatio, onis, f.

The Art or Science of Building, Architectura, æ, f.

A small Building, Ædificatiuncula, æ, f.

A building of pleasant prospects, as Galleries, &c. Menianum, i, n.

A Building made full of Grates for Men to look through, Dictyoton & Dictyota, orum.

A form of building where every thing is equal and straight, Isodomon.

A Building were the Walls are made of stones of an equal thickness, Pseudisodomon.

A Building with three Rooms on a Floor, Trichorum, i, n.

A Building made like a tower, Pyrgobaris.

Cross Building, Structura obliqua.

A Building that hath Pillars standing thick together as Cloisters, Pycnostylon.

A common Building kept in sufficient reparation, Sarta tecta.

A Platform (or description) of a Building, Sciagraphia, æ, f.

To draw together the materials of a Building, and lay the foundation, Præmolior, iri.

Built (or Built upon) Ædificatus, a, um.

Built about, Circumstructus, a, um.

Built up, Perædificatus, a, um.

Built with marble, Marmoratus, a, um.

B U L.

The bulk of a man from the neck to the middle, Thorax, acis, m.

Bulness *or* Bolness (in *Cumberland* upon the borders) Ablato-Bulgio, Blatum, Bulgium.

A Bull, Taurus, ri, m.

A little Bull, Bulliculus, li, m.

Of or belonging to a Bull, Taurinus, a, um. Taureus, a, um.

Like a Bull, Tauriformis, me.

Which beareth (or nourisheth) bulls, Taurifer, a, um.

Having bulls horns, Tauricornis, ne.

Bull baiting, Bubetiæ.

Bull baiters, Bubetii.

A bullery of Salt water, Bullaria aquæ salsæ. *Co. Entr.* 324. Buollariis, *Pry.* 180.

A bullet, Plumbata, æ, f. Glans Plumbea.

Bullion, Bullio, onis, m. (*i. e.*) Gold or Silver uncoined in the Lump. *Davis* 20.

A bullock (or heifer) Affrus, i, m. Affra, æ, f. Boviculus, i, m. Juvencus, i, m.

Bulrush, Scirpus, i, m. Juncus, ci, m.

Full of bulrushes, Juncosus, a, um.

Made of bulrushes, Junceus, a, um.

A bulwark (or strong hold, or place of defence) Propugnaculum, li, n.

Of or pertaining to a bulwark, Vallaris, re.

B U M.

Bumbast (or Cotton) Gossipium, ii, n.

Bumbasted (or bumbast) Xylinus, a, um.

B U N.

A bunch on the back, Gibbus, i, m.

A great bunch in the throat, Branchocele, Botium, ii, n.

A bunch or knot of a tree, Bruscum, ci, n. Tuber, ĕris, n.

A little bunch (or swelling) Tuberculum, li, n.

A bundle, Bundellus, li, m. *Co. Ent.* 416. *Pry.* 49.

A little bundle, Fasciculus, li, m.

Bundle wise, Fasciatim, adv.

Bungey (in *Norfolk*) Avona.

A bunghole of a barrel, Orificium, ii, n.

A bung (or stopple) Obthūrāmentum, ti, n.

A bunn (or little manchet) Collyra, æ, f. Libum, i, n.

B U Q.

Buquebam (in *Scotland*) Boghania, Buchania.

Buquebamness (in *Scotland*) Taizalum Promont.

B U R.

To burden (or load) Sarcĭno, are.

To be burdened, Sarcinor.

Burdened, Gravatus, a, um.

He that burdeneth, Sarcĭnātōr, oris, m.

A burden (or load) Sarcina, æ, f. Onus, ĕris, n.

A heavy burden, Moles, is, f. Grave onus.

A little burden, Onusculum, li, n. Sarcinula, æ, f.

Half a burden, Sēmĭpondus, ĕris, n.

Loaden with burdens, Sarcĭnatus, a, um.

That which serveth for a burden, Onerarius, a, um.

Of or for burdens, Sarcĭnālis, le.

Burgage, Burgagium, ii, n. *Ra. Ent.* 101. 486. *Burgagium* is derived of *Burgus*, a Town, and it is called a Burgh or Borough, because it sendeth Burgesses to Parliament. The termination of this word *Burgagium* signifieth the service whereby the Burgh is holden, *Cook on Lit. l.* 2. *c.* 10. *sect.* 162.

A burgess, Burgensis, is, m. *Lex.* 22. (*i. e.*) A Freeman of a Borough.

Burglary, Burglaria, æ, f. *Spel.* 110. It is derived of Burgh a House, and Laron a Thief. It is usually defined the Night-breaking of an House, with an intent to steal or kill, though none be killed, nor any thing stolen; and so it is of a Stable, parcel of a House, but not of breaking ones Close to kill him, nor ones House, if it be but to beat him, nor though it may be to kill him, if it be in the day time. It may be Burglary if one enter into a House and break

 it

it not, as if he come in at the Chimney, or by a falſe Key, and if he break the Houſe, tho' he enter not, as if one break down a Window to hook out any thing, *Cook* 4 *Rep*. *Richard Vaux* brings an Appeal of Burglary againſt *Thomas Brook*, and declares that the Defendant, *domum manſionalem prædictam Richardi Vaux felonice & burgaliter fregit*. The Declaration was found inſufficient, becauſe of this word *Burgaliter*, but it ought to be *Burgulariter*, or *Burglariter*, and the offence is called Burglary, or Burgulary, and not Burgale; *Burglariter eſt vox artis* as *felonice*, *murdravit*, *rapuit excambium warrantizare*, and divers others, which cannot be expreſſed by any Periphraſis or Circumlocution. If a man have a Manſion Houſe, and he and all his Family upon ſome accident are forth of the Houſe part of the Night, and at the ſame time one come and breaks the Houſe to commit Felony, this is Burglary, although no Man be there, for this is *Domus manſionalis*. So if a Man have two Houſes and inhabit ſometimes in one, and ſometimes in another, and hath Servants in both, and in the night when his Servants are forth, the Houſe is broke by Thieves, this is Burglary. All Indictments of Burglary, are *quod noctanter fregit*, and the night to this purpoſe begins at Sun ſetting, and continueth to the Sun riſing. *vid. Stamford.* Burglar ſhall not have his Clergy. *Dalton* 18. *Eliz. c.* 6.

A burgler, Effractor, oris, m. One that breaks open an Houſe to ſteal. Homo qui domum Burglariter frangit.

Burgh (in *Yorkſhire*) Bracchium.

Burgh *upon* Sands (in *Cumberland*) Exploratorum Caſtra.

Burgh *upon* Stanmore (in *Weſtmorland*) Verteræ, Verteris.

Burgſteed (in *Eſſex*) Cæſaromagus.

Burgh *or* Burk (the Family) De Burgo.

To bury (*or inter*) Funĕro, are. Sĕpĕlio, is, ivi, pultum.

To celebrate the burials of Parents and Anceſtors, Parento, are.

To be buried, Funeror, ari.

Buried (*or Interred*) Sepultus, a, um.

Bodies dead and buried, Conclamata corpora.

Not buried, Intumulatus, a, um.

A burier of dead bodies by night, Veſpillo, onis, m.

A burying (*or laying in earth*) Sepultūra, æ, f. Funĕrātio, onis, f.

A burial (*or funeral*) Funus, ĕris, n.

A burying place (*or vault*) Conditorium, ii, n.

A common place of burial, Calvaria, æ, f.

Solemnities at burials, Exequiæ, arum, f.

The coſts and charges of the burials, Lĭbĭtina, æ, f.

Of

Of the duties of burials, Justa funerum.

Pertaining to burials, Funerarius, a, um.

Buriable (or that may be buried) Sepelibilis, le.

To burl Cloath (as Fullers do) Enodo, are. Desquamo, are.

A burling iron, Forceps Fullonica.

To burn, Uro, ussi, ustum.

To burn (or set on fire) Crĕmo, are.

To burn sweet things, Adŏlĕo, ēs, ŭi, vel ēvi, ultum.

To burn in the hand, Cauterio, are.

To burn (or singe off the hair of a swine) Glabreo, es, ēre.

Burnt in the Cheek, Cauterizaus mala.

To be burned, Uror.

Burned, Ustus, a, um. Combustus, a, um.

A burning coal, Pruna, æ, f.

Much burned, Deustus, a, um.

Burned round about, Ambustus, a, um.

Burned to ashes, Cinefactus, a, um.

Burned like a coal, Carbonatus, a, um.

Burned in the fore-part, Præustus, a, um.

Burned in the end and hardned, Ustulatus, a, um.

Burned in the hand, Cauteriatus, a, um.

A burner, Ustor, oris, m.

A burning (or setting on fire) Combustio, onis, f. Ustio, onis, f.

A burning about, Ambustio, onis, f.

A burning flame, Incendium ii, n.

A thing burned, Caustum, i, n.

Meat burned on the spit, Subvernusta, æ, f.

That may be burned, Combustibilis, le.

Who hath power to burn, Causticus, a, um.

To burnish (or polish) Polio, is, ivi, itum, ire.

Burnished (or Polished) Politus, a, um.

A burnisher, Converritor, oris, m.

A burnishing (or pollishing) Politura, æ, f.

A burnishing about, Circumlinitio, onis, f.

Burrow *hill* (in *Leicestershire*) Vernemetum, Vernometum, Verometum.

Burrow bridge (in *Yorkshire*) Pons Burgensis.

A burse, Bursa, æ, f.

A burser of a College, Bursarius, ii, m.

Burst in sunder with a clap or noise, as a bladder full blown, Displosus, a, um.

Burstenness (or falling of the bowels into the cods, also the guts and the yard) Ramex, icis, m. Hernia, æ, f.

Bursten (or broken bellied) Herniosus, a, um. Ramicosus, a, um.

B U S.

A bushel, Modius, ii, m. Busellus, li, m.

Half a bushel, Dimidium modii Vet. Int. 57. *Spel.* 114. *Fleta* 71. *Stat. de mensuris & de Judicio*

Judicio Collistrigii, 2 *Monastic. Anglican.* 471. 971.

To be busied (or occupied) about a thing, Sătăgo, is, ēgi, ĕre. Sŏlĭcĭtor, aris.

To busie ones self, Solicito, are.

Busied (or busie) Occupatus, a, um.

Business (or affair) Negotium, li, n.

A little business, Negotiolum, ii, n.

Busie every where, Circumcurrens.

Full of business, Negotiosus, a, um.

A busk that Gentlewomen wear before the breast, to make them go upright, Pectorigium, ii, m.

A buskin coming up to the calf of the leg, Cothurnus, i, m.

He that weareth buskins, Cothurnatus, a, um.

A buss (ship) Bussa, æ, f. *Spel.* 114.

Bustleham (a place) Bustelli domus, Bisham.

B U T.

But, Sed, autem.

A butcher, Lanius, ii, m. Bovicida, æ, m. Sarcĭnātor, oris, m. Carnarius, ii, m.

A butchers shop (or shambles) Carnārium, ii, n. Lanarium, ii, n.

A butchers stall, Macĕra, æ, f.

Butchers meat, Caro Lanionia.

Of or belonging to a butcher, Laniarius, a, um.

Buth *Isle*, *or* Rothsay *near* Galloway (in *Scotland*) Rothesia.

A butler, Prōmus, mi, m. Pĕnārius, ii, m.

☞ *A butler (or he that waiteth on ones cup)* Pincĕrna, æ, c. g. Pocillator, oris, m.

An under butler, Suppromus, mi, m.

A butt, Butta, æ, f. Dolium, ii, n.

A little butt, Doliolum, li, n.

A butt of Wine, Butta vini, *Ra. Ent.* 168. So *Duo Dolia*, sive quatuor Pipas vini Rubei, *Monastic. Anglican. part* 1. *page* 976.

A butt (or mark to shoot at) Scopus, i, m. Meta, æ, f.

A little butt, Metula, æ, f.

Butter, Butyrum, ri, n.

A firkin of butter, Rusca butyri.

Buttered, Butyratus, a, um.

Butter milk, Lac serosum.

A buttery, Promptuarium, ii, n. Cella Cervisiaria, Cellŭla, æ, f. Pĕnaria, æ, f.

A buttock (or hanch) Clunis, is, d. g.

To button, Fibŭlo, are.

Buttoned underneath, Subfibulatus, a, um.

To button (or tye underneath) Subfibŭlo, are.

A button, Fibula, æ, f.

A buttoning, Fibŭlātio, onis, f.

A buttoner, Fibŭlātor, oris, m.

A button hole, Rĕtĭnācŭlum, i, n. Ansula, æ, f.

A button maker, Fibŭlārius, ii, m.

A place where buttons are made and sold, Fibŭlātorium, ii, n.

A button (or clasp) for a hat, Offendimentum, i, n.

A buttress, prop or pillar whereby buildings are stayed up, Anteris, idis, f. Fulcrum, i, n. Antes, ium, m.

Buttresses (*shore posts or props*) Erismæ, arum.

Buttrels, Buttria.

A Smiths buttress wherewith he pareth horses hoofs, Scaber, ri, m.

B U X.

Buxton (in *Derbyshire*) Bucostenum.

B U Y.

To buy, Emo, emi, emptum.

To buy together, Cŏēmo, mis.

To buy to the end to sell for gain, Prŏmercor, āris.

To buy beforehand (*or to buy out of ones hand*) Præmercor, are.

To buy under the price or value, or at a low rate, Ademo, emi, emptum.

To buy and sell and make merchandize, Mercor, aris.

To buy Meat (*or Victuals*) Opsŏno, as, āvi, āre.

To buy often, Empto, are.

To buy again, Redĭmo, is, ēmi, ere.

To have a list to buy, Empturio, is, ivi, itum, ire.

A buyer, Emptor, oris, m.

One that buyeth and selleth, Mercator, oris, m. Venundator, oris, m.

A great buyer, Emax, ācis, adj.

A buyer of forfeited Goods, Sector, oris, m.

He that buyeth any thing at great, and selleth it again for advantage, Manceps, cipis, c. g.

A buying, Emptio, onis, f.

A buying together, Coemptio, onis, f.

A buying or selling, Nundinatio, onis, f.

Communication of buying and selling, Commercium, ii, n.

Things bought at advantage to sell again, Promercalia, orum, n.

Which is often buying, Coemptionalis, le.

Affection or desire to buy, Emacitas, atis, f.

B Y.

By, Per.

A by-path, Devia, æ, f.

By (*or nigh together*) Juxta, prope.

By reason of, Propter.

By it self, Separatim, adv.

By some manner, means or reason, Aliquatenus.

By some place, way or means, Alĭqua, adv.

By what means, reason or sort soever, Quomodocunque.

By what way or place, Qua.

By chance, Casu, forte.

C A B.

A *Cabbage*, Brassica, æ, f.

A cole cabbage, Brassica capitata.

A cabinet, Capsula, æ, f. Phylaxa, æ, f. Scriniolum, li, n.

A little cabinet, Cistellula, æ, f.

A cabern (or cabin of a ship) Stega, æ, f.

A little narrow cabin (or dark lodging) Gurgustium, ii, n. Gurgustulum.

A cabin (or shepherds cottage) Tŭgŭrium, ii, n.

A cable rope, Rudens, entis, m. vel f.

Cables, Funes nautici.

Cablish, Cablicia, orum, n. pl. Among the Writers of the Forest-Laws, it signifieth Brush-wood, or Browse-wood, or rather wind-fallen-wood. *Manwood, pag.* 84. *Crompt. Jurisdict. fol.* 163.

C A E.

Caerdronack bay (in *Cumberland*) Moricamba, Moricambe, æstu.

Caerlaverock (in *Scotland*) Garbantorigum.

Caerleon (in *Glamorganshire*) Isca legio Augusta, Iscelegua Augusti. *Leg.* 11. Augusta.

Caermalei, Camaletum.

Caermarthen (in *Wales*) Caermardinia, Carmarthinia, Maridunum.

Caermarthenshire, Ager Maridunensis.

Caernarvan, Carnarvonia.

Caernarvanshire, Arvonia.

Caer-sejont, near to *Caernarvan*, Segontium.

Caerwent (in *Monmouthshire*) Venta silurum.

C A G.

A cage (or place to keep birds in) Cavea, æ, f. Aviarium, ii, n.

C A I.

Caishaw *Hundred* (in *Hartfordshire*) Cassi, Cassii.

C A K.

A cake, Placenta, æ, f. Pŏpanum, i, n.

A wheaten cake, Farreum, ei, n. Adŏrĕa, æ, f.

An oaten cake, Avenacia, æ, f.

A spice cake, Panis dulciarius.

A cake baked upon the hearth, Focarius panis.

A Cake-man (or Pastry Cook) Crustularius, ii, m.

C A L.

To calcinate (or bring metals into powder) Calcino, are.

Calcined (or done into powder) Calcinatus, a, um.

To calculate (or reckon) Calculo, are.

Calder *river* (in *Yorkshire*) Calderus.

Callis (in *France*) Britannicus portus. Callisia, Iccius portus.

A Calender (or Almanack) Calendarium, ii, n.

A Calender (or Calender book, or books declairing what is done every day, Hemerologium, ii, n. Diarium, ii, n.

The Calends (or first day of every month) Calendæ, arum, f. Sing. caret.

Pertain-

Pertaining to the Calends, Calendaris, re. Calendarius, a, um.

A calf, Vitulus, li, m.

Of or belonging to a calf, Vitulinus, a, um.

The calf of the leg, Sura, æ, f.

Calne (in *Wiltshire*) Calna.

A caliver, Sclopus, i, m. Æquilibrium, i, n. *i. e.* A hand-gun, a Piſtol or Snaphance. Equal weight, or ſtanding weight or equal heighth, becauſe the bore or hole of a Piece muſt be even or equal, or elſe the Piece will break.

To call, Voco, are. Appello, are.

To call back, Revoco, are.

To call upon, Invoco.

Called, Vŏcātus, a, um.

A calling (*or profeſſion*) Vocatio, onis, f.

Caltraps, Tribuli, orum, n. Murices, um, m. i. e. *Turn-pikes or great pricks of Iron, four ſquare, which are caſt in the Enemies way to keep off their horſe, or where the works or bulwarks are loweſt, in the Camp or Town of Garriſon. They are made with four Iron pricks, ſo joined, that being thrown, one ſtandeth upright.*

Pointed ſharp like a Caltrap, Muricatus, a, um.

To calumniate (*or accuſe craftily, falſly or maliciouſly*) Calumnior, aris.

Calumniation, Calumniatio, onis, f.

C A M.

Cambrick, Cameracum, ci, n. Syndon Cameracenſis.

Cambridge *Town*, Camboricum, Camboritum, Cantabrigia, Granta, Grantanus pons.

A camel, Cămēlus, li, m. & f.

A Keeper (*or Driver*) *of camels*, Cămēlārius, ii, m.

The Driving (*or Keeping*) *of camels*, Cămēlaſia ſive Camelaria, æ, f.

Of a camel, Cămēlinus, a, um.

Camelot (in *Scotland*) Coria vel Corta Damniorum.

To camp (*or pitch a camp*) Caſtrametator, aris.

Camvil (the Family) De Camvilla.

A camp, Caſtra, orum, n. pl.

A ſtanding camp (*or fortified place*, Stativa, æ, f.

The pitching of a camp, Caſtrămētatio, onis, f.

The camp maſter (*or he that pitcheth the camp*) Caſtrămētātor, oris, m. Præfectus caſtrorum.

Of or belonging to a camp, Caſtrenſis, ſe, adj.

One that followeth the camp, ready to do any thing, Lixābundus, a, um.

C A N.

To cancel (*or raſe out*) Cancello, are.

Cancelled, Cancellātus, a, um.

A cancelling, Cancellatura, æ, f. *Fle.* 426.

To make candles of tallow, Sevo, are.

A candle, Candela, æ, f.

A little candle, Lucernula, æ, f.

A wax candle, Cereus, ei, m.

A little wax candle, Cereolus, li, m.

A watch candle, Lucubra, æ, f. Vigiles lucernæ.

The wick, cotton or snuff of a candle, Ellychnium, ii, n. Emunctura, æ, f.

A candlestick, Candelābrum, i, n.

He that beareth (or holdeth a candle) Lucernarius, ii, m.

A candlestick whereon wax candles are set, Ceroferarium, ii, n.

He that beareth (or holdeth) a wax candle, Ceroferarius, ii, m.

A branch candlestick, Polycandelus, li, m. Lychnucus, ci, m.

A candle snuffer, Emunctorium, ii, n. Favillus, li, m.

A candle maker, Vid. *Chandler*.

Candlemas day, Festum Purificationis Beatæ Mariæ virginis.

A cane (or reed) Canna, æ, f. Calamus, i, m.

A little cane, Cannellum, li, n.

A cane bank, or place where canes grow, Cannetum, i, n.

Of or belonging to canes, Canneus, a, um.

A can (or pot) for beer or ale, Canna, æ, f. Olla, æ, f. So called because it is hollow, and in some fashion formed like a great Cane or Reed.

The cannel bone of the throat, Jŭgŭlum, li, n.

Cannions of breeches, Perixycnalia, orum, n.

A cannon (a piece of ordnance) Canna muralis. So called because they are cast long, after the manner of a great Reed.

A cannonier, Bombardicus, ci, m.

To shoot off a cannon, Exonerare cannam muralem. Emittere cannam muralem.

A canon resident in Cathedral churches, Canonicus, ci, m.

A canonship, Canonia, æ, f. Canonicatus, ûs, m.

A canopy, Canopium, ii, n. 10. *Co.* 130.

Canterbury *city* (in *Kent*) Cantuaria, Darvernum, Dorbernia, Dorobellum, Durorvernum, Durovernum.

Of Canterbury, Cantuariensis.

Arch-bishop of Canterbury, Episcopus Cantuariensis.

A cantle (or piece) Frustum, i, n. Offa, æ, f.

A cantred (or hundred of a shire in Wales) Cantredus, i, m.

Cantlow (the Family) De Cantelupo.

Canvas (or course linen) Canabium, ii, n.

C A P.

To wear or put on a cap, Pileo, are.

A cap, Cappa, æ, f. *Spel.* 137. Pileus, ei, m.

A little cap, Pileolus, li, m.

A night cap, Cuculio, onis, m. Pileus nocturnus.

A leather or furred cap, Cudo, onis, m. Cappa pellis.

A womans cap (or bonnet) Calyptra, æ, f.

A cap-

A capper (or maker of caps) Pilearius, ii, m.

A cap-case, Mantica, æ, f. Capsula pilea.

A cape : Vid. *bay*.

A cape of a garment, Capa, æ, f. Collare, is, n.

A Spanish *cape,* Chlămys, mydis, f. Chlamys hispanica.

Capers (a fruit used in sallets) Cappares, um. Inturis, is, f.

Capias, Is a Writ of two sorts, one before Judgment called (*capias ad respondendum*) and if the Sheriff return, *nihil habet in balliva sua,* &c. then the Process is, *alias capias,* and *pluries,* and an *exigent,* and they are called *capias ad respondendum* : Also the exigent shall be proclaimed five times, if the Party doth not appear he shall be Out-lawed. The other is a Writ of Execution after Judgment, being also of divers kinds, *viz.capias ad satisfaciendum,capias pro fine, capias utlagatum & inquiras de bonis & catallis,* which at large is declared in *Nat. Brev.*

Capias ad satisfaciendum, is a Writ of Execution, after Judgment, lying where a Man recovereth in an Action Personal, as debt or damages, or detinue in the King's Court; and he against whom the debt is recovered, and hath no Lands or Tenements, nor sufficient Goods whereof the debt may be levied; for in this case he that recovereth shall have his Writ to the Sheriff, commanding him that he take the body of him, against whom the debt is recovered, and he shall be put in Prison until satisfaction is made unto him that recovered.

Capias pro fine, Is where one being by Judgment fined unto the King, upon some offence committed against a Statute, doth not discharge it according to the Judgment; for by this is his body taken and committed to Prison until he content the King for his Fine, *Co. l. 3. c. 12. a.*

Capias Utlagatum, is a word of Execution, or after Judgment, which lieth against him which is Out-lawed upon any suit, by which the Sheriff upon the receipt thereof, apprehendeth the Party Out-lawed, for not appearing upon the Exigent, and keepeth him in safe Custody until the day of the return assigned in the Writ, and then presenteth him unto the Court, there further to be ordered for his contempt.

Capias Utlagatum & inquiras de bonis & catallis, Is a Writ all one with the former next before, but that it giveth a farther power to the Sheriff over and beside the apprehension of the body, to enquire of his Goods and Chattles, *Capias in withernamium de averiis, vid. withernam.*

Capias conductos ad proficiscendum, Is a Writ that lieth for the taking up of such as having received Prest-money to serve the King, slink away and come not in at their time assigned, *Regist. Orig. fol.* 191.

To capitulate, Capitulor, ari.

A capon, Capo, onis, m. Capus, i, m.

A caponet, Capunculus, li, m. Hesta, æ, f. *Spel.*

A capon fatted, Capus sāginātus.

A captain, Căpitāneus, ei, m. *Ra. Ent.* 492.

A captain general (or chief captain over an army) Dux primarius. Capitaneus Generalis, omnium armorum & exercituum Domini Regis in Anglia, &c.

The captain of a troop, Turmarcha, æ, f.

A captive (or prisoner) Captivus, a, um.

C A R.

A carravel (or swift bark) Dromo, onis, m. Celox, ocis, f.

A carbonado (or meat broiled on the coals) Carbonella, æ, f.

A carbuncle (or precious stone) Carbunculus, li, m.

A carcass (or dead body) Cadaver, ris, n. *Fle.* 169.

To card wooll or flax, &c. Carmino, are.

Carded, Pexus, a, um.

A card to comb wool withal, Carptarium, ii, n. Pecten lanaris vel lanarius.

A pair of cards for wool, Par hamorum.

A carder of wool, he or she, Carminator, oris, m. Carminatrix, icis, f.

The carding of wool, Carminatio, onis, f. Lanificium, ii, n.

Carding and Spinning, Lana ac Tela.

A card-maker, Carptarius, ii, m.

A pair of stock cards, Par chamarum: Vid. *Towns*.

Cards to play withal, Chartæ lusoriæ.

Coat cards, Chartæ pictæ.

A pair of cards, Fasciculus foliorum.

A single card that is no coat card, Charta simplex.

Card playing (or the game upon the cards) Chartarum seu foliorum pictorum ludus.

A suit or sort of cards, Familia, æ, f. Genus, eris, n.

An heart, Cor.

A diamond, Rhombus.

A club, Trimolium.

A spade, Vomerculus.

The king, Rex.

The queen, Regina.

The knave, Eques.

The ace, Monas.

The ten, Decas.

The nine, Enneas.

The eight, Ogdoas.

The seven, Heptas.

The six, Senio.

The five, Pentas.

The four, Quaternio.

The three, Trias.

The deuce (or two) Dyas.

The trump (or turned card) Index charta, Dominatrix.

The stock, Sponsio.

The small cards, Chartæ minores.

A card player, Chartarius, ii, m.

The

The dealer of the cards, Diſtributor.

Ruff at a ſuit of cards, Orbatus.

To deal the cards, Diſtribuere chartas. Impertire vel præbere.

To play at cards, Ludere pictis chartis.

To ſhuffle the cards, Chartas miſcere.

To cut the cards, Bipartire Chartas.

To pack the cards, Inſtruere vel Componere chartas.

A card (or map) Charta marina, mappa maritima.

Caradock *or* Cradock, *now called* Newton (the Family) Caradocus,

Cardigan (in *Wales*) Cardigania.

Cardiganſhire, Ceretica.

Carefully (or diligently) Induſtriè, adv. Diligenter, adv.

Careleſs (or negligent) Securus, a, um.

Careleſly (or negligently) Improvide, Officin. brev.

Caresbrook *caſtle* (*in the Iſle of* Wight) Keresburga.

Carleon: Vid. *Caerleon*.

Carliſle (in *Cumberland*) Carleolum, Caturactonium, Leucopibia, Luguballia, Luguballum, Luguvallum.

Biſhop of Carliſle, Epiſcopus Carlioleſis.

Carrict (in *Scotland*) Carricta.

To carry, Carrio, are.

To carry away, Abcarrio, are. *Dyer* 70. 1. *Fo.* 39.

To carry far off (or ſend away) Elongo, are.

To carry (or bear) Porto, are.

Carriage, Carriagium, ii, n. *Ra. Ent.* 115. 538. 2. *Mon.* 196. 231. *Pry.* 60.

Carriage over to a place, Advectus, ûs, m.

Money paid for carriage, Vectiva, æ, f.

Carried to, Advectus, a, um.

Carried in, Importatus, a, um.

Carried away, Abductus, a, um.

Carried out, Exportatus, a, um.

Carried from one place to another, Tranſportatus, a, um.

Carried (or Born) Vectus, a, um.

A carrier (or bearer) Portitor, oris, m. Advector, oris, m. Bajulus, li, m.

A carrier (or driver of horſes) Agaſo, onis, m. Vector, oris, m.

A carrier of Letters, Tabellarius, ii, m.

A carrier of a preſent, Dorophorus, ri, m.

A carrier that goeth on meſſages, Angărus, ri, m. Curſor, oris, m.

Belonging to carriers of Letters, Tabellarius, a, um.

Carriages, Vehicula, orum, n.

A carrying (or bearing) Vectio, onis, f. Portatio, onis, f.

A carrying away (or from one place to another) Aſportatio, onis, f. Exportatio, onis, f.

A carrying over, Tranſportatio, onis, f.

Of or belonging to carrying or carriage, Vecticarius, a, um.

A carpenter, Carpentarius, ii, m. Faber lignarius, ii, m.

A ma-

A master carpenter, Architector, oris, m.

A carpenters line, Linea, æ, f. Amussis, is, f.

A carpenters rule, Norma, æ, f. Rēgŭla, æ, f. Canon, ŏnis, f.

A carpenters plum-rule which he useth in squaring, Molorthus, i, m.

A carpenters ax, Dolabra, æ, f.

A carpenters shop, Fabrica, æ, f.

A carpenters timber frame for a house, Fabrica materia vel lignaria.

The carpenters art, Ars Fabrica.

Belonging to a carpenter, Carpentarius, a, um. Fabricus, a, um.

Belonging to a carpenters craft, Fabrilis, le, adj.

A carpet, Tapes, etis, m. Tapetum, i, n.

A Turkey *carpet*, Polymita phrygia.

A carpet for a table, Intĕga, æ, f.

A carpet, or cup-board cloath, Plagŭla, æ, f.

A carrack (or great ship) Carrucha, æ, f. Carraca, æ, f. Carca, æ, f. *Pry.* 341. Ter.

To guide or drive a cart (or wain) Aurigo, are.

A car (or cart) Carrus, i, m. Ra. Ent. 538. *Co. Ent.* 526. *Lex.* 19. Carecta, æ, f.

A dung cart, Benna, æ, f. Cœnivectorium, ii, n.

A cart to carry timber, Sarracum, ci, n.

A cart or wain load, Carectata, æ, f. *Pry.* 97. Careta, æ, f.

A carr room, Caruca Signata, 1. *Ro.* 525.

A carrman (or carter) Caretarius, ii, m. Carrucarius, ii, m.

The guiding of a cart, Aurigatio, onis, f.

The Axle-tree of a cart, Axis, is, m.

Cart harness, Helcium, ii, n.

The hoop or streak of a cart, Vietus, i, m.

A cart sadle, Dorsuale, lis, n.

A cart house, Domus Carucaria vel plaustraria.

The track of a cart, Orbita, æ, f.

Of or belonging to a cart, Carrucarius, a, um. Plaustrarius, a, um.

A carve of land, Carrucata terræ. It contains as much Land as may be Ploughed and Laboured in a year and a day with one Plough: And is also called *Hilda* or *Hida Terræ*, a word used in the old *Britain* Laws. Mr. *Lambert*, among his Presidents in the end of his *Eirenarchæ* Translateth *Carucatum terræ*, a Plough-land.

To carve (or grave) Cælo, are. Sculpo, is, psi, tum, ĕre.

Carved, Cælatus, a, um. Inscuptus, a, um. Incisus, a, um.

Carved with the Images of Beasts, Belluatus, a, um.

An instrument to carve with, Cælum, li, n.

That is, or may be carved, Sculptilis, le, adj.

A carver (or graver) Cælator, oris, m. Sculptor, oris, m. Incisor, oris, m.

A carving, Cælātūra, æ, f. Incisus, ûs, m. Sculptura, æ, f.

To carve meat, Exartuo, are.

So carved, Exartuatus, a, um.

A carver that cutteth up meat, Cibicida, æ, m.

A carving or engraving knife, Culter structorius.

C A S.

A case, cause, matter, Casus, ûs, m.

A case to put any thing in, Capsŭla, æ, f. Theca, æ, f.

A pin case, Acicularia, æ, f. Spinularium, ii, n.

A needle case, Acuarium, ii, n. Acutheca, æ, f.

The case of a looking-glass, Theca speculi.

A comb case, Pectinarium, ii, n.

A bow case, Corytus, i, m.

A knife case, Cultoria Theca.

A barbers case, Chirurgotheca, æ, f.

A casement, Transenna, æ, f. Porta fenestralis. Claustrum, tri, n.

To casheer or break up a company of soldiers, Elŏco, are. Exturmo, are.

A cask, Casca, æ, f. 1. *Fol.* 307.

A casket (or little coffer) Capsŭla, æ, f. Scrinium, ii, n.

A little casket, Scriniolum, li, n. Cistellula, æ, f.

Of Cassile (in *Ireland*) Cassilensis.

A cassock, Saga, æ, f. Sagum, i, n.

A little cassock, Sagulum, li, n.

One that weareth a cassock, Sagulatus, a, um.

A seller of cassocks, Sagarius, ii, m.

A selling of cassocks, Sagaria, æ, f.

To cast away, Abjicio, eci, ectum.

To cast away often with disdain, Abjecto, are.

To cast (or turn off) Abdico, are.

To cast darts (or arrows) Jacŭlor, aris.

To cast as a Jury casteth (or condemneth prisoners) Condemno, are.

To cast a meer or furrow with a plough, Urbo, are.

Cast, hurled or thrown down, Jactus, a, um.

Cast away, Abjectus, a, um.

A javelin cast or thrown, Lancea excussa lacertis.

A cast (or throw) at dice, Bōlus, i, m.

A cast (or draught) of a net, Jactus retis, bolus, i, m.

A cast (or throw) Jactus, ûs, m.

Caster (in *Norfolk*) Venta Icenorum.

He that casteth, Jăcŭlātor, oris, m.

She that casteth, Jăcŭlātrix, icis, f.

A casting against, Objectatio, onis, f.

A casting of an arrow (or dart) Jăcŭlātio, onis, f.

A casting by the Jury, Condemnatio, onis, f.

New-Castle *upon* Tine, Villa novi castri super Tinam.

Castle *or* Castel (the Family) De Castello.

The

The castle in the peak (in *Derbyshire*) De alto pecco.

Castleford (in *Yorkshire* near *Pontfract*, Lagecium, Legiolium.

A castle (*or fortress*) Castrum, i, n. No Subject can build a Castle or House of strength imbattelled, or other Fortress defensible, without the Licence of the King, for the danger which might ensue, if every man at his pleasure might do it. *Co. on Lit. p.* 5.

A little castle, Castellum, li, n. Castellain, Castellanus, i, m. (*i. e.*) *A captain or owner of a castle, sometime called Constable of a castle*, Brac. lib. 5. trac. 2. cap. 16. & lib. 2. cap. 32. num. 2. *Also An.* 3. Ed. 1. cap. 7. In the Books *de Feudis*, you may find *Guastaldus* to be almost of the same signification, but something more at large, because it extendeth to those that have the Custody of the Kings mansion houses, tho' they be not places of defence or strength. *Manwood* Part 1. of his Forest Laws. *pag.* 113. saith that there is an Officer of the Forest, called *Castellanus*.

Castel-ward, Castel-Gardum aut Wardum Castri. It is an Imposition laid upon such of the Kings Subjects as dwell within a certain compass of any Castle, toward the maintenance of such as do watch and ward the Castle. *Magn. Chart. cap.* 20. & *An.* 32. *H.* 8. *cap.* 48. It is used sometime for the very circuit it self, which is Inhabited by such as are Subject to this service, as in *Stow's Annals pag.* 632.

To castigate (*or punish*) Castigo, are.

Casual (*or that happeneth by chance*) Casualis, le, adj. Fortuitus, a, um.

Castinets (*or Rattles which Children play with*) Crembala, orum.

C A T.

A cat, Catus, i, m.

A cataract, Cataracta, æ, f. *i.* e. A Portcullis, a great fall of Water from a high place, a Flood gate: Also a Disease in the eyes, when any humour droppeth out like Gelly.

A catarr (*or rheum*) Catarrhus, i, m.

Catarrick Bridge, Cataractonium, Cataractuonium.

To catch, or snatch, Arripio, is, ui, eptum, ere.

To catch or draw as it were with an hook, Inunco, are.

To catch in a net, Retio, is.

A catch-pol (*serjeant or baily*) Cacepollus, li, m. Chacepollus, i, m.

Catched (*or caught*) Præhensus, a, um.

Catched in a net, Irretitus, a, um. Illaqueatus, a, um.

A catcher by violence, Raptor, oris, m.

A catching by fraud and violence, Raptio, onis, f.

Cate (*or cates, all kind of Victuals except bread*) Opsonium, ii, n.

A ca-

A cater (or provider of Victuals) Opsonātor, oris, m.

To do the office of a cater, Opsonor, ari.

Cathedraticum, i, n. i. e. The sum of two shillings paid to the Bishop by his Clergy, in acknowledgment of Subjection.

A cathedral church, Ecclesia Cathedralis, aut Episcopalis Ecclesia.

Cathness (in *Scotland*) Cathania.

Catholic (or universal) Catholicus, a, um.

Cattle, Averaria, orum, n. Averia, *Spel.* 60.

Cattle, Horses or Oxen, Averia, orum, n.

Cattle that draw (or bear) burdens, Jumenta, orum, n.

Of or belonging to such cattle, Jumentarius, a, um.

Full of cattle (or that hath much cattle) Pĕcŏrōsus, a, um.

Of or belonging to all manner of cattle, Pecorarius, a, um.

A taking in of cattle to a forest or other place, at a certain rate by the week, Agistamentum, i, n.

A stealer of cattle, Abactor, oris, m. Abigeatus, ûs, m.

A tender of cattle, Pĕcŭārius, ii, m.

The skill of ordering cattle, Ars pecuaria.

C A U.

A caudle, Sorbillum, li, n. Cyceon, onis, m.

A caveat, Cautela, æ, f.

A cave (or den) Caverna, æ, f.

A little cave, Cavernŭla, æ, f.

A cave for wild beasts in the wood, Lustrum, tri, n.

Caved (or made like a cave) Concavus, a, um.

Full of caves, Cavernosus, a, um.

Of or pertaining to a cave, or abiding in a cave, Căvāticus, a, um.

A cauldron, Caldarium, ii, n. Ahenum, i, n. Labes, etis, m. Cacabus, i, m.

A little cauldron, Caldariolum, li, n.

A cauldron maker, Lebetarius, ii, m.

A caul for womens heads, Căpillāre, is, n. Reticulum căpillāre.

The cawl or sewet which covereth the bowels, Omentum, i, n.

To caulk (or Cauk) a ship, Stipo, are. (i. e.) To fill the holes or chinks of a Ship with Okam and Tow.

A cause, matter or reason, Causa, æ, f.

To cause (or make) Causo, are.

To cause (or provoke) Incĭto, are.

To cause (or procure) Excĭto, are.

Caused, Causatus, a, um.

A causey (or paved place) Calcetum, i, n. Păvimentum, i, n.

A way causeyed, Via Calceata. *Spel.* 116.

A caustick, Causticum, ci, n.

A cauterie, searing or hot iron, Cauterium, ii, n.

To cauterize, sear, burn or close up with searing irons, ointments or medicines, Cauterizo, are.

A cau-

A caution, Cautio, onis, f.

Cautione admittenda, Is a Writ that lieth against a Bishop holding an Excommunicate Person in Prison for his Contempt, notwithstanding that he offereth sufficient caution or assurance to Obey the Commandments and Orders of holy Church from thenceforth: The form and further effect hereof, *vid. Regist. orig. p.* 66. & *Fitz Herb. nat. brev. fol.* 63.

C A W.

Cawood (in *Yorkshire*) Caveda.

C E A.

To cease (*or leave off*) Cesso, are.

Ceased, Cessatus, a, um.

C E L.

To celebrate, Celebro, are.

A cell, Cella, æ, f.

A cellar, Cellarium, ii, n. Hypogæum, i, n.

A privy cellar, Conclavia, æ, f.

A little cellar, Cellula, æ, f. Cellariolum, li, n.

A wine cellar, Vinearia, æ, f. Vini apotheca. Merotheca, æ, f.

He (*or she*) *that hath the charge of a cellar*, Cellarius, ii, m. Cellaria, æ, f.

Of or pertaining to a cellar, Cellaris, re, adj.

Celsitude, Celsitas, atis, f. Celsitudo, inis, f. (*i. e.*) Highness, Excellency, terms attributed to Princes.

C E M.

A cement wherewith stones are joyned together, Cementum, ti, n. Lithocolla, æ, f.

C E N.

A censer, Thuribulum, li, n. Igniculum, li, n.

A centre or center (*the middle of any thing*) Centrum, tri, n.

C E R.

Cerdicksford *or* Chardford (in *Hampshire*) Cerdici-vadum.

Ceremony, Ceremonia, æ, f.

Cern (in *Dorsetshire*) Cerneliense Cœnobium.

A cerot (*or sear cloath*) Cerotum, i, n.

Certain (*or sure*) Certus, a, um.

Certainty, Certitudo, inis, f.

Certainly (*or without doubt*) Certo, adv. Indubitanter, adv.

To certifie, Certifico, are.

A certificate, Certificatorium, ii, n.

Certiorari, Is a Writ issued out of the Chancery to an inferiour Court, to call up the Records of a Cause therein depending, that Conscionable Justice may be therein ministred, upon complaint made by Bill, that the Party which seeketh the said Writ hath received hard dealing in the said Court. *Terms of Law, vid.* the divers forms and uses of this in *Fitz. Her. nat. brev. fol.* 242. As also the Register both Original and Judicial in the Table *Certiorari.*

C E S.

Cessavit, A Writ that lieth where the Tenant hath not paid Rent, nor had distress upon his Land for two years.

Cession of a Benefice, Cessio Beneficii. Is when a Benefice is lost by taking of another (the Parson so taking the other not being qualified according to the Statute of 21. *H.* 8. *c.* 13.) and being Inducted into the second. *Whitlock's reading, p.* 4.

A cistern to put water in, Cisterna, æ, f. Sceptoria, æ, f.

A cistern cock by which the water cometh out, Mastus, i, m.

Pertaining to a cestern, Cisterninus, a, um.

C H A.

A chace, Chacea, æ, f.

To chace (or drive) Chacio, are.

A chafer (or chafing-dish) Ignitabulum, li, n. Fŏcŭlus, li, m. Authepsa, æ, f. Ignis receptaculum.

Chaff (or straw) Palea, æ, f.

A chaff-house, Palearium, ii, n.

Chaffie (or unclean) Acĕrātus, a, um.

Mingled with chaff, Paleatus, a, um.

Full of chaff, Acĕrosus, a, um.

A chaffern to heat water in, Fervŏrium, ii, n.

A chain, Cătena, æ, f. Torquis, is, f.

A little chain, Catenula, æ, f. Catella, æ, f.

A chain of Gold to wear about ones neck, Catena aurea. Torquis, is, f. Muræнula, æ, f.

A little chain of Gold, Torquillus, i, m.

That weareth a chain, Torquatus, a, um.

The chain or staple ring fastned to the yoke to draw by, Ampron, onis, m.

The ring of a chain, Ciclus, i, m.

Chained, Cătēnātus, a, um. Catenarius, a, um.

A chaining (or linking) Cătēnātio, onis, f.

To chain (or tye in with chains) Cătēno, are.

To chain together, Concateno, are.

A chair, Cathedra, æ, f. Sella, æ, f.

A chair of State, Sŏlĭum, ii, n.

A chair made with loose Joynts which may be turned every way, Trochum, i, n.

A compass, or half round chair, Hemicyclus, i, m.

A privy chair (or stool) Sella familiaris & familiarica.

A chair (or working) woman, Opĕrāria, æ, f.

Chaired (or stalled) Cathedratus, a, um.

Of or pertaining to a chair (or seat) Cathedralis, le. Cathedrarius, a, um.

Chalk, Creta, æ, f.

A chalk-pit, Cretarium, ii, n. Creta fodina.

Chalky, or full of chalk, Crētōsus, a, um.

Laid (or marked) with chalk, Cretatus, a, um.

Of or belonging to chalk, Cretaceus, a, um.

A chalker (or he that worketh in chalk) Cretarius, ii, m.

A piece of chalk, Crētŭla, æ, f.

A chaldron, Chaldra, æ, f. Celda, æ, f.

A chaldron of coals, Celda carbonum, *Pry.* 183.

To challenge, Calumpnio, are.

A challenge, Calumpnia, æ, f. *Spel.* 116. *Co. Lit.* 155. Calangium, ii, n. Challenge is a word common as well to the *English* as to the *French*, and sometimes signifieth to claim, sometimes in respect of Revenge, to challenge into the field: Sometimes in respect of Partiality or Insufficiency to Challenge in a Court, Persons returned on a Jury. Challenge made to the Jurors, is either made to the Array, or to the Polls. Challenge to the Array, is where exception is taken to the whole number, as Impannelled partialy; Challenge to or by the Poll, is where Exception is taken to one or more as not indifferent, *Co. on Lit. l.* 2. *c.* 12. *Sect.* 234. By the Common Law the Prisoner upon an Indictment or Appeal might Challenge peremptorily 35, which was under the number of three Juries: But now by the Statute of 22. *H.* 8. the number is reduced to 20 in Petty Treason, Murder and Felony. But by the Statute of 1 and 2 *Philip* and *Mary*, the Common Law is revived, for any Treasone, the Prisoner shall have his Challenge to the number of 35. But if he be a Lord of Parliament, and a Peer of the Realm, and is to be tried by his Peers; he shall not Challenge any of his Peers at all, for they are not sworn as other Jurors be, but find the Party Guilty or not Guilty; upon their Faith and Allegiance to the King, and they are Judges of the Fact, and every of them doth separately give his Judgment, beginning at the lowest. But a Subject under the degree of Nobility, may in case of Treason or Felony Challenge for just cause as many as he can, if he can alledge cause of Favour or Malice. Principal Challenges to the Poll may be reduced to four heads. 1. *Propter honoris respectum*, as any Peer of the Realm, or Lord of Parliament, for these in respect of Honour and Nobility, are not to be sworn on Juries; and if neither Party will Challenge him, he may Challenge himself, for by *Magna Charta* it is provided, *quod nec super eum ibimus, nec super eum mittemus, Nisi per legale Judicium parium suorum, aut per legem terræ.* A Peer of the Realm shall not be Impannelled, where any of the Commons is to have a Tryal, *Cook ubi supra.*

2 *Prop-*

2. *Propter defectum*, for want of default.

1. *Patriæ*, as Aliens born.

2. *Libertatis*, as Villains or Bondmen.

3. *Annui census*, i. e. *Liberi tenementi*, As if any of the Jury Impannelled cannot dispend 40 *s.* by the year of his own Freehold.

4. *Hundredorum, vicini vicinorum facta præsumuntur scire.*

3. *Propter Affectum*, for Affection or Partiality, as if the Juror be *consanguineus* of Blood or kindred to either Party: This is a principal Challenge; for the Law presumeth that one kinsman doth favour another before a stranger. If either Party labour the Juror, and give him any thing to give his Verdict, this is a Principal Challenge; but if either Party labour the Jury to appear, and do his Conscience; this is no Challenge at all: But Lawful for him to do it.

4. *Propter delictum*, For Crime, it being a Maxime in the Law, *Repellitur à sacramento infamis.*

To challenge (or take to himself) Arrogo, are. Vendico, are.

To challenge into the Field, Provoco, are. Provocare ad pugnam. Lacessere ad certamen.

A letter of challenge (or defiance) Literæ provocatoriæ. Charta provocationis ad certamen.

A challenge (or challenging) Provocatio, onis, f. Provocatio ad Pugnam.

Challenged, Provocatus, a, um.

A challenger, Provocator, oris, m.

A challenger at a Prize (or fighting with swords) Mirmillo, onis, m.

A challenger at all Games, Pantathlus, i, m.

Belonging to a challenge (or challenging) Provocatorius, a, um:

A chalice, challice (or cup) Calix, icis, m.

A chamber, Camera, æ, f.

A bed chamber, Cŭbicŭlum, i, n. Dormitorium, ii, n.

Of the bed chamber, Cŭbicŭlarius, a, um.

Belonging to a chamber, Cameralis, le, adj. *Spel.* 117. 2. *Mon.* 338.

A chamber of Presence in a King or Princes Court, Cubile Salutatorium. Solium Majestatis. Camera Regia Præcipua.

A bride chamber, Thalamus, i, m.

A chamberlain (he or she that waiteth in a chamber) Cubicularius, ii, m. Lectisterniatrix, icis, f.

Lord chamberlain, Dominus altus Camerariæ Angliæ.

Lord chamberlain of the Kings houshold, Dominus Camerarius hospitii Domini Regis.

A chamberlain of a City, Camerarius, ii, m. *Spel.* 116. There are two Officers of this name in the King's Exchequer, who were wont to keep a Controlment of the Pels of the Receits and Exitus, they keep the Keys of the Treasury,

 where

where the Leagues of the Kings Predeceſſors, and divers ancient Books do remain. There is mention of this Officer in the Statute *Anno* 34, & 35, *Hen.* 8. c. 16. Alſo Chamberlain of the Exchequer, *Anno* 51. *H.* 3. Stat. 5. And *Anno* 10. *Ed.* 3. c. 11. And *Anno* 14. *ejuſdem*, *cap.* 14. And *Anno* 26. *H.* 8. *cap.* 2.

Chamberlain to the Queen, Camerarius Dominæ Reginæ.

A Vice chamberlain, Vice-camarius, ii, m.

The joyning of chambers together, Conclavia, æ, f.

A chamber-maid, Pediſequa, æ, f. Ornatrix, icis, f.

A chamber-pot, Matula, æ, f. Scaphium, ii, n.

Chamblet, Sericum undulatum.

A garment of chamblet, Veſtis undulata vel cymatilis.

To make chamfering or rebats in ſtones or tombs, Strio, are.

Chamfered, Striatus, a, um.

A chamfer, or chamfering, Stria, æ, f. (i. e.) a Channel or Gutter in ſtones of Pillars or Tombs.

Champaigne (the Family) De Campania.

Champertie, or champerty, Campartia, æ, f. Co. Lit. 368. It is derived from the *French* word *Champarter*, which ſignifieth to divide a Field. In our Common Law it is a Bargain with the Demandant or Tenant, Plaintiff or Defendant to have part of the thing in Suit (be it Lands or Goods) if he prevail therein, for maintenance of him in that Suit, *Fitz. Her. nat. brev. fol.* 171. *Cook* 2 *part of Inſtit. c.* 3. Every Champertie is Maintenance, but every Maintenance not Champertie, for Champertie is but a ſpecies of Maintenance, which is the Genus, *Leigh Philolog. Com. fol.* 38. One may have a Writ of Champertie where 2 Men are Impleading, and one giveth the half, or part of the thing in Plea, to a third Man, to maintain him againſt the other, then the Party grieved may have this Writ of Champertie againſt this third Man. Vid. the *Stat. Articuli ſuper Chartas c.* 11.

A champerter, Cambiparticeps, ipis. *Spel.* 117. Champterers are thoſe that move ſuits, or cauſe to be moved, either by their own Procurement or by others, and ſue them at their own Coſts, to have part of the Land, Goods or Gains in variance, *Anno* 33. *Ed.* 1. *Cook on Lit. lib.* 3. *c.* 8. *Sect.* 500.

Champflour (the Family) De Campo Florido.

A champian (or valorous fighter) Campio, onis, m. *Spel.* 118. (i. e.) One that fights Combats in his own or anothers Quarrel.

Champion (or plain) ground, Fundus vel planities Campeſtris.

Chance-medley, Infortunium, ii, n.

Chance-medley, or Homicide, Per Infortunium, is when one is ſlain caſually, and by miſadventure, without the will of him that doth the Act, of this

no-

no Appeal doth lie. It is fitly so called, for in it Men are medled (or committed) together by meer chance, and upon some unlooked for occasion, without any former Malice. It is corrupted from *Chaudmelle*, which signifieth hot or suddain debate. *Rixa* in the Civil Law, whence in *Scotland Chaudmelle* is opposed against forethought Felony, as Manslaughter with us against Murder, *Selden's* notes upon *Hengham*. If a man casteth a stone, or shooteth an arrow, and another that passeth that way is killed, this manner of killing is manslaughter, by misadventure or chance medley, for he which killeth shall have his pardon of Course, as appeareth by the *Statute of 6 Ed.* 1. *c.* 9. and he shall forfeit his Goods in such manner, as he that shall kill a man in his own Defence: for the life of a man is a thing precious, and favoured in the Law, so that a man that killeth another in his own defence, or *per Infortunium*, without any intent, this is not Felony, and yet in such Cases, he shall forfeit his Goods and Chattels, for the great regard that the Law hath to the Life of a Man, *Cook* 5. *Rep.* Cases of Execution. But if he that committeth this manslaughter, was doing an unlawful Act, as casting stones in an Highway where men usually pass, or shooting Arrows in a Market place or such like, whereby a man is killed, it is Felony at least. *Leigh Phil.Com. fol.* 38, 39.

Chancing or happening by chance, Fortuitus, a, um.

By chance, Fortè, Fortuitò adv.

A Chancell of a Church, Cella, æ, f. Adytum, i, n.

A Chancellor, Cancellarius, ii, m.

Lord Chancellor of England, Dominus Cancellarius Angliæ. So called, because it is his part to Cancell if he find any Act, Matter or Decree obtained, which may any way prejudice his Prince or the Commonwealth which cancelling is made with lines drawn a cross like a Lettice, which in Latin is called *Cancelli*. In other Kingdoms, as also in ours Chancellor is a Title given to him that is the chief man, for matter of Justice, (in Civil causes especially) next unto the Prince. For whereas all other Justices in our Commonwealth, are tyed to the Law, and may not swerve from it in Judgment. The Chancellor hath in this a more absolute Power, to moderate and temperate the written Law, ordering all things *Juxta æquum & bonum*. And therefore *Stawnford Prærog. cap.* 20. *fol.* 65. saith that the Chancellor hath two powers, one Extraordinary, the other Ordinary, meaning, that tho' by his ordinary Power in some cases, he must observe the form of proceeding as other ordinary Judges, yet that in his extraordinary Power he is not limited by the written Law, but by Conſcience, and Equity, according to the circumſtances of the matters in Queſtion. He that beareth this Magiſtracy and High-Office, is called the Lord Chancellor of *England*. *Anno* 7. *R.* 2. *cap.* 14. and by the Statute *Anno* 5. *Eliz.* *cap.* 18. The Lord Chancellor and Keeper of the Great Seal of *England* have all one Power.

Chancellor of the Exchequer, Cancellarius & ſubtheſaurarius Scaccarii Domini Regis, *Anno* 6. *H.* 8. *cap.* 6. whoſe Office hath been thought by many to have been created for the qualifying of Extremities in the Exchequer; he ſitteth in the Court and in the Exchequer Chamber, and with the reſt of the Court, ordereth things to the Kings beſt benefit; he is always in Commiſſion with the Lord Treaſurer, for the letting of Lands that come to the Crown by the diſſolution of Abbies, and hath by Privy Seal from the King, Power with others, to compound for forfeiture of Bonds and forfeitures upon Penal Statutes, he hath alſo much to do in the Revenue come by the diſſolution and firſt fruits, as appeareth by the Acts and Statutes of uniting them to the Crown.

Chancellor of the Dutchy of Lancaſter, Cancellarius Ducatûs & Comitatûs Palatini Domini Regis Lancaſtriæ. *Anno* 3. *Ed.* 6. *cap. Anno* 5. *ejuſdem* *cap.* 26. Whoſe Office is principally in that Court to Judge and determine all Controverſies between the King and his Tenants of the Dutchy Land, and otherwiſe to direct all the King's affairs belonging to that Court.

The Chancery Court, Cancellaria, æ, f. Chancery is the Court of Equity and Conſcience, moderating the rigour of other Courts that are more ſtraightly tyed to the Letter of the Law, whereof the Lord Chancellor of *England* is the Chief Judge. *Cromp. Juriſdict. fol.* 41. or elſe the Lord Keeper of the Great Seal ſince the Stat. 5. *Eliz.* *cap.* 18. Mr. *Cambden* ſaith in his *Britannia p.* 114. of the 3*d.* Impreſſion that Chancery taketh the name of Chancellor. The Officers belonging to this Court are the Lord Chancellor or Keeper of the Broad or Great Seal, 12 Maſters of Chancery, whereof the Maſter of the Rolls is chief; next unto theſe 12 Maſters of the Chancery, are the 6 Clerks, the Examiners, a Sergeant at Arms, Uſher and Cryer of the Court, the Clerks of the Courts otherwiſe called Courſeters, the Clerks of the Petibag, and the Clerk of the Crown, the Clerk of the Hamper, or Hanaper, the Protonotary or Regiſter, the Comptroller of the Hamper, the Clerk of Appeals; the Sealer, the chaſe Wax, the Clerk of the Faculties, the Clerk of the Patents, Clerk of the Star-Chamber, the Clerk of Preſentations, the Clerk of Diſmiſſions, the Clerk of Licences to alienate

alienate, the Clerks of the Enrollments, the Clerk of the Protections, the Clerk of the Court of Wards, the Clerk of the Subpœnaes, the Clerks of the Chapel, now in number 7, which have the keeping of the Rolls, lying in the Chapel, adjoyning and belonging to the Mansion of the Master of the Rolls. All which see in their proper places and Alphabets.

A Tallow-Chandler (*or seller or maker of Tallow-Candles*) Sēbātor, ōris, m. Venditor Candelarum.

A Wax-Chandler, Cerarius, ii, m. Lychnopœus, i, m.

A Chanel, Canal (*or Gutter*) Canalis, is, f. vel m. Cloaca, æ, f. Imbrex, icis, m.

A little Chanel, Canaliculus, i, m. aqualiculus, i, m.

The Chanel of a River. Alveus, ei, m.

A change, Cambium, ii, n. Lex. 10.

To Change (*or exchange*) *moneys*, Cambire Denarios. Ry. 527.

Bills (or Letters) of change or Exchange, Literæ Cambitoriæ. Pry. 146.

Changed, Mutatus, a, um.

A Garment of changeable silk, Vestis Soriculata vel furculata.

Changeable of Colour, Discolor, oris, adj.

A Chanter (*or chief Singer*) *in a Church*, Cantor, oris, m. Præcentor, oris, m.

A chap (*or chink*) Rima, æ, f.

A little chap, Rimula, æ. f.

Chapped (*or chinked*) Rimatus, a, um.

Full of chaps, Rimosus, a, um.

The chapiter of a Pillar. Epistilium, ii, n.

A chaplain, Capellanus, i, m. Sacellanus, i, m. A Chaplain is he that performeth divine Service in a chapel, and it is used in our Common Law ordinarily for him that is depending upon the King or other Great Personages, for the Instruction of him and his Family, the executing of Prayers and Preaching in his private House, where commonly they have a Chapel for that purpose, as *Anno* 21. *H.* 8. *cap.* 13. where it is set down what persons may Priviledge one or more Chaplains to discontinue from their Benefices for the particular Service.

A chapman, Institor, oris, m.

Belonging to chapmanry, Institorius, a, um. Empŏrĕticus, a, um.

Chapmanship, Emporeuma, atis, n. Ars Institoria.

A chapel, Capella, æ, f.

A little chapel. Capellula, æ, f.

A chapelry (*or Hamlet with a chapel in it*) Capellania, æ, f. Capellaria, æ, f. Lex. 26. 1. Mon. 577.

A chapter of a Book, Caput, itis, n. capitulum, i, n.

A Dean and Chapter, Decanus & Capitulum. Chapter signifieth in the Common and Canon Law (whence it is borrowed) *Congregationem Clericorum in ecclesia cathedrali, conventuali, regulari, vel collegiata:* Why this Collegiate company ſhould be called *capitulum, i,* a little head of the Canoniſts, is for that this company, or corporation is a kind of head, not only to rule and govern the Dioceſs in the vacation of the Biſhoprick, but alſo in many things to adviſe the Biſhop when the See is full. *D. Cowell vid. Panormitan. in cap. extra, de reſcriptis.*

A Chapter-Houſe. Exedra, æ, f.

Charcoal (or coal made of wood,) Carbo, onis, m.

To charge (or command) Mando, are.

A charge or commandment, Mandatum, i, n.

He to whom a charge is given, Mandatarius, a, um.

An aſſignment to a charge (or Office) Delegatio, onis, f.

To lay to ones charge, Accuſo, are.

Laid to ones charge, Objectus, a, um.

A laying to ones charge, Objectio, onis, f.

Charged with, Accuſatus, a, um.

Charge (or coſt) Sumptus, i, m. Impenſa, æ, f.

Chargeable (or coſtly) Sumptŭōſus, a, um.

A charger (or great Platter) Lanx, cis, f. Pătina, æ, f. Catinus, i, m.

Charing croſs, Crux Chariniana.

A chariot, Currus, i, m. *Ra. Ent.* 538. *Co. Ent.* 526. *Lex.* 19.

The Axel-ree (or chief Tree of a chariot) Longale, is, n.

To charm (or inchant) Incanto, are.

A charm (or inchantment) Incantamentum, i, n.

A charmer, Incantator, oris, m.

A charter, Deed, or writing of Privilege, Charta, æ, f. Charter or Deed is ſo called from the Latin *charta,* quia ſcribi ſolebant. It is called Magna Charta, not for the length or largeneſs of it, (for it is but ſhort in reſpect of the Charters granted of private things to private perſons) but it is called the Great Charter, in reſpect of the great weightineſs, and weighty greatneſs of the matter contained in it, in few words, being the fountain of all the fundamental Laws of this Realm, and therefore it may be ſaid of it, that it is *magnum in parvo.* The Nobles and Great Officers were to be ſworn to the obſervation of it. *Cook on Lit. l.* 2. *c.* 4. *Sect.* 108. *and Epiſt.* 8. *Rep.* and *Proeme to his* 2. *part of Inſtitut.* It is called Magna Charta, in reſpect to the *Charta de Foreſta.* It is the quinteſſence of the whole bulk of the Politicks of our Nation, the Charter of the Peoples right, the hedge of their property, and the ſtrength of their ſecurity.

It

It hath been confirmed above 30 times, and commanded to be put in Execution, and was bought with the blood of our Nobility, and English Ancestors, in those troublesome times of King *John* and *Henry* his Son. It is in our books called, *charta libertatum, & communis libertas Angliæ,* or *Libertates Angliæ' charta delibertatibus.* Magna Charta. Judge *Doderidge. Cook* on *Lit. ubi Supra.*

Charters of Lands are writings, Deeds, Evidences and Instruments made from one man to another, upon some Estate conveyed or passed between them of Lands or Tenements, shewing the names, place, and quantity of the Land, and the Estate, time and manner of the doing thereof, the parties to the Estate delivered and taken, the witnesses presenr at the same with other circumstances. Terms of Law.

Charters are called Muniments, *à muniendo, quia muniunt, & defendunt hæreditatem.*

The purchaser of Land shall have all the Charters, Deeds and Evidences, as incident to the Lands, *& ratione terræ,* that he may the better defend the Land himself, having no warranty to recover in value, for the Evidences of it, are as it were the sinews of the Land, the Feoffer being not bound to warranty, hath no use of them, also he shall have all Deeds and Evidences, which are materials for the maintenance of the Title of the Land. *Cook on 9 Rep. Anna Bedingfield's* Case. *Cook on Lit. l. 1. c. 1. f. 1.* Lord *Buckhurst's* Case 1 *Rep.* 1.

A charter party, Chartapartita, æ, f.

A charter-party of affreightment, Chartapartita de affreëtamento.

Iron chases, Margines ferrei. *Townsand.*

Chattels, Catalla, orum, n. Chattels is a French word, and signifieth Goods, which by a word of art we call *Catalla*; it signifieth all Goods moveable, and unmoveable, except such as be of the nature of Freehold, or parcel thereof. *Cowell's Interp.* verb. cattals. *Kitchin fol.* 32. verb. *catalla.* Some hold that ready money is neither Goods nor Chattels, nor Hawks nor Hounds, because they be *feræ naturæ.* Dr. *Cowell* (in his Interpreter) gives this witty reason why money is not to be accounted Goods, or Chattels, because, saith he, Money of itself is not a thing of worth, but by the consent of men, and so for their easier Traffick or permutation of things necessary for their Life. *Cook on Lit. lib. 2. c. 11. Sect.* 177. but our Law accounts Money to be chattels. Goods or Chattels are either.

1. Personal, as Horses and other Beasts, household Stuffs, Bows, Weapons, *&c.* called personal, because for the most part they belong to the person of a man, or because they are to be recovered by personal actions.

2. Real,

2. Real, because they concern the reality, as terms for years of Lands or Tenements, Wardships.

The word Goods in the Common Law comprehends such things, as be either with, or without life, as a Horse or Bed Kitchin.

Bona dividuntur in mobilia & immobilia; mobilia rursum dividuntur in ea quæ se movent, & quæ ab aliis moventur, Cook on Lit. *ubi supra*, but by the Common Law no Estate of Inheritance or Freehold is comprehended under these words *Bona & Catalla, Leigh. Phil. Com. fol.* 42. The Civil Law sometimes puts a difference between *moventia* and *mobilia*, understanding by *moventia* such Goods as actively and by their own accord do move themselves, as Horses, Oxen, Sheep and Cattel, and by *mobilia* such Goods as passively are moveable, or removeable, from one place to another, as Apparel, Pots and Pans, yet regularly and for the most part, by moveables are indifferently understood goods both actively and passively moveable. Immoveables are those goods which otherwise be termed Chattels real; for that they do not immediately belong to the person, but to some other thing by way of dependency, as Trees growing on the Ground, or Fruit growing on the Trees, or a Lease or Rent for term of years, but not Lands, Tenements, or Frank-Tenement.

A chauntrey, Cantaria, æ, f.

Chaumont or Chaumond (the Family) De calvo monte.

Chaworth (the Family) De Cadurcis.

C H E.

To cheapen (or ask the price of any thing) Commercor, aris. Licitor, aci, Rogare pretium.

A cheapner of Wares, Licitātor, oris, m.

A cheapning, Lĭcĭtātio, onis, f.

Cheapness, Vilĭtas, ātis, f.

Cheap. Vilis, le, adj.

To cheat, cozen or deceive, Defraudo, are.

A Cheater (or Cozener, Fraudator, oris, m. Deceptor, oris, m. Ærufcator, oris, m.

To make chequer-work, or other little work with small pieces coloured, as in Tables, Boards and Pavements. Vermiculor, aris.

A small piece that men make checquer-work with, Tessella, æ, f.

Checquer-work, Tessellarium, ii, n. Opus Tessellatum.

Made checquerwise, or in checquer-work, Tessellātus, a, um.

A cheek, Gena, æ, f. Mala, æ, f.

Chelmsford (in Essex) Cononium. Cæsaromagus.

Chelsey, Schelsega.

Cheney (the Family) De Casineto. De Caneto.

Chensford or Chernford (in Essex) Canonium.

Cheese, Caseus, e, m.

Soft

Soft Cheese, Caseus recens. Metæ lactentes.

Cheese-Rennet (or the running which turneth milk into curds) Coagulum, i, n.

A cheese Press, Caseale, is, n.

A cheese Fat, (or cheese Vat) Fiscella, æ, f. Forma casearia.

A cheese Rack, Cremathra, æ, f.

Old salt cheese, Tyrotatichus, i, m.

A cheese-cake, Placenta galacticea. Quadra placentæ. Epityrum, i, n.

A cheesmonger, Casearius, ii, m.

Pertaining to cheese, Casearius, a, um.

Chepstow (in Monmouthshire) Strigulia.

To churn (or make butter) Butyrum agitare.

Chertsey (in Surry) Ceroti insula. Certesia. Cervi insula.

A Cherry, Cerasum, i, n.

A cherry-Tree, Cerasus, i, f.

A chest (or coffer) Cista, æ, f. Arca, æ, f. Capsa, æ, f.

A little chest, Cistula, æ, f. Cistella, æ, f.

A chest maker, Arcarius, ii, m. Scrinarius, ii, m.

Chester City, orWest-Chester(in Cheshire. Chestria. Chestrum. Deva & Devana urbs. Deunana. Duinana. Legio. x. x. Victrix.

Bishop of Chester, Episcopus Chestriensis vel Cestriensis.

Chester (the Family) DeCestria.

Chester on the Street (in the Bishoprick of Durham.) Condercum.

Cheverill, Aluta hædina. *(i. e.) Leather made from the Skin of a wild Goat.*

Chevage or chiefage, Chevagium, ii, n. It is a sum of Money paid by Villains to their Lords in acknowledgement of their Bondage, for their several heads, Chevage of the French word *Chief*, as if it were the service of the head, of which *Bracton* saith *Chivagium dicitur recognitio in signum subjectionis & Domini de Capite suo. Lambert* writeth it Chivage, but it is more properly written Chiefage.

A cheveron, Tignum, i, n. Cheverons, are the strong Rafters and chiefs that meet at the Top of the house to hold up the Tiles and covering of the House.

Chevisance, Chevisantia, æ, f. (i. e.) a bargain or contract, *Anno* 37. *H.* 8. cap. 9. & *Anno* 13. *Eliz.* cap. 5. & 8. *Anno* 10. R. 2. cap. 1. *Anno* 3. *H.* 7. cap. 5.

C H I.

A chibbol (or little Onion) Cepula, æ, f.

Chichester (in Sussex) Ciceastria. Cicestria.

Bishop of Chichester, Episcopus Cicestrensis.

A chick (or chicken) Gallinacus, i, m. Pullus gallinaceus. Gallinæ Pullus.

A chicken newly hatched. Pullicenus, i, m.

Breed of chickens or other Fowl, Pullities, ei, f.

A child, Infans, antis, c. g.

A little child, Infantulus, i, m.

Great with child, Prægnans, tis, adj. Gavida, æ, f.

A woman lying in child-bed, Puerpĕra, æ, f.

The time of a womans lying in child-bed, Puerpĕrium, ii, n.

Child-birth or child-bed, Partus, ûs, m.

Childhood (or infancy) Infantia, æ, f. Pueritia, æ, f.

Children, Liberi, orum, m. Sing. caret.

A chimney, Cāmīnus, i, m.

The shank or tunnel of a chimney, Infūmĭbŭlum, i, n. Fumarium, ii, n.

A chimney-sweeper, Mundator, sive Purgator caminorum.

To stop chinks, Obstipo, are.

A chink (or cleft) Rima, æ, f. Fissura, æ, f.

He that stoppeth chinks, Obstipātor, oris, m.

Having the chinks stopped, Obstipatus, a, um.

The chin, Mentum, i. n.

To chip bread, Distringere crustas Panis. Summas crustas panis distringere.

To chip with an Ax, Ascio, is, ivi. Dedolo, are.

To chip round about with an Ax, Circumdolo, are.

A chip (or chippings, such as Carpenters hew off) Segmen, inis, n. Segmentum, i, n. Assŭla, æ, f. Sĕcāmentum, i, n. Ramentum, i, n.

Chips to kindle fire, Fomes, itis, m.

The chipping of Bread, Resegmina Panis. Quisquiliæ crustarum.

A Chirographer, Chirographarius, ii, m. Chirographus Finium. Chirographator, oris, m. *Ry.* 19. (i. e.) An Officer of the Court of Common-Pleas that Ingrosseth the Fines. Chirographarius Finium & Concordiarum, signifieth in our Common Law him in *Communi Banco*, the Common Bench Office, that Ingrosseth Fines in that Court acknowledged, into a perpetual Record, after they be acknowledged and fully passed by those Officers, by whom they are formerly examined, and that writeth and delivereth the Indentures of them unto the Parties, *Anno* 2. *H.* 3. *c.* 8. *West*'s Symbol, *part* 2. Titulo Fines, Sect. 114. & 129. *Fitz. Herb.* Nat. Brev. fo. 147. A This Officer also maketh two Indentures, one for the buyer, another for the seller, and maketh one other Indented Piece, containing also the effect of the Fine, which he delivereth to the *Custos Brevium*, which indented piece is called the foot of the Fine. The Chirographer also or his Deputy, doth proclaim all the Fines in the Court, every Term, according to the Statute; and then repairing to the Office of the *Custos Brevium*, there endorseth the Proclamations on the backside of the foot thereof, and alway keepeth the Writ of Covenant, as also the note of the Fine.

The

The Chirograph of a fine, Chirographum Finis. 5. *Co.* 39.

A chirurgeon (or ſurgeon) Chirurgus, i, m.

Chirurgerie, Chirurgia, æ, f.

A chiſel, Scalper, ri, m. Scalprum, pri, n. Celtis, is, f.

A little chiſel, Scalpellum, i, n. Scalpulum, i, n.

A chitterling, Omăſum, ſi, n. Faliſcus venter.

A ſmall gut or chitterling ſalted, Hilla, æ, f. & Hilla, orum, n.

CHY.

A chymiſt (or Alchymiſt) Alchymiſta, æ, m.

CHO.

To choak (or ſtrangle) Strangulo, are. Suffoco, are.

Choaked (or ſtrangled) Strangulatus, a, um.

A choaker (or ſtrangler) Suffocator, oris, m.

A choaking, Suffocatio, onis, f.

To chooſe (or elect) Eligo, is, ĕgi, ctum, ĕre.

Choſen, Electus, a, um.

Choice (or election) Electio, onis, f.

To chop (or cut off) Trunco, are.

Chopped off, Truncatus, a, um.

A chopper off, Truncator, oris, m.

A chopping off, Truncatio, onis, f.

A chopping knife, Culter herbarius.

A chop, Diviſūra, æ, f.

A choiriſter (or queriſter) Choriſtarius, ii, m.

CHR.

A chriſolite, Cryſolithus, i, m. It is a kind of Jaſper ſtone, ſhining with a golden colour quite thorow.

Chriſtal, Cryſtallum, i, n.

Chriſt (our only anointed Lord and Saviour) Chriſtus, i, m.

Chriſtendom, Chriſtianiſmus, i, m. Chriſtianum dominium, ſeu Imperium. Orbis Chriſtianus.

To chriſten (or baptize) Baptizo, are.

A chriſtening (or baptizing) Baptiſmus, i, m.

A chriſtian, Chriſtianus, i, m.

Chriſtianity (or chriſtianiſm) Chriſtianitas, atis, f.

Chriſtmas day, Feſtum natalis Domini.

Chriſt-church (in *Hampſhire*) Interamna. Fanum Chriſti.

A chronicle or cronicle, Chronicum, ci, n. Sed potius Chronica, orum, n. Annāles, ium, m.

A chronicler (or writer of chronicles) Chronicus, i, m. Chronographus, i, m.

Chronographie, (or deſcription of time) Chronographia, æ, f.

Chronology, Chronologia, æ, f.

Chryſocolla (or Gold ſolder wherewith Goldſmiths ſolder Gold and other Metals) *Borax, acis*, f.

CHU.

A church (or temple) Eccleſia, æ, f.

A Pa-

A parish church with the Appurtenances, Rectoria, æ, f.

A collegiat church, Ecclesia Collegiata.

A church robber, Sacrilegus, i, m.

A church warden, Gardianus Ecclesiæ. Church Wardens are Officers yearly chosen by the consent of the Minister and Parishioners, according to the custom of every several place, to look to the Church, Church-yard, and such things as belong to both, and to observe the Behaviour of their Parishioners, for such faults as appertain to the Jurisdiction or Censure of the Court Ecclesiastical. These are a kind of Corporation enabled by Law to sue for any thing belonging to their Church, or poor of their Parish. Vid. *Lambert* in his Pamphlet of the duty of Church Wardens.

A church yard, Cœmeterium, ii, n. Sepulcretum, i, n.

Of or belonging to men of the Church, Sacerdotalis, le, adj.

Womens churchings, Puerperarum gratitudines.

C I C.

Cicely (or *Cecilia*) A Womans name, Cecilia, æ, f.

C I D.

Cider, Sicera Pomacea. Pomatium, ii, n. Vinum pomaceum.

C I L.

Cilerie, Silerium, ii, n. Voluta, æ, f. Or Drapery wrought on the heads of Pillars or Posts, and made like Cloth or Leaves turning divers ways.

A *cilinder* (*or round roller*) Cylindrus, i, m.

A cilinder (*or Geometrical round body*) Cylindrus, i, m.

C I M.

A cimbale (*or instrument of musick*) Cymbalum, i, n. Crotalum, i, n.

To play on the cimbals, Cymbalisso, are.

He that playeth on cimbals, Cymbalista, æ, m.

C I N.

Cinnamon, Cinnamomum, i, n.

Cinque Ports, Quinque Portus, i. e. Sea-Port Towns in which divers Courts and Privileges belong, of which Places and Ports to this day there is an especial Governour or Keeper, called by his Office Lord Warden of the Cinque-Ports, having the Authority, and all that Jurisdiction that the Lord Admiral of *England* hath in places not exempt, and sending out Writs in his own name: And further I find on Record in the Rolls, that *Henry* the Seventh respecting the dignity of this Office, thought it

not

not unworthy the Person of a Prince, but bestowed it upon his second Son, *Henry* the Eighth, who succeeded him in Name and Kingdom. The words of the Record are these expresly, *Hen. 7. Rex Angliæ*, &c. *quinto die aprilis, Anno regni sui octavo, secundo-genito filio suo Henrico, dedit officium Constabular. Castri Dover, ac custodiam quinque Portuum*, which Ports at this day are known by the names of *Hastings*, *Dover*, *Hich*, *Rumney*, *Sandwich*. The Inhabitants of these Ports, and of their Limbs or Members, enjoy divers and great Privileges above the rest of the Commons of that Country: They pay no Subsidies, besides, Suits at Law are commenced and answered within their own Towns and Liberties: Their Mayors have the credit of carrying the Canopy over the King or Queen at their Coronation, and for their greater Dignity they are placed then at a Table on the right hand of the King. *Crompton* in his Jurisdict. fol. 28. nameth the Cinque-Ports to be seven, adding *Rye* and *Winchelsey*, to the five before recited. *Rye* and *Winchelsey* are indeed Limbs or Members belonging to the Port of *Hastings*, as likewise *Lid* and old *Rumney*, are Limbs of the Port of new *Rumney* and not distinct Ports by themselves, *Quære statutum*, *Henr*. 8. *anno* 32. *cap*. 48. *in hunc finem*.

Lord Warden of the Cinque-Ports, Guardianus, sive custos quinque Portuum.

C I P.

Cipress (*or Cypress, a fine curled linen*) Bissus crispata. Carbăsus, i, m.

Cipress, or cypress the tree, also the wood thereof, Cyparissus, i, f. Cupressus, i, f.

Ciprian (*a mans name*) Ciprianus, i, m.

C I R.

Circester or *Cirencester* (in *Gloucestershire*) Cirencestria, Corinium. Durocornovium. Passerum urbs.

A circle (*or round compass*) Circulus, li, m. Orbis, is, m.

A little, or narrow circle, Sphærula, æ, f.

A half circle, Hemicyclus, i, m.

A circle (*or ring*) *of a cart*, Orbile, is, n.

Round, or belonging to a circle, Circŭlāris, re, adj.

Round like a circle, Orbĭcŭlatus, a, um.

Circle-wise, Circulatim, adv.

By circles, or like a circle, Zonatim, adv.

A circuit, Circuitus, ûs, m.

Circuit of action, Circuitus actionis, i. e. A longer course of Proceeding, to recover the thing sued for, than is needful.

Circular or round, Circŭlāris, re, adj.

A cir-

A circulation, Diſtillatio, onis, f. (i. e.) A ſubliming or extraction of Waters or Oil by an Alembick, ſo termed becauſe the vapour before it is reſolved, ſeemeth to go round or circlewiſe.

A circumference (or round compaſs about a center) Circumferentia, æ, f.

Circumlocution, Circumloquutio, onis, f.

Circumſpect (heedfull or wary) Circumſpectus, a, um.

Circumſtance (or quality that accompanieth a thing, as Time, Place, Perſon, &c.) Circumſtantia, æ, f.

A circumſtance (or circuit of words) Ambages, is, f.

Circumſtantibus, Signifies thoſe that ſtand about (a Law Term) for a Supply or making up the number of Jurors (if any Impanelled appear not, or appearing be Challenged by either Party) by adding to them ſo many other of thoſe that are preſent or ſtanding by, as will ſerve the turn, *anno* 35. *H.* 8. and *anno* 5 *Eliz. cap.* 25.

To circumvent, Circumvenio, ire.

C I S.

Ciſſors (or little ſheers) Forpex, icis, pl. Forpices. Forfex, icis, f. pl. Forfices.

A pair of ciſſors, Par forficum.

A little pair of ciſſors, Forficulus, li, m. Forpicula, æ, f.

C I T.

To cite (or ſummon) Cito, are.

A citation, Monitio, onis, f.

A city, Civitas, atis, f. Urbs, is, f.

A citizen, Civis, is, c. g.

A citadel (or cittadel) Arx urbis. (*i. e.*) A Caſtle or Forteſs of a City.

A citern (or harp) Cithăra, æ, f.

A citron (or pome citron) Citrus, i, f. Malum Heſperium, malum medicum.

Civet, Zibēthum, i, n.

C L A.

To clack wool, Picis Impreſſionem exſecare. To bard or beard Wool, is to cut the head and neck from the reſt of the Fleece, *Anno* 8. *H.* 6. *cap.* 22. To clack Wool is to cut off the Sheeps mark, which maketh it to weigh leſs, and ſo yield the leſs Cuſtom to the King. To force Wool is to clip off the upper and hairy part of it.

A clack, or clapper of a Mill, Crepitaculum molare.

Clad (or clothed in cloath) Veſtitus, a, um. Indutus, a, um.

To claim (or challenge) Clamo, are. *Spel.* 160. *Co. Lit.* 107. 291.

A claim (or challenge) Clameum, ei, n. Claim is a challenge of Intereſt in any thing that is in the Poſſeſſion of another, or at the leaſt out of his own, as claim by Charter, claim by Deſcent. *Old. nat. brev. fol.* 11. Si Dominus infra annum Clameum qualitercunque appoſuerit. *Brac. l.* 1. c. 10. See the definition and di-

vers

yers sorts of claim in *Plowden.* Casu Stowel f. 359. a.

A clapper of a bell, Campanæ malleus. Malleus Tintinnabuli.

A clapper of a door, Marculus ostii.

A clapper of a mill, Vid. clack.

A clapper wherein conies are kept, Vivarium, ii, n. Lŏcŭlāmentum, i, n.

Clare *county* (in *Ireland*) Clara, Claria.

Clare (the Family) De Claris vallibus, Claranus.

Clare (a Womans name) Clara, æ, f.

Claret wine, Vinum Rubellum.

To clarifie liquor, Despúmo, are.

Clarified, Despumatus, a, um. Clarificatus, a, um.

A clarifying, Clarificatio, onis, f.

To clasp or buckle together, Fibulo, are.

To clasp beneath, Subfibulo, are.

A clasp (or buckle) Fibula, æ, f. Rĕtĭnācŭlum, li, n.

A clasp or catch, Clavus uncinatus.

A little clasp, Spintherŭlum, li, n.

A clause, article, or conclusion, Clausula, æ, f.

A claw, Unguis aduncus.

To clay, cover or foul with clay, Deluto, are.

Clay, Lutum, i, n.

Potters clay, Argilla, æ, f.

Fullers clay (or earth) Creta vel Terra Cimolia. Argilla Fullonis.

Claying of Walls, or other Places, Dĕlŭtāmentum, i, n.

Clay ground, Figularis terra.

A clay-pit, Argilletum, i, n.

Made of clay, Lŭtĕus, a, um.

C L E.

Clean or pure, Limpidus, a, um. Mundus, a, um.

A maker clean of privies, Foricarius, ii, m.

To cleanse or make clean, Purifico, are. Mundo, are. Purgo, are.

A cleansing, Mundatio, onis, f.

Clear (or manifest) Clarus, a, um.

To cleave, cut or divide, Findo, idi, ssum, ere.

A cleaving (or cleft) Fissus, ûs, m. Fissura, æ, f.

A cleaving to, Adhæsio, onis, f.

Cleaving to, Glutinosus, a, um.

Cleft (or cloven) Fissus, a, um.

Cleft (or cut in two) Bifidus, a, um.

The cleft of a pen, Fissura calami.

Clemence (a Womans name) Clementia, æ, f.

Clement (a Mans name) Clemens, tis, m.

A clepsydre (or water dial) Clepsydra, æ, f.

The clergy, Clerus, i, m.

Privilege of clergy, Clerimonia, æ, f. 2 In. 63.

Clergy, Sometimes used for the whole number of those that are *de clero domini,* of the Lords lot or share, as the Tribe of *Levi* was in *Judæa,* sometime for a Plea to an Indictment an Appeal, an ancient Liberty confirmed in divers Parliaments, *Stamf. lib. 2. cap.*

41. It is when a Man is arraigned of Felony, and such like, before a Temporal Judge, and the Prisoner prayeth his Clergy, that is, to have his book, then the Judge shall command the Ordinary to try if he can read as a Clerk, in such a Book and Place, as the Judge shall appoint, and if the Ordinary certifie the Judge that he can, then the Prisoner shall not have Judgment for his Life, *Co. on Lit. lib.* 2. *cap.* 11. *sect.* 209. The Book was allowed to the Clergy for the scarcity of them to be disposed of in Religious Houses. It was allowable in ancient times for all Offences whatsoever they were, except Treason and robbing of Churches of their Goods and Ornaments. But by many Statutes made since, the Clergy is taken away, for Murder, Burglary, Robbery, Purse-cutting, Horse-stealing. Horse or Mare-stealers, shall not have their Clergy, because Horses are for Publick Service and Commerce. 2. The Thief by them is armed to do mischief. *Stamford Pl. of Cr. l.* 2. *c.* 43. Bacon's use of the Law, *p.* 22. *anno* 18. *Eliz. cap.* 7. If the Indictment be only *Murdravit*, without adding *ex malitia præcogitata*, the Offender shall have his Clergy, if he will read as a Clerk he ought to read all the verse, but although he do not read at the beginning, but first spell, and after read, yet he shall have Allowance as a Clerk, *in favorem vitæ. Fortescue* saith, that if a Felon fail to read, for which he is judged to be hanged, yet in *favorem vitæ*, if he demand a Book afterward under the Gallows, and read, he shall have the benefit of his Clergy. And yet it is to be supposed he had no Ordinary at that time to demand whether he could read, but this case ought to be specially taken, *viz.* where the Felon is judged before the Justices of the Kings Bench, for if he be judged before the Justices of Goal delivery it is otherwise, because their Commission ends with their Session. *Stamford Pl. of Cr. lib.* 2. *cap.* 45.

Clergy was allowed to an Accessory to the stealing of Horses and Mares, because the Statute shall be taken most strictly, which speaks expresly but of the Principal. *Dyer Term Pasch. ann Mariæ*, 1 p. 99. Although he hath been Instructed and taught in the Gaol to know his Letters, and to read, this shall serve him for his Life, but the Gaoler shall be punished for this. *Dyer Term Mich. annis* 3 & 4 *Reg. Eliz.* Clergy is grantable but once to one Person, except he be within holy Orders for such a Man may have it often, 4. *H.* 7. *c.* 13. and 1 *Ed.* 6. 12. *Lord Stamford.*

Articles of the clergy, Articuli Cleri, are certain Statutes made touching Persons and Causes Ecclesiastical, *Anno* 9 *Edw.*

Edw. 2. & *Anno* 14 *Edw.* 3. *Stat.* 3.

A clerk, Clericus, i, m. (i. e.) one that is in holy Orders of the Church, also those Persons that belong to the Courts of Judicature that use the Pen.

Belonging to such clerk, Clericalis, le, adj.

A parish clerk, Clericus Parochialis.

Clerkship (*the Office of a Clergyman*) Clericitas, atis, f.

Clerk of the Parliament Rolls, Clericus Rotulorum Parlamenti, Is he that Recordeth all things done in the High Court of Parlament, and Engrosseth them fair into Parchment Rolls, for their better keeping to all Posterity. Of these there be two, one of the Higher, another of the Lower House. *Crompt. Jurisdict. fol.* 4. *and* 8. *Sir Tho. Smith de Repub. Ang. pag.* 38. *Vid. also* Vowel's *Book touching the order of the Parliament.*

Clerk of the crown in the Chancery, Clericus Coronæ in Cancellaria, Is an Officer there, that by himself or his Deputy, is continually to attend the Lord Chancellor, or Lord Keeper, for special matters of Estate, by Commission, or the like, either immediately from his Majesty, or by order of his Privy Council, as well Ordinary as Extraordinary, *viz.* Commissions of Lieutenancies, of Justices Errant, i. e. Justices of Assizes, Justices of Oyer and Terminer, of Gaol delivery of the Peace, and such like, with their Writs of Association, and *Dedimus potestatem*, for taking of Oaths, also all general Pardons upon Grants of them at the Kings Coronation, or at a Parliament, with the names of Knights and Burgesses, which are to be returned into his Office. He hath also the making of all special Pardons, and Writs of Execution upon Bonds of Statute of the Staple forfeited: Which was annexed to his Office in the Reign of Queen *Mary*, in consideration of his continual and chargeable attendance, both these before being for every Cursitour and Clerk of Court to make.

Clerk of the crown, Clericus Coronæ, Is a Clerk or Officer in the Kings Bench, whose Function is to frame, Read and Record all Indictments against Traitors, Felons, and other Offenders there Arraigned, upon any publick Crime. He is otherwise termed Clerk of the Crown Office, and *Anno* 2 *H.* 4. *c.* 10. He is called Clerk of the Crown of the *Kings Bench*. The reason of his Denomination, is, because he Reads and Records Indictments against Traytors, Felons, &c. which are against the Kings Crown and Dignity.

Clerk of the extreats, Clericus Extractorum, Is a Clerk belonging to the Exchequer, who termly receiveth the Extreats out of the Lord Treasurers remembrancer his Office, and writeth them out to be Levied for the King. He also maketh Schedules for such Sums ex-treated, as are to be discharged.

Clerk of Assises, Clericus Assisæ, Is he that writeth all things judicially done by the Justices of Assises in their Circuits. *Crompt. Jurisdiction fo.* 227.

Clerk of the Pell, Clericus Pellis, Is a Clerk belonging to the Exchequer, whose Office is to enter every Tellers Bill into a Parchment Roll called *Pellis receptorum*, i. e. the Skin or Roll of Receipts, and also to make another Roll of Payments, which is called *Pellis exitum*, wherein he sets down by what Warrant the Money was paid, and thereof called *Pel*, or *Pell*, of the Latin *Pellis*, a Skin.

Clerk of the Warrants, Clericus Warrantorum & Extract. Cur. Is an Officer belonging to the Court of Common-Pleas, which entreth all Warrants of Attorney for Plaintiffs and Defendants, and Enrolleth all Deeds of Indenture of bargain and sale, which are acknowledged in the Court, or before any Judges out of the Court. And he doth Extreat into the Exchequer, all Issues, Fines and Amercements, which grow due to the King any way in that Court, and hath a standing Fee of 10 *l.* of the King for making the same Extreats. *Vid. Fitz. Nat. Brev. fo.* 76.

Clerk of the Petit bag, Clericus parvæ Bagiæ, Is an Officer in the Chancery, of which sort there are 3, and the Master of the Rolls is their chief. Their Office is to Record the return of all Inquisitions out of every Shire, all Liveries granted in the Court of Wards, *all Ouster les mains*, to make all Patents of Customers, Gawgers, Controllers and Aulnegers, all *Conge d' Eslires* for Bishops, all Liberateis upon Extent of Statute Staples, the recovery of Recognizances forfeited, and all Elegits upon them. The Summons of the Nobility, Clergy, and Burgesses of the Parliament. Commissions directed to Knights and others of every shire, for seising of the Subsidies, Writs for the nomination of Collectors, and all Traverses upon any Office, Bill, or otherwise, and to receive the Money due to the King for the same. This Officer is mentioned *Anno* 33, *H.* 8. *cap.* 22. and it is like had first this denomination and stile of Petie Bags, because having to do with so many Records of divers kinds, as above mentioned, they were put in sundry Leather bags, which were not so great as the Clerk of the Hamper now useth, and therefore might be called Petits Bags, small or little Bags.

Clerk of the Kings great Wardrobe, Clericus Magnæ Gardérobæ Regis, Is an Officer of the Kings house, that keepeth an Account or Inventory in Writing, of all things belonging to the Kings Wardrobe. This

This Officer is mentioned *An.* 1. *Ed.* 4. *ca.* 1.

Clerk or comptroller of a Market, Clericus Mercatus ſive Fori, Is an Officer in the King's Houſe, mentioned *Anno* 1 *Ed.* 4. *cap.* 1. and *Anno* 13 *R.* 2. *ca.* 4. whoſe duty is to take charge of the Kings Meaſures, and to keep the Standards of them (that is) the Examples or Patterns of all the Meaſures that ought to be thorow the Land, as of Elnes, Ells, Yards, Lagens, as Quarts, Pottles, Gallons, *&c.* of Weights, Buſhels and ſuch like, and to ſee that all Meaſures in every Place be anſwerable to the ſaid Standard or Pattern, *Fleta. lib.* 2. *cap.* 8,9,10,11,12. Of which Office, as alſo of our diverſity of Weights and Meaſures, you may there find a Treatiſe worth the reading. *Britton* alſo in his 30 Chapter, ſaith in the Kings Perſon to this effect, We will that none have Meaſures in the Realm, but we our ſelves, but that every Man take his Meaſure and Weights from our Standards, and ſo goeth on with a Tractate of this matter, that well ſheweth the Ancient Law and Practice in this point. Touching this Officers duty you have alſo a good Statute, *An.* 13 *R.* 2. *cap.* 4.

Clerk of the Kings ſilver, Clericus Argenti Regis Cur. *&c.* Is an Officer belonging to the Court of Common Pleas, unto whom every Fine is brought, after it hath been with the *Cuſtos Brevium*, and by whom the effect of the Writ of Covenant is entred into a Paper Book, and according to that Note, all the Fines of that Term are alſo recorded in the Rolls of the Court, and his entry is in this form, he putteth the Shire over the Margin, and then ſaith, *B. C. Dat Domino Regi dimidiam merkam* (or more, according to the value) *pro licentia concordandi D. cum D. E. pro talibus terris, in tali villa, & habet Chirographum per pacem admiſſum*, &c.

Clerk of the Peace, Clericus Pacis, Is an Officer belonging to the Seſſions of the Peace, his duty is in the Seſſions to read the Indictments, to Enroll the Acts, and draw the Proceſs, to Record the Proclamations of rates for Servants Wages, to Enroll the diſcharge of Apprentices, to keep the Conterpain of the Indenture of Armour, to keep the Regiſter book of Licences given to Badgers and Laders of Corn, and of thoſe that are licenc'd to ſhoot in Guns, and to certifie into the Kings Bench, Tranſcripts of Indictments, Outlawries, Attainders and Convictions, had before the Juſtices of Peace within the time limited by Statute. *Lambert Eirenarch. lib.* 4. *cap.* 3. *fol.* 379.

Clerk of the ſignet, Clericus Signetti, Is an Officer who continually attendant on his Majeſtys Secretary, who always hath the Cuſtody of the Privy Signet, as well for Sealing his

Majesties private Letters, as also such Grants as pass his Majesty's hands by Bill assigned. Of these there are four that attend in the Course, and were used to have their Diet at the Secretaries Table. You may read more largely of their Office in the Statute made *An.* 27. *H.* 8. *cap.* 11.

Clerk of the Privy Seal, Clericus Privati Sigilli, Is an Officer (whereof there are 4 in number) that attend the Lord Keeper of the Privy Seal, or if there be none such, upon the Principal Secretary, Writing and making out all things that are sent by Warrant from the Signet to the Privy Seal, and are to be passed to the Great Seal, as also to make out (as they are termed) Privy Seals, upon any special occasion of his Majesties Affairs, for loan or lending of Money, or such like. Of this Officer, and his Function, you may read the Statute *Anno.* 27. *H.* 8. *cap.* 11.

Clerk of the Juries, or Jurata Writs, Clericus Juratorum, Is an Officer belonging to the Court of Common Pleas, which maketh out the Writs called *Habeas corpora* and *Destringas*, for appearance of the Jury, either in Court, or at the Assizes, after that the Jury or Pannel is returned upon the *Venire facias.* He entreth also into the Rolls the awarding of these Writs, and maketh all the continuance from the going out of the *Habeas corpora*, until the Verdict be given.

Clerk of the Pipe, Clericus Pipæ vel Ingrassator magni Rotuli: Is an Officer in the Kings Exchequer, who having all accounts and debts due unto the K. delivered and drawn down out of the Remembrancers Offices, chargeth them down into the Great Roll, who also writeth Summons to the Sheriffs to Levy the said debts upon the Goods and Chattels of the said Debtors, and if they have no Goods then he doth draw them down to the Lord Treasurers Remembrancer, to write Extreats against their Land. The ancient Revenue of the Crown remaineth in Charge before him, and he seeth the same answered by the Farmers and Sheriffs to the King. He maketh a Charge to all Sheriffs of their Summons of the Pipe and Green Wax, and seeth it answered upon their Accompts. He hath the Ingrossing of all Leases of the Kings Lands, and it is likely that it was at the first called, and still hath denomination of Pipe, and Clerk of the Pipe, and Pipe Office, because their Records that are Registred, in their smallest Rolls, are altogether like Organ Pipes; but their great called the great Roll *Anno.* 37. *Ed.* 3. *cap.* 4. is of another Form.

Clerk

Clerk of the Hamper, or Hanaper, Clericus Hanaperii, Is an Officer in Chancery, *Anno* 2. *Ed.* 4. *cap.* 1. Otherwise called Warden of the Hamper, in the same Statute, whose Function is to receive all the Money due to the King for the Seals of Charters, Patents, Commissions and Writs, as also Fees due to the Officers for Enrolling and examining the same with such like. He is tied to attendance on the Lord Chancellor, or Lord Keeper, daily in the Term time, and at all times of Sealing, having with him Leather Bags wherein are put all Charters, &c. After they are Sealed by the Lord Chancellor, and those Bags being Sealed up with the Lord Chancellors Private Seal, are delivered to the Comptroller of the Hamper, or Hanaper. Whereas now the Clerk hath with him Leather Bags to put in the Charters. It is likely in old times they were Hampers or Baskets, and thereof called Clerk of the Hamper, or Hanaper. This Hanaper representeth a shadow of that which the Romans termed *Fiscum*, that contained the Emperors Treasure.

Clerk of the Pleas, Clericus Placitorum, Is an Officer in the Exchequer, in whose Office all the Officers of that Court (upon especial Privilege belonging unto them) ought to sue, or to be sued upon any Action, and thereof called Pleas, and Common Pleas, because Places whereupon Actions in Law are Impleaded and sued.

Clerk of the Treasury, Clericus Thesaurariæ, Is an Officer belonging to the Common Pleas, who hath the Charge of keeping the Records of that Court, and maketh out all Records of *Nisi prius*, hath the Fees due for all searches, and hath the certifying of all Records in the Kings Bench, when a Writ of Error is brought, and maketh out all Writs of *Supersedeas de non molestando*, which are granted for the Defendants, while the Writ of Error hangeth. Also he maketh all Exemplifications of Records being in the Treasury. He is taken to be Servant to the Chief Justice, but removeable at his Pleasure, whereas all other Officers are for term of Life. There is also a Secondary or under-Clerk of the Treasury, for assistance, which hath some allowances. There is likewise an under Keeper, who always keepeth one Key of the Treasury door, and the Chief Clerk of the Secondary another, so the one cannot come in without the other.

Clerk of the Essoines, Clericus Essoniorum, Is an Officer belonging to the Court of Common Pleas, who only keepeth the Essoin Rolls, and hath for entring every Essoin 6 *d.* and for every Exception to bar the Essoin 6*d.* He hath also the providing of Parchment, and Cutting it into Rolls, and making the numbers upon them, and the delivery out of all the Rolls to every Officer, and the receiving of them again when they are written, and the binding and making up of the whole Bundles of every Term, and this he doth as Servant to the Chief Justice, for the Chief Justice is at charge for all the Parchment of all the Rolls. The word *Essoines* cometh of the *French Essoin, Exoine*, m. i. e. An Essoin or Excuse or toleration for absence upon a lawful cause alledged upon Oath, *fortè à Lat. Exoneratus*, exempted.

Clerk of the Outlaries, Clericus Utlagiariarum, Is an Officer belonging to the Court of Common Pleas, being only the Servant or Deputy to the Kings Attorney General, for making out the Writs of *Capias Utlagatum*, after Outlary. And the Kings Attorneys name is to every one of these Writs, and whereas 7 *d.* is paid for the Seal of every other Writ, there is but a Penny paid for the Seal of this Writ, because it goeth out at the Kings Suit.

Clerk of the Sewers, Clericus Suerarum, Is an Officer pertaining to the Commissioners of Sewers, writing all things they do by vertue of their Commission, for which see the Statute, *Anno* 13. *Eliz. cap.* 9.

Clerk Comptroller of the Kings house (whereof there are two) Is an Officer in Court that hath Place and Seat in the Compting house, and Authority to allow or disallow the Charges and Demands of Pursuivants and Messengers of the Green-cloath, Purveyors, or other like. He hath also the oversight and Comptrolling of all defaults, defects and miscarriages of any Inferiour Officers, and to sit in the Compting-House, with the Superiour Officers, *viz.* the Lord Steward, the Treasurer, Comptroller, and Cofferer, Masters of the House-hold, and Clerks of the Green-cloath, either for correcting or bettering things out of order, and also for bringing in Country Provision requisite for the Kings houshold, and the censure for failing of Carriages and Carts, warned and charged for that purpose. This Office you have mentioned *An.* 33. *H.* 8. *cap.* 12.

Clerk of the Nihils, Clericus Nihilorum, Is an Officer in the Exchequer that maketh a Roll of all such Sums as are Nihiled by the Sheriffs upon their Extreats of Green Wax, and delivereth the same into the Lord Treasurers Remembrancer his Office, to have Execution done upon it for the King.

Clerk of the cheek, Is an Officer in Court, so called because he hath the Check and Comptrollment of the Yeomen of the Guard, and all other ordinary Yeomen Huissiers, belonging either to his Majesty, the

the Queen or the Prince, either giving leave or allowing their absences or defects in attendance, or diminishing their Wages for the same. He also nightly by himself or Deputy taketh the view of those that are to watch, in the Court, and hath the setting of the watch. This Officer is mentioned, *Anno* 33. *H.* 8. *cap.* 12.

Clerk marshal of the Kings house, Seemeth to be an Officer that attendeth the Marshal in his Court, and recordeth all his Proceedings, mentioned *Anno* 33. *H.* 8. *cap.* 12.

A clew (or bottom) of thread, Glŏmus, i, m.

Cleybrook, *or near to it* (in *Leicestershire*) Bennones, Vennones.

C L I.

A client, Cliens, entis, c. g.

Clientship, Clientela.

A woman client, Clienta, æ, f.

A Cliff, Rupes, is, f. Petra prærupta.

A cliff (or pitch) of a hill, Clivus, i, m.

A clift, vid. *cleft.*

A climate (or portion of the world) Clima, ătis, n.

Climacterical, Climactericus, a, um. The Climacterical year is every seventh or ninth, the fourteenth or eighteenth, the twenty one, twenty seven, till you come to sixty three, which is most dangerous of all, being seven times nine, or nine times seven, at which age divers worthy men have died.

To clinch (or draw together) as one doth the fist, or the Smith a nail, or the Carter his whip, Restringo, ere. Contraho, ere. Inflecto, ere.

A climbing, Scansio, onis, f.

Of or for climbing, Scansorius, a, um.

Clinton (the Family) De Clintona.

To clip (or shear) Tondeo, ere.

To clip with Cissors, Attondere Forfice.

A clipper (he or she) Tonsor, oris, m. Tonstrix, icis, f.

Clipped (or sheared) Tonsus, a, um.

That which is clipped off, Resegmen, inis, n.

A clipping, Tonsura, æ, f.

A clister (or washing purgation) Clyster, eris, m. Enema, atis, n.

A cliver (or Butchers chopping knife) Clunabulum, li, n. Clunaculum, li, n.

C L O.

To cloath and attire, Vestio, is, ivi, īre, itum.

A maker (or seller) of cloaths, Vestiarius, ii, m.

A place where cloaths are kept (or set out to be sold) Vestiarium, ii, n.

Embroidered cloaths, Vestes Barbaricæ.

Old cloaths, Veteramenta, orum, n.

A suit

A suit of cloaths, Series apparatus. Habitus Vestium.

An upper cloathing, Vestitus Superior.

Woollen cloaths, Drappi, orum, m.

Cloathed (or clad) Vestitus, a, um.

Cloathed with a long robe, Palliatus, a, um.

Cloathed with a Petticoat, Shirt, or Wastcoat, Indusiatus, a, um.

Cloathed with a robe of state, Prætextatus, a, um.

Cloathed with a russet or gray, Leucŏphæātus, a, um.

Cloathed with silk, Sericatus, a, um.

Cloathed with wool, Lanatus, a, um.

Cloathed with Gold (or Garments finely wrought) Segmentātus, a, um.

Cloathed with black mourning, Pullātus, a, um.

Cloathed with purple, Purpurātus, a, um.

Cloathed in white, Candĭdātus, a, um.

Cloathed with a linen vesture, Linteātus, a, um.

Cloathed with a coat of mail, Loricatus, a, um.

A clock, Cloca, æ, f.

A clock-house, Coclarium, ii, n. *Spel.* 160. 2. *Mon.* 210.

A clock-maker, Horologicus, i, m.

A clock-keeper, Nolæ curator,

A clod (or turf) of earth, Glēba, æ, f. Grumus, i, m.

Cloddy, Glēbōsus, a, um.

A clog (or wooden shooe) Calo, onis, m.

A clog for the neck of dogs or other beasts, Numella, æ, f.

A clog (or little log) Truncŭlus, i, m.

A cloister, Claustrum, i, n.

A little cloister, Claustellum, i, n.

A cloak, Pallium, ii, n. Penula, æ, f.

A shepherds cloak, Glomerum, i, n.

A cloak to keep from rain, Lacerna, æ, f.

A thread bare cloak, Tribon, onis, m.

A beggars patched cloak, Pannucia, æ, f.

A cloak-bag, Pera, æ, f. Penularium, ii, n.

Cloaked (or clad in a cloak) Palliatus, a, um.

A riding cloak, Casula, æ, f.

Clonmel (in Ireland) a Bishoprick, Cluanania. Episc. Clonensis.

To close (or shut up) Claudo, ere.

A close (or field enclosed) Clausum, i, n.

A close stool, Lăsānum, i, n. Sessibulum, i, n. Sella pertusa. Sella familiaris.

A closet, Conclave, is, n. Cellŭla, æ, f.

A little closet, Armāriŏlum, i, n.

Cloath, Pannus, i, m.

Fine cloath, Pannĭcŭlus, i, m.

London *cloath*, Pannus Londinensis.

Cloath

Cloath of Gold, Pannus auro intertextus.

Cloath of arras (or tapestry) Tapes, etis, m. Tapetum, i, n. Tapetia, orum. Aulæum, i, n.

Friez cloath, Pannus Villosus.

Woollen cloath, Pannus laneus.

Broad cloath, Pannus laneus latus, de quodam Panno laneo lato vocat.

A fine broad cloath with a narrow red list, Hil. 2. & 3. *Ed. 6.* rotulo 140. int Web. & Parker in C. B.

Thrums of cloth, Textivilitium, ii, n.

To Full cloth, Fullo, are.

A linen cloth, Linteum, ei, n.

Cloth wrought or friezed on both sides, Amphimallus, i, m.

Cloth of needle work, Acupicta vestis.

Course cloth of a low price, Levidensa, æ, f. Pannus pinguis.

Cloth with an high nap, as bays and cotton, Pannus villosus.

The nap or hair of cloth, Tumentum, i, n. Villus, i, m.

Searge cloth, Virga de Sargio. 1 *Mon.* 419. *Pry* 1[illegible]

A cloth (or garment) made of hair, or a hair cloth, Cilicium, ii, n. Pannum Cilicium.

A table cloth, Mappa, æ, f. Mantile, is, n.

A horse cloth, Stratum, i, n. Dorsuale, lis, n. Sudaria, æ, f.

A forehead cloth, Frontale, is, n.

A neck cloth, Amictorium, ii, n.

A wisp or rubbing cloth, Xystra, æ, f.

The art of making linen cloth, Linificium, ii, n.

The art of making woollen cloath, Lānĭficium, ii, n.

Fine linen clothes, Carbasa lina.

Course woollen cloths for package, Coactilia, rum, n.

Cloths to cover booths or tents, Velaria, orum, n.

Clothes of a bed, Strata, æ, f. Stragŭla, æ, f.

Clothing (or making of cloth) Lanicium, ii, n.

A clothier, or maker of cloth, Lanarus, ii, m. Pannifex, icis, m. Pannorum Opifex.

A clothier or linen weaver, Linteo, onis, m.

A cloth worker, Rasor Pannorum.

Of or belonging to cloth, Panneus, a, um.

Cloven (or cleft) Fissus, a, um.

Cloves (a spice so called) Caryophylli, orum, m.

To clout (or amend garments) Sarcĭo, is, si, tum, īre.

A clout (or rag) Panniculus, li, m. Linteolum, li, n.

A shooe clout or dish clout, Pēnĭcŭlum, li, n. Pēnĭcillum, li. n.

Childrens clouts, Panici, orum, n.

Clouts (or binders) Canthi ferrei.

C L U.

A club, Clava, æ, f. Fustis, is, m.

A little club, Clavicula, æ, f.

Bearing a club, Clāvĭger, a, um.

Cluid river (in *Denbighshire*) Cluida.

C O A.

A coach, Carrus, i, m. *Ra. Ent.* 538. *Co. Ent.* 526. *Lex.* 19.

A coal, Carbo, onis, m.

Sea coal (or Mineral coal) Carbo mineralis, Lapideus vel Fossilis.

A coal-mine, pit or coal-house, Carbonaria, æ, f. Domus Carbonaria.

Pertaining to coals, Carbonarius, a, um.

A coast (or shore) Costera, æ, f. *Ry* 38. 184. Costera Maris. *Magn. Chart.* 320. 10. *Co.* 138. 2. *Inst.* 38. *Spel.* 180.

The top of a coast, Summitas Costeræ. 1. *Mon.* 886.

A mountain near the sea coast, Costera Montis. 1. *Mon.* 835.

A coat, Tunica, æ, f.

A little coat, Sagŭlum, li, n.

An over (or upper) coat, Supertunica, æ, f. *Reg.* 93.

A riding coat, Penula, æ, f. Lacerna, æ, f.

A coat of mail, Lorica, æ, f.

A little coat of mail, Loricula, æ, f.

A coat armour, Pālūdamentum, i, n.

Clad in a coat armour, Pālūdātus, a, um.

That weareth a coat, Tunicatus, a, um.

A childs coat with long sleeves, Chlămys, mydis, f. Tunica manicata.

To put on a coat of mail, Lorico, are.

A tatter'd coat, Cento, onis, m.

A postillion, or post-boys leathern riding coat, Scortea, æ, f.

C O B.

Coberley (in *Gloucestershire*) Covi Berchilega.

A cobiron (whereon the spit doth turn) Cratenterium, ii, n. Crăteūta, æ, f.

To coble shoes, Resarcire Calceamenta.

A cobler of shooes, Calceari us, ii, m. Crepidarius, ii, m. Veteramentarius Sutor. Sarcinator, oris, m.

A coblers shop, Sutrina, æ, f. Cerdo, onis, m. Veterum calceorum consarcinator.

C O C.

Cocar *or* Cock (*a river in* Lancashire *and* Yorkshire) Cocarus, Cokarus.

A cock, Gallus, i, m.

A cock-pit, Gallipugnātōrium, ii, n.

Of or belonging to a cock, Gallinaceus, a, um.

Cockermouth (in ——) Novantum. Novantum Prom. Novantum Chersonessus.

The cock of a gun or piece, Serpentina, æ, f.

A cock (or heap) Tassum, i, n. *Lex.* 122.

To make into a cock (or heap) Tassari. *Fle.* 162.

A cock of hay, Fænum in Tassis, *Reg.* 94. *Meta Fæni.*

A cock

A cock or spout of a conduit, Epistomium, ii, n. Saliens, entis, m.

A little cock in a conduit, Papilla, æ, f.

A weather cock, Triton, onis, m.

A cock-boat, Scapha, æ, f.

A cocket, Cokettum, i, n. Is a Seal pertaining to the Kings Custom-house. *Regist. Orig. fol.* 192. *a,* and also a scrowl of Parchment, sealed and delivered by the Officers of the Custom-house to Merchants as a Warrant that their Merchandice be customed, *anno* 11. *H.* 6. *ca.* 16. which Parchment is otherwise called *Literæ de coketto,* or *Literæ testimoniales de coketto Regist.* 179, *a, ut Supra.* So is the word used, *anno* 5. & 6. *Ed.* 6. *c.* 14. & *anno* 14 *Ed.* 3. *Stat. cap.* 21. This word is also used for a distinction of Bread, in the Statutes of Bread and Ale made, *Anno* 51. *Hen.* 3. where there is mention of Cocket-bread, Wastel-bread, Bread of Trete, and Bread of Common-wheat.

C O D.

The cod or husk of any thing, or properly of Pease, Siliqua, æ, f.

The cod of a man or beast, Scrotum, i, n.

A cod-piece, Perizōma, atis, n.

A codicill, Cōdicillus, i, m. A Codicill is a just sentence of our will, touching that which any would have done after our death, without the appointing of an Executor, which definition doth agree with the definition of a Testament, *F. de Test. lib.* 1. Saving that some words are here expressed, which are there omitted, *viz. absque executoris institutione.* The writers conferring a Testament and a Codicil together, call a Testament a Great Will, and a Codicil a Little Will, and do compare a Testament to a Ship, and the Codicil to a Boat tied to the Ship. *D. D. de Codicil in prim.* and indeed when Codicils were first invented, they were used instead of a Testament, when the Testator had no opportunity to make a Testament, or else as additions to the Testament when any thing was omitted, which the Testator would add or put in, which the Testator upon better advice would direct, which Emendation was always done by way of Codicil, *Cujac. Cod. de Codicil. l. conficiuntur.* vid. *Swinburn in his Treatise of Testaments and Wills, Part* 1. *Sect.* 5. *num.* 2. 3. & *Sequent.*

C O F.

A coffer, Cofera, æ, f. *Ry.* 177. Coftis, is, f. 2 *Mon.* 473. Arca, æ, f. Capsa, æ, f.

A little coffer, Capsula, æ, f. Scrinium, ii, n.

Cofferer of the Kings houshold, Coferarius Domini Regis Hospitii, It is a principal Officer in the Kings Court next under the Controller, that in the

the Compting-house, and else-where, at other times, hath a special charge and over-sight of other Officers of the houshold, for their good demeanour and carriage in their Offices. To all which one and other, whether they are Serjeants, Yeomen, Grooms, Pages, or Children of the Kitchin, Bake-house, Buttery, or Cellar, or any other in any other room of his Majesty's Houshold, he payeth their wages. This Officer is mentioned, *anno* 39. *Elizab. cap.* 7.

A coffer (or chest) maker, Arcārius, ii, m. Capsārius, ii, m.

A coffin for the dead, Loculus, i, m. Sandapila, æ, f.

C O G.

A cog in a mill wheel, Scarioballum, i, n.

Cogs hall (in *Essex*) Ad Ansam.

Cognisance (or badge in arms) Insignia, orum, n.

Cognisance, *Cognizance*, *Conisancc*, *Conusance*, Cognitio, onis, f. *Spel.* 273. Is in the Common Law sometime taken for an acknowledgment of a Fine or Confession of a thing done, as *Cognoscens latro. Bract. Lib.* 3. *Tract.* 2. *cap.* 3. 20. 32. *Cognoscere se ad villanum*, *Id. lib.* 4. *tract.* 5. *cap.* 16. As also to make Cognizance of taking a Distress, sometime as an Audience or hearing of a matter judicially, as to take Cognizance, sometime Power or Jurisdiction, as Cognizance of a Plea, is an ability to call a Cause or a Plea out of another Court, which no man can do but the King, except he can shew Charter for it, *Manwood Part* 1. *of his Forest Laws p.* 68. The new Terms of Law hath these words Conusance of a Plea, is a Privilege that a City or Town hath of the Kings Grant, to hold Plea of all Contracts, and of Lands within the Precinct of the Franchises, and that when any man is Impleaded for any such thing, in the Court of the King at *Westminster*, the Major and Bailiffs of such Franchises, or their Attorney, may ask Conusance of the Plea, that is to say, that the Plea and the Matter shall be pleaded and determined before them. But if the Court at *Westminster* be lawfully of seized the Plea, before Conusance be demanded, then they shall not have Conusance for that Suit, because they have negligently surceased their time of demand thereof. But this shall be no bar to them to have Conusance in another Action; for they may demand Conusance in one Action, and omit it in another Action, at their pleasure; and that Conusance lieth not by Prescription, but it behoveth to shew the Kings Letters Patents for it, *vid. etiam*, the new Book of Entries in the word Conusance.

Cognisce, Cognisatus, i, m. or Conisee of a Fine, is he to whom the Fine is acknowledged.

A cognizor, or conisour, Cognitor, oris, m. Cognizarius, ii, m. One that passeth or acknowledgeth a Fine in Lands or Tenements, *vid. West part* 2 *Symbol. Tit. Fines, Sect.* 2.

Cognitionibus admittendis, Is a Writ to a Justice or other that hath power to take a Fine, who having taken knowledgment of a Fine, deferreth to certifie it into the Court of Common Pleas, commanding him to certifie it, *Regist. Orig.* 68. *b.*

C O H.

A coheir, Cohæres, idis, c. g.

Coherence or agreement, Cohærentia, æ, f.

C O I.

A serjeants coif, Coifo, onis, f. *Spel.* 99. 162. *Lex* 31. Coifa, æ, f.

A baron of the degree of the coif, Baro de gradu de la Coif.

A coif for a womans head, Capillare, is, n. Crinale, is, n.

To coin (or make) money, Cuno, are. *Crompt. Just. Peace*, f. 220.

Coin, Cuneus, ei, m. *Cav.* 62.

Coinage, Cunagium, ii, n. 8. *Co.* 21. Coinagium, ii, n. *Plo.* 328.

Coined, Cuneus, a, um.

A coiner, Cuneator, oris, m.

A coin (or corner) of a wall, Angulus, li, m.

C O K.

Cokers, Carbatinæ, arum, f. *i. e.* Hedgers or Plowmens Boots, or great thick Leather Mitins, to keep out Thorns and Briers.

C O L.

A collar, Collare, is, n. Capistrum, tri, n. Lorum, i, n.

A dogs collar, Mellium, ii, n.

A mastiffs collar made with leather and nails, Millum, i, n.

The studs or prickles in a dogs collar to keep off the biting of other dogs, Murices milli.

A horse collar whereby he draweth in the cart, Helcium, ii, n.

A collar put on horses necks stuffed with wool or hair to prevent hurting them, Tomex, icis, f.

A collar of iron that men are bound with, Collaria, æ, f.

A collar of SS. Collare humerorum, i. e. Such as great Councellours of State, Judges of the Land, &c. do wear on their shoulders on high and festival days, called SS. because they are made into the form of the Letter *S* round about their shoulders.

Collateral, Collateralis, le, adj. It is used in the Common Law for that which is not lineally or directly, but adhering of the side; as Collateral assurance, is that which is made over

over and beside the Deed it self, for example: If a Man Covenant with another, and enter a Bond for the performance of his Covenant, the Bond is termed Collateral assurance, because it is without the Nature and Essence of the Covenant. And *Crompton* in his *Jurisdict. fo.* 185. saith, that to be subject to the feeding of the Kings Deer, is Collateral to the soil within the Forest. In like manner to pitch Booths or Standings for a Fair, in another mans Ground, is Collateral to the Ground.

Collateral warranty, vid. Warranty.

Collation of benefice, Collatio Beneficii. It signifieth properly the bestowing of a Benefice by the Bishop, which he hath in his own Right or Patronage, and differeth from Institution in this, for that Institution into a Benefice, is performed by the Bishop, at the Motion or Presentation of another, who is Patron of the same, or hath the Patrons right for the time, *Extra de Institutionibus, & de concessione præbendarum*, &c. And yet *Anno* 25. *Ed.* 3. *Stat.* 6. is Collation used for Presentation.

Colebrook (in *Buckinghamshire*) Colunum Pontes.

Colchester (in *Essex*) Coleceastria. Colonia.

To collect (or gather together) Colligo, egi, ĕre.

A collection, Collectio, onis, f.

A college, Collegium, ii, n.

Collerford, or *Collerton (in Northumberland)* Cilurinum, Cilurnum.

The collet (or beazil) of a ring, Pala annuli.

The collick, Colica, æ, f. Colicus dolor. Colica passio (i. e.) A disease caused through wind in the belly.

He that is troubled with the collick, Collicus, a, um.

Colne river (in Middlesex, *another in* Shropshire) Colnius.

A collier, Carbonarius, ii, m. Anthracius, ii, m.

A colonel, Colonellus, i, m. *Spel.* 219.

A collop of bacon, Carbonella, æ, f.

A colony of men, Colonia, æ, f. i. e. The People that are sent to dwell in a Country uninhabited.

Colour, Color, oris, m. Colour signifieth in the Common Law, a probable Plea, but in truth false, and hath his end to draw the Tryal of the Cause from the Jury to the Judges. *Vid. new Terms of Law, in title colour:* Who also referreth you to *D. and Student, fol.* 158. *Vid. Brook. Tit. colour in assise, Trepass*, &c. *fol.* 190.

Coloured, Coloratus, a, um.

The tempering of colours, Harmŏge, es, f.

A colt (or little horse or nag) Equulus, li, m. Equuleus, ei, m. Pullus Equinus.

A mare colt, Equula, æ, f.

A colume or pillar, or column in a book, Columna, æ, f.

Colun-

Colunbrook, Vid. *Colebrook*.

C O M.

A combat, Pugna, æ, f.

To combat (or fight) Pugno, are.

A single combat, Duellum, li, n. i. e. when one Man fighteth against another single, hand to hand, or a fight between two Men only singled out by themselves. Combat in our Common Law is taken for a formal Tryal of a doubtful Cause or Quarrel, by the Sword or Bastons, of two Champions. Of this you may read at large, *Paris de Puteo de re militari & duello. Alciat de duello. Hotoman disput. feudalium, cap.* 42. As also in our Common Lawyers of *England*, namely, *Glanvile lib.* 14. *c.* 1. *Bract. lib.* 3. *tract.* 2. *cap.* 3. *Britton cap.* 22. Horns *mirrour of Justices*, *lib.* 3. *cap. des exceptions in fine proximè ante C. Juramentum Duelli, apud Dier fol.* 301. *num.* 41, 42. *Staunford*'s Pleas of the Crown, *lib.* 2. *fol.* 176. *B. and* 177. *A.* saith that it is an ancient Tryal in our Law, and much used in times past, as appeareth by divers Presidents in the times of *Edward* III. and *Henry* IV. which is not yet out of use, but may be by the Law in use at this day, if the Defendant will, and nothing can be drawn on Conter-plea thereto. And it is said *M.* 37. *H.* 6. *fol.* 3. That to wage Battle, or to Combat, is by the Civil Law: But *Moil* saith it is by our Common Law, and as *Staunford, Pleas of the Crown, fol.* 177. *a.* saith that they shall come armed into the Court, and join issue. The Plaintiff begins his Appeal, *&c.* and the Defendant pleads not Guilty, and (as *Britton* setteth it down, *fol.* 41.) undertakes to defend it with his Body, *&c.* and after, one taketh another by the hand, and first, the Defendant saith in this manner, Hear you this, you man whom I hold by the hand, which are called *John* by your Christian name, that I *Pierce*, such a year, such a day, in such a place, the aforesaid murder of *N.* neither did do, nor go about, neither purpose, nor assented to such a Felony, as you have alledged. So God help me, and his Saints. And after the Accuser saith, Hear you this, you man, whom I hold by the hand, which are called *P.* by your Christian name, you are Perjured: For on such a day, such a year, in such a place, you did such Treason, or such a Murder, which I have alledged against you, or whereof I challenge you. So God me help, and his Saints. Then they are both led into a certain place, where both further say, Hear you this, Justices, that we, *I.* and *P.* have neither eat nor drank, nor done any other deed whereby the Law of God should be abased, or the Law of the Devil advanced. And forthwith there ſhall be an Oyez or Proclamation made, That none ſhall be ſo bold but the Combatants, to ſpeak or do any thing that ſhall diſturb the Combat or Battle, and whoſoever ſhall do againſt this Proclamation, ſhall ſuffer Impriſonment for a year and a day. Then they ſhall fight with Weapons, but not with any Iron, but with two Staves or Baſtons tipt with horn of an ell long, both of equal length, and each of them a Target, and with no other Weapon may they enter the Liſts, and if the Defendant can defend himſelf till after Sun-ſet, and as my Author ſaith, till you may ſee the Stars in the Firmament, and demand Judgment if he ought to fight any longer, then muſt there be Judgment given on the Defendants ſide. And *Bracton* agreeth herewith in theſe words, *Quod ſi appellatus ſe defenderit contra appellantem, tota die, uſque ad horam qua ſtellæ incipiunt apparere, tunc recedat appellatus, quietus de Appello, ex quo appellatus ſe obligavit ad convincendum eum, una hora die, quod quidem non fecit.* When the Defendant doth Plead to the Appeal not Guilty, and undertakes to defend it with his body, he muſt thrown down his Gauntlet or Glove into the Court, and if the Plaintiff doth not enter Rejoinder to the Battle, then he muſt take up the Glove or Gauntlet, but if the Plaintiff doth Conterplead unto it, then muſt he ſuffer the Glove or Gauntlet to lie, and the other ſhall Demurr in Law, or void him of the Appeal, becauſe he refuſed his Glove or Gauntlet. When they are ſworn, they muſt produce Mainpriſers or Pledges to perform the Combat or Battle, and then the Court ſhall appoint them a day and place to fight, and as *Fitz. p.* 385. ſaith, that the Challenger ſhall be at liberty, but the Defendant in the Cuſtody of the Marſhal, and the Marſhal ſhall array them both at their own charge, and that muſt be the night before the Battle, that they may be ready in the Field or Liſts by Sunriſing. The Forms of Battle deſcribed 17. *Edw.* 3. & 9. *H.* 4. differ from that deſcribed by *Bracton* and *Britton*, and that deſcribed by *Dier Termino Trinitatis anno* 13. *Eliz.* As he ſets it down between one *Chevin*, and another *Paramour*, a *Kentiſh* Gentleman, about the Trial of Land, and Levying a Fine thereof; and on the iſſue *Paramour* choſe the Trial by Combat or Battle, and had a Champion one *George Thorn*, a Gentleman of *Kent*, and no doubt his deareſt Friend, that would enter the Liſts to ſuch a hazard of life, &c. And the other had one *Henry Nailer*, a Maſter of Fence, and the Court

Court awarded the Battle, and the Champions were Mainprised and sworn (*Quære formam Juramenti*) to perform the Combat or Battle, *Apud Totehill in Westm.* 18. *Junii, prox. post Crast. Trinitat.* which was the first day of the Utas of the Term, and on the day appointed there was a List made four-square on even ground, every square 60 foot, and East, West, North and South, and the place and seat of the Judges was made without, yet Close upon the Lists, and a Bar made for the Serjeants at Law, & *circa horam decimam ejusdem diei*, 3 Justices or Judges of the Common Pleas, *viz*, *Dier*, *Weston*, *Harper*, (the fourth, namely, *Welch*, was not there by reason he was sick) did repair to the place in their robes of Scarlet, with their other Habits and Coifs, and the Serjeants at Law also. And there a Proclamation being made with 3 Oyez, the Demandants were first called for, and they came not: After that the Mainpernours of the Champions were called to bring forth first the Champion of the Demandant or Challenger, which came into the place in rugged Sandals, bare legged from the knee downward, and bare headed, and bare arms to the elbow, being brought in by the hand of a Knight, Sir *Jerom Bowes* by name, who carried a red Baston, of an ell long, tipped with horn, and a Yeoman carrying the Target made of double Leather, and they were brought in at the North side of the Lists, and went about the side of the Lists, untill the middest of the Lists, and then came towards the Bar before the Judges with three solemn Congies, and there he was made to stand at the South side of the place, being the right side of the Court, and after that the other Champion was brought in, in like manner, at the South, or contrary side of the Lists, with like Congies, &c. by the hands of Sir *Henry Cheney*, Knight, &c. And was set on the North side of the Bar (quite opposite to the other Champion) and two Serjeants being of Councel of each Party, in the middest between them: This done, the Demandant was solemnly called again, and appeared not, but made default; upon which default, *Barham* Serjeant for the Tenant, prayeth the Court to record the Nonsuit; which was done: Then *Dier*, Chief Justice reciting the brief, the matter, and issue of the Battle or Combat, and the Oath of the Champions to perform it, and the prefixed day and place, gives final Judgment against the Demandant, and that the Tenant shall hold the Land, to him and to his Heirs for ever quietly, from the said Demandant or Challenger, and their Heirs for ever, and the Demandants and their Pledges, *de prosequendo*, to be at the mercy of the Queen, &c. And then there was solemn Proclamation made, that the Champions, and all others there present (which by Estimation were about 4000 persons) should depart in Gods Peace, and the Queens; and so they departed with a shout, *God save the Queen*. Vid. more at large in *Verstegan* in his Book entituled. A Restitution of decayed Intelligence, *Pag.* 64, &c.

A comb, Pecten, inis, m.

A horse comb (or curry comb) Strigilis, is, f.

A little curry comb (or scraper) Strigilĕcŭla, æ, f.

Combs of horn, Pectines cornei.

Combs of ivory, Pectines Eburnei.

Combs of wood, Pectines Lignei.

A comb-case, Pectinarium, ii, n.

A comb-maker, Pectinārius, ii, m.

To comb, Pecto, xi, xui, xum, ĕre.

To curry comb a horse, Strigilo, are. Equum stringere.

Combed, Pexus, a, um.

To comfort (or strengthen) Comforto, are. *Ra. Ent.* 486. Conforto, are. 1. *Mon.* 526.

Comitatu Commisso, Is a Writ or Commission whereby the Sheriff is authorised to take upon him the sway of the Country, *Regist. Orig. fo.* 295. *a.* & *b. Cooks Rep. lib.* 3. *fol.* 72. *a.*

Comitatu & Castro Commisso, Is a Writ whereby both the charge of the County, and the keeping of a Castle is Committed to the Sheriff. *Regist. Orig. fol.* 295. *a.*

A command or commandment, Mandatum, i, n. Præceptum, i, n. Commandment in the Common Law is taken either for the Commandment of the King, when upon his meer motion he commandeth any thing to be done, *Staunf. Plea Crown fol.* 72. or of the Justices, and that either ordinary, or absolute, as when upon their own Authority, in their Wisdom and Discretion, they commit a Man to Prison for a Punishment. Ordinary, when they commit one rather for safe custody than Imprisonment, and it is Replevizable, *Idem Pl. Cr. f.* 73.

Commandment, Is again used for the offence of him that willeth another to transgress the Law, or to do any such thing as is contrary to the Law, as Murder, Theft or such like, and he is accessary *Bract. Lib.* 3. *Tract.* 2. *cap.* 19. And this the *Civilians* call *Mandatum*, Vid. *Angelus de Maleficiis.*

To commemorate (or rehearse) Commemoro, are.

To commence (or begin) Commenso, are.

Commenda, æ, f. i. e. A Benefice which being void, is commited to the care of another Clerk, to supply the Cure, till it is full.

Commerce (or common traffique) Commercium, ii, n. A Commismissary, Commissarius, ii, m. Commissary is a Title of Ecclesiastical Jurisdiction, appertaining to such a one as exerciseth spiritual Jurisdiction (at the least so far as his Commission permitteth him) in Places of the Diocess so far distant from the chief City, as the Chancellor cannot call the Subjects to the Bishops principal Consistory, without their great molestation. This Commissary is by the Canonists termed *Commissarius* or *Officiales foraneus*, *Vid. Lynd. Provin.cap. de accus*, in the word *Mandat*, *Archiepiscopi*, in *Gloss*.

A commission, Commissio, onis, f.

A commissioner, Commissionarius, ii, m. *Lex.* 32.

To commit, Committo, ere.

A committee, Commissus, Is he to whom the Consideration or ordering of any matter is referred, either by some Court, or consent of Parties, to whom it belongeth: as in Parliament, a Bill being read, is either consented unto, and passed or denied, or neither of both, but referred to the consideration of some certain men appointed by the House further to examine it, who thereupon are called Commitees by *West. part.* 2.*Symb.Tit. Chancery Sect.* 144.

Committee of the King. This word seemeth to be somewhat strangely used in *Kitchin*, *fol.* 160. where the Widow of the Kings Tenant being dead, is called the Committee of the King, that is, one committed by ancient Law of the Land, to the Kings care and protection.

Committee of a Lunatic, is he to whom the care of the Lunatick and his Estate are committed.

Commodities, Commoditates. Bona res. mercimonia.

A common, Commune, is, n. Communia, æ, f. *Lex.* 32.

Common signifieth in our Common Law that soil or water whereof the use is Common to this or that Town, or Lordship, as Common of Pasture, *Communia pasturæ Brac. lib.* 4. *cap.* 19. & 40. Common of Fishing, *Communia piscariæ*, *Idem. lib.* 2. *cap.* 34. Common of Turbary (or digging of Turves) *Communia Turbariæ*, Common of Estovers, *Communia Estoviorum*, *Lex.* 32.

To common, Communio, are. *Ra. Ent.* 539.

A commoner, Communiarius, ii, m.

Common bench (*or court of common pleas*) Bancus communis vel Communia Placita, *An.* 2. *Ed.* 3. *cap.* 11. It is the Kings Court now held in *Westminster-Hall*, but in ancient time moveable, as appeareth by the Statute called *Mag. Chart. cap.* 11. As also *Anno* 2 *Ed.* 3. *cap.* 11. and *Pupilla oculi*, *part* 5. *cap.* 22. but Mr. *Gwin* in the Preface to his Readings saith, that untill the time that *Henry* III. granted the Charter, there were but two Courts of Justice in all, whereof one was the Exchequer, and the other the Kings Bench, which was then called *Curia Domini Regis*, and *Aula Regia*, because it followed the Court or King, and that upon the grant of that Charter, the Court of Common Pleas was erected and setled in one Place certain, *viz*. At *Westminster*, whereso-ever the King lay. Thereupon M. *Gwin, ut supra*, saith, that after all the Writs ran, *Quod sit coram Justiciariis meis, apud Westmonasterium*, whereas before, the Party was commanded by them to appear, *coram me, vel Justiciariis meis*, simply without addition of place, as he well observeth out of *Glanvile* and *Bracton*, the one Writing in *Henry* the Second's time, before this Court was erected, the other in the latter end of *Henry* the Third's time, who erected this Court. All civil Causes, both real and personal, are or were in former times tryed in this Court, according to the strict Law of this Realm. And by *Fortescue*, *cap*. 50. It seemeth to have been the only Court for real Causes.

Common Law, Communis Lex. Hath three divers significations, which see in the Author of the new Terms of Law.

Commons, Demensum, i, n. So called because it is meat in Common, among Societies, as Universities, Inns of Court, Doctors Commons, &c.

A company (or fellowship) Societas, atis, f.

A company of soldiers, Turma, æ, f.

To lead a company, Ordine deducere.

A compass, Circinus, i, m. An Instrument so called, because it serves to make a round circle or compass about.

A Pilot, or Mariners compass, Index nauticus. Pyxis nautica. Index viatorius.

To compass, or bring about, Compasso, are. *Co. Ent*. 351.

Competent (or sufficient) Competens, entis, n.

To complain, Queror, eris, vel ere, questus sum, queri.

A complaint, Questus, us, m. Querela, æ, f.

To compose, Compono, ere.

A compositor, or composer, Compŏsitor, oris, m. Typotheta, æ, f.

Comprised, Comprisatus, a, um.

A compound bolus, Compositus bolus.

De computo reddendo, Is a Writ so called of the effect, because it compelleth a Bailiff, Chamberlain, or Receiver, to yield his account, *Old nat. brev. fol*. 58. It is founded upon the Statute of *Westm*. 2 *Ca*. 2. *Anno* 13. *Edw*. 1. It lies also against Executors of Executors, *anno* 5 *Ed*. 3. *Stat. de Provis. Victual. ca*. 5. and against the Guardian in Soccage for wast made in the Minority of the heir, *Marbl. ca*. 17. and see further in what case it lyeth, *Regist. Orig. fol*. 135. *Old*

Old nat. brev. ubi supra, & *Fitz. Herb. nat. brev. f.* 126.

CON.

To conceal (or keep close) Concelo, are.

A concealment, Concelamentum, i, n. *Fle.* 22, 23.

Concealers, Concelatores, m. pl. In the Common Law are such at find out concealed Lands, that is, such Lands as privily are kept from the King by common persons, having nothing to shew for them, *An.* 39. *Eliz. cap.* 22. They are so called, *à Concelando,* of Concealing, by an Antiphrasis or contrary speaking, because indeed they do not conceal such Lands but reveal them, *Ut mons à movendo per Antiphrasim,* or rather they are so called because they enquire after concealed Land.

To concern, Concerno, are.

Concerning, Concernens, tis, f.

Concerned, Concernatus, a, um.

To conclude, Concludo, ere.

Concord (or agreement) Concordia, æ, f. Is in the Common Law by a peculiar signification defined to be the very agreement between Parties that intend the Levying of a Fine of Lands one to the other, how and in what manner the Land shall pass, for in the form thereof many things are to be considered. *West. part* 2. *Symb. Titul. Finis ad Concord. Sect.* 30, whom read at large. Concord is also an agreement made upon any Trespass committed between two or more, and it is divided into a Concord Executory, and a Concord executed, see *Plowden Casu Reniger,* & *Fogassa, fol.* 5, 6. where it appeareth by some opinion, that the one bindeth not, as being imperfect, and the other absolute, and tieth the parties, and yet by some other Opinion in the same case it is affirmed, that Agreements Executory are perfect, and do no less bind than agreements executed, *fol.* 8. *b.*

Concubinage, Concubinatus, ûs, m. In our Common Law it is an exception against her that sueth for her Dowry, whereby she is alledged that she was not a Wife lawfully married to the party in whose Lands she seeks to be endowed, but his Concubine. *Britton cap.* 107. *Bract. lib.* 4. *tract.* 6. *cap.* 8.

Condition, Conditio, onis, f. Condition is a restraint or Bridle annexed to a thing, so that by the not performance thereof the Party to the Condition shall receive prejudice and loss, and by doing of the same, Commodity and advantage. Terms of Law.

A conduit for water, Aquæductus, ûs, m. Aquagium, ii, n.

A conduit pipe, Colimbus, i, m.

To confederate, Confœdero, are.

A confectioner, Dulciarius Pistor. Opustorius, ii, m.

Confects, Confecta.

A confession, Confessio, onis, f.

Confidence (*or trust*) Confidentia, æ, f.

To have confidence (*or trust*) Confido, ere.

To confirm, Confirmo, are.

Confirmation, Confirmatio, onis, f. Confirmation cometh of the verb *Confirmare, quod est firmum facere*, and therefore it is said that *Confirmatio omnes supplet defectus*, *licet id quod actum est, ab initio non valuit*. It is a conveyance of an Estate or Right *in Esse*, whereby a voidable Estate is made sure and unavoidable, or whereby a particular Estate is increased. It is a strengthning of an Estate formerly had, and yet voidable though not presently void. *Cook on Lit. lib.* 3. *c.* 9. *Sect.* 5. 15. *Quælibet confirmatio aut est perficiens Crescens*, *aut diminuens*, *Fitz. nat. brev. fol.* 169. 1. *Perficiens*, As if Feoffee upon Condition make Feoffment over, and the Feoffer confirm the Estate of the second Feoffee; so if Disseisee confirm the Estate of the Disseisor, or his Feoffee. 2. *Crescens* doth enlarge the state of a Tenant, as Tenant at Will, to hold for years, or Tenant for years, to hold for life. 3. *Diminuens*, as where the Lord of whom the land is holden, confirms the Estate of his Tenant to hold by a less Rent, *Cook lib.* 9. *Rep. Beaumonts case*, 3. 142.

To confute (*or disprove*) Confuto, are.

Congleton (in *Cheshire*) Condate.

To conglutinate (*or joyn together*) Conglutino, are.

To congratulate, Congratulo, are.

A congregation (*or assembly*) Congregatio, onis, f.

A cony, Cuniculus, i, m.

A little cony, Cuniculina, æ, f.

A conjuration or conjuring (*an exorcising*) Conjuratio, onis, f.

Conjuration in the Common Law is used for such as have personal Conference with the Devil, or evil Spirit, to know any secret, or effect any purpose, *Anno* 5. *Eliz. cap.* 16. And the difference between Conjuration and Witchcraft, is, that the Conjurer seemeth by Prayers and Invocation of Gods powerful names to compel the Devil, to say or do what he commandeth him. The Witch dealeth rather by a friendly and voluntary conference or agreement between him or her and the Devil or Familiar to have his or her turn served in lieu or stead of blood, or other gift offered unto him, especially of his or her soul: So that a Conjurer compacts for curiosity to know secrets, and work miracles; and the witch of meer malice

malice to do mischief; and both these differ from Inchanters or Sorcerers, because the two former have personal Conference with the Devil, and the other meddles but with Medicines and Ceremonial Forms of words called Charms, without Apparition.

To conjure (or exorcise a spirit) Conjuro, are.

A conjurer, Conjurator, oris, m.

A conigree, Cunicularium, ii, n. *Fle.* 160.

Connaught Province (in *Ireland*) Conacta, Connatchtia.

Connor (in *Ireland*) Connaria, Conneria.

Conway river (in *Wales*) Conovius, Novius, Tœsobius, Toisobius, Toisovius.

To conquer, Conquestor, ari. *Pry.* 413.

A conqueror, Expugnator, oris, m. Superator, oris, m.

A conquest, Conquestus, i, m.

Consanguinity (or kindred by blood or birth) Consanguinitas, atis, f.

To consecrate (or make holy) Consecro, are. Sacro, are.

A consecrating, Consecratio, onis, f.

Consecrated, Consecratus, a, um.

Conservatour (or conserver of the peace) Conservator vel Custos pacis, Is he that hath an especial charge by vertue of his Office, to see the Kings Peace kept, which Peace Learned Mr. *Lamberd* defineth in effect, to be a with-holding or abstinence from that injurious force and violence, which boisterous and unruly persons are in their natures prone to use towards others, were they not restrained by Laws and fear of punishment. Of the Conservators he further saith thus, That before the time of King *Edward* III. who first erected Justices of Peace, there were sundry persons that by the Common Law had Interest in keeping of the Peace. Of these some had that charge, as incident to their Offices, which they did bear, and so included within the same, that they were nevertheless called by the name of their Office only. Some others had it simply, as of it self, and were thereof named *custodes pacis*, Wardens or Conservators of the Peace. The former and latter sort he again subdivideth, which read in his *Eirenarcha, lib.* 1. *cap.* 3.

To conserve (or keep) Conservo, are.

Conserves, Condita, Salgama, orum. i. e. Things Conserved or Condited to serve ones turn at time of need, as Grapes, Cherries, Plumbs, &c.

A consistory, Consistorium, ii, n. (i. e.) A Councel-house of Ecclesiastical Persons.

Consolidation, Consolidatio, onis, f. In our Common Law it is used for the combining and uniting of two benifices in one, *Vid. Brook. Tit. union.* The word is taken from the Civil Law, where it signifieth properly an uniting of the possession

ſion, occupation or profit with the property, for example, If a Man have by Legacy, *Uſufructum fundi*, and afterward I buy the Property or Fee-ſimple (as we call it) of the heir, *Hoc caſu conſolidatio fieri dicitur. Sect.* 3. *de uſufructu in Inſtit.*

Conſpiracy, Conſpiratio, onis, f. Though in Latin and French it is uſed for an Agreement of men to do any thing, either good or bad, yet in our Law Books it is always taken in the evil part, It is defined *Anno* 34. *Ed. prim. Statute* 2. To be an agreement of ſuch as doe confederate or bind themſelves, by Oath, Covenant or other Alliance, that every of them ſhall bear and aid the other falſly and maliciouſly to Indict, or falſly to move or maintain Pleas; and alſo ſuch as cauſe Children within age to appeal men of Felony, whereby they are Impriſoned and much grieved, and ſuch as receive men in the Countries with Liveries, or Fees to maintain their malicious enterpriſe; and this extendeth it ſelf as well to the takers as the givers, and Stewards and Bayliffs of great Lords, which by their Seignory, Office or Power, undertake to bear or maintain Quarrels, Pleas or Debates, that concern other Parties, than ſuch as touch the Eſtate of their Lords, or themſelves, *Anno* 4. *Ed.* 3. *cap.* 11. *Anno* 3. *H.* 7. *cap.* 13. Of this ſee more, *Anno* 1. *H.* 5. *c.* 3. and *Anno* 18. *H.* 6. *cap.* 12. As alſo in the new Book of Entries, *Vid.* Conſpiracy. And being thus taken as aforementioned, it is confounded with Maintenance and Champerty, but in a more ſpecial ſignification, it is taken for a Confederacy of two at the leaſt, falſly to Indict one, or to procure one to be Indicted of Felony. And the puniſhment of Conſpiracy upon an Indictment of Felony at the Kings ſuit, is that the Party attainted Leeſe his Frank Law, to the intent that he be not Impannelled upon Juries or Aſſiſes, or ſuch like employments for the teſtifying of Truth, and if he have to do in the Kings Court, that he make his Attorney, and that his Lands, Goods and Chattels, be ſeiſed into the Kings hands, his Lands Eſtreaped (if he find no better favour) his Trees razed, his Body committed to Priſon. 27. *lib. Aſſiſ.* 59. *Crompt. Juſt. of Peace*, *f.* 156. b. This is called Villanous Judgment, or Puniſhment. But if the Party grieved ſue upon the Writ of Conſpiracy, then ſee *Fitz. nat. brev. fol.* 114. *D.* 115. *I.* Conſpiracy may be alſo in caſes of leſs weight, *Idem fol.* 116. *a.* And ſee Frank Law.

Conſpiratione, Is a Writ that lieth againſt Conſpirators, *Fitz. nat. brev. fol.* 114. *D. Crompt. Juriſd. fol.* 209. See alſo the *Regiſt. fol.* 34.

To conſpire, Conſpiro, are.

A conſpirator, Conſpirator, oris, m.

A

A constable, Constabularius, ii, m. *Spel.* 170. *Lex.* 35. Constable comes of two old *Saxon* words, *Kinning*, which signifieth King, and *Stable*, Stability; as the Stability of the King and Kingdom. The common Law requireth that every Constable be *Idoneus homo*, i. e. apt and fit for exercise of the said Office; and he is said in Law to be *Idoneus*, which hath three things, Honesty, Science and Ability. 1. Honesty, to execute his Office truly without Malice, Affection or Partiality. 2. Science, to know what he ought to do duly. 3. Ability, as well in Substance or Estate as in Body, to execute his Office, when need is, diligently, and not through Impotency or Indigence to neglect it; for if poor men, which live by the labour of their hands, be elected to this Office, they will rather permit Felons and other Malefactors to escape, and neglect the execution of their Office in other points, than intermit their Labour, by which their Wife and Children live. The Office and Authority of High and Petty Constables remaineth, notwithstanding the death of the King, for their Authority is by the common Law, and not by Commission: So also of Mayors, Bailiffs in Towns corporate, &c. *Cook* 8 *Rep. Griesties case. Dalt. Just. of P. Leigh Philol. Com. f.* 47, 48.

Constable of Windsor *castle*, Constabularius Castri Domini Regis Regalis de Winsor, *Staunf. Pl. Cr. fol.* 152. and *Anno* 1. *H.* 4. *cap.* 13. Stow's *annals*, 812.

Constableship, Constabularia, æ, f. *Pry.* 71.

Of or belonging to a constable, Constabulariatus, a, um. *Pry.* 71.

A vice-constable, Vice-constabularius, ii, m.

Constance (a womans name) Constancia, æ, f.

Constantine (a mans name) Constantinus, i, m.

To constitute (or appoint) Constituo, ere.

Consuetudinibus & Servitiis, Is a Writ of right close, which lieth against the Tenant that deforceth his Lord of the Rent, or service due unto him, of this see more at large in *Old nat. brev. fol.* 77. *Fitz. eod. fol.* 151. and the *Regist. Orig. fol.* 159.

To consult, Consulto, are.

A consultation, Consultatio, onis, f.

Consultation, Is a Writ whereby a Cause being formerly removed by Prohibition from the Ecclesiastical Court (or Court Christian) to the Kings Court, is returned thither again: For the Judges of the Kings Court, if upon comparing the Libel with the suggestion of the Party, they do find the suggestion false, or not proved, and therefore the Cause to be wrongfully called from the Court Christian; then upon this Consultation or Deliberation,

tion, they Decree it to be returned again Whereupon the Writ in this caſe obtained, is called a Conſultation, of this read the *Regiſter fol* 44, 45, &c. *Uſque fol.* 58. *Old nat. brev. fol.* 32. and *Fitz. eodem, fol.* 50.

A conſulter, Conſultor, oris, m.

To conſume (or ſpend) Conſumo, ere.

To conſummate (or fully accompliſh) Conſummo, are.

A conſummation, Conſummatio, onis, f.

To contain, Contineo, ere.

Contenement, Contenementum, i, n. Seemeth to be the Freehold Land which lieth to a mans Tenement, or Dwelling-houſe that is in his own Occupation; for in *Magna Charta cap.* 14. you have theſe words, A Free man ſhall not be amerced for a ſmall fault, but after the quantity of the fault, and for a great fault, after the manner thereof, ſaving to him his Contenement, or Freehold. And a Merchant likewiſe ſhall be amerced, ſaving to him his Merchandiſe; And any other Villain than ours ſhall be amerced, ſaving his Wainage, if he take him to our mercy. *Vid.* alſo *Bracton, lib.* 3. *tract.* 2. *cap.* 1. *numb.* 3. *John Eimericus in Proceſſu judiciario, cap. de executione ſenten.* 79. *num.* 11.

The continent or firm main land, that is no iſle, nor ſeparated by ſea, Continens, entis, f.

To continue (or perſiſt) Continuo, are.

Continual, Continuus, a, um.

Continual claim, Continuum Clameum, Is a claim made from time to time, within every year and day, to Land or other thing, which in ſome reſpect we cannot attain without danger. For example, if I be diſſeiſed of Land, into which, tho' I have right unto it, I dare not enter for fear of beating, it behooveth me to hold on my right of entry to the beſt opportunity of me and mine Heirs, by approaching as near it as I can once every year, as long as I live, and ſo I ſave the right of entry to mine heirs, *vid. Terms of Law*, See more in *Littleton, verbo* continual Claim, and the new Book of Entries, *ibid.* and *Fleta, lib.* 6. *cap.* 53.

Continuance, Continuatio, onis, f. Continuance ſeemeth to be uſed in the Common Law, as *Prorogatio* in the Civil Law. For example, Continuance untill the next Aſſiſe, *Fitz. nat. brev. fol.* 154. *f.* and 244. *d.* in both which places it is ſaid, that if a Record in the Treaſury be alleged by the one Party, and denied by the other, a *Certiorari* ſhall be ſued to the Treaſurer, and the Chamberlain of the Exchequer: And if they certifie not in the Chancery, that ſuch a Record is there, or that it is likely to be in the Tower, the King ſhall ſend to the Juſtices repeating the

the *Certiorari*, and command them to continue the Assise. In this signification it is likewise used by *Kitchin, fol.* 202. and 199. and also *Anno* 11. *H.* 6. *cap.* 4.

Contract, Contractus, ûs, m. It is a Covenant or Agreement with a lawfull consideration or cause, *West. part. prim. Symbol. lib.* 1. *sect.* 10. Contract (called by the Civilians *Acceptilatio*) is an agreement between Parties concerning Goods or Lands for money or other recompence. It is called a Contract because by Covenanting *diversæ voluntates in unum contrahuntur*. It is a Bargain or Covenant between two Parties, where one thing is given for another, which is called *Quid pro quo*, as if you sell my Horse for 20 Shillings, you may keep the Horse till the other have paid the Money. The want of recompence causeth it to be but *nudum pactum, unde non oritur actio*, for if a man make promise to me that I shall have 20 Shillings, and after I ask it, and he will not deliver it, yet you shall never have any action to recover it, because this promise was no contract, but a bare promise; but if any thing were given for the 20 Shillings, tho' it were but to the value of a Penny, then it had been a good Contract. If he to whom the promise is made have a charge by reason of the promise, which he hath also performed, then in that case he shall have an Action for the thing that was promised, though he that made the promise have no Worldly profit by it. As if a man say to another, heal such a poor man of his Disease, or make an highway, and I shall give thee thus much; and if he do it, I think an Action lieth at the Common Law, *D. and Student, cap.* 4. This word *Pro* makes a Contract conditional, as if I Covenant to make an Estate *pro maritagio habendo*; if the Marriage take not effect, I shall be discharged of this Covenant. So if an annuity be granted, *pro consilio impendendo*, stop the Counsel giving, and stop the annuity; also if a man grant a way over his Land, and *pro chimino illo habendo*, he granteth to him a rent-charge: if one be stopped, the other is stopped; so it is in Contracts. As for a Hawk to be delivered me at such a day, you shall have my Horse at *Christmas*; if the Hawk be not delivered at the day, you shall not have an Action for the Horse. The Infants Contract for his Meat, Apparel, and necessaries is good, if he be of the age of fourteen years.

A contract of marriage, Sponsio, onis, f.

Contrary, Contrarius, a, um.

To do contrary, Contrario, are. *Ra. Ent.* 531. *Co. Lit.* 107.

A con-

A contribution, Contributio.

To contrive, Contrivo, are. *Ra. Ent.* 207.

Contrivances, Machinationes.

Controller of the houshold, Contrarotulator Hospitii Domini Regis, *Vid. Pl. Cor. fol.* 52. and *Anno* 6. *H.* 4. *cap.* 3.

Controller of the hamper, Contrarotulator Hamperii, He is an Officer in the Chancery, attending on the Lord Chancellor or Keeper daily, in Term time, and days appointed for sealing. His Office is to take all things sealed from the Clerk of the Hanaper, inclosed in Bags of Leather, as it is mentioned in the said Clerks Office, and opening the Bags to note the just number, and especial effects of all things so received, and to enter the same into a special Book, with all the duties appertaining to his Majesty, and other Officers for the same, and so chargeth the Clerk of the Hanaper or Hamper with the same.

Controller of the Pipe, Contrarotulator Pipæ, He is an Officer of the Exchequer that writeth out Summons twice every year to the Sheriffs to Levy the Farms and Debts of the Pipe, and also keepeth a Controlment of the Pipe.

Controller of the Pell, Contrarotulator Pellis. Is also an Officer of the Exchequer, of which sort there be two, *viz.* the two Chamberlains Clerks, that do or should keep a Controlment of the Pell of Receipts and goings out, and in one word this Officer was originally one that took notes of any other Officers Accounts, or Receipts, to the intent to discover him if he dealt amiss, and was ordained for the Princes better security: Howsoever the name since may be in some things otherwise applyed, *Vid. Fleta. lib.* 1. *cap.* 18. *in prin. Anno* 12. *Ed.* 3. *c.* 3. *Gregorii Syntag. lib.* 3. *cap.* 6. *num.* 6.

Controlment, Controllamentum, i, n.

Controversie, Controversia, æ, f.

Convenient, Conveniens, entis, Part.

Conveniencie, Convenientia, æ, f.

A conventicle, Conventiculum, i, n.

To convey, Conveio, are.

A conveyance, Conveiancia, æ, f. *Co. Ent.* 23. (*i. e.*) A Deed which transfers an Estate.

A conviction, Convictio, onis, f.

Conviction is either when a Man is Outlawed, and appeareth, and confesseth, or else is found Guilty by the Inquest, *Crompton* out of Judge *Dyer's Commentaries*, 275. Conviction and Attainder are often confounded. *Crompt. Just. of Peace*, *fol.* 9. 2. *lib.* 4. *fol.* 46. But *Staunford. Pl. Cor. fol.* 108. maketh a difference between Attainder and Conviction in these words, And note the diversity between Attainder and

Conviction

Conviction, &c. For Attainder is larger than Conviction. A Man by our ancient Laws was said to be Convicted presently upon the Verdict (Guilty) but not to be Attainted upon Conviction, until it appeared that he was no Clerk, or being a Clerk, and demanded of his Ordinary, could not purge himself. So that a Man was not Attainted upon Conviction, except he were no Clerk.

A convocation (or calling together) Convocatio, onis, f.

A convocation house, Domus Convocationis, It is the house wherein the whole Clergy is assembled for Consultation upon matters Ecclesiastical in time of Parliament, it consisteth of two distinct houses, one called the higher Convocation house, where the Archbishops and Bishops sit severally by themselves; the other the lower Convocation-house, where all the rest of the Clergy are bestowed, see *Prolocut.*

A convoy, Commeatus, us, m.

A convoy (or pass) Salvigardia, æ, f. Salvus conductus.

C O O.

A cook, Coquus, i, m.

A woman cook, Fuma, æ, f.

A ship cook, Fŏcarius, ii, m.

A cooks shop, Popina, æ, f.

A coop, where poultry are kept, Gallinarium, ii, n. Sāginārium, ii, n.

A cooper, Vietor, oris, m. Doliarĭus, ii, m.

C O P.

Coparcenary, Coparcenaria, æ, f.

A coparcener, Coparticeps, ĭpis, adj. *Co. Ent.* 477. 711. Otherwise called Parceners, and in Common Law are such, as have equal Portion in the Inheritance of their Ancestor, and as *Littleton* in the beginning of his third Book saith) Parceners be either by Law, or by Custom. Parceners by Law are the Issue Female, which (when there is no heir Male) come in equality to the Lands of their Ancestors, *Bract. lib.* 2. *cap.* 30. Parceners by custom, are those that by custom of the Country challenge equal part in such Lands, as in *Kent,* the custom called *Gavelkinde.* This is called *adæquatio,* amongst the *Feudists, Hot. in verbis feudal, verbo adæquatio,* and amongst the *Civilians,* it is termed *Familiæ judicium, quod inter cohæredes ideo redditur, ut & hæreditas dividatur, & quod alterum alteri dare facere oportebit, præstetur. Hotoman.* Of these two you may see *Littleton* at large in the first and second Chapters of his third Book. And *Britton, cap.* 27. intituled *De heritage devisable.* The Crown of *England* is not Subject to Coparcenary, *Anno* 25. *H.* 8. *cap.* 22.

A cope, Capa, æ, f. *Spil.* 137. *Cow.* 95.

A copy

A copy of a writing, Copia, æ, f.

To copy, Ad Copiandum. *Co. Lit.* 57. 1 *Mon.* 597. Transcribo, ere.

A printers first copy, Primum Exemplar.

A copy of the authors own hand, Autographum, i, n.

Copy-hold, Tenura per copiam rotulorum curiæ, Is a Tenure, for which the Tenant hath nothing to shew, but the Copies of the Rolls, made by the Steward of his Lords Court. For the Steward, as he enrolleth and maketh remembrances of all other things done in the Lords Court, so he doth also of such Tenants as are admitted in the Court, to any parcel of Land or Tenement, belonging to the Mannor, and the Transcript of this is called the Court-Roll, the Copy whereof the Tenant taketh from him, and keepeth as his only evidence. *Co. lib.* 4. *fol.* 25. *b.* This Tenure is called a base Tenure, because it holdeth at the will of the Lord, it was wont to be called *Tenure in Villenage*, *Kitchen fol.* 80. *cap.* Copy-holds. *Fitz. herb. nat. brev. fol.* 12. *B. C.* The doing of fealty by a Copy-holder, proveth, that a Copy-holder, so long as he observes the custom of the Mannor, and payeth his services, hath a fixed Estate, *Co. on Lit. p.* 63. Although in the Judgment of the Law, he hath but Estate for will, yet Custom hath so established and fixed his Estate, that by the custom of the Mannor, it is discendible to him and his Heirs; and therefore his Estate is not meerly *ad Voluntatem Domini*, but *secundum consuetudinem manerii*, and by keeping the Custom he shall inherit the Land, as well as he that hath Frank-Tenement at Common Law, for *Consuetudo est altera Lex.* The Stile of a Copy-holder imports three things.

1. *Nomen*, his name.
2. *Originem*, his beginning.
3. *Titulum*, his assurance.

1. His name is Tenant by Copy of Court Roll.

2. His beginning is, *Ad Voluntatem Domini*, for at the beginning he was but Tenant at the will of the Lord.

3. His Title or Assurance, *secundum consuetudinem manerii*, for the custom of the Mannor hath fixed his Estate, and assured the Land to him as long as he doth his service and duties, and performs the custom of the Mannor, *Cook* 4. *Rep. Copy-hold Case.* *Cook* 9. *Rep.* Combes *Case.* If a Copy-holder be a Popish Recusant, his Copy-hold is forfeit, for his life, to the Lord of the Mannor, if the Lord be not Recusant, and if the Lord be, then to the King. 35. *Eliz. c.* 1. *Kitchin, fol.* 81. *cap.* Tenants *per verge.*

Copy-holds, Custumaria Tenementa.

Copy-holders, Tenentes Custumarii, *Ra. Ent.* 131. *Co. Ent.* 645 657.

Copy-holder, or Tenant by Copy of Court Roll, is he which is admitted Tenant of any Lands, or Tenements within a Mannor, that time out of mind by use and custom of the said Mannor, have been demiseable and demised to such as will take the same in Fee, in Fee-tail, for Life, Years, or at Will, according to the custom of the said Mannor, by Copy of Court-Roll of the same Mannor. *West. part* 1. *Symb. lib.* 2. *Sect.* 646.

A copice (or little wood) Copicia, æ, f.

A coping, Summitas, atis, f.

Copper, Cuprum, i, n. Orichalcum, ci, n.

Of copper, Cupreus, a, um.

Pliant copper, Cuprum Ductitium.

Copper wire, Filum Orichalci.

Any copper or brass thing, Æramentum, i, n.

Copperas, Vitriolum, i, n. Chalcanthum, i, n.

C O Q.

Coquet *Isle, on the coast of* Northumberland, Coqueda Insula.

Coquet *river* (in *Northumberland*) Coqueda, Coquedus.

C O R.

Coral, Corallium, ii, n.

A corbell, corbet, or corbill, Mutulus, li, m. In Masonry it is a jutting out like a Bragget (as Carpenters call it) or shouldering piece in Timber work.

Cordage or tackle of a ship, Armamenta & Instrumenta navis.

A cord (or string) Corda, æ, f. 1 *Mon.* 850 *bis*, 2 *Mon.* 349.

The cord wherewith the foot of the sail is tied, Propes, is, m.

A cord at which any thing hangeth, Pendiculus, li, m.

The cord wherewith a sail is spread, Podea, æ, f.

A cord of wood, Corda ligni. *Co. Ent.* 36. Arcus sive Corda. Lex. 20.

Corebridge (in *Northumberland*) Coria, Corstopilti, Corstopitum, Curia, Curia Ottadinorum.

Cork *city* (in *Ireland*) Corcagia, Corragia.

Of Cork, Corcagiensis, Corcensis.

Cork, Suber, eris, n.

Corn on the ground in the blade, Bladum, i, n.

Land where corn grows, Terra bladata, *Ra. Ent.* 561.

Standing corn, Blada crescentia. Seges, etis, f.

An ear of corn, Spica, æ, f.

The beard of corn, Arista, æ, f.

Corn without beard, Spicæ muticæ.

Seed corn, Frumentum Sementicum.

Corn in swaths or straw, Blada in Garbis.

A sheaf of corn, Garba, æ, f. Fascis spicarum.

A gavel, or handful of corn, Palmata vel manipulus Bladi.

A thrave of corn, Trava Bladi, 2 *Mon.* 391. 1 *Mon.* 985.

A rick of corn, Strues Núbilarum.

A corn field, Arvum, i, n.

An heap of corn, Collecta Bladi, 1 *Mon.* 782.

Corn of all sorts, Frumentum, i, n.

A blasting of corn, Ustrigo, inis, f.

To mow or reap corn, Blada metere.

The knot in the bottom of a ear of corn, Uruncus, ci, m.

A corn-chandler, Frumentarius, ii, m.

A corner, Cornerium, ii, n. Angulus, i, m. 1 *Mon.* 408. 685. 817. 2 *Mon.* 1038.

Corners standing out, Anguli prostantes.

A corner jutting, Projectura Angularis.

Cornered, Angŭlatilis, le, adj.

Full of corners or nooks, Angŭlōsus, a, um.

Crooked having corners (or set in a corner) Angŭlāris, re, adj.

A triangle or figure with three corners, Triangŭlum, li, n.

Having three corners, Triangulus, a, um.

Six cornered, Sexangŭlātus, a, um.

Of six corners, Hexagonus, a, um.

A cornet, Buccina, æ, f.

A cornet of horsemen, and the ensign of the company of horse, Vexillatio, onis, f.

A cornet or coffin of Paper, such as Grocers bind up small Wares in, Cornus, ûs & i, f.

A cornice, Summitas fenestræ.

Cornwall, Corinea, Cornubia, Cornwallia, Occidua, Wallia.

A coroner, Coronator, oris, m. Coroner is an ancient Officer of Trust, and of great Authority, ordained to be a principal Conservator or keeper of the Peace, to bear Record of the Pleas of the Crown. Although by the Law the Coroner cannot enquire of any Felony; but the death of a man, yet it hath been said, that in *Northumberland* they enquire of all Felonies, but this Authority they maintain by Prescription. If a Man be killed or drowned in the Arms or Creeks of the Sea, where a Man may see Land from the one part to the other, the Coroner shall enquire thereof, and not the Admiral, because the Country thereof may well have knowledge. His name is derived a *Corona*, because he is an Officer of the Crown, and hath Conusance of some Pleas, which are called *Placita Coronæ*, *Cooks 2. part of instit. cap.* 17. See more there. He is so called, because he deals principally with Pleas of the matters

ters concerning the Crown, *Cooks* 4. *part of Instit. cap.* 59. Terms of Law. The Empannelling of the Inquest, and the view of the Body, and the giving of the Verdict, is commonly in the street, in an open place, and in *Corona populi*, but this name rather cometh because the death of every Subject by violence is accounted to touch the Crown of the Prince, and to be a detriment unto it, the Prince accounting that his Strength, Power and Crown doth consist in the force of his People, and the maintenance of them in Security and Peace, *Smith's Commonwealth of* England, *cap.* 24. Coroners remain Conservators of the Peace within the County where they are Coroners, notwithstanding the Kings death, for they are made by the Kings Writ, and not by Commission, as Justices are, whose Authority is determined by the death of the King, for by the Commission he maketh them, *Justiciarios suos*, so that he being once dead, they are no more his Justices. *Dalton's Just. of P.* The Statute giveth the Coroner thirteen Shillings and four pence for taking Inquisition, *Super visum corporis.*

A corporal in an army, Armorum Doctor.

Corpus cum causa, Is a Writ issuing out of the Chancery, to remove both the body and the Record, touching the cause of any man lying in Execution upon a Judgment for debt, into the Kings Bench, &c. there to lie untill he hath satisfied the Judgment, *Fitz. nat. brev. fol.* 251. *E.*

To correct (*or punish*) Corrigo, ere.

To correct (*or amend*) Emendo, are.

A corrector, Corrector, oris, m.

To corroborate (*or strengthen*) Corroboro, are.

Corroboratives, Roborantia.

Corroded (*gnawn or bitten about*) Corrosus, a, um.

Corrosive, Corrodens, sive Corrodendi vim habens.

A corslet, Lorica, æ, f. Thorax, acis, m.

Corslets, or Pikemen, Milites hastati.

C O S.

A cosmographer, Cosmographus, i, m.

Costs, Custagium, ii, n. Custus, i, m. *Spel.* 188. *Reg.* 112. *Try.* 49, 50.

Costs and charges of suit, Misæ & custagia sectæ.

Other costs and charges, Alia onera & custagia.

A costardmonger (*or fruiterer*) Pomarius, ii, m.

C O T.

A cot or cottage, Chota, æ, f. Cotagium, ii, n. *Spel.* 180.

A cottage (*or farm with some land belonging to it*) Cothlanda & Cothsethlanda, æ, f.

A cottager, Cotarius, ii, m. Coterellus, i, m. *Spel.* 180. A Cottager is ſuch a one as dwelleth in a Cottage, that is, a houſe without Land belonging to it, *Anno* 4 *Ed.* 1. *Stat.* 1. but by a later Statute no man may hold a Cottage, but he muſt lay 4 Acres of ground unto it. 31. *Eliz. cap.* 7.

Cottagers that hold bord lands, Bordarii, m. pl. Bores & Borduanni, m. pl.

Cottages of ſods, Tiguria cespitum.

Cotton or bombaſt, Xylum, i, n. Goſſipium, ii, n.

COV.

A covenant or bargain, Conventio. Covenant is an agreement made by Deed in Writing, and ſealed between two Parties. A Covenant in Law is that which the Law intendeth to be made, though in words it be not expreſſed. As if the *Leſſour* do deviſe and grant, &c. to the Leſſee for a certain time or term of years. The Law intendeth a Covenant on the Leſſours part, that the Leſſee ſhall, during his whole term, quietly enjoy his Leaſe againſt all lawfull encumbrance. Covenant in Fact, is that which is expreſly agreed between the Parties. There is alſo a Covenant meerly perſonal, and a Covenant real. *Fitz. nat. brev. fol.* 145. And he ſeems to ſay, that a Covenant real is whereby a Man tieth himſelf to paſs a thing real, as Land or Tenements, as a Covenant to Levy a Fine of Land, &c. A Covenant meerly Perſonal of the other ſide, is where a Man Covenanteth with another by Deed, to build him a houſe, or any other thing, or to ſerve him, or to Infeoffe him, &c. Inſtruments of Covenants you may ſee many in *Weſt. part* 1. *Symb. lib.* 2. *Sect.* 100. See alſo the new Book of Entries *verbo* Covenant.

Covenant is the name of a Writ that lieth for the breach of any Covenant in Writing, *Fitz. herb. nat. brev. fol.* 145.

A cover, Adopertorium, ii, n.

A cover (or covering) Obſtrāgŭlum, li, n. Operimentum, i, n.

A covering of a houſe, Tectum, i, n. Imbricium, ii, n.

To cover, Tĕgo, xi, ctum, ere.

A coverlet, Toral, ſive Torale, is, n. Strāgŭlum, li, n. Tĕges, ĕtis, f.

A covert for deer or other beaſts, Umbraculum, li, n. Lătĭbulum, li, n. Dumetum, ti, n.

Coverture, Coopertura, æ, f. Coverture is a *French* word, and ſignifieth any thing that covereth, a Apparel, a coverlet, &c. And cometh likewiſe from the French *Couvrir*, i. e. to cover. In the Common Law it is proper-

ly

ly applied to the Estate and Condition of a married Woman, who by the Laws of the Realm is *in potestate viri*, under-Covert Baron, and therefore disabled to make any bargain or contract without her Husbands consent or privity, or without his allowance or confirmation. *Broke, hoc Tit per totum.* And *Bracton* saith, that *Omnia quæ sunt uxoris, sunt ipsius viri, nec habet uxor potestatem sui, sed vir. lib.* 2. *cap.* 15. and that *Vir est caput mulieris, lib.* 4. *cap.* 24. And again, in any Law matter, *Sine viro illa respondere non potest, lib.* 5. *tract.* 2. *cap.* 3. And *Tract.* 5. *cap.* 25. *Ejusdem libri.* And if the Husband alienate the Wives Land, she cannot gainsay, during his life. *Vid. Cui ante divortium, & cui in vita.*

The cough, Tussis, is, f. pl. caret.

A covey, as a covey of Patridgges, Pullities, ei, f.

Covin, Covina, æ, f. It is a deceitful assent or agreement between two, or more, to the prejudice or hurt of another. *Vid. new terms of Law, Co. on Lit. lib.* 3. *cap.* 12.

Covinous, Covinosus, a, um. *Co. Lit.* 357. *Ra. Ent.* 207.

The coulter of a plough, or plough share, Dentāle, is, n. Culter, tri, m. Vomer & Vomis, eris.

One (not a Lord) of the council, Unus de privato Concilio, &c.

A Lord of the privy council, Dominus de privato concilio, Domini Regis.

A councel or council, or assembly of counsellors, Concilium, ii, n.

A council-house, Conciliābŭlum, li, n. Comitium, ii, n.

A counsellor, Consiliarius, ii, m.

A counsellor at Law, Barrasterius, ii, m. Apprenticius legis.

Counsel or advice, Consilium, ii, n.

To count or reckon, Computo, are.

Count, Narratio, onis, f. Chiefly in real Actions. Count cometh of the *French* word *Conter*, which in *Latin* is *Narratio*, and is vulgarly called a Declaration. The Original Writ is according to his name *Breve*, Brief and Short, but the Count which the Plaintiff or Demandant makes is more narrative and spacious, and certain both in Matter and Circumstance of time and place, that the Defendant may be compelled to make a more direct answer, so as the Writ may be compared to Logick, and the Count to Rhetorick. *Cook on Lit. lib.* 1. *cap.* 1. *sect.* 19. *Libellus* with the *Civilians*, comprehendeth both, and yet Count and Declaration is confounded sometimes, as *Count in debt, Kitchin, fol.* 281. Count or Declaration in Appeal, *Pl. cor. fol.* 78. Count in Trespass, *Britton, cap.* 26.

Count in an Action of Trespass upon the Case for a slander, *Kitch. fol.* 252.

The countenance or credit and reputation of a man, Contenementum, i, n. So it is used in *Old nat. brev. fol.* 111. in these words; Also the Attaint shall be granted to poor men that will swear that they have nothing whereof they may Fine, saving their Countenance, or to other by a reasonable Fine. So it is used *Anno* 1. *Ed.* 3. *Stat.* 2. *cap.* 4. in these words, Sheriffs shall charge the Kings Debtors with as much as they may Levy with their Oaths, without abating the Debtors Countenance.

A counter bond, Obligatio reciproca.

To counterfeit, Controfacio, ere.

A counterfeiting, Controfactura, æ, f. *Ry.* 542. *West. offences, fol.* 115. Ter. Controfactio, onis, f.

To counterfeit the Sheriffs Warrant upon a Writ, Controfacere Warrantum vicecomiti super aliquod breve.

A counter-plea, Contraplacitum, i, n.

A counter roll, Contrarotulus, i, m. *Fle.* 173.

A countess, Comĭtissa, æ, f.

A countess Dowager, Comitissa Dotissa.

A country, Rĕgio, ōnis, f.

Our country (or native soil) Patria, æ, f.

The country, Rus, ruris, n.

A country man (or a man of the Country) Rustĭcus, ci, m.

Of the country, Rŭrālis, le. Rusticus, a, um.

A county (or shire) Comitatus, ûs, m.

County signifieth as much as Shire, the one descending from the *French*, the other from the *Saxons*, both containing a compass or portion of the Realm, into the which all the Land is divided for the better Government thereof, and the more easie Administration of Justice, so that there is no Land but it is within some County, and every County is governed by a yearly Officer whom we call a Sheriff, *Cook on Lit. lib.* 2. *cap.* 10. *sect.* 124. Of these Counties there be four of especial note, which therefore are termed *County Palatines*, as the County Palatine of *Lancaster*, of *Chester*, of *Durham*, and of *Ely*, but *Ely* has been denied to be a County Palatine. And this County Palatine is a Jurisdiction of so high a Nature, that whereas all Pleas touching the Life or Maim of Man, called Pleas of the Crown, are ordinarily held and sped in the Kings name, and cannot pass in the name of any other. The chief Governours of these, by special Charter from the King, did heretofore send out all Writs in their own name, and did all things touching Justice, as absolutely as the Prince himself

in

in other Counties only acknowledging him their Superiour and Soveraign. But by the Statute *Anno* 27. *H.* 8. *cap.* 25. this power is much abridged. There are likewise Counties Corporate, as appeareth by the Statute *Anno* 3. *Ed.* 4. *cap.* 5. and these are certain Cities or ancient Boroughs of the Land, upon which the Princes of our Nation have thought good to bestow such extraordinary Liberties. Of these the famous City of *London* is one, and the principal. *York* another, *Anno* 32. *H.* 8. *cap.* 13. the City of *Chester* a third *Anno* 42. *Eliz.* *cap.* 15. *Canterbury* a fourth. *Lambert Eiren. lib.* 1. *cap.* 9. *Coventry*, and to these may be added many more, but I have only observed out of the Statutes and other Writers, the County of the Town of *Kingston* upon *Hull*, *Anno* 32. *H.* 8. *cap.* 26. and the County of *Litchfield*, *Crompt. Just. of P. fol.* 59. *a.* The County of the Town of *Haverford*, *West. Anno* 35. *H* 8. *cap.* 26. Of these Counties or Shires, one with another, there are reckoned in *England* 41, besides 12 in *Wales*.

The chief leading men in a county, Busones, m, pl.

County court, Curia Comitatus, by Mr. *Lambert* it is called *Curia Conventus*, in his Explication of *Saxon* words, and divided into two sorts, one retaining the general name, as the County-Court held every month by the Sheriff or his Deputy, the under Sheriff, whereof you may read in *Crompt. Jurisd. fol.* 231. The other called the *Turne* held twice every year, once after *Michaelmas*, and again once after *Easter*. *Magna Chart. cap.* 35. and that within one Month after each Feast. This County-Court had in old times the Cognition of great matters, as appears by *Glanvile*, *lib.* 1. *cap.* 2, 3, 4. From this Court are exempted only Arch-bishops, Bishops, Abbots, Priors, Earls, Barons, all Religious Men and Women, and all such as have hundreds of their own to be kept.

Couplings, Jŭgāmenta, orum, n. Copulæ, arum, f.

To couple or join together, Copulo, are.

A couple (or pair) Par, is, n.

A course, a running away or means, Cursus, ûs, m.

A water-course, Aquæductus, ûs, m.

A course, race or carreer, Curriculum, li, n.

A course or order, Sĕries, ei, f.

A course in serving at the table (or a mess or service of meat) Missus, ûs, m.

A course of fruit, Bellarium, ii, n.

By course (or turn) Alternè, alternatim.

Course or gross, not fine, Crassus, a, um.

 The

The court of a Prince, Aula, æ, f.

A courtier (one that follows the court) Aulicus, ci, m.

Court-like, Aulicus, a, um.

A court of judges, a court hall, gild-hall, or session house, Curia, æ, f. Court cometh of the *Latin Curia*, which also is fetched from *Cura* (as *Valla* writeth) whereby it is notified that heed and care ought to be taken in the deciding of Controversies. Court is diversly taken, sometimes for the House where the King remaineth with his ordinary retinue, and also the place where Justice is judicially administred, of which you may find 32 several sorts in *Crompt. Jurisdict.* well described, and of them most are Courts of Record, some are not, and therefore are accounted Base Courts in comparison of the rest. In times past the Courts and Benches followed the King and his Court, wheresoever he went, which thing especially shortly after the Conquest being found very cumbersome, painful and chargeable to the People, it was agreed by Parliament, that there should be a standing place where Judgment should be given, and it hath been long time used in *Westminster-Hall*, which K. *William Rufus* builded for the Hall of his own House. In that Hall are ordinarily seen three Tribunals or Judges Seats. At the entry on the right hand the Common Pleas, where Civil matters are to be Pleaded, specially such as touch Lands or Contracts. At the upper end of the Hall, on the right hand, the Kings Bench, where Pleas of the Crown have their place, and where Kings in former times have often personally sate. And on the left hand sitteth the Chancellor, accompanied with the Master of the Rolls, who in Latin may be called *Custos Archivorum Regis*, and certain men Learned in the Civil Law, called Masters of the Chancery, in Latin they may be called *Assessores*. There is also another Court of special Note, called the Star-chamber, *Camera Stellata*, or of the Latin word *Stellio*, a starry beast, whence Cosenage is called by the Civilians *Crimen Stellionatus*, because that sin is punished in this Court, *Lamb. Jur. of Cour.* Or it is called Star-chamber, either because it is full of Windows, or because at the first, all the roof thereof was decked and garnished with gilded Stars. But this Court is abolished by Act of Parliament. And many other Courts there are, of which some may Fine and not Imprison, as the Court Leet, some cannot Fine or Imprison but Amerce, as the Court-County, Hundred, Baron, for no Court may Fine or Imprison, which is not a Court of Record: Some may Imprison and not Fine, as the

Con-

Conſtables at the Petty Seſſions for any Affray made in diſturbance of the Court may Impriſon but not Fine: Some Courts can neither Impriſon, Fine nor Amerce, as Eccleſiaſtical Courts held before the Ordinary, Arch-Deacon, or other Commiſſaries, all which proceed according to Canon or Civil Law; and ſome may Impriſon, Fine and Amerce, as the Caſe ſhall require, as the Courts of Record at *Weſtminſter*, and elſewhere. Courts of Record are the Kings Courts, as he is King, thoſe have that Credit, that no Amercement can be taken againſt any thing there entred or done.

There are alſo Courts Chriſtian, *Curia Chriſtianitatis*, *Smith de Repub. Angl. lib.* 3. *cap.* 9. Which are ſo called becauſe they handle matters eſpecially concerning Chriſtianity, and ſuch as without good knowledge in Divinity, cannot be well Judged of, being held heretofore by Arch-Biſhops, and Biſhops, as from the Pope of *Rome*, becauſe he challenged the Superiority in all cauſes Spiritual, but ſince they hold them by the Kings Authority (*Virtute magiſtratus ſui*) as the Admiral of *England* doth his Court, whereupon it proceedeth that they ſend out their precepts in their own names, and not in the Kings, as the Juſtices of the Kings Courts do. And therefore as the Appeal from theſe Courts did lie to *Rome*, now by the Statute *Anno* 25. *H.* 8. *cap.* 19. It lieth to the King in his Chancery. *Leigh. Phil. Com. fol.* 54, 55. *Cook.* 11. *Rep. Godfreys Caſe.*

A court conſiſting of three hundreds, Trithingum, i, n.

The ſheriffs court, kept twice a year, Turnum, i, n.

The biſhops conſiſtory court, Conſiſtorium, ii, n.

Court baron, Curia Baronis, Is a Court that every Lord of a Mannor (which in ancient times were called Barons) hath within his own Precincts, *Vid. Kitchin, Sir Edward Cook in his 4th. book of Rep.* Amongſt his Copy-hold Caſes, *fol.* 26. *b.* ſaith, That this Court is of two ſorts, and therefore if a Man having a Mannor in a Town, and do grant the Inheritance of the Copy-holders thereunto belonging, unto another, this Grantee may keep a Court for the Cuſtomary Tenants, and accept ſurrenders to the uſe of others, and make both admittances and grants. The other Court is of Free holders, which is properly called the Court Baron, wherein the Suiters, that is, the Free-holders, be Judges, whereas of the other, the Lord or his Steward is Judge.

Court of pie-powder, Vid. *pie-powder*.

A court (or yard) Atrium, ii, n.

Couſenage (or deceit) Deceptio, onis, f. Fallacia, æ, f.

A cou-

A cousener (or deceiver) Deceptor, oris, m.

A cousin, Affinis, is, c. g.

A cousin by father, Patruelis, is, c. g.

A cousin by mother, Consobrinus, ni, m.

C O W.

A cow, Vacca, æ, f.

A barren cow, bearing no calf, Taura, æ, f.

A cow great with calf, Vacca prægnans. Vacca fœta. Forda, æ, f.

A milch cow, Vacca lactaria.

A cow-stall (or feeding place) Săginārium, ii, n. Bubile, is, n.

A cow-herd, Bubulcus, ci, m. Armentarius, ii, m.

A cow-house, Vaccaria, æ, f. *Cow.* 267. *Ry.* 341. 1. *Mon.* 527.

Cowbridge (in Glamorganshire) Bonnium. Bovium.

C R A.

A cradle, Cunæ, arum, f. Cūnăbŭla, orum, n.

Cradle cloaths, Stragula cunalia.

A craftsman, Artifex, icis, m.

Craft, Astutia, æ, f.

Crafty, or subtil, Astutus, a, um.

A crag, or rock, Rupes, is, f. Petra, æ, f.

Craggy (or rough) Petrosus, a, um.

A craggy or stony place, Rupina, æ, f.

To cram (or make fat) Sagino, are.

The cramp, Spasmus, i, m.

A cramperne (or cramp-iron) Subscus Ferrea.

Cranage, Cranagium, ii, n. *Ra. Ent.* 3. *Lex.* 39. i. e. A liberty, to use a Crane for the drawing up of Wares from the Vessels, at any Creek of the Sea or Wharf, unto the Land, and to make profit of it. It signifieth also the Money paid and taken for the same. *New books of Entries, fol.* 3. *col.* 3.

To crane, Crano, are.

Craneburn (in Dorsetshire) Cranburna.

A crane (an instrument to lift up heavy burdens) Grus, ŭis, f. Ergăta, æ, f.

The rope of a crane, Funis subductarius.

Hooks in the end of a cranes cable, Ansæ, arum, f.

A crayer, Craiera, æ, f. *Pry.* 402.

Craven (in Yorkshire) Cravena.

C R E.

The cream or best part of any Juice, Cremor, oris, m.

A creditor, Creditor, oris, m.

Crediton or *Kirton (in Devonshire)* Cridia.

A creek of the sea, Crepido, inis, f. Vorago incurva, Fossa verticosa. A Creek seemeth to be a part of a Haven, where any thing is landed or disburdened out of the Sea, so that

that when you are out of the main Sea within the Haven, look how many landing places you have, so many Creeks may be said to belong to that Haven, see *Crompt, Jurisdict. fol.* 110. *a.* This word is mentioned in the Statute as *Anno* 5. *Eliz. cap.* 5. and divers others. *Creca, æ, f. Crecum, ci, n. Ra. Ent.* 3. *Plow.* 1. *Lex.* 39.

Creeklade or *Creeklode* (in *Wiltshire*) Crecolada, Græcolada.

The crest of a helmet, Crista vel Conus galeæ.

A crewet or cruet, a narrow mouthed pot to keep oyl, or such like, Guttus, i, m.

A crevate (or band) Collare, is, n.

Crevecure or *Creveo* (the Family) De Crepito Corde. De Curceo. De Curci, De Cusância.

C R I.

To crisp (or curl) Crispo, are.

Crisped (or curled) Crispus, a, um.

A crisping or curling iron, Calamistrum, i, n.

To crisp locks with a curling iron, Crispare cincinnos calamistro.

Crystals a chymical preparation, Crystalli.

C R O.

Crooked, Curvus, a, um.

A croft, Croftum, i, n. *Spel.* 182. Crofta, æ, f. A little Close joyning to a House, that sometimes is used for a Hemp-plot, sometime for Corn, and sometime for Pasture, as the Owner pleaseth. It seemeth to come of the old *English* word *Creaft,* signifying Handy-craft, because such grounds are for the most part extraordinarily dressed and trimmed by the labour and skill of the Owner.

A crop, Proventus, ûs, m Messis, is, f.

A cross-bow, Balista, æ, Arcus crucialis, 1. *Fo.* 10.

A crosselet or frontlet, or cro cloth of linen, that Women w a cross upon the forepart of th head, Frontale, is, n.

Cross a river or way, E transverso rivuli, vel viæ.

Crowland (in *Lincolnshir* Crowlandia, Croylandia, Cr landia.

Of Crowland, Crulandens

Croydon (in *Surrey*) Neogus, Noviomagus.

C R U.

A crum, Mica, æ, f.

A crupper for a horse, Po na, æ, f. Postûla, æ, f. stella, æ, f.

A cruse (an earthen or pot or pitcher) Pocillum, Urceus, ei, m.

A crust (or hard piece of thing, as bread, or the like) stum, i, n.

A

A crust or shell (rough casting) Crusta, æ, f.

A cryer or bellman (one that cryeth things publickly in the market-place) Præco, onis, m.

A thing which is cryed, Præconium, ii, n.

C U C.

A cucumber, Cucumer, eris, m. Cucumis, is, m.

A cudgel, Baculum, i, n. Fustis, is, m.

Cudgelled, Fustigatus, a, um.

A cudgelling, Fustigatio, onis, f.

To cudgel, Fustigo, are.

C U F.

A cuff, or foresleeve, Manicula lintearia.

C U I.

Cui ante Divortium, Is a Writ that a Woman divorced from her Husband, hath to recover Lands or Tenements from him, to whom her Husband did alienate them during the Marriage, because during the Marriage she could not gainsay it. *Reg. Orig. fol.* 233. *Fitz-Herb. nat. brev. fol.* 204.

Cui in vita, Is a Writ of entry that a Widow hath against him to whom her Husband alienated her Lands or Tenements in his life time; which must contain in it, that during his life time she could not withstand it, *Reg. Orig. fol.* 232. *Fitz-Herb. nat. brev. fol.* 193. See the new Book of Entries, *Verbo Cui in vita.*

C U L.

A cullender (or strainer) Colum, i, n. Fiscella, æ, f.

Cullers, sheep culled, chosen and separated from those sheep that are good for meat, Oves rejiculæ.

Culverin (a piece of ordnance so called) Colleurina, æ, f.

Cumberland, Cumberlandia, Cumbria.

C U P.

A cup to drink in, Cupa vel Cuppa, æ, f. Poterium, ii, n. Cotina, æ, f. Poculum, li, n. Calix, icis, m. Crater, eris, m.

A small earthen cup, Pocillum fictile.

A wine cup, Pocillum, i, n.

The ear or handle of a cup, Ansa, æ, f.

A cup-bearer, Pocillator, oris, m.

A cup-bearer (or taster to a prince) Prægustator, oris, m. Pincerna, æ, c. g.

A cup-board, Abăcus, ci, m. Repositorium, ii, n. Vasarium, ii, n.

A cup-

A cup-board, or place to put cups and glasses in, Poteriotheca, æ, f.

The carved work of a cup-board, Abaci cymacium.

A cup-board keeper, Vasarii structor.

A cupping-glass. Ventosa, æ, f. Cucurbitula, æ, f.

C U R.

A curate (or priest) Curatus, i, m. Curio, onis, m.

Curdled, Densatus, a, um.

Curds and cream, Coagula liquefacta lacte.

A cure (or parish) Curionatus, ûs, m.

Curebridge, Vid. *Corebridge.*

Curia advisare vult, Is a deliberation that the Court purposeth to take, upon any point or points of a Cause, before Judgment be resolved on; for this see the new Book of Entries, *Verbo Curia advisare vult.*

Curia claudenda, Is a Writ that lieth against him who should fence and close up his ground, if he refuse, or defer to do it. *Reg. Orig. fol.* 155. *Fitz-Herb. nat. brev. fol.* 127. See also the new Book of Entries *Verbo Curia Claudenda.*

To curle (or frizle) Crispo, are.

To be curled, Crispor, ari.

Curled (or frizled) Crispus, a, um.

Somewhat curled, or curled into small rings, Crispulus, a, um.

A curling iron, Calamistrum, i, n.

Currance, Uvæ passulæ. Uvulæ Corinthiacæ.

A currier, Coriarius, ii, m. Alutarius, ii, m. Coriorum concinnator.

To curry leather, Coria concinnare. Tergora depsere.

A cursitor, Clericus de cursu, vel Curcista curiæ Cancellariæ. Cursitor, oris, m. They are called Cursitors, because they make *brevia de cursu*, Writs of course, so called, because they have a settled form prescribed in an ancient Book, therefore called the Register of Writs, *Judge Doderidge.* He is an Officer or Clerk belonging to the Chancery that maketh out Original Writs, *Anno* 14. & 15. *H.* 8. *cap.* 8. They are called Clerks of Course, in the Oath of the Clerks of the Chancery, appointed *Anno* 18. *Ed.* 3. *Stat.* 5. *cap. unico.* There are of these 24 in number, which have allotted unto every one of them certain Shires, into the which they make out such Original Writs as are by the Subject required, and are a Corporation among themselves. *Cowel, lib. de signif. verborum.*

A curtain (or hanging for beds or windows) Cortina, æ, f. *Ra. Ent.* 152. *Fle.* 71. Curtinus, i, m. *Co. Ent.* 162. Velum, i, n. Velarium, ii, n.

A curtain rod, Virga Ferrea.

A cur-

A curtilage, Curtilagium, ii, n. *Spel.* 187.

C U S.

A cushion, Pulvinus, i, m. Pulvinar, aris, n. Pulvinarium, ii, n.

A cushion to lean upon, Cubital, & tale, is, n.

A little cushion, Pulvinŭlus, li, m.

A custard, Artogala, æ, f. Artologanus, ni, m.

Custode admittendo & Custode amovendo, Are Writs for the admitting or removing of Guardians. *Regist. Orig. in indice.*

Custody (or keeping) Custodia, æ, f.

Customary Tenants, Tenentes per Consetudinem. Are such Tenants as hold by the Custom of their Mannor as their especial evidence, *Vid.* Copyhold.

A custom, Consuetudo, ĭnis, f. This word *Consuetudo* hath in Law divers significations. 1. It is taken for the Common Law, as *Consuetudo Angliæ.* 2. For Statute Law, as *contra consuetudinem, communi concilio regni, edit.* 3. For particular Customs, as Gavel kind, Borough *English*, and the like. 4. For Rents, Services due to the Lord, as *Consuetudines & Servitia.* 5. For Customs, Tributes or Impositions, as *de novis consuetudinibus levatis in regno, sive in terra, sive in aqua.* 6. Subsidies, or Customs granted by Common consent, that is by Authority of Parliament, *pro bono publico*, these be, *Antiquæ & rectæ consuetudines. Cook 2. part of the Instit. cap.* 30.

Custom is one of the main Triangles of the Laws of *England*, these Laws being divided into 1. Common Law. 2. Statute Law. 3. Custom. *Cook on Lit. lib.* 2. *c.* 10. *Sect.* 165. Custom is a reasonable act iterated, multiplied and continued by the People time out of mind. Of every Custom there are two essential parts, *time* and *usage*, time out of mind, and continual and peaceable usage without interruption. Sir *John Davis his Rep.* Some say there are three Essential qualities of a good Custom, 1. Certainty, 2. Reasonableness, 3. Use or Continuance. Others say, a good Custom ought to have four inseparable properties, 1. A reasonable Commencement (for every custom hath a Commencement, although that the memory of man extend not to this, as the river *Nilus* hath a Fountain (although the Geographers cannot find it) whence these Maximes in Law, *Obtemperandum est consuetudini rationabili tanquam legi. In consuetudinibus non diuturnitas temporis, sed soliditas rationis est consideranda.* For if the Custom be unreasonable in the Original, no use or continu-

ance

ance can make this good. *Quod ab initio non valuit, tractu temporis non convalescit.* A thing that is void *ab initio*, no Prescription of time can make this good. Every Custom is not unreasonable which is against the particular rule or maxim of the positive Law, as the custom of Gavel-kind and Borough *English* are against the maxim or descent of Inheritance, and the Custom of *Kent*, the Father to the Bough, the Son to the Plough, is against the maxim of *Escheats*, for *consuetudo ex certa causa rationabili usitata privat communem legem.* Besides, a Custom may be prejudicial to the Interest of a particular person;and yet reasonable where it is for the benefit of the Commonwealth in general, *Salus populi suprema lex esto.* As Custom to make Bulwarks upon the Land of another for defence of the Kingdom, 36. *H.* 8. *Dyer* 60. *b.* and to raze Houses, *in publico incendio*, 29. *H.* 8. *Dyer* 36. *B.* A Custom which is prejudicial and injurious to the Commonwealth, and begins only by Oppression and Extortion of Lords, hath no lawful Commencement, but is void: So by *Litleton, fol.* 46. Custom that the Lord shall have fine of his Frank Tenant for Marriage of his Daughter is held void: And Custom that the Lord of the Mannor shall detain distress taken upon his demeans untill a Fine be made to him for damage at his Will, is also void, 3. *Eliz. Dyer* 199. *B. Malus usus abolendus est.* 2. Custom ought to be certain, and not ambiguous, for *incerta pro malis habentur:* An uncertain thing may not be continued time out of mind without Interruption. 3. Custom ought to have continuance without interruption, time out of mind, for if it be discontinued within memory, the Custom is gone, *Consuetudo semel reprobata non potest amplius induci*; for as continuance makes custom, so discontinuance destroys it, *Nil tam conveniens naturali æquitati, quam unum quod quæ dissolvi eo ligamine quo ligatum est. Consuetudo* is nothing else, but *communis assuetudo.* 4. It ought to be submitted to the Prerogative of the King, and not exalt it self against it; for Prescription of time makes a custom, but *nullum tempus occurit Regi.* If a man hath Toll or Wreck, or stray by Prescription, this extends not to the Goods of the King: So Prescription to have Sanctuary for Treason, or to have *Catella felonum*, is void against the King; because that such a Privilege, *exaltat se in Prærogativam Regis*, 1. *H.* 7. 236. Custom is either, 1. General, which is currant through *England*, that which is used *per totam Angliam*, is Common Law, and *quod habetur consuetudo per totam angliam*, is not a a good manner, to alledge a Cuſtom, *Cook 9. Rep. Combes caſe*. If any general Cuſtom were directly againſt the Law of God, or if any Statute were made directly againſt it, as if it were ordained, that no Alms ſhould be given for no neceſſity the Cuſtom and Statute were void. 2. Particular is that which belongeth to this or that County, as Borough *Engliſh* in many places, *Gavelkind* to *Kent*, for all the Heirs Males to Inherit alike; Countries have their Cuſtoms according to the Conſtitution of the Place, as in *Kent*, *North-Wales*, becauſe thoſe Counties have been moſt ſubject to foreign Invaſions, that every man there may be of Power for reſiſtance; the Inheritances for the moſt part deſcend in Gavel-kind, *viz*. to every Brother alike. There are particular Cuſtoms alſo to this or that Lordſhip, City, or Town. The Cuſtom of the County of *Buckingham* is, and hath been time out of mind, that every Swan which hath her courſe in any water that runs to the *Thames* within the ſaid County, if the Swan come upon the Land of any Man, and make her Neſt, and hath Cignets upon the ſame, he that hath the property of the Swan, ſhall have two of the Cignets, and he whoſe Land it is, ſhall have the third Cignet, which ſhall be of leaſt value: This was held a good Cuſtom, becauſe the Owner of the Land ſuffered them to breed there, whereas he might have chaſed them out. *Cook 7. Rep. caſe of Swans*. In *London*, 1. If the Debtor be a fugitive the Creditor before the day of Payment may arreſt him to find better ſurety. 2. They may there enter a Mans Houſe with the Conſtable or Beadle upon ſuſpicion of Bawdery. 3. They may remove an Action before the Major, depending the Plea before the Sheriffs. Theſe Cuſtoms in *London*, though againſt the Rule of Common Law, are allowed *eo potius*, becauſe they have not only the force of a Cuſtom, but alſo are ſupported and fortified by Authority of Parliament. *Cook 8. Rep. caſe of the City of* London, *Leigh. Phil. Com. f.* 60. In ſome places within the County of *Glouceſter*, the Goods and Lands of condemned Perſons fall into the Kings hands for a year only and a day, and after that term expired (contrary to the Cuſtom of all *England* beſides) return to the next Heirs, *Conſuetudo loci eſt Obſervanda, Camb. Brit.* in *Glouceſterſhire*. *Baldwin le Pettour* held certain Lands in *Hemingſton* in *Suffolk* by Serjeantry, for which on *Chriſtmas* day every year before the King of *England*, he ſhould perform one *ſaltus* (that is, he ſhould dance) one *Suffletus* (puff up his Cheeks making therewith a ſound) and

and one *Bumbulus* (let a crack downward) *Cambden* in *Suffolk.* In ſome Country, an Infant when he is of the Age of fifteen years may make a Feoffment, and the Feoffment is good; and in ſome Country when he can mete an Ell of Cloth. *D. and Student. c.* 10. In ſome Places the Widow ſhall have the whole or half, *Dum ſola & caſta vixerit.* Sir *George Farmour* claimed by Cuſtom in his Mannor of *Torceſter* in *Northamptonſhire*, to have a Common-Bake-Houſe, and that none others ſhould Bake to ſell there; and it was adjudged a good Cuſtom *Cook*, 8 *Report*, Caſe of the City of *London*, ſee more there concerning particular Cuſtoms.

Cuſtom for Wares and Merchandize, Cuſtuma, æ, f. *Ry.* 327. 8. *Co.* 126. 11. *Co.* 98. *Spel.* 188. *Anno* 14. *Ed.* 3. *Stat.* 1. *cap.* 21. *Reg. Orig. fol.* 138. *a.* 129. *a.* This word *Cuſtuma* is alſo uſed for ſuch ſervices as Tenants of a Mannor owe unto their Lord, *Vid.* new Book of Entries, *verbo cuſtom.*

Cuſtomarily, Cuſtumabiliter, adv. *Ra. Ent.* 137.

Cuſtos Brevium, Is the Principal Clerk belonging to the Court of Common Pleas, whoſe Office is to receive and keep all the Writs, and put them upon Files, every return by it ſelf, and at the end of every Term, to receive of the Protonotaries, all the Records of *Niſi prius*, called the *Poſtea*, for they are firſt brought in by the Clerk of Aſſiſe of every Circuit to the Protonotary that entred the iſſue in that matter, for the entring of the Judgment, and then the Protonotaries do get of the Court peremptory day, for every Party to ſpeak what he hath to alledge in arreſt of Judgment: Which day being paſt, he entreth the Verdict, and Judgment thereupon into the Rolls of the Court; And that done, he doth in the end of the Term deliver over to the *Cuſtos brevium*, all the Records of *Niſi Prius*, which came to his hands that Term: which received, he bindeth into a bundle, and beſtoweth them. The *Cuſtos brevium* alſo maketh entry of the Writs of Covenant, and the Concord upon every Fine, and maketh forth Exemplifications and Copies of all Writs and Records in his Office and of all Fines Levied. The Fines after they are Ingroſſed, the parts thereof are divided between the *Cuſtos brevium*, and the Chirographer, whereof the Chirographer keeps always with him the Writ of Covenant, and the Note, the *Cuſtos brevium* keepeth the Concord, and the foot of the Fine, upon which foot the Chirographer doth cauſe the Proclamations to be endorſed, when they are all Proclaimed. This Office is in the

the Princes gift, and he is called *Custos brevium Domini Regis de banco.*

Custos Placitorum Coronæ, Master of the Crown Office, who is the chief Coroner of *England.*

Custos Rotulorum, Is he that hath the Custody of the Rolls or Records of the Sessions of Peace, and, as some think, of the Commission of the Peace it self, *Lamb. Eiren. lib. 4. cap. 3. 373.* He is always Justice of Peace and *Quorum* in the County where he hath his Office, he is usually called *Custos Rotulorum*, and not Master of the Rolls, the which see in Chancery.

C U T.

To cut, Seco, are.

A cut, Incisura, æ, f. Scissura, æ, f.

To cut or slice up, open, along or forward, Proseco, are.

A cutting up, Prosectus, ûs, m.

A cutting up or along, Proscissio, onis, f.

Cut up (or open) Prosectus, a, um.

A cutting (or lancing) Incisio, onis, f.

To cut the margent of books, Demargino, are.

A cutler, Cultrarius, ii, m.

A cut-purse (or cheat) Saccularius, ii, m. Marsupicida, æ, f. Crumenifeca, æ, f. Manticularius, ii, m. Zonarius sector.

Cutbert (a mans name) Cutbertus, i, m.

D A.

D A G.

A *Dag (or rag of cloath)* Fractura panni.

A dagger (or pistol) Sclopetum, i, n.

A dagger, Sica, æ, f. Pugio, onis, m. Daggarius, ii, m.

A little dagger (or pocket dagger) Pugiunculus, li, m.

A stab or thrust with a dagger, Pugionis ictus.

To stab with a dagger, Aliquem ictibus pugionis petere, vel Pugione confodere.

D A I.

A dairy (or milk-house) Daieria, æ, f. *Fle. 171. 172.* Lactarium, ii, n.

A dairy-man, Lactarius, ii, m.

A dairy maid, Lactaria, æ, f. Lactatrix, icis, f.

D A L.

Dalegrig (the Family) De Dalenrigius.

De La-Mare (the Family) De La-Mara.

D A M.

Damage, Damnum, i, n. Damage in the Common Law hath

hath a special signification, for the recompence that is given by the Jury, to the Plaintiff or Defendant, for the wrong done unto him, *Cook on Lit. lib. 3. c. 7. sect. 431. Damnum dicitur à demendo, cum diminutione res deterior sit. Cook lib. 10. Rep.* So costs of Suit are Damages to the Plaintiff, for by them his Substance is diminished.

Damage Feasant, Is when a strangers Beasts are in another mans grounds, without lawful Authority or Licence of the Tenant of the ground, and there do feed, tread and otherwise spoil the Corn, Grass, Woods, or such like, in which case the Tenant, whom they hurt, may therefore take, distrain, and impound them, as well in the night as in the day: But for Rent and Services none may distrain in the night season. He that hath the hurt may take the Beasts as a Distress, and put them in a pound overt, so it be within the same shire, and there let them remain till the Owner will make him amends for the hurt: But by the Statute of Queen *Mary*, the beasts must not be driven above three Miles out of the Hundred.

Damageable, Damnosus, a, um.

Damask (a kind of stuff) Damascenus pannus, Dalmaticum sericum.

A damask garment, Vestis Damascena.

A dam, Damma, æ, f. *Spel.* 44. 424. *Lex.* 8. Agger, ĕris, m.

To dam (or pen up) Aggero, are.

To damnifie, Damnifico, are.

D A N.

Dan or *Daven* river (in *Cheshire*) Danus.

A maurice dancer, Salisubsulus, i, m.

The chief maurice dancer, Præsultor, oris, m.

A rope-dancer, Funambulus, li, m. Schænŏbates, æ, m.

A dancer (or leaper) Saltator, oris, m.

Danger, Dangium, ii, n. 1. *Mon.* 723. 2. *Mon.* 1032. Daungium, ii, n. 1. *Mon.* 815. Periculum, li, n.

Dancaster (in *Yorkshire*) Doncaster, Danum.

Danes-end (in *Hertfordshire*) Dacorum Clades.

D A R.

Darby *town* (in *Darbyshire*) Darbia, Derbia.

Darbyshire, Darbiensis Comitatu Dorventania.

Darent *or* Dart *river* (in *Kent*) Darentus fluvius, Dorventa.

Darwent *river* (in *Darbyshire*, *Yorkshire* and *Cumberland*) Derventio, Derwentio, Doroventio, Dorventa.

A dart (*or Javelin*) Jaculum, li, n. Spicŭla, æ, f.
A darting, Jaculatio, onis, f.
To dart, Jaculor, ari.

D A S.

A dash, Nota, æ, f.

D A T.

The date of a deed or writing, Data, æ, f. *Bract.* 188. ter.
A date (*a kind of sweet fruit*) Dactylus, li, m.

D A U.

To daub, Dēlŭto, are.
A daubing, Cementum, i, n. 2. *Rol.* 816. Delutatio, onis, f.
Daven *river* : See *Dan.*
A daughter, Filia, æ, f.
A daughter-in-law, Nurus, ri, f. Filiastra, æ, f.
A daughter-in-law (*or daughter by a former bed*) Privigna, æ, f.
David (*a mans name*) David, idis, m.

D A Y.

A day, Dies, ei, m vel f.
Sunday, Dies Dominicus.
Monday, Dies Lunæ.
Tuesday, Dies Martis.
Wednesday, Dies Mercurii.
Thursday, Dies Jovis.
Friday, Dies Veneris.
Saturday, Dies Saturni vel Sabbati.
To day, Hodiè, adv.
The day before, Pridiè, adv.
Of the day before, Pridianus, a, um.
The day after (*or following*) Postridiè, adv.
In the day time (*or by day*) Interdiù, adv.
Daily (*every day*) Quotidiè, adv.
Two days space, Biduum, i, n.

D E A.

A deacon, Diaconus, ni, m.
A deaconship, Diaconatus, ûs, m.
A deacons vest or coat, Stica, æ, f.
Deaf, Surdus, a, um.
Deafness, Surditas, atis, f.
A false dealer (*or double dealer*) Prævaricator, oris, m.
False dealing, Prævaricatio, ons, f.
To use false dealing, Prævarico, ari.
A dean, Decanus, i, m. Dean is derived of the *Greek* word δέκα, that signifieth Ten, because he was anciently over Ten Prebends or Canons at the least in a Cathedral Church, and is head of his Chapter. *Cook on Lit.*
A deanry, or deanship, Decanatus, ûs, m. *Spel.* 104.
Dean forest (in *Gloucestershire*) Danubiæ vel Danica Sylva.
Deal (in *Kent*) Dela.
Dearness, Caristia, æ, f. *Pry.* 376. *Ry.* 527.

Dearth

Dearth (*or scarcity of corn and victuals*, Cāritas, atis, f.

Death (*decease or departure out of this life*) Mors, tis, f.

D E B.

A debate, Debatum, i, n. *Reg.* 111. *br. Judic.* 173. *Spel.* 194.

Debet & Solet, These words are divers times used in the Writers of the Common Law, and may trouble the mind of a young Student except he have some Advertisement of them; for example, it is said in the *Old nat. brev. fol.* 98. This Writ (*de secta molendini*) being in (the *debet & solet*) is a Writ of right, &c. And again, *fol.* 69. A Writ of (*Quod permittat*) may be pleaded in the County before the Sheriff, and it may be in the *debet*, and in the *solet*, or in the *debet* without the *solet*, according as the Demandant claimeth. Wherefore Note, that those Writs that are in this sort brought, have these words in them, as formal words not to be omitted, and according to the diversity of the Case, both *debet* and *solet* are used, or *debet* alone, that is, if a man sue to recover any right by a Writ, whereof his Ancestor was disseised by the Tenant or his Ancestor, then he useth only the word *Debet* in his Writ; because *Solet* is not fit, by reason his Ancestor was Disseised, and the Custom discontinued. But if he sue for any thing that is now first of all denied him, then he useth both these words (*Debet* and *Solet*) because his Ancestors before him, and he himself usually enjoyed the thing sued for, as *solet* to a Mill, or Common of Pasture, untill this present refusal of the Tenant. The like may be said of (*Debet*) and (*Detinet*) as appeareth by the Register Original, in the Writ *de debita fol.* 140. *a.*

Deborah (*a womans name*) Debora, æ, f.

Debts, Debita, orum, n. Debt is a Writ, and lieth where any sum of money is due to a Man, by reason of Accompt, Bargain, Contract, Obligation or other specialty, to be paid at a certain day, at which day, if he payeth not, then he shall have this Writ. But if any Sum of Money be due to any Lord by his Tenant for any Rent Service, the Lord shall never have Action of Debt, but he must always distrein. Also for Rent-charge or Rent-seek which any man hath for life, in tail, or in Fee, he shall not have any Action of Debt, as long as the Rent continueth, but his Executors may have an Action of Debt for the Arrearages of any of the said Rents due in the life of their Testator by the Statute 32. *H.* 8. *cap.* 37. But for the Arrearages of Rent reserved upon a Lease for term of of years, the Leasor is at his Election to have an Action of debt, or for to distrein. But if the Lease be determined, then he shall not distrein after for that Rent, but he must have an Action of Debt for the Arrearages, *New terms of Law*. Debts due by Obligation shall be paid by Executors before Debts by simple Contract, and Debts by simple Contract before Legacies, *Cook* 9. *Rep. Pinchens case*. If a man take a woman which is Indebted to other persons, the Husband and Wife shall be sued for this debt, the Wife living. But if she die, the Husband shall not be charged for this debt after her death, unless the Creditor of the Husband and Wife recover the debt during the Coverture, then, although the Wife die, yet the Husband shall be charged for to pay this debt, after the death of the Wife by this recovery, *Fitz. nat. brev. Tit. Debt*. If a Man Lease Land for Term of Life to a woman rendring Rent, and she taketh a Husband, and after the Rent is behind, and the Woman die, the Husband shall be charged by a Writ of Debt for this Rent behind, because that he takes the profit of the Land by reason of his Wife. By Law of the Realm debt only ariseth upon some Contract or penalty Imposed, upon some Statute, and not by other Offences, as in the Civil Law, *debitum ex delicto*. If a Tailor make a Garment for me, if we be not agreed before what I shall pay for the making, he cannot have an Action of Debt, otherwise it is for Victuals and Wine. But the Taylor may detain the Garment until he be paid, as an Inn-keeper may his Guests horse for meat, or he may have an Action upon the Case, upon an assumsit to pay him so much as he deserves, *Cook lib.* 8. *Rep. p.* 147. *Leigh Phil. Com. fol.* 63.

A debtor, Debitor, oris, m.

D E C.

To decay (or fall down) Decido, ere. Declino, are.

A decaying (or falling down) Lapsus, ûs, m. Câsus, ûs, m.

December, December, is, m.

Decies Tantum, Is a Writ that lieth against a Juror, which hath taken Money for giving of his Verdict; called so of the effect, because it is to recover ten times so much as he took. It lieth also against embracers that procure such an Inquest, *Anno* 38. *Ed.* 3. *cap.* 13. *Reg. Orig. fol.* 188. *Fitz-Herb. nat. brev. fol.* 171. New book of Entries *verbo Decies Tantum*.

To declare, Declaro, are.

A declaration, Declaratio, onis, f. 1. *Fo.* 236. 208. It is a shewing in writing of the Grief and Complaint of the Demand-

Demandant or Plaintiff, against the Tenant or Defendant, wherein he supposeth to have received wrong; and this Declaration ought to be plain and certain, both because it Impeacheth the Defendant or Tenant, and also compelleth him to make answer thereto. But note that such Declaration made by the Demandant against the Defendant in any action real, is properly called a Count, and the Declaration or Count ought to contain Demonstration, Declaration and Conclusion, and in Demonstration are contained three things, *viz.* who complaineth, and against whom, and for what matter: And in the Declaration what ought to be Comprised, how, and in what manner the Action rose between the Parties, and when, and what Day, Year and Place, and to whom the Action shall be given, and in conclusion, he ought to aver and proffer to prove his suit, and shew the damage which he hath sustained by the wrong done unto him.

A decoction (or boyling of herbs or other things) Decoctum, i, n. Decoctio, Apozema, tis, n.

A decoy, Illex, icis, c. g.

A decree, Decretum, i. n.

D E D.

Dedimus potestatem, Is a Writ whereby Commission is given to a private Man for the speeding of some Act appertaining to a Judge. The Civilians call it *Delegationem*, and it is granted most commonly upon suggestion that the Party, which is to do something before a Judge, or in Court, is so feeble that he cannot travel. It is used in divers Cases, as to make a personal answer to a Bill of Complaint in the Chancery, to make an Attorney for the following of a Suit in the County, Hundred, Wapentake, &c. *Old nat. brev. fol.* 20. To Levy a Fine, *West. part.* 1. *Symb. Tit. Fines.* And divers other effects, as you may see in *Fitz-Herb. nat. brev.* in divers places noted in the Index of the Book. In what diversity of Cases this Writ or Commission is used : See the Table of the *Regist. Orig. verbo Dedimus potestatem.*

To deduce or deduct, Deduco, ere.

A deduction, Deductio, onis, f.

Deducted, Deductus, a, um.

D E E.

A deed, Factum, i, n. This word in the understanding of the Common Law, is an Instrument written in Parchment or Paper, whereunto ten things are necessarily incident, 1. Writing. 2. In Parchment or Paper. 3. A Person able to Contract. 4. By a sufficient name.

5. A Person able to be Contracted with 6. By a sufficient name. 7. A thing to be Contracted for. 8. Apt words required by Law. 9. Sealing. 10. Delivery. *Cook on Lit. lib.* 1. *c.* 5. *sect.* 40. It is called of the Civilians *Literarum Obligatio.* In another place on *Lit.* (*viz. lib.* 3. *c.* 1. *sect.* 259.) Sir *Edward Cook* saith, a Deed is an Instrument consisting of three things, *viz.* Writing, Sealing and Delivery, comprehending a Bargain or Contract between Party and Party, Man or Woman. Also in *Goddards Case*, 2. *Rep.* He saith there are three things of the Essence and Substance of a Deed, *viz.* Writing in Paper or Parchment, Sealing or Delivery, and if it have these three, altho' it want in *cujus rei testimonium sigillum suum apposuit*, yet the Deed is sufficient, for (*Traditio loqui facit Chartam*) the delivery is as necessary to the Essence of a Deed, as putting of the Seal to it, and yet it is not necessary to express it in the Deed that it was delivered. The Date of the Deed is not of the Substance of it, for if it want Date, or if it be a false or impossible date, as the 30*th. day of* Febr. yet the Deed is good, for it takes effect by the Delivery and not the day of the date. The order of making a Deed is, 1. To write it, then to Seal it, and after to deliver it, and therefore it is not necessary, that the Sealing or Delivery be mentioned within the Writing, because they are to be done after, *Cook* 2. *Rep. Goddards Case.* *Cooks* 5. *Rep. Windham's Case.*

Of Deeds some be, 1. Indented, so called because they are cut to the fashion of the Teeth in the top or side, which are either *Bipartite*, when there are two Parts and Parties to the Deeds. *Tripartite*, when there are three Parts and Parties. *Quadripartite*, when there are four Parts and Parties. *Quinquepartite*, when there are five Parts and Parties: Which division groweth from the form or fashion of them, *West. part* 1. *symb.* 2. Polls which are plain without any Indenting, so called, because they are cut even or Polled, every Deed that is Pleaded, shall be intended to be a Deed Poll, unless it be alledged to be Indented, *Cook on Lit. lib.* 3. *c.* 5. *sect.* 370.

If a Deed beginneth *Hæc Indentura*, and the Parchment or Paper is not Indented, this is no Indenture, because words cannot make it Indented, and although there are no words of Indenture in the Deed, yet if it be Indented, it is an Indenture in Law, for it may be an Indenture without words, but not by words without Indenting, *Cook ubi supra*, and *Cook* 5. *Rep. Stiles Case.*

Dee *river* (in *Cheshire*) Deva.

Dee

Dee river (in *Scotland*) Dea, Diva, Ocasa.

Deemed, Existimatus, a, um. Reputatus, a, um.

A fallow deer, Dama, æ, c. g.

A red deer (*hart or stag*) Cervus, i, m.

The fawn of a fallow deer, Hinnulus, li, m.

The fawn of a red deer, Cervulus, li, m.

The skin of a deer, Nebris, idis, f.

D E F.

A default, Defalta, æ, f. *Reg. Indic.* 1.

A default of issue, Defectus exitus.

Default of payment, Defalta solutionis.

A defeat or overthrow, Clades, is, f.

A defect, Defectus, ûs, m.

Defective, Defectivus, a, um.

A defeisance, Defesantia, æ, f. *Co. Ent.* 147. Defeizantia, æ, f. (i. e.) A Condition that is in one Deed, whereby another Deed, &c. is made void.

A defence or defending, Tūtēla, æ, f. Defensio, onis, f. Munimentum, i, n.

To defend, Defendo, ere.

Undefended, Indefensus, a, um. *Lex.* 71.

A defendant in law, Impediens, tis, m. Defendens, tis, m. Is he that is sued in an Action Personal, as Tenant is he which is used in an Action Real, *Vid. new terms of Law.*

A defender, Defensor, oris, m. Protector, oris, m.

Defender or defendour of the faith, Defensor Fidei. It is a peculiar Title given to the Kings of *England* by the Pope (as *Catholicus*) to the Kings of *Spain*, and (*Christianissimus*) to the Kings of *France*. It was first given by *Leo Decimus* to King *Henry* VIII. for writing against *Martin Luther*, in the behalf of the Church of *Rome*, *Stows annals*, *pag.* 863.

Defensive, Defensorius, a, um.

Defiled (*stained or polluted*) Contaminatus, a, um.

To define, Defino, ire.

A definition, Definitio, onis, f.

Definitive, Definitivus, a, um.

Se Defendendo, Is not matter of Justification, because the Law intends it hath a Commencement upon an unlawful Case, for Quarrels are not presumed to grow without some wrongs, either in words or deeds; therefore the Law putteth him to sue out his Pardon of course, and punisheth him by forfeiture of Goods, *Vid. Bacons Collections of the Law.* If a Man kill another in his own defence, he shall not lose his Life nor his Lands, but he must lose his Goods, except the Party slain did first assault him, to kill, rob or trouble him by the High-way side, or in his own House, and then he shall lose nothing. *Id. use of the Law.*

Defeisible (*that may be undone*) Defesibilis, le, adj.

To bid defiance, Diffidio, are.

To deform (*or make deformed*) Deformo, are.

Deformed, Deformatus, a, um.

To deforce (*or keep one out of his own by force*) Deforcio, are.

A deforcer, Deforciator, oris, m. (i. e.) One that keepeth out the Right Heir.

A deforcement (*or taking away an Estate by force from the right owner*) Deforciamentum, i, n. *Lex.* 42.

To defraud, Defraudo, are.

D E G.

To degenerate (*or grow out of kind*) Degenero, are.

Degenerate (*or grown out of kind*) Degĕner, ris, adj.

A degree, Gradus, us, m.

To prefer to a degree, Ad honoris & dignitatis gradum promovere.

D E I.

Deirhurst (in *Gloucestershire*) Deirosylva.

Deirwald or *Beverly* (in *Yorkshire*) Deirorum Sylva.

D E L.

To delay (*defer or prolong from day to day*) Deffero, ers, tuli, latum, ferre. Prolongo, are. Craſtino, are.

A delay (*or delaying*) Dilatio, onis, f. Prolongatio, onis f.

A delegate, Delegatus, ûs, m.

To deliver, Delibero, are.

A delivery, Deliberatio, onis, f.

Delvin (in *West-meath* in *Ireland*) Delvinia.

D E M.

To demand, Demando, are. *Pry.* 278. *West.* 2. 9. *Co. Lit.* 281. *D. and Student* 57.

A demand, Demanda, æ, f. Demandum, i, n. It signifieth calling upon a Man for any thing due. It hath likewise a proper signification with the Common Lawyers opposite to Plaint: For the pursuit of all Civil Actions are either Demands or Plaints, and the Pursuer is called Demandant or Plaintiff, *viz.* Demandant in Actions real, and Plaintiff in personal, and where the Party pursuing is called Demandant, there the Party pursued is called Tenant; where Plaintiff, there Defendant. *New terms of Law, verbo* Demandant.

Demandant is he which is Actor in a Real Action, because he demandeth Lands; and Plaintiff, *Querens*, in Personal and mixt, *Quia queritur de injuria*; Tenant, *Tenens*, in real Actions; and Defendant, *Defendens*, in Actions Personal and mixt. *Leigh. Phil. Com. fo.* 67.

Demesn, Dominicum, ci, n. *Spel.* 214.

A demise (or letting of an Estate) Dimissio, onis, f.

Demised, Dimissus, a, um.

Demorage; Demoragium, ii, n.

To demur, Demurro, are. 1. *H.* 7. 13. *Morari in lege.* It signifieth in our Common Law, a kind of Pawse upon a point of difficulty in any Action, and is used substantively, for in every Action the Controversie consisteth, either in the Fact or in the Law: If in the Fact, that is tried by the Jury; if in Law then is the Case plain to the Judge, or so hard and rare, as it breedeth just doubt. I call that plain to the Judge, wherein he is assured of the Law, though perhaps the Party and his Counsel yield not unto it, and in such Case the Judge with his Assessors proceeds to Judgment without further work. But when it is doubtful to him and his Associates, then there is stay made, and a time taken, either for the Court to think further upon it, and to agree if they can: Or else for all the Justices to meet together in the Chequer Chamber, and upon hearing of that which the Serjeants shall say of both Parts, to advise and set down what is Law. And whatsoever they conclude, standeth firm without further remedy. *Smith de Repub. Angl. lib.* 2. *cap.* 13. *West* calleth it a Demurrer in Chancery likewise, when there is Question made whether a Parties Answer to a Bill of Complaint, &c. be defective or not, and thereof reference made to any of the Bench, for the Examination thereof, and report to be made to the Court, 2. *Symb. Tit. Chancery, sect.* 29.

A demurrer (or an abiding in the judgment of the Court) Moratio in Lege. Demurrer cometh of the *French* word *Demeurer*, Lat. *Demorari*, to abide, and therefore he which demurreth in Law, abideth in Law, *moratur* or *demoratur in lege, Minshew. Cook on Lit. lib.* 2. *cap.* 3. *sect.* 96.

Demy (or half) Dimidium, ii, n.

A demy hake, Tormentum, i, n. 1. *Fo.* 106.

D E N.

A den (cave or cell) Antrum, i, n. Specus, ci, & us, d. g.

The dens of wild beasts, Lustra, orum, n. pl. Sing. caret.

A denial (or denying) Negatio, onis, f.

To deny, Nĕgo, are.

Denied, Negatus, a, um.

A denizen, Denizatus, ûs, m. *Lex.* 43.

A dentifrice, Dentifricium, ii, n.

Denshire: See *Devonshire*.

Denbigh (in *Denbighshire*) Denbighia.

D E O.

A deodand, Deodandum, i, n. Deodand is when any Man by misfortune is slain by a Horse, or by a Cart, or by another thing that moveth to furher the death, then the thing that is the cause of his death, and which at the time of his misfortune did move, shall be forfeit to the King, and that is called Deodand, and pertains to the Kings Almoner for to dispose in Alms and deeds of Charity.

D E P.

To depart, Departo, ire. *Co. Ent.* 295. *Ra. Ent.* 162.

A departure, Departura, æ, f. *Departer* is a word properly used of him that first Pleading one thing in Bar of an Action and being replied thereunto, doth in his rejoinder shew another matter contrary to his first Plea, *Plowden in Reniger* and *Fogassa*, *fol.* 7. & 8. and of this see divers Examples in *Brook Tit. departer de son plee.*

To depart in despight of the court, In contemptum Curiæ discedere, Is when the Tenant or Defendant appeareth to the Action brought against him, and hath a day over in the same Term, or is called after, though he had no day given him, so that it be in the same Term, if he do not appear but makes default, it is a departure in despight of the Court, and therefore he shall be Condemned.

To depasture, Depasturo, are.

A depasturing, Depasturatio, onis, f.

To depend (or stay upon) Dependo, ere.

He that dependeth upon another, Accessarius, ii, m.

A depilatory (or medicine to take off hair) Dropax, acis, m.

To deprive, Privo, are.

A deprivation (or taking away of a benefice) Deprivatio, onis, f.

Deptford (in Kent) Profundum vadum.

To depute, Deputo, are.

A deputy (or substitute) Deputatus, i, m. Substitutus, i, m.

D E R.

Deraigne, Deraisnia, æ, f. It cometh of the *French* word *Derayer* or *Deraigner*, i. e. to displace, or to turn out of his order, and hereof cometh Deraignment, a displacing, or turning out of his Order. So when a Monk is deraigned, he is degraded and turned out of his order of Religion, and become a Lay-man, *Cook on Lit. lib.* 2. *c.* 11. *sect.* 202. *Rubigineus* in his grand Customary, *cap.* 122, & 123. maketh mention of (*Lex probabilis*) and (*Lex deraisnia*) *legem probabilem* or *probationem*, he defineth to be a Proof of a Mans own Fact, which he saith he hath done, and

and his adverſary denieth. His Example is this, *A.* ſueth *R.* for a Hog, ſaying thou ſhouldſt deliver me a Hog for two Shillings ſix Pence, which money *F.* paid thee, wherefore I demand my Hog, which I am ready to prove. *Deraiſnian* he defineth to be a proof of a thing that one denieth to be done by himſelf, which his adverſary ſaith was done, defeating or confounding of his Adverſaries Aſſertion (as you would ſay) and ſhewing it to be without and againſt reaſon or likelihood, which is avouched. In our Common Law it is uſed diverſly, firſt generally for to prove, as *Dirationabit Jus ſuum hæres propinquior. Glanvile lib.* 2. *cap.* 6. and *habeo probos homines, qui hoc viderunt & audierunt, & parati ſunt hoc dirationare. Idem, lib.* 4. *c.* 6. And (*Dirationavit terram illam in Curiâ meâ*) *Idem. lib.* 2. *cap.* 20. i. e. He proved that Land to be his own.

A deraignment or proof, Diſratiocinatio, onis, f.

To deraign (*or prove and make good*) Dirationo, are.

Dertford (in *Kent*) Derenti vadum.

D E S.

To deſcribe, Deſcribo, ere.

A deſcription, Deſcriptio, onis, f.

A desk to write upon, Deſca, æ, f. 2. *Mon.* 370. Pluteus, ei, m.

Le Deſpenſer or *Spencer* (*the Family*) Le Deſpenſer & Deſpenſator.

To deſtroy, Deſtruo, ere.

A deſtroyer, Deſtructor, oris, m. Devaſtator, oris, m. Perditor, oris, m.

A deſtroying (*or deſtruction*) Deſtructio, onis, f.

Deſmond (in *Ireland*) Deſmonia.

D E T.

To detain (*or cauſe to tarry*) Detineo, ere. Retardo, are.

To detect (*accuſe or bewray*) Detego, ere.

To determine, Determino, are.

Detinue, Dicitur à Detinendo, becauſe *Detinet* is the principal word in the Writ. It is a Writ that lieth againſt him who having Goods and Chattels delivered to him to keep refuſeth to deliver them again, and ſo detaineth them, *Fitz-Herb. nat. brev. fol.* 138. To this is anſwerable in ſome ſort (*actio depoſiti*) in the Civil Law. And he taketh his Action of *Detinue*, that intendeth to recover the thing delivered, and not the damage ſuſtained by the detinue, *Kitchin fol.* 176. See the new Book of Entries, *Verbo Detinue.* Upon general acceptance of Goods, to keep, or to keep ſafely, if the Goods be ſtolen, or otherwiſe periſh, the Bailiff or he that accepts them ſhall anſwer for them. Otherwiſe it is if he take them upon on special acceptance, to keep them as his own Goods, *Cook* 4. *Rep. Southcotes case.*

D E V.

Devastaverunt bona Testatoris, Is a Writ lying against Executors for paying Legacies and Debts without Specialties, before the debt upon the said Specialties be due, for in this case the Executors are as liable to Action as if they had wasted the Goods of the Testator riotously, or without cause: *Vid. new Terms of Law.*

To devide (or part) Divido, ere.

A deviding (or division) Divisio, onis, f.

Devises (in Wiltshire) Divisæ. Castrum de vies.

To devise (or bequeath by will) Deviso, are.

A devise (or request) Devisum, i, n. Devisatio, onis, f. Devisamentum, i, n. *Ra. Ent.* 486. 1 *Co.* 80.

Devonshire, Danmoniorum Regio. Devonia. Dommonia, Domnonia.

Of Devonshire, Dommucensis, Domnoniensis.

D I A.

A diadem, Diadema, atis, n.

A dial, Horarium, ii, n. Horoscopium, ii, n. Horologium, ii, n.

The rod, the gnomen or staff of a dial, Index, icis, m. Gnomon, onis, m.

A sun-dial, Solarium, ii, n.

The point in a dial (that which with his shadow showeth the hours) Sciatheras, æ, m.

A diameter (or line going thorough the middle point of any figure, dividing the same into equal parts) Diameter, tri, m.

A diamond (or adamant) Adamas, antis, m.

D I C.

A dice-box, Fritillus, li, m.

A die to play withal, plur. Dice, Taxellus, li, m. Talus, i, m. Alea, æ, f.

To play at dice, Astragalizo, are. Talis ludere. Ludere Taxillis.

A cast at dice, Bolus, i, m. Tesserarum jactus. Jactus Aleæ.

A player at dice, Aleator, oris, m.

A place where dice are laid up, Alearium, ii, n.

D I E.

To diet, Dietto, are.

Diet, Diæta, æ, f.

Diet drink, Potus diæteticus.

D I F.

Difficult, Difficilis, le, adj.

Difficulty, Difficultas, tis, f.

DIG.

D I G.

A digger of Mines, Metallicus fossor.

To dig or delve, Cavo, are. Fodio, ere. Ligonizo, are.

To dig about, Circumfodio, ere.

A digging, Fossio, onis, f. Cavatio, onis, f.

A plat of ground digged, Bescata, æ, f.

D I L.

To dilacerate (tear or rent in pieces) Dilacero, are.

To dilate, or make large, Dilato, are.

Dilatory (that causeth delay or stay) Dilatorius, a, um.

Diligent, Diligens, tis, adj.

Diligence, Diligentia, æ, f.

D I M.

A dimension (or measuring) Dimensio, onis, f.

To diminish, Diminuo, ere.

A diminution, Diminutio, onis, f.

D I N.

To dine, Prandeo, ere. Prandium edere.

A dinner, Prandium, ii, n.

A dining chamber, Pransorium, ii, n.

D I O.

Dionysius (a mans name) Dionysius, ii, m.

Dionysia (a womans name) Dionysia, æ, f.

D I R.

Direct, Directus, a, um.

To direct (or make streight) Dirigo, ere.

A directing or direction, Directio, onis, f.

A director, Director, oris, m.

D I S.

To disagree, Discordo, are.

To disanckor (or weigh the Anchor) Exancoro, are.

To disanull, Annihilo, are. Abrogo, are.

To disarm (or unarm) Exarmo, are. Dearmo, are.

To disburse, Enumero, are. Expendo, ere.

To disable, Dishabilito, are.

Disability, Dishabilitas, atis, f.

Disabled, Dishabilitatus, a, um.

To disavow, Deadvoco, are. *Spel.* 194.

Discent, Discensus, ûs, m. It signifieth in the Common Law an order or means, whereby Lands or Tenements are derived unto any Man from his Ancestors, *Old nat. brev. fol.* 201. And it is either Lineal or Collateral, Lineal discent

ſcent is when a deſcent is conveyed in the ſame line of the whole Blood, as Grandfather, Father, Son, Sons Son, and ſo downward. Collateral deſcent is out in another branch from above, of the whole Blood, as Grandfathers Brother, Fathers Brother, and ſo downward: Note, that if one die ſeized in Fee, or in Fee tail of Land, in which another hath right to enter, and that deſcendeth to his Heir, ſuch deſcent ſhall take away the entry of him which hath right to enter, for that the Heir hath them by diſcent from his Father and ſo came unto thoſe Tenements by the Law, and he that had right cannot put him out by entring upon him, but is put to ſue his Writ to demand the Land according to the nature of the Title, *Littleton lib.* 1. *c.* 1. & *lib.* 3. *cap.* 6. and *Stat.* 32. *H.* 1. *cap.* 33.

To diſcern, Diſcerno, ere.

To diſcharge, (*or disburden*) Exonero, are.

To diſcharge (*or acquit*) Quieto, are.

To diſcharge from being foreſt (*or to free and exempt from foreſt laws*) Deaforeſto, are.

To diſclaim (*or refuſe an intereſt*) Diſclamo, are.

A diſclaim, Diſclamium, ii, n. It is a Plea containing an expreſs denial or refuſal: As if the Tenant ſue a Replevin upon a diſtreſs taken by the Lord, and the Lord avow the taking of the Diſtreſs, ſaying that he holdeth of him, as of his Lord, and that he diſtreined for Rent not paid, or ſervice not performed: Then the Tenant denying himſelf to hold of ſuch Lord, is ſaid to diſclaim: And the Lord proving the Tenant to hold of him, the Tenant loſeth his Land. *Terms of Law.* Of this ſee *Skene de verborum ſignificatione, verbo Diſclamation.* Alſo if a Man deny himſelf to be of the Blood or Kindred of another in his Plea, he is ſaid to diſclaim his Blood, *Fitz-Herb. nat. brev. fol.* 197. *G.* See *Brook Titulo Diſclaimer.* If a Man Arraigned of Felony do diſclaim Goods, being cleared he leeſeth them, *Stawnford pl. Cor. fol.* 286. See the new book of Entries, *Verbo Diſclaimer.*

Diſcontinuance, Diſcontinuatio, onis f.

To diſcover, Detego, ere.

A diſcovering, Detectio, onis, f.

To diſcourſe, Diſcurro, ere.

A diſcourſe, Diſcurſus, ûs, m.

A diſeaſe, Morbus, i, m.

To disfranchiſe, Excivito, are. Exurbito, are.

Want of digeſtion, Indigeſtio, onis, f. Cruditas, atis, f.

A diſh, Diſcus, ci, m. Scuta, æ, f. Catinus, i, m. Ferculum, li, n.

A little diſh (*ſaucer or porringer*, &c.) Scutella, æ, f. Diſculus, li, m.

A diſh-bearer, Diſcophorus, ri, m.

Diſhoneſt, Inhoneſtus, a, um.

Diſ-

Dishonour, Dedecus, oris, n. Ignominia, æ, f.

To disinherit, Exhæredo, are.

A disinheriting, Exhæredatio, onis, f.

To dislodge (or put out of lodging) Demigro, are.

To dismember, Dismembro, are.

To dismiss, Dimitto, ere.

Disobedience, Inobedientia, æ, f.

Disobedient, Inobediens, ntis, adj.

To disobey, Inobedio, ire.

Disorder, Confusio, onis, f. Inordinatio, onis, f.

To disorder, Confundo, ere.

Disorderly, Confusè, adv.

Disparagement, Disparagatio, onis, f. *Spel.* 105. It is by our Common Lawyers used especially for matching an Heir in Marriage, under his or her degree, or against decency: See *Cowel Instit. de Nuptiis. sect.* 6. It cometh, as I take it, from the two *Latin* words *Dispar* (i. e.) unfit, inconvenient, disagreeing, and *Ago* to do, which is as much as to say, to do that which is not fit to be done.

To disparage, Disparago, are.

To dispark (or break down the inclosure) Dessepio, ire. Disparko, are.

To dispatch, Expedio, ire.

A dispatching (or dispatch) Expeditio, onis, f.

A dispensation, Dispensatio, onis, f.

To dispense with, Dispenso, are. Legibus solvere.

To dispose, order, or set in order, Dispono, ere.

To dispossess, Dispossessio, are.

Dispossessed, Dispossessionatus, a, um.

A disproof, Dirationamentum, i. n.

To disprove, Directiono, are. Placit Cor. 28. 2. *Mon.* 26. *Spel.* 204. Refello, ere.

To dispute, Disputo, are.

Disputable (or which may be the subject of disputation) Disputabilis, le, adj.

To disquiet, Inquieto, are. Molesto, are.

Disquiet or disquieting, Inquietatio, onis, f.

A dissection (or cutting asunder) Dissectio, onis, f.

Disseisin, Disseisina, æ, f. It signifieth in the Common Law an unlawful dispossessing of a man of his Land, Tenement, or other Immoveable or Incorporeal right, *Instit. of the Common Law, cap.* 15.

A disseisor, Disseisitor, oris, m.

To disseise, Disseiso.

A distaff, Colus, li & lûs, f.

A distaff, full of tow, flax or other such matter, which is spun, Pensum, i, n.

A distance, Distantia, æ, f.

To distill, Distillo, are.

A distilling (or distillation) Distillatio, onis, f.

By distilling, Distillando.

A distiller, Distillator, oris, m.

A seller of things distilled, Distillarius, ii, m.

Distinct, Distinctus, a, um.

Distinctly, Distinctè, adv.

To distinguish, Distinguo, ere.

A distinguishing (or distinction) Distinctio, onis, f.

To distrain, Distringo, ere.

Not distrainable, Indistringibilis, le, adj. 2 *Inst.* 402.

A distress, Districtio, onis, f. Angustia, æ, f. It signifieth most commonly in the Common Law, a compulsion in certain Real Actions whereby to bring a Man to appearance in Court, or to pay debt or duty denied. The effect whereof most commonly is to drive the Party distreined to Replevie the distress, and so take his Action of Trespass against the distreiner, or else to compound Neighbourly with him for the debt or duty, for which he distreineth. The *Civilians* call a distress, *Pignorum captionem*. *Brissonius de verbor. sign. lib.* 14. This compulsion is by *Britton, cap.* 71. divided into a distress Personal, and distress real; distress Personal is made by surprising a mans moveable Goods, and detaining them for the security of his appearance to the suit, and to make him Plaintiff. A distress real is made upon immoveable Goods, as the *Grand Cape*, and *Petit Cape*: And thus it is interpreted by *Hotoman de verb. feudal, verbo districtus*. This differeth from an attachment in this point (among others) that a distress cannot be taken by any Common Person, without the compass of his own Fee. *Fitz-Herb. nat. brev. fol.* 904. except it be presently after the Cattle or other thing is driven or born out of the ground by him that perceiveth it to be in danger to be distreined, *New terms of Law, Verbo* Distress. Distress is a *French* word, and it is called in Latin *Districtio* & *Angustia*, because the Cattle Distreined, are put into a streight which we call a Pound. One may distrein any where *intra feodum*, so that it be not in the High-way, nor Church-yard.

A distress must be, 1. of a thing whereof a valuable property is in some body, and therefore Dogs, Bucks, Conies, and the like, that are *feræ naturæ* cannot be distreined. 2. Although it be of valuable property, as a Horse (yet when a Man or Woman is riding on him) or an Ax in a Mans hand cutting of Wood, and the like, they are for that time Privileged, and cannot be distreined. 3. Valuable things shall not be distreined for Rent, for benefit and maintenance of Trades, which by consequence are for the Commonwealth, and are there by Authority of Law, as a Horse in a Smiths shop shall not be distreined for the Rent issuing out of the shop, nor the Horse in the Hostry, nor the materials in a Weavers shop for making of Cloath, nor Cloath or Garments in a Taylors shop, nor Sacks of Corn or Meal in a Mill, nor in a Market, nor any thing distreined for Damage Feasant, for it is in the Custody of the Law. 4. Nothing shall be distreined for Rent that cannot be rendred again in as good plight, as it was at the time of the distress taken, as sheaves or shocks of Corn cannot be distreined for Rent, but for damage feasant they may, but Carts with Corn may be distreined for Rent, for they may be safely restored. 5. Beasts belonging to the Plow, *Averia carucæ*, shall not be distreined, for no man shall be distreined by the Instruments of his Trade or Profession, as the Ax

Ax of a Carpenter, or the Books of a Scholar, but Goods or *Animalia otiosa* may be distreined. If the distress be of Utensils, of houshold or such like dead Goods, which may take harm by wet or weather, or be stollen away, there he must impound them in a house or other pound covert within three miles in the same County. 6. Furnaces, Cauldrons or the like fixed to the Freehold, or the doors or Windows of a house, or the like, cannot be distreined. 7. Beasts that escape may be distreined for Rent, though they have not been Levant and Couchant, he that distreins any thing that hath life must impound them in a Lawful Pound within three miles in the same County. The Common Law is, Men cannot distrein for rent or service in the night as is adjudged in the 12 of *E.* 3. *Tit.* Distress, but for damage Feasant he may distrein in the night for necessity of the Case, for otherwise peradventure he shall not distrein *omnino*, for before the day they may be taken or stray out of his Land, *Cook 7 Rep.* Cases upon the Statute, and 9. *Rep. Mackallyes case*, and *Co. on Lit. l.* 2. *c.* 12.

A grand distress that is which is made of all the Goods and Chattels which the Party hath within the County, *Britton c.* 26. *fol.* 52.

To distress, Angusto, are.

To distribute, Distribuo, ere.

A distributing (*or distribution*) Distributio, onis, f.

A district, Districtus, ûs, m. (i. e.) Liberties or Precincts of a place, the Territories or Circuit of a Country, within which a Lord or his Officers, may Judge, Compel, or call in Question the Inhabitant. *Ca. ne Romani, de Electio in Clem.* And *Cassan. de consuetud. Burgund. p.* 190. *Britton cap.* 120. And so likewise is *districtio* in the Register *Original fol. 6. b.* And so it seemeth to be used in *Pupilla oculi, parte* 5. *c.* 22. *Charta de Foresta*, see also *Mynsing* in the Chapter *licet causam.* 9. *extra de probationibus, Numb.* 5. And *Zasius* in his 16 Council, *Numb.* 47. Distress in the former signification is divided first into Finite and Infinite; Finite is that which is limited by Law, how often it shall be made to bring the Party to Tryal of the Action, as once or twice, *Old nat. brev. fol.* 43. Distress Infinite is without limitation until the Party come, as against a Jury that refuseth to appear, *super Certificatione Assisæ*, the Process is a (*Venire facias, habeas corpora*) and Distress Infinite *Old nat. brev. fol.* 113. Then it is divided into a grand Distress, *Anno* 52. *H.* 3. *cap.* 7. which *Fitz-Herbert* calleth in Latin, *Magnam districtionem, nat. brev. fol.* 126. And an ordinary Distress, of which see before in Distress. But see whether it be some time not all one with a Distress Infinite, *Britton cap.* 26. *fol.* 80. with whom also the Statute of *Marlbridge* seemeth to agree, *Anno* 52. *H.* 3. *cap.* 7. *cap.* 9. and *cap.* 12. See *Old nat. brev. fol.* 71. *b.* See grand Distress what things be distreinable, and for what Causes: See the new

Terms of Law, *verbo* Diſtreſs.

A diſturbance, Diſturbatio, onis, f. Diſturbantia, æ, f.

To diſturb, Diſturbo, are.

D I T.

A ditch, Foſſatum, i, n. *Spel.* 295. Foſſa, æ, f. Scrobs, ŏbis, f. & m.

A little ditch, Foſſula, æ, f. Scrobicŭlus, li, m. Lacuſcŭlus, li, m.

Ditched in, Infoſſatus, a, um. 1 *Mon.* 474.

Made hollow like a ditch, Lacunatus, a, um.

A ditcher, Foſſator, oris, m. Foſſarius, ii, m.

To make ditches, Lacūno, are.

D I U.

Divers, Diverſus, a, um. Varius, a, um.

A dividend, Dividenda, æ, f. *Stat. de Eſcaetor. Ry.* 230. Dividends in the Exchequer ſeemeth to be one part of an Indenture, *Anno* 10 *Ed.* 1. *cap.* 11. and *Anno* 28. *Ejuſdem Stat.* 3. *cap.* 2. A dividend in the Univerſity, is that ſhare that every one of the Fellows do equally and Juſtly divide either by an Arithmetical or Geometrical Proportion, of their Annual ſtipend.

A divine (or ſtudent of divinity) Theolŏgus, gi, m.

Divinity, Theologia, æ, f.

Diviſion, Diviſio, onis, f.

To divorce, Divortio, are.

A divorce, or divorcement, Divortium, ii, n. *Lex* 45. Divorce is ſo called either *à diverſitate mentium*, of the diverſity of minds of thoſe that are married, becauſe ſuch as are divorced, go one a divers way from the other, or from the verb *diverto*, which ſignifieth to return back, becauſe after the Divorce between the Husband and the Wife, he returneth her again to her Father or other Friends, or to the Place from whence he had her, *Ridley of the Civil Law*, *Cook on Lit.*

To divulge, or publiſh abroad, Divulgo, are.

D O.

A Do, or doe, Dama, æ, f.

D O C.

A dock where ſhips ſtand, are layed up, builded, repaired or made, Navale, is, n.

A docket, Docketta, æ, f. It is a Brief in Writing, *Anno* 2. & 3. *Phil. & Mariæ, c.* 6. It is a ſmall piece of Paper or Parchment containing the effect of a large Writing, *Weſt. Symbol. parte* 2. *Titulo Fines, ſect.* 106.

A doctor, Doctor, oris, m.

Doctorſhip, Doctura, æ, f. Doctoratus, ûs, m.

A doctors commencement or proceeding doctor in any art, Promotio Doctorum.

A doctor of divinity, Sacræ Theologiæ Doctor ſeu Profeſſor.

A doctor of law, Legum Doctor.

A doctor of physick, Medicinæ Doctor.

Doctrine, Doctrina, æ, f.

D O E.

To doe, Facio, ere.

A using to doe, Factitatio, onis, f.

He that useth to doe, Factitator, oris, m.

A doer, Factor, oris, m.

D O G.

A dog, Canis masculus.

A cur dog, Canis villaticus vel domesticus. Canis Rusticanus.

A mastiff dog, Mastivus, i, m. 1 *Mon.* 405. 175. *Spel.* 245. Molossus, ssi, m.

A shepherds dog, Canis Pecuarius.

A little dog, Catulus, li, m.

A dog collar, Collare, is, n. Millus, li, m.

D O L.

A dole, Dola, æ, f. *Spel.* 207. *Lex.* 46. Dolea, æ, f. *Ry.* 185. bis. It is a part or share in a Meadow.

A dole (or liberal gift of a prince) Largitas, atis. Congiarium, ii, n.

A dole (or distribution of bread, or raw flesh) such as is used at the death of rich men and great personages, Visceratio, onis, f.

Dole (sorrow or grief) Dolor, oris, m.

D O M.

Domestical (or domestick) Domesticus, a, um.

Domination, Dominatio, onis, f. Domo Reparanda, Is a Writ that lieth for one against his Neighbour, by the fall of whose house he feareth hurt toward his own house, *Regist. Orig. fol.* 153. for this point the Civilians have the Action, *de damno infecto*.

D O N.

Don or *Dune* river (in *Yorkshire*) Danus.

A donation (a gift, a giving) Donatio, onis, f.

A donative, Dōnātivum, i, n. It is a Benefice meerly given, and Collated by the Patron to a Man without either Presentation to the Ordinary, or Institution by the Ordinary, or Induction by his Commandment, *Fitz. nat. brev. fol.* 35. *E.* See the Statute, *Anno* 8. *R.* 2. *cap.* 4.

A donee, Donatus, i, m. 2. *Co.* 13.

A donor, Donator, oris, m. Donatorius, ii, m. *Brac.* 11, 13, 14. Sæpe. *Co. Lit.* 123.

Done, Actum, factum, transactum.

D O O.

A door, Ostium, ii, n. Foris, is, f. Porta, æ, f. Janua, æ, f.

A two leaved door, or folding doors, Valvæ, arum, f. pl. Sing. caret.

A fore door, Oſtium anticum.

Back doors, Oſtia retrorſa, Poſtica, orum, n.

Outward doors, Oſtia exteriora.

Inward doors, Oſtia interiora.

A door with leaves, Fores, ium, f.

A door that opens without the least noiſe, Taciturniſſimum Oſtium.

A falſe door, Pſeudoforum, i, n.

A garden door, Macellota, æ, f.

Having a double door, Bĭfŏris, re, adj.

A little door (or wicket) Foricula, æ, f. Forula, æ, f.

A little back door, Poſticŭla, æ, f. Poſticŭlum, li, n.

A door bolted, Oſtium oppeſſulatum.

The lintel of a door, Sublimen, inis, n. Hyperthyrum, ri, n.

Standings before a door, Statiunculæ, arum, f. 2. *Rol.* 814.

Door caſes, Thecæ Oſtiorum.

Archative door caſes, Thecæ Oſtiorum arcuatim.

A door keeper, Oſtii cuſtos, *vid.* Porter,

He that openeth the door, Apertularius, ii, m.

D O R.

Dor river (in Herefordſhire) Dorus.

*Dorcas (*a womans name*)* Dorcas, æ, f.

Dorcheſter City (in *Dorſetſhire)* Dorceſtria, Dorkceſtria, Dorkeceſtria, Dornſetta, Dunium, Durnium, Durnovaria *or* Durnonovaria.

Dorcheſter (in *Oxfordſhire*) Dorcinia Civitas, Durocaſtrum. Hydropolis.

Of *Dorcheſter (or Dorſetſhire)* Dorſatenſis, Dorcenſis, Dorſettenſis.

A dormer, Tignum, i, n. Culmen domus.

A dormer (or principal beam) Cŏlŭmen, inis, n.

Dornford near *Walmsford (in Huntingdonſhire)* Durobrivæ, Durobrivas.

Dorſetſhire, Dorſetania, Dorſettia. Duria provincia.

D O S.

A doſe, Doſis, is, f. The quantity of a Potion or Medicine which a Phyſician appoints his Patient to take at once, or the quantity of a Medicine that without danger may be given or taken.

Doſes of ſweating powder, Doſes Pulveris diaphoretici.

A doſſer, Doſſerum, i, n. *Pry.* 105. Corbis doſſuaria, Caniſtrum, i, n.

D O T.

Dote unde nihil habet, Is a Writ of Dower, that lieth for the Widow againſt the Tenant, which hath bought Land of her Husband in his Life time, whereof he was ſeized ſolely in Fee ſimple, or in Fee tail, in ſuch ſort as the iſſue of them both might have inherited it. *Fitz-Herb. nat. brev. fol.* 147. *Regiſt. fol.* 170.

D O U.

Double (or doubled) Duplus, a, um. Duplex, icis, adj.

Double

Double plea, Duplex Placitum, Is that wherein the Defendant alledgeth for himself two several matters, in barr of the Action, whereof either is sufficient to effect his desire in debarring the Plaintiff, and this is not to be admitted in the Common Law. Wherefore it is well to be observed when a Plea is double, and when it is not, for if a Man alledge several matters, the one nothing depending on the other, the Plea is accounted double. If they be mutually depending one of the other, then it is accounted but single. *Kitch. fol.* 223.

To double, Duplo, are. Duplico, are.

Doubles, Diploma, atis, n. *Anno* 14. *H.* 6. *cap.* 6. Signifieth as much as Letters Patents, it being a *French* word made of the Latin *Diploma*.

Double tongued, Bilinguis, e, adj.

A doublet, Diplois, idis, f. Ambiloquus, a, um.

A doubt, Dubium, ii, n. Dubitatio, onis, f.

To doubt, Dubito, are. Ambigo, ere.

Without doubt, Indubio, adv.

Doubtful, Dubius, a, um.

Doubtful speech, Ambilógium, ii, n. Ambiloquium, ii, n.

Doubtfully, Amphibolicè, adv.

A dove, Columba, æ, f.

A dove-house Columbārium, ii, n.

He that keepeth a dove-house, Columbarius, ii, m.

A ring-dove, Palumba, æ, f. Columba torquata.

A turtle-dove, Turtur, uris, m.

Dove river (in *Darbyshire*) Dovus.

Dough (*or paste*) Pasta, æ, f. Massa, æ, f. Tusculum, li, n. Farina mixtum & conspersum.

A dough-trough (*or kneading trough*) Mactra, æ, f. Artopta, æ, f. Alveus pistorius.

A dough scrape, Rādŭla, æ, f.

Dover (the family) De Dovera.

Dover (in *Kent*) Ad Portum Dubris, Dosris, Doris Cantiorum, Dorobrina, Dovoria, Dovorria, Doveria, Dubris, Durus.

Down feathers, Plumula, æ, f. Plumulæ molliores. Plumæ subalares.

Dousabel (a womans name) Dousabella, æ, f.

D O W.

A dowager, Dotissa, æ, f. (i. e.) A Widow endowed, or that hath a Joynture, a Title applied to the Widows of Princes and great Personages.

Down, a Bishops See (in *Ireland*) Dunum.

A down (*or hill*) Dunum, i, n. Duna, æ, f. Calveta, orum, n. Glabretum, i, n.

Dower, Dos, dotis, f. Dower in the Common Law, is taken for that Portion of Lands or Tenements which the Wife hath for Term of her Life of the Lands or Tenements of her Husband after his Decease, for the sustenance of her self, and the Nurture and Education of her Children. Dower is of five sorts or kinds, *viz.*

 1. Dow-

1. Dower *per legem communem.*

2. Dower *per consuetudinem.*

3. Dower *ex assensu patris.*

4. Dower *ad ostium Ecclesiæ.*

5. Dower *de la plus baile.*

To the Consummation of Dower three things are necessary, *viz.* Marriage, seisin, and the death of her Husband, *Cook on Lit. lib.* 1. *cap.* 5. *sect.* 36. *and Bingham's case,* 2. *Rep. Ubi nullum Matrimonium, nulla dos. Dos* is derived, *ex donatione, & est quasi donarium,* because the Law it self giveth it to her. Of a Castle that is maintained for the necessary defence of the Realm, a Woman shall not be indowed, because it ought not to be divided, and the Publick, shall be preferred before the Private, but of a Castle that is only maintained for the private use and habitation of the Owner, a Woman shall be endowed. A Woman may be endowed of a third part of the profit of a Dove-house, of the third part of a Piscary, viz. *Tertium Piscem vel Factum retis tertium.* The surest endowment of Tythes is of the third sheaf, for what Land shall be sown is uncertain. If the Wife be past the Age of nine years at the death of her Husband, she shall be endowed of what age soever her Husband be, albeit he were but four years old: for *Consensus non concubitus facit matrimonium,* and a Woman cannot consent before Twelve, nor a Man before Fourteen, yet this Inchoate, and Imperfect Marriage (from the which either of the Parties at the age of consent may disagree) after the death of the Husband shall give the Dower to the Wife, and therefore it is accounted in Law after the death of the Husband, *Legitimum matrimonium,* a Lawful Marriage, *quoad dotem.* If a Man taketh a Wife of the Age of 7 years, and after alien his Land, and after alienation the Wife attaineth to the age of nine years, and after the Husband dieth, the Wife shall be endowed, for albeit she was not absolutely dowable at the time of the Marriage, yet she was conditionally dowable, *viz.* she attained to the Age of nine years before the death of the Husband, for by his death the possibility of Dower is Consummate. So it is if the Husband alien his Land, and then the Wife is attainted of Felony, now she is disabled, but if she be pardoned before the death of the Husband, she shall be endowed. It is commonly said three things are favour'd in Law, Life, Liberty, Dower. With the Civilians Dower may be in Goods, and not in Lands, yet here in *England* it must be in Lands, and not in Goods, *Co. on Lit. Fulbecks pr. par.* If a Woman go away from her Husband with an Adulterer, and will not be reconciled, she loseth her Dower by the *Stat. of Westminster* 2. *C.* 34.

Dowry signifieth in the Common Law two things, 1. That which the Wife bringeth to her Husband in Marriage, otherwise called *Maritagium,* Marriage good; next and more commonly, that which she hath of her Husband after the Marriage determined, if ſhe outlive him, *Glanvile lib.* 7. *cap.* 2. *Bracton lib.* 2. *cap.* 38. *Britton cap.* 101. *in Prin.* and in *Scotland* (*Dos*) ſignifieth juſt as much, *Skene de verborum ſign. verbo Dos.* The former is in *French* called *Dot* or *Doſt*, the other *Dovayre*, and by them Latined, *Doarium* or *dowarium*. It is not unreaſonable to call the former a Dowry, and the other a Dower, but I find them confounded. For example, *Smith de Rep. Angl. p.* 105. calleth the latter a Dowry and Dower is ſometime uſed for the former, as in *Britton ubi ſupra*, yet it is not inconvenient to diſtinguiſh them, being ſo divers. The Civilians call the former (*Dotem*) and the latter (*Donationem propter nuptias*)

D O Z.

A dozen, Duodena, æ, f.

A dozen of bread, Duodena panis. *Vet. Inter.* 3. Duodena panni, *Pry.* 185. Duodena cannabi, 1 *Fol.* 157. Duo Duodenæ teniæ & tres duodenæ Ligularum, *Co. Ent.* 125.

A dozen (*or precinct of a leet*) Decenna, æ, f.

D R A.

A dragoon, Dirnacha, æ, m.

A drain, Drana, æ, f.

A dram (*the eighth part of an ounce*) Drachma, æ, f.

A draper, Draparius, ii, m. *Ry.* 294. Pannarius, ii, m. Pannicularius, ii, m.

A woollen-draper, Lanarius, ii, m.

A linen draper, Lintearius, ii, m.

A draught (*or model*) Idea, æ, f. Exemplar, aris, n. Schēma, atis, n. Modulus, i, m. Dēlineātio, onis, f.

He that makes the firſt draught, Dēlineātor, oris, m.

To make the firſt draught, Dēlineo, are.

A draught (*or caſt with a net*) Jactus, ûs, m.

A draught (*in drinking*) Tractus, ûs, m. Hauſtus, ûs, m.

Draughts (*or the play at draughts*) Luſus duodecim ſcruporum.

To play at draughts, Ludere ſcrupis.

To draw. Trăho, ere.

A drawer, Hauſtor, oris, m.

A drawer (*or tapſter*) Pincerna, æ, f.

To draw jointly, Protelo deducere.

A neſt of drawers, Arculæ loculatæ.

Drawers, Perizomata, orum, n.

Linen drawers, Subligacula linea interiora. Braccæ lineæ.

A pair of drawers, Par Subligacŭlorum.

A dray (*or ſled*) Traha, æ, f.

A ſmall dray, Trahŭla, æ, f.

A dray man, Traharius, ii, m.

Of a dray man, Traharius, a, um.

D R E.

Dregs (*or lees*) Fæx, æcis, f.

Small dregs, Fæcula, æ, f.

Dregs of wine, Flores.

Full of dregs, Fæculentus, a, um.

Dredg (*Bollmong*) Farrago, ĭnis, f.

A drench

A drench for horses or sick beasts, Salivatum, i, n.

Drenched, Salivatus, a, um.

To drench (or pour a drench) Să-livo, are.

The tenure of the drenges, Drengagium ii, n.

A dresser (or board to put meat upon) Abax, acis m. Asser coquinarius. Repositorium, ii, n.

Dressings, Capitalia lintea.

D R I.

To drie, Sicco, are.

To drie in the sun, Insolo, are.

To drie in the smoak, Infumo, are.

A drift of cattle depasturing in a common, Prisa, æ, f. *Ra. Entr.* 578.

To run a drift, Permittere Carinas turbinibus.

Drink, Poculenta, æ, f. *Ry.* 48. Potus, ûs, m.

A drink (or potion) Potio, onis, f.

Small drink, Potiuncula, æ, f. Cervisia tenuis.

A drinking together, Compotatio, onis, f.

To drip (or drop) Gutto, are.

A dripping-pan, Patella pingularia. Deguttorium, ii, n.

The dripping of meat, Eliquamen, inis, n.

To drive (or chase) Pello, ere.

To drive away, Abigo, ere. Depello, ere.

Driven away, Abactus, a, um.

A driving away, Abactus, ûs, m.

A driver (a coach man) Agitā-tor, oris, m.

To drive forth again, Rechacio, are.

D R O.

Drogheda (in Ireland) Pontana.

The Dropsie, Hydrops, ŏpis, m.

That hath the dropsie, Hydropicus, a, um.

Dross (or scum of metal) Scoria, æ, f.

A drover (or driver of cattle) Armentarius, ii, m.

To drown, Submergo, ere.

D R U.

A drum, Tympănum, ni, n.

To beat, or play on a drum, Tympanizo, are. PulsareTympanum, complodere Tympana.

A drummer (or player on the drum) Tympanista, æ, m.

A Kettle drummer, Æneator, oris, m.

D U B.

To dub a Knight, Decurio, are.

Dubbing, Decuriatio, onis, f.

Dublin or *Divilin (in Ireland)* Divilina, Dublinia, Dublinium, Eblana.

Dublin County, Dubliniensis Comitatus.

D U C.

Duces tecum, Is a Writ commanding one to appear at a day in the Chancery, and to bring with him some piece of evidence, or other thing that the Court would view. See the new Book of Entries, *Verbo Duces tecum*.

A duck,

A duck, Anas, ătis, d. g.

D U E.

Due (or owed) Debitus, a, um.
A duel, Duellum, li, n.

D U G.

A dug (or udder) Uber, eris, n.
A dug (or pap) Mamma, æ, f.

D U K.

A duke, Dux, ŭcis, m.

A little duke, Ducillus, li, m.

A dukedom (or dutchy) Dŭcātus, ûs, m. In ſome Nations at this day, the Sovereigns of the Country are called by this name, as Duke of *Savoy*, Duke of *Saxony*, &c. Here in *England* Duke is the next in ſecular dignity to the Prince of *Wales*, and (as Mr. *Cambden* ſaith) heretofore in the *Saxons* time, they were called Dukes without any Addition, being but meer Officers and Leaders of Armies. After the Conqueror came in, there were none of this Title until *Edward* I's. days, who made *Edward* his ſon Duke of *Aquitane*, and *Edward* III. made his Son Duke of *Cornwall* : After that there were more made, and in ſuch ſort that their Titles deſcended by inheritance unto their Poſterity. They were Created with ſolemnity (*per cincturam gladii, cappæque, & circuli aurei in capite impoſitionem, & traditionem virgæ aureæ*) *Cambd. Britan. Sub. Tit. Ordines Angliæ, pag.* 119.

D U L.

A dulcimer, Sambŭca, æ, f.

D U M.

Dumb, Mutus, a, um.

Dumfriſe (in Scotland) Corda ſelgovarum.

D U N.

Dunbriton (in Scotland) Britannodunum.

Dundee (in Scotland) Alectem, Allectum, Deidonum. Taodunum.

Dung, Fimus, i, m. Stercus, ŏris, n.

To dung (as to dung land) Letamo, are. Stercŏro, are.

Dunged, Stercŏrātus, a, um.

Dunging, Stercŏratio, onis, f.

Full of dung, Stercŏrōſus, a, um.

A dunghil (or mixen) Stercŏrārium, ii, n. Sterquilinium, ii, n. Fimetum, i, n.

A dunghil fork, Furcilla, æ, f.

A dungeon, Hypogæum, i, n. Barathrum, i, n.

Dunsbey or Danesby near Whitby (in Yorkſhire) Dunum. Dunus ſinus.

Dunsbey or Duncasbey (one of the three Northern Promontories of Scotland) Viervedrum, Virvedrum.

Dunstable (in *Bedfordshire*) Magnitum, Magionimum, Magovinium, Magiovintum.

Dunstan (a mans name) Dunstanus, i, m.

Dunstaphage (in *Scotland*) Evonium.

Dunstavile (the Family) Dunestanvilla.

Of *Dunwich* (in *Essex*) Domucensis.

D U R.

Dur river (in *Ireland*) Duri, Duris.

Duresse, Duritia, æ, f. It cometh of the *French* word *Dur* (i. e.) *durus*, *vel durete* (i. e.) *duritas*, and is where one is kept in Prison, or restrained from his Liberty, contrary to the Order of the Law: It is also an exception in Pleading to avoid the Deed, which a Man was enforced to seal to ransom himself from an unlawful Captivity, *vid. LeighPhil. Com. fol.* 81. *Brook* in his abridgment hath Duress and Manass together (i. e.) *duritiam & minas*, hardness and threatning. See the new Book of Entries, *verbo Duress*, and the new Terms of Law.

Durham City (*in the North*) Dunelmia, Dunelmum, Dunelmus, Dunholmus, Dunolmum.

Durham County, Dunelmensis Comitatus.

Bishop of *Durham*, Episcopus Dunelmensis.

D U S.

Dust, Scobs, obis, f. Pulvis, ĕris, d. g.

Saw dust, Scobis, is. f.

Smiths dust (*the sparks flying from hot iron*) Strictura, æ, f.

Mill-dust, Pollen, inis, n.

Dusty, Pulverulentus, a, um.

D U T.

A dutchess, Dŭcissa, æ, f.

A little dutchess, Ducilla, æ, f.

Dutchy Court, Curia Ducatûs, & Comitatûs Palatini Domini Regis Lancastriæ. It is a Court wherein all matters appertaining to the Dutchy of *Lancaster* are decided, by the decree of the Chancellour of that Court, and the original of it was in *Henry* IV's days, who obtaining the Crown, by deposing *Richard* II. and having the Dutchy of *Lancaster* by Descent in the right of his Mother, he was seized thereof as King, and not as Duke. So that all the Liberties, Franchises and Jurisdictions of the said Dutchy, passed from the King, by his grand Seal, and not by Livery or Atturnement, as the possession of *Everwick*, and of the Earldom of *March*, and such others did, which had descended to the King, by other Ancestors than Kings. But at the last, *Henry* IV. by Authority of Parliament passed a Charter whereby the Possessions, Liberties, &c. of the said Dutchy were severed from the Crown, yet *Henry* VII. reduced it to his former nature, as it was in *Henry* V.'s days. *Comptons Jurisdict. fol.* 136. The Officers belonging to this Court, are the Chancellor, the Attorney, Receiver

ceiver General, Clerk of the Court, the Messenger. Besides these, there are certain Assistants of this Court, as one Attorney in the Exchequer, one Attorney of the Dutchy in the Chancery, four Learned men in the Law, retained of Counsel with the King in the said Court.

Duty, Debitum, i, n.

Duties, Credita, orum, n.

Dutiful (or serviceable) Officiosus, a, um.

Dutifully, Officiosè, adv.

D W A.

A dwarf, Nanus, i, m. Pusillus, i, m.

A she-dwarf, Nana, æ, f.

D W E.

A dwelling, Mansum, i, n. Mansura, æ, f. *Cow.* 167. *Ra. Entr.* 610. *Reg.* 165. 1 *Mon.* 529. 598. Mansiones, 1 *Mon.* 523. 320, Mansio, onis, f. Habitaculum, li, n. Domicilium, ii, n.

To dwell, Moror, ari. Hăbĭto, are.

A dweller, Habitator, oris, m.

To go, or dwell in another place, Transmigro, are.

D Y E.

To dye in colours, Tingo, ere.

Dyed, Tinctus, a, um.

Double dyed, Dibaphus, a, um.

A dye-house, Tinctorium; ii, n. Officina tinctoria.

A dyer, Tinctor, oris, m.

A dyers wife, Tinctrix, icis, f.

A dyers vat. Cortina, æ, f. Ahenum Tinctorium.

A dying, Tinctura, æ, f. Tinctus, ûs, m.

The art of dying, Baphice, es, f.

Belonging to dying, Tinctorius, a, um.

E A C.

EAch and every, Alteruter & quilibet.

E A G.

An eagle, Aquila, æ, f.

An eaglet, Aquilæ pullus.

E A R.

An ear-ring, Inauris, is, f.

An ear, Auris, is, f.

An ear (or handle of a pot) Diota, æ, f.

An ear picker, Specillum, li, n. Auri-Scalpium, ii, n.

An ear of corn, Spica, æ, f.

To ear (or shoot forth ears) Spico, are.

Earings of corn, Azuræ. Bract.

The beard of the ear, Arista, æ, f.

An earl, Comes, itis, m. The manner of creating Earls is by Girding them with a Sword *Cam. pag.* 107. See the solemnity thereof of described more at large in *Stows* Annals, *p.* 1121. The occasion why these Earls in later time have had no sway over the County, whereof they bear their name, is not absurdly signified in Sir *Thomas Smith, lib.* 2. *cap.* 14. where he saith that the Sheriff is called Vicecomes, as (*Vicarius Comitis*) following all matters of Justice, as the Earl should do; and that because the Earl is most commonly attendant upon the King in his Wars, or otherwise. So that it seemeth that Earls by reason of their high Imployments, being not able to follow also the business of the County, were delivered of all that burthen, and only enjoyed the Honour, as now they do. And the Sheriff although he is still called *Vicecomes*, yet all he doth is immediately under the King, and not under the Earl. See *Hotoman de verb. feudal, verbo Comes* and *Cassan. de Consuetud. Burg. p.* 12.

Earnest money, Arrha, æ, f. Arrhabo, onis, m.

Earth, Terra, æ, f.

Formed of earth, Plasmatus, a, um.

Earthly, Terrenus. a, um.

An earth-quake, Terræmotus, ûs, m. Terræ quassatio.

Fullers earth, Creta cimolia.

E A S.

To ease (*lighten or disburthen*) Levo, are. Allevo, are.

Easement, Aisiamentum, i, n. *Spel.* 27. *Lex.* 48. *Reg.* 165.

Easement is a Service that one Neighbour hath of another by Charter, or Prescription without Profit, as a way through his ground a sink or such like, *Kitchin fol.* 105. which in the Civil Law is called *servitus predii.*

Easie (*or not difficult*) Facilis, le, adj.

The east where the sun riseth, Oriens, entis, m.

East part, Pars Orientalis.

Easter, Pascha, ătis, n.

The day after the octaves of Easter, Clausum Paschæ.

Eastonness (in *Suffolk*) Eminentior Extentio Prom.

Eastwick (in *Hertfordshire*) Vicus Orientalis.

E A T.

A great eater, Edulus, li, m.

Eaton (in *Berkshire*) Ætona.

E A V.

Eaves boards, Suggrundia. asseres imbricantes.

E B B.

An ebb, Ebba, æ, f. Ebba & Fluctus, *Bract.* 255. 338. *bis.* Flumen & Ebba. *Fle.* 216. Fluvius & Ebba. *Fle.* 383.

The ebb (*or ebbing of the sea*) Refluxus seu Recessus maris. Refusio maris.

E D E.

E D E.

Eden river (in *Cumberland* and *Westmorland*) Ituna.

Edenborough (in *Scotland*) Alata Castra. Alatum Castrum. Edenburgus, Edenburgum.

Edenborough Castle, Castrum Puellarum.

Edenborough Frith, Bodotria.

Ederington (in *Sussex*) Adurni portus.

E D I.

An edict (or statute) Edictum, i, n.

To edifie (or build) Ædifico, are.

An edifice (or building) Ædificium, ii, n.

An edition (setting forth or impression) Editio, onis, f.

Edith (a womans name) Editha, æ, f.

E D U.

To educate, Educo, are.

Education (nurture or bringing up) Educatio, onis, f.

E E L.

An Eel, Anguilla, æ, f.

An Eel-spear, Fuscina, æ, f. Stimulus, li, m. Hasta Triunguis.

E F F.

Effectual, Effectualis, le, adj. Efficax, acis, adj.

Effectually, Effectualitèr, adv.

Efficacy, Efficacia, æ, f.

Effusion (or pouring out) Effusio, onis, f.

E G G.

An egg, Ovum, i, n.

Poached eggs, Hapala ova. Ova sine tegmine cocta.

To poach eggs, Ova coctillare.

The yolk of an egg, Vitellus, i, m. Oviluteum, ei, n.

E G B.

Egbert (a mans name) Egbertus, i, m.

E G R.

Egress (or going forth) Egressus, ûs, m.

E I E.

Ejectione Firmæ, Is a Writ which lies where the Lessee for years is cast out of Possession.

E I G.

Eight, Octo, Indecl.

Belonging to eight, Octonarius, a, um.

Eight times, Octiès, adv.

The eighth, Octavus, a, um.

The eighth time, Octavum, adv.

Of the eighth year, Octennis, e, adj.

Gathering the eighth part of goods, Octonarii, orum, m.

The

The eight part above the whole, Sesquioctavus, a, um.
Eighthly, Octave, ad.
Eight fold, Octuplus, a, um.
Multiplied by eight, Octuplicatus, a, um.
The space of eight years, Octennium, ii, n.
Eighteen, Octodecim.
The eighteenth, Decimus octavus.
Eight and twenty times, Duodetricies, adv.
The eight and twentieth, Duodevicesimus, a, um.
Eighteen times, Duodevicies, adv.
Eight and thirty, Duodequadraginta, Indecl.
The eight and thirtieth, Duodequadragesimus, a, um.
Eight and fourty, Duodequinquaginta.
The eight and fourtieth, Duodequinquagesimus, a, um.
Eighty, Octoginta, Indecl.
The eightieth, Octogesimus, a, um.
Of eighty, Octogenarius, a, um.
Eighty times, Octogies.
Eight hundred, Octingenti.
Of eight hundred, Octingenarius, a, um.
Eight hundred times, Octingenties.

E I N.

Einsbury in St. *Neots* (in *Huntingdonshire*) Ernulphi curia.

E L A.

To elaborate (or labour diligently) Elaboro, are.

E L B.

An elbow, Cubitus, i, m.

E L D.

The elder sisters part of Lands, Enitia pars. *Co. Lit.* 166. *Kit.* 148.
Eldership (or birthright) Esnetria, æ, f. Einecia, æ, f.
Elder (or more ancient) Senior, oris.
Eldest, Maximus natu.

E L E.

To elect (or choose) Eligo, ere.
An electuary, Electuarium, ii, n. Which is a Confection made two ways, either liquid as in *forma opiatæ*, or whole, as in Lozenges, &c.
Elegancy in speech, Elegancia, æ, f.
An elegy, Elegia, æ, f.
Elegit, Is a Writ judicial and lieth for him that hath recovered debt or damages in the Kings Court against one not able in his Goods to satisfie; and directed to the Sheriff, commanding that he make delivery of half the Parties Lands or Tenements, and all his Goods, Oxen and Beasts for the Plough excepted. *Old nat. brev. fol.* 152. *Regist. Orig. fol.* 299. & 301. and the Table of the Register Judicial, which expresseth divers uses of this Writ. The Author of the new Terms of Law

Law ſaith, that this Writ ſhould be ſued within the year, whom read at large for the uſe of the ſame. *Elegit eſt nomen brevis, ſic dictum ab hoc verbo (Elegit) in eodem comprehenſo. Cowel Inſtit.*

Elenborough (in *Cumberland*) Olenacum.

Elen (a womans name) Elena, æ, f.

Elenborough or near it (in *Cumberland*) Volantium.

An elephant, Elephas, antis, m. Elephantus, i, m.

Eleven, Undecim.

Eleventh, Undecimus, a, um.

E L I.

Elias (a mans name) Elias, Indecl.

Elian (a womans name) Elianora, æ, f.

Elizeus (a mans name) Elizeus, ei, m.

E L L.

An ell, Ulna, æ, f.

E L M.

An elm-tree, Ulmus, i, f.

A grove of elms, Ulmārium, ii, n.

Elmesley (in *Yorkſhire*) Ulmetum.

E L O.

Elocution, Elocutio, onis, f.

An elogy (or teſtimonial of ones Praiſe and Commendations or Diſpraiſe) Elogium, ii, n.

Eloquence, Eloquentia, æ, f. Facundia, æ, f.

Eloquent, Eloquens, tis, adj. Facundus, a, um.

Eloquently, Facundè, adv.

To make eloquent, Facundo, are.

E L S.

Elſe (or otherwiſe) Aliàs, adv. Alitèr, adv.

Elſtree or *Egleſtree* (in *Hertfordſhire*) Nemus Aquilinum.

E L T.

Eltham (in *Kent*) Elteſhamum.

E L Y.

Ely Iſle (in *Cambridgeſhire*) Anguillaria Inſula.

Ely City (in *Cambridgeſhire*) Anguillarianum Monaſterium. Helienſe Cœnobium.

Of *Ely*, Elienſis.

E M A.

Emma (a Womans name) Emma, æ, f.

Emancipation, Emancipatio, onis, f.

E M B.

An embalming, Pollinctura, æ, f.

An emblem, Emblema, atis, n.

Embleaments (or the profits of lands ſowed) Embleamenta, orum, n.

An embrion (or child in the Womb before it is perfect) Embryo, onis, m.

To embroider, Phrygio, are. Acupingo, ere.

An embroiderer, Phrygio, onis, m. Acupictor, oris, m. Limbator, oris, m.

An embroideress, Limbatrix, icis, f.

An embroidering (or border of a garment embroidered) Acupigmentum, i, n. Opus Phrygium, Limbus Vestimenti.

Embroidering with eylet holes, Ocellatura, æ, f.

An embroidering needle, Acus Babylonica, Assyria.

Embroidered, Acupictus, a, um.

E M E.

An emendation (or amendment) Emendatio, onis, f.

An emerald (a pretious stone) Smaragdus, i, m.

E M I.

Eminent, Eminens, entis, adj.

E M O.

Emoluments, Emolumenta, orum, n.

E M P.

Empanel, (Impanellare, ponere in assisis & juratis) cometh of the *French* (*Panne*, i. e. *Pellis*) or of (*Panneau*) which signifieth sometime as much as a Pane with us, as a Pane of Glass, or of a Window. It signifieth the writing or entring the names of a Jury into a Parchment, Schedule, or Roll, or Paper by the Sheriff, which he hath summoned to appear for the performance of such publick service as Juries are imployed in.

Emparlance, cometh of the *French* word (*Parler*) and signifieth in our Common Law a desire or Petition in Court, of a day to pause what is best to do. *Cowel's Interp.* The Civilians call it (*Petitionem induciarum.*)

An empirick, Empiricus, i, m. i. e. A young and unskilfull Physician, which without regard either of the cause of the Disease, or of the Constitution of the Patient, applies those Medicines whereof either by observation of other mens Receipts, or by his own practice he hath had experience in some other, work how they will.

An emplaster (or salve) Emplastrum, i, n.

To empoverish (or make poor) Depaupero, are.

Empty, Vacuus, a, um.

To empty (or make empty) Vacuo, are. Evacuo, are.

Half empty, Sematus, a, um.

Emptiness, Exinanitio, onis, f.

E M R.

The emrods (or piles) Hæmorrhois, idis, f.

Of the emrods, Hæmorrhoidalis, le, adj.

E N A.

To enable (or give ability) Habilito, are.

Ena-

Enamel, Encaustrum, i, n.
To enamel, Encausto pingere.

E N C.

To enchaunt, Incanto, are.
An enchaunter, Incantator, oris, m.
An enchauntress, Incantatrix, icis, f.
An enchiridion (or small manual book that one may clasp in the hand) Enchiridium, ii, n.
To enclose (compass or shut in) Includo, ere. Concludo, ere.
An enclosure, Clausura, æ, f.
To encomber, Impedio, ire.
To encounter, Confligo, ere.
To encourage, Animo, are.
An encrease (or increasing) Incrementum, i, n.
An encroachment (or taking more than is due) Encrochamentum, i, n. Pourprestura, æ, f. (i. e.) when two Mens grounds lie together, the one presseth too far on the other; or when a Landlord hath gotten more Rent or Services of his Tenant, than of right is due.

E N D.

An end, Finis, is, m vel f.
To end, Finio, ire.
To endite, Endicto, are.
Endictment, Endictamentum, i, n. Signifieth in Law an Accusation found by an enquest of twelve or more, upon their Oath, and as the Appeal is always at the suit of the Party, so the Endictment, is always at the suit of the King. *Leigh. Phil. Com. fol.* 85. It is an Accusation, because the Jury that inquireth of the Offence, doth not receive it until the Party that offereth the Bill, appear so far in it as to subscribe his name. It differeth from an Accusation in this, that the preferrer of the Bill is no way tied to the proof thereof upon any Penalty if it be not proved, except there appear Conspiracy. Wherefore tho moved by Mr. *West*'s Authority, I call it an Accusation: Yet I take it to be rather, *Denunciatio*, because it is of Office due by the great Enquest, rather than of a free intent to accuse. Of this you may read, Sir *Thomas Smith de Repub. Angl. lib.* 2. *cap.* 19. & *Stawnf. pl. cor. lib.* 2. *cap.* 23, 24, 25, 26, &c. *usque* 34. And Mr. *Lamberd*'s *Eirenarch, lib.* 4. *cap.* 5. where you may receive good satisfaction in this matter. Endictment (saith Mr. *Lamberd*) signifieth in our Common Law, as much as (*Accusatio*) in the Civil Law, though it have not in all points the like effect. *West. part* 2. *Symb. Titulo Inditement*) defineth it thus. An Inditement is a Bill or Declaration made in form of Law (for the benefit of the Common-wealth) of an Accusation for some offence, either Criminal or Penal, exhibited unto Jurors, and by their Verdict found and presented to be true, before an Officer, having power to punish the same Offence. To make a good Endictment it is necessary to put in the day, year and place, when and where the Felony is done. It ought to be certain also in the matter, as appears *p.* 8. *e.* 4. *f.* 3. where a Bayliff was Endicted, be-

cause he took one for suspicion of Felony, and after, *eum felonicè & voluntariè ad largum ire permisit*, & did not shew in certain for what suspicion of Felony, so when one is Endicted that he made an hundred Shillings of Alchymy *ad instar pecuniæ domini Regis*, and alledged not what Money it was, Groats or Pennies; but in case a man be slain, and he is so mangled in the Visage that one cannot know him, but the Party which killed him is well known, there is no reason he should escape Punishment, therefore although no Appeal lieth against him in this case, yet an Endictment lies, and he shall be Endicted, *Quod interfecit quendam ignotum*, the same Law is, if one be Endicted that he stole the Goods, *Cujusdam ignoti*, or *bona cujusdam personæ*, the reason is, because the Indictment is not his which was the Owner of the Goods, but is the suit of the King, which is, to have the Goods, if none claim them.

An Endictment ought to express in certain, as well in what part the mortal wound is, as the profundity and latitude of it, and therefore it was moved that such an Endictment, *Quod unam plagam mortalem dedit, circiter pectus*, was insufficient, because altogether uncertain, for it might be in the neck or belly, but it was good Law, saith Sir *Edward Cook in Youngs case, lib.* 4. *Circiter Pectus* is uncertain and insufficient amongst the Cases of Appeals and Endictments, *Brooks Abridg.* 4. *Rep.* Cases of Appeals and Endictments.

Endictments of Treason, and of all other things are most curiously and certainly penned, *Cook* 7. *Rep. Calv.* case.

That Endictment is not good which ought to have an Argument or Implication to make it good, therefore that is not a good Endictment if it be *Quod furatus est unum equum*, and saith not *felonice*, and yet it is implied in this word *furatus est*. So if for Rape the Endictment be, *Quod eam carnaliter cognovit*, without saying *Rapuit*, this is not good. If one be Endicted *Super visum corporis*, before the Mayor of *London*, without adding this word *Coroner*, this is not good, and yet he which is Mayor of *London* is always Coroner, and therefore it is implyed. If one be Indicted, *Quod Felonice abduxit unum equum*. This is not good without saying *cepit & abduxit*, for it may be that it was delivered to him, and so he leadeth him, in which Case it is not Felony. *Stawnford Plea of Crown.*

In the Endictment it shall be supposed that a man such a day and place with force and arms, that is with staves, swords and knives feloniously stole the Horse, against the Kings Peace, and that form must be kept in every Endictment, though the Felon had neither Sword, nor other Weapon with him, yet this is no untruth in the Jury, for the form of an Endictment is, *Inquiratur pro Domino Rege, si à tali die & anno apud talem locum vi & armis, viz. Gladiis*, &c. *talem equum talis hominis cepit.* The twelve Men are only charged with the effect of the Bill, that is, whether he be Guilty

Guilty of the Felony or not, and not with the Form, and when they ſay *Billa vera*, they ſay true, as they take the effect of the Bill to be, for though there be falſe Latin in the Bill, and the Jury ſaith *Billa vera*, yet their Verdict is true, *Vi & armis*, muſt be in all Endictments of Treaſon, Murder, Felony, Treſpaſs, elſe it is not good, *Doctor and Student, cap.* 5. 4.

An Endictment of Murder found in this ſort that, *Eliz. fuit in pace quouſque, A. Vir.* 5. *Præfat. Eliz. de Pin. Com. S.* Yeoman did kill her, is good; for the addition Yeoman muſt of neceſſity refer to the Husband, becauſe a Woman cannot be a Yeoman, but an Endictment, *Quouſque Alicia, S. de Pin. in Com. S. uxor J. S.* Spinſter, is not good againſt *Alice S*, for there Spinſter, being an indifferent addition both for Man and Woman, muſt refer to *J. S.* which is the next antecedent, and ſo the Woman hath no addition, *Ad proximum antecedens fiat relatio*.

So if an Endictment againſt *J. S. Serviens J. P. de D. in Com. Mid.* Butcher. This is not good, for Servant is no addition, and *Butcher* referreth to the Maſter, which is the next antecedent.

If a Man take a Coat-armour which hangs over a dead mans Tomb in a Church, the Endictment muſt be *Bona executorum*, of the dead man, but if a Graveſtone be taken away, the Endictment muſt be *Bona Eccleſiæ, Lambert Eirenarch.* 494. 495.

To endow, Doto, are.

Endowment, Dotatio, onis, f. Cometh of the *French* (*Douer*) and ſignifieth the beſtowing or aſſuring of a Dower. See Dower. But it is ſometime uſed Metaphorically, for the ſetting forth or ſending of a ſufficient Portion for a Vicar toward his perpetual maintenance, when the benefice is appropriated. See the Statute *An.* 15. *Reg.* 2. *cap.* 6.

To endure, Enduro, are. *Co. Ent.* 205.

E N E.

An enemy, Inimicus, i, m. Hoſtis, is, c. 2.

Energy (*or effectual operation*) Energia, æ, f.

E N F.

An enforcement (*conſtraint or compulſion*) Coactus, ûs, m. Compulſio, onis, f.

E N G.

An engine, Machina, æ, f. Machinamentum, i, n.

Belonging to engines, Machinâlis, le, adj.

Of engines, Machinārius, a, um.

An inventer of engines, Machĭnātor, oris, m.

An engineer (*or worker of engines*) Machinārius, ii, m.

To deviſe an engine, Machĭnor, ari.

An engine to hoiſt packs in and out of ſhips, Mariſchăla, æ, f.

 Engines

Engines to draw ships on land, Remulcopæ, arum, f. pl.

Englecery (or *Englescbyrie*) Engleceria, æ, f. (i. e.) Ones being an *Englishman*.

England, Anglia, Britannia, Albion.

An Englishman man, Anglus, i, m.

English men (or *English Saxons*) Angli, Anglo-Saxones.

To engrave, Cœlo, are. Sculpo, ere.

Engraven (or *engraved*) Scalpratus, a, um. Sculptus, a, um.

An engraver, Sculptor, oris, m. Cælator, oris, m.

An engraving iron, Scalprum, ri, n.

To engross (or *ingross a writing*) Ingrosso, are. Inferre in Tabulas.

E N H.

To enhaunce the price of any thing, Augere pretium. Extollere pretium.

E N I.

An enigma (*a dark or hard question*) Ænigma, atis, n.

Enigmatical, Ænigmaticus, a, um.

Enisham (in *Oxfordshire*) Insula.

E N L.

To enlarge, Enlargio, are. Amplifico, are.

An enlargement, Enlargatio, onis, f. Enlargiamentum, i, n. *Reg.* 250. 255. *bis.* 8. *Co.* 109.

E N O.

Enormity, Enormitas, atis, f.

Enough, Satis, adv.

It is enough, Sufficit.

E N Q.

Enquest, Inquisitio, onis, f. Is all one with the *French* word, and all one in signification both with the *French* and *Latin*. It is especially taken for that Inquisition, that neither the *Romans* nor *French* men ever had use of that I can learn. And that is the Enquest of Jurors, or by Jury, which is the most usual Tryal of all Causes, both Civil and Criminal in our Realm, for in Causes Civil after proof is made of either side, so much as each Party thinketh for himself, if the doubt be in the Fact, it is referred to the discretion of twelve indifferent Men, Empanelled by the Sheriff for the Purpose: and as they bring in their Verdict, so Judgment passeth, for the Judge saith, the Jury finds the Fact thus: Then is the Law thus: And so we judge for the Inquest in causes Criminal. See Jury, and see Sir *Thomas Smith de Repub. Ang. lib.* 2. *cap.* 19. An Enquest is either of Office, or at the mise of the Party, *Stawnf. Pl. Cor. lib.* 3. *cap.* 12.

E N R.

To enrage (*or make angry*) Rabio, ire. Furio, are.

Enraged, Furiatus, a, um. Furore percitus.

To enrich (*or make rich*) Locupleto, are.

To enroll, Irrotulo, are.

An enrolling, Irrotulatio, onis, f.

An enrolment, Irrotulamentum, i, n. *Cow.* 145. *Spel.* 387.

E N S.

An ensign (*or banner*) Insigne, is, n.

An ensign-bearer, Vexillarius, ii, m.

To enstal, Installo, are.

E N T.

To entangle (*or ensnare*) Intrico, are.

To entail, Tallio, are. *Cow.* 99. 253. *Ry.* 110. 248. *Le.* 122.

An entail, Tallium, ii, n. Feudum Talliatum. It cometh of the French *entaille* (i. e.) *inscisus* and in our Common Law is a substantive abstract, signifying Fee-tail, or Fee-intailed. *Littleton* in the second Chapter of his book draweth Fee-tail from the verb *Talliare*, which must come from the *French Tailler*, i. e. *scindere*, *secare*. And the reason is manifest, because Fee tail in the Law is nothing but Fee abridged, scanted or curtailed (as I may say) or limited and tied to certain conditions. *Taille* in *France* is metaphorically taken for a Tribute or subsidy. Vid. *Lupanum de Magistratibus Francorum, lib.* 3. *cap. Talea.* Vid. *Fee & Tail* *Entenement*, cometh of the French *Entendement* (i. e.) *Intellectus ingenium.* It signifieth in our Common Law so much as the true meaning or signification of a word or sentence. See of this *Kitch. fol.* 224.

To enter (*or go in*) Intro, are.

To enterline, Interlineo, are. Interscribo, ere.

To enter (*or put into*) Introduco, ere. Intromitto, ere.

An enterprise, Imprisa, æ, f. *Ry.* 267. 287. Interprisa, æ, f. *Ra. Entr.* 467.

To entertain, Excipio, ere. Recipio, ere.

Entertained (*or entertaining*) Hospitus, a, um.

Entertainment of, or provision for the King for one night, Firma unius noctis.

An enticer, Abductor, oris, m.

Entire (*or whole*) Integer, a, um.

To entitle, Intitulo, are.

An entrance, Introitus, ûs, m. Ingressus, ûs, m.

To entrap, Intrico, are. Irretio, ire. Implico, are.

To entreat (*treat of or handle*) Tracto, are.

An entry, Ingressus, ûs, m. Cometh of the *French* (*Entree*, i. e. *Introitus, ingressus, aditus*) and properly signifieth in our Common Law the taking Possession of Lands or Tenements: See *Plowden Assise* of fresh force in *London*, and read *West* also, *part* 2. *Symbol. Titulo Recoveries, sect.* 2, & 3. who

3. Who there sheweth for what things it lieth, and for what it lieth not.

Entrusion, Intrusio, onis, f. It is a violent or unlawful entrance into Lands or Tenements, being utterly void of a Possessour, by him that hath no right, nor spark of right unto them. *Bract. lib.* 4.*ca.* 7. but it is most fitly applied to the Kings child.

E N V.

To envy, Invideo, ere.

Envious, Invidus, a, um.

To inviron (*or compass about*) Circundo, are. Circumcludo, ere.

To enure, Opero, are.

E P I.

The *Epigastrium*, or all the outward part of the Belly which covereth the entrails, from the Bulk down unto the Belly. Epigastrium, ii, n.

The *Epiglottis*, the cover or weasen of the Throat, the flap or little tongue, which by closing the amplitude of the Larynx, and the way of the Rough Artery, suffereth no meat or drink to slip down into the inner capacity thereof, and so to fall into the Lungs. Epiglottis, ĭdis, f.

An epigram, Epigramma, ătis, n.

An epigrammatist, Epigrammatographus, i, m.

The epilepsie (*or falling sickness*) Epilepsia, æ, f.

An epilogue, Epilogus, i, m.

An epistle, Epistola, æ, f.

An epitaph, Epitaphium, ii, n.

An epitome (*or abridgment*) Epitome, es, f.

To epitomize (*or abbreviate*) Epitomizo, are. Abbrevio, are. verb.

E Q U.

Equal, Equalis le, adj.

Equity (*right or justice*) Æquitas, atis, f.

Equivalent, Æquivalens, ntis, adj.

Equivocal, Æquivocus, a, um.

To equivocate, Æquivoco, are.

E R A.

To eradicate (*or pluck up by the root*) Eradico, are.

Erasmus (*a mans name*) Erasmus, i, m.

E R E.

To erect (*or set up*) Elevo, are. Erigo, ere.

E R M.

An ermine (*or ermines*) Mus Ponticus.

E R R.

To err, Erro, are.

E R U.

Erudition, Eruditio, onis, f.

An

An eruption (or breaking out) Eruptio, onis, f.

E S C.

Escambio, Is a Licence granted to one, for the making over a Bill of Exchange to a man over Sea. *Regist. Orig. fol.* 199. *a.*

To escape, Escapio, are. *Dr. and Student* 16. 1. *Fo.* 30. *Ra. Entr.* 583. *Co. Entr.* 532. Evado, ere.

An escape, Escapia, æ, f. Evasio, onis, f. Escape is where one that is arrested cometh to his Liberty before that he is delivered by award of any Justices, as by order of Law. If the arrest of him that escaped were for Felony, then that shall be Felony in him that did voluntarily suffer the escape, and if for Treason, then it shall be Treason in him, and if for Trespass, then Trespass. If Murder be made in the day, and the Murderer be not taken, then it is an escape, for the which the Town where the Murder was done shall be amerced, *Stawnf. Pl. of the Cr.* If a Man be robbed in the day, and the Thief escape, and be not taken within half a year after the robbery, the Town or Hundred shall answer it to the Party robbed. If he have made Hue and Cry. *Id. Pl. of Cr. lib.* 1. *c.* 33. The Township shall be amerced for an escape if it was *tempore diurno*, although the Murder was committed in the Town-field, or in a Lane, but it seemeth reasonable that complaint be made to the Justices, *L. Dyer Term. Hill. an.* 4. *Reg. Eliz.* Although the Prisoner which escapes be out of the view, yet if fresh suit be made, and he reprised in *recenti insecutione*, he shall be in Execution, for otherwise at the turning of a corner, or by an entry of an house, or by any other such means the Prisoner may be out of view, *Cook. Rigeways Case* 3. *Rep.* If a Sheriff or Bayliff of a Franchise Assent that one which is in Execution, and under their Custody shall go out of Gaol for a while, and then return, although that he return in the time, yet this is an escape, for the Sheriff or Bayliff ought to guard him in *salva & arcta custodia*, and the Statute of *Westm. c.* 11. saith, *Quod carceri mancipentur in ferris.* So that the Sheriff may keep them which are in Execution in Irons and Fetters, till they have satisfied their Creditors, *Cook Boytons case* 3 *Rep.* where the Sheriff dieth, and one in Execution breaketh the Gaol, and goeth at large, this is no escape, for when a Sheriff dieth, all the Prisoners are in the Custody of the Law, until a new Sheriff be made, *Leigh. Phil. Com. pag.* 90. If a Woman be Warden of the Fleet and a Prisoner in the Fleet marrieth her, this shall be Judged an escape in the Woman, and the Law judgeth the Prisoner to be at large. *Plowd. Commen. Plato's case.*

An escheat, Escaeta, æ, f. *Pry.* 66. *Cow.* 102. *Spel.* 235. Escheats happen two manner of ways, *Aut per defectum sanguinis*, as if the Tenant dies without Issue, *Aut per delictum tenentis*, that is for Felony. Escheta is derived of the

French

French word *Eschier*, *accidere*, for an Escheat is a casual profit, *Quod accidit Domino ex eventu & ex insperato*, which happeneth to the Lord by chance, and unlook'd for, in which Case we say the Fee is Escheated. Escheats by Civilians are called *Caduca*. *Co. on Lit. p.* 13 & 492. Those which are hanged by Martial Law, in *Furore Belli*, forfeit no Lands for Escheat · for Felony is three manner of ways.

1. *Aut quia suspensus per Collum.*

2. *Aut quia abjuravit Regnum.*

3. *Aut quia utlegatus est.*

The Father is seized of Lands in Fee holden of *J. S.* The Son is attainted of High-Treason, the Father dieth, the Land shall Escheat to *J. S. propter defectum sanguinis*. Because the Father dieth without Heir, and the King cannot have the Land, because the Son never had any thing to forfeit, but the King shall have the Escheat of all the Lands whereof the Person attainted of High Treason, was seized, of whomsoever they were holden. *Cook on Lit. lib.* 1. *sect.* 4.

An escheator, Escaetor, oris, m. Escheator cometh of (Escheat) he is so called because his Office is to observe the Escheats of the King in the County; whereof he is Escheator, and certifieth them into the Exchequer. This Officer is appointed by the Lord Treasurer, and by Letters Patents from him, and continueth in his Office but one year, neither can any be Escheator above once in three years, *Anno* 1 *H.* 8. *cap.* 8. and *Anno* 3. *ejusdem, cap.* 2. See more of this Officer and his Authority in *Crompton's Just. of Peace*: See *ep.* 29. *ed.* 1. the form of the Escheators Oath see in *Regist. Orig. fol.* 301. *Fitz* calleth him an Officer of Record. *Nat. brev. fol.* 100. *C.* because that which he certifieth by vertue of his Office, hath the Credit of a Record.

Escheatorship, Officium Escaetriæ. *Regist. Orig. fol.* 259. *b.*

Escripts, Escripta, orum, n. *Co. Ent.* 135. 146.

Escuage, Scutagium, ii, n.

E S D.

Esdras (a mans name) Esdras, æ, m.

E S K.

Esk river (in *Scotland*) Isca.

E S P.

Esplees (*or the full profits of land*) Expletia, orum, n.

E S Q.

An esquire, Armiger, ĕri, m.

E S S.

An essay, Assaia, æ, f. (i. e.) the Examination of Weights and Measures by the Clerk of the Market.

Essex,

Essex, East-Sexena. Essexia, Estsexa.

Essoin, Essonium, ii, n. And sometimes *Exonium*, and sometimes without *x*, or *s*, is a word forensecal, and cometh of an Obsolete *French* word *Essonier*, or *Exonier*, to excuse and free from care, from the word *Soingnier*. It is an excuse made for the Tenant or Defendant, who would not appear and be admitted in real Actions, or to Suiters in Court Baron for five Causes, 1. *De malo viæ sive veniendi*, where the Tenant would not come in respect of some impossibility, or durst not in regard of some eminent danger, and this is called *Essonium commune*. 2. *De malo lecti*, where some Disease hindereth, which according to its nature giveth longer or shorter day. *Glan. cap.* 19. 3. *Tenus mare*, which is cast on the behalf of the Tenant, when he is beyond the Seas, and this is for forty days at least, *Glanvillus cap.* 25. 4. *Servitium Regis*, when the Tenant is in the Kings Service, and then the Plea resteth without day untill he return, *Glanvil cap.* 27. 5. *De terra sancta*, where the Tenant or Defendant was in Pilgrimage to the Holy Land, or as Volunteer against the *Saracens*, and then a year and a day at the least was allowed by the Essoin. Essoin is sometimes taken for any excuse of Assize in *Clarendon tempore, H.* 2. *Forenden, p.* 549. *Nulli liceat hospitari aliquem extraneum ultra unam noctem in domo sua, nisi hospitatus ille essonium rationabile habuerit.* See *Cooks* 2. *part of Instit. c.* 12. *Leigh Phil. Com. fol.* 91, 92.

Essonio de malo lecti, Is a Writ directed to the Sheriff, for the sending of four lawful Knights to view one that hath Essoined himself, *de malo lecti Regist. Orig. fol.* 8. *b.*

E S T.

To establish, Stabilio, ire.

An establishment, Establiamentum, i, n. *Ry.* 195.

An estate (or condition) Status, ûs, m.

An estate left by ones father, Patrimonium, ii, n.

When the fee simple of an estate is in no person, as whilst a Parsonage is void, Abegancia, æ, f.

Esteem (or estimation) Æstimatio, onis, f.

To esteem (or account) Æstimo, are.

Esteemed, Æstimatus, a, um.

Estley or *Astley* (the Family) D'Estlega & Estlega.

Estoppel, Seemeth to come from the French *Estouper*, i. e. *Oppilare, obturare, stipare, obstipare*, to stop with a stopple, and signifieth in our Common Law, an Impediment or Bar of an Action growing from his own Fact, that hath or otherwise might have had his Action; for example, a Tenant maketh a Feoffment by Collusion to one: The Lord accepteth the services of the Feoffee, by this he debarreth himself of the Wardship of his Tenants Heir, *Fitz. nat. brev. fol.* 242. Divers other exemples might be shown out of him. Sir *Edward Cook lib.* 2. *Casu Goddard, fol.* 4. *b.* Defin th an *Estoppel* to be a Barr or hindrance

drance unto one to plead the Truth, and reftraineth it not to the Impediment given to a man by his own act only, but by anothers alfo, *Lib.* 3. *the cafe of Fines, fol.* 88. *a.* Jurors cannot be Eftopped, becaufe they are fworn to fay the Truth.

Eftoppels are three ways effected.

1. By matter of Record.

2. By bare writing.

3. By Fact in Paiis, *Leigh. Phil. Com. fol.* 92, 93.

Eftovers, Eftoveria, orum, n. 3. *Inft.* 229. *Spel.* 202. *Lex.* 51. *Eftoverium* cometh of the French *Eftover*, i. e. *fovere*, to fofter, and fignifieth in our Common Law nourifhment or maintenance, *Brac. lib.* 3. *tract.* 2. *cap.* 18. *num.* 2. ufeth it for that fuftenance which a man taken for Felony is to have out of his Lands or Goods for himfelf and his Family during his Imprifonment, and the Statute *Anno* 6. *Ed.* 1. *cap.* 3. ufeth it for an allowance in Meat or Cloth. It is alfo ufed for certain allowances of Wood, to be taken out of another mans wood, fo it is ufed *Weft.* 2. *cap.* 25. *Anno* 13. *Ed.* 1. *Weft. part* 2. *fymbol. Tit. Fines* §. 26. faith, that the name of Eftovers containeth houfe-boot, hay-boot, and plow-boot; as if he gave in his grant thefe general words, *De rationabili eftoverio in bofcis*, &c. He may thereby claim thefe three.

An eftranging, Abalienatio, onis, f.

To be eftranged, Abalienor, ari.

An eftray, Extrahura, æ, f.

An eftreat, Extractum, i, n. Extracta, æ, f. *Cow.* 105. *Ry.* 183. 285. *Lex.* 51. *Pry.* 30. 216. Eftreats are fhort Notes or Memorials, extracted or drawn out of the Records by the Clerk of the Peace, and by him Indented and Delivered funderly to the Sheriff, and to the Barons of the Exchequer, bearing this or the like Title, *Extracta finium amerciamentorum forisfactorum ad generalem feffionem pacis*, &c. *coram*, &c. For the form or making thereof, thence is full direction given to the Clerk of Eftreats by the *Stat.* 7. *H.* 4. *S.*

Eftrepement, Eftrepamentum, i, n. *Cow.* 104. *Spel.* 243. It cometh of the *French* word *Eftropier*, i. e. *Mutilare*, *Obtruncare*, which word the *French* men alfo borrowed of the *Italians*, or rather *Spaniards*, with whom *Eftropear* fignifieth to fet upon the rack. It fignifieth in our Common Law fpoil made by the Tenant for term of Life upon any Lands or Woods to the prejudice of him in the Reverfion, as namely in the Statute *Anno* 6. *Ed.* 1. *cap.* 13. and it may feem to be the derivation, that Eftrepement is properly the unmeafurable foaking or drawing of the heart of the Land by Ploughing or Sowing it continually, without manuring or other fuch ufage as is requifite in good Husbandry. And yet (*Eftropier* fignifying *mutilare*) it may no lefs be conveniently applied to thofe that cut down Trees or lopp them farther than the Law will bear. This fignifieth alfo a Writ, which lieth in two forts, the one is, when a Man having an Action on depending (as a *Foredome* or *dum fuit infra ætatem*, or Writ of Right, or any ſuch other) wherein the Demandant is not to recover damages, ſueth to Inhibit the Tenant for making waſt during the ſuit. The other ſort is, for the Demandant that is adjudged to recover ſeiſin of Land in queſtion, and before Execution ſued by the Writ *habere facias ſeiſinam*, for fear of waſt to be made before he can get poſſeſſion ſueth out this Writ: See more of this in *Fitz. nat. brev. fol.* 60, & 61. *Reg. Orig. fol.* 76. and the *Regiſt. Judicial fol.* 33.

E V A.

Evan (a mans name) Evanus, i, m.

E V E.

Eve (a womans name) Eva, æ, f.

The evening, Veſper, ri, m. Plur. caret. Veſperus, ri, m. Plur. caret.

Evenlode river (in *Oxfordſhire*) Evenlodus.

An event (*iſſue or ſucceſs*) Eventus, ûs, m.

Every one, Quiſque.

Every day, Quotidiè, adv.

Every year, Quotannis, adv.

Every where, Ubique.

Everard (a mans name) Everardus, i, m.

Eveſholm or *Eveſham* (in *Worceſterſhire*) Eoveſum, Eveſtamum.

Of *Eveſham*, Heoveſhamenſis.

E V I.

Evidence, Evidentia, æ, f. *Co. Lit.* 283. *Lex.* 51. Evidence is uſed in our Law, generally for any proof, be it teſtimony of Men or Inſtrument. See Sir *Tho. Smith lib.* 2. *cap.* 17. 23.

Evident, Evidens, entis, adj. Evidentalis, le, adj.

The Kings evil (a Diſeaſe) Scrofula, æ, f. Struma, æ, f.

Evilly, Malevolè, adv. *Br.* 1. 24. 254.

E U R.

D' Evreux (the Family) De Ebroicis.

E U S.

Euſebius (a mans name) Euſebius, ii, m.

Euſtace (a mans name) Euſtacius, ii, m.

E W E.

An ewe, Ovis matrix vel Fœmina.

An ewer, Aqualis, is, m. Gutturnium, ii, n.

E X A.

Exact (*perfect or exquiſite*) Exactus, a, um.

To

To exact (*or extort*) Exigo, ere.

To exaggerate (*or aggravate*) Exaggero, are.

To exalt (*or extol*) Sublimo, are.

To examine, Examino, are.

An examining (*or examination*) Examinatio, onis, f.

An examiner, Examinator, oris, m. Examiner in the Chancery is an Officer that examineth the Parties to any Suit upon their Oaths, and Witnesses producted of either side, in the Chancery are two Examiners.

An example, Exemplum, i, n.

To exanimate (*or astonish*) Exanimo, are.

To exasperate (*vex, or make more grievous*) Exaspero, are.

Ex river (in *Devonshire*) Exa, Isaca, Isca.

E X C.

To excel (*or exceed*) Excedo, ere. Præsto, are. Excello, ere.

Excellency, Excellentia, æ, f.

To except, Excepto, are.

Except before excepted, Exceptis præexceptis.

Except and always reserved all Trees, &c. Exceptis & Semper reservatis Omnibus arboribus, &c.

Exception, Exceptio, onis, f. It is a stop or stay to an Action, being used in the Civil and Common Law both alike, and in both divided into dilatory and peremptory: Of these see *Bract.* 5. *tract.* 5. *per Totum* & *Britton, cap.* 91, 92.

Excess, Excessus, ûs, m.

Excester City (in *Devonshire*) Exonia, Isca, Isca Danmoniorum, vel Dunmoniorum, Isca & Scudum Nunniorum.

To exchange, Excambio, ire. Cambio, are.

Exchange, Excambium, ii, n. Cambium, ii, n. Exchange hath a peculiar signification in our Common Law, and is used for that Compensation, which the Warranter must take to the Warrant value for value, if the Land Warranted be recovered from the Warrantees, *Bract. lib.* 2. *cap.* 16. and *lib.* 1. *cap.* 19. Exchange is where a man is seised of certain Land, and another man is seised of another Land, if they by a Deed indented or without Deed (the Lands being in one County) exchange their Lands, so that each of them shall have the others Lands to him so exchanged in Fee, Fee tail, or for term of life, that is called an exchange, and is good without Livery and Seisin. It behoveth alway that this word Exchange be in the Deed, or else nothing passeth by the Deed, except that he hath Livery and Seisin. For the word *Excambium*, only maketh an exchange, as the words *Liberum Maritagium*, only do make Frank Marriage. Every exchange ought to be made by this word *Excambium*, or by another word of the same effect, as *permutatio. Perkins.* Both the things exchanged ought to be in *Esse* at the time of the Exchange, and therefore an exchange of Land for Rent granted *de novo* is not good, but an exchange betwixt a Rent and a Common which are in *Esse* at the time of the exchange is good, and so it is of Land and Rent. If two Parsons of several Churches change their Benefices, and Resign them into the

the hands of the Ordinary to the ſame intent, and the Patrons make their Preſentations accordingly, and one of the Parſons is admitted, inſtituted and inducted, and the other Parſon is admitted and inſtituted, but dieth before induction, the other Parſon ſhall not retain the Benefice in which he is inducted, for the Exchange is not perfected, *Vid. Leigh Phil. Com. fol.* 94, 95.

Exchange ſignifieth generally as much as (*Permutatio*) with the Civilians, as the Kings Exchange, *Anno H.* 6. *cap.* 1. & 4. and *Anno* 9. *Ed.* 3. *Stat.* 2. *cap.* 7. which is nothing elſe but the Place appointed by the King for the exchange of Bullion, be it Gold or Silver, or Plate, &c. with the Kings Coin. Theſe places have been divers heretofore, as appears by the ſaid Statutes. But now there is only one, *viz.* The Tower of *London*, conjoyned with the Mint, which in time paſt might not be, as appeareth by *Anno* 1. *H.* 6. *cap.* 2.

An exchange (*or burſe*) Cambium, ii, n.

An exchanger (*of Land*) Excambiator, oris, m.

An exchanging, Cambitas, atis, f.

The exchequer, Scaccarium, ii, n. It cometh of the French *Eſchequier*, i. e. *Abacus, tabula luſoria*, a *Cheſſe* or *Chequer* board, and ſignifieth the Place or Court of all Receipts belonging to the Crown, and is ſo termed (as I take it) by reaſon that in ancient times, the accomptants in that Office uſed ſuch Tables as Arithmeticians uſe for their Calculations, for that is one ſignification of (*Abacus*) amongſt others, *Polydore Virgil lib.* 9. *Hiſtor. Angl.* ſaith that the true word in Latin is *ſcattarium*, and by abuſe called *ſcaccarium*. It may ſeem to be taken from the *German* word (*Schatz*) ſignifying as much as (*Theſaurus*) Treaſure, or (*Fiſcus*) and from this fountain, no doubt, ſpringeth the *Italian* word (*Zeccha*) ſignifying a Mint, and *Zeccherii*, alias *Zecchieri*, the Officers thereunto belonging, *Deſcis Genuin*, 134. Mr. *Cambden in his Britan. pag.* 113. ſaith that this Court or Office, took the name a *Tabula ad quam aſſidebant*, proving it out of *Gervaſius Tilburienſis*, whoſe words you may read in him. This Court is taken from the *Normans* as appeareth by the grand Cuſtomary, *cap.* 56. where you may find the Exchequer thus deſcribed. The Exchequer is called an Aſſembly of high Juſticiars, to whom it appertaineth to amend that which the Bailiffs, and other meaner Juſticiars have evil done, and unadviſedly judged; and to do right to all men without delay, as from the Princes mouth. *Skene de verbor. ſignificatione, verbo Scaccarium*, hath out of *Paulus Æmilius* theſe words, *Scaccarium dicitur quaſi ſtatarium, quod homines ibi in Jure ſiſtuntur, vel quod ſit ſtataria & perennis Curia, nam cæteræ curiæ eſſent indictivæ, nec loco nec tempore ſtatæ*, where he ſaith alſo of himſelf that in *Scotland* the Exchequer was ſtable, but the other Seſſion was *Deambulatory*, before *James* V. *Qui inſtituit ſtatariam Curiam, cum antea*

tea esset Indictiva. He addeth farther: Others think that *Scaccarium* is so called a *Similitudine ludi scaccorum*, that is, the play of the Chestes, because many persons meet in the Chequer, pleading their Causes, one against the other, as if they were fighting in an arrayed Battle: Others think that it cometh from an old *Saxon* word *(Scaza)* as writeth Sir *Tho. Smith*, which signifieth Treasure, Taxations or Imposts, whereof accompt is made in the Chequer. This Court consisteth as it were of two parts; whereof one is conversant, especially in the hearing and deciding of all Causes appertaining to the Princes coffers, anciently called *Scaccarium computorum*, as *Ockam* testifieth in his *Lucubrations*. The other is called the Receipt of the Exchequer which is properly imployed in the receiving and payment of money, *Cromp. in his Jurisdict. fol.* 105. defineth it to be a Court of Record, wherein all Causes touching the Revenues of the Crown are handled. The Officers belonging to both these, you may find named in *Camb. Britan. cap. Tribunalia Angliæ*, to whom I refer you. The Kings Exchequer which now is settled in *Westminster* was in divers Counties of *Wales*, *An.* 27. *H.* 8. *cap.* 5. but especially *cap.* 26.

Excise, Vectigal, ālis, n.

To exclaim (or cry out) Exclamo, are.

To exclude (or shut out) Excludo, ere.

To excogitate (or invent) Excogito, are.

To excommunicate, Excommunico, are. Anathematizo, are.

Excommunicato capiendo, Is a Writ directed to the Sheriff for the apprehension of him that standeth obstinately excommunicated for forty days, for such a one not seeking absolution, hath or may have his contempt certified or signified into the Chancery, whence issueth this Writ, for the laying of him up without Bail or Mainprise, until he conform himself, *Fitz. nat. brev. fol.* 62. and *Anno* 5. *Eliz. cap.* 23. and the *Regist. Orig. fol.* 95. 67. and 70.

Excommunicato deliberando, Is a Writ to the under Sheriff, for the delivery of an Excommunicate Person out of Prison: Upon certificate from the Ordinary of his Conformity to the Jurisdiction Ecclesiastical. *Fitz. nat. brev. fol.* 63. *A.* and the *Regist. fol.* 65 & 67.

Excommunicato recipiendo, Is a Writ whereby Persons Excommunicate being for their obstinacy committed to Prison, and unlawfully delivered thence, before they have given caution to obey the Authority of the Church, are commanded to be sought for and laid up again. *Reg. Orig. fol.* 67. *a.*

An excrescence, Excrescentia, æ, f.

An excursion, Excursio, onis, f.

To excuse, Excuso, are.

E X E.

To execute (or bring to pass) Finio, ire. Perficio, ere.

An

An execution, Executio, onis, f. In the Common Law it signifieth the last performance of an Act, as of a Fine, or of a Judgment, and the execution of a Fine, is the obtaining of actual Possession of the things contained in the same by virtue thereof; which is either by entry into the Lands, or by Writ, whereof see *West* at large, *p.* 2. *Sym. Tit. Fines*, *sect.* 136, 137, 138. Executing of Judgments and Statutes, and such like, see in *Fitz*, *nat. brev. in Indice* 2. *verbo Execution*. Sir *Edw. Cook*, *vol.* 6. *casu Blumfield*, *fol.* 87. *A.* maketh two sorts of Executions, one final, another with a (*Quousque*) tending to an end. An execution final is that which maketh money of the Defendants Goods or extendeth his Lands, and delivereth them to the Plaintiff, for this the Party accepteth in satisfaction; and this is the end of the suit, and all that the Kings Writ commandeth to be done. The other sort with a (*Quousque*) is tending to an end, and not final, as in the Case of (*Capias ad satisfaciendum*, &c.) this is not final. But the body of the Party is to be taken, to the intent and purpose to satisfie the Demandant; and his imprisonment is not absolute, but until the Defendant do satisfie, *Idem. ibidem*.

Execution for debt is four-fold. 1. of Goods only by *Fieri facias*, or of the moiety of Lands by *Elegit*, or upon the Reconusance of a Statute; or of the Body by *Capias ad satisfaciendum*. *Vid. Leigh. Phil. Com.* 95.

An executioner (*or hangman*) Carnifex, icis, m.

An executor, Executor, oris, m. Executor is he that is appointed by any Man in his last Will and Testament to have the disposing of all his substance, according to the Contents of the said Will. This Executor is either particular or universal. Particular, as if this or that thing only be committed to his charge. Universal, if all. And this is in the place of him whom the Civilians call *Hæres designatus*, or *Testamentarius*, and the Law accounteth one Person with the Party whose Executor he is, as having all advantages of Action against all men, that he had, so likewise being subject to every mans action, as far as himself was. This Executor had his beginning in the Civil Law, by the Constitutions of the Emperors, who first permitted those, that thought good by their wills to bestow any thing upon good and godly uses, to appoint whom they pleased to see the same performed: and if they appointed none, then they ordained, that the Bishop of the place should have Authority of course to effect it, *l.* 28. *C. de Episcopis & Clericis*, and from this time and experience hath wrought out the use of these universal Executors, as also brought the Administration of their Goods that die without will unto the Bishop.

An Executor is after three sorts.

1. *Executor Testamentarius à Testore constitutus.*

2. *Executor Legalis*, that is, the Ordinary.

3. *Dativus*, The Administrator, *Cook* 8. *Rep.* Sir *John Needham*'s case. An Executor or Administrator ought to execute his Office, and Administer the Goods of the dead lawfully, truly, and diligently. 1. Lawfully in paying all the Duties, Debts and Legacies in such precedency and order, as they ought to be paid by the Law. Debts due by Obligation, shall be paid by Executors before Debts by single Contract, and they before Legacies, *Cook* 9. *Rep. Duchon*'s *case*. 2. Truly to convert nothing to his own use, for an Executor or Administrator hath not Goods of the Dead to his own use, but in anothers Right, and to others uses, and he ought not to practise or devise any thing to hinder the Creditor of his Debt, but truly to execute his Office, according to the Trust reposed in him. 3. Diligently, *Quia negligentia semper habet comitem infortunium. Cook* 8. *Rep. Tamors case.*

1. *Necessitatis, ut funeralia.*

2. *Utilitatis*, that every one shall be paid in such precedency as ought to be.

3. *Voluntatis*, as Legacies. *Cook* 8. *Rep. Needham*'s *case.*

Executor de son tort, Is he that takes upon him the Office of an Executor by intrusion, not being so constituted by the Testator or Deceased, nor (for want of such Constitution) constituted by the Ordinary to Administer how far we shall become liable to Creditors, *Vide* 43. *Eliz. Cap.* 8. *Dyer* 166. 105. 6. *Dyer* 166, *Belknap.* 50. *Ed.* 3. 9. 13, 14. *Eliz. Dyer* 305. 306.

To make an executor, Constituere executorem.

To exemplifie, Exemplifico, are.

An exemplification (or copy of a Record under seal of the Court) Exemplificatio, onis, f.

Exemplificatione, Is a Writ granted for the Exemplification of an Original. See *Regist. Orig. fol.* 290.

To exempt (or take out, from, or away.) Eximo, ere.

Exempt (or free) Exemptus, a, um.

An exercise, Exercitium, ii, n. Exercitatio, onis, f.

To exercise, Exerceo, ere.

Ex gravi querela, Is a Writ that lieth for him, unto whom any Lands or Tenements in Fee within a City, Town or Borough being deviseable or devised by will, and the Heir of the devisor entreth into them and detaineth them from him, *Regist. Orig. fol.* 244. *Old nat. brev. fol.* 87. See *Fitz nat. brev. fol.* 198. *L.*

Bishop of Exeter, Episcopus Exoniensis.

E X H.

To exhibit, Exhibeo, ere.

To exhort, Exhorto, ari.

E X I.

Exigendary of the common Bank, Exigendarius de Banco communi. Is otherwise called Exigenter, *An.* 10. *H.* 6. *ca.* 4. and is an Officer belonging to that Court, for which see Exigenter.

An exigent, Exigenda, æ, f. Is a Writ that lieth where the Defendant in an Action personal cannot be found, nor any thing within the County, whereby to be attached or distreined, and is directed unto the Sheriff, to proclaim and call five County days one after another, charging him to appear under the pain of Outlawry. *Terms of Law.* This Writ lieth also in an Indictment of Felony, where the party Indicted cannot be found, *Smith de. Repub. Angl. lib. 2. cap. 19.* It seemeth to be called an Exigent because it exacteth the party, that is, requireth his appearance or forth-coming to answer the Law; for if he come not at the last days Proclamation, he is said to be *Quinquies exactus*, and then is Outlawed, *Crompt. Jurisd. fol.* 188. and this Mr. *Manwood* also setteth down for the Law of the Forest, *part 1. of his Forest Law, pag.* 71. See the new Book of entries, *verbo* Exigent.

An exigenter, Exigendarius, ii, m.

Unius Exigendariorum Curiæ, Anno 18. H. 6. cap. 9. Is an Officer of the Court of Common Pleas, of whom there are four in number, they make all Exigents and Proclamations in all Actions where process of Outlawry doth lie, and Writs of superſedeas as well as the Prothonotaries, upon such Exigents as were made in their Offices.

Exile (or banishment) Exilium, ii, n.

Ex mero motu, Are words formerly used in any Charter, or Letters Patents of the Prince, whereby he signifieth that he doth that which is contained in the Charter of his own will and motion, without Petition or Suggestion made by any other, and the effect of these words are to bar all exceptions that might be taken unto the Instrument wherein they are contained by alledging, that the Prince in passing that Charter was abused by any false suggestion, *Kitchin fol.* 151.

E X O.

Exorable (or easie to be intreated) Exorabilis, le, adj.

Exorbitant (things properly out of circle, square or rule, things irregular, enormous, and, in a manner, absurd) Exorbitans, antis, adj.

Exorcism, Exorcismus, i, m.

An exorcist (or conjurer) Exorcista, æ, m.

Exotick (foreign or strange) Exoticus, a, um.

E X P.

Ex parte talis, Is a Writ that lieth for a Bailiff or Receiver, that having Auditors assigned to hear his Account, can not obtain of them reasonable allowance, but is cast into Prison by them, *Regist. fol.* 137. *Fitz. nat. brev. fol.* 129. The manner in this Case is, to take this Writ out of the Chancery, directed to the Sheriff to take four Mainpernours to bring his body before the Barons of the Exchequer at a certain day, and to warn the Lord to appear at that time, *New Terms of Law verbo* Accompt.

To expect (or look for) Expecto, are.

Expedient (fit or convenient) Expediens, entis, adj.

Expedition (or dispatch) Expeditio, onis, f.

To expel (or drive away) Expello, ere. Exturbo, are.

Expence (or cost) Expensa, æ, f. Sumptus, ûs, m.

Experience (or experiment) Experientia, æ, f. Experimentum, i, n.

Expert (or skilfull) Expertus, a, um.

To expire (or die) Expiro, are.

An expiring, Expiratio, onis, f.

To explain (make plain or manifest) Explano, are.

To explicate (expound or unfold) Explico, are.

An exploit (or valiant act) Expletum, i, n. Facinus Nobile.

To expose (or set forth) Expono, ere.

To express (or utter) Exprimo, ere.

Express (or manifest) Expressus, a, um.

To exprobrate (or reproach) Exprobro, are.

An exprobration, Exprobratio, onis, f.

E X Q.

Exquisite (exact or elaborate) Exquisitus, a, um.

E X T.

Extant (appearing about, standing out) Extans, antis, adj.

To extend (or stretch out) Extendo, ere.

Extend, Extendere, Cometh of the *French (estendre)* i. e. *dilatare, dispandere, distendere*, and signifieth in our Common Law to value the Lands or Tenements of one bound by Statute, &c. that hath forfeited his Bond to such an indifferent rate, as by the yearly rent the Obliger may in time be paid his debt. The Course and Circumstance of this see in *Fitz. nat. brev. fol.* 131. Brief *D' execution* for Statute Merchant.

Extendi facias, Is a Writ ordinarily called a Writ of Extent, whereby the value of Lands, &c. is commanded to be made, and Levied in divers cases, which see in the Table of the *Register Original.*

Extent, Extenta, æ, f. *Cow.* 107. *Lex.* 52. Extent hath two significations, some time signifying a Writ or Commission to the Sheriff for the valuing of Lands or Tenements, *Register Judicial* in the Table of the Book, some time the act of the Sheriff or other Commissioner upon this Writ, *Brook Titulo Extent, fol.* 3. 13.

To extenuate (or make thin or small) Tenuo, are. Extenuo.

External (or outward) Externus, a, um.

To

To extinguiſh (*or quench*) Extinguo, ere.

Extinguiſhment, Extinguimentum, i, n. In our Common Law it ſignifieth an effect of Conſolidation: For example, if a Man have due unto him a yearly Rent out of any Lands, and afterwards purchaſe the ſame Lands, now both the Property aud Rent are Conſolidated, or united in one poſſeſſion, and therefore the Rent is ſaid to be extinguiſhed. In like manner it is, where a Man hath a Leaſe for years, and afterwards buyeth the Property, this is Conſolidation of the Property and the Fruits, and as an Extinguiſhment of the Leaſe. See the Terms of Law.

Extirpation, Extirpatio, onis, f. Extirpation is a Writ Judicial, that lieth againſt him, who after a Verdict found againſt him for Land, &c. doth maliciouſly overthrow any houſe upon it, &c. and it is twofold, one *Ante Judicium*, the other *Poſt Judicium*. *Regiſt. Judic. fol.* 13. 5. 6. 58.

To extort (*or take away by force a part*) Extorqueo, ere.

Extortion, Extortio, onis, f. Extortion is the unlawfull taking by any Officer, by colour of his Office, any money or valuable thing of or from any man, either that is not due, or more than is due, or before it be due. It is largely taken for any Oppreſſion, by Power, or by Colour, or Pretence of Right, from the verb *Extorqueo*, *Cook on Lit. lib.* 3. *c.* 13. *ſect.* 701. *Leigh. Phil. Com. fol.* 96. For example, if any Officer by terrifying any of the Kings Subjects in his Office take more than his ordinary duties he committeth and is Indictable of Extortion. To this (by Mr. *Weſt's* Judgment) may be referred the Exaction of unlawful Uſury, winning by unlawful Games, and (in one word) all taking of more than is due, by colour or pretence of Right, as exceſſive Toll in Millers, exceſſive prices of Ale, Bread, Victuals, Wares, &c. *Weſt part* 2. *Symb. Titulo, Indictments ſect.* 65. Mr. *Manwood* ſaith that Extortion, is *Colore Officii*, and not *Virtute Officii*, *part* 1 *of his Foreſt Laws*, *pag.* 216. Mr. *Crompton* in his Juſtice of Peace, *fol.* 8. hath theſe words in effect, Wrong done by any man is properly a treſpaſs: But exceſſive wrong done by any, is called Extortion, and this is moſt properly in Officers, as Sheriffs, Mayors, Bailiffs, Eſcheators, and other Officers whatſoever that by colour of their Office work great Oppreſſion, and exceſſive wrong unto the Kings Subjects, in taking exceſſive Reward or Fees for the Execution of their Office. Great diverſity of Caſes touching Extortion, you may ſee in *Cromptons* Juſtice of Peace, *fol.* 48. *b.* and 49. and 50. See the difference between *Colore Officii*, and *Virtute vel ratione Officii*. *Plowden Caſu Dives*, *f.* 64. *A.* This word is uſed in the ſame ſignification in *Italy* alſo. For, *Cavalcanus de brachio Regio part* 5. *num.* 21. thus deſcribeth it, *Extortio dicitur fieri, quando Judex cogit aliquid ſibi dari, quod non eſt debitum, vel quod eſt ultra debitum: Vel ante tempus petit id, quid poſt adminiſtratam Juſtitiam debetur.*

Extorſively, Extorſivè, 1 *Ro.* 544.

To extract (*or draw out*) Extraho, ere.

An extract (*or copy of any thing*) Extractum, i, n.

Extracts (*a Chymical preparation*) Extracta, orum, n.

Extraordinary, Extraordinarius, a, um.

Extravagant, Extravagans, antis, adj.

Extream (*or uttermoſt*) Extremus, a, um.

The extreamity (*or uttermoſt of any thing*) Extremitas, atis, f.

To exulcerate, Ulcero, are. Exulcero, are.

E Y E.

An eye, Oculus, li, m.

The eye ball or (*apple of the eye*) Pupilla, æ, f. Oculi orbis.

The eye brow, Supercilium, ii, n.

The eye lid, Palpebræ, arum, f.

The hair of the eye lids, Cilium, ii, n.

The white of the eye, Albugo, inis, f. Album oculi.

The corner of the eyes, Sinus oculorum.

Blear eyed, Lippus, a, um.

One eyed (*or hath but one eye*) Monoculus, i, m. Unoculus, i, m. Luſcus, a, um.

Gogle eyed (*or blinkard*) Pætus, i, m.

The web in the eye, Leucoma, æ, f.

The winking (*or twinkling of the eyes*) Nictatio, onis, f.

An eye witneſs, Teſtis Oculatus.

Eye ſalves, Collyria, orum, n.

Eyes, eylet-holes, Ocelli, orum, m.

E Y R.

Eyre, alias *Eyrel* (*Iter. Bracton lib.* 3. *cap.* 11. *in Rubrica*) It cometh of the old *French* word *Eire*, i. e. *Iter.* as a grand *Eire*, i. e. *Magnis Itineribus.* It ſignifieth in *Britton cap.* 2. the Court of Juſtices Itinerants: And Juſtices in Eyre are thoſe only which *Bracton* in many places calleth (*Juſticiarios Itinerantes*) of the Eyre, read *Britton, ubi ſupra*, who expreſſeth the whole courſe of it, and *Bracton lib.* 3. *Tractat.* 2. *cap.* 1. and 2. *Iter Foreſtæ.* The Eyre alſo of the Foreſt is nothing but the Juſtice Seat, otherwiſe ſo called: Which is or ſhould by ancient Cuſtom be held every three year by the Juſtices of the Foreſt, journing up and down to that purpoſe. *Crompton's Juriſdiction, fol.* 156. *Manwood parte prima of his Foreſt Laws, pag.* 121. See Juſtice in Eyre. Read *Skene de verborum ſignif. verbo Iter.* whereby, as by many other Places, you may ſee great affinity between theſe two Kingdoms of *England* and *Scotland*, in the Adminiſtration of Juſtice and Government.

FAB.

F A B.

FAbia (a womans name) Fabia, æ, f.

Fabian (a mans name) Fabianus, i, m.

Fabius (a mans name) Fabius, ii, m.

Fabritius (a mans name) Fabritius, ii, m.

F A C.

A face, Facies, ei, f.

Facility (*or easiness*) Facilitas, atis, f.

A faction (*or sect*) Factio, onis, f.

Factious (*leading a party*) Factiosus, a, um.

Factiously, Factiosè, adv.

A factor, Factor, oris, m. Institor, oris, m.

Factorage, Factoragium, ii, n.

A faculty, Facultas, atis, f.

F A G.

A faggot, Fagettus, i, m. 2 *Mon.* 542. Falcis, is, m.

F A I.

To fain (*or imagine*) Fingo, ere.

Fained, Fictus, a, um.

Faint Pleader, Falsa Placitatio, Cometh of the *French Feint*, a participle of the verb *Feindre*, i.e. *Simulare, fingere*, and *Pleidor*, i. e. *Placitare*. It signifieth with us a false covenous, or collusory manner of Pleading to the deceit of a third Party.

Faint (*or weak*) Languidus, a, um.

To faint (*or languish*) Langueo, ere.

A fair (*or mart*) Feria, æ, f. *Spel.* 264.

Fairs, Nundinæ, arum, f. pl.

The place where the fair is kept, Nundinarium, ii, n.

Money paid in fairs to the lord of the soil for breaking ground to set up booths, Piccagium, ii, n.

Fair Foreland (in Ireland) Rhobogdium.

Fairford (in *Gloucestershire*) Pulchrum vadum.

Fair Island, Dumna.

Fair Pleading, Pulchre Placitando. *Beau Pleader*, Is made of two *French* words, *beau*, i. e. *decorus*, *formosus*, *Pulcher*, and *Pleder*, i. e. *disputare & causam agere*. It signifieth in our Common Law a Writ upon the Statute of *Marlbridge*, made the 52 *d.* year of *H.* 3. *c.* 11. whereby it is provided, that neither in the Circuit of Justices, nor in Counties, Hundreds or Courts Baron, any Fines shall be taken of any Man for fair Pleading, that is, for not Pleading fairly, or aptly to the purpose. Upon which Statute this Writ was ordained against those that violate herein: See *Fitz. nat. brev. fol.* 270 *A. B. C.* whose definition is to this effect. The Writ upon the Statute of *Marlbridge* for not fair Pleading, lieth where the Sheriff or other Bailiff in his Court will take Fine of the Party,

Plaintiff or Defendant for that he Pleadeth not fairly.

A fairing, Penium, ii, n.

Faith, Fides, ei, f.

Faith (a womans name) Fides.

Faithful, Fidelis, le, adj.

F A L.

A falchion (*or short sword*) Falcatus Ensis.

A falcon, Falco,onis, m.

A falconer, Falconarius, ii, m. *Pry.* 71. Accipitrarius, ii, m.

Faldage (*or frankfold*) Faldagium, ii, n. *Spel.* 248. *Lex.* 53. Faldsoca, æ, f. (i. e.) the liberty of setting up sheep folds in any fields.

Falmouth (in *Cornwal*) Falensis portus. Voluba.

Fallen down, Prolapsus, a, um.

A falling (*or slipping down*) Prolapsio, onis, f.

A fall, Casus, ûs, m.

A fallacy, Fallacia, æ, f.

Fallow, Warectum, i, n. *Co. Lit.* 5. *Lex.* 133.

Time of fallowing, Terra jacens frisca & ad warectum. Tempus warectandi, *Fle.* 162.

False (*or untrue*) Falsus, a, um.

To falsifie (*or make false*) Falso, are.

Falso Judicio, Is a Writ that lies to remove a Judgment out of an Inferiour Court, that is not a Court of Record.

F A M.

Fame, Fama, æ, f.

Famous (*or renowned*) Famosus, a, um.

A family (*or houshold*) Fămĭlĭa, æ, f.

One of the family, Manupastus, i, m.

Familiar (*or acquainted*) Familiaris, re, adj.

A famine, Fames, is, f.

F A N.

A fan (*to cool the face*) Flabellum, i, n.

A fan to fan corn withal, Vannus, i, m. Ventilabrum, i, n.

To fan corn, Vanno, are. Ventilo, are.

Fanned (*winnowed*) Ventilatus, a, um.

A fanner of corn, Ventilator, oris, m.

A fanning (*or winnowing*) Ventilātio, onis, f.

Fantasie, Phantasia, æ, f.

Fantastick, Phantasticus, a, um.

F A R.

A fardel (*or farundel*) *of Land*, Farundella terræ. *Flo.* 78. *Lex.* 54. Quadrantata terræ. Fardella, æ, f. *Ra. Ent.* 15. *Fle.* 33. *Lex.* 53. i. e. The fourth part of an Acre. *Crompt. Jurisdict. fol.* 220. *Quadrantata terræ* is read in the *Regist. Orig. fol.* 1. *B.* where you have also *Denariata* and *Obolata*, *Solidata* and *Librata terræ*, which by probability must rise in proportion of quantity from the Farding-deal, as an half Penny, Penny, Shilling or Pound rise in Value and Estimation: Then must *Obolata* be half an Acre, *Denariata* the Acre, *Solidata* twelve Acres,

Acres, and *Librata* twelve ſcore Acres, and yet I find *Viginti Libratas terræ vel redditus, Regiſt. Orig. fol.* 94. *A.* and *fol.* 248. *B.* whereby it ſeemeth that *Librata terræ* is ſo much as yieldeth twenty ſhillings *per annum ad centum ſolidatas terrarum, tenementorum & redituum, fol.* 249. *A.* and in *Fitz. nat. brev. fol.* 87. *F.* I find theſe words, *Viginti libratas terræ vel reditus*, which argueth it to be ſo much Land as twenty Shillings *per annum* : See Furlong.

A fardle (*or pack*) Faſciculus, i, m.

Fare (*or fraught*) Naulum, i, n. Portorium, ii, n.

Fare money, Nautica ſors.

A farm, Firma, æ, f.

To let to farm, Ad firmam tradere. *Spel.* 274.

A farmer, Firmarius, ii, m.

A dung farmer, Rudiſta vel Ruderiſta, æ, m.

Far off, Longinquus, a, um.

To farrow (*as ſows do*) Fœto, are.

Farther, Ulteriùs, adv.

A farthing (*the fourth part of a penny*) Ferlingus, i, m. Quadrans, antis, m.

A farrier, Veterinarius, ii, m. Equitarius, ii, m. Mulomedicus, i, m.

F A S.

Faſhioned, Effigiâtus, a, um.

A faſhioning, Effigiâtio, onis, f. Formatura, æ, f.

A faſhioner, Effigiator, oris, m. Formator, oris, m.

To faſhion, Effingo, ĕre.

Faſt (*or firm*) Firmus, a, um.

To faſten (*or join*) Oppango, ĕre.

F A T.

Fate (*or deſtiny*) Fatum, i, n.

Fatal, Fatalis, le, adj.

A father, Pater, is, m.

A god-father, Pater Initialis.

A grand-father, Avus, i, m.

A father-in-law (*not by nature, but by the Law of marriage*) Socer, eri, m. Vitrĭcus, ci, m.

Fatherly, Paternus, a, um.

Fatherhood, Paternitas, atis, f.

A fathom, Orgya, æ, f. Hexapeda, æ, f.

Fat, Pinguis, e, adj.

Fat (*or fatneſs*) Pinguedo, inis, f.

To make fat, Pinguefacio, ere.

Fatted, Saginatus, a, um.

A fatting, Saginatio, onis, f.

Fatting meat, Sagina, æ, f.

A fatting place, Saginarium, ii, n.

Fatlings, Altilia.

F A U.

A fault, Culpa, æ, f.

Favorine (a mans name) Favorinus, i, m.

Favourably, Favorabilitèr, adv.

F A W.

A fawcet (*or tap*) Epiſtomium, ii, n.

A fawn (*or hind calf*) Hornŏtĭnus, i, m.

A fawn (or young deer) Hinnulus, li, m.

A fawning (or bringing forth young, as Does do) Faonatio, onis, f.

F E A.

Fealty, Fidelitas, atis, f. *Spel.* 267. It cometh of the French *Feaulte*, i. e. *Fides*, and signifieth in our Common Law an Oath taken at the admittance of every Tenant to be true to the Lord of whom he holdeth his Land, and he that holdeth Land by this only Oath of Fealty, holdeth in the freest manner that any man in *England* under the King may hold; because all with us that have Fee, hold *per fidem & fiduciam*, that is, by Fealty at the least, *Smith de Repub. Angl. lib.* 3. *c.* 8. Fealty is the most general service in the Common Law, for it is incident to every Tenure, unless it be a Tenure in *Frankelmoign*. It is also the most sacred, because it is done upon Oath, and the reason wherefore the Tenant is not sworn, in doing his homage to his Lord, is because no subject is sworn to another subject to become his man, of Life and Member, but to the King only, and that is called the Oath of Allegiance, *homagium ligeum*, and those words for that purpose are omitted out of Fealty, which is to be done upon Oath, *Cook lib.* 4. *Bert's Case*, and on *Lit. lib.* 2. *cap.* 2. *sect.* 91.

The doing of fealty to a Lord, Affidatio, onis, f.

A Tenant by fealty, Affidatus, i, m.

Fear or dread, Metus, ûs, m.

To fear (terrifie or make afraid) Terrefacio, ere.

Fearful (or afraid) Timidus, a, um.

A feasant cock, Phăsiānus, i, m.

A feasant hen, Phăsiāna, æ, f.

A feasant keeper, Phasiānārius, ii, m.

A feast (or banquet) Festum, i, n. Convivium, ii, n.

A feather, Pluma, æ, f.

F E B.

February, Februarius, ii, m.

F E E.

A fee, Feodum, i, n. Feudum, i, n. (i. e.) a Fee or Inheritance, also Money due to Officers for their Reward.

Fee-farm, Feodi firma, *Spel.* 263. *Lex.* 54. Feofirma, æ, f. Feudi firma.

To feed (graze or pasture as beasts do) Pasco, ere.

F E L.

Felix (a mans name) Felix, icis, m.

A fellmonger, Pellio, onis, m.

To fell (or cut down) Succido, ere.

A fellon (a sore in the body so called) Furunculus, i, m.

A fellon on the fingers, Rĕdŭvia, æ, f.

A

A fellow of a college, Socius, ii. m.

A fellowship, Consocietas, atis, f.

Felo de se, Is he that committeth Felony by murthering himself. *Crompt. Just. Peace, fol.* 28. *Lamb. Eirenarch. lib.* 2. *cap.* 7. *fol.* 243. If a man of *non sanæ memoriæ* give to himself a mortal wound, and before he dieth he become of sound memory, and after dieth of the same wound; in this case, although he die of sound memory, by reason of his proper stroke, yet because the Original cause was committed, being not of sound memory, he shall not be *Felo de se*, because the Death hath relation to the Original Act, *Cook* 1 *Rep. Shelly's Case*. By the Common Law if a Man kill himself, he is called *Felo de se*, and he doth only forfeit his Goods and Chattels, but not his Lands; neither doth this work Corruption of Blood, nor the Wife lose her Dower, because it is no Attainder in Deed. He that is *Felo de se*, shall not have Christian Burial, and all his Goods and Chattels are forfeited to the King, and by his Almoner are to be distributed to Pious uses (heretofore) *in salutem animæ. Leigh. Phil. Com. fol.* 103, 104.

Felony, Felonia, æ, f. *Spel.* 252. *Lex.* 54. Felony is so called either of the Latin word *Fel*, which is in English *Gall*, or of the ancient English word *Fell* or *Fierce*, because it is intended to be done with a cruel, bitter, fell, fierce or mischievous mind. *Significat quodlibet capitale crimen felleo animo perpetratum*, in which sense Murder is said to be done *per Feloniam*, and in ancient times this word (*Felonice*) was of so large an extent as it included High Treason, and by pardoning of all Felonies, High Treason was pardoned, *Cooks* 4. *Rep.* We account any offence Felony that is in degree next unto Petty Treason, and compriseth divers particulars under it, as Murder, Theft, killing a Mans self, Sodometry, Rape, willful burning of Houses, and divers such like, which are to be gathered especially out of Statutes, whereby many offences are daily made Felony that before were not. Felony is discovered from higher offences by this, that the punishment thereof is death. Yet this is not perpetual, for Petit Larceny which is the stealing of any thing under the value of twelve pence, is Felony, as appeareth by *Brook Tit. Coron. n.* 2. his reason is, because the Indictment against such a one must run with these words, *Felonicè cepit*, and yet this is not punished by Death, tho' it be loss of Goods a man may call that Felony which is under Petit Treason, and punished by Death; and of this there are two sorts, one higher, that for the first time may be relieved by Clergy, another that may not. The Cognition or knowing them is by Statutes, for Clergy is allowed where it is not expresly taken away. Of these matters read *Stawnf. lib.* 1. *pl. Cor. a fine, cap.* 2. *ad usque* 39. and the *Statutes. Lamb. Justice of Peace, cap.* 7. in a Table drawn for the

the purpose, as also *lib.* 4. *cap.* 4. *fol.* 404. *Crompt. in his Just. of P. fol.* 32, *&c.* Felony ordinarily worketh Corruption of Blood, tho' not where a Statute ordaineth an Offence to be Felony, and yet withal saith that it shall not work Corruption of Blood, as *Anno* 39. *Eliz. cap.* 17. Felony is also punished by loss of Lands not entailed, and Goods and Chattels as well real as personal, and yet by the Statute *Anno* 37. *H.* 8. *cap.* 6. a Man may have property of some things which are of so base nature that no Felony can be committed of them, and no Man shall lose for them Life or Member, as a Blood-hound and a Mastiff, *Cook on Lit. lib.* 3. *p.* 392. *Cooks* 7. *Rep. Cases of Swans.* To steal Fruit that hangeth on a Tree, to cut down and carry away the Tree it self, is not Felony, but these things are part of the Free-hold till they are severed, and cannot be reputed for any Chattels. But if I gather mine Apples, or cut down a tree of mine own, then may another become a Felon by taking away either of them. Felony cannot be committed by the taking of Beasts that be savage, if they be savage and untamed at the time of taking, nor for taking of Doves being out of a Dove-coat, nor for taking of Fishes being at large in a River, for such taking is not *Contrectatio rei alienæ, sed quæ est nullius in bonis*, but the stealing of a Doe which is tame and Domestical is Felony, but as Mr. *Stamford* well noteth, it seemeth that he that stealeth it should have certain knowledge that it is tame; but if the Doe be killed, and then stolen this is certainly Felony, saith he; so if one break a Dove coat and take out the young Pidgeons, which cannot go nor fly, this is Felony; or steal Fish out of a Pond or Trunk, or young Goshawks ingendred in my Park which cannot go nor fly. *Stawn-Pl. of Cr. p.* 1. *c.* 1. The Civil Laws do judge open Theft to be satisfied by the recompence of four-fold, and private Theft by the recompence of double. But the Laws of *England* suffer neither of these offences to be more favourably punished than with the Offenders death, if the value of the thing stolen be above twelve pence. *Leigh. Phil. Com. fol.* 103. If a Man be adjudged to be hanged, and the Sheriff be commanded that it be executed, and he behead him, this is Felony in the Sheriff, because the order of the Law is not observed. *Stawnf. l.* 1. *Pl. of Cr. c.* 4.

A felon, Felo, onis, m.

Feloniously, Felonicè, adv. *Spel.* 252. *Lex.* 54.

A felt, Feltrum, i, n. Pannus coactilis.

F E M.

A female, Fæmina, æ, f.

Female (of the female kind) Fæmineus, a, um.

F E N.

A fence (or inclosure) Fensura, æ, f.

A fencer (or master of fence) Gladiator, oris, m.

A fencing, Gladiatura, æ, f.

To fence, Digladior, aris.

F E O.

A feodary, Feodarius, ii, m. *Spel.* 263. *Lex.* 54. Is an Officer Authorised, and by the Master of the Court of Wards and Liveries, by Letters Patents under the seal of that Office. His Function is to be present with the Escheator at the finding of any Office, and give Evidence for the King, as well concerning the value as the Tenure, and also to survey the Land of the Ward, after the Office found, and to rate it. He is also to assign the Kings Widows their Dowers, and to receive all the Rents of the Wards Lands, within his Circuit, and to answer them to the receiver of the Court of Wards and Liveries. This Officer is mentioned, *Anno* 32. *H.* 8. *cap.* 46.

A feoffer, Feoffator, oris, m. i. e. the giver.

A feoffment (or giving of Lands in fee) Feoffamentum, i, n. Donatio feudi.

A feoffee (or receiver) Feoffatus, i, m. *Spel.* 263. *Lex.* 55. *Co. Ent.* 484.

Joint feoffees, Cofeoffati, orum, m. *Co. Ent.* 217.

F E R.

Fern, Filix, icis, f.

Ferdinand (a mans name) Ferdinandus, i, m.

A ferret, Viverra, æ, f.

Ferrars (the family) De Ferrariis.

A ferry (or passage by water) Feria, æ, f. *Spel.* 264. Trajectus, ûs, m.

A ferry-boat, Ponto, onis, m.

A ferry-man, Portitor, oris, m. Trajector, oris, m. Lintrarius, ii, m.

Fertil, Fertilis, le, adj.

F E S.

A fescue, Festuca, æ, f.

Festus (a mans name) Festus, i, m.

F E T.

Fetters (or gyves) Compĕdes, um, f. pl.

Fettered, Compeditus, a, um. Connexus, a, um. Compedibus vinctus.

Fettered horses, Equi Connexi. Co. Entr. 648.

Unfettered horses, Equi ad largum, *Co. Entr.* ibid.

F E U.

A feud (or deadly quarrel) Feuda, æ, f. Faida, æ, f.

A fever (or ague) Febris, is, f.

A hect-

A hectick fever, Hectica, æ, f.

A feverish distemper, Febricula, æ, f.

Feverish, Febriculosus, a, um.

F E W.

Few, Paucus, a, um.

Fewel, Fomes, itis, m.

F I C.

A fiction (or fained thing) Fictio, onis, f. Figmentum, i, n.

Fictitious, Fabulosus, a, um.

F I D.

A fidle, Fides, is, f. Vitulia, æ, f.

A fidlestick, Plectrum, i, n.

A fidler, Fidicen, inis, n. Citharœdus, i, m.

Fidelity (or faithfulness) Fidelitas, atis, f.

F I E.

A field, Campus, i, m.

The open field without a wood, Landa, æ, f.

A pease field, Campus pisaceus.

A wheat field, Campus Triticeus, *Co. Ent.* 648.

A little field, Agellus, i, m.

A hedge row about a field, Thenicium, ii, n.

Fieri facias, Is a Writ Judicial that lieth at all times within the year and day for him that hath recovered in an Action of Debt or Damages to the Sheriff to command him to Levy the Debt or Damages of his Goods, against whom the recovery was had. This Writ has beginning from *West.* 2. *c.* 18. *Anno* 13. *Ed.* 1. See old *Nat. brev. fol.* 150. See great diversity thereof in the Table of the *Regist. Judicial, verbo Fieri facias.*

Fierce (or outragius) Ferus, a, um.

F I F.

A fife, Buccina, æ, f.

A fifer, Buccinator, oris, m.

The fifth, Quintus, a, um.

Fifteen, Quindenus, a, um. Quindecim, adj. Indecl.

Fifteen times, Quindecies, adv.

Fifteen shillings, Quindecim solidi.

Fifteen pounds, Quindecim libræ.

Of fifteen, Quindenarius, a, um.

Fifty, Quinquaginta, adj. Indecl.

Fifty shillings, Quinquaginta solidi.

Fifty pounds, Quinquaginta libræ.

Fifty nine, Undesexaginta, pl. Indecl.

F I G.

A fig, Ficus, ci, & ûs, f.

A green fig, Grossus, si, d. g.

A dry fig, Carica, æ, f.

A fig-tree, Ficaria, æ, f.

A garden of figs, Ficetum, i, n.

To fight, Pugno, are.

To fight together, Interpugno, are. *Ry.* 156.

To fight hand to hand, Manum cum hoste conserere.

A fight, Pugna, æ, f.

A fight between two or more, Affraia, æ, f.

He that fights hand to hand, Consertor, oris, m.

A fight at sea, Naumachia, æ, f. Bellum Navale.

A forfeiture for fighting (or breaking the peace) Fightwita, æ, f.

A figure (or fashion) Figura, æ, f.

F I L.

A filazer, Filazarius, ii, m. *Spel.* 271. *Lex.* 76. *Filazarius* cometh of the French *Filace*, i. e. *Filum*. Filazer is an Officer in the Common Pleas, whereof there are 14 in number. They make out all Original Process, as well real as personal, and mixt; and in actions meerly personal, where the Defendants are returned or summoned, there goeth out the distress infinite until appearance. If he be returned *nihil*, then process of *capias* infinite, if the Plaintiff will, or after the third *Capias*, the Plaintiff may go to the Exigenter of the shire, where his Original is grounded, and have an Exigent and Proclamation made, and also the Filazer maketh forth all Writs in view in causes where the view is placed. He is also allowed to enter the Imparlance, or the general issue in Common Actions, where appearance is made with him, and also Judgment by Confession in any of them, before issue be joined: and make out Writs of Execution thereupon. But although they entred the issue, yet the Protonotary must enter the Judgment, if it be after Verdict. They also make Writs of *Supersedeas* in case where the Defendant appeareth in their Offices after the *Capias* awarded.

A filberd (or nut) Avellana, æ, f. Corylus, i, m.

File, Filacium, ii, n. (i. e.) a Thread or Wire whereon Writs or other Exhibits in Courts are filed or fastned for the more safe keeping of them, whence Filazers have their name.

A file, Lima, æ, f.

Filed, Limātus, a, um.

A filer, Limātor, oris, m.

A filing, Limātio, onis, f.

The filings, also a filing, Limatura, æ, f.

To file, Filo, are. Limo, are.

To fill, Pleo, ere. Impleo.

A fillet (or hair lace) Crinale, is, n. Texta, æ, f. Tænia, æ, f. Vitta crinalis. Fascia ligatoria.

To tie with a fillet, Vitto, are.

F I N.

A fine, Finis, is, m. *Spel.* 272. *Lex.* 56. Gersoma, vel Gersuma, æ, f. Fine cometh of the French *Fin*, and Latin *Finis*. This word *Finis* hath divers significations in the Law, *Quia aliquando significat pretium, aliquando pœnam, aliquando pacem*. For 1. The price or sum which is the cause of obtaining a benefit, is called a Fine, as a Fine for alienation, for admission

miſſion to a Copy-hold for obtaining of Leaſes. 2. What the Offender gives in ſatisfaction of his Offence, is called a Fine alſo, and in this ſence *dicitur pœna.* 3. The aſſurance which makes men to enjoy their Lands and Inheritance is called *Finis, Quia finem litibus imponit.* They are all ſo called becauſe they are the ends or cauſes of the ends of all ſuch buſineſs. Of Fines taken of Copy-holders, ſome be certain by Cuſtom, and ſome be uncertain. But that Fine tho' it be *incertus*, yet it muſt be *Rationabilis*, and that reaſonableneſs ſhall be diſcuſſed by the juſtices upon the true Circumſtances of the Caſe appearing unto them, and if the Court where the Cauſe dependeth, adjudgeth the Fine exacted unreaſonable, then is not the Copy-holder compellable to pay it, *Cook* 8. *Rep. Beechers caſe. Cook on Lit. lib.* 1. *cap.* 9. *ſect.* 74.

A fine (or amerciament) Geldum, i, n.

A fine for not purſuing a Thief, Overſameſſum, i, n.

Fine non capiendo pro pulcre placitando, Is a Writ to inhibit Officers of Courts to take Fines for fair Pleads.

A finger, Digitus, i, m.

The fore finger, Digitus Index.

The middle finger, Verpus, i, m. Digitus medius.

The ring finger, Digitus annŭlāris.

To finiſh (or end) Finio, ire.

F I R.

Fire, Ignis, is, m.

To ſtrike fire, Fugillo, āre.

A ſteel to ſtrike fire, Fugillus, i, m.

A fire brand, Fax, cis, f. Torris, is, m.

A coal-fire, Anthracia, æ, f.

A fire-ſhovel, Batillum, i, n.

A fire fork, Furca ignaria.

Fire buckets, Incendiarii Siphones.

Wild fire, Incendiarium oleum.

To ſet on fire, Incendo, ĕre.

Setting on fire, Incendiarius, a, um.

A firkin, Firkinus, i, m. Amphora, æ, f.

Fire-boat, Eſtoverium ardendi, *Co. Lit.* 41. *B.* of fire and boot; for the Compoſition look Hay-boot. It ſignifieth allowance or Eſtovers of Wood, to maintain Competent fire for the uſe of the Tenant.

Firm (or ſtedfaſt) Firmus, a, um.

A fir-tree, Abies, ietis, f.

The firſt, Primus, a, um.

Firſt, Primò, adv.

Firſt fruits, Primitiæ, arum, f. Sing. caret, (i. e.) the profits of every ſpiritual living for one year, given in ancient time to the Pope, throughout all Chriſtendom: But by the Statute, *Anno* 26. *H.* 8. *cap.* 3. tranſlated to the Prince, for the ordering whereof, there was a Court erected, *Anno* 32. *H.* 8. *cap.* 45. But this Court was diſſolved *Anno* 5. *M. Seſſ.* 2. *cap.* 10. and ſince that time, though thoſe profits be reduced again to the Crown by the Statute *Anno* 1. *Eliz. cap.* 4. Yet the Court was never reſtored, but all matters therein to be handled were transferred to the Exchequer.

Firſt

First born, Primogenitus, a, um.

F I S.

A fish, Piscis, is, m.
A little fish, Pisciculus, i, m.
The scale of a fish, Squama, æ, f.
The gills of a fish, Branchiæ, rum, f.
The fins of a fish, Pinnæ, arum, f.
A stock fish, Asellus arefactus, salpa, æ, f.
A fish market, Piscaria, æ, f. Forum piscarium.
A fish pond, Piscina, æ, f.
Holes in a fish pond, Cellæ Piscinales.
A master of fish ponds and pits, Piscinarius, ii, m.
Full of fish, Piscosus, a, um.
A fisher man, Piscator, oris, m. Navis Piscatoria.
A fisher woman, Piscatrix, icis, f.
A fishmonger (or seller of fish) Piscarius, ii, m.
A fishing, Piscatio, onis, f.
Of a fisher man, Piscatorius, a, um.
A little fry of fish, Pisciculi, orum, m.
A fishing basket, Fiscella, æ, f.
A shell fish, Concha, æ, f.
A last of barrel fish, Lasta piscis barellati.
Salt fish, Salsamenta, orum, n.
A fish hook, Hamus piscatorius.
A fishing line, Linea piscatoria.
A fishing net, Rete piscatorium.
A fishers boat, Lembus, bi, m.
To fish, Piscor, ari.
A fishery, Piscarium, ii, n.
To scale fish, Desquamare Pisces
A fist, Pugnus, i, m.
A fistula (a kind of running disease) Fistula, æ, f.

F I T.

Fit, Aptus, a, um.
A fit, Paroxysmus, i, m.
Fitz-Alan (the family) Filius Alani.
Fitz-Alured (the family) Filius Aluredi.
Fitz-Amand (the family) Filius Amandi.
Fitz-Andrew (the family) Filius Andrææ.
Fitz-Barnard (the family) Filius Bernardi.
Fitz-brian (the family) Filius Briani.
Fitz-Count (the family) Filius Comitis.
Fitz-Eustace (the family) Filius Eustachii.
Fitz-Fulk (the family) Filius Fulconis.
Fitz-Geofry (the family) Filius Galfredi.
Fitz-Gerrard (the family) Filius Gerrardi.
Fitz-Gilbert (the family) Filius Gilberti.
Fitz-Harding (the family) Filius Hardingi.
Fitz-Haimon (the family) Filius Haimonis.
Fitz-Henry (the family) Filius Henrici.
Fitz-Herbert (the family) Filius Herberti.
Fitz-Hugh (the family) Filius Hugonis.

Fitz-

Fitz-Humphry (the family) Filius Humphredi.

Fitz-James (the family) Filius Jacobi.

Fitz-John (the family) Filius Johannnis.

Fitz-Lucas (the family) Filius Lucæ.

Fitz-Maurice (the family) Filius Mauricii.

Fitz-Michael (the family) Filius Michaelis.

Fitz-Nichols (the family) Filius Nicholai.

Fitz-Oliver (the family) Filius Oliveri.

Fitz-Osburn (the family) Filius Osburni.

Fitz-Osmond (the family) Filius Osmondi.

Fitz-Otes (the family) Filius Odonis.

Fitz-Pain (the family) Filius Pagani.

Fitz-Patrick (the family) Filius Patricii.

Fitz-Peter, or Fitz-Piers (the family) Filius Petri.

Fitz-Ralph (the family) Filius Radulphi.

Fitz-Raynold (the family) Filius Reginaldi.

Fitz-Richard (the family) Filius Richardi.

Fitz-Robert (the family) Filius Roberti.

Fitz-Roger (the family) Filius Rogeri.

Fitz-Symon (the family) Filius Simeonis.

Fitz-Stephen (the family) Filius Stephani.

Fitz-Thomas (the family) Filius Thomasi.

Fitz-Walter (the family) Filius Walteri.

Fitz-Warren (the family) Filius Warreni.

Fitz-William (the family) Filius Gulielmi.

F I V.

Five, Quinque, adj. Indecl.

Five times, Quinquies, adv.

Five years old, Quinquennis, ne, adj.

The space of five years, Quinquennium ii, n. Spatium quinque annorum.

Into five parts, Quinquĕpartitò, adv.

Five pence, Quinque denarii.

Five shillings, Quinque solidi.

Five pounds, Quinque libræ.

Five hundred pounds, Quingentæ libræ.

Five thousand pounds, Quinque mille librarum.

F L A.

A flag (banner or ensign) Vexillum, i, n.

A flag on the top of the mast, Cheruchus, i, m.

A flag (or ornament of a ship) Aplaustrum, i, n.

Flags (or streamers) Fluitantia vela. Vexilla navalia.

Instruments drawn by Oxen, to draw up flags in meadows, Scirpines, ium, m.

A flagon, Lagēna, æ, f.

A flail, to thresh with, Trībŭla, æ, f.

A flame, Flamma, æ, f.

The flank, Ilia, um, n. pl.

A flap

A flap to kill or drive away flies, Muſcarium, ii, n.

The flap that covereth the weeſel of the Throat, Epigloſſis, idis, f.

A flask to keep Gun-powder in, Lagena pulveraria.

A flasket, Qualus, li, m.

A flatterer, Fuco, onis, m. Adulator, oris, m.

To flatter, ădūlo, are.

Flatulent (or windy) Flātulentus, a, um.

Flax, Linum, i, n.

Wrought flax, Linum factum.

Flax (or tasks) on the diſtaff, Penſum, i, n.

Fine flax, Byſſus, ſi, f.

A brake for flax or hemp, Linifrangibula, æ, f.

A flax plot, Linarium, ii, n.

He that ſells flax or cloath, Linarius, ii, n. Linipōla, æ, m.

A flax woman, Linifex, cis, f.

Made of fine flax, Carbaſeus, a, um.

An heap of flax, Linodium, ii, n.

To flay, Deglubo, ere. Excorio, are.

F L E.

A fleam (or Chyrurgions Inſtrument) Phlebotomum, i, n. Scalprum Chirurgicum.

A fleece of wool, Vellus, ĕris, n.

Fleſh, Caro, carnis, f.

Unſavory fleſh, Caro iners.

A fleſh fork (or hook to take up meat) Fuſcĭnŭla, æ, f.

A fleet (or navy) Claſſis, is, f.

The fleet priſon, Fleta, æ, f. So called of the river upon the ſide whereof it ſtandeth, *Camb. Brit. fol.* 137. The water out of the Thames flows up by it. Unto this none are uſually committed, but for contempt to the King and his Laws, or upon abſolute Commandement of the King, or ſome of his Courts, or laſtly upon debt, when men are unable or unwilling to ſatisfie their Creditors.

A fletcher (bowyer) Arcuarius, ii, m.

A fletchers ſhop, Fabrica Sagittaria.

F L I.

Flight, Fuga, æ, f.

A putting to flight, Fugatio, onis, f.

Put to flight, Fugatus, a, um.

A flint-ſtone, Silix, icis, d. g.

A quarry of flint, Cotonia, æ, f.

Flint (in Flintſhire) Flintia.

Flintſhire, Flintenſis Comitatus.

Flixton (in Suffolk) Dumwicus, alias, Felicis oppidum.

F L O.

A flock (or multitude of people), Turba, æ, f.

A flock of cattel, Grex, gregis, m.

A floodgate belonging to a Mill, Moles, is, f.

flo A floor of a barn (or threshing floor) Area, æ, f.

A floor for flooring, Area pro Tabulatione.

A boarded floor, Tabulata Area.

A rammed floor, Fistucata Area.

A paved floor, Tessellata Area.

Flora (a womans name) Flora, æ, f.

Florence (a mans name) Florentius, ii, m.

Florence (a womans name) Florentia, æ, f.

Flouer (or fine meal of corn) Simila, æ, f.

Fine flour, Pollen, inis, n.

The finest flour thrice sifted, Cribraria, æ, f,

Of fine flour, Pollinarius, a, um.

A flower, Flos, ris, m.

Floting, Flotans, antis, adj. *Co. Ent.* 536. *Pry.* 85. Flota navium. *Pry.* 118. 121.

F L U.

The flux (or loosness) Lienteria, æ, f.

The bloody flux, Dysenteria, æ, f.

F O A.

A foal, Pullus, i, m.

F O D.

Fodder, Foderum, i, n. *Spel.* 282. *Cow.* 117.

A foder (or fother) of lead, Fodera plumbi.

F O G.

Fog (or rank grass not eaten in summer) Fogagium, ii, n. *Spel* 283. *Lex.* 57.

F O L.

To fold (or pleat) Plico, are.

To fold (or wrap together) Obvolvo, ere.

A fold, Falda, æ, f. *Spel.* 248. *Lex.* 53.

A fold-sheep-coat, Ovile, lis, n.

A fold (or pleat) Plicatura, æ, f.

A folding together, Obvolutio, onis, f.

The folkmote, Folkmota, æ, f. (i. e.) the meeting of the people, the County Court, the Sheriffs turn.

Folkstone (in Kent) Pop. Lapis.

F O M.

A fomentation, Fomentatio, onis, f.

F O N.

A font, Baptisterium, ii, n.

F O O.

Food, Alimentum, i, n. Nutrimentum, i, n.

Pertaining to food, Alimentarius, a, um.

A foot, Pes, dis, m. Pedata, æ, f.

The sole of the foot, Planta, æ, f.

A footman, Pedes, itis, *c.* 2.

A footman that runs afore, Vantrarius, ii, m.

A footstool, Scabellum, i, n.

A foot pace, Vestigium foci.

A foot soldier, Pedes, itis, c. g.

F O R.

For, Pro, præp. Propter, præp.

Forage, Foragium, ii, n. *Lex.* 57.

To forbid, Veto, are. Prohibeo, ere.

A forbidding, Prohibitio, onis, f.

Forbidden, Prohibitus, a, um.

A forbidder, Prohibitor, oris, m.

Force (or, strength) Vis, vis, vi, vim.

Force, Forcia, æ, f. *Ra. Ent.* 73. *Cow.* 117. 2. *Inst.* 182. *Spel.* 249. Force is a French word, signifying *Vim, nervositatem, fortitudinem, virtutem.* In our Common Law it is most usually applied to the evil part, and signifieth unlawful violence: *West.* thus defineth it, Force is an offence, by which violence is used to things or persons, *P.* 2. *Symb. Tit. Inditements sect.* 65. Where also he divideth it thus, Force is either simple or compound, simple is that which is so committed that it hath no other Crime adjoined unto it, as if one by force do only enter into another Mans Possession, without doing any other unlawful act there. Mixt, is that violence which is committed with such a fact, as of it self only is Criminal; as if any by force enter into another mans possession, and kill a man, or ravish a woman there.

Force prohibited by the Statutes must be either *Manu forti*, with force or strong-hand, or *Multitudine*, with multitude of people.

The Counsellors and Committers of force are alike punished.

There is a difference in the Common Law betwixt publick and private force.

Fresh force done within forty days, Frisca fortia.

Forcible entry, Ingressus manu forti factus.

To forecast (or cast in ones mind before hand, or foresee) Prævideo, ere.

By force of an act of Parliament, Vigore.

A forehead, Frons, tis, f.

Foreign (or outlandish) Exterus, a, um.

Foreign, Forinsecus, a, um. It cometh of the French *Forain*, i. e. *Exterus, Externus*, It is used adjectively in our Common Law, and joineth with divers Substantives, as foreign matter, that is, matter triable in another County, *Pl. Cor. fol.* 154. or matter done in another County, *Kitch. fol.* 126.

Foreign plea, Forinsecum Placitum, Is a refusal of the Judge as Incompetent, because the matter in hand was not within his Precincts, *Kitchin fol.* 75. & *Anno* 4. *H.* 8. *cap.* 2. & *Anno* 22. *Ejusdem, cap.* 2. & 14.

Foreign answer, That is, such an answer as is not triable in the County where it was made, *An.* 16. *H.* 6. *cap.* 5.

Foreign service, Forinsecum servitium, That is, such service whereby a mean Lord holdeth over of another without the compass of his own Fee, *Brook. Tit. Tenures, fol.* 251. *n.* 12. and 28. *Kitch. fol.* 209. or else that which a Tenant performeth either to his own Lord, or to the Lord Paramount out of the Fee; of these services read *Bracton lib.* 2. *cap.* 16. *n.* 7. *Brook Tenures* 28. 95. Foreign service seemeth to be Knights service, or Escuage uncertain, *Perkins reservat.* 650.

Foreign attachment, Attachiamentum Forinsecum, Is an Attachment of Foreigners Goods found within a Liberty or City, for the satisfaction of some Citizen to whom the said Foreigner oweth money.

Foreign opposer, Forinsecarius oppositor, Is an Officer in the Exchequer, to whom all Sheriffs and Bailiffs do repair, by him to be opposed of their green wax, and from thence draweth down a charge upon the Sheriff and Bailiff to the Clerk of the Pipe.

Fore-judger, Foris judicatio, Abjudicatio, onis, f. Signifieth in the Common Law a Judgment, whereby a man is deprived or put by the thing in question. It seemeth to be compounded of *Fors*, i. e. *Præter*, and Juger, i. e. *Judicare*. See *Bracton*, *lib.* 4. *tract.* 3. *cap.* 5. *Kitchin fol.* 209. *Old nat. brev. fol.* 44. and 81. *Statute An.* 5. *Edw.* 3. *cap.* 9. and *anno* 21. *R.* 2. *cap.* 12.

To fore-judge, Foris-judico, are. Abjudico, are.

For ever, Imperpetuum.

A forehead cloath, Frontale, is, n.

Fore front (*or outside*) Frontispicium, ii, n.

A fore top, Caprona, æ, f.

Foreland, Forlandum, i, n.

To forestall, Forstallo, are.

A forestaller, Forstallator, oris, m.

Forestallment, Forstallamentum, i, n. *Spel.* 294. 2. *Ro.* 79. *Co. Lit.* 161. *Davis* 38. *Ry.* 26. 29.

A kind of forestalling the market, Abbrocamentum, i, n.

A forestall (*or stoppage of the way*) *also a forestalling of the market*, Forstallum, i, n.

A forest, Foresta, æ, f.

A forester, Forestarius, ii, m. *Spel.* 286. *Lex.* 58.

A Custom of foresters, &c. to take horse meat, mans meat, &c. gratis of Tenants and Inhabitants that lived thereabouts, Putura, æ, f. Qu. Portura.

A kind of club of forest Tenants at the Officer of the foresters house, Scotalium, ii, n. Scotalla, æ, f.

A forest bill, Hatchettum, i, n.

A principal Officer of the forest, Gruarius, ii, m.

Warden of a forest, Gardianus Forestæ Domini Regis de Waltham.

To turn ground to forest, Afforesto, are.

A duty to be paid to the Kings forester, Forestagium, ii, n.

To forfeit, Forisfacio, ere.

A forfeiture, Forisfactura, æ, f. *Spel.* 292. Forfeiture cometh from the French word *Forfaict*, i. e. *Scelus*, but signifieth in our Language rather the effect of transgressing a Penal Law, than the transgression it self, as forfeiture of Escheates, *Anno* 25. *Ed.* 3. *c.* 2. *Statute de prodition.* Goods confiscated, and Goods forfeited differ. *Stawnf. Pl. Cor. fol.* 186. where those seem to be forfeited that have a known Owner, having committed any thing, whereby he hath lost his Goods, and those confiscated that are disavowed by an Offender, as not his own, nor claimed by any other, or rather that forfeiture is more general, and confiscation particular to such as forfeit only to the Princes Exchequer, *Vi. cap.* 24. *lib.* 3. *per totum.*

Full forfeiture, Plena forisfactura, Otherwise called *Plena vita*, is forfeiture of Life and Member and all else that a man hath, *Manwood, p.* 1. *fol.* 341. The Canon Lawyers use allo this word, *Forisfacta sunt pecuniariæ Pœnæ delinquentum*, &c. *Cap. Presbyteri. Extr. pœn.*

To forge (as smiths do) Cudo, ere.

A forge, Forgea, æ, f. *Co.Lit.* 115. 1. *Mon.* 184.

A forge (or smiths forge) Fabrica ferraria.

To forge the Sheriffs warrant upon a Writ, Fabricare Warantum Vicecomitis super aliquod breve.

A forger of false deeds or writings, Fabricator falsarum Chartarum. It cometh of the French *Forger*, i. e. *Accudere, fabricare, conflare*, to beat on an Anvil, to fashion, to bring into shape, and signifieth in our Common Law, either him that fraudulently maketh and publisheth false writings, to the prejudice of any mans right, or else the Writ that lieth against him that committeth the offence. *Fitz. nat. brev. fol.* 96. *B. C.* calleth it a Writ of Deceit: See Terms of Law, *verbo Forger*, and *West. Symb. p.* 2. *Indictments, sect.* 66. See the new Book of Entries, *verbo forger de faits.* This is a branch of that which the Civilians call *Crimen falsi, vid. Hostiens & Azo in summ.*

A fork, Furca, æ, f. Fuscina, æ, f.

An iron fork, Furca ferrea.

A two grained fork, Bidens, tis, n.

A pack fork, Ærumna, æ, f.

A form, Forma, æ, f.

A form (or seat) Scamnum, i, n.

Forma donationis, Is a Writ whereby to recover Lands entailed. It is called *Formedon*, because the Writ doth comprehend the form of the gift. There are three kinds of Writs *Formedon*, *viz.* the first in the *Descender*, to be brought by Issue in tail, which claim by descent, *per formam doni.* The second is in the *Reverter*, which lieth for him in the Reversion, or his Heirs or Assigns after the state tail is spent. The third is the *remainder*, which the Law giveth to him in the Remainder, his Heirs or Assigns, after the determination of the Eſtate tail, *Cook on Lit. lib.* 3. *c.* 11. *ſect.* 595.

Fornication, Fornicatio, onis, f.

A fornicator, Fornicator, oris, m.

A forpriſe, Forpriſa, æ, f.

Forpriſed (*excepted or reſerved*) Forpriſatus, a, um. *Lex.* 59. Forpriſus, a, um.

A forrager, Frumentarius, ii, m.

To forrage (*or convoy corn into the camp*) Frumentor, ari.

To forſwear, Perjuro, are.

A fortlet (*or fortified place*) Fortuletum, i, n.

To fortifie (*or fence*) Munio, ire.

Fortified (*imbattelled as a caſtle is*) Kernellatus, a, um.

Fortunate, Fauſtus, a, um.

Fortune (a womans name) Fortuna, æ, f.

Forty, Quadraginta, pl. Indecl.

Fortieth, Quadrageſimus, a, um.

Forty ſhillings, Quadraginta ſolidi.

Forty pounds, Quadraginta libræ.

Forward, Antrorſum, adv.

F O S.

A foſter-father, Nutritor, oris, m.

A foſter-child, Alumnus, i, m.

A foſter-brother, Homogalactus, i, m.

F O T.

A fother (*or foder*) *of Lead*, Fothera Plumbi, *Pry.* 185.

F O U.

To found (*or cauſe to be built*) Fundo, are.

To found (*or melt*) Fundo, ere.

A founder, Fundator, oris, m.

A bell founder, Campanarius, ii, m. Fuſor aramentarius.

A metal founder, Fuſor, oris, m.

A foundation, Fundamentum, i, n.

A laying the foundation, Fundatio, onis, f. The foundation of a College or Hoſpital is called *Fundatio, quaſi fundi datio, vel fundamenti locatio. Cook lib.* 10. *Rep.*

A foundation made in a marſh, or in the water with piles of timber, Pālātio, onis, f.

A fountain, Fons, tis, m.

Four, Quatuor.

Four ſquare, Quadratus, a, um.

Four times, Quater, adv.

Four ſhillings, Quatuor ſolidi.

Four pounds, Quatuor libræ.

Four hundred pounds, Quadraginta libræ.

Four thouſand pounds, Quatuor mille librarum.

Of four years, Quadriennis, ne, adj.

The ſpace of four years, Quadriennium, ii, n.

Four cornered, Quadrangŭlus, a, um.

Made with four corners, Quadrangŭlātus, a, um.

Cleft into four parts, Quadrifidus, a, um.

Fourteen pounds, Quatuordecim libræ.

Fourteen ſhillings, Quatuordecim ſolidi.

Fourteen times, Quatuordecies, adv.

Fourſcore pounds, Octaginta libræ.

Four-

Fourscore and ten pounds, Nonaginta libræ.

The fourth, Quartus, a, um.

A fourm, Forma, æ, f. 1 *Mon.* 951. 2 *Mon.* 729.

F O W.

A fowler, Auceps, cupis, *c.* 2.

A fowlers call (or whistle) Fistula aucupatoria.

A fowling piece, Sclopus, i, m.

To go a fowling, Aucupor, ari.

F O X.

A fox, Vulpes, is, f.

F O Y.

Foy people (in *Cornwal*) Fawenses.

F R A.

A fragment (or piece) Fragmentum, i, n.

A fragment (or scrap) Frustum, i, n.

Fragrant, Fragrans, ntis, adj.

A frail (as for figs or raisins) Fiscella, æ, f. Quasillus, i, m.

To frame (or form) Formo, are.

A frame, Framea, æ, f. Fabrica, æ, f.

A framing (or making) Fabricatio, onis, f.

A framer, Fabricator, oris, m.

A franchise (or liberty) Franchesia, æ, f.

Frances (a woman's name) Francisca, æ, f.

Francis (a mans name) Franciscus, ci, m.

Franck (or free) Francus, a, um.

Frank Almoin, Libera Eleemosyna.

Fran bank (or free bench) Francus Bancus, *Brac.* 309.

Frank chase, Libera chasea.

Frank fee, Feudum francum seu liberum.

Frank firm, Firma libera.

Frank law, Libera lex.

Frank pledge, Franciplegium, ii, n. Francus plegius, Frideburgus, i, m.

View of frank pledge, Visus Franci Plegi. *Spel.* 296.

Frankfold, Faldagium, ii, n. *Spel.* 248. *Lex.* 53. Fald-soca, æ, f. i. e. The setting up sheepfolds in any fields.

Fraud (or deceit) Fraus, dis, f.

Fraw *or* Frome *river* (at *Dorchester*) Varia.

F R E.

Frederick (a mans name) Fredericus, i, m.

Free, Francus, a, um. Liber, a, um.

A free-man, Liber homo, A man may be a Free man in *London* three ways, 1. By Service, as he who hath served his Apprenticeship. 2. By Birth-right, as he which is the son of a Free man of *London*. 3. By Redemption, that is, allowance of the Court of the Mayor and Aldermen, *Co.* 8. *Rep. Case of the City of* London.

Freed, Liberatus, a, um, Franchisatus, a, um.

Free born, Francbordum, i, n. 2 *Mon.* 241. *Lex.* 60. (i. e.) the ſpace of two feet more or leſs, beyond ones fence.

Free bords, Fenſuræ, 1. *Fo.* 146.

To free (enfranchiſe or make free) Libero, are. Manumitto, ere.

Free coſt, Gratuitus, a, um.

Free chapel, Libera capella.

Free hold, Liberum Tenementum.

Of free hold, Liberæ Tenuræ.

To freight, Carco, are. *Ry.* 26. 891. 184.

To unfreight, Diſcarco, are. *Ry.* 26.

Freighted, Carcatus, a, um. *Ry.* 26. 891. 184. *Pry.* 112. Affrectatus, a, um. *Ra. Ent.* 409.

A freightment, Affrectamentum, i, n. *Ra. Ent.* 24. *Pry.* 402.

French, Lingua Francia vel Gallica.

Frequent, Frequens, ntis, adj.

To frequent, Frequento, are.

Freſh, Friſcus, a, um.

Freſhmarſh (the family) De Friſco Mariſco.

Freſh marſh, Mariſcus friſcus.

Land lying freſh and fallow, Terra jacens friſca & ad warectum. *Spel.* 300. *Lex.* 60. 163.

Freſh diſſeiſin, Friſca diſſeiſina.

Freſh ſuit, Recens Inſecutio, Although the priſoner which eſcapeth be out of view, yet if freſh ſuit be made, and he be taken in *recenti inſecutione*, he ſhall be in Execution, for otherwiſe at the turning of a corner, or by entry into a houſe, or by other means the priſoner may be out of view. *Cook* 3. *Rep. Rigeway's Caſe.*

Frevil (the family) De Frevilla.

F R I.

A friction, Frictio, onis, f.

Frideſwide (a womans name) Frideſwida, æ, f.

A diſcovery frigot, Cataſcōpium, ii, n.

A frith (or hedge) Haia, æ, f. Sepes, is, f. Sepimentum, i, n. *Brac. Engl. Preced.* 24.

A fritter, Frictilla, æ, f. Laganum, i, n.

Frivolous (or vain) Frivolus, a, um.

Frize, Phryxium, ii, n.

F R O.

From, De, A. Ab. Abs.

From (if from a place) Abinde.

From thence, Exinde.

From thence (if from a time) Ex tunc.

From thence next enſuing, Ex tunc proxime ſequens.

From thence forth for ever, Ex tunc deinceps (*or* de cætero) Imperpetuum.

From out to out, Ab extra ad extra.

Frome *river* (at *Briſtol*) Fromus.

Frome *river* (in *Dorſetſhire*) Fromus.

A front, Frontiſpicium, ii, n.

A frontlet (or frontail for a womans head) Frontale, is, n.

F R U.

Fruit, Fructus, ûs, m.

A fruit chamber, Oporotheca, æ, f.

A fruit-

A fruiterer, Arborator, oris, m.

Fruitful (*or fertil*) Fertilis, le, adj.

Frumenty(*pottage made of wheat*) Farraceum, ei, n.

To frustrate (*or deceive*) Fruſtro, are.

F R Y.

A frying-pan, Frixorium, ii, n. Sartāgo, ĭnis, f.

F U E.

Fuel, Focale, lis, n. *Pry*. 217.

F U G.

A fugitive (*or runaway*) Fugitivus, a, um.

Fugitives goods, Bona fugitivorum, Be the proper Goods of him that flieth upon felony, which after the flight lawfully found do belong to the King, *Cook vol. 6. fol.* 109. *B.*

F U L.

Full, Plenus, a, um.

To fulfill (*accompliſh or perform*) Perficio, ĕre. Conſummo, are.

To full a piece of cloath, Fullo, are.

Fulham (in *Middleſex*) Volucrum domus, Volucrum amius.

Fulk (a mans name) Fulco, onis, m.

A fuller (*or tucker*) Fullo, onis, m.

A fulling mill, Fullonia, æ, f.

A fulling, Fullatio, onis, f.

A fullers ſhop, Fullonicum, ci, n.

A fullers craft, Ars Fullonica.

Fullers earth, Terra fullonum.

Belonging to a fuller, Fullonicus, a, um.

Fulvius (a mans name) Fulvius, ii, m.

F U M.

A fumigation, Fumigatio, onis, f.

F U N.

A function, Functio, onis, f.

The fundament, Sedes, is, f.

A funeral, Funus, eris, n. Funerale, is, n.

Funeral ceremonies, Exequiæ, arum, f. pl.

Funeral rites, Juſta, orum, n. pl.

A funnel (*through which Liquors are poured into Veſſels*) Infundibulum, i, n.

F U R.

A furlong, Furlongus, i, m. *Spel.* 302. *Lex.* 61.

A furnace, Furnus, i, m. Fornax, acis, f.

To make a furnace, Furneo, are.

To take out of the furnace, Defurno, are.

A ſmall furnace, Fornacula, æ, f.

To furniſh (*or ſupply*) Adminiſtro, are.

Furniture, Furnitura, æ, f. *Co. Ent.* 13.

Travelling furniture, Equitatura, æ, f. *Reg.* 100. 2. *Ro.* 160.

Furr,

Furr, Pellicium, ii, n.

Furr, Furrura, æ, f. Cometh of the French *Fourer* (i. e.) *Pellicare*, to line with skins. Of Furr we find ſtrange kinds in the Statute *Anno* 24. *H.* 8. *cap.* 13. as of Sables, which is a rich Furr of colour black and brown, being the skin of a beaſt called a Sable, of quantity between a Pole Cat, and an Ordinary Cat, and of faſhion like a Pole Cat bred in *Ruſſia*, but moſt and the beſt in *Tartaria*. 2. *Lucerns*, which is the Skin of a Beaſt ſo called being near the bigneſs of a Wolf, of colour between red and brown ſomething mailed like a Cat, and mingled with black ſpots, bred in *Muſcovy* and *Ruſſia*, and is a very rich Furr. 3. *Genets*, that is, the Skin of a Beaſt ſo called, of bigneſs between a Cat and a Weſel, mailed like a Cat, and of the nature of a Cat bred in *Spain*, whereof there be two kinds, black and gray, and the black the more precious Furr, having black ſpots upon it hardly to be ſeen. 4. *Foines*, is a faſhion like the Sable, bred in *France* for the moſt part, the top of the Furr is black, and the ground whitiſh. 5. *Martern*, is a Beaſt very like the Sable, the skin ſomething courſer, it liveth in all Countries, that are not too cold, as *England*, *Ireland*, &c. and the beſt are in *Ireland*. 6. *Miniver*, is nothing but the Bellies of Squirrels, as ſome men ſay, others ſay it is a little Vermin like unto a Weſel, milk white, and cometh from *Muſcovy*. 7. *Fitch*, is that which we otherwiſe call the Polecat here in *England*. 8. *Shankes*, are the skin of the ſhank or leg of a kind of Kid, which beareth the Furr that we call Budge. 9. *Calaber*, is a little beaſt in bigneſs about the quantity of a Squirrel, of colour gray, and bred eſpecially in high *Germany*.

A furrier, Pellio, onis, m. Pelliculator, oris, m.

A furred gown, Toga pelliculata.

Furred caps, Pilei pellicei.

To furr gowns, Pelliculo, are.

Of furr, Pelliceus, a, um.

A furr (or hairy skin) Pellis, is, f.

Furious, Furialis, le, adj.

Furiouſly, Furioſè, adv. Furialitèr, adv.

A furrow, Sulcus, ci, m.

A water furrow (to convey water from the corn) Lacuna, æ, f. Colliquia, æ, f.

Furrow by Furrow, Sulcatìm, adv.

Under furrowed, Subaratus, a, um.

Fury (madneſs) Furor, oris, m.

Furze (or gorſe) Jampnum, i, n. *Lex.* 70.

Of furze, Jampnorum.

Fuſtian, Fuſtanum vel Fuſtagnum, i, n. Xylinum, i, n.

Future (which will be) Futurus, a, um.

G A B.

A *Gabardine (a rough* Iriſh *mantle, or horſe mans coat)* Læna, æ, f.

A ga-

A gabel (or custom upon lands) Gabella, æ, f. Gablum, i, n.

A gable end of a house, Gabalum, i, n. Fastigium, ii, n.

Gabriel (a mans name) Gabriel, elis, m.

G A G.

Gage, Vadium, ii, n. It signifieth with us a pawn or pledge. Use hath turned the *G.* into a *W.* so as it is often written Wage, as to wage deliverance, that is to give security that a thing shall be delivered, for if he that distreined, being sued, have not delivered the Cattle that were distrained, then he shall not only avow the distress, but Gager deliverance, i. e. put in surety that he will deliver the Cattle distreined, *Fitz-Herb. nat. brev. fol.* 74. *D.* and 67. *F. G.* Yet in some Cases he shall not be tied to make this security, as if the Cattle died in the Pound, *Kitchin fol.* 145. or if he claim a property in the Cattle sued for, *Terms of Law.* To wage Law, what it is, see in its place, *verbo* Law, *Vid.* Mortgage.

A gager, Gaugeator, oris, m. It signifieth with us an Officer of the Kings, appointed to examine all Tuns, Hogsheads, Pipes, Barrels, and Tercians of Wine, Oil, Honey, Butter, and to give them a mark of allowance before they are sold in any place, and because this mark is a Circle made with an Iron Instrument for that purpose, it seemeth that from thence he taketh his name, of the French *Gauchir*, that is, to wrie or turn. Of this Office you may find Statutes, the first whereof is *Anno* 27 *Edw.* 3. commonly called the Statute of Provision, or Purveyors, *cap.* 8.

A gagg to set open the mouth, Epistomium, ii, n. Linguarium, ii, n.

G A L.

The gall, Fel, fellis, n.

A gall (gall nut or oak apple) Galla, æ, f.

A gall (a chafe or galling) Intertrigo, inis, f.

A gallery, Galeria, æ, f. Pergula, æ, f. Porticus, ûs, f. Ambulacrum, i, n.

A small gallery, Porticŭla, æ, f.

An open gallery (or walk) Paradrŏmis, ĭdis, f.

An arched gallery, Macrena, æ, f.

A round gallery, Peribolatorium, ii, n.

A gally, Phaselus, i, m. & f. Galea, æ, f. *Pry.* 14. 134. 213. Actuarium, ii, n. Navis actuaria.

Gallimawfry, Tucetum, i, n.

A gally-pot, Alveolus, i, m. Cullullus, i, m.

A gallon, Galo, onis, f. Galona, æ, f. *Spel.* 305. Lagena, æ, f. *Co. Ent.* 370.

Galloway (in *Scotland*) Gaelwallia, Galweia, Gallovidia.

One that has been condemned to the gallows. Furcifer, i, m.

A place where a gallows stands (any place of execution) Gloaistowum, i, n.

A gallows (or gibbet) Gabalus, i, m.

Galba (a mans name) Galba, æ, m.

Galen (a mans name) Galenus, i, m.

Galfred (a mans name) Galfredus, i, m.

Galtres *forest* (in *Yorkshire*) Calaterium nemus.

Galway *bay* (in *Ireland*) Ansoba, Ausoba.

G A M.

Game, Præda, æ, f.

A game keeper, Custos ferarum.

A gammon of bacon, Perna, æ, f. Petaso, onis, m.

G A N.

A gangreen, Gangrena, æ, f.

G A O.

A gaol (or prison) Gaola, æ, f.

A goaler (or keeper of a gaol) Gaolarius, ii, m. Custos Gaolæ vel Prisonæ.

A gaolers fee, Carcerativum, i, n.

G A P.

A gap, as of a hedge or wall, Diruptio, onis, f.

G A R.

To garbage (or take out the entrails of any thing) Exentero, are.

To gard (or defend) Stipo, are.

A gard (or one that gardeth the person of a prince) Stipator, oris, m. Regii corporis custodes. Custodia Regis.

Gard, Custodia, æ, f.

A garden, Gardinum, i, n. Hortus, i, m.

A kitchin garden, Olitorium, ii, n.

A garden of pot herbs, Olitorius, ii, m. Herbuletum, i, n.

A gardiner, Hortulanus, i, m.

The art of gardening, Horticultura, æ, f.

Belonging to a garden, Hortensis, e, n.

A gardian, Gardianus, i, m. Custos, odis, m. It signifieth generally him that hath the charge or custody of any person or thing, but most notoriously him that hath the Education or Protection of such People as are not of sufficient discretion to guide themselves and their own Affairs, as Children and Ideots, being indeed as largely extended as being *Tutor* and *Curator* among the Civilians. For whereas Tutor is he that hath the Government of a Youth, until he come to 14 years of Age, and Curator is he that hath the disposition and ordering of his substance afterward, until he attain unto 21 years. Or that hath the charge of a Frantick person, during his Lunacy, the Common Lawyers use, but only Gardian for both these, and for the better understanding of our Common Law in this thing, you must know that as Tutor is either, *Testamentarius* or *a prætore datus*

datus ex l. Atilia, or laſtly *Legitimus*, ſo we have three ſorts of Gardians in *England*, one Ordained by the Father, in his laſt Will, another appointed by the Judge afterward, the third caſt upon the Minor by the Law and Cuſtom of the Land. Touching the firſt, a man having Goods and Chattels never ſo many, may appoint a Guardian to the Body or Perſon of his Child, by his laſt Will and Teſtament, until he come to the Age of 14 years, and ſo the diſpoſing and ordering of his ſubſtance until what time he thinketh meet, and that is moſt commonly the Age of 21 years. The ſame he may do, if he have Lands to never ſo great a value, ſo they hold not in *Capite* of the King, nor of any other Lord by Knights ſervice, but by a late Statute in *Ch.* Seconds time Liberty is given to deviſe the Pretection of the Child till 21. And in the former caſe, if the Father appoint no Guardian to his Child, the Ordinary may appoint one to order his Moveables and Chattle until the Age of 14 years, at which time he may choſe his Guardian himſelf, accordingly as by the Civil Law he may his Curator. For we hold all one rule with the Civilians in this Caſe: And that is, *invito Curator non datur*, and for his Lands, if he hold any by Copy of Court Roll, commonly the Lord of the Fee appointeth him a Gardian, until he come to the Age of 14 years, and that is one next of Kin to the Minor of that ſide that can hope for leaſt profit by his Death. If he hold by Charter in Socage, then the next of Kin on that ſide by which the land cometh not, is the Guardian, and hereupon called Guardian in Socage, and that which is ſaid here of Socage ſeemeth to be true likewiſe in *Petit Sergeanty*, *Anno* 28. *Ed.* 1. *Stat.* 1. and the reaſon of this *Forteſcue* giveth in his Book, intituled, a Commendation of the Politick Law of *England*, *c.* 44. *viz.* Becauſe there might be ſuſpicion if the next Kinſman on that ſide by which the Land deſcendeth ſhould have the Cuſtody and Education of the Child, that for deſire of his Land he might be inticed to work him ſome miſchief, Vid. *Forteſcue in Litera F.* If he hold of a Common Lord, it is either of one alone or more. If of one only, then is he Guardian of both Perſon and Lands, if of more, then the Lord of whom he holdeth by the elder Tenure, is Guardian of the perſon, and every one of the reſt hath the Cuſtody of the Land holden of himſelf. If the Priority of the Tenure cannot be diſcerned, then he is Gardian of the Perſon that firſt happeth him, *Trems of the Law* and *Stawnford*, which *fol.* 19. maketh mention of *Gardein in feit*, and *Gardein in Droit*, that is in Deed and in Law.

To gargarize (or gargle to waſh the mouth and throat) Gargarizo, are.

A gargariſm, Gargariſmus, i, m.

A ſanative gargariſm, Gargariſmus ſanativus.

A garland, Garlanda, æ, f. *Spel.* 67. Corolla, æ, f.

Garlick, Allium, ii, n.

A bed of garlick, Alliārium, ii, n.

A clove of garlick, Nucleus Allii.

A garment, Vestis, is, f. Vestitus, ûs, m. Vestimentum, i, n.

A garment made of hair, Cilicium, ii, n.

A course garment, Racana, æ, f.

A garment of cotton, Vestitus Xylinus.

A garment of leather, Vestitus coriaceus.

A garment of linen, Vestitus lineus.

A garment of skins, Vestitus pelliceus.

A garment of silk, Vestitus Sericus.

A garment of woollen, Vestitus laneus.

Garments all embroidered with gold, Rigentes auro Vestes.

A garment with many plaits, Multiplicia, arum, f.

A branched garment, Stauracina vestis.

A garment buttoned on both sides, Amphibulis, is, f.

An upper garment, Superula, æ, f.

A furred winter garment, Mastruca, æ, f.

A garment for the loins, Lumbare, is, n.

A kind of garment girt about the navel, Cinctĭcŭlus, i, m.

A garment fitted to half the body or breast, Præcinctus, ûs, m.

Old and worn garments, Scruta, orum, n.

The hem or border of a garment, Periclysis, is, f.

The gard (or fringe of a garment) Lacinea, æ, f.

The skirts of a garment, Peniculamentum, i, n.

A priests garment, Alba, æ, f. *Spel.* 27.

Garnesey *Isle*, Sarnia.

A garner, Granarium, ii, n. Cella penuaria.

Garnished with divers pictures or colours, Variegātus, a, um.

A garret in the top of a house, Cænaculum, i, n.

A garrison, Præsidium, ii, n.

A garrison about a city, Taxidium, ii, n.

A garter, Garterium, ii, n. *Spel.* 310. Genuale, lis, n. Fasciola, æ, f.

An hose garter, Ligula cruralis.

A Knight of the garter, Prænobilis ordinis Garterii miles.

G A T.

A gate, Porta, æ, f. Janua, æ, f.

A gate-house, Domus portuaria.

Gates-head (near Newcastle *upon* Tine) Gabrocentum, Gabrosentum, Capræ Caput.

To gather, Colligo, ere.

To gather together into one, Coaduno, are.

To gather goods or treasure, Thesaurizo, are.

To gather corn, Frumentor, ari.

To gather grapes in harvest, Vindemio, are.

Gate-bote, Estovium, Januarium, ii, n.

G A U.

Gaunless *a rivulet (in the Bishoprick of* Durham) Vinduglessus.

A gauntlet, Manica ferrea vel militaris.

Gauntlets for the arms, Brachialia ferrea.

Gauntlets for the shoulders, Humeralia ferrea.

Gaunt-

Gauntlets for the thighs, Femoralia ferrea.

Gaunt (the family) De Gandavo, & Gandavensis.

G A W.

Gawin (a mans name) Gawinus, i, m.

G E L.

To geld, Castro, are.

A gelding (*or gelded horse*) Canterius sive Cantherius, ii, m. Spado, onis, m.

A gelly, Gelatina, æ, f.

G E M.

A gem (*or precious stone*) Gemma, æ, f.

G E N.

A genealogy, Genealogia, æ, f.

General, Generalis, le, adj.

A general, Prætor castrensis, Dux Primarius.

A generation (*or procreation*) Generatio, onis, f. Genitura, æ, f.

A gentleman, Generosus, i, m.

G E O.

Geodesie (*or the art of measuring land*) Geodæsia, æ, f.

A geodesian (*or measurer of land*) Geodætes.

Geography, Geographia, æ, f.

A geographer, Geographus, i, m.

Geometry, Geometria, æ, f.

A geometrician (*or measurer of the earth*) Geometra, æ, m.

George (a mans name) Georgius, ii, m.

G E R.

Gerald (a mans name) Geraldus, i, m.

Gerard (a mans name) Gerardus, i, m.

German (a mans name) Germanus, i, m.

Gertrude (a womans name) Gertruda, æ, f.

Gervase (a mans name) Gervasius, ii, m.

G I B.

A gibbet, Gabalus, i, m.

Gibbeted (*staked*) Affurcillatus, a, um.

To hang on a gibbet, Furcillo, are.

G I D.

Giddy headed, Vertiginosus, a, um.

Giddiness, (*or dizziness*) *of the head*, Vertigo, inis, f.

Gideon (a mans name) Gideon, onis, m.

G I F.

A gift (*or present*) Donum, i, n.

A new years gift, Strena, æ, f.

A voluntary gift of the Subjects to the King, to maintain the charge of the Government, Benevolentia, æ, f.

G I L.

To gild, Auro, are. Inauro, are.

A gilder, Inaurator, oris, m.

A gilding, Inauratura, æ, f.

Gilt, Inauratus, a, um.

Gilbert (a mans name) Gilbertus, i, m.

Gildable (*liable to pay tax or tribute*) Geldabilis, le, adj.

Giles (a man's name) Egidius, ii, m.

A gill, Hemina, æ, f. Emina potus, 2 *Mon.* 727. 730.

Land held by paying a gilliflower, Gilliflorata terræ.

G I N.

Ginger, Gingiber, ĕris, n. Zinziber, ĕris, n.

A ginn (*or snare*) Laqueus, ei, m. Pedica, æ, f. Aucipula, æ, f.

G I R.

To gird, Cingo, ere.

Girded (*or girt*) Cinctus, a, um.

A girdle, Cingulum, i, n. Zona, æ, f.

A sword girdle, Baltheus, ei, m. Zona militaris.

A little girdle, Cingillum, li, n. Zonula, æ, f.

A womans girdle, Cinctus, ŭs, m.

A girdle about the loins, Renale, is, n.

Of a girdle, Zonarius, a, um.

A girdler (*or girdle maker*) Cingularius, ii, m. Zonarius, ii, m.

A girdle (*or girdling*) Præcinctura, æ, f.

A girding, Cinctura, æ, f.

To gird about, Circumcingo, ere.

Girders, Girdaria, orum, n. Junctoria, orum, n.

A girl, Puella, æ, f.

A girth, Cingula, æ, f.

G L A.

Glamorganshire, Glamorgania, Glamorgantia.

Glanvil (the family) de Glanvilla.

G L.

Glass, Vitrum, i, n.

A glass maker, Vitrarius, ii, m. Vitriarius, ii, m.

A looking glass, Speculum, i, n.

A drinking glass, Cyathus, i, m. Caucalium, ii, n. Baucalium, ii, n.

A prospective glass, Telescopium, ii, n.

A magnifying glass, Microscopium, ii, n.

Burning glasses, Specula urentia.

A glass furnace, Fornax vitraria.

A vessel of glass, Vitramen, ĭnis, n. Vas vitreum.

Glass bottles, Ampullæ vitreæ.

A glass case, Hyalotheca, æ, f. Theca vitrea.

Quarrels of glass, Rhombi vitri.

A glass house, Officina vitraria.

Of glass, Vitreus, a, um.

A glasier, Specularius, ii, m. Fenestrarius, ii, m. Hyalurgus, i, m.

To glaze with glass, Invitro, are.

Glascow *city* (in *Scotland*) Glascua.

Glastenbury (in *Somersetshire*) Avallonia, Glasconia, Glastonia, Glestonia, vitrea Insula.

Of Glastenbury, Glastoniensis, Glastingensis.

G L E.

To glean, Spicas colligere, Spicilegium facere.

A gleaner (*or leaser of corn*) Spicilegus, i, m. Spicarum Collector.

Glen *river* (in *Lincolnshire*) Glenus.

Glebe, Gleba, æ, f.

Glebe land, Terra Glebalis, *Ra. Ent.* 671. *Spel.* 318. (i. e.) Land belonging to the Church.

G L I.

GLI.

A glister, Clyster, ĕris, m. Enema, æ, f.

GLO.

Gloucester *city*, Claudia, Clevum, Claudiocestria, Glavorna, Glevum, Glocestria, Gloveceastria, Glovernia.

Gloucestershire, Glavornensis Provincia, Claudiana provincia.

Bishop of Gloucester, Episcopus Glocestrensis.

A glove, Chirŏthēca, æ, f.

The finger of a glove, Digitale, is, n.

A pair of gloves, Par Chirothecarum.

Gloved, Manicatus, a, um.

A glover, Chirothecarius, ii, m.

A glovers trade, Chirothecaria, æ, f.

GLU.

Glue, Gluten, inis, n. Gleatus, i, m.

To glue, Conglutino, are.

GOA.

A he-goat, Caper, pri, m. Hircus, ci, m.

A she goat, Capra, æ, f.

A wild goat, Rupicapra, æ, f.

A goat herd, Caprarius, ii, m. Caprarum Custos vel Pastor.

A stable for goats, Ægen, onis.

A herd (or market of goats) Æpolium, ii, n.

A goat house, Caprile, is, n.

GOB.

A goblet, Crater, ĕris, m.

GOD.

A god-daughter, Baptista, æ, f. Filia spiritualis.

A god-father, Susceptor, oris, m. Pater initialis.

A god-mother, Susceptrix, icis, f. Matrina, æ, f.

A god-son, Lustricus, ci, m. Filius initialis.

Godmanchester (in *Huntingdonshire*) Gumicastrum, Gumicaster.

Godmanham (in *Yorkshire*) Delgovitia.

Godfrey (a mans name) Godfridus, i, m.

Godstow (in *Oxfordshire*) Dei locum.

GOL.

Gold, aurum, i, n.

The making and finishing of gold, Aurificium, ii, n.

A gold mine, Aurifodina, æ, f.

Gold threads, Stamina aurea.

Vessels of gold, Vasa aurea.

A gold beater, Bracteator, oris, m. Petalurgus, i, m.

A goldsmith, Aurifaber, bri, m. Aurifex, icis, m.

A goldsmiths shop, Aurificina, æ, f.

A gold stealer, Aurifur, ŭris, m.

Goldcliff (in *Monmouthshire*) Rupis aurea.

Golden vale (in *Herefordshire*) Aurea vallis.

GOO.

Good abearing (or good behaviour) Bonus gestus.

Good country, Bona patria.

Goods, Bona, orum, n.

Goods belonging to the person of the Wife, which she has after her Husbands death besides her Dower, Paraphernalia, orum, n.

Goodwich *castle* (in *Hereford-shire*) Goderici castrum.

Goodwin *sands* (in *Kent*) Lomea.

A goose, Anser, ĕris, m.

A wild goose, Vulpanser, ĕris, m.

Goose giblets, Acrocolia anseris.

A goose house, Anserarium, ii, n.

G O R.

A gorget, Armatura pro collo.

A gorget (or neckerchief, or such thing worn about the neck) Mammillare, is, n. Strophium, ii, n.

Gormanchester (in *Huntindon-shire*) Durolipons, Durosipons.

Gornay (the family) De Gorniaco.

G O S.

A goss hawk, Auster, is, m. Austurcus, i, m.

G O U.

To govern, Guberno, are.

The gout, Arthritis, idis, f.

The gout in the hands, Chiragra, æ, f.

The gout in the hip, Sciatica, æ, f.

The gout in the knees, Gonagra, æ, f.

The gout in the feet, Podagra, æ, f.

G O W.

A gown, Toga, æ, f. Vestis pellicea.

A long sleeved gown, Toga manicata.

A loose gown, Stola, æ, f.

A womans gown, Palla, æ, f. Toga muliebris.

G R A.

Grace (a womans name) Gracia, æ, f.

A graduate, Graduatus, i, m. (i. e.) A Scholar that has taken degrees in the University, 8. *Co.* 113.

To graff, Insero ere.

To graff Cyons, Inserere Surculos.

A graff, shoot, &c. Insitum, i, n. Surculus, li, m. Clavŏla, æ, f.

Graffed, Insitus, a, um.

A graffer, Insitor, oris, m.

A graffing, Insitus, ûs, m.

A grain (the eighth part of an ounce) Granum, i, n.

A grain, Granum, i, n.

A granary, Granarium, ii, n.

Grains, Brasium madefactum.

Grand distress, Magna destrictio, It is a distress taken of all the Lands and Goods that a man hath within the County or Bailiwick, whence he is to be distrained. This word is used *Anno* 51. *H.* 3. *cap.* 9.

A grandfather, Avus, i, m.

A great grandfather, Proavus, i, m.

A grand mother, Avia, æ, f.

A great grandmother, Proavia, æ, f.

A great grand daughter, Proneptis, is, f.

Grandison *or* Grandisson (the family) De Grandisono & Grandissono.

A grange (or farm) Grangia, æ, f. *Spel.* 322. *Grangia*, is a house or building not only where Corn is laid up, as Barns be, but also where there are stables for Horses, stalls for Oxen and other Cattle, sties for Hogs, and other things necessary for Husbandry, *Lindwood.*

A grant, Grantum, i, n. *Glan.* 64. *Cow.* 132. Concessio, onis, f.

A grantor, Concessor, oris, m.

A grantee, Concessus, ûs, m.

Grant *river* (in *Cambridgeshire*) Granta.

Grantz-

Grantzbain (*a crooked mountain in Scotland*) Grampius mons.

Grantchester (see *Cambridge*)

A grapple of a ship, Harpago, inis, f.

A Grasier, Pĕcorārius, ii, m. (i.e.) one that buyeth Cattle and keepeth and fatteth them at grass to sell again.

Grass, Gramen, ĭnis, n.

A grass plot, Viridarium, ii, n.

A swath of grass, Serticulum, i, n.

To grate, Frio, are.

A grater (*to grate bread*) Radula, æ, f.

Grated on a grater, Tritus super Radulam.

A grate (*of iron or wood*) Crates, is, f. Clathrus, i, m.

Gratis (*freely, for nothing*) Gratis, adv.

Gratitude, Gratitudo, inis, f.

To grave, Cælo, are.

Graved (*carved*) Scalptus, a, um. Sculptilis, le, adj. Sculptus, a, um.

A Graver (*or carver*) Sculptor, oris, m. Scalptor, oris, m.

A graving (*or carving*) Scalptūra, æ, f. Sculptura, æ, f.

Gravel (*or course sand*) Glarea, æ, f. Săbŭlum, i, n.

A gravel pit, Săbŭlētum, i, n.

Gravesend (in *Kent*) Greva, Gravesenda, limes prætorius.

G R E.

Grease, Adeps, ĭpis, c. g.

Hogs grease, Axungia, æ, f. Porcinus adeps.

Great, Grandis, e, adj. magnus, a, um.

Great with young, Grăvĭdus, a, um.

Green, Viridis, de, adj.

The green cloath at court, Viridis pannus Hospitii Domini Regis. The name of a Court of Justice continually sitting in the Compting house within the Court of the King, whereat do sit these Officers following, *viz.* the Lord Steward, the Treasurer, the Comptroller and Cofferer of the Kings Houshold with the Master of the Houshold, two Clerks of the Green-cloth, and two Clerks Comptrollers. Of these the three first usually are (and sometimes the fourth hath been) of the Privy Council, and unto this, being (as some hold) the first and ancientest Court of Justice in *England*, is committed the charge and oversight of the Kings Court Royal for matter of Justice and Government, with the like Authority for maintaining of the Peace within 12 miles distance wheresoever the said Court be, and within the said House the Power of Correction over all the Servants therein with the Oeconomical charge of making Provisions, Payments and Accounts for all expences incident to the said house. It is called Green-cloath, of a Green-cloath, at which they always sit, whereon is embroidered the Kings Arms, under which they sit, and on each side thereof the Arms of the Compting-house, bearing *verte*, a Key and a Rod, or White Staff *Argent faulty*, signifying their power to reward and correct; as men for their great Wisdom and Experience, thought fit by his Majesty, to exercise both these Functions in his Royal House. The name of the Compting house where the Court of Green cloath is kept, is *Domus Computi.* Unto this Compting house, for the keeping of the place, for this Court of Green-cloath, are further allowed a Sergeant,

geant, Yeoman and Groom, with diet and allowance for keeping the ſame.

Greendon (the family) De Grendona.

Greenvil (the family) De Greenvilla.

Gregory (a mans name) Gregorius, ii, m.

A grey hound, Leporarius, ii, m. Canis Leporarius.

Greenwich (in *Kent*) Grenovicum, Grenovicus, Greenwicum, Viriduſinus.

G R I.

A gridiron, Craticula, æ, f.

Griffith (a mans name) Griffithus, i, m.

To grind, Molo, ere. Acuo, ere.

A grinder, Acuarius, ii, m.

A grinding, Exacuatio, onis, f.

A grinding-houſe, Molens domus.

A grindſtone, Molens lapis, Coticula, æ, f. Allo, onis, m.

Grieſt, Far, rris, n. Molitura, æ, f.

Grizel (a womans name) Grizelda, æ, f.

G R O.

A grocer, Aromatarius, ii, m. Aromatopola, æ, m.

A grocers ſhop, Aromatopolium, ii, n.

Grocery wares, Aromata, orum, n.

The groin (*or lower part of the belly*) Hypogaſtrium, ii, n. Inguen, inis, n.

A groom, Valectus, i, m. Valetus, i, m. *Cow.* 132. Gromettus, i, m. 1. *Co.* 29.

Groom of the ſtable, Gromettus ſtabuli.

The groom porter, Aleatorum arbiter.

A grove, Grova, æ, f. *Plo.* 269. *Co. Ent.* 111. Lucus, i, m. Arbuſtum, i, n.

A little grove, Grovetta, æ, f.

A grover of mines, Metallarius, ii, m.

Ground, Fundus, i, m.

Paſture ground, Fundus paſturalis, paſtura.

Meadow ground, Fundus pratalis. pratum.

Wood ground, Fundus boſcalis.

Heath ground, Fundus bruerallis.

Ruſhy ground, Juncaria, orum, n.

To break up ground, and beſtow the firſt tilling of it, Præcolo, ere.

A Tiller of the ground, Ruricola, æ, m.

A ground work, Fundamentum, i, n.

A ground pinning (*or under pinning*) Subſtructura, æ, f.

Groſmount *or* Gromount (the family) De Magroomonte.

Groſvenour, *corruptly* (*or* Gravenor, the family) Grandis venator.

A groſs, Groſſa, æ, f. 1. *Mon.* 118. Groſſum, i, n. *Ry.* 408.

Groſs, Groſſus, a, um.

Seiſed, as of any thing in groſs, Seiſitus ut de uno groſſo.

Groſs or thick trees, Arbores groſſæ, *Ry.* 408.

Selling by the groſs, Venditio in Groſſo, *Ry.* 400.

G R U.

De Grund-beof (the family) De Fronte Bovis.

G U E.

A gueſt, Hoſpes, itis, m.

G U I.

G U I.

A guide, Ductor, oris, m.

Guidage, Guidagium, ii, n. Guadagium, ii, n. (i. e.) Money given to a guide for safe conduct in a strange place.

A guild (*brotherhood or company incorporate*) Guilda, æ, f. 8 *Co.* 125. Gilda, æ, f. Sodalitium, ii, n.

The guild-hall, Guihalda, æ, f. Guildhalda, æ, f. (i. e.) the Common Hall of a City, a Town-house.

Guild-hall, Gildæ aula.

The Guild-hall of the high Dutch *or Easterly Merchants in* London (*called the* Stilliard) Guildehalla Teutonicorum.

Guildford *in* Surrey, Geldeforda, Guldeforda, Neomagus, Noiomagus, Noviomagus.

G U L.

The gule of August (*or first day of* August) Festum Sancti Petri ad Vincula, Gula augusti.

Gulf Island, Lisia.

G U M.

Gum, Gummi, n. Indecl.

The gums of the mouth, Gingiva, æ, f.

G U N.

A gun, Gunna, æ, f. *Spel.* 101. Pace Regis 36. Canna, æ, f. Bombarda, æ, f. Tormentum, i, n.

The cock of a gun, Serpentina, æ, f.

A gunner, Bombardius, i, m. Murifragus, i, m. Sclopetarius, ii, m.

A gun shot, Murifragium, ii, n.

A kind of gun, Burcheta, æ, f.

Gun-powder, Pulvis Bombardicus.

G U T.

A gutter, Guttera, æ, f. *Ra. Ent.* 129. *Reg.* 127. 199. 5. *Co.* 100. Guttura, æ, f. *Ra. Ent.* 10. *Co.* 141. Canalis, is, m. Colluviarium, ii, n.

A gutter tile, Imbrex, icis, d. g.

G U Y.

Guy (a mans name) Guido, onis, m.

G Y P.

A gypsie, Ægyptianus, i, m.

H A B.

A *Habberdasher of small wares*, Minutarius, ii, m. Mercularius, ii, m.

A habberdasher of hats and caps, Pileo, onis, m.

An habergeon, Habergettum, i, n. *Ry.* 53. Lorica, æ, f.

Habeas corpus, Is a Writ, the which a man indited of some Trespass, before Justices of Peace, or in a Court of any Franchise, and upon his apprehension being laid in Prison for the same, may have out of the Kings Bench, thereby to remove himself thither at his own costs, and to answer the Cause there, &c. *Fitz. nat. brev. fol.* 250. *H.* and the order in this Cause, first

first to procure a *Certiorari* out of the Chancery, directed to the said Justices for the removing of the Indictment into the Kings Bench, and upon that to procure this Writ to the Sheriff for the causing of his body to be brought at a day, *Reg. Judic. fol.* 81. where you may find divers cases wherein this Writ is used.

Habeas corpora, Is a Writ that lieth for the bringing in of a Jury, or so many of them as refuse to come upon the *Venire facias*, for the Trial of a Cause brought to Issue.

A scholars habit (or garment) Epitogium, ii, n.

An habitation (or dwelling) Habitatio, onis, f. Mansio, onis, f. Domicilium, ii, n.

Habitable, Habitabilis, e, adj.

H A D.

A hade, or hade of land, Hada, æ, f.

H A F.

A haft (or handle) Manubrium, ii, n. Capulum, i, n. Ansa, æ, f.

H A I.

The hair of the head, Capillus, i, m.

The hair of the body, Pilus, i, m.

False hair, Galericum, ci, n.

An hair lace, Vitta, æ, f.

H A K.

An hake, Bombarda, æ, f.

H A L.

A halbert, Framea, æ, f. Bipennis, is, f. Securis Amazonia.

Half. Dimidius, a. um.

A hall, Aula, æ, f.

A hall (or mansion house) Halla, æ, f.

A common hall (or dining room) Refectorium, ii, n.

A great porch hall, Paganica Pila.

Hallifax (in *Yorkshire*) Olicana, Sacra Sylva, Sacra Bosco.

Halm or hulm (the stem or stalk of corn from the root to the ear) Culmus, i, m.

A halster (he which haleth and draweth a ship or barge along the river by a rope) Helciarius, ii, m.

And halser (a rope wherewith Barks or boats are towed or haled along some channel or river) Helcium, ii, n.

A halter (or head-stall) Capistrum, stri, n.

H A M.

A hamlet, Hamlettum, i, n. Hamleta, æ, f. *Spel.* 330.

A hammer, Malleus, ei, m.

A little hammer, Malleolus, li, m.

A copper smiths hammer, Marculus, i, m.

A masons hammer, Asciculum, li, n.

A hammer (to knock at a door) Manulus Ostii, Annulus Ostii, Aut marculus ferreus quo pulsantur fores.

The hamper in the Chancery, Hanaperium, ii, n. *Cow.* 135. *Spel.* 331. *Lex.* 30.

A Ham-

A Hamper made of Twigs or Bull rushes, Scirpiculum, i, n.

Hampton Court. Avona. Avondunum.

H A N.

A hand, Manus, ûs, f.

The right hand, Dextra, æ, f.

The left hand, Siniſtra, æ, f.

The palm of the hand, Palma, æ, f.

The back of the hand, Metacarpium, ii, n.

The hollow of the hand, Vola, æ, f.

An hands breadth, Palma, æ, f.

A handfull Palmata, æ, f. Lex. 93. Manipulus, li, m. *A handfull is four Inches by the Standard*, anno 33. H. 8. cap. 5.

A hand Gun, Sclopus manualis.

A handicraft (or manual occupation, the Craft or Trade of the hand) Ars mechanica.

An handicrafts-man, Mechanicus, ci, m.

A handkerchief, Muccinium, ii, n. Sudarium, ii, n.

Ones own hand writing, Autŏgrăphum, i, n.

A hand-ſaw, Serrula, æ, f. Serra manuaria.

To handle, Tracto, are.

A handler, Tractator, oris, m.

A handling, Tractatio, onis, f.

A hand-gyve, Chiromanica, æ, f.

To hang Pendo, ere.

To hang down before Præpendeo, ere.

A hanger (or ſhort Sword) Enſis falcatus.

A wood-mans Hanger Culter venatorius.

A hang-man (or Executioner) Carnifex, ĭcis, m.

Hangings, Piſtromata camerarum. aulæa, orum, n.

Hanguſtald, or Hexham, (in Northumberland) Haguſtaldunum. Hanguſtaldunum.

Of Hanguſtald, Haguſtaldenſis.

Hannah (a womans Name) Hanna, æ, f.

Hans River (in Staffordſhire) Hanſus.

Hanton (the Family) D'Hantona.

Hantſhire, Hantonia.

H A P.

To happen, Fortuno, are. Co. Entr. 4. 8. 3.

By happ (or Chance) Fortè, adv. Fortuitò, adv.

H A R.

A harbinger (one that goeth before and provideth Lodging) Manſionarius, ii, m. Prodromus, i, m. He is an Officer of the Princes Court, that allotteth the Noble men and thoſe of the Houſhold their Lodgings in the time of Progreſs.

Hard, Durus, a, um.

To harden (or obdurate) Duro, are.

To wax hard or Brawny, to be hardned by Long uſe. Callo, ere.

A hardning Obfirmatio, onis, f.

A hardner, Obfirmator, oris, m.

A hare, Lepus, oris, m.

A hare-pipe, Harepipa, æ, f. *Ra. Ent.* 405. Leporicipula, æ,f.

A hare Warren, Lagotrophium, ii, n.

A harlot, Pellex, icis, f. Scortum, i, n. Prōseda, æ, f.

A young harlot, Scortillum, i, n.

To haunt or keep Company with Harlots, Scortor, ari.

Harman (a mans name) Harmanus, i, m.

Harkley, (the Family) D' Harcla.

Harmless, (Losseless and Indempnified) Indempnis, Innocuus, & Indempnificatus.

Harmony, Harmonia, æ, f.

Harness, Hernesia, æ, f. Harnesia, æ, f. Fitz. herb. Nat. brev. 94. Ry. 302. Fle. 78. Pry. 21.

An harness-maker, Frænarius, ii, m.

Harold (a mans name) Haroldus, i, m.

A harp, Lyra, æ, f.

A Jews Harp, Crembalum, li, n.

A harper, Lyricen, inis, m. Citharista, æ, m.

A harrow, Occa, æ, f.

Harrowed, Occatus, a, um.

A harrower, Occator, oris, m.

A harrowing, Occātio, onis, f.

To harrow, Occo, are, Hercio, ire. Lex. 68.

Harslets Offæ penitæ. Exta porcella.

A hart (or Stag) Cervus, i,m.

Hartlepool (in the Bishoprick of Durham) Cervi Insula.

H A S.

An hasp. Haspa, æ, f. *Co. Lit.* 48. *Spel.* 331. *Brac.* 40.

Hassey (the Family) De Hosata & Hosatus.

Hastings (in Sussex) Hastingæ.

H A T.

A hatch of a Door, Anticum, ci, n.

To hatch flax, Carmino, are. Pectino, are.

A hatchell (the Iron Comb wherewith the Flax is dressed) Pecten, inis, m.

The hatches of a Ship. Fori, orum, m.

A hatchet, Hatchettus, i, m. 4 Inst. 313. asciola, æ, f.

Hatred (ill will) Hatia, æ, f. Odium, ii, n.

A hat. Gaelrus, i, m.

A Beaver hat. Fibrinus Galerus.

An Hat-band, Spira, æ, f. Redimiculum Pilei.

An hat block, Globus Ligneus.

An hat and hat case, Galerus & Theca eundem Galerum continens.

A hatter (or maker or seller of Hats) Pileo, onis, m. Pilopæus, i, m.

Hatfield, or *Hantfield (in Hertfordshire,)* Campus altus.

H A U.

To have and to hold (If Inritance or Freehold, in the Common Pleas) *Habendum & Tenendum.*

To have and to hold (if a Lease for years, in the Common Pleas) *Habendum & occupandum.*

But

But in all Cases in the Kings Bench. Habendum & Tenendum.

A haven (or Port) Baia, æ, f. Heda, æ. f. Portus ûs, m.

A little haven (or Hyth) Hitha, æ, f.

H A W.

A hawk, Accipiter, ris, m.

A reclaimed hawk, Accipiter Reclamatus.

A hawks hood, Capitium, ii, n.

A hawks bell. Tintinnabulum, i, n.

An Airey of hawks, Aeria Accipitrum. Fle. 92.

Hawking Aucupium, ii, n.

To hawk, Aucupor, ari.

A Sparrow-hawk, Accipiter humipeta.

A goss-hawk, Palumbarius, ii, m.

H A Y.

Hay (the Family) De Haia.

Hay-bote, Estoverium, ii, n. *Co. Lit.* 41. B.

Hay, Fœnum, i, n.

Hay in swaths or Cocks. Fœnum in Tassis.

An hay cock, Meta Fœni.

An hay-mow, loft or stack. Fœnile, is, n. Strues Fœni.

A bottle of hay, Fasciculus Fœni. Batellus Fœni.

A truss of hay, Trussum Fœni.

Hay-harvest Fœnisecium, ii, n.

An hay (or net to take Conies) Cassiculus, i, m. Indago, inis f. Tendicula, æ, f.

An hayward Bedellus, i, m. Gre. 347. Custos agri.

H E.

He, Ipse, a, um. Ille, Illa, Illud, adj. Iste, ista, istud, adj.

H E A.

The head, Caput, itis, n.

The fore part of the head. Sinciput, itis, n.

The hinder part of the head, Occiput, itis, n.

The crown of the head, Vertex, icis, m.

A little head, Capitulum, li, n. Capitellum, i, n.

The head-ach. Cephalalgia, æ, f.

An arrow head (or head of a dart) Spiculum, i, n. Aculeus Sagittæ.

A broad arrow head. Uncinus, i, m.

An headborow, Capitalis plegius. Spel. 333.

Headlong, Præceps, ipis & ipitis.

An head-piece, Capillum ferreum. Ry. 53. Cassis, idis, f. Cassida, æ, f.

A head-land (or Hade Land) Forera, æ, f.

An headship, Præfectura, æ, f.

The headstall of a Bridle, Aurea, æ, f.

To heal (or cure) Sano, are, Curo, are.

Healed (or Cured) Sanatus, a, um. Curatus, a, um.

An healing, Sanatio, onis, f. Curatio, onis, f.

Health (or healthfulness) Sanitas, atis, f. Salus, ûtis, f.

Healthy (or healthfull) Saluber, a, um.

Healthfully, Salubritèr, adv.

To heap up, (or gather in heaps) Cumulo, are. Acervo, are.

An heap, Cumulus, i, m. Acervus, vi, m.

Heaped Cŭmŭlātus, a, um.

A heaping up, Cŭmŭlātio, onis. f.

A heard of Cattel, Armentum, i, n.

A heardsman, Armentarius, ii, m. Pecorarius, ii, m.

A cow-heard, Vaccarius, i, m.

A neat heard (or keeper of Oxen) Bubulcus, ci, m.

A swine-heard (or hog-heard) Porculator, oris, m. Porcarius, ii, m.

A shepheard, Opilio, onis, m.

To hear, Audio, ire.

Hearing, Auditus, ûs, m.

An hearse (or Monument of the dead) Cenotaphium, ii, n.

A hearse-cloath, Brandeum, ei, n.

The heart, Cor, dis, n.

The heart strings (or the film of the heart) Præcordia, orum, n, pl.

An hearth, Hertha, æ, f. Focus, i, m. Fŏcārium, ii, n.

Of a hearth, Focarius, a, um.

To heat, Calefacio, ere.

Heath, Erix, icis f. Erica, æ, f.

A heath, Ericetum, i, n. Bruera, æ, f.

An heath (or ground over run with Fern) Filicetum, i, n.

To heave (or lift up) Allevo, are.

Heavy (or weighty) Ponderosus, a, um.

H E B.

Hebe (a womans name) Heba, æ, f.

H E C.

A heckle (or Brake) for Hemp, Linibrium, ii, n. Hamus, i, m.

Hector (a mans name) Hector, oris, m.

H E D.

A dead hedge, Sepes, is, f.

A quick set-hedge, Haia, æ, f. Reg. 105. *bis*. Spel. 128. Sepes viva.

A hedge or Pale before a Gate, Hercæus, i, m.

To hedge, Sepio, ire. *To hedge or Fence round*, Circumsepio, ire.

To hedge in or divide by a Hedge, Intersepio, ire.

To hedge up Gaps, Contexere Interrupta.

Hedge Boot, Estoverium Claudendi.

Hedge-wood, Busca, æ, f.

H E E.

A heel, Calx, icis, m, *and* f.

H E I.

An heifer, Juvenca, æ. f.

An heir, Hæres, edis. c. 2. Although the word is borrowed of the Latin, yet it hath not altogether the same signification with us, that it hath with the Civilians. For whereas they call him

him *Hæredem, qui ex Testamento Succedit in universum jus Testatoris:* The Common Lawyers call him heir that succeedeth by right of blood in any mans Lands or Tenements in Fee, for there is nothing passeth with them, *jure Hæreditatis*, but only Fee. Moveables or Chatels immoveable, are given by Testament, to whom the Testator pleaseth, or else are at the disposition of the Ordinary.

Cassanæus in Consuetud Burg. pag. 909. hath a distinction of *Hæres*, which in some sort well accordeth with our CommonLaw. For he saith, there is *Hæres Sanguinis*, and *hæres hæreditatis.* And a man may be *hæres sanguinis*, that is, heir apparent to his Father or other Ancestor, by blood, and yet may upon displeasure be defeated of his Inheritance, or at the least the greatest part thereof.

Heir in the Legal understanding of the Common Law, implyeth that he is, justis nuptiis procreatus, *for* hæres legitimus est quem nuptiæ demonstrant, And is he to whom Lands, Tenements or Hereditaments, by the Act of God, and right of blood do descend, of some estate of Inheritance. *Cook on Lit. Lib.* 1. *cap.* 1. *Sect* 1. *Hæres dicitur ab Hærendo, quia qui hæres est hæret, id est, proximus est Sanguine illi cujus est hæres.*

Every Heir is either a Male or Female, or an Hermaphrodite, that is, both Male and Female, and an Hermaphrodite (which is also called *Androgynus*) shall be heir, either as Male or Female according to that kind of the Sex which doth prevail, *Hermaphrodita, tam masculo quam fæmina comparatur, secundum prævalescentiam sexus incalescentis.* and accordingly it ought to be baptized, *Id. Ib. Hæres est quintuplex.*

1. *Jure proprietatis*, so the Eldest Son shall Inherit only before all his brethren.

2. *Jure repræsentationis*, as where the Eldest Son dieth, his Issue shall Inherit before the younger Son, he represents the person of his Father.

3. *Jure propinquitatis, as* propinquus excludit remotum, *and* remotus remotiorem. Cook 3. Rep. Ratcliffs Case.

4. *Jure sanguinis*, so the daughter of the first venter shall Inherit before the Son of the second.

5. *Ratione Doni*, so the half blood shall Inherit, as if a Gift be made to one and the heirs of his body, and he hath Issue a Son, and a Daughter by one venter, and a Son by another venter. The Father dies, and the Eldest Son enters and dies, the young Son shall Inherit *per formam Doni*, for he claims as heir of the Body of the Donee, and not generally as heir of his Brother: otherwise where Land cometh by Descent, the Rule is, *Possessio fratris de fœodo Simplici facit sororem esse hæredem*, but the brother ought to be in actual Possession of the Fee

and Frank Tenement, either by his own possession, or the Possession of another, to make his Sister heir, and the reason is, because of all hæreditaments in Possession, he which claimeth as heir, ought to make himself Heir by him that was last actually seized. *Id. Ib. Soror est hæres facta*, therefore some act must be done to make her heir, and the younger brother is *hæres natus*, if no act be done to the contrary. But if the King by his Letters Patents make a Baron to him and his heirs, Possession in the Elder Brother of this dignity cannot make his Sister heir, but the Brother of the half blood shall Inherit, because no Possession can be gained of this dignity, *per pedis positionem*. *Cook ubi supra* and on *Lit. lib.* 1. *c.* 1. Sect 8.

In case of the Descent of the Crown, the half blood shall Inherit, so after the decease of King *Edward* the sixth, the Crown fell to Queen *Mary*, and from her to Queen *Elizabeth*, both which were of the half blood, and yet Inherited not only the Lands which King *Edward* or Queen *Mary* purchased, but the ancient Lands, parcel of the Crown also. *Cook Rep. Lib.* 7. *Calv. case.* and on *Lit. lib.* 1. c. 1. *Sect.* 8.

Hæres est pars antecessoris; therefore if Land be given to a man and his heirs, all his heirs, are so totally in him, as he may give the Lands to whom he will; one cannot be Heir till the death of his Ancestor; he is called *hæres apparens*, Heir apparent.

Every heir having Land, is bound by the binding acts of his Ancestors, if he be named, *qui sentit commodum sentire debet & incommodum sive Onus. Cook* on *Lit. Lib.* 1. *c.* 1. Sect. 1.

A man by the Common Law cannot be heir to Goods or Chattels; for *hæres dicitur ab hæreditate.* If a man buy divers Fishes, as Carps, Breams, Tenches, and put them into his Pond and dieth; in this case the heir shall have them, and not the Executors; but they shall goe with the Inheritance, because they were at Liberty, and could not be gotten without Industry, as by Nets and other Engines; and otherwise it is if they were in a Trunk. Likewise Deer in a Park, Conies in a warren, and Doves in a Dovehouse, young and old shall goe to the Heir. *Cook* on *Lit. Lib.* 1. c. 1. *Sect* 1.

An heir-loom, Principalium, ii, n. Lex. 67. It seemeth to be compounded of Heir and Loom, that is, a Frame, namely to weave in. The word by time is drawn to a more general signification than at the first it did bear, comprehending all Implements of houshold, as namely Tables, Presses, cupboards, Bedsteads, wainscots, &c. which by the custom of some Countries, having belonged to a house certain descents, are never Inventoried after the decease of the

the Owner, as Chatells, but accrew to the Heir with the house it self.

H E L.

The helm (the Rudder of the Ship) Ansa gubernaculi. Pars summa clavi.

A helmet, Galea, æ, f. Cassis, is, f. Calpes, is, f. Sila, æ, f.

Held in common, not divided, Indivisus, a, um. Lex. 71.

Helidorus (a mans name) Helidorus, i, m.

Hellen (a womans name) Helena, æ, f.

The crest of an helmet, Conus, i, m.

Help, Auxilium, ii, n.

To help, Juvo, are.

Helped, Auxiliatus, a, um. Adjutus, a, um.

An helper, Adjutor, oris, m.

An helping, Auxiliatio, onis, f. Juvatio, onis, f.

The Helve of an Ax, Securis manubrium.

H E M.

A hem or welt of a Garment, Limbus, i, m. Fimbria, æ, f. vestis extremitas.

To hem (or welt) Fimbrio, are.

That hath a hem, Frimbriatus, a, um.

A hemming, Prætextura, æ, f.

Hemp, Cannăbis, is, f.

A course part of hemp, Stupa, æ, f.

Of hemp, Cannăbaceus, a, um. Cannabinus, a, um.

A hempcroft (or Place to lay hemp in) Linarium, ii, n.

Hemp set on a Distaff, Stămen, ĭnis, n. Pensum, i, n.

A hemp cord, Tomex, icis, f.

H E N.

A hen, Gallina, æ, f.

A brood hen, Ovipara gallina. Gallina incubans.

One that keeps hens, Gallinarius, ii, m.

A hen-pen, Chors gallinaria.

Of a hen, Gallinaceus, a, um.

Hence, Hinc, adv.

Henceforth, Dehinc, abhinc, deinceps.

Hengist (a mans name) Hengistus, i, m.

Henly on Thames (in Oxfordshire) Henlega.

Henley hundred (in Oxfordshire) Ancalites.

Henry (a mans name) Henricus, i, m.

H E R.

Herbage, Herbagium, ii, n. It signifieth in our Common Law the fruit of the Earth provided by nature for the bitt or mouth of the Cattel. But it is most commonly used for a Liberty which a man hath to feed his Cattel in another mans ground, as in the Forest &c. *Crompt Jurisdict*: fol. 197.

An herb, Herba, æ, f.

Fruitful in herbs, Herbĭfer, a, um.

Full of herbs, Herbosus, a, um.

Of herbs, Herbarius, a, um.

Of (*or feeding*) *on Herbs*, Herbilis, e.

All kind of pot herbs, Lachanum, i, n.

The herb market, Lachanopolium, ii, n.

A ſeller of herbs, Lachanopoles, æ, m.

An herbal, Herbarium, ii, n.

An herbaliſt (*ſimpler*) Herbarius, ii, m. Botanicus, ci, m.

Herbert (*a mans name*) Herbertus, i, m.

An herald, Heraldus, i, m. Spel. 336. with us it ſignifieth an Officer at Arms whoſe Function is to denounce War, to Proclaim Peace, or otherwiſe to be employed by the King in martial meſſages or other buſineſs. They are the Judges and examiners of Gentlemens arms, they marſhall all the ſolemnities at the Coronation of Princes, manage Combats and ſuch like. With us three being the chief are called Kings at Arms, and of them *Garter* is the Principal, inſtituted and Created by *Henry* the fifth. *Stowes annals*, pag. 584. whoſe Office is to attend the Knights of the Garter at their ſolemnities, and to marſhal the ſolemnities of the Funerals of all the greater Nobility, as of Princes, Dukes, Marquiſes, Earls, Vicounts, and Barons, and in *Plowden*, *caſu Reniger & Fogaſſa*, is found, that *Edward* the Fourth granted the Office of the King of Heralds, to one called Garter, *cum feudis & proficuis ab antiquo, &c. fol.* 12. *b*.

The next is Clarentius, ordained by *Edward* the fourth, for attaining the Dukedom of *Clarence* by the death of *George* his Brother, whom he put to death for aſpiring to the Crown, made the Herald, which properly belonged to the Duke of *Clarence*, a King at arms, and called him *Clarentius*. His office is, to marſhall and diſpoſe the Funerals of all the leſſer Nobility, as Knights and Eſquires thorough the Realm of the South ſide of Trent.

The Third is *Norroy* or *Northroy*, whoſe Office is the ſame on the North-ſide of Trent, that *Clarentius* hath on this ſide, as may well appear by his name, ſignifying the Northern King, or King of the North parts. Beſides theſe, there are ſix others properly called Heralds according to their Original, as they were created to attend Dukes &c. in Martial Executions, viz. *York*, *Lancaſter*, *Somerſet*, *Richmond*, *Cheſter*, *Windſor*.

Laſtly there are 4 others called Marſhals or Purſuyvants at Arms, reckoned after a ſort in the number of Heralds, and doe commonly ſucceed in the place of the Heralds, as they die, or be preferred, and theſe are *Blew Mantle*, *Rouge croſs*, *Rougedragon*, and *Percullis*.

Hereafter, Ex tunc. Impoſterum.

Hercules (*a mans name*) Hercules, is, m.

Hereditary,

Hereditary, Hæreditarius, a, um.

Hereditaments, Hæreditamenta, orum, n. It signifieth all such things, as a man may have to himself and his Heirs, by way of Inheritance, or not being otherwise bequeathed, doe naturally and of course descend to him which is our next heir of blood, and fall not within the Compass of an Executor or administrator, as Chatels doe.

Heretofore, Præantea, ante tunc, olim, adv.

Hereunto or thereunto requested, Adinde, *or* ad hoc, *or* ad illud requisitus.

Hereford City, Herefordia, Harefordia.

Herefordshire, Herefordiæ Comitatus.

Bishop of hereford, Episcopus Herefordiensis.

Hermione (a womans name) Hermione, es, f.

An Hermitage (or solitary place) Hermitagium, ii, n.

A Chapel belonging to a Hermitage, Hermitorium, ii, n.

An Hermite, Eremita, æ, m.

An heresie, Hæresis, is, f.

The ring-leader of an heresie, Hæresiarcha, æ, *and* chus, i, m.

An heretick, Hærēticus, ci, m.

Heretical, Hærēticus, a, um.

Heretically, Hærēticè, adv.

A herring, Halec, ecis, f. & n.

An heriot, Heriotum, i, n. *Cow.* 135. 8. *Co.* 103. It is the best Beast a Tenant has at the time of his death due to the Lord, whether it be horse, Ox or any such like.

An heritage or inheritance, Hæreditas, atis, f.

Herod (a mans name) Herodes, is, m.

Hertford, Hertfordia.

Vadum { Rubrum. Corvinum.

Hertfordshire, Hertfordiæ comitatus.

Herty-point (in Devonshire) Herculis promontorium.

H E T.

Hethy Isle near Scotland (as some conjecture) Ocetis.

H E W.

To hew (or hack) Ascio, are. Dolabro, are.

A hewer of stones, Lapicida, æ, m.

A hewing, Dolatio, onis, f.

Hewed, Cæsus, a, um.

H E X.

Hexham (in Northumberland) Axelodunum.

Of hexham, Hangustaldensis.

H I D.

Hidage, Hidagium, ii, n. Spel. 352. It is an extraordinary Tax to be paid for every Hide of Land.

An hide of Land, Hida Terræ, Spel. 352. It is a certain measure or Quantity of Land, by some mens opinion, that may be Plowed with one Plough in a year *Terms of Law*. By other men it

It is an hundred Acres. By *Beda* (who calleth it *Familiam*) it is as much as will maintain a Family. *Crompton* ſaith, that it conſiſteth of an hundred acres, and eight Hides contain a Knights Fee.

Hide, or heth (in Kent) Portus Hintiuhs.

To hide, Abſcondo, ere.

A Hide (or Skin) Pellis, is, f. Tergus, ŏris, n.

A raw hide of a beaſt, Scortum, ti, n.

Made of hides, Pelliceus, a, um. Terginus, a, um.

Hidden, Abditus, a, um.

An hierarchy, Hierarchia, æ, f.

H I L.

Hilary (a mans name) Hilarius, ii, m.

A hill, Collis, is, m.

A hillock (or little hill) Colliculus, i, m. Grumus, i, m.

An hilt, (haft or handle) of a Sword, Capulum, i, n. Mannbrium, ii, n.

H I N.

An hind, Cerva, æ, f. Biſſa, æ, f. *Spel.* 99.

To hinder, Impĕdio, ire.

A hinge of a door, Cardo, inis, d. g. Gumphus, i, m.

Hinkſey (near Oxford) Hincheſega.

H I P.

The hip, Coxendix, ĭcis, f.

Hippocrates (a mans name) Hippocrates, is, m.

Hippolyte (a womans name) Hippolyta, æ, f.

H I R.

To hire (take to hire) Conduco, ere.

To let, or ſet to hire, Eloco, are, abloco, are.

An hireling, Mercenarius, ii, m. Stipendiarius, ii, m.

H I S.

His (or his own) Suus, a, um.

A hiſtory, Hiſtoria, æ, f.

An Hiſtorian (or Hiſtoriographer *)* Hiſtŏriogrăphus, i, m. Hiſtoricus, i, m.

A writing of hiſtory, Hiſtoriographia, æ, f.

Hiſtorical, Hiſtoricus, a, um.

H I T.

Hitchingham, (in) Vicanium.

Hithe, Hitha, æ, Lex. 70. i. e. *a ſmall haven to land wares out of Veſſels or Boats. New Book of Entries*, fol. 3. colum. 3.

Hitherto, Hactenus, adv.

H I U.

A bee-hive, Alveare, is, n.

H O B.

Hobelers, Hobelarii, Spel. 354. i. e. certain men that by their Tenure are tied to maintain a little light nag for the certifying of any Invaſion made by Enemies,

Enemies, or ſuch like Peril towards the Sea ſide, as *Portsmouth*, &c. of theſe you may read, Anno 18. Ed. 3. Stat. 2. cap. 7. & anno 25. ejuſdem, Stat. 5. cap. 8.

H O D.

A hodge-podge, Farraginaria, orum, n.

Hodney River (*in Buckinghamſhire*) Hodneius.

H O G.

A hog, Porcus, i, m.

An hogshead, Dolium, ii, n.

Hogs fleſh, Caro Suilla.

The belly piece in a hog, Sŭmen, inis, n.

The briſtle of an hog, Seta, æ, f.

Hogs dung, Succerda, æ, f.

An hogs trough, Aqualiculum, i, n.

An hogsſty, Porcarium, ii, n. Porcile, is, n. Suile, is, n. Hara, æ, f.

H O L.

Holderneſs (*in Yorkſhire*) Cavæ diræ peninſula.

A hole, Foramen, inis, n.

Holland (*a part of Lincolnſhire*) Hollandia. Houlandia, Hoylandia.

Hollow, Cavus, a, um.

To make hollow, Tumulo, are.

Firſt holyrood day (*the third of May*) Inventionis ſanctæ Crucis.

Second holyrood day (*the fourteenth of September*) Exaltationis ſanctæ Crucis.

H O.

H O M.

Homage, Homagium, ii, n. Spel. 356. Cow. 138.

Homicide (*Manſlaughter*) Homicidium, ii, n. *Homine Replegiando*, Is a writ to Replevy, or deliver a perſon out of priſon.

Homer (*a mans name*) Homerus, i, m.

H O N.

Honey, Mel, llis, n.

A honey comb, Favus, i, m.

Honour, Honor, is, m. alſo great Lorſhips, including other Mannors and Lordſhips.

H O O.

A hood, Cucullus, i, m. Capitium, ii, n.

A Graduates hood of the University, (*or ſuch a hood as thoſe of the Companies doe wear*) Humerale, is, n.

A French hood, Redimiculum, i, n.

A Travelling hood, Cucullio, onis, f.

A riding hood, Palliolum, i, n.

Hooded, Cucullatus, a, um.

A hoof of a horſe or beaſt, Ungula, æ, f.

A fiſhing hook, Hamus, i, m.

A hook to cut withal, Falx, cis, f.

A Fleſh hook, Fuſcinula, æ, f.

A hook to pull down houſes on Fire. Hāma, æ, f.

Of a hook, Hămātilis, le. adj.

Hooked

Hooked, Falcatus, a, um. Hămātus, a, um.

A Hooker (Catcher) Hămātor, oris, m.

To weed with a hook, Sarcŭlo, are.

A hoop, Circulus, li, m.

Twig hoops, Circuli Viminei.

An Iron hoop, or band, such as Chests are bound withall, Stegestris, is, f.

H O P.

Hop (or Hops) Lŭpŭlus, i, m.

An Hop merchant, Lupularius, ii, m.

H O R.

Horace (a mans Name) Horatius, ii, m.

A horn, Cornum, i, n.

A Tax within a Forest to be paid for Horned Beasts, Horngelda, æ, f.

A Shooe-horn, Cornu calceatorium.

An Ink-horn, Atramentarium, ii, n.

A Horse, Equus, i, m. Caballus, i, m.

An ambling horse, Equus Gradarius, asturco, onis, m.

A little ambling Nag, Mannus, i, m.

A Trotting horse, Succussator, oris, m.

A Stone-horse, Burbo, onis, m.

A Pack-horse, Sarcinarium jumentum, *vel* Clitellarium.

A War-horse, Equus agminalis.

A Sumpter horse, Equus Sarcinarius vel Clitellarius.

A Wincing horse, Calcuro, onis, m.

A Stallion (or horse kept for breed) Equus Admissarius.

A Hackney horse, Equus conductitius. Equus Tolutarius, Equus meritorius.

A broken winded horse, Equus Suspiriosus.

A mill horse, jumentum molarium.

A light horse, veredus, i, m.

A sadle horse, Equus vectarius.

A cart horse, Jumentum plaustrarium.

A hobbie (or Irish horse) Equus Hybernicus.

A post horse, Veredus, i, m.

A light horse man, Veredarius, ii, m.

An hard mouthed Restiff horse, Equus Refractarius.

The crupper of an horse, Subtela, æ, f.

A breed (or store) of horses, Restaurus Equorum, Ry. 253.

Of the races or breed of horses, Decimæ de araciis equorum, 2 Mon. 967.

A stud or race of horses, Equitium, ii, n.

A horse stable, Equile, is, n.

A horse Courser, Mango equorum.

A horse man, Equestris, is, m. Eques, itis, c. 2.

A horse litter, Vehiculum cameratum, Lectuarium gestatorium.

A horse rider, or breaker, Equisso, onis, m.

A horse

A horse keeper, Equipaſtor, oris, m.

Horse harneſs, Phalaræ Equinæ.

Horses harneſſed, Funales Equi.

An horse cloath, Dorſuale, is, n.

A horse ſhooe, Solea Equina.

Horse bread, Panis Equinus.

To ſhooe an horse, Affigere Soleas Equo. Calceo, are.

A Smiths Buttreſs to pare horse Hoofs, Scaber, ri, m.

A horses reins, Laximina, orum, n.

A horse load, Summagium, ii, n. Rol. 103. Cow. 250, Pry. 184. Ry. 104, 105. Lex. 114. 120.

Barnacles for a horses Noſe, Poſtmodis, dis, f.

A troop of horse, Equeſtre agmen.

The art of horsemanſhip, ars Equeſtris.

An Horse race, certamen Equeſtre.

A drench for an horse, Salivatum, i, n.

He that gives a drench to a horse, Salivarius, ii, m.

The maſter of the Horse, Magiſter Equorum Domini Regis.

A horse to ſaw wood on, Cantherius, ii, m. Equus durateus.

Horn Church (in Eſſex,) Cornutum Monaſterium.

Hortenſia (a Womans name) Hortenſia, æ, f.

H O S.

A hose, Hoſa, æ, f. Caliga, æ, f.

Hoſea (a mans name,) Hoſeas, æ, m.

A Hoſier (one that maketh or ſelleth hose or ſtockings,) Căligārius, ii, m.

Ancle-hose, Caligæ talares.

Hose tops, Summitates caligarum.

Hose garters, Faſciæ crurales.

Pertaining to hose, Caligarius, a, um.

Hosed Caligatus, a, um,

An Hoſpital, Hoſpitalium, ii. n.

An Hoſpital for Poor Children, Epitrophium, ii, n.

An Hoſpital for Sick people, Valetudinarium, ii, n.

Hoſpitality, Hoſpitalitas, atis, f.

An Hoſtage (or Pledge in war) Obſes, idis, c. 2.

An Hoſt, which receiveth Strangers, Hoſpes, itis, m.

An Hoſtler (or Inn-keeper) Hoſtellarius, ii, m. anno 9. Ed. 3. Stat. 2. cap. 11.

An Hoſtler that keepeth a ſtable, Stabularius, ii, m.

H O T.

A Hot houſe, Vaporarium, ii, n. Sudatorium, ii, n.

H O U.

A Hovel or Shed, wherein Husbandmen ſet their Ploughs and Carts, out of the Rain or Sun, Mandra, æ, f. Appendix, icis, f.

A Hound, Venaticus, ci, m.

A Blood hound, Canis Sagax.

An

An Houlster, Theca pro Sclopo.

An hour, Hora, æ, f.

An hour-glass, Horarium, ii, n. Clepsydra, æ, f.

Half an hour Semihora, æ, f.

During an hour, Horarius, a, um.

A house, Domus, i, or, ûs, f.

A *dwelling house*, Domus Mansionalis. Haga, æ, f.

A little house, Domuncula, æ, f. Domicilium, ii, n.

A Cow-house, vaccaria, æ, f. Cow. 267. Ry. 341. 1 Mon. 527.

An Ox-house, Boveria, æ, f. Lex. 21. 2 Mon. 210.

A Hay-house, Fœnile, is, n.

A Gate-house, Domus portuaria. Co. Ent. 696.

Front-houses, Frontana messuagia. Domus frontalis.

A Tan-house, or Heath-house, Barcaria, æ, f. Ra. Ent. 69. 697.

A wood-house, Lignile, is, n.

A Sheep-house, Ovile, is, n.

A Goat-house, Caprile, is, n.

A Lamb-house, Agnile, is, n.

A Cart-house, Domus Carucaria.

A Cart-hovel (*or Wain-house*,) Domus Plaustraria.

A Goose-house, anserarium, ii, n.

A Poultry-house, Aviarium, ii, n.

A Fatting-house, Saginarium, ii, n.

A Coal-house, Domus Carbonaria.

A Treasure-house, Ærarium, ii, n.

A Council-house, Conciliabulum, i, n.

A Store-house, Repositorium, ii, n. Reconditorium, ii, n.

A Malt-house, Brasitorium, ii, n.

A Brew-house, Pandoxatorium, ii, n.

A Work-house, Domus operaria.

A Milk-house, Domus Lactearia.

A Dairy-house, Lactarium, ii. n.

A Bake-house, Pistrinum, i, n.

A Slaughter-house, Laniena, æ, f.

A Wash-house, Lavatrina, æ, f.

A Pent house, Compluvium, ii, n, Imbricamentum, i, n.

House and Land sufficient to maintain one Family, Cassatum, i, n.

The freedom of a mans own house, Hamsora, æ, f.

A Summer or country house, Suburbanum, i, n.

A Summer-house, Sellio, onis, m.

A Sunning house, Heliocamanus, i, m.

The Stories of an house, Tăbŭlāta, orum, n.

The back side of an house, Posticium, ii, n.

A Thatched-house Top, Culmen, inis, n.

The jetting out of an house where it joyns to another, Protectum, i, n.

The house eaves, Subgrunda, æ, f.

A making of house eaves, Subgrundatio, onis, f.

Living

Living in the same house, Homocapnus, a, um.

Pertaining to a house, Domesticus, a, um. Oeconomicus, a, um.

Houshold stuff, Supellex, ctilis, f. Utensilia, bona mobilia. Penates, um, *m. pl. Sing. caret.*

A place where houshold stuff is sold, Arctorium, ii, n.

Houshold, Domestici, orum, m.

To make a floor of a house, Paviclo, are.

House-bote, Esto verium Ædificandi. Co. Lit. 41. B. Brac. 407.

It is necessary Timber that the Lessee for Years, or for Life, of common right may take upon the Ground, to repair the houses, upon the same ground to him Leased, although it be not expressed in the Lease, and although it be a Lease paroll, by words without deed. But if he take more than is needful, he may be Punished by an action of Wast.

H O W.

Howard (the Family) Howerdus, Havertus.

Howel (a mans name) Howelus, i, m.

H O Y.

Hoyes (Catches, Mongers) Navigiola, æ, f.

H U B.

Hubert (a mans name) Hubertus, i, m.

H U C.

A Huckster, Propola, æ, m.

H U E.

Hue and Cry, Hutesium & clamor. Spel 370. Cow. 141. Lex 70. *Hue and Cry is derived of two* French *words*, Huyer *and* Cryer, *both signifying to Shout or Cry aloud. In Legal understanding*, Hue *and* Cry *is all one. See* Cook 3. part *of* Institutes, c. 52.

This Hue and Cry, may be by Horn and by voice. He that goeth not at the Commandment of the Sheriff or Constable, upon Hue and Cry, shall be grievously Fined and Imprisoned. *Cook* 52. part of his *Institutes*, c. 9.

It signifies a pursuit of one having committed Felony by the High-way, for if the party robbed, or any in the Company of one murdered or robbed, come to the Constable of the next Town, and will him to raise Hue and Cry, or to make pursuit after the offender, describing the Party, and shewing as near as he can, which way he is gone: the Constable ought forthwith to call upon the Parish for aid in seeking the Felon, and if he be not found there, then to give the next Constable warning, and he the next, untill the Offender be apprehended, or at the least, untill he be thus pursued to the Sea Side, of this read *Bract. lib.* 3. *tract.* 2. *cap.* 5. *Smith de Repub. angl. Lib.* 2. *cap.* 20.

20. and the *Stat. Anno* 13. *Ed.* 1. *Stat. of Winchester cap.* 3. *&* *anno* 28. *Ed.* 3. *cap.* 11. *& anno* 27. *Ed. cap.* 13. *Crompt. Justice of Peace. fol.* 160. *B.*

H U G.

Hugh (*a mans name*) Hugo, onis, m.

H U L.

A Hulk (*a kind of Ship Broad and Great*) Stlata, æ, f.

Hull River (*in Yorkshire*) Hullus.

H U M.

Humane, Humanus, a, um.

Humanity, Humanitas, atis, f.

Humber River (*in Yorkshire,*) Abus Æstuarium, Humber, Humbra, Umber.

Humidity (*or moistness*) Humiditas, atis, f.

Humble River (*over against the Isle of Wight,*) Homelea.

Humphrey (*a mans name*) Humphridus.

H U N.

An hundred (*or part of a shire,*) Hundredum, i, n.

An hundreder, Hundredarius, ii, m. Spel. 364. Reg. 174.

A hundred (*in number,*) Centena, æ, f.

On hundred of Fish, Centena Piscium. Pry. 303.

One hundred of hides (*or skins*) Centena Pellium. Pry. 185.

One hundred weight, Centena, æ, f. Pondus unius Centenæ Ra. Ent. 3.

A hundred weight of madder, Centena de madder, Kit. 252. Pry. 185.

Hundredeskelde, Centum Fontes.

A hundred, Centum, adj. indecl.

A hundred times, Centies, adv.

A hundred fold, Cĕntŭplex, icis, adj. Centŭplus, a, um.

Two hundred, Ducenti, Ducentus, a, um.

Two hundred fold, Ducentuplus, a, um.

Two hundred times, Ducenties, adv.

Of two hundred, Ducenarius, a, um.

Three hundred, Trecenti.

Three hundred times, Trecenties, adv.

The three hundredth, Trecentenus, a, um.

Of or concerning three hundred Trecenarius, a, um.

Four hundred, Quadriginti.

Five hundred, Quigenti.

Five hundred (*in weight, number or age*) Quingenārius, a, um.

The five hundredth, Quingentēsimus, a, um.

Five hundred times so much, Quingentŭplus, a, um.

Which weigheth five hundred Pounds, Quingentilibrālis, le, adj.

Six hundred, Sexcenti.

Six hundred times, Sexcenties, adv.

The six hundredth, Sexcentēsimus, a, um.

Seven

Seven hundred, Septingenti.

The number of seven hundred, Septingēnārius, a, um.

Of or belonging to seven hundred, Septingentārius, a, um.

The seven hundredth, Septingentēsĭmus, a, um.

Seven hundred times, Septingenties, adv.

Seven hundred fold, Septingentŭplus, a, um.

Eight hundred, Octingenti.

Containing eight hundred, Octingenarius, a, um.

The eighth hundredth, Octingentesimus, a, um.

Eight hundred times, Octingenties, adv.

Eight hundred fold, Octingentuplus, a, um.

Nine hundred, Nongenti.

Of or concerning Nine hundred, Nongenarius, a, um.

The nine hundredth, Nongentesimus, a, um.

Nine hundred times, Nongenties, adv.

Hunger, Fames, is, f. pl. caret.

To hunt, Venor, ari.

To go a hunting, Ire venatum.

A Hunter (or Huntsman) Vēnātor, oris, m.

A Huntress, Vēnatrix, icis, f.

A hunting, Vēnatio, ōnis, f.

Gotten *with hunting*, Venatitius, a, um.

Of, or belonging to, or serving for hunting, Venatorius, a, um.

A kind of hunting by taking stands at several places, Trista, æ, f.

A hunting staff, Venabulum, i, n.

A hunting horn (a Bugle,) Cornu venatorium.

Hunting-nets, Plagæ, ārum, f. sing. caret.

Huntingdon, Huntingdonia. Venantodunum.

Huntingdonshire, Huntingdonensis comitatus, vel ager Venantodunensis.

Hungerford (in Berkshire) Hungerforda.

Hunsdon (in Hertfordshire) Hundesdena. Hunsdona.

H U R.

A Hurdle, Crates Lignea.

Hurds, Lini floccus. Stupa, æ, f.

Hovels or hurdles, Gurgustia, orum, n.

Made of Reeds, Rods or Sticks in manner of a hurdle, and daubed with loam or clay, *Cratitius, a, um.*

To cover with hurdles, Cratio, ere.

To hurt, Noceo, ere. Lædo, ire.

Hurt, Læsus, a um.

Hurt (or annoyed,) Offensus, a, um.

Hurt (or marred) Corruptus, a, um.

Hurt (or mischief) Malum, i, n. Nocumentum, i, n.

Hurt (or Injury,) Maleficium, ii, n.

Hurt, (Loss, or damage) Damnum, i, n. Detrimentum, i, n.

A hurt, Læsura, æ, f.

A hurting, Læsio onis, f.

Hurtfulness, Noxietas, atis, f. hence comes the word *Annoyance*.

Hurtful (or that hurteth) Nocuus, a, um. Noxius, a, um.

Hurtful (or mischievous) Perniciosus, a, um.

Hurtful (or that causeth hurt or Loss,) Dispendiosus, a, um.

Hurtful (or noisom) Maleficus, a, um.

Very hurtful, Noxiosus, a, um.

Hurtfully, Nocenter, adv.

Hurtfully (or mischievously,) Perniciosè, adv. Malitiose, adv.

Hurtfully (*or against Profit*) Damnosè, adv. Incommodè, adv.

Hurst Castle (*in Hantshire*) Hurstanum castellum.

Hursteley (*in Hantshire*,) Hurstelega.

H U S.

A husband, Mărītus, i, m. Conjux, jugis, c. 2. Vir, viri, m.

A husbandman, Agricola, æ, c. 2. Agricolator, oris, m. Agricultor, oris, m.

In husband-like manner, More Colonico.

Husbandry, Husbandria, æ, f. *Ra. Ent.* 162. 421. *Dyer.* 35. Agricultura, æ, f. Agricolatio, onis, f.

Implements of husbandry, Implementa husbandriæ.

To practice husbandry, Rusticor, ari. Villico, are.

The husk (*or hull of Grains*,) Folliculus, i, m. Siliqua, æ, f.

Hustings, Hustingum, i, n. Spel. 369, (*i. e.*) the chief Court in the City of *London*, *anno* 11. *H.* 7. *cap.* 21. *Fitz. nat. brev. fol.* 23. *anno* 9. *Ed.* 1. *cap. unico.*

H U T.

A hutch (*or Bin*) *to keep Bread in*, Mactra, æ, f. Cardopus, i, m.

H Y P.

Hypsipile, (*a Womans name*) Hypsipila, æ, f.

H Y R.

Hyrtha Isle, Hyrtha.

J A C.

Jacinth (*a precious Stone*) Hyacinthus, i, m.

A jack, Veruversorium, ii, n.

A jack (*ancient, or colours hanged out of a Ship*,) Aplustrum, i, n.

A jacket (*Coat*) Jackettus, i, m. Supertunica, æ, f. Exomis, ĭdis, f. Exuvis, is, f.

A short jacket, Colobium, ii, n.

A little jacket, Tunicula, æ, f. Tunicella, æ, f.

Jacob (*a mans name*) Jacob, Indecl.

J A G.

A jagg, Lacinea, æ, f. Incisura, æ, f.

J A K.

A jakes, Cloăca, æ, f. Sentina, æ, f. Forĭca, æ, f. Lătrina, æ, f.

A jakes Farmer (*or Gold finder*) Foricarius, ii, m. Coprophorus, i, m.

J A M.

James (*a mans name*) Jacobus, i, m.

Jambes (*Cheeks, or side posts of a door*, Antæ, arum, f.

J A N.

January, Januarius, ii, m.

Janus (*a mans name*) Janus, i, m.

Jane (*a Womans name*,) Jana, æ, f.

J A R.

A little jar (*or Pot*) Seriola, æ, f.

Jarrs of Oyl, Seriæ oleares.

Jarrow

Jarrow (in the Bishoprick of Durham,) Ingirvum.

Jarsey Isle, Cæsarea.

J A S.

Jason (a mans name,) Jason, onis, m.

Jasper (a mans name,) Gaspa-rus, i, m.

J A U.

A javelin, Hasta, æ, f. Lancea, æ, f. Pilum, i, n.

A little javelin, Hastula, æ, f.

A javelin, with a barbed head, Tragula, æ, f.

He that beareth a Javelin, Lancearius, ii, m.

The shaft and steel of a Javelin, Hastile, is, n.

The Jaundice, Icterus, i, m.

That is sick of the Jaundice, Ictericus, a, um.

J A W.

The Jaw or gum wherein the Teeth are set, Gingiva, æ, f.

The Jaws, Faucis, is, f.

The Jaw-bone, Mandibula, æ, f. Maxilla, æ, f.

Belonging to the Jaw bone, Mandibularis, re, adj.

I C B.

Icborrow (in Norfolk,) Iciani, Isianos.

I D E.

Identitate nominis. Is a writ that lyeth for him who is upon a *Capias* or *Exigent*, taken and committed to Prison, for another man of the same name, whereof see the form and further use, in *Fitz. nat. brev. fol.* 267. *Regist. Orig. fol.* 194.

The Ides of every month, Idus, uum, f. pl. Sing. caret.

An Ideot (or fool,) Ideota, æ, m.

An Ideot and he that afterward becometh of Insane memory, differeth in divers cases. *Cook fol.* 154. *b. lib.* 4.

Ideota Inquirenda vel examinanda. Is a writ that is directed to the Escheator or the Sheriff of any County, where the King understanding that there is an Ideot, naturally born, so weak of understanding, that he cannot govern or manage his Inheritance, to call before him the Parties suspected of Ideocie, and examine him: and also to enquire by the Oaths of twelve men, whether he is sufficiently witted to dispose of his own lands with discretion or not, and to certifie accordingly into the Chancery. For the King hath the Protection of his subjects, and by his Prerogative the Government of their Lands and substance, that are naturally defective in their own discretion. *Stat. de Prerogativa Regis editum anno.* 17. *Ed.* 2. *cap.* 8. *Stawnford Prærog. cap.* 9. *Fitz. nat. brev. fol.* 231. *Regist. Orig. fol.* 267. The Author of the new Terms of Law, saith thus. An Ideot is he that is a fool naturally, from his birth, and knoweth not how to account or number twenty pence, or cannot name his Father or mother, nor of what age himself is, or such like easie or common matters. But if he have so much knowledge that he can read, or learn to read, or can measure an an Ell of Cloth, or name the days of the week, &c. then (ſaith he) it appeareth ſuch a one is no Ideot.

I D L.

Idle, Otioſus, a, um.

Idleneſs, Otium, ii, n.

Idleton (in —) Segelocum. Segelogum.

J E L.

Jelly, Gelatina, æ, f. Coactum, i, n.

J E N.

Jenkin (*a mans name*) Jenkinus, i, m.

J E R.

A jerkin (*or Jacket*) Tunicula, æ, f.

A jerkin of Leather, Colobium Scorteum.

A Frize jerkin uſed in Winter, Endromis, is, f.

A jerkin with ſleeves, Succinctorium, ii, n.

Jerom (a mans name) Jeronymus, i, m.

J E S.

Jeſſes, *for Hawks*, Lemniſci, orum, m.

A Jeſter, Jocator, oris ,m. Mimus, i, m.

J E T.

A jetting out, Projectus, ûs, m.

A jetty, Projectura, æ, f. Superpendiculum, Plac. 27.

J E W.

A jewel, Jocale, is, n. Gemma, æ, f. Clinodium, ii, n.

Jewels, Jocalia, orum, n. Pry. 142. 160. Ra. Entr. 486. Fle. 341.

A jewel to hang about ones Neck. Monile, is, n. Torquis, is, m, vel f.

A jewel hanging at the Ear, Inauris, is, f. Ellobium, ii, n.

A jewel for the Arms, Armilla, æ, f.

A jewel for the hands, Annulus purus.

A Jeweller, Clinodarius, ii, m. Gemmarius, ii, m.

I F.

If, Si, conj.

I G N.

Ignoramus, is a word properly uſed by the Grand Inqueſt, Impanelled in the Inquiſition of cauſes, criminal and publick, and written upon the Bill, whereby any Crime is offered to their conſideration, when as they miſlike their evidence as defective, or too weak to make good the preſentment. The effect of which word ſo written, is, that all farther inquiry upon that party for that fault, is thereby ſtopped, and he delivered without farther anſwer.

Ignorance, Ignorantia, æ, f.

Ignorance of art, Inſcitia, æ, f.

Ignorant, Ignarus, a, um.

Ignorantly, Ignarè, adv.

I L A.

Ila Iſle, (*near Cantire in Scotland,*) *or Cantire it ſelf*, Caledonium, Epidia, Epidium.

I L L.

*Ill-street(in Cheshire)*Mala Platea.

Ill-will (hatred) Atia, æ,f. *Vid. West. de Odio & Atia.*

Illegal, Illicitus, a, um.

Illegitimate, Illegitimus, a, um.

Illiterate, Illiteratus, a, um.

To illustrate, Illustro, are.

I M A.

An Image (form or likeness) Imago, inis, f.

An Image of Metal, Ivory, or Stone, Statua, æ, f.

Images bearing up Posts or Pillars in Building, Telamones, f. pl.

The place where Images are sold, Hermopolium, ii, n.

The Craft of Carving Images, Statuaria, æ, f.

A Carver (or maker) of Images, Statuarius, ii, m. Hermoglyphus, i, m.

He that maketh Poppets (or little Images,) Coroplathus, i, m.

He that maketh images of Wax, Ceroplastes, is, m. Cerarius, ii, m.

He that beareth an Image, Signifer, a, um.

Full of Images, Imaginosus, a,um.

Of or belonging to images, Statuarius, a, um.

To imagine, Imagino, are. Imaginor, ari.

Imaginary, Imaginarius, a, um.

An imagination, Imiginatio,onis,f.

A Crafty and Subtile imagination, Machina,æ,f.

I M B.

To Imbark (or Embark) Ascendere seu Conscendere navem,Nāvigo, are.

Imbecility, Imbicilitas, atis, f.

To imbesil, Imbesilo, are. Ra. Entr. 186. 446. Plo. 118.

An imbesiling,Imbesilatio, onis,f.

To imboss (or cut in Plates) Lamino, are, Cœlo, are.

An imboss (or imbossment) Dejectus, ûs, m.

Imbossed work, in Metal or Stone, made with bosses or bunches, Toreuma, æ, f. Toreumatum, i, n. Opus cœlatum.

An imbosser of Plate, Toreutes, is, m.

I M M.

Immaculate, Immaculatus,a,um.

Immediately, Immediatè, adv.

Immedicable, Immedicabilis, le, adj.

Immemorable (or not worthy to be remembred) Immemorabilis, le, adj.

Imminent (at hand, or hanging over, ready to fall) Imminens, tis, part.

Immoderate, Immoderatus,a,um.

Immoderately, Immoderatè, adv.

Immunity, Immunitas, atis, f.

Immutable, Immutabilis, le, adj.

I M P.

To impanel, Impanello, are.

Imparlance, Interloquela, Licentia interloquendi. It is a Petition made in Court, upon the account of the Demandant by the Tenant, or Declaration of the Plaintiff, by the Defendant, whereby he craveth respite, or another day to put in his answer, that is a day to parle or speak about his answer.

Impatience, Impatientia, æ, f.

To impeach, Impeto, ere.

An impeachment (or hindrance) Impetitio, onis, f. Pry. 34, 35.

Impeachment of Waſt, Impetitio vaſti, (i. e.) A Reſtraint from committing of Waſt upon Lands or Tenements.

An impediment, Impedimentum, i, n.

Impentirable, Impenitrabilis, le, adj.

Imperfect, Imperfectus, a, um.

Imperfectly, Semè, adv.

Impertinent, Impertinens, tis, adj.

Impetuous, Impetuoſus, a, um.

To implant, Implanto, are.

To implead, (*ſue, to Proſecute*) Implacito, are.

Implements within a houſe, Implementa, orum, n.

Implements (*or Tools*) Inſtrumenta, orum, n.

To implie (*or import*) Implico, are. Importo, are.

To implore, Imploro, are.

Importance, Importantia, æ, f. Co. Ent. 204. Momentum, i, n.

Importunate, Importunus, a, um.

Importunity, Importunitas, atis, f.

Importunately, Importunè, adv.

To be employed, Implicandum. 1 Fol. 252.

In the hands and imployment, In manibus & uſu. 1 Rol. 454.

To impoſe, Impono, ere.

Impoſſible, Impoſſibilis, le, adj.

Impoſt, Vectigal, lis, n. Tributum, i, n.

It ſignifieth with us, the Tax received by the Prince, for ſuch merchandize as are brought into any Haven from other Nations. *anno* 31. *Eliz. cap.* 5. and I think it may in ſome ſort be diſtinguiſhed from Cuſtoms, becauſe Cuſtom is rather that profit which the Prince maketh of Wares Shipped out of the Land, yet they may be confounded.

An impoſtume (*or Courſe of evil humours gathered to ſome part of the Body*,) Apoſtema, atis, n. Abſceſſus, ûs, m.

Opening Impoſtumes, Aperibens abſceſſus.

An impoſtor (*or cozener*,) Impoſtor, oris, m.

Impoſture, Impoſtura, æ, f.

To impound, Imparco, are.

Impoundment (*or put into a Pound*) Imparcamentum, i, n. 1 Mon. 119. Spel. 373.

Impreſſion, Impreſſio, onis, f.

Impreſt-money, Auctoramentum, i, n.

To Impriſon, Impriſono, are.

An impriſonment, Impriſonamentum, i, n.

Hardſhip of impriſonment, Duritia Impriſonamenti.

Improbable, Improbabilis, le, adj.

Improperly, Impropriè, adv.

Improper, Improprius, a, um.

Impropriation, Impropriatio, onis, f. (i. e.) an annexing an Eccleſiaſtical benefice, to the uſe of a Biſhoprick, *&c. Abbes.* 5.

To improve, Appruo, are.

An improvement, Appruamentum, i, n. Reg. 8. Lex. 8. 2 Mon. 255. Appruatio, onis, f.

Improvident, Improvidus, a um.

Imprudence, Imprudentia, æ, f.

To impugne, Impugno, are.

Impulſion, Impulſio, onis, f.

Impunity (*or Pardon*) Impunitas, atis, f.

To impute, attribute, or aſcribe, Imputo, are.

I N.

In as much, In quantum.

I N A.

Inacceſſible, Inacceſſibilis, le, adj.

I N C.

I N C.

An incendiary (*or ſetter of houſes on Fire*) Incendiarius, ii, m.

To Incenſe, Incendo, ere. Stimulo, are. Incito, are.

Inceſſantly (*or continually*) Indeſinenter, adv.

An inch, Pollex, ĭcis, m. Stat. de admenſuratione terræ.

Inch-Keith Iſle, near Scotland, Victoria.

Incident, Incidens, tis, adj. It ſignifieth a thing neceſſarily depending upon another, as more principal: for example, A Court Baron is ſo incident to a Mannor, and a Court of Pie-powder to a Fair, that they cannot be ſevered by Grant, for if a Mannor or Fair be granted, theſe Courts cannot be reſerved, *Kitchin fol.* 36.

An inciſion, Inciſio, onis, f.

To make an inciſion, Incīdo, ere.

To incite, Incito, are.

To incline (*or bend to*) Inclino, are.

To incloſe, Includo, ere.

An incloſure, Inclauſura, æ, f. Clauſus, ûs, m.

An income, or revenue, Proventus, ûs, m. Reventio, onis, f.

An income (*or Fine*) Landa, æ, f. Landicinia, æ, f.

Incommodious, Incommodus, a, um.

Incomparable, Incomparabilis, le, adj.

Incompatibility of Benefices, Incompatibilitas Beneficiorum. Is when Benefices cannot ſtand one with another, if they be with Cure, and of Eight pound value in the Kings book, or above. *Whitlocks Reading, Pag.* 4.

Incongruity, Incongruentia, æ, f.

Inconvenient, Inconveniens, tis, adj.

To incorporate, Incorporo, are.

Incorrigible, Incorrigibilis, le, adj.

Incredible (*or not to be believed*) Incredibilis, le, adj.

Incredulous (*or hard of belief*) Incredulus, a, um.

To incroach, Incrochio, are, Spel. 375. Cow. 143.

An incroachment, Incroachamentum, i, n.

To inculcate (*or repeat often one thing*) Inculco, are.

Inculpable, Inculpabilis, le, adj.

An incumbent, Incumbens, tis, n.

To incumber, Incombro, are.

An incombrance, Incombrantia, æ, f. 1 Ro. 536. Incumbramentum, i, n. Brac. 261. 392.

An incurring, Incurramentum, i, n. Ry. 204, 205.

I N D.

Indeed, In facto.

Indefatigable, Indefatigabilis, le, adj.

Indefinite (*undefined, not limited*) Indefinitus, a, um.

Indepted, Indebitatus, a, um.

Indefecible, Indefecibilis, le, adj, Co. Ent. 64. 83.

To Indemnifie, Indempnem conſervare.

An indenture, Indentura, æ, f.

Indicavit. Is a writ or prohibition that lieth for a Patron of a Church, whoſe Clerk is defendant in Court Chriſtian, in an action of Tithes commenced by another Clerk, and extending to the fourth part of the Church, or of the Tithes belonging unto it. For in this caſe the ſuit belongeth to the Kings Court, by the *Stat. Weſtm.* 2. *cap.* 5. wherefore the Patron of the defendant being like to be prejudiced in his Church and Advowzen, if the Plaintiff obtain in the Court Christian, hath this means to remove it to the Kings Court. *Regist. Orig. fol.* 35. *b. Old Nat. brev. fol.* 31. *The Register fol.* 35. & *Britton Cap.* 109. *fol.* 260. *A.*

To indite, Indicto, are.

An inditement (or charge in Law) Indictamentum, i, n. Spel. 375. Fle. 30. Lex. 49.

Individual, Individuus, a, um.

Individuals (or particulars) Individua, orum, n.

Indivisum. Is used in the Common Law, for that which two hold in Common without partition. *Kitchin fol.* 241. in these words, he holdeth *pro Indiviso*, &c.

To indorse (or write upon the back of any thing) Indorso, are.

An indorsement (a writing on the backside) Indorsamentum, i, n.

Indorsed. Indorsatus, a, um.

To *indow*, Doto, are.

An induction, Inductio, onis, f. *(i. e.)* the giving a Clerk possession of a Benefice.

Inducted, Impersonatus, a, um. *(i. e.)* put in possession of a Benefice.

Industry, Industria, æ, f.

I N E.

Inequality, Inæqualitas, atis, f.

Inestimable (or which cannot be valued) Inæstimabilis, le, adj.

Inevitable, Inevitabilis, le, adj.

I N F.

Infallible. Infallibilis, le, adj.

Infamy, Infamia, æ, f.

Infamous (also absurd, unlikely, improbable) Adoxus, a, um.

An infant (a person under the age of One and Twenty Years) Infans, tis, m.

Infatigable, Infatigabilis, le, adj.

To infeoffe, Feoffo, are, *(i. e.) grant in Fee.*

Infelicity, Infelicitas, atis, f.

Inferiour, Inferior, ius, adj.

Infertil, Infertilis, le, adj.

Infirmity, Infirmitas, atis, f.

To inflame, Inflammo, are.

Inflammation, Inflammatio, onis, f.

Influence, Influentia, æ, f.

Informatus non Sum. Is a formal answer, or of Course made by an Attorney that is commanded by the Court, to say what he thinketh good in the defence of his Client, by which he is deemed to leave his Client undefended, and so Judgment passeth for the adverse party. See the new book of *Entries, Titulo, non sum informatus*, and Judgment, 12.

To inform, Informo, are.

An informer, Informator, oris, m. He is an Officer belonging to the Exchequer, Kings Bench, and Common Pleas, that complaineth of those that offend against any Penal Statute. They are otherwise called Promoters, but the men do blush at this name. These among the *Civilians* are called *Delatores*.

Infortunate, Infortunatus, a, um.

To infringe, Infringo, ere.

An infusion, infusio, onis, f.

I N G.

To ingage, Suscipio, ere.

An ingot (a small Mass or Wedge of Gold) Palacra, æ, f.

Ingratitude, Ingratitudo, inis, f.

Ingrailed, Engrallatus, a, um. 1 Mon. 930.

An ingredient, or going in, a beginning (in Physick) when a medicine is made) one of the Simples put into the Medicine compounded, Ingrediens, tis, n.

Ingress, Egress, and Regress, Ingressus, Egressus & Regressus.

To ingross, Ingrosso, are, (*i. e.*) to buy in great Quantities of Provisions and Victuals; also to write in great hand.

An ingrosser, Ingrossator, oris, m. Cow. 145. Spel. 382. Lex. 30. It signifieth in the Common Law, one that buyeth Corn growing, or dead Victual, to sell again, except Barley for Mault, Oats for Oatmeal, or Victuals to retail, badging by Licence, and buying of Oils, Spices and Victuals, other than Fish or Salt. *Anno* 5. *Ed.* 6. *cap.* 14. *anno* 5. *Eliz. cap.* 14. *anno* 13. *Eliz. cap.* 25. these are Mr. *West*'s words, part. 2. *Symbol. Titulo, Indictments Sect.* 64. yet this definition rather doth belong to unlawful Ingrossing, than to the word in general.

I N H.

To inhabite, Inhabito, are.

Inhabitable, Inhabitabilis, le, adj.

An inhabitant, Habitator, oris, m.

To inherit, Hæredito, are.

An inheritance, Hæreditas, atis, f. It is a perpetuity in Lands or Tenements to a Man and his Heirs. *Littleton, cap.* 1. *Lib.* 1. and it is to be understood, that this word (Inheritance) is not only understood where a man hath Inheritance of Lands and Tenements by descent of heritage, but also every Fee simple, or Fee tail, that a man hath by his purchase, may be said Inheritance, for that his heirs may Inherit him.

Several Inheritance, is that which two or more hold severally; as if two men have Land given them, to them and the heirs of their two Bodies, these have Joynt Estate during their Lives, but their heirs have several inheritance. *Kitchin fol.* 155. See the new Terms of Law, *verbo Inheritance.*

A man may have an Inheritance in Title of Nobility and Dignity three manner of ways. That is, first by Creation, Secondly by descent, Thirdly by Prescription.

By Creation two manner of ordinary ways. First, by *Writ.* Second, by *Letters Patents.* Creation by writ is the ancienter way; yet that by Letters Patents is the surer. If he be generally called by a writ to the Parliament, he hath a Fee-Simple in the Barony without words of Inheritance. But if he be created by Letters Patents, the State of Inheritance must be limited by apt words, or else the Grant is void; but a man must not only have the writ delivered to him, but sit in Parliament, to make him noble that way; and thereupon a Baron is called a Peer of Parliament: Therefore a Duke, Earl, &c. of another Kingdom are not to be sued by these names here, for they are not Peers of our Parliament. *Cook on Lit. L.* 1. *c.* 1. *Sect.* 9.

Some have an Inheritance, and have it neither by deſcent, nor properly by Purchace, but by Creation; as when the King doth Create any Man a Duke, a Marqueſs, Earl, Viſcount, or Baron to him and his Heirs, or to the Heirs Males of his Body, he hath an Inheritance therein by Creation, *Id. Ib.*

A Demanding of an inheritance, Petæredium, ii, n.

A Diſinheritance, Exhæredatio, onis, f.

To inhibit (or forbid) Inhibeo, ere.

An inhibition (or prohibition) Inhibitio, onis, f.

Inhumane, Inhumanus, a, um.

Inhumanity, Inhumanitas, atis, f.

I N I.

An injection, Injectio, onis, f.

A Reſtringent Injection, Reſtringens injectio.

An injunction, Injunctio, onis, f. It is an Interlocutory Decree out of the Chancery, ſometime to give Poſſeſſion unto the Plaintiff, for want of appearance in the Defendant, ſometime to the Kings ordinary Court, and ſometime to the Court Chriſtian, to ſtay proceeding in a Cauſe upon Suggeſtion made, that the rigour of the Law, if it take place, is againſt Equity and Conſcience in that caſe. *Weſt. part.* 2. *Symb. Titulo, Proceeding* in *Chancery, Sect.* 25.

To injure (or wrong) Injurior, ari.

Injury, Injuria, æ, f.

Injuſtice, Injuſtitia, æ, f.

I N K.

Ink, Atramentum, i, n.

An ink-horn, Atramentarium, ii, n. Cornugraphium, ii, n.

Printers ink, Atramentum Typographicum vel Fuligineum.

I N L.

Inlagary, Inlagatio, onis, f. as it were to bring one within the Laws as a Subject. It is a Reſtitution of one out-lawed, to the Kings Protection, and to the benefit or Eſtate of a Subject. *Bract. Lib.* 3. *Tract.* 2. *cap.* 14. *num.* 6, 7, 8. *Britton cap.* 13.

Inlawed, Inlagatus, a, um. *Brac.* 131. 421. *Spel.* 382. (i. e.) one that is in Franckpledge, and lives under the Protection of the Law.

The Inland or Demeſnes of a Lord, as the Outland were the Tenancies, Inlandum, i, n.

An inlargement, Inlargiamentum, i, n. Elargatio, onis, f.

I N N.

An Inn, Diverſorium, ii, n.

An inn-holder, or inn-keeper, Diverſoriarius, ii, m. Hoſpitator, oris, m.

An inn-holder his Wife, Hoſpita, æ, f.

Inner or more within, Interior, us, adj. Interius, adv.

An inner Parlour, Conclave, is, n.

Innerlothy, (in Scotland) Innerlothea.

Innerneſs (in Scotland) Innerneſſus.

Innocent (*a mans name*) Innocentius, ii, m.

To innovate, Innovo, are.

Innovation, Innovatio, onis, f.

Innuendo, a word uſed in declarations to aſcertain the perſon, or thing that was doubtfull before.

Inquirendo, is an authority given to a perſon or perſons, to inquire into ſomething for the Kings advantage, which in what caſes it lyeth, *See the Regiſt. Orig. fol.* 72. 85. 124. 265. 266. 179. 267.

An inquiſition, Inquiſitio, onis, f. 8. Co. 108.

An inqueſt, Inqueſtum, i, n.

An inqueſt (*or Jury*) Duodæna, æ, f. Jurata.

I N R.

To inroll, Inrrotulo, are.

An inrollment, Irrotulatio, onis, f. Irrotulamentum, i, n. Cow. 145. Spel. 387.

I N S.

To inſinuate, Inſinuo, are.

To inſiſt, Inſiſto, ere.

In ſomuch, In tantum.

Inſpection, Inſpectio, onis, f.

To inſtall, Inſtallo, are.

An inſtalment, Inſtallagium, ii, n. 2 Mon. 26. Ry. 333.

An inſtance (*or particular example*) Inſtantia, æ, f.

An inſtant (*or preſent time*) Inſtans, tis, Articulus temporis.

Inſtantly, Inſtantèr, adv.

To inſtigate, Inſtigo, are.

To inſtill, Inſtillo, are.

To inſtitute, Inſtituo, ere.

Inſtitutes, Lord Coke's *Books of Law.*

To inſtruct, Inſtruo, ere.

An inſtrument to doe or make any thing with, Inſtrumentum, i, n.

A Kitchin inſtrument, wherewith the Pot is removed, Toryna, æ, f.

Inſufficient, Inſufficiens, tis, adj.

An inſurer, Aſſecurator, oris, m.

An inſurrection, Inſurrectio, onis, f.

I N T.

An intail, Feodum talliatum.

Intacks (*or Cattle taken in to be fed*) Animalia introcapta. Spel. 383.

To intercommon, Intercommunico, are.

Interchangeably, Alternatim, adv. Mutualitèr, adv.

To interdict, Interdico, ere.

An interdiction, Interdictio, onis, f.

Intereſt of money, alſo an intereſt in any thing, Intereſſe.

An intereſt in a Term not begun, Intereſſe Termini.

Interledged, Conſertus, a, um.

Intermiſſion, Intermiſſio, onis, f.

To intermit, Intermitto, ere.

Interpoſition, Interpoſitio, onis, f.

An interpreter, Interpres, ĕtis, c. 2.

To interrogate, Interrogo, are.

An interrogation, Interrogatio, onis, f.

To interrupt, Interrumpo, ere.

Interruption, Interruptio, onis, f.

To intervene, Intervenio, ire.

Inteſtate (*or dying without a will*) Inteſtatus, a, um.

Intricate, Intricatus, a, um.

Introduction, Introductio, onis, f.

To intrude, Intrudo, ere.

In truth, Revera.

I N V.

To invent, Invenio, ire.

An inventory, Inventorium, ii, n. Fle. 159. Inventarium, ii, n. Cow. 146. Ry. 148. Lex. 73. (*i.e.*) An account and value ſet down in writing of the Goods of a Perſon deceaſed.

To inveſt, Inveſto, ire, Cow. 146. Spel. 385.

An inveſtiture, Inveſtitura, æ, f. Inveſtatio, onis, f. Weſt, Sect. 565.

Inviolable, Inviolabilis, le, adj.

An inundation (or deluge) Innundatio, onis, f.

To involve, Involvo, ere.

To inure, Opero, are. Operor, ari.

An invoice, Nota Onerationis.

J O A.

Joan (a Womans name) Joanna, æ, f.

J O B.

Job (a mans name) Job, Indecl.

J O C.

Joceline (a mans name) Jocelinus, i, m.

J O E.

Joel (a mans name) Joel, lis, m.

J O H.

St. *Johns day*, Feſtum, Sancti-Johannis Evangeliſtæ.

J O I.

Joint Tenants, Simul tenentes.

Jointure, Junctura, æ, f. Cow. 147. Lex. 73. It is a Covenant whereby the Husband, or ſome other Friend in his behalf, aſſureth unto his Wife, in reſpect of Marriage, Lands or Tenements for Term of her Life, or otherwiſe. See *Weſt part* 2. *Symb. lib.* 2. *Tit. Covenants*, *Sect.* 128. It is called a Jointure, either becauſe it is granted *ratione juncturæ in Matrimonio*, or becauſe the Land in Frank Marriage is given jointly to the Husband and the Wife, and after to the Heirs of their Bodies, whereby the Husband and the Wife are made Joynt-Tenants, during the Coverture. *Cook. Lib.* 3. *Rep. the Marqueſs of Wincheſters caſe, fol.* 3. *a. b.*

J O N.

Jonah (a mans name) Jonas, æ, m.

Jonathan (a mans name) Jonathan, Indeclin.

J O R.

Jorval (in Yorkſhire) Urivallis.

J O S.

Joſeph (a mans name) Joſephus, i, m.

Joſhua (a mans name) Joſhua, æ, m.

Joſiah (a mans name) Joſias, æ, m.

J O U.

A Journal (or Day-book) Diarium, ii, n.

A Journey, Iter, itineris, n.

A days Journey, Dieta, æ, f. Diurnata, æ, f.

To go, or take a Journey, Itineror, ari.

J O Y.

Joyce (a Womans Name) Jocosa, æ, f.

To joyn, Jungo, ere.

To joyn together, Conjungo, ere.

A joyner, Junctor, oris, m. Adjŭgator, oris, m.

A joynt, Articulus, i. m.

A putting out of joynt, Luxātio, onis, f.

Out of joynt, Luxatus, a, um.

To put out of joynt, Luxo, are. Exarticulo, are.

To set Limbs out of joynt, Reponere locis suis membra luxata.

Joynts in Timber, Jugamenta, orum, n.

Joysts, Asseres, m. pl.

I P R.

De Ipres (the Family) De Ipra.

I R E.

Ireland, Bernia, Hibernia, Ibernia, Jerne, Jernis, Insula Britanica, Inernia, Iris, Inernis, Juverna, Ogygia, Vernia.

Of Ireland, Hybernicus, a, um.

I R O.

Iron, Ferrum, ri, n.

An iron Mine, Ferraria, æ, f.

A branding iron, Cauterium ii, n.

Dog irons, Sustentacula ferrea.

Cramp irons, Ansæ ferreæ.

To sear with a hot iron, Cauterio, are.

A searing iron, Cauter, ēris, m.

A scalping iron, for a Chirurgeon, Scalprum, i, n.

A marking iron, Tudicula, æ, f.

Iron-work, Ferramentum, i, n.

A dog of iron, Catellus ferreus.

Iron-wire, Filum ferrum, Ferrum netum.

Dressed with iron, Ferratus, a, um.

Old iron, Ferramenta detrita, vel rupta.

Of iron, as hard as iron, Ferreus, a, um.

An iron (or black) Smith, Faber Ferrarius.

An ironmonger, Ferramentarius, ii, m.

Irregular, Irregularis, re, adj.

Irreparable, Irreparabilis, le, adj.

Irrevocable, Irrevocabilis, le, Adj.

I S L.

An island, Insula, æ, f.

An islander, Insulaneus, ei, m.

I S S.

To issue forth, Exeo, ire.

An issue, Fluxio, onis, f.

An issue in the body, Fontanella, æ, f.

An issue, or the end of a matter, Exitus, ûs, m. It hath divers applications in the Common Law, sometime being used for the Children begotten between a man and his Wife, sometime for profits growing from an amercement or Fine, or expences of Suit, sometime for profits of Lands or Tenements. *West 2. anno 13. Ed. 1. cap. 39.* Sometime for that point of matter depending in Sute, whereby the parties

parties join and put their Cause to the Trial, of the Jury, and this is called *Junctio Exitus*. In all these it hath but one signification, which is an effect of a Cause proceeding, as the Children be the effect of the Marriage between the Parents, the Profits growing to the King or Lord, from the Punishment of any mans offence, is the effect of his Transgression, the Point referred to the Trial of twelve Men, is the effect of Pleading or Process.

Ithancester (in Essex) Ad ansam, Othona.

I T I.

An itinerary, Itinerarium, ii, n. (*i. e.*) a Commentary concerning things fallen out in Journeys; also the Kalendar of Miles, with the distances of Places, and the time of abode in every Place, like to the Guests of Princes.

J U D.

To Judge (or give Sentence) Judico, are.

Leisurely to consider and Judge, Sentito, are.

A Judge, Judex, icis.

Judgment, Jūdĭcium, ii, n.

Strict judgment according to the Letter of the Law, Acribodicæum, æi, n.

A judgment place (or Seat) Tribunal, lis, n.

Judicial (or pertaining to judgment) Judicialis, le, adj.

Judicious, Judiciosus, a, um.

Judith (a Womans name) Juditha, æ, f.

J U G.

A jug to drink in, Cantharus, i, m.

A jugler, Præstigiator, oris, m. Circulator, oris, m. Pililūdius, ii, m.

J U I.

Juice, Succus, i, m.

Scorbutick Juices, Succi Scorbutici.

J U L.

A Julep, Julepus, i. m.

A Cordial julep, Potio corroborans.

Julia (a womans name) Julia, æ, f.

Julian (a womans name) Juliana, æ, f.

Julianus (a mans name) Julianus, i, m.

Juliet (a womans name) Julietta, æ, f.

Julius (a mans name) Julius, ii, m.

July (Month) Julius, ii, m.

J U N.

June (Month) Junius, ii, m.

J U O.

Ivory, Ebur, oris, n.

Made of Ivory, Ebŏreus, a, um.

Overlaid with ivory, Eboratus, a, um.

Set with small pieces of ivory, Eburnĕŏlus, a, um.

Covered with ivory, Ebŏrātus, a, um.

A wor-

A worker in ivory, Eburarius, ii, m.

Of ivory (*as white as ivory*) Eburneus, *and* nus, a, um.

J U R.

A jury, Jurata, æ, f. Cow. 147. Spel. 397. Lex. 73. It signifieth in our Common-Law, a Company of men, as 24 or 12 ſworn to deliver a truth upon ſuch evidence, as ſhall be delivered them, touching the matter in Queſtion, of which Trial you may, and who may not be Empanelled. *Vid. Fitz. Herb. Nat. brev. fol.* 165. *D.*

For better underſtanding of this point, it is to be known. That there are three manner of Trials in *England.* One by *Parliament*, another by *Battle*, and the third by *Aſſize* or *Jury. Smith de Repub. Angl. Lib.* 2. *cap.* 5, 6, 7. *Vid. Combat*, *&* *Parliament.* The Trial by Aſſize or Jury (be the action Civil or Criminal, Publick or Private, Perſonal or Real) is referred for the Fact to a Jury, and as they find it, ſo paſſeth the Judgment.

Jurata, *Juratores*, and *Jury*, are ſo called, a *Jurando*, they are called in *legibus antiquis*, *Sacramentales à Sacramento præſtando.* There are divers ſorts of Jurors, according to the variety of ancient matters, and the nature of the Courts, of which there are two ſorts more eſpecially eminent, *viz.*
1. *Jurata delatoria*, is which inquires out offenders againſt Law, and preſents their names together with their offences to the Judge. *Ut in examen vocati juris ſubeant Sententiam*, *Sive ad condemnationem*, *Sive ad deliberationem*, and this is called an Inqueſt, and is twofold.

1. *Major*, cui totius Comitatus luſtratio, ut in aſſiſis, & ſeſſionibus pacis, nec non in Curia Regii tribunalis demandatur, and is called the *Grand Jury*, or *Grand Inqueſt.*

2. *Minor*, cui minor jurisdictio, ut unius Hundredi in ſeſſionibus pacis creditur.

2. *Jurata judiciaria*, Is that Jury which determineth *de ſumma litis*, or the matter of Fact in iſſue before the Judge, doth *punire de jure*, and this *Jurata*, or Jury is alſo two-fold.

1. *Civilis*, which takes Cognizance of Civil actions between Subject and Subject.

2. *Criminalis*, which takes Cognizance of actions Criminal *de vita & membris*, and is always betwixt the King and the Subject, commonly called the Jury of Life and Death.

This Jury though it appertain to moſt Courts of the Common Law, yet it is moſt notorious, in the half Year Courts of the *Juſtices Errants*, commonly called the Great aſſizes, and in the Quarter Seſſions, and in them it is moſt ordinarily called a Jury: And that in Civil cauſes, whereas in other Courts, it is oftner termed an *Inqueſt*, and in the Court Baron the *Homage*. Vid. Homage.

In the General aſſize, there are uſually many Juries, becauſe there are ſtore of Cauſes both Civil and Criminal, commonly to be tryed, whereof one is called the *Grand-Jury*, and the reſt *Petit-Juries*, whereof there ſhould be one for every

every Hundred. *Lamb. Eirenar. Lib.* 4. *cap.* 3. *pag.* 384.

The Grand Jury consisteth ordinarily of twenty four Grave and Substantial Gentlemen, or some of them Yeomen, chosen indifferently out of the whole Shire by the Sheriff, to consider of all Bills of indictment preferred to the Court, which they do either approve by writing upon them these words, *Billa vera*, or disallow by writing *Ignoramus*, such as they do approve, if they touch Life and Death, are further referred to another Jury to be considered of, because the Case is of such importance; but others of lighter moment, are upon their allowance, without more adoe, Fined by the Bench, except the Party Traverse the Indictment, or Challenge it for insufficiency, or remove the Cause to an Higher Court by *Certiorari*, in which two former cases it is referred to another Jury, and in the latter transmitted to the Higher. *Lambert. Eiren. Lib.* 4. *cap.* 7.

And presently upon the allowance of this Bill by the *Grand-Inquest*, a man is said to be Indicted. Such as they disallow, are delivered to the Bench, by whom they are forthwith cancelled or torn.

The Petit Jury consisteth of twelve men at the least, and are Empanelled, as well upon Criminal as upon Civil Causes as aforesaid.

The Determination of the Jury is called sometimes *Duodecim virorum judicium*, for that the number of men to make up a Jury are for the most part but twelve, which custom for the tryal of matter of Fact is very ancient, and was used amongst the *Saxons*. *Ut e L. L. Etheldredi in frequenti Senatu apud Panatingum editis cap.* 4. *refert Lambertus. In Singulis (inquit) Centuriis Comitia sunto, atque liberæ conditionis viri duodeni ætate superiores una cum præposito sacra tenentes jurento se adeo virum aliquem innocentem, haud damnaturos, sontemve absoluturos.* The like to which memorial is in *consulto de Monticulis Walliæ sub ævo ejusdem Etheldredi, cap.* 3. *de pignore ablato, viri duodecim jure consulti (seu legales) Anglis & Wallis jus dicunto, Sc. Angli Sex, Walli totidem*, which we call *medietas linguæ*, which is a Privilege or Curtesie afforded by the Law to Strangers, aliens, whose King is in League with us, in Suits about things personal, namely, that the Jury shall consist of six *English*, and six of the Aliens own Country-men, if so many can be found, if not Aliens of any other Country, who by League are capable. The office of the Jury is to find *Veritatem facti*, and of the Judge to declare *Veritatem juris*.

It is a Maxim in the Law, Quod ibi semper fieri debet triatio, ubi juratores meliorem possunt habere notitiam.

Their finding is called veredictum, quasi dictum veritatis. Cook 4. Rep. Cases of appeals and Indictments.

By the Law of *England*, a Jury after their evidence given upon the Issue, ought to be kept in some convenient Place, without meat or drink, fire or candle, which some books call an Imprisonment, and without Speech with any

any unless it be the Bailiff, and with him only if they be agreed. *Cook* on *Lit. lib.* 3. *c.* 5. *Sect.* 366.

After they are agreed, they may in Causes between Party and Party give a Verdict before any of the Judges of the Court, and then they may eat and drink, and the next morning, in open Court they may either affirm or alter their privy Verdict, and that which is given in Court shall stand.

If the Jury after their Evidence given unto them at the Bar, do at their own Charges eat or drink either before or after they be agreed on their Verdict, it is finable, but it shall not avoid the Verdict; but if before they be agreed upon their Verdict, they eat or drink at the Charge of the Plaintiff, if the Verdict be given for him, it shall avoid the Verdict, but if it be given for the Defendant it shall not avoid it, *& sic è converso.* But if after they be agreed on their Verdict, they eat and drink at the Charge of him for whom they do pass, it shall not avoid the Verdict.

If A. be Appealed or Indicted for Murder, *viz.* that he of Malice prepensed, kills J. A. pleadeth that he is not Guilty, *modo & forma*, yet the Jury may find the Defendant guilty of Man-slaughter without Malice prepensed, because the killing of J. is the matter, and malice prepensed is but a circumstance. *Cook* on *Lit. Lib.* 3. *cap.* 8. *Sect.* 484.

A sufficient man (or a good man of the Jury) Legamannus, i, m.

A Jury man in an Assize, Recognitor, oris, m.

A Juror (or person sworn on a Jury, Jurator, oris, m.

A supply, or addition of men to a jury, Tales. *Tales de circumstantibus*, A Tales of the By-standers.

Juris utrum, Is a writ that lyeth for the Incumbent, whose Predecessor hath alienated his Lands or Tenements: the divers uses of which writ, *See in Fitz-Herb. Nat. brev. fol.* 48.

Jurisdiction (or authority to Minister and execute Laws) Jurisdictio, onis, f.

JUS.

Just, Justus, a, um.

Justice (or Equity) Justitia, æ, f.

A Justice, Justiciarius, ii, m. (*i. e.*) one that has the Kings Commission to do Justice. They are called Justices *per Metonymiam Subjecti*, because they do or should do Law and Justice, *Cook on Lit.* All the Commissions of the Justices of the Assize, are bounded with this express limitation. *Facturi quod ad justitiam pertinet secundum legem, & consuetudinem Angliæ.*

Lord Chief Justice of England. Capitalis Justiciarius Domini Regis ad Placita coram ipso Rege Tenenda assignatus.

His Office especially is to hear and Determine all Pleas of the Crown; that is, such as concern offences committed against the Crown, Dignity and Peace of the King, as Treasons, Felonies, Mayhems, &c. which you may see in *Bracton Lib.* 3. *Tract.* 2. *per totum*, and in *Stawnford's* Pleas of the Crown, from the first Chapter to the fifty first of the first book. But either it was from the beginning, or by time it is come to pass, that he with his Assistants, heareth all Personal actions, and real also, if they be incident to any Personal action depending before them. *Crompt. Jurisdict. fol.* 67, &c. This Court was first called the Kings Bench, because the King sat as Judge in it, in his Proper person, and it was moveable with the Court. *Anno* 9. *H.* 3. *cap.* 11. Of the Jurisdiction you may see more in *Crompton ubi supra.* Vide also Kings Bench.

A Justice of the Kings Bench, Unus Justiciarius Domini Regis ad Placita coram ipso Rege tenenda assignatus.

Lord Chief Justice of the Common Pleas, Capitalis Justiciarius Domini Regis de Banco.

He with his assistants did Originally hear and determine all Causes at Common Law, that is, all Civil causes between common persons, as well personal as real, for which causes it was called the Court of Common Pleas, in opposition to the Pleas of the Crown, or the Kings Pleas, which are special, and pertaining to him only. Of this Court and the Jurisdiction hereof *Vid. Cromptons Jurisdiction, fol* 91. This Court was always settled in a Place, as appeareth by the Statute *Anno* 9. *H.*3.*cap.* 11.

Justice of the Forest. Capitalis Justiciarius itinerans omnium Forestarum & Parcorum Domini Regis circa Trentam. He is also a Lord by his Office, and hath the hearing and determining of all Offences within the Kings Forest, committed against Venison or Vert. Of these there be two, whereof the one hath Jurisdiction over all the Forests on this side *Trent*, the other of all beyond. The chiefest part of their Jurisdiction, consisteth upon the Articles of the Kings Charter, called *Charta de Foresta* made *anno* 9. *H.* 3. which was by the Barons hardly drawn from him, to the mitigation of over cruel Ordinances made by his Predecessors.

The Court where this Justice sitteth and determineth, is called the Justice Seat of the Forest, held every three years once, whereof you may read at large in Mr. *Manwoods* first part of *Forest* Laws, *pag.* 121. *&* 154. *& pag.* 76. He is sometimes called Justice in Eyre of the Forest, see the reason in Justice in Eyre. This is the only Justice that may appoint a Deputy, *per Statutum anno* 32. *H.* 8. *c.* 35.

Justices of Assise, Justicarii ad capiendas Assisas, are such as were wont by special Commission to be sent (as occasion was offered) into this or that County to takes Assises: The Ground of which Policy was the ease of the Subjects. For whereas these actions pass alway by Jury, so many Men might not without great hindrance be brought to *London*, and therefore Justices for this purpose were by Commission particularly authorised and sent down to them. When they come to this Dignity, they give over Practice. *Anno* 8. *Ric.* 2. *cap.* 3. But this alway to be remembred, that neither Justice of either Bench (nor any other) may be Justice of Assise in his own Country, *Anno* 8. *Ric.* 2. *cap.* 2. *& anno* 33. *H.* 8. *cap.* 24.

Justices of Oyer *and* Terminer, Justiciarii ad audiendum & terminandum, were Justices deputed upon some especial or extraordinary

nary occasion, to hear and determine some or more Causes. *Fitz-Herb.* in his *Nat. Brev.* saith the Commission, D' *Oyer* and *Terminer*, is directed to certain persons upon any great Assembly, Insurrection, heinous Demeanour, or Trespass committed. And because the occasion of granting this commission should be maturely weighed, It is provided by the Statute, *anno* 2. *Ed.* 3. *cap.* 2. that no such Commission ought to be granted, but that they shall be dispatched before the Justices of the one Bench or other, or Justices Errants, except for horrible trespasses, and that by the especial favour of the King. The form of this Commission, see in *Fitz-Herb. Nat. brev. fol.* 110.

Justices in Eyre, Justiciarii Itinerantes. The use of these in ancient time, was to send them with Commission into divers Countries to hear such causes especially, as were termed the Pleas of the Crown: and therefore one may imagine they were so sent abroad for the ease of the Subjects, who must else have come to the Kings Bench if the Cause were too high for the County Court. They differed from the Justices of *Oyer* and *Terminer*, because they (as is above said) were sent uncertainly, upon any uproar or other occasion in the Country, but these in Eyre, (as Mr. *Gwin* setteth down in the preface to his Reading) were sent but every seven Year once. These were Instituted by *Henry* the Second, as Mr. *Cambden* in his *Britannia* witnesseth.

Justices of Gaol delivery, Justiciarii ad Gaolas deliberandas, are such as are sent with Commission to hear and determine all Causes appertaining to such, as for any Offence are cast into the Gaol part of whose authority is, to punish such as let to mainprise, those Prisoners that by Law are not bailable, by the Statute *de Finibus*, *cap.* 3. *Fitz. Nat. brev. fol.* 251. I. These by Likelyhood, in ancient time, were sent to Countries upon several occasions. But afterward Justices of Assise were likewise authorised to this *anno* 4. *Ed.* 3. *cap.* 3.

Justices of Peace, Justiciarii ad Pacem. Are they that are appointed by the Kings Commission, with others, to attend the Peace in the County where they dwell; of whom some upon special respect are made of the *Quorum*, because some business of importance may not be dealt in, without the presence or assent of them, or one of them; they are called of the *Quorum*, because the King in their Commissions thus chuseth or chargeth them. *Quorum vos A. B. C. D. E. F, unum esse volumus*, for the special trust in them reposed: They were called Guardians of the Peace, until the 36*th*. Year of King *Edward* the IIId. *cap.* 12. where they be called Justices. *Lamb. Eirenarcha, Lib.* 4. *cap.* 19. *pag.* 578. Sir *Tho. Smyth de Repub. angl. Lib.* 2. *cap.* 19.

Justices of Peace within Liberties, Justiciarii ad Pacem infra libertates, be such in Cities and other Corporate Towns, as those others be of any County; and their authority or Power is all one within their several Precincts, *Anno* 27. *H.* 8. *cap.* 25.

Justicies, It is a writ giving the Sheriff authority, to hold Plea, where otherwise he could not; it is called a Justicies, because it is a Commission to the Sheriff, *ad Justiciandum aliquem*, to do a man right, and requireth no Return of any Certificate of what he hath done. *Bract. Lib.* 4. *tract.* 6. *cap.* 13. *nu.* 2. maketh mention of a Justicies to the Sheriff of *London*, in a case of Dower, see the new book of Entries, *Justicies*.

To Justify or make Just, Justifico, are.

Justification, Justificatio, onis, f.

Justin (a mans name) Justinus, i, m.

Justinian (a mans name) Justinianus, i, m.

J U T.

Jutties of houses, or other buildings, Jutting or standing out further than the Residue, Projecta, orum, n. Prominentiæ, arum, f. Protecta, orum, n. Columna Meniana.

J U V.

Juvenal (a mans name) Juvenalis, is, m.

K E E.

A *Keel, (or bottom of a Ship)* Carina, æ, f.

A Keel, a Vessel to Cool wort or new brewed Ale and Beer, Labrum, i, n.

To keep, Servo, are.

A keeper, Custos, ōdis, m.

Lord keeper, Dominus custos Magni Sigilli Angliæ. He is Lord Keeper of the Great Seal of *England*, and is of the Kings Privy Council, under whose hands pass all Charters, Commissions, and Grants of the King, strengthened by the Great or Broad Seal of *England*, without which Seal, all such Instruments, by Law are of no force: For the King is in Interpretation and Intendment of Law, a Corporation, and therefore passeth nothing firmly, but under the said Seal. This Lord Keeper by the Statute *Anno* 5. *Eliz. cap.* 18. hath the same and the like Place, Authority, Pre-eminence, Jurisdiction, Execution of Laws, and all other customs, commodities and advantages, as hath the Lord Chancellor of *England* for the time being.

Lord Keeper of the Privy Seal, Dominus Custos privati Sigilli Domini Regis. Under his hands pass all Charters Signed by the King, before they come to the broad or Great Seal of *England*. He is also one of the Kings most Honourable Privy Counsel.

Keeper of the Forest, Custos Forestæ. He is also called Chief Warden of the Forest. *Manwood part* 1. of his Forest Laws, pag. 156, &c. and hath the Principal Government of all things belonging thereunto, as also the Check of all Officers belonging to the Forest. And the Lord Chief Justice in Eyre of the Forest, when it pleaseth him to keep his Justice Seat, doth forty days before, send out his General summons to him, for the warning of all under Officers, to appear before him at a day assigned in the Summons, vid. *Manwood ubi Supra*.

K E G.

K E G.

A Kegg of Sturgion, Sturionarium, ii, n. Turfionarium, ii, n.

K E L.

Kelnsey (in Yorkshire) Ocellum Promontorium.

K E N.

Ken river (in Scotland) Jena.

Kenchester (near Hertford) Ariconium.

Kendal (in Westmorland) Candalia.

Kendal Barony, Concangium.

Kened River (in Wiltshire) Keneta.

Kenelm (a mans name) Kenelmus, i, m.

Kenelworth Castle (in Warwickshire) Chinegliſſi caſtrum.

A kennel for Dogs, Canile, is, n.

A kennel-raker, Lacunarius, ii, m. Carinarius, ii, m.

Kenet River (in Wiltshire) Cunetio.

Kent, Cantia, Cantium.

Kentish Saxons, Cantuaritæ.

K E R.

A Kerchief for women, Rica, æ, f. Calantica, æ, f.

A Kernel, properly in nuts, Nucleus, ei, m.

A Kernel in Grapes, Acinus, i, m.

A kertle, (or kirtle) Supparus, i, m.

Kerry County (in Ireland) Kerriensis Comitatus.

K E S.

Kester (a mans name) Keſterus, i, m.

Kesteven a part of Lincolnshire, Keſtevena.

K E T.

A kettle, Caldārium, ii, n. Cacabus, i, m. Cŏcŭlum, i, n.

K E W.

Kew (in Surrey) Cheva.

K E Y.

A key, Clavis, is, f.

A little key, Clāvĭcŭla, æ f.

Of a key, Clāvĭcŭlarius, a, um.

A key (or wharf) Kaia, æ, f.

A duty paid for loading or unloading of Goods, at a Key (or Wharf) Kaiagium, ii, n. Ry. 400. Spel. 419. Lex. 75.

K I D.

A kid (or young goat) Hœdus, i, m.

A young kid, Hœdulus, i, m.

A place where kids are kept, Hœdile, is, n.

Of a kid, Hœdinus, a, um.

A kidnapper, (one that steals Children) Laucus, i, m.

A kidney, Ren, renis, m.

K I L.

To kill, Occido, ere.

Kildare (in Ireland) Kildaria.

Of Kildare, Kildarienſis.

Kildare Bishoprick, Darensis Episcopatus.

Killair Castle (in Meath in Ireland) Laberus.

Killalo Bishoprick in Ireland, Ladensis Episcopatus.

Killage, Killagium, ii, n. Ry. 169.

A kilderkin, Semicadus, i, m. Cadiolus, i, m.

A kiln for lime (or lime kiln) Calcaria fornax.

Killigrew (the Family) Cheligrevus.

K I M.

Kimbolton Castle (in Huntingtonshire) Kinebantum castrum.

K I N.

The Kings Majesty, Dominus Rex. Regia Majestas. Rex, regis, m. The King hath in the Right of his Crown, many Prerogatives above any person whatsoever, be he never so Potent or Honourable, whereof you may read in *Stawnford tract.* upon the Statute thereof made, *Anno* 17. *Ed.* 2. what the Kings Power is, *Vid. Bract. Lib.* 2. *cap.* 24. *numb.* 1, and 2.

Kings County (in Ireland) Regis comitatus.

Death of the King, Dimissio Regis.

The Kings Evil, Scrofula, æ, f.

A Kingdom, Regnum, i, n.

Kings Bench, Bancus Regius. It is the Court or Judgment Seat, where the King of *England* was wont to sit in his own Person, and therefore it was moveable with the Court or Kings Houshold, and call'd *Cura Domini Regis*, or *Aula Regia*; as Mr. *Gwin* reporteth in the Preface to his Readings, and that, in that and the Exchequer, which were the only Courts of the King, until *H.* 3. his days, were handled all matters of Justice, as well Civil as Criminal; whereas the Court of Common Pleas might not be so by the Statute, *anno* 9. *H.* 3. *cap.* 11. or rather by Mr. *Gwin*'s opinion, was presently upon the Grant of the Great Charter severally Erected. This Court of the Kings Bench, was wont in Ancient times to be especially exercised in all Criminal matters and Pleas of the Crown, leaving the handling of private contracts to the County Court. *Glanv. Lib.* 1. *cap.* 2, 3, 4. & *L.* 10. *cap.* 18. *Smith de Repub. Angl. lib.* 2. *cap.* 11. and hath president of it, the Lord Chief Justice of *England*, with three or four Justices assistants, and Officers thereunto belonging. The Clerk of the Crown, a Protonotary, and other six inferior Ministers or Attorneys. *Camd. Britan. pag.* 112. How long this Court was moveable, I find not in any writer, but in *Britons* time, who wrote in King *Edw.* the first his days. It appeareth it followed the Court, as Mr. *Gwin* in his said Preface well observeth out of him.

Kingston upon Hull (in Yorkshire) Regiodunum Hullinum.

Kingston upon Thames (in Surrey) Regiodunum Thamesinum.

Kin by blood, Cognatus, i, m.

Kin by Marriage, Affinis, is, c. 2.

A kinsman, Propinquus, i, m.

K I R.

Kirby (the Family) Chirchebeius.

Kirkby-Stephen (in Westmorland) Fanum Sancti Stephani.

Kirton (in Devonshire) See Crediton.

K I T.

A kitchin, Culina, æ, f. Coquina, æ, f.

A kitchin boy, Puer culinarius.

A kitchin maid, Focaria, æ, f.

Of the kitchin, Culinarius, a, um.

K N E.

To knead, Depso, ere.

A kneading Trough, Mactra, æ, f. Alveus pistorius.

A knee, Genu, n. Indecl.

K N I.

A knife, Culter, tri, m.

A little knife, Cultellus, i, m.

A childs bone knife, Cicilicula, æ, f.

A chopping knife, Culter herbarius, Culter panarius.

A Butchers chopping knife, Clunaculum, li, n.

A scraping knife, Radula, æ, f. Radens Culter.

A pairing knife, Culter sutorius.

A wood knife, Scrama, æ, f.

A Shooe-makers round cutting knife, Smilium Sutorium.

A Pen-knife, Pennarius cultellus.

Made sharp, like a knife, Cultratus, a, um.

Of a knife, Cultrarius, a, um.

The back of a knife, Ebiculum, i, n.

A grinder or whetter of knifes, Cotiarius, i, m.

A Knight, Miles, itis, m.

A Knight of the Garter, Prænobilis Ordinis Garterii Miles. It signifieth with us, both in divers Statutes and otherwise, one Especial Garter, being the Ensign of a Great and Noble Society of Knights, called Knights of the Garter. This High Order as appeareth by Mr. *Camden* and many others, was first instituted by that Famous King *Edward* the Third, upon good Success, in a Skirmish wherein the Kings Garter (I know not upon what occasion) was used for a token. But I know that *Polydore Virgil* casteth in another suspicion of the Original, his ground by his own confession grew from the vulgar opinion, yet as it is, take it as I have read it. *Edward* the third King of *England*, after he had obtained many great Victories, King *John* of *France*, King *James* of *Scotland*, being both Prisoners in the Tower of *London* at one time, and King *Henry* of *Castile*, the Bastard expulsed, and Don *Pedro* restored by the Prince of *Wales* and Duke of *Aquitane*, called the black Prince, did upon no weighty occasion first Erect this Order in *anno* 1350. *viz.* he dancing with the Queen, and other Ladies of the Court, took up a Garter that happened to fall from one of them, whereat some of the Lords smiling, the King said unto them, that ere it were long, he would make that Garter to be of high Reputation, and

 shortly

ſhortly after Inſtituted this Order of the Blue Garter, which every one of the order is bound daily to wear on the left Leg, being richly deckt with Gold and Precious Stones, with a buckle of Gold, and having theſe words written or wrought upon it, *Honi Soit qui maly penſe.* Which is, ſhame take him that thinketh evil. Mr. *Fearne* in his Glory of Generoſity, agreeth with Mr. *Camden*, and expreſlier ſetteth down the Victories, whence this order was occaſioned. Whatſoever beginning it had, it need not ſeem a baſe Original, ſeeing as one ſaith, *Nobilitas ſub amore jacet*, Nobility lies under love.

The Order is inferior to none in the world, conſiſting of twenty ſix Martial and Heroical Nobles, whereof the King of *England* is the Chief, and the reſt be either Nobles of the Realm, or Princes of other Countries, friends and Confederates with this Realm, the Honour being ſuch, as Emperors and Kings of other Nations have deſired and thankfully accepted it. The Ceremonies of the Chapter proceeding to Election of the Inveſtitures, and Robes of his Inſtallation, of his Vow, with all ſuch other Obſervances. See in Mr. *Segar*'s book intituled Honour Military and Civil, *Lib.* 2. *cap.* 9. *fol.* 65.

There are depending on this Honourable Order twenty ſix Poor Knights, that have no other Suſtenance or means of Living, but the allowance of this Houſe, which is given them in reſpect of their daily Prayer to the honour of God, and (according to the courſe of thoſe times) of St. *George*.

There are alſo certain officers belonging to this Order, as namely the Prelate of the Garter, which office is Inherent to the Biſhop of *Wincheſter* for the time being, the Chancellor of the Garter, the Regiſter who is always Dean of *Windſor*. The Principal King at Arms called Garter, which ſee in Herald, whoſe chief Function is to manage and marſhal their ſolemnities at their Yearly Feaſts and Inſtallations.

Laſtly, the Uſher of the Garter, which (as I have heard) belongeth to an Uſher of the Princes Chamber, called *Black Rod*. The Seat of this College, is the Caſtle of *Windſor*, with the Chappel of St. *George*, Erected by *Edward* the Third, and the Chapter-houſe in the ſaid Caſtle.

Garter, ſignifieth alſo the Principal King at Arms among our *Engliſh* Heralds, created by King *Henry* the Fifth, *Vid. Stow. pag.* 584.

A Knight Baneret, Banerettus. Which dignity is more than an ordinary Knight, equal with that of King *James*'s lately erected of Baronets, yet Inferior to a Baron. It was given at the firſt by the Kings of *England* and *France*, to ſuch Gentlemen that Valiantly carried themſelves in two Royal Battles, or to ſuch as had ten Vaſſals, and means to maintain a Troop of Horſe at their own Charge. Sr. *Thom. Smith de Repub. Angl. lib.* 1. *c.* 18. Saith that a Baneret is a Knight made in the Field, with the Ceremonies of the cutting of the Point of his Standard, and making it as it were a Banner, and they being before Batchelor

Knights, are now of greater degree, allowed to display their Arms in a Banner in the Kings Army as Barons do. Of Creating a Knight Baneret, you may read more in Mr. *Segar Norrey* his Book.

Mr. *Camden* saith he cannot fetch the Antiquity of these Knights from further, than King *Edward* the third, when *Englishmen* as he there saith, were renowned for Chivalry.

A Knight of the Bath, Miles Balnei. They are the Order of Knights made within the Lists of the Bath, girded with a Sword, in the Ceremonies of his Creation. These are spoken of *Anno* 8. *Ed.* 4. *cap.* 2. But I have heard that these Knights, were so called of a Bath, into the which (after they had been shaved and trimmed by a Barber) they Entred, and thence, the night before they were Knighted, being well bathed, were taken again by two Esquires commanded to attend them, dried with fine Linen Cloaths, and so apparelled in a Hermits gray-weed, with a Hood and a Linen Coif, and booted withal, and led through many Solemn ceremonies, *viz.* confessing their Sins, watching and praying all Night in a Church or Chappel, as though they would begin their Warfare, in employing their service for God especially, with many other, to the Order of Knighthood the next day.

Knight Marshal, Marescallus hospitii. Is an Officer in the Kings house, having Jurisdiction and Cognizance of any Transgression within the Kings House, and Verge; as also, all Contracts made within the same, whereunto one of the House is party. *Regist. Orig. fol.* 185. *a. b. u. fol.* 191. *b.* whereof you may read there more at large.

Knights of the Shire, Milites Comitatus; otherwise be called Knights of the Parliament, and be two Knights, or other Gentlemen of worth, that are chosen in *Pleno comitatu*, by the Free-holders of every County that can dispend forty Shillings, *per annum*, and be Resident in the Shire, *Anno* 10. *H.* 6. *cap.* 2. *&* *anno* 1. *H.* 5. *cap.* 1. upon the Kings writ to be sent to the Parliament, and there by their Counsel, to assist the common proceedings of the whole Realm. These when every man that had a Knights Fee, were customarily constrained to be a Knight, were of necessity to be *Milites gladio cincti*, for so runneth the Tenour of the writ at this day. *Crompt. Jurisdict. fol.* 1. But now there being but few Knights in comparison of former times, and many men of great living in every County. Custom beareth that Esquires may be chosen to this Office, so that they be Resident within the County, for the observation in the choice of these Knights, see the Statutes, and the new book of Entries, *verbo Parlamentum.* Their Expences, during the Parliament, are born by the County or Shire. *Anno* 35. *H.* 8. *cap.* 11.

Knight-hood, Militaris ordo.

To Knit, Necto, ere.

K N O.

A Knot, Nodus, i, m.

Full of knots, Condylŏmăticus, a, um.

To

To know, Cognoſco, ere.

To cauſe to know, Scirefacio, ere.

To ſhew cauſe. 2. Inſt. 473. Ry. 52.

K N U.

A Knuckle, Condylus, i, m.

K R E.

Kreckhornwell (*in* ——) Uxela.

L A B.

L*Abour*, Labor, oris, m.

To labour, Operor, ari.

To labour with Child (*or to be in Labour or Travail*) Parturio, ire.

A labourer, Laborarius, ii, m. Operarius, ii, m.

L A C.

A lace (*or riband*) Aſtrigmentum, i, n. Tenia, æ, f.

Lace, Lacinia, æ, f. Inſtita, æ, f.

Bone-lace, Tæniola, æ, f.

A Hair-lace, Faſcia crinalis.

A Neck-lace, Monile, is, n.

To lace, Conſtringo, ere.

A lackey, Pediſſequus, i, m.

L A D.

A Ladder, Scala, æ, f. Climax, acis, f.

A ſhort ladder, Eriſma, atis, n.

A ladder-ſtaff, Interſcalare, is, n.

Ladder-ſtaffs, Scalæ gradus.

A Lady, Domina, æ, f.

A little Lady, Dominula, æ, f.

Our Lady, the bleſſed Virgin, Beata virgo. Virgo Maria.

The Feaſt of the Annunciation of the Bleſſed Virgin, commonly called Lady day, always the 25th. of March. Feſtum Annunciationis beatæ Mariæ Virginis.

Lady-day in Harveſt (*or the aſſumption of our Lady*) Feſtum aſſumptionis beatæ Mariæ Virginis.

The conception of our Lady, Feſtum Conceptionis beatæ Mariæ Virginis.

Ladings, Carcationes.

Unladings, Diſcarcationes, Ry. 30.

Laden (*overcharged*) Onĕrātus, a, um.

A ladle, Cucchiara, æ, f. Spatha, æ, f. Capula, æ, f. Futum, i, n.

L A I.

To laie (*as one layeth a foundation*) Loco, are.

To laie a part, Sepono, ere.

To laie aſide, Repono, ere.

To laie down, Depono, ere.

To laie under, Sub-mitto, ere.

To laie out (*Disburſe or ſpend*) Expono, ere.

Laid aſide, Poſtpoſitus, a, um.

A Laie-man, Laicus, i, m.

Lairwite (*or Laherwite*) Legergildum, i, n. (*i. e.*) a kind of Fine for Fornication or Adultery, 4 Inſt. 206.

L A K.

A Lake or Pool, Lacus, ûs, m.

A little Lake, Lacunculus, i, m.

L A M.

A lamb, Agnus, i, m.

A lamb newly yeaned, Avilla, æ, f.

A little lamb, Agnellus, i, m.

A lean lamb, Curiosus agnus.

Lamb, Caro agnina.

Lambard (the Family) Lambardus.

Lambert (a mans name) Lambertus, i, m.

Lambeth (in Surrey) Lamitha, Lomithis.

Lammas day (the Gule or first day of August) Festum Sancti Petri ad Vincula. Gula Augusti.

A lamp, Lampas, ădis, f.

L A N.

Lancaster Town, Alion, Alione, Alone, Lancastria, Loncastria, Longovicum.

Lancashire, Lancastrensis comitatus.

Of Lancaster, Mediolanensis.

A lance, Lancea, æ, f.

A lancier (one that serves on horse-back with a lance) Lancearius, ii, m. Doryphorus, i, m.

A Chirurgeons lance or fleam, (an instrument used in letting Blood) Scalprum, i, n.

To lance, cut, or open a sore, Scarifico, are.

To be lanced, Scarificor, ari.

A lancing or opening of a Sore, Scarificatio, onis, f.

Land, Fundus, i, m.

Fallow land, Vervactium, i, n.

New broken land, Novale, is, n.

Arable land, Arvum, i, n. Terra Arrabilis.

Land covered with water, Terra aqua cooperta.

A rood of land, Rodata, æ, f.

A ridge of land, Selio terræ.

A neck of land, Isthmus, i, m.

A hide of land, (100 acres) Hida terræ. Swolinga, æ, f.

A Teem of Land, Quadrugata terræ.

A Yard-land (40 acres) Virgata terræ.

Twelve acres of land, Solidata terræ.

As much land as one Plough can till in a year, Sulinga & Solinga, æ, f.

A small piece of land, Frustum terræ.

Land that may be tilled or ploughed, Excultabilis terra.

Fresh land that hath not been long Ploughed, Terra frisca.

A field or land to be manured, Terrenum, i, n.

The crop or profits of land, Vestura terræ, Vestitura Bosci. 1 Mon. 780.

Going forth and Issuing out of land, Egrediens, & Exeuns è Terris.

To levy (or raise money) on lands, Levo, are.

Landaffe, Landava.

Bishop of Landaffe, Episcopus Landavensis.

A quarter of a yard land, Ferlingata terræ, Lex. 55. Ferdellum terræ Spel. 250.

A lane, Venella, æ, f.

Langdon (the Family) Dē Langdona, & Landa.

A lantern, Laterna, æ, f.

A dark lantern (or thieves lantern) Laterna Secreta.

The lantern of a Ship or Gally, also a great lantern on the top of a Tower to light & guide Ships into a Harbor, Pharus, i, m.

A lan-

A lantern-maker, Cornificus, i, m.

Lanvethlin (in Montgomeryshire) Mediolanum.

Lands end Cape, Antivesteum, Belerium, Bolerium, Helenum Prom.

L A O.

Laon, See Killalo.

L A P.

A lapidary (or Jeweller) Lapidarius, ii, m.

Lapse, Lapsus, ûs, m. It is a slip or departure of a Right of Presenting to avoid a Benefice from the Original Patron, neglecting to present within six Months unto the Ordinary. For we say, that Benefice is in Lapse, or Lapsed, whereunto he that ought to present, hath omitted or slipped his opportunity. *Anno* 13. *Eliz. cap.* 12. This Lapse groweth as well, the Patron being Ignorant of the avoidance, as privy, except only upon the Resignation of the former Incumbent, or the deprivation upon any Cause comprehended in the Statute. *Anno* 13. *Eliz. cap.* 12. in which cases the Bishop ought to give Notice to the Patron.

L A R.

Larcenie, Laricinium, Latrocinium, ii, n. In respect of things stollen, it is either great or small, Great Larcenie, is wherein the things stollen, though severally, exceed the value of twelve pence. And Petit Larcenie, is when the Goods stollen, exceed not the value of twelve pence, then it is not felony. *Vid. Stawnford.*

Lard, Lardum, i, n.

A lardery (or larder) Lardarium, ii, n. Carnarium, ii, n. Promptuarium, ii, n.

Large (or broad) Largus, a, um.

To go at large (to be set at Liberty, or to make an Escape) Ire ad Largum.

A hanging larum with minutes, Horologium pendens cum momentis.

L A S.

A last of Fish, Lasta vel Halecium Piscis. Ra. Entr. 161. Spel. 426. Lex. 78. Pry 25. A Last of Hering containeth ten Thousand, *Anno* 31. *Ed.* 3. *Stat.* 2. *cap.* 2. A Last of Pitch and Tar, or of Ashes containeth fourteen Barrels, *anno* 32. *H.* 8. *cap.* 14. A Last of Hides, *anno* 1 *Jac. cap.* 33. containeth twelve Dozen of Hides or Skins.

A last for shooe-makers, Calus, i, m. Mustricula, æ, f.

Lastage, Lastagium ii, n. *(i. e.)* a Custom in Fairs and Markets, paid for Carrying of things, or for wares sold by the Last, also the Balast of a Ship.

L A T.

A latch of a door, Clostrum, i, n.

The latchet of a shooe, Corigia, æ, f.

Late, Tardus a, um.

Lately, Nuper.

A lath

A lath (or little board) Assula, æ, f. Asserculus, i, m.

A lath (or shingle) Scindula, æ, f.

A lath (or great part of a County) Læstrum, i, n.

A lath (or part of a County, containing three or more hundreds) Leda, æ, f.

The Latin tongue, Lingua Latina.

Latitat, is the name of a writ, whereby all men in Personal actions are called Originally to the Kings Bench, and it hath the name from this, because in respect of their better Expedition, a man is supposed *Latitare*, (*i. e.*) to Lurk and lie hidden; therefore being served with this writ, he must put in security for his appearance at the day; therefore the form of this writ is after the Return. *Non est Inventus in Balliva, &c. Ut in curia nostra coram nobis sufficienter testatum est quod prædict. &c. latitat & discurrit in commitatu tuo. Id circo tibi præcipimus quod capias prædict. T. Si inventus fuerit in Balliva tua, & eum salvum custodias, ita quod habeas corpus ejus coram nobis apud Westm. die, &c. ad respond. &c.*

A lattise (or, a window with barrs) Transenna, æ, f. Clathrus, i, m.

L A U.

A lavacre (or washing place) Lavacrum, i, n. Lavatorium, ii, n.

Lauden, or Lothien (in Scotland) Laudenia, Laudonia.

To lavish, Absumo, ere.

A laundress, Lotrix, icis, f. Candidatrix, icis, f.

L A W.

A Law, Laga, æ, f. Lex, legis, f.

A by-law, Ordinatio plebiscitum.

To thwart the laws, Oblego, are.

A Doctor of law, Legisdoctor, oris, m. Legum Doctor.

A law-giver, Legifer, eri, m. Legislator, oris, m.

Lawful, Legitimus, a, um. Legalis, le, adj.

Law of arms, Jus militare. Is a Law that giveth precepts, and rules how rightly to Proclaim War, to make and observe Leagues and Truce, to set upon the Enemy, to retire, to punish offenders in the Camp, to appoint Soldiers their Pay, to give every one dignity to his desert, to divide Spoils in proportion, &c. *Vide Martial* Law, *sub voce Martial.*

Law day, Dies Juridicus.

The civil Law, Jus civile.

Lawing of Dogs, Expeditatio canum.

Mastiffs must be lawed every third year, Crompt. Jurisdict. fol. 163.

A lawyer, Jurisconsultus, i, m.

A civil lawyer, Civilista, æ, m. Dyer 267.

Lawful money of England, Legalis moneta angliæ.

It shall and may be lawful, Liberet & licitum foret, *or* Liceret *alone*, *or* licitum foret *only*.

A lawless person, Exlex, legis, c. 2. Illex, legis, c. 2.

A lawnd (or open field) Landa, æ, f. Lex. 77. Fle. 90. Ry. 636. Landa, æ, f. 2 Mon. 969.

Lawn (or fine linen cloth) Syndon, ŏnis, f.

Lawrence (*a mans name*) Laurentius, ii, m.

L A Y.

An underlaying, Fulcimentum, i, m.

L A Z.

Lazarus (*a mans name*) Lazarus, i, m.

L E A.

Lead, Plumbum, i, n.
Black lead, Plumbum nigrum.
Read lead, Minium, ii, n. Plumbum rubrum.
White lead, Cerussa, æ, f. Plumbum album.
Of lead, Plumbeus, a, um.
Full of lead (*or mixt with lead*) Plumbosus, a, um.
Lead oar, Plumbago, inis, f. Molybdena, æ, f.
Leading, Plumbatio, onis, f.
Soddering with lead, Plumbatura, æ, f.
Sodder of lead, Ferrumen, inis, n.
A pipe of lead, Pipa Plumbea.
A roof covered with lead, Tectum plumbo obductum.
A Sow of lead, Plumbi lamina.
A pellet of lead, Plumbata, æ, f. Glans plumbea.
To lead (*cover with lead*, *or ſodder together*) Plumbo, are. Plumbo conglutinare.
A ſheet of lead, Charta Plumbea.
Leah (*a womans name*) Læa, æ, f.
A leaf fallen, Folium, ii, n.
The green leaf of a tree, Frons, ndis, f.
A leaf of paper, Folium chartæ.
A league (*ordinarily two miles, in ſome Countries more*) Leuca, æ, f. 2 Mon. 853.
A league (*or agreement*) Fœdus, eris, n.
Leakey, Futilis, le, adj.
A leaking, Futilitas, atis, f.
Lean, Macilentus, a, um.
Leanneſs, Macies, ei, f.
A leaning ſtock, (*as a rail, ſtay, or reſt to lean on*) Fulcimentum, i, n.
Learned, Doctus, a, um.
Learning, Doctrina, æ, f.
A Leaſe, Lessa, æ, f. Dimissio, onis, f.
Leaſed, Traditus, a, um. Dimisſus, a, um.
A leaſh (*or line to hold a Dog in*) Lorum caninum.
A leaſowe, Lesura, æ, f. 1 Fo. 144.
At leaſt, Ad minus, Ad minimum.
Leather, Corium, ii, n.
Of leather, Coriaceus, a, um.
A thong of leather, Lorum, i, n.
Of Buff leather, Bubulinus, a, um.
Made of Leather, Scorteus, a, um. Coriaceus, a, um.
Covered with leather, Pellitus, a, um.
Utenſils of leather, Corium tannatum.
A leather dreſſer, Allutarius, ii, m.
A leather ſeller, Pellio, onis, m.
A leather ſellers trade, Pelliparia, æ, f.
To tan leather, Tanno, are.
To dreſs leather, Concinnare Coria.
Upper leather, Obstragulum, i, n.
To leave, Relinquo, ere.
Leave (*or permiſſion*) Permissio, onis, f.

To leavel at (or aim at) Collimo, are.

To leavel (or make plain) Plano, are: Complano, are.

Leaven, Fermentum, i, n.

To leaven, Fermento, are.

Unleavened, Infermentatus, a, um.

A leaver (or bar to lift, or bear up Timber) Palanga, æ, f.

Using a leaver, Vecticularius, a, um.

He that turns a wine-press with a leaver, Vectiarius, ii, m.

A lewn or levy, Levina, æ, f. Assessmentum, i, n.

L E C.

Lechlade (in Gloucestershire) Lechenlada, Lechelada, Lathelada.

L E D.

Ledah (a womans name) Læda, æ, f.

L E E.

Leeds (in Kent) Ledanum. Castrum Lodanum.

Lees (or Dregs) of Wine, Floces.

Lees (or Dregs) of oyl, Fraces, ium, f.

A leet Court, Leta, æ, f. Reg. 134. Spel. 431. Visus francus plegii.

L E F.

Left, Relictus, a, um.

L E G.

Legacester (in--) Legionum civitas. *See* Isca.

A legacy, Legatum, i, n.

Legal, Legalis, le, adj.

A legate (or ambassador) Legatus, i, m.

The leg, Crus, cruris, n.

The calf of the leg, Sura, æ, f.

Legible (or to be read) Legibilis, le, adj.

Legitimate, Legitimus, a, um.

L E I.

Leicester town, Legacestria, Legecestria, Leiceastria, Licestria, Legoria, Leogoria, Ratæ.

Leicester, or Lester, (the Family) De Leicestria.

Leighlin in Caterlough (in Ireland) Lechlinia.

Leith Town (in Scotland) Letha.

Leiton, in Essex (or near it) Durolitum.

L E M.

Lemster (in Herefordshire) Leofense & Leovense Cœnobium, Leonis monasterium, Leonense cœnobium.

L E N.

Lenister province (in Ireland) Lagenia.

Leneham (in Kent) Durolenum, Durolevum.

Lenitives, Mitigatoria.

Lent, or lent season, Quadragesima.

L E O.

Leonard (*a mans name*) Leonardus, i, m.

Leominster (*in*) Fanum Leonis. Vide *Lempster.*

Leopold (*a mans name*) Leopoldus, i, m.

L E P.

The leprosie, Lepra, æ, f.

L E S.

Leskard (*in Cornwall*) Sebasta altera Legio.

A lessee, Firmarius, ii, m. Terminarius, ii, m. Captor, oris, m. Conductor, oris, m. (*i. e.*) he to whom the Lease is made for term of years, for Life or at will.

A lessor (*or landlord*) Locator, oris, m. Lessor, oris, m. (*i. e.*) he that leaseth or letteth Lands, *&c.*

L E T.

The lethargy (*a sleepy disease*) Lethargia, æ, f.

A letter without a seal, Indiculus, i, m.

A letter of attorney, Litera attornati. It is a writing authorizing an Attorney, that is a man appointed to do a lawful act in our Steads. *West part* 1. *Symb. Lib.* 2. *Sect.* 559. It is called in the Civil Law, *Mandatum* or *Procuratorium.* There seemeth to be some difference between a Letter of Attorney, and a Warrant of Attorney, for whereas a Letter of Attorney is sufficient if it be sealed and delivered before sufficient Witness, a Warrant of Attorney must be acknowledged and certified before such Persons, as Fines be acknowledged in the Country, or at least before some Justice or Serjeant. *West part* 2. *Symb. Tit. recoveries. Sect.* 1. *F.* See the Statute, Anno 7. *R.* 2. *cap.* 14.

Letters of Exchange, Literæ Cambitoriæ, *vel* Literæ Cambij.

Letters Patents, Literæ Patentes. Be Writings Sealed with the Broad Seal of *England*, whereby a Man is authorized to do or enjoy any thing, that otherwise of himself he could not. *Anno* 19. *H.* 7. *cap.* 7. and they are so termed of their form because they are Patents, (*i.e.*) open with the seal hanging, ready to be shewed for the confirmation of the authority given by them. If any will say, that Letters patents may be granted by common Persons, you may find to that effect in *Fitz-Herb. Nat. brev. fol.* 35. E. Howbeit they be rather called Patents in our common speech, than Letters Patents.

Letters of recommendation, Literæ Recommendatitiæ.

Lettered (*or well learned*) Literatus, a, um.

Lettley (*the Family*) De Læto, Loco.

L E V.

Levant and Couchant, Levans & cubans. (*i. e.*) when Beasts or Cattle of a stranger, are come into another mans ground, and there have remained a good space, have Layen and Risen.

Levari facias, Is a writ directed to the Sheriff, for the levying of a

Sum of money upon Lands and Tenements, of him that hath forfeited a Recognizance, &c. *Regist. Orig. fol.* 298. *b.* & 300 *b.*

Levari facias damna de disseisitoribus. Is a writ directed to the Sheriff for the Levying of damages, wherein the Disseisor hath formerly been condemned to the disseised. *Regist. fol.* 214. *b.*

Levari facias residuum debiti. Is a writ directed to the Sheriff, for the Levying of a remnant of a debt upon Lands and Tenements, or Chattels of the Debtor, that hath in part satisfied before. *Regist. Orig. fol.* 299.

Levari facias quando vice-comes returnavit quod non habuit emptores. Is a writ commanding the Sheriff to sell the Goods of the Debtor, which he hath already taken, and returned that he could not sell them, and as much more of the Debtors goods, as will satisfie the whole Debt. *Regist. Orig. fol.* 300. *a.*

A level, Levella, æ, f. Co. Entr. 293.

A level, Plumb-line, Perpendiculum, i, n.

By line and level, Ad Perpendiculum.

A measurer by a level, Perpendiculator, oris, m.

Leviable, Leviabilis, le, adj. Ra. Ent. 513.

Leveney (in Brecknockshire, or near it) Loventium.

Levin river (in Scotland) Lelanonius, Levinus.

Levie, Levare. It is used in our Common Law, for to set up any thing, as to levy a mill, *Kitchin fol.* 180. or to cast up, as to Levy a Ditch. *Old Nat. brev. fol.* 110. or to gather and exact, as to Levy money, *Vide Levari facias.*

L E W.

Lewis Island, the largest of the Hebrides, Ebuda vel Hebuda Secunda, Hebuda occidentalior. Levissa.

Lewis (a mans name) Ludovicus, i, m.

Llewellin (a mans name) Leonellus, i, m.

Lewkin (the Family) Leuchenorius.

L E X.

Lexington (the Family) De Lexintuna.

L E Y.

A ley, Terra Subcessiva.

L H E.

Lheyne Promontory (in Caernarvanshire) Canganum, Canganorum, Ganganorum, Ganganum, Langanum prom.

L I A.

Liable (chargeable) Onerabilis, le, adj. Responsibilis, le, adj.

L I B.

A libel, Libellus, i, m. Lex. 80. It literally signifieth a little book, but by use it is the Original Declaration of any action in the Civil Law, *Anno* 2. *H.* 5. *cap* 3. & *anno* 2. *Ed.* 6. *cap.* 13. It signifieth also a criminous or scandalous Report of any man cast abroad, or otherwise unlawfully Published in writing, but then for difference sake, it is called an Infamous Libel. *famosus Libellus*.

Libera Chasea habenda, Is a Writ Judicial granted to a man for a free chase belonging to his Manor, after he hath by a Jury proved it to belong unto him, *Regist. Judic. fol.* 36, & 37.

Liberal, Liberalis, le, adj.

Liberate, Is a warrant Issuing out of the Chancery to the Treasurer, Chamberlains and Barons of the Exchequer, or Clerk of the Hamper, &c. for the Payments of any annual Pension, or other sums granted under the Broad Seal. *Vid. Brook Tit.* Taye D' *Exchequer, num.* 4. *Regist. Orig. fol.* 193. a. b. or sometime to the Sheriff, &c. *Nat. brev. fol.* 132. for the delivery of any Lands or Goods taken upon forfeits of a Recognizance. It is also to a Goaler from the Justices for the delivery of a Prisoner, that hath put in Bail for his appearance. *Lamb. Eiren. lib.* 3. *cap.* 2.

Libertas, Is a privilege held by Grant or prescription, whereby men enjoy some benefit or favour beyond the ordinary subject. Liberties Royal what they be, see in *Bract. Lib.* 2. *cap.* 5. *Brook hoc Titulo.*

Libertatibus allocandis, Is a writ that lyeth for a Citizen or Burgess of any City, that contrarily to the Liberties of the City or Town whereof he is, is Impleaded before the Kings Justices, or Justices Errants, or Justice of the Forest, &c. that refuseth or deferreth to allow his Privilege. *Regist. Orig. fol.* 262. *Fitz. Herb. Nat. brev. fol.* 229.

Liberty, Libertas, atis, f.

To set one at liberty, Libero, are.

A liberty (or Franchise) Socna, æ, f.

A library, Bibliotheca, æ, f.

A library keeper, Librarius, ii, m. Bibliothecarius, ii, m.

Librata terræ, containeth four Ox-gangs, and every Ox-gang thirteen acres. *Skene de verb. Signif. verbo Bovata terræ*, See *Farding Deal* of Land.

L I C.

Lichfield (in Staffordshire) Lichfeldia, Lychefeldia.

Of Lichfield, Lecefeldensis, Licetfeldensis.

Licentia transfretandi, Is a writ or warrant directed to the Keepers of the Port at Dover, &c. willing them to let some pass quietly over Sea, that hath formerly obtained the Kings licence thereunto. *Regist. Orig. fol.* 193. *b*.

Licentious, Licentiosus, a, um.

A licking medicine, Linctus, i, m.

L I D.

Lidford (in Devonshire) Lideforda.

L I E.

Lie, made of ashes, Lixivium, ii, n.

Lieftenant, Locum tenens. It signifieth with us sometimes, him that occupieth the Kings Place, or representeth his Person, and then he is called the Kings Lieftenant, *anno* 4. *H.* 5. *cap.* 6. So it is used *anno* 2. & 3. *Ed.* 6. *cap.* 2. whence that Officer seemeth to take his beginning, you may read also in Mr.

Mr. *Manwood's* first part of Forest Laws, pag. 113. that the Lord Chief Justice in Eyre of the Forest, and the Chief warden also, have their Lieftenants in the Forest.

A lieftenant of a shire, Præfectus limitaneus, Custos limitis.

A liege-man, Ligeus, ei, m. Spel. 448. Lex. 8. Co. postnati. 2.

In lieu, In loco, compensatione.

L I F.

Life, Vita, æ, f.

Liffy river (in Ireland) Libnius.

To lift up, Levo, are.

L I G.

A ligature (any thing to tie with) Ligamentum, i, n.

Ligeance, Ligeantia, æ, f. It sometime signifieth the Dominions or Territory of the Liege Lord, as *anno* 25. *Ed.* 3. *Stat.* 2.

Light horse-men, Equites levis armaturæ.

A lighter-boat, Epholcium, ii, n.

A lighter, Ratiaria, æ, f. Remulus, i, m. Pontonium, ii, n.

The lights or lungs, Pulmo, onis, f.

Ligon Isle on the coasts of France, Liga.

L I M.

A limbeck, Alembicus, ci, m.

Bird-lime, Viscum, ci, n.

Lime Twigs, Calamus aucupatorius, virga, viscata, Festuca viscata.

Lime to make mortar, Calx, cis, f.

A lime Kill, Calcifurnium, ii, n. Spel. 116.

Lime pits, Foveæ calcariæ.

A lime burner (or lime maker) Calcarius, ii, m.

Limitation of assize, Limitatio assisæ. It is a certain time set down by Statute, within the which a man must alledge himself or his Ancestor to have been seised of Lands, sued for by a writ of assise, *vid.* the Statute of *Merton*, *cap.* 8. *anno* 20. *H.* 3. and *West*, 1. *cap.* 38. and *anno* 32. *H.* 8. *cap.* 2. & *anno* 1. *M.* 1. *p.* c. 5.

A limit or bound, Limes, itis, m.

To limit (or set bounds) Limito, are.

Lime, or Limen (in Kent) Ad Portum Lemanis. Lemanis portus, Novus portus.

Lime-house near London, Limo domus.

Lime-hill. *See Lime.*

Limerick county (in Ireland) Limiricensis comitatus.

To limn (or paint with colours) Miniculor, ari.

A limner, Miniculator, oris, m. Miniator, oris, m.

A limning, Miniatura, æ, f.

A limon, Malum limonicum Limones, num, m.

Limsie (the Family) De Limesi.

L I N.

Lin river (in Nottinghamshire) Linus.

A lineage (or stock) Prosapia, æ, f.

Lineal (as lineal descent successive) Linealis, le, adj.

A linck is the tenth part of a Pole, Longitudo & latitudo acræ terræ. Dyer 303. 11 Mon. 313. Stat. de Terris mensurand.

Lincoln City, Caerlincoit, Lincolnia, Lindecolina, Lindecollina civitas,

civitas, Lindecollinum, Lidocolina, Lindocollinum, Lindon, Lindum.

Bishop of Lincoln, Episcopus Lincolniensis.

Lindsey (*a part of Lincolnshire*) Lindesia, Lindisi, Lindisgia.

A line (*which Masons or Carpenters use*) Linea, æ, f.

A line with a plummet, Perpendiculum, li, n.

A slope line, Hypothenusa, æ, f.

A plumb-line (*or level*) Amussis, is, f.

To line, draw, or square out by line or level, Lævigo, are.

To draw a line about, Circumscribo, ere.

A line (*as in writing*) Linea, æ, f.

Line (*or flax*) Linum, i, n.

To line a Garment, Duplico, are. Adduplico, are.

The lining of a garment, Pannus subductitius. Suffultura, æ, f.

To link, Cateno, are. Concateno, are.

A link or Torch, , Funale, lis, n. Fax, acis, f.

Linen, Linteum, i, n.

Fine linen, Linteum tenue, Sindon, ŏnis, f.

Linen wore next the skin, Interula, æ, f.

Cloathed with linen, Linteatus, a, um.

Wearing linen, Liniger, a, um.

A linen wearer, Linteo, onis, m.

A linen work, Linificium, ii, n.

Of linen, Linteus, a, um.

To make linen, Linifico, are.

A linen draper, Lintearius, ii, m.

Linne (*the Family*) De Linna.

Linne (*in Norfolk*) Linum, Linum Regis.

Linsie-woolsie, Linostema, atis, n. Vestis ex Lino & Lana.

Lint (*or rags of linen*) Linteum, i, n.

L I O.

A lion, Leo, ōnis, m.

A lioness, Leæna, æ, f.

Lionel (*a mans name*) Lionellus, li, m.

L I Q.

English liquorish, Glycyrrhiza Britannica.

Spanish liquorish, Glycyrrhiza Hispanica.

Liquor, Liquor, oris, m.

L I S.

A list (*or line*) Lista, æ, f. Spel. 119. 449.

L I T.

Lithquo (*in Scotland*) Lindum.

Litter (*or straw for horses, &c.*) Littera, æ, f. Substramen, ĭnis, n. 1 Fo. 141.

A horse litter, Lectica, æ, f. Vehiculum cameratum.

Litter-bearers, Liburni, orum, m.

Little, Parvus, a, um.

A little while, Parum, adv.

By little and little, Paulatim.

Littlebourough (*in Nottinghamshire*) Agelocum, Segelocum, Segelogum.

L I U.

Livelihood (*or way of living*) Victus, ûs, m. Ars vivendi, Facultas vivendi, Vitalitium, ii, n.

A living (*or benefice*) *Spiritual or Ecclesiastical*, Victus Ecclesiasticus, Beneficium.

The liver, Jecur, ŏris, n. Hēpar, atis, n.

Hardness of the liver, Scirrhoma, ătis, n.

Of the liver, Hepaticus, a, um.

A livery of cloth, Liberatura, æ, f. Cow. 162. Spel. 445. Liberata, æ, f. West Indictments 183. Livery hath three significations. In one it is used for a suit of Cloth or other Stuff, that a Gentleman giveth in Coats, Cloaks, Hats or Gowns, with cognisance or without, to his servants or followers. *Anno* 1. *Ric*. 2. *cap*. 7. *&* *anno* 20. *Ejusdem*, *cap*. 1. *anno* 8. *H*. 6. *&* *anno* 8. *Ed*. 4. *cap*. 3. *&* *anno* 3. *H*. 7. *cap*. 1, &c.

In the other signification it betokeneth a delivery of Possession.

Livery in the third signification, is the writ which lieth for the heir to obtain the Possession, or seising of his Lands at the Kings hands, which see in *Fitz*. *nat*. *brev*. *fol*. 155.

Livery of seisin, Liberatio seisinæ. Livery of Seisin, is a solemnity that the Law requireth for the passing of a Free-hold, or Lands or Tenements, by delivery of Seisin thereof. There are two kinds of Livery of Seisin, *viz*. a Livery in Deed, and a Livery in Law.

A Livery in Deed, is when the Feoffer taketh the Ring of the Door, or Turf, or Twig of the Land, and delivereth the same upon the Land to the Feoffee, in the name of Seisin of the Land.

A Livery in Deed may be two manner of ways, by a solemn act and words, as by delivery of the Ring, or hasp of the Door, or by a branch or twig of a Tree, or by a turf of the Land, and with these, or the like words, the Feoffer and Feoffee, both holding the Deed of the Feoffment, and the ring of the door, hasp, branch, twig, or turff, and the Feoffer saying, Here I deliver you Seisin and Possession of this House, in the name of Seisin, and Possession of all the Lands contained in this Deed; or, Enter you into this House or Land, and have and enjoy it according to the Deed; or, Enter into the House or Land, and God give you joy; or, I am content you shall enjoy this Land, according to the Deed, or the like. *Cook on Lit*. *l*. 1. *c*. 7. *Sect*. 59.

A Livery in Law, is when the Feoffer saith to the Feoffee, being in view of the House or Land (I give to you yonder Land, to you and your Heirs, and therefore enter into the same, and take Possession thereof accordingly) and the Feoffee doth accordingly in the life of the Feoffer enter; This is a good Feoffment, for *Signatio pro traditione habetur*. But if either Feoffer or the Feoffee die before the entry, the Livery is void, and delivery within the view is good, where there is no Deed of Feoffment: and such a Livery is good, albeit the Land lie in another County. *Cook on Lit*. *l*. 1. *c*. 7. *Sect*. 59. and 5. *Rep*. *Sharps case*.

There is a diversity between the Livery of Seisin of Land, and the delivery of a Deed; for if a man deliver a Deed without saying of any thing, it is a good delivery; but to a Livery of Seisin of Land, words are necessary; as taking in his hand the Deed, and the Ring or the Door (if it be an House) or a Turf or Twig, (if it be of Land) and the Feoffee laying his hand on it, the Feoffer says to the

the Feoffee, Here I deliver to you Seisin of this House, or of this Land, in the name of all the Land contained in this Deed, according to the Form and effect of the Deed; and if it be without Deed, then the words may be, Here I deliver you Seisin of this House or Land, to have and to hold to you for Life, or to you, and the heirs of your body, or to you and your heirs for ever. When one makes Livery of Seisin, this Livery shall be taken most strong against him.

And therefore if one give Land to a man *& hæredibus*, this shall be a Fee-simple to him, although *suis* be left out, and yet he gives not Fee-simple expresly, but because every Livery shall be taken most strongly against him that makes it. *Plowden, Colthrist* against *Beinshin.*

Livia (a Womans name) Livia, æ, f.

L I Z.

Lizard point (in Cornwall) Danmoniorum prom. Ocrinum prom.

L O A.

A load (or burthen) Onus, ĕris, n.

A load to avoid water, Lada, æ, f. Spel. 4.

To load, Onero, are.

A loader, Onĕrātor, oris, m.

A load-stone, Magnes, etis, m.

A loaf of bread, Unus panis. Collyra, æ, f.

Loam (or mudwall) Lutamentum, i, n.

Loam tempered with Chopt straw, Lutum paleatum.

L O B.

A lobby (or antichamber) Antithalamus, i, m.

L O C.

Local, Localis, le, adj. It signifieth in our Common Law, as much as fixed or annexed to a place certain, Example, The thing is local, and annexed to the Freehold. *Kitchin fol.* 180. And again in the same place:

An Action of Trespass for Battery, &c. is transitory and not local; that is, not needful, that the place of the Battery should be set down as material, in the Declaration: or if it be set down, that the Defendant should traverse the Place set down, by saying he did not commit the Battery in the place mentioned in the Declaration, and so avoid the Action. And again, *fol.* 230. The Place is not local, that is, not material to be set down in certainty; and the guard of the Person and of the Lands differeth in this, because the person being transitory, the Lord may have his Ravishment *de garde*, before he be seised of him, but not of the Land, because it is *local*, *Perkins Graunts*. 30.

Locus partitus, Signifieth a division made between two Towns or Counties, to make Trial in whether the Land or Place in Question lieth. *Fleta lib.* 4. *cap.* 15. *num.* 1.

Locii (the Family) De Lasey.

A lock of a door, Sera, æ, f.

A spring-lock, Sera laconica.

The

The key of a ſpring-lock, Clavis laconica.

To lock, Sero, are.

A lock-ſmith, Faber Serarius.

A lock (or flock) of wool, Floccus, i, m.

A lock of hair, Cirrus, i, m.

A curled lock of hair, Cincinnus, i, m.

Locks and Tores, Capilli intorti.

L O D.

To lodge (or ſojourn) Hoſpitor, ari.

A lodge, Logia, æ, f. 1 Mon. 759. 880. 2 Lon. 610. Logia, æ, f. Co. Ent. 71. Tugurium, ii, n.

A little lodge, Tuguriolum, i, n.

A lodge (or ſummer-houſe) Nubilarium, ii, n. Suffugium Imbris & ſolis.

A lodging, Diverſorium, i, n. 1 Fo. 32. Lectus, i, m. 1. Fo. 63. Hoſpitium, ii, n. 1 Fo. 74. Hoſpitatio, onis, f.

Lodowick (a mans name) Lodovicus, i, m.

L O F.

A loft, Tabulatum i, n.

An upper loft, Piſaculum, i, n.

L O G.

Logick (the art of reaſoning and of Diſputation) Logica, æ, f.

A Logician, Logicus, i, m.

Logh, Luthea, or Louthea (in Scotland) Louthea, Leutea.

Loghor (in South-wales) Leucarum.

L O N.

London, Londinenſe oppidum, Londinia, Londinium, Londinum, Londonia, Lundinum, Lundonia, Lundonium.

Biſhop of London, Epiſcopus Londonienſis.

Longchamp (the Family) De longo campo.

Longſpee (the Family) De Longa Spatha.

Longuille (the Family) De longa Villa.

L O O.

A weavers loom, Jugum Textoris.

A loop hole for a button or ſuch like, Tranſenna, æ, f.

To looſe (or unty, or make looſe) Solvo, ere.

L O P.

To lopp, (top, or ſhred trees) Amputo, are.

Lopped, Loppatus,a,um. Plo.469. Ra. Entr. 490.

Lopping, Amputatio, onis, f.

L O R.

A Lord, Dominus, i, m. It is a word of Honour with us, and is uſed diverſely. Sometime being attributed to a man, that is Noble by Birth or Creation, which ſort are otherwiſe called Lords of the Parliament. Alſo to the ſons of a Duke, or the eldeſt Son of an Earl, &c. Sometime to men honourable by Office, as Lord Chief Juſtice, &c. and ſometime to a mean man that hath Fee, and ſo conſequently the Homage of Tenants within his mannor; for by his Tenants he is called Lord, and by none other; and in ſome places, for diſtinction ſake, he is called Landlord. It is uſed nevertheleſs by the writers of the Common Law, moſt uſually in this ſignification: And ſo it is divided into Lord above, and Lord *Meſne*; Lord *Meſne* is he that is owner of a Mannor, and by Vertue thereof, hath Tenants holding of him in Fee; and by Copy of Court roll, and yet holdeth himſelf under a ſuperior Lord, who is called Lord above, or Lord *Paramount*, *Old nat. brev. fol.* 79.

A young Lord, Dominulus, li, m.

Titular Lords, Domini Honorarii.

Lordſhip (or Signiory) Dominium, ii, n.

A Lordſhip or Privileged place with Power to keep Courts, Soca, æ, f.

Lordly (or ſtately) Imperioſus, a, um.

L O S.

Loſs, Deperditum, i, n. Amiſſus, ûs, m.

Loſt, Amiſſus, a, um.

L O U.

Lovel (the Family) Lupellus.

A lover (or tunnel on the top of a [illegible] *or houſe to let out the ſmoake)* [illegible]mentum, i, n. Fumarium, [illegible]

Lovet (the Family) Lupellus.

Loughborough (in Leiceſterſhire) *See Lutterworth.*

Lough Corbes (in Ireland) Anſoba, Auſoba.

Lough der (in Ireland) Logia fluvia.

Lough Erne (in Ireland) Lacus Ernus.

Lough longus (in Scotland) Longus Fluvius.

Louth County (in Ireland) Luva. Luda.

L O W.

A low bell, Campanola, æ, f.

A low beller, Campanolator, oris, m.

L U C.

Lucan (a mans name) Lucanus, i, m.

Luce (a womans name) Lucina, æ, f.

Good luck, Fauſtitas, atis, f.

Luckily, (happily) Fauſtè, adv.

Lucrece (a womans name) Lucretia, æ, f.

L U G.

Lug river (in Herefordſhire) Lugus fluvius.

L U K.

Luke (a mans name) Lucas, æ, m.

St. Lukes day, Feſtum Sancti Lucæ Evangeliſtæ.

L U M.

A lump (heap, or maſs) Cumulus, i, m.

L U N.

LUN.

The lungs (or lights) Pulmo, onis, m.

LUR.

A lurcher (Dog) Lurco onis, m. Lurcherius, ii, m.

A lure for a hawk, Illubra, æ, f. Revocatorium accipitrum, Scapus pinnarum.

To lure a hawk, Affuefacere accipitrem revocatorio.

LUT.

A lute, Teſtudo, inis, f. Barbiton, ti, n.

A lutaniſt, Barbitiſta, æ, m.

A lute ſtring, Chorda, æ, f.

Lutterworth (in Leiceſterſhire) Lactodorum, Lactodurum, Lactorodum, Lactorudum.

LYC.

Lycaſte (a womans name) Lycaſte, es, f.

Lycurgus (a mans name) Lycurgus, i, m.

LYD.

Lydia (a womans name) Lydia, æ, f.

LYN.

Lyned, Duplicatus, a, um.

MAB.

M*Abel (a womans name)* Mabella, æ, f.

MAC.

A mace, Clava, æ, f. Geſtamen, inis, n.

A ſerjeant at mace, Serviens ad Clavam.

Macegriefs, Macherarii, orum, m. (*i. e.*) thoſe that wittingly buy and ſell ſtoln fleſh. *Crompt. Juſt. Peace, f.* 193. *a.*

Mace (a ſpice) Macis, is, f.

Maclenith (in Montgomeryſhire) Maglova, Maglona.

MAD.

Mad, Inſanus, a, um.

Madam (a title given to a Lady) Domina mea.

Madneſs, Inſania, æ, f.

Made (or done) Factus, a, um.

A magician, Magus, i, m.

Magick, Magica, æ, f.

Magdalen (a womans name) Magdalena, æ, f.

Magiſtracy (the Office of a Magiſtrate) Magiſtratus, ûs, m.

A Magiſtrate, Magiſtratus, i, m.

The chief Magiſtrate of a City, Major, oris, m.

Magiſteries, Magiſteria, orum, m. (*i. e.*) a Chymical Preparation.

Magna Charta, called in *Engliſh*, the Great Charter, Is a Charter containing a number of Laws, ordained the ninth year of *Henry* the third, and confirmed by *Edward* the firſt. The reaſon why it was termed *Magna Charta*, was either for that it contained the ſum of all the written Laws in *England*, or elſe that there was another Charter call'd the Charter of the Foreſt, eſtabliſhed with it, which in quantity was the leſſer of the

the two. We have now no ancienter written Law than this, which was thought to be so beneficial to the Subjects, and a Law of so great Equity, in comparison of those, which were formerly in use, that King *Henry* the third was brought but hardly to yield unto it, and had the fifteenth peny of all the moveable goods, both of the Spirituality and Temporalty throughout his Realm. *Holinshed* in *H.* 3. and though his Charter consist not of above 37 Chapters or Laws; yet it is of such extent, as all, or the most part of the Law we have, is thought in some sort to depend upon it. *Vid Polydorus*, and *Holinshed ubi supra.*

Magnanimous, Magnanimus, a, um.

Magnificence, Magnificentia, æ, f.

Magnificent, Magnificus, a, um.

Mago (a mans name) Mago, onis, m.

M A I.

A maid, Virgo, inis, f.

Maid Isle (on the east of Scotland) Emonia.

A maid servant, Serva, æ, f.

A chamber (or waiting) maid, Cubicularia, æ, f. Ancilla Cubicularia.

Maidenhead (in Berkshire) Alaunodunum.

Maidstone (in Kent) Madus vagniacæ, Vagniacum.

Maim, Mahemium, ii, n. Is a Corporal hurt whereby a man loseth the use of any member, that is or might be any defence unto him in Battle. The Canonists call it *Membri Mutilatio* or *Obtruncatio*, as the eye, the hand, the foot, the scalp of the head, his fore teeth, or as some say of any finger of his hand. *Glanvil lib.* 14. *cap.* 7. See *Bracton* at large, *& Brit. cap.* 25. *& Stawnf. pl. cor. lib.* 1. *cap.* 41. and the Law Terms who saith thus; Maim is, where by the wrongful act of another, any Member is hurt, or taken away, whereby the Party so hurt, is made unperfect to fight; as if a Bone be taken out of the Head, or a Bone be broken in any other part, or a foot, or a hand, or finger, or joynt of a foot, or any member be cut, or by some wound the Sinews be made to shrink, or the fingers, or other member made more Crooked, or an Eye be put out, or the fore teeth broken, or any other thing hurt in a mans Body, by means whereof he is made the less able to defend himself, or offend his Enemy. But the cutting off an Ear or Nose, or breaking of the hinder teeth, is no Maim, but rather a Deformity of body, than diminution of Strength; by a maim a member is hurt, or taken away, by reason whereof the Party is less able, and made unperfect to fight.

This offence of Maim is under all Felonies deserving death, and above all other inferiour offences, so as it may be truly said of it, that it is *inter crimina majora minimum & inter minora maximum, vita & membra sunt in potestate Regis.* The life and members of every subject are under the Protection of the King. *Cook on Lit.*

In my Circuit (saith Sir *Edward Cook*) in *anno* 11. *Jacobi Regis*, in the County of *Leicestershire*, one *Wright*, a young, strong, and lusty Rogue, to make himself Impotent, there by thereby to have the more colour to beg, or to be relieved without putting himself to any Labour, caused his Companion to strike off his left hand, and both of them were Indicted, fined, and ransomed therefore. *Cook on Lit. L.* 2. *c.*11. *Sect.* 194.

The Party only shall recover damages in Maim. *Leigh. Phil. Com. fo.*155.*Vide*, the Act of Parliament, call'd the Lord *Coventry*'s Act. In some Cases it is made Felony.

To maim, Mahemio, are. Cow. 164. Co. Lit. 126. Mutilo, are.

Mainprise, Manucaptio, onis, f. It signifieth in our Common Law, the taking or receiving a man into friendly custody, that otherwise is or might, be committed to Prison, and so upon security given for his forth coming at a day assigned.

A mainpernor, Manucaptor, oris, m. (*i.e.*) He that doth thus undertake for any, and receive him into their hands, a Surety, or Bail.

To maintain (*or uphold*) Manuteneo, ere.

Maintenance, Manutenentia, æ. f. In our Common Law it is used in the evil part, for him that secondeth a Cause depending in suit between others, either by Lending of money, or making friends for either party towards his help. *Anno* 32. *H.* 8. *cap.* 9.

Maintenance is most usually done by the hand, either by delivery of money, or other reward, or by writing on the behalf of one of the parties, in a suit depending. *Cooks* 2. *part. of Instit. c.* 28.

When one laboureth the Jury, if it be put to appear, or if he Instruct them to put them in fear, or the like, he is a maintainer, and an action of maintenance lyeth against him.

Manutenentia est duplex. 1. *Curialis*, in Courts of Justice, *pendente placito.* 2. *Ruralis*, to stirr up and maintain complaints, suits, and parts in the County, other than their own, though the same depend not in Plea. *Cooks* 2. *part of Instit. c.* 28.

And when a mans Act in this kind is by Law accounted maintenance, and when not, *vid. Broke titulo* maintenance, and *Kitchin fol.* 202. *& seq. Fitz. nat. brev. fol.* 172. and *Crompt. Jurisdict. fol.*38. The writ that lieth against a man for this offence is likewise called a writ of Maintenance.

A maintainer, Manutentor, oris, m. Lex. 83. Ry. 600. Ra. Entr. 24. *vid. Maintenance.*

M A K.

To make good, Firmam facere. 2 Rol. 738.

M A L.

Malachy (*a mans name*) Malachias, æ, m.

A male (*or satchel*) Bulga, æ, f.

A malefactor, Malefactor oris, m.

Malice, Malitia, æ, f.

Malc on the river Shannon (*in Ireland*) Macolicum.

Maldon (*in Essex*) Colonia victricensis, Camalodunum, Camolodunum, Camoludunum, Camudolanum, Camulodunum, Mealdunum.

A mal-

A malkin (*an Instrument to make an Oven clean*) Peniculus, i, m. Penicillus, i, m. Peniculus furnarius.

A mallet, Tudes, is, f. Busalia, æ, f. Malleolus ligneus.

Mallieure, *commonly Mallyvery* (*the Family*) Malus Leporarius.

Mallovell (*the Family*) Malus Lupellus.

Malmsbury (*in Wiltshire*) Bladunum; fortasse à noto nemore vicino. Maidulphi curia, Maidulphi urbs, Maldunense Monasterium, Malmesburium, Meldunum.

Of Malmsbury, Meldunensis.

Malpas (*in Cheshire*) Malus passus.

Malpas (*the Family*) De Mala Platea & De malo passu.

Malverne (*in Worcestershire*) Malvernia, Malvernum.

M A N.

A Man, Homo, inis, m. Vir, viri, m.

The chief man of a Town or Parish, Sitheundus, i, m. Custos paganus.

The chief man in a rank, Cardinatus, i, m.

A young man, Juvenis, is, c. 2.

A man slayer, Homicida, æ, m.

Man-slaughter, Homicidium, ii, n.

The kindred of a man that is slain, Wallesheria & Wallecheria, æ, f.

The price of a mans Life, Wera, æ, f.

Manhood, Pubertas, atis, f.

Man Island, Eubonia, Mannia, Menavia, Menavia Secunda, Mevania, Mona ulterior (*to distinguish it from Anglesey*) Monabia, Monœda.

Bishop of the Isle of man, Episcopus Menevensis.

Manasses (*a mans name*) Manasses, is, m.

Mancastle (*in Lancashire*) Manucium.

Manchester (*in Warwickshire*) Manduessedum.

Manchester (*in Lancashire*) Mammucium, Mancunium.

To manage, Administro, are.

A Manciple, Opsonator, oris, m. Ash. 188. (*i. e.*) a Caterer, one that in Colleges buyeth Victuals, and common Provisions into the House.

Mandamus, Is a writ that lies to restore a person put out of his Office.

Mandatum. Is a Commandment judicial of the King, or his Justices, to have any thing done for the dispatch of Justice, see more in the Table of the Register Judicial, *verbo Mandatum*.

Mandevil (*the Family*) De Magna Villa & De Mandavilla.

The mandible (*or Jaw*) Mandibulum, i, n.

The mane of a beast, Juba, æ, f. Coma equi.

Manicles (*or Manacles, wherewith Prisoners are bound by the hands*) Manicæ, arum, f.

Many, Multus, a, um.

Manufacture, Manufactura, æ, f.

Manifest, Manifestus, a, um.

A manger, Præsepe, is, n.

A manning (*or mans days work*) Manopera, æ, f.

A Mannor or Lordship, Manerium, ii, n.

A mannor house, Domus Manerialis. Cow. 166. 2 Mon. 348.

A free mannor, Alodium, ii, n.

A Lord of a mannor, Alodarius, ii, m. Dominus Manerii.

Mannours or Mannors (the Family) De Maneriis.

A mantle, Mantelium, ii, n.

A flowred Silk mantle, Loricum Sericum floratum.

Manual, Manualis, le, adj.

A manual (or small portable Volume, a book which may be carried in ones hand) Manuale, is, n.

Manumission, Manumissio, onis, f. (*i. e.*) a freeing of a slave or Villain from his slavery.

Manurance, Manurancia, æ, f.

M A P.

A plank of maple, Mollufcum, ci, n.

A map, for description of Countries or of the whole world, Tabula Cosmographica.

M A R.

March (in Scotland) Marchia.

The month of March, Martius, ii, m.

Marble, Marmor, oris, n.

A slate of marble, a thin Pill crust, or cream, Crustula, æ, f.

A march pane (or spice Cake) Laguneulus, li, m. Panis Dulciarius.

A marching, Expeditio onis, f.

The marches or borders of Wales, Marchiæ Walliæ, Cow. 168. Lex. 21. Pry. 33.

A Marchioness, Marchionissa, æ, f.

Of the Marches (or March the Family) De Marchia.

Marcella (a womans name) Marcella, æ, f.

A mare, Equa, æ, f. Caballa, æ, f.

A mare-colt, Equula, æ, f.

A margin, Margo, inis, d. g.

A mariner, Nauta, æ, f.

Maritime (or by the Sea) Maritimus, a, um.

A mark (note or sign) Stigma, æ, f. (*i. e.*) a mark made with a burning iron, such as Rogues are burned in the hand with, and horses on the buttock or foreshoulder to be known by.

A mark to shoot at, Meta, æ, f.

A sea mark (or Beacon with a light, to direct ships into the Haven in dark night) Pharus, i, m.

A Mark of money in Silver, 13 s. 4 d. in Gold eight Ounces, Marca, æ, f. We use ordinarily, *Tredecim Solidos & quatuor Denarios*, unless in translation of Deeds.

A Mark of Silver, Mancusa, æ, f.

Mark (a mans name) Marcus, i, m.

St. *Marks day*, Festum sancti Marci Evangelistæ.

To mark upon the edge, Præsigno, are.

A market, Mercatum, i, n. Cow. 169.

A fish-market, Piscaria, æ, f. Macellum, i, n. Cetariorum, i, n.

A market-woman, Foraria, æ, f.

Money given for standing in the market. Mesiticum, ci, n.

To forestall the market, Præmercor, ari.

A forestaller of the Market, Præmercator, oris, m. Propola, æ, m.

Margery (a womans name) Margeria, æ, f.

Marleborough (in Wiltshire) Cunetio, Marlebrigia.

Marle, Marlera, æ, f. Carta de Foreſt. Ra. Ent. 690. 697. Marla, æ, f. Lex. 84. Marlia, æ, f. Reg. Indic. 23. 25. Terra marlanda vel melioranda. 1 Mon. 722. Marga, æ, f.

A marle-pit, Marlerium, ii, n. Lex. 84. Margarium, ii, n.

Marmaduke (a mans name) Marmaducus, i, m.

Marmalade, Cotoneatum, i, n. Gelatina Cydoniorum.

A Marqueſs, Marchio, onis, m. They are Lords of dignity, and are in Honour and account next unto Dukes.

A marquiſate (or marquiſhip) Marchionatus, ûs m.

Marriable (or Marriageable) Nūbilis, le.

The Marriage bed, Lectus jugalis.

Marriage, Maritagium, ii, n.

A Marriage (or wedding) Nuptiæ, arum, f.

A contract of marriage, Pactio nuptialis.

To marry, Marito, are.

Married, Maritatus, a, um.

A fine to the Lord for the marriage of a tenants daughter, Marchetum, i, n.

Marrow, Medula, æ, f.

A marſh or watery ground, Mariſcus, i, m.

Freſh marſh, Mariſcus friſcus.

Salt marſh, Mariſcus falſus.

Lord marſhal of England, Magnus Mareſchallus Angliæ. Mention is made in divers Statutes of this Lord or Earl Marſhal of *England*. *Anno* 1. *H*. 4. *cap*. 7. *&* 14. *& anno* 13. *R*. 2. *ca*. 2. His Office conſiſteth eſpecially in matters of War and Arms, as well with us, as in other Countries, whereof you may read in *Lupanus*, and *Tilius*, *Lib*. 2. *ca. de Coneſtabili*, *mariſcallo*, *&c*. But he that will know the Office of our Lord Marſhall, beſide the few Statutes which concern him, muſt read his Commiſſion, and alſo have acceſs to the Heralds, who out of their Antiquities are able to diſcover much, that by preſcription belongeth unto this Office.

A Vice-Marſhal, Vice-mareſchallus, i, m.

A marſhals man that ſcourges offenders, Lorarius, ii, m.

March (the Family) Mariſca.

Le marſhal (the Family) Mareſcallus.

The marſhalſee, Mareſcaltia, æ, f. It is the Court of the Marſhal (or word for word) the ſeat of the Marſhal, of whom ſee *Crompt. Juriſdict. fol*. 102. It is alſo uſed for the Priſon in Southwark the reaſon whereof may be, becauſe the Marſhall of the Kings houſe was wont perhaps to ſit there in Judgment. See the Statute *anno* 9. *R*. 2. *cap*. 5. *& anno* 2. *H*. 4. *ca*. 23.

Letters of mart or marque, Literæ repriſatoriæ.

Mart, Literæ priſales.

Counter mart, Repriſales.

Martha (a womans name) Martha, æ, f.

Martin (a mans name) Martinus, i, m.

St. Martins day, Feſtum Sancti Martini Epiſcopi.

Martial Law, Lex Martialis, Jus Militare. Is the Law that dependeth upon the voice of the King, or the Kings Lieutenant in Wars, for although the King for the Indifferent and equal temper of Laws, to to all his ſubjects, do not in time of Peace make any Laws, but by the conſent of the three Eſtates in Parliament; yet in Wars, by reaſon of great dangers, riſing of ſmall occaſions, he uſeth abſolute Power; in ſo much as his word goeth for Law; and this is called Martial Law. *Smith de Rep. angl. lib.* 2. *cap*. 3. See Law of Arms.

Marre (in Scotland) Marria.

Martlemas (or Martimas) beef, Caro fumo durata, Caro infumata.

Mary (a Womans name) Maria, æ, f.

M A S.

Maſham bridge (in Yorkſhire) Maſſamenſis pons.

The maſh (or meſh) of a net, Macula retis, foramen retis.

A mask, Maſca, æ, f. 1 Fo. 89. Larva, æ, f.

Maſlin (or meſlin) Wheat and Rye, Mixtilio, onis, f. Farrago, inis, f.

A maſon, Cœmentarius, ii, m. Lapicida, æ, m. Macerio, onis, m.

Maſons, that work upon ſcaffolds, Machiones, m. pl.

A maſs (or lump of any thing) but properly of Dough in the Kneading Trough, Maſſa, æ, f.

The maſt of a ſhip, Malus, i, m.

The top of the maſt, (or ſcuttel of the maſt) Carcheſium, ii, n.

Maſt of Oak, &c. Hogs meat, Glans, dis, f.

To feed hogs with maſt, Maſto, are. Paſch 9. H. 8. *in C. B.*

Feeding with maſt, Maſtatio, onis, f. ibid.

A maſter, Magiſter, tri, m.

A ſchool maſter, Ludimagiſter, tri, m.

A maſter of arts, Magiſter artium, in artibus Magiſter.

Maſter of the rolls, Magiſter Rotulorum Curiæ Cancellariæ Domini Regis. He is an aſſiſtant to the Lord Chancellor of *England*, in the high Court of Chancery, and in his abſence heareth Cauſes there, and giveth Orders. *Cromp. Juriſdict.* fol. 41. his Title in his Patents (as I have heard) is *Clericus parvæ bagæ, cuſtos Rotulorum & domus converſorum*. This *Domus converſorum*, is the place where the Rolls are Kept, ſo called, becauſe the *Jews* in ancient times, as they were any of them brought to Chriſtianity, were beſtowed in that houſe, ſeparately from the reſt of their Nation by King *Henry* the third, who erected this houſe. Vid. *Cambden*, and King *Edward* the third appointed it afterward for Rolls and Records. At this day it is ſtill called the Rolls. Sir *Thomas Smith lib.* 2. *cap.* 10. *de Repub. Angl.* ſaith, that he might not unfitly be called *Cuſtos archivorum*. He ſeemeth to bear the beſtowing of the Offices of the ſix Clerks, *anno* 14. & 15. *H. cap.* 8. *Vid.* Chancery.

Maſters of the Chancery, Magiſtri Cancellarii. They are aſſiſtants in Chancery to the Lord Chancelor, or Lord keeper of the Great Seal in matters of Judgment, of theſe there be ſome Ordinary, and ſome extraordinary. Of Ordinary, there are twelve in number, whereof the Maſter of the Rolls is chief; whereof ſome ſit in Court every day of the term, and have committed unto them (at the Lord Chancelors diſcretion) the Interlocutory report, and ſome-

ſometime the final determination of Cauſes there depending.

Maſter of the Court of Wards and Liveries, Magiſter Curiæ Wardi & Liberaturæ. He is the chief and Principal Officer of the Court of Wards and Liveries, named and aſſigned by the King, to whoſe Cuſtody the Seal of the Court is committed. He at the entring upon his Office, taketh an Oath before the Lord Chancelor of *England*, well and truly to ſerve the King in his Office, to Miniſter equal Juſtice to Rich and Poor to the beſt of his Cunning, Wit, and Power, diligently to procure all things, which may honeſtly and juſtly be to the Kings advantage and Profit, and to the Augmentation of the Rights and Prerogative of the Crown, truly to uſe the Kings Seal appointed to his Office, to endeavour to the uttermoſt of his Power, to ſee the King juſtly anſwered, of all ſuch Profits, rents and revenues, and Iſſues, as ſhall yearly riſe, grow or be due to the King in his Office, from time to time, to deliver with ſpeed ſuch as have to do before him, not to take or receive of any perſon any Gift or reward, in any caſe or matter depending before him, or wherein the King ſhall be Party, whereby any prejudice, loſs, hindrance, or diſheriſion, ſhall be or grow to the King, *Anno* 33. *H.* 8. *cap.* 33.

Maſter of the Horſe, Magiſter Equorum Domini Regis. Is he that hath the Rule and Charge of the Kings ſtable, being an office of high account, and always beſtowed upon ſome Nobleman, both valiant and Wiſe. The Maſter of the Horſe is mentioned *Anno* 39. *Eliz. cap.* 7. *&* *anno* 1. *Ed.* 6. *cap.* 5.

Maſter of the Poſts, (*or Poſt-maſter of England*) Magiſter curſorum Angliæ. Is an officer of the Kings Court, that hath the appointing, placing, and diſplacing of all ſuch through *England*, as provide Poſt-horſes for the ſpeedy paſſing of the Kings Meſſengers, and other buſineſs, in the through fair Towns where they dwell; as alſo to ſee that they keep a certain number of convenient horſes of their own, and when occaſion is, that they provide others, wherewith to furniſh ſuch as have warrant from him to take Poſt-horſes, either from or to the Sea, or other borders, or places within the Realm. He likewiſe hath the Care to pay them their wages, and make their allowance accordingly, as he ſhall think meet. This Officer is mentioned *Anno* 2. *Ed.* 6. *cap.* 3. but now altered by the late Statutes.

Maſter of the Ordinance, Magiſter Machinariorum Domini Regis. Is a great Officer, to whoſe care all the Kings Ordnance and Artillery is committed, being ſome great man of the Realm. *Anno* 39. *Eliz. cap.* 7.

Maſter of the Armory, Magiſter Armamentarii Domini Regis. Is he that hath the Care and overſight of his Majeſties Armour, for his Perſon or Horſes, or any other Proviſion or ſtore thereof in any ſtanding Armories; with command, and placing and diſplacing of all inferior Officers thereunto appertaining. Mention is made of him *Anno* 39. *Eliz. cap.* 7.

Maſter of the Kings Muſter, Magiſter & Recenſor Militum Domini

Regis.

Regis. Is a martial officer, in all Royal Armies most necessary, as well for the maintaining the forces complete, well armed and trained, as also for prevention of such frauds, as otherwise may exceedingly wast the Princes treasure, and extreamly weaken the Forces. He hath the Oversight of all the Captains and Bands, and ought to have at the beginning delivered unto him by the Lord General, perfect Lists and Rolls of all the forces, both horse and foot, Officers, *&c.* with the rates of their allowances signed by the Lord General, for his direction and discharge, in signing warrants for their full Pay. This Officer is mentioned in the Statute *Anno* 2. *Ed.* 6. *cap.* 2. and Muster Master General, *anno* 35. *Eliz. cap.* 4. If you desire to read more of him, see Mr. *Digs* his *Stratioticos.*

Master of nhe Wardrobe, Magister Garderobæ Domini Regis. Is a great and Principal Office in Court, having his habitation and dwelling house belonging to that Office call'd the Wardrobe, near Puddle wharf in *London*; he hath the Charge and Custody of all former Kings and Queens ancient Robes, remaining in the Tower of *London*, and all hangings of Arras, Tapestry or the like, for his Majesties houses, with the bedding remaining in standing Wardrobes, as *Hampton-Court*, *Richmond*, &c. he hath also the charge and delivering out, of all either Velvet or Scarlet, allowed for Liveries to any of his Majesties servants of the Privy Chamber, or others. Mention is made of this Office, *Anno* 39. *Eliz. cap.* 7.

Master of the Kings houshold, Magister Hospitii Domini Regis. Is in his Just Title called Grand Master or Great Master of the Kings Houshold, and beareth the same Office that he did, that was wont to be called Lord Steward of the Kings most honourable houshold, *Anno* 32. *Hen.* 8. *cap.* 39. whereby it appeareth that thename of this Office was then changed.

Master of the Jewel house, Magister Domus Jocalium Domini Regis. Is an Officer in the Kings houshold of great Credit, being allowed Bouge of Court, that is, closet diet for himself and the Inferiour Officers, *viz.* Clerks of the Jewel house, and a special Lodging or Chamber in the Court, having charge of all Plate of Gold, of Silver double or parcel gilt, used or occupied for the King or Queens board, or to any Officer of account, attendant in Court, and of all Plate remaining in the Tower of *London*, of chains and loose Jewels not fixed to any Garment, mention is made of this Officer, *Anno* 39. *Eliz. cap.* 7.

Master of the Mint, Magister Monetarii Domini Regis. Anno 2. Hen. 6. cap. 14. he is now called Warden of the mint, who is the Chief of the Officers belonging to the mint, and is by his Office to receive the Silver of the Goldsmiths, and to pay them for it, and to oversee all the rest belonging to this Function, his Fee is a hundred Pounds *per annum.*

Master of the revels and masques, Magister Jocorum, Revellorum & Mascarum.

Master-ship, Magisterium, ii, n.

The master of a ship, Patronus, i, m.

The masters mate, Optio gubernatoris, Socius Magistri, Proreta, æ, m.

One that runs from his master, Herifuga, æ, m.

A mastiff dog, Molossus, i, m.

A mastiffs collar, made with leather and nails, Millum, i, n.

M A T.

A matt, Storea, æ, f. Teges, itis, f.

A match to keep fire, commonly made of a fine kind of cord, Myxus, i, m. Fomes igniarius.

A match (or wiek of a candle) Fungus Lucernæ, Lucernarium, ii, n.

A match made of Brimstone, or like matter, and a card apt to take fire, Sulphuratum, i, n.

Materialed, Materiatus, a, um.

A matricide (one that killeth his own Mother, Matricida, æ, m.

A matron, Matrona, æ, f.

Matter (or substance whereof any thing is made) Materia, æ, f.

It makes no matter, Nihil refert.

Material, Materialis, le, adj.

Matthew (a mans name) Matthæus, i, m.

Matthias (a mans name) Matthias, æ, m.

St. *Matthews day*, Festum Sancti Matthæi Apostoli.

A mathematician, Mathematicus, i, m.

A mattock (or pick-axe) Marra, æ, f. Bipalium, ii, n.

Matrafal (in Montgomerishire) Mediolanum.

M A U.

A maund (or great basket) Canistrum, i, n.

Mault, Brasium, ii, n.

Sweetish mault, Brasium dulciculum.

Maulting (or mault making) Granificium ii, n.

A mault-house, Brasitorium, ii, n.

A mault kiln, Fumarium farrarium.

Mault, meal (or flour) Polenta, æ, f.

A maulster, Brasiator, oris, m.

Mauley (the Family) De Malo Lacu.

Maurice (a mans name) Mauritius, ii, m.

M A W.

Mawd (a womans name) Matilda, æ, f.

Mawdlin (a womans name) Magdalena, æ, f.

M A X.

Maximilian (a mans name) Maximilianus, i, m.

M A Y.

The month of may, Maius, i, m.

M E A.

A mead or meadow, Pratum, i, n.

Meal of wheat, Farina triticea.

Meal of barley, Farina hordeacea.

Meal of oats, Farina avenacea.

The refuse of meal, Bultellum, i, n. Lex. 22.

To sift meal, Subcerno, ere.

A meal

A meal ſive, Cribrum pollinarium.

A meal-trough, Farinarium, ii, n.

Mean (*or meſne*) Medius, ii, m.

Mean rates, Mediæ ratæ.

Mean profits, Media proficua.

The meaſels (*a diſeaſe*) Morbilli, orum, m.

A meaſh-vat, Vas Pandoxatorium.

A meaſure, Menſura, æ, f.

A meaſure of ten buſhels, Mitta, æ, f.

Heaped meaſure, Cumulus, i, m.

To meaſure, Menſuro, are.

To meaſure out by feet, Podiſmo, are.

The meaſuring of ſolid things, Stereometrica, æ, f.

Meat (*food or victuals*) Eſculenta, æ, f. Ry. 48.

Baked meat, Pinſum, i, n.

Dainty meat, Daps, apis, f.

Roaſt meet, Aſſum, i, n. Aſſatura, æ, f.

Boiled meat, Elixum, i, n. Caro elixa.

A meſs of meat, Geſtarius, ii, m. Ferculum, i, n.

A diſh of ſeveral ſorts of Meat, Sătūra, æ, f.

Diſhes of meat, Vaſa eſcharia.

White meats, made of milk, cream, butter, &c. Lactaria, orum, n. Lacticinia, orum, n.

Minced meat, Minutal, alis, n.

A chop of meat, Offa, æ, f.

A tid bit, meat well dreſſed, Pulpamentum, i, n.

To dreſs meat, Coquinor, ari.

A dreſſing of meat, Coctura, æ, f.

One that brings in meat and ſets it on the Table, Infertor, oris, m.

Meath county (*in Ireland*) Media, Midia.

Of Meath, Midenſis.

Meaux abby (*in Yorkſhire*) Monaſterium de Melſa.

M E C.

Mechanical, Mechanicus, a, um.

M E D.

Medemenham (*in —*) Mediamnis.

A Medicine, Drug or Phyſick, Medicina, æ, f. Pharmacum, i, n.

Medway River (*in Kent*) Medegnaia, Medweagus.

A meer, Mera, æ, f. Spel. 425. Lex. 21.

M E G.

The megrim (*a pain in the Temples of the Head*) Hemicrania, æ, f.

M E L.

Mela, one of the Hebrides (*in Scotland*) Maleos.

Melchiſedeck (*a mans name*) Melchiſedecus, i, m.

Melius inquirendo, Is a writ that lyeth for a ſecond Inquiry, as what Lands and Tenements a man died ſeiſed of, where partial dealing is ſuſpected upon the writ, *Diem clauſit extremum. Fitz. nat. brev. fol.* 255.

To melt (or make soft by Fire) Liquesco, ere. Liquefacio, ere.

A melter, Fusor, oris, m. Liquefactor, oris, m.

Melted, Fusus, a, um. Liquatus, a, um.

A melting, Fusura, æ, f.

A melting-house for metal, Ustrina, æ, f.

M E M.

A member (or part of the body properly) Membrum, i, n.

Memorable (or worthy of remembrance) Memorabilis, le, adj. Memorandus, a, um.

A memorial (sign or Monument of remembrance) Memoriale, lis, n.

M E N.

A mender (or repairer) Refector, oris, m.

A mending (or repairing) Refectio, onis, f.

A menial servant, Menialis Serviens.

Mention (or a mentioning of any thing) Mentio, onis, f.

Fit to be mentioned, Commĕmŏrandus, a, um.

To make mention, Memoro, are. Mentionem facere.

M E R.

Mercenary, Mercenarius, a, um.

A Mercer that selleth all kinds of small wares by retail, Tabernarius, ii, m. Propola, æ, m.

A Mercer that selleth Silks and Velvets as in London, Mercerus, i, m. Metaxarius, ii, m. Serico-pola, æ, m.

M E.

Mercery, Mercimonia, æ, f. Merceria, æ, f. Pry. 157.

A merchant, Mercator, oris, m.

A merchant adventurer, Mercator & negotiator.

A merchant Taylor, Mercator scissor.

To deal as a merchant (to sell) Merchandizo, are.

A society of Merchants, Hausa, æ, f.

Merchandize, Mercandiza, æ, f.

Mercury (a mans name) Mercurius, ii, m.

Mercy, Misericordia, æ, f.

Merionithshire (in Wales) Merionithia, Mervinia, Terra filiorum Canæni.

M E S.

Meschines (the Family) De Micenis.

The mesentery (or midle of the Bowels or Entrails) Mesenterium, ii, n.

A message (or errand) Nuncium, ii, n. Nunciatum, i, n.

A mess of pottage, Ferculum jusculi.

A messenger, Veredarius, ii, m. Nunciator, oris, m. Fero, onis, m. Nuncius, ii, m.

A mesuage, Mesuagium, ii, n. Co. Lit. 56. Is a dwelling house, *West part* 2.*Symb. Tit. Fines Sect.* 26. But by the name of a mesuage may pass also a Courtilage, a Garden, an Orchard, a Dove-house, a Shop, a Mill as parcel of an house, as he himself confirmeth out of *Bract. Lib.* 5.*cap.* 28. *Sect.* 1. and *Plowd. fol.* 199, 170, 171. and of himself, he avoucheth the like of a Cottage, a Toft, a Chamber, a Cellar, &c. yet

yet they may be demanded by their single names.

M E T.

Metal, Metallum, i, n.
Latten-metal, Orichalcum, i, n.
A method (or order) Methodus, i, f.
A metropolis, mother city, chief city or town, Metropolis, is, f.
A metropolitan (or Arch-bishop) Metropolitanus, i, m.

M E W.

Mews (the Family) De Melsa.

M I C.

Michael (a mans name) Michael, lis, m.
Michaels mount (in Cornwal) Mons Michaelis.
Michelney (in Somersetshire) Michelnia.
Michaelmas day, Festum Sancti Michaelis archangeli.

M I D.

The middle, Medium, ii, n.
The midriffe, separating the heart and lights from the other nether Bowels, Diaphragma, atis, n.
Middle England, Mercia.
Middle english-men, Mercii.
Middleham (in Yorkshire) Mediolanium.
Middleton (in Dorsetshire) Middletunensis, Mildetunensis.
Middlesex, Middlesexia.
Midsummer day, Festum Nativitatis Sancti Johannis Baptistæ.
A midwife, Obstetrix, icis, f. Umbilisesca, æ, f.
The midwifes fee, Maotrum, i, n.

M I L.

Mildred (a womans name) Mildreda, æ, f.
A mile, Milliare, is, n. It is a quantity of a thousand paces, otherwise described to contain eight furlongs, and every furlong to contain forty Lugges or Poles, and every Lugge or Pole to contain sixteen foot and a half, *Anno 35. Eliz. cap. 6.*
Miles (a mans name) Milo, onis, m.
Military (or pertaining to War) Militaris, re, adj.
Milk, Lac, lactis, n. pl. caret.
To milk, Mulgeo, ere.
Sowre milk, Lac acidum seu acetosum.
Butter-milk, Lac Butyraceum, Lac pressum, Lac agitatum.
Almond-milk, Lac Amygdalinum.
Turned milk (or milk turned to curds) Lac coagulatum.
A milk-house, vid. *House.*
A milk-maid, Lactaria, æ, f.
A milk-pail, Mulctra, æ, f. Sinum, i, n. Mulgarium vas.
Of milk, Lactarius, a, um.
A milk seller, Galactopola, æ, m.
A mill, Molendinum, i, m.
A wind-mill, Mola alata. Molendinum ventriticum.
A water-mill, Mola aquaria. Molendinum aquaticum.
A hand-mill, Mola manualis vel Trusatilis, Moletrina, æ, f.

A horse or ass mill, Mola Asinaria, Mola Equaria.

An oyl-mill (or a mill for oyl) Trapetum, i, n.

A fulling mill, Molendinum Fullonicum, Multo, onis, m.

A sider-mill, Molendinum Pomarium.

A mault-mill, Molendinum Brasitorium.

A corn-mill, Bladonicum Molendinum.

A smelting-mill, Molendinum plumbarium.

A mill-house, Domus molendinaria.

The hopper of a mill, Infundibulum, i, n.

The upper mill-stone, Catillus, li, m.

The under milstone, Meta, æ, f.

A milstone, Mola pro Molendino Pry. 185. Saxum molare Lapis molaris.

A mill clapper, Crepitaculum molare, Taratantarium, ii, n.

A pair of mill clappers, Par Malleorum.

The site of a mill, Situs Molendini.

Ground or running Work, tackling for mills, Instrumenta currentia.

A mill door, Janua molendinaria.

Fenders belonging to a mill, Emissaria, orum, n.

Locks belonging to a mill, Fluvialia, orum, n.

The trendle of a mill, Molucrum, i, n.

A mill Pool (or Pond) Stagnum, i, n.

A pond head belonging to a mill, Caput Stagni.

A mill dam, Castellum, i, n. Commatum, i, n.

A milleate, Emissarium, ii, n.

Mill-dust, Pollen inis, n.

Pertaining to a mill, Molaris, re, adj. Molarius, a, um.

A miller, Molitor, oris, m. Molendarius, ii, m. Pollinctor, oris, m.

A millers wife, Molitrix, icis, f.

The millers toll, Multura, æ, f.

Millet (Corn) Milium, ii, n.

Millicent (a womans name) Milicentia, æ, f.

The milt, Lien, is, m.

Milford haven (in Wales) Alaunicus portus.

A million (a thousand times) Decies centum millia.

M I N.

A mine, Minera, æ, f. Fodina, æ, f.

A mine of gold, Aurifodina, æ, f. Auraria, æ, f.

A silver mine, Argenti-fodina, æ, f.

A miner, Minerarius, ii, m. 2. Ro. 547. Minetarius, ii, m. 2 Inst. 578.

A mine of brass, Æraria, æ, f. Ærifodina, æ, f.

A mine of iron, Ferri-fodina, æ, f. Ferraria, æ, f.

A Mine, Cave or Trench digged under ground, whereby to undermine the walls of a City, &c. Cuniculus, li, m.

To undermine, Subruo, ere. Cuniculos agere.

Undermined, Subrutus, a, um.

Mineral (or any thing that grows in mines, and contains metal) Minerale, lis, adj. Fossilis, le, adj.

To mingle (or mix together) Misceo, ere.

A mi-

A minister, Minister, tri, m. Clericus, ci, m.

The ministry, Ministerium, ii, n.

A minstrell (or fidler) Menestrallus, i, m. Co. Lit. 59. 94. Ry. 553. Fle. 81. Minstrellus, i, m. Tibicen, inis, m.

Minours (the Family) De Mineriis.

A mint (or place were money is coined) Monetarium, ii, n. 1 Mon. 65. 1 Mon. 417. It is the Place where the Kings coin is formed, be it Gold or Silver, which is at this present, and long hath been, *viz.* the Tower of *London*. The Officers belonging to the Mint have not been always alike. At this present they seem to be these. The warden, who is the chief of the rest, whose Office see in Master of the mint. 2. The master worker, who receiveth the Silver from the warden, causeth it to be melted, and delivereth it to the Moniers, and taketh it from them again, when it is made, his allowance is not any set Fee, but according to the Pound weight. The third is the Controller, who is to see that the money be made the Just assize, to oversee the Officers, and control them, if the money be not as it ought to be, his Fee is 100 Marks *per annum*. The Fourth is the Master of the assay, who weigheth the Silver, and seeth whether it be according to Standard, his yearly Fee is also 100 Marks. Fifthly the Auditor to take the accompts, and make them up auditor-like. Sixthly, the Surveyor of the melting, who is to see the Silver cast out, and not to be altered after it is delivered to the melter; which is after the Assay master hath made tryal of it' Seventhly, the Clerk of the Irons who seeth that the Irons be clean and fit to work with. Eighthly the Graver, who graveth the stamps for the money. Ninthly the smiter of Irons, who after they be graven, smiteth them upon the money. Tenthly the melters that melt the Bullion, before it come to the Coyning. Eleventhly the Blanchers, who do aneal, boyle and cleanse the money. Twelfthly the Porter, who keepeth the Gate of the Mint. Thirteen the Provost of the mint, who is to provide for all the Moniers, and to oversee them. Lastly the Moniers, who are some to Sheer the money, some to forge it, some to beat it abroad, some to round it, some to Stamp or Coin it. Their wages is not by the day or year, but uncertain, according to the weight of the money coined by them.

M I R.

A miracle, Miraculum, i. n.

Miraculous, Miraculosus, a, um.

A Quag-mire (or bogg) Palus, i, m.

M I S.

Mischief, Infortunium, ii, n. Pernicies, ei, f.

Mischievous, Perditus, a, um. Perniciosus, a, um.

To misconstrue, Detorqueo, ere.

A misdeed, Male-factum, i, n.

To misdo, Malefacio, ere.

A misdoer, Malefactor, oris, m.

Misery (or adversity) Miseria, æ, f.

The misne (or misen Sail of a ship) Epidromus, i, m.

Misprision, Missprisio, onis, f. It signifieth in our Common Law, neglect, or negligence, or oversight, Vid. *Stawnf. pl. cor. Lib. 1. cap. 19.* which read at large. *Anno 8. H. 6. cap. 15. Anno 14. Ed. 3. cap. 6. Stat. 1. Crompt.* Just. Peace, *fol. 40. West. part. 2. Symb. Tit.* Indictments, *Sect. 63.* in fine, *anno 14. Eliz. cap. 3. Crompt. Jurisdict. fol. 238.*

A mistery (or Trade) Mysterium, ii, n.

MIT.

A mitre (a Bishops attire of the head) Mitra, æ, f.

Mittimus. A writ whereby Records are sent from one Court to another. *West. part 2. Symb. Tit. Fines, Sect. 138. F. & 154. B.* of divers other uses and applications of this mittimus. See *Regist. Orig.* in the Table of the Book.

MIX.

A mixture, Mixtura, æ, f.

The mixture of other metals with Gold or Silver, Allaia, æ, f.

MOD.

A model (or frame of any thing) Modulus, li, m.

To moderate (or keep a mean) Moderor, ari.

A moderator, Moderator, oris, m.

Modern (or of late time) Modernus, a, um.

Modo & Forma, are words of art in a Process, and namely in the answer of the Defendant, whereby he denyeth himself to have done the thing laid to his charge, *Modo & forma declarata*, in the manner and form declared. *Kitchin fol. 232.* It signifieth as much as that clause in the Civil Law. *Negat allegata, prout allegantur, esse vera.*

MOE.

Moelles (the Family) De Moelis.

MOI.

Le Moigne, or Monk (the Family) De Mona, Monachus.

A moiety (or half part) Medietas, atis, f. Pars media.

MOL.

A mole-catcher, Talpicidus, i, m.

Mole river (in Surrey) Molis.

To molest, Molesto, are.

Molestation, Molestatio, onis, f.

Molines (the Family) De Molendinis, Molendinarius.

MOM.

A moment, Momentum, i, n.

MON.

A monarch, Monarcha, æ, f.

A monarchy (or state of the Commonwealth governed by a Monarch) Monarchia, æ, f.

A monastery, Monasterium, ii, n.

Monday, Dies Lunæ.

A month, Mensis, is, m.

Monthly, Menstruatim, adv. Mensatim, adv.

Money, Moneta, æ, f. Pecunia, æ, f. Yet for moneys we commonly

monly use, *Denarii*, as *Possessionatus de decem libris in Pecuniis numeratis ut de Denariis suis propriis.*

Advance money, Pecunia præparatoria.

Press-money, Auctoramentum, i, n.

Currant money, Pecunia ambulans, æquæ à contrahentibus datur & accipitur.

Ready money, Pecuniæ numeratæ, Præsens pecunia, Argentum præsentaneum.

In ready money, In pecuniis numeratis.

The right or art of coining money, Monetagium, ii, n.

One that maketh the Kings money, Monetarius, ii, m.

To pay ready money, Numerare Pecuniam.

Well monied, Nummosus, a, um.

Money lying unimproved, Sterilis Pecunia.

To judge what a thing is worth in money, Æstimare pecunia.

A money bag, Sparteum, ei, n. Saccus nummarius, Theca nummularia.

Moniers, Monetarii, orum, m. (*i.e.*) Ministers of the Mint, which make and Coin the Kings money. *Regist. Orig. fol.* 262. 6. & *anno* 1. *Ed.* 6. *cap.* 15.

A monk, Monachus, i, m.

Monkery (*the profession of a Monk*) Monachatus, i, m. *Whitlocks* reading in the middle Temple, 2*d. August*, 161[illegible]. upon the *Stat.* 21. *H.* 21. *c.* 13. *de facultatibus Beneficiorum fo.* 23. *his verbis* —— *Defectus.* 1. *Natalium*, as Bastards, Villains, &c. 2. *Morum, ut Criminosi Perjurii.* 3. *Scientiæ*, want of Learning. 4. Civil capacity, as *Monachatus*, *Utlaria*.

A monky, Cercopithecus, i, m.

Monmouth (*in Wales*) Monmuthia, Monumetha, Monumuthia.

Of Monmouth, Monumethensis.

A monopoly (*a sole buying or selling*) Monopolia, æ, f.

Montacute (*in Somersetshire*) Mons acutus.

Montacute (*the Family*) De Monte acuto.

Mont-eagle (*the Family*) De Monte aquilæ.

Montchensey (*the Family*) De Monte Canisio.

Montfichet (*the Family*) De Monte Fixo.

Montgomery (*the Family*) De Monte Gomerico.

Montgomery (*in Wales*) Mons Gomericus, Montgomeria.

Monthermer (*the Family*) De Monte Hermerii.

Montjoy (*the Family*) De Monte Jovis.

Mont-Pesson (*the Family*) De Monte Pessonis.

Mont-pisson (*the Family*) De Monte Pisserio.

Montrose (*in Scotland*) Celurca, Mons rosarum.

A monument, Monumentum, i, n.

M O O.

Moorish ground, Mora, æ, f.

To moor a ship (*or to fasten her that she stick in the mudd*) *to tye or bind her in some Creek or harbour with Cables, or great Ropes.* Navem continenti alligare, navem sistere in Portu, navem deducere, appellere ad Portum.

A moot, Mota, æ, f. (i.e.) a Court or Convention, a Plea, also a Castle, also a Moat or Ditch of water.

M O R.

Moral (or pertaining to manners) Moralis, le, adj.

Morgan (a mans name) Morganus, i, m.

The morning, Aurora, æ, f.

A morsel (or bit) Morsellum i, n.

Mortal, Mortalis, le, adj.

Mortality, Mortalitas, atis, f.

Morter, Intritum, i, n. Lutum, i, n. Cæmentum, i, n.

White morter, Albarium, ii, u.

A tray of morter, Qualus Cæmenti.

To stop with morter, Lio, are.

A mortar, Mortarium, ii, n.

A mortar to pound spice, Fracellium, ii, n.

To bray in a mortar, Pinso, are.

To pound in a mortar, Pinso, ere.

A morgage, Mortgagium, ii, n. Ra. Ent. 3. Co. Ent. 114. Co. Lit. 205. Morganizand. Ra. Entr. 4.

Mortuum vadium, It signifieth in our Common Law, a Pawn of Land or Tenement, or any thing moveable laid or bound for money borrowed, peremptorily to be the Creditors for ever, if the money be not paid at the day agreed upon; and the Creditor holding Land or Tenement upon this bargain, is in the mean time called Tenant in Mortgage. The Cause why it is called Mortgage, is for that it standeth in doubt, whether the Feoffer or the borrower (as you may call him) will pay the money at the day appointed, or not, and if he fail to pay, then the Land which he laid in Gage upon condition of payment of the money, is gone from him for ever, and so dead to him upon Condition. But if he Pay the Money, then is the Gage dead to the Feoffee or Tenant, and for this cause called *Mortuum vadium*, Mortgage, to distinguish it from that which is called *Vivum vadium*. As if a man borrow an hundred Pounds of another, and maketh an Estate of Lands unto him, untill he hath received the said sum of the Issues and profits of the Lands, so as in this case, neither Money nor Land dieth or is lost, and therefore it is called *Vivum vadium*. *Cook on Lit. L.* 3. *c.* 5. *Sect.* 332.

To mortgage, Invadio, are.

A mortgaging, Invadiatio, onis, f. 1. Mon. 478. Ry. 272. Glan. 79. Lex. 73.

Mortimer (the Family) De Mortuo mari.

A mortise, Incastratura, æ, f. Cubilia, um, n. Columbaria, orum, n.

Mortmain, Manus mortua. (*i.e.*) a giving of Lands to a Corporation that never dies.

A mortuary, Mortuarium, ii, n. It is a Gift left by a man at his Death to his Parish Church, for the recompense of his personal Tithes and Offerings, not duly paid in his Life time.

Morpit (in Northumberland) Corstopilum, Corstopitum Curia.

Morsby (in Cumberland) Morbium.

Mortlake (in Surrey) Mortuus lacus.

M O S.

Mosaical work (a work of small inlaid pieces) Mosaicum, i, n. Tessalatum, i, n. Segmentatum, i, n.

Moses (a mans name) Moses, is, m.

A moss,

A moss, Mossa, æ, f. 2. Mon. 632. 636.

Mossy-ground, Mossetum, i, n.

MOT.

A mote round a house, Fossa, æ, f.

A mother, Mater, tris, f.

A mother in law (my wives or husbands mother) Socrus, cri, f.

A mother in law (or a step mother) Matrastra, æ, f. Materiastra, æ, f.

A grand-mother, Avia, æ, f.

The grand-fathers, or grand-mothers Mother, Abavia, æ, f.

The mother tongue (or language) Lingua vulgaris, Lingua Vernacula.

A motion (or moving) Motus, ûs, m. Motio, onis, f.

A motto, Emblema, atis, n.

MOV.

Moveables (or any Goods that can be removed from place to place) Bona mobilia.

To move, Moveo, ere.

A mould (or Form, wherein any thing is framed) Modulus, li, m. Proplasma, atis, n.

Moulds (or patterns) Formamenta, orum.

A moulding board for bread, Tabula pistoria.

The art of making moulds for Image work of clay, Proplastice, es, f.

A mound, Sepimentum, i, n.

Mounds, Clausuræ.

A mountain (or mount) Mons tis, m.

Mountains (in Ossery in Ireland) Bladinæ montes.

A mountebank, Medicaster, tri, m. Circulator, oris, m.

Mounthault (the Family) De Monte Alto.

Mountfort (the Family) De Monte Forti.

A mouse trapp, Muscipula, æ, f.

A mouse catcher, Muscio, onis, m.

The mouth, Os, oris, n.

The mouth (or entrance) Orificium, ii, n.

Things moving alone, Semoventia. 2. Mon. 511. Some watches are called movements.

MOW.

To mowe (or cut Corn, or Hay) Meto, ere. Demeto, ere.

A mow (stack or pile of hay, corn, &c.) Tassa, æ, f. Strues, is, f. Moles, is, f.

Mowbray (the Family) De Mowbraia.

A mower, Messarius, ii, m. Falcarius, ii, m. Fœniseca, æ, m.

Mowings, Messuræ, arum, f. Brac. 35.

To mow grass, Herbam falcare.

To mow or reap corn, Blada metere.

MUE.

A mue for hawks, Mutatorium, ii, n.

MUF.

A womans muffler, Focale, is, n.

MUL.

Mula Island, Maleos, Mula.

The mul of Cantire (a promontory in Scotland) Epidium, Epidiorum.

The mul of Galloway (a promontory in Scotland) Novantum Chersonessus, Novantum Promontorium.

A mule, Mulus, i, m. Mula, æ, f. (*i. e.*) a mule engendred of an ass and a mare.

A mule (*engendred of a horse and she ass*) Burdo, onis, m. Hinnus, i, m.

A muletier (*or mule driver*) Mulio, onis, m. Mulicurius, ii, m.

M U N.

Muncorn, Olicastrum, i, n.

A muniment, Munimentum, i, n. (*i. e.*) a Deed or writing, whereby to defend an Estate.

A muniment house for the keeping of Records, &c. Munimen, inis, n.

A mungrel (*Dog*) Hybrida, æ, m.

Munster (*in Ireland*) Momonia.

M U R.

Murage, Muragium, ii, n. It is a Toll or Tribute to be levied for the building or repairing of publick Edifices or Walls. *Fitz. nat. brev. fol.* 227. *D.* It seemeth also to be a Liberty granted by the King to a Town, for the gathering of money, toward walling of the same. *Anno* 3. *Ed.* 1. *cap.* 30.

To murder, Murdero, are. Ra. Entr. 11. Cow. 177. Brac. 134. Cow. 84. Co. Entr. 24. Murdro, are.

Murder, Murdrum, i, n. It signifieth in our Common Law a wilful and fellonious killing of any other upon prepensed Malice. *Anno* 52. *H.* 3. *cap.* 25. *West part.* 2. *Symb. Tit. Indictments Sect.* 47.

Fleta saith that it was not murder, except it were proved that the party slain were *English*, and no stranger. But as *Stawnford* saith. *Pl. Cor. lib.* 1. *cap.* 2. the Law in this point is altered by the Stat. *Anno* 14. *Ed.* 3. *cap.* 4. and murder is now otherwise to be defined. When a man upon prepensed malice killeth another, whether secretly or openly, it mamaketh no matter, whether he be an *Englishman* or a foreigner, living under the Kings Protection. And prepensed malice is here either express or implied: Express when it may be evidently proved, that there was formerly some evil design implied; when one killeth another suddenly, having no time to defend himself; as going over a stile, &c. *Crompt.* Justice of Peace in the Chapter of murder, *fol.* 19. *B.*

If upon an affray made, the Constable and others in his assistance come to suppress the Fray, and to preserve the Peace, and in doing their Office, the Constable or any of his assistants is slain, this is murder in the Law, although the murderer knew not the party which was killed, and although the affray was suddain, because the Constable and his assistants, came by authority of the Law to keep the Peace, and to prevent the danger which may ensue by breaking of it, and for this the Law adjudgeth it murder, and that the murderer had malice prepensed, because he opposeth himself against the Justice of the Realm. *Cook* 4. *Rep.* Cases of Appeals and Indictments. *fol.* 10.

So if the Sheriff, or any of his Bailiffs, or other Officers be slain in the Execution of the Process of the Law, or in doing their Office; or if a watchman be killed in doing his Office, this is murder.

The

The like is in 9. *Rep. Mackallies Case*, and this reason given, for this is *contra potestatem Regis & Legis*.

If a Thief, which offers to rob a true man, kill him in resisting the Thief, this is murder of malice prepensed; or if one kill another without any provocation, the Law implyeth malice. *Cook*. 9. *Rep. Mackallies Case*.

The Statute 1 *Jac. Reg. c.* 8. hath well provided, that that party that stabbeth, or thrusteth any person (not having a weapon drawn, or that hath not first stricken him) so as he dye thereof within six months after, shall suffer death as a wilfull murderer.

A. hath wounded B. in fight, and after they meet suddenly and fight again, and B. killeth A. this seemeth murder, and malice shall be intended in B. upon the former hurt; but now if A. had killed B. this seemeth but manslaughter in A. for his former malice shall be thought to be appeased by the hurt he first did to B. *Leigh Phil. Com. fol.* 163.

If two fall out upon a sudden occasion, and agree to fight in such a field, and each of them go and fetch their weapon, and go into the field, and therein fight, the one killeth the other: here is no malice prepensed, for the fetching of the weapon and going into the field, is but a continuance of the sudden falling out, and the blood was never Cooled; (cave: this not Law now) but if they appoint to fight the next day, that is malice prepensed. Sir *Edward Cookes* 3. *part of Institutes c.* 1.

If *A.* put Poison in a pot of Wine, to the intent to Poison *B.* and lay it in a place where he supposeth *B.* will come and drink of it, and by accident one *C.* (to whom *A.* hath no malice) come and of his own head take the pot and drink off this, of which Poison he dies, this is murder in *A.* for he coupleth the Event with the Intention, and the end with the Cause. But if one prepare Ratsbane, to kill Rats and Mice, or other Vermine, and leave this in some place to this purpose, and with no ill intent; and one finding this, eat of it, this is not felony, because he which prepared the Poison, had no evil or felonious intent. *Cook*. 9. *Rep. Agnes Gores case*.

John Sanders had a purpose to kill his Wife, to the intent he might marry another whom he better affected, and opens his intent to *Alexander Archer*, and prays his aid and Counsel how he might effect it; he Counsels him to Poison her. And to this purpose the said *Alexander* buys the Poison, *viz*. Arsenick and Rose-acre, and gives this to *Sanders* to minister to his Wife; afterwards he gives his Wife this in a roasted Apple, and the Wife eats a little part of it, and gives the remnant to her young Child about three years old, and the said *John Sanders* seeing this, reprehends his Wife, and saith that apples were not good for such children, and she saith it was better for the Child than for her, and the Child eats the impoisoned apple, which the Father permits to avoid suspicion, afterwards the woman recovers, and the Child dies of the said Poison. This was murder in *Sanders*, though he bore no malice to his Child, because he had an Intent to kill a person. Here *Sanders* was adjudged a Principal, and hanged; but whether *Archer* was accessary here, was a great doubt, for his offence was in Counselling, and procuring him to kill his Wife, and no other, for no mention was made of the Daughter. So if one lie in wait in a place to kill one, and another cometh to the place, and he which lies in wait mistakes him, and kills him; this is murder, being founded upon prepensed malice, *Plowdens Comment. Sanders Case.*

If a Peer of the Realm be Arraigned at the suit of the King, upon an Indictment of murder, he shall be tryed by his Peers, that is Nobles; but if he be appealed of murder by a Subject, his Tryal shall be an ordinary Jury of twelve Freeholders, as appears 10. *Edw.* 4. 6. 33. *Hen.* 8. *Cook.* 9. *Rep.*

The Township shall be amerced for the Escape of a murderer, *tempore diurno*, although the murder was committed in the Town-field, or lane. *L. Dyer p.* 210. *B.*

If a man be attainted of murder, he shall suffer pain of death, and shall forfeit Lands, Goods and Chattels. *Leigh. Phil. Com. fol.* 165.

A murderer, Murditor, oris m.

The murrain, Morina, æ, f. Fle. 169.

Murrey (*in Scotland*) Moravia, Murevia.

Murrey bay (*in Scotland*) Varar, Vararis æstuarium.

M U S.

Muschamp (*the Family*) De Musco campo.

A musician, Musicus, ci, m.

Musical, Musicus, a, um.

Musical instruments, Organa musica.

Musick, Musica, æ, f.

The distance or time in musick, Intervallum, i, n.

A musician that composes or sets songs and Lessons, Componista, æ, m.

A musk ball (*or a Ball made of divers odoriferous Gums, Powders and Spices, wherein Pomander is the chief*) Pastillus, li, m.

A musket (*or Gun*) Palumbarius, ii, m. Sclopus major, Tormentum minus, Sclopeta peditis.

A musketeer, Sclopetarius, ii, m. Ferentarius, ii, m.

Mustard, Sinapis, is, f.

A mustard (*or pepper*) *mill*, Fraxillus, i, m. Fritillum, i, n.

To muster, Mustro, are.

A muster, Mustrum, i, n.

A muster master, Diribitor, oris, m.

Muster rolls, Rotuli Lustratorii.

A mustering, Mustratio, onis, f.

Musters (*the Family*) De Monasteriis.

M U T.

Mute, Mutus, a, um. Is one that will not plead, or that will not put himself upon his Countrey in a criminal Cause.

Mutton, Caro vervecina, Caro ovilla, vel Ovina.

A shoulder of mutton, Armus Ovillus.

A leg

A leg of mutton, Clunis ovina.

A neck of mutton, Cervix vervecina.

M U Z.

A muzle (or head-stall) Fiscella, æ, f.

N A G.

A *Nagg*, Mannus, i, m. Equus pumilus.

A saddle nag, Equus vectarius.

A nail (or measure) Unguis, is, m. Unum Le Nail. Co. Ent. 125.

A nail, Clavus, i, m.

A horse nail, Clavus Equinus.

A little nail, Clavulus, li, m.

The nail of the fingers, or toes, Unguis, is, m.

N A K.

Naked, Nudus, a, um.

To strip naked, Nudo, are. Vestes exuere.

A naked promise without any consideration, which is void in Law, Nudum pactum.

N A M.

A name, Nomen, inis, n.

The first name (or Christian name) Prænomen, inis, n.

A surname, Cognomen, inis, n.

A nick name, Improperium, ii, n.

To name (or nominate) Nomino, are.

N A.

One that knoweth the names of things, and calleth them by their several names. Nomenclator, oris, m.

Namptwich (in Cheshire) Vicus malhanus.

N A P.

The nape, neck or middle of the neck, Cervix, icis, f.

A napkin, Mantile, is, n. Mantelium, ii, n. Manupiarium, ii, n.

A napkin to wipe the face, Facitergium, ii, n.

N A R.

A Narration, Narratio, onis, f.

N A S.

Nasaret (a womans name) Nasareta, æ, f.

Naseby (in Northamptonshire) Navesbeia.

N A T.

Nathan (a mans name) Nathan, Indecl.

Nathaniel (a mans name) Nathaniel, lis, m.

A nation, Natio, onis, f.

Native, Nativus, a, um.

The feast of the nativity of the blessed Virgin, Festum nativitatis Beatæ mariæ virginis.

Nativity, Nativitas, atis, f.

To calculate ones nativity, Horoscŏpo, are.

A caster or calculator of nativities, Horoscopus, i, m. Genethliacus, i, m.

Nature, Natura, æ, f.

Natural,

Natural, Naturalis, le, adj.

A naturalist, Physiologus, i, m.

Naturalization, Naturalizatio, onis, f.

N A U.

The nave of a cart wheel, Medium Rotæ, Mediolus Rotæ.

The navel, Umbilicus, i, m.

A navy, fleet or army of ships, Classis, is, f.

Navigation, Navigatio, onis, f. Navalis disciplina.

N E.

Ne admittas, Is a writ that lyeth for the Plaintiff in a *Quare Impedit*, or him that hath an action of *Darein presentement* depending in the Common Bench, and feareth that the Bishop will admit the Clerk of the Defendant, during the suit between them, and this writ must be sued within six Months after the avoidance, because after the six months, the Bishop may present by Lapse. *Regist. Orig. fol.* 31. *Fitz. nat. brev. fol.* 37.

N E A.

Near, Propinquus, a, um.

Near at hand, In promptu.

Near to, Prope, adv.

Neath (in Glamorganshire) Nidum, Nidus.

Neats leather, Pellis bovina.

N E C.

Necessary, necessarius, a, um.

Necessity (or want) Necessitas, atis, f.

The neck, Collum, i, n.

A neckcloth, Strophium, ii, n.

A necklace, Torquis, is, d. g.

A necklace with three rows of Pearl, Trifilum, i, n.

Necromancy (or divination by calling up deceased bodies) Necromantia, æ, f.

A necromancer, Necromanticus, ci, m.

N E E.

A neece, Neptis, is, f.

A needle, Acus, us, f.

A little needle, Acutella, æ, f.

A needles eye, Foramen acus.

A needle case, Acutheca, æ, f. Aciarium, ii, n.

A garment of needle work, Vestis acupicta, Vestis Phrygia.

The needle of a ship-mans compass, used in a ship, or of a dial, Versoria, æ, f.

A needle-maker, Acicularius, ii, m.

N E G.

Negative, Negativus, a, um.

A negative that implies an affirmative, a Negative pregnant, Negativum, i, n. Negativa pregnans.

To neglect, Negligo, ere.

Neglected, Neglectus, a, um.

Negligence, Negligentia, æ, f.

Negligent, Negligens, tis, Part.

Negligently, Negligentèr, adv.

A neighbour, Vicinus, i, m.

Of a neighbour, Vicinalis, le, adj.

The Neighbourhood, Vicinetum, i, n, Cow. 238. 268. Co. Lit. 155. 11. Co. 25.

N E P.

A nephew, Nepos, otis, m.
The nephews wife, Prōnŭrus, ûs, f.

N E R.

Nero (a mans name) Nero, onis, m.

N E S.

A neſt, Nidus, i, m.

N E T.

A nett, Rete, is, n. Caſſis, is, m.

A ſweep-net, or drag net to catch fiſh, Tragum, i, n. Tragula, æ, f. Verriculum, i, n. Sagena, æ, f.

A caſting net, Funda, æ, f.

A broad net to catch fowls, Pantherum, i, n. Rete aucupatorium.

A wheel or bow-net, Naſſa, æ, f.

A ſmall float net, Rete jaculum.

A hay-net, Obvolutorium, ii, n.

A wide net with great maſhes, Rete latum, Grandimacula, æ, f.

A purſe-net, Excipulum, i, n.

The arming or croſs maſhing a net, Semplagium, ii, n.

Cords or nets wherewith fowlers intangle birds, Reſtricæ, arum, f.

A maſh or hole of a net, Macula, æ, f.

An arming of a net, Epidromis, is, f. Plagæ, arum, f.

A net maker, Retiarius, ii, m.

Net-work, Reticulatum opus.

N E U.

Never, Nunquam, adv.

Never after, Nunquam dehinc.

N E.

Nevertheleſs, Nihilo minus, tamen, conjunct.

Nevil (the Family) De Nova villa & de Nevilla.

Neuter (or Neutral) Neutrālis, le, adj.

N E W.

New, Novus, a, um.

To make new, Novo, are. Renovo, are. Novello, are.

Newburgh (the Family) De Novo Burgo.

Newark (the Family) De Novo loco.

Newbury (in Berkſhire) Nubiria Spiriæ.

Newcaſtle upon Tine (in Northumberland) Monarchapol, Novum Caſtellum.

Newcaſtle (the Family) De Novo Caſtello.

New hall (a ſtately houſe in Eſſex) Locus. Nova aula.

Newenden (in Kent) Anderida. Noviodunum.

Newington (in Kent or near it) Durolevum.

Newmarket (in Suffolk) Novum forum, Novus mercatus.

Newmarket heath, Campus Novoforenſis.

Newmarch (the Family) De Novo Mercatu.

Newnham (in Hertfordſhire) Villa nova.

Newport, Novus portus.

Newport (in the Iſle of Wight) Medena, Novus Burgus.

Newport Pagnel (in Buckinghamſhire) Neoportus Paganellicus.

New years day, Feſtum Circumciſionis domini.

A News-monger, Famigerator, oris, m.

To forge or carry about news, Famigero, are.

N E X.

Next, Proximus, a, um.
Next after, Inde, deinde, adv.

N I C.

Nicholas (*a mans name*) Nicolaus, i, m.
Nicola (*a womans name*) Nicola, æ, f.

N I E.

Niele or Neal (*the Family*) Nigellus.

N I G.

A night, Nox, tis, f.
A night guard, Excubitum, i, n.
To lodge all night, Pernocto, are.
A night cap, Galericulus, li, m. Pileus nocturnus.
To wax night, Noctesco, ere.
Nightly (*night by night*) Noctuatim adv. West Indictments 239.
In the night, Noctanter. in Indictments.

N I H.

Nihil dicit. Is a failing to put in answer to the Plea of the Plaintiff by the day assigned, which if a man do omit, Judgment passeth against him, as saying nothing why it should not.

N I N.

Nine, Novem, adj. Indecl.
Nineteen, Novendecim, adv.
Nine times, Novies, adv.
Ninety, Nonaginta, adv.
Nineteenth, Nonogesimus, a, um.
The ninth, Nonus, a, um.

N I P.

A nipple of the breast, Papilla, æ, f.

N I S.

Nisi prius, Is a writ judicial, which lyeth in case where the Enquest is panelled, and returned before the Justices of the Bank, the one party, or the other, making Petition, to have this writ for the ease of the Country. It is directed to the Sheriff, commanding that he cause the men Impanelled to come before the Justices in the same County, for the determination of the Cause there, except it be so difficult, that it need great deliberation. In which case it is sent again to the Bank. *Anno* 14. *Ed.* 3. *cap.* 15. The form of the Writ, see in old *Nat. brev. fol.* 159. and in the *Regist Indic. fol.* 7. & 28. & 75. See the new book of Entries, *verbo, nisi prius.* And it is called *nisi prius*, of these words comprised in the same, whereby the Sheriff is willed to bring to *Westminster* the men Impanelled at a certain day, or before the Justices of the next Assizes: *Nisi die Lunæ apud talem locum prius venerint*, &c. whereby it appeareth that Justices of Assizes, and Justices of *nisi prius* are differing. And Justices of *nisi prius* must be one of them, before whom the cause is depending in the Bench, with some other good man of the County associated unto him. *Fitz. nat. brev. fol.* 240. E. which he taketh from

from the Statute of *York*, *Anno* 12. *Ed.* 2. See *Westm.* 2. *cap.* 30. *anno* 13. *Ed.* 1. *& anno* 27. *ejusd. cap.* 4. *& anno* 2. *Ed.* 3. *cap.* 17. *& anno* 4. *Ejusd. cap.* 11. *& anno* 14. *Ejusd. cap.* 16. *& anno* 7. *Rich.* 2. *cap.* 7. *& anno* 18. *Eliz. cap.* 12.

NOB.

Noble, Nobilis, le, adj. Illustris, tre, adj.

A noble (in money) Merka, æ, f. Nobile, is, n.

A noble-man, Heros, ois, m.

To make noble, Nobilito, are.

Noblenefs (or nobiilty) Nobilitas, atis, f.

Nobly, Nobilitèr, adv.

NOC.

The nock in horn of a bow or arrow, Crena, æ, f.

NOG.

A noggin (a kind of cup with two ears) Diota, æ, f.

NOM.

Nomination, Nominatio, onis, f.

Nominated, Nominatus, a, um.

NON.

Nonage (or minority) Minoritas, atis, f. It is all the time of a mans age under one and twenty years in some cases, or fourteen in some, as marriage. See *Brook Tit. Age*.

Non Compos mentis, is a man of no found memory, many times the Latin word explaineth the true sense, and calleth him *Amens*, *Demens*, *Furiosus*, *Lunaticus*, *Fatuus*, *Stultus* or the like: but *non compos mentis* is most sure and legal.

Non compos mentis is of four Sorts. 1. *Ideota*, which from his Nativity by a perpetual Infirmity is *non compos mentis*. 2. He that by sicknefs, grief or other accident wholly loseth his memory and understanding. 3. A Lunatick, that hath sometime his understanding, and sometime not, *aliquando gaudet lucidis intervallis*: and therefore he is called *non Compos mentis*, so long as he hath not understanding. *Cook on Lit. lib.* 3. *cap.* 6. *Sect.* 405. *&* 4. *Rep.*

Beverlies case, Lastly, he that by his own vitious act for a time depriveth himself of his memory and understanding, as he that is drunken, but that kind of *Non Compos mentis* shall give no privilege or benefit to him or his heirs; and a descent shall take away the entry of an Ideot, albeit the want of understanding was perpetual.

So likewise if a man that becomes *Non Compos mentis*, by accident be disseised and suffer a descent, albeit he recover his memory and understanding again, yet he shall never avoid the Descent, and so it is *à fortiori* of one that hath *Lucida intervalla*. *Id. Ib.*

If an Ideot make a Feoffment in Fee, he shall in pleading never avoid it, saying that he was an Ideot at the time of his Feoffment, and so had been from his Nativity. But upon an Office found for the King, the King shall avoid the

Feoffment for the benefit of the Ideot, whose custody the Law giveth to the King; so it is of a *Non Compos mentis*, and so it is of him *qui Gaudet lucidis intervallis*, of an Estate made during his Lunacy; for albeit the parties themselves cannot be deceived to disable themselves, yet twelve men upon this Office may find the Truth of the matter: But if any of them alien by fine or recovery, this shall not only bind himself, but his Heirs also.

Non Compos mentis cannot commit Felony, because he cannot have a Felonious intent. *Furiosus* (saith *Bracton*) *non intelligit quid agit, & animo & ratione caret, & non multum distat à brutis.* Neither can he commit Petty Treason. As if a woman *Non Compos mentis* kill her husband; but in some cases, *non Compos mentis* may commit High Treason, as if he kill, or offer to kill the King, for he is *Caput & salus reipublicæ, & à capite bona valetudo transit in omnes*; and for this cause their persons are privileged, that none ought to offer violence to them, but he is *reus criminis læsæ Majestatis*, and *pereat unus ne pereant omnes*. *Cooks* 4th. *Rep. Beverly's Case.*

Of an Ideot which is so *à Nativitate* the King hath *Custodiam*, of *Non compos mentis* he hath only Provision. That is, of a natural Ideot, the King hath his Lands to his own use; but of *Non compos mentis*, he hath not to his own use, but shall with the Profits of the Land maintain him, his Wife, Children and Houshold. *Cooks* 4*th. Rep. Beverly's* Case.

Non distringendo, Is a writ comprising under it divers particulars, according to divers cases; all which you may see in the Table of the *Regist. Orig. verbo*, *Non distringendo.*

Non est Culpabilis. Is the general answer to an action of Trespass, whereby the Defendant doth absolutely deny the fact imputed unto him by the Plaintiff. Whereas in other special answers, the Defendant granteth the Fact to be done, and alledgeth some reason in his defence, why he lawfully might do it. And therefore whereas the Rhetoricians comprise all the substance of their discourses under three questions. *An sit, quid sit, quale sit*: This answer falleth under the first of the three; all other answers are under one of the other two. And as this is the general answer in an action of Trespass, that is, an action criminal civilly prosecuted; so is it also in all actions criminally followed, either at the suit of the King, or other, wherein the Defendant denyeth the Crime objected unto him, see the new book of Entries. *Tit. non culpabilis*, and *Stawnf. Pl. Cor. lib.* 2. *cap.* 62.

Non est Factum, Is an answer to a Declaration, whereby a man denyeth that to be his Deed, whereupon he is Impleaded. *Broke hoc Titulo.*

Non Implacitando aliquem de libero tenemento sine brevi. Is a writ to inhibit Bayliffs, &c. from distraining any man without the Kings writ, touching his Free-hold. *Regist. fol.* 171. *B.*

Non omittas, Is a writ lying where the Sheriff delivereth a former

mer writ to a Bailiff of a franchise, within the which the Party, on whom it is to be served, dwelleth, and the Bayliff neglecteth to serve it, for in this case, the Sheriff returning, that he delivered it to the Bayliff, this shall be directed to the Sheriff, charging him himself to execute the Kings Commandment. *Old nat. brev. fol.* 44. Of this the *Regist. Orig.* hath three sorts, *fol.* 82. *b.* & 151. & *Reg. Judic. fol.* 5. & 56.

Non ponendo in Assisis & Juratis. Is a writ founded upon *Stat. Westm.* 2. *cap.* 38. & the *Stat. Articuli super chartas*, *cap.* 9. which is granted upon divers causes to men, for the freeing them from Assises and Juries. *Fitz. nat. brev. fol.* 165. See the *Regist. fol.* 179. 100. 181. 183.

Non residentia pro Clericis Regis. Is a writ directed to the Ordinary, charging him not to molest a Clerk, Imployed in the Kings service, by reason of his Non-residence. *Regist. Orig. fol.* 58. *b.*

Non sanæ memoriæ, (not of sound memory) Is an exception taken to any act declared by the Plaintiff or demandant to be done by another, whereupon he granteth his plaint or demand. And the Contents of this exception are, that the Party that did that act (being himself or any other) was not well in his wits, or mad, when he did it. See the new book of Entries, *Tit. non sanæ memoriæ*, and *dum non fuit compos mentis.* See also *Non Compos mentis.*

Non Term, Non Terminus. Is the time of vacation between Term and Term. It was wont to be called the times or days of the Kings Peace. *Lamb. Archaion. fol.* 126. and what these were in the time of King *Edward the Confessor*, see there.

None, Nullus, a, um.

The nones of every month, Nonæ, arum, f, pl. Sing. caret.

Nonsuit, Non prosecutus est breve. Is a Renunciation of the suit by the Plaintiff or Demandant, when the matter is so far proceeded in, as the Jury is ready at the Bar, to deliver their Verdict. *Anno* 2. *H.* 4. *cap.* 7. See the new book of Entries, *verbo Nonsuit.* The *Civilians* term it *Litis renunciationem.*

N O O.

A nook of land, Noca terræ. 2. Mon. 254. bis, 331. Noka Terræ Lex. 90.

Noon, Meridies, ei, m.

N O R.

Norfolk, Nordovolca, Norfolcia.

Norham (in Northumberland) Ubbanforda.

Norris (the Family) Norrisius.

The north, Septentrio, onis, m. Boreas, æ, m.

The north part, Pars Borealis.

The north-east part, Pars Euroaquilonica.

North-west part, Borea Zephyralis.

The north pole (or pole artick) Polus Articus.

Northampton town, Bannavenna, Bannaventa, Bennaventa, Isannavantia, Isannavaria, Isannavatia, Northamptonia.

Northamptonshire, Northantoniensis ager vel comitatus.

North-hall (in Hertfordshire) Nemus Boreale.

Northforeland (in Kent) Cantium Prom. Carion.

Norton hall (in Yorkshire) Nortobricum.

Northumberland, Nordhumbria, Northanimbria, Northimbria, Northumbria.

Norwick City, Norwicus, Nordovicum, Venta.

Bishop of Norwich, Episcopus Norwicensis.

Norwich (the Family) De Norwico.

N O S.

The nose, Nasus, i, m.

The nostrils, Nares, ium, f.

N O T.

A notary, Nŏtārius, ii, m.

A notch (or slit) Crena, æ, f. Divisura, æ, f.

To note (mark or observe any thing) Nŏto, are.

A note (or annotation) Nota, æ, f. Annotatio, onis, f.

A note (mark or star in a book) Stellula, æ, f. Asteriscus, ci, m.

Note of a fine, Nota Finis. It is a Brief of a Fine made by the Chirographer, before it is engrossed. The form whereof, see in *West. part 2. symb. Tit. Fines. sect.* 117.

Noted, Notatus, a, um.

Nothing, Nihil, n. Indecl.

Notice, Notitia, æ, f.

To notify, Notifico, are.

A notion, Notio, onis, f.

Notorious, Notorius, a, um.

Nottingham, Nottinghamia.

Nottinghamshire, Nottinghamiensis ager vel comitatus.

Notwithstanding, Non obstante.

N O V.

The month November, November, bris, m.

A novice, Novitius, ii, m.

Nourished, Nutritus, a, um.

A nourisher, Nutritor, oris, m.

A nourishing, Nutritio onis, f. Nutricatio, onis, f.

Nourishment, Nutrimentum, i, n. Alimentum, i, n.

To nourish, Nutrio, ire.

N O W.

Nowres (the Family) De Nodoriis.

N U L.

To null, Nullo, are. Adnullo.

N U M.

A number, Numerus, i, m.

To number, Numero, are.

Of number, Numeralis, le, adj.

N U N.

A Nun, Monacha, æ, f.

A Nunnery, Absterium, ii, n.

N U R.

A nurse, Nutrix, icis, f. Alumna, æ, f.

A nursery, Alimoniarium, ii, n. Nutriciarium, ii, n.

A nursery of trees, Seminarium ii, n.

N U S.

Nusance, Nocumentum, i, n. It signifieth in our Common Law not only a thing done, whereby another

ther man is annoyed in his Free-Lands or Tenements, but especially the assise or writ lying for the same. *Fitz. nat. brev. fol.* 183. And this writ *de Nocumento*, or of Nusance, is either simply *de Nocumento*, or *de parvo Nocumento*, and then it is Vicountiel. *Old. nat. brev. fol.* 108, *&* 109. *& Fitz. nat. brev. ubi supra & fol.* 184.

Mr. *Manwood* part 2. of his Forest Laws *cap.* 17. maketh three sorts of Nusance in the forest. The first is *Nocumentum commune*. The second *Nocumentum speciale*. The third *Nocumentum generale*; which read with the rest of that whole chapter. See the *Regist. Orig. fol.* 197, *&* 199.

A Man shall not have an action upon the case for a Nusance done in the High-way, for it is a common Nusance, and then it is not reason that a particular person should have an Action. For by the same Reason that one Person should have an Action for this. Every one may have an Action for it, and then he shall be punished a hundred times for one and the same cause. But if any particular person after the Nusance made, hath a more particular damage than any other, for this particular injury he shall have a particular Action upon the Case. *Cooks 5th. Rep. Williams Case.*

NUT.

A nut, Nux, nucis, f.

A hazel nut (or filberd) Avellana, æ, f. Corylum, li, n.

A wall-nut, Juglans, dis, f.

A nutmeg, Nux moschata vel Myristica.

A nut-cracker, Nucifrangibulum, i, n.

A place where nuts grow, Nucetum, i, n.

OAK.

AN oak, Quercus, ûs, f.

A grove of oaks, Quercetum, i, n.

Oaken (of oak) Querceus, a, um.

OAR.

The oar of a ship or boat, Remus, i, m.

An iron oar, Strictura, æ, f.

The handle of an oar, Manubrium, ii, n.

The broadest part, or blade of the oar, Palmula, æ, f. Tonsa, æ, f.

A round piece of wood whereat the Oars do hang by a Leather thong, Scalmus, i, m.

Oar of a mine, Ora, æ, f. 2 Inst. 579. Ura, æ, f. F. b. p. 1. part Second Edition fol. 337. Quædam venæ sive mineræ & Plumbagines Sive Metallacupri, aurum vel argentum in se continentes Anglice dicta. *Mines and Oars of Copper, containing in themselves Gold or Silver.* Plowd Com. fo. 310. Infor. pur *Mynes*.

Lead oar, Ura plumbea.

The space between the oar in a Galley, Interscalmium, ii, n.

OAT.

Oats, Avēna, æ, f.

Of oats, Avenācĕus, a, um. Avēnārius, a, um.

Wild oats, Bromus sterilis. Festucago, inis, f. Lolium, ii, n.

Oat-meal, Farina avenacea.

An oaten field, Avenarium, ii, n.

An oath, Affidavit, idem per omnes casus. n. Sacramentum, i, n. Depositio, onis, f. juramentum.

O B E.

Obedience, Obedientia, æ, f.

An obeliske, Obeliscus, ci, m.

The ground work of an obelisk, Crepidines Obelisci.

O B I.

To object (or lay against) Objicio, ere.

An object, Objectum, i, n.

An objection, Objectio, onis, f.

Objected, Objectus, a, um.

O B L.

An oblation (or offering) Oblatio, onis, f.

An obligation, Obligatio, onis, f. Obligation is a word of his own Nature, of large extent, but it is commonly taken in the Common Law, for a Bond containing a penalty, with condition for payment of money, or to do or suffer any Act or thing, and a Bill is most commonly taken for a single Bond without Condition. *Cook on Lit. lib.* 3. *cap.* 1. *Sect.* 259.

If a man be bound in an Obligation with Condition, that if the Obligor do go from the Church of St. *Peter* in *Westminster*, to the Church of St. *Peter* in *Rome* within three hours, that then that Obligation shall be void; the Condition is void, and impossible. *Cook on Lit. Lib.* 3. *c.* 5.

If a man be bound to Pay twenty Pound at any time at a Place certain, the Obligor cannot tender the money at that place when he will, for then the obligee should be bound to perpetual attendance, and therefore the Obligor in respect of the incertainty of the time, must give the Obligee Notice, that on such a day at the place limited he will Pay the money, and then the Obligee must attend there to receive it; for if the Obligor pay the money, he shall save the Penalty of the Bond for ever. *Cook on Lit. Lib.* 3. *c.* 5. *Sect.* 340.

Whereas a man is bound to pay ten Pound at such a day and place, if the Obligee accept a less sum at the same day and place, this appears to the Court to be no satisfaction of the greater, but acceptance of the less at a day before it is due, or at another place, or of some other thing (as of an horse) may be a satisfaction, *Cooks 5th. Rep. Pinnels Case.*

When any act to be done by Condition, is to be done by the Sole act, or Labour, or Industry of a Stranger, which act in no manner concerns the Obligor, Obligee, or any other person, and no time is limited when this shall be done, it sufficeth the Obligor, if the act be done in the Life of him which ought to do this. As if I am obliged to you on Condition, that *J. S.* shall go to *Rome* or *Jerusalem*, or that such a Student in Divinity at the *University* shall preach at *Pauls*, or in the Law, shall argue the matter in Law in *Westminster*-Hall, in these cases no time being limited, they have time to do it during their Lives. *Cooks 6th. Rep. Bothies Case.*

Obligatory

Obligatory (obliging or binding) Obligatorius, a, um.

To oblige (or bind by obligation) Obligo, are.

To obliterate (blot out or abolish) Oblitero, are.

To observe (or mark diligently) Obſervo, are.

An obſtacle, Obſtaculum, li, n.

Obſtinate (or wilfull) Obſtinatus, a, um.

Obſtruction, Obſtructio, onis, f.

To obtain, Obtineo, ere.

To obtain by requeſt, Impetro, are.

To obtrude, Obtrudo, ere.

O C C.

Occaſion, Occaſio, onis, f.

An occupation (or uſing) Occupatio, onis, f.

To occupy (or uſe) Occupo, are.

An occurrence (or accident, a thing or matter happened by chance) Occurrentia, æ, f.

The ocean ſea that compaſſeth the world, Oceanus, i, m.

O C K.

Ock river (in Devonſhire) Ockus.

Ockhampton (in Devonſhire) Ochamptonia.

O C T.

The month of October, October, bris, m.

O C U.

An Oculiſt, Ophthalmicus, i, m.

O D O.

Odoriferous, Odoriferus, a, um.

O E C.

Oeconomy (or adminiſtration of a Family) Oeconomia, æ, f.

Oeconomical (belonging to Goverment of a houſe) Oeconomicus, a, um.

O F F.

Of, De, Præp.

Offal (of any thing ſifted or ſearſed) Excretum, i, n.

Offal (or refuſe cut off) Reſegmen, inis, n.

Offal (or refuſe) Palea, æ, f.

An offence, Offenſa, æ, f.

Charged with an offence, Rectatus, a, um. Arrectatus, a, um. Lex. 9. Ry. 85. Rettum, Rectatus, Reg. 77. 8. 3. Fin. 130. 2. Inſt. 42. 151. 1 Mon. 763.

To offend, Offendo, ere.

Offending (going againſt) Contraveniens. Ra. Ent. 467.

To offer (or preſent) Offero, erre.

An office, Officium, ii, n.

An officer (a miniſter of a Court) Officiarius, ii, m.

An officer belonging to the King, that provides Oats for his horſes, Avenator, oris, m.

To be prickt down or appointed for an Office (or for Pay) Adpunctor, aris.

A Jack out of Office, Ethronus, i, m. Officiperda, æ, m.

An official (Commiſſary or Chancelor to a Biſhop) Officialis. Official in our Statute and Common Law, ſignifieth him whom the Archdeacon Subſtituteth in the executing of his Juriſdiction, as appeareth by the Statute, *Anno* 32. *H.* 8. *cap.* 15.

Officious, Officioſus, a, um.

An offspring (or progeny) Soboles, is, f. plur. Nom. acc. voc. Soboles.

O F T.

Often, Sæpè, frequenter, adv.
When and as often, Quando & quoties.
Then and so often, Tunc & toties.
So often as, or as often as, Toties quoties.
Very often, Sæpiusculè, Sæpissimè, adv.
Very oft (or frequent) Sæpissimus, a, um.
Oftentimes, Sæpenumero, adv.

O G I.

An ogive (or Ogee, a wreath, circlet or round band in architecture) Corona, æ, f. Præcinctura, æ, f. Projectura, æ, f.

O I L.

Oil, Oleum, i, n.
To oil (or anoint with oil) Ungere Oleo.
An oil seller (or oil maker) Olearius, ii, m.
A penniworth of oil, Denarata Olei. Spel. 198.
An oil glass, Lecythus, thi, d. g.
Made or mixed with oil, Oleatus, a, um.
Oiled, Oleo unctus.
Pertaining to oil, Olearius, a, um.
Oily, Oleaceus, a, um. Oleorsus, a, um.
D'oily (the Family) De Oileio, & Oili, & Oilius.
An oilet hole (or button hole) Fibularium, ii, n.

O I N.

Ointment, Unguentum, i, n.
He that maketh or selleth ointments, Unguentarius, ii, m.
The art of making ointment, Unguentaria, æ, f.

O I S.

An oister, Ostrea, æ, f.
An oister-pit, Ostrearia, æ, f.
An oister-man, Ostrearius, ii, m.
An oister-woman, Ostreatrix, icis, f.
Full of oisters, Ostreosus, a, um.
Of or belonging to oisters, Ostrearius, a, um.

O K E.

Okenyate (in Shropshire) Usoccona, Usocona.
Oker that painters do use, Ochra, æ, f.

O L D.

Old, Vetus, eris, adj.
An old man, Senex, is, c. 2.
An old woman, Anus, ûs, f.
To be old (or wax old) Seneo, ere. Senesco, ere.
Old age, Senecta, æ, f.
Old Carlile (See Burghupon Sands.)
Old Perith (in Cumberland) Voreda.
Old Radnor, Magæ, Magi, Magnæ, Magni, & Magnis.
Old town (in Herefordshire) Blestium.

O L E.

Oleron isle (in France) Ulcarus.

O L I.

O L I.

Olive (a womans name) Oliva,æ,f.
Oliver (a mans name) Oliverus, i, m.

O M I.

Ominous, Ominosus, a, um.
An omission, Omissio, onis, f.
To omit (or let pass) Omitto,ere.

O N E.

One, Unus, a, um.
Of one, Unalis, le, adj.

O P E.

Open law, Lex manifesta, Lex apparens. It is making of Law, which by *Magna Charta, cap.* 28. Bayliffs may not put men unto, upon their own bare assertions, except they have witnesses to prove their Imputation.
Operation (or working) Operatio, onis, f.

O P P.

Opportunity, Opportunitas, atis,f.
To oppose (or object) Oppono, ere.
An opposite (contrary or Antagonist) Oppositus, ûs, m. Antagonista, æ, m.
To oppress, Opprimo, ere.
Opprobrious, Opprobriosus, a,um.

O R.

Or, Aut, vel, sive, seu. (aut) should be used in the beginning of a Sentence. (*vel*) in Connexion of words. (*sive, seu*) in further proceeding of a thing pleaded, seldom using the same word twice together.

O R A.

An oration, Oratio, onis, f.
Oratory (or belonging to an Orator) Oratorius, a, um.
An Orator, Orator, oris, m.

O R B.

An orb (a sphere, or round compass) Orbis, is, m.

O R C.

An orchard, Pomarium, ii, n.
A young orchard, Plantarium, ii, n.

O R D.

To ordain (or appoint) Ordino, are.
An ordaining (or ordination) Ordinatio, onis, f.
The tryal by ordel, Ordalium, ii, n. Judicium ignis & aquæ.
Order, Ordo, inis, m.
Orderly, Ordinate, Ordinatim, adv.
An ordinance (law, decree or statute) Decretum, i, n. Statutum, i, n. Edictum, i, n.
Ordinary (or usual) Ordinarius, a, um.
An ordinary, Ordinarius, ii, m. Ordinary, is he that hath ordinary Jurisdiction in causes Ecclesiastical, immediate to the King and his Courts of Common Law, for the better execution of Justice; as the Bishop or any other that hath exempt and immediate Jurisdiction in Causes Ecclesiastical. It is derived *ab ordine* to put him in mind of the Duty of his Place, and of that Order and Office that he is called unto. *Cook on Lit. Lib.* 3. *c.* 11.

c. 11. *Sect.* 641. *Cooks* 2 *part of Institutes. cap.* 19.

Ordinarily, Ordinariè, adv.

Ordnance, Tormenta bellica.

O R E.

Ore river (*in Suffolk*) Orus.

O R G.

An organ (*or musical instrument*) Organum, i, n.

Organ pipes, Cantes, f. pl.

The keys of the organ, Epitoniorum manubria.

An organ player (*or organist*) Organista, æ, m.

O R I.

The orifice (*mouth or brim of any thing*) Orificium, ii, n.

Origen (*a mans name*) Origenes, is, m.

The original (*or first pattern*) Archetypum, i, n.

An original (*or beginning*) Origo, inis, f. Principium, ii, n.

Originally, Originalitèr, adv.

O R K.

Orkeney islands (*on the coasts of Scotland*) Orcades Insulæ. Orchadia.

Orkeney island, Orkeneia.

O R M.

Ormond (*in Ireland*) Ormandia.

O R N.

An ornament, Ornamentum, i, n.

An ornament upon the jambs of doors, Autarium, ii, n.

O R P.

An orphan (*or fatherless child*) Orphanus, i, m.

Orpington (*in Kent*) Dorpendunum.

O R T.

Orthodox (*or true and right opinion*) Orthodoxia, æ, f.

Orthography (*or the manner of true and right writing*) Orthographia, æ, f.

O R Y.

Orythia (*a womans name*) Orythia, æ, f.

O S E.

Osbert (*a mans name*) Osbertus, i, m.

O S T.

Ostentation (*or vain boasting*) Ostentatio, onis, f.

O S W.

Oswald (*a mans name*) Oswaldus, i, m.

O T F.

Otford (*in Kent*) Ottaforda.

O T H.

A little otherwise, Aliquo secius, adv.

Otho (*a mans name*) Otho, onis, m.

O V E.

An oven, Furnus, i, m.

An ovens mouth, Præfurnium, ii, n.

To heat an oven, Infurno, are.

To make an oven, Furneo, are.

Belonging to an oven (*or made like an oven*) Furnaceus, a, um.

Over or croſs a bank, Ex tranſverſo Ripæ. Ry. 552.

Over or croſs a valley, Ex tranſverſo vallis. 2 Mon. 649.

Over or croſs the water, Ex tranſverſo aquæ. Reg. 95. Ra. Entr. 616.

Over or croſs a way, Ex tranſverſo viæ. 1 Cro. 302. Eundo in tranſverſo uſque ad 2 Mon. 425.

Overborough (*in Lancaſhire*) Calacum, Brementonacum.

To overflow, Superfluo, ere.

Overflowed, Superfuſus, a, um.

An overflowing (*or inundation*) Inundatio, onis, f.

To overload (*or overcharge*) Prægravo, are. Degravo, are.

Overloaded, Prægravatus, a, um.

The overmoſt part (*or ſurface of any thing*) Superficies, ei, f.

To over reckon, Numerando fallere.

Over ſea, Tranſmarinus, a, um.

To overſee, Inſpicio, ere.

A overſeer (*as he that overſeeth workmen*) Inſpector, oris, m. Antiſtitor, oris, m.

The overſight (*of workmen, &c.*) Inſpectio, onis, f.

An overſight (*or Error*) Error, oris, m.

To overthrow (*or caſt down*) Diruo, ere Everto, ere.

Overthrown (*or turned up ſide down*) Dirutus, a um. Everſus, a, um.

Overthrown (*or deſtroyed*) Profligatus, a, um. Conſternatus a, um.

An overthrowing, Everſio, onis, f. Subverſio, onis, f.

An overthrower, Everſor, oris, m.

To over-weigh, Superpondero, are.

To overwhelm, Obruo, ere.

O U G.

It ought (*or it behoveth*) Oportet, debet.

O U I.

Ovid (*a mans name*) Ovidius, ii, m.

O U N.

An ounce weight, Unciata, æ, f. Uncia, æ, f.

Half an ounce, dimidium unius Unciæ.

A quarter of an ounce, Quarteria unius unciæ.

O U R.

Our. Noſter, a, um.

O U S.

Ouſeburn, Iſiburna.

Ouſe river (*in Yorkſhire*) Ouſa.

Ouſe river (*in Buckinghamſhire*) Uſa.

Ouſeford (*or Oxford*) Iſidis vadum

Ouſeney or Oſney (*near Oxford*) Iſidis Inſula.

O U T.

An out cry, Vociferatio, onis, f.

An out cry of goods to be ſold, Auctio, onis, f.

An out-law, Utlagatus, i, m.

An

An outlawry, Utlagaria, æ, f. It is the loss or deprivation of the benefit belonging to a subject, that is of the Kings Protection and the Realm. Heretofore none could be outlawedbut for felony,the Punishment whereof was death, but now the Law is changed: An outlawed man had then *Caput lupinum*, because he might be put to death by any man, as a Wolf that hateful beast might. *Dictus utlagatus quasi extra legem positus. Leigh. Phil. Com. fol.* 175.

Outlawed, Utlagatus, a, um.

An outlawing, Utlagatio, onis, f.

The restoring of an outlawed person to the benefit of the Law, Inlagatio, onis, f.

An out-standing, Podium, ii, n.

The outward, Externus, a, um.

O W E.

To owe, Debeo, ere.

Owed (or that is owed) Debitus, a, um. Creditus, a, um.

To pay money that is owed, Creditas solvere pecunias.

An owing, Debitum, i, n. Debitio, onis, f.

Owen (a mans name) Owenus, i, m.

O W N.

An owner, Proprietarius, ii, m.

A part owner, Parte proprietarius, ii, m.

An other mans own, Alienus, a, am.

O X E.

An oxe, Bos, ovis, m.

Large fat oxen, Larini Boves.

A yoke of oxen, Celænia, æ, f.

A team of oxen, Protelum, i, n.

An oxe-house: See *house*.

An oxe-stall, Bovellium, ii, n.

Oxe-keepers, Bovarii, orum, m, plur. Monast. Anglic. part 1. fo. 1021.

An Oxgang of land, Bovata terræ Spel. 104. It is as much Land as one Oxe can Plow. By the Grant of an Oxgang of Land may pass Meadow and Pasture. *Le Phil. Com. fo.* 174.

A piece of ground containing four Oxgangs, Librata terræ.

About four Oxgangs of land, Masura terræ.

O X F.

Oxford City, where is also the most famous University in the World, Bellositum, Isidis vadum, Oxenforda, Oxfordia, Oxonia, Oxonium.

Bishop of Oxford, Episcopus Oxoniensis.

O X N.

Oxney isle (in Kent) Oxinega.

O Y E.

Oyer and terminer, Audiendo & terminando. Is in the Intendment of our Law, a Commission especially granted to certain men, for the hearing and determining of one or more Causes. This was wont to be in use upon some suddain Outrage or Insurrection in any place. *Crompt. Jurisdict. fol.* 131, & 132. See the Statute of Westm. 2. *cap.* 29. *anno* 13. *Ed.* 1. who might grant this Commission, and See *Fitz. nat. brev. fol.* 100, for the form and occasion of the writ, as also to whom it is to be granted

granted and whom not. See *Broke Tit. Oyer and determiner.*

P A C.

A *Pace*, Paſſus, ûs, m. Gradus, ûs, m. Veſtigium, ii, n.

A pace of five feet, containing two ſteps, and by this pace are miles meaſured, Paſſus major.

A pace of two feet and a half, a ſtep, which is the diſtance from the heel of the hinder foot, to the toe of the forefoot, Paſſus minor.

To pacify (or appeaſe) Pacifico, are.

A pack, Sarcina, æ, f. Sagma, æ, f.

A ſmall pack, Sarcinŭla, æ, f.

To make packs, Sarcino, are.

Burdened with packs, Sarcinatus, a, um.

Of or belonging to packs, Sarcĭnā-lis, le.

A pack-cloth, Segeſtria, æ, f. Involucrum mercium.

A pack-horſe, Jumentum, i, n.

A pack-ſadle, Sagma, atis, n. Clitellæ, arum, f. Dorſuarium, ii, n.

A pack of mercery wares, Paccum merceriæ. Pry. 197.

Packthread, Filum Sarcinarium.

P A D.

A padlock, Sera catenata.

P A G.

A page, Pagius, ii, m. 1 Mon. 816. 2 Mon. 935. Garcio, onis, m. Spel. 309. Ry. 92. 156, 177. Aſſecla, æ, m. Pediſſequus, i, m.

A page of a book, Pagina, æ, f.

A pageant, Caſtellulum, li, n.

P A.

P A I.

A pail to carry water in, Sĭtŭla, æ, f.

A milk-pail, Mulctrum, i, n.

A wreath under a pail, Ceſticillus, i, m.

Pain, Dolor, oris, m.

Pain fort and dure, Pœna fortis & dura. It is a puniſhment for thoſe arraigned for Felony that ſtand mute.

Painels (the Family) Pagenelli.

To paint, Pingo, ere.

To paint out, Delineo, are.

Painted, Pictus, a, um.

Half painted, Semipictus, a, um.

Painted colours, Pigmentum, i, n.

A maker (or ſeller) of painted colours, Pigmentarius, ii, m.

A painter, Pictor, oris, m.

A painting, Pigmentatio, onis, f. Pictio, onis, f.

Of or for painting, Pictōrius, a, um.

Paint for the cheeks (or womens painting) Fucus, i, m.

A pair, Par, ăris, m.

P A L.

A palace (or court of a King) Palatium, ii, n. Regia, æ, f.

Palace at Greenwich built by Humphrey Duke of Glouceſter, Placentia.

A county palatine, Comitatus Palatinus. Spel. 168.

A pale, Palus, i, m. Pry. 383. Ra. Ent. 646. Palicium, ii, n. 2 Mon. 420.

To pale (or hedge in with pales) Vallo, are.

A palfrey (Horſe) Palafredus, m. Palfredus, i, m. Palefridus, i, m.

A pal-

A palfrey-keeper, Agaſo, onis, m. Equiſo, onis, m.

Pallas (a womans name) Pallas, adis, f.

A pallet-bed, Palea, æ, f. Stratum, i, n. Grabatus, i, m.

The palm of the hand, Palma, æ, f. Canum manus, Vola manus.

A palm in meaſure the breadth of four fingers, Palmus, i, m.

Palm Sunday, Dominica palmarum.

The palmer (or feruler) Ferula, æ, f.

A palmiſter (or diviner by the palm of the hand) Chirŏmantes, is, m.

Palmiſtry, Chiromantia, æ, f.

The palſy, Părălyſis, is, f.

Sick of the palſy, Paraliticus, a, um,

P A M.

A pamphlet, Pampletum, i, n.

P A N.

A pan, Patella, æ, f.

A warming-pan, Calefactorium, ii, n. Thermoclinium, ii, n.

A dripping-pan, Deguttorium, ii, n.

A frying-pan, Sartago, inis, f. Frictorium, ii, n.

A cloſe-ſtool-pan, Laſanum, i, n.

A chafing-diſh-pan, Ignitabulum, i, n.

A pancake, Lăgănum, i, n. Panis teſtuaceus.

The panch (or lower part of the belly) Abdomen, inis, n. Alvus, i, f, & m. Omaſum, i, n.

A pane of glaſs, Quadra vitrea.

A pane of wainſcot, Quadra lignea.

A Pannel, Panellum, i, n. It is an *Engliſh* word, and ſignifieth a little part, for a Pane is a part, and a Pannel a little part (as a Pannel of wainſcot, a Pannel of a ſaddle, and a Pannel of a Parchment, wherein the Jurors names are written and annexed to the writ,) and a Jury is ſaid to be impannelled when the Sheriff hath entred their names into the Pannel, or little piece of Parchment, *in Pannello aſſiſæ. Cook on Lit. Lib.* 2. c. 2. *Sect.* 234.

The pannel of a horſe, Dorſuale, lis, n. Stratum, i, n.

A pannier, Fiſcina, æ, f. Caniſtrum, i, n. Panarium, ii, n.

Pant (river in eſſex) Pente fluvius.

A pantler, Panarius, ii, m. Panitorius, ii, m.

A pantry, Panarium, ii, n. Paniſtra, æ, f. Cerealium, ii, n.

P A P.

Paper, Papyrus, i, f. Charta, æ, f.

Fine paper, Charta auguſta.

Paper imperial (or royal) Charta Claudiana, Charta Regia, vel Imperialis.

Blotting, ſinking paper, Charta Bibula.

Brown (or cap) paper, to wrap wares in, Charta Emporetica.

Paper not written on, Charta pura.

Waſt paper, Schediaſma, atis, n.

A ſheet of paper, Scheda, æ, f.

A leaf of paper, Schedula, folium.

A quire or ream of paper, Scapus, i, m.

A coronet of paper uſed by Grocers, Cuculium, ii, n.

A ſmall piece of paper, Chartŭla, æ, f.

Paper mills, Chartariæ officinæ.

A maker

A maker of paper, Chartarius, ii, m. Papyri confector.

A paper merchant, Chartularius, ii, m.

A seller of paper, Păpyrŏpōla, æ, m. Chartŏpōla, æ, m.

Made of paper, Chartaceus, a, um.

Belonging to paper, Chartarius, a, um.

A pap, Mamma, æ, f.

Pap castle (in Cumberland) Apiacum, Epeiacum, Epiacum.

P A R.

A paradox (or matter contrary unto common opinion) Paradoxum, i, n.

A paragraph in writing, whatsoever is contained in one sentence, Paragraphus, i, m.

A parapet, Lorica, æ, f. Vallum paris pectori altitudinis.

A paraphrase (or plain interpretation of a thing) Paraphrasis, is, f.

A paraphrast, Paraphrasta, æ, m.

To parboil, Semicoquo, ere.

Parboiled, Semicoctus, a, um.

A parcel, Parcella, æ, f. Particula, æ, f.

To parcel out, Parcello, are. Ra. Entr. 2.

By parcels, Particulatim, adv.

Parcenary (or joynt tenancy) Paragium, ii, n. Participatio, onis, f.

Parchment (or vellum) Pergămēna, æ, f. Membrana, æ, f.

A little skin (or piece of parchment) Membranula, æ, f.

A parchment maker, Membranarius, ii, m.

Parchment making, or the place where parchment is sold, Membranaria, æ, f.

Of or belonging to parchment, Membranaceus, a, um.

Parco Fracto. Is a writ that lyeth against him that violently breaketh a Pound, and taketh out Beasts thence, which upon some trespass done upon another mans ground, are lawfully impounded. *Regist. Orig. fol. 166. Fitz. nat. brev. fol.* 100.

To pardon, Pardono, are.

A pardon, Pardonatio, onis, f. Perdonatio, onis, f. It is the forgiving of an offence against the King.

To pare, Decortico, are.

To pare or clipp, Reseco, are.

To pare or scrape away, Abrado, ere.

A parent (father or mother) Parens, tis, c. g.

Parentage (or kindred) Parentela, æ, f.

To parget (or plaister) Crusto, are.

To new parget (or white line) Interpolo, are.

Parget (or plaister) Cæmentum, i, n.

Marble parget, Crustæ Numidæ.

Pargeted (covered with thin slates of marble thin shelled) Crustatus, a, um.

A pargeter (or plaisterer) Cæmentarius, ii, m. Crustarius, ii, m.

A pargeting of walls, Incrustatio, onis, f.

A paring (shred, or that which is pared off) Resegmen, inis, n.

A parish, Parochia, æ, f.

A parishioner, Parœcus, ci, m. Parochianus, i, m.

A park, Parcus, i, m.

The keeper of a park, Parcarius, ii, m. Ra. Entr. 75. Placit. Cor. 18. Stat. de Malefactoribus in Parcis.

The game of a park, Venaria Parci. Ra. Entr. 75.

Parliament, Parlamentum, i, n. It is the Assembly of the King and the three Estates of the Realm, *viz.* The Lords Spiritual, the Lords Temporal, and Commons, for the debating of matters touching the Common wealth, and especially the

 making

making and correcting of Laws, which assembly or Court is of all others the highest, and of greatest authority, as you may read in Sir *Thomas Smith de Rep. Angl. Lib.* 2. *cap.* 1. *Cambd. Brit.* and *Crompt. Jurisdict. fol.* 1. *& seq.* The institution of this Court *Polydor. Virgil. lib.* 11. of his Chronicles, referreth after a sort to *Hen.* 1. yet confessing that it was used before, though very seldom. See more of the course & order of this Parliament, *In Crompt. Jurisdict. fol.* 1. *& seq.* and *Powel alias Hooker* in his book purposely written of this matter.

A parlour (or inner room) Parloria, æ, f. Conclavium, ii, m. Cœnaculum, li, n.

A waiter in the parlour, Triclinarius, ii, m.

Parnel (a womans name) Petronella, æ, f.

Parole, Loquela, æ, f. It is a *French* word, signifying as much as *Dictio*, *Allocutio*, *Sermo*, *Vox*, It is used in *Kitchin fol.* 193. for a Plea in Court. It is also some time joyned with Lease, as Lease parol, that is Lease *per parole*, a Lease by word of mouth.

A parricide (a killer of his father or mother) Patricida, æ, m.

A parson (or rector of a Church) Persona, æ, f.

A parsonage, Personatus, ûs, m.

A partner in a parsonage, Porcionarius pro portionaris.

Partable, Partibilis, le.

To partake (of part and take) Participo, are.

A part (piece or share) Pars, rtis, f.

A small part (or portion) Portiuncula, æ, f.

Parted, Partitus, a, um.

Parthenia (a womans name) Parthenia, æ, f.

Partial, Partialis, le, adj.

Particular, Particularis, re, adj.

A partition, Partitio onis, f.

A partition wall which belongeth to two rooms, Paries intergerinus.

Partitione faciendo. Is a writ that lyeth for those that hold Lands or Tenements *pro indiviso*, and would sever to every one his part, against him or them that refuse to join in partition, as Coparceners, and Tenants in Gavel kind. *Old nat. brev. fol.* 142. *Fitz. nat. brev. fol.* 61. *Regist Orig. fol.* 76. 316. and *Regist. Judic. fol.* 80. and the new book of Entries *verbo* Partition.

A partlet (or neckerchief) Mammillare, is, n. Amiculum, li, n.

A partner (or a complice) Particeps, ipis, adj. Partiarius, ii, m.

A joint partner with an other in office and duty, Jugales.

Part owner, Parte proprietarius, ii, m.

Party-peers, Columnæ partibiles.

P A S.

Paschal (a mans name) Paschalis, m.

Passage, Passagium, ii, n. Co. Ent. 521. Brac. 163. 8. Co. 46. Ry. 258. 344. Lex. 94. It signifieth in our Common Law, the hire that a man payeth for being transported over Sea. *Anno* 4. *Ed.* 3. *cap.* 7. or over any river. *West.* 2. *cap.* 25. *anno* 13. *Ed.* 1.

Safepassage (guidage) Guidagium, ii, n.

To pass (or go by) Prætereo, ire. Transmeo, are.

To pass at present till further examination, Debere esse.

To pass, Passo, are.

A passenger (or way-faring man) Viator, oris, m.

A passenger, Vector, oris, m.

Past (or dough) Massa, æ, f.

Puff-past, Crustulata, æ, f.

Stationers

Stationers past, Colla, æ, f.

The pasterns of a horse, Suffrago, inis, f.

All kind of pastery work, pies or baked meats, Dulcia, æ, f.

A pasty or pye, Artocreas, atis, n. Minutal dulciarium, Crustulatum, i, n.

A pastler (or maker of cakes) Crustularius, ii, n. Cupedinarius, ii, m.

A pastry, Artocrearium, ii, n.

A grasing or pasturing of cattle, Pascuagium, ii, n.

Pasturing, Pasturatio, onis, f.

A depasturing, Depasturatio, onis, f.

To pasture, Pasturo, are.

To depasture, Depasturo, are.

Pasture ground, Pascuum, ui, n.

P A T.

To patch (or repair) Sarcio, ire.

A patent (or letter patent of a Prince) Literæ Patentes. (*i. e.*) Grants made by the King under the Great Seal.

A patentee, Concessus per literas patentes.

A pattern (or example) Exemplar, aris, n.

A path (or foot way) Semita, æ, f. Callis, is, m.

A patriarch (or chief father) Patriarcha, æ, m.

Patrick (a mans name) Patricius, ii, m.

Patrimony (or inheritance) Patrimonium, ii, n.

Patrington (in Yorkshire) Prætorium.

A patron, Patronus, i, m. Is one that hath the advowson or Presentation to a Church.

Patronage, Patronagium, ii, n.

A patten (or wooden shooe) Calopodium, ii, n. Cuspus, i, m. Solea lignea.

P A U.

To pave (or make pavements) Pavio, ire. Pavimento, are. Strastumino, are. Pavimentum Sternere Lapidibus.

A pavement, Pavimentum, i, n.

Paved, Pavimentatus, a, um. Stratus, a, um.

To pave all through, Persterno, ere.

Paved all through, Perstratus, a, um.

Paving (as of causeys and ways) Pavimentatio, onis, f. Stratura, æ, f.

Money for paving of streets (or highways) Paviagium, ii, n.

A paving Beetle or such like thing wherewith they trim pavements. Pavicula, æ, f. Fistuca, æ, f.

To pave the floors, Ruderare Pavimenta.

A paver, Pavitor, oris, m.

A pavillion (or tent) Pavilio, onis, f. Pry. 196. Sæpe. Tentorium, ii, n. Papilio, onis, f.

A pavillion (or canopy over a bed) Conopeum, ei, n.

Paul (a mans name) Paulus, i, m.

The conversion of St. Paul, Festum Conversionis Sancti Pauli.

To paunch (or unbowel) Exentero, are.

Paunton (in Lincolnshire) ad Pontem.

To pause (or rest) Pauso, are. Spatium interponere.

A pause, Pausa, æ, f.

P A W.

A paw (or foot of a beast) Ungula, æ, f.

A pawn (or pledge) Pignus, eris, & oris, n.

To pawn, Oppignero, are. Pignero, are.

A pawning, Oppigneratio, onis, f.

Laid to pawn, Pigneratitius, a, um.

A Pawn-broker, Hypothecarius, ii, m. Pigneratitius creditor. Pignerator, oris, m.

P A Y.

To pay, Paio, are. 2 Inst. 456. Solvo, ere.

 A

A soldiers pay (*or wages*) Stipendium, ii, n.

A pay-master, Diribitor, oris, m.

Payment, Paiagia, æ, f. Ry. 565. Solutio, onis, f.

A payment of corn to the King by way of purveyance, Coragium, ii, n.

P E A.

Peace (*or concord*) Pax, acis, f.

To make peace, Pacifico, are.

A peace maker, Pacificator, oris, m. Pacarius, ii, m.

Peace-making, Pacificatio,onis,f.

A Peach, Malum Persicum.

A Peacock, Pavo, onis, m.

A Pea-hen, Pava, æ, f.

A Pearch (*for a Hawk or Bird*) Ames, is, f.

A Peak, Velamen pro fronte.

A Pear, Pyrum, i, n.

A Katern Pear, Pyrum crustumium.

A Pear Apple, Melapium, ii, n.

A Pear Tree, Pyrus, i, f.

A Choke-Pear-Tree, Pirafter, tri, m.

A Pearl, Margarita, æ, f.

A Necklace of Pearls, Monile Margaritarum.

A Seller of Pearls, Margaritarius, ii, m.

Pease(*a kind of Pulse*) Pisum,i,n.

P E B.

A Pebble-Stone,Calculus, li, m.

P E C.

Peche (*the Family*) De Peccato.

A Peck, Modiolus, i, m.

Peckirk near *Crowland*, Pegelandia.

Peculiar (*or proper*) Peculiaris, re, adj.

Peculiarly (*or properly*) Peculiter, adv.

P E D.

The half round elevations upon the pedestal, Scamilli impares.

A Pedler (*he that maketh merchandice of little things*) Cocio, onis, m. Particus, i, m. Frivolarius, ii, m. Perpola, æ,m.

A Pedlers trade in going from town to town to sell wares, Vellatura, æ, f.

Pedlers Packs, Ægina, orum, n.

P E E.

A Peel to set bread in the oven, Infurnibulum, li, n.

A Peer (*as at Dover*) Pera, æ, f.

A Peer or Lantherne by the shore side, Pharus, i, m.

Peers (*or States of the Realm*) Pares. (*i. e.*) those that be of the Nobility of the Realm, and Lords of the Parliament,See *Stawnford Pl. Cor. Lib.* 3. *cap. Trial per les Peers*, The Reason whereof is, because there is a distinction of Degrees in our Nobility, yet in all publick actions they are equal: as in their voices in Parliament, and in passing upon the Trial of any Nobleman,*&c.*We have no set number of them, because the number of our Nobles may be more or less as it pleaseth the King.

P E I.

Peirce (*a mans name*) Piercius, ii, m.

To peirce (*or bore*) Foro, are. Perforo, are.

A peircer (*or wimble*) Terebra,æ,f.

A Peice (*or gobbet*) Frustum,i,n.

A Peice (*or fragment of any thing*) Fragmentum, i, n. Pecia, æ, f.

To peice one thing with another, Assuo, ere.

To pull in peices, Discerpo, ere.

A Fowling peice (*or hand Gun*) Avium Bombarda.

Peiton (*the Family*) De Pavilliano. Pietonus.

A peitrel (*or breast leather of a horse*)

horse) Antilena, æ, f.

P E L.

Pelf (goods and chattels) Palfra, æ, f.

A Pellet (or Plummet) Glans, dis, f.

A Pellet of Lead, Plumbata, æ, f.

Pellets of bread or past, wherewith Capons or other Fowls are crammed, Turunda, æ, f.

Pelt, Pellicea, æ, f.

A Pelt (or Hide) Pellis, is, f. Tergus, oris, n. Melota, æ, f.

A Pelt-man, Pelliparius, ii, m. Pellio, onis, m.

A Pelt-mans trade, Pelliparium, ii, n.

P E N.

Penance, Pœnitentia, æ, f. Pœna, æ, f.

A Pencil, Penicillum, i, n.

Pendants, Pensilia, ium, n.

Penelope (a womans name) Penelope, Indecl.

A Penn to write withal, Penna, æ, f. Calamus, i, m.

A Pen-case, Pennarium, ii, n. Calamarium, ii, n. Forulus, i, m.

A Pen-man, Librariolus, li, n.

A Pen-knife, Scalpellum, i, n.

Of a Pen, Pennarius, a, um.

A Penny, Denarius, ii, m. Denariolus, i, m. 2 Inst. 172.

A Pension (or ordinary Payment) Pensio, onis, f.

A Pensioner, Pensionarius, ii, m.

A Penthouse (to keep off rain) Subgrunda, æ, f. Imbricamentum, i, n. Compluvium, ii, n. Stillarium, ii, n. Appendix, icis, f.

A Pentice (or shed covered with boards) Penticia, æ, f.

Penury, Penuria, æ, f.

P E O.

People of Assinshire (in Scotland) Cerones.

People of Atterith or Atheury (in Ireland) Auterii.

People of Belgium about Monstreul, Morini.

People of Berkshire, &c. Attrebatii.

People of Britain, Britanni, Britones.

People of Britany (in France) Veneti.

People of Buquhan (in Scotland) Taizali.

People of Buckingham, Bedford and Hertfordshires, Cattidudani, Catticuclani, Cathicludani, Catuellani, Cattieuchlani.

People of Cardiganshire, Ceretici.

People of Caermarthenshire, Muredunenses.

People of Carrick (in Scotland) Novantes.

People of Cathness (in Scotland) Catini.

People about Cork (in Ireland) Vodiæ & Udiæ, Corionei.

People of Cheshire, or adjoining to it, Cangi, Ceangi, Conganii.

People of Donegal or Tyrconel (in Ireland) Rhobogdii, Vennicnii.

People of Cumberland, Cumbri.

People of Desmond (in Ireland) Iberni, Outerni.

People of Cluidesdale (in Scotland) Damnii.

People of Dorsetshire Dorotenses, Durotriges, Murotriges, Sumotriges.

People of Galloway in Scotland and Cunningham, Novantæ, Novantes.

People of Conaght (in Ireland) Gangani.

People of Devonshire and Cornwall, Damnonii, Danmonii, Dumnonii, Dunmonii, Ostæi, Ostiones.

People of Eskedale, &c. (in Scotland) Horesti, Horresti.

People of the Fennes, Girvii.

People of Fermanagh (in Ireland) Erdini.

People of France towards the British Sea, Osisini, Osismii.

People of Glocestershire and Oxfordshire, Dobuni, Boduni.

People of Hantshire, Meandari.

People of Holderness (in Yorkshire) Parisi.

People of Ireland, Cauci, Chaugi, Eblani, Iberi, Iverni, Simeni, Uterni.

People of Lancashire, &c. Brigantes,

People of Lennox (in Scotland, &c.) Canovaci, Carnonacæ.

People of Liddesdale, &c. (in Scotland) Elgovæ, Selgovæ.

People of man island, Mannenses.

People of Meanborow, East and West Mean (in Hampshire) Meanvari.

People of Mernis (in Scotland) Vernicones.

People of Middlesex, Hertfordshire, &c. Trinoantes, Trinobantes, Trinovantes.

People of Mounster (in Ireland) Concani.

People of West Mounster, Luceni, Velabri.

People of Murrey (in Scotland) Vacomagi.

People of Northamptonshire, Leicester, Rutland, Lincoln, Darby and Nottinghamshire, Coritani, Coritavi.

A Petty People in Northumberland or adjoining to it, Fisburgingi.

People of Northumberland, Hymbrionenses, Meatæ, Nordhumbri, Northanimbri, Northimbri, Ottadeni, Ottadini, Taizales, Vernicones.

People of north Wales. Geminii, Ordevices, Ordolucæ, Ordovices.

People of Radnorshire, Magesetæ.

People of Ross in Scotland Cantæ.

People of Scotland, Scoti, Ducalidonii, Vecturiones.

People of Scilly Islands, Melanchlani.

People of Somersetshire, Wiltshire, and Hampshire, Belgæ, Somerseti.

People of South-Wales, Silures.

People of Staffordshire, Cornavii, Mediterranei angli.

People of Strathnaverne (in Scotland) Cornabii, Cornabui Logi.

People of Suffolk, Norfolk, Cambridge, Huntingtonshires, Iceni, Cenimagni, Icini.

People of Surrey and the Sea coasts of Hampshire, Regni, Southregienses.

People of Teifidale, Twedale, &c. (in Scotland) Gadeni, Ladeni.

People of Ulster (in Ireland) Voluntii, Darni.

People of Warwick, Worcester, Stafford, Shropshire, Cheshire, Cornavii.

People of waterford, Kilkenny, art of Wesford (in Ireland) Brigantes.

People of West-Wales, Demetæ, Dimetæ.

People of Worcestershire, Wiccii, Hwiccii.

People of Yorkshire, Westmorland, Durham, Lancashire, Cumberland, Brigantes, Brigæ, Jugantes.

People of Wiltshire, Wilsati, Wiltenses.

People over against the Isle of Wight, Gevissi.

People (or Nation) Populus, li, m. Plebs, is, f.

The Common People, Vulgus, gi, m. &c. n.

P E P.

Pepper, Piper, ĕris, n. plur. caret.

P E R.

Peradventure, Fortè, adv.

A perch or pole (a measure) Pertica, æ, f. Stat. de Terris mensurand. Pertica 16. Pedum. 2 Mon. 1012.

1012. 15. Pedum & dimidium. 2 Mon. 157. 18. Pedum. 2. Mon. 157. 18. Pedum & dimidium 1. Mon. 828. 20. pedum. 2. Mon. 21. 204. Ry. 349. 24. pedum. 2. Mon. 608. 25. pedum. 2. Mon. 1007.

A perch of land, Pertica vel Perticata terræ.

Perdition (or destruction) Perditio, onis, f.

Perdonatio Utlagariæ. Is the form of Pardon for him, that for not coming to the Kings Court is Outlawed, and afterwards of his own accord yieldeth himself to Prison. *Regist. Judicial. fol.* 28.

Peregrine (a mans name) Peregrinus, i, m.

Peremptory, Peremptorius, a, um.

Perfect (exact or compleat) Perfectus, a, um.

To perfect (or make perfect) Perficio, ere. Consummo, are.

To perform, Performo, are.

Performance, Performatio, onis, f.

To perfume, Odoro, are. Suffumigo, are.

A perfume, Suffimentum, i, n. Odoramen, inis, n.

Perfumed, Suffitus, a, um. Odoratus, a, um.

A maker of perfumes, Odorarius, ii, m. Suffitor, oris, m.

A perfumer (or seller of perfumes) Unguentarius, ii, m. Seplasiarius, ii, m.

A perfuming pan, Acerra, æ, f. Thuribulum, li, n.

Perinde valere. Is a dispensation granted to a Clerk, that being defective in his Capacity to a Benefice, or other Ecclesiastical Function, is *de Facto* admitted unto it, and it hath the Appellation of the words which make the faculty as effectual to the party dispensed with at the time of his admission.

To perish, Pereo, ire.

Old Perith (in Cumberland) Petrianæ, Voreda.

To perjure, Perjuro, are.

Perjured, Perjuratus, a, um.

Perjury, Perjuratio, onis, f. Perjurium, ii, n. If a man swear to one that he will pay to him twenty Pound which he oweth him at a certain day, and at the day faileth of the Payment, he may not be sued in the Spiritual Court for the Perjury, because an action of debt lyeth at the Common Law for the Principal. But 34. *H.* 6. It is said, That if a man buy a horse for five Pound, *Solvendum*, such a day, and sweareth to make Payment at the day, but when the day is come, faileth of Payment, an action of debt lyeth at the Common Law, and another at the Spiritual Law, *pro Læsione fidei.* If a man calleth another Perjured man, he may have his Action upon his Case, because it must be intended contrary to his oath in a Judicial Proceeding: but for calling him a forsworn man, no action doth lie, because the forswearing, may be Extra judicial. *Cooks* 3. *part* of his *Instit. c.* 74.

To permit (suffer, or let) Permitto, ere. Sino, ere.

It is permitted, Licet, licuit, *and* Licitum est.

Permutation, Permutatio, onis, f.

Permutatione Archidiaconatus & Ecclesiæ eidem annexæ, cum Ecclesia & prebenda. Is a writ to an Ordinary commanding him to admit a Clerk to a Benefice, upon Exchange made with another. *Regist. Orig. fol.* 307. *A.*

Pernicious (or very hurtful) Perniciosus, a, um.

A perpendicular (or plumb-line) Perpendiculum, li, n.

Perpetual, Perpetuus, a, um.

Perplexed, Perplexus, a, um.

Perplexity, Perplexitas, atis, f.

A person, Persona, æ, f.

Persons cast away at Sea, Naufraga corpora.

Personable, Personabilis, le, adj. One who may maintain a Plea in a Court, *qui habet personam Standi in Judicio*.

Personal, Personalis, le, adj. It hath in our Common Law one strange signification, being joined with the Substantive, Things, Goods, or Chattels, as Things personal, Goods Personal, Chattels personal; for thus it signifieth any Corporeal and moveable thing belonging to any man, be it quick or dead. So it is used in *West Part* 2, *Symb. Tit.* Indictments *Sect.* 58. in these words. Theft is an unknown felonious taking away of another mans moveable personable Goods, and again *fol.* 61. Larceny is a felonious taking away of another mans moveable personal Goods. And *Kitchin fol.* 139. in these words where personal things shall be given to a Corporation; as a Horse, a Cow, an Oxe, Sheep, Hogs, or other Goods, &c. *Stawnf. pl. Cor. fol.* 25. *Contrectatio rei alienæ* is to be understood of things personal, for in things real it is not Felony; as the cutting of a Tree is not felony.

To perswade (induce, or move to do a thing) Perswadeo, ere.

To peruse (or over-look) Recognosco, ere.

A perwig (or perriwig) Galericulum, li, n. Capillamentum factitium. Coma Adoptiva.

P E S.

A pessary or other suppository of soft wool, Pessus, i, m.

A pestle (or pounder) Pistillum, i, n. Fractillum, i, n. Teratrum, i, m. Tritorium, ii, n.

To beat or pound with a pestle, Pinso, ere. Tero, ere.

P E T.

Peter (a mans name) Petrus i, m.

St. *Peters chair*, Festum Sancti Petri in Cathedra.

St. *Peter, and* St. *Pauls day*, Festum Sanctorum Petri & Pauli Apostolorum.

Peterborow, Petriburgus, Petropolis.

Bishop of Peterborow, Episcopus Petriburgensis.

A peticoat for a woman, Indusium, ii, n. Subucula muliebris.

Petit Larceny, Parvum Latrocinium.

Petit Treason, Parva Proditio. In true *French*, is *Petite Trahaison*, (*i. e.*) *Proditio minor*, Treason in a lesser or lower kind; for whereas Treason in the Highest Kind, is an Offence done against the security of the Common-wealth. *West part* 2. *Symb. Tit.* Inditements. *Sect.* 63. Petit Treason is of this nature, though not so expresly as the other. Petit Treason is a Killing of any to whom Private Obedience is due; as for a Servant to kill his Master or Mistress, a Wife her Husband, a Child her Father or Mother, a Clerk his Ordinary, to whom he oweth Canonical Obedience. *Stawnf. Pl. cor. Lib.* 1. *c.* 44.

If a Servant procure another to kill his Master, and he kill him in his Servants presence, this is Petty Treason in the Servant, and murder

der in the other; but if it be in his absence, the Servant is only accessary to the Murder, because the Principal is not a Traytor, and the Accessary should not be in worse condition than the principal. *Leigh. Phil. Com. fol.* 229. 230.

A maid conspired with a stranger to rob her Mistress, and in the night time let him in at the door, and led him to her Mistress's bed with a Candle, and the stranger killed her, the servant saying or doing nothing but holding the Candle, this was Petty Treason in her. *L. Dyer Ter. Hil. Anno* 2. *&* 3. *P. & M.* See *Crompt. Justice* of Peace, *fo.* 2. where he addeth divers other Examples to those of *Stawnford* for the Punishment of Petty Treason. See also the Statute *anno* 22. *H.* 8. *cap.* 14.

Petition, Petitio, onis, f. It hath a General Signification, for all Intreaties, made by an inferiour to a Superiour, and especially to one having Jurisdiction; but most especially it is used for that remedy, which the Subject hath to help a wrong done by the King: For the King hath it by Prerogative, that he may not be sued upon a writ, *Stawnford prærog. c.* 15. whom also read *cap.* 22. And a Petition in this Case, is either general or special. It is called General of the General Conclusion, set down in the same, *viz.* that the King do him Right and Reason, whereupon followeth a General Indorsement upon the same, let Right be done to the parties. Petition special is where the Conclusion is special for this or that; and the Indorsement to that is likewise special. See the rest *Chap.* 22.

Peto (the Family) De Pictavia, & Peto.

P E W.

A pew in a Church, Podium, ii, n. Subsellium templorum, Sedile, lis, n.

Pewter, Plumbum argentarium vel candidum. Stannum, i, n.

Pewter vessels, Vasa Stannea.

A pewterer, Stannarius, ii, m.

P H E.

A pheasant, Phasianus, i, m.

A pheasant hen, Phasiana, æ, f.

He that keepeth or breadeth pheasants, Phasianarius, ii, m.

Belonging to a pheasant, Phasianus, a, um.

P H I.

Philibert (a mans name) Philibertus, i, m.

Phillida (a womans name) Phillida, æ, f.

Philip (a mans name) Philippus, i, m.

Philip (a womans name) Philippa, æ, f.

St. *Philip and Jacobs day*, Festum Sanctorum Philippi & Jacobi Apostolorum.

Phillis (a womans name) Phillis, is, f.

Philomela (a womans name) Philomela, æ, f.

Philosophy, Philosophia, æ, f.

A philosopher, Philosophus, i, m.

Phineas (a mans name) Phineas, æ, m.

P H L.

Phlebotomy (or letting of blood) Phlebotomia, æ, f.

P H Y.

Physick, Medicina, æ, f. Ars medica.

To minister physick, Potiono, are. Curo, are.

A doctor of physick, Medicinæ Doctor.

A phy-

A physician, Medicus, i, m.

A physicians fee, Sostrum, tri, n.

Piccage, Piccagium, ii, n. (*i.e.*) Money paid in Fairs to the Lord of the Soil for breaking ground to set up Booths or Standings.

A pick-ax, Marra, æ, f. Rutum, i, n.

An ear-picker, Auriscalpium, ii, n.

A tooth picker, Dentiscalpium, ii, n.

Pickle (or Brine) Salsilago inis, f. Salsugo, inis, f. Liquamentum Salsum, Salsamentorum liquor.

A pickling (or saucing) Conditura, æ, f.

Pickle (or sauce) Condimentum, i, n.

To pickle, Salio, ire. Muria sive Salsugine condire.

One that sells pickles, Liquaminarius, ii, m. Condimentarius, ii m.

Pickle for fish, Tharia, æ, f.

Pickled herrings, Halec muriâ durata, sive Conditanea, Halec Muriatica.

Serving for pickle, Condimentarius, a, um.

A picture, Pictura, æ, f.

To picture (or make pictures) Picturo, are. Delineo, are.

The first draught of a picture, Catagraphe, es, f.

A picture drawer, Delineator, oris, m.

Adorned with pictures, Picturatus, a, um.

Of a picture, Picturālis, le.

Picts (a people of Britain) Picti.

Picts Country, Pictavia, Pictandia.

Picts wall, Hadriani murus, Murus picticus, Vallum.

P I E.

A piece, Pecia, æ, f.

Pie-powder Court, Curia pedis pulverizati. It signifieth a Court held in Fairs, for the Redress of all disorders committed within them: which because it is summary, *De plano & sine figura judicii*; It hath the name of dusty feet, which we commonly get by sitting near the ground, or rather from the Country mens dusty shoes, of this see *Crompt. Jurisd. fol.* 221. Of this Court read the Statute *anno* 17. *Ed.* 4. *cap.* 2. The stile of the Pie-powder Court held in the Close of St. *Bartholomew* the Great, near West *Smithfield London*, with the Licence granted by the Steward of that Court, for selling meat and drink during three days, is thus. *Curia pedis pulverizati Domini Regis tenta infra præcinctum Sancti Bartholomei magni juxta West Smithfield London, tempore Feriæ ibidem, videlicet in Vigilia Festi Sancti Bartholomei, in Festum Sancti Bartholomei, & in crastino die post Festum prædictum. Anno Regni Regis Gulielmi Tertii Dei Gratia Angliæ, &c. Undecimo, Egidius Wilks venit hic in Curia & petiit licentiam Curiæ pro venditione Esculenti & Poculenti infra jurisdictionem Feriæ pro tempore prædicto, & super se bene habendum ei conceditur, &c. per. Cur.*

To pierce (or bore) Penetro, are.

Pierced, Penetrātus, a, um.

A piercer, Penetrator, oris, m.

A piercing, Penetratio, onis, f.

Pierpont (the Family) De Petra Ponte.

P I G.

A pigeon, Columba, æ, f.

A pigeon house, Columbarium, ii, n.

A pig (or little young swine) Porculus, i, m. Porcellus, i, m.

A sow pig, Sūcŭla, æ, f.

A boar pig, Verres, is, m.

A shot or pig, Nefrens, tis, m.

A pigs-trough, Lapista porcina.

A pightell, Pightellum, ni, n.

Fo.

Fo. 144. Lex. 9. Pictellum, i, n. (*i. e.*) a Pingle or little Close.

P I K.

A pike (or spear) Lancea, æ, f. Hasta, æ, f.

A pike-man, Hastātus, i, m. Lancearius, ii, m.

P I L.

A pile (or heap) of wood, Moles, is, f. Strues, is, f. Meta Lignorum.

A pile, Sublica, æ, f. Pila, æ, f.

The piles (or emeroids) in the Fundament of a man, Hæmorrhois, idis, f.

A pilgrimage, Peregrinatio, onis, f.

To pill (or take off the bark) Decortico, are.

A pill (in physick) Pillula, æ, f.

A pillar, Columna, æ, f. Pila, æ, f.

A little pillar, Columella, æ, f.

A little pillar set on a greater, Epystilium, ii, n.

A chief pillar, or buttress, Anteris, idis, f. Erismæ, arum, f.

Chief pillars, Antes, ium, m.

A square or flat sided pillar, Stela, æ, f. Pila, æ, f.

The foot of a pillar that sustaineth any thing, Basis, is, f.

The place between two pillars, Intercolumnium, ii, n.

The shaft of a pillar between the Chapiter and the Base, Scapus, i, m.

The nether part of a pillars foot bearing the form of a four square tile stone, Plinthis, is, f.

The blunter part of a pillar, in the very top like a goats nose, Sima, æ, f.

Those parts in furrowed pillars which stand up higher than the furrows or gutters, Striæ, arum, f.

The rundle in the bottom of a pillar, Scotia, æ, f.

The border above the Chapiter of a pillar (the Freese) Zophŏrus, i, m.

The footstool of a pillar, Stylobata, æ, f.

The main body of the pillar, Hypotrachelium, ii, n.

A part of a pillar whereon an arch standeth especially, Incumba, æ, f.

The pillar of a stair-case, Scāpus, i, m.

A place set about with pillars, Circumcolumnium, ii, n.

A kind of pillars so graven that the carved work resembleth the rowling waves, Cymatium, ii, n.

The making of pillars small towards the top, Contractura, æ, f.

The part of a Chapiter of a pillar which is cut and graven like Teeth, Denticulus, li, m.

Building or proping with pillars, Columnatio, onis, f.

Pillar by pillar, in close order, Pīlātim, adv.

A pillion, Dorsuale, is, n.

A pillory, Pillorium, ii, n. Stat. de Collistrigio, vet. Entr. 107. Pilloria, æ, f. Ra. Entr. 259. 540. Collistrigium, ii, n.

Belonging to a pillory, Pilloralis, le, adj. Bract. 101. Co. Lit. 287.

A pillow to lay the head on, Pulvinar, aris, n. Pulvinus, i, m. Pulvinarium, ii, n. Cervicale, lis, n. Pulvinarium de down Ra. Entr. 53.

A pillober, Theca pulvinaria.

A pilot (or conductor of a ship) Naviculārius, ii, m. Navarchus, i, m. Nauclerus, i, m. Naustrologus, i, m.

P I N.

A pin, Acicula, æ, f. Spinula, æ, f.

A pin of wood, Clavus ligneus, Impages.

A pin that keepeth on the wheel of the axle-tree, Humerillus, i, m. Embolium, ii, n.

A Rowling-pin used to make pie-lids, Artopta, æ, f.

Pins or wedges wherewith one piece of

of wood is fastned to another, Epigri.

A pin of wood or ivory to trim or crisp the hair with, Calamistrum, i, n. Discerniculum, i, n.

A pin of a beam, Clavus trabalis.

The pin of a table book, Stylus, i, m.

A pin-case, Theca acicularis. Acicularium, ii, n. Spinularium, ii, n.

Pin-dust (or the dust of filed metal) Limatura, æ, f. Ramentum, i, n.

A maker of pins, Acicularius, ii, m. Spinularius, ii, m.

A pinning of houses, Substructio, onis, f.

A pair of pincers, Forceps, ipis, m. Forcipula, æ, f.

Pincers to draw teeth with, Odontagra, æ, f. Dentarpagra, æ, f.

A pinfold (or pound) Pynfolda, æ, f. Parcus, i, m.

A pinnace (or swift ship) Liburna, æ, f. Actuariolum, li, n. Celo, onis, f.

A pinnacle, Pinnaculum, li, n. Fastigium, ii, n. Acroteria, orum, n.

Laced pinners, Frontalia Fibulata.

A pint, Pinta, æ, f. 1 Fo. 259.

P I O.

A pioneer (or underminer) Cunicularius, ii, m.

P I P.

A pipe (or measure of 126 Gallons) Pipa, æ, f. It is also a Roll in the Exchequer. *Anno 27. Ed. 3.*

A pipe of wine, Pipa vel butta vini, Ra. Entr. 168. Spel. 114. Cadus, i, m.

A pipe to play on, Tibia, æ, f. Fistula, æ, f.

A short pipe with a small sound, Cingria, æ, f.

A bag-pipe, Tibia utricularis.

A conduit pipe, Aquæductus, ûs, m. Canalis, is, d. g. Tŭbus, i, m.

A small conduit pipe, Tŭbŭlus, li, m.

A pipe to conveigh water into houses, Paragogia, æ, f.

A water pipe of a small size, so made that the water may mount aloft, Euripus, i, m.

Made hollow like a Conduit Pipe, Tubulātus, a, um.

A making hollow like a Pipe, Tubulatio, onis, f.

A piper, Fistulator, oris, m. Tibicen, inis, m.

A bag-piper, Utricularius, ii, m.

A pipkin (or little pot) Ollŭla, æ, f. Chytra, æ, f.

P I R.

A pirate (or Sea robber) Pirata, æ, m. Pirea, æ, m.

An arch pirate, Archipirāta, æ, m.

A pirates ship, Navis prædatoria.

A place where Pirates resort unto, Piraterium, ii, n.

Piracy, Piratica, æ, f.

P I S.

Piscary, Piscaria, æ, f. *(i. e.)* a Liberty of fishing in another mans water.

A pispot, Matula, æ, f.

A pistol (or pistolet) Bombardula, æ, f. Sclopus, i, m.

P I T.

A Pit (or deep hole made in the ground) Puteus, ei, m. Fossa, æ, f. Lăcūna, æ, f.

A little pit, Puteolus, li, m.

A pit or ditch to avoid water, Agoga, æ, f.

A pit where potters clay is digged, Argilletum, i, n.

A sand-pit, Arenarium, ii, n.

A bird-lime pit, Viscarium, ii, n.

A pitch-fork, Furca, æ, f.

Pitch, Pix, picis, f. plur. caret.

To pitch, or cover over with pitch, Pico, are. Oppico, are.

A pitch-pit, Picaria, æ, f.

Having pitch hanging to it, Piceatus, a, um.

Of Pitch, Picarius, a, um.

To

To pitch tents (or pavillions) Castrametor, ari. Tentoria figere.

A pitcher (or pot) Situla, æ, f. Haustum, i, n. Urna, æ, f. Hydra, æ, f. Urceus, ei, m.

A great pitcher, Culullus, i, m.

A little pitcher, Urceŏlus, i, m.

A dresser or other board to set pitchers or pots on, Urnarium, ii, n.

A pitfal (or trap) Dēcĭpŭla, æ, f. Fŏvea, æ, f.

A pittance (or small repast) Pitancia, æ, f. Dimensum, i, n.

P L A.

A placard of a Prince, Placitum, i, n. vid. Patent and Letters Patents.

A place, Locus, ci, m.

A secret place, Abditum, i, n.

An open place to walk in, Subdiale, is, n.

A little place (a piece or parcel) Placitum, i, n.

A place where Lawyers meet in afternoons to moot, or to talk with their Clients, or as some, a Court or Yard before a Palace, Pervisus, i, m.

A place of Land, Placea terræ. Ra. Entr. 145. 155. 539. 618.

The plague, Pestis, is, f.

To plaight, Plico, are. Complico, are.

Plain (manifest) Planus, a, um.

A plain (down or Champion ground) Plānĭties, ei, f.

A Joyners plain, Rādŭla, æ, f. Planula, æ, f. Dolabra, æ, f.

A little plain, Dolabella, æ, f.

To plain with a plain, Deplanare planula. Plano, are. Cutello, are.

To shave with a plain, Runcino, are.

Plained, Dedolatus, a, um. Complanatus, a, um.

A plaint (or pleynt) Querula, æ, f.

To plaister, Gypso, are. Trullisso, are.

To plaister, rough cast, cover with thin slates of Marble, Crusto, are.

Plaister (Plaistering or Pargetting) Piastra, æ, f. Gypsum, i, n. Intritum, i, n. Incrustatio, onis, f.

A plaister (or salve) Emplastrum, i, n.

Plaistering (rough casting) Trullissatio, onis, f. Tectorium, ii, n. Cœmentatio, onis, f.

Plaistered, Tectoriatus, a, um.

A plaisterer (or pargeter) Cæmentarius, ii, m. Crustarius, ii, m.

A plaisterers brush, Penicillum tectorium.

A plank (or board) Planca, æ, f. Assamentum, i, n. Tabula, æ, f.

Joynts of planks, Assamentorium commissuræ.

To plank a house, Tabulo, are.

To plank or joyn planks and boards, Coasso, are.

Overthwart boards or planks laid a cross, Transversaria, orum, n.

A planking, Coassatio, onis, f.

A plant, Planta, æ, f.

To plant, Planto, are.

A plate of metal, Lamina, æ, f. Bractea, æ, f.

A plate (or plate trencher) Scutella, æ, f. Orbis, is, m.

A plate of iron, Lamina, æ, f.

To plate with iron, Lamino, are.

Plate, Argentum factum, Argentum escarium.

Well wrought plate, benefactum argentum.

A platform, Ichnographia, æ, f.

A platter (or dish) Patina, æ, f. Catinus, i, m. Discus ci, m. Scutula, æ, f.

A little platter, Patella, æ, f. Catillus, i, m.

A platter maker, Patinarius, ii, m.

Belonging to a platter, Patellarius, a, um.

Plato (*a mans name*) Plato, onis, m.

A Stage player, Histrio, onis, m. Scenicus, ci, m.

A playing the whore, Putagium, ii, n.

P L E.

A plea, Placitum, i, n. It signifieth in our Common Law, that which either party alledgeth for himself in Court, and this was wont to be done in *French*, from the Conquest until *Edward* the Third, who ordained them to be done in *English*, *Anno* 36. *cap*. 15 All pursuits and actions (we call them in our *English* Tongue Pleas) and in barbarous (but now usual Latin) *Placita*, taking the name abusive, of the definitive Sentence, which may well be called *Placitum*. The *French* call it *Arrest*, in which word after their custom, they do not sound *s*. but we call *Placitum* the Action, not the Sentence: and *Placitare* barbarously for to plead, in *English agere*, or *litigare*. Vid. *Smiths* Commonwealth of *England*, c. 9.

Pleas are divided into Pleas of the Crown, and into Common or Civil Pleas. Pleas of the Crown are all suits in the Kings name, against offences committed against his Crown and Dignity. *Stawnf. pl. cor. cap*. 1. or against his Crown and Peace. *Smith de Rep. Angl. lib*. 2. *cap*. 9. and these are Treasons, Felonies, misprisions of either and Mayhem, for those only doth that Reverend Judge *Stawnford* mention in that Tractate.

Communia Placita. Common Pleas are those that are held between Common persons, They are *Communia placita*, not in respect of the Persons, but in respect of the Quality of the Pleas. *Cooks* 4*th*. *part* of *Instit*. *cap*. 10.

All those Pleas which touch the Life or Mutilation of man are called Pleas of the Crown, and cannot be done in the name of any Inferiour person, than he or she that holdeth the Crown of *England*, and likewise no man can give Pardon thereof, but the Prince only. *Cooks* 4*th*. *part of Instit*. *cap*. 4.

Plea may further be divided into as many Branches as Action; which see, for they signifie all one. Then there is a Foreign Plea, whereby matter is alledged in any Court that must be tried in another. As if one should lay Bastardie to another in a Court Baron, *Kitch. fol*. 75.

A pleader, Placitatorius, ii, m.

A pleading, Placitatio, onis, f.

A Court where Lawyers pleadings are, Placitatorium, ii, n.

To plead, Placito, are.

A pledge (*or surety*) Plegius, ii, m.

A pledge (*an earnest*) Arrha, æ, f.

One that is in Frank-pledge and lies under the protection of the Law, Inlagatus, a, um.

Plegiis acquietandis, Is a writ that lyeth for a surety, against him for whom he is surety, if he pay not the money at the day. *Fitz. nat. brev. fol*. 137. *Regist. Orig*. 158. *a*.

Plenty, Plentitudo, inis, f

Plevin (*or Replevin*) Plevina, æ, f. Lex. 97. 109. Placit. Cor. 45. Brac. 365. bis.

The pleurisie (*an inward shooting pain*) Pleuritis, idis, f.

P L O.

A plough, Aratrum, i, n.

Ploughings (*or earings*) Aruræ, arum, f.

A ploughman, Arator, oris, m. Glebarius, ii, m.

He

He that holdeth the plough, Stivatius, ii, m.

One that plougheth under, Subatator, oris, m.

The plough tail (or handle) Stiva, æ, f. Bura, æ, f.

A plough-ſhare, Vomer, eris, m. Dens aratri.

A beam of a plough, Temo, onis, m.

A plough-ſtaff, Rallum, i, n.

Plough-bote, Eſtoverium arandi. Co. Lit. 41. B.

A plough-wright, Aratrifaber, bri, m.

To yoke the bulls to the plough, Tauros aratro adjungere.

To plough, Aro, are.

To plough over a field, Peraro, are.

Ready to plough, ărātūrus, a, um.

He that driveth the plough drawn with Oxen, Jugarius, ii, m.

Ploughed, Aratus, a, um.

The heads of ploughed lands, Chevifæ, arum, f.

Ploughed throughout, Peraratus, a, um.

A plough-land, Caruchata, æ, f. alſo a wain Load.

Ploughing and Harrowing, Arrura, æ, f. Aratura, æ, f.

P L U.

A plummer (or plumber) Plumbarius, ii, m.

A plummers ſhop, Shopa Plumbaria.

A plume of feathers, Coſta, æ, f.

A plum, Prunum, i, n.

A plummet, Plumbata, æ, f.

A plummet or weight of Lead that leapers or dancers on Cords, hold in their hands to countervail their weight, Halter, eris.

A plummet and line let down into the water to ſound the depth thereof Bŏlis, idis, f.

A plummet (or plumb rule for Maſons and Carpenters) Libella, æ, f. Perpendiculum, li, n. Amuſſis, is, f.

To plunder, Prædor, ari.

Plunder, Prædātum, i, n.

A ſelling plundered goods by outcry, Haſtarium, ii, n.

A plunderer, Prædator, oris, m. Depopulator, oris, m. Prædo, onis, m.

A plundering, Prædatio, onis, f. Depopulatio, onis, f.

Pluries, Is a writ that goeth out in the third place, for firſt goeth out the Original *Capias*, which if it ſpeed not, then goeth out the *ſicut alias*, and if that fail, then the *Pluries*. See *Old. nat. brev. fol.* 33. in the writ *de Excom. capiendo*. See in what diverſity of Caſes this is uſed in the Table of the *Regiſt. Orig.*

P O C.

A pocket, Saccellus, li, m. Loculus, li, m. Sacculus, li, m.

P O E.

A poet, Poeta, æ, m.

P O I.

The point of a weapon, Cuſpis, idis, f.

A point or tittle, Punctus, i, m.

A point to truſs withal, Ligŭla, æ, f.

To point or make ſharp at the end, Cuſpido, are.

A point maker, Corigiarius, ii, m.

A poiſe (or weight) Peiſa, æ, f.

To poiſon, Impoiſono, are. 2. Inſt. 634.

P O L.

A polcat, Putorius, ii, m. Martes, is, f.

A pole or perch to meaſure land with, Pola, æ, f. Lex. 46. Pertica, æ, f.

The pole which Ropedancers uſe, Halter, eris, m.

A pole or thwart piece laid croſs way, Longurius, ii, m.

To pole up, Palo, are.

Policy (or civil government) Politia, æ, f.

To polish, Polio, ire.

Polished, Politus, a, um.

P O M.

A pomander, Magma, atis, n. Diapasma, atis, n.

A pomegranat, Malum aut Pomum Granatum.

P O N.

A pond, Stagnum, i, n.

A fish pond, Vivarium, ii, n. Lex. 130. 2 Inst. 100.

Pone is a writ whereby a Cause depending in the County Court is removed to the Common Bank. *Old nat. brev. fol.* 2. It is also a writ to the Sheriff to take security of the Defendant for his appearance. See in what diversity of Cases it is used, in the Table of the *Register Original*. Of this writ, see five sorts in the Table of the *Regist. Judic. verbo Pone per vadium*.

Ponendis in Assisis, Is a writ founded upon the Statute of *Westm.* 2. *cap.* 38. and upon the Statute *Articuli Super Chartas cap.* 9. which Statutes do shew, what persons Viscounts ought to Impanel upon Assises and Juries, and what not; as also what number he should Impanel upon Juries and Inquests. Which see in the *Regist. Orig. fol.* 178. *a*, and in *Fitz. Nat. brev. fol.* 165.

Ponendo in Ballium, Is a writ whereby to Will a Prisoner held in Prison to be committed to Bayl in cases Bayleable. *Regist. Orig. fol.* 133. *b.*

Ponendo Sigillum ad Exceptionem. Is a writ whereby the King willeth Justices, according to the Statute of *Westm.* 2. to put their Seals to exceptions laid in against the Plaintiffs Declaration by the Defendant.

Pontage, Pontagium, ii, n. 8. Co. 46. Ry. 252. 303. 336. It is a Contribution towards the Maintenance, or re-edifying of Bridges. *Westm.* 2. *cap.* 2. *anno* 13. *Ed.* 1. It may be also Toll taken to this purpose of those that pass over the Bridges. *Anno* 39. *Eliz. cap.* 24. *anno* 1. *H.* 8. *cap.* 9. and see the Statute *anno* 22. *H.* 8. *cap.* 5.

Pontibus reparandis. Is a writ directed to the Sheriff, &c. willing him to charge one or more to repair a Bridge, to whom it belongeth. *Regist. Orig. fol.* 153. *b.*

P O O.

The poop or hindeck of a ship, Puppis, f.

Pool (the Family) Polus.

Poor (or needy) Pauper, eris, adj.

Poorness (or poverty) Paupertas, atis, f.

P O P.

Popularity, Popularitas, atis, f.

Populous (or full of people) Populosus, a um.

P O R.

A porch (or Gallery) Porticus, ûs, f.

A Church porch, Vestibulum, i, n. Pronaus, i, m. Limen Sacrum.

Pork, Caro porcina.

A loin of pork, Penita Ossa.

A pestle of pork, Petaso, onis, m.

A port or haven, Portus, ûs, m.

Portchester, Caer peris.

A portcullis, Cataracta, æ, f.

A porter (or burden bearer) Bajulus, li, m. Portitor, oris, m. Corbulo, onis, m. Gestor, oris, m.

Porters fare (or carriers hire) Commistrum, i, n.

A

A porter (or door keeper) Janitor, oris, m. Ostiarius, ii, m. Pataginarius, ii, m.

The place of porter, Porteria, æ, f. 8. Co. 47.

A port town, Villa portum habens. Villa portuaria. 1 Fo. 64.

A porringer (or little dish) Catillus, i, m.

Portgreve, Portgrevius, ii, m. Spel. 68.

A portmantle (or cloak bag) Hippopera, æ, f. Mantica, æ, f.

A portion (or part) Portio, onis, f.

Portsmouth (in Hampshire) Magnus portus, Portesmutha, Portus ostium.

Portland Isle, Portlandia, Portuna.

Portmuck, Isamnium, Isanium, Isannium.

P O S.

A position, Positio, onis, f.

A posnet, Ollula, æ, f.

To possess, Possideo, ere.

A possession, Possessio, onis, f.

A possessor, Possessor, oris, m.

Postea, The return of the Justices of assises, made on the Record of *Nisi prius*, and called so from the word *Postea*, wherewith it begins.

Post diem, Is a return of a Writ after the day assigned for the Return, for the which the *Custos brevium* hath four pence, whereas he has nothing, if it be returned at the day, or it may be the Fee taken for the same.

Post disseisin, Post disseisina, æ, f. Is a writ given by the Satute of *Westm.* 2. *cap.* 26. and lyeth for him that having recovered Lands or Tenements by (*præcipue quod reddat*) upon default, or reddition, is again disseised by the former disseisor. *Fitz. nat. brev. fol.* 190. See the writ that lyeth for this, in the *Regist. Orig. fol.* 208. *a.*

Post fine, Is a Duty belonging to the King for a Fine formerly acknowledged before him in his Court, which is paid by the Cognizee after the Fine is fully passed, and all things touching the same wholly accomplished. The Rate thereof is so much, and half so much, as was payed to the King for the Fine, and is gathered by the Sheriff of the County where the Land, &c. lyeth, whereof the Fine was Levyed to be answered by him into the Exchequer.

Posterminus, Post Term, is a return of a writ, not only after the day assigned for the Return thereof, but after the term also, which may not be received by the *Custos brevium*, but by the Consent of one of the Judges. It may be also the Fee which the *Custos brevium* taketh for the Return thereof, which is twenty Pence.

A post (or Stake) Postis, is, m.

A post (or prop) Statumen, inis, n.

The side post on which the door turns, Scapus Cardinalis.

A post (or Messenger in hast) Veredarius, ii, m. Angarius, ii, m.

A post (or messenger between parties) Commeator, oris, m.

A post horse, Veredus, i, m. Equus viatorius, Equus decursorius. Pegasus, i, m. Noy 114.

A post-master, Magister Cursorum, Veredarius, ii, m.

Posteriority, Posterioritas, atis, f. Is a word of Comparison and relation in Tenure, the Correlative whereof is priority. For a man holding Lands or Tenements of two Lords, holdeth of his Antienter Lord by Priority, and of his latter

latter Lord by Posteriority, &c. *Stawnf. Prærog. fol.* 10 and 11. When one Tenant holdeth of two Lords, of the one by Priority, of the other by Posteriority, &c. *Old. nat. brev. fol.* 94.

Posterity (or off-spring) Posteritas, atis, f. Minores, m. pl.

A postern gate, Posticum, ci, n.

Posthumus (a mans name) Posthumus, i, m. One so called that is born after his fathers decease.

P O T.

A drinking pot (or pot to drink in) Poculum, li, n.

A pot to seeth meat in, Olla,æ,f.

A garden (or watering pot) Clepsydra, æ, f. Harpagium, ii, n.

An earthen pot, Catinus tuscus.

A braß pot (or kettle) Ahenum, i, n. Incoctilis, le.

A flax pot, Linarium, ii, n.

A brass pot, Olla ærea.

An iron pot, Olla ferrea.

To stir or lade the pot seething, Truo, are.

A little pot, Chytrĭdium, ii, n.

Pot-hangers (or pot-hooks) Cremathra, æ, f. Climacter, ris, m.

Potherbs, Olus, i, m. Lachanum, i, n.

A pot-lid, Aular, aris. Operculum, li, n.

A pot seller, Aulularius, ii, m. Chytrŏpōla, æ, m.

A potter, Figulus, li, m. Urnarius, ii, m.

A potters trade, Figulina, æ, f.

A potters wheel, Rota figulina.

Belonging to a potter, Figlinus, a, um.

Potters clay, Argilla, æ, f.

Pottage, Potagium, ii, n. Lex. 83.

A pottle, Potellus, i, m. 1 Fo. 259. Cabus, i, m.

P O U.

A pouch, Pera, æ, f. Pungium, ii, n.

A poudring tub, Cupa, æ, f. Alveus, ei, m.

A poultess, Cataplasma, atis, n.

A poulterer, Pullinarius, ii, m. Pullarius, ii, m. Aviarius, ii, m.

Poultry (or Fowls) Aves villaticæ. Pulletria, æ, f.

Poultry compter (or a prison in London) Computatorium in Pulletria. Co. Entr. 345.

Poultney (the Family) Poultenius.

A pound (or twenty shillings) Libra, æ, f.

A pound weight, Libratа, æ, f.

Half a pound, Dimidium unius libratæ.

A quarter of a pound, Quarterium unius libratæ.

Half a quarter of a pound, Dimidium Quarterii unius libratæ.

Poundage (or a payment of twelve in the pound) Pondagium, ii, n. Davis. 7.

A pounder in a mortar, Pinsor, oris, m.

Pounded (bruised) Pinsus, a, um.

To pour (spill or shed) Fundo, ere. Effundo, ere.

Pourparty, Propars, tis, f. Propartia, æ, f. Lex. 98. Ra. Entr. 447. 515, 516, 517. It is contrary to *(Pro indiviso)* for to make Pourparty, is to divide and sever the Lands that fall to Partners, which before Partition they hold jointly, and *pro indiviso. Old. nat. brev. fol.* 11.

Pourpresture, Pourprestura, æ, f. Porprestura, æ, f. Paraprestura, æ, f.

A Pourveyour, Provisor, oris, m. It signifieth an Officer of the King, Queen, or other Great Personage, that provideth Corn and other Victual for the house of him whose Officer he is. See *Magna Charta. cap.* 22. & 3. *Ed.* 1. *cap.* 7. & 31.

&

& anno 28. *ejusdem. Articuli super Chartas.* 2. and many other Statutes gathered by *Rastal* under this Title.

P O W.

Powder, Pulvis, eris, m, vel f.

Gun powder, Pulvis tormentarius vel Bombardicus, Pulvis Nitri. us.

Power of the county, Posse comitatus. By Mr. *Lamberts* opinion in his *Eirenarch*, *lib.* 3. *cap.* 1. *fol* 309. containeth the aid and attendance of all Knights, Gentlemen, Yeomen, Labourers, Servants, Apprentices, and Villains. And likewise of Wards, and of other young Men about the age of fifteen Years, within the County, because all of that age are bound to have harness by the Statute of *Winchester*. But women, Ecclesiastical Persons, and such as be decripit, or do labour of any continual Infirmity, shall not be compelled to attend; for the Statute 2. *H.* 5. *cap.* 8. (which also worketh upon the same ground saith) that Persons sufficient to travel shall be assistant in this Service.

A Pownd, Parcus, i, m. It signifieth a Place of strength to restrain Cattel, being distrained or put in for any Trespass done by them, untill they be Replevied or Redeemed; and in this signification it is called a Pownd Overt (*i. e.*) *apertus* or open Pownd, being builded upon the Wast of some Lord, within his Fee, and is called the Lords Pownd, for he provideth it to his use, and the use of his Tenants. See *Kitch. fol.* 144. It is divided into Pownd open and Pownd close. Pownd open or Overt, is not only the Lords Pownd, but a Back-side, Court, Yard, Pasture or else whatsoever, where the Owner of any Beasts Impounded may come to give them meat and drink without Trespass to any other, and there the Cattel must be sustained at the Peril of the owner.

Pownd Close or Covert, is as if one Impownd the Cattel in some part of his House, or Close, and then the Owner cannot come unto it, to the purpose aforesaid without Offence, but the Cattel are to be sustained with Meat and Drink at the peril of him that distreineth, and he shall not have any satisfaction therefore.

If a man destrein Cattel for damage Feasant, and put them in the Pownd, and the owner that had Common there make fresh suit, and find the door unlocked, he may justifie the taking away of his Cattel in the writ of *à Parco fracto*. If the owner break the Pownd, and take away his Goods, the party distraining may have his Action *de Parco fracto*, and he may also take his Goods that were distreined wheresoever he find them, and Impownd them again. *Cook on Lit. lib.* 1. *cap.* 7. *Sect.* 58.

Powis (*a part of Wales*) Powisa.

P R A.

To practice, Practizo, are.

Practice, Practica, æ, f. Praxis, eos, f.

P R E.

To preach, Prædico, are.

A preacher, Prædicator oris, m.

A preaching, Prædicatio, onis, f.

A preamble, Præambulum, li, n. Præludium, ii, n. Procœmium, ii, n.

A prebend, Præbenda, æ, m. It is the Portion which every member or Canon of a Cathedral Church receiveth in the Right of his Place, for his Maintenance.

A prebendary, Prebendarius, ii, m. Lex. 98.

A precedent, Præcedens, tis, part.

A Precept (or Instruction) Præceptum, i, n. Precept is diversely taken in the Common Law, sometime for a Commandment in writing sent out by a Justice of Peace, or other, for the bringing of a Person, one or more, or Records before him. There are divers Examples of this in the table of the Register Judicial. Sometime it is taken for the Provocation whereby one Man inciteth another to commit a Felony, as Theft or Murder. *Stawnf. pl. Cor. fol.* 105.

Bracton calleth it *Præceptum* or *Mandatum lib.* 3. *tract.* 2. *cap.* 19. whence a Man may observe three diversities of Offending in Murder: *Præceptum, fortia, consilium. Præceptum* being the Instigation used before hand. *Fortia* the Assistance in the Fact, as help to bind the party Murdered or Robbed: *Consilium,* advice either before or in the Deed. The *Civilians* use *Mandatum* in this case, *vid. Angelus in tractat de Maleficiis. vers. Sempronium mandatorem.*

A precinct, Præcinctus, ûs, m.

Precious, Preciosus, a, um.

Præcipe quod reddat. Is a writ of great diversity, touching both the form and use, This form is extended as well to a writ of Right, as to other writs of Entry or Possession. *Old nat. brev. fol.* 13. *&* *Fitz, nat. brev. fol.* 5. and it is called sometime a writ of Right close, as a *Præcipe in Capite,* when it Issueth out of the Court of Common Pleas for a tenant holding of the King in chief, as of his Crown, and not of the King, as of any Honour, Castle, or Manor. *Regist. Orig. fol.* 4. *b. Fitz. nat. brev. fol.* 5. *F.* Sometime a Writ of Right patent, as when it Issueth out of any Lords Court, for any of his Tenants deforced, against the deforcer, and must be determined there. Of this read more at large in *Fitz. nat. brev.* in the first Chapter.

A precipice (or break-neck) Præcipitium, ii, n.

To precipitate, Præcipito, are.

A predecessor, Antecessor, oris, m.

Prædial tithes, tithes of Corn, Hay, &c. growing out of the earth, Prædiales decimæ.

Pre-eminence, Pre-eminentia, æ, f.

De pree (the Family) De Pratellis, De Prato.

A preface, Præfatio, onis, f.

To preferr (or advance) Præfero, ere.

Preferment, Præferamentum, i, n. Co. Entr. 36. Præferementum, i, n. 1 *Co.* 78.

Preference, Preferentia, æ, f. Co. Entr. 664. 1 Co. 161.

To prefix, Præfigo, ere.

The prefiction or assigning of a day, Præfictio diei.

Prejudice, Præjudicium, ii, n.

A prelate, Prælatus, i, m.

Prelacy, Prælatia, æ, f. 14. H. 4. 10.

To premeditate, Præmeditor, ari.

Præmunire. Is taken either for a writ, or for the Offence whereupon the writ is granted. Whosoever sueth, for any thing to *Rome,* or in any Spiritual Court, for that Cause or Action which may be Pleaded in the Temporal Court of the Realm, by an old Law of *England,* he falleth into a

Præmu-

Præmunire, that is, forfeiteth all his Goods to the Prince, and his body to remain in Prison, during the Princes pleasure, and not that only, but the Judge, the Scribe, the Procurer, and the Asseſſor or Abettor which receiveth, or maintaineth that uſurped Pleading doth incurr the ſame danger. Sr. *Thomas Smith de Repub. Angl. lib.* 3. *cap.* 9.

Some Statutes do caſt this Puniſhment upon other Offenders, as namely the Statute *Anno* 1. *Eliz. cap.* 1. upon him that denyeth the Kings Supremacy the ſecond time, *&c.* and the Statute *anno* 13. *cap.* 2. upon him that affirmeth the Authority of the Pope, or that refuſeth to take the Oath of Supremacy. And the Statute *anno* 13. *Eliz. cap.* 1. Such as be ſeditious talkers of the Inheritance of the Crown, or affirm the Kings Majeſty to be an Heretick.

Some hold an Opinion that the Writ is ſo called a *Præmunire*, becauſe it doth fortify *Jurisdictionem jurium regionum coronæ ſuæ*; the Kingly Laws of the Crown againſt Foreign Juriſdiction, and againſt the Uſurpers upon them, as by divers acts of Parliament appear. But in truth it is ſo called of a word in the Writ, for the words of the Writ are, *Præmunire facias præfatum A.B. quod tunc ſit coram nobis.* where *Præmunire* is uſed for *Præmonere*, and ſo do divers Interpreters of the Civil and Canon Law uſe it, for they are *Præmuniti* that are *Præmoniti. Cook on Lit. lib.* 2 *cap.* 11. *Sect.* 199.

So odious was this offence of *Præmunire*, that a Man that was attainted of the ſame, might have been ſlain by any Man without danger of Law, becauſe it was provided by Law, that a Man might do to him as to the Kings Enemy, and any man may Lawfully kill an Enemy. But Queen *Elizabeth* and her Parliament, liking not the extream and Inhumane rigour of the Law in that Point, did provide, that it ſhould not be Lawful for any Perſon to ſlay any Perſon in any manner attainted, upon any *Præmunire*, 5. of *Eliz. c.* 1.

If a man kill one which is attainted by a *Præmunire*, this is not Felony for he is out of the Kings Protection, but it is contrary if one kill another, that is attainted of Felony, and Judged to die, but now by the Statute of *Eliz.* It is Felony, to kill one attainted by a *Præmunire. Brooks abridg. fol.* 181. *B.*

Præmunire, Is to be adjudged out of the Kings Protection, to loſe all their Lands and Goods, and to ſuffer perpetual Impriſonment, *Cook on Lit.* and Preface to the 7*th. Rep.*

To premoniſh (*or warn before hand*) Præmoneo, ere.

To prepare, Præparo, are.

Prepared, Præparatus, a, um.

Preparatory, Præparatorius, a, um.

Prepoſterous (*out of order*) Præpoſterus, a, um.

Prerogative, Prærogativa, æ, f. Lex. 99.

To preſcribe, Præſcribo, ere.

A preſcription, Præſcriptio, onis, f. Lex. 100. A Right averred to have been from the time, whereof the memory of man is not to the contrary.

Presbytery, Presbyteratus, ûs, m. Fle. 211.

The chamber of presence in a Princes Court, Præsentia Majestatis, Solium Majestatis.

In ones presence, In Præsentia.

To present, Præsento, are.

A present (or token) Xenium, ii, n.

Presents given by the suitor when he came to see his Mistreß, Opteria, orum, n.

A presentation, Præsentatio, onis, f. It is the offering of a Clerk to a Bishop, to be put into a Benefice.

Presently, Statim, confestim.

Things preserved (as pears, plumbs, &c.) Salgăma, orum, n.

To preserve and keep from corruption, Condio, ire.

Preserved, Condititius, a, um. Conditus.

To preserve (or keep) Præservo, are.

Preserved, Præservatus, a, um.

A president, Præsidens, tis, m. Ra. Entr. 443. Præses, idis, c. 2.

Lord president of the councel, Dominus Præsidens privati concilii Domini Regis. Anno 22. H. 8. cap. 3. &. 14.

To preß (or squeeze) Premo, ere.

Pressed, Pressus, a, um.

A wine preß, Torculum, i, n.

A preß (or case for books) Pluteus, ei, m.

A press where apparel is laid, Vestiarium, ii, n. Pressorium, ii, n. Zaberna, æ, f.

A printers press, Impressorium, ii, n. Prælum, i, n.

A presser, he that works at a press, Torcularius, ii, m.

A pressing, Pressura, æ, f.

A pressing board, Calotriticatorium, ii, n.

A pressing iron, Ferramentum pressorium.

Preß money, Auctoramentum, i, n. Pecunia præparatoria.

To press Soldiers, Auctionor, ari. Conscribere vel Colligere milites.

To presume, Præsumo, ere.

Presumption, Præsumptio, onis, f.

A pretence, Prætextus, ûs, m.

By pretence of an Attornment, a Licence, &c. Prætextu.

To prevent, Prævenio, ire.

A prevention, Anticipatio, onis, f. Præoccupatio, onis, f.

A prey (or booty) Præda, æ, f.

P R I.

Price (or value) Pretium, ii, n. Valor, oris, m.

To set a price upon, Apprecio, are.

A priest, Presbyter, ri, m. Sacerdos, ōtis, c. 2.

Priesthood, Sacerdotium, ii, n.

Primacy, Primatus, ûs, m.

A primate, Primas, atis, m.

A Prince, Princeps, ipis, *c. g.* Is taken with us diversly, some time for the King himself, but more properly for the Kings Eldest Son, who is Prince of *Wales*; as the Eldest Son of the *French* King is called Dauphine, both being Princes by their Nativity. Mr. *Fearn* in the *Glory of Generosity* pag. 138. for *Edward* the First to appease the tumultuous Spirits of the *Welchmen*, who being the Antient *Indigenæ* of this Land, could not in long time bear the Yoke of us who they call Strangers; sent his Wife and Queen, being with Child into *Wales*, where at *Carnarvan* she was delivered of a Son, thereupon called *Edward* of *Carnarvan*, and afterward asked the *Welchmen*, seeing they thought much to be governed by Strangers, if they would be quietly rul'd by one of their own Nation, who answering, him, Yea. Then (saith he) I will appoint you one of your own Country-try-men that cannot ſpeak one word of *Engliſh*, and againſt whoſe Life you can take no juſt exception, and ſo named unto them his Son born in *Carnarvan* not long before; from which time it hath continued that the Kings Eldeſt Son (who was before called Lord Prince, *Stawnſ. Prærog. c.* 22. *fo.* 75.) hath been called Prince of *Wales*, *Stows Annals pag.* 303. See *Anno* 27. *H.* 8. *c.* 26. and *Anno* 28. *ejusd. c.* 3.

Principality, Principalitas, atis, f.

To print, Imprimo, ere.

Printed, Impreſſus, a, um.

A printer, Impreſſor, oris, m. Typographus, i, m.

Printers ink, Atramentum Typographicum *vel* Impreſſorium.

A letter caſt to print with, Typus, i, m.

Printers ink-balls wherewith they beat the letters in the form lying upon the Preſs, Tudes, itis, m.

Printing, Impreſſio, onis, f. Typographia, æ, f.

Priority, Prioritas, atis, f.

Priſage, Priſagium, ii, n. Lex. 100. It is that cuſtom or ſhare that belongeth to the King, out of ſuch Merchandize as are taken at Sea by way of Lawful Prize. *Anno* 31. *Eliz. cap.* 5.

Priſe, Priſa, æ, f.

A priſon, Priſona, æ, f. Every ſuffering of a Priſoner to eſcape is a breach of Priſon. If a man Arreſt one for Felony, and after let him go at large whither he will, if he be Arreſted for Felony, it is Felony; if for Treaſon, it is Treaſon: if for Treſpaſs, it is a Treſpaſs; & *ſic de Singulis. Stawnſ. Lib.* 1. *c.* 26. Impriſonment is the putting of any perſon from his own liberty, into the Cuſtody of the Law, to anſwer to that which is Objected; and therefore to break the Priſon is to fly from the Tryal of the Law, and is adjudged a Publick Felony, if he were impriſoned for Felony, otherwiſe not, as the *Stat. de frangent priſonam. Lamb. Juſt. of Peace.*

Out of this one fact, there groweth ſometime a treble offence and felony. *viz.* 1. in the Priſoner himſelf, which is moſt properly called the breaking of Priſon: 2. another in him that helpeth the Priſoner to get away, which is commonly termed Reſcuſs: 3. in the Officer or party whatſoever, by whoſe wilful default he is ſuffered to go, and that is termed an Eſcape. *Id. ib.*

A man impriſoned by Proceſs of Law, ought to be kept *in Salva & arcta cuſtodia*, and by the Law ought not to go out though it be with a Keeper, and with the leave and ſufferance of the Gaoler; but yet Impriſonment muſt be *cuſtodia non pœna*, for *Carcer ad homines cuſtodiendos, non ad puniendos dari debet. Cook* on *Lit. L.* 3. *c.* 7. *Sect.* 438.

He which is Impriſoned by Judgment of the Law, ought to be kept in *Salva & arcta cuſtodia, Salva* becauſe he ought to be in a Priſon ſo ſtrong, that he cannot eſcape, and *arcta* in reſpect that he ought to be kept cloſe without conference with others, or Intelligence of things at large. *Cook Lechfords Caſe* 8. *Rep.*

A priſoner, Priſonarius, ii, m.

Private, Privatus, a, um.

Privately, Privatim, adv.

Privity, Scientia, æ, f.

Privy, Sciens, tis, adj.

Privy Seal, Privatum ſigillum. Is a Seal that the King uſeth ſometime for a Warrant, whereby things passed the Privy Signet, and brought to it, are sent further to be confirmed by the Great Seal of *England*: Sometime for the strength or credit of other things written upon occasions more transitory, and of less continuance than those be that pass the Great Seal. *Vid.* Keeper of the Privy Seal, *Sub voce* Keeper.

A privy (or house of Office) Latrina, æ, f. Forica, æ, f. Cloaca, æ, f.

A Cleanser of Privies, Foricarius, ii, m. Coprophorus, i, m.

Privilege, Privilegium, ii, n. It is *Jus singulare*, whereby a Private man, or a particular Corporation is exempted from the Rigour of the Common Law, for that which is now called *Proprium*, hath been called of old writers, *privum*.

Privilege is either Personal or Real. A Personal Privilege is that which is granted to any person, either against or beside the Course of the Common Law: as for example, a Person called to be one of the Parliament may not be arrested either himself, or any of his attendance, during the time of the Parliament. A Privilege Real is that, which is granted to a Place, as to the Universities, that none of either many be called to *Westminster-Hall*, upon any Contract made within their own Precincts. And one toward the Court of Chancery, cannot originally be called to any Court, but to the Chancery, certain cases excepted. If he be, he will remove it by a Writ of Privilege grounded upon the Statute, *Anno* 18. *Edw.* 3. See the new book of Entries, *verbo Privilege*.

P R O.

Pro Indiviso, Is a Possession and Occupation of Lands or Tenements, belonging to two or more persons, whereof none knoweth his several portion, as Coparceners before partition. *Brac. lib.* 5. *Tract.* 2. *cap.* 1. *num.* 7.

Pro partibus liberandis, Is a writ for the partition of Lands between Co-heirs. *Regist. Orig. fol.* 316.

Probable (or like to be true) Probabilis, le, adj.

Probability (or likely-hood) Probabilitas, atis, f.

Probat of Testaments, Probatio Testamentorum. Is the Producting and Insinuating of dead Mens Wills before the Ecclesiastical Judge, Ordinary of the Place, where the Party dieth. And the Ordinary in this case is known by the quantity of the Goods that the party deceased hath out of the diocess where he departed, for if all his goods be in the same Diocess, then the Bishop of the Diocess, or the Arch-Deacon (according as their composition or prescription is) hath the Probate of the Testament. If the Goods be dispersed in divers Diocesses, so that there be any sum of Note (as five pounds ordinarily) out of the Diocess where the party led his Life: Then is the Archbishop of *Canterbury* the Ordinary in this case by his Prerogative; for whereas in old time the Will was to be proved in every Diocess, wherein the Party deceased had any Goods: it was thought convenient both to the Subject, and to the Archiepiscopal See, to make one Proof for all before him, who was and is of all, the General Ordinary of his Province. But there may

may be anciently ſome Compoſition between the Archbiſhop and an Inferiour Ordinary, whereby the ſum that maketh the Prerogative, is above five pound.

This Probate is made in two ſorts, either in common form, or *per teſtes*, the proof in common form, is only by the Oath of the Executor, or party exhibiting the Will who ſweareth upon his credulity, that the Will by him exhibited, is the Laſt Will and Teſtament of the party deceaſed. The proof *per teſtes*, is when over and beſide his Oath, he alſo produceth witneſſes, or maketh other proof, to confirm the ſame, aud that in the preſence of ſuch as may pretend any intereſt in the Goods of the deceaſed, or at the leaſt in their abſence, after they have been lawfully ſummon'd to ſee ſuch a Will proved, if they think good; and the latter courſe is taken moſt commonly where there is fear of ſtrife and contention between the kindred and friends of the party deceaſed about his Goods. For a Will prov'd only in common form, may be called into queſtion any time within 30 Years after by common Opinion, before it work preſcription.

A probationer, Probaticus. Is one that is to be approved and allowed of in the College for his Doctrine and Manners before they chooſe him Fellow, and this in ſome Colleges is 12 Months proof or tryal; in ſome 6, and in others more or leſs, according to their Cuſtoms.

A Chirurgeons Probe, Cathĕter, ĕris, m.

To proceed (or go forward) Procedo, ere.

Procedendo. Is Writ, whereby a Plea, or cauſe formerly called from a baſe Court, to the Chancery, Kings-Bench, or Common-Pleas, by Writ of Privilege, or Certiorari is releaſed, and ſent down again to the ſame Court, to by proceeded in there, after it appeareth that the defendant hath no cauſe of Privilege, or that the matter comprized in the Bill, is not well proved. *Brook hoc titulo*, and terms of Law, *Cook vol. 6. fol 63. a.* See *anno* 21. *R.* 2. *cap.* 11. *in fine.* See in what diverſity it is uſed in the Table of the *Orig. Regiſt.* and alſo of the Judicial.

Proceſſe, Proceſſus, ûs, m. It is called Proceſs, becauſe it proceedeth (or goeth out) upon former matter, either Original or Judicial.

This word Proceſs hath two ſignifications. It is largely taken for all proceeding in all Real and Perſonal actions, and in all criminal and Common Pleas, and *Proceſſus derivatur à Procedendo uſque ad finem.* 2. For the proceeding after the Originals is Plea before Judgment. See the Table of *Fitz. nat. brev. verbo Proceſs*, and *Brooks abridgment hoc Titulo.* And whereas the writings of our Common Lawyers ſometime call that the Proceſs, by which a man is called into the Court, and no more. The reaſon thereof may be given, becauſe it is the beginning or the Principal part thereof, by which the reſt of the buſineſs is directed.

The difference between Proceſs and the precept or warrant of the Juſtices. The Precept or warrant is only to attach and Convent the Party before any Indictment or Conviction, and may be made either

ther in the name of the King or of the Justice. Process is always in the name of the King, and usually after an Indictment found, or other Conviction; and because the King is a party, it must also be with a *Non omittas propter aliquam libertatem. Cooks 8th. Rep. Blackmores Case.*

Divers kinds of Process upon Indictments before Justices of Peace. See in *Crompt.* Justice of Peace, *fol.* 133. *b.* 134, 135. but for Orders sake, I referr you rather to Mr. *Lambert* in his Treatise of Processes adjoined to his Eirenarchy, who according to his Subject in hand, divideth criminal Process, either into Process touching causes of Treason or Felony, and Process touching inferiour offences. The former is usually a *Capias*, *Capias aliàs*, and *Exigi facias.* The second is either upon Indictment, or Presentment, or Information: That upon Indictment or Presentment, is all one, and is either general, and that is a *venire facias*, upon which if the party be returned sufficient, then is sent out a *Distringas* infinite untill he come. If he be returned with *Nihil habet*, then Issueth out a *Capias*, *Capias aliàs*, *Capias pluries*, and lastly an *Exigi facias.* The special Process is that, which is especially appointed for the offence by Statute; for the which he referreth his Reader to the 8th. Chapter of his 4th. book, being very different.

A procession, Processio, onis, f.

Processum continuando. Is a writ for continuance of a Process, after the death of the Chief Justice, in the writ of Oyer and Terminer. *Regist. Orig. fol.* 128. *a.*

To proclaim (or make a proclamation) Proclamo, are.

A proclamation, Proclamatio, onis, f. It signifieth a notice publickly given of any thing, whereof the King thinketh good to advertize his Subjects. So it is used *anno* 7. *R.* 2. *cap.* 6.

Proclamation of Rebellion is a publick notice given by the Officer, that a man not appearing upon a Subpæna, nor an Attachment in Chancery, shall be reputed a Rebel, except he render himself by a day assigned. *Crompt. Jurisd. fol.* 92.

Proclamation of a fine, Proclamatio Finis. It is a Notice openly and solemnly given at all the assises that shall be holden in the County within one Year after the Ingrossing of the Fine, and not at the four General Quarter Sessions. And these Proclamations be made upon transcripts of the Fine, sent by the Justices of the Common Pleas, to the Justices of Assize, and the Justices of Peace. *West. part.* 2. *Symb. Tit. Fines. Sect.* 132. where also you may see the form of the Proclamation. I read in *Fitz. nat. brev. fol.* 85. *C.* that the Kings Proclamation is sufficient to stay a subject from going out of the Realm. See the force of Proclamations. *Anno* 31. *H.* 8. *cap.* 8. New book of Entries, *verbo* Proclamation.

A proctor, Procurator, oris, m.

Proctors of the Clergy, Procuratores Cleri.

To procure, Procuro, are.

To produce, Produco, ere.

Proffer, Profrum, i, n. It is the time appointed for the accompts of Sheriffs and other Officers in the

the Exchequer, which is twice in the Year. *Anno* 51. *H.* 3. *Stat.* 5. and it may be gathered alſo out of the *Regiſt. fol.* 139. in the writ *de atturnato vicecomitis pro proffro faciendo.*

To profeſs, Profiteor, eri.

Profeſſion, Profeſſio, onis, f.

A profeſſor (or a publick Reader of Lectures in open Schools) Profeſſor, oris, m.

Profitable, Utilis, le, adj.

Profit, Profectus, ûs, m. Utilitas, atis, f.

To profit, Proficio, ere.

Profuſe (or waſtful) Profuſus, a, um.

Profuſely, Profuſè, adv.

A progeny, Progenies, ei, f.

The progenitors, Progenitores, m, pl.

To prognoſticate, Prognoſtico, are.

Prognoſtication, Prognoſticon, ci, n. Præſagium, ii, n.

A progreſs, Progreſſio, onis, f.

To prohibit, Prohibeo, ere. Prohibitio de vaſto directa parti. Is a writ Judicial directed to the Tenant, and Prohibiting him from making waſt upon the Land in Controverſy, during the ſuit. *Regiſt. Judic. fol.* 21. It is ſometime made to the Sheriff, the example whereof you have there next following.

Prohibition, Prohibitio, onis, f. It is a writ framed for the forbidding of any Court, either ſpiritual or ſecular, to proceed in any Cauſe there depending, upon ſuggeſtion, that the Cognition thereof belongeth not to the ſaid Court. *Fitz. nat. brev. fol.* 39. but it is moſt uſually taken for that writ which lyeth for one which is Impleaded in the Court Chriſtian, for a Cauſe belonging to the Temporal Juriſdiction, or the Cognizance of the Kings Court, whereby as well the Party and his Councel, as the Judge himſelf, and the Regiſter, are forbidden to proceed any further in that Cauſe: for that it appertaineth to the diſinheriting of the Crown of ſuch right as belongeth to it. In how many Caſes this lyeth, See *Broke hoc Tit.* and *Fitz. nat. brev. fol.* 39. *& ſeq. Regiſt. Orig.* See the new book of Entries *verbo* Prohibition and *Fitz. nat. brev. fol.* 39.

Prolocutor of the Convocation houſe, Prolocutor domus Convocationis. Is an Officer choſen by Perſons Eccleſiaſtical, publickly aſſembled by the Kings writ at every Parliament, and as there are two Houſes of Convocation, ſo there are two Prolocutors, one of the Higher houſe, the other of the Lower houſe, who preſently upon the firſt aſſembly, is by the motion of the Biſhops, choſen by the Lower houſe, and preſented to the Biſhops for their Prolocutor. That is the man by whom they mean to deliver their Reſolutions to the Higher houſe, and to have their own houſe eſpecially ordered and governed. His Office is to cauſe the Clerk to call the names of ſuch as are of that houſe, when he ſeeth cauſe, to cauſe all things propounded to be read by him, to gather the ſuffrages, and ſuch like.

Promiſcuous (one with another) Promiſcuus, a, um.

A promiſe, Promiſſio, onis, f. Promiſſum, i, n.

To promiſe, Promitto, ere.

Promiſed, Promiſſus, a, um.

A promiſer, Promiſſor, oris, m.

A promontory (or brow of a hill hanging over the Sea) Promontōrium, ii, n.

A promoter, Inquiſitor, oris, m.

Promoters, Promotores, m, pl. Are thoſe which in popular and penal actions do deferr the names, or complain of Offenders, having part of the profit for their Reward, they belong eſpecially to the Exchequer, and the Kings Bench. *Smith de Repub. Angl. lib.* 2. *cap.* 14.

A prong (or pitch fork) Merga, æ, f.

A proof of Inſtruments before playing, Incentivum, i, n.

To prove (or try) Probo, are.

A proof (or tryal) Probatio, onis, f.

Proper, Proprius, a, um.

A property (or propriety) Proprietas, atis, f.

To whom the property of a thing belongs, Proprietarius, a, um.

To proportion, Proportiono, are. Ry. 52.

Proportion, Proportio, onis, f.

Proportionable, Proportionabilis. le, adj. Co. Ent. 5.

Proportioned, Proportionatus, a, um.

A propoſal (or propoſition) Propoſitio, onis, f.

To propoſe, Propono, ere.

To prop, Suſtineo, ere. Fulcio, ire.

A prop, Suſtentaculum, li, n. Fulcimentum, i, n. Fulcrum. i, n. Adminiculum, li, n.

Propped, Fultus, a, um,

A vine prop (or hop pole) Ridica, æ, f.

Proprietary, Proprietarius, a, um.

A prorogation, Prorogatio, onis, f.

Prorogued, Prorogatus, a, um.

A proſecutor, Proſecutor, oris, m.

A proſpect, Proſpectus, ûs, m.

To proſper (or make proſperous) Proſpero, are.

Proſperity, Proſperitas, atis, f.

To protect, Protego, ere.

Protection, Protectio, onis, f. Guardia, æ, f.

To proteſt, Proteſtor, ari.

A proteſtant, Proteſtans.

Proteſtation, Proteſtatio, onis, f.

A Prothonotary of the Common Pleas, Unus Prothonotariorum Curiæ Domini Regis De Banco. There are three of them in the Common Pleas. *Anno* 5. *H.* 4. *cap.* 14. He is termed the chief Clerk of that Court. His Office is to enter and Inroll all manner of Declarations, Pleadings, Aſſizes, and Judgments, and all Actions, the ſame term that the appearance is made. He alſo makes out all Judicial writs, *venire facias*, after iſſues joined, and *habeas corpus* for the bringing in of the Jury, after it is returned upon the *venire facias*. He alſo maketh forth writs of Executions, and of Seiſin, writs of *Superſedeas* for appearance to Exigents, as well as the Exigents, and writs of Privileges, for removing of Cauſes from other Inferiour Courts of Record, in Caſe where the party hath cauſe of Privilege. Alſo writs of *Procedendo*, of *ſcire facias*, in all caſes, writs to enquire of damages, and all Proceſs upon Prohibitions, and upon writs of *audita querela* and falſe Judgment. Finally, he Inrolls all Recognizances acknowledged in that Court, and all Common Recoveries, and may make exemplifications of any Records the ſame Term, before the Rolls are delivered from them.

A Prothonotary of the Kings Bench, Protonotarius de Banco Regis, Is an Officer in the Kings Bench that recordeth all Actions Civil

Civil sued in that Court, as the Clerk of the Crown Office doth all continual Causes.

Provender, Præbenda, æ, f. Lex. 37. 49.

To provide, Provideo, ere.

A province, Provincia æ, f.

Provided, Proviso. 1 Co. 109.

Provision, Provisio, onis, f.

Proviso. Is a condition inserted into any deed, upon the Observance whereof the Validity of the deed consisteth, which form of condition, seemeth to be borrowed from *France* for (*Pourueu Gallicum*) *semper conditionem inducit*. Or rather from the *Lat. Provideo*. Our Common Lawyers say, that it sometime signifieth but a Covenant, whereof you have a large dispute in the second Book of the Lord *Cook*'s *Reports*, in the Lord *Cromwell*'s case. It hath also another signification in matters judicial: as if the Plaintiff or defendent desist in Prosecuting an Action, by bringing it to a Tryal, the Defendant or Tenant may take out the *venire facias* to the Sheriff, which hath it in these words, *Proviso quod*, &c. to this end, that if the Plaintiff take out any Writ to that purpose, the Sheriff shall summon but one Jury upon them both. *See Old Nat. Brev. in the Writ Nisi Prius. fol.* 159.

Provocation, Provocatio, onis, f.

To provoke, Provoco, are.

A provost, Præpositus, i, m.

The provost of a provostship, Præpositus præpositura, 2. *H.* 5. 9.

A provost martial, Præfectus, i, m.

The prow (*or fore-castel*) *of a Ship*, Prora, æ, f.

P R U.

Prudence, Prudentia, æ, f.

Prudhow or Prodhow(*Castel in Northumberland*) Procolitia. Protolitia.

To prune (*or lop*) *trees*, Puto, are.

Pruned, Putatus, a, um, Sarptus, a, um.

To prune young shots with a pruning hook; Scalpro putare germina.

A prune (*or plum*) Prunum, i, n.

A pruning iron, Scirpicula, æ, f.

Of or for pruning, Putatorius, a, um.

P S A.

A psaltery, Psalterium, ii, n. Nablium, ii, n.

P U B.

Publick, Publicus, a, um.

To publish, Publico, are. Promulgo, are.

Published, Promulgatus, a, um.

A publisher, Promulgator, oris, m.

A publishing, Promulgatio, onis, f.

P U C.

Pucellage (*or maiden-head*) Pucellagium, ii, n.

P U D.

A pudding, Fartum, i, n. Botulus, i, m.

A dry pudding (*or dumpling*) Globulus, li, m.

A black pudding (*or bludding*) Apexabo, inis, f. Faliscus, ci, m.

A bag pudding, Fundulum, li, n. Farreum, ei, n.

A hasty pudding, Fugetatio, onis, f. Maza, æ, f. Massula, æ, f.

A pan pudding, Minutal, lis, n. Libum Testulaceum.

A pudding maker, Fartor, oris, m. Offarius, ii, m.

Pudsey (*the Family*) De Puteaco.

P U L.

A pullet (*or young hen*) Pullastra, æ, f. Pulletra, æ, f. Gallina Minuscula.

A pulley wherein a cord runneth to draw any thing, Trochlea, æ, f. Orbiculus, li, m. Artemon, onis, m.

A pulpit, Pulpitum, i, n. Subsellium, i, n. Lectrum, i, n. Suggestum, i, n. Analogium, ii, n.

Pulse (*as Beans and Pease*) Legumen, inis, n.

The pulse (*or beating of the Arteries*) Pulsus, ûs, m.

P U M.

A pumice stone, Pumex, icis, m.

Smoothed with a pumice stone Pumicatus, a, tum.

To pumice (*or make smooth with a pumice stone*) Pumico, are.

A pump to draw water with, Antlia, æ, f.

To pump, Exantlo, are.

The pump of a ship, Sentina, æ, f.

To pump water out of a ship, Sentino, are.

A pair of pumps, Endromides, um, pl.

P U N.

To punish, Punio, ire,

Punished, Punitus, a, um.

A punishment, Pœna, æ, f.

P U R.

Purcels (*the Family*) De Purcellis.

To purchase, Perquiro, ere.

A purchase, Acquisitum, i, n. perquisitum, i, n. Spel. 22. Adquisitum, i, n. 2. Mon. 380. Perquisitio, onis, f. Purchasia, æ, f.

Purchased, Perquisitus, a, um.

A purchaser, Perquisitor, oris, m.

Purgation, Purgatio, onis, f.

Purple, Purpura, æ, f.

Purple Coloured, Purpureus, a, um.

Purpresture, Purprestura, æ, f. Ra. *Ent.* 135. Co. *Lit.* 277.

A purprise, Purprisa, æ, f. Purprisum, i, n. Ra. *Ent.* 533.

A purport, Purporta, æ, f.

Purporting, Purportans, Co. *Ent.* 196. 35. 1. Mon. 754.

A purse, Bursa, æ, f. Crumēna, æ, f. Perulà, æ, f.

A little purse, Bursella, æ, f.

The strings of a purse, Astrigmenta Bursæ.

A purse bearer, Bursarius, ii, m.

A purse maker, Crumenarius, ii, m. Marsupiarius, ii, m.

A pursevant, Apparitor, oris, m.

A purveyour, Provisor, oris, m.

Q U A.

A *Quacksalver* (*or pedling physician*) Mediculus circumforaneus. Circulator, oris, m.

Quacksalvery, Medicina unguentaria.

A quadrangle (*having four corners*) Quadrangulus, li, m.

Quadrangular (*four square*) Quadrangularis, re adj.

The Quadrant (*a Mathematical Instrument*) Quadrans, tis, m.

Quadrate (*or four square*) Quadratus, a, um.

A quadrate (*or geometrical Instrument*) *whereby the distance and height of a place is known a far off, by looking through a certain little hole therein*, Dioptra æ, f.

Quadripartite (*or of four parts*) Quadripartitus, a, um.

To quadruplate, Quadruplico, are.

Quadruple (*or four fold*) Quadruplus, a um.

Quæ plura. Is a Writ that lyeth where an inquisition hath been made by the Escheatour in any County, of such Lands, or Tenements as any man died seized of, and all that was in his possession be not thought to be found by the Office. The form whereof see in the *Regist. Orig. fol.* 293. and in *Fitz. Nat. brev.* fol. 255. It differeth from the writ called *Melius Inquirendo*

quirendo as *Fitz-herbert* there saith, because this is granted where the Escheatour formerly proceeded by vertue of his Office, and the other, where he found the first Office by vertue of the writ called *Diem clausit extremum*. See the new book of Entries, *verbo que plura*.

Quæ servitia. Is a Writ Judicial, issuing from the Note of a Fine, and lyeth for the Cognizee of a Mannor, Seignory, chief rent or other services, to compel him that is Tenant of the Land, at the time of note of the Fine levied, to Attorne unto him. *West. part* 2. *Symb. Tit. Fines, Sect.* 826. To the same effect speaketh the *Old Nat. brev.* fol. 155. See the new Book of Entries *verbo Per quæ servitia*.

Quærens non invenit Plegium. Is a return made by the Sheriff, upon this Condition inserted. *Si A. fecerit B. Securum de Loquela Sua prosequenda*, &c. *Fitz. Nat. brev. fol.* 38. *O*.

Quale Jus. Is a Writ Judicial, that lyeth where a man of Religion hath Judgment to recover Land, before Execution be made of the Judgment, for this Writ must between Judgment and Execution, go forth to the Eschreatour, to enquire whether the Religious Parson hath right to recover, or the Judgment is obtained by Collusion, between the Demandant and the Tenant, to the intent the true Lord be not defrauded. See *Westm.* 2. *cap.* 32. *Cum Viri Relig.* &c. The form of this Writ you may have, in the *Regist. Judic. fol.* 8. 16, 17. & 46. and in *Old Nat. brev. fol.* 161. See the new Book of Entries *verbo Quale Jus*.

To qualifie, Qualifico, are.

Qualified, Qualificatus, a, um.

Quality, Qualitas, atis, f.

A contrariety of natural qualities, Antipathia, æ, f.

A quality or property conceived by nature or exercises, Habitus, ûs, m.

A quality or degree, Gradus, ûs, m.

Of what quality, Qualis, le, adj.

A quantity, Quantitas, atis, f.

Of what quantity, Quantus, a, um.

Quantum meruit. An Action brought upon a promise to pay the Plaintiff what he deserves.

Quare Ejecit Infra terminum. Is a Writ that lyeth for a Lessee in case where he is cast out of his Farm, before his term is expired, against the Feoffee of the Leassor that ejecteth him, and it differeth from the *Ejectione Firmæ*, because this lyeth, where the Leassor after the Lease made, in feoffeth another, which ejecteth the Leassee. And the *Ejectione Firmæ* lyeth against any other Stranger that ejecteth him. The effect of both is all one: and that is, to recover the residue of the Term. See *Fitz-herb. Nat. Brev. fol.* 197. See the *Reg. Orig. fol.* 227. and the new Book of Entries *verbo Quare Ejecit infra terminum*.

Quare impedit. Is a writ that lyeth for him that hath purchased a Mannor, with an Advowson thereunto belonging against him that disturbeth him in the right of his Advowson, by presenting a Clerk thereunto, when the Church is void. And it differeth from the Writ called, *Assisa ultimæ præsentationis*, because that lyeth where a man or his ancestors, formerly presented, and this for him that is the Purchaser himself. See the expositor

of

of the Terms of Law, and *Old Nat. brev. fol.* 27. *Bract. Lib.* 4. *tract.* 2. *cap.* 6. *Brit. cap.* 92: and *Fitz. Nat. brev. fol.* 32. and the *Regist. Orig. fol.* 30. where it is said that a *Quare impedit* is of a higher nature than *Assisa ultimæ præsentationis*; because it supposeth a Possession and a Right. See at large the new book of Entries *verbo Quare impedit.*

Quare non permittit. Is a Writ that lyeth for one that hath Right to present for a Turn against the Proprietary. *Fleta. Lib.* 5. *cap.* 16.

Quare non admisit. Is a Writ that lyeth against a Bishop refusing to admit his Clerk, that hath recovered in a Plea of Advowson, the further use whereof see, in *Fitz. nat. brev. fol.* 47. and *Regist. Orig. fol.* 32. See the new Book of Entries *verbo Quare non admisit.*

Quare Obstruxit. Is a Writ that lyeth for him who having a Servitude to pass through his Neighbours ground, cannot enjoy his Right, for that the owner hath so straitned it, *Fleta Lib.* 4. *cap.* 26.

A quarentine (or quantity of Land containing 40 *perches)* Quarentena terræ. 1 Mon.313.2 Mon. 547. 555.

A quarentin, Quarentena, æ, f.

Quarentina Mulieris, *Lex* 104. *Brac.* 60. *Stat. De Merton.* It is a benefit allowed by the Law of *England* to the Widow of a Landed-Man deceased, whereby she may challenge to continue in his capital Messuage(*or chief Mansion House*) by the space of forty days, after his decease. Of this see *Brac. Lib.*2.*c.* 40. And if the Heir, or any other attempt to eject her, she may have the Writ *de Quarentena habenda. Fitz.Nat.brev.fol.*161.*Regist.Orig.fol.* 175. *Anno* 9. *Hen.* 3. *cap.* 7. and *Anno* 20. *cap.* 1. and *Brit. cap.* 103. Mr. *Skene*, *de verb. signif. verbo Quarentina Viduarum*, deriveth this word from the *French*, *Quaresme*, (*i. e.*) Lent 40 days, who also have this Custom, called *Le Quaresme des vefues*, granted to Widows after the decease of their Husbands: as he proveth out of *Papon* in his Arrests, *Lib.* 15. *Tit. des dotes. cap.* 7. *Lib.* 10. *Tit. Substitutiones cap.* 30. Of this read *Fleta* also, *Lib.* 5. *c.* 23.

A quarrel or strife, Quĕrēla, æ, f. Briga, æ, f. This properly concerneth Personal Actions, or mixt at the highest, for the Plaintiff in them is called *Querens*, and in most of the Writs it is said *Queritur.* And yet if a man Release all Quarrels (a mans deed being taken most strongly against himself) It is as beneficial as all Actions, for by it all Actions Real and Personal are Released. *Cook on Lit. Lib.* 3. *cap.* 8. *Sect.* 511. *Litis nomen actionem significat sive in rem sive in Personam.*

To quarrel, Litigo, are. Cavillor, arc.

A quareller, Cavillator, oris, m.

Quarrellous, Litigiosus, a, um.

A quarrell of glass, Rhombus vitri, vitrum quadratum fenestræ.

A quarrel, bolt or dart shot out of an Engine, Cătăpultarium pilum.

A quarry of stones, Quarera, æ, f. Reg. 105. 1 Mon. 707. 811. 2 Mon. 281. 252. Quareria, æ, f. Lapidicina, æ, f. Latumia, æ, f.

A quarry of whet-stones, Cotaria, æ, f.

A quarry-man (or he that worketh in a quarry) Lapicida, æ, m. Latomus, i, m.

A

A Quart measure, *Quarta, æ, f. Vet. Intr.* 178. *Quartarius, ii, m.*

Quartain, *Quadrinus, a, um.*

A Quartain Fever, *Quartana, æ, f. Febris quartana.*

He that hath such a Fever, *Quartanarius, a, um.*

A Quarter (or eight Bushels) *Quarterium, ii, n.*

A Quarter or fourth part of any thing, *Quarta, æ, f.*

A Quarter of Wheat, *Quarterium Tritici*, Brac. 35.

Of a Quarter, *Quarterialis, le, adj. Quarteriatus, a, um.* Spel. 51.

Quarterly, *Quarteriatim, adv.*

A Quarter (a Piece of Timber four Inches Thick) commonly four Square, as it wear a quarter or fourth Part of a Beam, *Trabs quadrata. Trientalis materia.*

A Quarter of a Foot, *Quadrans pedis.*

A Quarter of a Year, *Trimestre Spatium, tempestas anni.*

Quarters for Soldiers, *Stativa, æ, f.*

Quarters or Rafters cross a Transome, *Transumsaria.*

A double Quarter, *Trabs crassior.*

A Quarter Master, *Metator oris, m. Campometator, oris, m. Quartus Magister.*

Quarter Sessions, *Generalis Quarterialis Sessio pacis.* Is a Court held by the Justices of Peace in every County, once every Quarter. The Jurisdiction whereof how far it extendeth, is to be learned out of *Lamb. Eirenar.*

Sir *Thomas Smith*, de Rep. Angl. lib. 2. cap. 19. But to these you must add the late Statutes of the Realm, for their Power daily encreaseth. Originally it seemeth to have been erected only for Matters touching the Peace. But in these days it extendeth much further. That these Sessions should be held Quarterly was first of all Ordained (so far as I can learn) by the Statute *Anno* 25. *Ed.* 3. *Stat.* 1 *Cap* 8. Of these read *Lamb Eirenar. Lib.* 4. where he setteth them out, both Learnedly and at large.

To Quarter (or Dismember) *Deartuo, are. Artuo, are. Disseco, are.*

Quartered, *Exartuatus, a, um. Excarnificatus, a, um. Dissectus, a, um.*

To Quash, *Quasso, are, Casso, are.* It signifieth in our Common Law to over-throw. *Bract. Lib.* 5. *Tract.* 2. *cap.* 3. *num.* 4.

QUE.

A Queen, *Regina, æ, f. Domina Regina.* Is either she that holdeth the Crown of this Realm by Right of Blood, or else she that is Married to the King. In the former signification, she is in all Construction the same that the King is, and hath the same Power in all respects. In the

the other signification she is Inferiour, and a Person exempt from the King, for she may sue and be sued in her own Name: Yet that she hath, is the Kings; and look what she loseth, so much departeth from the King. *Stawnf. Prærog.* cap. 2. *fol.* 10. in *fine. Kitchin fol.* 1. *b.* *Cook, Lib.* 4. Copy-hold Cases, *fol.* 23. *b.*

Quem Redditum reddit. Is a writ Judicial, that lyeth for him, to whom a Rent Seck, or Rent Charge is granted, by Fine Livied in the King's Court, against the Tenant of the Land, that refuseth to attурn unto him, thereby to cause him to attурn. See *Old Nat. Brev.* fol. 156. and *West part* 2. *Symbol.* Tit. *Fines*, Sect. 125. See the New Book of *Entries verbo, Quem redditum reddit.*

To Quench (or Extinguish) *Extinguo, ere.*

Quenched (or put out) *Extinctus, a, um.*

A Quenching, *Extinctio, onis, f.*

A Quencher, *Extinctor, oris, m.*

Querela coram Rege, & Consilio discutienda & terminanda, Is a Writ, whereby one is called to Justifie a Complaint of a Trespass made to the King and himself, before the King and his Council, *Regist. Orig. fol.* 124. *b.*

A Querister (or Choirester) *Chorista, æ, m.*

A Quern (or hand Mill) *Molitrina, a, f. Mola manualis.*

A Pepper Quern (or Mustard Quern) *Mola Piperaria. Fraxillus, li, m.*

A Querry for the King's Horses, *Stabulum Principis.*

A Quest (Inquest or Inquisition) *Duodena, æ, f. Inquisitio, onis, f. Duodecemviratus, i, m.* Thereof in *London*, in the *Christmas* Holidays, the Citizens in every Ward hold a Quest, and a Quest-House, as they call it, to Enquire and be informed, what Misdemeans or Annoyance is made or done within the Ward.

A Quest (or the Office of a Questor) *Quæstura, æ, f.*

A Question (or demand) *Quæstio, onis, f.*

A Dark, or subtle Question, *Ænigma, atis, n.*

Questionless (without all Question) *Indubius, a, um. Indubitatus, a, um. Indubitantèr adv.*

To Question, or ask a Question, *Quæstionor, ari. Quæstionem agere.* To call one in Question, *In Crimen vocare.*

A Questioner (or Examiner) *Quæstionarius, ii, m.* *Quæstus est Nobis*, &c. is the form of a Writ of nuisance, which by the Statute, *Anno* 13. *Ed.* 1. *cap.* 24. lieth against him, to whom the House or other thing that breedeth the Nuisance, is alienated, whereas before that Statute, this Action lay only against him that first levied the thing, to the hurt of his Neighbour. See the Statute.

QUI.

Quia Improvide, seemeth to be a Supersedeas granted, in the behalf of a Clerk of the Chancery, sued against the Privilege of that Court, in the Common Pleas, and pursued to the Exigend. See *Dyer*, fol. 33. n. 18.

Quickgrass, *Gramen caninum*.

Quick (or lively) *Vivificus a, um. Agilis, le, adj.*

Quickness, *Celeritas, atis, f. Agilitas, atis, f*

Quickly, *Cito, Celeriter, adv.*

Quicksands, *Sabulum vivum, Insidæ & rapaces arenæ. Syrtes, f.*

A Quick-set Hedge, *Sepes viva, Sepimentum virgulteum.*

Quicksilver, *Hydrargyrum i, m. Argentum vivum.*

Quid pro quo, Is an Artificial Speech in the Common-Law, signifying a mutual Protestation or Performance of both Parties to a Contract: As a Horse and ten Pound between the Buyer and the Seller. *Kitch.* fol. 184. but used in our common Speech one for another, as to render one *Quid pro quo*, (i.e.) to give him as good as he brings.

Quid Juris clamat, Is a Writ Judicial, issuing out of the Record of the Fine, which remaineth with the *Custos Brevium* of the Common-Pleas, before it be Ingrossed (for afterward it cannot be had) and it lieth for the Grantee of a Reversion or remainder, when the particular Tenant will not attutn. *West part.* 2. *Symb. Tit. Fines, Sect.* 218. whom see further. see the *Register* Judicial fol. 36, 37. and the new Book of Entries, *verbo*, *Quid Juris clamat*.

Quiet, *Quietus, a, um.*

A Quill, *Calamus, i. m. Calamus pennæ.*

A Quill (or bow to play on the Harp, Rebeck or Dulcimer) *Plectrum, i, n.*

A Quilt, (or quilted counter-point, or covering for a Bed) *Culcitra, æ, f. Stragulum, li. n.*

A little Quilt of many Pieces, *Centunculus, li, m.*

A Quilt made of Leather, *Salganum. i, n.*

A Quilt maker for Beds, *Plumarius, ii, m.*

Quilted, *Culcitratus, a, um.*

A Quill-turn (*i.e.*) that turns the Quills or Spoiling Wheel, *Harpedone, is, f. Rota Glomeratoria, quæ fila rotando conglomerantur.*

A Quince (a kind of Fruit) *Malum cotoneum, Cydonium malum.*

Quinborough (in *Kent*) *Regis Burgus.*

The Quinsey (a Disease in the Throat) *Angina, æ, f. Synanche, is, f.*

Quintane, *Quintana, a, f.* (*i e*) an Exercise on Horseback, used at Weddings.

A Quintal, (or hundred Weight) *Centupondium, ii, n.*

Quintilian (a Man's Name) *Quintilianus, i. m.*

Quintus (a Man's Name) *Quintus, i, m.*

A Quire or Choire in a Church, *Chorus, i, m.*

The Master of the Quire, *Phonascus, ci, m. Magister Chori.*

To Quit (or discharge) *Quieto, are. Exonero, are.*

A Quit-claim (or Release) *Quieta clamantia.*

Quittance, *Quietantia, æ, f.*

Quit-Rent, *Quietus redditus.*

A Quiver of Arrows, *Pharetra, æ, f. Solennarium, ii, n.*

Wearing a Quiver, *Pharetratus, a, um.*

QUO.

Quo Jure, Is a Writ that lieth for him that hath Land, wherein another challengeth common of Pasture, time out of Mind, and it is to compel him to shew by what Title he challengeth this common of Pasture, *Fitz. Nat. Brev. fol.* 128. Of this see *Brit.* more at Large, *Cap.* 29. see the *Regist. Orig.* fol. 156. and the new Book of Entries, *verbo, Quo Jure.*

A Quoif, *Capital, alis, n.*

Quo minus, Is a Writ that lieth for him which hath a Grant of House-bote, and Hey-bote, in another Man's Woods, against the Granter making such Wast, as the Grantee cannot enjoy his Grant, *Old Nat. Brev. fol.* 148. Terms of Law, see *Brook hoc titulo, Kitchin,* fol 178. *b.* This Writ also lieth for the King's Farmer in the Exchequer, against him to whom he selleth any thing by way of Bargain touching his Farm, *Perkin's Grants* 5. for he supposeth, that by the Breach of the Vendee, he is disabled to pay the King his Rent.

Quo Warranto, Is a Writ that lieth against him, which usurpeth any Franchise or Liberty against the King, as to have Wayf, Stray, Fair, Market, Court Baron, or such like without good Title, *Old Nat. Brev. fol.* 149. Or else against him that intrudeth himself as heir into Land, *Bract. Lib.* 4. *Tract.* 1. *cap.* 2. *num.* 3. See *Brook hoc. Tit.* read also *Anno* 18. *Ed.* 1. *Stat.* 2, and 3. and *Anno* 30. *Ejusdem,* and the new Book of Enteries, *Quo Warranto.*

Quod Clerici non eligantur in Officio Ballivi, &c. Is a Writ that lieth for a Clerk, which by reason of some Land he hath, is made, or in doubt to be made, either Bayliff, Beedle or Reeve, or some such like Officer, See *Regist. Orig. fol.* 187. *Fitz nat. brev. fol.* 175.

Quod Clerici beneficiati de Cancellaria, &c. Is a Writ to exempt a Clerk of the Chancery from Contribution, toward the procters of the Clergy in Parliament, *Regist. Orig. fol.* 261. a.

Quod ei deforciat, Is a Writ that lieth for the Tenant in Tail, Tenant in Dower, or Tenant for Term of Life, having lost by the default, against him that recovered, or against his Heir, exposition of Terms, see

see *Brook, hoc Tit. Regist. Orig. fol.* 171. and the new Book of Entries, *verbo, Quod ei deforciat*.

Quod permittat, Is a Writ that lieth for him, that is disseized of his common of Pasture, against the Heir of the Disseisor being Dead. Terms of Law, *Brit. cap.*8. saith, that this Writ lieth for him, whose Ancestor dyed seized of common of Pasture, or other like thing annexed to his Inheritance, against the Deforceor, see *Crook, hoc Tit. Regist. Orig. fol.* 155. and the new Book of Entries, *verbo, Quod permittat.*

Quod persone nec prebendarii, &c. Is a Writ that lieth for Spiritual Persons, that are distrained in their Spiritual Possessions, for the payment of the fifteenth with the rest of the Parish, *Fitz. nat. brev. fol.* 176.

A Quoit, *Discus, ci, m.*

A Quoit Caster, *Discobolus, li, m.*

Quotidian (or daily) *Quotidianus, a. um.*

To Quote (or Cite) *Allego, are. Cito, are.*

A Quoting, *Citatio, onis, f.*

Q U U.

Quunster (in *Ireland*) *Hultonia.*

R A B.

A Rabbet (or Young Cony) *Cuniculus, li, m.*

R A C.

A Race, Stock or Lineage, *Prosapia, æ, f. Progenies, ei, f.*

A Race (or Course) *Cursus, ûs, m.*

A Race place (or Course) *Hippodromus, i, m.*

Rachel (a Woman's Name) *Rachel, lis, f.*

To Rack, *Torqueo, ere.*

A Rack (or Manger) *Crates pabularis*

A Cheese Rack, *Crates casearia.*

A Rack or Cobiron, to lay the Broach in at the Fire, *Cratenterium, ii, n.*

A Rack for a Cross-Bow. *Harpago, inis, f.*

A Rack (or Wooden Horse) *Equuleus, ei, m.*

The Racks or sides of a Chariot, *Lorica plaustri.*

A Racker of Wine, *Saccellator, oris, m.*

A Racking of Wine, *Saccellatio, onis, f.*

A Racket to play with at Tennis, *Reticulum, li, n.*

Racline Isle, one of the *Hebrides*, the least and next to *Ireland, Ricina, Ricluna, Ricnea, Riduna.*

R A D.

Radcot Bridge (in *Oxfordshire*) *Radecotanus Pons.*

Radigund (a Woman's Name) *Radigunda, æ, f.*

Radnor (in *Radnorshire*) *Radnoria.*

Radnorshire, *Radnoriæ comitatus*.

Old Radnor, *Magæ*, *Magi*, *Magna*, *Magnis*.

R A F.

A Raft, *Ratis, is, f.*

A Rafter, *Tignum, i, n. Trabs, abis, f.*

Rafters set a Cross, *Transversaria lignea.*

A little Rafter, *Tigillum, i, n.*

The Raftering of an House, *Contignatio, onis, f.*

The space between the Rafters, *Intertignium, ii, n.*

A laying of Rafters from one Wall to another, *Immissum, i, n.*

Belonging to a Rafter, *Tignarius, a, um.*

R A G.

To Rage, *Furo, ere*, *Sævio, ire.*

A Rag, *Panniculus, li, m.*

A linen Rag, *Linteolum, li, n.*

Rags, *Panni, orum, m. Frusta pannorum.*

R A I.

A Raie or thin leaf of Gold, Silver or other Metal, *Bractea, æ, f. Bracteola, æ, f.*

To Rail, *Maledico, ere.*

A Railer, *Maledicus, a, um. Maledictor, oris, m. Rabula, æ, m.*

A Rail of fine Linen, *Ralla, æ, f. Anabolagium, ii, n. Amictorium, i, n.*

A Rail or Stake to bear up a Vine, *Cantherium, ii, n.*

A Rail whereupon the Vine runneth, made like an Arbour, *Pergula, æ, f.*

A Rail or Rails to inclose any thing. *Vacerra, æ, f. Tigillum, i, n.*

Rails on each side of a Gallery, *Lorica, æ, f.*

To set with Rails *Longuriis circundare.*

Rain, *Pluvia, æ, f.*

The Rem (or Rein of a Bridle) *Habena, æ, f.*

A Raising-Piece, *Pecia struens.*

A Raisin, *Uvæ passæ.*

R A K.

A Rake, *Rastrum, i, n. Sarculus, li, m.*

An Iron Rake, or an Iron Tool serving to Rake, *Scalpratum ferramentum.*

A Rake with two Teeth wherewith they pull up Weeds and Herbs by the Root, *Irpex, cis, m.*

A Rake for an Oven, called a Cole-Rake, *Rutabulum, li, n.*

A little Rake, *Rastellum, i, n.*

To Rake, *Sarrio, ire.*

A Raking, *Sarritio, onis, f.*

R A L.

Ralegh (in *Essex*) *Raganeia.*

Ralegh (the Family) *De Ralega.*

Ralph (a Man's Names) *Radulphus, i, m.*

R A M.

R A M.

A Ram, *Aries, ëtis, m.*

A Rammer, *Fistuca, æ, f. Pavicula, æ, f. Trudes, is, f.*

To Ram, (or beat in Stones) *Fistuco, are.*

To Ram in Piles, *Depango, ere.*

A Ramming of Piles, *Oppactio, onis, f.*

A Ramming of the Ground, *Fistucatio, onis, f.*

Ramesbury (in *Wiltshire*) *Ramesburia.*

Ramsey (in *Huntingdonshire*) *Ramesia.*

Ramsey Island, *Limnos, Silimnus.*

Rams-head (a Promontory in *Ireland*) *Vennicnium Promont.*

A Rampire (*Trench* or Bulwark) *Munimentum, i, n. Agger, eris, m.*

A Rampire made of Wood, *Vallum, i, n.*

To Rampire a City round about, *Circumvallo, are, Vallo, are.*

The making of a Rampire, *Circumaggeratio, onis, f. Aggestio terræ.*

R A N.

Randolph (a Man's Name) *Randolphus, i, m.*

A Range of Land, *Rengia terræ,* 1 *Mon.* 515.

Ranges of Butchers Stalls, *Rengi famellorum Carnificum,* 1. *Mon.* 113.

To Range, (as Meal through a Sieve is Ranged) *Cribro, are. Succerno, ere.*

Ranged, *Ordinatus, a, um. Dispositus, a, um.*

A Ranging Sieve, *Subcerniculum, li, n. Cribrum rarum.*

A Range or Beam, between two Horses in a Coach, *Limo, onis, m.*

A Ransome, *Redemptio, onis, f.*

R A P.

A Rape, *Rapa, æ, f. Raptus, ûs, m.* also a part of a Shire.

Raphael (a Man's Name) *Raphael, lis, m.*

R A S.

To Rase (Cancel or Cross out) *Deleo, ere. Erado, ere.*

Rased (or put out) *Erasus, a, um, Cancellatus, a, um.*

Rasing (or Crossing out) *Abolitio, onis, f.*

A Rasour (such as Barbers use) *Nŏvăcŭla, æ, f. Culter Rasorius vel tonsorius.*

A Rasour-case, *Xyrŏthēca,*

A Rasp (or File) *Scŏbina, æ, f. Radula, æ, f.*

R A T.

A Rate, *Rata, æ, f. Ratum, i, n. Dyer* 82.

Rating, *Ratando, Ra. Entr.* 505.

To Rate, *Arrento, are.*

A Rate (or Rent) *Arrentatio, onis, f. Reg.* 252. 254. 255. *Ry.* 302. *Stat. de Marl. cap.* 11. *Stat. de Prærogativa, cap.* 7.

A Rat-catcher, *Musiarius, ii, m.*

Rateby (in) *Raga*, *Rage.*

Ratification, *Ratificatio*, *onis*, *f.* Is used for the confirmation of a Clerk in a Prebend, *&c.* formerly given him by the Bishop, *&c.* where the Right of Patronage is doubted to be in the King. Of this, see the *Regist. Orig. fol.* 304.

To Ratifie, *Ratum facere*

Rationabili parte bonorum, Is a Writ that lieth for the Wife, against the Executors of her Husband, denying her the third part of her Husbands Goods, after Debts and funeral Charges defrayed, *Fitz.nat.brev.fol.* 222. who there citeth *cap.*18. of *magna charta*. And *Glanvile*, to prove that according to the Common Law of *England*, the Goods of the deceased, his Debts first paid, should be divided into three parts, (whereof his Wife to have one, his Children the second, and the Executors the third, *Fitz* saith also, that this Writ lieth as well for the Children, as for the Wife, and the same appeareth by the *Regist. Orig. fol.* 142. but I take it that this Writ, hath no use but in *London*, and where the Custom of the Country serveth for it. See the new Book of Entries, *Verbo*, *Rationabili parte & Rationabili parte bonorum.*

R A V.

To Ravish (or force a Woman) *Rapio*, *ere.*

Ravished, *Raptus*, *a*, *um.*

A Ravisher, *Raptor*, *oris*, *m.* *Stuprator*, *oris*, *m.*

R A Y.

A Ray (or Water-Lock) *Gaya*, *æ*, *f.*

R E A.

To Reach, *Porrigo*, *ere.* *Exporrigo*, *ere.*

Reached, *Porrectus*, *a*, *um.*

To Read, *Lego*, *ere*

To Read over, *Perlego*, *ere.*

A Reader, *Lector*, *oris*, *m.*

A Reader in Schools, *Professor*, *oris*, *m.*

A Reader to Scholars, *Prælector*, *oris*, *m.*

A Reading, *Lectio*, *onis*, *f.* *Lectura*, *æ*, *f.*

Ready (or present at hand) *Promptus*, *a*, *um.* *Paratus*, *a*, *um.*

Reading (in *Berkshire*) *Pontes*, *Readingum.*

Readily, *Promptè*, *adv.*

Real (or that is indeed) *Realis*, *le*, *adj.*

Really, *Realiter*, adv.

A Realm, *Regio*, *onis*, *f.* *Regnum*, *i*, *n.*

To Reap, *Meto*, *ere.* *Tondeo*, *ere.*

A Reap-hook, *Falx Messoria.*

Reaped, *Messus*, *a*, *um*,

A Reaper, *Messor*, *oris*, *m.* *Falcator*, *oris*, *m.*

A Reaping, *Falcatio*, *onis*, *f.* *Brac.* 35. *Messio*, *onis*, f.

Pertaining to Reaping, *Messorius*, *a*, *um.*

A Reason, *Ratio*, *onis*, *f.*

Reasonable, *Rationabilis*, *le*, *adj.*

Reasonable

Reasonable Ayd, *Rationabile Auxilium.*

Reattachment *Reattachiamentum, i, n.*

Reather-Hithe, *Nauticus sinus.*

R E B.

Rebecca (a Woman's Name) *Rebecca, æ, f.*

To Rebel, *Rebello, are.*

Rebellion, *Rebellio, onis, f.*

Rebellio, *Breve Rebellionis,* A Writ of Rebellion, to bring a Person in Contempt into the Court of Chancery.

Rebutter, *Repellere* (i. e.) to Repel or Bar; that is in the understanding of the Common Law, the action of the Heir by the Warranty of his Anceстor, and this is called to Rebut, or Repel, *Cook on Lit. Lib.* 3. *cap.* 12.

A Man giveth Land, which he hath to him and the Issue of his Body, to another in Fee with Warranty: And the Donee leaseth out this Land to a third for Years: The Heir of the Donor Impleadeth the Tenant, alledging, that the Land was entailed to him, the Donee cometh in, and by vertue of the Warranty made by the Donor repelleth the Heir, because though the Land were intailed to him, yet he is Heir to the Warranty likewise: And this is called a *Rebutter*, see *Brook, Tit.* Barre *Numb.* °13.

And again, If I grant to my Tenant to hold, *Sine impetitione vasti,* and afterward I implead him for wast made, he may debar me of this Action, by shewing my Grant, and this is likewise a Rebutter, *Idem, eod num.* 25. see the new Book of Entries, *verbo Rebutter.*

R E C.

To Recant, *Recanto, are. Reclamo, are.*

A Recantation, *Recantatio, onis, f.*

Recaption, *Recaptio, onis, f.*

Recaptio, Breve Recaptionis, A Writ of Recaption which lies where a Second distress is taken pending a Suit for a former.

To Receive, *Recepto, are. West. Indict.* 81. *Recipio, ere.*

Received, *Receptus a, um.*

A Receiving (Entertaining or Harbouring) *Receptamentum, i, n. Reg.* 80. 2. *Inst.* 645. *Bract.* 157. *Fle.* 57.

A Physicians Receipt, *Dosis, is, f.*

A Receiver, *Receptor, oris, m. Receptator, oris, m.*

A Receptacle (a Place to receive, a Store-House, or Ware-House, *Receptaculum, li, n.*

To Recite, *Recito, are.*

Reciting, *Recitando.*

To Reckon, *Supputo, are. Computo, are.*

Reckonings, (accounts) *Raciocinia, Recensiones, Calculi, Computi.*

A shot, or Reckoning, *Commissa, æ, f.*

Reckoned, *Recensus, a, um. numeratus, a, um.*

That may be Reckoned, *Computabilis, le, adj.*

A

A Recognisance, *Recognitio, onis, f.* (*i. e.*) an Obligation acknowledged of Record: Also an acknowledgment.

Recognitores, *Recognitores*, Is a Word used for the Jury impaneled upon on assize, the reason why they are so called may be, because they acknowledge a Disseisin by their Verdict, see *Bract.* Lib. 5. *tract.* 2. cap. 9. *num.* 2. and lib. 3. *tract.* 1. cap. 11. num. 16.

To Recommend, *Recommendo, are.*

To Recompence (or requite) *Recompenso, are.*

To Reconcile, *Reconcilio, are.*

A Record, *Recordum, i, n.*

To Record, Vide to Register, *Recordare Facias* or *Recordari facias*, Is a Writ directed to the Sheriff, to remove a cause depending in an Inferiour Court to the King's Bench, or Common Pleas, as out of a Court of Ancient Demesne, Hundred or County, *Fitz, nat. brev. fol.* 71. *b.* Out of the County Court, *Idem*, fol. 46. B. or other Courts of Record, *Idem*, fol. 71. C. and 119 K. But if you would learn more exactly, where, and in what Cases this Writ lieth, read *Brook* in his Abridgement, *Titulo, Recordare & pone.* It seemeth to be called a *Recordare*, because the form is such, that it commandeth the Sheriff to whom it is directed, to make a Record of the Proceeding by himself and others, and then to send up the Cause. See *Regist. verbo, Recordare*, in the Table of the Original Writs.

A Recorder, *Recordator, oris, m.* (*i. e.*) a Judge of a Town Court of Record. He is one whom the Mayor, or other Magistrate of any City or Town Corporate, having Jurisdiction, or a Court of Record within their Precincts by the King's Grant doth associate unto him for his better direction in Matters of Justice, and Proceedings according to Law.

A Recorder (or Flute) *Tibia Sarrana Recordo & processu mittendis*, Is a Writ to call a Record, together with the whole Proceeding in the Cause, out of one Court into the King's Bench, which see in the Table of the *Regist. Orig.* how diversly it is used.

To Recover, *Recupero, are.*

Recovery, *Recuperatio, onis, f.* It signifieth in our Common Law, an obtaining of any thing by Judgment or Trial of Law: But you must observe there is a true Recovery and a Feigned.

A true Recovery, Is an actual or real Recovery, of any thing or the value thereof, by Judgment, as if a Man sued for any Land, or other thing moveable or immoveable, and have a Verdict and Judgment for him.

A Feigned Recovery is (as the Civilians call it) *Quadam fictio Juris*, a certain form or course set down by Law, to be observed, for the better assuring of Lands or Tenements to us.

For the better understanding of this, read *West.* part 2. Symb. Tit. Recoveries, Sect 1. who

saith

ſaith that the end and effect of a Recovery, is to diſcontinue and deſtroy Eſtates, Tails, Remainders, and Reverſions, and to bar the former Owners thereof, and in this formality, there are required three Parties, *viz.* the Demandant, the Tenant, and the Vouchee. The Demandant is he, that bringeth the Writ of Entry, and may be termed the Recoverer. The Tenant is he, againſt whom the Writ is brought, and may be termed the Recoveree. The Vouchee is he, whom the Tenant Voucheth or calleth to Warranty, for the Land in demand, *Weſt ubi ſupra*, in whom you may read more touching this Matter.

But for Example to explain this Point. A Man that is deſirous to cut off an Eſtate tail in Lands or Tenements, to the end, to ſell, give, or bequeath it, as himſelf ſeeth good, uſeth his Friend to bring a Writ againſt him for this Land. He appearing to the Writ, ſaith for himſelf, that the Land in Queſtion came to him or his Anceſtors, from ſuch a Man or his Anceſtor, who in the Conveyance thereof, bound himſelf and his heirs, to make good the Title to him, or to them to whom it was conveyed. And ſo he is allowed by the Court, to call in his third Man to ſay what he can for the juſtifying of his Right to this Land, before he ſo conveyed it. The third Man cometh not; whereupon the Land is recovered by him that brought the Writ, and the Tenant of the Land is left for his Remedy to the third Man that was called, and came not in to defend the Tenant, and by this means the Entail which was made by the Tenant or his Anceſtor, is Cut off by Judgment hereupon given, for that he is pretended to have no Power to entail that Land, whereunto he had no juſt Title, as now it appeareth: Becauſe it is evicted or recovered from him. This kind of Recovery, is by good Opinion, but a ſnare to deceive the People, *Doct. & Stud.* cap. 32. dial. 1. fol. 56. a.

This feigned Recovery is alſo called a common Recovery, and the reaſon of that Epitheton is, becauſe it is a beaten and common path to that end, for which it is ordained, *viz.* to cut off the Eſtates above ſpecifyed, ſee the new Book of Entries, *verbo Recovery.*

A True Recovery is as well of the value, as of the thing: For the better underſtanding whereof, know, that (in value) ſignifieth as much as (*Illud quod Intereſt*) with the Civilians; for Example, if a Man buy Land of another with Warranty, which Land a third Perſon afterward by Suit of Law recovereth againſt me, I have my Remedy againſt him that ſold it me, to recover in value, that is, to recover ſo much in Money as the Land is worth, or ſo much other Land by way of Exchange.

Fitz.

Fitz. nat. brev. fol. 134. K. To recovery a Warranty, *Old nat. brev.* fol. 146. is to prove by Judgment, that a Man was his Warrant against all Men for such a thing.

To Recourse (or have recourse) *Recurro, ere.*

Recto, Is a Writ called in *English*, a Writ of Right, which is of so high a Nature, that whereas other Writs in real actions, are only to recover the Possession of the Land or Tenements in Question, which have been lost by our Ancestors or our selves, this aimeth to recover both the Seisin, which some of our Ancestors or we had, and also the Property of the thing, whereof our Ancestors died not seized, as of Fee: And whereby are Pleaded and tried both the Rights together: *viz.* as well of Possession as Property. Insomuch, as if a Man once lose his cause upon this Writ, either by Judgment, by Assize, or Battel, he is without all Remedy, and shall be excluded (*per exceptionem rei Judicatæ*) *Bract.* Lib. 5. tract. 1. cap. 1. & seq. where you may read more at large concerning this Writ. It is divided into two Species, *Rectum patens*, a Writ of Right patent, and *Rectum Clausum*, a Writ of Right Close. This the Civilians call *Judicium petitorium.*

The Writ of Right Patent is so called, because it is sent open, and is in Nature the highest Writ of all others, lying always for him, that hath fee simple in the Lands or Tenements sued for, and not for any other, and when it lyeth for him that Challengeth fee simple, or in what Cases, see *Fitz nat. brev. fol.* 1. C. whom see also *fol.* 6. of a special Writ of Right in *London*, otherwise called, a Writ of Right according to the Custom of *London.* This Writ is also called, *Breve magnum de Recto. Regist. Orig. fol.* 9. *A. B.* and *Fleta*, Lib. 5. cap. 32. Sect 1.

A Writ of Right close, is a Writ directed to a Lord of Ancient Demesne, and lieth for those which hold their Lands and Tenements by Charter in Fee simple, or in Fee-tail, or for Term of Life, or in Dower, if they be ejected out of such Lands, *&c.* or disseized. In this case a Man or his heir, may sue out this Writ of Right Close directed to the Lord of the Ancient Demesne, commanding him to do him right, *&c.* in his Court. This is also called a small Writ of Right, *Breve parvum. Regist. Orig.* fol. 9. *A. B.* and *Brit.* cap. 120. *in fine.* Of this see *Fitz*, likewise at large *Nat. brev.* fol. 11. & seq.

Yet Note, that the Writ of Right Patent seemeth further to be extended in use, than the Original invention served, for a Writ of Right of Dower, and only for Term of Life, is patent, as appeareth by *Fitz nat. brev.* fol. 7. E. The like may be said of divers others that do hereafter

hereafter follow. Of these see also the Table of the *Regist. Orig. verbo Recto.* This Writ is properly tried in the Lord's Court, between Kinsmen that claim by one Title from their Ancestor. But how it may be thence removed, and brought either to the County, or the King's Court, see *Fleta*, Lib. 6. cap. 3. 4, and 5. *Glanvile* seemeth to make every Writ, whereby a Man sueth for any thing due to him, a Writ of Right, *Lib.* 10. *Cap.* 1. *Lib.* 11. *Cap.* 1. *Lib.* 12. *Cap.* 1.

Recto de Dote, Is a Writ of right of Dower, which lieth for a Woman, that hath received part of her Dower, and purposeth to demand the remanent in the same Town, against the Heir, or his Guardian, if he be Ward. Of this see more in Old *nat. brev.* fol. 5. and *Fitz nat. brev.* fol. 7. E. *Regist. Orig.* fol. 3. and the new Book of Entries, *Verbo Droyt.*

Recto de dote unde nihil habet, Is a Writ of Right, which lieth in case, where the Husband having divers Lands or Tenements, hath assured no Dower to his Wife, and she thereby is drawn to sue for her Thirds, against the Heir or his Guardian, *Old nat. brev. fol. Regist, Orig. fol.* 170.

Recto de Rationabili parte, Is a Writ that lieth always between Privies in Blood, as Brothers in Gavelkind, or Sisters or other Coparceners, as Nephews or Neeces, and for Land in Fee simple, for Example. If a Man lease his Land for Term of Life, and afterwards dieth, the one Sister entring upon all the Land, and so deforcing the other, the Sister so deforced, shall have this Writ to recover her part, *Fitz, nat. brev. fol.* 9. *Regist. Orig. fol.* 3.

Recto quando Dominus remisit, Is a Writ of Right, which lieth in case, where Lands or Tenements that be in the Seigneury of any Lord, are in demand by a Writ of Right, for if the Lord hold no Court, or otherwise at the Prayer of the Demandant or Tenant, shall send to the Court of the King his Writ, to put the cause thither for that time (saving to him another time the Right of his Seigneury) then this Writ Issueth out for the other party, and hath this Name from the Words therein comprized, being the true occasion thereof. This Writ is close, and must be returned before the Justices of the Common Bank, *Old nat. brev. fol.* 16. *Regist. Orig. fol.* 4.

Recto de Advocatione Ecclesiæ, Is a Writ of Right lying where a Man hath Right of advowzen, and the Parson of the Church dying, a Stranger presenteth his Clerk to the Church, and he not having moved his Action of *Quare Impedit*, nor *Darrein presentment*, within six Months, but suffered the Stranger to Usurp upon him, and this Writ he only may have, that claimeth the Advowzen, to himself and to his Heirs in Fee, and as it lieth for the whole Advowzen, so it lieth also for the half, the third, the fourth part, *Old nat. brev. fol.* 14. *Regist. Orig. fol.* 29.

A Rector, *Rector, oris, m. Rector Ecclesiæ parochialis.*

A Rectory, *Rectoria, æ, f.*

A Rectory Impropriate, *Rectoria Impropriata.*

Rectus in Curia, Is he that standeth at the Bar, and hath no Man to object any Offence against him, *Smith de Repub. Angl. Lib.* 2. *Cap.* 3. see *Anno* 6. *R.* 2. *Stat.* 1. *Cap.* 12.

Reculver (in *Kent*) *Reculsum. Regulbium.*

Red, *Ruber, bra, brum.*

Redbridge (in *Hampshire*) *Arundinis vadum.*

Redburn (in *Hertfordshire*) *Aqua rubra, Durocobrivæ.*

Redcliff (near *London*) *Ruber clivus.*

Reddendum, The Clause in a Lease that Reserves the Rent.

Reddition, *Redditio, onis, f.*

Redisseisin, *Redisseisina, æ, f.*

Redisseisina, Is a Writ lying for a Redisseisin, *Regist. Orig. fol.* 206, and 207.

To Redound, *Redundo, are.*

To Redress, *Emendo, are. Reformo, are.*

To Reduce, *Reduco, ere.*

Redvers or Rivers, (the Family) *De Redveriis*, *De Ripariis, Rigidii. De Riperia.*

R E E.

To Reedify, *Reædifico, are.*

A Reel to wind Yarn or Thread on, *Girgillus, li, m. Rhombus, i, m. Alabrum, i, n.*

To Reel Yarn, *Alabro, are. Glomero, are.*

A Realing, *Alabratio, onis, f.*

A Reeler of Yarn, *Alabrator, oris, m.*

Reeled (or wound up) *Alabratus, a, um.*

To Re-enter (to take Possession again) *Reentro, are.*

A Reeve of a Mannor, *Præfectus Manerii*, *Grevius Manerii.*

Re-extent, *Re-extentum, i, n.* It is a second Extent made upon Lands or Tenements, upon complaint made, that the former Extent was partially performed, *Brook. Tit. Extent. fol.* 313.

R E F.

To Refer, *Refero, ferre.*

To put a thing into a thirds hand, to refer it to him, *Intertio, are.*

To Refine, *Fino, are. Plo.* 320.

A Refiner (or Purifier of Metals) *Aurifex, icis, m.*

Refined (Racked) *Fæcatus, a, um.*

A Refuge, *Refugium, ii, n. Sepedium, ii, n. Perfugium, ii, n.*

To Refuse, *Recuso, are. Detracto, are.*

The Refuse, *Recrementum, i, n. Excrementum, i, n.*

R E G.

Regard, *Regardum, i, n. Rewardum, i, n.* 3. *Bul.* 91.

Regardum Forestæ, *Ry.* 2. 24. 651. *Rewardum Forestæ*, *Ry.* 2. 1. *Mon.* 513. 2. *Mon.* 631. (*i. e.*) the Compass of a Regarders Ground in a Forest.

A Regarder, *Regardator, oris, m.* Is an Officer of the Forest, who is to view it and inquire into Offences.

Regarding, *Regardans, tis, adj.* West *Indict.* 239.

A Regiment, *Regimentum.*

A Register, *Registrarius, ii, m. Lex.* 108.

The Register, *Registrum, i, n.* Lex. 108.

A Regrater, *Regratarius, ii, m. Stat. de Collistrigio. Ry.* 248. One who buys and sells in the same Market or Fair.

Regular, *Regularis, re, adj.*

Regularly, *Regulariter, adv.*

R E I.

To Reject (or cast off) *Rejicio, ere. Rejecto, are.*

Rejected, *Rejectus, a, um.*

To Reign (or Rule) *Regno, are.*

The Reins, *Renes, um, m.*

To Reinfeoffe, *Refeoffo, are. Co. Entr.* 291.

A Rejoinder, *Rejunctio, onis, f.* It signifieth in our Common Law, as much as *Duplicatio* with the Civilians, that is, an Exception to a Replication. For the first answer of the defendant to the Plantiffs Bill, is called an Exception, the Plaintiffs answer to that, is called a Replication, and the Defendants to that, Duplication in the Civil Law, and a Rejoinder with us, especially in Chancery, *West par.* 2. *Symb. tit.* Chanry, *Sect* 56. where he citeth these words out of *Spigelius. Est autem rejunctio seu duplicatio, allegatio, quæ datur reo ad infirmandam replicationem actoris, & confirmandam actionem rei.*

R E L.

A Relapse into Sickness, *Recidivatio, onis, f.*

A Relation (or rehearsing) *Relatio, onis, f.*

To Release, *Relaxo, are.*

A Release, *Relaxatio, onis, f.* It is an Instrument whereby Estates, Rights, Titles, Entries, Actions, and other things are sometime extinguish'd, sometime transferred, sometime abridged, and sometime enlarged, *West, part.* 1. *Symb. Lib.* 2. *Sect.* 50.

Release is the giving or discharging of the Right or Action, which any hath or claimeth against another, or his Land. *Laxare* is properly to put Prisoners in Fetters at Liberty, and *Relaxare* is to do this often, and *Metaphorice relaxare* is to put at Liberty fettered Estates and Interests, and to make them absolute, *Cook's* 10. *Rep. Hampet's* case.

There is a Release in Fact, and a Release in Law, *Perk. Grants* 71. A Release in Fact, seemeth to be that, which the very words expresly declare. A Release in Law, is that which doth acquit by way of consequent or intendment of Law, an Example whereof you have in *Perk. ubi Supra.* Of these how they be

available,

available, and how not, see *Littleton* at large, *Lib.* 3. *Cap.* 8. *f. fol.* 94. Of divers sorts of these Releases, see the new Book of Entries, *verbo* Release.

Relief, *Relevium, ii, n.* (*i. e.*) a kind of fine paid by the Heir at a Tenant's Death.

To Relieve, *Relevo, are. Erigo, ere.*

Religion, *Religio, onis, f.*

Religious, *Religiosus, a, um.*

R E M.

A Remainder, *Remanere, is, n. Co. Lit.* 49. The Remainder of an Estate.

Remainders, *Remaneria.*

To Remain, *Remaneo, ere.*

Remarkable, *Notabilis, le, adj.*

A Remedy, *Remedium, ii, n.*

To Remedy, *Remedio, are. Reg.* 80.

Remedied, *Remediatus, a, um. Ra. Entr.* 24.

Be it Remembred, *Memorandum.*

A Remembrance, *Remembrancia, æ, f. Memoranda.*

A Remembracer, *Rememorator, oris, m.*

To Remit, *Remitto, ere.*

Remission, *Remissio, onis, f.*

Remote (or far distant) *Remotus, a, um.*

To Remove (withdraw or put aside) *Removeo, ere*

Removeable, *Amotibilis, le, adj. Bract.* 12. *Sæpe.*

R E N.

To Render (give or Payback) *Reddo, ere.*

A Rendring, *Redditio, onis,*

To Renew, *Renovo, are.*

Renet, *Coagulum, li, n.*

To Renounce, *Renuncio, are.*

Rent, *Redditus, ûs, m.* It cometh of the French Rent, (*i. e*) *Vectigal, pensitatio annua.* And signifieth with us, a sum of Money, or other consideration, issuing Yearly out of Lands or Tenements, *Plowden casu Browning, fol.* 132. b. and *fol.* 138. a. and 141. b.

There are three sorts of Rents observed by our Common Lawyers, that is Rent Service, Rent charge, and Rent seck. Rent Service is where a Man holdeth his Land of his Lord by Fealty, and certain Rent; or by fealty, Service, and certain Rent, *Littlet. Lib.* 2. *Cap.* 12. *fol.* 44. or that which a Man, making a Lease to another for Term of Years, reserveth Yearly to be paid him for the same. Terms of Law, *verbo* Rents, who giveth this Reason thereof, because it is in his Liberty, whether he will distrain, or bring an Action of Debt.

A Rent Charge is that, which a Man, making over an Estate of his Lands or Tenements to another, by deed indented either in Fee, or Fee tail, or for Term of Life, reserveth to himself by the said Indenture, a summ of Money Yearly to be paid to him with Clause of distress, or to him and his heirs, see *Littlet. Ubi supra.*

A Rent seck, otherwise a dry Rent, is that which a Man, making over an Estate of his Land or Tenement, by Deed indented, reserveth Yearly to be paid him without Clause of distress mentioned in the Indenture, *Littl. Ubi supra*, and Terms of the Law, *verbo* Rents. See the new Expositor of Law Terms, see *Plowden casu*, *Browning*, *fol.* 132. *b.* See the differences between a Rent and an Annuity, *Doct.* & *Stud. Cap.* 30. *Dial.* 1. Tenure by Rents is called, *vivi redditus*, because the Lord's and the Owners thereof, do live by them, *Cook* on *Lit.* A Feme sole Lessee for Life rendring Rent, takes a Husband, the Rent Arere, the Wife dieth, though here be no recovery in the Wives Life time, yet because the Baron took the profit, he is still chargeable in a Writ of Debt for the Rent, for *qui sentit commodum sentire debet & Onus*, Wom. Law.

For Rent payable at a Day, the party hath all the Day till Night to pay it, but if it be a great summ, as five hundred or a thousand Pound, he must be ready as long before the sunset, as the Money may be told: For the other is not bound to tell it in the Night, *Cook's fifth Rep. Wade's Case.*

A Penny Rent, *Denarata Redditus*, Reg. 1.

A Rent payable by, and chargeable on the Grantor and his Heirs, and not on Lands, *Annuus redditus.*

Rent paid to the Lord of the Hundred in Silver Coin, *Alba firma.*

Rent is demanded by the Name of *sex libratas, decem soliditas, sex denariatas, & unam obolatam redditus.*

A Rent (or Tatter) *Scissura, æ, f. Ruptio, onis, f.*

To Rent (or Tear) *Frango, ere. Lanio, are. Lacero, are.*

A Rental (or an account of Rents in Writing) *Rentale, is, n. Ra. Entr.* 209. *Co. Entr.* 146.

A Rent Master (Collector or Baily) *Quæstor ærarius. Præfectus ærarii.*

R E P.

To Repair, *Reparo, are. Restauro, are.*

Repassage, *Repassagium, ii, n. Ra. Entr.* 335.

To Repeal, *Repello, ere.*

Repealed, *Repellatus, a, um.* 2. *mon.* 702.

A Repealing, *Repellatio, onis, f. Co. Entr.* 204. *Repellum, i, n.*

Repleader (*Replacitare*) is to Plead again that which was once pleaded before, *Rastal Tit. Repleader*, see the New Book of Entries, *Verbo*, Repleader.

Replegiare de averiis, Is a Writ brought by one, whose Cattle are destrained or put in Pound upon any cause by another, upon surety given to the Sheriff to pursue the Action in Law, *anno* 7. *H.* 8. *cap* 4. *Fitz nat. brev. fol.* 68. see the *Regist. Orig.*

Orig. of divers ſorts of this Writ called *Replegiare*, in the Table, *verbo eodem.* See alſo the *Regiſt. Judic.* fol. 58. and 70. ſee alſo the New Book of Entries, *verbo, Replevin, Dyer fol.* 173. *num.* 14.

A Replevin, *Replegiamentum, i, n.*

To Replevin, *Replegio, are. Reg.* 180.

To be Replevied, *Replegior, ari.*

That cannot be Replevied, *Irreplegiabilis, le, adj.*

A Replication, *Replicatio, onis, f.* Is an Exception of the ſecond degree made by the Plaintiff upon the firſt Anſwer of the Defendant, *Weſt part.* 2. *Symb. Tit.* Chancery, *ſect.* 55. and *Weſtm.* 2. *anno* 13. *Ed.* 1. *cap.* 36. this is borrowed from the Civilians, *De Replicationibus, Lib.* 4. *Inſtit. Tit.* 14.

To Reply, *Replico, are.*

A Report, *Reportus, i, m. Cow.* 226. *Dyer* 166. It is in our Common Law a Relation or repetition of a Caſe debated or argued, which is ſometime made to the Court, upon reference from the Court to the Reporter, ſometime to the World, voluntarily as *Plowden*'s Reports, the Lord *Cook*'s Reports, *&c.*

To Report, *Reporto, are. Ra. Entr.* 14 *Ry.* 259. *Pry.* 420.

To Reprehend, *Reprehendo, ere.*

A Reprehenſion, *Reprehenſio, onis, f.*

To Repreſs, *Reprimo, ere.*

A Repriſe, *Repriſa, æ, f. Lex.* 110.

A Repriſal, *Repriſale, is, n. Cow.* 226. 10. *Cow.* 133.

Repriſes (charges to be deducted) *Repriſæ, arum, f.*

To Reprive, *Reprendo, ere.*

To Reproach, *Exprobro, are. Infamo, are. Inculpo, are.*

A Reproach, *Probrum, i, n. Contumelia, æ, f.*

Reproachful, *Contumelioſus, a, um.*

Reproachfully, *Contumelioſè, adv.*

To Reprove, *Reprobo, are.*

Reptaceſter, Richberg, Richborow near Sandwich (in *Kent*) *ad Portum Rutupas, Rhutubi Portus, Rhutupiæ Statio, Rhitupus portus, Rutupinus portus, Rutupinum Littus, Rhutupiæ Trutulenſis portus, urbs Rutupina.*

Repton (in *Darbyſhire*) *Ripadium, Repandunum.*

A Repulſe, *Repulſa, æ, f. Repulſio, onis, f.*

Reputation, *Reputatio, onis, f.*

R E Q.

To Requeſt (or require) *Requiro, ere. Peto, ere.*

A Requeſt, *Requeſta, æ f.*

Requiſite, *Requiſitus, a, um.*

The Rereward of an Army, *Retrogardia, æ, f. Kit.* 208. *Retaguardia, æ, f. Tergum exercitus.*

R E S.

Reſceit, *Receptio, onis, f.*

Reſceit is in the Civil Law called, *admiſſio tertiæ Perſonæ pro intereſſe*, In our Law when one is ſued, whoſe Eſtate is ſo weak

weak that he cannot defend full suit, then is another who is better able admitted upon Prayer: Sometimes Refceit is Sur Refceit, this is againft Rule, as a Wife being Tenant for Life, is received upon the default of her Husband, and after makes default, he in Reverfion fhall be received; fo if Baron and Feme be received; and after Baron make default, the Feme fhall be received, 2. *p.* of *Inftit. fol.* 345. If a Tenant for Term of Life, or Tenant for Term of Years bring an Action, he in the Reverfion cometh in, and Prayeth to be received to defend the Land, and to Plead with the Demandant, *vid.* Terms of Law; many more you may have in *Brook Tit. Refceit*, *fol.* 205. fee *Perkin*'s *Dower* 448.

Refceit is alfo applied to an admittance of Plea, tho' the controverfie be but between two only, *Brook* Eftopel. in many Places.

Refcous, *Refcuffus*, *i*, *m.* It is an Ancient *French* Word, coming from *Refcourrer*, that is, *Recuperare* to take from, to refcue or recover. Refcous, is a taking away and fetting at Liberty againft Law, a Diftrefs taken, or a Perfon Arrefted by the Procefs or Courfe of the Law, *Cook* on *Lit. Lib.* 2. *cap.* 12. *Sect* 237. There is a Refcous in deed, and a Refcous in Law: Of the firft hath been fpoken.

A Refcous in Law is when a Man hath taken a diftrefs, and the Cattel diftreined, as he is driving of them to the Pound, do go into the Houfe of the Owner, if he that took the diftrefs, demand them of the Owner, and he deliver them not, this is a Refcous in Law.

It is alfo ufed for a Writ which lieth for this Act, called, *Breve de Refcuffu*, whereof you may fee both the form and ufe, in *Fitz*, *nat. brev. fol.* 101. and the *Regift. Orig. fol.* 125. fee the new Book of Entries, *verbo Refcous*. This Refcous in fome cafes is Treafon, & in fome Felony, *Crompt. Juftice*, fol. 54. b.

To Refcue, *Recupero*, *are.*

A Refcue, *Refcuffus*, *i*, *m.* *Lex* 109. *Co. Lit.* 160.

A Refcuer, *Refcuffor*, *oris*, *m.*

To Refeife, *Refeifio*, *ire.*

Refervation, *Refervatio*, *onis*, *f.*

To Referve, *Refervo*, *are.*

Refidence (or Abode) *Refidentia*, *æ*, *f.* *Refiantia*, *æ*, *f.* *Refeantifa*, *æ*, *f.* *Brac.* 337.

To Refide, *Refido*, *ere.* *Lex.* 110. *Cow.* 227.

A Refiant (or Tenant to a Mannor) *Refians*, *tis*, *m.* *Plo.* 119.

The Refidue, *Refiduum*, *ui*, *n.*

Refignation, *Refignatio*, *onis*, *f.*

To Refift, *Refifto*, *ere.*

To Refolve, *Refolvo*, *ere.*

Refolution, *Refolutio*, *onis*, *f.*

To Refort, *Reforto*, *are.* *Weft. Indict.* 199.

The Right did Refort, *Refortiebatur Jus. Ra. Entr.* 29. *bis.*

Refort (the Authority of a Court) *Refortum*, *i*, *n.*

To Refpect (or have refpect) *Refpicio*, *ere.*

A Refpect, *Refpectus*, *ûs*, *m.*

Refpight of Homage, *Refpectus Homagii.*

A Refpight (Paufe or Stop) *Spatium*, *ii*, *n.* *Intervallum*, *i*, *n.*

The Reft and Refidue, *Remanere & Refiduum.*

A Refting place, *Quietorium*, *ii*, *n.*

Reftitution, *Reftitutio*, *onis*, *f.*

 To

To Restore, Restituo, ere. Reddo, ere.

To Restrain, Restringo, ere. Coerceo, ere.

To Resume, Resumo, ere.

Resummons, Resummonitio, onis, f. It is a second Summons, and calling of a Man to Answer an Action, where the first Summons is defeated by any occasion, as the Death of the Party or such like, *Brook*, *Tit. Resummons*, *fol.* 214. See of these four sorts, according to the four divers cases in the Table of the Regist. Judicial, *fol.* 1. See also the new Book of Entries *verbo*, re-attachment and resummons.

Resumption, Resumptio, onis, f.

R E T.

Retail, Retallium, ii, n. Retallia, æ, f. *Reg.* 184. *Ry.* 400.

To retail, Renumero, are.

A retailer, Propola, æ, m.

To retain, Retineo, ere.

Retained, Retentus, a, um.

A Retaining, (*or keeping back*) Retenementum, i, n. Retentio, onis, f.

A retinue, Retinentia, æ, f. *Pry.* 309.

To retire, Retiro, are. *West. Indict.* 74.

Retraxit, It is so called, because that word is the effectual word in the Entry. It is an exception against one that formerly commenced an Action, and withdrew it, or was Non-suite before Trial, *Brook*, *Tit.* departure in despight, and *Retraxit*, *fol.* 216. See also the new Book of Entries, *verbo* Departure, and *verbo*, Retraxit. The difference between a Non-suit and a *Retraxit*; a Retraxit is ever when the Demandant or Plaintiff is present in Court. A Non-suit is ever upon a demand made, when the Demandant or Plaintiff should appear, and he makes default, *Cook on Lit. l.* 2. *c.* 11. *sect.* 288.

A *retraxit*, is a Barr of all other Actions, of Like or Inferiour Nature, *Qui semel actionem renunciavit, amplius repetere non potest.* But regularly Non-suit is not so, but that he may commence an Action of like Nature again, for it may be that he hath mistaken somewhat in that Action, or was not provided of his Proofs, or mistook the Day, or the like, *Leigh. Phil. Com fol.* 205, 206.

To retreat, Pedem referre.

To return, Redeo, ire.

To return back (*or restore*) Refundo, ere.

Return (*as of a Writ*) Retorna, æ, f. Retornum, i, n. Retornum brevis. In our Common Law it hath two particular Applications, as namely, the return of a Writ by Sheriffs and Bailiffs, which is nothing but a Certificate made to the Court, whereupon the Writ directeth him, of that which he hath done, touching the serving of the same Writ, and this among the Civilians is called *Certificatorium.* Of returns in this signification, speak the Statutes of *West.* 2. *Cap.* 39. *Anno.* 13. *Ed.* 1. and *Tract. contra vice-comites & clericos*, with divers other, collected by *Rastal. Tit.* return of Sheriffs, so is the return of an Office, *Stawnf. Prærog. fol.* 70. A Certificate into the Court, of that which is done by by vertue of his Office, See the Statutes of Daies in Bank, *Anno* 51. *H.* 3. and *Anno* 32. *H.* 8. *Cap.* 21. And in this signification *Hilary* Term is said to have four returns, *viz. Octabis Hilarii*, *Quindena Hilarii*, *Crastino Purificationis*, *Octabis Purificationis*; and *Easter* Term to have five returns, *viz. Quindena Pascha*, *Tres Pascha*, *Mense Pascha*, *Quinque Pascha*, and *Crastino Ascensionis*; and *Trinity* Term four returns, *viz. Crastino Trinitatis*, *Octabis Trinitatis*, *Quindena Trinitatis*, *Tres Trinitatis*; and *Michaelmas* Term eight returns, *viz. Octabis Michaelis*, *Quindena Michaelis*, *Tres Michaelis*, *Mense Michaelis*, *Crastino Animarum*, *Crastino Martini*, *Octabis Martini*, *Quindena Martini*.

The other Application of this word is in case of Replevy, for if a Man distrain Cattel for Rent, *&c.* and afterward justifie or avow his Act, that it be found Lawful, the Cattel before delivered to him that was distrained upon security, given to follow the Action, shall now be returned to him that distrained them, *Brook*, *Tit. Return. d' Avers*, and *Hommes*, *fol.* 218. You may find this word often used in *Fitz, nat. brev.* as appeareth in the word Return in his Table: But in all those Places, it hath the one or other of these two significations---

To return, Retorno, are.

A return from a place, Reditus a loco.

Returnum Averiorum, Is a Writ Judcial, granted to one impleaded for taking the Cattel of another, and unjustly detaining of them, *contra vadium & Plegios*, and appearing upon Summons is dismissed without Day, by reason that the Plaintiff maketh default, and it lieth for the return of the Cattel unto the defendant, whereby he was summoned, or which were taken for the security of his appearance upon the Summons, *Regist. Judic. fol.* 4. a.

Returnum Irreplegiabile, Is a Writ Judicial sent out of the Common Pleas to the Sheriff, for the final Restitution or return of Cattel to the Owner, unjustly taken by another, as damage feisant, and so found by the Jury before Justices of Assize in the County, for which see the Regist. Judicial, *fol.* 27. a. *b.*

R E V.

Reuben (*a man's Name*) Reuben, Indecl.

Revels, Revella, orum, n. 1. *fol* 89. (*i. e.*) sports of Dancing, Masking, Comedies, Tragedies, *&c.* used in the King's House, the Inns of Court, or Houses of other Great Personages.

Reverend, Reverendus, a, um.

To reverse, Everto, ere. Abrogo, are.

Reversion, Reversio, onis, f.

To revert, Reverto, ere.

Revived, Redivivus, a, um.

Revocation, Revocation, onis. f.

To revoke (*or call back*) Revoco, are.

R E W.

A reward, Præmium, ii, n.

To reward, Præimor, ari.

R E Y.

A reyn (or drain for the avoiding of superfluous moisture) Obex Aquarius.

Reynold (a man's Name) Reynoldus, i, m.

R H E.

Rhead River (in Northumberland) Rheadus.

Rhetorick, Rhetorica, æ, f.

A rhetorician, Rhetor, oris, m.

Rhetorically, Rhetoricè, adv.

Of or belonging to Rhetorick, Rhetoricus, a, um.

R I B.

A riband, Lemniscus, ci, m. Vitta, æ, f.

A rib, Costa, æ, f.

Ribel river, or Rhibel mouth (in Lancashire) Belisama, Bellisama.

Ribblechester (in Lancashire) Coccium, Goccium, Ribodunum, Rigodunum.

R I C.

Rice (a kind of grain) Olyra, æ, f. Oriza, æ, f.

Rice (a man's Name) Ricius, ii, m.

Rich (or Wealthy) Dives, tis, adj.

Riches, Divitiæ, arum, f.

Richberge, Richborough. See *Reptacester.*

Richmond in the North, Richmundia.

Richmond (in Surrey) Richmondia, Richmundia Shenum.

R I D.

A ridle, Ænigma, atis, n.

To ride, Equito, are.

To ride away, Abequito, are.

A rider, Equitator, oris, m.

A rider of a horse (or Stable boy) Equiso, onis, m.

A riding, Equitatio, onis, f.

A riding Cap, Galericulum, li, n.

A ridge of Land, Riga, æ, f. *Lex.* 111. Porca, æ, f.

The ridge (or top of an Hill, or House) Fastigium, ii, n.

R I E.

Rie River (in Yorkshire) Rhius.

R I F.

Rifling, Riflura, æ, f. *Placita, Cor.* 79. *Brac.* 144.

R I G.

Right. Jus, juris, n.

By Colour of a supposed Estate or Right (usually taken in the worst part) *Colore.*

Right (or just) Rectus, a, um.

Right against (or Opposite) Contra, Adversum.

R I M.

A rime, Rima, æ, f. *Lex.* 111.

R I N.

A ring, Annulus, li, m.

A little ring, Annellus, li, m.

A wedding ring, Annulus pronubus.

A sealing

A sealing ring, Annulus Sigillaris.

A ring box, Annularium, ii, n.

A ring which Women wear on their Fore Finger, Corianus, i, m.

A seller of rings, Annularius, ii, m.

A ring with a Sapphire, Annulus aureus cum Sapphiro in eodem fixo.

A ring that Smiths tie Horses to, Balbatum, i, n.

The staple ring or chain that fastneth to Yokes, Ampron,onis,m.

A ring of a door (or hammer wherewith men knock at the door) Cornix, cis, f.

The Iron rings in which the gudgeons of a wheel Spindle turn, Armillæ, arum, f.

An ear-ring, Inauris, is, f.

Of or belonging to a ring, Annularis,re, adj. Annularius, a, um.

Ringed (wearing Rings) as Dogs when they are tyed up, Annulatus,a,um.

A ring leader, Præsultor, oris, m. Coryphæus, i, m.

A ring-worm (or tetter) Impetigo, inis, f.

R I O.

A riot, Riottum, i, n. *Cow.* 23[illegible]. *Pace Regis.* 30. Riotum, i, n *Keil.* 194. *Pace Regis.* 26. Riota, æ, f. Riot is where three at the least or more do some unlawful act, it comes from the French word *Riottor*, *id est*, *Rixari*, to scold or brawl, *Cook on Lit. lib.* 3. *sect.* 50.

It signifieth in our common Law the forcible doing of an unlawful act, by three or more Persons assembled together for that purpose, *West. part.* 2. *Symb. Tit.* Inditements, *sect.* 65. *p.* The Differences and Agreements between a Riot, a Rout, and unlawful assembly, see in *Lamb. Eirenar. lib.* 2. *cap.* 5. *&c.* see the *Statute* 1. *m.* 1. *cap.* 12. and *Kitch. fol.* 19. who giveth these Examples of Riots: The breach of inclosures or banks, or Conduits, Parks, Pounds, Houses, Barns, the burning of stacks of Corn, *Lamb. ubi supra*, useth these examples, to beat a Man, to enter upon a Possession forcible, see *Rout*. See also *Crompt.* Justice of Peace, divers cases of Riots, *&c. fol* 53.

Riotously, Riotose, adv. *Pace Regis.* 30.

To rip (that which is sewed) Dissuo, ere. Resuo, ere.

Ripped, Dissutus, a, um. Resutus, a, um.

A ripier (one that carries fish about) Riparius, ii, m.

R I T.

A rite (or Custom) Ritus, ûs, m.

Rites, Justa, orum, n.

Riton upon Dunsmore (in Warwickshire) Rugnitunia, Rutunia, Ruitonia.

R I V.

To Rive in Pieces, Discerpo, ere, Proscindo, ere. Lacero, are.

A River, Rivus, vi, m. Fluvius, ii, m. Flumen, inis, n. Amnis, is, m.

The mouth of a River (or the place whereat it runneth into the Sea) Ostium, ii, n. Faucis, is, f.

The middle of the breadth of a River, Filum aquæ, *Davis*, 57. 2. *Mon.* 205. *Ra. Entr.* 666.

The Bank of a River (*or the River it self*) Riparia, æ, f. 2. *Inst* 30. 474, 478. 2. *H.* 4. 8. *Pry.* 189. *bis*, 383.

Places before the River banks, Paripia, orum, n.

A little river (*or brook*) Rivulus, i, m.

The Chanel of a river, Affluens, ior, issimus, adj. Alveus, ei, m.

A river that floweth over the banks, Expanditor amnis.

The turning of a River another way, Diverticulum fluminis.

Of a river, Fluvialis, le, adj.

Full of rivers, Fluminosus, a, um.

River by River, Rivatim, adv.

To rivet, Depango, ere.

Riveted, Depactus, a, um. Impetratus, a, um.

A Riveting, Depactio, onis, f.

Rivets, (*or splints in harness*) Clavi, orum, m.

R O A.

A Road for Ships, Navale, is, n. Statio, onis, f.

Road (*or high way*) Via Regia.

To roast, Asso, are. Torreo, ere. Torrefacio, ere.

Roasted, Assatus. a, um. Assus, a, um.

Roasted meat, Assatura, æ, f. Carnes assatæ.

Roast beaf, Bubula assa.

Throughly roasted, Inassatus, a, um.

Roasted under ashes, Subcinericius, a, um.

A roasting, Assatio, onis, f. Adustio, onis, f.

A roaster, Assator, oris, m.

R O B.

A robe, Roba, æ, f. Brac. 60.

A robe or kirtle worn by Kings under their Mantles of Estate, Trabea, æ, f.

To Rob (*or spoil*) Rapio, ere. Spolio, are. Latrocinor, ari.

He hath robbed, Robbaverit, *Pry.* 153. *Brac.* 102, 112.

A robber, Robator, oris, m. Terms *de Ley*. *Cow.* 84.

Robbers, Robberatores, m. *Pl. Ry.* 178.

A robbery, Roboria, æ. f. Roberia, æ, f. *Reg.* 272. *Co. Lit.* 288. *Dyer*, 213.

Robaria, æ, f. In our common Law is a Felonious taking away of another Man's goods from his Person or presence, against his will, putting him in fear, and of purpose to steal the same goods, *West. Part.* 2. *Symb. Tit.* Inditements, *sect.* 60. This is sometime called violent Theft, *Idem, eod.* which is Felony for two pence, *Kitch. fol.* 26. and 22. *lib. assis.* 39.

Robbery is so called, because goods are taken as it were *de la robe*, from the Robe, that is from the Person, *Leigh. Phil. Com. fol.* 207. Either because they bereaved the true Man of some of his Robes or Garments, or because his Money or Goods were taken out of some part of his Garment or Rob about his Person, Sir *Edward Cook's third part* of *Instit. ch.* 16.

A robbery was done in *January*, after the sun-setting, during twilight, and it was adjudged that the Hundred should answer for it, because it was convenient time for Men to Travel, or be about their Works or businesses, and with this accords the Book in 3. *Ed.* 3. *Tit. Coronne* 293.

That

That if one kill another at the hour of the Evening and escape, by the common Law the Town shall be amerced, for this is counted in the Law part of the Day, *Cook 7th Rep. Ashpoole's case.* A Man in time of Divine Service, upon the Sabbath-day was rob'd, *Mountague* Chief Justice was of Opinion, that the Hundred should not be charged, but *Doderidge*, Sir *John Crook*, and *Hawtain* Justices, were of contrary Opinion, that the Hundred should be charged, and so it was adjudged, *termino Michaelis.* This is altered alate, although the thing so taken, be not to the value but of a penny, yet it is felony, for which the offender shall suffer Death, and shall not have the benefit of his Clergy, not so much for the value of the goods taken, as for terrifying the party robbed, a putting him in dread and fear of his Life. *Stawnford, Dr. & Stud.*

He that robbeth any dwelling House, or out House belonging to it in the Day time, of the value of 5*s.* whether it be Money, Goods or Cattels, shall not have his Clergy, 39, *Eliz.* 15. *c.*

If a Bailiff of a Mannor, or a Receiver, or a Factor of a Merchant, or the like accountant be robbed, he shall be discharged thereof upon his account. But otherwise it is of a Carrier, for he hath his hire, and thereby implicitely, undertaketh the safe delivery of the Goods delivered to him, and therefore he shall answer the value of them, if he be robbed of them, *Cook, 4th. Rep. Southcot's case.* 83. *B.* and on *Lit. lib.* 2, *cap.* 5. *sect.* 123.

So if Goods be delivered to a Man to be safely kept, and after those goods are stollen from him, this shall not excuse him, because by the acceptance, he undertook to keep them safely, and therefore he must keep them at his Peril.

So it is if Goods be delivered to one to be kept: For to be kept, and to be safely kept is all one in Law. But if Goods be delivered to him to be kept, as he would keep his own, there if they be stollen from him without his default or negligence, he shall be discharged, *Idem ibid.*

So if Goods be delivered to one as a gage or pledge, and they be stollen, he shall be discharged, because he hath a property in them, and therefore he ought to keep them no otherwise than his own: But if he that gaged them tendred the Money before the stealing, and the other refused to deliver them, then for this default in him he shall be charged.

If *A.* leave a Chest locked, with *B.* to be kept, and taketh away the Key with him, and acquainteth not *B.* what is in the Chest, and the Chest together with the Goods of *A.* are stolen away, *B.* shall not be chargeld therewith, because *A.* did not trust *B.* with them, as this case is.

R O C.

Roch (the Family) De Rupe *and* Rupibus. Rupinus.

Rochester (in Northumberland) Bramenium, Bremenium.

Rochester City (in Kent) Darvernum, Dorobrevum, Durobrevis, Durobrevum, Durobrius, Durobrovæ.

Durobrovæ, Duropronis, Duroprovis, Hrofi vel Rhefi Civitas, Roffa, Roibis, Roffi civitas.

Bishop of Rochester, Episcopus Roffensis.

A Rochet, Rochetum, i, n.

A Rock, Rupes, is f. Petra, æ, f.

R O D.

A Rod, Virga, æ, f.

A rod or pearch of Land, Roda terræ.

Rodney (the Family) De Radeona.

R O E.

A roe or roebuck, Caprea, æ, f. Capreolus, li, m.

R O G.

Roger (a man's Name) Rogerus, i, m.

A rogue, Rogus, i, m, *Lex.* 112. Vagrants.

R O L.

To roll, Volvo, ere.

To roll (or wrapabout) Circumvolvo, ere. Circumplico, are.

To roll from a Place, Evolvo, ere.

To roll smooth Lands (or break clods with a Roller) Deocco, are.

To drive a thing on rolls, Phalango, are.

Rolled, Volutus, a, um.

A rolling, Volutatio, onis, f.

Rollers on which Ships are run a shoar, or into the Sea, Phalangæ, arum, f.

One that turns great Weights on Rollers, Phalangarius, ii, m.

A roller of timber to break Clods with, and make the Ground even, Cylindrus, i, m. Volvulus, li, m.

A roll or wreath for a Woman's head to bear Water, or Milk on. Arculus, li, m.

A muster roll, Censura, æ, f.

Master of the rolls, Magister rotulorum Curiæ Cancellariæ Domini Regis.

To roll (or enroll) Irrotulo, are.

A roll or strickle, to strike any measure even, Hostorium, ii, n.

A rolling Pin, Magis, idis, f.

A roll (or catalogue) Rotulus, li, m. *Lex.* 112. It signifieth with us a Schedule of Paper or Parchment, turned or wound up with the hand, to the Fashion of a Pipe. So it is used in *Stawnf.* Pleas of the Crown, *fol.* 11. The Chequer Roll of the King's house out of the Statute, *Anno* 3. *H.* 7. *cap.* 13. which signifieth nothing but the Catalogue wherein the Names of the Kings Houshold Servants are set down, and *Anno* 5. *R* 2. *cap.* 14. *Stat.* 1. there is mention made of the Great Roll of the Exchequer, which seemeth otherwise to be called the Pipe. The Rolls is also a place destinated by *Edward* the Third, to the keeping of the Rolls or Records of the Chancery, the Master whereof is the second Man in Chancery, and in the absence of the Lord Chancellor or Keeper, sitteth as Judge, being commonly called the Master of the Rolls See Master of the Rolls, and Chancery.

R O O.

A rood, Roda, æ, f.

A rood of Land, Rodata terræ. It is ten Pearches, the fourth part

part of an Acre, *Eliz.* 5. *c.* 5.

A Roof (or covering of a House) Tectum, i, n.

A Vaulted roof of an house, Laquear, aris, n.

A roof (or cieling) boarded, Tabulatum laqueatum.

A roof or cieling fretted, Vermiculatum Laquear.

A bending roof, Testudinatum, i, n.

A roof of tiles, Tectum Tegulaneum.

A room, Romea, æ, f.

A inner room, Conclave, is, n. Penetral, alis, n.

A withdrawing room, Poscenium, ii, n.

Dining rooms, Romeæ pransoriæ.

A roost (or Hen-roost) Gallinarium, ii, n.

A root, Radix, icis, f.

R O P.

A rope (or cord) Funis, is, m. Restis, is, m.

A litle rope (or cord) Funiculus, li, m.

A cable rope, Cucurba, æ, f. Rudens, tis, m. vel, f. Funis Anchorarius.

A rope like a Chaplet, Serta, æ, f.

A Dancing rope, Cătădrŏmus, i, m.

A Walker on a rope, or rope-dancer, Funambulus, li, m. Petaurista, æ, m.

A rope, wherewith Ships are tyed to a Post or Stone, Prymnesium, ii, n.

The rope, wherewith the Sail is bound to the Mast, Anquina, æ, f. Axifera, æ, f.

The rope of a Pulley, Ductarius funis.

A rope in the fore-deck of a Ship, Saphon, onis, f.

The cable ropes of Ships, Habenæ, arum, f.

An instrument wherewith ropes are made, Medipontus, i, m.

A roper (or rope maker) Restio, onis, m. Restiarius, ii, m.

A rope seller, Spartarius, ii, m.

To make ropes, Funes torquere.

Pertaining to Ropes, Funalis, le, adj.

R O S.

Rosamund (a Woman's name) Rosamunda, æ, f.

Rose (a Woman's name) Rosa, æ, f.

Rosemary (a Woman's name) Rosamaria, æ, f.

Rosin, Rossinum, i, n. *Dyer*, 75. Resina, æ, f.

Rossland (in Cornwall) and Ross (in Pembrookshire) Rossia.

Ross Bishoprick (in Scotland) Rossia.

R O T.

Rotherbridge (in Sussex) Robertinus Pons.

Rother river, Limenus fluvius.

Rothsay an Island in Scotland, *which formerly gave the Title of a Duke to the Prince of Scotland*, Rothesia.

Rotler river, Lemanus, alias Lelienus.

R O U.

Rough timber, Maeremium impolitum.

Round

Round, Rotundus, a, um.

A round thing, Orbis, is, m.

A rout, Routum, i, n *Keil.* 194. *Pace Reg.* 26. Routa, æ, f. It is so called because they do move and proceed in Routs and Numbers. It signifieth in our Common Law, an Assembly of three Persons or more going on about forcibly to commit an unlawful act, but yet do it not, *West. part.* 2. *Symb. Tit.* Indictments, *fol.* 65. *Lamb.* thus saith of it. A Rout is the same which the *Germans* yet call Rot, meaning a Band, or great Company of Men gathered together, and going about to execute, or executing indeed, any Riot or unlawful act, and saith more, that it is said properly of the multitude that Assembleth themselves in such disorderly sort for their common Quarrels. As if the Inhabitants of a Township, do assemble to pull down a Hedge or Pale, to have their Common, where they ought to have none, or to beat a Man that hath done them some publick offence or displeasure. But the Statute of 18 *Ed.* 3. *Stat.* 1. *Cap. unico*, which giveth Process of Outlawry against such as bring Routs into the presence of the Justice, or in a fray of the People, and in the Statute of 2. *Rich.* 2. *cap.* 6. that speaketh of riding in great Routs, to make entry into Lands, and to beat others, and to take their Wives, *&c.* do seem to understand it more largely.

It is a Rout whether they put their purpose in execution or not: If so be, that they do go, ride, or move forward their meeting, *Brook, Tit. Riot.* 4, and 5.

So that a Rout is a special kind of unlawful assembly, and a Riot the disorderly fact committed generally by any unlawful Assembly. The one that three Persons at the least be gathered together, the other that they being together, do breed disturbance of the Peace, either by signification of Speech, shew of armor, turbulent gesture, or actual and express violence. So that either the Peaceable sort of Men be unquieted and feared by the Fact, or the lighter sort, and busie Bodies emboldened by the Example. Thus far *Lambert* in his *Eirenar. Lib.* 2. *Cap.* 5. where you may read more worth the noting, *Kitchin* giveth the same definition of a Rout, *fol.* 20. An unlawful Assembly may well be called an Introduction, a Rout, a Persecution, and a Riot, an Execution.

Routously, Routosè, adv.

R O W.

To row, Remigo, are.

Rowed, Remigatus, a, um.

A rower of a Ship, Remex, igis, m.

The master Rower, Pausarius, ii, m.

Seats for the rowers, Transtra, orum, n.

A rowing, Remigatio, onis, f.

A rowel, Stimulus, li, m.

Rowland (a Man's name) Rolandus, i, m.

A Rowney, Runcinus, i, m. (*i. e.*) a Load Horse, sumpter Horse or Cart Horse.

Rowton, (*in Shropshire*) Rutunium.

R O X.

R O X.

Roxburg in Teifidale (in Scotland) Marchidunum.

R O Y.

Royal, Regalis, le, adj. Basilicus, a, um.

Royal Assent, Regius Assensus. Is that approbation which the King giveth to a thing formerly done by others, as to the Election of a Bishop by Dean and Chapter, which given, then he sendeth the especial Writ to some Person for the taking of his fealty; the form of which Writ you may see in *Fitz. nat. brev. fol.* 170. *chap.* and also to a Bill passed by both the Houses of Parliament, *Crompt, Jurisd. fol.* 8. which assent being once given, the Bill is indorsed with these words, *Le Roy veult*, it pleaseth the King. If he refuse to agree unto it, then thus *Le Roy advisera*, the King will yet think of it.

Royalities, Regalia, orum, n. *Ra. Ent.* 468. *Pry.* 146. Regalitates, um, f. It is the Rights of the King, *Jura Regis*, or the Kings Prerogative, and some of these are such as the King may grant to common Persons, some so high, as may not be separated from his own Crown *Privative*, as the Civilians term it, though *Cumulative* he may, see *Bracton, Lib.* 2. *cap.* 5. These are in some sort expressed in the first of *Samuel, chap* 8. but these Generalities are specified more at large by those Lawyers that Write of this Point, of whom I especally commend *Matth. de afflictis* upon the Title of the Feuds, *Quæ sint Regalia* being the 33 Title of the third Book, as some divide them, but according to others the 56 of the second Book, where are named in the Text 25. specialties of Royalties: See also *Hottomans* Commentaries in *Lib.* 2. *feudor. cap.* 56. see also *Stawnf. Prærog.*

The Royal Exchange, Cambium Regale, Bursa, Excambium Regium. Peristilium.

Royston, Cambridgeshire, Roisiæ oppidum.

R U B.

To rub, Frico, are.

Rubbed, Frictus, a, um.

Rubbidge, Rubbosa, æ, f. *Pry.* 415. bis.

R U D.

A rudder or stirrer belonging to Brewers, Motaculum, li, n.

A rudder of a Ship, Clavus, i, m. Camax, cis, f.

Rudiment, Rudimentum, i, n.

R U F.

A ruffian (or debashe) Leccator, oris, m. Meretricarius, ii, m.

R U G.

A Rugg, Opimentum, i, n.

A frieze rugg, Gausapina, æ, f.

R U I.

To Ruinate, Ruino, are.

Ruine, (or fall) Ruina, æ, f.

R U L.

To rule (*or govern*) Rego, ere.

Rule (*or domination*) Dominatio, onis, f.

To rule (*or have Sovereign Anthority*) Regno, are.

A rule to rule by, Regula, æ, f. Norma, æ, f.

A carpenters (*or Masons*) *Rule* Amussis, is, f.

A rule or instrument to measure Land, Gnoma, æ, f.

Made even or right by Rule or Square, Normalis, le, adj. Regularis, re, adj.

Rule by Rule, Regulatim, adv.

A Rule (*or direction*) Præscriptum, i, n.

R U M.

To Ruminate, Rumino, are.

A rumor, Rumor, oris, m.

A Rumor-raiser, Coryphæus, i, m. Auctor turbarum.

R U N.

A runaway, Transfuga, æ, c. 2.

A running away, Fugitas, atis, f.

To run, Curro, ere.

Runners (*or Coursers*) Proclastæ.

The runner (*or upper Stone in a Mill*) Cattillus, li, m.

Runnet, Quactum, i, n.

A runlet, Orcula, æ, f. Amphora, æ, f.

R U P.

A Rupture, Ruptura, æ, f.

A Rupture, (*or Burstenness*) Hernia, æ, f.

R U S.

Rushden (*in Hertforshire*) Vallæ Scirpinæ.

The rust of Iron, Rubigo, inis, f. Ferrugo, inis, f.

To rust, Rubigino, are.

Russet, Russetum, i, n. 2 *Mon.* 337.

Of Russet Cloth, Russetorum pannorum, *mag. Chart. cap.* 25. 2 *Inst.* 41.

Somewhat Russet, Russulus, a, um.

R U T.

Rutland, Rutlandia.

R Y E.

Rye, Secale, is, n. Typha Cerealis.

S A B.

SAbin (*a Woman's name*) Sabina, æ, f.

Sabrina (*a Woman's name*) Sabrina, æ, f.

S A C.

A sack, Saccus, i, m.

A little sack, Sacculus, li, m.

A Leather sack, Culeus, ei, m.

The Mouth of a sack, Lura, f.

Merchandize of sacks, Saccaria, æ, f.

A bearer of sacks, Saccarius, ii, m.

Put in a sack, Saccatus, a, um.

Of a sack, Saccarius, a, um.

A

A sack-cloth, Cilicium, ii, n.

A sachel, Saccipium, ii, n.

Sack (a wine that cometh out of Spain) Vinum Hispanense.

To sack (or wast Countries or Cities) Diripio, ere. Depopulor, ari.

Sacked (or wasted) Direptus, a, um. Populatus, a, um.

A sacker (or waster) Depopulator, oris, m. Direptor, oris, m.

A sacking, Direptio, onis, f.

To strain through a sack, Saccello, are.

Sacred (or holy) Sacer, ra, rum. Consecratus, a, um.

To make sacred, Sacro, are.

Sacrilege (stealing of holy things) Sacrilegium, ii, n.

A Sacrilegious Person, Sacrilegus, i, m.

S A D.

A saddle, Ephippium, ii, n. Sella Equi. Scordiscus, ci, m.

A pack-saddle, Clitellæ, arum, f. Sagina, æ, f.

A side-saddle, Sella muliebris.

A saddle-cloath, Instratum, i, n.

The fore part of the saddle, Antella, æ, f.

The saddle-bow, Sellæ arcus.

A saddle-tree, Sellæ lignea forma.

To saddle an Horse, Equum sternere, Equo Ephippium imponere.

Saddled, Ephippiatus, a, um. Instratus Ephippiis.

A saddler, Ephippiarius, ii, m. Sellarius, ii, m. Scordiscarius, ii, m.

S A F.

Safe, Salvus, a, um.

Safety, Salus, utis, f. Sanitas, atis, f.

Saffron-Walden (in Essex) Waldena.

S A I.

Said, Idem, Eadem, Idem, *Pron. Rel.* usually and most properly, *Idem* in Declarations or Pleadings is attributed to Plaintiffs or Demandants, declaring or Pleading; *Prædictus*, to Defendants or Tenants, Places, Towns or Lands; *Præfatus* to Persons named not being actors; yet if the same Persons, Lands, *&c.* come very nearly again to be named or mentioned in Pleadings usually and most properly *Idem* is used.

Said is sometimes omitted in Pleadings, and *quidem* used instead thereof, especially in the beginning of a Sentence; as *Qui quidem Finis*, for which said fine, *Quæ quidem Indentura*, which said Indenture, *Quod quidem Recordum*, which said Record, *Qui quidem locus*, which said place.

To sail, Navigo, are.

To sail beyond, Præternavigo, are.

To sail by or before, Prænavigo, are.

To sail to, Adnavigo, are.

To sail through, Pernavigo, are.

To sail forward, Provehor, eris.

To sail over, Trajicio, ere.

To hoise sail, Dare vela, Pandere sive extendere vela, velifico, are.

To strike sail, velum contrahere, vela demittere.

A sail of a Ship, velum, i, n. Linteum, ei, n.

The

The main sail, Artemon, onis, f. Scatium, ii, n.

The top-sail, Thoracium, ii, n. Supparus, i, m.

A sail wherewith the Course of a Ship is holpen, when the Wind is weak, Acatium, ii, n.

The sail in the fore part of a Ship, called the sprit-sail, Mendicium, ii, n.

A small sail called a Trinket, Dolo, onis, m.

The third sail behind, or the misen-sail, Epidromus, i, m.

The sail-yard, Antenna, æ, f.

The two ends of the sail-yard, Ceruchus, i, m. Cornua, n.

The bonnet or enlargment of the sail, Orthiax.

The band or cord wherewith the sail of a Ship is tyed to the Mast. Anquina, æ, f.

Of a sail, Velaris, re, adj.

Sailed, Navigatus, a, um.

Sailed through, Pernavigatus, a, um.

A sailer, Navigator, oris, m.

A sailing, Navigatio, onis, f.

A sailing by, Prænavigatio, onis, f.

A sailing beyond, Præternavigatio, onis, f.

A sailing through, Pernavigatio, onis, f.

A sailing to a place, Adnavigatio, onis, f.

A sailing about, Pĕrĭplous.

Saint *Alban* (*the Family*) De Sanct. Albano.

St. *Albans* (*in Hertfordshire*) Fanum Sancti Albani. Villa Albani.

St. *Andrews* (*in Scotland*) Andreapolis. Fanum Reguli.

Of St. *Asaphs* (*in Flintshire*) Asaphensis.

St. *Barbara, contracted to* St. *Barb, and corruptly Simbarb* (*the Family*) De Sancta Barbara.

St. *Clare, corruptly*, Synclere (*the Family*) De Sancta Clara.

St. *Davids* (*in Wales*) Menevia, Oppidum Sti. Davidis.

St. *David's head, a Promontory* (*in Pembrokeshire*) Octopitarum Promont.

Of St. *Davids*, Menevensis.

St. *Edmondsbury in Suffolk*, Curia Edmundi Burgus. Villa Faustini. Villa Regia.

St. *Faith* (*the Family*) De Sancta Fide.

St. *Foster* (*the Family*) De Sancto Vedasto.

St. *Hellen's head*, Boræum Prom.

St. *John's foreland* (*in Ireland*) Isamnium, Isanium. Isannium.

St. *John town* (*in Ireland*) Sti. Johannis Fanum, Pertha, Perthum.

St. *Ives* (*in Huntingdonshire*) Fanum Ivonis Persiæ. Slepa.

St. *Lantwit* (*in Glamorganshire*) Fanum Sti Iltuti.

St. *Laud, commonly Sentlo* (*the Family*) De Sancto Laudo.

St. *Leger or Sellenger* (*the Family*) De Sancto Leodogario.

St. *Lis* (*the Family*) De Sancto Lizio, & Sylvanectensis.

St. *Mark* (*the Family*) De Sancto Marco.

St. *Maur or Semour* (*the Family*) De Sancto Mauro.

St. *Mawes Castle* (*in Cornwall*) Mauditi Castrum.

St. *Michael's Mount* (*in Cornwall*) Mons Michaelis.

St. *Morrice* (*the Family*) De Sancto Mauricio.

St. *Neots* (*in Huntingdonshire*) Fanum Neoti.

St. *Omer* (*the Family*) De Sancto Audomaro.

St. *Owen* (*the Family*) De Sancto Audoeno.

St. *Patricks Purgatory* (*in Ireland*) Regia Regalis.

St. *Quintin* (*the Family*) De Sancto Quintino.

St. *Semarc* (*the Family*) De Sancto Medardo.

St. *Sentlow* (*the Family*) De Sancto Lupo.

St. *Singlis in Ireland* (*the Family*) De Sancto Gelasio.

St. *Alban Woodstreet*, *St.* Albani in vico Ligneo Parochia.

St. *Alphage*, *St.* Alphagii.

St. *Andrew Holborn*, *St.* Andreæ in Holborn.

St. *Andrew Hubbard*, *St.* Andreas Hubbardus.

St. *Andrew Undershaft*, *St.* Andreæ ad Sub malo cereali.

St. Andrew Wardrobe, *St.* Andreæ ad Vestiarium.

St. *Ann Aldersgate*, *St.* Annæ intra Portam Alneam.

St. *Ann Black-Fryers*, *St.* Annæ nigrorum Monachorum.

St. *Ann Westminster*, *St.* Annæ Westm.

St. *Antholin*, alias *Anthonia*, *St.* Anthonii.

St. *Austins*, *St.* Augustini.

St. *Bartholomew-Exchange*, *St.* Bartholomæi pone Peristylium.

St. *Bartholomew the Great*, *St.* Bartholomæi magni.

St. *Bartholomew the Less*, *St.* Bartholomæi Parvi.

St. *Bennet-Fink*, *St.* Benedictus Finchus.

St. *Bennet Grace Church*, *St.* Benedictus in Graminoso vico.

St. *Bennet Paul's-Wharf*, St. Benedictus ad Ripam Paulinam.

St. *Bennet Shere-hog*, *St.* Benedictus Sherhogus.

St. *Botolph Aldersgate*, *St.* Botolphi Alneæ portæ.

St. *Botolph Aldgate*, *St.* Botolphi ad veterem portam.

St. *Botolph Billingsgate*, *St.* Botolphi ad Portam Belini.

St. *Botolph Bishopsgate*, *St.* Botolphi ad Episcopi portam.

St. *Bridget* alias *Bride*. *St.* Bridgettæ.

St. *Christophers*, *St.* Christopheri.

St. *Clement Danes*, *St.* Clementis Danorum, Dacorum.

St. *Clement East-Cheap*, *St.* Clementis in foro Orientali.

St. *Dionys Back-Church*, *St.* Dionysius Ecclesiæ Back-Church.

St. *Dunstan East*, *St.* Dunstani in Oriente.

St. *Dunstans West*, *St.* Dunstani in Occidente.

St. *Edmund Lumbard-Street*, *St.* Edmundi in Lumbard-Street.

St. *Ethelburg*, *St.* Ethelbora virgo.

St. *Faith*, *St.* Fidei.

St. *Gabriel Fen-Church*, *St.* Gabriel in vico Palustri.

St. *George Botolph Lane*, *St.* Georgius in Botolphi viculo.

St. *George's Southwark*, *St.* Georgii in Australi opere.

St. *Giles Cripplegate*, *St.* Ægidii ad Portam membris captorum.

St. *Giles in the Fields*, *St.* Ægidii in Campis.

St. *Gregories by Pauls*, *St.* Gregorii juxta Templum Paulinum.

St. *James Clerkenwell*, *St.* Jacobus ad Clericorum fontem.

St. *James Dukes place*, *St.* Jacobus ad Ducis hospitium.

St. *James Garlickhyth*. *St.* Jacobi ad Montem allii.

St. *John Baptist Walbrook*, *St.* Johannes Baptista prope Galli torrentem.

St. *John Evangelist*, *St.* Johannis Evangelistæ.

St. *John Zachary*, *St.* Johannis Zachary.

St. *John at Hackney*, *St.* Johannis de Hackney in Com. Middlesex.

St. *John Wapping*, St. Johannis apud Wapping.

St. *Katherine Coleman-Street*, *St.* Catharina Colmanni.

St. *Katherine Cree-Church*, *St.* Catharina Christi Ecclesiæ.

St. *Katherines Tower*, *St.* Catharina juxta Turrim.

St. *Lawrence Jewry*, *St.* Laurentius in Judaismo.

St. *Lawrence Pountney*, *St.* Laurentii Pountneius.

St. *Leonard East-Cheap*, *St.* Leonardi East-cheap.

St. *Leonard Foster-Lane*, *St.* Leonardi Foster-Lane.

St. *Magdalen Bermondsey*, *St.* Magdalene de Bermondi insula.

St. *Magnus*, *St.* Magnetis.

St. *Margaret Lothbury*, *St.* Margaritæ in Lothbury.

St. *Margaret Moses's*, *St.* Margaritæ Mosis.

St. *Margaret New-fish-street*, *St.* Margarita in Novo foro piscario.

St. *Margarets Pattons*, *St.* Margarita à Gallicarum venditione.

St. *Margarets Westminster*, *St.* Margaritæ Westmonasteriensis.

St. *Martins Ironmonger-Lane*, *St.* Martini in Ferrariorum viculo.

St. *Martins Ludgate*, *St.* Martini ad Luddi portam.

St. *Martins Orgars*, *St.* Martini Orgari.

St. *Martins Outwich*, *St.* Martini Outwichi.

St. *Martins Vintrey*, *St.* Martini in Vinariis.

St. *Martins in the Fields*, St. Martini in Campis.

St. *Mary Abchurch Parish*, Parochia *St.* Mariæ abbatis Ecclesiæ.

St. *Mary Aldermanbury*, *St.* Mariæ in Aldermannorum burgo.

St. *Mary Aldermary*, *St.* Mariæ senioris Mariæ.

St. *Mary Le-Bow*, *St.* Mariæ de Arcubus.

St. *Mary Bothaw*, *St.* Mariæ à lintris Statione.

St. *Mary Cole-church*, *St.* Mariæ Cole-church.

St. *Mary Hill*, *St.* Mariæ in Collem.

St. *Mary Islington*, *St.* Mariæ Illington ad villam insularem.

St. *Mary Monthaw*, *St.* Mariæ de Monte alto.

St. *Mary Newington*, *St.* Mariæ ad villam novam.

St. *Mary Savoy*, *St.* Mariæ de Sabaudiâ.

St. *Mary Somerset*, *St.* Mariæ Somerseti.

St. *Mary Staining*, *St.* Mariæ Staining.

St. *Mary White-Chappel*, *St.* Mariæ de alba Capella.

St. *Mary Woolchurch*, *St.* Mariæ ad lanæ trutinam.

St. *Mary Woolnoth*, *St.* Mariæ Woolnothi.

St. *Matthew Friday-Street*, *St.* Matthæi in Friday-Street.

St. *Maudlins Milk-Street*, *St.* Magdalenæ in vico lacteo.

St. *Maudlins Old-fish-Street*, *St.* Magdalenæ in veteri piscario foro.

St. *Michael Bassishaw*, *St.* Michaelis Bassishaw.

St.

St. Michaels Cornhill, St. Michaelis in hordeaceum collem.

St. Michaels Crooked-Lane, St. Michaelis in curvo viculo.

St. Michael Queen-hyth, St. Mariæ ad Ripam Reginalem.

St. Michael Quern, St. Mariæ ad Pladum.

St. Michael Royal, St. Maræ in Riola.

St. Mildred Poultrey, St. Mildredæ in Foro Gallinario.

St. Nicholas Acorns, St. Nicholai de Acona.

St. Nicholas Coleabby, St. Nicholai aureæ abbatiæ.

St. Nicholas Olaves, St. Nicholai Olavi.

St. Olaves Hart-Street, St. Olavi in Cervina platea.

St. Olave Jewry, St. Olavi in Le Jewry.

St. Olave Southwark, St. Olavi in Auſtrali opere.

St. Olaves Silver-Street, St. Olavi in argenteo vico.

St. Paul Shadwel, St. Pauli Shadwel.

St. Pancras Soper-Lane, St. Pancraſii in vico Smegmatico.

St. Pauls Covent-Garden, St. Pauli in Conventuali horto.

St. Peters Cheap, St. Petri in foro.

St. Peters Cornhill, St. Petri in Cornhill.

St. Peter Pauls Wharf, St. Petri prope Pauls Wharf.

St. Peters Poor, St. Petri pauperis.

St. Saviours Southwark, St. Mariæ Salvatoris in Auſtrali opere.

St. Sepulchres Pariſh, St. Sepulchrorum Parochia.

St. Stephens Coleman-ſtreet, St. Stephani in vico Colmanni.

St. Swithin, St. Swithini.

St. Thomas the Apoſtle, St. Thomæ Apoſtoli.

St. Thomas Southwark, St. Thomæ in Auſtrali opere.

St. Vedaſt alias *Foſter, St.* Vedaſti.

S A K.

Cauſe or ſake, Saca vel Sacha, æ, f. *(i. e.)* a Plea in a Court, alſo a forfeiture or amerciament.

A ſaker (or a piece of Ordnance called a ſaker) Hierax.

S A L.

A ſalary, Salarium, ii, n.

A ſale (or ſelling) Venditio, onis, f.

To ſtand or be ſet out to ſale or hire, Proſto, are.

Any thing that is ſet to ſale, Promercalis, le.

Saleable or that may be ſold, Ædibilis, le, adj.

Sale Cloathes, Veſtes promercales.

Salisbury City (in Wiltſhire) Salesburia, Salisburia, Saresberia, Sarisburia, Severia.

Old Sarum (or Salisbury) Sorbiodunum, Sorviodunum, Sorurodunum.

Biſhop of Salisbury, Epiſcopus Salisburienſis.

A ſallet of herbs, Acetaria, orum, n.

To ſally out, Erumpo, ere. Excurro, ere.

Sallies, Excurſiones.

Salt, Sal, alis, m & n.

To ſalt or ſeaſon with ſalt, Salio, ire.

Bay-ſal

Bay-salt, Sal popularis, Sal communis.
The Sea salt, Salum, i, n.
A corn of salt, Grumus salis, Mica salis, Granum salis.
Salt digged out of the Ground, Sal fossilis, Sal fossititius.
White salt, Salis flos, Sal purus.
Salt making, Salsaria, æ, f.
Salt-petre, Sal petræ.
A salt-pit, Salina, æ, f.
Salt-water, Aqua Salsa.
Any thing that is salt, either Fish or Flesh, Salsamentum, i, n.
A Garner, or Room to keep salt in, Salis repositorium.
Salt meats, Salsiuscula, orum, n.
Saltness, Salsitudo, inis, f.
Salt Liquor (or Brine) Salsilago, inis, f.
Salt springs, Salsulæ, arum, f.
Full of salt, Salsuginosus, a, um.
A salting (or seasoning) Salsura, æ, f. Salitura, æ, f.
Salt, Salsus, a, um.
Salted, Salitus, a, um.
A salter (or seller of salt) Salsamentarius, ii, m. Salitor, oris, n.
A salt-seller, Salinum, i, n. Salsarium, ii, n. 2. *mon.* 666.
A little salt seller, Salillum, li, n.
A salting Tub, Vas Salsamentarium.
Belonging to salt, Salinarius, a, um.
Of or for salting, Salsamentarius, a, um.
Saltmarsh (the Family) De Salso Marisco.
Salvage, Salvagium, ii, n (*i e*) Money allowed for rescuing a Ship from Enemies.
Salva guardia, Is a security given by the King to a stranger, fearing the violence of some of his Subjects, for seeking his Right by course of Law. The form whereof see *Reg Orig. fol. 26. a.b.*
A salve (or Ointment) Unguentum, i, n.
A salve (or Plaister) Emplastrum, i, n. Cerotum, i, n. Linimentum, i, n.
A salve for the Eyes, Collirium, ii, n.
Salmey Isle near Milford-haven, Sylimnos.
Saludy (in Bedfordshire) Salenæ, Salinæ.
Salwarp River (in Worcestershire) Salwarpus.

S A N.

Sand, Arena, æ, f.
Sandwich (the Family) De Sandwico.
Sandwich (in Kent) Portus Ammonis, Sabulovicum, Sandicum, Sandovicus, Sanwicum.
Sanden (in Hertfordshire) Mons Arenosus, Caer Severus.
A sand Box, Pyxidula Arenaria.
A sand Pit, Sabuletum, i, n. Arenifodina, æ, f.

S A P.

Sapp, Sappum, i, n. *Fle.* 163. Succus, ci, m. Alburnum, i, n.

S A R.

Sarah (a Womans Name) Sara, æ, f.
A Sarplar, Sarplera lanæ (*i. e.*) a Pocket of Wool, being half a sack, 40. Tods.

S A T.

A satchel (or snapsack) Sacculus,

lus, li, m. Saccellus, li, m. Pera, æ, f.

Satin, Tramosericum, ci, n.

Figured Satin, Tramosericum Palmatum.

A satisfaction, Satisfactio, onis, f.

To satisfie, Satisfacio, ere.

Saturday, Dies Sabbati.

S A U.

Savage (the Family) Salvagius.

A sausage, made of Pork, &c. Tucetum, i, n. Lucanica, æ, f. Salsicia, æ, f. Farcimen, inis, n.

A maker of sausages, Tucerarius, ii, m. Botularius, ii, m.

Sause, Condimentum, i, n.

All kind of sharp sauses, Embamma, atis, n.

A dish full of sause, Uncta Patella.

To sause, Condio, ire.

To dip in the sause, Intingo, ere.

A seller of sharp sause, Oxypŏrŏpola, æ, m.

Saused, Conditus, a, um.

A sauser, Scutella, æ, f. Tryblium, ii, n. Acetabulum, i, n.

Saul (a Man's Name) Saulus, i, m.

Savoy (the Family) De Sabaudia.

The Savoy (in London) Sabaudia.

S A W.

To saw, Serro, are. Serra Secare.

To saw asunder, Serra dissecare.

A saw, Serra, æ, f.

A little saw (or hand saw) Serrula, æ, f.

A whip-saw, Runcina, æ, f.

Sawed, Serratus, a, um. Runcinatus, a, um.

Saw-dust, Serrago, inis, f.

A sawyer, Serrarius, ii, m.

A sawing, Serratura, æ, f.

Sawtrey (in Huntingdonshire) Saltria.

S A Y.

Say (the Family) De Saio.

Of Say-Abbey, Sagiensis.

Sayne Isle near Brest in Brittany, Sena, Sonnos.

S C A.

A scab, Scabies, ei, f.

A scabbard of a Sword, Vagina, æ, f.

A little scabbard, Vaginula, æ, f.

A scaffold, Fala, æ, f. Catasta, æ, f. Fori visorium.

To scald, Glabro, are.

To scale Walls, Scando, ere.

The scale of a fish or Beast, Squama, æ, f.

Scales (the Family) De Scalariis.

A scalping Iron for a Surgeon, Scalprum, i, n. Runcina, æ, f.

Scandalum Magnatum. Is the especial name of a wrong done to any high Personage of the Land, as Prelates, Dukes, Earls, Barons, and other Nobles, and also of the Chancelor, Treasurer, the Privy Seal, Stewards of the King's House, Justice of the one Bench or of the other, and other Great Officers of the Realm by false News, or horrible or false Messages, whereby debates and discords betwixt them and the Commons, or any scandals to their Persons might arise, *Anno* 2. *Rich.* I. *cap.* 5.

A scandal, Scandalum, li, n.

A scar, Cicatrix, icis, f.

A scarf, Mitella, æ, f.

Scarlet, Scarletum, i, n. *Pry.* 25. Coccum, i, n.

Scavage, Scavagium, ii, n. *Cow.* 234. Money paid for offering or shewing Merchandize for sale.

A scavinger, Purgator Luti de viis.

S C E.

A Scepter, Sceptrum, i, n.

S C H.

A schism, Schisma, atis, n.

Schismatical, Schismaticus, a, um.

A school, Schola, æ, f.

A schoolmaster, Ludimagister, tri, m.

A school-fellow, Condiscipulus, li, m.

A school-fellowship, Condiscipulatus, ûs, m.

Of a school, Scholaris, re, adj.

A scholar, Discipulus, li, m. Scholaris, is, m.

Scholar like, Scholasticè adv.

Scholars commons, Victulus, li, m.

S C I.

The sciatica (or gout in the hip) Ischias, adis, f. Ischiadicus dolor.

Science, Scientia, æ, f.

Scire facias. Is a Writ Judicial most commonly to call a Man to shew cause unto the Court, whence it is sent, why Execution of a Judgment passed, should not be made. This Writ is not granted before a Year and a Day be passed, after the Judgment given. *Old nat. brev. fol.* 151.

Scire facias, Upon a Fine, lieth after a Year and a Day, from the Fine levyed, otherwise it is all one with the Writ *Habere facias Seisinam. West part* 2. *Symb. Titulo Fines, Sect.* 137. See *Anno* 25. *Ed.* 3. *Stat.* 5. *cap.* 1. *Anno* 39. *Eliz. cap.* 7. the Register Original and Judicial, also in the Table sheweth many other diversities of this Writ, which read. See also the New Book of Entries, *verbo Scire facias.*

Scituated, Situatus, a, um.

A scite, Situs, i, m. *Lex.* 117.

S C O.

A scoffer, Scurra, æ, m.

To sconce, Mulctare pecunia.

Scone, (in Scotland) Scona.

A scoop for Corn, or such like, Rutellum, i, n.

The scoop wherewith they draw up water to wet the sails, Haustrum, i, n. Hauritorium, ii, n.

A Scot, Scota, æ, m. 1 *Mon.* 413. 1006.

A scot, custom or tollage, Scotum vel Scottum, i, n.

A scot or reckoning, Symbolum, li, n.

Scotch, Scoticus, a, um.

Scotland, Albania, Caledonia, Scotia, æ, f.

Scottish Sea, Caledonius Oceanus.

Scots, Scoti.

To scour or cleanse, Escuro, are. mundo, are. Polio, ire.

Scoured, Detersus, a, um.

New scoured (or polished) Interpolus, a, um.

A scourer (or Polisher) Interpolator, oris, m.

An harness scourer, Armarius, ii, m.

He that scoureth Rust, Æruginator, oris, m.

A scouring, Depurgatio, onis, f.

A scouring or polishing of things, Interpolatio, onis, f.

To scourge, Flagello, are.

A scourge, Flagellum, i, n.

A scourge made with Leather thongs, Scutica, æ, f.

A scourge made of Neats Leather, Taurea, æ, f.

scourged, Flagellatus, a, um.

A scout, Explorator, oris, m. Emissarius, ii, m. Antecursor, oris, m.

Scout-watches, Excubiæ,arum, f.

S C R.

To scrape, Scalpo, ere,Rado,ere.

To scrape off, as with a horse Comb, Distringo, ere.

Scraped, Rasus, a, um.

Scraped out, Obliteratus, a, um.

A scraper, Rasor, oris, m.

A scraping, Rasura, æ, f.

A scraping out, Obliteratio, onis, f.

Scraps (or Reliques of Victuals) Fragmenta, orum, n.

A screen, Umbraculum, li, n.

A screw (or vice to wind up and down, Coclea, æ, f.

A scripp, Scirpus, i, m.

A scrivener, Scriba, æ, m. Scriptor, oris, m. Librarius, ii, m. Bibliographus, i, m.

A scriveners shop, Trapeza, æ,f.

A scroll (or Bill) Scheda, æ, f.

A scruple (or doubt) Scrupulus, li, m.

A scruple (the third part of a dram, scrupulus, li, m.

A scrutiny (or search) Scrutinium, ii, n. Rumor, oris, m.

S C U.

The scull of the Head, Cranium, ii, n. Calvaria, æ, f.

A sculler (or boat so called) Linter, tris, m.

A sculler (or he that driveth such a Boat) Navicularius, ii, m. Remex singularis.

A little scull to Row with, Tonsæ, arum, f.

The scullery (or place where the Vessel is laid) Scutellarium, ii, n.

A scullion, Lixa, æ, m. Fumarius, ii, m.

Scullions, Focarii servi.

A scullion Wench, Furnaria, æ, f.

The scullery, Lavatrina, æ, f.

Scumm, Spuma, æ, f. Excrementum, i, n.

To scumm, or take away the scumm, Despumo, are. Defæco, are.

A scummer, Despumatorium, i, n. Spatha, æ, f.

Scurf in the Head, Porrigo,inis,f.

The scurf (or scab of a wound) Crusta, æ, f.

The scurvy, Scorbutus, i, m.

A scutcheon in the midst of a Timber wall, where the Posts do rest, Tholus, i, m.

A scutcheon, Coat of Arms, or shield, Scutum, i, n. Scutulum, i, n. Stemma, æ, f.

A scuttle, Sportula, æ, f. Scutula, æ, f. Corbis, is, f.

The scuttles (or Hatches of a Ship) Pergula, æ, f.

The scuttle of the mast of a Ship, Carchesium, ii, n.

S E.

Se Defendendo. Is a Plea for him, that is charged with the Death of another, saying that he was driven unto that which he did, in his own defence: The other so assaulting, that if he had not done, as he did, he must have been in peril of his own Life: Which danger ought to be so great, as it appears inevitable, *Stawnf.* Pleas of the Crown, *Lib.* 1. *Cap.* 7. and if he do Justifie it to be done, in his own defence, yet he is forced to procure his Pardon of Course from the Lord Chancellor, and forfeiteth his goods to the King, as the Author saith in the same Place.

SEA.

The sea, Mare, is, n. Salum, i, n. Fretum, i, n. Pontus, i, m. pl. caret.

The main sea, Altum, i, n.

A Bosom (or gulf of the sea) Hadria, æ, f.

The sea which encompasseth the Earth, Oceanus, i, m.

The deep sea, Profundum pelagus.

The deep Channel of the sea, Vectes, is, m.

An arm of the sea, Æstuarium, ii, n.

The sea-bank, Coast, shoar or side, Littus, oris, n. Ora maritima.

The sea-coast, Acta, æ, f.

A sea-bank, Ægialus, li, m.

A narrow sea, Fretum, i, n.

A dangerous sea, in which wrecks often happen, Naufragium Mare.

To sail over the sea, Transfreto, are. Perfreto, are.

The first day of putting to Sea, Navigationis natalia.

A passing over the sea, Perfretatio, onis, f.

Sea sickness, Nausea, æ, f.

One apt to be sick at sea, Nauseator, oris, m.

Which belongeth to the Sea, Marinus, a, um.

Of or belonging to the sea bank, Littorosus, n, um.

On the sea side or coast, Maritimus, a, um.

Partly belonging to the sea, and partly to the Land, Semimarinus, a, um.

That cometh from beyond sea, Transmarinus, a, um.

Between two Seas, Bimaris, re, adj.

Sea charts, Chartæ marinæ.

Seamen (or Mariners) that look to the Ports or Heavens, Buscarli, orum, m.

Sea-coals (or Pit-coals) Carbones fossiles.

A seal, Sigillum, i, n.

To seal or sign, Sigillo, are.

To seal (or set to his sign or seal) Subsigno, are, Subscribo, ere.

The print of a seal, Signăcŭlum, li, n.

Sealed, Sigillatus, a, um. Signatus, a, um.

A sealer, Sigillator, oris, m. Is an Officer in Chancery, whose duty is to seal the Writs and Instruments there made.

A seal-ring, Annulus signatorius.

A sealing, Sigillatio, onis, f.

Seam-rent (or ripped) Vestis dissuta.

A seam, Sutura, æ, f. Sarcimen, inis, n.

Seamed (or that hath seams) Sutus, a, um, Consutilis, le, adj.

Without seam, Inconsutilis, le, adj.

To seam-rent or rip, Resuo, ere.

A seam (or closure of any thing) Commissura, æ, f.

A seam of coals, Cursus Carbonum.

A seamster, Sutrix, icis, f. Filatrix, icis, f.

A

A seamsters shop, Suternum, i, n.

To search, Scrutor, ari. Exploro, are.

To search (or examine diligently) Excutio, ere.

A search (or searching) Scrutinium, ii, n.

A searcher, Scrutator, oris, m.

To sear, Sicco, are.

To sear with a searing Candle, Cero, are. Incero, are.

A searing-iron, Cauterium, ii, n.

A searing, Ustio, onis, f.

Seared, Cauteriatus, a, um.

A searcloth, Cerotum, i, n.

An embalming searcloth, Cerotum funerarium.

To line a Coffin with searcloth, Linire loculum cum ceroto.

A searce (or sieve to sift withal) Cribrum, i, n.

Searge (or sarge) a kind of Cloth, Rasulus pannus.

To season (as to season meat) Condio, ire.

Seasoned Conditus, a, um. Saporatus, a, um.

A seasoner, Conditor, oris, m.

A seasoning, Conditura, æ, f. Condimentum, i, n.

Season (or time convenient) Opportunitas, atis, f.

Seaton (in Devonshire) Moridunum, Ridunum.

A seat, Sedes, is, f.

A seat of a King, Solium, ii, n. Sella eburnea.

A seat or seats whereon one only may sit, Sella, æ, f.

A seat (or bench) of marble, Abacus, ci, m.

A seat in a Porch or other such like place, Præstega, æ, f.

A seat or the seats in a Barge, Boat or Ship, wherein the Mariners do sit, Transtrum, i, n.

Seasonable time, Tempus seasonabile, *Ra. Entr.* 667.

Seaven, Septem, adj. Indecl.

The seaventh, Septimus, a, um.

Seaventeen, Septendecim, adj. Indecl.

Seaventy, Septuaginta, adj. Indecl.

Seaventieth, Septuagesimus, a, um,

S E B.

Sebastian (a man's name) Sebastianus, i, m.

S E C.

Seckington (in Warwickshire) Secandunum.

Secluded, Seclusus, a, um.

The second, Secundus, a, um.

Second deliverance, Secunda deliberatione. Is a Writ that lieth for him, that after a Return of Cattel replevied, adjudged to him that distrained them, by reason of a default in the party that replevied, for there plevying of the same Cattel again, upon security put in for the Redelivery of them, if in case the distress be justified. New book of Entries, *verbo Replevia*, in second deliverance, *fol.* 522. *col.* 2. *V. Dier. fol.* 41. *n.* 4. 5.

The secondine or after-birth, the three skins wherein an Infant lieth, while it is in the Womb, or when it cometh into the World, Secundæ, arum, f.

Secret, Secretus, a, um. Arcanus, a, um.

A secret, Arcanum, i, n. Secretum, i, n.

A publisher of secrets, Vulgātor, oris, m.

Secretly, Secretò, Arcanè, abditè, adv.

A Secretary, Secretarius, ii, m.

A chief secretary, Primarius secretarius Domini Regis.

A principal secretary, Unus principalium secretariorum Domini Regis.

A sect, Secta, æ, f.

A sectary, Sectarius, ii, m. Multarius, ii, m.

Secta ad Curiam. Is a Writ that lieth against him, who refuseth to perform his suit, either to the County or Court Baron, *Fitz. nat. brev. fol.* 158.

Secta facienda per Illum qui habet eniciam partem. Is a Writ to compel him, the Heir that hath the Elders part of the Co-heirs, to perform service for all the Co-parceners, *Regist. Orig. fol.* 177. *a*.

Secta molendini. Is a Writ lying against him that hath used to grind at the Mill of *A*, and after goeth to another Mill with his Corn, *Regist. Orig. fol.* 153. *Fitz. nat. brev. fol.* 122. but it seemeth by him that this Writ lyeth especally for the Lord against his frank Tenant, who holds of him by making suit to his Mill, *eodem. Vid.* the new Book of Entries, *verbo*, *Secta ad Molendinum*.

Secular, Secularis, re, adj.

A secundary, Secundarius, ii, m. Is the Name of an Officer next unto the Chief Officer, as the secundary of the Fine Office, the secundary of the Counter, which is (as I take it) next to the Sheriff of *London*, in each of the two Counters. Secundary of the Office of the Privy Seal. *Anno Ed.* 4. *cap.* 1. Secundaries of the Pipe two, Secundaries to the Remembrancers two, which be Officers in the Exchequer, *Cambd. Brit*.

Secure, Securus, a, um.

To secure, Securo, are. *Co. Ent.* 30.

A securing, Securantia, æ, f.

To give faith and security to a thing, Affido, are, Affiducio, are.

S E D.

A sedan, Carpentum, i, n. Sella Gestatoria.

Sedge (*or shear grass*) Carex, icis, f.

A sedge-bush, Carectum, i, n.

Sedition, Seditio, onis, f.

To Seduce, Seduco, ere.

S E E.

To see, Video, ere.

Seed, Semen, inis, n.

A seed-plot, Seminarium, ii, n.

To bring forth seed, Semento, are.

A bringing forth seed, Sementatio, onis, f.

Seed sown (*or seed time*) Sementis, is, f.

To seel, Camero, are. Laqueo, are.

Sealed, Cameratus, a, um. Laqueatus, a, um.

A seeling, Concameratio, onis, f.

The seeling of a Parlor or other like place, Laquearium, ii, n.

S E G.

Seg-hill (*in Northumberland*) Segedunum.

S E I.

Sejanus (a Man's Name) Sejanus, i, m.

Seignior, Dominus, i, m. It ſignifieth in the general ſignification, as much as Lord: But parcularly, it is uſed for the Lord of the Fee, or of a mannor, even as *Dominus* or (Senior) among the Feudiſts, is he who granteth a Fee or Benefit, out of his Land to another, and the reaſon is (as *Hotman* ſaith) becauſe having granted the uſe and profit of the Land to another, yet the property (*i. e.*) *Dominium*, he ſtill retaineth in himſelf, ſee *Hotman* in *verbis feudal. verb. Dominus & Senior.* Seignior in groſs, ſeemeth to be he that is Lord, but of no mannor, and therefore can keep no Court, *Fitz. nat. brev. fol.* 3. 6.

Seignory, Dominium, ii, n. It ſignifieth peculiarly with us a Mannor or Lordſhip. Seignory de *Sokemans, Kitch fol.* 80. Seignory in Groſs ſeemeth to be, the Title of him that is not Lord by means of any Mannor, but immediately in his own Perſon, *&c.*

To ſeiſe (take hold on, or take into Poſſeſſion) Seiſo, ire.

To be ſeiſed of Lands, &c. Seiſor, iris.

Seiſed or Poſſeſſed of Lands, &c. Seiſitus, a, um.

Seiſin, Seiſina, æ, f. Seiſin or Seiſon, is common as well to the Engliſh or French, as ſignifieth in the Common-Law Poſſeſſion, *Cook on Lit. Lib.* 2. *cap.* 12. *ſect.* 233. *Seiſina* is derived of *Sedendo*, for untill he have ſeiſin, all is labour and grief, but when he hath ſeiſin, he may *ſedere & acquieſcere*, *Cook's 6th. Rep. Brediman's caſe*.

S E L.

Selbury Hill (in Wiltſhire) Selburgi Tumulus.

Seldom, Rarus, a, um. Inſolens, tis, adj.

Seldomneſs, Inſolentia, æ, f.

A ſelion of Land, Selio, onis, f. Sometime it containeth an Acre of Land, ſometime half an Acre, ſometime more, ſometime leſs, *Weſt. part.* 2. *Symb. Tit. Recovery, ſect.* 3. There *Crompton* in his Juriſdiction, *fol.* 221. ſaith, that a Selion of Land cannot be in demand, becauſe it is a thing uncertain.

To ſell, Vendo, ere. Venundo, are.

To ſell at an outcry, Subhaſto, are. Auctionor, aris.

To ſell Wine and other Victuals, Cauponor, ari.

To buy at firſt hand to ſell again by retail, Promercor, ari.

A ſeller, Venditor, oris, m.

A turning back upon the ſeller, Redhibitorius, a, um.

A ſelling, Venundatio, onis, f.

The ſelling of old things, Scrutaria, æ, f.

Selſey (in Suſſex or Kent) Seoleſia. Vituli Inſula.

S E M.

A ſeme of corn, Summa, æ, f. (*i. e.*) Eight Buſhels, an horſeload.

A

A seme of fish, Sema Piscium *Ra. Ent*. 256.

Semiramis (*a Woman's Name*) Semiramis, is, f.

A semitar or short Persian Sword, Acinacis, is, f.

Sempiternal, Sempiternus, a, um.

S E N.

The senate, Senatus, ûs, m.

A senator, Senator, oris, m.

To send, Mando, are. Mitto, ere.

A seneschal (*or steward*) Seneschallus, i, m. Seneshallus, i, m.

Seneca (*a Man's Name*) Seneca, æ, f.

Senseless, Insensatus, a, um.

To sentence, Sententio, are, *Ra. Entr*. 413.

A sentence (*or judgment*) Sententia, æ, f.

S E O.

Seolsey (*in Sussex*) *a Bishop's See*, Silesia.

S E P.

To separate, Separo, are.

September, September, bris, m.

A sepulchre, Sepulchrum, i, n.

S E Q.

A sequele, Sequela, æ, f.

To sequester, Sequestro, are.

A sequestration, Sequestratio, onis, f. Sequestrum, i, n. 2 *Inst*. 624.

S E R.

A Sergeant at Law, Serviens ad Legem.

The King's Sergeant at Law, Unus Servientium Domini Regis ad Legem. This word Sergeant is diversly used in our common Law, and applied to sundry Offices and Callings. First a Sergeant at Law, or of the Coife, is the highest degree taken in that Profession next to the Judges, as a Doctor in Divinity, or the Civil Law, *&c*. and to these as Men best learned, and best experience of others, there is one Court severed to plead by themselves, *viz*. the Common Pleas, where the Common Law of *England* is most strictly observed. These are made by the King's Mandate or Writ directed unto them, commanding them upon a great Penalty, to take upon them that degree, by a day certain therein assigned, *Dyer fol*. 72. *Num*. 1.

And of these one or two, are the King's Sergeants, being commonly chosen by the King out of the Rest, in respect of their great Learning, to Plead for him in all his Causes, as namely in Causes of Treason, *Stawnf. Pl Cor. Lib*. 3. *cap*. 1. and of these there may be more, if it please the King.

Concerning the Antiquity of Sergeants at Law, the Lord *Cook* in the Preface to one of his Reports, saith thus. It is evident by the Book of the Mirror of Justices, *Lib*. 2. *cap. des loiers*, which treateth of the Laws of this Realm, and the Ministers thereof, long before the Conquest, that Sergeants at Law, were of Ancient times called, Narratores, Countors or Counteurs, because the Count or Declaration comprehended the substance of the Original

ginal Writs, and the very Foundation of the ſuit, of which part, as of the worthyeſt, they took their Denomination, and is all one in effect with that which in the Civil Law is called *Libellus*, and they loſt not that Name in the Raign of King *Edward* the Firſt, as it appeareth by the Statute of *W.* 1. *c.* 29. *Anno* 3. *Ed.* 1. for there he is called Serjeant Counter, *Serviens narrator*: And by the Statute of *Articuli ſuper chartas*, *cap.* 11. *Anno.* 28. *Ed.* 1. they are called Counters, that is Sergeants at Law, and until this day, when any proceedeth Sergeant, he doth Count in ſome real Action at the Bar of the Court of Common Pleas. But ſince the Raign of *Ed.* 1. they have always been called *Servientes ad Legem*, for their good ſervice to the Common Wealth, by their ſound advice in Law.

A ſergeant at Arms, Serviens ad Arma. Whoſe Office is to attend the Perſon of the King. *Anno* 7. *H* 7. *cap.* 3. to arreſt Traitors or Great Men that do, or are like to contemn Meſſengers of ordinary condition for other cauſes, and to attend the Lord High Steward of *England*, ſitting in Judgment upon any Traitor and ſuch like, *Stawnf. Pl. Cor. lib.* 3. *cap.* 1. of theſe by the Statute, *Anno* 13. *R.* 2. *cap.* 6. there may not be above 30. in the Realm.

There are alſo two of theſe Sergeants of the Parliament, one of the upper, and another of the lower Houſe, whoſe Office ſeemeth to be for the Execution of ſuch Commandments, eſpecially touching the apprehenſion of any Offender, as either Houſe ſhall think good to enjoin them. See *Crompt.* Juriſdict. *fol.* 9. See alſo *Vowel*'s alias *Hooker*'s Book of the Order of the Parliament.

There is one Sergeant at Arms that belongeth to the Chancery who is called *Serviens ad Clavam*, Serjeant of the Mace, as the reſt may be, becauſe they carry Maces by their Office. He of the Chancery attendeth the Lord Chancellor, or Lord Keeper in that Court, for the means to call all Men into that Court, is either by that Officer or by *Subpœna*, *Weſt. part.* 2. *Symb. Tit. Chancery. Sect.* 17.

Then there are Sergeants that be the Chief Officers in their ſeveral Functions, within the Kings Houſhold, which are chief in their places, of which ſort you may read many named in the Statute, *Anno* 33. *H.* 8. *cap.* 12.

In War alſo there are Sergeants of every Band or Company.

There is alſo an Inferior Sergeant of the Mace, whereof there is a Troop in the City of *London* (and other Towns Corporate) that ſerve the Lord Major or other head Officer, both for Meſnial attendance and matters of Juſtice, *Kitch. fol.* 143. and theſe are called, *Servientes ad Clavam*, Serjeants of the Club or Mace. New Book of Entries, *verbo Scire facias in Mainpernors*, *fol.* 538. *cap.* 3. and may rightly be called in all the Tongues, firſt in this word mentioned Sergeant, *quaſi ſerrer les gens*, to Lock or ſhut up ſuch as they meet with.

A.

A sergeant that arrests Persons, Rabduchus, i, m. Apparitor, oris, m.

Sergeantry, Serjantia, æ, f. (*i. e.*) a kind of Tenure, by doing some service to the King.

A sermon, Concio, onis, f.

A servant, Servus, i, m. Famulus, li, m.

A woman servant, Serva, æ, f.

An under servant, Subministrator, oris, m.

Servants that wait at Table, Panthectæ, orum, m.

A servant in Ordinary, Ordinarius Serviens—*Per nomen Thomæ Twist de Eltham, in Com Canc. unius* Ordinarius Serviens *Serenissimæ Dominæ Reginæ Elizabethæ,* &c. *Wi. Tit. Dower inter Twist & Cotton.*

To serve, Servio, ire.

Service, Servitium, ii, n.

Servientibus are certain Writs, touching Servants and their Masters, violating the Statutes made against their abuses, which see in the *Regist. Orig. fol.* 189, and 190, and 191.

S E S.

Sessions, Sessiones, signifieth in our Common Law, a sitting of Justices in Court upon their Commission: As the Sessions of *Oyer* and *Terminer* Quarter Sessions, otherwise called General Sessions, *Anno* 5. *Eliz. cap.* 4. or Open Sessions, *ibidem.*

Opposite thereunto are especial, otherwise called Privy Sessions, which are procured upon some special occasion, for the more speedy Expedition of Justice in some Causes, *Crompt.* Justice of Peace, *fol.* 110. What things be inquirable at General Sessions, see *Crompt. fol.* 109. *Petit Sessions* or Statute Sessions, are kept by the High Constable of every Hundred, for the placing of Servants, *Anno* 5. *Eliz. cap.* 2. 4. *in fine.*

S E V.

A seuer, drain or Gutter to convey Water in Fen-lands, Severa vel Sewera, æ, f.

Sevenshale (*in Northumberland*) Hunnum.

Severn River, Sabriana, Sabrina, Saverna.

Severn sea, Mare Sabrinianum.

To sever (*or set apart*) Severo, are.

Several, Separalis, le, adj.

A severer, Discretor, oris, m.

Severe, Severus, a, um.

Severity, Severitas, atis, f.

S E W.

A sewer, Sewera, æ, f. *Cow.* 240. 10. *Co.* 143. *Lex.* 115. Suera, æ, f. *Lex.* 116. 10. *Co.* 141. It hath two significations with us: One applyed to him that Issueth or cometh in before the Meat of the King, or other great Personage, and placeth it upon the Table; the other to such passages, or gutters, as carry Water into the Sea or River, *Anno* 6. *H.* 6. *cap.* 5. which is also used in Common speech for Commissioners Authorized under the Great Seal, to see Drains and Ditches well kept and maintained in the Marish and Fen Countries, for the better conveyance of the Water into the Sea, and the preserving

of

of the grafs for food of Cattle, *Stat. Anno 6. H. 6. cap.* 5.

To few (or ftitch) as Cloth or Leather, Suo, ere. Confuo, ere.

To few up again, Refuo, ere.

Sued, Sutus, a, um. Confutus, a, um.

Sewed unto (or together) Affutus, a, um.

A fewing, Sutura, æ, f.

Sewet, Sevum, i, n.

S E X.

A fexton of a Church, Æditus, i, m. Sacrifta, æ, m.

The Sextry (or Veftry in the Church) Sacrarium, ii, n. Sacriftia, æ, f.

S H A.

A fhale, Siliqua. æ, f.

A fhallop, Paro, onis, f.

A fhallow place, Vadum, i, n.

The fhambles (or place where Flefh meat is fold) Carnarium, ii, n. Macellum, i, n. Laniarium, ii, n.

Of the fhambles, Macellarius, a, um.

Shame (or difhonefty) Ignominia æ, f.

Paft fhame, Expudoratus, a, um.

The fhanck (or the Legg from knee to Ankle) Tibia, æ, f.

The fhanck, fhaft or Body of a Candleftick or Pillar between the Chapter and the Bafe, the fpindle that winding ftairs go about, Scapus, i, m.

Shanon River (in Ireland) Sacana, Sena, Senus, Siambis, Sineus, Socinos.

A fhape, Species, ei, f.

To fet the fhape of a thing before one, Præfiguro, are.

To fhare (or divide into fhares) Partio, ire.

Shared, Partitus, a, um.

A fharer, Partitor, oris, m.

A fhare (or portion) Portio, onis, f.

Sharp crees, imbrices lapidei.

To fharpen, Acuo, ere.

To fhave (or fcrape) Rado, ere.

A Joyners Plane, or inftrument to fhave with a Rafor, Detondere Novaculâ.

To fhave thin (or clofe) Rafito, are.

Shaven, Rafus, a, um. Radulanus, a, um. Tonfus, a, um.

A fhaver, Rafor, oris, m.

A fhaving, Rafura, æ, f.

A fhaving cloth, Linteum tonforium.

The fhaving of any thing, Ramen, inis, n.

A fhaving inftrument, Radula, æ, f.

A fhaving Knife, Scalprum, i, n.

Any thing that is fhaved of, Ramentum, i, n.

Belonging to fhaving, Raforius, a, um.

S H E.

A fheaf, Garba, æ, f.

A fheaf of arrows, Pharetra, æ, f.

He that carrieth a fheaf of arrows, Pharetratus, a, um.

To fhear (or clip) Tondeo, ere.

A fhearer, Tonfor, oris, m.

A fhearman, Pannitonfor, oris, m.

A pair of fhears, Forfex, icis, f.

A little pair of fhears, Forficula, æ, f.

A

A shearing, Tonsura, æ, f.

A sheath (*or scabbard*) Vagina, æ, f.

A little sheath, Vaginula, æ, f.

To sheath (*or put into a sheath*) Vagino, are. Recondere in Vaginam.

A sheath maker, Vaginarius, ii, m.

Sheathed, Vagina tectus vel clausus.

S H E.

A shed, Casale, lis, n.

A little shed, Castitium, ii, n.

She, Illa, æ, f.

A sheep, Ovis, is, f.

A little sheep. Ovicula, æ, f.

A *flock of sheep*, Collecta Ovium. *Reg.* 120.

A sheep coat, *also a sheep walk*, Ovile, is, n.

A sheep-hook, Pedum, i, n.

A shepherd, Pastor, oris, m Opilio, onis, m.

Of, *or belonging to sheep*, Ovinus, a, um.

Sheep shearing, Ovitonsura, æ, f.

A sheet, Lodix Linea, Linteamen, inis, n.

A sheet of Paper, vid. *Paper.*

A sheet of Lead, Lamina plumbi.

A shell, Testa, æ, f.

A shelf, Abacus, ci, m. Repositorium, ii, n.

Shelney (*in Hertfordshire*) Sulloniacæ, Sullonicæ.

Shene (*or Richmond in Surry*) Shenum

Sheppey Island (*in Kent*) Counos, Insula Ovium, Ovinia insula, Toliapis, Toliatis.

A sheriff, Vicecomes, itis, m.

Sheriff or Shrieve, is derived of two Saxon Words, *viz.* Shire, *comitatus*, which cometh of the Saxon verb, shiram, *id est*, *partiri*, because the whole Realm is parted, and divided into Shires, and Reve, *præfectus*, or *præpositus*, so as Sheriff is *præfectus provinciæ*, or *Comitatus*, keeper of the Shire or County. The words of his Patent be, *Commisimus vobis custodiam comitatus nostri*, and he hath *triplicem custodiam*, a three fold Custody.

1. *Vitæ Justitiæ*, for no suit begins, and no Process is served but by the Sheriff.

2. *Vitæ Legis*, he is after long suits, and chargeable to make Execution, which is the Life and Fruit of the Law.

3. *Vitæ Reipublicæ*, he is *Principalis conservator pacis* within the County, which is the Life of the Common-Wealth. He is called in Latin *Vice-comes id est*, *Vice-comitis*, that is instead of the Earl of the County, who in Ancient times had the Regiment of the County under the King. Sheriffs were great Officers, and Ministers of Justice long before the Conquest, and Justices of Peace had not their being until almost 300. Years after, *viz.* in the first Year of *Edward* the Third, *Cook on Lit. Lib.* 3. *cap.* 1. *sect.* 248. *Cook's* Preface to third Rep.

When the King makes a Sheriff, *Durante bene placito*, although he may determine his Office at his pleasure, yet he cannot determine this in part, nor abridge the Sheriff of any thing incident or appurtenant to his Office,

Office, for the Office is intire, and it ought to continue ſo without any fraction or diminution, unleſs it be by Act of Parliament, *Cook fourth Rep. Mitton's caſe.*

The Sheriff's turn, Turnum vicecomitis.

A Sheriffwick, Vicecomitatus, ûs, m. Henricus, *&c.* Archiepiſcopus, *&c.* Sciatis nos conceſſiſſe & præſenti Charta noſtra confirmaſſe civibus Londōn. Vicecomitatum Londōn, & Middleſexiæ cum omnibus rebus, & conſuetudinibus quæ pertinent ad prædictum Vicecomitatum infra Civitatem & Extra, *&c. Chart. conceſſ. Civibus Londōn, Anno* 11. *H.* 3.

Sherburn (in Dorſetſhire) Clarafontanus, Clarus fons, Schirburnia.

Sherwood Foreſt (in Nottinghamſhire) Limpida Sylva.

Shetland Iſles, Thule.

To ſhew, Monſtro, are. Oſtendo, ere.

S H I.

A Shiēld, Scutum, i, n.

The handle of a Shield (or Buckler) Ochanus, i, m.

Service of the Shield (or Knights Service) Scutagium, ii, n.

Shift, Machina, æ, f. Verſutia, æ, f.

Shifted, Verſutus, a, um. Excambiatus, a, um.

A Shilling, Solidus, i, m.

A Shingle (or Tilē of Cleft wood) Scandula, æ, f.

Covered with Shingles, Scindularis, re, adj.

The Shingles (a Diſeaſe) Herpes, etis.

The Shin-bone, Tibia, æ, f.

The Shin, Crea, æ, f.

A Ship, Navis, is, f.

A little Ship Navicula, æ, f.

A Ship of Burden, Navis Oneraria.

A Pinace (or Swift Ship) Legia, æ, f.

A little Shear-Ship, Actula, æ, f.

A Smack (or ſmall Ship) Halias, ădos, f.

The Admirals Ship, Navarchis, dis, f.

A Ship to tranſport Soldiers, Navis Militaris.

A great Ship, Cyrſerum, i, n.

A great Ship ſlow to ſail, Corbita, æ, f. Gaulus, i, m.

A Ship of War, Præſidiaria Navis.

A little Ship called a Galeot, Phaſelus, li, d. g.

A little Ship called a Foiſt, Liburna, æ, f.

A Ship (or Barge) that Noblemen uſe for Pleaſure, with Gorgeous Chambers, and other Ornaments, Navithalamus, i, m.

A Ship (or Veſſel) for Paſſage that goeth with Oars and Sails together, Navis actuaria.

An open or uncovered Ship, a Ship without a Deck, Aphractus, i, m. Navis aperta.

A covered Ship, a Ship with a Deck, Navis conſtrata.

A Ship Stemm'd, beaked, or pointed with braſs, or having an Iron noſe, Navis Roſtrata.

A Pirats Ship, Myopara, æ, f. Navis prædatoria vel Piratica.

A ſpial Ship, Cataſcopium, ii, n. Navis Speculatoria.

A well rigged Ship, Decentrix, icis, f.

A Ship having two Ranges of Oars, Biremis, is, f.

A Ship having three Oars on aside, Quadriremis, is, f.

A Ship boat, Scapha, æ, f.

To Ship, Shippo, are. 2. R. 3. 11. Eskippo, are. *Ra. Entr.* 409.

A Ship Laden, Navis cartata.

A Ship unladen, Navis difcarcata, *Ry* 251. 184.

A Ship calked, Serilla, æ, f.

A Ship Master, Naviculator, oris, m. Navarchus, i, m. Nauclerus, i, m.

He that draweth a Ship or Barge by a Rope, or that draweth Packs into a Ship, Helciarius, ii, m.

He that holdeth the stern (a Master or Governor of a Ship) Gubernator, oris, m.

A Ship-wright (or he that maketh Ships) Naupegus, i, m. Barcarius, ii, m.

The art of governing a Ship, Navicularia, æ, f.

To be Pilot (or go out Master of a Ship) Naviculariam facere.

A Ship Boy, Drudge or slave in a Ship, Mesonauta, æ, m.

The hind-deck, tail or steerage of a Ship, Puppis, is, f.

The fore-deck of a Ship, Prora, æ, f.

The upper deck of a Ship, Catastrōma, ătis, n.

The Hatches of a Ship, Agea, æ, f. Pergula, æ, f.

The Rowers seats in Ships, Transtra, orum, n.

The stern of a Ship, Clavus, i, m. Serraculum, li, n. Gubernaculum, i, n.

The stemm of a Ship, Rostrum, i, n. Corymbus, i, m.

A Ships Company, Navis conventus.

The keel of a Ship, Carina, æ, f. Ceola fregatina, *Spel.* 156. Tropis, is, *or*, ios, f.

A Purser of a Ship, Quæstor, oris, m. Receptor generalis.

A Navy of Ships, Classis, is, f.

A Ship Rope, Curcuba, æ, f.

A Stool, wont to stand in the forepart of a Ship, Selis, is, f.

The Helm of a Ship, Servaculum, li, n.

The Helm Stock, Ansa gubernaculi.

The Ships Rudder, Adminicula gubernandi.

A Ship Victualled, Tacked and apparelled, Cibata, Velata & Parata, 1. *Fo.* 136.

The Sail-yard belonging to a Ship, Antenna, æ, f.

The shrowds of a Ship, Funes, ium, m. *pl.*

To slack the shrowds, Funes laxare.

To set the shrowds to rights (or aright) Funes intendere.

The Pump of a Ship, Sentina, æ, f.

All the Tackling of Ships, Armamenta navis, hernesia ad Navem spectantia, *Ry.* 188.

The Grapple of a Ship, Harpăgo, onis, m.

A Pole belonging to a Ship, Contus, i, m.

A Pully belonging to a Ship, Trochlea, æ, f.

The sail of a Ship, Velum, i, n.

Sail-cloths, Vela, orum, n. pl.

To set sail, Vela dare.

The Mast of a ship, Malus, i, m. Mamilla, æ, f.

The mizzen mast sail, Dalum, i, n.

The main ends of the ſail-yard, Cornua antennarum.

Bands faſtning the ſail-yard to the maſt, Anchoræ.

The utmoſt part of the ſhip that lies upon the water, Cuba, æ, f.

The Foot Oaks of Ships, Statumina navium.

The Holes in the Tops of the maſts to receive the Ropes, Liæ, f. *Pl.*

The tryal of a Ship after Launching, Tyrocinium navium.

The Galleries or other adornments of ſhips, alſo the Beaks of fore-decks, Acroſtolia, orum, n.

A fleet of ſhips, Claſſis, is. f.

A Haven for Ships, Nauſtibulum, li, n.

A ſhip-cook, Focarius, ii. m.

The Tranſomes in a ſhip whereon the Hatches are made, Canonia, orum, n.

The laying of a Ship in the Dock to be repaired, Culagium, ii, n.

The filth coming out of the ſhips Pump, Nautea, æ, f

The ſounding line of a ſhip, Bolis, is, f.

The Lading of a ſhip, Mercatura, æ, f.

To ballaſt a ſhip, Săburro, are.

The Ballaſt of a ſhip, Săburra, æ, f.

To carene ſhips, Rates inficere.

To navigate a ſhip (ſail, cruiſe under,) Naviculor, ari.

To go a ſhip-board, Navem conſcendere.

To joyn ſhips together in a Navy, alſo to call together, Conclaſſo, are.

Ship-wreck, Naufragium, ii, n.

Ship-wrecked, Naufragus, a, um.

Goods ſhip-wrecked, Bona Wreccata. 5. *Co.* 106.

To make ſhip-wreck, Naufragor, ari.

One eſcaped out of ſhip-wreck, Naufragus, i, m.

To ſink a ſhip, Deprimere navem.

Belonging to a ſhip (or mariner) Nauticus, a, um. Navalis, le, adj.

A ſhire (or County) Shira, æ, f. *Lex.* 116.

A ſhirt, Camiſia, æ, f. Subucula, æ, f. Surcarium, ii, n. Supparum, i, n. Induſium, ii, n.

A half ſhirt, Curtum induſium.

S H O.

A ſhock of Corn, Acervus, i, m.

A ſhooe, Calceus, i, m.

A ſhooe-ſole, Solea, æ, f. Fulmenta, æ, f.

The upper Leather of a ſhooe, Obſtrigillum, i, n.

A ſingle ſoled ſhooe, Endromides, is, f.

A high ſhooe, Pero, onis, f.

One wearing a high ſhooe, Peronatus, a, um.

A wooden ſhooe, Calopodium, ii, n. Crepida, æ, f.

A horſe-ſhooe, Solea ferrea, Calceus equinus.

To put off (or pull off) the ſhooes, Diſcalceo, are.

To put on a ſhooe (or ſhooes) Calceo, are.

To ſhooe a Horſe, Ferreis ſoleis Equum munire.

A ſhooe-buckle, Ligŭla calceorum.

A ſhooe-ſtring (or Latchet) Corrigia, æ, f.

A Country ſhooe with one ſo[illegible] Carbatina, æ, f.

A ſhooe-laſt, Muſtricŭla, æ, f.

A Patch that is ſet on a ſhooe, Pictariuncula, æ, f. Suppagmentum, i, n.

A Shooe-maker (*or Cordwainer*) Sutor, oris, m. Calcearius, ii, m. Crepidarius, ii, m. Calceolarius, ii, m.

A maker of shooes, either horse shooes or pattins, Sŏlĕārius, ii, m.

The King's shooe-maker, Zangarius, ii, m.

A shooe-makers thread with a bristle at the end, Cheleuma, æ, f.

To bristle a shooe-makers Thread, Inseto, are.

Shooe-maker's Wax, Cerotum Sutorium.

A shooe-makers paring Knife, Smilium, ii, n. Scalprum Sutorium.

A Shooe-makers round cutting Knife, Arbella, æ, f.

A shooing-horn, Cornu calceatorium, Calcipes, is, f. Calceatorium, ii, n.

To underlay shooes, Resarcire calceamenta.

To shoot an Arrow, Sagitto, are. Jaculor, ari.

A shoot (*or young twig*) Surculus, i, m.

A shooter (*or Archer*) Sagittarius, ii, m.

The shooter of a Lock, Pessulus, li, m.

A shop, Shopa, æ, f. 10. *Co.* 133. *Lex.* 116. Officina, æ, f.

A shop, stall, shed or standing, Selda, æ, f. *Lex.* 114. Shopa sive selda, *Ra. Entr.* 558. Solda, æ, f.

The shore about Kent, Totonesium.

A shore, Litus, oris, n. Acta, æ, f.

Short, Curtus, a, um, Brevis, ve, adj.

A cutting short, Abbreviatio, onis, f.

A shot or reckoning, Symbolum, i, n.

Shot to shoot with, Glans, dis, f.

A shovel (*or spade*) Pala, æ, f. Rutrum, i, n.

A fire shovel, Batillus, li, m.

A little shovel, Rutellum, li, n.

A shoulder, Humerus, i, m.

The shoulder-blade, Scapula, æ, f.

Mantles to throw about the shoulders, Vestes Scapulares.

Showre River (*in Ireland at Waterford*) Suirius.

S H R.

A shred (*any thing cut or pared away*) Resegmen, inis, n.

Shrewsbury (*in Shropshire*) Penguernum, Salopesbiria, Salopia, Scrobberia, Scrobbesbiria, Slopesbaria.

Shropshire, Salopiæ Comitatus.

Shrovetide, Carnisprivium, ii, n. Carnivale, is, n.

A shrub, Arbuscula, æ, f.

A shut belonging to a Mill, Canalis, is, c. g.

Shuts, Secluforia Claustra.

A Weavers shuttle, Liciatorium, ii, n. Radius textoris.

A small shuttle, Radiolus, li, m.

S I B.

Sibyl (*a Woman's Name*) Sibylla, æ, f.

Sick, Ægrotus, a, um. Morbidus, a, um. Infirmus, a, um.

One that looks to Sick People, Infirmarius, ii, m.

To be sick, Ægroto, are.

Sickness, Ægrotatio, onis, f. Morbus, i, m.

Sickly, Ægrotè, adv.

A sickle (*or Sythe*) Falx, cis, f. Saturni dens.

A

A little sickle (or Hook) Falcula, æ, f. Falcicula, æ, f.

Sicut alias. Is a Writ sent out in the second place, whereas the first sped not, *Cook. Lib.* 4. *fol.* 55. *B.* It is so called of these words expressed in it, as for example. *Gulielmus Dei Gratia,* &c. *Vicecomiti Kanc. salutem. Præcepimus tibi (sicut alias præcepimus) quod non omittas propter aliquam libertatem in Balliva tua, quin etiam ingrediaris & capias, A. B,* &c. *de C. in Comitatu tuo Labourer,* &c. as in the first *Capias. Lamb.* in his Tractate of Processes in the end of his *Eirenarchia.*

S I D.

A side, Latus, ĕris, n. Costa, æ, f.

A side of a leaf in a Book, Pagina, æ, f.

A sidesman, Gardianis Ecclesiæ assistens, or Questmen be these that are yearly chosen according to the Custom of every Parish, to assist the ChurchWardens in the Inquiry, and presenting such Offenders to the Ordinary, as are punishable in the CourtChristian.

He that is on both sides, Ambidexter, tri, m.

Sider (drink made of Apples) Sicera, æ, f. Pomatium, ii, n.

S I E.

A sieve, Cribrum, i, n.

A meal sieve, Subcerniculum, li, n.

A ranging sieve, Sisactea, æ, f. Ruderarium, ii, n.

An hair sieve, Cribrum Setaceum.

A sieve to Winnow vetch, Cribrum viciarium.

A sieve to Winnow darnel, Cribrum Lolliarium.

A very fine sieve, Nebula linea.

A boulting sieve, Cribrum farinarium.

A little sieve, Cribrellum, i, n.

A sieve maker, Cribrarius, ii, m. Rudiarius, ii, m.

Of a sieve, Cribrarius, a, um.

S I G.

A signal that the Master gives the Mariners to do any thing, Chirembolum, li, n.

A signature, Signatura, æ, f. (*i. e.*) a signing, subscribing, a sign manuel, ones hand or mark set unto a writing, a signing of a notary, and among Printers the signature is the mark or Letters that they set at the bottom of every Sheet printed, as A. B. C. *&c.* to tell their Quires by, and thereby to know whether their Books be perfect when they are fully Printed.

A sign or token, Signum, i, n.

To sign, or subscribe a Letter, Writing or Bill, to set his Mark, stamp, or hand unto, Signo, are.

The King's signet, Signetum Regis. *Ra. Entr.* 443. 2. *An.* 120. *Signettum Regis Pry.* 36.

Significavit, Is a certificate made by the Bishop into the Chancery Court, that a Person stands Excommunicate, which is thence transmitted into the King's Bench and thereon an *Excommunicato cap.* issues.

Sigismund (a Man's Name) Sigismundus, i, m.

Silceaster

Silceaster or Silcester (in Hampshire) Murimintum, Murivindum, Seguntium, Vindonum, Vindonus.

Silence, Silentium, ii, n.

To keep silence, Sileo, ere.

Silent, Silens, tis, adj.

Silently, Tacitè, adv.

Silk. Sericum, ci, n.

Course Silk, Plocum, ci, n.

A Garment of Silk, Vestis Serica.

A Silk weaver (or Silk Merchant) Sericarius textor.

A Silk man, Sericarius, ii, m.

A Silk Woman, Sericaria, æ, f.

Clothed in Silk, Sericatus, a, um.

Silken or of Silk, Sericus, a, um.

One that worketh in Silk twisted with Gold, Polymitarius, ii, m.

A sillabub, Oxygala, æ, f.

Silvanus (a Man's Name) Silvanus, i, m.

Silver, Argentum, i, n.

Pure silver, Merum argentum.

Quick-silver, Argentum vivum, Hydrargyrum, i, n.

A silver-smith, Argentarius, ii, m. Argentifex, icis, m.

A silver-mine, Argentifodina, æ, f.

Silver Foam (or spume) Argyritis, idis, f.

To cover (or over-lay) with silver, Argento, are.

Covered with silver, Argentatus, a, um.

Vessels of silver, Vasa Argentea.

Silver Spoons, Cochlearia Argentea.

Silvester (a Man's Name) Silvester, tri, m.

S I M.

A Simbal Cymbalum, li, n.

A simnel (bun, or cracknel) Colyra, æ, f. Simila, æ, f. Crustulum, li, n. Simnellus, i, m.

Simeon (a Man's Name) Simeon, onis, m.

Simon (a Man's name) Simon, onis, m.

St. *Simon and Judes day,* Festum Sanctorum Simonis & Judæ Apostolorum.

Simony, Simonia, æ, f.

S I N.

Since, Post, præp.

Since that, Siquidem.

Not long since, Paulo ante, non ita pridem.

A sinew, Nervus, i, m.

A singer of merry Songs, Hilarœdus, i, m.

A Woman that sings Ballads (or Shows any sights) Circŭlātrix, icis, f.

A sink, Sentina, æ, f. Latrina, æ, f.

The sink of a Kitchin, Lavatrina, æ, f.

The sink or Gutter of a Town, Cloaca, æ, f. Colluviarium, ii, n.

A sink-hole, Fusorium, ii, n. Os latrinæ.

Sinodun-hill, near Wallingford (in Berkshire) Sinnodunum.

S I R.

A Sirrop, Syrupus, i, m.

A Sirringe (or Squirt) Syringa, æ, f.

S I S.

A Sister, Soror, oris, f.

A Sister in Law, Glos, otis, f.

A Sisters Son (*or Cousin-German by the Mother*) Consobrinus, i, m.

A Sisters daughter (*or Cousin German by the Mother*) Consobrina, æ, f.

S I T.

Sitfilt (*or Cecil, the Family*) Sitfiltus, *alias* Cecilius.

A sith, Falx fœnaria, Fœnisecа.

A sith to cut Bushes, Runeo, onis, m.

A sith maker, Faber falcarius.

To sit, Sedeo, ere.

Six (*in number*) Sex, adj. Indecl.

Six times, Sexies, adv.

Sixth, Sextus, a, um.

Sixteen, Sexdecim, Indecl.

Sixty, Sexaginta.

Sixtieth, Sexagesimus, a, um.

S K I.

Skie Island, one of the Hebrydes, Ebuda, Hebuda, Hebuda prima, Hebuda Orientalior.

A skillet, Ollula, æ, f. Cacabus, i, m.

A skin (*or hide*) Pellis, is, f.

The skin of a Man or Woman, Cutis, is, f.

The skin of a Beast, Corium, ii, n.

A skinner, Pellio, onis, m.

A skinners-trade, Coriaria, æ, f.

A little skin, Pellicula, æ, f.

Of a skin, Pelliceus, a, um.

A skirt, Fimbria, æ, f.

A skreen, Umbraculum, li, n.

A hand skreen, Antifera, æ, f.

S L A.

To slander, Scandalizo, are.

Slander, Scandalum, li, n.

A slanderer, Famicida, æ, m. Obtrectator, oris, m.

A slate (*or shingle*) Scandula, æ, f.

He that slates Houses, Scandularius, ii, m.

A slaughter-house, Laniena, æ, f. Carnificina, æ, f.

S L E.

Sleep, Somnus, ni, m.

A sleeve, Manica æ, f.

Slegah-bay (*in Ireland*) Liboeus.

Slight of hand, Astutia, æ, f.

S L I.

A slice, Rudicula, æ, f.

A slice (*or shred*) Segmentum, i, n.

A sling, Funda, æ, f. Balistrum, i, n.

To sling, Balistro, are.

A slinger, Funditor, oris, m.

A slipper (*or Pantoffle*) Crepida, æ, f. Sandalium, ii, n.

A slipper-maker, Crepidarius, ii, m.

A slit, Fissura, æ, Rima, æ, f.

A slokster, Plagiarius, ii, m. Mango, onis, m. (*i. e.*) One that enticeth Men's Servants away.

S L U.

A sluce to let in or out Water, Exclusa, æ, f. *Ra. Entr.* 9. *Reg.* 96. bis. Exclusagia molendini, 1. *Mon.* 587. 720. 760. 2. *Mon.* 8. Emissarium, ii, n.

S M E.

A sweet smell, Fragrantia, æ, f.

S M I.

An Iron-smith, Ferrarius Faber.

A smith that Works on an Anvil, Incudo, onis, m.

A Copper-smith, Ærarius, ii, m.

A Lock-smith, Serarius, ii, m. Faber Clavicularius.

A smiths buttress to pare horse Hoofs, Scaber, ri, m.

A smiths shop, Shopa Ferraria.

S M O.

To smoak (or dry in the smoak) Infumo, are.

A smoaker, Fumator, oris, m.

Smoaked, Fumatus, a, um.

A smock, Subucula muliebris, Camisia seu Indusium mulieris.

S N A.

A snafle (that part of the bridle which the horse Champs, Salevare, is, n.

A snapsack, Saccipium, ii, n.

A snare, Laqueus, ei, m. Pedica, æ, f. Decipula, æ, f.

S N O.

A snout, Rostrum, tri, n.

Snowden hills (in Caernarvanshire) Nivicollini.

Snowden forest (in Caernarvanshire) Snaudonia.

S N U.

To snuff a Candle, Emungo, ere.

Snuffers, Emunctorium, ii, n.

S O.

So, Ita, adv.

So as, so that, Ita quod.

So much, so far, In tantum, *Reg.* 94. 97. Sæpe, 106. In tantum, *Reg.* 92. 94.

So often as, Toties, quoties.

So that they could not, or might the less, Quominus potuerunt, *Reg.* 106.

S O C.

Soccage, Socagium, ii, n. *Lex.* 117. Soccagium, ii, n. a Tenure of Lands for some small Services of Husbandry performed to the Lord.

Society, Societas, atis, f.

Society and Company, Societas & Communitas.

A Woollen sock, Soccus, ci, m. Sculponea, æ, f. Udo Silicius.

A Linen sock, Linipidium, ii, m.

A sock-man (or Tenant in soccage) Socmannus, i, m.

S O D.

Sod (or sodden) Coctus, a, um.

Sodomy (or Buggery) Sodomia, æ, f.

A sodomite (or buggerer) Sodomita, æ, m. Pæderastes.

S O K.

A soke, Soca, æ, f.

S O L.

A solar (Garret, or upper Room) Solarium, ii, n. *Lex.* 117. Sollarium

rium, ii, n. 10. *Co.* 133. *Co. Entr.* 377.

Solder, Ferrumen, inis, n.

To solder, Ferrumino, are, Solido, are.

A Solderer, Ferruminator, oris, m.

A soldering, Ferruminatio, onis, f.

Sold, Venditus, a, um.

A thing, set out to be sold, Promercium, ii, n.

To solemnize, Solempnizo, are,

A solemnization, Solempnizatio, onis, f.

To solicite, Solicito, are.

A solicitor, Solicitator, oris m. *Lex.* 117.

The Solicitor General, Solicitator Domini Regis Generalis.

Solwayfryth (in Scotland) Solvathianum æstuarium.

S O M.

Sommer, Æstas, atis, f.

Somersetshire, Somersata Semerseta, Somersetania, Somersettensis comitatus, Somertunensis comitatus.

Somerton (in Lincolnshire) Somaridunum.

S O N.

A son, Filius, ii, m.

A son-in-law, Gener, ri, m.

A son-in-law (or son by a former Bed) Privignes, is, m.

S O O.

A soothsayer. Auspex, icis, m. Hariolator, oris, m.

S O P.

A little sop (or sippet) Ofella, æ, f.

Sope, Sapo, onis, m. Smegma, atis, n.

Sope-balls, Mattiacæ pilæ.

To sope, Smegmate obluere.

Washed with sope, Smegmate Oblitus.

A sope boiler, Saponarius, ii, m.

Of or belonging to sope, Smegmaticus, a, um.

Sophia (a Womans Name) Sophia, æ. f.

A sophister, Sophista, æ, m.

S O R.

A sorcerer, Veneficus, i, m.

Sorcery, Veneficium, ii, n.

A sore, Ulcus, eris, n.

S O U.

Soveraign, Supremus, a, um.

Soveraignty, Primātus, us, m. Principatus, us, m.

Souldier, Soldarius, ii, m. *Ra. Entr.* 493. *Co. Entr.* 436.

A souldier under a Captain, Soldarius sub conductu Capitanei.

A Company of souldiers under one standard, Vexillatio, onis, f.

A Band of souldiers, Banda, æ, f. & Bandus, i, m. Turma, æ, f.

An host of souldiers, Exercitus, us, m. Acies, ei, m.

An Old or Weather beaten souldier, Miles Veteranus.

A heartless Souldier, Socors Miles.

Souldiers Postures, Armaturæ gestus.

To make a souldier, Quirinor, aris.

To List souldiers, Scribere Milites.

The discharging of a souldier from service, Emertio, onis, f.

The place where Common souldiers are Mustered and Paid, Diribitorium, ii, n.

An Engin made of boards and covered with Raw Hides to defend

the

the Souldiers at a Siege, Teſtudo Militaris.

The Watchword (a Private token among Souldiers,) Teſſera Militaris.

A Bringer or Giver of the Watchword to Souldiers, Teſſerarius, ii, m.

South, Auſter, tri, m.

South part, Pars Auſtralis, Meridionalis.

South-Eaſt part, Pars Euronotalis.

South-Weſt part, Pars Notozephyralis.

South Weſternly, Africius.

Southampton Town (in Hampſhire) Avondunum, Clauſentum, Hamptuna, Southamptonia, Triſanton, Triſantonis portus.

Of Southampton, Southantunenſis.

Southerland (in Scotland,) Southerlandia.

South Eske River (in Scotland) Tavus.

Southwark (in Surrey) Suderverça.

S O W.

A ſow, Sus, ſuis, c. g.

A ſow great with Pig, Sus prægnans.

A ſow that never farrowed but once, Porcetra, æ, f.

A ſow that hath had Pigs more than once, Scrofa, æ, f.

A little ſow, Porcula, æ, f. Porcella, æ, f.

A ſow-pig, Suilla, æ, f. Sucula, æ, f.

Of or belonging to a ſow, Suillus, a, um.

To ſow (as to ſow Corn, &c.) Semino, are.

To ſow (as to ſow ſeeds) Sero, ere.

To ſow (or ſet in Beds) Conſero, ere.

Sown (Planted) Satus, a, um.

A ſower, Sator, oris, m. Seminator, oris, m.

A ſowing (or planting) Satus, ûs, m. Satio, onis, f.

Of or belonging to ſowing, Seminalis, le, adj.

Of or belonging to a ſower, Satorius, a, um.

Sowſe, Omaſum, i, n. Succedia, æ, f.

A ſowſe-ſeller, Oxyporopola, æ, m. Omaſarius, ii, m.

S P A.

A ſpace, Spatium, ii, n.

A ſpade, Ligo, onis, f. Pala, æ, f. Beſca, æ, f. Sappa, æ, f.

A ſpangle, Bractea, æ, f.

A ſpan, from the Thumb to the fore Fingers end ſtretched out, Spithama, æ, f. Palmus, i, m.

A ſpaniel, Hiſpaniolus, li, m.

A Water ſpaniel, Canis Anatinus.

To ſpar (or ſhut), Obdo, dere. Oppeſſulo, are.

A ſpar (or bar of wood,) Vectis, is, m.

The ſpar or bolt of a door, Obex, cis, d. g. Repagulum, li, n. Peſſulum, li, n.

To ſpare (or forbear) Parco, ere.

A ſpark, Scintilla, æ, f.

A ſparrow Hawk, Eſparvarius, ii, m.

S P E.

To ſpeak, Loquor, eris.

A ſpeaker, Loquutor, oris, m. Locutor, oris, m.

A ſpear, Haſta, æ, f. Lancea, æ, f.

A little ſpear, Haſtula, æ, f.

A long ſpear, Sariſſa, æ, f.

A bore ſpear, Excipulum, li, n. Venabulum, li, n.

A spear with a barbed head, Tragula, æ, f.

A French spear, Materis, is, f.

A Trout or Eel speer, Fuscina, æ, f. Tridens, tis, m.

A spear (or long Pole to Gage water) Contus, i, m.

A Spear Staff, Hastile, lis, n.

A spear with an Iron head, Hasta præferrata.

The Point (or head) of a spear, Cuspis idis, f.

A spear-man, Lancearius, ii, m. Hastarius, ii, m.

Special, Specialis, le, adj.

A specialty (or writing under seal) Specialitas, ātis, f.

To specifie, Specifico, are.

A spectacle, Spectaculum, li, n.

A Pair of Spectacles, Specillum, li, n. Ocularium Specillum.

A spectacle-maker, Specularius, ii, m. Faber ocularius.

Speculation, Speculatio, onis, f.

A speech, Sermo, onis, m.

To spell, Syllabico, are.

Spencer or Le Despenser (the Family) Le Despencer & Dispensator.

To spend, Dispendo, ere.

Spey River (in Scotland) Spea.

S P I.

Spice, Aroma, atis, n.

Spiced sause or Pickle, Conditura, æ, f.

A spicer, Aromatopola, æ, m.

A spicery (box or place to keep spice in) Narthecium, ii, n.

A spie, Speculator, oris, m. Catascopus, i, m. Emissarius, ii, m.

A spigot, Siphon, onis, f. Epistomium, ii, n.

A spike, Clavus trabalis.

A spindle, Fusus, si, m.

A little spindle, Fusillus, li, m.

A spindle to wind yarn on, Alabrum, i, n.

A spindle-full, Pensum, i, n.

A spindle-maker, Fusarius, ii, m.

Spine (the Family) De Spineto.

To spin, Neo, ere, Filo, are.

A spinner, Lanifica, æ, f. Filacissa, æ, f. Lanipendia, æ, f.

A spinning of Wool, Lanificium, ii, n.

Spinning and Carding, Lana & Tela.

A spinning Wheel Rhombus, i, m.

A spire (or steeple) Pyramis, idis, f.

A spit, Veru, n. Obelus, li, m.

A spitting Box, Salivarium, ii, n.

A spittle for sick folks, Hospitium, ii, n. Abso, onis, m.

S P L.

The spleen (or milt) Lien, ēnis, m. Splen, ēnis, m.

Splits (or splents) of wood, Assulæ, arum, f. Schidia, orum, n.

S P O.

To spoil. Spolio, are.

Spoil, Spolium, ii, n.

Spoiled, Spoliatus, a, um. Depopulatus, a, um.

A spoiling, Spoliatio, onis, f. Depopulatio, onis, f.

A spoke of a Wheel, Radius, ii, m.

A Weavers spole, Spola, æ, f. Panus, i, m.

Spoliation, Spoliatio, onis, f. Is a Writ that lieth for an Incumbent against another Incumbent. in case where the Right of the Patronage cometh not in debate. As if a Parson be made a Bishop, and hath a Dispensation to keep his Benefice still, and afterward the Patron present another to the Church, which is Instituted and Inducted, the Bishop shall have against this Incumbent a Writ of Spoliation in Court

Christian. *Fitz. Nat. brev. fol.* 36. See more in New Terms of Law.

A ſponge, Spongia, æ, f.

A ſpoon, Cochlear, aris, n.

A ſpoon maker, Cochlearius, ii, m.

A ſpot, Labes, is, f.

A ſpouſe (bridegroom, or new Married Man) Sponſus, i, m.

A Spouſe or Bride, Sponſa, æ, f.

A ſpout or cock in a Conduit, Epiſtomium, ii, n.

Spouts (or Gutters) by which water cometh down from Houſes, Colliquiæ, vel Colliciæ, arum, f.

The mouth of ſpouts in buildings like Anticks or Leopards faces, Perſonæ, arum, f.

S P R.

A ſpring or fountain head, Fons, tis, m. Scatebra, æ, f.

A little ſpring, Fonticulus, li, m.

A ſpring tide where the water riſeth, Eluvio, onis, f.

The ſpring, Ver, veris, n. plur caret.

S P U.

Spun, Netus, a, um.

A ſpur, Calcar, aris, n. Stimulus, li, m.

Spurs ſet on a fighting Cock that wanted ſpurs, Plectrum, tri, n.

An Ice-ſpur, or ſhooe with Iron Nails, to walk upon the Ice withal, Encentris, is, f.

To ſpur, Extimulare cum Calcaribus.

S Q U.

A ſquadron, Agmen quadratum.

To make ſquare, Quadro, are.

A ſquare, Quadra, æ, f. Norma, æ, f.

A ſquare Court, Impluvium, ii, n.

A ſquare at the bottom of a Pillar, Abacus, ci, m.

Thin ſquares of Marble, Cruſta Marmoris.

Square (or ſquared) Quadratus a, um.

A ſquaring, Quadratūra, æ, f.

A ſquirel, Sciūrus, i, m.

S T A.

To ſtab with a Dagger or ſuch like. pungo, ere. Confodere pugione.

Stabbed, Confoſſus, a, um. Sica confectus.

A ſtable, Stabulum, li, n.

To ſtable (or houſe Cattel in a ſtable) Stabulo, are.

To be ſet up in a ſtable, Stabulor, ari.

A groom of a ſtable, Equiſo, onis, m.

A groop in ſtables, Minthorium, ii, n.

A ſtack, Acervus, i, m.

A ſtack of Hay, Striga vel meta fœni.

A ſtaff, Baculum, li, n.

A little ſtaff, Bacillum, li, n.

A walking ſtaff, Scipio, onis, f. Manutentum, i, n.

A Hunting ſtaff, Venabulum, li, n.

A ſtaff to drive Cattel with, Agolum, li, n.

A bearing-ſtaff, Geſtatorium, ii, n.

A Biſhops ſtaff (or Croſier) Lituus, ui, m.

A ſtaff to beat Flax with, Scutula, æ, f.

A Plough-mans ſtaff to cleanſe the Coulter, Rulla, æ, f.

Stafford Town, Staffordia.

Staffordſhire, Staffordiæ comitatus.

A ſtage, Theatrum, tri, n. Scena, æ, f. Proſcenium, ii, n.

The Box near the Stage, Podium, ii, n.

A ſtage whereon Pageants are ſet, Pegma, atis, n.

A ſtage-Player, Hiſtrio, onis, m.

Belonging

Belonging to the Stage, Scenalis, le, adj.

A ſtair, Scala, æ, f. Gradus, us, m.

A winding ſtair, Scala Annularia, Cockleum, ei, n.

A pair of ſtairs, Par Scalarum.

Half paced ſtairs, Scalæ Dimidiatæ.

The top of ſtairs, Culmen ſcalarum.

The back ſtairs, Poſtica pars Palatii.

A ſtair-caſe, Foramen ſcalarum.

A ſtake, Palus, i, m. Sudes, is, f.

Stake-bote, EſtoveriumSurorum.

A ſtake or poſt whereunto they bind Cattel in ſtables, Vacerra, æ, f

A ſtake or fork for the hurdles of a Fold, Cervus, vi, m.

Staked, Palatus, a, um

A ſtall, Stalla, æ, f. *Ra. Entr.* 667. *Lex* 119. Stallum, i, n. 2. *mon.* 657. (*i. e*) a ſtall in a Fair or Market.

Stallage, Stallagium, ii, n. *Lex.* 118 *Cow.* 24. 5. Is money paid for Pitching of Stalls in Fair or Markets.

An Ox-ſtall, Bovile, lis, n. Saginarium, ii, n.

A Butchers-ſtall, Macera, æ, f.

A ſtalling of Cattel, Stabulatio, onis, f

To ſtamp (or beat ſmall) Contundo, ere.

Stamped (or Pounded) Contuſus, a, um.

A ſtandard, Standarda, æ, f. *Ry.* 555, 568, 569. Standardum, i, n. *Spel.* 71. *Pry.* 24. *Fle.* 71. Vexillum, li, n.

A ſtandard bearer, Vexillarius, ii, m.

He that goeth before the ſtandard to defend it, Anteſignanus, i, m.

A ſtand for Ale or Beer, Talea, æ, f. Fulcrum, i, n. Seſſibulum, li, n.

A little ſtanding out, Prominulus, a, um.

A ſtandiſh, Atramentarium, ii, n.

Standrope or Steinthorp (in the Biſhoprick of Durham) Vicus Saxeus.

Stanford (in Lincolnſhire) Stanfordia.

A ſtaple for Wares, Stapula, æ, f. *Cow.* 245. *Lex.* 118. Statutum ſtapulæ, *Reg.* 151. 152.

Starboard (or right ſide of the Ship) Dextra Navigii, Latus dextrum Navigii quod Naucleres occupat locus Naucleri.

Starch, Amylum, li. n.

A ſtationer, Bibliopola, æ, m. Librarius, ii, m.

A ſtatuary (a carver or maker of Statues or Images) Statuarius, ii, m.

A ſtatue (or ſtanding Image) Statua, æ, f.

A ſtatue without hands, Hermula, æ

A ſtatute, Statutum, i, n. *Statuto Stapulæ and Statuto Mercatorio*, are Writs for the Impriſoning of them that have forfeited Statute Staples, or Statute Merchant.

S T E.

A diſh of ſteakes, Cremium, ii, n.

To ſteal, Furor, ari.

A ſtealer, Furator, oris, m.

A ſtealing, Furatio, onis, f. Furtum, i, n.

A ſteed or great horſe for ſervice in Wars or other ways, Equus Bellator.

Steel, Chalybs, ybis, m.

A ſteel to ſtrike fire with, Ignitabulum, li, n. Fugillus, li, m.

The ſteel-yard in London, Guildhalda Teutonicorum.

To ſteep, Stipo, are.

A ſteeple (or ſpire) Campanile, lis, n. Turris Campanaria.

A

A steer, Juvencus, i, m.

A stemm or stalk of any Herb Caulis, is, m.

Stene (in Northamptonshire) Stenum.

A step-father, Vitricus, ci, m.

A step-mother, Noverca, æ, f.

A step-son, Privignus, i, m.

A step-daughter, Privigna, æ, f.

Stephen (a man's Name) Stephanus, i, m.

St. *Stephens day*, Festum sancti Stephani Protomartyris.

Sterling (in Scotland) Strivillina.

Sterling Money, fine Silver Money, Sterlingum, i, n.

The stern of a Ship, Gubernaculum, i, n.

A stern-man (or steer-man) Gubernator, oris, m.

A Steward, Dispensator, oris, m, Oeconomus, i, m. Vicedominus, i, m. Massarius, ii, m.

A Steward or Bailiff, Ballivus, i, m.

Lord Steward of the Kings Houshold, Dominus Seneschallus Hospitii Domini Regis. See *Anno* 1. *Mar.* 2. *Parlam. cap.* 4. where you may at large read divers things touching his Office, as also in *Fitz Nat. Brev. fol.* 241. *B. Of this Officers ancient Power read*, Fleta, *lib.* 2. *cap.* 3.

The Stewardship or Governance of a House, Oeconomia, æ, f.

To stew (or boil to pieces) Macero, are.

Stewed in Broath, Jurulentus, a, um.

A Stew (hot-house or bath) Calidarium, ii, n. Vaporarium, ii, n.

S T I.

A stick, Bacillus, li, m.

A stick for setting, Pastinum, i, n.

A stick (or bow) to play upon a Viol with, Dædala, æ, f.

Small sticks or any dry brush to kindle the Fire Quickly, Cremia, orum, n. Cocula, orum, n.

A stick of Eeles, Stica anguillarum. 1. *Mon.* 137, 329. Sticcus, 2. *Mon.* 815.

A stie, or swine stie, Hara, æ, f.

A stile to go over, Agrestis Scala, Climax, acis, f.

A stile (the Pin of a pair of writing Tables) Stylus, i, m.

Stile-bote, Estoverium Climacum.

A Still, Clibanus, i, m. Stillatorium, ii, n.

A Lembick still, Alembicus, ci, m.

Stilts to go upon, Grallæ, arum, f.

A stilt man (or goer on stilts) Grallator, oris, m.

A stipend (or Wages) Stipendium, ii, n. Salarium, ii, n.

A stipendiary (he to whom a stipend is paid) Stipendiarius, ii, m. Salariarius, ii, m. Pensionarius, ii, m.

Stipulation, Stipulatio, onis, f.

A stirrop, Stapes, edis, f. Pedestella, æ, f. Strapia, æ, f. Strepa, æ, f.

An Iron stirrop, Encentris, is, f. Stapes ferreus.

The Yeoman of the stirrop, Strator, oris, m.

A stock, Instaurum, ri, n.

A stocking, Instauramentum, i, n. *Fle.* 157, 159. 1. *Mon.* 548, 924, 112, 604.

To stock, Instauro, are. *Fle.* 164.

A stock of a Tree, Truncus, ci, m.

A pair of stocks, Cippus, i, m.

A pair of stocks with a Whipping Post, Bitus, i, m.

A stocking (or pair of stockings) Caliga, æ, f. Par Caligarum.

Linnen stockings, Caligæ lineæ

A pair of silk stockings, Par caligarum byssinarum.

A pair of Thread stockings, Par Caligarum de filo.

stolen, Furatus, a, um.

The stomach, Stomachus, i, m.

A stomacher, Pectorale, lis, n. Thorax, acis, m. Strophium, ii, n. Cingillus, li, m.

A stomacher (or Bib) Fascia pectoralis.

A stone, Lapis, idis, m.

A stone (weight) Petra, æ, f. *Fle.* 73.

A quarry of stones Lapidum fodina.

An old stone put into a new building, Lapis Redivivus.

A pumice stone, Lapis bibulus.

A sleek stone, Lapis Lævigatorius.

Hard and rough hewn stones, Jantilia, orum, n.

Free-stone, Saxum quadratum.

Wrought stone, Saxa dedolata.

Stone dust, Pulvis Lapideus.

A stone that serveth to work withal, Lapis Operarius.

Made of square stones, Tesserarius, a, um.

A stone-cutter, Lapidicæsor, oris, m.

The stone or gravel in the Reins, Calculus, li, m.

Stony-Stratford (in Buckinghamshire) Lactodorum Lactodurum, Lactorodum, Lactorudum, Stratfordia Stenica.

Stoneham (in Hampshire) Ad Lapidem.

Stonor (in the Isle of Thanet in Kent) Lapis Tituli.

A stool, Sella, æ, f. Sedile, lis, n. Tripodium, ii, n.

A close-stool, Scaphium, ii, n. Sella Familiaris.

A cucking-stool, Terbichetum, i, n.

A foot-stool, Scabellum, li, n.

A folding-stool (or chair) Sella plicatilis.

A place where stools are kept for Men to sit upon, Sellaria, æ, f.

A cover of a stool, Episellium, ii, n.

Joined stools, Juncta Sedilia.

To stop (or shut up) Oppilo, are.

A stopping (or shutting up) Oppilatio, onis, f. Obstructio, onis, f.

A stoppel, Obthuramentum, i, n. Obstructorium, ii, n.

A store (or stock) Staurus, i, m. 2. *Cro.* 567. 1. *Mon.* 944.

To have in store, Habere repositum. 1. *fo.* 116.

A store-house, Promptuarium mercium, Repositorium, ii, n.

A store house for Armour and Ordinance, Armamentarium, ii, n.

A store house for Tackling of Ships, Casteria, æ, f.

Two stories, Distega, orum, n.

Three stories, Tristega, orum, n.

A stove (or hot house) Thermæ, arum, f. Hypocaustrum, i, n. Stuba, æ, f.

The place where smoak comes forth in an hot-house, Vaporarium, ii, n.

Stoven (or dry withered stump of a Tree) Zuchus & Zucheus, ei, m.

Stour River (in Darbyshire) Sturus.

Stour River (in Dorsetshire) Durus, Starus.

Stourmouth (in Kent) Ostium Sturæ.

Stourton or Sturminster (in Dorsetshire) Sturodunum.

S T R.

To strain Liquor, Colo, are.

To strain through a Cloth, Sacco, are.

A strainer, Colum, i, n.

A strake or hoop of a Cart-Wheel wherein the spoaks be set, Absis, is, f. Canthus, i, m. Vietus, i, m.

A strand or high shoar, Acta, æ, f.

A stranger, Peregrinus, i, m. Alienigena, æ, f. It signifieth in our Common Law a Man born out

out of the Land, or unknown: But in the Law it hath an especial signification for him that is not privy or party to an Act, as a Stranger to a Judgment, *Old nat. brev. fol.* 128. Is he to whom a Judgment doth not belong, and in this signification it is directly contrary to party or privy.

Le strange (*the Family*) Extraneus.

To strangle, Strangulo, are.

The strangury (*a Disease*) Stranguria, æ, f.

A stratagem, Stratagêma, atis, n.

Strat-flower or strat-fleur (*in Cardiganshire*) Stata florida.

Stratton (*the Family*) De Strattone.

Stratonice (*a Woman's name*) Stratonice, es, f.

Straw, Stramen, inis, n. Stramentum, i, n.

To be covered with straw, Straminor, ari. *Fle.* 164.

A straw (*or Chaffe*) *house* Palearium, ii, n.

A straw-bed, Stratum Stramineum.

A stack of straw, Meta Straminis.

Strays (*Estrays*) Extrahuræ, arum, f.

A streak, Tractus, us, m. Lineamentum, i, n.

A streamer in a Ship, Supparum, i, n. Aplustre, is, n.

A street (*or paved way*) Strata, æ, f. *Reg.* 98. Platea, æ, f. 2 *Inst.* 38. Vicus, ci, m.

A little street, Viculus, li, m. 1. *Mon.* 138

The streights of Callis, Fretum Britannicum, Fretum Gallicum, Fretum Morinorum.

The streights of Gibralter, Fretum de Gibralter.

Stress of Weather, Tempestas Naufraga.

To strike (*or smite*) ferio, ire. Verbero, are.

To strike or pluck down sails, Vela contrahere, destringere carbasa.

A strikle or strichel, *wherewith the measure of Corn or Grain being filled, is striked and made even*, Hostorium, ii, n. Radius, ii, m.

A string of a Harp (*or other Instrument*) Chorda, æ, f Nervus, vi, m.

The string of a Dart, Amentum, i, n.

A Leather string, Corrigia, æ, f. Stropha, æ, f. Lorum, i, n.

To strip or make naked, Nudo, are.

Stript or stripped, Nudatus, a, um.

A stroak, Verber, eris, n. Plaga, æ, f. Ictus, us, &, i, m.

The mark or print of a stroak, Vibex, icis, f.

Strong, fortis, ior, issimus, Robustus, a, um.

A structure, fabrick, frame, or building, Structura, æ, f.

S T U.

Stubble, Stubula, æ, f. *Fle.* 162. 166. Stipula, æ, f.

A stud in girdles, or such like, Bulla, æ, f.

A little stud, Bullula, æ, f.

A stud for a Robe, Clavus, i, m.

Studded, or garnished with studs, Clavatus, a, um, Bullatus, a, um.

A stud-maker, Bullarius, ii, m.

The studs of a Buckler, Militares Claviculæ.

Studs driven into Souldiers Buskins, Clavi caligares.

A stud or breed of horses, Equariæ, arum, f.

A student (*or Scholar*) Studiosus, a, um, Scholaster, tri, m. Scholasticus, a, um.

Study, Studium, ii, n.

To study, Studeo, ere, Studium adhibere.

A study, Musæum, i, n.

Studious, Studiosus, a, um.

To stuff, Farcio, ire.

A stuffing, Stuffura, æ, f. *Vet. Intr.* 228.

S U B.

A Sub-Deacon, Subdiaconus, ni, m.

Sub-Deaconship, Subdiaconatus, ûs, m.

A Subject, Subjectus, a, um. Subditus, a, um.

A Liege Subject, Ligius, ij, m.

Subjection, Subjectio, onis, f.

A Sub-Marshal, Submarescallus, i, m. Is an Officer in the Marshalsea, that is Deputy to the Chief or Lord Marshal of the Kings house, commonly call'd the Knight Marshal, and hath the Custody of the Prisoners there. *Compt. Jurisd.* fol. 104. He is otherwise call'd under Marshal.

Submission, Submissio, onis, f.

To Submit, Submitto, ere.

To Suborn (or bring in false Witness) Suborno, are.

Suborned, Subornatus, a, um.

A Suborner (or he that Suborneth) Subornator, oris, m. Prævaricator, oris, m.

A Suborning, Prævaricatio, onis, *f.* A Writ of *Subpœna*, *Breve de Subpœna*, *Doct. & Stud.* 48. It is a Writ to call a Man into the Chancery, upon such Case only as the Common Law faileth in, and hath not provided for: so as the Party who hath wrong, can have no ordinary remedy by the Rules and course of the Common Law, *West part.* 2. *Symbol. Titulo* Proceedings in Chancery, *Sect.* 18. where you may read many Examples of such Cases as *Subpœna* lyeth in.

There is also a *Subpœna ad Testificandum*, which lyeth for the calling in of Witnesses to testify in a Cause, as well in Chancery as in other Courts. And the name of both these proceed from Words in the Writ, which charge the Party call'd to appear at the Day and Place assign'd, *Sub pœna centum librarum, &c.*

There is mention of a Common *Subpœna* in *Cromptons Jurisd.* fol. 33. which signifieth nothing else but such a *Subpœna* as every Common Person is call'd by into the Chancery: Whereas any Lord of Parliament is call'd by the Lord Chancellors Letters, giving him notice of the Suit intended against him, and Requiring him to appear. *Crompton eodem.*

The service of a Subpæna *or other Writ*, Executio, onis, f. Servitus.

To Subscribe, Subscribo, ere.

Subsidy, Subsidium, ij, n.

Substance, Substantia, æ, f.

To Substitute, Substituo, ere.

To Substract, Subtraho, ere. Deduco, ere.

To Subvert, Subverto, ere.

The suburbs of a City, Suburbia, orum, n.

S U C.

To succeed, Succedo, ere.

Success (or event of a thing) Successus, ûs, m. Eventus, ûs, m.

A successour, Successor, oris, m.

Succour, Succursus, ûs, m.

To succour, Succurro, ere.

S U D.

Sudbury (the Family) de Sudburia.

S U E.

To sue (in Law) Secto, are.

Suerby (in Yorkshire) Eilimenom, Gabrantonicorum, Gabrantotorucorum, Salutaris portus, Sinus Portuosus & Salutaris.

Suet, Sevum, i, n.

Melted suet, Liquamen, inis, n.

S U F.

To suffer (*or bear*) Suffero, ferre.

To suffer (*or permit*,) Permitto, ere.

To suffice, Sufficio, ere.

Sufficient, Sufficiens, tis, adj.

To suffocate (*or Choak*) Suffoco, are.

Suffolk, Suffolcia, Suffolicia, Sudovolca.

A suffragan, Suffraganeus, ei, m.

A suffrage, Suffragi[illegible]m, ij, n.

S U G.

Sugar, Saccharum, ri, n.

A sugar-loaf, Collyra Sacchari, Albanus Pileus, ——Dedit & deliberasset eidem J. J. filio unam Saccharam Collyram (anglice *a sugar-loaf*.)

A sugar-sop (*or Hony sop*) Offa Saporata.

To suggest, Suggero, ere.

S U I.

A Suit of Apparel, Vestimentum, i, n.

A Suit at Law, *Secta*, *æ*, *f*. It cometh of the French *Suit* (*i. e.*) following, and so it is taken in our Common Law, but in divers senses. The first is a Suit in Law, and is divided into Suit Real and Personal, which is all one with Action Real and Personal.

Then there is Suit of Court, or Suit Service, that is, an attendance which a Tenant oweth at the Court of the Lord.

The New Expositor of the Law Terms, maketh mention of Four sorts of Suits, *viz.* Suit Covenant, Suit Custom, Suit Real, and Suit Service. Suit Covenant he defineth to be when your Ancestor hath Covenanted with my Ancestor to Sue to the Court of my Ancestors. Suit Custom, when I and my Ancestors have been seised of your own Suit and your Ancestors, time out of mind, *&c.* Suit Real, when Men come to the Sheriff's Turn or Leet, to which Court all Men are compell'd to come to know the Laws, so that they may not be Ignorant of things declar'd there, how they ought to be Govern'd, and it is call'd Real, because of their Allegiance, and this appeareth by Common Experience. When one is sworn; his Oath is, that he shall be a Loyal Subject to the King. And this Suit is not for the Land that he holdeth within the County, but by Reason of his Person and his abode there, and ought to be done twice a Year; for default thereof he shall be Amerc'd and not Distrained. Suit Service, is to Sue to the Sheriff's Turn or Leet, or to the Lords Court from three Weeks to three Weeks, by the whole Year, and for default thereof a Man shall be Distrain'd, and not Amerc'd. And this Suit Service is by reason of the Tenure of a Mans Land. Moreover, Suit signifieth, the following of one in Chase, as fresh Suit. Lastly, it signifieth a Petition made to the Prince or Great Personage.

A

A Wife is disabl'd to Sue without her husband, as much as a Monk is without his Sovereign. But by the Common Law, the Wife of the King of *England* is an Exempt Person from the King, and is capable of Lands or Tenement of the Gift of the King, as no other Feme covert is, and may Sue, and be Su'd without the King, as a Feme Sole by the Common Law, but where the Husband is Banish'd, the Wife may Sue and be Su'd. *Cook on Lit. Lib.* 2. *cap* 11. *Sect.* 200. *Cook Ib. fol.* 132, 133.

Suit of the King's Peace, *Secta Pacis Regis.* It is the pursuing of a Man for breach of the King's Peace, by Treasons, Insurrections, Rebellions, Trespasses, *Ann.* 6, *R.* 2. *Stat.* 2. *cap.* 1. & *Ann.* 21. *ejusdem cap.* 15. & *Ann.* 5. *H.* 4. *cap.* 15.

S U L.

Sulwath, see Solwey.

S U M.

A Summary (*or Abridgment*) Summarium, ij, n.

A Sum of Mony, Summa, æ, f.

To Sum, Summo, are.

To Summon to appear (*to Cite*) Cito, are.

A Summoner, Summonitor, oris, m.

A Sumpter Horse, Equus Onerarius, Equus Sarcinarius, Equus Sagmarius.

Sumptuous, Sumptuosus, a, um.

S U N.

The Sun, Sol, solis, m.

S U.

Sun-rising, Exortus, ûs, m.

Sun-setting, Occasus, ûs, m.

To Sun (*or dry in the Sun*) Insolo, are.

A Sun-dial, Solarium, ij, n.

S U P.

Superfluity, Superfluitas, atis, f.

Superfluous, Ex abundanti, Smith *and* Peases *Case*. Leon Hughs *grand Abridgment*, 484. *Tit. Covenants.* Superfluus, a, um.

Superiority, Superioritas, atis, f.

Superiors, Superiores.

A Superscription, Superscriptio, onis, f.

Supersedeas, Is a Writ commanding to forbear the doing a thing, or to discharge a Person.

A Supper, Cæna, æ, f.

A Funeral Supper, Pollinctum, i, n.

To Supplant, Supplanto, are.

A Supplement, Supplementum, i, n.

A Suppliant, Supplex, icis, adj.

A Supplication, Supplicatio, onis, f.

To make a Supplication, Supplico, are.

Supplicavit, Is a Writ Issuing out of the Chancery for taking the Security of the Peace against a Man. It is directed to the Justices of the Peace of the County and the Sheriff, and is grounded upon the Statute, *An.* 1. *Ed.* 3. *cap.* 16. which ordaineth that certain Persons in Chancery shall be assign'd to take care of the Peace, *Fitz. nat. brev. fol.* This Writ was of Old call'd, *Breve de minis*, a Writ of Threatnings, as Mr. *Lambert*, in his *Eirenarcha* noteth out of the Register Original, fol. 88.

To Supply, Suppleo, ere.

To Support (or uphold) Supporto, are.

A Suppository, Suppositorium, ij, n.

To Suppress, Supprimo, ere.

Supremacy, Suprematus, ûs, m.

S U R.

Sur cui in vita, Is a Writ that lieth for the Heir of that Woman, whose Husband having alienated her Land in Fee, She bringeth not the Writ *Cui in vita* for the Recovery of her own Land, for in this Case her Heir may take this Writ against the Tenant after her decease, *Fitz. nat. brev.* fol. 193. b.

Surety ship, Plegiagium, ij, n. Plegiatio, onis, f. Lex. 97. Ra. Entr. 467. Reg. 158. 180. Vadium, ij, n. Reg. 93. Ra. Entr. 59. Ry. 247.

A Surety (or Pledge) Plegius, ij, m. Vadius, ij, m. Ra. Ent. 561. 4. Co. 6.

Entred into Surety ship, Vadiatus, a, um.

A Surfeit, Crapula, æ, f.

A Surgeon (or Chirurgeon) Chirurgus, i, m.

Surgery, Chirurgia, æ, f.

A Surname, Cognomen, inis, n.

A Surplice, Superpellicium, ij, n. Camisiola, æ, f. Vestis Linea Religiosa.

A Surplusage, Surplusagium, ij, n.

To Surprize, Deprehendo, ere.

A Surrejoynder, Surrejunctio, onis, f.

To Surrender, Resigno, are.

A Surrender of an Estate, Sursumredditio, onis, f.

Surteyes (the Family) Super Teisam.

To Survey (or over see) Inspicio ere, Lustro, are, Curo, are.

A Survey, Supervisus, ûs m.

A Surveyor, Supervisor, oris, m.

Surveyors to go before the Camp, Antecensores.

A Surveyor (or Master of Works) Fabricensis, is, m. Curator, oris, m.

A Surveyor of the High ways. Viaculus, li, m. Viocurus, ri, m.

To Survive, Supervivo, ere.

Surviving, Superstes, itis, adj.

Surrey County, Southeria, Southriona, Southria, Sudria, Sudurheia, Surria, Suthria, Suthriona.

Of Surrey, Southeriensis, Sudriensis.

S U S.

Susan (a Womans name) Susanna, æ, f.

To Suspect (or mistrust) Suspicio, ere. Suspecto, are.

Suspected (accused) Arrectatus, a, um. Rectatus, a, um. Spel. 53.

Suspension, Suspensio, onis, f.

Suspicion, Suspicio, onis, f.

Sussex County, Sussexia, Southsexena, Southsexia.

The Wild of Sussex, Wilda Sussexiæ, Hob. 266. Walda.

S U T.

A Suture (or Seam) Sutura, æ, f.

Suthley or Sudley (the Family) de Suthleia, & Sutleia.

S W A.

To Swadle (or Swath) Fascio, are.

Swadled, Fasciatus, a, um.

Swadling (or Swathing) Clouts Fasciæ, arum, f. Spargana, orum, n.

A Swainmote, Swainmotus, i, m. Swainmotum, i, n. *a Court kept thrice a Year for matters of the Forest.*

A

A Swarm of Bees, Examen, inis, n.

Swale River (in Richmondshire) Cataracta, Sualva, Swala.

A Swallow-tail or Dovetail to join Timber together, Subscus, udis, f.

A Swan, Cygnum, i, n.

A Swan-mark, Cygninota, æ, f. 7. Co. 17.

A Swath, Fascia, æ, f.

A little Swath, Fasciola, æ, f.

A Swath of Grass, &c. *in Mowing*, Andena, æ, f. Per nomen sex andenarum prati. Wi. Tit. Action Sur le Case.

To Swath, Sparganizo, are.

S W E.

To Swear, Juro, are.

To Sweep, Scopo, are.

A Sweeper of the House, Scoparius, ij, m.

She that sweeps the House, Scoparia, æ, f.

Sweet-meats, Bellaria, orum, n. Tragemata, tum, n.

S W I.

Swift River (in Leicestershire) Swiftus.

Swilley lake (in Ireland*)* Argita.

To Swim, No, nare; Nato, are.

A Swimmer, Nattator, oris, m.

A Swimming, Natatio, onis, f.

A Swimming place, Natatoria, æ, f

A Swine, Sus, Suis, c. g. Porcus, i, m.

A breed or stock of Swine, Haratium, ij, n.

A Swine herd (or keeper of Swine, Subulcus, ci, m, Suarius, ij, m.

A Swine-fly, Porcistetum, i, n.

A Swingle-staff (or bat to beat Flax) Scutula, æ, f.

A swingle-foot, Excudipes.

A swingle-head, Excudia, æ, f. Excussorium, ij, n.

A swingle-tree, Projectorium, ij, n. Excudides, dis, f.

Swithin (a Mans name) Swithinus, i, m.

S W O.

A Sword, Gladius, ij, m. Ensis, is, m.

A little sword, Gladiolus, li, m.

A short sword, Sica, æ, f. Semispathium, ij, n.

An Executioners sword, Clunabulum, li, n.

A sword hanger, Scalmus, i, m.

An arming sword, Bellatorius Ensis.

A two edged sword, Gladius anceps.

A sword-maker, Faber gladiarius.

The Pummel of a sword, Milum, li, n.

A riding sword, Parazonium, ij, n.

A sword player, Gladiator, oris, m.

A master which teacheth to play at sword, Lanista, æ, m.

A sword bearer, Ensifer, ri, m.

The act or feat of fighting with a sword, Gladiatura, æ, f.

Pertaining to fighting or sword plays, Gladiatorius, a, um.

S Y R.

A Syringe for the Ears, Otenthites, æ, m.

A Syrup, Syrupus, i, m.

T A B.

A Taber or Tabret, Tympanum, i, n.

To play on the Taber, Tympanizo, are. Tympanum pulsare.

A Taberer (or he that plays on the Taber) Tympanista, æ, m.

A Tabernacle, Tabernaculum, li, n.

Tabitha (a Womans name) Tabithæ, æ, f.

A Table, Tabula, æ, f. Mensa, æ, f.

A little Table, Mensula, æ, f.

A round Table, Cibilla, æ, f.

A Table to set drinking Glasses upon, Hialotheca, æ, f.

A Table with one foot, Monopodium, ij, n.

A three footed, or round Table, Mensa delphica, Mensa tripedanea.

A folding Table with divers leaves, Caudex, ecis, f.

A wainscot Table, Mensa undulata, Mensa undatim crispa.

The setting of little pieces of painted Horn or Ivory into Tables, Cerostrotum, i, n.

A Table whereon Bankers tell their mony, Trapeza, æ, f.

A poor mans Table, Tenabula, æ, f.

A Table book, Pugillares, um, m, pl.

To lay (or cover) the Table, Sternere mensam.

To wait at the Table, Præministro, are.

A Table Cloth, Mappa, æ, f. Mantile, lis, n.

A little Table cloth, Mappella, æ, f.

A Table (or Index) in a Book, Index, icis, c. g. Elenchus, i, m.

A pair of Tables to play, Tabularium, ij, n. Tabula lusoria, alveus lusorius.

To play at Tables, Latrunculis vel scrupis ludere.

A Table man, Latrunculus, li, m.

A Tablet or Jewel which hangeth about the Neck, Monile, lis, n. Bulla aurea.

A little Tablet, Bullula, æ, f.

Garnish'd with Tablets, Bullatus, a, um.

T A C.

A Tack (Hook or Clasp) Uncus, ci, m.

T A D.

Tadcaster (in Yorkshire) Cacaria, Calatum, Calcaria, Galatum, Tadecastrum.

T A F.

Taff river (in Glamorganshire) Ratostatibius, Rhatostatibius, Taffus.

Taffety, Taffeta, æ, f. Multitia, orum, n, pl.

Tuff taffety, Villosa multitia.

Striped-Taffety, Scutulata, æ, f.

T A I.

Taiesborough (in Norfolk) Ad Taum.

A Tail, Cauda, æ, f.

A fee Tail, Taliatum feudum, *an Estate entail'd* (i. e.) *curtail'd and limited to conditions.*

The Plough tail, Bura, æ, f.

To

T A K.

To Take, Capio, ere.

To take away, Abripio, ere. Eripio, ere.

A Taking away by violence or force, Direptio, onis, f.

T A L.

Tallage, Tallagium, ij, n. Cow. 253. Ry. 254. Lex. 122. (i. e.) *any kind of Toll or Tax.*

A Talley (or cleft piece of Wood to nick up an account on) Tallia, æ, f. Cow. 258. Ry. 450. Pry. 7. Lex. 122. 133.

Tallow, Sevum, i, n. Sebum, i, n.

Talshide, Taliatura, æ, f. (i. e.) *Talwood or fire-wood cleft, and cut into Billets of a certain size.*

T A M.

Tame river (in Oxfordshire) another in Staffordshire, Tama.

Tame town (in Oxforshire) Tama Opidum.

Tamar river (in Cornwall) Tamara, Tamarus, Tambra.

Tamerton (in Cornwall) Tamarus.

Tamworth (in Staffordshire) Tamawordina, Tamworthia.

T A N.

Tanet, *see Thanet.*

Tanfield (in Yorkshire) Tanfelda.

A Tankard, Cantharus, i, m. amphora, æ, f.

A water Tankard, Anclatorium, ij, n. Passacriatium, ij, n.

A Tankard bearer, Cantharius, ij, m. Amphorarius, ij, m.

A Tanner or Tawer of Leather, Tannarius, ij, m. Ra. Enter. 602. Coriarius, ij, m.

A Tan-house (or house to keep bark in) Barkaria, æ, f.

A Tanners Craft, Tannaria, æ, f.

To tann, Tanno, are. Reg. 602. Ry. 27.

A Tann vat, Labrum coriarium.

Tanned Leather, Corium Tannatum.

T A P.

A Tap or faucet whereout liquor runneth, Epistomium, ij, n. Fistula, æ, f. Tappa, æ, f. 2 Mon. 746. Lex. 20.

To tap a vessel, Relinere dolium.

The spiggot of a tap, Siphonis obturaculum.

The Cock in a brazen tap, Vertibulum, li, n.

A tap-house, Caupona, æ, f.

A tapster, Promus, i, m. Caupo, onis, m.

A tape to bind the apron about, Ligatorium, ij, n. Fascia, æ f.

A taper (or waxcandle) Cerius, ei, m.

A taper-bearer, Cerocerarius, ij, m. Cerophérarius, ij, m.

A Candlestick whereupon tapers are set, Ceroferarium, ij, m.

Tapestry (or Hangings) Plagæ, arum, f. Aulæum, æi, n. Peristroma, atis, n. Peripetasma, atis, n.

Tapestry or Cloth in which are pictures wrought with divers colors, Tapes, etis, m. Tapetum, i, n.

Tapestry wrought with pictures of Beasts, Belluata tapetia.

Thick tapeſtry, Attallica Peripetaſmata.

A tapeſtry-maker, Phrygio, onis, m.

T A R.

Tares, Zizania, æ, f. Lolium, ij, n.

A target (or ſhield) Scutum, i, n. Parma, æ, f.

A target like an half Moon, Pelta, æ, f.

He that uſeth ſuch a Target, Peltatus, a, um. Peltaſta, æ, m.

A ſhort Target, Ancyle, lis, n.

A little round Target, Parmula, æ, f. Scutulum, li, n.

A target made of Leather thongs without Wood, Scetra, æ, f.

A target made of a Bulls hide, Taurea, æ, f.

Armed with a target (or ſhield) Scutatus, a, um.

A target maker, Scutarius, ij, m.

A target makers ſhop, Shopa vel fabrica Scutaria.

Of or belonging to targets (or ſhields) Scutarius, a, um.

A Tart, Scriblita vel Streblita, æ, f. Chanona, æ, f.

A tart-maker, Scriblitarius, ij, m.

T A S.

A Task (or charge) that one is enjoyn'd to do, Penſum, i, n.

A taſſel, Apex, icis, f.

A taſter to a Prince, or great Perſon, Prægustator, oris, m.

A little cup or taſter, Cupillum, li, n. Guſtatorium, ij, n.

A wine taſter, Meraria, æ, f.

T A.

T A U.

A Tavern, œnopolium, ij, n. Caupona, æ, f.

A wine tavern, Taberna vinaria.

A taverner, Tabernarius, ij, m. Caupo, onis, m.

A little Tavern, Tabernula, æ, f.

A tavern haunter, Attabernio, onis, m. Ociſtrio, onis, m.

Taveſtock (in Devonſhire) Taviſtokia.

Taunton (in Somerſetſhire) Thonodunum.

T A W.

Taw River (in Devonſhire) Tawus.

Soft tawed Leather wherewith they make Gloves and Purſes, Aluta, æ, f.

Any thing made of tawed leather, Alutamen, & Alutamentum, i, n.

A tawing, Alutatio, onis, f.

A tawer, Alutarius, ij, m. Coriarius, ij, m.

T A X.

To Tax, Taxo, are.

A tax, Taxa, æ, f.

A taxing, Taxatio, onis, f. Lex. 122. 1. Mon. 976.

A tax by Plough-land, Carucagium, ij, n.

Taxors, Taxatores, Ry. 250.

A Land tax, Terragium, ij, n.

A ſervice of Plowing, Reaping, &c. which ſome Tenants perform to the Lord.

A

T A Y.

A Taylor, Sartor, oris, m. Vestiarius, ij, m. Sutor Vestiarius.

A taylor of Rich Cloaths (a Womans Taylor) Patagiarius, ij, m.

Merchant taylors of London, Armirarij Linearum Armiturarum, Mon. 576.

T E A.

A Teasel (or shear-mans Bur) Hippophas.

T E E.

A Teem (or Team) of Oxen to draw the Plough, Temo, onis, f. Protelum, li, n.

Tees river (in the Bishoprick of Durham) Athesis, Tesa, Teisis, Tesis, Teisa.

A Row or set of Teeth, Sepes dentium.

The Fore-teeth, Primores vel incisores dentes.

The upper or over teeth, Superiores dentes.

The Jaw or Cheek teeth, Gemini dentes, Dentes maxillares vel molares.

The sharp or Eye teeth, Dentes Canini.

Tusks or tushes of teeth, Dentes exerti.

A Growing or breeding of teeth, Dentitio, onis, f.

T E M.

Temperance (a Womans name) Temperantia, æ, f.

A tempest (or great storm) Tempestas, atis, f.

The Temple within temple Bar, Templum pacis seu concordiæ, *so call'd from the Knights Templars.*

A temple, Templum, i, n.

The temples of the head, Tempora, rum, n.

Temporal (or that lasteth but for a time) Temporalis, le, adj.

The temporalties, Temporalia, ium, n. (i. e.) *Lay Fees that belong to Bishopricks.*

To tempt or intice, Tento, are.

A tempter, Tentator, oris, m.

T E N.

A Tenancy, Tenentia, æ, f. Ry. 219. 376.

A tenant, Tenens.

Tenants in free soccage, Coleberti.

A tenement, Tenementum, i, n.

Tenantable, or fit to be Inhabited, Tenentabilis, le, adj. Tenente aptus.

Ten, Decem. Indecl.

Tennis play, Sphæromachia, æ, f. Pilæ lusoriæ certamen.

A tennis Court, Sphæristerium, ij, n.

A tenon to put into a Mortis, Impages, is, f. Lingula edolata, cardo, inis, m & f.

That hath a tenon, Lingulatus, a, um.

A tent or Pavillion, Tentorium, ij, n.

A little tent, Tentoriolum, li, n.

A Souldiers tent, Castra, orum, n.

Merchants tents, Tentoria mercatoria. 1 Mon. 987.

A tent in a Fair or Market, Velabrum, i, n.

A tent-maker, Scenofactorius, ij, m.

Of or belonging to a tent, Tentorius, a, um.

To pitch their tents one against another, Castra castris conferre.

To make tents, Scenofacio, ere.

A tent for a Wound, Turunda, æ, f. Penicillus, li m.

A long tent for a Wound, Lemniscus, ci, m.

A tenture or tenter for Cloth, Pannitendium, ij, n.

The tenth, or number of ten, Decimus, a, um.

Tenths, Decimæ, arum, f.

A tenure, Tenura, æ, f.

T E R.

Term, Terminus, i, m. Signifieth with us commonly the bounds and Limits of time, as a Lease for term of Life, or term of Years. Also it is used for the time wherein the Tribunals or places of Judgment are open to all, that have cause of Complaints of Wrongs, to seek their Right by course of Law or Action. The rest of the year is called Vacation. Of these Terms there be four in the Year; during which matters of Justice, (for the most part) are dispatch'd.

Termor, a Lessee, Terminarius, ij, m Reg. 197.

A terrace or terras, Agger, eris, m Vallum Terraceum.

A terrace of hard and even'd Earth, as in a Bowling alley, Pavimentum, i, n.

To make a Terrace or Floor, Pavimento, are.

Tern river, in Shropshire, Terna.

A Terrar, Terrarium, ij, n, (i e) *a writing describing Lands*.

Terretenant, Terra tenens.

Terriors, Terraria, orum, Co. Ent. 146.

A territory, Territorium, ij, n. 1 Mon. 500. 594. 2 Mon. 99, 132.

T E S.

A Testament, Testamentum, i, n.

A Testator, Testator, oris, m.

Teste is a word used for the last part of every Writ, as *teste meipso, &c.* if it be an Original Writ; or if Judicial, *teste Edwardo Cook*, or *Henrico Hobart*, according to the Court from whence it cometh.

Testification, Testificatio, onis, f.

To testify, Testificor, ari.

Testified, Testificatus, a, um.

A testimonial, or Certificate, Testificatio, onis, f. literæ testimoniales.

A testimony, or Witness, Testimonium, ij, n.

T E T.

Tetbury, in Gloucestershire, Tetocuria.

A Tetter, or Ringworm, Impetigo, inis, f. Lichen, enis, m.

T E W.

Tewkesbury, in Gloucestershire, Theoci curia, Theokesberia.

T H A.

Thames river, Jamesa, Jamissa, Tamesis, Tamensis, Thamesis.

Thames Mouth, Estuarium Tamesæ vel Temesæ.

A

A Thane, Thanus, i, m. Thingus, i, m. (*i. e.*) a Noble Man, the Son of an Earl, alſo an Officer or Miniſter of the King.

A part of the Kings *lands whereof the Governour was called Thane*, Thanagium, ij, n.

Thanet or tanet Iſle, in Kent, Athanatos, Tanathos, Teno, Thanatos, Thanaton, Toliapis.

To Thatch, Intego, ere.

Thatched, Intectus, a, um.

Thatched houſes, Cannitiæ, arum, f. Stramineum tectum, Tectum culmis conſtratum.

A Thatching, Tectura, æ, f.

A thatcher, Tector. oris, m. Calamarius, ij, m.

Thatch, Culmen, inis, n. Stipula, æ, f.

T H E.

A Theater, Theatrum, tri, n.

Theft, Furtum, i, n. Latrocinium, ij, n.

Then next enſuing, Tunc Proxime ſequens.

Then and ſo often, Tunc & toties.

Theobalds or Tibbalds, in Hertfordſhire, Theobaldenſes ædes.

Theobald, a mans name, Theobaldus, i, m.

Theodora, a womans name, Theodora, æ, f.

Theodore, a mans name, Theodorus, i, m.

Theodoſia, a womans name, Theodoſia, æ, f.

Theophilus, a mans name. Theophilus, li, m.

Theorie, Contemplation or Speculation, Theoria, æ, f.

Theorie or theorique, Speculation of an Art without Practiſe, Theorica.

Thetford, in Norfolk, Simomagus, Sinomagus, Sitomagus, Tedfordia, Theodfordum.

Of thetford, Tetfordenſis, Thetfordenſis.

T H I.

A Thicket, Silva, æ, f. Fruticetum, i, n. Dumetum, i, n.

A thief, Fur, Furis, c. 2. Latro, onis, m.

Thief-boat, Rachetum, i, n. (i e) *the Ranſom of a thief.*

The thigh, Femur, oris, n. Femen, inis, n. Coxendix, icis, f.

A thiller, or thill horſe, Veredus, i, m.

A thimble, Digitale, lis, n. Digitabulum, li, n. Tramellum, li, n.

The third, Tertius, a, um.

Thirteen, Tredecim.

The thirteenth, Decimus tertius.

Thirty, Triginta.

The thirtieth, Triceſimus, a, um.

T H R.

A Thrave of Corn, Trava, æ, f. It contains 12 Sheaves, in ſome places 24.

Thread, Filum, i, n.

Thread ſpun or Yarn made ready to ſtuff in the Loom. Stamen, inis, n.

Silk Thread, which Silk Women do Weave in Lintles or Stools. Licium, ij, n.

A skain of Thread, Schænos, i, m. Globus fili.

Waxed Thread, Filum paratum.

To ſpin or make Thread, Filo, are.

To thread a Needle, Acum filo trajicere.

To wind Thread in a Bottom, Glomero, are.

A winder of Thread, Glomerator, oris, m.

A winding of Thread, Glomeratio, onis, f.

Thread wound up, Glomeratum, filum.

Thread in a Needle to sow withal, Acia, æ, f. Aciarium, ij, n.

Threads of Gold, Aurea ſtamina.

Thread by thread, Filatim.

To threaten, or Menace, Minor, ari, Minas proponere.

A Threatner, Minator, oris, m.

A threatning, Minatio, onis, m.

Three, Tres.

Three months ſpace, Trimeſtre ſpatium Ry. 299.

To threſh, Trituro, are, tribulo, are.

Threſhed, Tritus, a um. Trituratus, a, um.

A threſher Triturator, oris, m. Tritor, oris, m, Flagellator, oris, m.

A threſhing, Tritura, æ, f. Trituratio, onis, f.

A place where Threſhing inſtruments are laid up, Tribularium, ij, n.

A threſhold, Limen, inis, n. Liminare, is, n. Hypothirum, i, n.

To make a Threſhold, Limino, are.

A throne, Thronus & Thronum, i, n. Solium, ij, n.

The throat, Guttur, uris, n. Gula, æ, f. Jugulum, li, m.

T H U.

Thule Iſle, Thule, Tilæ.

A Thumb, Pollex, icis, m.

Thurſday, Dies Jovis.

T I B.

Tibbals, ſee Theobalds.

T I D.

The Tide, when the water Ebbeth and Floweth, Fluxus & refluxus Maris. Venilia.

A ſpring Tide, Æſtus Marinus, malina, æ. f.

T I K.

The Tick of a Bed, Culcitra, æ, f.

T I L.

A Tile. Tegula, æ, f.

A gutter Tile or roof tile being half crooked, Imbrex, icis, m.

A Tiler or tile maker, Imbricarius, ij. m.

Tiled, Tegulatus, a, um.

In manner of a Roof Tile, Imbricatim, adv.

A Tiling, Tegulatio, onis, f.

To cover with Tile, Imbrico, are.

A Tile Kiln, Fornax Tegularis.

A ſquare paving Tile, Teſſera, æ, f.

A wooden Tile, or Shingle, Scandula, æ, f.

To Till, Colo, ere, Terram vel agrum ſubigere.

Tillage, Tillagium, ij. n. Cultura, æ, f. Agricultura, æ, f.

A piece of Foreſt or woodland grubbed up; and cleared of Buſhes and fitted for Tillage, Aſſartum, i, n.

A Tiller of Land, Cultor, oris, m.

Till or until, Donec.

Till now, Adhuc, adv.

A Till in a Cheſt, Capſella, æ, f. Capſula, æ, f.

To Tilt a Barrel, Cadum inclinare

A Tiltyard, Catadromus, i, m.

Tim-

T I M.

Timber, Maeremium, ij, n. Co Lit. 53. Lex. 81. Materies, ei, f.

Any Timber to build with, Tignum, i, n.

Any great piece of Timber, the upright piece of timber in the Inner side, which by some are call'd Footstocks, Stamina, orum, n.

The laying of Timber over the Brow or Coping of a Wall, Projectura, æ, f.

A roller laid under Timber for the more easy conveying of it, Hypomochlium, ij. n.

Timbred, or made of Timber, Materiatus, a, um.

A Timbring, or work made of Timber, Materiatio, onis, f.

A sawer of Timber, Pristes, is, m.

To cut Timber, or wood, for work, Materior, ari.

A Timbrel, Tympanum, i, n. Crepitaculum, i, n. Cruma, atis, n.

A Timbrel whereon maids play with their Fingers, Crusma, atis, n.

A brazen or Iron Timbrel, Sistrum, i. n.

To play on a Timbrel, Tympanizo, are.

A Timbrel player, Tympanista, æ, m.

Time, Tempus, oris, n.

For a long Time, à diu.

Time out of mind, à Condito ævo.

Timothy, a mans name, Timotheus, ei, m.

T I N.

A Tincture, Tinctura, æ, f.

Tinder, Fomes, itis, m.

A Tinder box Igniarium, ij, n.

Tine river, in the North, Tina, Tinna, Tinus.

Tinmoth near Newcastle, Tinemutha, Tunnocellum, Tunocellum,

A Tinker, Sercitor ahenorum Sartor vel circuitor ærarius.

Tinkers work, Æramentum, i, n.

Tinn, Stannum, i, n.

A mine of Tinn, Minera tinnei, Plo. 319. Stagnarium, ij, n.

Tinn work, Opus Stannarium.

To Tin or cover with tin, Stanno linere vel inducere.

Made of Tin, Stanneus, a, um.

A Tinner, Stannarius, ij, m.

T I P.

Tipperary County, in Ireland, Tipperariensis comitatus.

A Tippet, Flammeolum, li, n.

A Tipling house, Domus Tipularia. cauponula, æ, f.

T I R.

Tirconel, in Ireland, Conallea.

T I S.

Tissue, Cloth of Gold or silver tissue, made of three threads of divers colours, Trilix, icis, f. Textile, lis, n.

T I T.

Titchfield, in Hampshire, Titchfelda.

Tithes, Decimæ, arum, f.

To Tithe, or take away the tenth part, Decimo, are.

A Tithing, Tithinga, æ, f. 2. Inst. 73. Decenna, æ, f.

A

A Tithing-man, Decennarius, ij m.
A Title, Titulus, li, m.
Intituled, Intitulatus, a, um.
A Title, or speck, Punctum, i, n.

TO.

To, ad, præp.

TOB.

Tobacco, Petum, i, n. Nicotiana, æ, f.
A Tobacconist, Nicotianista, æ, m.
A Tobacco-pipe maker, Tubularius, ij, m.
Toby a mans name, Tobias, æ, m.

TOD.

A Tod, Todda, æ, f, 1 Bul. 131.
A Todd of Wool, containing 28 *pound*, Todda lanæ, Ash. 88.

TOE.

A Toe, Digitus pedis.
The great Toe, Hallus, i, m. Pollex pedis.

TOF.

A Toft, Toftum, i, n. 10 Co. 133. (i. e.) *a Messuage or rather the ground where the old Messuage stood.*
The Owner of a Toft, Toftmannus, i, m.

TOG.

Together, Insimul.
Together with, Simul cum, una cum.

TOI.

Toils, Nets or Haies, wherewith Woods, Parks or Forests are beset to take Wild beasts, Indago, inis, f.

TOL.

Toll at Markets, Tolnetum, *i, n.* 8 *Co.* 46. *Lex.* 125. *Ry.* 10. 16. 127. *Theolonium, ij, n.* 8 *Co.* 96. *Ry.* 11. 13. 48. 195. In our Common Law it hath two significations, First, it is used for a Liberty to buy and sell within the Precincts of a Mannor, *Lamb. Archainom fol.* 132. which seemeth to Import so much as a Fair or a Market. The words are these. *Thol (quod nos dicimus Tholonium) est scilicet quod habeat libertatem vendendi & emendi in Terra sua.* In the second signification, it is used for a Tribute or a Custom paid for Passage, *&c. Bracton.*

The Expositor of the Terms of Law saith thus. *Toll* or *Tolne*, is most properly a payment used, in Cities, Towns, Markets, and Fairs, for Goods and Cattels brought thither to be bought and sold, and is always to be paid by the Buyer, and not by the Seller, except there be some custom otherwise.

Toll for Grist, Multura, æ, f. Reg. 153. 127. Lex. 88. Mulctura, æ, f. Ra. Ent. 9.
A Toll for carrying on horseback, Summagium, ij, n.
Toll paid for weighing Wool, Tronagium, ij, n.
Toll paid by Merchants for Passage, Diabaticum, ci, n.

A

(*i e*) a Duty paid by Barge-men to the owner of the ground where they towed their Barge.

A Towel, Mantile, lis, n. Manutergium, ii, n. Mantelium, ij, n. Extergimentarium, ij, n.

A Tower, or steeple, Turris, is, f.

A little Tower, or Turret, Turricula, æ, f.

A watch Tower, Specula, æ, f. Pharus, ri, d. g.

Womens Towers, or hairs hanging over the forehead, Ananſiæ & anantiæ, arum, f.

A Town, Villa, æ, f.

A Country Town or Village, Villata, æ, f.

A little Town, Oppidulum, li, n.

A Town Incorporate having their proper and especial Officers, Laws, Liberties, and Privileges, Municipium, ij, n.

A Townſman, Oppidanus, i, m.

Towers, the Family, de Turri.

T R A.

A Trace, or tract, Tracea, æ, f. Brac. 106. bis. Veſtigium, ij, n.

To Trace, track, or ſeek out by the footing, Inveſtigo, are

Traced, Inveſtigatus, a, um.

A Tracer, Inveſtigator, oris, m.

To Trade, Mercandizo, are.

A Trade, Ars, tis, f. Negotium, ij. n.

Trades, Myſteria, orum, n.

A Tradeſman, Opifex, icis, m. Negotiator, oris, m.

Trading, Mercatura, æ, f.

A Tradition, Traditio, onis, f.

Traffick, Commercium, ij, n.

To Traffick, Negotior, ari, Mercaturam facere. Negotium tractare.

A Tragedy, Tragœdia, æ, f.

A writer of Tragedies, Tragicus, i, m.

A Traie, whereon meat ſodden or roſted is put, Trulla, æ, f. Concha, æ, f. Alveolus, li, m.

A Traie uſed to carry Mortar in to Maſons, Quailus, i m.

A Trail or border about a Womans Gown, &c. Segmentum, i, n.

Trailed, or that hath Trails or borders finely wrought, with many ſmall pieces, Segmentatus, a, um.

A Trainband, Cohors diſciplinata vel ſelecta.

A Train or Company of ſervants attending on a Prince or Nobleman, Strepitus, ûs, & ti, m. Pompa, æ, f.

The Train of a Womans Gown, Sirma, atis, n

He that beareth a Noble womans Train, Sirmatophorus, ri, m.

The Train of an Army, Impedimenta, orum, n.

To Train up, Trano, are, Inſtruo, ere.

Trained up, Inſtructus, a, um.

A Training up, Diſciplina, æ, f.

A Traitor, betrayer, or he that uſeth Treachery, Traditor, oris, m. Proditor, oris, m.

A Traitor to his Father, Antipater, tris, m.

A Traitor which flieth from his Captain in Battle, and fleeth to his Enemies, Transfuga, æ, c. g.

Traiterous, treacherous, or full of Diſloyalty, Perfidioſus, um.

Pertaining to a Traitor, Proditorius, a, um.

Traiterouſly or diſloyally, Perfidioſe, Proditorie.

A

A Toll for going through a Forest with Carts or Horses loaded, Chiminagium, ij, n.

A Toll for Passage through another mans ground, Paagium, ij, n.

A Toll for the repairing of walls, Muragium, ij, n.

A Toll gatherer, Telonarius, ij, m.

A Tolt, Tolta, æ, f. 1 Mon. 763. Lex. 125.

TOM.

A Tome, a Part, or one Volume of a Book, Tomus, i, m.

TON.

A pair of Tongs, Par forcipium.

The Tongue, Lingua, æ, f.

Tonnage, Tonnagium, ij, n. It is a Custom or Import for Merchandize brought or carry'd in Tonns and such like Vessels from or to other Nations, after a certain Rate in every Tonn. *An.* 12 *Edw.* 4. *c.* 3. *An.* 6 *H.* 8. *c.* 14. *An.* 1 *Jac. c.* 33.

TOO.

A Tooth, Dens, tis, m.

A Tooth-picker or scraper, Dentiscalpium, ij, n.

The Tooth-ach, Odontalgia, æ, f.

Pinchers to pluck out a Tooth, Odontagra, æ, f.

TOP.

The Top, height, or sharp end of a thing, Summitas, atis, f. Culmen, inis, n.

A Top to play withal, Trochus, i, m.

The Top head of a Pillar, Capitellum, i, n.

The Top of the Mast of a Ship, Carchesium, ij, n. Thoracium, ij, n.

Topicks, Books that speak and treat of Places of Invention touching Logick, Topica, orum, n.

TOR.

Torcester, in Northamtonshire, Torcestria, Tripontium.

A Torch, Torcherus, i, m. 4 Co. 98. Fax, facis, f.

A little Torch, Facula, æ, f.

A Torch or Taper-bearer, Facularius, ij, m.

A Torch-maker, Lichnopæus, i, m.

TOS.

To Tost, Torreo, ere.

A Tost, Tostus panis.

Tosted, Tostus, a, um.

A Tosting Iron, Tostorium, ij, n. Artopta, æ, f.

TOT.

Totnes, in Devonshire, Totonesium.

TOU.

A Touch-stone, Lydius lapis.

Tournament, a Marshal exercise on Horseback, Torneamentum, i, n.

TOW.

To Tow a ship, Remulco, are.

A Tower, Helciarius, ij, m.

Tow or hirds, Stupa, æ, f. Lini floccus, Lina stupa.

Little Tow or hirds, Stupula, æ, f.

Towage, Towagium, ij, n. *Ry.* 29. *Thowagium batellorum*, *Ry.* 27.

(*i e*)

A Tramel net, Tragum, i, n. Tragula, æ, f.

A Tramel for a Pot-hanger, Cremaſter, ſteris

To Tranſcribe or Copy-out of one thing into another, Tranſcribo, ere.

To Tranſlate from one Language to another, Interpretor, aris. Verto, ere.

Tranſlated, Tranſlatus, a, um. Verſus, a, um.

A Tranſlator, or Interpreter, Tranſlator, oris, m.

A Tranſlation, Tranſlatio, onis, f. Interpretamentum, i, n. Verſio, onis, f.

To Tranſmit, Tranſmitto, ere.

Tranſmutation, Tranſmutatio, onis, f.

A Tranſom, or beam going overthwart an Houſe, Tranſtrum, i, n.

The Tranſom, or croſs piece of a Jacobs ſtaff, Tranſverſarium, ii, n.

A Tranſom, or Lintle over a door, Superliminare, is, n.

A Tranſom, or piece of Timber four Inches thick, Trientalis materia.

The Tranſoms in a Ship whereon the Hatches be made, Canonia.

To Tranſport, carry or conveigh over, Tranſporto, are.

Tranſported, Tranſportatus, a, um.

To Trap, barb or dreſs Horſes with Trappers, Ephippio, are.

Trapped, barbed or dreſſed with Trappers, Ephippiatus, a um. Phaleratus, a, um.

Trappers, trappings or barbs for Horſes, Phaleræ, arum, f. Lorica equi, Strata, orum, n.

They that have Sadles on their Horſes Trapped with Coſtly harneſſes, Ephippiarij, orum, n.

To Trap, or take in a trap, Irretio, ire.

Trapped, or taken in a Gin or Snare, Irretitus, a, um. Captus, a, um.

A Trap, Snare or Gin, Decipula, æ, f. Tendicula, æ, f.

The ſnare or fall of a Trap, Rupius, ii, m.

A Trap for Mice or Rats, Muſcipula, æ, f. Muriſtrecula, æ, f.

A Traverſe, Traverſia, æ, f. It took the name of the French *de Traverſe*, which is no other than *de traverſo* in Latin, ſignifying, on the other ſide, becauſe as the Indictment on the One ſide chargeth the Party, ſo he on the other ſide cometh in to diſcharge himſelf. *Leigh Phil. Com.* fol. 228. It ſignifieth in our Common Law ſome time to deny, ſome time to overthrow or undo a thing, as by Denying and Traverſing a Bill, or the material parts thereof, and the formal words of this Traverſe are in Lawyers French *Sanſceo*; and *abſq; hoc*, in *Latin*. See *Kitchin*, fol. 227. *Titulo affirmationis & negationis.*

To Traverſe an Indictment, is nothing elſe but to make Contradiction, or to deny the point of the Indictment. As in a Preſentment againſt *A.* for a High way over flown with Water, for default of ſcouring a Ditch, *&c.* *A.* may Traverſe either the matter, *viz.* that there is no High-way there, or that the Ditch is ſufficiently ſcoured, or otherwiſe he may Traverſe the Cauſe that he hath not the ground. *Lamb. Eirenarch. Lib.* 4. *cap.* 13. *pag.* 521, 522. Of Traverſe ſee a whole Chapter in *Kitch.* fol. 240.

See new book of Entries *Verbo* Traverſe.

To Traverſe, Traverſo, are. Diſrationo, are.

A Traveller of Countrys or Journys; Viator, oris, m.

A Traveller on the High-way, Hadœporus, i, m.

To Travel, or go on a Journy, Itineror, ari.

T R E.

Treacle, Theriaca, æ, f.

The Treadle of a Weavers Loom, Inſile, lis, n.

Treaſon, Proditio, onis, f Treaſon is deriv'd from *Trahir*, which is Treacherouſly to betray, *Trahiſon, per contractionem*, Treaſon.

If a Man be arraign'd for High-Treaſon, and ſtands Mute, or will not directly anſwer to the Crime, Judgment ſhall be given upon him, as upon a Traitor Convict. Fatetur facinus qui Judicium fugit *L. Dyer.*

In Treaſon concealment is as Capital as the Practice. Here are no acceſſaries, all are in a like Predicament of offence and danger of Law, *in Majori proditione omnes ſunt principales.*

It is either High or Petty-Treaſon. It is call'd High in reſpect of the King which is the Higheſt Perſon: Petty in regard of the Inferiority of the Perſons againſt whom it is committed. *Voluntas non reputabitur pro facto niſi in cauſa proditionis.*

To Intend or Imagin the Death of the King or Queen, though it be not effected, yet if this be declar'd, by an Open Act, or utter'd by words, or Letters, it is Treaſon.

Proditorie *muſt neceſſarily be uſed in every Inditement of Treaſon.*

A Man that is a Traitor Convicted and Attainted, hath his Judgment to be drawn upon a Hurdle from his Priſon to the Place of Execution as being unworthy to Tread any more upon Mother Earth, and that Backward, with his Head downward, for that he hath been Retrograde to Natural Courſes; after hang'd up by the Neck between Heaven and Earth, as deem'd unworthy of both; his Privy parts are cut off, as being unprofitably begotten, and unfit to leave any Generation after him: his Bowels and Intrals burned, which Inwardly had conceived and concealed ſuch horrible Treaſon; Then his Head cut off that Imagin'd the miſchief. *Stawnf. pl.* of Cr. *lib.* 3. cap. 19. with Dr. *Boys* his Gloſs. vid. Petit Treaſon.

Treaſonably, Proditionaliter, adv. Reg. 102.

Treaſure(or abundance of Riches) Theſaurus, ri, m.

A Treaſure houſe, Theſauraria, æ, f. Ry. 96. Domus Theſauraria.

Lord Treaſurer, Dominus Summus Theſaurarius Angliæ. He is a Lord by his Office, and one of the greateſt Men in the Land, under whoſe charge and Government is all the Princes Wealth contain'd in the Exchequer, as alſo the Check of all Officers any way Imployed in the Collecting of the Impoſts, Tributes, or other Revenues belonging to the Crown. Sir *Thomas Smith, de Rep. Angl. lib.* 2. *cap.* 14. alſo more belonging to his Office, ſee *Anno* 20. *Ed.* 3. *c.* 6. & *Anno* 31. *H.* 6. *cap.* 5. & *Anno* 4. *Ed.* 4. *cap.* 1.

1. *& Anno* 17. *ejusdem cap.* 5. *& Anno* 1. *R.* 2. *cap.* 8. *& Anno* 21. *H.* 8. *cap.* 20. *& Anno* 1. *Ed.* 6. *cap.* 13.

This High Officer hath by vertue of his Office, the nomination of the Escheators yearly throughout *England*, and giveth the places of all Customers, Comptrollers, and Searchers in all the Ports of the Realm. He sitteth in the Exchequer Chamber, and with the rest of the Court ordereth things to the Kings best Benefit. He with the Barons may by Statute Stall Debts of 3000 *l.* and under; and by Commission from his Majesty, he with others joyned with him, letteth Leases for Lives or Years of the Lands that came to the Crown by the Dissolution of Abbeys: He by his Office giveth Warrant to certain Men to have their Wine without Impost. He taketh declaration of all the Mony paid into the Receipt of the Exchequer, and of all Receivers accounts.

Treasurer of the Kings Houshold, Thesaurarius Hospitij Domini Regis. He is always of the Privy Council, and in the absence of the Steward of the Kings Houshold, hath power with the Comptroller, and the Steward of the Marshalsea to hear and determine Treasons, Misprisions of Treason, Murder, Homicide, Bloodshed committed within the Kings Palace. *Stawnf. pl. Cor. lib.* 3. *ca.* 5.

To Treat of, or handle a matter, Tracto, are.

A Treatise, or handling of the matter, Tractatus, ûs, m.

A Treaty, or truce after Battel, Fœdus, eris, n.

A Tree, Arbor, oris, f.

A little Tree, Arbuscula, æ, f.

The twig of a Tree, Virga, æ, f.

The stock or main body of a Tree, Caudex, icis, m.

The stock or stump of a Tree without Boughs, Truncus, ci, m.

The main bough or branch of a Tree, Ramus, i, m. Brachium arboris.

A seared or dead bough cut off, and lopt from the Tree, Ramale, lis, n.

A bough or branch broken, or pluckt away with the fruit thereupon, Termes, itis, m.

The bark, or outward rind of a Tree, Cortex, icis, m.

The inner Pill, or rind, of a Tree, Liber, bri, m.

The Pith, sap or life, of a Tree, Medulla arboris, Fructus, matrix.

A Tree with young fruit on it, Arbor Prægnans.

A low Tree, Humilis Arbor.

To set a place with Trees for Vines to grow by, Arbusto, are.

To top Trees, Toppare arbores, Plo. 469. Ra. Entr. 490.

To grow to the bigness of a Tree, Arboresco, ere.

A Nursery of young Trees, Arboretum, i, n.

A Lopper of Trees, a Dresser or Planter of Trees, Arborator, oris, m.

A Grove of Trees, Arbustum, i, n.

An Alder-Tree, Alnus, i, f.

An Apple-Tree, Malus, li, f.

An Ash-Tree, Fraxinus, i, f.

A Wild-ash-Tree with broad leaves, Ornus, i, f.

The Place where ash-Trees grow, Fraxinetum, i, n.

A Beach-Tree, Fagus, gi, f.

A Grove where Beach-Trees grow, Faginetum, i, n.

A Birch Tree, Betula & Betulla, æ, f.

The Box tree, Buxus, i, f.

A Broom-tree, Genista, æ, f.

A Cherry-tree, Cerasus, i, f.

A Chestnut-tree, Castanea, æ, f.

A Cypress-tree, Cupressus, si, vel, ûs, f.

A Damson tree, Prunus, i, f.

An Elder-tree, Sambucus, ci, f.

An Elm-tree, Ulmus, i, f.

An Elm Grove, or Place set full of Elms, Ulmarium, ij, n.

The Ivie-tree, Hedera, æ, f.

A Juniper-Tree, Juniperus, ri, f.

A Maple Tree, Acer, eris, n.

A Medler-Tree, Mespilus, li, f.

An Oak-Tree, Quercus, ci, f.

The Place where Okes grow, Quercetum vel Querquetum, i, n.

An Osier or Twig, Vimen, inis, n.

The Place where Osiers and Twigs are set to bind Vines, Virgetum, i, n.

A Peach-Tree, Malus Persica.

A Pear Tree, Pyrus, i, f.

A Plum-Tree, Prunus, i, f.

A Place set about with Plumb-Trees, Prunetum, i, n.

A Poplar Tree, Populus, li, f.

The white Poplar-Tree, Farfugium, ij, n.

A Place where Poplar Trees grow, Populetum, i, n.

A Quince-Tree, Cydonia, æ, f.

A Sallow-Tree, Salix, icis, f.

A Grove of Sallow Trees, Salictum, i, n.

A Servise-Tree, Sorbus, bi, f.

A Place where servise Trees grow, Sorbetum, i, n.

A Tamarisk-Tree, Myrica, æ, f.

A Vine-Tree, Vitis, is, f. Vinea, æ, f.

A Walnut Tree, Juglans, dis. f.

A Place where Walnut Trees grow, Juglandiarium, ij, n.

A Warden Tree, Volemum, i, n.

A Willow Tree, Salix, icis, f.

A Place where Willow Trees grow, Salicetum vel Salictum, i, n.

A Withe (or Osier) Tree, Siler, eris, n.

A Yew Tree, Smilax, acis, f. Taxus, xi, f.

A Treen (or Wooden dish) Catinus ligneus.

A Trench, Trenchea, æ, f. Ra. Entr. 441. Reg. 127. 252. 10. Co. 143. Trenchia, æ, f. Fo. 369. 1 Mon. 911. Militare Sepimentum. Vallum, i, n. Aplectum, i, n.

To Fortify and inclose with a Trench, Vallo, are. Prævallo, are.

A Trencher (to eat meat on) Quadra, æ, f.

A round Trencher, Orbis mensarius.

A Plate Trencher, Scutella, æ, f.

A Trendel of a Mill, Moluchrum, i, n.

Trent River, Trehenta, Trenta, Terentus.

A Trespass, Transgressio, onis, f. The Law adjudgeth every Trespass to be done with Force and Arms; therefore the Plaintiff, that saith the Defendant took his Horse with Force and Arms (tho he came without Weapons) saith truly that he took him with Force, as the Law meaneth force. *Dr.* and *Stud. cap.* 14. If *vi & armis* be not in the Writ, it shall abate. *Fitz. Nat. Brev.*

The Law accounteth all to be *vi* which is contrary to *Jus*. I do but Hawk or Walk for my pastime or Recreation over another Man's Ground,

Ground, he may have his Action of Trespass against me, *quare vi & armis*, for tho I meant no harm to him or his, yet I might not Pass upon his Ground without Licence, *Leigh Phil. Com. fol.* 228.

The form of a Writ for living things, as Horses, is, *cepœrunt & abduxerunt*; for a dead thing, *cœperunt & asportaverunt. Fitz Herb. Nat. Brev. Tit. Tresp. Transgressio dicitur à transgrediendo*, because it over passeth that which is Right. *Cook* on *Lit p.* 57.

A Tressel (or three footed stool) Tripus, i, m.

A Tressel for a table, Trapezophorus, i, m.

Tressels, Trestoria, orum, n. Fle. 79.

Womens Tresses, Tressoria Mulierum, Fle. 69.

T R I.

A Triangle (a figure that hath three Corners) Triangulus, i, m.

Triangular (or having three Corners) Triangulus, a, um. Triangularis.

Tribute, Tributum, i, n. Vectigal, alis, n.

A Trigger (or Instrument put in the Cart wheel, least the Cart be overthrown) Sufflamen, inis, n.

To Trim (as Barbers do) Tondeo, ere. Ornare comam & barbam.

To Trim up a thing to make it seem fairer, Mangonizo, are.

Trinity House. Domus Trinitatis. Is a certain House at *Deptford* which belongeth to a Company or Corporation of Sea-faring Men, that have power by the King's Charter, to take knowledge of those that destroy Sea-marks, and to Redress their doings, as also to Correct the faults of Saylers, *&c.* and to take Care of divers other things belonging to Navigation and the Seas. *Anno* 8. *Eliz. cap.* 13. *Anno* 35. *ejusd. cap.* 6.

A Tripe, Omasum, i, n.

A Tripe laid in souse, Omasum conditum.

A Tripe woman (she that sells Tripes) Allantopolis, is, f.

The Place where Tripes are sold (such as Field lane) Allantopolium, ij, n.

A Triumph, Triumphus, i, m.

To Triumph, Triumpho, are.

Tristram, a mans name, Tristramus, i, m.

T R O.

A Trochisk, a Medicine made round like a Top, or Bunn of Bread, Trochiscus, ci, m.

A Troop or Company of Souldiers, Agmen, inis, n. Turma, æ, f.

To Trouble, or molest, Vexo, are. Disturbo, are. Turbo, are.

Troubled, Turbatus, a, um.

A Kneading Trough, Artopta, æ, f. Mactra, æ, f.

A Trough, or Binn, to keep Corn in, Alveus, ei, m.

A Trough to feed Swine, Aqualiculus, i, m.

A Trough of Stone, Lapista, æ, f.

A Trowell, Trulla, æ, f.

T R U.

A Truant, or Loyterer, Emansor, oris, m.

A Truce, Treuga, æ, f. Armistitium,

um, ij, n. Indufiæ, arum, f. pugnæ ceſſatio.

True, Verus, a, um.

Truly, Quidem, adv.

Trumpery, or old Baggage, Scruta, orum, n.

A Trumpet, Tuba, æ, f. Buccina, æ, f.

To ſound a Trumpet, Buccino, are. Clango, ere.

The ſtopple of a Trumpet (or wind Inſtrument) Tappa, æ, f.

A Trumpeter, Buccinator, oris, m. Tubicen, cinis, m. Salpicta, æ, m.

A Trumpet maker, Æreator, oris, m. Tubarius, ij, m.

To ſound the alarm on the Trumpet, Signum dare buccinâ, Claſſicum canere.

The ſound of the Trumpet when they blow to the Battel or Alarm, Bellicum, ci, n. Claſſicum, ci, n.

The ſound of the Trumpet, Clangor Tubæ.

A Writhed or Crooked Trumpet, Lituus, ui, m. Concha, æ, f.

A Truncheon, or Stake, Talea, æ, f. Clava, æ, f.

A little Truncheon, Taleola, æ, f.

A Trunk or Cheſt covered with Leather, Riſcus, ci, m.

A Trunk-maker, Riſcarius, ij, m.

To Truſs or tye up, Subſtringo, ere. Ligulas ſtringere.

To Truſs up the Hair, Crinem nodo cohibere.

To Truſs, Stuff, or make a Fardel, Suffarcino, are. Convaſo, are.

Truſſed up together, Suffarcinatus, a, um.

Truſſed, or girt about, Succinctus, a, um.

A Truſſing point, Ligula, æ, f. Strigmentum, i, n.

A Truſs, Fardel or Burden, Sarcina, æ, f.

A Truſs of Hay, Fœni manipulus.

A Truſs for ſuch as are burſten, Hernioſorum Faſcia.

A Truſs whereunto a mans horſe is tyed, Exomis, is, f.

A Truſſing up, Subligatura, æ, f. Sarcinatio, onis, f.

To Truſt, or have a ſure confidence, Fido, ere. Confido, ere.

Truſt, or Fealty, Fidelitas.

Truſted, Fiſus, a, um. Creditus, a, um.

Truſtees, Fiduciarij.

Truſty, Sure or faithful, Fidus, a, um. Fidelis, le, adj.

T R Y.

To Try a Cauſe, Trio, are.

A Tryal, Triatio, onis, f. (i. e.) the Tryal of a Cauſe.

Ready to Try, Paratus Sacramento Recognoſcere.

A Tryer, Triator, oris, m. (i. e.) one Choſen by the Court, to Examine whether a Challenge made to the Panel, or any of the Panel, or Jury, be Juſt, yea, or no. *vid. Brook titulo* challenge, *fol.* 122. & *Old Nat. Brev. fol.* 158. *Spel.* 204. *Doct & Stud.* 20.

T U B.

A Tub, or great Vatt, Cupa, æ, f. Vaſ, aſis, n.

A Tub fit for ſerviceable waſhing or to be bathed in, Labrum, i, n. Baptiſterium, ij, n. Solium, ij, n.

A Bucking (or Bathing) Tub, Cucuma, æ, f. Liximatorium, ij, n.

A Tub ſet under the tap to Receive

ceive Droppings, Sinum, i, n. Excipulum, li, n.

A meal Tub, Cumera, æ, f.

A powderimg Tub, Orca, æ, f. Carnarium, ij, n.

An open Tub or Stand, Aquiminarium, ij, n.

T U C.

A Tucker, or Fuller, Fullo, onis, m.

Tuckers, or Fullers Earth, Fullonica, æ, f. Fullonium, ij, n.

T U E.

Tuede or Tees, in the Bishoprick of Durham, Tuefis.

Tuesday, Dies Martis.

T U F.

A Tuft or Crest, Crista, æ, f. Apex, icis, f.

A Tuft of Grass, Cespes, itis, m.

T U I.

Tuition, or safe keeping, Tutela, æ, f. Tuitio, onis, f.

T U M.

A Tumb, Tumba, æ, f. Tumulus, li, m. Sepulchrum, i, n.

To put in a tumb, Intumbo, are. Tumulo, are.

A tumbler, Hister, ri, m.

A tumbler which danceth through a Hoop, Petaurista, æ, m. Cybister, ri, m.

A tumbler that walketh on a Rope, &c. Neurobata, æ, m. Funambulus, li, m.

A tumbler, or Dog so called, Vertagus, gi, m.

A tumbrel, or Cucking-stool, Tumbrellum, i, n. Ra. Ent. 540. Cow. 265. Terbichetum, i, n. Tribithetum, i, n. Turbichetum, i, n.

It is an Engine of Punishment which ought to be in every Liberty that hath view of Franck Pledge, for the bridling of Scolds and Unquiet Women. *Kitchin fol.* 13.*a.*

A tumor, or swelling, Tumor, oris.

A tumult, Tumultus, ûs, m.

Tumultuously, Tumultuose, adv.

T U N.

A Tune, Tonus, i, m.

To Tune (or Measure, also to tune or accent) Modulor, ari.

To set a Tune to One, Præmodulor, ari

Tuned, Modulatus, a, um.

He that Tuneth in measure, Modulator, oris, m.

A Tuning of the Voice, Modulatio vocis.

A Tunn, Tonna, æ, f. 2 Mon. 528. (i. e.) a Measure containing 252. Gallons.

Tunnage, Tunnagium, ij, n. Lex. 127. a Custom or Impost for Merchandize brought or carried in Tunns or such like Vessels, from or to other Nations after a certain Rate in every Tunn. *anno* 12. *Ed.* 4. *cap.* 3. *anno* 6. *H.* 8. *cap.* 14. *anno* 1. *Jac. cap.* 33. also a Duty due to the Mariners for unloading their Ship arriv'd in any Haven, after the Rate of every Tunn.

A Tunnel where thro' Liquor is poured into Vessels, Infundibulum, li, n. Infusorium, ij, n. Tonelius, ij, m.

Tunnel of a Chimney, Fumarium, ij, n. Spiramentum, i, n.

A Tunnel in the Roof to let out Smoak, Epigaustorium, ij, n.

T U R.

Turbary, Turbaria, æ, f. Co. 265. Ry. 339 Ra. Ent. 540. Liberty of digging Turves.

Common of Turbary, Communia Turbariæ.

Turbage, Turbagium, i, n. Lex. 127. 1 Mon. 632.

Turbervil (the Family) de Turbida villa.

Turchill (the Family) Turchetiffus.

A Turf, Turba, æ, f. Gleba, æ, f. Terricidium, ij, n.

A Turky Cock, Gallus Numidicus.

A Turky Hen, Gallina Numidica.

To turn (as turners do) Torno, are.

A Turner, Tornator, oris, m.

A Turners Instrument, wherewith they make things smooth by turning up and down, Tornus, i, m.

That is wrought (or made with a wheel or Turn) Tornatus, a, um. Tornatilis, le, adj.

Turners works, Opera Tornatilia Toreumatum, ti, n.

A Turn-broach, Tornarius, ij, m.

To turn up and down, Affurcillo, are.

A Turn-key, Clavicularius, ij, m.

Turn, Turnum, i, n. Is the Sheriff's Court kept every Year twice, once after Easter, and again after Michaelmas, *Mag. Charta cap.* 35. and that within one month after each Feast *An.* 3. *Ed.* 3. *c.* 25. from this Court are Exempted only Arch-Bishops, Bishops, Abbots, Priors, Earls, Barons, all Religious Men and Women, and all such that have hundreds of their own to be kept.

Turno Vicecomitum. Is a Writ that lyeth for those that are called to the Sheriffs Turn out of their own hundred. *Regist. Orig. fol.* 174.

A Turret of Wood, Fala, æ, f.

T U T.

A Tutor, Tutor, oris, m.

Tutors and Overseers of Orphans, Authores Pupillorum.

A Tutor or Guardian not bound to give an account of his Ward, Analogista, æ, m.

T W E.

Twede River (in the North) Tueda, Tuesis, Tweda.

Twelve, Duodecim, Indecl.

Twelve times, Duodecies, adv.

The twelfth, Duodecimus, a, um.

The Feast of twelftide, Festum Epiphaniæ Domini.

Twenty, Vigenti, Indecl.

The twentieth, Vicesimus, a, um.

T W I.

A Twibill (or Ax) Bipennis, is, f.

A young Twig (or Osier) Vimen, inis, n. Surculus, li, m.

The twig of a tree cut off, Sarmentum, i, n.

Twilight, Crepusculum, li, n.

Twinhamburn (in Dorsetshire) Interamna.

A Twin, Gemellus, li m.

To twist, Torqueo, ere.

Twisted, Tortus, a um.

T W O.

Two, Duo.

Two-

Twomond (in Ireland) Thuetmonia, Twomondia.

T Y R.

A Tyrant, Tyrannus, i, m.
Tyranny, Tyrannis, idis, f.

T Y T.

Offerings and all small Tythes due to the Priest, Altaragium, ij, n. Obventio Altaris.
Not Tythable, Indecimabilis, le. vid. *Tithes.*

V A C.

A Vacation (or the time between the Terms) Vacatio, onis, f.

V A G.

A Vagabund, Vagabundus, a, um.

V A I.

A Vail, Velum, i, n. Velamen, inis, n.
Belonging to a Vail, Velaris, re, adj.

V A L.

Vale River (in Cornwall) Fala.
Valemouth (or Falmouth, in Cornwall) Voluba.
Vale of the Cross (in Denbighshire) Vallis Crucis.
Valence, the Family, de Valentia.
Valentine, a Man's name, Valentinus, i, m.
Valentine's day, Festum sancti Valentinj Episcopi & Martyris.
A Valet, or Gentleman of the Privy Chamber, Valettus, i, m. Valecta, æ, f. also a Benchers Clerk.
Valetor, or Vautor, the Family, de Valle Torta.
A Valley, or Dale, Vallis, is, f.
Value, the worth of any thing, Valentia, æ. f.
Valuable, Valibilis, le, adj. Vet. Intr. 185.

V A N.

A Vane, or weather cock, Triton, onis, m.
Vandeles, in the Bishoprick of Durham, Vinduglessus.
A Van-guard, or the fore-ward in Battail. Antegardia, æ, f. Kit. 208.

V A S.

A Vassal, one that holdeth Land in Fee of his Lord, Vassallus, li, m.
A kind of Vassal, Alpimanus, i, m.

V A T.

A Vate, or Fat, Vas, asis, n. Labrum, i, n. Vas pressorium.
A Great dying Vate, Ahenum, i, n.
A Cheese Vate, Casearium, ij, n.

V A V.

A Vavasour, one in Dignity next a Baron, Vavasor, & Valvasor, oris, m.
The Estate, or Lordship of such a one, Vavasoria, æ, f.
A Vault, or Roof, Fornix, icis, m.
A Vault low in the Ground, Crypta, æ, f. Hypogæum, i, n.
Made like an arch or Vault, Testudineatus, a, um.

To

To make a Vault, Fornico, are.

Vaux (the Family) de Valibus.

U D D.

An Udder, Uber, eris, n.

V E A.

Veal, Caro vitulina.

To Vear a Cable or to Roll it up in a round Circle, Gyrare Rudentem.

V E I.

A Vein, Vena, æ, f.

V E L.

Velum, Membrana, æ, f. Pergamena, æ, f.

Velvet, Velvetum, i, n. Ra. Ent. 3. Velvettum, i, n. Co Entr. 565. Holosericum, ci, n.

V E N.

Vendible, Vendibilis, le, adj.

Venial (or pardonable) Venialis, le, adj. Venire facias, Is a Writ Judicial and goeth out of the Record lying where two parties plead and come to Issue, *scilicet*, upon the saying of the Country, for then the party Plaintiff or Defendant shall have this Writ directed to the Sheriff, that he cause to come 12 Lawful men of the same Country to say the Truth upon the said Issue taken. And if they come not at the day of this Writ returned, then shall go out a *Habeas Corpora*, and after a distress, until they come. *Old. Nat. brev. fol.* 157.

Venison, Caro Ferina.

Venison season in Winter, Ferisona, æ, f.

A Vent-hole, Spiraculum, li, n.

Ventre *Inspiciendo*, is a Writ for the Search of a Woman, that saith she is with Child, and thereby withholdeth Land from him that is the next Heir at Common Law. *Regist. Orig. fol.* 227. a.

Venus (a Womans name) Venus, eris, f.

V E R.

A Verderor, Viridarius, ij, m. Co. 168. 1 Mon. 574.

A Verdict, Veredictum, i, n. It is the answer of a Jury or Inquest made upon any Cause Civil or Criminal, committed by the Court to their Consideration or Tryal.

The Verge (or Compass of the Kings Court being 12 *miles about)* Virgata, æ, f.

Vergers, Virgatores, Lex 129.

Vergivian, or Western Sea, Oceanus Vergivius. Vergivium Mare.

To Verify a thing, Verifico, are.

Verily (or Truly) Vere, adv.

Verjuice, Omphacium, ij, n.

Vernish, Vernix, icis.

By Vertue of a Deed, Feoffment, Lease, &c. Virtute.

Vertuous, Virtuosus, a, um.

Verulam, an ancient City near St. Albans (in Hertfordshire) Cassivelauni oppidum. Verolamium. Verulamium. Virolamium. Urolamium. Urolanium.

V E S.

Vescy (the Family) de Vesci.

A Vessel of what kind so ever, Vas, vasis, n.

A little Vessel, Vasculum, li, n.

An

An Oyl Vessel made of Leather, Scortia, æ, f.

A wine Vessel, Vinarium, ij, n.

A great Vessel for Wine as a Vat, Orca, æ, f.

A Vessel with Cold water to Rinse Cups in, Luterium, ij, n. Baucalis, is, f.

A Vessel to wash Feet, Podoniptrum, i, n.

A Vessel used by Goldsmiths to wash away Dross, Thermastris.

He that makes Vessels of Silver or Gold, Vascularius, ij, m.

A vessel of any sort to Sail in, Navigium, ij, n.

A Vessel or Ship to Carry Anchors in, Ancyromachus, chi, m.

The Master (or owner of a Vessel) Ratiarius, ij, m.

A Vestry in a Church, Vestiarium, ij, n. Sacrarium, ij, n.

A Vestry keeper, Sacrista, æ, m.

A Vestment (or Garment) Vestimentum, i, n.

Vesture, Vestura, æ, f. (i. e.) Possession or admittance to a Possession. West 2 chap. 25. Anno 13. Ed. 1.

The Corn that grows on it, Vestura terræ.

A Vetch, Vicia, æ, f.

A Place sowed with Vetches, Viciarium, ij, n.

Of Vetches, Viciarius, a, um.

V I A.

A Viage, Viagium, ij, n. Reg. 191. Pry. 85. 121. 2 Mon. 367.

A Vial (or Glass) Phiala, æ, f. Lecythus, i, m.

A Vial with a Big Belly, Ampulla, æ, f.

A Vial maker, Ampullarius, ij, m.

V I C.

A Vicar, Vicarius, ij, m.

A Vicarage, Vicaria, æ, f.

Vice-Chamberlain, Vicecamerarius Hospitij Domini Regis, An. 13. R. 2. Stat. 2. cap. 1. Is a great Officer in Court next under the Lord Chamberlain, and in his absence hath the Command and Controlment of all Officers appertaining to that part of his Majesty's Household which is call'd the Chamber, wherein is concluded as well the Bed-chamber, as the Privy-chamber, the Presence and the Great-chamber, and all other Rooms and Galleries, &c. thereunto belonging, with the Council chamber, Privy-closet, &c. and in the Lord Chamberlains absence, he Commandeth and Overseeth the Attendants of all to whom it appertaineth to be ready and waiting on his Majesty going to the Chappel, or to Speak with Ambassadors, or else Walking or Riding forth.

A Vicechancellor, Vicecancellarius, ij, m.

A vicecount (or viscount) Vicecomes, itis, m. It is a degree of Nobility next unto an Earl, which as Mr. Cambden saith, is an old name of Office, but a new name of dignity never heard of amongst us until H. 6. his days, but this Degree of Honour is more ancient far in other Countries. Cassan. in gloria mundi. part. 5. consid. 55.

A vicegerent, Vicegerens.

A viceroy, Prorex, egis, m. Surregulus, li, m. Vicarius Regis.

A victory, Victoria, æ, f.

Victuals, Victualia, orum, n.

A victualler, one that sells victuals, Victualarius, ij, m. Lex. 130. Vitellarius, ij, m. Opsopœus, œi, m.

A victualling, Vitellatio, onis, f. Ra. Ent. 211.

A Victualling House, Domus victualaria, Caupona, æ, f.

A victualling (or ale) house, Gutturilla, æ, f.

V I E.

Vies or Devises (in Wiltshire) Castrum de vies, Devisæ, Divisio.

A viewing of Urin, Inspectio lotij.

A View of Frank Pledge, Visus Franci Plegij.

V I G.

By Vigor, or force, Vigore.

V I L.

A Village belonging to some town or Mannor, Berwica, æ, f. Villa Frumentaria.

A little village, Villula, æ, f. 1 Mon. 599. 650. 2 Mon. 610

A Villein, Villanus, i, m.

Villenage, Villenagium, ij, n. (i. e.) *Servile Tenure.*

V I N.

Vincent, a man's name, Vincentius, ij, m.

A vine, Vitis, is, f.

A vine running upon a Latteſſed frame, Brachiata vinea.

A vineyard, Vinetum, i, n. vinea, æ, f.

A vine dresser, Vinitor, oris, m.

To Prune a vine, Castrare vitem.

Vinegar, Acetum, i, n.

A vinegar-maker, Acetarius, ij, m.

A vintener, Vintenarius, ij, m. *Stat. de Collistrigio*, Vinarius, ij, m.

V I O.

A Viol to play on, Pandura, æ, f. Cithara, æ, f.

A viol maker, or he that playeth on a Viol. Pandurarius, ij, m.

To Play on a Viol, Pandurifo, are.

V I P.

Vipont or vipount, the Family, de vetei P onte.

V I R.

The Virginals, Clavecymbalum, i, n.

A virgin, Virgo, inis, f.

The Feast of the visitation of the blessed virgin, Festum visitationis beatæ Mariæ virginis.

Virgil, a man's name, Virgilius, ij, m.

V I S.

A Visne, or venew, Visnetum, i, n. Vicinetum, i, n. (i. e.) a Neighbour place, or a place near at hand, *An 16. R. 2. cap. 6.*

V I T.

Vital, a man's name, Vitalis, lis, m.

Vitsan, in France near Callis, Iccius portus, Itius, Itium Galliæ. Itinus portus.

A

V I Z.

A Vizard, or mask, Larva, æ, f.

U L C.

An Ulcer, Ulcus, eris, n.

The Cavities of an Ulcer, Sinus Ulceris.

An Ulceration breaking out in Scab or Sore, Ulceratio, onis, f.

To Ulcerate, Ulcero, are.

U L S.

Ulster (in Ireland) Ulidia. Ultonia.

U M P.

An Umpirage (or award made by an Umpire) Umpiragium, ij, n.

An Umpire. Umpirator, oris, m.

U N A.

Unaccustomed, Insuetus, a, um.

Unadvised, Inconsideratus, a, um.

Unarmed, Inermus, a, um.

U N C.

An Uncle, Avunculus, i, m. (*i e*) *an Uncle by the Mothers side*.

An Uncle (or Fathers Brother) Patruus, ui, m.

The Great Uncle (or Grandfathers Brother) Propatruus, ui, m.

The Great Uncle (or Grandmothers Brother) Proavunculus, li, m.

U N D.

To Underprop, Præfulcio, ire.

An Underproping (or undersetting) Suffultura, æ, f. Fulcrum, i, n.

To Underset (or set under) Suppono, ere.

To Understand, Intelligo, ere.

An Understanding, Intellectus, ûs, m.

Under-Treasurer of England, Vicethesaurarius Angliæ An. 39. Eliz. cap. 7. & An. 43 ejusdem. This Officer as some think was first Created in the time of King *Henry* the Seventh, to Chest up the King's Treasure at the end of every Term, and to Note the Content of the mony in each Chest, and to see it carried to the Kings Treasury in the Tower, for the ease of the Lord Treasurer as being a thing too mean for him to be troubled withal, and yet meet to be performed by a man of great Service and Trust. This Officer in others Judgment is far more ancient than King *Henry* the Sevenths days, yet not named Treasurer of the Exchequer till Q. *Elizabeths*'s time, where he is termed Under-Treasurer of *England*, notwithstanding *Anno* 35. *Eliz*. he is also written Treasurer of the Exchequer. Read the Statutes. *Anno* 18. *Ed*. 3. *Stat*. 2. *cap*. 17. & 27. *ejusd*. *Stat*. 2. *cap* 18. 1 *Rich*. 2. *cap*. 5. 4. *Hen*. 4. *cap*. 18. 8 *Hen*. 6. *cap*. 17. 27 *Hen*. 8. *cap*. 11. with divers other Places that seem to approve this to be true.

U N I.

Universal, Universalis, le, adj.

An University, Academia, æ, f. Universitas, atis, f.

Unjust, Injustus, a, um.

Unjustly, Injuste adv.

U N K.

Unknown, Incognitus, a, um.

U N L.

Unlawful, Illicitus, a, um.
Unlearned, Indoctus, a, um.
Unlike, Dissimilis, le, adj.
Unlimited, Interminatus, a, um.
To Unload, Discarco, are. Ra. Entr. 3. 409. Lex. 44.
An Unloading, Discarcatio, onis, f.

U N P.

Unplowed, Inaratus, a, um.

U N S.

Unsold, Invenditus, a, um.

U N T.

Untouch'd, Intactus, a, um.
Untrue, Falsus, a, um.

V O I.

A voidance, Vacatio, onis, f. It is a want of Incumbence upon a Benefice, and this Voidance is double: either in Law, or in Fait or Deed: In Law, as when a man hath more Benefices incompetible; in Fait, or in Deed, as when the Incumbent is dead, or actually deprived, *Brook Titulo, Quare impedit.* 51.

Void, Vacuus, a, um.

To make void, Frustro, are. Frustratoria dilatio. Ra. Entr. 603.

V O L.

A volunteer, Voluntarius, ii, m.

V O U.

To Vouch (Call, or Warrant) Voco, are.

A Voucher (or he that voucheth) Vocans, tis, m. Advocator, oris, m. Spel. 23. It is a calling in of one into the Court, at the Petition of a Party that hopeth to be helped thereby. New book of Entries *verbo voucher. Voucher de Garrantie. Britton. cap.* 75. *in Latin, Advocatio ad Warrantizandum*, is a Petition in Court made by the Defendant to have him call'd, of whom he or his Ancestor bought the Land or Tenement in Question, and received Warranty for the secure enjoying thereof against all men, that he may either defend the Right against the Demandant, or to yield him other Land. *Bracton* writeth a large Treatise of it, *Lib.* 5. *Tract.* 4. *per totum.* See *Littleton* in the last Chapter of his Tenures, *Fitz. Horb. Nat. Brev. fol.* 134 *de Warrantia Chartæ.*

There is a Common Voucher and a double voucher. Cook Lib. 2. *Sir.* Hugh Cholmleys *case, fol.* 50. *b.* This is very answerable to the Contract in the Civil Law, whereby the Buyer bindeth the Seller, sometime in the simple value of the thing bought, sometime in the double, to Warrant his secure enjoying of the thing bought. But this difference is between the Civil and Common Law, that whereas the Civil Law bindeth every Man to Warrant the security of that which he selleth, the Common Law doth not so, except it be especially Covenanted. The Party that voucheth in this Case, is called the Tenant; The Party vouched is termed the *vouchee*; The Writ whereby he is call'd, is termed *Summoneas ad Warrantizandum, vid.* Terms of Law, *verbo voucher.* and *Lambert* in his Explication of Saxon Words, *verbo advocare.* *vide Warranty.*

A vouchee, Advocatus, i, m Spel. 23.

U P H.

An Upholster, Culcitrarius, ij. m. Tapetiarius, ij, m. Plumarius, ij, m.

An Upholsters Trade, Plumarium, ij, n.

U P L.

Upland (Highland) Uplanda, æ, f.

U R B.

Urban (a man's name) Urbanus, i, m.

U R D.

Urdhead a Promontory (in Scotland) Berubium.

U R E.

Ure river, in Yorkshire, Urus.

U R I.

Urine, Urina, æ, f.

An Urinal, Urinarium, ij, n.

The sediment at the bottom of an Urinal, Hypotasis, is, f.

U R S.

Ursly, a Womans name, Ursula, æ, f.

U S A.

An Usage, Usagium, ij, n. 1 Mon. 502. 978. 2 Mon. 1016. Usuagium, ii, n. 1 Mon. 504 981.

U S H.

Ushant Isle on the Coast of France, Axantos, Uxantissena.

An Usher of a School, Hypodidascalus, li, m. Subpræceptor, oris, m.

U S K.

Uske Town, in Monmouthshire, Castrum Oscæ, Burrium.

Uske river, in Monmouthshire, Isca, Osca.

U S U.

Usury, Usura, æ, f.

To lend upon Usury, Usuro, are.

An Usurer, Usurarius, ij, m.

A Griping Usurer, Ærarius mergus.

Usurpation, Usurpatio, onis, f.

U T E.

Utensils, Utensilia.

To Utlaw, Utlago, are.

Utlawed, Utlagatus, a, um.

An Utlawry, Utlagaria, æ, f. Utlagatio, onis, f. Placit. Cor. 18. Lex. 131. It is a Punishment for such as being called in Law and Lawfully sought, do contemptuously refuse to appear. He that is sued, must be called at five Counties, a Month being between every County, to answer to the Law, and if he come not within that time, *pro exlege tenebitur, cum Principi non obediat, nec legi, & extunc utlagabitur*, and shall lose all his Goods and Chattels to the King: If upon Felony, his Lands and Tenements. *vide* Terms of Law, *Titulo* Utlagarie. *vid* Outlawry.

To

UTT.

To Utter, Uttero, are.

The Uttermost, Extremus, a, um.

Uttoxiter (in Staffordshire) Etocetum.

VUL.

Vulgar, Vulgaris, re, adj.

The vulgar Tongue, Lingua Vulgaris, Lingua vernacula.

UVU.

The Uvula, or Palate of the Mouth, Uvula, æ, f.

UXB.

Uxbridge, in Middlesex, Uxinus Pons.

WAD.

TO *Wade, also to Wade over*, Vado, are.

WAF.

A Wafer, Libum, i, n.

Wafters, Waftores, m, pl. Officers that Guarded our Fishermen chiefly on the Coast of *Norfolk* and *Suffolk*.

WAG.

To Wage, or put in Pledges to do any thing, Vadio, are.

To Wage Law, Vadiare Legem.

To Wage deliverance, Vadiare Liberationem averiorum.

Wager, a giving Security, or putting in Pledges to do a thing, Vadiatio, onis, f.

Wager of Law, Vadiatio Legis.

Wager of Battel, Vadiatio duelli.

To lay a Wager, Fortunæ deponere.

Wages, Salarium, ij, n. Stipendium, ij, n. Merces, edis f.

A Wagon, Rheda, æ, f.

W A.

A Wagoner, Rhedarius, ij, n.

The Rack staves of a Wagon, Scirpiculus, li, m.

A seat in a Wagon Esseda, æ, f.

WAI.

A Waife, Waivium, ij, n. 2 Inst. 163. Brac. 8. Wavium, ij, n. It is properly when a Thief being pursued and having Stollen Goods about him, doth leave or forsake them, that he may fly away. *Cook. 5. Rep. Foxleys* Case.

Wainage, Wainagium, ij, n. (i e) the Furniture and appurtenances of the Wain, also Land Tilled, and the Profits arising from it.

A Wain, Plaustrum, i, n.

A Wain driver, Plaustrarius, ij, m.

A Wain-house, Wannagium, ij, n.

Wainscot, Tabulatum, i, n. Opus Intestinum.

To Wainscot, Contabulo, are. Opere intestino vestire parietes, Tabulis parietes vestire.

A Wainscotting, Incrustatio materiaria.

A Waiter, Anclator, oris, m.

A Waiting Woman, or Gentlewomans maid, Pedissequa, æ, f.

To Waive, Waivio, are.

Waive, the waiving of a Woman, as outlawing is of a Man, Waiviaria, æ, f. Waive is a Woman that is Outlaw'd, and she is called Waive, as left out or forsaken of the Law, and not an Outlaw, as a Man is, for Women are not sworn in Leets to the King as Men are, which be of the age of 12 Years or more. *Cook on Lit. Lib. 2. cap. 11. Sect. 186.*

A

A Woman waived, Fæmina waiviata, *Reg.* 132, 135, 277. This word waived belongeth to a Woman, that being sued in Law, contemptuously refuseth to appear, as the word Outlawed doth to a Man, for a Man is said in such contempt Outlawed, and a Woman waived, *Regist. Orig. fol.* 132. *b.* and 277. *a.* the reason whereof see in *Fitz. nat. brev. fol* 161. *a.*

Goods waived, Bona waiviata. 1 *Co.* 29.

W A K.

Wakefield (in Yorkshire) Wakefeldia.

W A L.

A wald (plain or down) Walda, æ, f.

Walden, *See* Saffron Walden.

Wales, Wallia, æ, f. *Davis*, 35. Cambria, Gualæ, Guinethia Gwallia.

A walk (or walking place) Ambulacrum, cri, n.

A private walk, Ambulatorium, ii, n.

A walk or cloyster before a Church, Propylæum, i, n.

An open walking-place, to walk in out of the Rain or Sun, Xystus, sti, m.

Walking under Piazza's, Subbasilicanus, a, um.

A night-walker, Noctuabundus, a, um.

To wall in or about, Muro, are. Circummunio, ire. Cingere Muro.

To make walls, Parieto, are.

A wall, Paries, etis, m. Wallia, æ, f. *Reg.* 92, 108, 127. 5. *Co.* 100. *Ry.* 548. Ac walliæ videlicet decem virgatæ in Longitudine & tres virgatæ latitudine Walliarum duorum molendinorum aquaticorum fuerunt fractæ, diruptæ & spoliatæ, *&c.* Hill 14. and 15. *Car.* 2. *Rotulo* 726. *Modus Intrandi*, fol. 120.

A wall about a House, Dissepium, ii, n.

A brick wall, Paries testaceus, Paries lateritius, Muri coctiles.

A wall of stones heaped together without mortar, Maceria, æ, f.

A partition-wall, Paries Intergerinus, Muri dividentes.

A mid-wall serving for Rooms, Paries medianus.

A mud wall, Lutamentum, i, n.

A wall made of flint stone, Silicatus Murus.

A rough wall, made of Lime and Sand, Paries cæmentitius.

Walls made of Laths, Splints and Studs, Parietes arrectarii, Concratitii, vel Cratitii.

The Toothing of a wall, Dentatio, onis, f

The utter wall before a House, Promurale, lis, n.

An arched wall, Paries fornicatus.

An enclosure made with walls unartificially built, Rudis parietum circumjectus.

The wall in Staffordshire a Mile from Litchfield, Etocetum.

Wall of Adrian, Hadriani murus.

Walled about, Armata muris.

A wallet, Mantica, æ, f. Bisaccus, ci, m.

A wallet to put Victuals in, Corycium, ii, m.

Bearing or carrying of a wallet, Manticatus, a, um.

Wallingford (in Berkshire) Calena, Caleva, Galeva, Gallena, Galleva.

Walsingham (*in Norfolk*) Parathalassia.

Walls end near Newcastle, Vindobala, Vindomara.

Walter (*a man's name*) Walterus, i, m.

Waltown (*in—*) Ad-murum.

Walwick (*in Northumberland*) Galava, Gallava.

W A N.

Wandle River (*in Surrey*) Vandalis.

Wandlesbury, a Fort on the Hills near Cambridge, Vandelbiria.

Wantage or Wanting (*in Berkshire*) Vanatinga.

W A P.

A wapentake (*or Hundred*) Wapentakium, ii, n. *Cow.* 277. Wapentagium, ii, n. 2 *Inst.* 99.

W A R.

A ward, Warda, æ, f. Warda in Civitate. Ward hath divers applications as a Ward in *London*, which is a Portion of the City committed to the special Charge of one of the four and twenty Aldermen of the City, in such sort that every one knoweth the Ward assigned unto him, and hath dwelling within the same compass some Grave Citizen for the good Government thereof, who is in that respect a Deputy unto the said Alderman, and called the Alderman's Deputy. Of these Wards there are five and twenty within the City, and one without, besides other Liberties and the Suburbs, *Stowes Survey of London.*

A ward (*or rather a Valet*, Quasi Vassalatus) Vallettus, i, m.

Wardmote, Wardemotus, i, m. The Court of every Ward in *London.*

Wardpenny, Wardagium, ii, n. (*i e*) Money paid for the Warding of a Castle.

A Warden, Guardianus, i, m. *Cow.* 128. *Spel.* 324.

Warden of the Cinque Ports, Gardianus quinque Portuum.

Warden of the Fleet, Gardianus Prisonæ Domini Regis de le Fleet.

Warden of a Forest, Gardianus Forestæ Domini Regis de Waltham.

A Church-warden, Gardianus Ecclesiæ.

A warden (*Fruit*) Volemum, i, n.

The King's Wardrobe, Garderoba, æ, f. Vestiarium, ii, n.

Keeper of the Wardrobe, Custos Garderobæ Domini Regis.

Ware Town (*in Hertfordshire*) Wara.

Ware that is bought and sold, Mercimonium, ii, n. Merx, cis, f.

A ware-house, Repositorium, ii, n. Receptaculum, ii, n.

A ware-house-man, Solidarius, ii, m.

Earthen ware, Figlinum, i, n.

A seller of Wares, Venditor, oris, m.

A warming pan, Thermoclinium, ii, n, Caleficium Lectuale.

Warminster (*in Wiltshire*) Verlucio.

A warrant, Warrantum, i, m.

A warranty, Warrantia, æ, f. 2 *Inst.* 137. *Ry.* 92. *Co. Lit.* 383. *Lex.* 131.

A warranty is a Covenant real annexed to Lands or Tenements whereby a Man and his Heirs are bound to warrant the same.

There are two kinds of warranties, *viz.* Express by deed, Lineal, Collateral, Implyed by Law, *viz* that commenceth by Disseisin, *Co.* 1. *Inst.* 365. *a.* It is called a Lineal warranty not because it must descend upon the Lineal Heir, for be the Heir Lineal or Collateral if by Possibility he might claim the Land from him that made the warranty, it is a Lineal warranty, but if the Title to the Land be Collateral (*i. e.*) if one claims the Land not as Heir to him that made the warranty, in respect of the Title, it is a Collateral warranty, *Co.* 1. *Inst.* 370. *a.*

A warranty is not called Collateral in respect of the Blood, for the warranty may be Collateral albeit the Blood be Lineal, and the warranty may be Lineal albeit the Blood be Collateral, but it is in Law deemed a Collateral warranty, in respect that he that maketh the warranty is Collateral to the Title of him upon whom the warranty doth fall. *Co.* 1 *Inst.* 376. *a.*

A warranty that commenceth by Disseisin is Regularly when the Conveiance whereunto the warranty is annexed doth work a Disseisin. *Co.* 1. *Inst.* 366. *b*

To warrant, Warrantizo, are.

A warranty in deed or an Express warranty is Created only by this word, Warrantizo, but warranties in Law are created by many other words, *Co.* 1. *Inst.* 384. *a.*

He that makes a warranty, Warrantus, i, m.

Warrantia chartæ, Is a Writ that lies to compel the defendant to warrant Lands, *&c.*

To Warrant (or take upon him the Guarranty) Guaranto, are

War, Guerra, æ, f. Bellum, i, n.

In warlike manner, Modo Guerrino, *Ry.* [illegible]. 253. *Spel.* 314. *Pry.* 6[illegible]

To make war, Bello, are. Belligero, are.

A civil war, Bellum Intestinum

A jack (or horse man's Coat of defence) in war, Wambasium, ii, n.

A warriour (or man of war) Bellator, oris, m. Duellator, oris, m. Prœliator, oris, m.

Men of war always about the standard, Campigeni milites.

A man of war upon the Seas, Classiarius, ii, m. Navis præsidiaria

Goods got by service in war, Peculium castrense

A Council of war, Prætorium, ii, n.

A nimble charger in the war, Concursator, oris, m.

To prepare for a new war, Redintegrare Bellum.

All the Points of war, Armaturæ omnes numeri.

A war-horse, Bellator Equus, Equus agminalis.

A gally for war, Bellatrix triremis.

Ordnance or furniture of war, Instrumentum Bellicum.

Warlike, Bellicus, a, um.

Pertaining to war, Bellatarius, a, um.

Warren (the Family) De Warenna.

Warren (a man's name) Warinus, i, m.

A warren, Warenna, æ, f. *Reg.* 109. 93, 96. 110. Vivarium, ii, n. *Lex.* 130. 2. *Inst.* 100.

A warrener, Warrennarius, ii, m. *Placit. Cor.* 140. *Stat. de Malefac. in parcis.*

Warwick Town (in Warwickshire) Præsidium, Verovicum, Vervicus, Warwicus.

Warwickshire, Warwicana Provincia, Warwici comitatus.

W A S.

A wase (or wreath) to be laid under a Vessel, that is born on the Head, Cesticillus, i, m.

To wash, Lavo, are.

To wash all over, or clean, Diluo, ere.

A wash ball, Smegma, atis, n.

A seller of wash-balls, Smegmatopola, æ, m.

Washed, Lotus, a, um. Lavatus, a, um.

A washer, Lotor, oris, m.

A wash house, Lavatrina, æ, f.

A washing, Lavatio, onis, f. Lotio, onis, f.

A washing place, Aquarium, ii, n.

A washing beetle, Pala lotoria.

The Washes (in Norfolk) Metaris æstuarium.

The wast (or midle) Cinctura, æ, f. Cingulum, li, n.

To wast (usually applyed to Executors) Devasto, are.

Wast made upon Lands or Woods by a Tenant for Life, Estrepamentum, i, n.

The wast of woods and hedgerows that Cattle feed on, Pennagium, ii, n. Panagium vel Pannagium, ii, n. It also signifieth the Money that is given for it.

A wasting or consuming of Goods, Imbesilatio, onis, f.

Wast, Vastum, i, n. Wast is where Tenant for term of years, Tenant for term of Life, or for term of anothers Life, Tenant in Dower, or Tenant by the Courtesie, *&c.* commit wast to the prejudice of the Heir, or of him in the reversion or remainder, *Kitchin* fol. 168, &c. *usque* 172. doth make wast or spoil of Houses, Woods, Gardens, Orchards, *viz.* by pulling down the House, cutting down Timber, or suffering the House to fall, or diggeth up the ground, then he in the reversion shall have a Writ of wast, and shall recover the place where the wast is done and treble damages. But if a Man cut down Timber and repaireth old Houses, this is no wast. But if he with the Timber build a new House, then the cutting down of the Timber is wast.

A wast in the Forest is, where a Man cutteth down his own Woods without Licence of the King or of the Lord Chief Justice in *Eyre* of the Forest, *Manwood.* 1. *part.* Forest Laws, *pag* 172. Or in the Forest Plough up his own Meadow or Pasture and converts it into Tillage, *part.* 2. *cap* 8 *num.* 4. and 5.

Brook holds that the Executors shall have glass, for the House (saith he) is perfect without it. *Brooks abridg. Tit. Chattels, pag.* 135. *B.* Yet it was adjudged in the common Pleas, that a wast may be committed in Glass, annexed to the Windows, for it is parcel

parcel of the House, and shall descend as parcel of the Inheritance to the Heir, and Executors shall not have it, and although that the Lessee himself at his own Costs, put the glass in the Windows, yet this being once parcel of the House, he cannot take away this, or wast it. *Cook on Lit. Lib.* 1. *cap.* 7. *Sect.* 67. Glass annexed to the Windows by nails, or after other manner by the Lessor or Lessee, cannot be removed by the Lessee, for without glass it is no perfect House, and by a Lease or Grant of a House this shall pass as parcel of it, and the Heir shall have it, and not the Executors, and peradventure a great part of the Costs of a House consists of Glass, and if they be open in a Tempest and Rain, wast of the Timber of the House will follow. *Cook Rep. Harlakenden's case, fol.* 63, 64.

Also it was resolved, that if Wainscot be annexed to a House by the Lessor or Lessee, it is part of the House, and there is no difference in the Law whether it be fastned with great or little nails, or by Screws or Irons put through Posts or Walls. But if it be any of these ways, or any other fixed to the Posts or Walls of the House, the Lessee cannot remove this, but he is punishable in an action of wast, for this is part of the House, and by Lease, or Grant of the House shall pass as parcel.

By an Action of wast at our Law, the Plaintiff if it be found for him, shall recover Treble damages, *Fitz. nat. brev. fol.* 58. *b.*

For permissive wast no action lies against Tenant at Will, but for Voluntary wast, a general action of Trespass lies, *Cook lib.* 5. *Rep. Countes. de Salop fol.* 13.

If a House be uncovered (whereby the Sparrs or Rafters, or other Timber of the House are Rotten) when the Tenant cometh in, it is no wast in the Tenant to suffer the same to fall down. But though the House he Ruinous at the Tenants coming in, yet if he pull it down, it is wast, unless he re-edifie it again.

Though there be no Timber growing upon the ground, yet the Tenant at his peril, must keep the Houses from wasting. If the Tenant do, or suffer wast to be done in Houses, yet if he repair them before any action brought, there lieth no action of wast against him; but he cannot plead *quod non fecit vastum*, but the special matter, *Cook on Lit. Lib.* 1. *cap.* 7. *sect.* 67.

A wall uncovered when the Tenant cometh in, is no wast, if it be suffered to decay. If the Tenant cut down, or destroy any fruit Trees growing in the Garden or Orchard, it is no wast. *Id. ib.*

If the Tenant build a new House it is wast, and if he suffer it to be wasted, it is a new wast.

Wast properly is in Houses, Gardens, in Timber Trees, *viz.* Oak, Ash and Elm; either by cutting of them down, or Topping of them, or doing any act whereby the Timber may decay. *Cook. Id. ib.*

 If

If a House be ruinous at the time of the Lease made, if the Lessee suffer the House to fall down, he is not punishable, for he is not bound by Law to repair a House in that Case, and if he cut down Timber upon the ground so letten, and repair it, he may well justifie it; and the reason is, because the Law doth favour the supportation and maintenance of Houses of Habitation for Mankind, *Cook id. ib.*

Wast in another signification as Year, Day, and Wast, *annus, dies & vastum*, is a punishment or forfeiture belonging to Petit Treason, or Felony, whereof you may read, *Stawnf. pl.cor.lib. 3. cap. 30.*

A wast-coat, Subucula, æ, f. Inducula, æ, f. Esophorium, ii, n.

W A T.

To watch, Vigilo, are.

To watch and work by candle light, Lucubro, are.

A watch-man, Vigilarius, ii, m.

A scout watch, Speculator, oris, m.

A watch-word, Symbolum, li, n.

He that bringeth or giveth the watch word, Tesserarius, ii, m

A watch-tower, Specula, æ, f

To watch about the King whilst asleep, Advigilare somno Regis.

A watch house, Vigilarium, ii, n.

A watch (or Clock that strikes not) Horarium, ii, n Horologium Viatorium.

A watch going seven days, Horologium motionem habens per septem dies.

A watch with the days of the month, &c, Horologium monstrans dies mensis, ætatem Lunæ, ac Fluxus & Refluxus maris.

Water, Aqua, æ f

River water, Aqua fluminea.

Spring water. Aqua fontana.

Well water, Aqua puteana.

An instrument to gage water, Watergagium, ii, n.

A water-gang (or water-course) Watergangia, æ, f. Watergangia, æ, f. Watergangium, ii, n. Aquarum cursus.

A little current of water dry in the Summer, Sikettus, i, m.

An overflow of water, Rufullum aquæ, *Fle 268. 2. mon. 913.*

A vessel of water, Soricula, æ, f.

A thing to sprinkle water with, Aspergillum, li, n.

A water Conduit, Cancello, onis, m.

A water wheel, Rota aquatica.

A water-course to a Mill, Gurges molaris.

A water-pot, Aqualis, is, m.

The water pot or thing that Birds drink in, being fastned to their Cage, Potristris, is, m.

A water-trough, Aqualiculum, li, n. Alveus aquarius.

He that searches and scours water-channels, Hydrophanta, æ, m.

A water-man (or boat-man) Remex, igis, m.

A water-man's Pole, Contus, i, m.

Waterdone (in——) Aquadunensis saltus.

Waterford (in Ireland) Batilfordia, Dunum, Manapia, Waterfordia.

The County of Waterford (in Ireland) Waterfordiensis Comitatus.

Watling-street-way, Vetilingiana via, via Consularis.

W A V.

Waveney river (*in Norfolk*) Avona.

W A X.

Wax, Cera, æ, f.

To wax (*or dress with wax*) Cero, are.

Covered with wax, or waxed, Ceratus, a, um.

A wax-chandler, Cerarius, ii, m.

A wax-chandlers wife, Ceraria, æ, f.

W A Y.

A way, Chiminus, i, m. Via, æ, f. It is the high-way where every Man goeth, which is called *Via Regia*, and yet the King hath no other thing there, but the passage for him and his People: For the Freehold is in the Lord of the soil, and all the profit growing there, as Trees and other things. It is divided into two sorts, the Kings high way and a private way, *Kitch fol* 35. The King's high way is that, by which the King's Subjects and all others under his Protection, have free liberty to pass, though the property of the soil of each side where the way lieth, may perhaps belong to some private Man.

A way private is that, by which one Man or more have liberty to pass either by Prescription or by Charter, thorough another Man's ground.

A stopping or blocking up of the way, Forestallamentum, i, n.

A cross-way, a way where many ways do meet, Compitum, i, n.

A way having two Paths, Bivium, ii, n.

A place where three ways meet, Trivium, ii, n.

W E A.

Weadon on the street (*in Northamptonshire*) Bannavenna, Bannaventa, Issannavantia, Issannavaria, Issannavatia.

Weald of Kent, Saltus Andred. It is the woody part of the Country. Master *Verstegan* saith, that *Wald*, *Weald*, and *Wold*, differing in vowel, signifie one thing, *viz.* a Wood or Forest.

Wealth (*goods or substance*) Copia, æ, f. vid. Riches, Goods.

Wealthy (*or full of wealth*) Copiosus, a, um, Locuples, pletis, &, ior, us, adj.

A common-wealth (*or weal publick*) Respublica, æ, f.

To wean, Ablacto, are.

Weaned, Ablactatus, a, um.

A weaning, Ablactatio, onis, f.

To furnish ones self with weapons, Armo, are.

Weapons, Arma, orum, n. *pl.* Armamenta, orum, n.

Defensive weapons, Arma defensiva.

Offence weapons, Arma offensiva.

The use of weapons, Armatura, æ, f.

A weapon made wholly of Iron, Soliferreum, ei, n.

A weapon having three points, Tridens, tis, m

A weapon like a Boar spear, Sabina, æ, f.

Weaponed, Armatus, a, um.

 Weaponless,

Weaponless (or without weapons) Inermis, e, adj.

℞ *Which beareth weapons*, Tēlifer, ra, rum, adj.

To wear (or wast by wearing) Variego, are Tero, ere.

To wear a Garment, Gesto, are.

A wear (or dam) Wera, æ, f. 1. *Mon.* 590. 983. *Lex.* 133. Wara, æ, f.

A wear in a River, Boera, æ, f. pro Wera. Moles, is, f. Cataracta, æ, f.

A wear (or Kidle) with a cut in it for laying of Weels to catch fish in, Kidellus, i, m. 2. *Inst.* 38. *mag. Chart. cap.* 23. *Spel.* 420. *Lex.* 75.

Wear River (in the Bishoprick of Durham) Wirus.

The weasand of a man's Throat, Gurgulio, onis, f. Gula, æ, f.

The weasand or wind-pipe of the Lungs, Trachea vel Trachia, æ, f.

A weasel, Mustela, æ, f.

Weather, Aura, æ, f. 1. *Fo.* 135.

Fairness of Weather, Serenitas, atis, f.

A weather (or gelded Sheep) Vervex, ecis, m.

Weathers, Muttones, 2. *Cow.* 39. Verveces.

A weather-cock (or vane) Triton, onis, m. Versoria, æ, f. Penniculum, li, n. Index venti, Ventilogium, ii, n.

To weave, Texo, ere.

To weave to the end, Pertexo, ere.

To weave in, or with another thing, Intexo, ere.

To twist or weave together, Contexo, ere.

To weave round about, Circumtexo, ere.

To weave or joyn to after, Subtexo, ere.

To weave Silk, Bombycino, are. Bombycinum facere

Weaved (or woven) Textus, a, um.

Weaved (or wrought between) Intertextus, a, um.

A Weaver, Textor, oris, m.

A woman Weaver, Textrix, icis, f.

A Silk-weaver, Sericarius, ii, m.

A Linen-weaver, Linteo, onis, m.

A Weaver's Shop, Textrina, æ, f.

A Weaver's Beam or Rundle whereon they turn their Web at hand, Jugum, i, n Jugum Textorium.

A Weaver's Loom, Machina Textoria.

A Weaver's Shuttle (the Yarn-Beam, Liciatorium, ii, n.

A Weaver's Spole, Panus, i, m.

A Weaver's Warp, Stamen, inis, n.

The Thread in weaving called the Woof or West, whereunto the Warp is tyed, Subtegmen, inis, n.

A Weaver's Slay in his Loom, having Teeth like a Comb, Pecten, inis, m.

A Woof in weaving, (or the Weaver's Tram) Trama, æ, f.

The Tredle of a Weaver's Loom, Insile is, n.

A Weaver's Shuttle-threads, Licia, orum, n.

A Weaver's bottom of Yarn, Glomus, i, m. vel, eris, n.

Stuff fit for weaving, Linutum, i, n.

A weaving, Textus, ûs, m. Textura, æ, f

Of or belonging to a weaver or weaving, Textorius, a, um.

W E B.

A Webb of Cloath, Tela, æ, f.

The long roughness of the webb, Pexitas, atis, f.

A webb of Lead, Charta plumbea.

The webb (or pearl) in the Eye, Albugo, inis, f.

Webley Town (in Herefordshire) Weableia.

W E D.

To wed. Vide, *to marry.*

A wedding-house, Nuptorium, ii, n.

A wedge, Cuneus, ei, m.

An Iron wedge, Cuneus ferreus.

To cleave with a wedge, Cuneo, are.

A little wedge, Cuneolus, li, m.

A great wedge or ingot of Gold, Palacra, æ, f.

A little wedge of Gold, Pala, æ, f.

Wedged, Cuneatus, a, um.

Wedge-wise, Cuneatim, adv.

Wedlock, Matrimonium, ii, n. Conjugium, ii, n.

Wednesday, Dies Mercurii.

W E E.

To weed, Sarrio, ire, Sarculo, are.

To weed again, Resarrio, ire.

To weed or pull up weeds, Erunco, are.

To weed with a weeding-hook, Runco, are.

A weeder, Sarritor, oris, m. Runcator, oris, m.

A weeder-woman, Poastria, æ, f.

A weeding, Sarritio, onis, f. Runcatio, onis, f.

A weeding-hook, Runcina, æ, f. Sarculum, li, n.

A weed, Gramen noxium.

A week, Septimana, æ, f. Hebdomada, æ, f.

Weekly, Septimanatim, adv.

He that waits in his week, Hepdomarius, ii, m.

Of a week, Hebdomarius, a, um.

W E.

The week or match in a Candle, Myxus, i, m. Ellychnium, ii, n.

A weel or gin to take or keep Fish in, Nassa, æ, f. Excipulum, li, n.

Weels to take Eels, Caudecæ.

A little weel, Tendicula, æ, f. Scirpulus, li, m.

W E I.

To weigh, Pondero, are. Libro, are.

A weigh (of Cheese, Wool, &c. of 256 pounds) Waga, æ, f. Spel. 226. Lex. 134. 1 Mon. 515. Weya, æ, f. Pry. 303. Waya, æ, f. Fle. 73. Wayea, æ, f. Cypha, æ, f. Spel. 426. Vaga, æ, f. Vet. Intr. 235. and so used in the Exchequer.

To weigh for tryal, Pensiculo, are.

An officer to weigh wool, Tronator, oris, m.

A weighing, Pensura, æ, f. Librario, onis, f.

The art of weighing, Statice, es, f.

Of weighing, Staticus, a, um.

A Toll paid for weighing, Trona, æ, f. Tronagium, ii, n.

A weight (or poise) Pondus, eris, n.

A pound weight, Librata, æ, f.

Too much weight, Nimietas ponderis Reg. 100.

That which is put into the Scale to make up even weight, a Counterpoise, Tergimentum, i, n. Sacoma, atis, n.

The difference of weight between the buyer and seller, Interpondium, ii, n.

Equality of weight, Æquilibritas, tatis, f.

Of equal weight, Æquilibris, bre, adj.

Gold weight, Æquilibrium, ii, n. Libramentum, i, n.

To try by weight, Penso, are.

A weight to jump with, Halter, eris, m.

A pair of Weights to weigh Wool, Bilancium, ii, n.

Weights,

Weights, Pondera. There are two sorts in use with us, the one called *Troy* weight, which containeth twelve Ounces in the Pound and no more, by which Pearl, Precious stones, Gold, Silver, Bread, *&c.* are weighed. The other is called *Averdupois*, which containeth sixteen Ounces in the Pound. By this all other things are weighed that pass between Man and Man by weight, saving only those above named. All our weights and measures have their first composition from the Penny Sterling, which ought to weigh 32 wheat Corns of a middle sort, twenty of which Pence make an Ounce, and 12 such Ounces a Pound or 60 Shillings, but 15 Ounces make the Merchants Pound, though an Ounce less, should be all one in signification with the Pound of *Averdupois*, and the other Pound called by *Fleta Trone* weight, plainly appeareth to be all one with that we call *Troy* weight, *Fleta*, *Lib.* 2. *cap.* 12.

Weisford (in Ireland) Menapa, Menapia, Wassordia, Weshfordia.

W E L.

Weland River (*in Northamptonshire*) Welandus.

Welch Maylor or Bromfield (*in Denbighshire*) Mailoria Wallica.

Welch-men, Walani, Wallenses.

A welch man, Wallus, i, m.

A well, Puteus, ei, m.

A little well, Puteolus, li, m.

The cover of a well, Puteal, ālis, n.

A wells mouth, or brim, Crepido, inis, f.

A Digger or searcher of a well, Putearius, ii, m.

Of or belonging to a Well, Puteālis, le, adj.

Wells City (*in Somersetshire*) Fontanenses Ecclesiæ, Theodorodunum, Wellæ.

Of wells, Wellensis.

Bishop of Bath and Wells, Episcopus Bathoniensis & Wellensis.

The welt of a Garment, Limbus, i, m. Fimbria, æ, f.

A little welt, Laciniola, æ, f.

To welt or hemm, Prætexto, are.

A welting, Prætextura, æ, f.

The welt of a Shooe, Intercutium, ii, n.

W E N.

Wentsbeck, or upon the River Wentsbeck, Clamoventa, Clanoventa, Glannibanta, Glanoventa.

Wentworth (*a mans name*) Wentworthius, ii, m.

W E R.

Were River (*the Bishoprick of Durham*) Vedra, Verus, Wirus.

Wereburgh (*a woman's name*) Wereburga, æ, f.

Wergild, Wergildus, i, m (*i.e.*) the price of a Man's Life, so much as one paid in ancient times for killing a Man.

Werwick on Eden (*in Cumberland*) Virosidum.

W E S.

The West, Occidens, ntis, m.

Western, Hesperius, a, um.

West-

West-part, Pars occidentalis.
A western-wind, Ventus occidentalis.
Western Britains, Occidentales Britones.
Western Islands of Scotland, Ebudæ, Incades, Hebrides, Lucades.
Westminster, Visimonasterium, Westmonasterium.
Westmorland (see People of Westmorland) Westmaria, Westmoria, Westmorlandia.
West-saxons, Visi-Saxones.
West-wales, Demetia.

W E V.

Wever River (in Cheshire) Weverus.

W H A.

A whale, Cœtus, i, m.
Wharfe River (in Yorkshire) Guersa, Verbeia, Wherfus.
A wharfe, Wharfa, æ, f. 1. *Co.* 19. *Co. En.* 536. *Lex.* 134. It is a broad plain place near to a Creek or Hith of the Water, to lay wares upon, that are brought to or from the Water, to be transported to any other place. New Book of Entries. 3. *Col.* 3.
Wharfage, Wharfagium, ii, n. Kaiagium, ii, n. (*i. e.*) Money paid for loading or unloading goods at a Wharfe.
A wharl or whern to put on a spindle to spin with, Verticulum, li, n.

W H E.

Whealp castle (in Cumberland) Calacum, Gallatum, Gallagum.
Wheat, Triticum, ci, n. Frumentum, n.
Wheat yielding very white flower, Frumenta Lactentia.
Of or belonging to Wheat, Triticeus, a, um.
Wheatly Bridge (in Oxfordshire) Veteleganus pons.
A wheel, Rota, æ, f.
A little wheel, Rotula, æ, f.
The strake of a Wheel, which is either the Iron bound about the Wheel, or the Round hoop of wood, in which the spoaks are put, peradventure so called, because it makes a strake in the gound as it goeth, *Canthus, i, m.*
A water-wheel to draw water, Haustrum, i, n. Hauritorium, ii, n.
A spinners wheel, Rhombus, i, m.
The spoke of a wheel, Radius rotæ.
A Turners wheel, Tornus, i, m.
A Cart-wheel, Orbita, æ, f.
A water-mill wheel, Tympanum, ni, n.
The great wheel of a Crane wherein Men raise up burdens and packs, Tympanum versatile.
The spoling or weavers wheel, Harpedone, is, n.
A potters wheel, Rota figularis.
The circles of a Cart wheel, Orbile, is, n.
The wheel of a windlas or gin, in the which the Rope runneth, Trochlea, æ, f.
To work with the wheel as turners do, Torno, are.
To shooe wheels, Ferrare rotas.
A cog-wheel belonging to a mill, Rota denticulata.
Of or belonging to a wheel, Rotalis, le, adj.

Wheelage,

Wheelage, Rotaticum, ci, n. a Custom paid for the Passage of Wains and Carts.

A wheel wright, Rotarius, ii, m.

A wheel barrow, Pabo, onis. Vehiculum trusatile.

A Whelp, Catulus, li, m.

When and as often, Quando & quoties.

Whereof, Unde, cujus, quorum, de quibus.

Whereby, of a Descent, a Right, Per quod.

A wherl that women put on their Spindle Harpax, agos, m.

A Wherry or Ferry boat, Ponto, onis, m.

To whet, Acuo, ere.

Whetted, Acutus, a, um.

A whetting, Exacuatio, onis, f.

A Whetstone, Cos, cotis, f.

Whey, Serum, i, n. Serum lactis.

W H I.

Which shall first happen, Utrum prius acciderit.

A whip. Flagellum, li, n. Scutica, æ, f.

A Dog-whip Libriffa, æ, f.

Whip-cord, Resticula, æ, f.

A whipping-stock, Statua verbera, Flagri Subiculum.

To whip, Verbero, are. Flagello, are.

Whipped, Flagellatus, a, um. Verberatus, a, um.

A whipping, Flagellatio, onis, f. Verberatio, onis, f.

A whip saw wherewith Timber is sawed, Runcina, æ, f. Runca, æ, f.

A whirl-pool, Vortex, icis, m.

A whisk, Scopæ vimineæ.

A whistle, Fistula, æ, f.

A whistler, Fistulator, oris, m.

White, Albus, a, um.

Whitby Castle (in Cumberland) Alion, Alione, Alone.

Whitchurch (in Shropshire) Album monasterium.

Whitchurch (the Family) De Albo monasterio.

A white-pot (or Custard) Oogala, actis, n.

Whithern or Whitberne (in Scotland) Candida casa, Lucopibia.

The feast of Whitsontide, Pentecoste, es, f.

A whitster, Insolator, oris, m.

W H O

A playing the whore, Putagium, ii, n.

A whore (or Harlot) Meretrix, icis, f. Scortum, i, n.

A whoring, Scortatio, onis, f.

A whoremonger, Meretricarius, ii, m. Admissarius, ii, m. Fornicator, oris, m.

W I B.

Wiburton, Wiburti villa.

W I C.

Wicked, Sceleratus, a, um. Impius, a, um.

Wickedly, Scelerate, adv. Impiè, adv.

A wicket, Festra, æ, f. Forula, æ, f. Porticula, æ, f.

A wicket (or little Door beside the Gate) Parapertium, ii, n.

Wickham (in Buckinghamshire) Wichcombia.

Wich (in Worcestershire) Wichum.

Wide,

W I D.

Wide, Latus, a, um.

A widow, Vidua, æ, f.

A widow that hath been twice married, Bivita, æ, f. Bivira, æ, f.

A widower, Viduus, ui, m.

Widowhood, Viduitas, atis, f.

W I F.

A Wife, Uxor, oris, f. After marriage, all the Will of the Wife in Judgment of the Law is subject to the Will of her Husband; and it is commonly said, a Feme covert hath no Will. *Cook* 4. *Rep. Forse*, and *Hembling*'s case.

If she have any Tenure at all, she holds in *Capite*, and she hath no Title but by her Husband: the Maxim of the Lawyers is, *Uxor fulget radiis mariti*, the Wife shines with her Husband's Beams.

Where Baron and Feme commit Felony, the Feme can neither be principal, nor accessary, because the Law intends her to have no Will, in regard of her Subjection and Obedience she owes to her Husband. Our Law saith, That every Gift, Grant, or Disposition, of Goods, Lands, or other thing whatsoever, made by a Woman-Covert, and all, and every Obligation and Feoffment made by her, and Recovery suffered, if they be done without her Husband's consent, are void, 45 *Edw*. 3. *Fitz*. Coven. 18. 1 *H*. 5. 12. 6. *Perk. cap. de Grant. nat. brev. fol.* 120.

Yea, if she do wrong to another, she hath not any thing to make satisfaction during Coverture, either her Husband must do it, or by Imprisonment of her person must it be done. *Nat. brev. fol.* 188. 11.

And though she have Inheritance of her own, yet can she not grant any Annuity out of it during her Coverture without her Husband: If any Deed be made to that purpose without his Consent, or in her Name alone, it is void in Law. Yea, if there be debate between the Husband and his Wife, whereby certain Lands of the Husband's be assigned to the Wife with his Consent, if out of such Lands she grant an Annuity to a Stranger, the Grant is void. *Perk. fol.* 2. *A. Perk. fol.* 2. *B.*

And if he Covenant to give her yearly such and such apparel, she cannot dispose it as she list without his consent, but only use and wear it her self 27 *H*. 8 27. p. 12.

Neither can she Lease her own Land for Years, for life; if she do, it is void, and the Lessee entring by force thereof, is a Disseisor to the Husband, and a Tresspasser. *Perk. fol.* 3, 4.

If she sell any thing, the Sale is void, except she be a Merchant, where by the Custom she is inabled to merchandize, 21 *H*. 7. 18. p. 29. *Nat. brev. fol.* 12.

Finally, she cannot make Executors without the consent of her Husband, nor a Devise or Will, *Cook* 4. *Rep. Ognel's Case.*

If she make a Will, and thereby devise her own Inheritance; and her Husband die, and she after die without any new publication of it, it is of no force, but it was void at first. *Plowd. Comment*. 344. *A. Bret*, and *Rigdon's Case.*

Suppose

Suppose a Woman at the time of her Marriage have a lease for Years, or the Wardship of the Body and Lands of an Infant, or have it by gift or purchase, after Marriage she cannot give it away whatsoever the extremity be, but her Husband may at any time during coverture dispose of it, and such his disposition shall cut off the Wives interest, *Dr.* and *Stud* f. 13. *Plowd. Comment.* fol. 418. 8.

By the common Law Marriage is a gift of all the goods and chattels Personal of the Wife to her Husband; so that no kind of property in the same remaineth in her, 12. *H.* 7. 22. *Cook.* 5. *Rep. fol* 36. *H.* 8 *Dyer. Fol.* 6.

And all Personal Goods and Chattels during Marriage given to the Wife, are presently *Ipso facto* tranferred (as to the property of them) to the Husband, *Dr.* and *Stud. fol.* 13. *Plowd. Comment. fol.* 36.

By our Law her necessary apparel is not hers in property; while she remaineth a Wife, she is (to use the Law Phrase) under covert Baron: She can neither Let, Set, Alien, Give, nor otherwise of right make any thing away, 4. *H.* 6. 31.

Money allowed to the Wife for maintenance, after separation from her Husband, *Alimonia, æ,* f.

A new Married wife, Sponsa, æ, f.

An old wife, Vetula, æ, f. Anicula, æ, f.

An house-wife, Mater familias.

The sons-wife, Nurus, ûs, f.

The wives of two Brethren, Janitrices, vel Lautrices.

A brothers wife, Fratria, æ, f.

The wife of my son, or my daughters son, Pronurus, ûs, f.

The wife of two husbands, Bigamia, æ, f. *Bigamist* is one who hath two wives one after another.

Belonging to a wife, Uxorius, a, um.

W I G.

Wight Island by the Britains anciently Guith, *whence probably all its other names.* Icta, Vecta, Vectis, Vectesis, Victesis, Wotha.

The wild of Sussex, Wilda Sussexiæ, *Hob.* 266. Walda, æ, f.

A wilderness (or desert) Desertum, i, n. Eremus, mi, f.

A wilderness in a Garden, Sylva conseminea.

Wilfrid (a mans name) Wilfridus, i, m.

A will, Voluntas, atis, f.

A last will (or testament) Supremum arbitrium, Ultima Voluntas.

To make his last will and testament in writing, Condere Testamentum & Ultimam Voluntatem suam Scriptis.

Having made no will (not proved by witnesses) Intestatus, a, um.

Without a will, Intestatò, adv.

An imperfect will, Improbum Testamentum.

A will that holds not good, Testamentum ruptum.

An Addition to a will or other writing, Codicillus, li, m.

He that maketh a will (or Testament) Testator, oris, m.

She that maketh a will (or Testament) Testatrix, icis, f.

Of or belonging to a will (or Testament) Testamentarius, a, um.

William (a mans name) Guliemus, i, m.

Willingly,

Willingly, Voluntariè, adv.

Willoughby (the Family) De warnevilla, Willoughbæus.

Wiltshire, Vilugiana provincia, Wiltonia.

Of wiltshire, Wiltunensis.

Wilton (in Wiltshire) Ellandunum.

W I M.

Wimundham, now Windham (in Norfolk) Wimundhamia.

A wimble, Terebrum, bri, n.

A little wimble, Terebellum, li, n.

A boring with a wimble or other like Instrument, Terebratio, onis, f.

W I N.

Winander mere (in Lancashire) Setantiorum palus

Winburn (in Dorsetshire) Vindogladia, Vinduglacia, Winburna.

Winchomb (in Gloucestershire) Wincelcumba. Winchelcumba.

Winchelsey (in Sussex) Winchelsega.

Old Winchelsey, Vindelis.

Winchester City (in Hampshire) Vent abelgarum, Venta Simenorum, Wentana Civitas, Wincestria.

Of Winchester, Wenlanus.

Winchester in the wall (in—) Tindolana

Winchester House (in Southwark) Avonii Palatium.

Old Winchester (in Northumberland) Vindolana.

Bishop of Winchester, Episcopus Wintoniensis.

The wind, Ventus, i, m.

The East-wind, Eurus, i, m. Subsolanus, i, m. Ventus Orientalis.

The West-wind, Zephyrus, ri, m. Favonius, ii, m.

The South-wind, Auster, tri, m. Ventus Australis, notus, i, m.

The North-wind, Aquilo, onis, m. Ventus Borealis, septentrio, onis, m.

The East-north-east-wind, Cæcias, æ, m.

The North-east-wind, Euro-aquilo, onis, m.

North-North-west-wind, Thrascias, æ, m.

North-west-wind, Boreazephyrus, i, m. Corus, i, m.

West-north-west wind, Argestes, æ, m.

West-south-west wind, Lybs, bis, m. Africus, ci, m.

The south-south-west wind, Libonotus, i, m. Austroafricus, ci, m.

The South-south-east wind, Carbas, æ, m.

The South-east wind, Euronotus, i, m. Euroauster, tri, m. Notozephyrus, i, m

A gentle wind, Aura, æ, f.

A contrary wind. Reflatus, ûs, m.

A whirl-wind, Turbo, onis, m.

Belonging to the East wind, Orientalis, le, adj.

Of or belonging to the North wind, Aquilonaris, re, adj.

Of or belonging to the West wind, Zephyrius, a, um.

Of the south, wind, Austrinus a, um.

A wind-mill, Mola alata, Mola Pneumatica.

A wind mill sail, Alæ Molares.

A wind Beam of an house, Sustentaculum, li, n. Columen, inis, n.

A winding-sheet, Sudarium, ii, n. Ferale, lis, n. Involucrum, i, n.

A

A window, Feneſtra, æ, f. Repagulum, li, n. Specularium, ii, n.

A little window, Feneſtella, æ, f. Feneſtricula, æ, f.

Bay windows, Cavæ feneſtræ.

A cellar window, Spiraculum, li, n.

Dormer windows, Tectorum feneſtræ.

Luthern windows, Solariorum feneſtræ.

A flap window, Feneſtra pendula.

A window-caſe, Feneſtræ defenſaculum.

Window Beams, Feneſtralia.

A Glaſs window, Vitrea feneſtra.

A lattice window, Clathrum, i, n. Tranſenna, æ, f.

Windows made with croſs Barrs with many holes to look out, Cancelli, orum, m.

To make windows, Feneſtro, are.

Wine, Vinum, i, n.

New wine, Muſtum, i, n.

Claret wine, Vinum rubellum.

French wine, Vinum Gallicum.

White wine, Vinum album.

Rheniſh wine, Vinum Rhenenſe.

Red wine, Vinum rubrum.

Spaniſh wine (or Sack) Vinum Hiſpanicum.

New wine ſodden till the third part is boiled away, Defrutum, i, n. Sapa, æ, f.

Decayed or dead wine, Vappa, æ, f.

To boil or burn wine, Defruto, are.

To allay wine, Vinum diluere.

Wine allayed, Vinum dilutum.

Wine of a year old, Annotinum, i, n.

To taſt wine, Taſtare Vinum. Ry. 295 Pry. 196.

A Cup to taſt new wine, Acrătŏphŏrum, ri, n.

A wine pot, Oenophorum, ri, n.

A wine veſſel, Colatum, i, n.

A Flask of wine, Flaſca, æ, f.

A wine cellar, Cella vinaria.

He that ſelleth wine, Vinarius, ii, m.

She that ſelleth wine by the pot, Decupa, æ, f.

A wine bearer (one which bringeth wine to the Board) Oenophŏrus, ri, m.

Pertaining to wine, Vinaceus, a, um. Vinarius, a, um.

Belonging to Muſt or new wine, Muſtarius, a, um.

Pertaining to the boiling of new wine, Defrutarius, a, um.

A wine preſs, Torcular, aris, n.

A wine preſſer, Vectarius, ii, m.

Winifred (a woman's name) Winifrida, æ, f.

The wing of a Bird, Ala, æ, f. Penna, æ, f.

The wing of an Army, Cornu, n. Cornu tibi cura ſiniſtri. *Lucan.*

To winn, (or Game, as in Play) Lucror, aris. Lucrifacio, ere.

To winn by aſſault, Expugno, are.

To winnow or fan Corn, Vanno, are. Ventilo, are.

Winnowed, Ventilatus, a, um.

Not well winnowed, Exaceratus, a, um.

A winnower, Ventilator, oris, m.

A winnowing, Ventilatio, onis, f.

Winter, Hyems, emis, f.

The winter ſeaſon for ſowing of Corn, Yvernagium, ii, n.

W I P.

To wipe (or make clean) Tergo, ere. Mundo, are.

To wipe away, Abſtergo, ere.
To wipe out, Deleo, ere.
To wipe clean with a Sponge, Spongio, are.
Wiped, Abſterſus, a, um.
Wiped out, Deletus, a, um. Eraſus, a, um.
A wiper, Abſterſor, oris, m.
A wiping, Abſterſio, onis, f.
A wiping clout, Muccinium, ii, n.

W I R.

Gold wire, Aurum netum.
Copper wire, Filum orichalci.

W I S.

Wisk River (*in Yorkſhire*) Wiſkus.
A wiſp (*or wreath*) Peniculus, li, m.

W I T.

A Witch, (*Sorcereſs, or Enchantreſs*) Saga, æ. f. Faſcinatrix, icis, f.
Witchcraft, Magia, æ, f. Faſcinium, ii, n. Veneficium, ii, n.
Witching, Faſcinatio, onis, f.
Pertaining to Witchcraft, Magicus, a, um.
With, Cum, *Præp.*
Within few days, Cis paucos dies.
A with (*or Faggot-band*) Vinculum, li, n.
To withdraw, Retraho, ere. Subtraho, ere. Subduco, ere.
A withdrawer, Subductor, oris, m.
Withernam, Withernamium, ii, n. Vetitum namium, is in the Common Law, when a Diſtreſs is taken and driven into a Hold, or out of the County, ſo that the Sheriff cannot upon the Replevin make delivery thereof to the party diſtreined. In which caſe this Writ of *Withernam*, or *de vetito namio*, is directed to the Sheriff, for the taking of as many of his Beaſts, that did thus unlawfully diſtrain, or as much Goods of his into his keeping, till he hath made deliverance of the firſt Diſtreſs.

The form of the Writ is thus, *Fitz. nat. brev. fol.* 73. *Tibi præcipimus quod averia prædicti B. in balliva tua capias in Withernam*, &c. and the *Regiſt. Orig. fol.* 82. & 83. & 79. *a* & 80. *a.* and in the *Reſt. Judic. fol.* 29. *a.* & 30. *a.* whereby it appeareth, that the Sheriff by theſe words is commanded to take Compenſation and Recompence of the former, taking ſo many Cattle, &c.

Withernam comes from two old and outworn *Saxon* words, *Wither alterum* and *nam pignus, quaſi altera pignoris oblatio.* Some derive it of the German *Wider* (i. e.) *rurſus*, again, and *nam* or *namp*, (i. e.) *Captio*, a taking, of *Nemen*, (i. e) *Capere*, to take, as it were a taking again, as the old Latin word, *Repræſalia*, a Repriſal. When one taking of me a Diſtreſs, which in Latin is called *Pignus*, or any other thing, and carrying it away out of the Juriſdiction where I dwell, I take by order of him that hath Juriſdiction, another Diſtreſs of him again, or of ſome other of that Juriſdiction, and do bring it into the Juriſdiction wherein I dwell; that by equal wrong, I may come by equal right.

Alſo *Withernam* in *Bract. lib* 3. *Tract.* 2. *cap.* 37. and alſo in *Weſt.* 2. *cap.* 2. ſeemeth to ſignifie an unlawful Diſtreſs made by him that hath no right to diſtrein,

Anno 13 *Ed.* 1. *cap.* 2. New Book of Entries, *Verbo Withernam*, whereof is made this Latin word, *Vetitum namium*, a forbidden taking, or an unlawful taking; *viz.* in the first taking or distress, to take away the Mervaile of Mr. *Lamberd* in his Explication of Saxon words. How *Withernam*, which is a taking again, should be latined *Vetitum namium*, a forbidden taking, is nothing else, but that the first taking or distress was unlawful, and so in Law forbidden, and thereof called, *Vetitum namium*.

To with-hold, Retineo, ere. Detineo, ere.

With holden, Detentus, a, um. Retentus, a um.

A with holder, Detentor, oris, m. Retentor, oris, m.

A with-holding, Detentio, onis, f.

A witness, Testis, is, c. 2.

To witness, Testificor, ari.

To call to witness, Contestor, ari.

A calling to witness, Contestatio, onis, f.

Capable of bearing witness, Testabilis, le, adj.

An Ear-witness, Testis auritus.

An Eye-witness, Testis oculatus.

Before witness, Contestatò, adv.

Which by Law can make no Testament, or be taken for a witness, intestabilis, le, adj.

When a man is put down as a witness though not present, Testimonium cœcum.

Witnessed, Contestatus, a, um.

Wittingly, Scienter, adv.

W I Z.

A wizard, Magus, i, m. Augur, uris, m.

W O A.

Woad wherewith Cloth is dyed, Guadium, vel potius, Gualdum, i, n. Glastum, i, n.

W O L.

A wolf, Lupus, i, m.

A female wolf, Lupa, æ, f.

A little wolf, Lupulus, li, m.

A little she wolf, Lupula, æ, f.

Wolf (the Family) Lupus.

Wolley (the Family) Wollæus.

Wolsey (the Family) Wolsæus, Volvesius.

W O M.

A woman, Mulier, eris, f.

A single woman (Spinster) Femina marito expers.

A free woman, Frea, æ, f.

A woman in Childbirth, Puerpera, æ, f.

A woman new married, Sponsa, æ, f.

A woman great with child, Mulier pregnans.

An old woman, Anus, ûs. f.

A grave, sober, motherly woman, Matrona, æ, f.

A woman that lies but with one man, Unicuba, æ, f.

A woman that hath two Husbands, Digama, æ, f.

A working woman, Operaria, æ, f.

A woman Servant, Ancilla, æ, f.

A woman that hath brought forth twice, Bipara, æ, f.

A woman's Bonnet, Cap, or Hood, Calyptra, æ, f.

A woman's Gown with a Train, Cyclas, adis, f.

Of

Of or belonging to a woman Mulierosus, a, um.

The womb (or Matrix) Uterus, ri. Hystera, orum.

Wood cut (or dead wood) Lignum, i, n.

A wood (or wood growing) Boscus, ci, m.

A little wood, Bosculus, li, m. 2 Mon. 239. 242. Lex. 20. Grava, æ, f.

Hedging wood, Busca, æ, f. Reg. 105. bis.

Under wood growing, Subboscus, ci, m.

A heap of Fire wood, Redulus, li, m.

Coppice-wood, wood cut under 20 years growth, Sylva cædua.

A turning of wood Lands into Arable or Pasture, Disboscatio, onis, f.

Woodcot (in Surry near Crayford) Neomagus, Noviomagus, Noiomagus.

A wood of Ash trees, Fraxinetum, i, n.

A wood-house, Boscarium, ii, n. Lignarium, ii, n.

Splits or Billets of wood, Gremia, orum.

A Carrier of wood, Caletarius, ii, m.

A Hewer of wood, Lignarius, ii, m. Ligniseca, æ, m. Ligniciffinus, i, m. Frondator, oris, m.

To cut wood, Ligniseco, are.

A wood-knife, Culter venatorius.

Woodgeld, Woodgeldum, i, n. (*i. e.*) Money paid for gathering or cutting of wood in Forests.

A woodmonger, Lignator, oris, m. Xylopola, æ, m.

A wood Pile, Strues vel meta lignorum.

A Turret of wood, Fala, æ, f.

A hewing of wood, Lignisecatio, onis, f.

To gather wood, Lignor, ari.

Made of wood, Ligneus, a, um.

Belonging to wood, Lignarius, a, um.

A woodward (or under Officer in a Forest) Woodwardus, i, m.

To wooe, Proco, are.

A wooer, Procus, ci, m.

The woof of Cloth, Trama, æ, f. Linium, ii, n.

The woof of a web, Subtegmen, inis, n.

Wool, Lana, æ, f.

Unwashed wool, Lana succida.

Carded or spun wool, Lana facta vel Neta.

Wool unspun, Lana infecta.

Course refuse wool, Solox, Solocis, m. Lana recusata.

A lock of wool, Haspeum, ei, n. Hapsus, i, m.

A flock of wool, (loose lint) Floccus, ci, m.

A fleece of wool, Vellus, ĕris, n. Apsum, i, n.

A carder of wool, Carminator, oris, m.

A woman carder of wool, Carminatrix, icis, f. Xantria, æ, f.

A wool-winder or weaver (any one that selleth or occupieth wool, as a Clothier, Draper, or Weaver) Lanarius, ii, m. Lanificus, ci, m.

A spinner of wool (or maker of Yarn; she that worketh wool to make it serviceable to the Clothier) Lanifica, æ, f.

A spinning (or carding) of wool, Lanificium, ii, n.

Wool-combs, Pectines.

A pair of wool-cards, Par carptariorum.

A wool Market, Eriopolium, ii, n.

A thing which makes the Dye sink into the wool, Turbistrum, tri, n.

A Store house for wool, Lanarium, ii, n. Lanæ repositorium.

A Stone of wool, Petra lanæ.

A tod of wool, Laniscus, ci, m.

A weight of wool (or Cheese) of two hundred fifty six pounds, Uvaga, æ, f.

He that weigheth wool, Lanipendius, ii, m.

Of or belonging to wool, Lanarius, a, um.

W O R.

Worcester City, Branovium, Brannovium, Bravinum, Bravonium, Vigornia, Wigornia.

Of Worcester, Wigorniensis.

Worcestershire, Wiccia, Wigorniæ comitatus.

Bishop of Worcester, Episcopus Wigorniensis.

A word, Verbum, i, n.

Work, Opus, eris, n.

To work, Operor, ari.

To work, forge, or frame, Fabrico, are.

Carved work, Opus incisum.

Lime work, Opus albarium.

Mosaick work, Pavimentum Scalpturatum.

Handy-work. Manopera, æ, f.

To take work by the great, Opus redimere faciendum.

A Surveyor, or taker of work by the great, Redemptor, oris, m.

A Master of Work, Architector, oris, m.

A day's work, Præcaria, æ, f. Lex. 99. Brac. 160.

A worker, Operator, oris, m.

A worker with a hammer, (a Smith or Coiner) Malleator, oris, m.

A work-house, Opificina, æ, f. Artificina, æ, f. Domus operaria.

To cast up works round about (or trench about) Circumvallo, are.

One that works sitting, Sellularius, ii, m.

A working, Operatio, onis, f.

A workman, Opifex, icis, m. Artifex, icis, m. Faber, ri, m.

Workman-like, Fabriliter, adv.

Workmanship, Opificium, ii, n. Fabia, æ, f. Artificium, ii, n.

Pertaining to a workman, Operarius, a, um.

The world, Mundus, i, m. Cosmus, i, m.

The description of the world, Cosmographia, æ, f.

Wort, Mustea cervisiæ.

Worshipful, Venerabilis, le, adj.

Worthy, Dignus, a, um.

Worthiness, Dignitas, atis, f.

W O V.

Woven, Textus, a, um. Textilis, le, adj.

A wound, Vulnus, eris, n.

A little wound, Vulnusculum, li, n.

The Scurf of a wound, Crusta vulneris.

The Crust upon a seared wound, Escara, æ, f.

Causing a Crust upon a seared wound, Escaroticus, a, um.

To wound. Vulnero, are.

Wounded, Vulneratus, a, um.

W R A.

To wrangle, Litigo, are. Alterco, are.

A wrangler, Altercator, oris, m. Litigator, oris, m.

A wrangling. Altercatio, onis, f.

To wrap (or wind about) Circumplico, are.

Wrapped about, Circumligatus, a, um. Intortus, a, um. Circumvolutus, a, um.

Wrapped (or folded in) Implicitus, a, um. Involutus, a, um.

Wrapped together, Obvolutus, a, um. Complicatus, a, um.

A wrapper, Involucrum, cri, n.

Wrapping-Paper, Cucullus, li, m.

To wrap or roll about, Circumvolvo, ere.

One that wraps or rolls together, Obvolutor, oris, m.

To wrastle, Luctor, ari.

A wrastler, Luctator, oris, m.

A great wrastler, Athleta, æ, m.

A wrastling, Luctatio, onis, f.

A wrastling-place, Palæstra, æ, f. Hermathena, æ, f. Xystus, i, m.

The art of wrastling, Athletica, æ, f.

Pertaining to wrastling, Athleticus, a, um.

W R E.

To wreath, crisp, curle, turn a Pin round, Torqueo, ere.

A whirling or wreathing, Torsio, onis, f.

To wreath about, Contorqueo, ere.

Wreathed, Obtortus, a, um.

A wreathing, Contorsio, onis, f. Convolutio, onis, f.

A wreck of the Sea, Wreccum, i, n. Cow. 285. 5. Co. 106. 2 Inst. 167. Wreccum maris.

Goods Shipwreckt, Bona wreccata, 5. Co 106.

Wreck River (in Leicestershire) Wrekus.

Wreshil (in Yorkshire) Urosullum.

W R I.

A wrinckle, Ruga, æ, f.

To wrinckle, Rugo, are.

To wring, Stringo, ere.

A wristband (or Sleeve) Brachiale, lis, n.

The wrist (or Joynt between the Hand and the Arm) Carpus, i, m.

A writ, Breve, is, n. *Spel.* 104. A Writ is a formal Letter, or Epistle of the King in a Parchment sealed with a Seal, directed to some Judge, Officer, Minister, or other Subject, at their Suit, or the Suit or Plaint of a Subject, commanding or authorizing something contained in the same Letter to be done for the cause briefly (and therefore called a Brief) in that Letter expressed, which is to be discussed in some Court according to Law. *Leigh. Phil. Com. fol.* 243.

The Civilians call it, *Actionem sive formulam*, but *actio* seemeth rather the Parties whole suit, and *Breve* is the King's Precept, whereby any thing is Commanded to be done touching the Suit of Action; as the Defendant to be summoned, a Distress to be taken, a Disseisin to be redressed, &c.

And these Writs are diversly divided in divers respects. Some in respect of their Order, or manner of Granting, are termed Original, and some Judicial.

Original Writs are those that are sent out for the summoning of the Defendant in a Personal, or Tenant in a Real Action, or other like purpose, before the Suit beginneth, or to begin the Suit thereby.

Those are *Judicial*, that are sent out by order of the Court where the Cause dependeth, upon occasion growing after Suit begun. *Old Nat. Brev. fol.* 51. And Judicial is thus by one sign

known

known from the Original, because the Teste beareth the Name of the chief Justice of that Court whence it cometh, where the Original beareth in the Teste the Name of the King.

Then according to the nature of the Action, they are Personal or Real; and Real are either touching the Possession, called Writs of Entry, or the Property, called Writs of Right. *Fitz. Nat. brev. sparsim per totum.*

Some Writs are at the Suit of a Party, some of Office. *Old. nat. brev. fol.* 147. Some Ordinary, some of Privilege.

A Writ of Privilege is that, which a privileged Person bringeth to the Court for his Exemption, by reason of some Privilege. See *Procedendo.* See the new Book of Entries *Verbo* Privilege.

To write, Scribo, ere.

To write much, or often, Scriptito, are.

To write in, or upon, Inscribo, ere

To write between, Interscribo, ere.

To write (or make) a Book, Compono, ere.

To write over, Superscribo, ere.

To write an Answer, Rescribo, ere.

To write out a Copy, Transcribo, ere. Exscribo, ere.

A writer, Scriptor, oris, m. Præscriptor, oris, m

A writing, Scriptio, onis, f. Scriptura, æ, f.

Short writing, Tachygraphia, æ, f. Stenographia, æ, f.

A short writing referring to a longer, Docketta, æ, f.

Of or for writing, Scriptorius, a, um.

A writer of the Tallies, Scriptor Taliarum. Is an Officer of the Exchequer, being Clerk to the Auditor of the Receipt, who writeth upon the Tallies the whole Letters of the Tellers Bills.

Written, Scriptus, a, um.

Written over, Superscriptus, a, um.

Written out, Exscriptus, a, um.

W R O.

To do wrong, Tortum facere. *Co. Lit.* 158.

Wrong, Tortitudo, inis, f 1. *Mon.* 580. Injuria, æ, f. Wrong or Injury is in French aptly called *Tort*, because Injury and Wrong is wrested or crooked, being contrary to that which is Right and Straight. Injury is derived of *In* and *Jus*, because it is contrary to Right. *Cook on Lit. Lib.* 2. *cap* 1.

Wronged violently, Oppressus, a, um

Wrongfully, Injuriè, Injustè, adv.

Wrotham (in Kent) Vagniacæ, Vagniacum.

Wroxcester (in Shropshire) Virecinum, Virecium, Viroconium, Uriconium.

W U L.

Wulstan (a man's name) Wulstanus, i, m.

W Y D.

A Wydraught for a Privy, Fotica, æ, f. Latrina, æ, f. Sentina, æ, f. Cloaca, æ f. Colluviarium, ii, n. Stercidium, ii, n.

W Y E.

Wye River, Vaga, Waya.

W Y K.

A Wyke or little Village, Wyka, æ, f.

Y A R.

A *Yard to measure with*, Yarda, æ, f. *Co. Ent.* 377. Virgata, æ, f. Virga, æ, f.

A man's Yard (or Privities) Penis, is, m. Veretrum, i, n.

The Sail-yard (or cross piece whereunto the Sail is fastened) Antenna, æ, f.

Yard-land, Virgata terræ. The *Saxons* called it *Girdland*. It is a proportion of Land. In some Countries it is Ten Acres, in some Twenty, some Twenty four, and some Thirty Acres of Land.

Yare (in Yorkshire) Yarum.

Yare River (in Norfolk) Garrienis, Garryenus.

Yarmouth (in Norfolk) Garonum, Garienis ostium.

Yarn, Lana neta. *Mich.* 14. *Car.* 2. *in* C. *B.* Lana facta.

A Bottom of Yarn, Glomus, i, m. vel, eris, n.

A Skain of Yarn (Thread or Silk) Forago, inis, m. Mataxa, æ, f.

A Quill of Yarn, Panus, i, m.

A Spindle to wind Yarn, Alabrum, i, n.

To reel Yarn, Alabro, are.

To wind Bottoms of Yarn, Glomerare Glomos.

Y E A.

A Year, Annus, i, m.

Year and Day, Annus & Dies. Is a time thought in Construction of our Common Law, fit in many Cases to determine a Right in one, and an Usurpation or Prescription in another: As in case of an Estray, if the Owner (Proclamation being made) challenge it not within that time, it is forfeit. So is the Year and Day given in case of Appeal, in case of Descent after Entry or Claim; or of no Claim; upon a Fine or Writ of Right at the Common Law. So of a Villain remaining in ancient Demesn; of the Death of a Man sore bruised and wounded; Of Protections; Essoines in respect of the King's service; of Wreck, and divers other Cases. *Cook, Vol.* 6. *fol.* 107. *B* and that touching the Death of a Man likewise in the Civil Law. *Nam si mortifere fuerit vulneratus, & postea post longum intervallum mortuus sit inde annum numerabimus secundum Julianum.*

Year, Day, and Wast, Annus, Dies, & Vastum. Is a part of the King's Prerogative, whereby he challengeth the Profits of their Lands and Tenements, for a Year and a Day, that are attainted of Petty Treason or Felony, whosoever be Lord of the Manner, whereunto the Lands or Tenements do belong; and not only so, but in the End wasteth the Tenement, destroyeth the Houses, rooteth up the Woods, Gardens, Pastures, and ploweth up Meadows, except the Lord of the

Fee agree with him for the Redemption of ſuch Waſt, afterward reſtoring it to the Lord of the Fee; whereof you may read at large in *Stawnf. Prærog. Cap.* 16. *fol.* 44. *& ſeq.*

The Leap year, Biſſextilis, le.

Yearly (or year by year) Quotannis, adv. annuatim, adv.

Yeaſt (or Barm) Giſtum, i, n. Spel. 317. Spuma vel flos Cereviſiæ.

Y E L.

Yellow, Flavus, a, um. Citrinus, a, um.

Y E O.

A Yeoman, Homo ingenuus. *Spel.* 361, 381.

A Yeoman of the Guard, Stipator corporis.

Y O A.

A Yoak, Jugum, i, n.

The Band faſtening the Yoak about the Neck, Subjugium, ii, n.

Unaccuſtomed to the Yoak, Subjugis, e, adj.

To Yoak, Jugo, are. Subjugo, are.

Y O R.

York City, Brigantium, Eboracum, Eburacum. Legio VI. Nicephorica. Legio VI. Victrix. Urovicum.

Yorkſhire, Eboracenſis ager vel comitatus. Iſuria.

Of Yorkſhire, Iſurovicanus.

Archbiſhop of York, Archiepiſcopus Eboracenſis.

Y O U.

The Young of any Tame Beaſt or Bird, Pullus, i, m.

A young man, Juvenis, adj.

Youth, Juventus, utis, f.

Z A C.

Z*Achary (a Man's name)* Zacharias, æ, m.

F I N I S.

www.ingramcontent.com/pod-product-compliance
Lightning Source LLC
Chambersburg PA
CBHW030252100426
42812CB00002B/410

* 9 7 8 1 5 8 4 7 7 3 7 7 1 *